Volume Six

Motif Programming Manual

---

by Dan Heller

Reference Appendices by Daniel Gilly

O'Reilly & Associates, Inc.

Motif Programming Manual

Motif Programming Manual
by Dan Heller
Reference appendices by Daniel Gilly

X Series Editor: Tim O'Reilly

Printing History:

        September 1991:   First Printing

Printed on recycled paper.

Volume 6: ISBN 0–937175–70–6

Table of Contents

Figures

Examples

Tables

Preface

By convention, a preface describes the book itself, while the introduction describes the subject matter. You should read through the preface to get an idea of how the book is organized, the conventions it follows, and so on.

In This Chapter:

Preface

This book describes how to write applications using the Motif toolkit from the Open Software Foundation (OSF). The Motif toolkit is based on the X Toolkit Intrinsics (Xt), which is the standard mechanism on which many of the toolkits written for the X Window System are based. Xt provides a library of user-interface objects called *widgets* and *gadgets*, which provide a convenient interface for creating and manipulating X windows, colormaps, events, and other cosmetic attributes of the display. In short, widgets can be thought of as building blocks that the programmer uses to construct a complete application.

However, the widgets that Xt provides are generic in nature and impose no user-interface policy whatsoever. That is the job of a user-interface toolkit such as Motif. Motif provides a complete set of widgets designed to implement the application look and feel specified in the *Motif Style Guide* and the *Motif Application Environment Specification*.

This book provides a complete programmer's guide to the Motif toolkit. While the OSF/Motif toolkit is based on Xt, the focus of the book is on Motif itself, not on the Toolkit Intrinsics. Detailed information about Xt is provided by Volume Four, *X Toolkit Intrinsics Programming Manual*, and references are made to that volume throughout the course of this book. You are not required to have Volume Four, however, in order to use this book effectively. They are not companion volumes, but complementary ones. However, truly robust applications will require a depth of knowledge about Xt and Xlib, the layer on which Xt itself is based, that is not addressed in this book alone. We will never leave you completely in the dark about Xt functions or Xlib that we use or reference, but you won't learn everything there is to know about them through this particular volume.

The Plot

There are several plots and subplots in this book and the stories told are intertwined. Our primary goal is to help you learn about the Motif environment from both the programmer's and the user's perspectives. However, we are talking to you as a programmer, not as a user. We treat the user as a third party who is not with us now. But in order to create an application for the user, you sometimes have to assume his role. At times, we may ask you to play such a role to help you think about things from the user's perspective and not the programmer's.

Each chapter begins by discussing the goals that Motif is trying to achieve using a particular widget or gadget. For example, before we describe how to create a FileSelectionDialog, we introduce the object visually and conceptually; we discuss its features, drawbacks, main elements of focus; and we put you in the role of the user. Once you understand what the user is going to work with, you should have a better perspective on how you want to approach your task of presenting it to him.

The next subplot is that of designing applications. Whether or not you are designing a Motif application, many concepts transcend the graphical user interface (GUI) and are common to all programs that interact with users. You could even interpret this book as a programmer's guide that happens to use Motif as an example. As you read the material, you should always stop and think about how you might be approaching a particular interface method if you weren't using Motif, but another toolkit instead. A wild concept, perhaps. But this approach is the key not only to better application design, but to toolkit independence. If Motif changes in later releases, or if you decide to port your application to another toolkit or even another windowing system, the more generalized your code is, the easier it will be to successfully bring it into a new realm.

The last story we are telling is that of general programming technique. By providing you with examples of good programming habits, styles, and usages, we hope to propagate a programming methodology that has proven to be successful over the years. These techniques have been applied to applications that have ported to multiple architectures and operating systems. As an added bonus, we have thrown in a number of interesting programming tricks. No, these are not hacks, but conveniences that are particular to C, to UNIX, or even to the X Window System. We don't focus on these things, but they are made available to you in passing—you should have no problem identifying them when they come up. And when they do, we hope your reaction will be "Oh! That's neat! Or, I didn't know you could do that."

Stories Not Told

This book is intended to be used as a programmer's manual—not a reference manual. Although there is a reference appendix that describes every Motif library function, every widget, and every gadget, we do not discuss every aspect of the Motif toolkit in the body of the book. While we try to keep this practice to a minimum, we have tried to identify those features of the toolkit that are most important for general discussion. While overly simple or uninteresting items (usually obscure resources) are not discussed, you may also find that other, perhaps major features are also left out. This is usually done for one of several reasons:

- *Expected or Announced Changes.* In some cases, OSF has already announced that a particular feature or design is going to change. Accordingly, we may have chosen not to address those particular features if we felt that there were reasonable alternatives we could provide in the interim.

- *Bugs.* There are many bugs in the Motif toolkit that have not yet been worked out. This is not to imply that the toolkit is poorly written or is riddled with errors. *Any* major software development effort, especially in its early stages, has bugs that prevent certain features from being used. In most cases, we alert you to potential problems. In those cases where bugs are too severe, we merely do not discuss the particular issue due to expected *application programmer's interface* (API) or design changes.

- *Design Errors.* In some cases, there are things that work in Motif, but they are poorly designed, and we don't recommend that you use them. Again, we will provide an explanation of what's going on and possibly an alternative to the mis-feature.

- *Lack of Support.* There are a great number of features, resources, and functions available in the toolkit that are not supported by OSF. OSF reserves the right to change anything not publicly documented. Rather than discuss undocumented features, we simply ignore them.

Despite these omissions, this book should tell you everything you need to know in order to get a good start on just about any development effort. In fact, you will very likely be able to see your whole way through your application using only this book.

We should also point out that this book is not intended to solve all your problems or answer all your questions concerning Motif or its toolkit. It is not going to spoon-feed you by giving you step-by-step instructions on how to achieve a particular task. You are encouraged, even expected, to experiment on your own with the example applications or, better yet, with your own programs. We want to provide you with discussion and examples that provoke you into asking questions like, "What would happen if I changed this program to do this?" It would be unrealistic to believe that we could address every problem that might come up, so rather than approaching situations using overly specific examples, we discuss them in an abstract and generalized way that should be applicable to many different scenarios. It is your responsibility to think about how the technique we demonstrate can be applied to your application(s).

Alternatives to the Motif Toolkit

As you will no doubt learn, building a GUI is a time-consuming process that requires a great deal of precise knowledge and design skill. The application designer must have not only the creative expertise to build an effective interface, but also a considerable amount of technical skill in using the toolkit (or lower-level libraries)—not to mention an understanding of the actual application beneath the interface.

As a result, many organizations are exploring alternative approaches to building a Motif interface for an application. These approaches come in the form of *user-interface languages*, or as separate products known as *user interface management systems* (UIMS).

User-interface languages and UIMSs have two goals. The first is to make it possible for less sophisticated people (those who do not or cannot program in C) to build and design GUI applications easily. The second is to reduce development time.

There are some advantages and disadvantages to each of these approaches. Let's take a closer look at each.

User-interface Languages

A user-interface language is a meta-programming language that is designed to be much simpler than a structured programming language such as C. The user typically edits some kind of text file that defines the objects in the interface, and then a language compiler or interpreter makes the lower-level calls to the C language Motif toolkit.

One advantage to interface languages is that they can be interpreted, which means that you don't have to go through the process of recompiling a file every time you want to make a change. Also, by having a fixed file online, your changes are always saved and available.

The greatest disadvantage to user-interface languages is that they lack structure and inhibit good application design techniques. In order to make them simple enough for nontechnical people, these languages tend not to support looping constructs, variables, conditional expressions, and many other features that software engineers take for granted. As a result, the interface generated by such languages tend to be quite inflexible. Furthermore, because the implementation is incomplete, once the language is out of the picture, you must resort to using the C language Motif toolkit anyway, to provide additional features.

OSF provides a user-interface language called UIL. UIL is a complex language that attempts to overcome many of the disadvantages described above. However, in doing so, it has also removed many of the advantages of using an interface language. UIL is almost as complicated as C. In fact, most nontechnical people can no more use UIL than they can program in C. Furthermore, UIL does not fully recover from the other problems these languages have, like their lack of looping constructs and structured programming techniques.

While it is an interpreted language, the UIL interpreter only loads the data once; there are no functions to execute or conditional statements that act differently based on different states of the application. Despite that, UIL must still be compiled and linked with the main application. While it does not take as long to compile UIL as it does C code, it is a more complicated and time consuming process than it should be.

Another user-interface language that is available, and considerably better designed than UIL, is the *Widget Creation Library* (WCL), which is freely available on the Internet.[1] WCL was written by David Smythe at the Jet Propulsion Labs (JPL) in Pasadena, California, and is widget-set independent. WCL works with the Motif toolkit or any other widget set because it abstracts the method by which widgets are created, manipulated, and destroyed. You can write separate C functions and link them directly to widgets defined and built by WCL. The package does have similar disadvantages to UIL in that there are no looping constructs or other control flow mechanisms. Nonetheless, the language is very simple and much easier for nontechnical people to use than most others. It is perfect for what it was intended to be used for: prototyping a user interface.

---

[1] WCL can be obtained from any *comp.sources.x* archive site or uunet.uu.net. See *Obtaining Motif*, in the Preface, for more information.

UIMS Packages

UIMS packages take another approach to simplifying GUI design. These programs provide blank windows and a palette of user-interface objects to place on them. You can point and click on the types of objects you want to create, and then move them around on the screen. When you want to save what you've done, most programs output standard C code (or UIL) to a file.

Unfortunately, mechanically-generated C code does not incorporate any reasonable programming style or technique. As a result, these programs tend to be enormous and quite inefficient. This is not what you want from the part of the application that needs to perform most efficiently.

Also, consider what it's like to read someone else's code. Imagine providing support for a customer who's having a problem with your application, if the user-interface code was written by a UIMS. You are at a double disadvantage here: first, not having written the code, you are as lost as if you were trying to read and debug someone else's program; second, if you didn't write the code, chances are you aren't familiar enough with the Motif toolkit to know how to fix the problem.

UIMS products can be quite sophisticated, and they are quite fun to use. But don't let these products get the better of you; they are best for *prototyping* what you want your application to look like. UIMS packages definitely serve one important purpose: to cut down on development time in the initial design stages. Once done, you should build the application from scratch strictly using the Motif widget set and toolkit described by this book. Trying to find a quick way to build a complex application will only cause you more grief later. Sooner or later, you're going to have to learn Motif, so you might as well do it right the first time.

In short, using the Motif toolkit is definitely the best way to address your design and implementation goals for your Motif-based applications. We do not address UIL or UIMS in this book.

Assumptions

The basic methods for creating simple applications in Motif is conceptually simple and straightforward. Even those who *dabble* in C can understand the concepts well enough to do most things. However, unless you have a strong handle on the C programming language, there is an upper limit to what you will be able to do when you try to create a full-featured, functioning application. After all, the user-interface portion of most applications should make up no more than 30-40% of the total code. The rest of it is up to you and is not discussed here. Without a strong background with C, or some other structured programming language, you might have a problem keeping up with the material presented here.

This book uses the standard K&R-style[2] C programming language. Recently, there has been a wider use of ANSI-C, a newer version of the C language that imposes tighter type-checking, function prototyping, and other newer conventions in the language. While you are

---

[2] K&R stands for Kernighan and Ritchie, developers of C and authors of *The C Programming Language*.

advised to use the ANSI-C programming style whenever possible, most computers still use the older K&R version of the language, which is the primary reason we chose to use that programming style.

How This Book is Organized

While this book attempts to serve the widest possible audience, that does not imply that the material is so simple that it is only useful by novice programmers. In fact, this book might even be considered to be an advanced programmer's handbook, since in many places, it assumes a fairly sophisticated knowledge of many features of the X Window System.

Each chapter is organized in such a way that it gets more demanding on the reader as he progresses. Each chapter begins with a short introduction on the particular Motif element that is the subject of the chapter. Next, the basic mechanics involved with creating and manipulating the object are addressed. The intermediate sections deal with the resources and other configurable aspects of the object, including possible convenience functions and other related material. The ending usually encapsulates what we have covered. Many chapters include exercises intended to suggest how the material can be adapted for uses not directly discussed in the text.

While the chapters may be read sequentially, it is certainly not required or expected that you do so. As you will soon find, there are many circular dependencies that justify skipping around between chapters. Since no other organization would reduce this necessary evil, the material is not organized so that you learn-as-you-go. Rather, the book is organized in a "top-down" manner, starting with several chapters that provide a general introduction to the Motif application look and feel, followed by chapters organized on a widget-by-widget basis. The larger, higher-level manager widgets are discussed first, followed by the primitive widgets and gadgets. General material is positioned towards the end of the book, since the details are not of paramount importance to the earlier material.

In short, everything is used everywhere. Starting at the beginning, however, means that we won't necessarily assume you know about the material that is referenced in later chapters. On the other hand, the later chapters may make the assumption that you are aware of material in earlier chapters.

The book is broken down into twenty chapters and four appendices, as follows:

Chapter 1,   *You, Motif, and Everything*, answers the question "Why Motif?" in terms of the development of applications that are "easy enough for your mother to use." It suggests some of the complexities that the programmer has to master in order to make his applications simple.

Chapter 2,   *The Motif Programming Model*, teaches the fundamentals of Motif by example. It dissects a simple "Hello, World" program, showing the program structure and style common to all Motif programs. Because much of this material is already covered in detail in Volume Four, *X Toolkit Intrinsics Programming Manual, Motif Edition*, this chapter can be seen as a refresher, or a light introduction for those who haven't read the earlier book. It makes reference to Volume One and the Motif edition of Volume Four to point out areas that the programmer will need to understand (windows, widgets, events, callbacks, resources, translations) before he can progress with Motif.

Chapter 3, *Overview of Motif Widgets*, helps the reader understand what has to go into a real application: details of geometry management of primitive widgets within some kind of main window, when to fit things into the main window and when to use popups (dialog boxes and menus), and how applications relate to the window manager. After reading this chapter, the programmer should have a solid overview of Motif application programming, and should be able to read the remaining chapters in any order.

Chapter 4, *The Main Window*, describes the Motif MainWindow widget, which can be used to frame many types of applications. The MainWindow is a manager widget that provides a menubar, scrollable work area, and various other optional display and control areas.

Chapter 5, *Introduction to Dialogs*, describes the fundamental concepts that underly all Motif dialogs. It provides a foundation for the more advanced material in the following chapters. In the course of the introduction, this chapter also provides details on Motif's predefined MessageDialog classes.

Chapter 6, *Selection Dialogs*, describes the more complex Motif-supplied dialogs for displaying selection lists (such as lists of files or commands) to the user.

Chapter 7, *Custom Dialogs*, describes how to create new dialog types, either by customizing Motif dialogs or by creating entirely new dialogs.

Chapter 8, *Manager Widgets*, provides detailed descriptions of the various classes of Motif manager widgets. Useful examples explore the limits of the various methods of Form and RowColumn positioning.

Chapter 9, *ScrolledWindows and Scrollbars*, describes the ins and outs of scrolling, with particular attention to application-defined scrolling, which is often required when the simple scrolling provided by the ScrolledWindow widget is insufficient.

Chapter 10, *The DrawingArea Widget*, describes the Motif DrawingArea widget, which provides a canvas for interactive drawing. Rather than trying to teach Xlib drawing, the chapter simply highlights, with numerous code examples, the difficulties that may be encountered when working with this widget. (Some knowledge of Xlib is assumed; we direct the user to Volume One, *Xlib Programming Manual*, for additional information.)

Chapter 11, *Labels and Buttons*, provides an in-depth look at labels and buttons, the most commonly-used primitive widgets. It also suggests techniques for interpreting multiple button clicks, which are not supported by the default translations for the PushButton widget.

Chapter 12, *Toggle Widgets*, describes both ToggleButtons and the special configurations of the RowColumn widget used to manage Toggles in either a CheckBox or RadioBox format.

Chapter 13, *List Widgets*, describes yet another method for the user to exert control over an application. List widgets display a series of text choices that the user can select interactively.

Chapter 14,   *Scale Widgets*, describes how to use scales to display ranges of data.

Chapter 15,   *Text Widgets*, explains how the Text and TextField widgets can be used to provide anything from a single data-entry field to a full-fledged text editor. Special attention is paid to problems such as how to mask or convert data input by the user so as to control its format.

Chapter 16,   *Menus*, describes the Motif menu system in greater detail than was presented in the simple menus used with the MainWindow widget.

Chapter 17,   *Interacting with the Window Manager*, provides additional information on the relationship between shell widgets and the Motif window manager. It discusses shell widget resources, and how to use Motif's functions for adding or modifying window manager protocols.

Chapter 18,   *The Clipboard*, describes a way for the application to interact with other applications. Data is placed on the Clipboard, where it can be accessed by other windows on the desktop, regardless of the applications with which they are associated.

Chapter 19,   *Compound Strings*, describes Motif's technology for encoding font changes and character directions (for use with foreign languages) in the strings that are used by almost all Motif widgets.

Chapter 20,   *Advanced Dialog Programming*, describes Motif features that have not been described (at least not completely) in earlier chapters, including issues involved in creating multi-stage help systems, in creating WorkingDialogs that allow you to interrupt a long-running task, and a method for dynamically changing the pixmaps displayed in a dialog.

Appendix A,   *Motif Functions and Macros*, lists the syntax of every Motif library function.

Appendix B,   *Xt and Motif Widget Classes*, describes the resources, callbacks, and translations associated with every Motif user-interface object.

Appendix C,   *Data Types*, describes any special data types used by Motif functions, including Xt or Xlib data types where necessary.

Appendix D,   *Additional Examples*, provides several additional examples that illustrate techniques not discussed in the body of the book.

The Index   should help you to find what you need to know.

Conventions Used in This Book

Italic is used for:

- UNIX pathnames, filenames, program names, user command names, and options for user commands.

- New terms where they are defined or introduced.

`Typewriter Font` is used for:

- Anything that would be typed verbatim into code, such as examples of source code and text on the screen.

- Variables, data structures (and fields), symbols (defined constants and bit flags), functions, macros, and a general assortment of anything relating to the C programming language.

- All functions relating to Motif, Xt, and Xlib.

`Italic Typewriter Font` is used for:

- Arguments to functions, since they could be typed in code as shown but are arbitrary.

Helvetica Italic is used for:

- Titles of examples, figures, and tables.

Boldface is used for:

- Chapter headings, section headings, and the names of buttons and menus.

Request for Comments

To help us provide you with the best documentation possible, please write to tell us about any problems you find in this manual or how you think it could be improved.

Our U.S. mail address, e-mail address, and phone numbers are as follows:

O'Reilly & Associates, Inc.
632 Petaluma Avenue
Sebastopol, CA 95472
800-338-6887
international +1 707-829-0515

UUCP: uunet!ora!motif   Internet: motif@ora.com

Obtaining Motif

If your hardware vendor is an OSF member, they may be able to provide Motif binaries for your machine. Various independent vendors also provide binaries for some machines. Source licenses must be obtained directly from OSF:

> Motif Support Administration
> Open Software Foundation
> 11 Cambridge Center
> Cambridge, MA 02142
> USA
>
> +1 617 621-8990

Obtaining the Example Programs

You can obtain copies of the programs in this book from UUNET and other Internet sites that archive freely distributable source code. (That is, free except for any system's possible connect-time charges.)

If you have access to UUNET, you can retrieve the source code using *uucp* or *ftp*. For *uucp*, find a machine with direct access to UUNET, and type the following command:

```
uucp uunet\!~/nutshell/motif/examples.tar.Z yourhost\!~/yourname/
```

If you are directly connected to the Internet, you can use *ftp* to obtain sources from UUNET or *export.lcs.mit.edu*. To use *ftp* to *uunet.uu.net*, for example, use *anonymous* as your user name and *guest* as your password. Then type the following:

```
ftp> cd nutshell/motif
ftp> binary (you must specify binary transfer for compressed files)
ftp> get examples.tar.Z
lots of output
ftp> bye
```

On *export.lcs.mit.edu*, the compressed tar file is stored in *contrib/OReilly*. The other directions are the same as for UUNET.

The file is a compressed tar archive. To extract files once you have retrieved the archive, type:

```
uncompress examples.tar
tar xvf examples.tar
```

The examples will be installed in subdirectories under the current directory, one for each chapter in the book.

The backslashes can be omitted if you use the Bourne shell (*sh*) instead of *csh*. The file should appear some time later (up to a day or more) in the directory */usr/spool/uucppublic/yourname*.

In addition to being placed in the "nutshell" hierarchy at *uunet.uu.net* and the "contrib" hierarchy at *export.lcs.mit.edu*, the examples will be posted to comp.sources.x, the usenet newsgroup for freely-available X software. Postings to this newsgroup are distributed worldwide, and are archived by many sites. You can obtain a current listing of archive sites by sending a request to:

```
comp-sources-x@uunet.uu.net
```

You don't need to be on the Internet, or to have a UUCP account with UUNET to be able to access their archives (either the in the nutshell directory described above, or in the comp.sources.x archives). By calling 1-900-468-7727 and using the login "uucp" with no password, anyone within the United States of America may uucp any of UUNET's online source collection.

If you want to see everything that's available, start by copying *uunet!/usr/spool/ftp/ls-lR.Z*, which is a compressed (but still huge) index of every file in the archives. As of this writing, the cost is 40 cents per minute. The charges will appear on your next telephone bill.

Most other comp.sources.x archive sites provide free connect charges, although you must pay for the phone call. If such an archive site is in your local area, this might be an advantage over UUNET.

Copyright

The example programs are all written by Dan Heller for the *Motif Programming Manual*, Copyright 1991 O'Reilly & Associates, Inc. Permission to use, copy, and modify these programs without restriction is hereby granted, as long as this copyright notice appears in each copy of the program source code.

For the purposes of making the book easier to read, the above copyright notice does not appear in the program examples. However, the copyright does exist in the electronic form of the programs available on the Internet.

Notes on Z-Mail

Many of the screenshots in this book that are not based on the example programs are of Z-Mail, an electronic mail program. Z-Mail is the culmination of years of work, starting with a freely-distributed program called Mail User's Shell (Mush). Mush's only GUI interface was SunView, although it also supported tty and curses interfaces. Over the course of writing this book, I developed the Motif interface for Z-Mail that you see here. This was my reality-check that what I preach really does work. :-)

It should be mentioned that Z-Mail also supports an OPEN LOOK interface. To do the OPEN LOOK version, I chose to use OLIT (OPEN LOOK Intrinsics Toolkit) because, like Motif, it is based on the X Toolkit Intrinsics. Xt is a great environment for developing applications for the X environment. I also believe that the best applications are those whose user interfaces can be abstracted, generalized, and modularized so that you can unplug one interface and plug in another. My approach to how to do that is also reflected in this book, although not as a major topic.

Finally, Z-Mail is my first break into the commercial software market, and it remains to be seen whether the product will be a success. But if this book has helped you develop successful software, please contact me and let me know. That's the real purpose of this book.

Use of Sexist Language

On another personal note, it is important to me to discuss a topic of growing social importance, and that is the use of "sexist" language, or more specifically, gender-oriented pronouns, when neither or both genders were intended.

While I always try to choose alternative sentence constructions, sometimes the only way to properly express a point is in a "generic" way, even though the actual content does not suggest (or preclude) one gender over another. Over the years, the social climate of the world has changed to include women in higher social, political, and economic roles than ever before, which is a very good thing. Naturally, such social conditions affect the way we use speech. As a result, there has been a trend to use terms like "she" and "her" in a generic way, so as to suggest that women can be just as generic as the next guy. :-)

However, I am not fond of using "she" or "her" in a generic sense because it is no less sexist than using "he" or "him." I also don't like being inconsistent by using one type of pronoun and then the other sporadically throughout a discussion. I also believe it to be overly distracting to use phrases like "he or she," "him or her," or contractions like "he/she," or "s/he," as is done in other O'Reilly & Associates books.

The only acceptable alternative with respect to sexism that I have ever been comfortable with is the incorporation of people's names into examples. For example, consider the following segment:

> "...to change the foreground color of a widget, the user could add the following line to his .Xdefaults file...either that, or he could use the -xrm command line option to the X program..."

This could be changed to the following without sounding awkward:

> "...to change the foreground color of a widget, Mary could add the following to her .Xdefaults file...either that, or she could use her own command-line options parsed by XtAppInitialize( )..."

When I did this kind of thing in college, I was then chastized for being racist because I was *clearly* using white, Anglo-Saxon names. I even had one teacher's assistant think I was highly religious when I tried using biblical names!

There are too many people in the world to offend, and no matter what you do, someone is going to be offended by something. It just depends on what issues the reader happens to be sensitive to. I can just imagine trying to translate this portion of the book to other languages where the cultures are clearly not in tune with American ideas.

I sincerely hope that in time, our culture adopts a new set of terms that everyone can feel comfortable with. But until then, I'm going to use the generic "he." **: – (**

Acknowledgements

This book took over a year to write and compile. It would take another appendix to properly acknowledge everyone involved. These people deserve at least a page, and I don't know how long this will turn out to be, but I'm not holding back.

Tim O'Reilly's usual spendid job of editing was certainly appreciated, but I learned a lot more from him about life, business, myself, and other things that exceed what I ever expected to get out of this project.

Those who worked most closely with me on the project include Irene Jacobson, who dedicated long hours to meticulous editing and support. Her intuition and insistence on proper use of words saved many cuts of Tim O'Reilly's scalpel. David Lewis also gets super-high marks for his excellent feedback, for his technical expertise, and for helping take care of certain Z-Mail ports while I was busy hunched over this computer. More thanks go to the great folks at Z-Code Software, Bart Schaefer and Don Hatch, for not laughing at me when I told people for at least six months that the book would take "just two more weeks now." (I really meant it, too!) Actually, they helped quite a bit with reading nroff'ed manuscripts, and by taking care of the business whenever I was at O'Reilly & Associates' offices in "Bahston."

The figures in this book come in two forms: screendumps and hand-generated figures done by Chris Reilly. What a super job he did—and always on time. And how can I thank Kismet McDonough, Lenny Muellner, Rosanne Wagger, Mike Sierra, Eileen Kramer, and the other production folks at O'Reilly & Associates, who did a wonderful job of copyediting, proofing, page layout, and all the other things that make the difference between a manuscript and a finished book. And that's not all: Ellie Cutler wrote the index; Tony Marotto of Cambridge Computer Associates and Steve Talbott figured out how to scale screen dumps without the moire patterns you see in many books; and, of course, Daniel Gilly took on the enormous job of developing the reference appendices when it became clear that I wouldn't have time.

Enthusiastic applause goes to Libby Hanna (do I get a *real* official OSF/Motif decoder ring now!!??), David Brooks, Scott Meeks, Susan Thompson, Carl Scholz, Benjamin Ellsworth, and the entire cast at OSF in Cambridge for their support. And, of course, *everyone* on the motif-talk mailing list. (I wish I could remember all your names!)

People I can't forget: Bill "Rock" Petro, Akkana, Mike Harrigan at NCD for the terminal, Danny Backx at BIM (sorry I didn't get you any review copies!), John Harkin, and certain folks at Sun that I'd love to mention, but I can't because they're into that *OL-thang* and they wouldn't want to be associated with the *M-word*, Jordan Hayes, Paula "The Associate" Ferguson, and Kee Hinckley (just because he's cool). Also thanks to Ralph Swick and Donna Converse at the X Consortium for being somewhat patient with me.

Added thanks to Lynn Vaughn at CNN for keeping me informed about what's going on in the world, since I have no time to look out the window; to Short Attention-Span Theatre, for keeping me amused; and to Yogurt World, for keeping me fed.

This book was written using a Sun workstation, the *vi* editor (for which I guess I ought to thank Bill Joy), SoftQuad's *sqtroff*, X11R4 and various versions of Motif (1.0 through 1.1.3). The screendumps of Motif programs were done using *xwd*; the output was converted to Post-Script using the Portable BitMap (PBM) library by Jeff Poskanzer.

Dan Heller
August 16, 1991

1

You, Motif, and Everything

This chapter answers the question "Why Motif?" in terms of the development of applications that are "easy enough for your mother to use." It suggests some of the complexities that the programmer has to master in order to make his applications simple.

In This Chapter:

You, Motif, and Everything

1
You, Motif, and Everything

Congratulations! After slaving behind the computer for months, fighting a deadline that seemed impossible to meet, you've finished your software product and it's a big hit. The critics love it, you're in the money, and everyone, including your mother, is buying your new product. Just as everything seems to be going your way, your worst nightmare comes true: your mother calls and asks you how to use it.

An unlikely scenario? Not if you're developing applications to run under the Motif Graphical User Interface (GUI). As a proposed standard for graphical user interfaces, Motif may be implemented on a wide range of computer platforms from large IBM mainframes right down to the PC that your mom may be using. The Open Software Foundation (OSF), developer of the Motif GUI, hopes to reach all kinds of computers and computer users no matter how advanced (or limited) their computer skills may be.

So, will your mom really call you for help? Well, mine did. In fact, she did something worse. She wanted me to explain how to use a software product I *didn't* write. I didn't know how her software worked or even what it was. Fortunately, though, the software was based on Microsoft Windows, which has more than a passing similarity to Motif. The experience of providing technical support to my mother reminded me of some of the fundamental concepts behind the design of a user interface and the role of the application programmer in carrying out that design.

1.1 A True Story

Before I tell my story, let me start with a little background. I have been developing software for the X Window System for several years. Every now and then, when the family gets together for dinner someone always asks the same thing, "So, explain it to me again: just what *is* it that you do?" I launch into my usual speech: "It's called *X Windows*, dad ... uh, no, mom, it's computer software ... it's rather hard to explain, but ..." The attention span lasts only until the next course is served, at which time the discussion turns to new ways for cooking eggplant. Little did I realize that something actually registered with someone in my family, because shortly thereafter, I got a call from my mom.

Mom: Guess what?!

Me: What?

Mom: Our company is switching to a new line of software based on *your* work!

Me: Really? You're going to use electronic mail?

Mom: No, all of our insurance packages use this new software that runs under *Windows*. You wrote that, didn't you?

Me: No, mom. I write software using *X Windows* — and I didn't write X, I just use it. I think you're talking about *Microsoft Windows*. You're using it with your PC, right?

Mom: That's right, but it looks exactly like your software, so I figured you could show me how to use it. I have never seen this stuff before.

(Uh, oh... I see it coming now. Last time she wanted me to help her explain her computer to her, I ended up translating the entire DOS 2.0 user's guide into English, which she conveniently forgot in about a week.)

Me: Mom, I don't know Microsoft Windows, I know *X Windows* and they're not the same . . .

Mom: You mean you won't help me?

Me: You don't understand — I *can't* help you. MS-Windows has nothing to do with X . . .

Silence.

Me: I don't think I'm getting through to you.

Silence.

Me: Ok, I'll be right over . . .

Despite all my explanations of the X Window System, the only keyword my mom remembered was *Windows*. I had high hopes, though, because I was actually going to teach her something related to what I do for a living. And this time she had to listen because her job depended on it.

After some fidgeting with diskettes and other necessary start-up procedures, I finally got Microsoft Windows 3.0 up and running. Sure enough, it looked just like Motif. Several applications came up by default: a clock, an editor of some sort, and a little calendar program. Immediately, the questions started flying at me:

Mom: How do you access those buttons at the top of the window?

Me: Those are called *Pulldown Menus*, and every application has them. They are located in what is called a *MenuBar*.

Mom: What does "F1" mean?

Me: The "F" denotes a *function key* and the "1" indicates it's the *first* function key. Pressing it gives you help depending on where the cursor is. For example ...

Mom (*interrupting*): Why are these keys labeled "ALT?" What do they do?

Me: Oh, those are used in conjunction with other keys. You press "ALT" and then some other key and you get special attention, like ...

Mom (*growing frustrated*): Look what you did. Now there are too many windows up. How do I get back to the one I was using?

Me (*fighting for words*): Well, you see, you can move from one window to the next or between elements *within* a window by using the "TAB" key and possibly some other key like the *control key*, the *shift key*, or the *Alt key* or maybe a combination of several of these keys depending on where you want to go ...

Mom (*sitting back and sighing*): Oh, that's way too complicated, I'll never remember all that. And just *look* at those colors—they're awful.

Me (*trying to sound encouraging*): You can change them using this tool ...

It was a long grueling day, but she eventually figured out how to do most of what she had to do. After she memorized those actions she used most frequently, she seemed quite capable and no longer needed my supervision. Her favorite trick was **Alt-F3**, which closed a window and terminated a program. Because she had several things figured out, I thought I'd dare teach her something new.

Me: You know, if you don't want to use that key sequence, you can define it yourself by ...

Mom (*protecting the computer like it was her only child*): NO! Don't touch anything! I know how to use it now, so don't confuse me any more!

My fault. I figured that since she was pleased that she could change window colors, she'd be eager to make other aesthetic alterations. Her reaction to my offer to teach her how to change keyboard input foreshadowed what was about to come. I was in the other room when I heard a screech: "The computer is broken! The *Alt-F3* thingy you showed me doesn't work any more!" Sure enough, it didn't work on the window she was trying to use it on, but as we discovered, that was the only window on the screen where it didn't work. It turned out that the program she tried it on didn't understand the *Alt-F3 thingy*. It was devastating for my mom and, needless to say, she will never run *that* program again.

We never did get to her new insurance software; we didn't have to. All she needed to learn was how to use the graphical user interface. She now reports having figured out her company's software "all by herself" and I can't take credit for teaching her.

1.2 Basic User-interface Concepts

There are many lessons an application designer can learn from this story. As it so happens, the designer and the application programmer are often the same person. But whether you are the designer of the software or an engineer responsible for implementing someone else's design, there are still some basic principles that will benefit you in your work. Let's begin with the basics drawn from this particular story.

1. All applications running on a user's workstation should have a consistent interface design. Programs that deviate from the expected design will almost assuredly confuse the user even if the changes were intended for the user's benefit. Chances are also high that the user will not want to use the questionable software again.

2. Users rely on rote memory; they will remember seemingly complicated interface interaction techniques provided that the functions they perform are useful and are invoked frequently. There is a limit, however, to how much users want to remember. It is important that essential or frequently used functions follow memorable patterns.

3. Users, especially novices, will probably not want to customize or alter their applications in any way. If they do, the available methods must be as easy and painless as possible.

If you are a cast-in-stone UNIX software engineer, you may be quite skeptical about this last point. It is true that, traditionally, UNIX applications are extremely flexible, offering the user many options for modifying functional or aesthetic details. One of the first things the hard-core X programmer learns is that "the user is always right; if he wants to customize his interface, by God you had better let him."

This principle is absolutely correct. Unfortunately, many early X applications carry it too far and end up "spineless." Many such programs actually require the user to make certain customizations in order for the program to be usable or attractive. For some programs, the problem worsens if unreasonable customization settings are given (because there is no sanity-checking for unreasonable configuration).

So far, such customization issues have not gotten out of hand because UNIX and X applications are used almost exclusively by technical people who understand the environment and know how to work within it. But it is now time to consider users who know absolutely nothing about computers and don't want to—they are only using your software because they *have* to.

1.3 What is Motif?

So, back to Motif. What is it and how can it help you solve your user-interface design goals? To start, Motif is a set of guidelines that specifies how a user interface for graphical computers should *look and feel*. This term describes how an application appears on the screen (the look) and how the user interacts with it (the feel).

Figure 1-1 shows a Motif application.

Figure 1-1. A Motif application

The user interacts with the application by typing at the keyboard, and by *clicking*, *selecting*, and *dragging* various graphic elements of the application with the mouse. For example, any application window can be moved on the screen by moving the pointer to the top of the window's frame (the titlebar), pressing and holding down a button on the mouse, and dragging the window to a new location. The window can be made larger or smaller by dragging any of the resize corners with a press of a mouse button.

Most applications sport "buttons" that can be clicked with the mouse to initiate application actions. Motif uses clever highlighting and shadowing to make buttons (and the border around the application window) look three-dimensional. Buttons appear to be actually pressed in and released when they are clicked on.

A row of buttons across the top of most applications forms a *menu bar*. Clicking on any of the titles in the menu bar pops up a menu of additional buttons. Buttons can also be arranged in palettes that are always visible on the screen. When a button is clicked, the application can take immediate action, or it can pop up an additional window called a *dialog box* that asks the user for more information or presents additional options.

This style of application interaction isn't new to most people, since the Apple MacIntosh popularized it years ago. What is different about Motif is that the graphical user interface specification is designed to be independent of the computer on which the application is running.

Motif was designed by the Open Software Foundation (OSF), a non-profit consortium of companies such as Hewlett-Packard, Digital, IBM, and dozens of other corporations. OSF's charter calls for the development of technologies that will enhance interoperability between computers from different manufacturers. Targeted technologies range from user interfaces to operating systems.

Part of OSF's charter was to choose an appropriate windowing system environment that would enable the technology to exist on as wide a range of computers as possible. It was decided that the OSF/Motif toolkit should be based on the X Window System, a network-based windowing system that has been implemented for UNIX, VMS, DOS, Macintosh, and other operating systems. X provides an extremely flexible foundation for any kind of graphical user interface.

When used properly, the Motif toolkit enables you to produce completely Motif-compliant applications in a relatively short amount of time. At its heart, though, Motif is a *specification* rather than an *implementation*. While most Motif applications are implemented using the Motif toolkit provided by OSF, it would be quite possible for an application implemented in a completely different way to comply with the Motif GUI. The specification is captured in two documents: the *Motif Style Guide*, which defines the external look and feel of applications, and the *Application Environment Specification*, which defines the application programmer's interface (API).[1]

The Motif specifications don't have a whole lot to say about the overall layout of applications. Instead, they focus mainly on the design of the objects that make up a user interface—the menus, buttons, dialog boxes, text entry, and display areas. There are some general rules ("Every application should provide online help, and the help menu should always be the rightmost entry on a menu bar"), but for the most part, the consistency of the user interface relies on the consistent behavior of the objects used to make it up, rather than their precise arrangement.

---

[1] Both have been published for OSF by Prentice-Hall, and are available in most technical bookstores.

The Motif specification is broken down into two basic parts:

1. The output model describes what the objects on the screen look like. This model includes the shapes of buttons, the use of three-dimensional effects, the use of cursors and bitmaps, and the positioning of windows and subwindows. Although some recommendations are given concerning the use of fonts and other visual features of the desktop's, Motif is flexible in most of these recommendations.

2. The input model specifies how the user interacts with the elements on the screen.

The key point of the specification is that consistency should be maintained across all applications. Similar user-interface elements should look and act similarly regardless of the application that contains them.

Motif can be used for virtually any application that interacts with a computer user. Programs as conceptually different as a CAD/CAM package or an electronic mail application will still use the same types of user-interface elements. When the user interface is standardized, the user gets more quickly to the point where he is working with the application, rather than just mastering its mechanics.

My experience with Microsoft Windows and my mother's new software demonstrates how far Motif has come in reaching this goal. I was faced with a window system that I had literally never seen before and an operating system I rarely use (DOS), but that didn't prevent me from using the application. This is not a coincidence; I knew how to use MS-Windows because its user-interface is based on the same principles as Motif. Motif can be seen as a superset of both MS-Windows and Presentation Manager. Even though the others came first, Motif views them as specific implementations of an abstract specification.

The Motif interface was intentionally modeled after the Microsoft's Common User Access (CUA) specifications, which define the interface for Microsoft Windows. The reason for this is twofold: first, there is a proven business model for profiting from an "open systems" philosophy; second, the level of success and acceptance of Micrsoft Windows in the PC world is expected to be quite substantial. As a result, more and more vendors are jumping on the bandwagon, and are supporting Motif as their native graphical interface environment.

Just as my mom becomes more and more familiar with how to use Windows-based software, so too are thousands of other PC users. As the PC world migrates to UNIX and other larger-scale computers, so too will their applications. In order to keep their customer base, the developers of those PC applications will adopt Motif as the GUI for the UNIX versions of their software. As a result, the next few years will see the number of Motif users and developers grow astronomically as Motif becomes the focal point for software and hardware companies alike.

You have two options for making applications Motif-compliant. You can write the entire application yourself (making sure that all your user-interface features conform to the Motif GUI specifications), or you can choose a more realistic option by using a programmer's aid or *toolkit*. This is a collection of prewritten functions that implement all the features and specifications of a particular GUI.

However, toolkits cannot write applications for you, nor can they enforce good programming techniques. They aren't going to tell you that there are too many objects on the screen or that your use of colors is outrageous. The job of Motif is solely to provide consistent appearance and behavior for user-interface controls. So, before we jump into the mechanics of the Motif toolkit, let's take a moment longer with the philosophy of graphical user interfaces.

1.4 Designing User Interfaces

The principles behind an effective user interface cannot be captured in the specifications for Motif or any other GUI. Even though the Motif toolkit specifies how to create and use its interface elements, there is still quite a bit left unsaid. You, the programmer, must take the responsibility to use those elements effectively, helping the user to be as productive as possible. You must take care to keep things simple for the beginner. At the same time, you cannot restrict the more experienced user. This is perhaps the most difficult task facing the programmer in application design.

There is frequently no right or wrong way to design an interface. Good user-interface design is usually a result of years of practice: you throw something at a user, he plays with it, complains, and throws it back at you. Experience will teach you many lessons, although we hope to guide you in the right direction to avoid many of the mistakes and to make the rest of them less painful.

So, rather than having absolute commandments, we rely on *heuristics*, or rules of thumb. Here is a rough list to start with:

* Keep the interface as simple as possible.

* Make direct connections to real-world objects or concepts.

* If real-world metaphors are not available, improvise.

* Don't forget to keep the interface simple.

* Don't restrict functionality to accommodate simplicity.

This may sound flippant, but this is precisely what makes designing an interface so frustrating. Keeping an interface as simple as possible relies on various other factors, the most basic of which is intuition. The user is working with your application because he wants to solve a particular problem or accomplish a specific task. He is going to be looking for clues to spark that connection between the user interface and the preconceived task in his mind. Strive to make the use of an application obvious by helping the user form a mental mapping between the application and real-world concepts or objects. For example, a calculator program can use PushButtons and Text areas to graphically represent the keypad and the one-line display on a calculator. Most simple calculators have the common digit and arithmetic operator keys; a graphical display can easily mimic this appearance. Other examples include a programmatic interface to a cassette player, telephone, or FAX machine. All of these could have graphical equivalents to their real-world counterparts.

The reason these seemingly obvious examples are successful interface approaches is because they take advantage of the fact that most people are already familiar with their real-life counterparts. But there is another, less obvious quality inherent to those objects: they are simple. This is where we get into the major problem concerning interface design: not everything is simple. There isn't always a real-world counterpart to use as a crutch. In the most frustrating cases, the concept itself may be simple, but there may not be an obvious way to present the interaction. Of course, once someone thinks of the obvious solution, it seems odd that it should have been difficult in the first place.

Consider the VCR. Conceptually, a VCR is a simple device, yet statistics say that 70% of VCR owners don't know how to program one. How many times have you seen the familiar **12:00-AM** flashing in someone's living room? Researchers say that this is because most VCRs are poorly designed and are "too featureful." They're half-right; the problem is not that they are too featureful, but that the ways to control those features are too complicated. Reducing the capabilities of a VCR isn't going to make it easier to use; it's just going to make it less useful. The problem with VCRs is that their designers focused on functionality and not enough on usability.

How do you design an interface for a VCR when there is no other object like it? You improvise.

Sure, the VCR is a simple device; everyone understands how one is supposed to work, but few have actually designed one that is easy to use until recently. Maybe you've heard about the new device that, when connected to your VCR, enables you to have a complete TV program guide displayed on your screen in the bar-graph layout similar to the nightly newspaper listings. All you have to do is point and click on the program you want to record and that's it — you're done. No more buttons to press, levels of features to browse through, dials to adjust or manuals to read. At last, the right interface has been constructed. None of the machine's features have been removed. It's just that they are now organized in an intuitive way and are accessible in an simple manner.

This *black box* for VCRs satisfies heuristics 4 and 5. Functionality has not been reduced, yet simplicity has been heightened because a creative person thought of a new way to approach the interface. The lesson here is that no object should be difficult to use no matter how featureful it is or how complex it may seem. You must rely heavily on your intuition and creativity to produce truly innovative interfaces.

Let's return to computer software and how these principles apply to the user-interface design model. The first heuristic is simplicity. This typically involves fewer, rather than more, user-interface elements on the screen. PushButtons, popup menus, colors, and fonts, should all be used sparingly in an application. Often, the availability of hundreds of colors and font styles along with the attractiveness of a three-dimensional interface compels many application programmers to feel prompted, even justified, in using all the bells and whistles. Overuse of these resources will quickly fatigue the user and overload his ability to recognize useful and important information.

Ironically, the potential drawbacks to simplicity are those that are also found in complexity. By oversimplifying an interface, you may introduce ambiguity. If you reduce the number of elements on your screen or make your iconic representations too simple, you may be providing too little information to the user about what a particular interface element is supposed to do. Underuse of visual cues may make an application look bland and uninteresting.

One of Motif's strengths is the degree of configurability that you can pass on to the end user. Colors, fonts, and a wide variety of other resources can be set specifically by the user. This leaves a wide margin of error. You should be aware, however, that once your application ships, its default state is likely to be the interface most people use, no matter how customizable it may be. While it is true that more sophisticated users may customize their environment, you are in ultimate control of how flexible it is. Also, novice users quickly become experts in a well-designed system, so you must not restrict the user from growth.

There is another side to the user-interface coin. That is, not only are many applications complex, but they are intended to be. Such applications are only supposed to be used by sophisticated users. Consider a 747 aircraft, for example. Obviously, these planes are intended to be flown by experts who have years of experience. In this case, aesthetics is not the goal of the interior design of a cockpit; the goal is that of functionality.

In summary, you must evaluate both the goals of your particular application and your intended audience before you can really determine the best interface to use. Remember, your mom just might call you for help.

2

The Motif Programming Model

This chapter teaches the fundamentals of Motif by example. It dissects a simple "Hello, World" program, showing the program structure and style common to all Motif programs. Because much of this material is already covered in detail in Volume Four, X Toolkit Intrinsics Programming Manual, Motif Edition, this chapter can be seen as a refresher, or a light introduction for those who haven't read the earlier book. It makes reference to Volume One and the Motif edition of Volume Four to point out areas that the programmer will need to understand (windows, widgets, events, callbacks, resources, translations), before he can progress with Motif.

In This Chapter:

2

The Motif Programming Model

Though we expect most readers of this book to be familiar with the X Toolkit Intrinsics, this chapter briefly reviews the foundations of Motif in Xt. We do this for several reasons. First, for completeness, we define our terms, so a reader who is unfamiliar with Xt will not be completely at sea if he forges ahead. Second, there are many important aspects of the X Toolkit Intrinsics that we aren't going to cover in this book; this review gives us a chance to direct you to other sources of information about these areas. Third, Motif diverges from Xt in some important ways. A brief review of Xt allows us to point these out up front. Finally, any programmer has his own peculiarities; we can similarly point out some of the particular choices we have made when Xt or Motif provides more than one way to do the same thing.

If you are unfamiliar with any of the concepts introduced in this chapter, please read the first few chapters of Volume Four, *X Toolkit Intrinsics Programming Manual*. Portions of Volume One, *Xlib Programming Manual* (for basic X Window System concepts) and Volume Three, *X Window System User's Guide*, may also be appropriate.

2.1 Basic X Toolkit Terminology and Concepts

As discussed in Chapter 1, *You, Motif, and Everything*, the Motif user-interface specification is completely implementation-independent. In other words, one does not have to use the X Window System to implement a Motif-style graphical user interface (GUI). However, to enhance portability and robustness, the Open Software Foundation chose to implement the Motif GUI using X as the window system and the *X Toolkit Intrinsics* (also known as Xt) as the platform for the application programmer's interface (API).

Xt provides an object-oriented framework for creating reusable, configurable user-interface components called *widgets*. Motif provides widgets for such common user-interface elements as labels, pushbuttons, menus, dialog boxes, scrollbars, and text-entry or display areas. In addition, there are widgets called managers, whose only job is to control the layout of other widgets, so that the application doesn't have to worry about details of widget placement when the application is moved or resized.

A widget operates independently of the application, except through prearranged interactions. For example, a pushbutton widget knows how to draw itself, how to highlight itself when it is clicked on with the mouse, and how to respond to a mouse click (or other user-defined action) by calling an application function.

The general behavior of a widget such as a pushbutton is defined as part of the Motif library. Xt defines certain base *classes* of widgets, whose behavior can be inherited and augmented or modified by other widget classes (its *subclasses*). The base widget classes provide a common foundation for all Xt-based widget sets. A *widget set*, such as Motif's Xm library, defines a complete set of widget classes, sufficient for most user-interface needs. Xt also supports mechanisms for creating new widgets or for modifying existing ones.

Xt also supports lighter-weight objects called *gadgets*, which for the most part look and act just like widgets, but whose behavior is actually provided by a manager widget that contains them. (For example, a pulldown menu pane is made up of pushbutton gadgets rather than pushbutton widgets, with the menu pane doing much of the work that would normally be done by the pushbutton widgets.)

Most widgets and gadgets inherit characteristics from objects "above" them in the class hierarchy. For example, the Motif PushButton class inherits the ability to display a label from the Label widget class, which in turn inherits even more basic widget behavior from its own superclasses. (See Volume Four, *X Toolkit Intrinsics Programming Manual*, for a complete discussion of Xt's classing mechanisms; see Chapter 3, *Overview of Motif Widgets*, for details of the Motif widget class hierarchy.)

The object-oriented approach of Xt means that the application programmer is completely insulated from the code inside of widgets. All he has access to are functions to create, manage, and destroy widgets, plus certain public widget variables known as *resources*. In short, the internal implementation of a widget can change, without requiring changes to the API. A further benefit is that an object-oriented approach forces the programmer to think about the application in a more abstract and generalized fashion, which leads to better design in the long run, and fewer bugs in the short run.

Creating a widget is also referred to as *instantiating* it; that is, you ask the Toolkit for an *instance* of a particular widget class, which can be customized by setting its resources. All Motif PushButton widgets have the ability to display a label; an instance of the PushButton widget class actually *has* a label.

Creating widgets is a lot like buying a car: first you choose the model (class) of car you want, then you choose the options you want, and then you drive an actual car off the lot. There may exist many cars exactly like yours, others that are similar, and others still that are completely different. You can create widgets, destroy them, and even change their attributes just as you can buy, sell, or modify a car by painting it, adding a new stereo, and so on.

Widgets are designed so that many of their resources can be modified by the user at runtime. When an application is run, Xt automatically loads data from a number of system and user-specific files collectively referred to as the *resource database*, and uses it to configure the widgets in the application.

If the application programmer wants to keep the user from modifying resources, he can set their values for a widget when he creates it. This is commonly referred to as *hard-coding* resources.

It is generally considered good practice to hard-code only those resource values that are essential to program operation, and to leave the others configurable. Default values for configurable resources are typically specified in what is called an application-defaults file (more colloquially referred to as the *app-defaults file*), which by convention has the same name as the application, with the first letter capitalized, and is stored in the directory */usr/lib/X11/app-defaults*. The app-defaults file is loaded into the resource database along with other files that may contain different values set by the system administrator or the user. A complex set of precedence rules determines what value a resource will actually get, in the event of conflicts between different settings. See Volume Four for more information on how to set resources in app-defaults files or other resource files.

Whether resource values are read from the resource database or hard-coded in the application, they can usually can be changed "on the fly" from the application via a call to the Xt function `XtVaSetValues( )`.

Motif widgets are prolific in their use of resources. For each widget class, there are many resources that neither the application nor the user will ever need to change. Some of these resources provide fine control over the three-dimensional appearance of Motif widgets (which should typically not be modified, since that would violate the quest for a common application look); others are used internally by Motif to make one large, complex widget appear to the user in a variety of guises.

A particularly important class of resource, which must be set from the application, is a widget's *callback lists*. Each widget that expects to interact with an application publishes one or more callback resources. The application must associate with that resource a pointer to the application function(s) that will be invoked when certain things happen in the widget. For example, a PushButton calls an application function when the user clicks the mouse on the button.

Note, however, that not every event that occurs in a widget results in a callback to an application function. Widgets are designed to handle many events themselves, with no interaction from the application. All widgets know how to draw themselves, for example. They may even provide application-like functionality. For example, a Text widget provides a complete set of editing commands via internal widget functions called *actions*.

Actions are mapped to events in *translation tables*, which can be augmented, selectively overridden, or completely replaced by settings in the widget class, the application, or in a user's resource files.

In the basic Xt design, translations are intended to be configurable by the user. However, the purpose of Xt was to provide mechanism, not impose user-interface policy. In Motif, translations are not typically modified by either the user or the application programmer. While it is possible for an application to install event handlers or new translations and actions, most Motif widgets expect that application interaction will occur only through callbacks.

Because Motif widgets generally disallow changes to their translation tables, translations are discussed very little in this book. At first, the experienced Xt programmer's response is that Motif's limitations on the configurability of translations violates Xt. But consider that Xt is a library for building toolkits, not a toolkit itself. Motif has the further job of ensuring consistent user-interface behavior across applications.

Whether this is sufficient justification for OSF's implementation is a matter of judgement, but it should at least be taken into account. At any rate, you should be aware of this when configuring Motif widgets. Motif provides callback resources to support all of the expected behavior; you should not add actions or modify translations if a widget doesn't have a callback associated with an event you want your application to respond to.

2.2 Motif and Xt Libraries

You create a Motif user interface using both the Motif Xm library and the Intrinsics' Xt library. Xt provides functions for creating and setting resources on widgets. Xm provides the widgets themselves, plus an array of utility and *convenience functions* for creating groups of widgets that are used collectively as a single type of user-interface element. (The Motif MenuBar, for example, is not implemented as one particular widget, but as a collection of smaller widgets put together by one convenience function.)

An application may also need to make calls to the Xlib layer to render graphics or get events from the window system. In the application itself (rather than in the user-interface), you may also be expected to make lower-level system calls into the operating system, filesystem, or hardware-specific drivers. Thus, the whole application may have calls to various libraries within the system. Figure 2-1 represents the model for interfacing to these libraries.

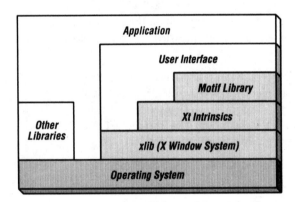

Figure 2-1. User-interface library model

As illustrated above, the application itself may interact with all layers of the windowing system, the operating system, and other libraries (math libraries, rpc, database) as needed. On the other hand, the user-interface portion of the application should restrict itself to the Motif, Xt, and Xlib libraries whenever possible. This will aid in the portability of (at least) the user-interface across multiple computers and operating systems. Since X is a distributed windowing system, once the application runs on a particular computer, it can be displayed on any computer running X—even across a local or wide-area network.

A programmer's hint: in addition to restricting yourself to using the Motif, Xt, and Xlib libraries, you should always try to use the higher-level libraries whenever possible. That is, focus on using the Motif-specific widgets and functions rather than trying to implement equivalent functionality using Xt or Xlib.[1] Higher-level libraries hide a great number of details you would otherwise have to handle yourself. By following these guidelines, you'll find that code complexity and size will be greatly reduced and applications more easily maintained.

In situations where the Motif library does not provide the functionality you need, you may attempt to "borrow" widgets from other toolkits or write your own. This is possible and made relatively simple because Motif is based on Xt.[2] For example, an application might make good use of a general-purpose graphing widget.

Whatever libraries you use, be sure to keep your application modular. The first and most important step in application development is its design. You should always identify the parts of the application that are "functional" (do what the application is supposed to do for the user), and the parts that are the user interface.

Well-designed applications keep the user-interface code separate from the functional code. You should be able to "unplug" the Motif code and replace it with another user-interface widget set based on Xt merely by writing corresponding code that mirrors the Motif implementation.

2.3 Programming Using Xt and Motif

The quickest way to understand the basic programming model for Motif is to look at Example 2-1, a version of the classic "hello world" based on Motif widgets.

Example 2-1. The hello.c program

```
/* hello.c --
 * Initialize the toolkit using an application context and a toplevel
 * shell widget, then create a pushbutton that says Hello using
 * the R4 varargs interface.
 */
#include <Xm/Xm.h>
#include <Xm/PushB.h>

main(argc, argv)
char *argv[ ];
{
    Widget       toplevel, button;
    XtAppContext app;
    void i_was_pushed();
    XmString label;
```

---

[1] An exception to this rule is the use of convenience functions for creating simple widgets, as discussed later in the chapter.

[2] While this book discusses certain methods for extending the Motif library, you should refer to Volume Four, *X Toolkit Intrinsics Manual*, for a general discussion of how to build your own widgets.

Example 2-1. The hello.c program (continued)

```
    toplevel = XtVaAppInitialize(&app, "Hello", NULL, 0,
        &argc, argv, NULL, NULL);

    label = XmStringCreateSimple("Push here to say hello");
    button = XtVaCreateManagedWidget("pushme",
        xmPushButtonWidgetClass, toplevel,
        XmNlabelString, label,
        NULL);
    XmStringFree(label);
    XtAddCallback(button, XmNactivateCallback, i_was_pushed, NULL);

    XtRealizeWidget(toplevel);
    XtAppMainLoop(app);
}
void
i_was_pushed(w, client_data, cbs)
Widget w;
XtPointer client_data;
XmPushButtonCallbackStruct *cbs;
{
    printf("Hello Yourself!\n");
}
```

The output of the program is shown in Figure 2-2.

Figure 2-2. Output of hello.c

Let's take a look at this program step by step, noting elements of both the underlying Xt model and where Motif differs from it.

2.3.1 Header Files

All applications using the OSF/Motif toolkit must include header files for each widget you use in your application. For example, because *hello.c* uses a PushButton widget, we include *<Xm/PushB.h>*. The appropriate header file for each Motif widget class is described in Appendix B, *Xt and Motif Widget Classes*.

If you simply browse through */usr/include/Xm* (or wherever you have installed your Motif distribution) trying to find the appropriate header file to include, you will find that each widget class actually has two header files there. The one whose name ends in a "P" (e.g., *PushBP.h*) is the widget's *private header file*, and should never be included directly by applications. It is used only by the code that implements each widget class (and its subclasses).

Xt uses two header files to hide the details of the widget implementation from the application, thus providing object-oriented encapsulation and data hiding in a language (C) that isn't designed to support object-oriented programming. (See Volume Four for additional information on the object-oriented design of widgets.)

For some types of objects, you may see another pair of header files, each containing a capital G at the end of their names (for example, *PushBG.h* and *PushBGP.h*). The "G" header files are for the gadget version of the object. For the most part, when we talk about widgets, we mean widgets or gadgets. Later chapters will make it clear when to use gadgets and when to use widgets.

In addition to the widget header files, you may of course need other include files specific to your application, such as *<stdio.h>* or *<ctype.h>*.

Multiple Header File Inclusions

A quick examination of the **#include** directives in each of the Motif widget or gadget header files reveals that each of them includes *<Xm/Xm.h>*, the general header file for the Motif library. *<Xm/Xm.h>* in turn includes the following files:

```
#include <X11/Intrinsic.h>
#include <X11/Vendor.h>
#include <Xm/VirtKeys.h>
#include <Xm/VendorE.h>
```

Therefore, none of these files ever need to be included by your application, as long as you include *<Xm/Xm.h>*. This is in contrast to the way you may have been used to in dealing with other toolkits like the Athena toolkit or OLIT (OPEN LOOK Intrinsics Toolkit), which are both Xt-based toolkits.

Further investigation shows that *<Xm/VendorE.h>* includes the following files:

```
#include <Xm/ExtObject.h>
#include <X11/Shell.h>
#include <X11/Vendor.h>
```

If you look closely at the code, you'll see that just about every necessary header file is included the moment you include your widget header files.

We recommend against duplicating the inclusion of header files for two reasons. First, if you include only the header files you need, whoever has to maintain your code will know which widgets you're dealing with in your source files. Second, duplicating header files is generally bad practice because you risk the possibility of redeclaration of macros, functions, variables and so on.

However, it isn't always easy to prevent multiple inclusions. Some files, like *<X11/Vendor.h>*, would be included twice if you expand everything *<Xm/Xm.h>* includes. There is a way to protect files from multiple inclusion that we recommend you incorporate into your own header files as well. This is a method called *ifdef-wrapping*. For example, the ifdef-wrapper for *<X11/Vendor.h>* has:

```
#ifndef _XtVendor_h
#define _XtVendor_h

/* Include whatever is necessary for the file... */
#endif /* _XtVendor_h */
```

The "wrapper" defines **_XtVendor_h** when that file is first included, so if during the course of compiling the *same* source (**.c**) file, the file is ever included again, the **#ifdef** will prevent anything from being redeclared or redefined.

Of course, the wrapper prevents inclusion only on a per-source file basis; the next source file that gets compiled and includes the same files goes through the same test. Here, the same macros, definitions, data types, and function declarations happen again for the benefit of the new file. For this reason, you should *never write functions in header files*. This would be equivalent to having the same function exist in every source file. (Function *declarations* are acceptable and expected.)

The order of inclusion is generally not important unless certain types or declarations required by one file are declared in another. In this case, you should include the files in order of necessity. Application-specific header files are usually included first, UI-specific header files next (with Xt header files, if any, preceding Motif header files), followed by system-specific files.

2.3.2 Initializing the Toolkit

Before any widgets are ever created, you must initialize the toolkit. There are many ways to do this, most of which include performing a number of other related tasks such as opening a connection to the server, loading the resource database, etc. Here's a list of some of the things that are almost always done:

1. Open the application's connection to the X display.

2. Parse the command line for any of a dozen or so standard X Toolkit command-line options plus any custom command-line options you define for your own program.

3. Load the resource database from the app-defaults file, if any, as well as from a number of user, host, and language- or locale-specific resource files.

4. Create the application's top-level window, a Shell class widget that will handle all of the application's interaction with the Motif window manager, *mwm*, and act as the "parent" of all the other widgets in the application.

There are several functions available to do toolkit initialization. The one you'll see us use most often is `XtVaAppInitialize( )`, since it performs all of the functions listed above in one convenient call. Here's the call we used in Example 2-1:

```
Widget          toplevel;
XtAppContext    app;

toplevel = XtVaAppInitialize(&app, "Hello", NULL, 0,
    &argc, argv, NULL, NULL);
```

The widget that is returned by `XtVaAppInitialize( )` is a Shell widget. Shell widgets handle the application's interaction with the window manager, and act as the "top level" window of the application. All other widgets created by the application are created as "children" of the shell (or children of its children). We'll talk more about the implications of this statement later in this chapter.

The Application Context

The first argument to `XtVaAppInitialize( )` is the address of an application context, a structure in which Xt will manage some data internal to Xt that is associated with the application. Most applications do little more with the application context than receive an opaque pointer to it in the toolkit initialization call, and pass that pointer to a few other toolkit functions that require it as an argument. The fact that the application context is a public variable rather than hidden in the toolkit internals is a forward-looking feature of Xt, designed to support multiple threads of control.

The simpler Release 3 initialization call, `XtInitialize( )`, is still supported, but its use is discouraged to provide a greater degree of upward compatibility with future Xt-based applications. This simpler function creates an application context, but it is held by Xt and is generally assumed to be uninteresting to the programmer.

The Application Class

The second argument to `XtVaAppInitialize( )` is a string that defines the *class name* of the application. A class name is used in the resource database to specify values that will apply to all instances of an application, a widget, or a resource. (See Volume Three, *X Window System User's Guide*, and Volume Four, *X Toolkit Intrinsics Programming Manual*, for details.) For many applications, application classes are rarely used, and the class name is important only because it is also used as the name of the application's app-defaults file.

(Recall that whenever widgets are created in Xt, their resources must have certain initial (or default) values. You may either hard-code values, allow them to default to widget-defined values, or you can specify what the default values should be, provided that the user hasn't provided his own default settings. This is where the app-defaults file comes in.)

By convention, the class name is the same as the name of the application itself, except that the first letter is capitalized.[3] For example, a program named *draw* would have a class name

---

[3] Some applications follow the convention that if the application's name begins with an "X", the X is "silent" and so the second letter is capitalized as well. So, for example, the class name of *xterm* is *XTerm*.

of *Draw*, and an app-defaults filename of */usr/lib/X11/app-defaults/Draw*. (Note, however, that there is no requirement that an app-defaults file with this name actually be installed.)

Exceptions can be made to this convention, as long as you document it. For example, all the example programs in this book have the class name of **Demos**, which allows us to set certain common defaults in a single file. This technique might be useful whenever you have a large collection of independent programs that are part of the same suite of applications.

Command-line Arguments

The third and fourth arguments specify an array of command-line arguments defined for your program, if any, and the number of arguments in the array. These arguments are unused in most of the examples in this book, and are specified as **NULL** and **0**, respectively.

The program *xshowbitmap.c* in Appendix D, *More Example Programs*, provides an example of using command-line arguments. See Volume Four, *X Toolkit Intrinsics Programming Manual*, for a more complete discussion.

The fifth and sixth arguments contain the value and count of any actual command-line arguments. The initialization call actually removes (and acts on) any arguments it recognizes (such as the standard X Toolkit command-line options, and any options you've defined in the third argument), so after this call, **argv** should contain only the application name (and any expected arguments such as filenames). You may want to check the argument count at this point, and issue an error message if any spurious arguments are found.

Fallback Resources

The seventh argument is the start of a **NULL**-terminated list of *fallback resources* for the toplevel shell widget created by the initialization call. Fallback resources are a kind of "belt and suspenders" protection against the possibility that an app-defaults file isn't installed. They are ignored if the app-defaults file (or any other explicit resource settings) is found.

It is generally a good idea to provide fallbacks for resources that are essential for your application's operation. An example of how they may be used by an application is shown in the following code fragment:

```
String fallbacks[ ] = {
    "Demos*background: grey",
    "Demos*XmList.fontList: -*-courier-medium-r-*--12-*",
    "Demos*XmText.fontList: -*-courier-medium-r-*--12-*",
    /* list the rest of the app-defaults resources here ... */
    NULL
};
    .
    .
    .
toplevel = XtVaAppInitialize(&app, "Demos", NULL, 0,
    &argc, argv, fallbacks, NULL);
    .
    .
    .
```

When no fallback resources are specified, the seventh argument should be NULL.

Fallback resources will protect your application against a missing app-defaults file, but they won't protect against one that's modified incorrectly or otherwise corrupted, since they aren't used if the app-defaults file is present in any form. This implementation leaves something to be desired. Fortunately, X11 Release 5 introduces a new function called **XrmCombine-Databases( )**, which allows you to provide "real" fallbacks in case the user or the system administrator misconfigures the app-defaults file.

Additional Initialization Parameters

The eighth parameter is the first of a NULL-terminated list of resource-value pairs that are applied to the toplevel widget returned by **XtVaAppInitialize( )**. If there are none (which is often the case for this function), you can pass NULL as the eighth parameter.

If you were to pass any parameters, this would be done just as we will describe for **Xt-VaCreateWidget( )** later in this chapter. All of the functions whose names begin with **XtVa** support the same type of varargs-style (variadic) argument lists that we will demonstrate in that discussion.

NOTE

The X11 Release 4 implementation of **XtVaAppInitialize( )** and other varargs functions may not work entirely as expected for some *non-ANSI* compilers due to a bug in the way the X Toolkit Intrinsics declare variadic functions. *This is only true for some compilers that do not understand function prototypes.* The problem is rare, for the most part, since it is compiler-dependent and only happens on older compilers. This is not a compiler error; it is an Xt error, since you are not supposed to mix fixed parameter declarations with variadic declarations when writing functions. **XtVaAppInitialize( )** is one such function because the first seven parameters are fixed, whereas the eighth-through-nth arguments are variadic. (ANSI allows, and even *requires* this sort of specification.)

If you experience problems such as segmentation faults or bus errors as a result of using **Xt-VaAppInitialize( )**, you can try passing an extra NULL parameter after the final NULL. Another option is to use **XtAppInitialize( )**, which is identical to **XtVaApp-Initialize( )**, but does not contain a variable argument list of resource-values pairs. Instead, it uses the old-style **args** and **num_args** method described in .

2.3.3 Creating Widgets

There is a "convenience function" for creating every class of widget and gadget supported by the Motif toolkit. For example, to create a PushButton widget, you can use the function **Xm-CreatePushButton( )**. To create the corresponding gadget, you'd use **XmCreate-PushButtonGadget( )**. In addition, there are convenience functions for creating objects that are not single widgets, but really collections of other widgets. For example, a

ScrolledList is really a List widget inside a ScrolledWindow widget; `XmCreate-ScrolledList( )` creates both widgets.

The convenience functions for creating each class of widget are listed in Appendix A, *Motif Functions and Macros*. In the body of the book, however, we typically use the Xt functions `XtVaCreateWidget( )` and `XtVaCreateManagedWidget( )` for creating simple widgets. We do this for two reasons. First, these functions allow you to make your own choice of whether to create the widget as *managed* or *unmanaged*. (The Motif convenience functions always create unmanaged widgets.) Second, they allow you to set resources for the widgets using a varargs interface, which is more convenient.

To understand what is meant by managed and unmanaged widgets, consider that X nests windows using a parent-child model. A display screen is defined as the root window; every application has a top-level window that is a child of the root. That top-level window in turn has subwindows, which overlay it, but cannot extend beyond its boundaries without clipping.

Because every widget has its own X window, widgets follow a similar parent-child model. Whenever a widget is created, it is created as the child of some other widget. The shell widget returned by the call to `XtVaAppInitialize( )` is the top-level window of the application. It is usually overlaid with a special class of widget called a *manager*, which implements rules for controlling the size and placement of widget children. For example, the Motif RowColumn widget is a manager that allows widgets to be laid out in regular rows and columns, while a Form is a manager that allows widgets to be placed at precise positions relative to one another. Managers can contain both other managers and the *primitive* widgets that are used to implement actual user-interface controls. Some managers also support *gadgets*, which are lighter-weight objects identical to widgets in appearance, but which do not have their own windows.

In Example 2-1, the button was created as a child of the toplevel window. (Because this is a very simple application containing only one visible widget, no manager was used. Shells are themselves extremely simple managers, understanding only to make themselves exactly the same size as their only child, so as to remain invisible behind it.) Here's the call:

```
button = XtVaCreateManagedWidget("pushme", xmPushButtonWidgetClass, toplevel,
    XmNlabelString, label,
    NULL);
```

The first argument is a string to use as the name of the widget in the resource database. That is, if a user wanted to configure the color of the label in the button in *hello.c*, he would specify it as:

```
hello.pushme.foreground:  blue
```

not as:

```
hello.button.foreground:  blue
```

The resource name of the widget thus need not be identical to the variable name given the widget inside the program, though to minimize confusion, most programmers make them the same. You should always be sure to include in your documentation the names of any widgets that you want the user to be able to configure via resources.

The second argument is the class of the widget to be created. This name is defined in the public header file for the widget, and you can find out what it is for each widget class by referring to Appendix B, *Xt and Motif Widget Classes.*

The third argument is the parent, which must be a manager widget that has already been created. In this example, the parent of the PushButton widget is **toplevel**, the shell widget returned by the call to **XtVaAppInitialize( )**.

The remainder of the argument list is a variable-length list of resource settings. We'll talk about the format of these resource settings in the next section.

2.3.4 Setting and Getting Widget Resources

The Motif convenience functions (and the older Xt functions **XtCreateWidget( )** and **XtCreateManagedWidget( )**) require you to declare resources in a static array, which you pass to the function, along with the number of items in the array. By contrast, the varargs-style functions introduced in X11R4 allow you to specify resources directly in the creation call, as a **NULL**-terminated list of resource-value pairs.

In the **XtVaCreateManagedWidget( )** call from *hello.c,* the only resource set was the string displayed as the PushButton's label. However, other resources could have been set in the same call, as follows:

```
button = XtVaCreateManagedWidget("pushme", xmPushButtonWidgetClass, toplevel,
    XmNlabelString, label,
    XmNwidth, 200,
    XmNheight, 50,
    NULL);
```

which sets the widget to be **200** pixels wide by **50** pixels high, rather than its default, which is to be just big enough to display its label.

There are several things worthy of note here:

- Each widget may define resources of its own, and it inherits resources from its superclass. The names of the resources each widget class provides (whether new or inherited) are documented in Appendix B, *Xt and Motif Widget Classes.* The most useful of the resources are described in detail in the individual chapters on each of the Motif widget classes.

- When you are setting resources in your program, each resource name begins with the prefix **XmN**; these names are *mnemonic constants* that correspond to actual C strings that have the same name without the **XmN** prefix. For example, the actual resource name associated with **XmNlabelString** is **labelString**. The **Xm** identifies the resource as being a Motif-related resource. Xt uses the prefix **XtN** for any resources its base widget classes define; however, Motif also provides corresponding **XmN** names for most of them.[4] The main purpose of the macro definitions for resource names is to allow the C

_____

[4] Some toolkits use the **XtN** prefix even though the resource is not common to all Xt toolkits. The convention has not been used long enough for all vendors to conform to it. If you find that you need access to an Xt-based resource that has no **XmN** constant defined for it, you will need to include the file *<X11/StringDefs.h>.*

preprocessor to catch spelling errors. If you were to use the string `width` rather than the constant `XmNwidth`, your program would still work. However, if you typed `widdth`, the compiler would happily compile away, but your program wouldn't work, and you'd have a difficult time trying to find out why. (Neither Xt nor Motif reports errors or warnings when an unknown resource name is encountered.) On the other hand, if you use `XmNwiddth`, then the compiler would catch the error, and complain that the token is an undefined variable.

When resources are specified from a resource file, or when using the `-xrm` option to specify resources on the command line, the `XmN` is omitted.

- When you set resources in the call to create the widget, those resources are no longer configurable by the user. Such resources are said to be *hard-coded*. For example, because we've set the width and height of the PushButton in the call to `XtVaCreate-ManagedWidget( )`, a user resource specification of the form:

```
*pushme.width:  250
*pushme.height: 100
```

would be ignored. It is generally recommended that you hard-code only those resources that are absolutely required by your program. Most widgets have reasonable defaults for many of their resources, and those that do not should be set in an app-defaults file. (As mentioned earlier, every Xt-based application will look for default application resource settings in a file in the directory */usr/lib/X11/app-defaults*, where the file's name is the same as the "class name" argument to the toolkit initialization function. There are numerous other sources of resource values; see Volume Three or Volume Four for additional details.)

Despite this admonition, to simplify the presentation, most of the examples in this book set their resources directly in the application. Don't take this as an example of recommended practice, but rather, of pedagogical convenience.

- Each resource has a data type, which is defined by the widget class (or inherited from a superclass). When resources are specified in a resource file, Xt automatically converts the resource value from a string (which is the only way it can be specified in a text file) to the appropriate type. However, when you set a resource in your program, you must provide the value in the appropriate type. For example, the PushButton widget expects its label to be a compound string (see Chapter 19, *Compound Strings*), so we had to allocate the string and free it when we were done:

```
label = XmStringCreateSimple("Push here to say hello");
    .
    .
    .
XmStringFree(label);
```

It is possible to invoke Xt's resource type converters from within a varargs list by using the keyword `XtVaTypedArg` followed by four additional parameters: the resource whose value is going to be set, the type of value you are providing (Xt will figure out the type it needs to be converted to), the value itself, and the size of the value's data in bytes. As an example, if we wanted to specify the background color directly in our program, and didn't want to call Xlib functions to allocate a colormap entry, we could say:

```
button = XtVaCreateManagedWidget("pushme", xmPushButtonWidgetClass,
    toplevel, XmNlabelString, label,
        XtVaTypedArg, XmNbackground, XmRString, "red", strlen("red")+1,
    NULL);
```

The data type is specified in this construct not using the familiar C types, but using a special symbol called a *representation type*, which is defined by Xt.

These symbols are defined in just the same way as the **XmN** symbols used for resource names. It is the **N** that identifies the symbol as being a resource *name*. An **XmR** prefix identifies a name to be a representation type.[5] See Volume Four for more information on resource type conversion and the possible values for representation types.

Setting Resources After Widget Creation

Resources may be set after a widget has been created using **XtVaSetValues( )**. The values set by this function will override any values set in either the widget creation call or in the resource database (which are applied when the widget is created).

The syntax for using **XtVaSetValues( )** is:

```
XtVaSetValues(widget_id,
    attribute-value list,
    NULL);
```

The **widget_id** is the value returned from a widget-creation call and the *attribute-value list* is a NULL-terminated list of resource names and associated value pairs (the last resource "name" is the NULL pointer).

Some Motif widget classes also provide convenience routines for setting some of their resources. For example, **XmToggleButtonSetState( )** sets a ToggleButton's **Xm-Nset** resource to either **True** or **False**. Those convenience functions that are available are listed in Appendix A, *Motif Functions and Macros*, or in the chapters on each widget class.

The primary advantage of using convenience functions over the more generic **XtVaSet-Values( )** function is that the convenience functions have direct access to the internal fields in the widget's data structures, and so they might have slightly better performance. Functionally, however, the two methods should be interchangeable.

---

[5] You may also see symbols with the prefix **XmC** or **XtC**. These symbols identify resource *classes*.

Getting Resource Values

The routine used to *get* values for a widget resource is **XtVaGetValues( )**. Its syntax is exactly the same as **XtVaSetValues( )** except that the value part of the attribute-value pair is the *address* of a variable that will assume the widget's resource value. For example:

```
extern Widget    label;
XmString         str;
Dimension        width;
...
XtVaGetValues(label,
    XmNlabelString, &str,
    XtNwidth,        &width,
    NULL);
```

This call gets the label string and the width for a Label widget.

There are some things to be very careful about when getting resource values from widgets. First, always pass the *address* of the type of object you are getting. Notice that we passed the address of the **str** variable even though it is already an address by definition. That is, do *not* do the following:

```
extern Widget label;
char          buf[ 80 ];
int           width;

XtVaGetValues(label,
    XmNlabelString,  buf,      /* do not do this */
    XtNwidth,        &width,
    NULL);
```

Programmers new to Xt and Motif do this with the expectation that **XtVaGetValues( )** will "fill in" **buf** with the appropriate value. This is not the case—values represented by pointers are not copied into address space. What the get routine does is set the value for the address of a pointer to the position of the internal variable that is holding the desired value. Because **buf** is an array, not a pointer, the get routine cannot move its address. By passing the address of a pointer (that does not point to any actual data space), **XtVaGetValues( )** is able to reset the pointer to the correct internal value.[6] This is not the case for the **width** value because that value is an **int** and its value is copied accordingly.

Another thing to be careful about is changing the values of variables that have been returned by **XtVaGetValues( )**. In the case of variables of type **int** (or any type whose size is less than or equal to the size of the typedef **XtArgVal**), the value can be changed since the variable does not point to the internal data for the widget. However, if the variable is a string or data structure pointer and you passed the address of that pointer, you must be sure not to change the contents dereferenced by the pointer or you will change the internal contents of the widget.

---

[6] The Motif toolkit deviates from the Xt specifications and sometimes sets the given address to allocated data, which must be freed when no longer needed. This occurs when getting "compound string" resources from widgets and when getting the "text" (a **char** pointer) from Text widgets. These cases are discussed in Chapter 15, *Text Widgets*, and Chapter 19, *Compound Strings*.

There are many pitfalls for the unwary in Xt and Motif.

To set a widget variable, you should be using **XtVaSetValues( )** on an approved resource name. This ensures that the widget can redraw and manage itself appropriately.

Motif also provides convenience routines for getting the resource values from certain widget classes. For the most part, these functions correspond directly to those functions that set values, but they usually allocate memory that is returned. For example, **XmTextGetString( )** allocates space for and returns a pointer to the text in the Text widget.

You might wonder why the convenience routines allocate space, when the **XtVaGetValues( )** function doesn't. The reason is that the convenience routines are defined by Motif. Motif has no right to redefine the behavior of standard Xt functions, but it has every right to define its own behavior.

When a convenience function is available, we recommend using it.

Using Argument Lists

While we use the variadic functions almost exclusively in this book, you should know how to use the old-style argument lists needed by the Motif widget-creation functions.

The Motif convenience functions (and some Xt functions like **XtCreateWidget( )** and **XtCreateManagedWidget( )**) require you to set resources in a separately declared array of objects of type **Arg**. You pass this array to the appropriate function you are using, along with the number of items in the array. For example, the following code fragment creates a PushButton widget similar to that shown in *hello.c*, but this time using a Motif convenience routine:

```
Arg args[1];

XtSetArg(args[0], XmNlabelString, label);
button = XmCreatePushButton(toplevel, "pushme", args, 1);
XtManageChild(button);
```

For all Motif convenience routines, the first argument is the parent of the widget about to be created, the second argument is the widget's name, the third and fourth arguments are the array of resource specifications and the number of resources given in the array. The widget class being created is reflected in the name of the convenience function, and so doesn't need to be specified as an argument. For example, **XmCreateLabel( )** creates a Label widget.

There are also generic (but non-varargs) Xt functions that can be used to create widgets. These functions take a different set of parameters:

```
Arg args[ 1 ];

XtSetArg(args[ 0 ], XmNlabelString, label);
button = XtCreateWidget("pushme", xmPushButtonWidgetClass, toplevel, args, 1);
XtManageChild(button);
```

Here, the name of the widget is the *first* parameter, the widget class to use is the *second* parameter, and the parent is the *third* parameter. The fourth and fifth parameters are resource specifications, as in the Motif convenience routines.

The `Arg` method of setting resources is quite clumsy and error-prone, since it requires you to declare an array beforehand (either locally or statically) and make sure it has enough elements. It is quite common for programmers to forget to increase the size of the array when new resource-value pairs are added, which usually results in a segmentation fault.

However, in spite of the disadvantages of this method for setting resources, there are still cases where the convenience routines may be useful. This is especially true when the routine creates several widgets and arranges them in some predefined way consistent with the *Motif Style Guide*.

Another situation where the `Arg`-style functions might be useful is when you have a number of different resources that should be set depending on runtime constraints. For example, the following code fragment creates a widget whose foreground color is set only if the application knows it is using a color display:

```
extern Widget parent;
Arg args[5];
Pixel red;
int n = 0;

XtSetArg(args[n], XmNlabelString, label);
n++;
if (using_color) {
    XtSetArg(args[n], XmNforeground, red);
    n++;
}
    .
    .
    .
widget = XtCreateManagedWidget("name", xmLabelWidgetClass, parent, args, n);
```

If the `using_color` Boolean variable were `False`, then the `XmNforeground` resource would not be set.

Last, using the old-style routines allows you to pass the exact same set of resources to more than one widget. Since the contents of the array are unchanged, you can reuse it for as long as the array is still available. (Be careful of scoping problems like using a local variable outside of the function where it was declared.) For example, the following loop creates a number of widgets that all have the same hard-coded resources:

```
static char *labels[ ] = { "A Label", "Another Label", "Yet a third" };
XmString xm_label;
Widget widget, rc;
Arg args[ 3 ];
int i;

/* Create an unmanaged RowColumn widget parent */
rc = XtCreateWidget("rc", xmRowColumnWidgetClass, parent, NULL, 0);

/* Create RowColumn's children -- all 50x50 with different labels */
XtSetArg(args[ 0 ], XmNwidth, 50);
XtSetArg(args[ 1 ], XmNheight, 50);
for (i = 0; i < XtNumber(labels); i++) {
    xm_label = XmStringCreateSimple(labels[ i ]);
    XtSetArg(args[ 2 ], XmNlabelString, xm_label);
    widget =
        XtCreateManagedWidget("label", xmLabelWidgetClass, rc, args, 3);
    XmStringFree(xm_label);
}

/* Now that all the children are created, manage RowColumn */
XtManageChild(rc);
```

Each Label widget is created with the same width and height hard-coded in its resource settings. Each widget's **XmNlabelString** resource is also hard-coded, but is distinct from
the others. All other resource settings can be set in resource files. You may note that to set
resources in external files, you need to specify the widgets' names, which in this case are all
set to the same value: **"label"**. Yes, it is perfectly legal to give the same name to more
than one widget. By doing so, all resource values specified outside of the application will
affect all widgets with that name, provided that the widget tree matches the resource specification. For example, you can set all the above Labels' foreground colors to "red" using the
following resource specification:

```
*rc.label.foreground: red
```

If there were other widgets in the application that had the widget name of "label" (and they
weren't children of a widget by the name of "rc"), their foreground colors would not be
affected by this specification.

Obviously, whether you really want to do something like this is dependent on your application. The names of the widgets you choose to use may make certain things easier for your
application to handle (e.g., maintaining consistency). For example, the resource name of the
widget is rarely identical to the variable name given the widget inside the program, though to
minimize confusion, some programmers make them the same anyway. (In fact, this is what
we did with the **rc** widget.)

Note that we could have used the elements of the **labels** array as widget names, but in this
example, these array elements contain spaces, which by definition are "illegal" widget
names. If you want to allow the user to specify resources on a per-widget basis, then you
cannot use spaces (or other non-alphanumeric characters other than the hyphen (-) and the
underscore (_)). If that is not a concern, then you can give your widgets any name you like
— even **NULL** or the null string (" ").

Be careful, though, since giving a widget an illegal name does not prevent the user from specifying resources on those widgets entirely; he can still set resources on widget *classes*:

```
*rc.XmLabel.foreground: red
```

This resource setting will cause all Label widgets to have a foreground color of red, regardless of the names of those widgets (and provided that each widget instance doesn't have a hard-coded value for `XmNforeground`). See Volume Four for a discussion of appropriate widget names and further details of resource specification syntax.

Whatever you do, you should always be sure to include in your documentation the names of any widgets that you want the user to be able to configure via resources.

2.3.5 Event Handling for Widgets

Once widgets have been created and configured, they must be hooked up to application functions. This is done by means of widget resources known as *callback resources*.

Before we can talk about callback resources and callback functions, though, we need to say more about events.

In one sense, the essence of X programming is the handling of asynchronous events. Events can occur in any order, in any window, as the user moves the pointer, switches between the mouse and the keyboard, moves and resizes windows, or invokes functions available through graphical user interface elements.

You can think of X as a system for demultiplexing a continuous stream of events that occur on a workstation or X terminal, and dispatching the events to the appropriate applications, and to the separate windows that make up each application.

Xlib provides many low-level functions for handling events. There are special cases in which you may need to dip down to this level, which are described appropriately later in this book. Xt simplifies event-handling because widgets handle many events for you, without any application interaction. For example, widgets know how to redraw themselves, so they respond automatically to exposure (the event that is generated when one window is covered up by another, and then uncovered). These kind of "widget survival skills" are handled by functions called *methods* deep in the widget internals. Methods typically include code to redraw the widget, to respond to changes in resource settings resulting from calls to `Xt-VaSetValues( )`, and to free any allocated storage when the widget is destroyed.

Actual widget functionality—the kinds of things that the user-interface specifications requires the widget to do in response to user events—is typically handled by *action functions*. Each widget defines a table of events that it will respond to (a *translation table*), and maps each event, or sequence of events, to one or more actions.

Consider the PushButton in *hello.c*. Run the program, and note how the widget highlights its border as the pointer moves into it; watch how it displays in inverse video when you click on it, and switches back when you release the button. See how the highlighting disappears when you move the pointer out of the widget. Also, notice how pressing RETURN or the SPACEBAR while the pointer is in the widget has the same effect as clicking on it. These are the kinds of things that are captured in the widget's translation table:

```
<Btn1Down>:                         Arm( )
<Btn1Down>,<Btn1Up>:                Activate( ) Disarm( )
<Btn1Down>(2+):                     MultiArm( )
<Btn1Up>(2+):                       MultiActivate( )
<Btn1Up>:                           Activate( )
                                    Disarm( )
<Key>osfSelect:                     ArmAndActivate( )
<Key>osfActivate:                   ArmAndActivate( )
<Key>osfHelp:                       Help( )
~Shift ~Meta ~Alt <Key>Return:     ArmAndActivate( )
~Shift ~Meta ~Alt <Key>space:      ArmAndActivate( )
<EnterWindow>:                      Enter( )
<LeaveWindow>:                      Leave( )
```

The translation table contains a list of *event translations* on the left side, with a set of *action functions* on the right side. If any of the events specified on the left occur, the action function on the right is invoked. As we described earlier, moving in and out of the PushButton causes some visual feedback. The events generated were `<EnterWindow>` and `<Leave-Window>`, and the actions they invoke are `Enter( )` and `Leave( )`, respectively.

As another example, if the first (left) mouse button is pressed down, the `Arm( )` action routine is called, which contains the code to display the button as if it were "pressed in" (as opposed to "pushed out"). A release of the same button invokes both the `Activate( )` and `Disarm( )` routines (in that order), which contain code to redraw the button.

Here is where your application actually steps in: if your application has provided an appropriate callback function, the widget's `Activate( )` action will call it.

2.3.6 Event Specifications

In the Xt syntax, events are specified using symbols that are tied fairly closely to pure X hardware events, such as "ButtonPress" or "EnterWindow." For example, the way to specify a Button 1 press is `<Btn1Down>`. KeyPress events are indicated by symbols called *keysyms*, which are hardware-independent symbols representing individual keystrokes. (Different keyboards may produce different hardware *keycodes* for the same key; the X server uses keysyms as a portable representation, based on the common labels found on the tops of keys.)

Motif provides a further level of indirection in the form of *virtual keysyms*, which describe key events in a completely device-independent manner. For example, `osfActivate` simply means that the user invoked some sort of action that Motif considers to be an "activating action." This typically corresponds to the RETURN key being pressed. Similarly, `osfHelp` corresponds to any one of several possible user requests for help (the HELP or F1 keys on the keyboard).

Virtual keysyms are supposed to be provided by the vendor of the user's hardware based on the keys on the keyboard, but some X vendors also provide keysym databases to support multiple keyboards. The X Consortium will also provide a virtual keysym database in the file */usr/lib/X11/XKeysymDB* by default as of X11 Release 5. This file contains a number of predefined key bindings that OSF has registered with the X Consortium to support actions in the Motif toolkit.

Virtual keysyms are usually invoked by physical events, but the Motif toolkit goes one step further and defines them in the form of *virtual bindings*. Here's the translation table for the PushButton widget expressed using virtual bindings:

```
BSelect Press:          Arm( )
BSelect Click:          Activate( ) Disarm( )
BSelect Release:        Activate( ) Disarm( )
BSelect Press 2+:       MultiArm( )
BSelect Release 2+:     MultiActivate( ) Disarm( )
KActivate:              ArmAndActivate( )
KSelect:                ArmAndActivate( )
KHelp:                  Help( )
```

Examples of virtual bindings are **BSelect,** which corresponds to the first (leftmost) mouse button, and **KHelp** which is usually the HELP key on the keyboard. (The rule of thumb is that any virtual binding beginning with a "B" involves a mouse button event, and any binding beginning with a "K" involves a keyboard event.) More than one event can be bound to a single virtual keysym. For example, because the *Motif Style Guide* also permits F1 to be the "help key," that key is also virtually bound to **KHelp**.

Virtual bindings can be specified by the system administrator, by the user, or by applications using resources. The user has the additional flexibility of having a file called *.motifbind* in his home directory. For example, some people use keyboards on which the BACKSPACE key is in a particularly difficult location for frequent access. They might prefer using the DELETE key to do their backspacing (or vice-versa). These people find the default actions taken by the Motif Text widget annoying, since they cannot backspace using their "normal" backspace key.

Since Xt allows the application or the user to override, augment, or replace translation tables, the first thing most people familiar with Xt think of doing is specifying a new translation for the delete key to invoke the function that "backspaces" in a Text widget. However, this is not the right approach. The Text widget has the following translation:

```
<Key>osfBackSpace:  delete-previous-char( )
```

That is, the *virtual keysym* **osfBackSpace** is bound to **delete-previous-char( )** (which is the backspace action). The solution is not to change the translation table to specify that the **<Key>Delete** event should invoke this action, but for the user to redefine the virtual event to match the translation table. The following virtual binding can be placed in the user's *.motifbind* file:

```
osfBackSpace : <Key>Delete
```

This binding specifies that the physical DELETE key is mapped to the **osfBackSpace** virtual binding. That way, the virtual keysym will be activated and perform the desired function. Better yet, the Text widget is not the only place that is affected; any widget in the Motif toolkit that might want to use the **osfBackSpace** key will now work with the physical DELETE key. The interface now remains consistent and nothing in the toolkit or the application needs to change.

Virtual bindings can also be set using the resource **XmNdefaultVirtualBindings**. The value of this resource is the same as that of the motifbind file:

```
*defaultVirtualBindings: \
    osfBackSpace : <Key>Delete    \n\
    other bindings
```

The one difference from the syntax of the *.motifbind* file is that the resource value specification must have a newline character (in the form of \n) between each entry.

The complete syntax of Motif virtual bindings is explained in the introduction to Appendix B, *Xt and Motif Widget Classes*.

Callbacks

Translations and actions allow a widget class to define associations between events and widget functions. But beyond a certain point, a widget is helpless. A complex widget, such as the Motif text widget, is almost an application in itself. (Its actions provide a complete set of editing functions.) Yet somewhere along the line, control must be passed from the widget to the application.

A widget that expects to call an application function defines one or more callback resources. This is the hook on which the application can hang its functions. For example, the Push-Button widget defines resources called **XmNactivateCallback**, **XmNarmCallback**, and **XmNdisarmCallback**.

That the callback resource names bear a resemblance to the names of the widget's actions is no accident: in addition to doing its job of highlighting the widget, each action also calls an application function, if any, that is associated with a callback of the same name. Note that there is no intrinsic reason why callbacks should be called by actions; a widget could install low-level event handlers to do the same thing. However, you will find that this convention is followed by most widgets.

Figure 2-3 illustrates the event-handling path that results in an application callback being invoked. The widget's translation table registers the widget's "interest" in a particular type of event. When the Intrinsics receive an event (such as a button press) that happens in a widget's window, they test the event against the translation table. If there is no match, the event is thrown away. If there is a match, the event is passed to the widget, and one of its action functions is invoked. (As mentioned earlier, certain events, such as exposure, are handled by lower-level functions called widget methods.)

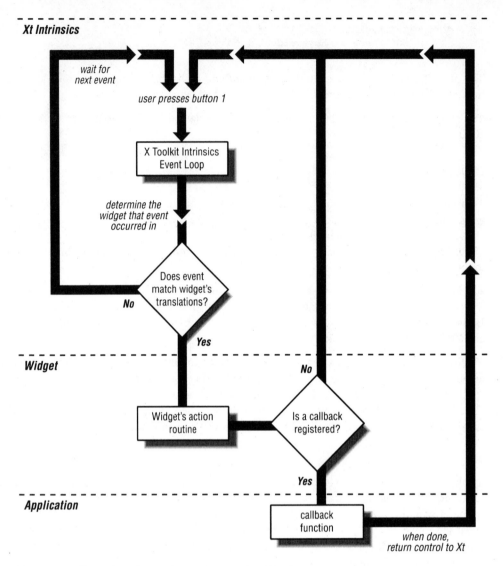

Xt Intrinsics

wait for
next event

user presses button 1

X Toolkit Intrinsics
Event Loop

determine the
widget that event
occurred in

Does event
match widget's
translations?

No

Yes

Widget

No

Widget's action
routine

Is a callback
registered?

Yes

Application

callback
function

when done,
return control to Xt

Figure 2-3. Event-handling using actions and callbacks

The action may perform a function internal to the widget, such as changing the widget's appearance (for example, highlighting a button). Depending on its design, it may then pass control back to an application callback function. If an action is associated with a callback resource, it checks to see if a callback function has been add for that resource, and if so, dispatches the callback.

There are several ways to connect an application function to a callback resource. The most common is to call `XtAddCallback( )`, as demonstrated in *hello.c*:

```
void i_was_pushed( );
                    .
                    .
                    .
XtAddCallback(button, XmNactivateCallback, i_was_pushed, NULL);
```

The first argument is the widget in which the callback is to be installed; the second is the name of the callback resource; and the third a pointer to the callback function. The fourth argument is referred to as "client data." It will be passed to the callback function when it is called. Here, the client data is `NULL`.

The type of the client data is technically any value that has the same size as `XtPointer`. `XtPointer` is a type that is usually the same as a `char` pointer, and is typically represented by a 32-bit value. Thus, you usually pass pointers to variables, data structures, arrays and so on. You may *not* pass actual data structures; you'll get undefined results if you try this. Also, you may pass variables of type `int` or `char`, but understand that you are only passing the data by *value*, not by *reference*. If you want to pass variables and have the callback routine be able to change the variable's value, then you must pass the address of the variable. If you do this, also take care that the variable is a global, not a local. Local variables lose their scope once you return from the routine that calls `XtAddCallback( )`.

As for the callback function itself, it is passed the widget, the client data, if any, and a third argument, generically referred to as "call data."

The *signature* of the callback function can be expressed in one of two ways: as an *ANSI-compliant function prototype*, or using the older style conventions of K&R C. The ANSI-style function declaration is as follows:

```
i_was_pushed(Widget w, XtPointer client_data, XtPointer call_data)
```

In the strictest sense, this is the proper way to handle function declarations and signatures (declaring the types of the parameters to the function). However, while this convention is good style and recommended for upwards compatibility for the future, most compilers today will still understand the older style conventions:

```
i_was_pushed(w, client_data, call_data)
    Widget w; XtPointer client_data; XtPointer call_data;
```

Since this is the least common denominator, your best bet is to use the second, more portable method. In the course of the book, we usually know the types of the parameters being passed to the function, so we declare them right up front in the declarations. For example, the `i_was_pushed( )` function is known to have the following values:

```
void
i_was_pushed(w, client_data, cbs)
Widget w;
XtPointer client_data; /* unused */
XmPushButtonCallbackStruct *cbs;
{
    printf("Hello Yourself!\n");
}
```

The first parameter is known to be a **Widget,** so it is declared as such. The second parameter is known to be unused, so we give it its default type of **XtPointer** and never reference it in the function. The third parameter is always the same for Motif-based callback functions: it is a structure containing information specific to the widget class that invoked the callback function, as well as information about the event that triggered the callback. There is a generic form, **XmAnyCallbackStruct,** with variations for each widget class. The **XmAny-CallbackStruct** is as follows:

```
typedef struct {
    int       reason;
    XEvent *event;
} XmAnyCallbackStruct;
```

The callback structures for each widget class are documented in their associated chapters and in Appendix C, *Motif Data Types.* For example, the **XmPushButtonCallbackStruct** is defined as follows:

```
typedef struct {
    int       reason;
    XEvent *event;
    int       click_count;
} XmPushButtonCallbackStruct;
```

All of the callback structures contain at least the two fields found in **XmAnyCallback-Struct.** The **reason** field is always filled in with a symbolic value that indicates why the callback was called. These values are defined in */usr/include/Xm/Xm.h,* and are usually self-explanatory. For example, in the case of an **XmPushButtonCallbackStruct, reason** is going to be **XmCR_ACTIVATE** when the button is clicked. Obviously, if you already know that the callback is from a PushButton, this is small news; however, it does make it easy to write callback routines that could be called by more than one type of widget. Testing the **reason** field can then help you determine the appropriate response to take.

Similarly, because the widget is always passed in to the callback function, you can always find out what widget caused the function to be invoked. Furthermore, you are passed the actual event, which can provide a great deal more useful information. See Volume Four, *X Toolkit Intrinsics Programming Manual,* for information on how to interpret the contents of events; that subject is not discussed at length in this book (though our examples frequently take advantage of events that are passed in).

The Event Loop

Once all the widgets are created and managed, and all callbacks registered, it's time to start the application running. This is the purpose of the final two calls in **main( ):**

```
XtRealizeWidget(toplevel);
XtAppMainLoop(app);
```

Realizing a widget means to actually create its window. When you call *XtRealizeWidget( )* on the top-level widget of the application (the one returned by the call to **XtVaApp-Initialize( )**), Xt recursively traverses the hierarchy of widgets in the application, creating windows for each one. Until that point, the widgets exist only as data structures on the client side of the X connection. After this call, the widgets are fully instantiated, with windows, fonts, and other X server data in place. What's more, that first **Expose** event (bane of beginning Xlib programmers), without which no drawing will actually appear on the screen, is actually generated, and the application is displayed.

The call to **XtAppMainLoop( )** turns control of the application over to the X Toolkit Intrinsics. Xt handles the dispatching of events to the appropriate widgets, which in turn pass them to the application via callbacks. The application code is idle until summoned to life by user-generated events.

2.4 Summary

We've looked at the skeleton of a simple Motif program. Every application follows more or less the same plan:

1. Initialize the X Toolkit Intrinsics.

2. Create and manage widgets.

3. Configure widgets by setting their resources.

4. Register callbacks to application functions (and of course, write those functions, the meat of the application!).

5. Realize the widgets, and turn control over to Xt's event loop.

How this skeleton is fleshed out in a real application is the subject of the next chapter. Chapter 3 addresses the role of manager widgets in laying out the user interface, the use of dialog boxes and other popups for transient interactions with the user, the many specialized types of widgets available in Motif, and other essential concepts. Once you've read that chapter, you should have sufficient foundation to read the remaining chapters in any order.

Motif Programming Model

3

Overview of Motif Widgets

This chapter helps the reader understand what has to go into a real application: details of geometry management of primitive widgets within some kind of main window, when to fit things into the main window and when to use popups (dialog boxes and menus), and how applications relate to the window manager. After reading this chapter, the programmer should have a solid overview of Motif application programming, and should be able to read the remaining chapters in any order.

In This Chapter:

3

Overview of Motif Widgets

In Chapter 2, *The Motif Programming Model*, we talked about the basic structure of Xt-based programs—how to initialize the toolkit, create and configure widgets, link them to the application, and turn control over to Xt's main loop. In this chapter, we discuss what widgets there are in the Motif toolkit, and how you put them together into an effective application.

If you already have a sense of what the widgets are, you can jump ahead to any of the later chapters in the book, which focus on individual widget classes. However, this chapter does provide some insight about the intended design of the widgets and a general overview of the Motif style and methodology.

3.1 The Motif Style

You don't build a house by nailing together a bunch of boards; you have to design it from the ground up before you really get started. Even with a prefabricated house, where many of the components have already been built, you need a master plan for putting them together.

When programming a GUI, you have to think about the tasks your application is going to perform. Then you must envision the interface, and learn to use your tools effectively so you can create what you've envisioned.

Motif's "toolbox" contains basic items that you can assemble into a graphical user interface. However, without design schematics, the process of assembling the user-interface elements may become ad hoc or inconsistent. Here is where the *Motif Style Guide* comes in—it presents a set of guidelines for how widgets should be assembled and grouped as well as how they function and interact with the user.

All Motif programmers should be intimately familiar with the *Style Guide*. This book is not a replacement for it. While we do make recommendations for Motif style from time to time, and the toolkit itself enforces many aspects of this style, there are many aspects of the Motif style that are not covered in detail here, because they involve the content of the application, rather than just the mechanics.

On the other hand, neither is the *Motif Style Guide* an instructional manual for the Motif toolkit. In fact, many of the objects described in the *Style Guide* are not even widgets, but are higher-level, more complex objects that may be made up of many widgets. For example, the *Style Guide* describes an object called a menu bar, which spans the top of the application's main window. The menubar contains menu titles that, when clicked on, display pulldown menus. Figure 3-1 shows a typical menubar and a pulldown menu.

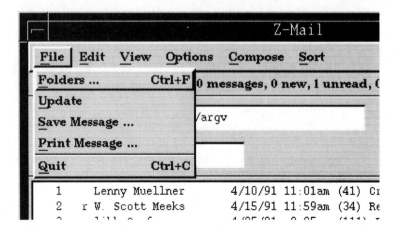

Figure 3-1. A MenuBar provides pulldown menus

The Motif toolkit doesn't implement menus as a distinct widget class, nor, in fact, does the *Style Guide* make any recommendations for how a menu object should be implemented.

What the *Style Guide* does talk about (albeit somewhat loosely) is the actions that are taken by the items on the menu: they may invoke application functions, popup *dialog boxes* that have yet more options and commands, or they may display other *cascading menus* (also known as *pullright menus*).

The *Style Guide* also makes recommendations about what menus an application should provide. For example, most applications should have a **File** menu that provides items such as a **Quit** button to exit the application and a **Save** button that pops up a dialog to prompt for a filename. It also specifies details of presentation, such as that you should provide an ellipsis (**. . .**) as part of the label for a menu item that generates a dialog box rather than executing an immediate action.

How the Motif toolkit goes about supporting the recommendations of the *Motif Style Guide* opens up some interesting points, particularly in relation to some of the underlying principles of the X Toolkit Intrinsics.

In Xt, widgets are envisioned as self-contained objects, each of which is designed to carry out a specific, clearly-defined function. This is the case with many of the Motif widgets. Labels, PushButtons, Scrollbars, and many other common interface objects are implemented as separate widgets. In other cases, Motif creates compound objects out of several widgets, and expects you to treat them as if they were a single object. For example, Motif provides ScrolledText and ScrolledList objects, which combine Text or List widgets with a Scrolled-Window widget (which in turn automatically manages horizontal and vertical scrollbars).

In still other cases, the Motif toolkit provides complex, general-purpose widgets that can be configured to appear in several guises. For example, there is no MenuBar widget class, and no PulldownMenu widget class. Instead, the RowColumn widget (which also serves as a general-purpose manager widget) has resources that allow it to be configured as either a menu bar or a pulldown menu pane.

In order to allow the programmer to think of ScrolledTexts, MenuBars, and pulldown menus as distinct objects, the Motif toolkit provides convenience functions that make it appear as though you are creating discrete objects when, in fact, you aren't. For example, `Xm-CreateMenuBar()` and `XmCreateSimpleOptionMenu()` automatically create and configure a RowColumn widget as a MenuBar or a pulldown menu, respectively. Similarly, there are convenience routines for creating various types of predefined dialog boxes (which may be assembled from four or five separate widget classes).

In short, convenience routines emphasize the functional side of user-interface objects, and hide their implementation. However, because Motif is not truly an object-oriented system, it behooves you to understand what you're really dealing with. (For example, if you wanted to use resource classes to configure all MenuBars to have one color, and all pulldown menus another, you couldn't do so, because they are not actually distinct widget classes. The class name for both items would be `RowColumn`.)

In the remainder of this chapter we'll be looking at Motif user-interface objects from the side of both the "functional object" illusion and the actual widget implementation. In the body of the book, we use the Motif convenience routines for creating most complex objects, but stick to the underlying Xt routines for creating objects made up of single widgets or gadgets. Even with the complex objects, we show you how to pierce the veil of Motif's convenience functions, and work directly with the underlying widgets when necessary.

We'll begin by taking a closer look at the Motif user-interface elements that the user typically interacts with. Then we'll see how manager widget classes are used to hold together and arrange the more visible application controls. After that, we will see how we can use all these objects to create functioning windows and dialogs that make up a real application.

3.2 Giving Choices to the User

In many ways, application *controls* are the heart of a graphical user interface. Rather than controlling an application by typing commands, the user is presented with choices using graphical elements. He no longer needs to remember the syntax of commands, since his choices are presented to him as he goes along.

As we've seen, some of Motif's application controls (such as menus) are complex objects assembled by convenience routines. Others are simple, single-purpose widgets that you can create directly.

The widgets in this latter group are collectively referred to as *primitive* widgets—not because they are simple, but because they are designed to work alone. The contrast is not between "primitive" and "sophisticated" widgets, but between primitive and manager widgets.

3.2.1 The Primitive Widget Class

The Primitive widget class is a superclass for all the Motif primitive widgets. This widget serves only to define certain common behavior used by all its subclasses, so one never instantiates a widget directly from the Primitive class. This is somewhat like saying that "Hammer" is a class of object, but that you never really have a generic hammer; you can only have a "claw hammer," a "ball peen hammer," or a "sledge hammer."[1]

Just as all hammers have particular characteristics that qualify them as hammers, the Primitive widget class provides its subclasses with common resources such as window border attributes, highlighting, and help with keyboard traversal (so the user can navigate through the controls in a window using the keyboard and avoid the mouse). The actual widget classes that you use are subclassed from the Primitive class as shown in Figure 3-2.

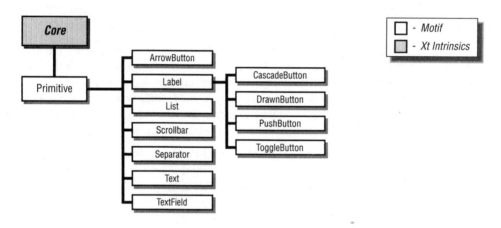

Figure 3-2. The class hierarchy of Primitive widgets

Primitive itself inherits even more basic widget behavior from the Xt-defined Core widget class, which establishes the basic nature of "widgetness." The Core class provides widgets with the capability to have windows and background colors, as well as translations, actions, and so on. You could actually use a simple Core widget as an instance and define your own translations and action routines, although this is not done frequently. (See the *Summary* section of Chapter 10, *The DrawingArea Widget*, for a short discussion of this topic. Complete details are provided in Volume Four, *X Toolkit Intrinsics Programming Manual*.)

---

[1] The "claw hammer" has the prongs in the back behind the hammer-head that allow you to pull nails out of a wall; the "ball peen" hammer has a round corner where the "claw" would be otherwise be; and a sledge hammer is the large, heavyweight hammer used to drive thick nails through concrete or to destroy things.

The Label Class

The Label widget provides a visual label either as text (in any font or using multiple fonts) or as an image (in the form of a `Pixmap`). Its text is a *compound string* and can be oriented from left-to-right or right-to-left. Compound strings can also be multilined, multifont or any combination of these. Most Motif widgets that use text must use compound strings to facilitate internationalization.[2] Chapter 19, *Compound Strings*, discusses functions that convert between `char *` text and compound strings along with other functions to manipulate them.

The Label widget does not provide for any callback routines, but using Xt, one could install event translations and action routines to make them respond to user input. However, the Label widget is not intended to be used this way. Rather, it is only intended to be used to display labels or other visual aids. Figure 3-3 displays a Label with multiple lines using multiple fonts.

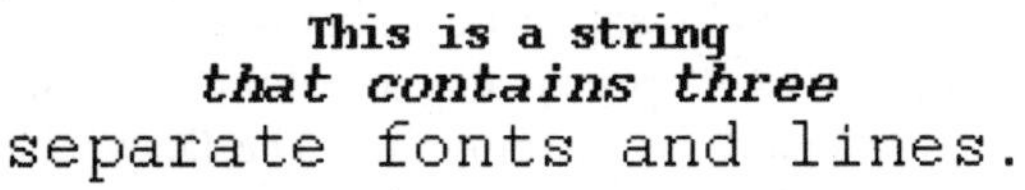

This is a string
that contains three
`separate fonts and lines.`

Figure 3-3. A Label widget with multiple lines and fonts

Label widgets are described in detail in Chapter 11, *Labels and Buttons*.

The PushButton Class

PushButtons support the same visual display capabilities as Labels, since they are subclassed from them. However, the PushButton also provides resources for the programmer to install callback routines that will be called when the user "activates" the button (clicks on it, or executes some other user-defined action). Additionally, the PushButton displays a shadow border that changes in appearance to indicate when the pointer is in the widget, and when it has been activated.

When the PushButton is not selected, it appears to project out towards the user. The button's border is highlighted when the pointer moves into the button; in this state, the button is said to be "armed." When the user actually selects the button by pressing the pointer on the armed button, it appears to be "pushed in." The user actually "activates" a PushButton by releasing the mouse button while the button is in a "selected" state. Figure 3-4 shows some examples of PushButtons.

---

[2] Of course, internationalization requires more involved design considerations than simply whether or not text can be represented from right-to-left and using an arbitrary character set. Chapter 19, *Compound Strings*, discusses this in more detail.

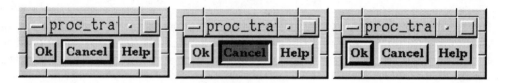

Figure 3-4. Examples of the PushButton widget

PushButton widgets are described in detail in Chapter 11, *Labels and Buttons*.

The DrawnButton Class

The DrawnButton widget is similar to a PushButton in functionality and its three-dimensional appearance. However, the DrawnButton is used by applications that wish to draw the text or image directly into the widget's window itself, presumably because the image is dynamic and may change frequently during the course of the program. The DrawnButton provides additional callback resources for when it is resized or exposed, and also contains extended ways to draw an outlined border. DrawnButton widgets are described in detail in Chapter 11, *Labels and Buttons*. Figure 3-5 shows some drawn buttons.

Figure 3-5. DrawnButtons display more complex or dynamic graphics

The ToggleButton Class

This widget displays text or graphics similarly to a Label widget, but has an additional *indicator* box (a square or diamond shape) placed to the left of the label. The indicator box shows the state of the toggle button: on or off. When on, the indicator is colored and appears to be pushed in. When off, it appears to project outward.

Toggles are often used to set application state, so their callback routines typically set simple Boolean variables internal to the application.

Toggles may be configured so that only one in a group of buttons can be chosen (in which case they are referred to as *radio buttons*), or they can act like *check boxes*, where the user can select any option that applies. Figure 3-6 shows how ToggleButtons may be used and displayed together.

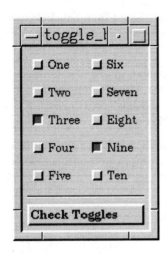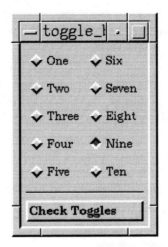

Figure 3-6. Example uses of ToggleButtons

ToggleButton widgets are described in detail in Chapter 12, *Toggle Widgets*.

The CascadeButton Class

The CascadeButton is a special kind of button used to pop up menus. It can only be used as a child of a RowColumn widget: in a MenuBar as the title of a pulldown menu, in a pulldown menu pane as an item that has a cascading pullright menu associated with it, or as the label of an option menu.

The CascadeButton's menu is not a part of the widget itself, but is associated with the button abstractly in the implementation of the toolkit. The CascadeButton merely provides a label and other visual aids that support the appearance that a menu can pop up from the object.

Even though the CascadeButton widget class is subclassed from Label, and so could inherit all of its functionality, Motif imposes restrictions on the labels a CascadeButton can display. CascadeButton labels cannot contain multiple lines or fonts.

Because CascadeButtons are typically used in menus, they don't have the same "pushbutton" border as other buttons. They do have similar highlighting behavior when activated, however.

The labels in the menu bar in Figure 3-1 were actually CascadeButtons.

CascadeButton widgets are described in detail in Chapter 4, *The Main Window*, and Chapter 16, *Menus*.

The ArrowButton Class

Despite the similarity in its name, the ArrowButton is not subclassed from Label along with the other button widgets. Like the remaining widgets in this section, it is subclassed directly from the Primitive widget class.

The ArrowButton widget contains an image of an arrow pointing in one of four directions: up, down, left, or right. When the user selects this widget, the ArrowButton provides visual feedback giving the illusion that the button is pressed in, and invokes a callback routine, which the application can use to do application-defined positioning.

In most respects, the ArrowButton is no different from a PushButton, since it would be easy enough to provide "arrow" pixmaps for a PushButton. But since directional arrows are a commonly-used user-interface element, ArrowButton is provided as a separate widget class for simplicity. Figure 3-7 shows several ArrowButtons.

ArrowButton widgets are described in detail in Chapter 11, *Labels and Buttons*.

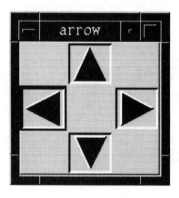

Figure 3-7. ArrowButtons

The List Class

The List widget provides a mechanism for the programmer to make a list of text items available to the user for selection. The user selects items from it using the mouse or keyboard. Lists are not usually created as primitive widgets. Instead, you typically create a ScrolledList object using a Motif convenience function, since this allows a scrollbar to be added if the list exceeds the size of the visible area. Figure 3-8 shows a List widget in context with other interface elements.

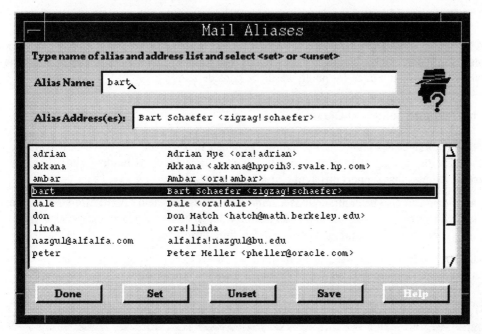

Figure 3-8. A List widget in a mail application

List widgets are described in detail in Chapter 13, *List Widgets*.

The Scrollbar Class

The Scrollbar is one of the more intuitive user-interface elements in the Motif toolkit. It is almost always attached to a ScrolledWindow widget, which may display the contents of any arbitrarily large window, or another widget.

When the contents of the window are too big to be displayed in a smaller area, the Scrollbar allows the user to scroll the window to view other portions of the contents. Figure 3-9 shows a vertical and horizontal scrollbar. Scrollbar widgets are described in Chapter 9, *Scrolled-Windows and Scrollbars*.

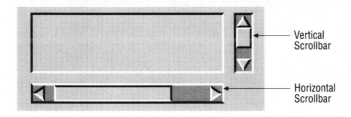

Figure 3-9. Motif Scrollbars

The Separator Class

A Separator is used as a visual aid to separate adjacent items in a display. It may be found in menus to separate menu items, in dialog boxes to separate discrete areas of control, or at various points in the interface for purely aesthetic consideration.

The Text and TextField Classes

The Text widget is a complete text editor contained in a widget. Resources are available to configure the editing style of the widget, which usually involves binding key sequences to action routines that support different text-editing capabilities.

The widget can also be configured as a single-line data entry field. As of Motif 1.1, the Text-Field widget class is also available, as a somewhat lighter-weight version. (Other than the single versus multiline editing support, there is little difference between the two classes.)

The Text widget can be used in many different ways to support an application's text entry requirements. Figure 3-10 shows an application using various forms of the Text widget.

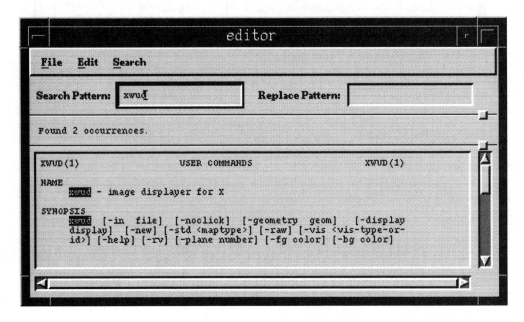

Figure 3-10. Text widgets

Text and TextField widgets are described in detail in Chapter 15, *Text Widgets*.

3.2.2 Other Application Controls

As suggested earlier, Motif provides a number of application controls that are not implemented as single primitive widget classes. There are several cases where the toolkit makes
use of smaller, more primitive widgets in order to construct a larger, more abstract user-
interface element described by the Motif GUI.

Because a proper discussion of how these compound objects work is dependent on a better
understanding of the Motif manager and shell widgets, we will postpone their discussion till
later in the chapter. However, you should feel free, as Motif does, to think of these interface
elements as "objects," just as you do with the various primitive widgets.

Another set of controls is provided in the form of gadgets. There are gadgets equivalent to
many of the primitive widgets, including Labels, Separators, PushButtons, CascadeButtons,
ToggleButtons, and ArrowButtons. Their behavior, for the most part, is identical to that of
the corresponding widgets.

All of the gadgets are subclassed from the Gadget class, which, like Primitive, is never
instantiated.

Gadgets are not widgets. In fact, they are subclassed not from the Core widget class, which
defines basic widget behavior, but from an even earlier precursor, called RectObj. Figure
3-11 shows the class hierarchy for gadgets.

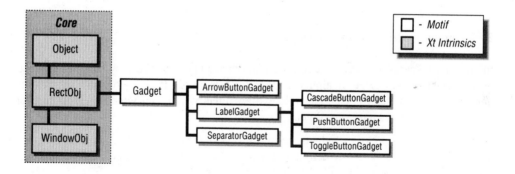

Figure 3-11. Gadget class hierarchy

Because an understanding of how gadgets work is dependent on an understanding of the managers that support them, we will return to this topic later in the chapter.

3.3 Manager Widgets

While the controls are the most obvious part of a Graphical User Interface, these elements alone don't make an effective interface. A random collection of buttons, or endless nested menus, can make an application as obscure and difficult to use as one that has only a command-line interface. It's the arrangement of the controls that makes all the difference.

This brings us to a more general discussion about how to lay out your application and the tools available to help you do that—manager widgets.[3] You can almost think of manager widgets as boxes that you put things in. These boxes, however, can grow or shrink as necessary to provide the best fit possible for the items they contain. You can place boxes inside of other boxes, whether or not they also contain other items. By using differently sized boxes, you can find many different ways to organize things.

Unlike primitive widgets such as PushButtons, Scrollbars, and Labels, whose usefulness depends on their visual appearance and interaction with the user, manager widgets provide no visual feedback and have few callback routines that react to user input.

Manager widgets have two purposes:

1. To manage the sizes and positions of the widgets they contain.

2. To provide special support for gadgets.

In all other respects, manager widgets are like other widgets in that they have windows, can receive events, and can be manipulated directly through Motif or X Toolkit Intrinsics functions. This means that you can, if you like, draw directly into their windows, look for events in them, or specify resources for them.

When it comes to supporting gadgets, all manager widgets are created equal. However, when it comes to widget layout, they definitely are not. (Gadget support is defined by the Manager widget class, and inherited by all of the other managers.)

---

[3] Xt uses the more general term *composite widgets*. Technically speaking, the Xt Composite widget class defines the characteristics of widgets that are able to manage the size or position of other widgets. The Motif Manager widget class is a subclass of the Xt Constraint class (which in turn is a subclass of Composite) that adds Motif-specific management features, such as support for keyboard traversal, gadget event handling, and so on.

There are many manager widget classes, each of which is tuned especially for different kinds of widget layout. The superclass for all these subclasses is the Manager widget class. Manager is subclassed from the Xt Constraint class, which in turn is subclassed from the Xt Composite class. The Composite widget class defines the basic characteristics of widgets that are able to manage children, while the Constraint class adds the additional capability for the parent to provide additional resources for the children that "constrain" their position. Constraint resources can be thought of as "hints" about how the children would like to be laid out.

As with the Primitive widget class and the Gadget class, you never create an instance of a Manager widget; you create an instance of one of its subclasses.

The relationship between manager widgets and the widgets they manage is commonly referred to as the *parent-child* model. The manager acts as the parent and the other widgets are its children.

Motif provides a number of very narrowly focused manager widgets such as the Main-Window and certain "dialog" classes, which can almost be treated as if they were single user-interface elements, since they create and manage their children with only minimal help from the application. We sometimes refer to these widgets as *compound widgets*, since they include both a manager and one or more children.

However, Motif also provides an array of general-purpose manager widgets, which allow the programmer to manage the size and arrangement of an arbitrary number of children. In some ways, you can consider the art of Motif programming to be the design of effective widget layouts, using these particular manager widgets.

Manager widgets may manage other managers as well as primitive widgets like Labels and PushButtons. In fact, the layout of a typical application can be thought of as a kind of tree structure. As discussed in Chapter 2, *The Motif Programming Model*, at the top of the tree is always a shell widget like that returned by `XtVaAppInitialize( )`. Shells always have a single managed child, which is usually a general-purpose manager widget. This manager then contains other managers and primitive widgets that make up the entire window (and thus, the branches of the tree).

For example, the dialog box shown in Figure 3-12 contains a number of different managers and primitive widgets, but appears to the user as a single, conceptually focused user-interface object.

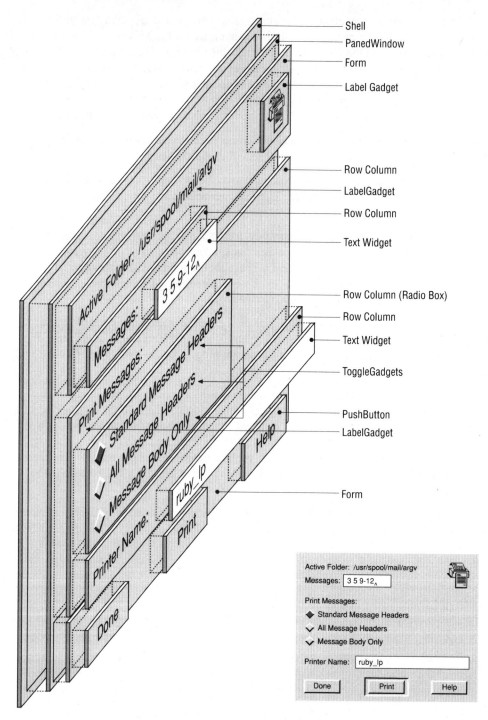

Figure 3-12. *A window that uses managers within managers*

The parent-child relationships between the widgets in this dialog can be graphically illustrated using the tree-structure shown in Figure 3-13.

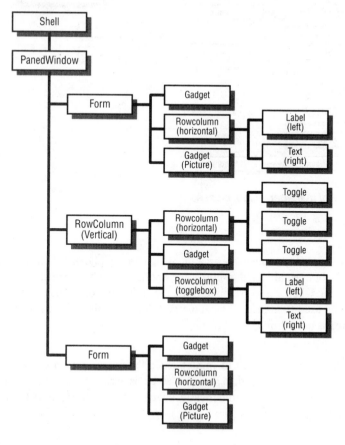

Figure 3-13. Parent-child relationships between widgets

3.3.1 Manager Widget Classes

This section lists the manager widgets provided by the Motif toolkit. A more detailed description of these widgets is given in Chapter 8, *Manager Widgets*. Figure 3-14 shows the class hierarchy of the manager widget classes.

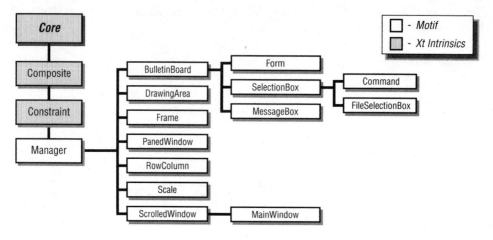

Figure 3-14. Class hierarchy of manager widget classes

DrawingArea

The DrawingArea widget provides an area in which the application can display graphics. Callback routines are used to notify the application when expose or resize events take place, or when there is input from the keyboard or mouse. While a DrawingArea can be used to manage the geometry layout for child widgets, its functionality in this area is quite limited.

ScrolledWindow

The ScrolledWindow widget is used to implement a "window" into a data object (such as text or graphics). If the data being viewed is larger than the Scrolled-Window object, scrollbars can be automatically attached to enable the user to view portions of the window interactively.

MainWindow

The MainWindow widget acts as the standard layout manager for the main application's window (base frame). It is tuned specifically to pay attention to the existence of a MenuBar, Command window, a work region, and Scrollbars, although all these areas are optional. This widget is subclassed from the ScrolledWindow widget.

RowColumn

The RowColumn Widget is perhaps the most widely used and robust of all the manager widgets. As its name suggests, the widget lays out its children in a rows and columns. It may contain widgets of any type and requires no special knowledge about how those children function. The RowColumn widget is used by many different parts of the toolkit to implement more abstract objects like the Menubar, menus, ToggleBoxes, and RadioBoxes.

Frame The Frame widget provides a three-dimensional border for widgets that normally have no borders. It is also useful if you want to enhance the style of border for a widget. The Frame widget may only have one child, but you can use another manager widget (which in turn contains many children) as that child.

PanedWindow

The PanedWindow widget manages its children in a vertically tiled format. Its width fluctuates with the widest widget in its list of managed children and forces all children to stretch to the same width as that widget. Each *pane* in the PanedWindow contains a child and a *control sash* (or *grip*) that allows the user to change the height of the pane interactively. Resizing a pane with the grip may cause the widgets in other panes to become more or less visible.

BulletinBoard

BulletinBoard widgets do not impose much of a layout policy for the widgets they manage. These widgets act as "bulletin-boards"—the application posts a widget on the bulletin board and it sticks where it is placed. The BulletinBoard does impose margins, and has a resource that controls whether or not children can overlap. However, if the BulletinBoard is resized, it doesn't move its children, nor does it resize them. BulletinBoard widgets are most widely used by the predefined Motif dialog widget classes, which are implemented internally by the toolkit.

Form Subclassed from the BulletinBoard widget, the Form widget class provides a great deal of control over the placement and sizing of widgets it manages. Forms may lay out children in a grid-like manner or may allow their children to "link" themselves to one another in a chain-like fashion.

Scale The Scale widget displays a slider object somewhat similar in appearance and functionality to a Scrollbar. It provides feedback to the user about the value or setting of a particular state of the application. This widget class is not really intended to be used as a general manager. It creates and manages its own widgets, which are needed to construct the Scale "object." The only children you can add to a Scale widget are Label widgets, which are used to represent tickmarks.

3.3.2 Geometry Management

Almost any kind of widget can be contained by managers—even other managers. Children are always placed within the geometrical boundaries of their parents. A child may not move or resize itself without requesting permission from its parent, which may, if it chooses, deny the request. The manager, acting as the parent, may even force the child into arbitrary sizes or positions. However, like any good parent, managers should be fair at all times and not deny reasonable requests made by their children. As you might expect, geometry management can be quite complex in an application with several levels of managers.

For example, let's say that we have a List widget to which we have just added a new item. In order to display the new item, the List widget must grow vertically (since Lists display their items vertically). Hence, it makes a request to its own manager widget regarding its new potential size. If that parent has the room (or some other mechanism for satisfying the request, such as scrollbars), it can approve the request. However, if the manager itself must also grow to honor its child's request, it will have to negotiate with its own parent. This chain reaction may go all the way up to the shell widget. The shell must communicate with the window manager (if it hasn't done so already) concerning the new size. If the window manager and the shell agree to the new size, the acknowledgement filters back down through the widget tree to the List widget, which may now grow to its requested size. If any of the parents in the widget tree refuse to resize, the original child's request will be denied (or only partially fulfilled).

Most of the time, this type of interaction executes successfully, as there is rarely a dispute among children about resizing negotiations or positional boundaries. That is, children usually go wherever their managers put them, and make few requests of their own. Exceptions might be RowColumns acting as MenuBars, since they must be situated at the top of the window and spread to both extents horizontally. Another is the Scrollbar, which is typically positioned on an edge of a ScrolledWindow widget.

Constraints

So, how do children make such requests to their parents? The answer to this question can be rather complicated, since the X Toolkit Intrinsics support a large selection of functions that enable two-way communication. The child may use specific functions such as `XtMove-Widget( )` and `XtResizeWidget( )` to request permission from its parent to be a specific size or in a particular position. Likewise, the parent may use functions like `XtQuery-Geometry( )` to give the child the opportunity to announce its preferred geometry.

Some of these functions and methods are described in Chapter 8, *Manager Widgets*, but a detailed treatment of such custom geometry management techniques is beyond the scope of this book. These functions are commonly used only by the internals of composite and constraint widgets. See Volume Four, *X Toolkit Intrinsics Programming Manual*, for a more detailed discussion.

In the Motif toolkit, geometry management cannot work without cooperation. The easiest way for children to cooperate with their parents and siblings is simply to comply with whatever layout policies are already supported by their particular manager widget parents. (That is, a child should not try to force itself into sizes or positions that are not supported by the manager widget class used as the parent.) Each of the manager widget classes described above are implemented to support a specific layout style. For example, the RowColumn widget lays out its children in rows and columns; the Form widget allows children to specify relative or absolute positions to other widgets within the form; and the PanedWindow widget gives children the opportunity to inform their parents of their desired maximum and minimum heights. The methods by which a particular manager widget accomplishes this are made available publicly to its children through constraint resources.

Constraint resources are generically defined by Xt's Constraint widget class, from which the manager widgets are subclassed. Unlike other resources, constraints are applied to the *children* of the manager, not to the manager itself. Examples include specifications for maximum and minimum heights, relative sizes and positions, specific positional constraints or even absolute x,y coordinates.

Here's how constraints work. When the parent needs to size or position its children, it goes to each child and checks to see if it is *managed* (if not, it goes on to the next child).[4] It then examines the child's constraint resources and, depending on those constraints, enforces the geometric change or negotiates with its own parent to see if it can comply with the new size. Much of this depends on whether the child's needs require the parent to be resized as well. Therefore, *all* widgets, including manager widgets, have an extra internal data structure that contains only constraint resources that are only used by the widget's constraining parent widget to aid it in geometry management.

3.3.3 How Gadgets Are Managed

Besides geometry management, manager widgets also have a responsibility for their gadget children. Before we can discuss how they do this, we need to more clearly define what a gadget is.

Every widget has its own X window. This simplifies many aspects of programming, since each widget can take responsibility for repainting itself, selecting its own events, and in general being as self-sufficient as possible. Historically, however, windows have been perceived as heavyweight objects; system performance would slip if the application used too many windows. This is especially important for GUI applications that use widgets because there are frequently hundreds of widgets per application—perhaps thousands for very large programs.

Gadgets (windowless widgets) were originally developed as a part of Motif, and added to Xt as of X11 Release 4. There are gadget versions of many common primitive widgets, such as PushButtons and Labels. Like widgets, they can be created using either Motif convenience functions or Xt's `XtCreateManagedWidget()`. The widget and gadget versions of an object are functionally very similar, but there are small but important differences.

Because gadgets do not have their own windows, they are entirely dependent on their parents (manager widgets) for redrawing on exposure, highlighting as a result of keyboard traversal, notification of event activity, and so on. Without windows, gadgets have no control over the colors they use (foreground, background, three-dimensional shading) or other window-based attributes normally associated with widgets. For this reason, gadgets can only be used in managers that support them. How closely gadgets emulate their widget counterparts is largely dependent on the capabilities of the manager widget parent.

The Motif Manager class has limitations that require all gadgets to inherit the same background colors as the manager widget acting as its parent; they must also use the same foreground color specified by the parent, and so on. (Gadgets may, on the other hand, specify their own fonts.) These restrictions are not inherent in generic Composite widgets or Xt-based gadgets; they are specific to *Motif managers only*. (That is, one could hypothetically write a Composite widget that allowed a gadget to specify what kind of background

---

[4] The PanedWindow has a bug where it queries the sizes of its unmanaged children as well as its managed children.

By the way, while this discussion is chiefly given in terms of constraint resources for size and position, constraint resources can be used for any arbitrary information that needs to be kept on a per-child basis.

color it would like to have. The manager would then paint the area of its own window obscured by the gadget's boundaries in that color, giving the user the impression that the gadget was indeed a separately colored widget.)

You can use Motif's manager/gadget restrictions to your advantage by using them to impose a level of consistency and conformity throughout your application. For example, it is easy to require that all PushButtons in a particular window maintain the same colors simply by using gadgets intead of widgets. Here, the user can only provide color resources on the manager rather than on the PushButtons themselves (since gadgets have no color resources).

Despite the original reason for the development of gadgets, you should no longer automatically use gadgets if you are looking for performance improvement in an application that has many widgets. In X11 Release 4 (and more so in Release 5), X windows have become substantially lighter weight objects than they were when gadgets were first developed. If anything, at this point you could say that gadgets are "worse" than widgets from a performance perspective because the Motif managers take a very simplistic approach to the way they handle events for gadgets: they track for *all* events (such as **MotionNotify**) whether or not the gadget expresses interest in the events. As a result, gadgets typically generate a great deal more network traffic. Those with X terminals might find a noticable network performance drop as a result.

We will bring up complications in using gadgets whenever it is appropriate in the course of this book.

3.3.4 Keyboard Traversal and Tab Groups

Keyboard traversal is a feature of the Motif GUI that requires all applications to support movement between user-interface elements using only the keyboard (not the mouse). This feature is part of the Motif specification because not every display will have a mouse or other pointing device. (It is also possible that for some applications, such as data entry, keyboard traversal will be more useful than mouse actions.)

Keyboard traversal is based on an underlying model known as *tab groups*—that is, groups of widgets that are considered to be "related" for purposes of keyboard traversal. For example, all the items in a menu are considered a tab group, since they are grouped together, and possibly perform related functions.

Within a tab group, a particular widget always has input focus regardless of the location of the pointer. This is the *current* item, and is usually identified by a "highlight," which is typically a black border around the boundaries of the widget. The user can change the current item with the pointer. But if he wants to make another item current using only the keyboard, he can do so with one of the arrow keys. When the user finds the item he wants, he presses RETURN to activate it.

If the user wants to move from one tab group to another, he uses the TAB key. (The CTRL key must be used with TAB if the current item is a multiline Text widget; otherwise, there would be no way to insert a tab character.) To traverse tab groups in reverse, the SHIFT key is used with the TAB key.

In switching both between and within tab groups, traversal goes in a circle, starting with the first widget in the group, and returning to it when focus has passed to each of the other widgets in turn.

Although keyboard traversal is not a direct function of manager widgets, they do play a pivotal role in implementing it. Most of the time, a manager is typically initialized as a tab group and primitive widgets are typically members or elements of that group. There are exceptions, though. For example, Text and List widgets are normally set up as their own tab groups. This allows keyboard traversal to be used, for example, to move among the selections in the List widget.

Within tab groups, there is no sense of a manager-within-manager structure; the widget hierarchy is flattened out so that it appears (to the user) that all the controls in a window are at the same "depth." (The user has no knowledge of a widget tree.)

Keyboard traversal can only be accomplished if each widget in the tree cooperates; if a PushButton has keyboard focus and the user presses the $\boxed{\text{TAB}}$ key, the internals of the PushButton widget are responsible for directing focus to the next tab group.

Managers play a key role in keyboard traversal because they are responsible for the events that take place within gadgets (since gadgets have no windows of their own to receive events). If an event occurs within a PushButton gadget, then the manager is responsible for directing input focus to the next tab group.

While the whole process of keyboard traversal may seem complex and difficult, it is automated by the Motif toolkit and does not require application intervention. There are escape mechanisms, however, that allow *you*, rather than the toolkit, to control the keyboard traversal. There are functions that allow you to specify exactly which widgets *are* tab groups, which widgets should be *in* tab groups, and which widgets should neither be tab groups nor in one. Such fine-tuning is considered to be an exception rather than the rule.

3.4 How an Application Hangs Together

Managers and primitive widgets provide the basic mechanisms with which you can build a graphical user interface from the ground up. However, Motif also provides several important classes of objects that address the larger-scale organization of the application.

In particular, Motif provides a specialized manager widget called the MainWindow, which is intended to be used as the organizing frame for an application. It also provides transient dialog boxes, in which the application can provide or request information that does not need to be displayed all the time.

In the course of exploring these objects, we'll also need to take a deeper look at shell widgets than we did in Chapter 2.

3.4.1 The Main Window

Every application is different. A word processor, paint program, or spreadsheet has a single main work area, with controls taking on a peripheral role, perhaps in a pulldown menu. More sophisticated or intricate programs, on the other hand, may have several main work areas. An electronic mail program, for example, may have a work area in which the user reviews and selects from a list of incoming messages, another where he reads and responds to messages, and yet another where he issues commands to organize, delete, or otherwise affect groups of messages.

Still other applications—and this includes a large number of commercial, data-entry type applications—really have no separate work area. The work area is really just a collection of controls, such as checkboxes and text fields which are repetitively filled in.

It is quite conceivable that an application could provide multiple windows for performing different tasks. For example, an order entry program might use one window for looking up a customer record, another for checking stock on hand, and yet another for entering the current order. Motif allows for the creation of multiple top-level application windows as well as transient dialog boxes that provide additional information or ask for confirmation or option settings before carrying out a command.

Nonetheless, every application has at least one main window. The main window is the most visible window in an application. It is the home-plate for the application's user interface; the first window the user sees and the location where he interacts with the program most of the time. No matter how small or large an application may be, there must be a focal point that ties it all together. As a program grows more complex, the main window may grow more abstract and perform fewer functions, but it never becomes obsolete or defocused. Rather, it is transformed into a hub, where the user starts, finishes, and returns again and again as he goes from one function to the next.

It is possible to create a custom main window, using the general-purpose manager widgets Motif provides. However, the *Motif Style Guide* suggests a particular layout that applications should follow, unless they have a compelling reason not to. This recommended layout is shown in Figure 3-15.

The main window should have a menu bar across the top, with the *work area* immediately below. The work area usually contains the main interface object of the application. For example, a paint or draw application might provide a DrawingArea widget as a canvas, an electronic mail application might provide a ScrolledList of message summaries from which the user can make selections, or a Text editor might place a Text widget in the work area. It is also quite possible that the application work area might require a custom widget or a non-widget-based X window, as described in detail in Volume Four, *X Toolkit Intrinsics Programming Manual*.

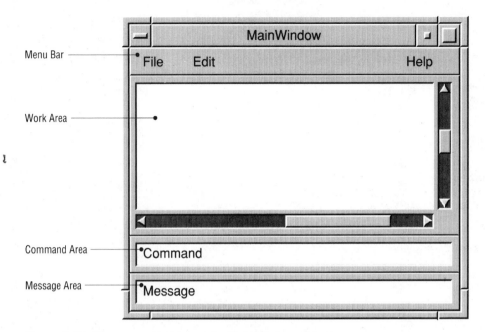

Menu Bar

Work Area

Command Area

Message Area

Figure 3-15. Recommended layout for MainWindow widget

The work area should have both horizontal and vertical scrollbars. Beneath the work area (or optionally, above it, but below the menu bar) can be an optional *command area* for entering typed commands. (This is designed to aid in porting character-based applications to the Motif GUI, but can be useful in other applications as well.)

At the bottom of the main window is an optional *message area*. This area is typically not used for error messages or any type of message that requires a response from the user. (Messages requiring a response usually cause a transient window called a *dialog box* to be displayed.) The Message Area is usually a text widget that does not accept input, but you can implement it as any widget you choose (for example, a Label widget).

While it is entirely possible to construct your own main window (and in fact, this is done quite frequently), the Motif toolkit provides a special MainWindow widget (described in detail in Chapter 4) to support the recommended style. Unfortunately, the MainWindow widget is a little ungainly, as shown in Figure 3-16.

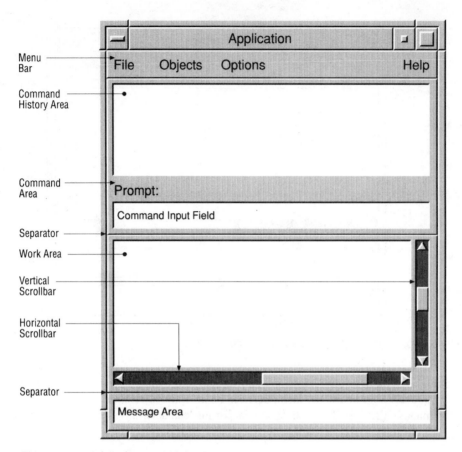

Menu Bar

Command History Area

Command Area

Separator

Work Area

Vertical Scrollbar

Horizontal Scrollbar

Separator

Figure 3-16. A fully featured MainWindow widget

The command area is placed above the work area. This might not be so bad, but it is typically implemented by a Command widget, which is very poorly laid out, and takes up far too much room for most applications. It includes a TextField widget for entering commands, a prompt string that takes up an entirely separate line above the TextField, and a large scrolling list that contains the history of all commands that have been typed. Fortunately, the Command widget can be replaced by a single-line TextField widget. In fact, the MainWindow widget is configurable to display or suppress each of the sub-areas it contains.

All of the elements in the main window are optional, including, to a lesser degree, the order of the components. In actual practice, main windows can be as varied as the applications they support. Figure 3-17 graphically demonstrates this point.

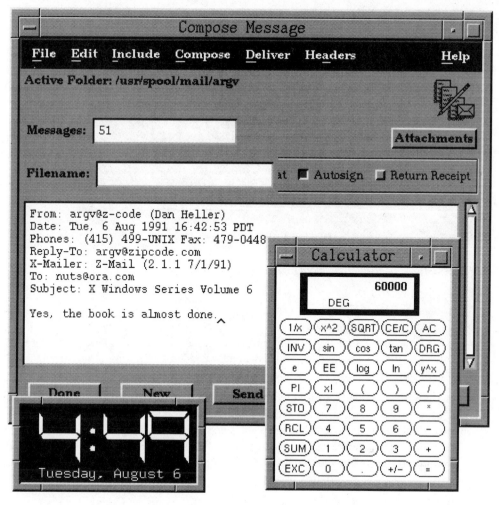

Figure 3-17. A miscellany of main windows

3.4.2 Menus

The MenuBar and pulldown menus supported by the MainWindow are not the only style of menus supported by Motif.

First of all, *cascading* menus allow a menu to "pull right," as shown in Figure 3-18. Thus, these are sometimes referred to as *pullright* menus.

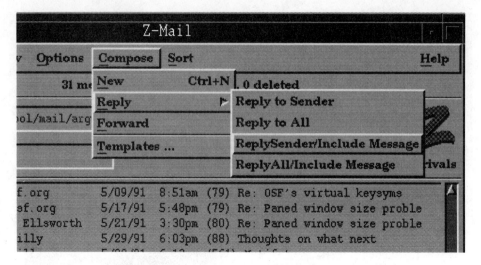

Figure 3-18. A cascading pullright menu

Menu bars, pulldown menus, and cascading menus are all created in similar ways. Special convenience functions are used to create a specially configured RowColumn widget. This widget is then populated with PushButtons, CascadeButtons, ToggleButtons, Labels, and Separators (or their gadget equivalents), which are added as children of the manager widget returned by the menu creation functions.

In the case of a menubar, all of the children must be CascadeButtons, since each button will bring up a separate menu. In the pulldown menu pane, many of the buttons will be Push-Buttons or PushButtonGadgets, though Labels and Separators might also be used for clarity. In order to have another cascading menu with further sub-options, one of the items needs to be a CascadeButton. The additional menu needs to be created separately, populated with its own buttons, and attached to the CascadeButton.

Motif also supports a construct called an OptionMenu. Again, an OptionMenu is a specially configured RowColumn that manages an array of buttons. However, the behavior is quite different; a CascadeButton is displayed somewhere in the application, with its label typically appearing as a data or choice value following a prompt of some kind. Clicking on the button pops up a menu containing the other choices, directly on top of the CascadeButton. Choosing an item from the menu rotates the items in the menu, so that the currently chosen item now appears as the label of visible CascadeButton.

Figure 3-19 shows an OptionMenu popped up from a CascadeButton.

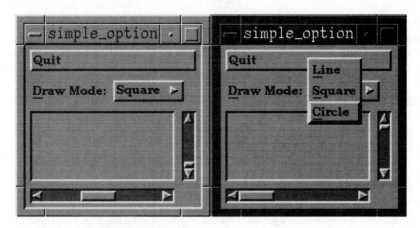

Figure 3-19. A CascadeButton popping up an option menu

In addition, Motif provides true popup menus, which are not attached to any visible interface element, but can be popped up at any arbitrary location in the application, usually as a result of some combination of keyboard and/or mouse button presses.

3.4.3 The Role of the Window Manager

To the unsophisticated user, the Main window looks like the "top-level" window of the application. In window-system talk, a top-level window resides at the top of the window (and widget) tree hierarchy for the application. Its parent is the *root window*, which is what the user perceives as the background behind all the windows on the desktop. In the Xt-world, however, things are a little different. Behind every visible top-level application window is a special kind of widget known as a shell widget.

Every window that can be placed independently on the screen, including top-level windows and dialog boxes, has as its parent an invisible shell widget. (It's not really invisible; it's just obscured by all the widgets contained inside of it.) Typically, shell widgets contain only one managed child widget (such as the Motif MainWindow widget) whose job it is to manage the layout of more primitive components such as Labels, Text widgets, Scrollbars, and Push-Buttons. These are the items that the user actually sees and interacts with on the screen. These objects are really descendants of the shell widget because they are contained within its boundaries. However, the actual geometry management (layout) is turned over to the shell's single child, which is typically a manager widget of some kind. (The shell widget is "shrink-wrapped" around this widget, which is why we referred to the shell as being invisible.)

Aside from managing its single child, one of the shell's main jobs is to communicate with the *window manager* on behalf of the application. Without the shell, the application has no idea what else is happening on the desktop.

It is very important for you to understand the fact that *the window manager is a separate application from your own.* This can be very confusing because the visual and physical interaction between your application and the window manager is usually so close that most users cannot tell the difference between the two.

To get an idea of the relationship between the window manager and an application, let's compare them with the way a bed is built and how it fits into someone's room. A bed is made up of a frame, a mattress, and as many accessories as you want to pile on top of it. The main window is the mattress, and the sheets, pillows, blankets and stuffed animals you throw on it represent the user-interface controls inside the main window. The whole lot sits on top of the bed frame—this is the shell widget. When you push a bed around the room, you're really pushing the bed's frame. The rest just happens to go along with it. The same is true for windows on the screen. The user never moves an application window, he moves the window manager frame. The application just happens to move with it.

You may have to stretch your imagination a little to visualize the bed resizing itself with the frame, but this is precisely what happens when the user resizes an application. It is the window manager that the user interacts with during a resizing operation. It is only when the user is done resizing that the window manager informs the application of the new size through the shell widget. The shell then communicates the new size to its child, which filters down to the widgets in the application.

This window manager frame is made up of *window decorations* that the window manager places on all toplevel windows (which are the windows associated with shell widgets). The controls allow the user to interactively move windows, resize them, cause them to redraw themselves, or even to close them down. Figure 3-20 shows the standard Motif window manager decorations.

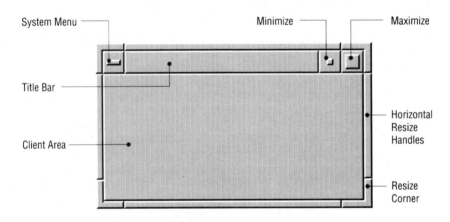

Figure 3-20. Standard Motif window manager elements

The *window menu* displays a list of window manager functions that allow the user to move, resize or even exit the application. You do not have access to the menu itself or the items within it; similarly, you cannot get handles to the "minimize" and "maximize" buttons. These objects act independently from your application because they are a part of another application—the window manager.

Motif provides *window manager protocols* that allow menu items like these to affect the application. You can manipulate the window manager's window menu by using many of the same types of protocols. You can specify which of the items in the window menu you want to appear, whether there are resize handles on the frame or whether you want to allow the user to iconify the window.

At the same time, the user is also expecting a consistent interaction between the window manager and all the applications on the desktop. This expectation is magnified by the fact that the user probably has quite a few user-settable resources for the window manager, and unexpected interference from the application rarely makes users happy. All things considered, you should leave the window manager alone. A technical discussion of the window manager can be found in Chapter 17, *Interacting with the Window Manager*.

Types of Shell Widgets

As we've pointed out earlier, it is possible for an application to have more than one independent window. In addition to the main window, there are may be one or more dialog boxes, as well as popup windows, and perhaps even independent application windows that co-exist with the main window. Each of these cases requires different handling by the window manager, and as a result, there are several different classes of shell widgets. Figure 3-21 shows the class hierarchy of the different types of shell widgets that are available in the Motif toolkit.[5]

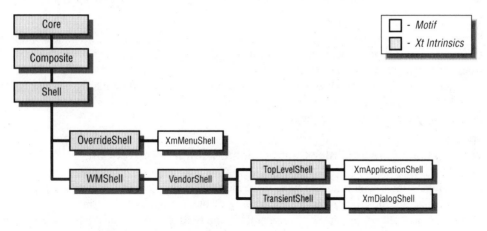

Figure 3-21. Shell widget class hierarchy

Because dealing with the window manager is a complex problem, there are quite a few Shell widget classes. Fortunately, you typically need use only those classes at the bottom of the tree; the others are used internally by Xt and Motif, or their behavior is inherited by the classes you do need to use.

---

[5] In the figure, shell classes designated with an Xm are Motif-specific. All others are defined by the X Toolkit Intrinsics. The basic template for VendorShell is defined by Xt, but it is typically replaced by each vendor.

Shells for Popup and Pulldown Menus

There are cases in which an application needs to put up a temporary window that is completely free of window manager interaction.

Menus are such a case. When a user pops up a menu, he typically wants to make a choice immediately, and he wants that choice to take precedence over any other window system activity. The window manager need not be involved, either to decorate or to place the menu. This is entirely up to the application.

As its name suggests, the OverrideShell widget class provides for windows that bypass the window manager. OverrideShells are like futons; you can place them on the floor without using a bed-frame (and without being tasteless).

The OverrideShell is a generic Xt-based widget class, so the Motif toolkit introduces the MenuShell to service the special interface needs required by the *Motif Style Guide*. That is, the MenuShell's translation table is set to support keyboard traversal, its **XmNfocus-Policy** is set to **XmPOINTER**, and its **XmNallowShellResize** resource is set to **True** and makes sure that its solely managed child is a RowColumn widget. Menus are discussed later in this chapter, but for an in-depth discussion on the various types of menus you can use in Motif, see Chapter 16, *Menus*. (However, there is little more to be said about MenuShells.) For information and discussion on *modal dialogs*, see Chapter 6, *Selection Dialogs*.

OverrideShells are seldomly used as the main window for an application. One exception to this is possibly a screen locking application whose purpose is to prevent other applications from appearing on the screen while the computer is left unattended. Because the window manager is unaware of the OverrideShell, it does not provide window manager controls, and does not interpret certain window manager accelerators (like "close this window"), or other possible methods for bypassing the lock.

Window Managers and Inter-Client Communications Conventions

Shell widgets must communicate with the window manager to negotiate screen real estate (window size and positions) and a wide variety of other properties. The information that is exchanged is defined by the X Consortium's Inter-Client Communications Conventions (ICCC). The WMShell widget class implements ICCC-compliant behavior as a standard part of the X Toolkit Intrinsics, so that it will be available to all vendors providing Xt-based widget sets and window managers. This is what allows Motif applications to work correctly with virtually any ICCC-compliant window manager.

In our analogy, WMShells are simple, wire bed-frames that have no special attributes—no wheels, rollers, or anything else.

The VendorShell widget class is subclassed from the WMShell class so that vendors (such as OSF) can define attributes that are specific to their own window managers. In our analogy, this is like having a bed frame that has attached cabinets, shelves above the headboard, or nice wheels that glide on the carpet. In this case, the role of the VendorShell is to be cognizant of the special features of the vendor's specific window manager. In other words, the VendorShell does not actually add any additional functionality to the window manager, but it is written specifically for applications (toolkits) that wish to interact with it. All the attributes of the window manager decorations can be modified or controlled through resources specific to the VendorShell. Thus, the VendorShell can be used by the application to communicate to the window manager.

WMShells and VendorShells are never implemented directly by an application, but the features they provide may be made available to the application. For example, the Motif Vendor-Shell allows the application to specify the items in the window menu, or what happens when the user *closes* a shell window from the outside. Examples of what the Motif VendorShell can do are given throughout this and other chapters. Chapter 17, *Interacting with the Window Manager*, discusses window manager interactions in more detail.

TransientShells and DialogShells

While dialog boxes are not typically decorated by the window manager, neither are they completely independent, like popup menus. If an application is iconified, its dialog boxes are typically iconified as well.

You can think of dialog boxes as an application's *secondary windows*. Dialog boxes are usually implemented in Xt using TransientShells. The DialogShell is a Motif-defined widget class subclassed from the TransientShell and VendorShell classes. See Chapter 5, *Introduction to Dialogs*, for details on Motif dialogs.

Motif functions for creating dialog boxes tend to hide the shell widget side of the dialog. When you make a call like **XmCreateMessageDialog( )**, you are actually creating a MessageBox widget as a child of a DialogShell widget.

TopLevelShells and ApplicationShells

When you initialize the X Toolkit with a call such as **XtAppInitialize( )**, you are automatically returned an ApplicationShell widget to use as the top-level widget in your application. If secondary top-level windows are desired (as described earlier where an application might support both text and picture editors in separate windows at the same time), the secondary top-level window is typically a TopLevelShell. The differences between these classes are subtle and deal mostly with how resources are specified in the user's resource database. In Chapter 7, *Custom Dialogs*, we review this concept and explore many ways where TopLevelShells are used as primary windows apart from the main window.

3.4.4 Dialogs

Some applications can get all their work done in one main window. Others may require multiple windows. For example, an electronic mail application might include its own text editor for composing new messages. Also consider the design if a mail program provides "multimedia" support (e.g., graphics and sound as well as text); it might need to provide its own paint-style application, while maintaining it as part of the single program. Under these circumstances, it is conceivable that the application would want to separate each of these functions into separate top-level windows that are controlled separately.

Motif actually allows an application to have multiple true top-level windows. (A true top-level window is one that can be iconified, moved, resized, or otherwise manipulated by the window manager.) However, even applications without this level of complexity will at least want to display transient windows called dialog boxes.

Motif provides two main types of dialog box: MessageDialogs and SelectionDialogs. It is also possible to create custom dialogs.

MessageDialogs

MessageDialogs simply provide some kind of message to the user, and typically include buttons that allow the user to respond to the message. For example, a menu item to delete a file might issue a dialog with the message, "Are you sure?" with PushButtons labeled **Yes**, **No**, and **Cancel**.

The Motif MessageDialog widget actually comes in six different guises. Depending on the value of a particular resource, it can display any of five symbols defined by the *Motif Style Guide* (or no symbol at all). Motif provides convenience routines for creating Message-Dialogs with each symbol, so they are often referred to as if they were distinct widget classes:

ErrorDialog

> A *do not enter* symbol (a circle with a diagonal line through it) is displayed with a message informing the user that he made an error in a user-interface component or that a selection was a invalid. For example, he may have pressed a PushButton at the wrong time, made an invalid selection in a List widget or entered an unknown filename for a Text widget.

InformationDialog

> The international information symbol (an "i" with a circle around it) is displayed with a helpful message providing help of some kind. An InformationDialog is usually displayed in response to a request for help.

QuestionDialog

> A question mark symbol is displayed with an interrogative statement (a *question*). The possible answers should be limited to Yes, No, Cancel, or a derivative of these. You should avoid asking questions that require answers in the form of text or a selection from a list of some kind.

WarningDialog

> An exclamation mark is displayed with a warning message indicating that something has unexpectedly gone wrong with the interface, the computer system, or some other urgent error condition.

WorkingDialog

> An hourglass is displayed with a message indicating that the application is busy processing a lengthy computation or anything that requires the user to wait.

Two of the different message dialog types are illustrated in Figure 3-22, along with the symbols for the other three.

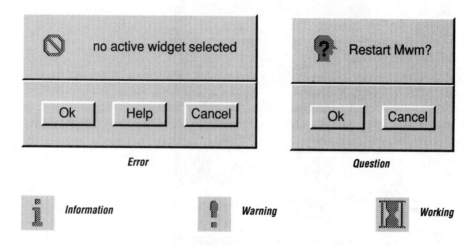

Figure 3-22. MessageDialogs with the five standard symbols

SelectionDialogs

SelectionDialogs are used when the user needs to provide more than a yes or no answer. For example, a SelectionDialog presents a ScrolledList containing an arbitrary list of choices that can be selected with the mouse, plus a TextField widget that can be used to type in a choice (which may or may not also be on the list). Figure 3-23 shows a SelectionDialog.

Figure 3-23. A SelectionDialog is useful for presenting a dynamic list of choices

A FileSelectionDialog is a more complex cousin to the SelectionDialog that is used to select a file to be read or written. This is shown in Figure 3-24.

Figure 3-24. A FileSelectionDialog is arcane but frequently needed

A PromptDialog, shown in Figure 3-25, is useful for prompting for any arbitrary text data.

Figure 3-25. A PromptDialog

A CommandDialog is an extension of the PromptDialog in that items input to the text entry field are stored in a scrolling list region. This widget is based on the Command widget, which is also an optional part of the MainWindow.

The intent is for the user to provide the application with commands; the list region contains a history of the commands already given. The user can select from the items in the history list to reissue previous commands. Figure 3-26 shows an example of a CommandDialog.

Figure 3-26. A CommandDialog

Custom Dialog Boxes

There are many cases where a popup dialog is useful, but none of the standard Motif dialog types applies. It is easy enough to create your own dialogs; however, there are some guidelines that the *Motif Style Guide* asks that you follow if you do so. These guidelines also apply to the configuration and labeling of buttons in the standard Motif dialogs.

At the highest level, all dialogs are broken down into two major components: the *control area* (or *work area*) and the *action area*. Each of these areas are conceptual regions which may be represented by multiple subwidgets.

In MessageDialogs, the control area is used only to display messages, but as you can see if you look back at the illustrations of the SelectionDialogs, this area can provide other optional control elements. SelectionDialogs display Lists and TextField widgets; it is also very common for a custom dialog to display an array of PushButtons or Toggles. For example, a communications program might have a setup dialog, which allowed the user to set parameters such as baud rate, parity, start and stop bits, and so on, using arrays of toggle buttons.

These controls provide information that will be used by the application once an action area button is invoked. In a typical MessageDialog, the control area displays the question while the action area provides PushButtons associated with the possible answers. Figure 3-27 shows a more complicated dialog with a control area that contains many items. Chapter 7, *Custom Dialogs*, discusses how to build customized dialogs, which may require the direct creation of widgets in the control area. Motif dialogs, on the other hand, do not require you to create any of the objects in the control area. The widgets displayed in that part of the dialog are always predefined and automatically created.

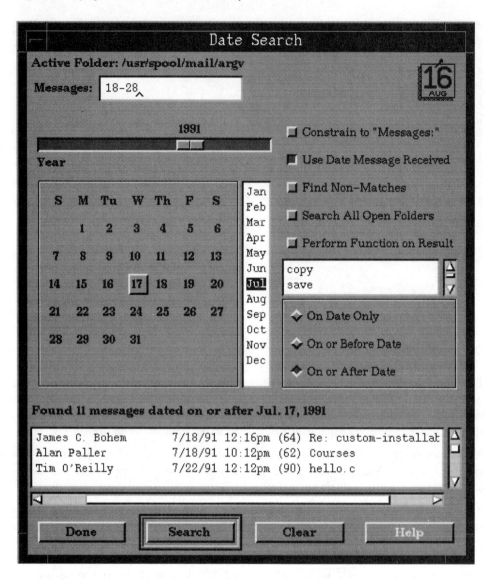

Figure 3-27. A custom dialog

Dialog Modality

One important concept to be aware of when it comes to dialogs is *modality*. In general, GUI-based programs are expected to be modeless. What this ultimately means is that the user, not the application, should be in control. The user should be able to choose from an array of application functions at any time, rather than stepping through them in a prearranged sequence, under the application's control.

Of course, there are limits to modelessness. Sometimes one thing has to happen before another. Often, sequencing is taken care of simply by the nesting of graphical user interface elements. For example, faced with the main window, the user may have only a choice of menu titles; once he pulls down the file menu, he may have a choice of opening, closing, saving, renaming, or printing the contents of a file. At some point, though, he goes far enough down a particular path that his choices need to be constrained.

Specifically, some dialog boxes require an answer before the user can go back to the application. For example, if the user asks to load a file, he may need to specify a filename via a dialog before he can go on to edit the file. A modal dialog requires an answer, by disallowing input to any other part of the application until it is either satisfied or cancelled.

There may be other cases, though, where dialogs are modeless. They can be left up on the screen without an immediate response, while the user goes back to the application's main window or another dialog.

3.5 Summary

Motif's rich widget set gives you a great deal of flexibility in designing your application. But with flexibility frequently comes indecision, or even confusion about the most effective way to use these objects.

If you want to give a user a set of exclusive choices, should you use a pulldown menu, a dialog box containing a group of exclusive ToggleButtons, or a List widget? There is no right answer—or perhaps it is better to say that the right answer depends on the nature of the choices and the flow of control in your application.

Effective user-interface design is an art. Only experience and experimentation, can teach you the most effective way to organize your application. What we can do in this book is to teach you how to use each widget class, and to give you a sense of the tradeoffs involved in using one class rather than another.

In this chapter, we've given you a broad overview of the Motif toolkit. Subsequent chapters delve into each widget class in detail. You should be able to read the chapters in any order, as the needs of your application dictate.

4

The Main Window

This chapter describes the Motif MainWindow widget, which can be used to frame many types of applications. The MainWindow is a manager widget that provides a menubar, scrollable work area, and various other optional display and control areas.

In This Chapter:

4
The Main Window

As discussed in Chapter 3, *Overview of Motif Widgets*, an application's main window is the most visible and most used of all the windows in an application. It is the focal point of the user's interactions with the program, and is typically the place where the application provides most of its visual feedback. To encourage consistency across the desktop, the *Motif Style Guide* suggests a generic main window layout, which can vary from application to application, but is generally followed by most Motif applications. Such a layout is shown in Figure 4-1.

In an effort to facilitate the task of building a main window, the Motif toolkit provides a MainWindow widget.

The MainWindow widget is not the only option for handling the application's main window layout; you are not required to use the MainWindow widget, nor should you feel you need to follow the Motif specifications to the letter. The main window layout is a strong recommendation, but many applications simply don't fit into the standard GUI design. For example, a clock application, a terminal emulator, a calculator, and a host of other desktop applications do not follow the Motif specifications in this regard, but they can still have Motif elements within them and can still be regarded as Motif-compliant. If you already have your application in mind, chances are you already know whether the main window layout applies to your situation; if in doubt, you are better off complying with the *Motif Style Guide*.

Before we get into a discussion of the MainWindow widget, realize that this widget class does not create any of the widgets it manages. What it does do is provide a facility for managing those widgets in a manner consistent with the *Style Guide*. Therefore, in order to properly discuss the MainWindow widget, we are going to have to discuss many other widget classes and use them in examples. As a beginning chapter in a large book on Motif programming, this might seem like a bit much to handle—especially if you are completely unfamiliar with the Motif toolkit. If this is the case, we encourage you to branch off into other chapters whenever you find it necessary to do so. However, recognize that it is not our intention to explain these other widgets ahead of time, nor is it our assumption that you already do. The lack of discussion of other widgets should not interfere with the main goal of this chapter: the MainWindow widget and how it fits into the design of an application.

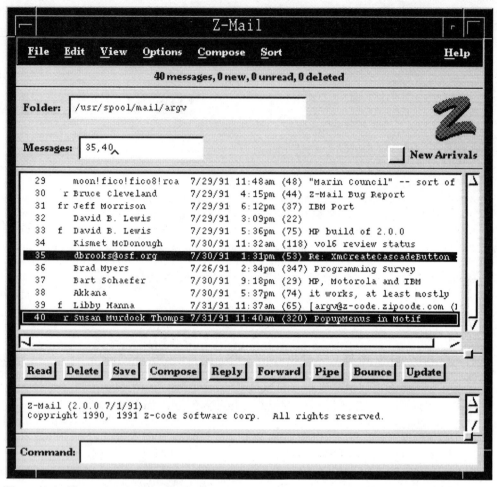

Figure 4-1. The main window of a Motif program

4.1 Creating a MainWindow

The MainWindow widget class is defined in *<Xm/MainW.h>*, which must be included whenever you create a MainWindow widget. As mentioned in Chapter 2, *The Motif Programming Model*, you should probably use an ApplicationShell or TopLevelShell widget as the Main-Window's parent. Assuming that you are using a MainWindow for the main application window, you typically use the ApplicationShell returned from `XtVaAppInitialize()` (or other similar toolkit initialization functions). The function `XtVaCreateManaged-Widget( )` is used to create an instance of the MainWindow widget, as shown in the following code fragment:

```
#include <Xm/MainW.h>
    .
    .
    .
main(argc, argv)
int argc;
char *argv[ ];
{
    Widget toplevel, main_w;
    XtAppContext app;

    toplevel = XtAppInitialize(&app, "App-Class",
        NULL, 0, &argc, argv, NULL, NULL);
    main_w = XtVaCreateManagedWidget("name", xmMainWindowWidgetClass, toplevel,
        resource-value list,
        NULL);

    XtRealizeWidget(toplevel);
    XtMainLoop(app);
}
```

The MainWindow class is subclassed from the ScrolledWindow class, which means that it has all the attributes of a ScrolledWindow, including all its resources. The ScrolledWindow allows the user to view an arbitrary widget of any size by attaching horizontal and vertical Scrollbars to it. In fact, you can think of a MainWindow as a ScrolledWindow with the additional ability to have an optional MenuBar, Command, and Message area. Unlike the ScrolledWindow widget, which can only manage one child widget (its *work window*), the MainWindow is also like a manager widget in that it can control the size and positions of other child widgets.

Because the MainWindow is subclassed from the ScrolledWindow widget, we will be referencing many ScrolledWindow resources and disclosing many facts about the ScrolledWindow before their time (Chapter 9, *ScrolledWindows and Scrollbars*). Eventually, you will need to learn more about the ScrolledWindow widget to best make use of the MainWindow. This chapter doesn't focus on the ScrolledWindow as much as it tries to present fundamental concepts about how the MainWindow operates on its children.

While the MainWindow does control the sizes and positions of other widget children (normally the duties of a manager widget), the geometry management it performs is not the classic management style of other manager widgets; the MainWindow is a special-case object that can handle only certain types of children, and can perform only simple widget positioning. Specifically, it can only handle cases that serve the generic main window layout specifications of the *Motif Style Guide*. We'll discuss this further after the upcoming example.

Let's take a look at how the MainWindow can be used in an actual application. Example 4-1 demonstrates how resource-value pairs can be used as well as how the MainWindow widget fits into a typical application design.

Example 4-1. Using a MainWindow widget in an application

```
/* show_pix.c -- a minimal MainWindow.  Use Label as the workWindow
 * to display a bitmap specified on the command line.
 */
#include <Xm/MainW.h>
#include <Xm/Label.h>

main(argc, argv)
int argc;
char *argv[ ];
{
    Widget toplevel, main_w, label;
    XtAppContext app;
    Pixmap pixmap;

    toplevel = XtVaAppInitialize(&app, "Demos",
        NULL, 0, &argc, argv, NULL, NULL);

    if (!argv[1]) {
        printf("usage: %s bitmap-file\n", *argv);
        exit(1);
    }

    main_w = XtVaCreateManagedWidget("main_window",
        xmMainWindowWidgetClass,   toplevel,
        XmNscrollBarDisplayPolicy, XmAS_NEEDED,
        XmNscrollingPolicy,        XmAUTOMATIC,
        NULL);

    /* Load bitmap given in argv[1] */
    pixmap = XmGetPixmap(XtScreen(toplevel), argv[1],
        BlackPixelOfScreen(XtScreen(toplevel)),
        WhitePixelOfScreen(XtScreen(toplevel)));

    if (pixmap == XmUNSPECIFIED_PIXMAP) {
        printf("can't create pixmap from %s\n", argv[1]);
        exit(1);
    }

    /* Now create label using pixmap */
    label = XtVaCreateManagedWidget("label", xmLabelWidgetClass, main_w,
        XmNlabelType,   XmPIXMAP,
        XmNlabelPixmap, pixmap,
        NULL);

    /* set the label as the "work area" of the main window */
    XtVaSetValues(main_w,
        XmNworkWindow, label,
        NULL);
    XtRealizeWidget(toplevel);
    XtAppMainLoop(app);
}
```

In this example, the MainWindow widget is not exploited to its fullest potential; it only contains one other widget, a Label widget, which is used to display a bitmap from the file specified as the first argument on the command line (`argv[1]`).[1] The Label widget is used as the work area window for the MainWindow. We did this intentionally to focus your attention on the *scrolled-window* aspect of the MainWindow widget. The following command line:

```
% show_pix /usr/include/X11/bitmaps/xlogo64
```

produces the output shown in Figure 4-2.

Figure 4-2. Output of 'show_pix xlogo64'

The file specified on the command line should contain X11 bitmap data so the application can create a pixmap. The pixmap is then displayed in a Label widget, which is set in the MainWindow as the value for the **XmNworkWindow** resource.

As shown in Figure 4-2, the bitmap is simply displayed in the window. However, if a larger bitmap was specified, only a portion of the bitmap is displayed, and scrollbars are provided so the user can view the rest. The output of the command:

```
% show_pix /usr/include/X11/bitmaps/escherknot
```

is shown in Figure 4-3.

---

[1] **XtVaAppInitialize( )** parses the command-line arguments the user gave when he ran the program. Those command-line options that are specific to Xlib or Xt are evaluated and removed from the argument list. What is not parsed is left in **argv**; our program reads **argv[1]** as the name of a bitmap to display in the MainWindow.

Figure 4-3. A large bitmap in a MainWindow widget

In this figure, we see that the bitmap is obviously too big to be placed in the MainWindow without either clipping the pixmap or enlarging the window. Rather than resizing its own window to unreasonable sizes, the MainWindow displays Scrollbars. This behavior was enabled by setting the following resource-value pairs for the MainWindow:

```
XmNscrollBarDisplayPolicy,  XmAS_NEEDED,
XmNscrollingPolicy,         XmAUTOMATIC,
```

These values automate the process whereby Scrollbars are managed when they are needed. If there is enough room for the entire area to be displayed, the Scrollbars are removed. The obvious question is, *what's its default size?* The answer is undefined; the internals to the toolkit set the width and height both to be **100** pixels. However, this is not a documented feature. In fact, both the MainWindow and the ScrolledWindow widget suffer from the same problem: unless you specifically set the **XmNwidth** and **XmNheight** resources, the default size is not very useful.

In any event, try resizing the *show_pix* window and see how the Scrollbars appear and disappear as needed. This is a result of the **XmNscrollBarDisplayPolicy** being set to **XmAS_NEEDED**.

As noted earlier, the **XmNscrollingPolicy** resource is inherited from the Scrolled-Window widget class. Another possible value that can be used is **Xm-APPLICATION_DEFINED**, which implies that some other entity is going to create, manage, and control (through callback routines) all the aspects of the MainWindow's Scrollbars. Application-defined scrolling happens to be the default for the MainWindow widget, but it is unlikely that you're going to want to leave it this way. Automatic scrolling is far easier to manage at this stage of the game. For complete details see Chapter 9, *ScrolledWindows and Scrollbars*.

Of course, setting the scrolling policy to be application-defined does not necessarily require you to provide your own scrolling mechanisms. It simply relieves the MainWindow widget from assuming the responsibility. If you use a ScrolledList or ScrolledText widget as the work area, you should definitely leave the **XmNscrollingPolicy** to be **Xm-APPLICATION_DEFINED**. This is because those widgets manage their own Scrollbars and will assume the scrolling behavior from the MainWindow. Example 4-2 provides an example of a program that uses a ScrolledList in a MainWindow widget.

Example 4-2. The main_list.c program

```
/* main_list.c -- use the ScrolledList window as the feature
 * component of a MainWindow widget.
 */
#include <Xm/MainW.h>
#include <Xm/List.h>

main(argc, argv)
char *argv[ ];
{
    Widget toplevel, main_w, list_w;
    XtAppContext app;
    Pixmap pixmap;

    toplevel = XtVaAppInitialize(&app, "Demos",
        NULL, 0, &argc, argv, NULL, NULL);

    main_w = XtVaCreateManagedWidget("main_window",
        xmMainWindowWidgetClass,    toplevel,
        NULL);

    list_w = XmCreateScrolledList(main_w, "main_list", NULL, 0);
    XtVaSetValues(list_w,
        XtVaTypedArg, XmNitems, XmRString,
            "Red, Green, Blue, Orange, Maroon, Grey, Black, White", 53,
        XmNitemCount, 8,
        XmNvisibleItemCount, 5,
        NULL);
    XtManageChild(list_w);

    /* set the list_w as the "work area" of the main window */
    XtVaSetValues(main_w, XmNworkWindow, XtParent(list_w), NULL);
    XtRealizeWidget(toplevel);
    XtAppMainLoop(app);
}
```

The most important thing to note about this program is that because **XmCreate-ScrolledList( )** creates both a ScrolledWindow and a List widget and returns a handle to the List widget, we must use **XtParent( )** to return a handle to the ScrolledWindow widget, so that it can be made the work area of the MainWindow. The most common error programmers make with ScrolledText and ScrolledList widgets is to use the actual Text or List widgets themselves rather than their ScrolledWindow parents. Again, we refer you to Chapter 9, *ScrolledWindows and Scrollbars*, for a complete discussion of how ScrolledText and ScrolledList objects should be used with the ScrolledWindow widget.

In order to simplify this application, we provided the items in the ScrolledList as a single string:

```
XtVaSetValues(list_w,
    XtVaTypedArg, XmNitems, XmRString,
        "Red, Green, Blue, Orange, Maroon, Grey, Black, White", 53,
    XmNitemCount, 8,
    XmNvisibleItemCount, 5,
    NULL);
```

This was done primarily because it was the easiest way to provide the list of colors for the List widget. Briefly, the items in the List widget must be specified as an array of compound strings. However, if we took the time to create this list separately, we would have had to create an array of **XmString** objects, create each string separately, set those strings in the List widget, then free each string separately after the widget was created. By using **Xt-VaTypedArg**, the whole list was created in one line without any complications because the List widget's type converter was used to convert the string into a list of compound strings. (This is the purpose of **XtVaTypedArg**).

The value of **53** represents the length of the string (containing the color names), plus the null terminator.

We use this form of resource specification frequently in this book to facilitate examples. See Volume Four, *X Toolkit Intrinsics Programmer's Manual*, for a complete discussion and details on how this kind of type conversion is done. See Chapter 13 for details on the List widget; see Chapter 19 for details on compound strings.

4.2 MenuBars

Creating a MenuBar is a fairly complex operation, and one that is completely independent of the MainWindow itself. However, the MenuBar is one of the principal reasons for using the MainWindow widget. We demonstrate the simplest way of implementing MenuBars in this section. Once they have been created, you simply tell the MainWindow to include the Menu-Bar in its window layout by providing a handle to it as the value of the MainWindow's **Xm-NmenuBar** resource.

In the Motif toolkit, a MenuBar is not implemented as a special widget. Rather, it is composed of a set of CascadeButtons arranged horizontally (under normal circumstances) by a RowColumn widget. Each CascadeButton is associated with a pulldown menu that contains PushButtons, Toggles, Labels, and Separators. The managing RowColumn widget has an internal flag set so that it knows when it is being used as a MenuBar. You do not need to know specific details about any of these widgets in order to create a functional MenuBar, as they are usually self-sufficient and handle themselves automatically. While the specifics for creating popup menus, pulldown menus, and MenuBars are covered in more detail in Chapter 16, *Menus*, the basic case is extremely simple.

There are various methods for creating and managing MenuBars, but the easiest is to use the simple convenience menu routines available from the Motif toolkit: `XmVaCreateSimpleMenuBar()` and `XmVaCreateSimplePulldownMenu()`.[2] These functions are demonstrated in the following code fragment:

```
XmString file, edit, help;
Widget menubar, main_w;
    .
    .
    .
/* Create a simple MenuBar that contains three menus */
file = XmStringCreateSimple("File");
edit = XmStringCreateSimple("Edit");
help = XmStringCreateSimple("Help");
menubar = XmVaCreateSimpleMenuBar(main_w, "menubar",
    XmVaCASCADEBUTTON, file, 'F',
    XmVaCASCADEBUTTON, edit, 'E',
    XmVaCASCADEBUTTON, help, 'H',
    NULL);
XmStringFree(file);
XmStringFree(edit);
XmStringFree(help);
    .
    .
    .
```

We show an extended example of using these functions later in the chapter. The output that this code generates is shown in Figure 4-4.

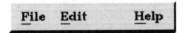

Figure 4-4. A simple MenuBar

The MenuBar is created using the convenience routine `XmVaCreateSimpleMenuBar()`. Like `XtVaSetValues()` and `XtVaCreateWidget()`, this function takes a variable argument list of configuration parameters. However, in addition to resource-value pairs, it may also take special arguments that define the types of items in the MenuBar. The first parameter is a symbolic constant that identifies the type of element to be added. Because a MenuBar is really just a special case of a RowColumn widget, most of the symbolic values possible here are not appropriate.

Each item in the MenuBar is a CascadeButton, since that is the only type of item that can display a pulldown menu. Therefore, the first parameter should always be set to `XmVaCASCADEBUTTON` unless you are passing RowColumn-specific resource-value pairs.

The label of the CascadeButton is given by the second parameter. In the first CascadeButton definition in the example, the variable `file` contains a compound string that represents the text `File`.[3] Compound strings have the ability to use multiple fonts and multiple lines, but

---

[2] There are also non-varargs versions of these functions, which require you to create each of the buttons individually, and associate them with the Menu via resources. However, the varargs functions are much easier to use.

[3] The only Motif widgets that display text and do not use compound strings are the Text and TextField widgets.

you should be careful not to abuse this flexibility. Each item in the MenuBar should be consistent in its font style, size, and color. A MenuBar is definitely not the place to be using multiple font techniques. This is why we use the simple compound string creation function, `XmStringCreateSimple( )`. This function creates a compound string using the default character set associated with the widget in which the string is rendered. For a complete discussion of compound strings, see Chapter 19, *Compound Strings*.

If you want to specify a global font for MenuBars and their menus, it would be better to specify them as resources (fallbacks or app-defaults). We'll discuss this towards the end of the chapter.

Since you are not creating each CascadeButton using the normal creation routines, you are not returned a handle to each button. You might hope that the label string you assign might serve as the widget's name, but in fact, since the buttons are created automatically and sequentially, the MenuBar assigns the name "button_*n*" to each, where *n* is the index into the MenuBar where it exists.[4] The third parameter defines the mnemonic, if any, for the CascadeButton on the MenuBar. The mnemonic used to pull down the **File** menu from the keyboard is "F". By convention, the first letter of the menu or menu item label is used as the mnemonic.

4.2.1 Creating the PullDown Menus

A similar method is used to create the items in the pulldown menu associated with each CascadeButton. The pulldown menu is created using the function `XmVaCreateSimplePulldownMenu( )`. This function is slightly more involved than `XmVaCreatSimpleMenuBar( )`. The parameters are:

```
Widget
XmVaCreateSimplePulldownMenu(menubar, name, post_from_button,callback, ...)
    Widget    menubar;
    char      *name;
    int        post_from_button;
    void      (*callback)( );
    ...
```

The CascadeButton associated with the menu is the `post_from_button` index (starting at zero) into the array of CascadeButtons held by the **menubar** parameter. This is going to be the same button that is going to display the pulldown menu. The **name** parameter is used strictly as the widget name for the RowColumn widget that is used to manage all the menu items in the menu. This name is *not* the title of the CascadeButton associated with it. The actual MenuShell that *is* the menu uses the same name with the suffix `_popup` appended to it. The name of the pulldown menu or its RowColumn widget child that manages the menu items are not of particular interest, since you should not (nor expect the user to) provide resource specifications for them. However, the widget hierarchy in resource specifications

---

[4] The names given to the CascadeButtons (e.g., *Button_0*) are subject to change in future releases of the Motif toolkit.

for these menus starts at the MenuBar, goes through the MenuShell to the RowColumn "pull-down menu" and finally to the menu items.

The `callback` parameter specifies a function that will be invoked whenever the user activates any of the items in the menu. We'll get back to this function in a moment.

Unlike MenuBars, which can only contain CascadeButtons, there are many possible types of elements that can be put into a pulldown menu. As was the case with `XmVaCreate-SimpleMenuBar()`, these elements are created by specifying a symbolic constant identifying the type of item to be added, followed by a variable number of additional parameters, depending on the type of menu item.

The types of menu items to be added are specified using one of the following variable argument list parameters:

`XmVaPUSHBUTTON`

> The item is a standard PushButton, as shown in the example code fragment. It takes four additional parameters: a label, a mnemonic, an accelerator, and a compound string that displays what the accelerator is. Selection of this item causes the `callback` routine to be called. Its `client_data` parameter is an integer value from `0` to `n-1`, indicating the index into the pulldown menu that the item represents. That is, if the `client_data` value is two, then the third item in the menu was selected.

`XmVaTOGGLEBUTTON`

> The item is a ToggleButton and takes the same four extra parameters as described by `XmVaPUSHBUTTON`. Selecting this item toggles the value of the button and causes the `callback` routine to be called. The `client_data` passed to the callback routine is also handled similarly.

`XmVaCHECKBUTTON`

> This value is identical to `XmVaTOGGLEBUTTON`.

`XmVaRADIOBUTTON`

> The item is a ToggleButton with RadioBox characteristics, as discussed in Chapter 12, *Toggle Widgets*. That is, only one item in the menu may be set at a time. *Note: the pulldown menu does not enforce this behavior.* You must either handle this yourself, or pass extra parameters to the menu for it to function like a normal Radio-Box. Creating a menu with RadioBox behavior is demonstrated later in the Chapter.

`XmVaCASCADEBUTTON`

> The item is a CascadeButton that usually contains a pullright menu. This value only has two additional parameters: a compound string label and a mnemonic. Pullright menus are, ironically, more easily implemented and managed using the not-so-simple menu creation routines described in Chapter 16, *Menus*. `XmVaCreateSimplePulldownMenu()` is only intended to be used in very simple cases.

`XmVaSEPARATOR`

> The item is a Separator gadget, and since separators cannot be selected, the callback routine cannot be called for this item. There are no additional parameters for this

item. Furthermore, adding a separator does *not* affect the item count with respect to the `client_data` values passed to the callback routine for other menu items.

XmVaSINGLE_SEPARATOR

This value is identical to **XmVaSEPARATOR**.

XmVaDOUBLE_SEPARATOR

This is similar to **XmVaSEPARATOR**, except that the separator widget displays a double line.

XmVaTITLE

This value causes a simple Label widget to be created as a title (perhaps for a group of other items). The item is not selectable, so it does not have a mnemonic associated with it.

Once all the items in a MenuBar have been created, it must be managed using **XtManage-Child( )**. However, the widgets returned by **XmVaCreateSimplePulldown-Menu( )** should not be managed until they are ready to be popped up. This process happens automatically, though, so you needn't worry about managing them.

The following code fragment shows how **XmCreateSimpleMenuBar( )** can be used:

```
/* First menu is the File menu -- callback is file_cb() */
new = XmStringCreateSimple("New ...");
save = XmStringCreateSimple("Save ...");
quit = XmStringCreateSimple("Quit");
quit_acc = XmStringCreateSimple("Ctrl+C");
XmVaCreateSimplePulldownMenu(menubar, "file_menu", 0, file_cb,
    XmVaPUSHBUTTON, new, 'N', NULL, NULL,
    XmVaPUSHBUTTON, save, 'S', NULL, NULL,
    XmVaSEPARATOR,
    XmVaPUSHBUTTON, quit, 'Q', "Ctrl<Key>c", quit_acc,
    NULL);
XmStringFree(new);
XmStringFree(save);
XmStringFree(quit);
```

General Comments on MenuBars

*   The MenuBar should be handled using a completely straightforward implementation of menus and menu items. You may use the methods described here, or the more sophisticated ones discussed in Chapter 16, *Menus*.

*   Do not attempt to install callback routines on the CascadeButtons themselves. People sometimes do this because they want to know when a particular menu was popped up. This should be handled using **XtNpopupCallback** functions on the MenuShell itself. Popup and popdown callback lists are mentioned in Chapter 7, *Custom Dialogs*; for greater detail, see Volume Four, *X Toolkit Intrinsics Programmer's Manual*.

*   All CascadeButtons must have menus associated with them.

*   Menus are not intended to be dynamically changed; do not attempt to add, delete, or modify menus or menu items once the program has started (with the exception that you can change menu items' sensitivities using **XmNsensitive**). The MenuBar is intended

to be static in the user's eyes; changing the menus in the MenuBar would be like changing the functionality of the program while the user is running it.

Note that the labels associated with each menu item are just like the labels associated with the CascadeButtons on the MenuBar—they are not the names of the widgets themselves. And, just like the CascadeButtons, the *names* of these widgets are "button_*n*", where *n* is the index into the menu with which the item is associated.

Later, we'll examine how you can modify MenuBars and menu items through X resources. Using fallback resources, for example, you can specify the labels, mnemonics, and accelerators for all menus and menu items used in the MenuBar.

4.2.2 SimpleMenu Callback Routines

The callback routine associated with the **File** menu shown earlier is invoked whenever the user selects any of the buttons in the menu. You can write the callback routine in the form:

```
void
file_cb(menu_item, item_no, cbs)
    Widget menu_item;          /* the menu item selected */
    int item_no;               /* pulldown menu item number */
    XmAnyCallbackStruct *cbs;  /* unused here */
```

The **menu_item** parameter is a handle to the widget that was selected in the menu. The **client_data** parameter is the menu item's index into its parent menu. The **cbs** parameter (short for "CallBack Structure") is a pointer to a structure of type **XmAnyCallbackStruct**. This is the simplest version of a wide variety of callback structures associated with all Motif callback routines. In actuality, the callback structure is an **XmPushButtonCallbackStruct** because the menu item that invoked it was a PushButton. Later, we'll see that this button could have been a ToggleButton, in which case the callback structure would be of type **XmToggleButtonCallbackStruct**. It is because we don't really know which type of widget class was used as the menu item that we declare the **cbs** parameter as the generic *any* callback structure.

This particular structure has the following form:

```
typedef struct {
    int      reason;
    XEvent *event;
} XmAnyCallbackStruct;
```

All callback structures have these fields as well, but they also contain more detailed information about why the callback function was invoked. In the case of **XmPushButtonCallbackStruct**, the structure has the following form:

```
typedef struct {
    int      reason;
    XEvent *event;
    int      click_count;
} XmPushButtonCallbackStruct;
```

The **click_count** field is normally used when PushButtons are not in menus. See Chapter 11, *Labels and Buttons*, for details.

The `XmToggleButtonCallbackStruct` is also quite similar; it takes the following form:

```
typedef struct {
    int      reason;
    XEvent *event;
    int      set;
} XmToggleButtonCallbackStruct;
```

The `set` field indicates whether the item was *selected* (turned on) or deselected (turned off). We will get into this topic in more detail later in the chapter. The way to determine which of the two callback structures the `cbs` parameter points to is by examining its `reason` field. Since all callback structures have this field, it is always safe to query it. This field has a wide range of possible values that indicate why the callback routine was invoked, which also may lead to an indication of the type of widget that invoked us. While we could always check the `widget` parameter (menu item) itself by using the macro `XtIsSubClass()` to determine from which widget class it is subclassed, the task can be much simpler and more straightforward.

In our example, the value will always be `XmCR_ACTIVATE`, since we know that there are only PushButtons as the menu items. If, however, there happened to be ToggleButtons in the menu, and the callback was invoked by a Toggle, the value would be `Xm-CR_VALUE_CHANGED`.

The `event` field is a pointer to an `XEvent` structure that identifies the actual event that caused the callback routine to be invoked. In this example, the event is not of particular interest.

In the callback function, you can choose to do whatever is appropriate for the item that was selected. The callback structure is probably not going to help much for the common case. However, the `client_data` can be used to identify which of the menu items was selected. The following code fragment demonstrates how this is done:

```
/* a menu item from the "File" pulldown menu was selected */
void
file_cb(w, item_no, cbs)
Widget w;                    /* menu item selected (unused here) */
int item_no;                 /* pulldown menu item number */
XmAnyCallbackStruct *cbs;    /* unused here */
{
    extern void OpenNewFile(), SaveFile();

    if (item_no == 2)      /* the "Quit" button */
        exit(0);

    if (item_no == 0)      /* the "new" button */
        OpenNewFile();
    else if (item_no == 1) /* the "save" button */
        SaveFile();
}
```

The callback routines for menu items should be as simple as possible from a structural point of view. If your application is designed well, you should have application-specific entry points such as `OpenNewFile()` and `SaveFile()`, as shown in the previous example, defined in separate files not necessarily associated with the GUI portion of the program. This will help considerably if your program must be maintained by a large group of people or you expect to port it to other user interfaces.

4.2.3 A Sample Application

Let's examine an example program that integrates what we have discussed so far. Example 4-3 modifies the behavior of our first example, which displayed an arbitrary pixmap, by allowing the user to change the bitmap dynamically using a Motif FileSelectionDialog. The program also offers the user the ability to dynamically change the bitmap's color using a pulldown menu. As you can see by the size of the program, adding these two simple features is not trivial. Many functions and widgets are required in order to make the program functional. As you read the example, don't worry about unknown widgets or details that we haven't addressed just yet; we will discuss them afterwards. For now, try to identify the familiar parts and see how everything works together.

Example 4-3. The dynapix.c program

```
/* dynapix.c -- Display a bitmap in a MainWindow, but allow the user
 * to change the bitmap and its color dynamically.  The design of the
 * program is structured on the pulldown menus of the menubar and the
 * callback routines associated with them.  To allow the user to choose
 * a new bitmap, the "New" button popsup a FileSelectionDialog where
 * a new bitmap file can be chosen.
 */
#include <Xm/MainW.h>
#include <Xm/Label.h>
#include <Xm/MessageB.h>
#include <Xm/FileSB.h>

/* Globals: the toplevel window/widget and the label for the bitmap.
 * "colors" defines the colors we use, "cur_color" is the current
 * color being used, and "cur_bitmap" references the current bitmap file.
 */
Widget toplevel, label;
String colors[ ] = { "Black", "Red", "Green", "Blue" };
Pixel cur_color;
char cur_bitmap[ 1024 ] = "xlogo64"; /* make large enough for full pathnames */

main(argc, argv)
int argc;
char *argv[ ];
{
    Widget main_w, menubar, menu, widget;
    XtAppContext app;
    Pixmap pixmap;
    XmString file, edit, help, new, quit, red, green, blue, black;
    void file_cb(), change_color(), help_cb();

    /* Initialize toolkit and parse command line options. */
    toplevel = XtVaAppInitialize(&app, "Demos",
        NULL, 0, &argc, argv, NULL, NULL);

    /* main window contains a MenuBar and a Label displaying a pixmap */
    main_w = XtVaCreateManagedWidget("main_window",
        xmMainWindowWidgetClass,    toplevel,
```

Example 4-3. The dynapix.c program (continued)

```
            XmNscrollBarDisplayPolicy, XmAS_NEEDED,
            XmNscrollingPolicy,        XmAUTOMATIC,
            NULL);

    /* Create a simple MenuBar that contains three menus */
    file = XmStringCreateSimple("File");
    edit = XmStringCreateSimple("Edit");
    help = XmStringCreateSimple("Help");
    menubar = XmVaCreateSimpleMenuBar(main_w, "menubar",
        XmVaCASCADEBUTTON, file, 'F',
        XmVaCASCADEBUTTON, edit, 'E',
        XmVaCASCADEBUTTON, help, 'H',
        NULL);
    XmStringFree(file);
    XmStringFree(edit);
    /* don't free "help" compound string yet -- reuse it later */

    /* Tell the menubar which button is the help menu  */
    if (widget = XtNameToWidget(menubar, "button_2"))
        XtVaSetValues(menubar, XmNmenuHelpWidget, widget, NULL);

    /* First menu is the File menu -- callback is file_cb() */
    new = XmStringCreateSimple("New ...");
    quit = XmStringCreateSimple("Quit");
    XmVaCreateSimplePulldownMenu(menubar, "file_menu", 0, file_cb,
        XmVaPUSHBUTTON, new, 'N', NULL, NULL,
        XmVaSEPARATOR,
        XmVaPUSHBUTTON, quit, 'Q', NULL, NULL,
        NULL);
    XmStringFree(new);
    XmStringFree(quit);

    /* Second menu is the Edit menu -- callback is change_color() */
    black = XmStringCreateSimple(colors[0]);
    red = XmStringCreateSimple(colors[1]);
    green = XmStringCreateSimple(colors[2]);
    blue = XmStringCreateSimple(colors[3]);
    menu = XmVaCreateSimplePulldownMenu(menubar, "edit_menu", 1, change_color,
        XmVaRADIOBUTTON, black, 'k', NULL, NULL,
        XmVaRADIOBUTTON, red, 'R', NULL, NULL,
        XmVaRADIOBUTTON, green, 'G', NULL, NULL,
        XmVaRADIOBUTTON, blue, 'B', NULL, NULL,
        XmNradioBehavior, True,      /* RowColumn resources to enforce */
        XmNradioAlwaysOne, True,     /* radio behavior in Menu */
        NULL);
    XmStringFree(black);
    XmStringFree(red);
    XmStringFree(green);
    XmStringFree(blue);

    /* Initialize menu so that "black" is selected. */
    if (widget = XtNameToWidget(menu, "button_0"))
        XtVaSetValues(widget, XmNset, True, NULL);

    /* Third menu is the help menu -- callback is help_cb() */
    XmVaCreateSimplePulldownMenu(menubar, "help_menu", 2, help_cb,
        XmVaPUSHBUTTON, help, 'H', NULL, NULL,
        NULL);
```

Example 4-3. The dynapix.c program (continued)

```
        XmStringFree(help); /* we're done with it; now we can free it */

        XtManageChild(menubar);

    /* user can still specify the initial bitmap */
    if (argv[1])
        strcpy(cur_bitmap, argv[1]);
    /* initialize color */
    cur_color = BlackPixelOfScreen(XtScreen(toplevel)),

    /* create initial bitmap */
    pixmap = XmGetPixmap(XtScreen(toplevel), cur_bitmap,
        cur_color, WhitePixelOfScreen(XtScreen(toplevel)));

    if (pixmap == XmUNSPECIFIED_PIXMAP) {
        puts("can't create initial pixmap");
        exit(1);
    }

    /* Now create label using pixmap */
    label = XtVaCreateManagedWidget("label", xmLabelWidgetClass, main_w,
        XmNlabelType,    XmPIXMAP,
        XmNlabelPixmap, pixmap,
        NULL);

    /* set the label as the "work area" of the main window */
    XtVaSetValues(main_w,
        XmNmenuBar,     menubar,
        XmNworkWindow, label,
        NULL);

    XtRealizeWidget(toplevel);
    XtAppMainLoop(app);
}
/* Any item the user selects from the File menu calls this function.
 * It will either be "New" (item_no == 0) or "Quit" (item_no == 1).
 */
void
file_cb(w, item_no)
Widget w;       /* menu item that was selected */
int item_no;    /* the index into the menu */
{
    static Widget dialog; /* make it static for reuse */
    extern void load_pixmap();

    if (item_no == 1) /* the "quit" item */
        exit(0);

    /* "New" was selected.  Create a Motif FileSelectionDialog w/callback */
    if (!dialog) {
        dialog = XmCreateFileSelectionDialog(toplevel, "file_sel", NULL, 0);
        XtAddCallback(dialog, XmNokCallback, load_pixmap, NULL);
        XtAddCallback(dialog, XmNcancelCallback, XtUnmanageChild, NULL);
    }
    XtManageChild(dialog);
    XtPopup(XtParent(dialog), XtGrabNone);
}

/* The Ok button was selected from the FileSelectionDialog (or, the user
 * double-clicked on a file selection).  Try to read the file as a bitmap.
```

Example 4-3. The dynapix.c program (continued)

```
 * If the user changed colors, we call this function directly from change_color()
 * to reload the pixmap.  In this case, we pass NULL as the callback struct
 * so we can identify this special case.
 */
void
load_pixmap(dialog, client_data, cbs)
Widget dialog;             /* Ok button was pressed in "dialog" (unused) */
XtPointer client_data;      /* ignored -- NULL passed to XtAddCallback() */
XmFileSelectionBoxCallbackStruct *cbs; /* NULL if called from change_color() */
{
    Pixmap pixmap;
    char *file = NULL;

    if (cbs) {
        if (!XmStringGetLtoR(cbs->value, XmSTRING_DEFAULT_CHARSET, &file))
            return; /* internal error */
        (void) strcpy(cur_bitmap, file);
        XtFree(file); /* free allocated data from XmStringGetLtoR() */
    }

    pixmap = XmGetPixmap(XtScreen(toplevel), cur_bitmap,
        cur_color, WhitePixelOfScreen(XtScreen(toplevel)));

    if (pixmap == XmUNSPECIFIED_PIXMAP)
        printf("can't create pixmap from %s\n", cur_bitmap);
    else {
        Pixmap old;
        XtVaGetValues(label, XmNlabelPixmap, &old, NULL);
        XmDestroyPixmap(old);
        XtVaSetValues(label,
            XmNlabelType,    XmPIXMAP,
            XmNlabelPixmap, pixmap,
            NULL);
    }
}

/* called from any of the "Edit" menu items.  Change the color of the
 * current bitmap being displayed.  Do this by calling load_pixmap().
 */
void
change_color(w, item_no)
Widget w;     /* menu item that was selected */
int item_no;  /* the index into the menu */
{
    XColor xcolor, unused;
    Display *dpy = XtDisplay(label);
    Colormap cmap = DefaultColormapOfScreen(XtScreen(label));

    if (XAllocNamedColor(dpy, cmap, colors[item_no], &xcolor, &unused) == 0 ||
        cur_color == xcolor.pixel)
        return;

    cur_color = xcolor.pixel;
    load_pixmap(w, NULL, NULL);
}

#define MSG \n
"Use the FileSelection dialog to find bitmap files to\n
display in the scrolling area in the main window.  Use\n
```

Example 4-3. The dynapix.c program (continued)

```
the edit menu to display the bitmap in different colors."

/* The help button in the help menu from the menubar was selected.
 * Display help information defined above for how to use the program.
 * This is done by creating a Motif information dialog box.  Again,
 * make the dialog static so we can reuse it.
 */
void
help_cb()
{
    static Widget dialog;

    if (!dialog) {
        Arg args[1];
        XmString msg = XmStringCreateLtoR(MSG, XmSTRING_DEFAULT_CHARSET);
        XtSetArg(args[0], XmNmessageString, msg);
        dialog = XmCreateInformationDialog(toplevel, "help_dialog", args, 1);
    }
    XtManageChild(dialog);
    XtPopup(XtParent(dialog), XtGrabNone);
}
```

The output of the program is shown in Figure 4-5.

Figure 4-5. Output of dynapix.c

The beginning of the program is pretty much as expected. After the Toolkit is initialized, the MainWindow and the MenuBar are created the same way as in the previous examples. Just after the MenuBar is created, however, we make the following calls:

```
    if (widget = XtNameToWidget(menubar, "button_2"))
        XtVaSetValues(menubar, XmNmenuHelpWidget, widget, NULL);
```

The purpose of these statements is to inform the MenuBar which of its CascadeButtons contains the **Help** menu. By setting the MenuBar's **XmNmenuHelpWidget** resource to the CascadeButton returned by **XtNameToWidget( )**, the MenuBar knows that this button should be treated specially. (It should be right-adjusted at all times.) This is necessary for the appearance of the application to conform to the Motif guidelines. For details on how to support a help system, see Chapter 7, *Custom Dialogs*, and Chapter 20, *Advanced Dialog Programming*.

Pulldown menus are created next in the expected manner. However, for the **Edit** menu, something new is added. The effect we want to give is shown in Figure 4-6.

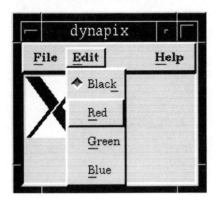

Figure 4-6. The Edit menu for dynapix.c

Here, each item in the menu represents a color; the color that is currently being used is marked with a diamond shape inset into the menu. In order to get this *radio-box* behavior, we must set each menu item in the pulldown menu to be an **XmVaRADIOBUTTON** and tell the menu to treat the entire menu as a RadioBox. The analogy is that of an old car radio where selecting a new station causes the other selectors to pop out. Just as you can only have the radio tuned to one station at a time, you may only have one color set at a time. This is all managed automatically by the RowColumn widget, which is used by the Motif toolkit to implement the layout of menu items in MenuShells. When a RowColumn widget's **Xm-NradioBehavior** and **XmNradioAlwaysOne** resources are set to **True**, then you get the RadioBox behavior. See Chapter 12, *Toggle Widgets*, for a complete description and further examples of how this works.

We're not quite done with this menu, though. The RowColumn can manage the RadioBox provided that the "radio" has been turned on. That is, we need to initialize one of the buttons to the initial color. In the next statement, the menu (RadioBox) is initialized to have its first item selected, which is the same color we are using as the initial color. (We know ahead of time that the color will be black.) The function **XtNameToWidget( )** is used again to get the appropriate button from the menu. Since the menu items were created using **Xm-VaRADIOBUTTON**, the widget returned must be a ToggleButton. The resource **XmNset** can be used on that button to turn it on. Once the menu has been initialized, the Motif toolkit handles the rest automatically.

To clarify an important point, although **XmVaCreateSimplePulldownMenu( )** creates an entire pulldown menu, the function actually returns a RowColumn widget that manages the menu's items; it does not return the MenuShell widget that is actually popped up and down when the menu is used. To get a handle to that widget, you need to use **XtParent( )** on the RowColumn widget. This is good design, since you need access to the RowColumn widget more than you need access to the MenuShell. (In fact, you should never need access to the MenuShell, except in rare cases.)

The final task is to create the **Help** menu. Note, however, that even though there is only one item in the menu (the **Help** item), it must still be installed; you cannot have an empty pulldown menu in a MenuBar.

Once all the items are installed, the MenuBar is managed using `XtManageChild( )`. While the whole approach to creating MenuBars, menus, menu items, and their associated callback routines may seem simple and straightforward, you may find that you are still quite limited. For instance, you cannot specify different labels and callback routines for different items in the same menu; you cannot provide different client data to the callback routines; and you cannot name the widgets individually. Of course, you may not need this flexibility. Still, the most inconvenient aspect of this method is that there is so much redundant code you have to write in order to build a realistically sized MenuBar. For the time being, the intent is to introduce to the concept and demonstrate the recommended design approach for applications. You can learn about how the process can be generalized for large quantities of menus, menu items, and so forth in Chapter 16, *Menus*.

The rest of Example 4-3 is composed of callback routines used by the pulldown menu items and other objects created within those callbacks. For example, when the user selects either of the items in the **File** menu, the function `file_cb( )` is called. If the **Quit** item is selected, the `item_no` parameter will be 1, and the program will exit. If the **New** item is selected, the `item_no` will be 0, and a FileSelectionDialog will pop up, allowing the user to select a new bitmap file to display. This is done using the convenience routine `XmCreateFileSelectionDialog( )`, and produces the results found in Figure 4-7. Two callback routines are installed for the dialog: `load_pixmap( )`, called when the user presses the **Ok** button (confirming a file selection); and `XtUnmanageChild( )`, called when the **Cancel** button is selected. This indicates that the dialog may be dismissed. For more detailed information on the FileSelectionDialog, see Chapter 6, *Selection Dialogs*.

The `load_pixmap( )` function actually loads a new bitmap from a file into the Label widget. This function uses the same method for loading a pixmap as was used earlier in `main( )`. However, because the function may be called from the FileSelectionDialog, we need to get the value of the file selection. Since the filename is represented as a compound string, it must be converted into a C string. The value is taken from the **value** field of the FileSelectionDialog's callback structure, `XmFileSelectionBoxCallbackStruct`. The conversion is done using `XmStringGetLtoR( )`, which creates a regular C string for use by `XmGetPixmap( )`. Yet, because `load_pixmap( )` may be called artificially from `change_color( )`, we check the `cbs` parameter. If the function was called artificially, `cbs` will be NULL.

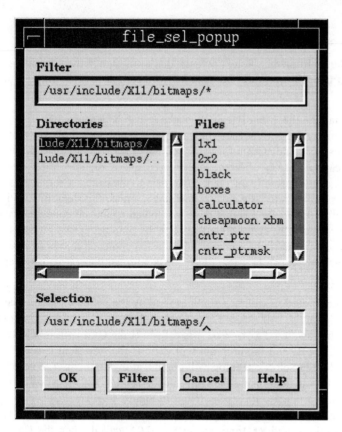

Figure 4-7. FileSelectionDialog used to specify bitmap files

If `XmGetPixmap( )` succeeds, then we need to get the old pixmap and "destroy" it using `XmDestroyPixmap( )` before installing the new one. This function is the companion function to `XmGetPixmap( )`, which loads and caches each pixmap it is given. If you call the function more than once for a given image, then it returns the same image each time. This saves space by not having to allocate a new version of the pixmap for each call. `Xm-DestroyPixmap( )` decrements the reference count for the image; if the reference count goes to zero, then the pixmap is actually destroyed. Otherwise, another reference to it may exist, in which case, nothing is done. It is always important to use these functions in pairs. If you need to use other pixmap-loading functions to create pixmaps, you cannot use `Xm-DestroyPixmap( )` to free it.

The function `change_color( )` is used as the callback routine for items in the **Edit** menu. The name of the chosen color is stored in the `colors` array of `String` types. The index into the array is the same as the index into the menu of the menu item selected. The color name is parsed and loaded using `XAllocNamedColor( )` provided the string exists in the RGB database (usually */usr/lib/X11/rgb.txt*). If successful, the function returns a non-zero status and the `XColor` structure is filled with RGB data and the pixel values. (The pixel is the index into the colormap for the color.) If the function returns zero, or if the pixel value returned happens to be the same as the one currently used, `change_color( )` returns, as there is no point in reloading an identical pixmap. For additional information about loading and using colors, see Volume One, *Xlib Programmer's Manual*, and Volume Two, *Xlib Reference Manual*.

The last function of the file is `help_cb( )`, the callback routine for when the **Help** menu item is selected from the **Help** menu on the MenuBar. It simply displays an Information-Dialog containing a message describing how to use the program. See Chapter 6, *Selection Dialogs*, for a complete description of these dialogs and suggestions on implementing a functional help system.

NOTE

The next section deals with the Command and Message Areas. However, most of what you need to know about the main window of an application has already been discussed. This chapter deals with the MainWindow widget, and Chapter 3, *Overview of Motif Widgets*, dealt with more general issues concerning the way Motif specifies the main window of the application. Hypothetically, you could skip the next section and be relatively secure in moving on to the next chapter. However, there are more details of the MainWindow widget that need to be discussed in order to make this chapter complete. Therefore, this section is considered "advanced" and, regrettably, imprecise. Examples in later chapters should clarify some of the material used here.

4.3 The Command and Message Areas

The greatest difficulty with the Command and Message Areas of the MainWindow is that these objects are better defined in the Motif specification than in the Motif toolkit. By definition, the Command Area is intended to support a tty-style command-line interface to the application. This is not to suggest that the Command Area is supposed to act like *xterm* or any sort of terminal emulator. It is just a single-line text area for entering individually typed commands for the application.

The Message Area is just a Text widget used for outputting error and status messages as needed by the application.

While both of these are optional MainWindow elements, the Message Area is usually more common than the Command Area. Nevertheless, let's begin with the Command Area.

Command Areas are most convenient for applications that have command-line interpreters. This is usually necessary for programs that have been converted from a tty interface where the program responds to typed commands. Properly converted, such applications can do rather well as GUI-based programs, although this is frequently more difficult than what most people expect. On the other hand, there are some cases that are somewhat unrealistic, although possible. For example, a PostScript interpreter could be implemented using a Command Area in the MainWindow. However, PostScript is a very verbose and lengthy language that does not work well with single-line text entry fields.

Example 4-4 shows how the Command Area can be used to allow the user to input standard UNIX commands. The output of the commands is displayed in the ScrolledText object (the work area of the MainWindow). For brevity, we've kept the MenuBar smaller so as to dedicate most of the program to the use of the Command Area.

Example 4-4. The cmd_area.c program

```
/* cmd_area.c -- use a ScrolledText object to view the
 * putput of commands input by the user in a Command window.
 */
#include <Xm/Text.h>
#include <Xm/MainW.h>
#include <Xm/Command.h>
#include <stdio.h>              /* For popen() */

/* main() -- initialize toolkit, create a main window, menubar,
 * a Command Area and a ScrolledText to view the output of commands.
 */
main(argc, argv)
int argc;
char *argv[ ];
{
    Widget        top, main_w, menubar, menu, command_w, text_w;
    XtAppContext  app;
    XmString      file, quit;
    extern void   exec_cmd(), exit();
    Arg           args[4];

    /* initialize toolkit and create toplevel shell */
    top = XtVaAppInitialize(&app, "Demos",
        NULL, 0, &argc, argv, NULL, NULL);

    (void) close(0); /* don't let commands read from stdin */

    /* MainWindow for the application -- contains menubar, ScrolledText
     * and CommandArea (which prompts for filename).
     */
    main_w = XtVaCreateManagedWidget("main_w",
        xmMainWindowWidgetClass, top,
        NULL);

    /* Create a simple MenuBar that contains one menu */
    file = XmStringCreateSimple("File");
    menubar = XmVaCreateSimpleMenuBar(main_w, "menubar",
        XmVaCASCADEBUTTON, file, 'F',
        NULL);
    XmStringFree(file);

    /* "File" menu has only one item (Quit), so make callback exit() */
    quit = XmStringCreateSimple("Quit");
    menu = XmVaCreateSimplePulldownMenu(menubar, "file_menu", 0, exit,
        XmVaPUSHBUTTON, quit, 'Q', NULL, NULL,
        NULL);
    XmStringFree(quit);

    /* Menubar is done -- manage it */
    XtManageChild(menubar);

    /* Create ScrolledText -- this is work area for the MainWindow */
    XtSetArg(args[0], XmNrows,        24);
```

Example 4-4. The cmd_area.c program (continued)

```
    XtSetArg(args[1], XmNcolumns,    80);
    XtSetArg(args[2], XmNeditable,   False);
    XtSetArg(args[3], XmNeditMode,   XmMULTI_LINE_EDIT);
    text_w = XmCreateScrolledText(main_w, "text_w", args, 4);
    XtManageChild(text_w);

    /* store text_w as user data in "File" menu for file_cb() callback */
    XtVaSetValues(menu, XmNuserData, text_w, NULL);

    /* Create the command area -- this must be a Command class widget */
    file = XmStringCreateSimple("Command:");
    command_w = XtVaCreateWidget("command_w", xmCommandWidgetClass, main_w,
        XmNpromptString, file,
        NULL);
    XmStringFree(file);
    XtAddCallback(command_w, XmNcommandEnteredCallback, exec_cmd, text_w);
    XtManageChild(command_w);

    XmMainWindowSetAreas(main_w, menubar, command_w,
        NULL, NULL, XtParent(text_w));
    XtRealizeWidget(top);
    XtAppMainLoop(app);
}
/* execute the command and redirect output to the ScrolledText window */
void
exec_cmd(cmd_widget, text_w, cbs)
Widget cmd_widget;  /* the command widget itself, not its Text widget */
Widget text_w; /* passed the text_w as client_data */
XmCommandCallbackStruct *cbs;
{
    char *cmd, buf[BUFSIZ];
    XmTextPosition pos;
    FILE *pp;

    XmStringGetLtoR(cbs->value, XmSTRING_DEFAULT_CHARSET, &cmd);

    if (!cmd || !*cmd) { /* nothing typed? */
        if (cmd)
            XtFree(cmd);
        return;
    }

    /* make sure the file is a regular text file and open it */
    if (!(pp = popen(cmd, "r")))
        perror(cmd);
    XtFree(cmd);
    if (!pp)
        return;

    /* put the output of the command in the Text widget by reading
     * until EOF (meaning that the command has terminated).
     */
    for (pos = 0; fgets(buf, sizeof buf, pp); pos += strlen(buf))
        XmTextReplace(text_w, pos, pos, buf);

    pclose(pp);
}
```

When using the MainWindow widget strictly as written, the CommandArea can *only* be a CommandWidget. Attempting to use any other type of widget class will result in a warning message. Thus, you will most likely come out with a window layout resembling that shown in Figure 4-8. Visually, the Command widget has a *history area* that contains at least one visible item. However, in the general case, you don't necessarily have to use a Command widget. You could avoid this by specifying a manager widget as the "work window" of the MainWindow widget and providing a TextField widget in that manager to (at least visually) represent the command area.

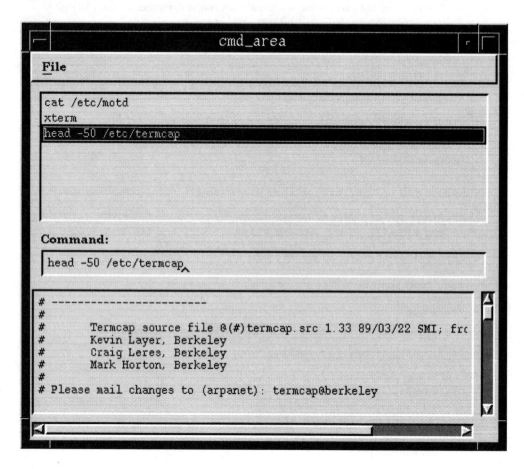

Figure 4-8. Output of cmd_area.c

Some particular notes of interest about Example 4-4: rather than using the natural scrolling area of the MainWindow, we are relying on the ScrolledWindow that is created automatically by `XmCreateScrolledText( )`. Because of this, we are careful to make the *parent* of the Text widget returned by this function the `XmNworkWindow` of the MainWindow. This is done using `XmMainWindowSetAreas( )`, which is merely a convenience function for informing the MainWindow widget which widgets should be used as predefined areas of the main window. The form of the function is as follows:

```
void
XmMainWindowSetAreas(main_w, menubar, cmd_w, h_scroll, v_scroll, work_w)
    Widget main_w;
    Widget menubar;
    Widget cmd_w;
    Widget h_scroll;
    Widget v_scroll;
    Widget work_w;
```

The function is really a front end for **XmScrolledWindowSetAreas()**. Basically, these functions remanage all the appropriate widgets so that they all appear in the correct order in the MainWindow, while making sure there is enough space for them all to be visible. Neither function is entirely necessary, though. First of all, whenever you create widgets as children of a MainWindow widget, the internals of the MainWindow check the type of the widget you are adding. If the new widget is a RowColumn, and it is being used as a Menu-Bar (its **XmNrowColumnType** is **XmMENU_BAR**), then the MainWindow automatically sets it as the *MenuBar* widget. This is also true for the Command Area. Simple enough—yet it happens automatically, so **XmMainWindowSetAreas()** isn't going to provide much help for us yet. Alternatively, you could also accomplish the same thing using **XtVaSet-Values()**. The resources you can use are:

```
XmNmenuBar
XmNcommandWindow
XmNverticalScrollBar
XmNhorizonalScrollBar
XmNworkWindow
XmNmessageWindow
```

Once these values are set, you cannot reset them to NULL, although you can reset them to other widgets, provided they are of the appropriate types. Conversely, this is also why **Xm-MainWindowSetAreas()** is used. Yet, dynamically changing the major elements of the MainWindow is rarely done.

You might notice, however, that the convenience function does not have a parameter specifying the Message Area. Yet, even though there is a resource to support it, the current version of the toolkit does not automatically manage and lay out the Message Area properly.

This is why we have avoided an in-depth discussion of the Message Area so far in this chapter. Briefly, the Message Area is very important for most applications, as it is typically the place where error messages and other brief status messages are displayed. It is customary to make the Message Area a read-only, ScrolledText object. The way to handle the Message Area is also the way you can provide a Command Area that is not implemented using a Command widget. You must create either object manually by placing them inside of a manager widget and using that manager as the work area (the **XmNworkWindow**). But, this gets out of the realm of the MainWindow and into manager and Text widget details. They can, as any other widget can, legitimately act as the work area of the MainWindow widget. Chapter 15, *Text Widgets*, discusses how to create a Message Area for the main window of an application in detail in Section 15.3.3, *Output-only Text Areas*.

4.4 Using Resources

Resources specific to the MainWindow and its subelements can be useful when configuring your application's default appearance while also providing a framework for users to follow when they want to set their own configuration parameters. Even those users sophisticated enough to figure out how X resource files work still copy existing files and modify them to their own tastes. Thus, app-defaults files for your applications should be informative and complete, even though they might be lengthy. Of course, the first step in such a procedure is to determine exactly which aspects of the program you want to be configurable. Remember, consistency is the only way to keep from completely confusing a user.

Once you have decided which portions of the application you would like to be configurable, you can specify widget hierarchies that access widget instances and resources. Let's start with the MenuBar from *dynapix.c*. The application creates the **File** menu in the following way:

```
XmVaCreateSimplePulldownMenu(menubar, "file_menu", 0, file_cb,
    XmVaPUSHBUTTON, new, 'N', NULL, NULL,
    XmVaSEPARATOR,
    XmVaPUSHBUTTON, quit, 'Q', NULL, NULL,
    NULL);
```

We can add accelerators to both the **New** and **Quit** menu items using the following resource specifications:

```
dynapix.main_window.menubar*button_0.accelerator: Ctrl<Key>N
dynapix.main_window.menubar*button_0.acceleratorText: Ctrl+N
dynapix.main_window.menubar*button_1.accelerator: Ctrl<Key>C
dynapix.main_window.menubar*button_1.acceleratorText: Ctrl+C
```

The result is shown in Figure 4-9.

Figure 4-9. Output of resource settings to add accelerators to the File menu

The reason this was possible is that the accelerator and accelerator text parameters were set to NULL—they were not hard-coded values. For the same reason, *the labels of the MenuBar titles and the menu items in pulldown menus are hard-coded values that cannot be modified through resources.* To relax this restriction, you must do one of two things: first, you could try setting the `label` and `mnemonic` parameters to `NULL` in the function `XmVaCreate-SimplePulldownMenu( )`, but then the resource specification itself becomes awfully messy. Recall that the CascadeButtons in the MenuBar are named with the "button_*n*" method, just as the menu items are. This basically leaves you with the second alternative: use more advanced methods of MenuBar and pulldown menu creation described in Chapter 16, *Menus.*

Other resources specific to the MainWindow that may be used are more trivial attributes such as `XmNshowSeparator`, `XmNmainWindowMarginWidth`, and `XmNmainWindow-MarginHeight`. These resources control whether or not the Separator widgets should be shown, and the width and height of the MainWindow's margins. However, these resources should generally not be set by the application, but left to the user to specify. Examples include:

```
*XmMainWindow.showSeparator: On
*XmMainWindow.mainWindowMarginWidth: 10
*XmMainWindow.mainWindowMarginHeight: 10
```

The class name for the MainWindow widget is *XmMainWindow*, so these resource settings would set the associated resource values to all MainWindow widgets in the application, if these settings were made in a resource file. If the user had these settings in his *.Xdefaults* file, then they would apply to all MainWindow widgets in all applications.

Resource settings for other widgets are discussed in other chapters.

4.5 Summary

This chapter introduced you to the concepts involved in the main windows of applications. To a lesser degree, we show how the MainWindow widget can be used to achieve some of the necessary tasks. You can identify the control areas involved and even use some convenience routines to build some adequate prototypes. However, the MainWindow is frequently misunderstood because of its capabilities as a ScrolledWindow, and because it also supports the management of so many other objects such as the MenuBar and the Command and Message areas.

The MainWindow's work area can, and usually does, contain a manager widget that contains other widgets, including (possibly) another ScrolledWindow. Because of the MainWindow widget's problems in supporting some of its auxiliary elements (Command and Message areas), you are not necessarily encouraged to use all its features. For larger, production-style applications, you would probably be much better off using MainWindows for the MenuBars' sake and placing the rest of the main window's layout in the hands of a reasonable manager widget. These are described in Chapter 8, *Manager Widgets.*

And finally, if you decide not to use the MainWindow widget at all, you could probably use another manager widget class described in Chapter 8 and still be Motif-compliant. Depending on your application, you might even find this easier to manage than the MainWindow widget.

4.6 Exercises

Based on the material in this chapter, you should be able to do the following exercises.

1. Modify *dynapix.c* by adding a new pulldown menu that controls the background color of the pixmap.

2. Modify *dynapix.c* so that it has a Command Area. The callback for the Command widget should understand either file names or color names. If you feel adventurous, try to have it understand both the command "file" and the command "color". Each command would take a second argument indicating the file or color to use.

5

Introduction to Dialogs

This chapter describes the fundamental concepts that underly all Motif dialogs. It provides a foundation for the more advanced material in the following chapters. In the course of the introduction, this chapter also provides details on Motif's predefined MessageDialog classes.

In This Chapter:

5
Introduction to Dialogs

In Chapter 4, *The Main Window*, we discussed top-level widgets, free-floating windows managed by the window manager that provide the overall framework for the application. However, most applications are too complex to do everything in one main top-level window. Situations arise that call for individual, secondary, or *transient windows* that serve specific purposes. These windows are commonly referred to as *dialog boxes* and are implemented as PopupShells from primary windows.

Dialog boxes play an integral role in every GUI-based interface such as Motif. The examples in this book use dialogs in many ways, so just about every chapter can be used to learn more about dialogs. We've already explored some of the basic concepts in Chapter 2, *Fundamentals of Motif Programming* and Chapter 3, *Real Motif Applications*. However, the use of dialogs in Motif is quite complex, and we need more detail to proceed further.

First, the *Motif Style Guide* makes a set of generic recommendations for how all dialogs should look. But then it goes on to specify precisely how *certain* dialogs should look and respond to user events, and under which circumstances those dialogs should be used. We call these *predefined Motif dialogs* because not only is the *Motif Style Guide* specific about them, but the Motif toolkit implements each of them for you. Given the right context, you should be able to create the necessary dialog using a single convenience routine and you're done. They are completely self-sufficient, opaque objects that require very little interaction from your application. If you need more than what is required by a predefined Motif dialog, you may have to create your own *customized dialog*, where you must take a completely different approach to building and handling dialogs.

For these reasons, there are three chapters on basic dialog usage—two on predefined Motif dialogs and one on customized dialogs. There is also an additional chapter later in the book that deals with more advanced topics. This chapter discusses the most common class of Motif dialogs called MessageDialogs. These are the simplest kinds of dialogs because they are usually used to display a single, short message and require one of a very small set of responses (typically, "**Ok**," "**Yes**," or "**No**"). As such, these are very *transient* dialogs; they are intended to be thrown away immediately after use. MessageDialogs define resources and attributes that are shared by most other dialogs in the toolkit, and provide a foundation for us to build upon in the later dialog chapters. And while Motif dialogs tend to be opaque objects, to really understand how they work, we look around inside and dissect their implementation and behavior. This will be very helpful for understanding not only what is happening in your application, but also how you can create customized dialogs.

Chapter 6, *Selection Dialogs*, goes into detail on SelectionDialogs, although most of the material in this chapter still applies. Also a set of predefined Motif dialogs, SelectionDialogs are the next step in the evolution of dialogs. They typically provide a large list of responses for the user to choose from and are usually less transient on the screen. (They may remain displayed for repeated use.) Chapter 7, *Custom Dialogs*, addresses the issues of creating customized dialogs, and Chapter 20, *Advanced Dialog Programming*, discusses some advanced topics in X and Motif programming using dialogs as a backdrop.

Let's begin by examining the main purpose of dialog widgets and analyzing the anatomy of a dialog.

5.1 The Dialog's Main Purpose

For most applications, it would be impossible to develop an interface for all of the application's functions in a single main window, so the interface is typically broken up into discrete functional modules, each represented by different dialog boxes. Consider an electronic mail application whose broad range of different functions include searching for messages according to patterns, composing messages, editing an address book, reporting error messages, and so on.

Dialog boxes are used for a variety of purposes ranging from displaying a simple message (shown in Figure 5-1), to prompting the user for simple questions (shown in Figure 5-2), to presenting a highly interactive dialog (shown in Figure 5-3).

Figure 5-1. A message dialog

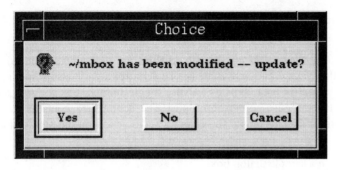

Figure 5-2. A question dialog

Figure 5-3. A customized dialog box

Dialogs are typically customized by the application programmer. In Figure 5-3, many different widget classes are used to provide the user with a template for sorting e-mail messages according to different criteria. The purpose of a dialog is to focus on one particular aspect of the application. Since the scope of these tasks is usually quite limited, most applications have dialog boxes separate from their main windows.

5.2 Dialog Widget Anatomy

As described in Chapter 3, *Overview of Motif Widgets*, dialogs are typically broken down into two regions known as the *control* and *action* areas. The control area is also sometimes known as the *work area*. The control area contains Labels, ToggleButtons, List widgets, and other widgets for the user to configure application state. The action area contains Push-Buttons whose callback routines actually apply the changes (take action on the application) indicated in the control area.

Figure 5-4 shows these areas in a sample dialog box.

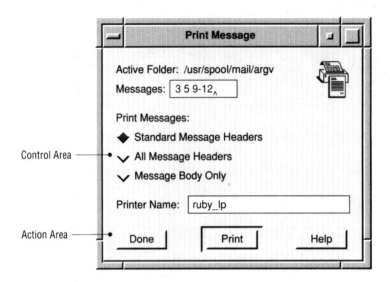

Figure 5-4. A sample dialog box

While most dialogs follow this pattern, it is important to realize that these two regions represent a user-interface concept, and do not necessarily reflect how Motif dialogs are implemented. It is helpful to understand the actual "widget anatomy" of dialogs, since you will need to know this to customize dialogs or create your own.

To start with, there is actually no such thing as a "dialog" widget class. A dialog is actually made up of a DialogShell widget, which persuades the window manager to allow the "transient window" behavior required of dialogs, plus a manager widget child that implements the visible part of the dialog. When you write custom dialogs, you simply create and manage the children of the DialogShell in the same way that you might create and manage children of a top-level application shell.

The predefined Motif dialogs follow the same sort of approach, but the toolkit creates the dialog widget and all its children internally. Most of the standard Motif dialogs are composed of a DialogShell and either a *MessageBox* or *SelectionBox* widget. Each of these widget classes creates and manages a number of internal widgets without application intervention. Variations on each of these types of dialog widgets are configurable through a resource. See Chapter 3, *Overview of Motif Widgets*, to review the various types of dialogs.

All the predefined Motif dialogs are subclassed from the BulletinBoard widget class. As such, BulletinBoards may be thought of as the generic dialog widget class, although they can certainly be used as generic manager widgets (see Chapter 8, *Manager Widgets*). Indeed, dialog widgets *are* manager widgets, but they are usually not treated as such by the application. What the BulletinBoard widget provides is the keyboard traversal mechanism that supports tab groups. But since BulletinBoard widgets are used as the superclass for Motif dialogs, many dialog-specific resources have been incorporated into the class, as we will soon see.

What's important to note about predefined Motif dialogs is that each dialog is implemented as a single widget class even though there are smaller, primitive widgets under the hood. When you create a MessageBox widget, you automatically get a set of Labels and Push-Buttons that are laid out in conformance with the *Motif Style Guide*. What is *not* created automatically is the shell widget that is managed by the MessageBox widget. This leaves you with three options: create the shell yourself and place the MessageBox in it, use a predefined Motif convenience routine that also creates the shell and places the dialog widget in it, or place the MessageBox widget inside some other (larger) manager widget. While this latter case may seem awkward at first, it is possible, although not very common.

For now, let's concentrate on the more common case: dialog widgets that are immediate children of shell widgets. The Motif toolkit provides the DialogShell widget class, which acts as the parent for all predefined Motif dialogs. In this context, a MessageBox widget combined with a DialogShell widget creates what the Motif toolkit calls a *MessageDialog*. A careful look at terminology can help you to remember this point: the name of the actual widget class ends in *Box*. A name that ends in *Dialog* refers to the compound object: *somethingBox* plus DialogShell.

So, for example, the convenience function **XmCreateMessageBox( )** creates a Message-Box widget, which you will be expected to put under parental management in the normal way. **XmCreateMessageDialog( )** creates a MessageBox *and* a DialogShell.

Just to keep the terminology straight, the commonly-used term *dialog box* should be considered a colloquial form of the *-dialog* usage employed by the Motif toolkit. So, do not be confused when we use the term "dialog box" to describe an object on the screen. (You may find this term used in other references as well.) This typically means a dialog widget plus a DialogShell widget.

There is another important reason for discriminating between one of the "box" widgets and its "dialog" equivalent. For example, the *Motif Style Guide* says that clicking on the **Ok** button in the action area of a MessageDialog causes the application to take an "action" and then dismiss the dialog. Furthermore, pressing the $\boxed{\text{RETURN}}$ key anywhere in the dialog is equivalent to clicking on the **Ok** button. (Again, an action is taken and the dialog is dismissed.) However, none of this takes place when the MessageBox widget is not a direct child of the DialogShell.

Similarly, for the predefined Motif SelectionDialogs, if the object contains a single-line text field, pressing RETURN in the TextField widget automatically activates the **Ok** button and the dialog is dismissed. However, when the SelectionBox is not an immediate child of a DialogShell, this action does not take place automatically. These sorts of subtleties inevitably confuse the beginning Motif programmer, when he tries to place dialog widgets inside shells that are not DialogShell widgets, or within other manager widgets.

Perhaps the most important thing to remember is how the Motif toolkit treats dialogs. Once a dialog *widget* is placed in a dialog *shell*, the toolkit tends to treat the entire dialog—the widgets in the control area, the action area and the shell widget—as a single entity. In fact, as we move on, you'll find that the toolkit's use of convenience routines, callback functions, and popup-widget techniques all hide the fact that the dialog is composed of these discrete elements.

While the Motif dialogs are really composed of many primitive widgets such as PushButtons and TextFields, the single-entity approach to dialogs implies that you never access those subwidgets directly. If you want to change a button's label or the text in a Text widget, you do not get the handles to those widgets and change their resources; you set resources specific to that dialog class. Similarly, you always install callbacks on the dialog widget itself rather than on any of the buttons in the control or action areas.

This approach may be confusing for those already familiar with Xt programming, but not yet familiar with the Motif toolkit. Similarly, those who learn Xt programming though experiences with the Motif toolkit might get a misconception of what Xt programming is all about. For these reasons, we will point out those inconsistencies so that you will understand the boundaries between the Motif toolkit and its Xt foundations.

Remember not to lose perspective on the relationship between predefined Motif dialogs and customized dialogs. That is, once you get into customized dialogs, you should no longer expect the kind of behavior found in Motif dialogs.

5.2.1 Action Area Buttons

The *Motif Style Guide* describes in a general fashion how the control and action areas for all dialogs should be laid out. For predefined Motif dialogs, the control area is rigidly specified. For customized dialogs, there is only a general set of guidelines to follow. The action area, on the other hand, tends to be more specific (yet flexible) for both the predefined Motif dialogs and customized dialogs. The action area is always made up of PushButtons whose callback routines take action on the application using data provided by the controls in the control area.

The predefined Motif dialogs have three buttons, normally labeled (from left-to-right) **Ok**, **Cancel**, and **Help**. SelectionDialogs (and their subclasses) have a fourth button labeled **Apply**, which is placed between the **Ok** and **Cancel** buttons. This button is created but not managed. (It will not be visible unless the application explicitly manages it.)

When you are creating custom dialogs, or even when using the predefined Motif dialogs, you may need to relabel the buttons so that the action the user is going to take is intuitively obvious. We will address this issue as it comes up in discussion, but it is usually not a problem until you create your own customized dialogs (discussed in Chapter 7, *Custom Dialogs*).

5.3 Creating Motif Dialogs

Under most circumstances, creating a predefined Motif dialog box is very simple. All Motif dialog types have corresponding convenience routines that simplify the task of creating and managing them. For example, a standard MessageDialog may be created as shown in Example 5-1.

Example 5-1. A 'Hello World' code fragment

```
#include <Xm/MessageB.h>

extern Widget parent;
Widget dialog;
Arg arg[1];
XmString t;

t = XmStringCreateSimple("Hello World");
XtSetArg(arg[0], XmNmessageString, t);
dialog = XmCreateMessageDialog(parent, "message", arg, 1);
XmStringFree(t);

XtManageChild(dialog);
```

The result of this code is shown in Figure 5-5.

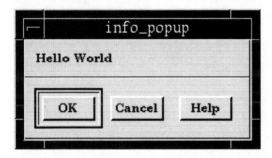

Figure 5-5. A 'Hello World' MessageDialog

The convenience routine does almost everything automatically. The only thing we have to do is specify the message we want to display. Once the dialog is managed using **Xt-ManageChild( )**, it is displayed on the screen. (We should mention that technically, according to Xt specifications, we should use **XtPopup( )** to pop up any PopupShell such as this, but the Motif toolkit provides for this internally.)

Let's examine more closely the process for creating a complete, functioning Motif dialog. The following procedure is used to set up most dialogs:

1. Include proper header files for the type of dialog desired.

2. Create the desired dialog using the appropriate convenience routine.

3. Set resources and create callback functions for the possible responses in the action area.

4. Manage the dialog widget returned by the convenience function.

5.3.1 Dialog Header Files

As we mentioned earlier, there are two basic types of predefined Motif dialog boxes: MessageDialogs and SelectionDialogs. MessageDialogs present a simple message, to which a yes or no (Ok/Cancel) response usually suffices. SelectionDialogs allow for more complicated interactions, in which the user selects an item from a list, or types in an entry in a Text-Field widget, before acting on the dialog.

As described in Chapter 3, *Overview of Motif Widgets*, there are five subtypes of Message-Dialog: ErrorDialog, InformationDialog, QuestionDialog, WarningDialog, and Working-Dialog. These are not actually separate widget classes, but simply instances of the generic MessageDialog configured to display a different graphic symbol. The symbols are illustrated in Figure 3-11.

Similarly, a PromptDialog is just a specially configured SelectionBox. Command and File-SelectionBox, on the other hand, are separate widget classes. However, they are subclassed from SelectionBox and share many of its features. When we use the general term *selection dialogs*, we are referring to any of these three widget classes (plus their associated dialog shell.)

For MessageDialogs, you must include the file, *<Xm/MessageB.h>*. For selection dialogs, you must include both that file and *<Xm/SelectioB.h>*.[1]

5.3.2 Creating the Dialog

You can use any of the following convenience routines to create a dialog box. They are listed according to the header file in which they are declared:

---
[1] Yes, you read that right. It does, in fact, read *SelectioB.h*. The reason for the missing *n* is there is a fourteen character filename limit on UNIX System V machines.

<Xm/MessageB.h>:

```
XmCreateMessageDialog( )
XmCreateMessageBox( )
XmCreateErrorDialog( )
XmCreateInformationDialog( )
XmCreateQuestionDialog( )
XmCreateWarningDialog( )
XmCreateWorkingDialog( )
```

<Xm/SelectioB.h>:

```
XmCreateSelectionDialog( )
XmCreateSelectionBox( )
XmCreatePromptDialog( )
XmCreateCommandDialog( )
```

Each of these routines creates a dialog widget; those that end in *Dialog*, however, also create a DialogShell automatically.

All the convenience functions for creating dialogs use a similar format. For example:

```
Widget
XmCreateMessageDialog(parent, name, args, num_args)
    Widget parent;
    char   *name;
    Arg    args[ ];
    int    num_args;
```

In this case, we are creating a common MessageDialog (the kind that creates the DialogShell automatically). The `parent` parameter is another widget (Shell, PushButton, etc.) that acts as the owner or parent of the DialogShell. Note that the parent must *not* be a gadget, since the parent must have a window associated with it. The dialog widget itself is a child of the DialogShell. You are returned a handle to a newly created dialog widget, not the DialogShell parent.

For the routines that create dialog widgets without the shell, the `parent` is just another manager widget, which is not automatically created of course. (It must already exist.)

The `args` and `num_args` parameters for these functions are given in the old-style `ArgList` format which is similar to other Motif convenience routines. A *varargs* interface is not available for creating dialogs, but you can use the varargs style interface for setting resources on dialogs after dialogs are created using `XtVaSetValues( )`. (See Chapter 2, *The Motif Programming Model*, for a discussion of how to set resources using ArgLists.)

5.3.3 Setting Resources

There are many resources that apply only to specific types of dialogs. However, there are many resources and callback functions that apply to almost all Motif dialogs. These resources affect the action area buttons and other parts of the widget including its Labels, Texts, and List widgets (depending on the type of dialog used). Some of these resources are listed below:

Available in all Motif dialogs
XmNokLabelString	XmNokCallback
XmNcancelLabelString	XmNcancelCallback
XmNhelpLabelString	XmNhelpCallback

Common to MessageDialogs
XmNmessageString	XmNsymbolPixmap

Common to selection dialogs
XmNapplyLabelString	XmNapplyCallback
XmNselectionLabelString	XmNlistLabelString
XmNpromptString	

XmNmessageString specifies the message to be displayed by any of the MessageDialog types. **XmNsymbolPixmap** displays the iconic symbol associated with each of the MessageDialog types. This resource is rarely changed, so discussion is deferred until Chapter 20, *Advanced Dialog Programming*.

The labels and callbacks of the various buttons are specified by resources based on the standard Motif dialog button names. For example, the **XmNokLabelString** is used to set the label for the **Ok** button. **XmNokCallback** is used to specify the callback routine(s) the dialog should call when that button is activated. As discussed in Section 5.2.1, *Action Area Buttons*, it may be appropriate to change the labels of these buttons, but the resource and callback names will always have names that correspond to their default labels.

The other resources apply only to selection dialogs; for example, **XmNselectionLabelString** sets the label that is placed above the list area in the selection dialog. This is discussed in Chapter 6, *Selection Dialogs*.

All these resources apply to the Labels and PushButtons in the dialog, but are different from the usual resources that Labels and PushButtons take when used on their own. The Label resource **XmNlabelString** would normally be used to specify the label for both the Label and the PushButton widgets, yet dialogs use their own resources to maintain the abstraction of the dialog widget as a single discrete user-interface object.

Another important thing to know about the resources that refer to widget labels is that their values must be given as *compound strings*. Compound strings allow labels to be rendered in arbitrary fonts or use multiple lines. See Chapter 19, *Compound Strings*, for more information.

Setting a dialog's buttons and callback routines is demonstrated by the code fragment in Example 5-2.

Example 5-2. Setting buttons and callback routines for a dialog

```
Widget dialog;
XmString msg, yes, no;
extern void my_callback( );

dialog = XmCreateQuestionDialog(parent, "dialog", NULL, 0);
yes = XmStringCreateSimple("Yes");
no = XmStringCreateSimple("No");
```

Example 5-2. Setting buttons and callback routines for a dialog (continued)

```
msg = XmStringCreateSimple("Do you want to quit?");

XtVaSetValues(dialog,
    XmNmessageString,      msg,
    XmNokLabelString,      yes,
    XmNcancelLabelString,  no,
    NULL);
XtAddCallback(dialog, XmNokCallback, my_callback, NULL);
XtAddCallback(dialog, XmNcancelCallback, my_callback, NULL);

XmStringFree(yes);
XmStringFree(no);
XmStringFree(msg);

XtManageChild(dialog);
XtPopup(XtParent(dialog), XtGrabNone);
```

5.3.4 Motif Dialog Management

None of the Motif toolkit convenience functions manage widgets by default, so the application must call **XtManageChild( )** explicitly. It just so happens that managing a dialog widget that is an immediate child of a DialogShell widget, causes the entire dialog to *pop up*. Similarly, unmanaging the same dialog widget causes it (and its DialogShell parent) to *pop down*. This is intended to maintain consistency with the toolkit's treatment of the dialog/shell combination as a single object abstraction. Since the Motif toolkit itself is treating its own dialog widgets as opaque objects, it is trying to "hide" the fact that there is a DialogShell associated with it. There is also an assumption being made by the Motif toolkit that if the programmer is creating a dialog, he (apparently) wants it to immediately pop up.

This practice is a little too presumptuous and contrasts directly with the specifications for the X Toolkit Intrinsics. That is, the specifications say that when the programmer wants to map a popup shell to the screen, **XtPopup( )** should be used. Similarly, when the dialog is to be dismissed, the programmer should call **XtPopdown( )**. The fact that **XtManage-Child( )** happens to pop up the shell and that **XtUnmanageChild( )** causes it to pop down is often misleading to the new Motif programmer (and especially to the experienced Xt programmer).

NOTE

None of this applies to customized dialogs you create yourself. It only applies to predefined Motif dialog widgets that are immediate children of DialogShells. For the curious, the reason the Motif toolkit uses this method is that it has been around for so long and must be supported for backwards compatibility with older versions. Furthermore, using **XtPopup( )** requires access to the dialog widget's DialogShell parent, breaking the single-object abstraction.

In short, there are two ways to manage Motif dialogs. You can use the Motif toolkit conventions of using `XtManageChild( )` and `XtUnmanageChild( )` to pop up and down dialog widgets, or you can use `XtPopup( )` and `XtPopdown( )` on the dialog's parent to do the same job. Whatever you do, it is good practice to pick one method and be consistent throughout the application. It is frequently possible to mix and match the methods, but there may be undesirable side effects that we'll address through the next few sections. (This is not the final word on the subject.)

In an effort to make our applications more easily portable to other Xt-based toolkits, we follow the established convention of using `XtPopup( )`. This can easily co-exist with `XtManageChild( )`, since popping up an already popped-up shell has no effect.

The form of `XtPopup( )` is:

```
void
XtPopup(shell, grab_kind)
    Widget shell;
    XtGrabKind grab_kind;
```

The `shell` parameter to the function must be a shell widget, which, in this case, happens to be a DialogShell. If you created the dialog using one of the Motif-supplied convenience routines, then you can get a handle to the DialogShell easily by calling `XtParent( )` of the dialog widget. Remember, this can (and should) only be done if the dialog widget is an immediate child of the DialogShell (or other shell widget subclassed from the TransientShell widget class).

The `grab_kind` parameter can be one of `XtGrabNone`, `XtGrabNonexclusive`, or `XtGrabExclusive`. We almost always use `XtGrabNone`, since the other values imply a *server grab*. That is, other windows on the desktop will be "locked out." (Grabbing the server results in what is called *modality*; it implies that the user cannot interact with anything but the dialog.) While a grab might be desirable behavior in some cases, the Motif toolkit provides some predefined resources that handle grab for you automatically. The advantages to using those alternate methods is to allow the client to communicate more closely with the Motif window manager (*mwm*), and to provide for different kinds of modality. These methods are discussed in Section 5.7.1, *Implementing Modal Dialogs*. For detailed information on `XtPopup( )` and the different uses of `XtGrabKind`, see Volume Four, *X Toolkit Intrinsics Programming Manual*.

Note again that calling `XtPopup( )` on a dialog widget that has already been popped up using `XtManageChild( )` will have no effect. Thus, if you attempt to use a grab kind other than `XtGrabNone`, it will have no effect either.

The counterpart to `XtPopup( )` is `XtPopdown( )`. That is, any time you wish to pop down a shell, you can use this function:

```
void
XtPopdown(shell)
    Widget shell;
```

Again, the `shell` parameter should be the `XtParent( )` of the dialog widget. If you use `XtUnmanageChild( )` to pop down a dialog, `XtPopdown( )` is not necessary, although (as before) it is advised for correctness and good form. However, it is important to note that if you used `XtUnmanageChild( )` to pop down a dialog, you *must* use

XtManageChild( ) to redisplay it again. Don't forget that the dialog widget itself is not a shell, so managing or unmanaging it still takes place when you use the manage and unmanage functions.

Let's now take a closer look at how dialogs are used in an application and examine not only the overall design, but the mechanics involved. This will help clarify a number of issues about managing and unmanaging dialogs and DialogShells. The program listed in Example 5-3 displays an InformationDialog when the user presses a PushButton in the application's main window.

Example 5-3. The hello.c program

```
/* hello.c -- your typical Hello World program using
 * an InformationDialog.
 */
#include <Xm/RowColumn.h>
#include <Xm/MessageB.h>
#include <Xm/PushB.h>

main(argc, argv)
int argc;
char *argv[ ];
{
    XtAppContext app;
    Widget toplevel, rc, pb;
    extern void popup(); /* callback for the pushbuttons.  pops up dialog */

    toplevel = XtVaAppInitialize(&app, "Demos", NULL, 0,
        &argc, argv, NULL, NULL);

    rc = XtVaCreateWidget("rowcol",
        xmRowColumnWidgetClass, toplevel, NULL);
    pb = XtVaCreateManagedWidget("Hello", xmPushButtonWidgetClass, rc, NULL);
    XtAddCallback(pb, XmNactivateCallback, popup, "Hello World");

    XtManageChild(rc);
    XtRealizeWidget(toplevel);
    XtAppMainLoop(app);
}
/* callback for the PushButtons.  Popup an InformationDialog displaying
 * the text passed as the client data parameter.
 */
void
popup(push_button, text, cbs)
Widget push_button;
char *text;
XmPushButtonCallbackStruct *cbs; /* unused */
{
    Widget dialog;
    XmString xm_string;
    extern void activate();
    Arg args[1];

    /* set the label for the dialog */
    xm_string = XmStringCreateSimple(text);
    XtSetArg(args[0], XmNmessageString, xm_string);

    /* Create the InformationDialog as child of push_button */
```

Example 5-3. The hello.c program (continued)

```
    dialog = XmCreateInformationDialog(push_button, "info", args, 1);

    /* no longer need the compound string, free it */
    XmStringFree(xm_string);

    /* add the callback routine */
    XtAddCallback(dialog, XmNokCallback, activate, NULL);

    /* manage the dialog */
    XtManageChild(dialog);
    XtPopup(XtParent(dialog), XtGrabNone);
}
/* callback routine for when the user presses the Ok button.
 * Yes, despite the fact that the Ok button was pressed, the
 * widget passed to this callback routine is the dialog!
 */
void
activate(dialog)
Widget dialog;
{
    puts("Ok was pressed.");
}
```

The output of this program is shown in Figure 5-6.

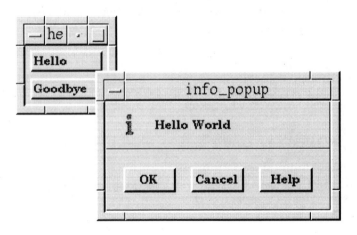

Figure 5-6. Output of hello.c

Dialogs are often invoked from callback routines attached to PushButtons or other interactive widgets. Once the dialog is created and popped up, control of the program is returned to the toplevel event-handling loop (i.e., **XtAppMainLoop( )**) where normal event processing resumes. At this point, if the user interacts with the dialog by selecting controls or activating one of the action buttons, the dialog's callback routine(s) are invoked. In Example 5-3, we happen to use an InformationDialog, but the type of dialog used is irrelevant to the model.

When the PushButton in the main window is pressed, **popup( )** is called, passing a text string to use as the message to display in an InformationDialog. This dialog contains a single callback routine, **activate( )**, for the **XmNokCallback** resource. This function is invoked when the user presses the **Ok** button. (Similar callback routines can be installed for the **Cancel** and **Help** buttons through the resources `XmNcancelCallback` and `Xm-NhelpCallback`.) Here, the callback simply prints a message to standard output that the button has been pressed.

You might also notice that activating either the **Ok** or **Cancel** buttons will cause the dialog to be automatically popped down. This summarizes the idea behind Motif dialogs—they are completely self-contained and self-sufficient objects. They manage everything about themselves from their displays to their interactions with the user. And when it's time to go away, they unmanage themselves. Your application does not have to do anything to cause any of this to happen. While this may be fine for the most naive programmer, there is clearly more that needs to be done for any real application to make serious use of dialog widgets. For example, let's take a closer look at the practice of automatically popping down the Dialog-Shell widget and unmanaging the dialog widget when the **Ok** button is activated.

5.3.5 Closing the Dialog

The *Motif Style Guide* says that when any button in the action area of a predefined Motif dialog is pressed (except for the **Help** button), the dialog should be dismissed. The Motif toolkit, therefore, takes the specification at face value and enforces this default behavior. However, this does not take into account error conditions or other exceptional events that may not necessarily justify the dialog's dismissal. For example, if pressing **Ok** causes a file to be updated, but the operation fails, you may not want the dialog to be dismissed. If the dialog is still displayed, the user can try again without having to repeat the actions that led to popping up the dialog. There is a way out, though.

The `XmNautoUnmanage` resource controls whether the entire dialog box is automatically unmanaged when the user selects one of the action area buttons (except for the **Help** button). If `XmNautoUnmanage` is `True`, after the callback routine associated with an action area button that was pressed gets called, the DialogShell is popped down and the dialog widget is unmanaged—automatically.

The value of this resource defaults to `True` for MessageDialogs and `False` for File-SelectionDialogs.

The **Help** button is immune to automatic popdown, even if `XmNautoUnmanage` is `True`. However, as noted earlier, even with the other buttons, it may not always be a good idea for this behavior to happen automatically. It is frequently much easier to manage dialog behavior when you are in control of the display state. Therefore, it turns out to be easier to set `Xm-NautoUnmanage` to `False` so that the toolkit does not indiscriminately dismiss the dialog simply because an action button was activated.

While it is true that we could program around this situation by calling `XtPopdown( )` or `XtManageChild( )` from the callback routine, rather than resetting `XmNauto-Unmanage`, this type of activity is confusing because of the "double-negative" action it implies. In other words, it's much easier to understand code that invokes a single positive action than code that invokes a negative action intended solely to undo another negative action.

Reusing Dialog Widgets

This discussion brings up several questions and issues about when a dialog should be unmanaged and when it should be destroyed. If you expect the user to have an abundant supply of computer memory, you may reuse dialogs by retaining a handle to the dialog as shown in Example 5-8 later in this chapter. There are also performance considerations that may affect whether you choose to destroy or reuse dialogs. It takes less time to reuse a dialog than it does to create a new one, provided that your application isn't so big that it consumes all the computer's resources already.

If you do not retain a handle to the dialog and if you feel you need to conserve on memory and other resources, you should destroy dialogs whenever you take them down. Of course, whichever approach you choose may not affect how you set **XmNautoUnmanage**. However, by setting it to **False**, you, not the Motif toolkit, are in control of the dialog's fate.

Dialogs and the Window Manager

Another method the user might use to close a dialog is by selecting the **Close** item from the *window menu* that can be pulled down from a window's titlebar. This menu does not belong to either the shell widget or the application; it belongs to the window manager, so you cannot install a callback routine for its menu items. You can, however, use the resource **Xm-NdeleteResponse** to control how the DialogShell responds to a **Close** action.[2] It can have any of the following values:

XmUNMAP

> Causes the dialog to be unmapped. That is, the dialog disappears from the screen, but it is not destroyed, nor is it iconified. The dialog widget and its windows are still intact and can be redisplayed using **XtPopup( )**. (This is the default value.)

XmDESTROY

> Destroys the DialogShell and calls its **XmNdestroyCallback**. Note that all of the shell's children are also destroyed, including the dialog widget and its subwidgets. If destroyed, you cannot redisplay the dialog or reference its handle. If you need the dialog again, you must create another one.

XmDO_NOTHING

> The toolkit takes no action. This value should only be given in circumstances where you want to handle this event on your own. However, this requires much more than installing a simple callback routine; it involves building lower-level mechanisms that interpret the proper events sent by the window manager. The most common thing to do in such cases is to activate the dialog's *default action*, or to interpose a prompting mechanism to verify the user's action. A complete discussion of how this can be done is found in Chapter 17, *Interacting with the Window Manager*.

---

[2] It is really Motif's VendorShell (from which the DialogShell is subclassed) that traps the notification and determines what to do next based on the value of this resource.

An example of using **XmNdestroyCallback** in this context is found in the discussion of Help dialogs in Chapter 20, *Advanced Dialog Programming*.

Popup and Popdown Callbacks

As an aside, it may be convenient for your application to know when a dialog has been popped up or down. If so, you can install callbacks that will be invoked whenever either of these events take place. The actions of popping up and down dialogs can be monitored through special callback routines associated with the resources **XtNpopupCallback** and **XtNpopdownCallback**. These Xt resources are not explicitly supported by Motif. That is, the resources themselves are defined by the Shell widget class, but their resource names are not defined in *<Xm/Xm.h>* as the other Motif-specific resources are. The Xt include file *<X11/StringDefs.h>* must be included for these resource names to be used.

When the functions associated with **XtNpopupCallback** is invoked, for example, you can position dialogs automatically, rather than allowing the window manager to place them wherever it likes. See Chapter 7, *Custom Dialogs*, for more information on how this is done.

5.4 Miscellaneous Resources for Dialogs

The following subsections discuss resources that are specific to Motif dialogs. In all cases, these are BulletinBoard widget resources, since all Motif dialogs are subclassed from this class. However, this does not mean that these resources can be used on generic Bulletin-Board widgets; they only apply when the widget is an immediate child of a DialogShell widget and are really only intended to be used by the predefined Motif dialog classes. (They must be set on the dialog widget, not the DialogShell.) Consult Chapter 8, *Manager Widgets*, for details on other BulletinBoard resources.

5.4.1 The Default Button

All predefined Motif dialogs have a *default button* in their action area, which indicates which button is activated when the user presses the RETURN key in the dialog. The **Ok** button is normally the default button, but the default can be changed interactively by the user with the arrow keys. Since the default button can change dynamically, which button is the default is only important when the dialog is initially displayed. This is particularly true in dangerous interactions where you want to influence the user's default response.

You can only change the default button on MessageDialogs (not on any of the Selection-Dialogs) by setting the **XmNdefaultButtonType** resource on the dialog widget. This resource may have any of the following values:

XmDIALOG_OK_BUTTON
> The default button will be the furthest button on the left. By default, this is the **Ok** button, although its label may have been changed to another string.

XmDIALOG_CANCEL_BUTTON

> The **Cancel** button should be the default in situations where the actions of the dialog are definitely destructive. This would be a good choice for WarningDialogs that are posted in order to warn the user of a possibly destructive action.

XmDIALOG_HELP_BUTTON

> The **Help** button is always the last action area button on the right in a Motif dialog. It is rarely set as the default button.

An example of how the default button type can be used is shown in Example 5-4.

Example 5-4. The WarningMsg() function

```
/*
 * WarningMsg() -- Inform the user that he is about to embark on a
 * dangerous mission and give him the opportunity to back out.
 */
void
WarningMsg(parent, msg)
Widget parent;
char *msg;
{
    static Widget dialog;
    char buf[256];
    XmString text, ok_str, cancel_str;

    if (!dialog)
        dialog = XmCreateWarningDialog(parent, "warning", NULL, 0);
    sprintf(buf, "WARNING:\n%s", msg);
    text = XmStringCreateLtoR(buf);
    ok_str = XmStringCreateSimple("Yes, I'm Sure");
    cancel_str = XmStringCreateSimple("Nope. I'm chicken");
    XtVaSetValues(dialog,
        XmNmessageString,     text,
        XmNokLabelString,     ok_str,
        XmNcancelLabelString, cancel_str,
        XmNdefaultButtonType, XmDIALOG_CANCEL_BUTTON,
        NULL);
    XmStringFree(text);
    XmStringFree(ok_str);
    XmStringFree(cancel_str);

    XtManageChild(dialog);
    XtPopup(XtParent(dialog), XtGrabNone);
}
```

The intent of this function is to discourage the user from doing the wrong thing. By using the WarningDialog (which displays the '!' symbol), using negative language in the PushButtons, and by making the **Cancel** button the default choice, we have given the user adequate warning that the action may have dangerous consequences. The output of a program running this code fragment is shown in Figure 5-7.

Figure 5-7. Output of WarningMsg()

The values for `XmNdefaultButtonType` will come again later, when we discuss `Xm-MessageBoxGetChild( )` and again in Chapter 6, *Selection Dialogs*, for `Xm-SelectionBoxGetChild( )`.

5.4.2 Button Sizes

The `XmNminimizeButtons` resource specifies how the action area buttons' widths are sized by the dialog. If `True`, each button's width is set so that it is as small as possible while still enclosing its entire label. (Each button will probably have a different width.) The default value of `False` indicates that each PushButton has the same width (that of the widest one). By default, the label is centered in the button.

5.4.3 The Dialog Title

Whenever a new shell widget is mapped to the screen, the window manager creates its own window (to contain the titlebar, resize handles, and other window decorations) and makes the DialogShell's window the child of another, new window. This is called "reparenting" a window, and is only done by the window manager in order to add shell decorations. The only time this isn't done is for OverrideShells (popup, pulldown, and pullright menus).

Most window managers that reparent shell windows print a text message in the window's titlebar. This is known as the shell's *title*. For predefined Motif dialogs, the Motif toolkit sets the default title to be the dialog widget's *name*, followed by the string *_popup*. This is almost assuredly a string that you do not want the user to see, since it makes no sense whatsoever, so you can change the title explicitly using the `XmNdialogTitle` resource. (This title should not be confused with the message displayed in a MessageDialog's message area set by `XmNmessageString`.) The value for `XmNdialogTitle` is an `XmString` and is a resource of the BulletinBoard widget, since it is the superclass for all predefined Motif dialog widgets. The BulletinBoard in turn sets the DialogShell's `XtNtitle` resource, which is a regular C string. `XtNtitle` is a Toolkit Intrinsics resource (not a Motif-specific resource) that is understood by the Shell widget (the base class for the DialogShell and other shell widget classes) which communicates with the window manager. (`XtNtitle` is defined in *<X11/Shell.h>*.)

So, you can set the window manager's titlebar string in two ways. You can set the **Xm-NdialogTitle** resource:

```
XmString title_string;

title_string = XmStringCreateSimple("Dialog Box");
dialog = XmCreateMessageDialog(parent, "dialog_name", NULL, 0);
XtVaSetValues(dialog,
    XmNdialogTitle, title_string,
    NULL);
XmStringFree(title_string);
```

Or, you can use the **XtNtitle** resource directly on the dialog's parent:

```
dialog = XmCreateMessageDialog(parent, "dialog_name", NULL, 0);
XtVaSetValues(XtParent(dialog),
    XtNtitle, "Dialog Box",
    NULL);
```

Clearly, the latter method is easier and doesn't require creating and freeing a compound string.

5.4.4 Dialog Resizing

Another resource that can be set on dialogs that affects the window manager is **XmNno-Resize**. This resource controls whether or not the resize handles for the shell of the dialog are available. The default value is **True**. However, some dialogs cannot handle resize events very well, and you may find it more aesthetic if the user didn't bother resizing them.

Again, this is a resource of the BulletinBoard widget, not of the shell widget, but it is available as a convenience to the programmer. Since all Motif dialogs are subclassed (eventually) from the BulletinBoard widget, it makes sense to provide this functionality, rather than requiring the programmer to get a handle to the DialogShell. See Chapter 17, *Interacting with the Window Manager*, for details on how you can set this resource directly on the DialogShell (or any shell widget).

5.4.5 Button Fonts

BulletinBoard widgets have various resources that enable you to specify the fonts to use for all Labels, PushButtons, or Text widgets. Since Motif dialog widgets are subclassed from BulletinBoards, these resources can be used to make all items within dialogs consistent.

For example, **XmNbuttonFontList** specifies the default font to use for all the Push-Buttons and DrawnButtons (widgets and gadgets) within dialog or BulletinBoard widgets. This resource is set on the dialog widget itself, not on its individual children. Similarly, the resource **XmNlabelFontList** is used to set the font for all the Labels (widgets and gadgets), and the resource **XmNtextFontList** is used for all Text and TextField widgets in the dialog or BulletinBoard.

If all of these resources are not set, the others will be checked to see if there are any font preferences set for the other types. For example, if a dialog has a Label widget, the font it uses will be first derived from the dialog's **XmNlabelFontList,** if it exists (is not NULL). Otherwise, the **XmNbuttonFontList** is used. If that resource is also NULL, the value for **XmNtextFontList** is then used.

You can override this behavior on a per-widget basis by setting the **XmNfontList** resource directly on the individual widgets. Of course, this means that you must pierce the dialog abstraction and retrieve the widgets internal to the dialog itself. How to do this is described in Section 5.5, *Piercing the Dialog Abstraction.*

All in all, however, you probably shouldn't be configuring dialogs down to this level of detail unless it is pertinent to your application. Arbitrarily changing such resources should not be done simply to please the application designer's personal taste.

5.5 Piercing the Dialog Abstraction

As described earlier, Motif treats dialogs as if they were single user-interface objects. However, there are times when you need to penetrate this abstraction, and work with some of the individual widgets that make up a dialog. This section describes how convenience routines work, how to work directly with the DialogShell, and how to get widgets internal to dialogs.

5.5.1 How Convenience Routines Work

The fact that Motif dialogs are self-sufficient does not imply that they are "black boxes" that perform magic that you couldn't perform yourself. The convenience routines for the MessageDialog types, for example, follow these basic steps:

*   A popup widget of type **xmDialogShellWidgetClass** is created using **Xt-CreatePopupShell( ).**

*   A widget of type **xmMessageBoxWidgetClass** is created as its child.

*   The **XmNdialogType** resource for the dialog is set to one of the following values:

    > XmDIALOG_ERROR
    > XmDIALOG_INFORMATION
    > XmDIALOG_MESSAGE
    > XmDIALOG_QUESTION
    > XmDIALOG_WARNING
    > XmDIALOG_WORKING

    Remember that the dialog's type, in this sense, does not affect the kind of widget that is created. The only thing the type affects is the graphic symbol displayed in the control area. (See Figure 3-11.) The convenience routines set this automatically based on the value of **XmNdialogType.** (You can change a dialog's type after creation using **Xt-VaSetValues( ),** which will effectively change the dialog symbol displayed.) You may find this useful for developing large applications that reuse the same dialog to display different runtime messages, help information, error messages, and so on. A method of dialog reuse is discussed later.

- A callback routine for the **XmNdestroyCallback** resource is set for the MessageBox widget to automatically destroy its DialogShell parent.

The Motif toolkit's convenience routines internally create DialogShells to support the overall dialog/DialogShell abstraction. When using these functions, the responsibility for the DialogShell is the Motif toolkit's, not yours. Thus, the dialog widget's use of **XmNdestroyCallback** is to destroy its parent upon its own destruction. If the dialog is unmapped or unmanaged, so too is its DialogShell parent. Yet the convenience routines aren't adding any resources or calling any functions to support this special relationship between the dialog widget and the DialogShell. Most of this interaction is written into the internals of the BulletinBoard.

The DialogShell, on the other hand, has other properties that affect its relationship with its dialog widget child. The DialogShell is subclassed from the TransientShell and VendorShell classes. Shells subclassed from TransientShell cannot be iconified. However, if its parent is iconified or unmapped, the DialogShell will be unmapped as well. If its parent is destroyed, so is the DialogShell (and the dialog within it). Remember, the parent of the DialogShell is another widget somewhere in the application—a Label, PushButton, ApplicationShell, or even another DialogShell. This particular parent-child relationship is different from the classic case where the parent actually *contains* the child within its geometrical bounds. That is, widgets may have "popup widget" children, which does not imply the usual geometry-management relationship parents have with their children. Nonetheless, the parent must be managed in order for the child to be. (If a widget has popup children, those children are not mapped to the screen if their parents are not managed.)

An additional constraint the Motif window manager imposes is the stacking order of the DialogShell and its parent. That is, the Motif window manager *always forces the DialogShell to be directly on top of its parent*. The result is that the shell that contains the widget acting as the DialogShell's parent cannot be placed on top of the dialog.

NOTE

This behavior is defined by the *Motif Style Guide* and is therefore enforced by the Motif window manager and the Motif toolkit. Many end-users have been known to report this as an application-design bug, so it might be a good idea to describe this behavior explicitly in your program's end-user documentation in order to prepare the user ahead of time.

As mentioned earlier, the parent of a DialogShell must be mapped to the screen in order for the dialog to be mapped. (Therefore, you must never make a menu item the parent for a DialogShell widget.) Assuming the parent is displayed, the window manager will attempt to place the DialogShell near the parent (usually centered on top of it). The value for **XmNdefaultPosition** controls whether or not this happens. If set to **True** and the DialogShell's immediate child is a BulletinBoard (as is the case for all Motif Dialogs), the shell is positioned directly over the parent. Otherwise, the application and window manager negotiate where the dialog is placed (although the stacking order *cannot* be changed). If you want, you can position the dialog by setting the dialog widget's `XmNx` and `XmNy` values. Positioning the dialog on the screen must be done through a `XmNmap-Callback` routine, which is called whenever the application calls `XtManageChild( )`. See Chapter 7, *Custom Dialogs*, for a discussion and examples of how automatic positioning is handled.

5.5.2 DialogShell Widgets

As your programs become more complex, you may eventually have to access a dialog widget's DialogShell parent in order to get certain things done. This section examines DialogShells as independent widgets and describes how they are different from other shell widgets.

There are three main features of DialogShells that differentiate them from ApplicationShells and other TopLevelShells.

- DialogShells cannot be iconified by the user or by the application.

- DialogShells are *always* placed on top of the shell widget that owns the parent of your new dialog. (Remember the relationship between the owner of the DialogShell and the shell itself.)

- When the DialogShell's parent is iconified, withdrawn, unmapped, or destroyed, all DialogShells that are children of that window are withdrawn or destroyed. (In other words, if the callback for PushButton created a dialog and the PushButton was designated as the owner of the dialog, if the PushButton's shell iconifies, the dialog will be withdrawn from the screen; if the PushButton's shell or the PushButton itself is destroyed, so will the dialog.)

Internally, DialogShells communicate frequently with dialog (BulletinBoard) widgets in order to support the single-entity abstraction that Motif tries to promote.

However, you may find you need to access the DialogShell part of the Motif dialogs in order to perform certain actions on the shell or even to just query information from it. In such cases, you must include the file *<Xm/DialogS.h>*:[3] This file provides a convenient macro for identifying whether a particular widget is a DialogShell.

```
#define XmIsDialogShell(w) \
    XtIsSubclass(w, xmDialogShellWidgetClass)
```

This macro is useful if you want to determine whether or not a dialog widget is the direct child of a DialogShell. For example, earlier in this chapter, we mentioned that the *Motif Style Guide* suggests that if the user activates the **Ok** button in a MessageDialog, the entire dialog should be popped down. However, if you have created a MessageDialog without using `XmCreateMessageDialog( )` and you want to be sure that the same thing happens when the user presses the **Ok** button in that dialog, then you need to test whether or not

---

[3] You do not have to include *<Xm/DialogS.h>* unless you need to use any of the macros defined in that file.

the parent is a DialogShell before you bother performing the "magic" yourself (popping down the dialog).

```
/* traverse up widget tree till we find a window manager shell. */
Widget
GetTopShell(widget)
Widget widget;
{
    while (widget && !XmIsMShell(widget))
        widget = XtParent(widget));

    return widget;
}

void
ok_callback(dialog, client_data, cbs)
Widget dialog;
XtPointer client_data;
XmAnyCallbackStruct *cbs;
{
    /* do whatever the callback needs to do ... */

    /* if immediate parent is not a DialogShell, mimic the same
     * behavior as if it were (i.e., pop down the parent.)
     */
    if (!XmIsDialogShell(XtParent(dialog_w)))
        XtPopdown(GetTopShell(dialog_w));
}
```

Similar functions are also available for the dialog widgets themselves from their respective header files. For example, *<Xm/MessageB.h>* defines the macro **XmIsMessageBox( )**:

```
#define XmIsMessageBox(w) \
    XtIsSubclass (w, xmMessageBoxWidgetClass)
```

This macro determines whether or not a particular widget is or is not subclassed from a MessageBox. This includes all the different types of MessageDialogs there are and returns the same value whether or not the widget is an immediate child of a DialogShell. The macro does *not* return **True** if the widget is a DialogShell.

There is no similar macro associated with any of the SelectionBox dialogs (although it is easy enough to construct one).

5.5.3 Getting Widgets Internal to Dialogs

Earlier, we discussed ways to set the default button for a dialog, and to set the fonts used for labels and buttons. If necessary, it is also possible to set these values by getting handles to the widgets internal to the dialog.

For example, another way to set the default button for a dialog is to use the **XmNdefault-Button** resource. However, the value must be a widget ID, not a predefined **int** as shown in the previous section. This is one of those times when it is necessary to get a handle to the actual subwidgets contained within a dialog. For predefined Motif MessageDialogs, you can do this using `XmMessageBoxGetChild( )`:

```
Widget
XmMessageBoxGetChild (widget, child)
    Widget          widget;
    unsigned char   child;
```

For SelectionDialogs, you can use `XmSelectionBoxGetChild( )`; the two functions are otherwise identical. The `widget` parameter is a handle to a dialog widget (not its DialogShell parent) and the child is a value represented by a value similar to that used with `XmNdefaultButtonType`. The following is a complete list of values you can use with this resource:

```
XmDIALOG_OK_BUTTON
XmDIALOG_APPLY_BUTTON
XmDIALOG_CANCEL_BUTTON
XmDIALOG_HELP_BUTTON
XmDIALOG_DEFAULT_BUTTON
XmDIALOG_MESSAGE_LABEL
```

The items in this list are used by each of the different dialog types and by both the Message-Dialog and SelectionDialog classes to reference their Labels, PushButtons, and other subwidgets. For example, to make the **Help** button unavailable in a dialog box is demonstrated in the following code fragment:

```
text = XmStringCreateSimple(dialog, "You have new mail.");
XtSetArg(args[0], XmNmessageString, text);
dialog = XmCreateMessageDialog(parent, "message", args, 1);
XmStringFree(text);

XtSetSensitive(
    XmMessageBoxGetChild(dialog, XmDIALOG_HELP_BUTTON), False);
XtUnmanageChild(
    XmMessageBoxGetChild(dialog, XmDIALOG_CANCEL_BUTTON));

XtManageChild(dialog);
XtPopup(XtParent(dialog), XtGrabNone);
```

The function `XtSetSensitive( )` is used to set a widget's sensitivity. The widget being set is that returned by `XmMessageBoxGetChild( )`. The output of this code fragment is shown in Figure 5-8.

Figure 5-8. Action area with Cancel unmanaged and Help insensitive

The message in this dialog is simple and clear: "You have new mail." It doesn't make sense to have both an **Ok** and a **Cancel** button, so we unmanage the latter. On the other hand, it makes sense to have a **Help** button, it's just that we have no help available at this time. So, rather than making it completely invisible, we merely make it unselectable by desensitizing it.

5.6 Generalizing Dialog Creation

Posting dialogs that display informative messages is something just about every application is going to do frequently. Rather than writing a separate routine for each case where a message should be displayed, we can generalize the process by writing a single routine that handles most, if not all cases. Let's begin with the following simple code fragment that creates a MessageDialog of a given type and displays an arbitrary message. Rather than using the convenience functions provided by Motif for each of the MessageDialog types, we use the generic function `XmCreateMessageDialog( )`, and configure the symbol to be displayed by setting `XmNdialogType`.

Example 5-5. The PostDialog() routine

```
    ...
    if (!(fp = fopen(filename, "r"))) {
        char buf[BUFSIZ];
        sprintf(buf, "Cannot open %s", filename);
        PostDialog(widget, XmDIALOG_ERROR, buf);
        return;
    }
    ...
/*
 * PostDialog() -- a generalized routine that allows the programmer
 * to specify a dialog type (message, information, error, help, etc..),
 * and the message to display.
 */
Widget
PostDialog(parent, dialog_type, msg)
Widget parent;
int dialog_type;
char *msg;
```

Example 5-5. The PostDialog() routine (continued)

```
{
    Widget dialog;
    XmString text;

    dialog = XmCreateMessageDialog(parent, "dialog", NULL, 0);
    text = XmStringCreateSimple(dialog, msg);
    XtVaSetValues(dialog,
        XmNdialogType,    dialog_type,
        XmNmessageString, text,
        NULL);
    XmStringFree(text);

    XtManageChild(dialog);
    XtPopup(XtParent(dialog), XtGrabNone);

    return dialog;
}
```

This routine is generic in nature because it allows the user to specify several parameters: the parent widget, the type of dialog to use and the message to display. The function returns the new dialog widget in case the calling routine wishes to modify it, unmanage it, or whatever it likes. In actuality, you may have additional requirements that this simplified example does not provide. For instance, there are no provisions for the caller to specify his own callback functions for the items in the action area. Also, there is no proper destruction method for the dialog when it is no longer needed. These may or may not be the kinds of things you want to control yourself outside of the context of the function. You may also want to extend it to possibly reuse the same dialog each time or to disable one or more of the action area buttons.

All these issues are brought up again in Chapter 6, *Selection Dialogs*, and in Chapter 20, *Advanced Dialog Programming*. For now, we need to clearly understand how dialog callback routines work in order to be able to use them effectively.

5.6.1 Dialog Callback Routines

As mentioned earlier, predefined Motif dialogs have their own resources to reference the action area's PushButton labels and callback routines. You typically avoid accessing the PushButton widgets in the action area to install those callbacks. Instead, you use the resources **XmNokCallback**, **XmNcancelCallback**, and **XmNhelpCallback** on the dialog widget itself. These correspond to each of the three buttons, **Ok, Cancel**, and **Help**.

Installing callbacks for dialogs is no different than for any other type of Motif widget; it may just seem different because the dialog widgets contain so many subwidgets. Example 5-6 demonstrates an extremely simplified way to install callbacks for a MessageDialog.

Example 5-6. Installing callbacks for the action area

```
    ...
    dialog = XmCreateMessageDialog(w, "notice", NULL, 0);
    ...
    XtAddCallback(dialog, XmNokCallback, ok_pushed, "Hi");
    XtAddCallback(dialog, XmNcancelCallback, cancel_pushed, "Foo");
    XtAddCallback(dialog, XmNhelpCallback, help_pushed, NULL);
```

Example 5-6. Installing callbacks for the action area (continued)

```
    XtManageChild(dialog);
    ...

/* ok_pushed() --the OK button was selected.  The "widget" passed
 * to this function is the dialog widget, not the pushbutton actually
 * selected by the user.
 */
void
ok_pushed(w, client_data, reason)
Widget w;
XtPointer client_data;
XmAnyCallbackStruct *reason;
{
    printf("Ok was selected: %s\n", client_data);
}

/* cancel_pushed() --the Cancel button was selected. */
void
cancel_pushed(w, client_data, reason)
Widget w;
XtPointer client_data;
XmAnyCallbackStruct *reason;
{
    printf("Cancel was selected: %s\n", client_data);
}

/* help_pushed() --the Help button was selected. */
void
help_pushed(w, client_data, reason)
Widget w;
XtPointer client_data;
XmAnyCallbackStruct *reason;
{
    puts("Help was selected");
}
```

In this example, a dialog is created and callback routines for each of the three responses are added using **XtAddCallback( )**. We also provide simple "client data" to demonstrate how the data is passed to the callback routines. These callback routines simply print the fact that they have been activated. The messages they print are taken from the client data. The **widget** parameter to the callback routines is the dialog manager widget; it is not the DialogShell widget (its parent) or the PushButton that the user selected from the action area.

Because the **client_data** parameter is of type **XtPointer**, we can pass arbitrary values to the function, depending on what we need. You cannot pass **float** or **double** types or actual data structures. If you need to pass such values, you need to pass the *address* of the variable (or a pointer to a data structure). In keeping with the philosophy of abstracting and generalizing our code, we want to exploit the client data parameter as much as possible. In so doing, we eliminate the need for some global variables and keep the structure of the application modular.

5.6.2 Callback Reasons

All callback routines have three parameters: the first is the *dialog* widget that contains the button that was selected; the second is the `client_data` supplied to `XtAdd-Callback( )`; and the third is the `call_data`, provided by the internals of the widget that performed the callback. For predefined Motif dialogs, the `call_data` is a pointer to a data structure filled in by the dialog box that indicates which button was selected and the event that invoked the callback. The structure is of type `XmAnyCallbackStruct` and is declared as:

```
typedef struct {
    int     reason;
    XEvent  *event;
} XmAnyCallbackStruct;
```

The value of the `reason` field is an integer value that can be any one of `XmCR_HELP`, `Xm-CR_OK`, or `XmCR_CANCEL`. There are many other values that `reason` could have, but these are the only values that could be returned by action area buttons in MessageDialogs. Each of the selections' values for `reason` remains the same no matter how you change their callback routines or button labels. For example, you can change the label for the **Ok** button to say "Help" using the resource `XmNokLabelString`, but the `reason` parameter will remain to be `XmCR_OK` when that button is activated.

The `XmAnyCallbackStruct` is the simplest of a large number of similar data types that provide information to widget callback routines. These other callback structure types are discussed in the appropriate chapters and sections that address callback functions for the various Motif widgets. All of the different types of callback structures contain both the `reason` and `event` fields.

Because the `reason` parameter provides information about the nature of the user's response (e.g., which button was pushed), we can greatly simplify Example 5-6 by having one callback function for all of the possible actions. The callback function can determine which button was selected by examining `reason`. Example 5-7 demonstrates this simplification.

Example 5-7. The reason.c program

```
/* reason.c -- examine the reason field of the callback structure
 * passed as the call_data of the callback function.  This field
 * indicates which action area button in the dialog was pressed.
 */
#include <Xm/RowColumn.h>
#include <Xm/MessageB.h>
#include <Xm/PushB.h>

/* main() --create a pushbutton whose callback pops up a dialog box */
main(argc, argv)
char *argv[ ];
{
    XtAppContext app;
    Widget toplevel, rc, pb;
    extern void pushed();

    toplevel = XtVaAppInitialize(&app, "Demos", NULL, 0,
        &argc, argv, NULL, NULL);
```

Example 5-7. The reason.c program (continued)

```
        rc = XtVaCreateWidget("rowcol", xmRowColumnWidgetClass, toplevel, NULL);

        pb = XtVaCreateManagedWidget("Hello", xmPushButtonWidgetClass, rc, NULL);
        XtAddCallback(pb, XmNactivateCallback, pushed, "Hello World");

        pb = XtVaCreateManagedWidget("Goodbye", xmPushButtonWidgetClass, rc, NULL);
        XtAddCallback(pb, XmNactivateCallback, pushed, "Goodbye World");

        XtManageChild(rc);
        XtRealizeWidget(toplevel);
        XtAppMainLoop(app);
}

/* pushed() --the callback routine for the main app's pushbuttons.
 * Create and popup a dialog box that has callback functions for
 * the Ok, Cancel and Help buttons.
 */
void
pushed(w, message)
Widget w;
char *message; /* really: client_data, but we know what it is */
{
    static Widget dialog;
    XmString t = XmStringCreateSimple(message);

    /* See if we've already created this dialog -- if so,
     * we don't need to create it again.  Just set the message
     * and manage it (repop it up).
     */
    if (!dialog) {
        extern void callback();
        Arg args[1];

        XtSetArg(args[0], XmNautoUnmanage,  False);
        dialog = XmCreateMessageDialog(w, "notice", args, 1);
        XtAddCallback(dialog, XmNokCallback, callback, "Hi");
        XtAddCallback(dialog, XmNcancelCallback, callback, "Foo");
        XtAddCallback(dialog, XmNhelpCallback, callback, "Bar");
    }
    XtVaSetValues(dialog, XmNmessageString, t, NULL);
    XmStringFree(t);
    XtManageChild(dialog);

    XtPopup(XtParent(dialog), XtGrabNone);
}

/* callback() --One of the dialog buttons was selected.
 * Determine which one by examining the "reason" parameter.
 */
void
callback(w, client_data, cbs)
Widget w;
XtPointer client_data;
XmAnyCallbackStruct *cbs;
{
    char *button;

    switch (cbs->reason) {
        case XmCR_OK : button = "OK"; break;
```

Example 5-7. The reason.c program (continued)

```
            case XmCR_CANCEL : button = "Cancel"; break;
            case XmCR_HELP : button = "Help";
    }
    printf("%s was selected: %s\n", button, client_data);
    if (cbs->reason != XmCR_HELP) {
        /* the ok and cancel buttons "close" the widget */
        XtPopdown(XtParent(w));
    }
}
```

This program uses only one callback routine for each of the selections in the action area. The **reason** is examined to determine which was selected.

Another interesting change in this application is the way **pushed( )** determines if the dialog has already been created. By making the dialog widget handle **static** to the **pushed( )** callback function, we retain a handle to this object across multiple button presses. Upon each invocation, the dialog's message is reset and is re-popped up.

Considering style guide issues again, it may be important to know when it is appropriate to dismiss a popped-up dialog. As noted earlier, the toolkit automatically unmanages dialogs whenever any of the action area buttons are activated (except for the **Help** button and the FileSelectionDialog). This is controlled by **XmNautoUnmanage**, which defaults to **True**. However, if you set this resource to **False**, the callback routines for the buttons in the action area may have to control this behavior on their own. In Example 5-7, the callback routine pops down the dialog when the reason is **XmCR_OK** or **XmCR_CANCEL**, but not when it is **XmCR_HELP**.

5.7 Dialog Modality

Once you begin working with dialogs, there are many questions that typically come up, such as, "How can I prevent the user from interacting with other dialogs until he responds to the one currently open?" Restricting the user to the current dialog is a concept known as *modality*.

Modality governs whether or not (and to what degree) the user may interact with other windows on the desktop while a particular dialog is active. Dialogs are either modal or modeless; modal dialogs have three levels: *primary-application-modal*, *full-application-modal*, and *system-modal*. In all cases, the user must interact with a modal dialog before control is released and normal input is resumed. In a system-modal dialog, the user is prevented from interacting with any other window on the display. Full-application-modal dialogs allow the user to interact with any window on the desktop except those that are part of the same application as the modal window. Primary-application-modal dialogs allow the user to interact with any other window on the display except for the window that is acting as the parent for this particular dialog. That is, if the user selected an action that caused an error that generates an error dialog box, the new dialog could be primary-application-modal so that the user must acknowledge the error before he interacts with the same window again. This does not restrict his ability to interact with other windows in the same application, provided that that window is not the one acting as the parent for the modal dialog.

Modal dialogs are perhaps the most frequently misused feature of graphical user interface design. Programmers who fail to grasp the concept of event-driven programming and design ("the user is in control!") often fall into the convenient escape route that modal dialogs provide. The problem is difficult to detect, let alone cure, because there are just as many right ways to invoke modal dialogs as there are wrong ways. Modality should be used in moderation and consistently. Let's present a few scenarios for discussion. (Note that the examples we are about to give won't necessarily represent cases favoring dialog modality—they are only used as reference points to the types of things people are used to doing in tty-based programs.)

Your text editor program has a function that allows the user to save its text to a file. In order to do so, you need to have a filename. Once you have that, you need to check that the user has sufficient permission to open or create the file and whether or not there is already some text in it. If you have an error condition, you need to notify the user of the error, ask him for a new filename, or get permission to overwrite the file's contents. Whatever the case, some interaction with the user is necessary in order to proceed. If this were a typical terminal-based application, the program flow would be similar to that in Example 5-8.

Example 5-8. Typical tty-based program flow to prompt the user for input

```
FILE *fp;
char buf[BUFSIZ], file[BUFSIZ];
extern char *index();

printf("What file would you like to use? ");
if (!(fgets(file, sizeof file, stdin)) || file[0] == 0) {
    puts("cancelled.");
    return;
}

*(index(file, '\n')) = 0; /* get rid of newline terminator */

/* "a+" creates file if it doesn't exist */
if (!(fp = fopen(file, "a+"))) {
    perror(file);
    return;
}

if (ftell(fp) > 0) { /* There's junk in the file already */
    printf("Overwrite contents of %s? ", file);
    buf[0] = 0;
    if (!(fgets(buf, sizeof buf, stdin)) || buf[0] == 0 ||
            buf[0] == 'n' || buf[0] == 'N') {
        puts("cancelled.");
        fclose(fp);
        return;
    }
}

rewind(fp);

/* continue */
```

This style of program flow is still possible in a window system using modal dialogs. In fact, it is frequently used by engineers who are trying to port tty-based applications to Motif. It is also a logical approach to programming—do one task followed by another, asking only for what you need when you need it.

However, in a graphical user interface and event-driven environment where the user can interact with many different parts of the program simultaneously, displaying a sequential series of modal dialogs is not the best way to handle input. Frequently, it's just plain wrong as a design approach. You must adopt a new paradigm in interface design that conforms to the abilities of the window system and thus, to the expectations of the user. It is essential that you understand the event-driven model, if you want to create well-written and popular applications (let alone if you want to use model dialogs correctly).

Window-based applications should be modeled on the behavior of a person filling out an application for employment or a medical questionnaire for a doctor. (Any similar situation will do.)

You are given a form asking various questions. You take it to your seat and fill it out however you choose. If it asks for your license number, you get out your driver's license and copy it down; if it asks for your checking account number, you can examine your checkbook for that information. The order in which you fill out the application is entirely up to you. You are free to examine the entire form, filling out whatever portions you like, in whatever order you like.

When the form is complete, you return it to the person who gave it to you. The attendant may check it over to see if you forgot something. If there are errors, you typically take it back and continue until it's right. The attendant can simply ask you the question straight out and write down whatever you say, but this prevents him from doing other work or dealing with other people. Furthermore, if you don't know the answer to the question right away, then you have to take the form back and fill it out the way you were doing it before. No matter how you look at it, this is not an interview where you are asked questions in sequence and must answer them that way. You are supposed to prepare the form "off-line," without requiring interaction from anyone else.

Window-based applications should be treated no differently. Each window (dialog) may be considered to be a form of some sort. Allow the user to fill out the form at his own convenience and however he chooses. If he wants to interact with other parts of the application or other programs on the desktop, he should be allowed to do so. When the user selects one of the buttons in the action area, this is his way of returning the form. At this time, you may either accept it or reject it. So far, at no point in the process do we ever need modal dialogs.

Once a form (dialog) has been submitted (an action area button was activated), you then take whatever action is appropriate (your callback routine). If there are errors in any section of the dialog, you may need to notify the user of the error. Here is where modal dialogs are used legitimately. For example, if the user is using a FileSelectionDialog to specify the file he wants to read and the file is unreadable, then you must notify him somehow so he can make another selection. In this case, the notification usually consists of a dialog that says, "Error: permission denied" and an **Ok** button. The user reads the message and presses the button acknowledging the error.

It is often difficult to judge whether the types of questions you ask or the amount of information you state is appropriate. The rule of thumb is that modal dialogs should be limited to yes/no questions, but even this is vague. Most likely, you should not prompt for anything already available through an existing dialog. In that case, you would want to bring up that dialog and instruct (or cue) the user to provide the necessary information. You should also avoid posting dialogs that prompt for filenames or anything that requires typing. This is the type of information you should be making available through text fields of normal dialog boxes.

All this is not to suggest that modal dialogs are rare or that you should avoid them at all costs. On the contrary, they are extremely useful, are very common and are used in a wide variety of ways—even those that we might not recommend. (There are always exceptions to the rule.) However, dialogs are frequently misused and programs that use fewer of them are usually better than those that use more of them.

As for the issue of forcing the user to fill out forms (dialogs) in a particular order, it may be perfectly reasonable to require this type of interaction. The implementation of this restriction, however, should be handled by managing and unmanaging separate dialogs rather than preventing interaction with all but the one you want him to use (e.g., by using modal dialogs).

Let the programmer beware: Motif will allow you to do whatever you like—there is no sanity checking to prevent you from misusing dialogs. It is up to you to keep the use of modal dialogs to a minimum.

5.7.1 Implementing Modal Dialogs

Once you have determined that you need to implement a modal dialog, you can set its modality using the resource `XmNdialogStyle`. It can be set to one of the following values:[4]

```
XmDIALOG_FULL_APPLICATION_MODAL
XmDIALOG_PRIMARY_APPLICATION_MODAL
XmDIALOG_SYSTEM_MODAL
```

When you use one of these values, the user has no choice but to respond to your dialog box before continuing to interact with the application. If you use modality at all, you would probably want to avoid using system-modal dialogs because it is usually not necessary to restrict the user from interacting with other applications on the desktop. However, this style of modality is commonly used to inform the user of an urgent message or some other condition that requires immediate attention. When a system-modal dialog is up, if the user moves the mouse outside of the modal dialog, the cursor turns into the international "do not enter" symbol (commonly found on street signs). Attempts to interact with other windows cause the server to beep.

Example 5-9 shows a sample program that displays a dialog box that the user must reply to before continuing to interact with the application.

Example 5-9. The modal.c program

```
/* modal.c -- demonstrate modal dialogs.  Display two pushbuttons
 * each activating a modal dialog.
 */
#include <Xm/RowColumn.h>
#include <Xm/MessageB.h>
#include <Xm/PushB.h>
```

---

[4] The value `XmDIALOG_APPLICATION_MODAL` is used for backwards compatibility with Motif version 1.0 and is defined to be `XmDIALOG_PRIMARY_APPLICATION_MODAL`.

Example 5-9. The modal.c program (continued)

```
/* main() --create a pushbutton whose callback pops up a dialog box */
main(argc, argv)
char *argv[ ];
{
    XtAppContext app;
    Widget toplevel, button, rowcolumn;
    void pushed();

    toplevel = XtVaAppInitialize(&app, "Demos",
        NULL, 0, &argc, argv, NULL, NULL);

    rowcolumn = XtCreateManagedWidget("rowcolumn",
        xmRowColumnWidgetClass, toplevel, NULL, 0);

    button = XtCreateManagedWidget("application-modal",
        xmPushButtonWidgetClass, rowcolumn, NULL, 0);
    XtAddCallback(button, XmNactivateCallback,
        pushed, XmDIALOG_FULL_APPLICATION_MODAL);
    button = XtCreateManagedWidget("system-modal",
        xmPushButtonWidgetClass, rowcolumn, NULL, 0);
    XtAddCallback(button, XmNactivateCallback, pushed,
        XmDIALOG_SYSTEM_MODAL);

    XtRealizeWidget(toplevel);
    XtAppMainLoop(app);
}

/* pushed() --the callback routine for the main app's pushbutton.
 * Create either a full-application or system modal dialog box.
 */
void
pushed(w, modality)
Widget w;
unsigned char modality;
{
    static Widget dialog;
    XmString t;
    extern void dlg_callback();

    /* See if we've already created this dialog -- if so,
     * we don't need to create it again.  Just re-pop it up.
     */
    if (!dialog) {
        Arg args[2];
        XmString ok = XmStringCreateSimple("OK");
        XtSetArg(args[0], XmNautoUnmanage, False);
        XtSetArg(args[1], XmNcancelLabelString, ok);
        dialog = XmCreateInformationDialog(w, "notice", args, 2);
        XtAddCallback(dialog, XmNcancelCallback, dlg_callback, NULL);
        XtUnmanageChild(
            XmMessageBoxGetChild(dialog, XmDIALOG_OK_BUTTON));
        XtUnmanageChild(
            XmMessageBoxGetChild(dialog, XmDIALOG_HELP_BUTTON));
    }
    t = XmStringCreateSimple("You must reply to this message now!");
    XtVaSetValues(dialog,
        XmNmessageString,    t,
        XmNdialogStyle,      modality,
```

Example 5-9. The modal.c program (continued)

```
            NULL);
        XmStringFree(t);
        XtManageChild(dialog);
        XtPopup(XtParent(dialog), XtGrabNone);
}

void
dlg_callback(dialog, client_data, cbs)
Widget dialog;
XtPointer client_data;
XmAnyCallbackStruct *cbs;
{
        XtPopdown(XtParent(dialog));
}
```

The output of this program is shown in Figure 5-9.

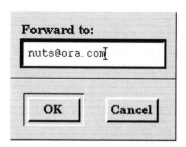

Figure 5-9. Output of modal.c

Functionally, the program is not much different than *reason.c* (Example 5-8).

Since we have two PushButtons, we are required to use a manager widget since the toplevel shell can only manage one child. We chose to use the RowColumn widget because its default layout policy is simple and does not require us to do extensive geometry management. (The choice is otherwise arbitrary).

The PushButtons are then created and their associated callback routines are installed. While the routines for both buttons are the same, the client data is different. In each case, we are passing the modality for the dialog box to use when it is popped up. Note that in the callback routine itself (**pushed( )**), the value for **XmNdialogStyle** is an **unsigned char**. Note that this will be a problem for ANSI compilers that are looking for **XtPointer** as the second parameter to this function. You may have to change this type appropriately and cast it to an **unsigned char** later in the function.[5]

The callback routine for the action area buttons is left unchanged from *reason.c*.

---

[5] See Chapter 2, *The Motif Programming Model,* for a discussion on ANSI compilers and why we don't use the ANSI standards in this book.

5.7.2 Immediate Response

In Example 5-9, once the dialog is posted, the function must return so that **XtAppMain-Loop( )** will continue to process the user's events. If this is not done, the application will fail to respond to button-clicks or other events. For that matter, the dialog won't even be displayed. (Just because a dialog is realized and managed does not mean it exists on the screen—events must be processed in order to allow this to happen. See Chapter 20, *Advanced Dialog Programming,* for more discussion on this phenomenon; see Volume One, *Xlib Programming Manual,* if you don't understand this concept.) We would like to be able to avoid this problem and have the events that display and manage the dialog be processed without our having to return to the main loop.

Furthermore, it would be nice not to have to return from the function, breaking its flow of control. But in order for the user to be able to reply to the dialog (which would cause our callback routines to be activated), event processing must still be going on. Again, this is a problem that is typically solved by returning back to the main event loop.

Consider the following scenario: you have a function that allows the user to perform a particularly dangerous action such as removing or overwriting a file. What you'd like to do is prompt the user first, allowing him to reconsider his action before proceeding. If he confirms the action, you'd like to continue from within the same function without having to return in order to process events.

Let us assume that the hypothetical function we're talking about is called **AskUser( )**. This is how it might be used:

```
if (AskUser("Are you sure you want to do this?") == YES) {
    /* proceed with action... */
}
```

The function **AskUser( )** should post a MessageDialog that is full-application-modal and return some predefined value for **YES** and **NO**. The magic of the function is to get around the requirement that events can only be read and processed directly from **XtAppMain-Loop( )**. The code for the function is shown in Example 5-10.

Example 5-10. The askuser() routine

```
#define YES  1
#define NO   2
/*
 * AskUser() -- a generalized routine that asks the user a question
 * and returns the Yes/No response.
 */
int
AskUser(parent, question)
Widget parent;
char *question;
{
    static Widget dialog;
    XmString text, yes, no;
    int answer = 0;
    extern void response();
    extern XtAppContext app;
```

Example 5-10. The askuser() routine (continued)

```
    if (!dialog) {
        dialog = XmCreateQuestionDialog(parent, "dialog", NULL, 0);
        yes = XmStr("Yes");
        no = XmStr("No");
        XtVaSetValues(dialog,
            XmNdialogStyle,         XmDIALOG_FULL_APPLICATION_MODAL,
            XmNokLabelString,       yes,
            XmNcancelLabelString,   no,
            NULL);
        XtSetSensitive(
            XmMessageBoxGetChild(dialog, XmDIALOG_HELP_BUTTON),
          False);
        XtAddCallback(dialog, XmNokCallback, response, &answer);
        XtAddCallback(dialog, XmNcancelCallback, response, &answer);
    }
    text = XmStr(question);
    XtVaSetValues(dialog,
        XmNmessageString,       text,
        NULL);
    XmStringFree(text);
    XtManageChild(dialog);

    /* while the user hasn't provided an answer, simulate main loop.
     * The answer changes as soon as the user selects one of the
     * buttons and the callback routine changes its value.  Don't
     * break loop until XtPending() also returns False to assure
     * widget destruction.
     */
    while (answer == 0)
        XtAppProcessEvents(app, XtIMAll);
    XtUnmanageChild(XtParent(w));
    return answer;
}
/* response() --The user made some sort of response to the
 * question posed in AskUser().  Set the answer (client_data)
 * accordingly and destroy the dialog.
 */
void
response(w, answer, cbs)
Widget w;
int *answer;
XmAnyCallbackStruct *cbs;
{
    switch (cbs->reason) {
        case XmCR_OK:
            *answer = YES;
            break;
        case XmCR_CANCEL:
            *answer = NO;
            break;
    }
}
```

The function takes two parameters: the first is a widget that acts as the new dialog's owner or parent. It is important to choose this widget wisely. It must not be a gadget or an unrealized widget and should be one that is currently mapped to the screen. Widgets that are items in

MenuBar menus are not good candidates since they are not mapped to the screen for very long. A good choice is typically the toplevel shell widget of the widget that caused the callback function to be invoked.

The second parameter is a string (prompt) to display. Because the function intends to ask a Yes/No question, we want to change the **Ok** and **Cancel** labels to say "Yes" and "No", respectively. A QuestionDialog box (`dialog`) is created as a static `Widget`. This allows us to reuse the same dialog box repeatedly rather than re-creating it all the time. This may be a significant performance improvement for some computers. The modality and labels for the PushButtons in the action area are set at creation time, but the actual message string is set independently each time the function is called (obviously, since the message changes).

The callback routines for the buttons are installed next. We use the *address* of the `answer` variable as the client data for the callback routine. When the dialog is displayed and the user responds to the question by selecting the **Yes** or **No** button, the callback routine will have access to the variable and change its value accordingly.

The `while` loop is where the application waits for the user to make a selection. The loop exits when the variable `answer` is changed from its initial value (0) to either `YES` (1) or `NO` (2) by the callback routine. We have effectively reproduced the `XtAppMainLoop( )` function used in the main application. Rather than returning to that level and breaking our flow of control, we introduce a mini main loop right here.

Generalizing AskUser()

We now have all the knowledge we need to generalize `AskUser( )` to be more useful. By pooling together bits and pieces of everything we've learned in this chapter—setting resources on dialogs, getting dialog widget children, passing `client_data` to callback routines, using dialog modality, and generalizing and abstracting code and algorithms, we can come up with a simple, yet extremely robust interface for prompting for responses to questions without breaking a natural flow of control for the application.

Example 5-11 demonstrates all of these concepts. The program *ask_user2.c* provides a simple design that allows the user to execute UNIX commands. Here, we use it to create or remove a temporary file. This version of `AskUser( )` is included in a complete application.

Example 5-11. The ask_user2.c program

```
/* ask_user2.c -- advanced version of ask_user.c.
 * The user is presented with two pushbuttons.  The first creates
 * a file (/tmp/foo) and the second removes it.  In each case,
 * a dialog pops up asking for verification of the action.
 *
 * This program is intended to demonstrate an advanced implementation
 * of the AskUser() function.  This time, the function is passed the
 * strings to use for the Ok button and the Cancel button as well as
 * the button to use as the default value.
 */
#include <Xm/DialogS.h>
#include <Xm/SelectioB.h>
#include <Xm/RowColumn.h>
#include <Xm/MessageB.h>
```

Example 5-11. The ask_user2.c program (continued)

```
#include <Xm/PushB.h>

#define YES 1
#define NO  2

/* Generalize the question/answer process by creating a data structure
 * that has the necessary labels, questions and everything needed to
 * execute a command.
 */
typedef struct {
    char *label;    /* label for pushbutton used to invoke cmd */
    char *question; /* question for dialog box to confirm cmd */
    char *yes;      /* what the "ok" button says */
    char *no;       /* what the "cancel" button says */
    int  dflt;      /* which should be the default answer */
    char *cmd;      /* actual command to execute (using system()) */
} QandA;

QandA touch_foo = {
    "Create", "Create /tmp/foo?", "Yes", "No", YES, "touch /tmp/foo"
};
QandA rm_foo = {
    "Remove", "Remove /tmp/foo?", "Do", "Don't", NO, "rm /tmp/foo"
};

XtAppContext app;

main(argc, argv)
int argc;
char *argv[ ];
{
    Widget toplevel, button, rowcolumn;
    XmString label;
    void pushed();

    toplevel = XtVaAppInitialize(&app, "Demos",
        NULL, 0, &argc, argv, NULL, NULL);

    rowcolumn = XtVaCreateManagedWidget("rowcolumn",
        xmRowColumnWidgetClass, toplevel, NULL);

    label = XmStringCreateSimple(touch_foo.label);
    button = XtVaCreateManagedWidget("button",
        xmPushButtonWidgetClass, rowcolumn,
        XmNlabelString,         label,
        NULL);
    XtAddCallback(button, XmNactivateCallback, pushed, &touch_foo);
    XmStringFree(label);

    label = XmStringCreateSimple(rm_foo.label);
    button = XtVaCreateManagedWidget("button",
        xmPushButtonWidgetClass, rowcolumn,
        XmNlabelString,         label,
        NULL);
    XtAddCallback(button, XmNactivateCallback, pushed, &rm_foo);
    XmStringFree(label);

    XtManageChild(rowcolumn);
    XtRealizeWidget(toplevel);
    XtAppMainLoop(app);
```

Example 5-11. The ask_user2.c program (continued)

```
}

/* pushed() --when a button is pressed, ask the question described
 * by the QandA parameter (client_data).  Execute the cmd if YES.
 */
void
pushed(w, quest)
Widget w;
QandA *quest;
{
    if (AskUser(w, quest->question, quest->yes, quest->no,
                quest->dflt) == YES) {
        printf("executing: %s\n", quest->cmd);
        system(quest->cmd);
    } else
        printf("not executing: %s\n", quest->cmd);
}

/*
 * AskUser() -- a generalized routine that asks the user a question
 * and returns a response.  Parameters are: the question, the labels
 * for the "Yes" and "No" buttons, and the default selection to use.
 */
AskUser(parent, question, ans1, ans2, default_ans)
char *question, *ans1, *ans2;
int default_ans;
{
    static Widget dialog; /* static to avoid multiple creation */
    XmString text, yes, no;
    int answer = 0;
    extern void response();

    if (!dialog) {
        dialog = XmCreateQuestionDialog(parent, "dialog", NULL, 0);
        XtVaSetValues(dialog,
            XmNdialogStyle,          XmDIALOG_FULL_APPLICATION_MODAL,
            NULL);
        XtSetSensitive(
            XmMessageBoxGetChild(dialog, XmDIALOG_HELP_BUTTON),
            False);
        XtAddCallback(dialog, XmNokCallback, response, &answer);
        XtAddCallback(dialog, XmNcancelCallback, response, &answer);
    }
    text = XmStringCreateSimple(question);
    yes = XmStringCreateSimple(ans1);
    no = XmStringCreateSimple(ans2);
    XtVaSetValues(dialog,
        XmNmessageString,      text,
        XmNokLabelString,      yes,
        XmNcancelLabelString,  no,
        XmNdefaultButtonType,  default_ans == YES?
                    XmDIALOG_OK_BUTTON : XmDIALOG_CANCEL_BUTTON,
        NULL);
    XmStringFree(text);
    XmStringFree(ans1);
    XmStringFree(ans2);
    XtManageChild(dialog);
```

Example 5-11. The ask_user2.c program (continued)

```
    while (answer == 0) {
        XtAppProcessEvent(app, XtIMAll);
        XSync(XtDisplay(dialog), 0);
    }

    XtUnmanageChild(dialog);
    XSync(XtDisplay(dialog), 0);
    XmUpdateDisplay(dialog);

    return answer;
}

/* response() --The user made some sort of response to the
 * question posed in AskUser().  Set the answer (client_data)
 * accordingly.
 */
void
response(w, answer, cbs)
Widget w;
int *answer;
XmAnyCallbackStruct *cbs;
{
    if (cbs->reason == XmCR_OK)
        *answer = YES;
    else if (cbs->reason == XmCR_CANCEL)
        *answer = NO;
}
```

The new version of **AskUser( )** is more dynamic than before, since more of the dialog is configurable upon each invocation of the function. This is achieved at the cost of a few more source code lines and additional parameters to the function. The performance of the function or the application is completely unaffected.

Food for Thought

As another example, what if you wanted to provide a **Cancel** button in addition to the Yes/No answers? Consider the following scenario: the user has selected the **Quit** button in your text editor application. He has yet to update his changes to the file he'd been editing, so you ask the user:

> Do you want to update your changes?

His response could be:

- Yes, update the changes (**Yes**).

- No, don't update the changes, but quit anyway (**No**).

- Don't update the changes, and don't quit the application (**Cancel**).

The easiest way to provide these three choices is to set the label for the **Help** selection using `XmNhelpLabelString` to be "Cancel" and have the callback function set the `*answer` to be a new `#define`:

```
#define CANCEL    3
```

However, if you wish to provide help in addition to these choices, you run into a problem because MessageDialogs only provide for three selections in the action area. Try to figure out how you might create this dialog based on the information presented in this chapter so far. If you get stuck, you can refer to Chapter 7, *Custom Dialogs*.

5.8 Summary

Dialogs are very heavily used in all window-oriented applications and their uses are quite diverse. Because of this, it is impossible to provide extensive examples of any one particular style of dialog. This chapter introduced the implementation of Motif dialogs using the default MessageDialog widgets as examples. The next chapter deals with SelectionDialogs, which are a group of Motif dialogs that allow you to provide a selection of choices to the user. Chapter 7, *Custom Dialogs*, discusses dialogs you can build on your own, breaking away from the default Motif specifications and implementations. Chapter 20, *Advanced Dialog Programming*, gets into advanced topics in Xt and Motif programming, using various forms of MessageDialogs as examples. In particular, you will find in that chapter a discussion of how to use dialogs in a help system.

6

Selection Dialogs

This chapter describes the more complex Motif-supplied dialogs for displaying selection lists (such as lists of files or commands) to the user.

In This Chapter:

6
Selection Dialogs

In Chapter 5, *Introduction to Dialogs*, we introduced the general idea behind dialog widgets—that they are transient windows that perform a single, discrete task. The kinds of tasks dialogs may perform range from displaying a simple message, to asking a question, to providing a highly interactive window that obtains information from the user. That chapter also introduced MessageDialogs and discussed how they are used by the Motif toolkit. This chapter discusses the next level of complexity in dialogs predefined by Motif: SelectionDialogs.

In general, SelectionDialogs are used to present the user with a list of choices; alternatively, he can provide a new selection or edit an existing one by typing in a text field. Selection-Dialogs are appropriate when the user is supposed to respond to the dialog with more than just a simple yes or no answer. With respect to the action area, SelectionDialogs have the same default buttons as MessageBoxes (e.g., **Ok, Cancel,** and **Help**). (An **Apply** button is also available, but it is not managed by default.) Obviously, this form of dialog is less transient than MessageDialogs, since the user is expected to do more than read message and click a button.

6.1 SelectionDialog Types

As mentioned in Chapter 5, *Introduction to Dialogs*, there are four kinds of SelectionBoxes: the standard SelectionBox, a FileSelectionBox, a PromptBox, and a CommandBox. You can create each of these types using the associated convenience routines:

```
XmCreateSelectionDialog( )
XmCreateFileSelectionDialog( )
XmCreatePromptDialog( )
XmCreateCommand( )
```

Which type of SelectionDialog has been created is always available in the **XmNdialog-Type** resource, which may have one of the following values:

```
XmDIALOG_WORK_AREA
XmDIALOG_PROMPT
XmDIALOG_SELECTION
XmDIALOG_COMMAND
XmDIALOG_FILE_SELECTION
```

These values should be intuitively obvious, except for **XmDIALOG_WORK_AREA**. This value is set when a SelectionDialog is not a child of a DialogShell, and is not one of the other types. When you create a SelectionDialog using **XmCreateSelectionDialog( )**, the type is **XmDIALOG_SELECTION**. But if you use **XmCreateSelectionBox( )**, it will be **XmDIALOG_WORK_AREA**. In the latter case, the **Apply** button will be automatically managed. (This makes sense; in a transient dialog, the selection value will typically be applied by the **Ok** button, which will also make the dialog go away. If the SelectionBox is not transient, an **Apply** button makes more sense.)

The value for **XmNdialogType** is automatically set by the convenience routine that creates the dialog. However, this is a read-only resource. Unlike the MessageDialogs, you cannot dynamically change this resource once the dialog has been created.

Like the MessageDialog convenience routines, the SelectionDialog routines also create the DialogShell for you. CommandDialogs, however, do not have corresponding DialogShells created for them by their convenience routine. To put a Command box into a DialogShell, you must create the DialogShell yourself.

Whether or not a list of selections is available does not affect the default functionality of the SelectionBox. The user can select from the list and/or type in new or existing values in the text entry field, but nothing happens unless the user presses the $\boxed{\text{RETURN}}$ key or selects one of the buttons in the action area. (If a List is displayed, double-clicking on an item fills in the Text widget with the associated value and automatically selects the **Ok** button.)

Let's examine the basics of how SelectionDialogs work by looking at the most basic type: the PromptDialog. We'll come back to each of the other SelectionDialogs in turn.

6.2 PromptDialogs

The PromptDialog is unique among the SelectionDialogs in that it does not create a Scrolled-List object. (The user must always generate a new selection.) By default, this dialog allows the user to type a text string and then enter it by selecting the **Ok** button or by pressing $\boxed{\text{RETURN}}$.[1] Example 6-1 shows an example of how such a dialog box is created.

---

[1] One very frustrating feature of the predefined Motif dialogs is that the TextField widget doesn't receive the keyboard focus by default. If the user isn't paying attention, he could well type away without any effect, and then press $\boxed{\text{RETURN}}$. All the keystrokes will be thrown away except the $\boxed{\text{RETURN}}$, which will activate the **Ok** button—even though the text for the selection was never specified. This is a design flaw that you will need to warn your users about or program around. As described in Chapter 8, *Manager Widgets*, you can use **XmProcessTraversal( )** to set the focus to a particular widget; whether or not this is taking license with the approved Motif style is left to your judgement. We certainly don't think users will complain.

Example 6-1. The prompt_dlg.c program

```c
/* prompt_dlg.c -- prompt the user for a string.  Two PushButtons
 * are displayed.  When one is selected, a PromptDialog is displayed
 * allowing the user to type a string.  When done, the PushButton's
 * label changes to the string.
 */
#include <Xm/SelectioB.h>
#include <Xm/RowColumn.h>
#include <Xm/PushB.h>

main(argc, argv)
char *argv[ ];
{
    XtAppContext app;
    Widget toplevel, rc, button;
    void pushed();

    /* Initialize toolkit and create toplevel shell */
    toplevel = XtVaAppInitialize(&app, "Demos", NULL, 0,
        &argc, argv, NULL, NULL);

    /* RowColumn managed both PushButtons */
    rc = XtVaCreateWidget("rowcol", xmRowColumnWidgetClass, toplevel,
        NULL);
    /* Create two pushbuttons -- both have the same callback */
    button = XtVaCreateManagedWidget("PushMe-1",
        xmPushButtonWidgetClass, rc, NULL);
    XtAddCallback(button, XmNactivateCallback, pushed, NULL);
    button = XtVaCreateManagedWidget("PushMe-2",
        xmPushButtonWidgetClass, rc, NULL);
    XtAddCallback(button, XmNactivateCallback, pushed, NULL);

    XtManageChild(rc);
    XtRealizeWidget(toplevel);
    XtAppMainLoop(app);
}

/* pushed() --the callback routine for the main app's pushbuttons.
 * Create a dialog that prompts for a new button name.
 */
void
pushed(pb)
Widget pb;
{
    static Widget dialog;
    XmString t = XmStringCreateSimple("Enter New Button Name:");
    extern void read_name();
    Arg args[2];

    /* Create the dialog -- the PushButton acts as the DialogShell's
     * parent (not the parent of the PromptDialog).
     */
    XtSetArg(args[0], XmNselectionLabelString, t);
    XtSetArg(args[1], XmNautoUnmanage, False);
    dialog = XmCreatePromptDialog(pb, "prompt", args, 2);
    XmStringFree(t); /* always destroy compound strings when done */

    /* When the user types the name, call read_name() ... */
    XtAddCallback(dialog, XmNokCallback, read_name, pb);
```

Example 6-1. The prompt_dlg.c program (continued)

```
    /* If the user selects cancel, just destroy the dialog */
    XtAddCallback(dialog, XmNcancelCallback, XtDestroyWidget, NULL);

    /* No help is available... */
    XtSetSensitive(
        XmSelectionBoxGetChild(dialog, XmDIALOG_HELP_BUTTON), False);
    XtManageChild(dialog);

    XtPopup(XtParent(dialog), XtGrabNone);
}

/* read_name() --the text field has been filled in. */
void
read_name(w, push_button, cbs)
Widget w;
Widget push_button;  /* the "client_data" parameter to XtAddCallback */
XmSelectionBoxCallbackStruct *cbs;
{
    XtVaSetValues(push_button, XmNlabelString, cbs->value, NULL);
    /* Name's fine -- go ahead and enter it */
    XtDestroyWidget(w);
}
```

The output of the program is shown in Figure 6-1.

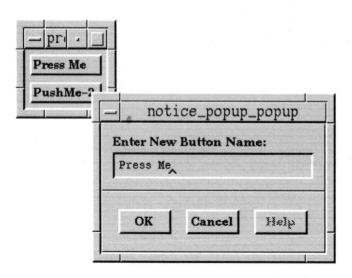

Figure 6-1. Output of prompt_dlg.c

The PushButtons' callback routine (**pushed( )**) creates a PromptDialog that prompts the user to enter a new name for the PushButton. The PushButton acts as the parent for the PromptDialog. It is also passed as the **client_data** for the **XmNokCallback** routine, **read_name( )**, so it can set the name of the PushButton directly from inside the callback. The function also destroys the dialog, since it is no longer needed.

If **Cancel** is pressed, the text isn't needed, so we can just destroy the dialog. Since the first parameter to dialog callback routines is the dialog widget, we can use `XtDestroyWidget` *as* the callback routine. Since it only takes one parameter, and the widget to destroy is passed to the callback routine as the first parameter, no client data is needed. For both cases (**Ok** and **Cancel**), the application is assuming the responsibility of the dialog's management state, so we don't need to let Motif handle it for us. Thus, we set `XmNautoUnmanage` to `False` upon creation.

Because there is no help for this item, the **Help** button is disabled by setting its sensitivity to `False`.

6.2.1 SelectionDialog Callback Structure

The callback structure (`cbs` parameter) for the PromptDialog's callback routine is of type `XmSelectionBoxCallbackStruct`, since the PromptDialog is really a special form of SelectionDialog. This structure is similar to the one used by MessageDialogs, but has more fields. The structure is declared as follows:

```
typedef struct {
    int          reason;
    XEvent       *event;
    XmString     value;
    int          length;
} XmSelectionBoxCallbackStruct;
```

The `value` and `length` fields represent the compound string version of the text that the user typed. Since we want to set the label for a PushButton, this value is adequate. However, in order to get the actual `char` version of this text, we would have to use the function `XmStringGetLtoR( )`. (See Chapter 19 for a discussion of compound strings.)

The `reason` may be any of the values used by the MessageDialog with the addition of `XmCR_APPLY`. Thus, the possible values for the `reason` field are:

```
XmCR_HELP
XmCR_OK
XmCR_CANCEL
XmCR_APPLY
```

The **Apply** button is available to the PromptDialog, but it is unmanaged by default. To use this button, you must manage it and specify an `XmNapplyCallback` routine. For example:

```
XtAddCallback(dialog, XmNapplyCallback, read_name, NULL);
XtManageChild(XmSelectionBoxGetChild(dialog, XmDIALOG_APPLY_BUTTON));
```

The callback routine is the same as the one set for the **Ok** button, but the `reason` will indicate that it was called as a result of the **Apply** button being pushed.

6.2.2 The Prompt's Text

Since the editable text field is a Text widget, you can get a handle to it and set Text widget resources accordingly. However, there are two resources that you can set directly onto any SelectionDialog that affect its Text widget's *value* (the text it displays) as well as its width. These values can be set using the `XmNtextString` and `XmNtextColumns` resources. The `XmNtextString` resource value must be of type `XmString` and the `XmNtext-Columns` resource must be of type `int`.

6.3 SelectionDialogs

The SelectionDialog is slightly more complex than a PromptBox with the difference being the addition of a ScrolledList that allows the user to select from an array of choices. In the default case, the user can input text, just as he would with a PromptBox, ignoring the selections in the List widget. However, you can restrict the user to the set of existing choices using the `XmNmustMatch` resource. When this resource is set to `True`, the dialog does not accept input unless the user's response matches one of the items in the list. If the response doesn't match, the routine associated with the `XmNnoMatchCallback` resource is called. Example 6-2 demonstrates these and other resources for the SelectionDialog.

Example 6-2. The select_dlg.c program

```
/* select_dlg.c -- display two pushbuttons: days and months.
 * When the user selects one of them, post a selection
 * dialog that displays the actual days or months accordingly.
 * When the user selects or types a selection, post a dialog
 * that identifies which item was selected and whether or not
 * the item is in the list.
 *
 * This program demonstrates how to use selection boxes,
 * methods for creating generic callbacks for action area
 * selections, abstraction of data structures, and a generic
 * MessageDialogBox posting routine.
 */
#include <Xm/SelectioB.h>
#include <Xm/RowColumn.h>
#include <Xm/MessageB.h>
#include <Xm/PushB.h>

Widget PostDialog();

char *days[ ] = {
    "Sunday", "Monday", "Tuesday", "Wednesday",
    "Thursday", "Friday", "Saturday"
};
char *months[ ] = {
    "January", "February", "March", "April", "May", "June",
    "July", "August", "September", "October", "November", "December"
};
typedef struct {
    char *label;
    char **strings;
```

Example 6-2. The select_dlg.c program (continued)

```
    int size;
} ListItem;

ListItem month_items = { "Months", months, XtNumber(months) };
ListItem days_items = { "Days", days, XtNumber(days) };

/* main() --create two pushbuttons whose callbacks pop up a dialog */
main(argc, argv)
char *argv[ ];
{
    Widget toplevel, button, rc;
    XtAppContext app;
    void pushed();

    toplevel = XtVaAppInitialize(&app, "Demos", NULL, 0,
        &argc, argv, NULL, NULL);

    rc = XtVaCreateWidget("rowcolumn", xmRowColumnWidgetClass, toplevel, NULL);

    button = XtVaCreateManagedWidget(month_items.label,
        xmPushButtonWidgetClass, rc, NULL);
    XtAddCallback(button, XmNactivateCallback, pushed, &month_items);

    button = XtVaCreateManagedWidget(days_items.label,
        xmPushButtonWidgetClass, rc, NULL);
    XtAddCallback(button, XmNactivateCallback, pushed, &days_items);

    XtManageChild(rc);
    XtRealizeWidget(toplevel);
    XtAppMainLoop(app);
}

/* pushed() --the callback routine for the main app's pushbutton.
 * Create a dialog containing the list in the items parameter.
 */
void
pushed(w, items)
Widget w;
ListItem *items;
{
    Widget dialog;
    XmString t, *str;
    int i;
    extern void dialog_callback();

    str = (XmString *)XtMalloc(items->size * sizeof(XmString));
    t = XmStringCreateSimple(items->label);
    for (i = 0; i < items->size; i++)
        str[i] = XmStringCreateSimple(items->strings[i]);
    dialog = XmCreateSelectionDialog(w, "selection", NULL, 0);
    XtVaSetValues(dialog,
        XmNlistLabelString, t,
        XmNlistItems,       str,
        XmNlistItemCount,   items->size,
        XmNmustMatch,       True,
        NULL);
    XtSetSensitive(
        XmSelectionBoxGetChild(dialog, XmDIALOG_HELP_BUTTON), False);
    XtAddCallback(dialog, XmNokCallback, dialog_callback, NULL);
    XtAddCallback(dialog, XmNnoMatchCallback, dialog_callback, NULL);
```

Example 6-2. The select_dlg.c program (continued)

```
        XmStringFree(t);
        while (--i >= 0)
            XmStringFree(str[i]); /* free elements of array */
        XtFree(str); /* now free array pointer */
        XtManageChild(dialog);
}

/* dialog_callback() --The Ok button was selected or the user
 * input a name by himself.  Determine whether the result is
 * a valid name by looking at the "reason" field.
 */
void
dialog_callback(w, client_data, cbs)
Widget w;
XtPointer client_data;
XmSelectionBoxCallbackStruct *cbs;
{
    char msg[256], *prompt, *value;
    int dialog_type;

    switch (cbs->reason) {
        case XmCR_OK:
            prompt = "Selection:\n    ";
            dialog_type = XmDIALOG_MESSAGE;
            break;
        case XmCR_NO_MATCH:
            prompt = "Not a valid selection:\n";
            dialog_type = XmDIALOG_ERROR;
            break;
        default:
            prompt = "Unknown selection:\n";
            dialog_type = XmDIALOG_ERROR;
    }
    XmStringGetLtoR(cbs->value, XmSTRING_DEFAULT_CHARSET, &value);
    sprintf(msg, "%s%s", prompt, value);
    XtFree(value);
    (void) PostDialog(XtParent(XtParent(w)), dialog_type, msg);
    XmStringFree(prompt);
    if (cbs->reason != XmCR_NO_MATCH)
        XtDestroyWidget(w); /* doesn't work for pre-Motif 1.1.1 */
}

/*
 * PostDialog() -- a generalized routine that allows the programmer
 * to specify a dialog type (message, information, error, help,
 * etc..), and the message to show.
 */
Widget
PostDialog(parent, dialog_type, msg)
int dialog_type;
char *msg;
{
    Widget dialog;
    XmString text;

    dialog = XmCreateMessageDialog(parent, "dialog", NULL, 0);
    text = XmStringCreateLtoR(msg);
    XtVaSetValues(dialog,
```

Example 6-2. The select_dlg.c program (continued)

```
        XmNdialogType,    dialog_type,
        XmNmessageString, text,
        NULL);
    XmStringFree(text);
    XtUnmanageChild(
        XmMessageBoxGetChild(dialog, XmDIALOG_CANCEL_BUTTON));
    XtSetSensitive(
        XmMessageBoxGetChild(dialog, XmDIALOG_HELP_BUTTON), False);
    XtAddCallback(dialog, XmNokCallback, XtDestroyWidget, NULL);
    XtManageChild(dialog);
    return dialog;
}
```

The output of *select_dlg.c* is shown in Figure 6-2.

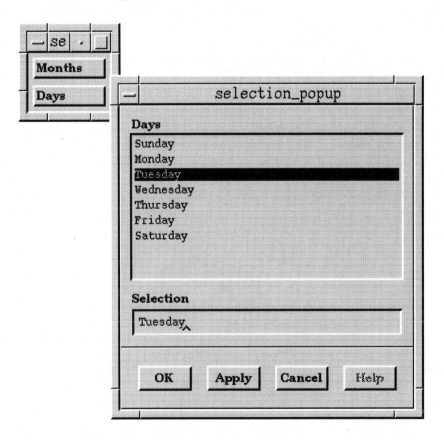

Figure 6-2. Output of select_dlg.c

The program displays two PushButtons, one representing the months and the other representing the days of the week. When either button is activated, a SelectionDialog appears showing a list of all the items from the list corresponding to the widget selected. The user may select an item from the list or type one in manually. Because the **XmNmustMatch** resource is set, when the user activates the **Ok** button or hits RETURN , the widget checks the selection against those in the list. If the selection doesn't match any of the selections in the list, a dialog pops up indicating the error.

Keeping in line with the philosophy of generalized and object-oriented programming techniques, we have broken down the application's task into three routines—two callbacks and one general-purpose message posting function. The list of day and month names is stored as an array of strings. We know that we are going to have to provide the label for the list and the number of items ahead of time, so we declare a data structure (**ListItem**) to contain this information. Two instances of this data structure are initialized to the correct values for the "months" and "days" array. This is the generalized data structure we use as the **client_data** for the callback function (**pushed( )**) that actually generates the Selection-Dialog. This callback function is associated with the PushButtons in the main application.

The **pushed( )** callback function creates the SelectionDialog. Since the list for the dialog must be given as an array of **XmString** values, the list given in the **items** parameter (e.g., the **client_data**) must be converted. So, we create an array of **XmString** the size of the list and copy each item into the new array using **XmStringCreateSimple( )**.[2] The resulting list is used as the value for the **XmNlistItems** resource. The number of items in the list is given as the value for the **XmNlistItemCount** resource. This value must be given in order for the list to be displayed. It must be less than or equal to the actual number of items in the list.

Finally, we set the **XmNmustMatch** resource to **True**, indicating that the user cannot make up his own month or day names; his input must match one of the items in the list or an error is generated. Once the dialog is created, we desensitize its **Help** button (because we are not providing help), and install the callback routine for the **Ok** button and the "no-match" error. The routine **dialog_callback( )** is used to handle both cases.

Since the intent of this application, is simply to display a dialog box indicating the response that the user gave and indicate whether or not there was an error, we can use the generalized function we provided in Example 5-6, **PostDialog( )** (with some minor modifications).

The **dialog_callback( )** function is generalized for any SelectionBox widget. The reason the function was called is given in the **reason** field of the callback structure, and it may be either **XmCR_OK** or **XmCR_NO_MATCH**. Of course, its functionality and generalization can be extended by adding more cases to the **switch** statement. The routine constructs a message to pass to **PostDialog( )** by building one based on the **value** field from the **reason** parameter. Since this value is in **XmString** format, it is first converted to **char** format before posting.

Don't forget to destroy the dialog using **XtDestroyWidget( )**.

Just as a point of discussion, it was an arbitrary decision to have the **PostDialog( )** function accept **char** strings rather than **XmStrings**. As it turns out, both functions could be modified to use **XmStrings** as parameters, but doing so doesn't buy us anything. You may find that your application deals with one type of string format more often than another and you may wish to modify your routines accordingly. However, be aware that converting from one type of string to another is expensive; if done frequently, you may see a performance

---

[2] Hint: foresight indicates that this functionality should be generalized to a convenience function.

drop. Another option is for your routine to accept both types as different parameters. Pass a valid value as one parameter and NULL as the other parameter and deal with them accordingly. For more information on handling compound strings, see Chapter 19, *Compound Strings*.

6.4 CommandDialogs

A Command widget allows the user to enter commands and have them saved in a "history" list widget for later reference. This is a convenient interface for applications that have a command-driven interface such as a debugger. The Command widget class is subclassed from SelectionBox, and is similar in that the user has the ability to select from items in a list. However, the list is composed of text previously input. As the user enters new strings (presumably commands), each entry is added to the list. A CommandBox is usually found in a MainWindow (see Chapter 4, *The Main Window*) and is not commonly used in its own DialogShell.

You can use the convenience routine `XmCreateCommand( )` for creating an instance of a CommandBox. Alternately, you can create one using `XtVaCreateWidget( )` with the class `xmCommandWidgetClass`. However, there is no convenience routine for creating a CommandBox in its own DialogShell. The rationale for this is that CommandBoxes are intended to be used on a more permanent basis, because they are accumulating a history of command input. Therefore, if you want to create a CommandDialog, you'll need to create your own DialogShell widget and make the CommandBox its immediate child. See Section 5.5.1, *How Convenience Routines Work*, in Chapter 5, *Introduction to Dialogs*.

Subwidgets of the CommandBox include a List widget, a Text widget, and all the standard widgets that make up the action area. You can get a handle to these widgets using the function `XmCommandGetChild( )`. The function takes the form:

```
Widget
XmCommandGetChild(cw, child)
    Widget          cw;
    unsigned char   child;
```

The `child` parameter may be one of the following:

XmDIALOG_COMMAND_TEXT
Returns a handle to the Text widget where input is provided.

XmDIALOG_HISTORY_LIST
Returns a handle to the List widget containing the command history. This is a ScrolledList, so the parent of this widget is a ScrolledWindow widget. See Chapter 9, *ScrolledWindows and Scrollbars*, for a discussion of ScrolledLists.

XmDIALOG_PROMPT_LABEL
Returns the Label widget that displays a message above the Text widget.

6.4.1 Command Callback Routines

The resources to specify callback routines for the CommandDialog are the same as for the SelectionDialog with the addition of:

```
XmNcommandEnteredCallback
XmNcommandChangedCallback
```

Because of the nature of the CommandBox, it doesn't make sense to use the **XmNnoMatch-Callback** callback resource. In each case, the callback routine specified gets the usual parameters:

```
void
command_callback(cw, client_data, cbs)
    Widget                  cw;
    XtPointer               client_data;
    XmCommandCallbackStruct *cbs;
```

The difference is the callback structure (**call_data**) parameter is of type **XmCommand-CallbackStruct**, which is identical to the **XmSelectionBoxCallbackStruct**. The values for the **reason** field of the structure include:

```
XmCR_OK
XmCR_CANCEL
XmCR_HELP
XmCR_APPLY
XmCR_COMMAND_ENTERED
XmCR_COMMAND_CHANGED
```

6.4.2 Other Command Routines

If you want to add an element to the history items in the CommandBox, you can use the routine **XmCommandAppendValue( )**. The function takes the following form:

```
void
XmCommandAppendValue(cw, command)
    Widget                  cw;
    XmString                command;
```

The **command** is added to the history list immediately.

The function **XmCommandError( )** displays an error message in the history area of the CommandBox. The function takes the following form:

```
void
XmCommandError(cw, msg)
    Widget                  cw;
    XmString                msg;
```

The error message remains until the user enters the next command.

The convenience function **XmCommandSetValue( )** is used to set the text in the Text widget of the CommandBox. The function takes the following form:

```
void
XmCommandSetValue(cw, text)
    Widget          cw;
    XmString        text;
```

You could alternatively use **XmTextSetString( )** on the **XmDIALOG_COM-MAND_TEXT** widget. Note, however, that the string you specify to this function is not a **Xm-String**, it is a **char** string.

Except for the new convenience routines, the CommandBox is not very different from the SelectionBox.

6.5 FileSelectionDialogs

Like Command, the FileSelectionBox is subclassed from SelectionBox rather than simply configured within the same widget class. It breaks the mold used by the other Selection-Dialogs because of its complexity and unusual widget layout and architecture. Functionally, the FileSelectionDialog displays the filesystem hierarchy so that the user can select a file or directory for use by the application. The dialog provides the ability for the user to specify a *filter* to indicate which files from a directory he is interested in. This filter is generally given as a "regular expression" reminiscent of the classic UNIX meta-characters (e.g., "*" matches all files, while "*.c" matches all files that end in ".c").

Figure 6-3 shows a FileSelectionDialog.

The dialog is broken down into three main components. The directory *mask* identifies the directory to use and a filter or pattern-matching string (described in a moment); the **Directories** and **Files** List widgets break down the mask into two lists (a list of directories and a list of files within the selected item from the directory list); and the **Selection** Text widget identifies a file to use when the **Ok** button is activated.

The **filter** button acts on the directory and pattern specified in the **Filter** Text widget. For example:

```
/usr/src/motif/lib/Xm/*
```

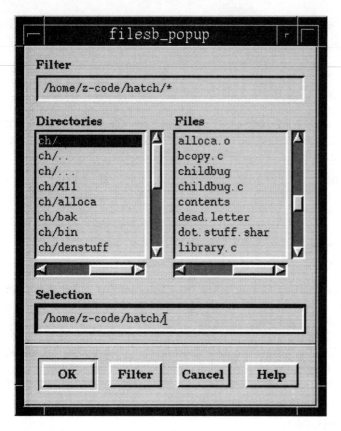

Figure 6-3. A typical file selection dialog

Since directories are delimited by the "/" character, the very last segment (*) is the *pattern* and is treated as a filter for the directory preceding it (*/usr/src/motif/lib/Xm*). When the user selects the **Filter** button or presses RETURN in the filter's Text widget, the directory part of the filter is searched and all the directories within that directory are displayed in the **Directories** list. The pattern part is then used to find all matching files within the directory; the result is listed in the `Files` list. *Only files are placed in this list; directories are excluded, since they are listed separately.*

While this seems straightforward, the issue can become very confusing for users and programmers alike. For example, consider the following string:

```
/usr/src/motif/lib/Xm
```

This pathname appears to be a common directory path, but in fact, the directory is */usr/src/motif/lib* and the pattern is *Xm*. If searched, the **Directory** list will contain all the directories in */usr/src/motif/lib* and the **Files** part won't contain anything because **Xm** is a directory—not a pattern that will match any other files. This is one of the most common mistakes made by users, so your application should be accompanied by detailed documentation as to how to use this part of the FileSelectionBox. Likewise, programmers are also at a disadvantage, since they frequently try to compensate for the confused user by attempting to second guess what the user *intended* as opposed to what he *did*.

Therefore, the convention is to use the last "/" in the filter's pathname to separate the directory part from the pattern part. Fortunately, the Motif toolkit provides resources and other mechanisms to retrieve the proper parts of the pathname/filter specification. We will demonstrate proper usage in the next few subsections.

6.5.1 Creating FileSelectionDialogs

The convenience function for creating a FileSelectionDialog is **XmCreateFile-SelectionDialog( )** and is declared in *<Xm/FileSB.h>*. It creates a FileSelectionBox widget and its DialogShell parent and returns the FileSelectionBox itself (not the parent). Alternatively, you can create the FileSelectionBox widget (without the parent) using either **XmCreateFileSelectionBox( )** or **XtVaCreateWidget( )** with the widget class specified as **xmFileSelectionBoxWidgetClass**. In this case, you could install the widget in a DialogShell that contains more objects than just the FileSelectionBox.

Example 6-3 demonstrates how the FileSelectionDialog can be created. This program was used to produce the dialog shown in Figure 6-3. The intent of this program is to display a single FileSelectionDialog and print the selection made. We will provide more realistic examples in a moment. For now, notice how little is required to create the dialog itself.

Example 6-3. The show_files.c program

```
/* file.c -- introduce FileSelectionDialog; print the file
 * selected by the user.
 */
#include <Xm/FileSB.h>

#define charset XmSTRING_DEFAULT_CHARSET

main(argc, argv)
int argc;
char *argv[ ];
{
    Widget        toplevel, text_w, dialog;
    XtAppContext  app;
    extern void   exit(), echo_file();

    toplevel = XtVaAppInitialize(&app, "Demos",
        NULL, 0, &argc, argv, NULL, NULL);

    /* Create a simple FileSelectionDialog -- no frills */
    dialog = XmCreateFileSelectionDialog(toplevel, "filesb", NULL, 0);
    XtAddCallback(dialog, XmNcancelCallback, exit, NULL);
    XtAddCallback(dialog, XmNokCallback, echo_file, NULL);
    XtManageChild(dialog);

    XtAppMainLoop(app);
}
/* callback routine when the user selects Ok in the FileSelection
 * Dialog.  Just print the file name selected.
 */
```

Example 6-3. The show_files.c program (continued)

```
void
echo_file(fs, client_data, cbs)
Widget fs;  /* file selection box */
XtPointer client_data;
XmFileSelectionBoxCallbackStruct *cbs;
{
    char *filename;

    if (!XmStringGetLtoR(cbs->value, charset, &filename))
        return; /* must have been an internal error */

    if (!*filename) { /* nothing typed? */
        puts("No file selected.");
        XtFree(filename); /* even "" is an allocated byte */
        return;
    }

    printf("Filename given: \"%s\"\n", filename);
    XtFree(filename);
}
```

The program simply prints the filename selected in the Text widget labeled **Selection**. The user can change the file by selecting an item in the **Files** List widget, or he can directly select one by double-clicking on an item. The FileSelectionDialog itself is very simple to create; most of the work of this program is done in the **Ok** button's callback. Before we discuss the callback routines, let's take a closer look at all the widgets that make up a FileSelection-Dialog.

A FileSelectionDialog is made up of a number of subwidgets, including Text, List, and Push-Button widgets. You can get the handles to these children using the routine **XmFile-SelectionBoxGetChild( )**. The function takes the following form:

```
Widget
XmFileSelectionBoxGetChild (fs, child)
    XmFileSelectionBox  fs;
    unsigned char       child;
```

The **child** parameter indicates which child widget to return. It may be one of:

```
XmDIALOG_APPLY_BUTTON
XmDIALOG_CANCEL_BUTTON
XmDIALOG_DEFAULT_BUTTON
XmDIALOG_DIR_LIST
XmDIALOG_DIR_LIST_LABEL
XmDIALOG_FILTER_LABEL
XmDIALOG_FILTER_TEXT
XmDIALOG_HELP_BUTTON
XmDIALOG_LIST_LABEL
XmDIALOG_OK_BUTTON
XmDIALOG_SELECTION_LABEL
XmDIALOG_SEPARATOR
XmDIALOG_TEXT
XmDIALOG_WORK_AREA
```

When you use **XmFileSelectionBoxGetChild( )**, you should not assume that the widgets returned will be of any particular class. The widget returned to you should be treated as an opaque object as much as possible. Getting FileSelectionDialog children is not very useful in any event because you can access most of the important information held by these children through other FileSelectionDialog resources. You should only get handles to these children if you need to change resources on those widgets that are not involved with the file-selection mechanisms.

6.5.2 FileSelectionDialog Callback Routines

The default `XmNokCallback`, `XmNcancelCallback`, `XmNhelpCallback`, and `XmNnoMatchCallback` callbacks can be specified for FileSelectionBoxes as they are for SelectionBoxes. The callback routines take the usual parameters, but the callback structure given in the `call_data` parameter takes a new form:

```
typedef struct {
    int         reason;
    XEvent      *event;
    XmString    value;
    int         length;
    XmString    mask;
    int         mask_length;
    XmString    dir;
    int         dir_length;
    XmString    pattern;
    int         pattern_length;
} XmFileSelectionBoxCallbackStruct;
```

This structure is passed as the third parameter to all callback routines associated with the FileSelectionBox regardless of the reason it was called. The **value** field represents the string displayed in the **Selection** Text widget. This value may or may not match what currently exists in the **Directory** or **Files** lists.

The **mask** field corresponds to the `XmNdirMask` resource and represents a combination of the entire pathname specification in the filter. The **dir** and pattern fields represent the two components that make up the mask. All of the compound strings can be converted to a **char** string using `XmStringGetLtoR( )`:

```
void
my_callback(fs, client_data, cbs)
Widget      fs;             /* the file selection box widget */
caddr_t     client_data;    /* data provided by the application */
XmFileSelectionBoxCallbackStruct *cbs; /* callback structure */
{
    char *text;

    if (!XmStringGetLtoR(cbs->value, charset, &text))
        my_error("Can't get value.  Possibly wrong charset?");
    /* ... */
    XtFree(text);
}
```

The compound string (`cbs->value`) is converted into text and the **text** variable now points to that newly allocated space. You must be sure to free this space (using `XtFree( )`) when you're done with it.

The value for the **reason** field matches those that can be set for the SelectionDialog:

XmCR_OK
XmCR_APPLY
XmCR_CANCEL
XmCR_HELP
XmCR_NO_MATCH

The value passed depends on which item was selected in the FileSelectionBox's action area. The **XmCR_NO_MATCH** value is used if the function is being called as a result of a no-match error discussed earlier.

The callback structure passed to the callback routine may also be used if you provide your own file-searching routines, as discussed in the next section.

6.5.3 File Searching

You can force the FileSelectionBox to reinitialize itself (e.g., reread the directory part of the mask text) by calling **XmFileSelectionDoSearch( )**. This is useful if you are going to set the mask directly. The function takes the following form:

```
void
XmFileSelectionDoSearch(fs, dirmask)
    XmFileSelectionBoxWidget  fs;
    XmString                  dirmask;
```

Once called, the widget will call its directory search procedure and set the mask Text widget to the **dirmask** parameter.

By default, this function tells the FileSelectionBox to search the directory specified in the mask according to its internal searching algorithm. You can write your own file-searching procedure by specifying a callback routine associated with the resource **XmNfile-SearchProc**. Note that this is not a callback list, just a single procedure. Therefore, you do not install it by calling **XtAddCallback( )**; you specify it as you would any other resource—as a value.

```
extern void my_search_proc( );

XtVaSetValues(file_selection_dialog,
    XmNfileSearchProc, my_search_proc,
    NULL);
```

Whenever the user selects the **Filter** button, and whenever **XmFileSelection-DoSearch( )** is called, your routine will be used to provide the list of filenames given in the **Files** portion of the dialog box.

The form of the routine is:

```
void
file_search_proc(fs, search_data)
    XmFileSelectionBoxWidget           fs;
    XmFileSelectionBoxCallbackStruct *search_data;
```

The **fs** parameter is the actual widget and the **search_data** is the same callback structure used in the callback routines discussed in the previous section. You should not be concerned with the value for **search_data->reason** in this situation because none of the routines along the way use this value.

The function should scan the directory denoted by the **dir** field of the **search_data** parameter. The **pattern** should be used to filter the files within the directory. You can get the complete directory and **pattern** value concatenated together through the **mask** field.

After the search procedure has determined the new list of files that it is going to use, it must set the resources **XmNfileListItems** and **XmNfileListItemCount** to store the list into the List widget used by the selection box. It must also set the resource **XmNlist-Updated** to **True** to indicate that it has indeed done something, whether or not any files are found. The function may also optionally set the **XmNdirSpec** resource to reflect the full file specification in the **Selection** Text widget. This way, if the user selects **Ok**, that file would be used. This is optional, but recommended in case the old value is no longer valid.

To understand why it may be necessary to have your own file search procedure, consider how you would customize a file selection box that only displayed the writable files in an arbitrary directory. This might come in handy for an electronic mail application's save dialog—the user invokes a **Save** action which displays a FileSelectionDialog that lists files in which the user can save messages. Files that can't be written to should not be listed. Example 6-4 shows an example of how this might be accomplished.

Example 6-4. The file_sel.c program

```
/* file_sel.c --a single pushbutton, when selected, creates a
 * file selection dialog that displays a list of all the writable
 * files in the directory described by the XmNmask of the dialog.
 * This program demonstrates how to use the XmNfileSearchProc for
 * file selection dialog widgets.
 */
#include <stdio.h>
#include <Xm/Xm.h>
#include <Xm/FileSB.h>
#include <Xm/DialogS.h>
#include <Xm/PushBG.h>
#include <Xm/PushB.h>
#include <sys/stat.h> /* may also have to include file.h */

void do_search(), new_file_cb();
XmStringCharSet charset = XmSTRING_DEFAULT_CHARSET;

/* routined to determine if a file is accessible, a directory,
 * or writable.  Return -1 on all errors or if the file is not
 * writable.  Return 0 if it's a directory or 1 if it's a plain
 * writable file.
 */
int
is_writable(file)
char *file;
{
    struct stat s_buf;

    /* if file can't be accessed (via stat()) return. */
    if (stat(file, &s_buf) == -1)
        return -1;
    else if ((s_buf.st_mode & S_IFMT) == S_IFDIR)
```

Example 6-4. The file_sel.c program (continued)

```
            return 0; /* a directory */
        else if (!(s_buf.st_mode & S_IFREG) || access(file, W_OK) == -1)
            /* not a normal file or it is not writable */
            return -1;
        /* legitimate file */
        return 1;
}

/* main() -- create a FileSelectionDialog */
main(argc, argv)
int argc;
char *argv[ ];
{
    Widget toplevel, dialog;
    XtAppContext app;
    extern void exit();
    Arg args[1];

    toplevel = XtVaAppInitialize(&app, "Demos",
        NULL, 0, &argc, argv, NULL, NULL);

    XtSetArg(args[0], XmNfileSearchProc, do_search);
    dialog = XmCreateFileSelectionDialog(toplevel, "Files", args, 1);
    XtSetSensitive(
        XmFileSelectionBoxGetChild(dialog,
            XmDIALOG_HELP_BUTTON), False);
    /* if user presses Ok button, call new_file_cb() */
    XtAddCallback(dialog, XmNokCallback, new_file_cb, NULL);
    /* if user presses Cancel button, exit program */
    XtAddCallback(dialog, XmNcancelCallback, exit, NULL);

    XtManageChild(dialog);

    /* XtRealizeWidget(toplevel); */
    XtAppMainLoop(app);
}

/* a new file was selected -- check to see if it's readable and not
 * a directory.  If it's not readable, report an error.  If it's a
 * directory, scan it just as tho the user had typed it in the mask
 * Text field and selected "Search".
 */
void
new_file_cb(w, client_data, cbs)
Widget w;
XmFileSelectionBoxCallbackStruct *cbs;
{
    char *file;

    /* get the string typed in the text field in char * format */
    if (!XmStringGetLtoR(cbs->value, charset, &file))
        return;
    if (*file != '/') {
        /* if it's not a directory, determine the full pathname
         * of the selection by concatenating it to the "dir" part
         */
        char *dir, *newfile;
        if (XmStringGetLtoR(cbs->dir, charset, &dir)) {
            newfile = XtMalloc(strlen(dir) + 1 + strlen(file) + 1);
```

Example 6-4. The file_sel.c program (continued)

```
            sprintf(newfile, "%s/%s", dir, file);
            XtFree(file);
            XtFree(dir);
            file = newfile;
        }
    }
    switch (is_writable(file)) {
        case 1 :
            puts(file); /* or do anything you want */
            break;
        case 0 : {
            /* a directory was selected, scan it */
            XmString str = XmStringCreateSimple(file);
            XmFileSelectionDoSearch(w, str);
            XmStringFree(str);
            break;
        }
        case -1 :
            /* a system error on this file */
            perror(file);
    }
    XtFree(file);
}
/* do_search() -- scan a directory and report only those files that
 * are writable.  Here, we let the shell expand the (possible)
 * wildcards and return a directory listing by using popen().
 * A *real* application should -not- do this; it should use the
 * system's directory routines: opendir(), readdir() and closedir().
 */
void
do_search(fs, cbs)
Widget fs; /* file selection box widget */
XmFileSelectionBoxCallbackStruct *cbs;
{
    char        *mask, buf[BUFSIZ], *p;
    XmString     names[256]; /* maximum of 256 files in dir */
    int          i = 0;
    FILE        *pp;

    if (!XmStringGetLtoR(cbs->mask, charset, &mask))
        return; /* can't do anything */

    sprintf(buf, "/bin/ls %s", mask);
    XtFree(mask);
    /* let the shell read the directory and expand the filenames */
    if (!(pp = popen(buf, "r")))
        return;
    /* read output from popen() -- this will be the list of files */
    while (fgets(buf, sizeof buf, pp)) {
        if (p = index(buf, '\n'))
            *p = 0;
        /* only list files that are writable and not directories */
        if (is_writable(buf) == 1 &&
            (names[i] = XmStringCreateSimple(buf)))
            i++;
    }
```

Example 6-4. The file_sel.c program (continued)

```
    pclose(pp);
    if (i) {
        XtVaSetValues(fs,
            XmNfileListItems,        names,
            XmNfileListItemCount,    i,
            XmNdirSpec,              names[0],
            XmNlistUpdated,          True,
            NULL);
        while (i > 0)
            XmStringFree(names[--i]);
    } else
        XtVaSetValues(fs,
            XmNfileListItems,        NULL,
            XmNfileListItemCount,    0,
            XmNlistUpdated,          True,
            NULL);
}
```

The program simply displays a FileSelectionDialog that lists only files that are writable by the user. The directories listed may or may not be writable; we aren't testing that case here as it is handled in another routine specifically for directories (discussed in the next section). The `XmNfileSearchProc` is set to `do_search( )`, our own routine used to fill the list of files in the **Files** List widget. The function calls `is_writable( )` to determine if a file is accessible (which may or may not indicate if it's writable), if it is a directory, or if it is a plain file that is writable.

The callback routine for the **Ok** button is set to `new_file_cb( )` through the resource `XmNokCallback`. This is the function that is called when a new file is selected in the **Files** list, the **Ok** button is pressed, or new text is entered using the **Selection** Text widget. The file given is evaluated using `is_writable( )` and acted on accordingly: if it's a directory, that directory is scanned as if it were entered on the **Filter** Text widget. If the file can't be read, an error message is printed. Otherwise, it's a legitimate selection and, for demonstration purposes, it is printed to `stdout`.

A "real" application should do something different with the information in each case; errors should be reported using ErrorDialogs and legitimate values should be dealt with appropriately. An example of such a program is given in Chapter 15, *Text Widgets*, as *file_browser.c*. This program is an extension of Example 6-4 that takes a more realistic approach to how the application itself might work. Of course, the intent of that program is to show how Text widgets work, but its use of dialogs is consistent with the approach we are taking here.

6.5.4 Directory Searching

The FileSelectionBox also provides for a directory searching function analogous to the file-searching function described in the previous section. While file searching may be necessary for some applications as described in the previous section, it is less likely that a directory searching function will be as useful, since the default action taken by the toolkit should cover all common usages. However, it is impossible to second-guess the requirements of all applications, so Motif allows you to specify a directory searching function through the **XmNdir-SearchProc** resource.

The procedure is used to list directories rather than files. The method used by this procedure is virtually identical to the file-searching method except for the resources it sets. For example, **XmNdirListItems** and **XmNdirListItemCount** set the contents of the **Directory** List widget. The value for **XmNlistUpdated** must be set just as it is for the file selection routine, but **XmNdirectoryValid** must also be set to either **True** or **False**. If the directory cannot be read, then **XmNdirectoryValid** is set to **False** to prevent the **XmNfileSearchProc** from being called. As you can see, the file-searching procedure is protected from getting invalid directories through the directory searching procedure.

6.5.5 Miscellaneous Notes on Filesystem Searches

The material in this subsection is rather advanced and is mostly for use by those writing advanced file and/or directory searching routines. Presented here is an overview of the design for file and directory searching functions and how the functions we've described in the previous sections play a part in the grand scheme.

The following list describes the steps taken by the FileSelectionDialog when the user or the application invokes a directory search.

1. The List widgets are unmapped to give the user feedback that something is happening. This way, if a file and/or directory search takes a long time, the user will have a visual cue that the application isn't waiting for input. Of course, you always have the option of providing additional feedback, like changing the mouse image, etc.

2. All the items are deleted from the List widgets.

3. The widget's *qualify search* procedure is called to construct a proper pair of file selection box callback structures based on the value of the **Filter** Text widget. That is, the text in that widget is parsed for the *directory* and *pattern* portions and placed into their appropriate fields of the **XmFileSelectionBoxCallbackStruct**. These are used to pass to the directory and file-searching routines.

   You can write your own qualify search procedure and install it as the value for **Xm-NqualifySearchProc**. However, replacing the widget's own procedure will change the default behavior of the FileSelectionBox described by Motif.

4. The **XmNdirSearchProc** function is called with one of the callback structures constructed in the qualify search procedure. This function will check to be sure that the directory it was given can in fact be searched. If so, it fills the **Directory** List widget with a complete set of directories that reside within the given directory. If not, it sets **XmNdirectoryValid** to **False**.

5. Next, the **XmNfileSearchProc** is called if **XmNdirectoryValid** was set to **True** in the previous step (otherwise, the file list remains empty).

The **XmNfileTypeMask** resource indicates the types of files that a particular search routine should look for. It can be set to one of the following values:

```
XmFILE_REGULAR
XmFILE_DIRECTORY
XmFILE_ANY_TYPE    (XmFILE_REGULAR and XmFILE_DIRECTORY)
```

If you are using the same routine for both the **XmNdirSearchProc** and the **XmNfileSearchProc**, then this resource can be queried to determine which type of file you should be searching for.

6.6 Summary

The material in Chapter 5, *Introduction to Dialogs*, introduced the concept of dialogs and discussed the basic mechanisms that implement them. This chapter addressed how dialogs work in real applications by focusing on some of the more difficult problems facing engineers in the development process. While the material in this chapter specifically addressed Motif dialogs, much of it applies to all dialogs—even those you create yourself. Creating your own dialogs is discussed in Chapter 7, *Custom Dialogs*. Chapter 20, *Advanced Dialog Programming*, provides additional information regarding special case situations involved in using dialogs.

7

Custom Dialogs

This chapter describes how to create new dialog types, either by customizing Motif dialogs or by creating entirely new dialogs.

In This Chapter:

7

Custom Dialogs

In this chapter, we examine methods for creating your own dialogs. The need for such dialogs exists when those provided by Motif are too limited in functionality or are not specialized enough for your application. However, it's not always clear when this is the case. In some situations, you may find that Motif dialogs are just fine *if only they did this one little thing.* Fortunately, you may still be able to use predefined Motif dialogs with some small adjustments rather than building an entirely new dialog box from scratch.

There are some issues to consider before deciding on how you want to approach the problem. For example, do you want to do your own widget layout management or use a layout other than that of a defined Motif dialog? Do you have specialized user-interface appearance or functionality needs that go beyond what Motif describes? The answers to these questions may affect your application's design and how you should proceed. The discussion and examples provided in this chapter addresss both scenarios.

Before we get started, we should mention that creating your own dialogs makes heavy use of manager widgets such as Forms, BulletinBoards, RowColumns, and PanedWindows. While we use and describe manager widgets in context, you may want to consult Chapter 8, *Manager Widgets*, for specific details about those widgets.

7.1 Modifying Motif Dialogs

We begin by discussing the simpler case of modifying existing Motif dialogs. In Chapter 5, *Introduction to Dialogs*, we showed how dialogs can be modified somewhat by changing the default labels on buttons in the action area or by unmanaging or desensitizing certain elements. However, we have yet to suggest that you can add new items (widgets, gadgets) to dialog boxes, expanding on their functionality. All the predefined Motif dialog widgets can have more children added to them; these children are referred to as the dialogs' *work windows*. In this sense, you can virtually treat these dialogs as "manager" widgets in that you can create new widgets as children of the dialog widgets. You may have more or less success with various dialogs, depending on what you try to do, but the basic method for handling this problem is the same for all.

Let's start with an example where you'd like to add additional controls to a PromptDialog like the one used in the program *prompt_dlg.c* from Chapter 6, *Selection Dialogs*. In this program, the dialog prompts the user for a new label for the PushButton that activated the dialog. By adding another widget to the dialog, we can expand its functionality to prompt for either a label name or a button color. The user uses the same text area to input either value, but how the text is used is determined by the value of new ToggleButtons added to the PromptDialog. The new dialog is shown in Figure 7-1 and the program that produced the figure is shown in Example 7-1.

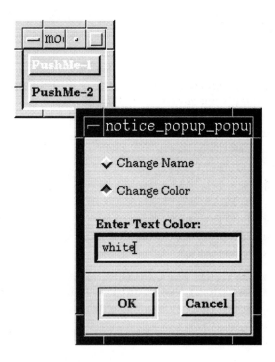

Figure 7-1. Output of modify_btn.c

Example 7-1. The modify_btn.c program

```
/* modify_bnt.c -- demonstrate how a default Motif dialog can be
 * modified to support additional items that extend the usability
 * of the dialog itself.  This is a modification of the prompt_dlg.c
 * program.
 */
#include <Xm/SelectioB.h>
#include <Xm/RowColumn.h>
#include <Xm/PushB.h>

main(argc, argv)
char *argv[ ];
{
    XtAppContext app;
    Widget toplevel, rc, button;
```

Example 7-1. The modify_btn.c program (continued)

```
    void pushed();

    /* Initialize toolkit and create toplevel shell */
    toplevel = XtVaAppInitialize(&app, "Demos", NULL, 0,
        &argc, argv, NULL, NULL);

    /* RowColumn managed both PushButtons */
    rc = XtVaCreateWidget("rowcol", xmRowColumnWidgetClass, toplevel,
        NULL);
    /* Create two pushbuttons -- both have the same callback */
    button = XtVaCreateManagedWidget("PushMe-1",
        xmPushButtonWidgetClass, rc, NULL);
    XtAddCallback(button, XmNactivateCallback, pushed, NULL);
    button = XtVaCreateManagedWidget("PushMe-2",
        xmPushButtonWidgetClass, rc, NULL);
    XtAddCallback(button, XmNactivateCallback, pushed, NULL);

    XtManageChild(rc);
    XtRealizeWidget(toplevel);
    XtAppMainLoop(app);
}

/* pushed() --the callback routine for the main app's pushbuttons.
 * Create a dialog that prompts for a new button name or color.
 * A RadioBox is attached to the dialog.  Which button is selected
 * in this box is held as an int (0 or 1) in the XmNuserData resource
 * of the dialog itself.  This value is changed when selecting either
 * of the buttons in the ToggleBox and is queried in the dialog's
 * XmNokCallback function.
 */
void
pushed(pb)
Widget pb;
{
    static Widget dialog;
    XmString t = XmStringCreateSimple("Enter New Button Name:");
    extern void read_name(), toggle_callback();
    Arg args[3];

    /* Create the dialog -- the PushButton acts as the DialogShell's
     * parent (not the parent of the PromptDialog).  The "userData"
     * is used to store the value
     */
    XtSetArg(args[0], XmNselectionLabelString, t);
    XtSetArg(args[1], XmNautoUnmanage, False);
    XtSetArg(args[2], XmNuserData, 0);
    dialog = XmCreatePromptDialog(pb, "notice_popup", args, 3);
    XmStringFree(t); /* always destroy compound strings when done */

    /* When the user types the name, call read_name() ... */
    XtAddCallback(dialog, XmNokCallback, read_name, pb);

    /* If the user selects cancel, just destroy the dialog */
    XtAddCallback(dialog, XmNcancelCallback, XtDestroyWidget, NULL);

    /* No help is available... */
    XtUnmanageChild(
        XmSelectionBoxGetChild(dialog, XmDIALOG_HELP_BUTTON));

    /* Create a toggle box -- callback routine is toggle_callback() */
```

Example 7-1. The modify_btn.c program (continued)

```
    {
        XmString btn1 = XmStringCreateSimple("Change Name");
        XmString btn2 = XmStringCreateSimple("Change Color");
        Widget toggle_box = XmVaCreateSimpleRadioBox(dialog,
            "radio_box", 0 /* inital value */, toggle_callback,
            XmVaRADIOBUTTON, btn1, 0, NULL, NULL,
            XmVaRADIOBUTTON, btn2, 0, NULL, NULL,
            NULL);
        XtManageChild(toggle_box);
    }
    XtManageChild(dialog);
    XtPopup(XtParent(dialog), XtGrabNone);
}

/* callback for the items in the toggle box -- the "client data" is
 * the item number selected.  Since the function gets called whenever
 * either of the buttons changes from true to false or back again,
 * it will always be called in pairs -- ignore the "False" settings.
 * When cbs->set is true, set the dialog's label string accordingly.
 */
void
toggle_callback(toggle_box, n, cbs)
Widget toggle_box;
int n;
XmToggleButtonCallbackStruct *cbs;
{
    Widget dialog = XtParent(XtParent(toggle_box));
    XmString str;

    if (cbs->set == False)
        return; /* wait for the one that toggles "on" */
    if (n == 0)
        str = XmStringCreateSimple("Enter New Button Name:");
    else
        str = XmStringCreateSimple("Enter Text Color:");
    XtVaSetValues(dialog,
        XmNselectionLabelString, str,
        XmNuserData, n, /* reset the user data to reflect new value */
        NULL);
    XmStringFree(str);
}

/* read_name() --the text field has been filled in.  Get the userData
 * from the dialog widget and set the PushButton's name or color.
 */
void
read_name(dialog, push_button, cbs)
Widget dialog;
Widget push_button;  /* the "client_data" from XtAddCallback */
XmSelectionBoxCallbackStruct *cbs;
{
    char *text;
    int n;

    /* userData: n == 0 -> Button Label, n == 1 -> Button Color */
    XtVaGetValues(dialog, XmNuserData, &n, NULL);

    if (n == 0)
```

Example 7-1. The modify_btn.c program (continued)

```
        XtVaSetValues(push_button, XmNlabelString, cbs->value, NULL);
    else {
        /* convert compound string into regular text string */
        XmStringGetLtoR(cbs->value, XmSTRING_DEFAULT_CHARSET, &text);
        XtVaSetValues(push_button,
            XtVaTypedArg, XmNforeground,
                XmRString, text, strlen(text) + 1,
            NULL);
        XtFree(text); /* must free text gotten from XmStringGetLtoR() */
    }
}
```

The task of adding a new widget to the PromptDialog is solved by simply calling **Xt-VaCreateSimpleRadioBox( )** with the parent of the RadioBox being the Prompt-Dialog widget. In other words, we are treating the PromptDialog just as if it were any manager widget.

The toggle items within the RadioBox indicate whether the input text is supposed to change the name of the PushButton's label, or its text color. To determine which of these attributes to change, we use the callback routine **toggle_callback( )**. Rather than storing the toggle value in a global variable, we store the value in the **XmNuserData** resource of the dialog widget. That way, we can retrieve it anytime we wish and maintain a minimum number of global variables in the program. The **XmNuserData** resource is available in all Motif widgets (except for shells) so it is a convenient storage area for arbitrary values. The type of value that **XmNuserData** takes is any type whose size is less than or equal to the size of a **XtPointer** (typically defined as a **char** pointer). That is, **int** works just fine; if you want to store data structures in this resource, you may only store a *pointer* to the structure. The size or type of the structure is irrelevant, since pointers are the same size.[1]

When the user enters new text and presses RETURN or activates the **Ok** button, **read_name( )** (the **XmNokCallback**) is called, which gets the **XmNuserData** from the dialog widget. If the value is **0**, the PushButton's label is reset using the **XmNlabel-String** resource. Since the callback routine provides the text typed in compound string format, it is already in the correct format for the PushButton's label.

If the **XmNuserData** is **1**, then the text describes a color name for the PushButton. Rather than converting the string into an actual color (which isn't particularly difficult, but we like to use as many shortcuts as possible), the **XtVaTypedArg** feature is used in **XtVaSet-Values( )** to do the conversion for us. This special resource converts any value to the format needed by the specified resource. Here, it's **XmNforeground**, which takes a variable of type **Pixel** as a value. This conversion will work provided there is an underlying conversion function to support it.[2] Motif does not supply a conversion function to change a compound string into a **Pixel** value, but there is one for converting C strings into **Pixels**. So,

---

[1] You might run into problems if your computer is an unusual architecture whose pointers of different types are not the same size (like DOS). For example, there is a remote possibility that you would have a problem if you attempted to store a pointer to a function, but even then the chances of error are remote.

[2] For more information on conversion functions, how to write them, or how to install your own, see Volume Four, *X Toolkit Intrinsics Programming Manual*.

we convert the compound string into a C string first using **XmStringGetLtoR( )** (see Chapter 19, *Compound Strings*) and set the foreground color using:

```
XtVaSetValues(push_button,
    XtVaTypedArg, XmNforeground,
        XmRString, text, strlen(text) + 1,
    NULL);
```

For more ways of converting strings into colors, see Chapter 11, *Labels and Buttons*.

Example 7-1 gives one example of how you can add new widgets to predefined Motif dialogs. However, in general, you will have different results depending on the dialog type you use, so experimentation is advised. However, there is nothing more to the process than what we've shown in this brief section. As noted before, dialog widgets are no different from other manager widgets except that you don't have certain constraint resources available to lay out the new children. Basically, they just fall where the dialog wants them. If your layout needs are more specific, and you can't allow the dialog to use its defaults, you should consider building your own dialogs from scratch.

7.2 Building New Dialogs

In this section, we introduce the methods for building dialogs entirely from scratch. To do this, you need to follow basically the same steps used by the Motif convenience routines as described in 5.5.1, *Introduction to Dialogs* . However, for our purposes here, we've modified the list due to the flexibility you have in controlling the kind of dialog you wish to make. Here are the steps you need to follow:

1. Choose a shell widget that most appropriately fits the needs of your dialog. You may continue to use a DialogShell if you like.

2. Choose an appropriate manager widget as the dialog's child. You do not have to use a BulletinBoard or Form widget if you don't want to, but again, this is your option. The manager widget you choose greatly affects how the dialog is laid out.[3]

3. Create the control area, which may include any of the primitive or Composite widgets. This is pretty much the same thing that Motif dialogs do, but you must create this area yourself.

4. Create an action area with PushButtons such as **Ok, Cancel, Help**, etc. Motif dialogs do this entire step automatically. Because you are creating the control area yourself, you cannot use **XmNokCallback** and other resources specific to the predefined Motif dialogs; you must use the callback resources appropriate for the widgets you use in the dialog.

5. Pop up the new shell.

---

[3] If you do want to use both a DialogShell and either a Form or BulletinBoard widget as the manager, you can use either of the Motif convenience routines **XmCreateBulletinBoardDialog( )** or **XmCreateFormDialog( )**. This will give you the starting point for a custom dialog. However, in this chapter, we create each of the widgets explicitly, so that you have a complete sense of what goes into the dialog.

7.2.1 Choosing and Creating a Shell

In step one, using TopLevelShells or even ApplicationShells as dialogs is very useful and common, but implies a different set of goals than what we have been discussing so far. In Chapter 4, *The Main Window*, we demonstrated the purpose of a main window in an application and the kinds of widgets you use in toplevel windows. Dialog boxes, as they were introduced in Chapter 5, *Introduction to Dialogs*, were thought of as transient windows that acted as satellites to toplevel shells. Transient dialogs should use DialogShell widgets. However, not all dialogs can be categorically placed in this role. Many dialogs, especially in larger applications, may act as secondary application windows that remain on display for an extended period. Even the MainWindow widget can be used in many dialog boxes. Thus, we relax the limitation that DialogShells must be used in step one.

However, choosing the shell widget now becomes an interesting problem, since it depends so much on the activities carried out in the dialog. This is a judgment call that's entirely up to you; it's difficult, if not impossible, to provide rules or even heuristics in choosing the type of shell to use.

There are three points about DialogShells discussed in Chapter 5, *Introduction to Dialogs*, that will probably have the greatest influence on whether you decide to choose this particular widget class. That is, DialogShells cannot be iconified, they are *always* placed on top of the shell widget that owns the parent of your new dialog, and they are always destroyed or withdrawn from the screen if their parents are destroyed or withdrawn.

ApplicationShells and TopLevelShells, on the other hand, are always "independent" of other windows, so you can change their stacking order (raise one over the top of another), iconify them separately, or withdraw them completely without affecting other TopLevel shells. (The exception, of course, is that if a TopLevel shell has any transient dialogs as its children, then they will be similarly treated.)

The difference between an ApplicationShell and a TopLevelShell is that an ApplicationShell is designed to start a completely new widget tree, as if it were a completely separate application. (Among other things, this means that resource specifications can no longer be applied to the entire application.) It is recommended that most applications have only one ApplicationShell.[4]

Once you have chosen which shell widget you want to use, you need to determine how you want it created. While DialogShells can only be created using `XtCreatePopupShell( )` or `XtVaCreatePopupShell( )`,[5] ApplicationShells and TopLevelShells can be created using either of those functions or using `XtAppCreateShell( )` or `XtVaAppCreateShell( )`. The difference is whether the newly-created shell is treated like

---

[4] For some applications, you'd really like a shell with characteristics of several of the available shell classes. Unfortunately, you can't intermix the capabilities of DialogShells with those of the ApplicationShells and TopLevelShells without doing quite a bit of intricate window manager interaction. Having ultimate control over the activities of a shell widget requires setting up a number of event handlers on the shells themselves, and monitoring certain window property event state changes. Aside from being very complicated, you run the risk of breaking Motif compliance. See Chapter 17, *Interacting with the Window Manager*, for details on how this might be done.

[5] DialogShells may also be created using the Motif convenience routine `XmCreateDialogShell( )`.

a popup shell or as a less transient window on the desktop. The choice of which function you use is just as complex as choosing the type of shell widget class to use.

Using the popup shell method requires that you select an adequate parent, which may affect your decision. The parent for DialogShells, as discussed in Chapter 5, *Introduction to Dialogs*, must be an initialized and realized widget. It can be any kind of widget, but it may *not* be a gadget because the parent must contain a *Window*. (Gadgets have no windows associated with them.) This is true for all widgets that are created using `XtCreatePopupShell( )` or `XtVaCreatePopupShell( )`, even if they aren't DialogShells.

In addition, certain attributes about the dialog are inherited from the parent. For example, if the parent is insensitive (`XmNsensitive` is set to `False`), the entire dialog will be insensitive as well. Other resources, such as the position of the dialog, are determined from the parent. This is discussed in .

7.2.2 The Dialog's Manager Child

In step two, you must choose a manager widget as the solely managed child of the shell widget. This widget must contain (manage) both the control and action areas of the dialog. (That is, the action area should be below the control area.) The predefined Motif dialog widgets handle this positioning automatically, but your own dialogs are responsible for managing this aspect of the window. Since this is entirely a manager widget issue, you should consult Chapter 8, *Manager Widgets*, for details.

In step two, you must choose a manager widget as the solely managed child of the shell widget. Therefore, this widget must contain both the control area and the action area of the dialog and manage the relationship between them. (That is, the action area should be below the control area.) Motif dialog widgets handle this positioning automatically, but your own dialogs are responsible for managing this aspect of the window. Since this is entirely a manager widget issue, you should consult Chapter 8, *Manager Widgets*, for details.

For general dialog layout design, we recommend using PanedWindow widgets for the reasons described here and illustrated in Figure 7-2.

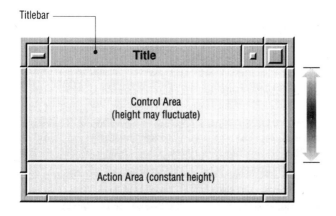

Figure 7-2. General layout of dialogs

Recall that the *Motif Style Guide* suggests that dialogs be composed of two main areas: the control area and the action area. Both of these areas extend to the left and right sides of the dialog, and are vertically stacked. (The control area is always on top.) Furthermore, the action area usually does not fluctuate in size as the shell is resized, while the control area may be resized in any way. PanedWindows allow you to emulate this behavior. This widget class supports vertically stacked windows (or *panes*) each of which may or may not be resizable, depending on the constraint resources of each pane. Thus, you could have a PanedWindow as the main manager widget of a dialog, which manages in turn two other managers acting as the control and action areas. The control area may be resizable, while the action area is not. As an added bonus, PanedWindows also provide separators between each pane, fulfilling the style guide's recommendation that a Separator widget lie between the control and action areas.

Generally speaking, of course, you can use whatever manager widget you like. If you use BulletinBoard or Form widgets, then you may be able to take advantage of the special interaction these widgets have with DialogShells, if you find those particular features advantageous. RowColumn widgets can also lay out their children vertically; you could use one to manage the control and action areas of the dialog, but then there is a problem with resizing the dialog. There is no way to tell the RowColumn widget to keep the bottom partition a constant height while allowing the top to fluctuate as necessary. The same is true for other manager widgets as well, unless you introduce external code to influence this behavior.

7.2.3 Control Area

Step three involves creating the control area and its underlying widgets. This is entirely application-defined. You may choose virtually any Motif widget, including other managers, to fill the control area of the dialog. Obviously, you will want to include only those controls that are pertinent to the functionality of the dialog.

7.2.4 Action Area

The last major step in constructing a dialog is actually producing an action area for the dialog. This includes choosing the button labels and callback routines, and determining the best way to get the information from the control area of the dialog.

According to the *Motif Style Guide*, the action area should consist entirely of PushButtons laid out horizontally. Button labels, and the actions they take, should be taken from the following list. (This list is provided only as a recommendation; you are not required to use these particular labels, but you should consider them first, rather than arbitrary alternatives.)

Yes   Indicates a positive response and implies that the dialog should be subsequently dismissed ("popped down," or removed from the screen).

No   Indicates a negative response and that the dialog should be dismissed.

Apply   Applies any changes reflected in the control area but leaves the dialog open for further interaction.

Ok	Same as Apply, but the dialog box is dismissed.
Retry	This label is commonly found in dialog boxes that report errors. If an error is reported as a result of some kind of interaction with the user, activating this button would cause the action to be retried.
Stop	If the user initiates a time-consuming process, you could display a dialog box that tells the user that the application is "busy." This dialog box might contain a **Stop** button that terminates the ongoing process. The dialog is removed either when the user selects this button or when the process is complete.
Reset	Resets the controls in the work area to the values they had at the time the dialog was originally opened.
Cancel	Resets the controls in the work area and dismisses the dialog from the screen.
Help ...	Pops up a new dialog displaying help corresponding to the task being performed by the host dialog. The ellipsis (...) should not be used if help is given without popping up a new dialog. To be completely thorough, and to provide even more context-sensitive help, you may also choose to install `XmNhelpCallback` routines in case the user presses the $\boxed{\text{HELP}}$ key on any of the items in the dialog box. Information on installing help callbacks is discussed in Chapter 20, *Advanced Dialog Programming*.

The following heuristics can help in designing action areas for general or customized dialog boxes:

- Lay out the action area as a single horizontal row at the bottom of the dialog. The action area should also be set apart from the rest of the dialog using a separator.

- Use single-word labels.

- Choose command-style verbs over nouns when possible. Some words can be interpreted in more than one way, so be careful to avoid ambiguity.

- Positive actions should be placed farthest to the left (or to the right for right-to-left languages), followed by negative actions, followed by cancel actions (open to interpretation). For example, **Yes** should be to the left of **No**.

- **Help,** if available, should always be placed farthest to the right (or left, if the language is read from right-to-left).

Depending on your application, you may be forced to overlook some of these guidelines. Even the recommended defaults listed here could be very confusing if used inappropriately. Figure 7-3 shows a complex dialog that illustrates how alternate labels may be more effective.

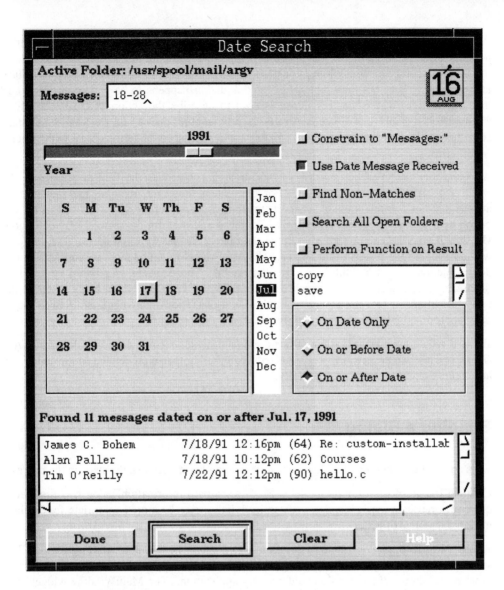

Figure 7-3. A complex dialog

This custom dialog from an e-mail application demonstrates some considerations involved in designing effective dialogs.

Here, the **Help** button is the only one with a label recommended by Motif. The other recommended labels did not effectively represent the actions taken by activating the buttons. We did not choose to use the **Cancel** label, for example, because we don't want to combine the actions of **Reset** and **Close** in one single button. Instead, we separate the functionality into two separate actions: the **Done** button closes the window and the **Clear** button resets the controls.

A button labeled **Done** suggests that the dialog will be dismissed. **Cancel,** the recommended Motif label, implies that the action specified by the dialog should not be taken. Here, selecting **Done** does not cancel anything, it just dismisses the dialog. You might suggest that **Close** is more appropriate, but the problem is that this dialog happens to be part of an electronic mail application, where the term *close* is used to describe the action of closing a folder. Therefore, it is likely that **Close** is already used by another dialog and we wish to maintain consistency. It is important to avoid mixing application-specific terminology with general Motif terms.

Also consider the **Ok** label and the specification that it applies the control settings in the work area and dismisses the dialog. For our dialog, however, imagine the sequence of actions that the user might take: he selects the date to search for messages and selects the **Ok** button as if to say, "I've set my controls. Go ahead and perform the search." By definition, **Ok** should take the action and bring down the dialog. If that were to happen here, the user would never see the results of the search. The **Apply** label might be more appropriate for our desired action. So, why didn't we use that label? The decision was based on creative license; that is, it seemed that **Search** was more descriptive of the action being taken by the user's selection. It was the author's intuition (and discretion) that suggested **Search** was a more appropriate label to use than **Apply**.

While it would have been feasible to use the default labels recommended by the *Motif Style Guide*, because we are creating a customized dialog rather than a predefined Motif dialog, we have more flexibility available for clarity.

7.3 Building a Dialog

Let's now put together a real dialog from scratch and identify each of the steps in the process.

Consider the problem of providing help. Motif's standard InformationDialog is entirely adequate for brief help messages, but a customized dialog may be more appropriate for displaying large amounts of text.

As shown in Example 7-2, the best solution is to display the text in a scrolling region. The structure of this example is fairly straightforward. A main application window is used as a generic backdrop—the example could use any application. The MainWindow widget contains a MenuBar that has two common elements: a **File** and a **Help** menu. The latter contains several items that, when selected, pop up their own dialog window displaying the associated help text. While the default text is not very lengthy, the dialog is capable of handling arbitrarily large amounts of data. The text we provide happens to be predefined in the program, but you may choose to incorporate information from anywhere else (e.g., a database or an external file). The output of the program is shown in Figure 7-4.

Example 7-2. The help_text.c program

```
/* help_text.c:
 * Create a simple main window that contains a sample (dummy) work
 * area and a menubar.  The menubar contains two items: File and Help.
 * The items in the Help pulldown call help_cb(), which pops up a
 * home-made dialog that displays predefined help texts.  The purpose
```

Example 7-2. The help_text.c program (continued)

```
 * of this program is to demonstrate how one might approach the
 * problem displaying a large amount of text in a dialog box.
 */
#include <stdio.h>
#include <ctype.h>
#include <Xm/DialogS.h>
#include <Xm/MainW.h>
#include <Xm/RowColumn.h>
#include <Xm/Form.h>
#include <Xm/Text.h>
#include <Xm/PushBG.h>
#include <Xm/LabelG.h>
#include <Xm/PanedW.h>

/* The following help text information is a continuous stream of characters
 * that will all be placed in a single ScrolledText object.  If a specific
 * newline is desired, you must do that yourself.  See "index_help" below.
 */
String context_help[ ] = {
    "This is context-sensitive help.  Well, not really, but such",
    "help text could easily be generated by a real help system.",
    "All you really need to do is obtain information from the user",
    "about the widget from which he needs help, or perhaps prompt",
    "for other application-specific contexts.",
    NULL
};

String window_help[ ] = {
    "Each of the windows in your application should have an",
    "XmNhelpCallback associated with it so you can monitor when",
    "the user presses the Help key over any particular widget.",
    "This is another way to provide context-sensitive help.",
    "The MenuBar should always have a Help entry at the far right",
    "that provides help for most aspects of the program, including",
    "the user interface.  By providing different levels of help",
    "indexing, you can provide multiple stages of help, making the",
    "entire help system easier to use.",
    NULL
};

String index_help[ ] = {
    "This is a small demonstration program, so there is very little",
    "material to provide an index.  However, an index should contain",
    "a summary of the type of help available.  For example, we have:\n",
    "    Help On Context\n",
    "    Help On Windows\n",
    "    This Index\n",
    "\n",
    "Higher-end applications might also provide a tutorial.",
    NULL
};

String *help_texts[ ] = {
    context_help,
    window_help,
    index_help
};
```

Example 7-2. The help_text.c program (continued)

```
main(argc, argv)
int argc;
char *argv[ ];
{
    XtAppContext app;
    Widget toplevel, rc, main_w, menubar, w;
    extern void help_cb(), file_cb();
    XmString str1, str2, str3;

    toplevel = XtVaAppInitialize(&app, "Demos", NULL, 0,
        &argc, argv, NULL, NULL);

    /* the main window contains the work area and the menubar */
    main_w = XtVaCreateWidget("main_w",
        xmMainWindowWidgetClass, toplevel, NULL);

    /* Create a simple MenuBar that contains two cascade buttons */
    str1 = XmStringCreateSimple("File");
    str2 = XmStringCreateSimple("Help");
    menubar = XmVaCreateSimpleMenuBar(main_w, "main_w",
        XmVaCASCADEBUTTON, str1, 'F',
        XmVaCASCADEBUTTON, str2, 'H',
        NULL);
    XmStringFree(str1);
    XmStringFree(str2);

    /* create the "File" pulldown menu -- callback is file_cb() */
    str1 = XmStringCreateSimple("New");
    str2 = XmStringCreateSimple("Open");
    str3 = XmStringCreateSimple("Quit");
    XmVaCreateSimplePulldownMenu(menubar, "file_menu", 0, file_cb,
        XmVaPUSHBUTTON, str1, 'N', NULL, NULL,
        XmVaPUSHBUTTON, str2, 'O', NULL, NULL,
        XmVaSEPARATOR,
        XmVaPUSHBUTTON, str3, 'Q', NULL, NULL,
        NULL);
    XmStringFree(str1);
    XmStringFree(str2);
    XmStringFree(str3);

    /* create the "Help" menu -- callback is help_cb() */
    str1 = XmStringCreateSimple("On Context");
    str2 = XmStringCreateSimple("On Window");
    str3 = XmStringCreateSimple("Index");
    w = XmVaCreateSimplePulldownMenu(menubar, "help_menu", 1, help_cb,
        XmVaPUSHBUTTON, str1, 'C', NULL, NULL,
        XmVaPUSHBUTTON, str2, 'W', NULL, NULL,
        XmVaPUSHBUTTON, str3, 'I', NULL, NULL,
        NULL);
    XmStringFree(str1);
    XmStringFree(str2);
    XmStringFree(str3);

    {
        /* Identify the Help Menu for the MenuBar */
        Widget *cascade_btns;
        int num_btns;
        XtVaGetValues(menubar,
```

Example 7-2. The help_text.c program (continued)

```
                XmNchildren,          &cascade_btns,
                XmNnumChildren,       &num_btns,
                NULL);
            XtVaSetValues(menubar,
                XmNmenuHelpWidget, cascade_btns[num_btns-1],
                NULL);
        }
        XtManageChild(menubar);

        /* the work area for the main window -- just create dummy stuff */
        rc = XtVaCreateWidget("rc", xmRowColumnWidgetClass, main_w, NULL);
        str1 = XmStringCreateLtoR("\n  This is an Empty\nSample Control Area\n ",
            XmSTRING_DEFAULT_CHARSET);
        XtVaCreateManagedWidget("label", xmLabelGadgetClass, rc,
            XmNlabelString,  str1,
            NULL);
        XmStringFree(str1);
        XtManageChild(rc);
        XtManageChild(main_w);

        XtRealizeWidget(toplevel);
        XtAppMainLoop(app);
}

/* callback for all the entries in the File pulldown menu. */
void
file_cb(w, item_no)
Widget w;
int item_no;  /* pulldown menu item number offset from 0 */
{
    if (item_no == 2) /* the Quit menu button */
        exit(0);
    printf("Item %d (%s) selected\n", item_no + 1, XtName(w));
}

/* climb widget tree until we get to the top.  Return the Shell */
Widget
GetTopShell(w)
Widget w;
{
    while (w && !XtIsWMShell(w))
        w = XtParent(w);
    return w;
}

#include "info.xbm"  /* bitmap data used by our dialog */

/* callback for all the entries in the Help pulldown menu.
 * Create a dialog box that contains control and action areas.
 */
void
help_cb(w, item_no)
Widget w;
int item_no;  /* pulldown menu item number offset from 0 */
{
    Widget help_dialog, pane, text_w, form, sep, widget, label;
    extern void DestroyShell();
    Pixmap pixmap;
```

Example 7-2. The help_text.c program (continued)

```
    Pixel fg, bg;
    Arg args[9];
    int i;
    char *p, buf[BUFSIZ];

    /* Set up a DialogShell as a popup window.  Set the delete
     * window protocol response to XmDESTROY to make sure that
     * the window goes away appropriately.  Otherwise, it's XmUNMAP
     * which means it'd be lost forever, since we're not storing
     * the widget globally or statically to this function.
     */
    help_dialog = XtVaCreatePopupShell("Help",
        xmDialogShellWidgetClass, GetTopShell(w),
        XmNdeleteResponse, XmDESTROY,
        NULL);

    /* Create a PanedWindow to manage the stuff in this dialog. */
    pane = XtVaCreateWidget("pane", xmPanedWindowWidgetClass, help_dialog,
        /* XmNsashWidth,  1, /* PanedWindow won't let us set these to 0! */
        /* XmNsashHeight, 1, /* Make small so user doesn't try to resize */
        NULL);

    /* Create a RowColumn in the form for Label and Text widgets.
     * This is the control area.
     */
    form = XtVaCreateWidget("form1", xmFormWidgetClass, pane, NULL);
    XtVaGetValues(form,  /* once created, we can get its colors */
        XmNforeground, &fg,
        XmNbackground, &bg,
        NULL);

    /* create the pixmap of the appropriate depth using the colors
     * that will be used by the parent (form).
     */
    pixmap = XCreatePixmapFromBitmapData(XtDisplay(form),
        RootWindowOfScreen(XtScreen(form)),
        info_bits, info_width, info_height,
        fg, bg, DefaultDepthOfScreen(XtScreen(form)));

    /* Create a label gadget using this pixmap */
    label = XtVaCreateManagedWidget("label", xmLabelGadgetClass, form,
        XmNlabelType,          XmPIXMAP,
        XmNlabelPixmap,        pixmap,
        XmNleftAttachment,     XmATTACH_FORM,
        XmNtopAttachment,      XmATTACH_FORM,
        XmNbottomAttachment,   XmATTACH_FORM,
        NULL);

    /* prepare the text for display in the ScrolledText object
     * we are about to create.
     */
    for (p = buf, i = 0; help_texts[item_no][i]; i++) {
        p += strlen(strcpy(p, help_texts[item_no][i]));
        if (!isspace(p[-1])) /* spaces tabs and newlines are spaces.. */
            *p++ = ' '; /* lines are concatenated together, insert a space */
    }
    *--p = 0; /* get rid of trailing space... */

    XtSetArg(args[0], XmNscrollVertical,          True);
```

Example 7-2. The help_text.c program (continued)

```
    XtSetArg(args[1], XmNscrollHorizontal,        False);
    XtSetArg(args[2], XmNeditMode,                XmMULTI_LINE_EDIT);
    XtSetArg(args[3], XmNeditable,                False);
    XtSetArg(args[4], XmNcursorPositionVisible,   False);
    XtSetArg(args[5], XmNwordWrap,                True);
    XtSetArg(args[6], XmNvalue,                   buf);
    XtSetArg(args[7], XmNrows,                    5);
    text_w = XmCreateScrolledText(form, "help_text", args, 8);
    /* Attachment values must be set on the Text widget's PARENT,
     * the ScrolledWindow. This is the object that is positioned.
     */
    XtVaSetValues(XtParent(text_w),
        XmNleftAttachment,      XmATTACH_WIDGET,
        XmNleftWidget,          label,
        XmNtopAttachment,       XmATTACH_FORM,
        XmNrightAttachment,     XmATTACH_FORM,
        XmNbottomAttachment,    XmATTACH_FORM,
        NULL);
    XtManageChild(text_w);
    XtManageChild(form);

    /* Create another form to act as the action area for the dialog */
    form = XtVaCreateWidget("form2", xmFormWidgetClass, pane,
        XmNfractionBase,    5,
        NULL);

    /* The Ok button is under the pane's separator and is
     * attached to the left edge of the form.  It spreads from
     * position 0 to 1 along the bottom (the form is split into
     * 5 separate grids ala XmNfractionBase upon creation).
     */
    widget = XtVaCreateManagedWidget("Ok",
        xmPushButtonGadgetClass, form,
        XmNtopAttachment,       XmATTACH_FORM,
        XmNbottomAttachment,    XmATTACH_FORM,
        XmNleftAttachment,      XmATTACH_POSITION,
        XmNleftPosition,        1,
        XmNrightAttachment,     XmATTACH_POSITION,
        XmNrightPosition,       2,
        XmNshowAsDefault,       True,
        XmNdefaultButtonShadowThickness, 1,
        NULL);
    XtAddCallback(widget, XmNactivateCallback, DestroyShell, help_dialog);

    /* This is created with its XmNsensitive resource set to False
     * because we don't support "more" help.  However, this is the
     * place to attach it to if there were any more.
     */
    widget = XtVaCreateManagedWidget("More",
        xmPushButtonGadgetClass, form,
        XmNsensitive,           False,
        XmNtopAttachment,       XmATTACH_FORM,
        XmNbottomAttachment,    XmATTACH_FORM,
        XmNleftAttachment,      XmATTACH_POSITION,
        XmNleftPosition,        3,
        XmNrightAttachment,     XmATTACH_POSITION,
        XmNrightPosition,       4,
```

Example 7-2. The help_text.c program (continued)

```
            XmNshowAsDefault,              False,
            XmNdefaultButtonShadowThickness, 1,
            NULL);

    /* Fix the action area pane to its current height -- never let it resize */
    XtManageChild(form);
    {
        Dimension h;
        XtVaGetValues(widget, XmNheight, &h, NULL);
        XtVaSetValues(form, XmNpaneMaximum, h, XmNpaneMinimum, h, NULL);
    }
    XtManageChild(pane);

    XtPopup(help_dialog, XtGrabNone);
}

/* The callback function for the "Ok" button.  Since this is not a
 * predefined Motif dialog, the "widget" parameter is not the dialog
 * itself.  That is only done by Motif dialog callbacks.  Here in the
 * real world, the callback routine is called directly by the widget
 * that was invoked.  Thus, we must pass the dialog as the client
 * data to get its handle.  (We could get it using GetTopShell(),
 * but this way is quicker, since it's immediately available.)
 */
void
DestroyShell(widget, shell)
Widget widget, shell;
{
    XtDestroyWidget(shell);
}
```

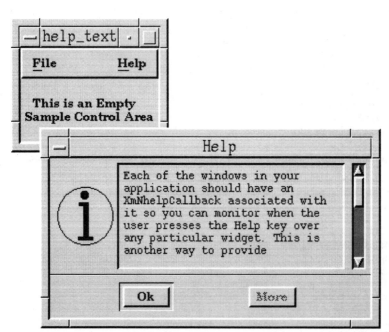

Figure 7-4. Output of help_text.c

The function **help_cb( )** is the callback routine that is invoked from any of the **Help** menu items. Here, we follow the steps listed earlier to create the dialog box. In this case, it's a standard DialogShell:

```
help_dialog = XtVaCreatePopupShell("Help",
    xmDialogShellWidgetClass, parent,
    XmNdeleteResponse, XmDESTROY,
    NULL);
```

Instead of using **XtVaCreatePopupShell( )**, we could have used a convenience routine and achieved the same result:

```
XtSetArg(args[0], XmNdeleteResponse, XmDESTROY);
help_dialog = XmCreateDialogShell(parent, "title", args, 1);
```

Either method returns the same kind of DialogShell. The **XmNdeleteResponse** resource is set to **XmDESTROY** because we want the **Close** item from the window menu in the window manager's titlebar for the shell to destroy the shell and its children. The default value for this resource is **XmUNMAP**; had we wanted to reuse the same dialog upon each invocation, we would have used **XmUNMAP** and retained a handle to the dialog widget.

7.3.1 Dialog Titles

The dialog's *name* is **Help**, since that is the first parameter to the call to **XtVaCreate-PopupShell( )** (or, the second parameter to **XmCreateDialogShell( )**). Resource specifications in the resource database that pertain to this dialog should therefore use **Help** as the widget name:

```
*Help*foreground: green
```

The string displayed in the titlebar of a dialog defaults to the name of the widget itself. So, even though the name of the dialog is set to **Help**, this is a soft-coded value as far as the dialog's *title* is concerned; it may still be changed by the user or the application defaults file. For example:

```
*Help.title: Help Dialog
```

We could alternatively set the **XmNtitle** resource to the same or another C string.[6] In this case, we would have to provide it as a parameter to the calling function:

```
help_dialog = XtVaCreatePopupShell("Help",
    xmDialogShellWidgetClass, parent,
    XmNtitle,    "title",
    NULL);
```

When the title is hard-coded like this, resource specifications made by the user or the application defaults files are ignored.

---

[6] **XmNtitle** is defined identically to **XtNtitle**, which is a Toolkit Intrinsics (Xt) resource, not a Motif resource. Thus, the value is not given as a compound string.

7.3.2 DialogShell Children

The next task is to create a manager widget that acts as the sole child of the DialogShell (remember, shell widgets may only have one managed child). We should point out up front that this section deals heavily with manager widget issues, which may prompt you to look ahead to Chapter 8, *Manager Widgets*, if you have problems keeping up. However, the main point of this section is simply to provide enough context for you to understand Example 7-2.

For the main child of the DialogShell, we are using a PanedWindow widget, as per our earlier recommendations. It is created as follows:

```
pane = XtVaCreateWidget("pane", xmPanedWindowWidgetClass, help_dialog,
    XmNsashWidth,  1,
    XmNsashHeight, 1,
    NULL);
```

The PanedWindow manages two Form widget children, one each for the control area and the action area. These are also called the PanedWindow's *panes*. Normally, in a PanedWindow, the user can resize one or the other of the panes by clicking-and-dragging the control sashes. However, we don't want that to happen because in a dialog, the action area isn't supposed to grow or shrink in size.

There are really two issues involved here: the user might try to resize the panes individually, or he might resize the entire dialog, causing the PanedWindow itself to resize them.

You can prevent the PanedWindow from resizing (or adjusting) the action area when it is itself resized by setting the pane's `XmNskipAdjust` resource to `True`. However, this will still allow the user to resize the individual panes. To prevent the user from resizing a pane, you must disable its control sashes.

The best way to prevent both undesirable resize possibilities is to set the action area pane's maximum and minimum allowed heights to the same value. When you do this, the Paned-Window is supposed to disable the sashes for that particular pane. However, this rarely works due to a bug in the PanedWindow widget class. To compensate, we can try to make the sashes invisible. Unfortunately, the PanedWindow won't let you set a sash's size to `0`, so we set the values for `XmNsashWidth` and `XmNsashHeight` to `1`, so they won't be readily visible.[7]

The PanedWindow is created *unmanaged* using `XtVaCreateWidget()`. As pointed out in Chapter 8, *Manager Widgets*, manager widgets should not be "managed" until all their children have been created and managed first. This is so that the children's desired sizes and positions can be specified before the manager widget tries to renegotiate (or mandate) other sizes or positions.

---

[7] The only other problem that might come up is that keyboard traversal will still allow the user to reach the sash widgets; you may wish to remove them from the traversal list by setting their `XmNtraversalOn` resources to `False`. This specific case is described in Chapter 8, *Manager Widgets*.

Since the action area goes below the ScrolledText, we create the Text widget first, followed by the action area (so it can be placed under it). The next thing to do is create the control area so we can place the Text widget in it:

```
form = XtVaCreateWidget("form1", xmFormWidgetClass, pane, NULL);
```

The Form widget is going to be the control area, so it is created as a child of the Paned-Window. As far as the pane is concerned, the Form widget is a single child whose width will be stretched to the left and right edges of the shell. Within the Form, we add two widgets: a Label widget that contains the pixmap (as shown in Figure 7-4), and the ScrolledText. In order to create the Label, we must first create the pixmap it is going to use, which cannot be done until we know what the foreground and background colors are going to be. Our approach works for either monochrome or color screens:

```
XtVaGetValues(rowcol,
    XmNforeground, &fg,
    XmNbackground, &bg,
    NULL);
pixmap = XCreatePixmapFromBitmapData(XtDisplay(form),
    RootWindowOfScreen(XtScreen(form)),
    bitmap_bits, bitmap_width, bitmap_height,
    fg, bg, DefaultDepthOfScreen(XtScreen(parent)));
label = XtVaCreateManagedWidget("label", xmLabelGadgetClass, form,
    XmNlabelType,        XmPIXMAP,
    XmNlabelPixmap,      pixmap,
    XmNleftAttachment,   XmATTACH_FORM,
    XmNtopAttachment,    XmATTACH_FORM,
    XmNbottomAttachment, XmATTACH_FORM,
    NULL);
```

The foreground and background colors may be gotten from the root window, since it is guaranteed to be a valid window and contain a valid colormap. We use these values as the foreground and background for the pixmap we create in the call to **XCreatePixmap-FromBitmapData( )**. The bitmap's bits, width, and height are predefined in the X bitmap file included earlier in the program (*info.xbm*). The Label is created based on this pixmap by setting the resources **XmNlabelType** and **XmNlabelPixmap** (see Chapter 11, *Labels and Buttons*, for details on these resources).

While we could have used **XmGetPixmap( )**, the function is more complicated because it does not provide an easy method for loading pixmaps directly from bitmap data as we have done here. To use **XmGetPixmap( )** effectively, we would have to have relied on the file that contains the bitmap data to exist at runtime or we'd have to load the bitmap data directly into a static **XImage** type. All things considered, this is more complicated than the method we used previously. (See Chapter 11, *Labels and Buttons*, for details of **XmGet-Pixmap( )**.)

NOTE

Just as a note for those developing larger-scale applications: distributing software with bitmaps stored in separate files that are loaded at runtime is an administrative nightmare for anyone who has to install and maintain your program at any given site. You are also burdened with the responsibility to test and recover adequately from errors (e.g., the file(s) do not exist), and to provide a backup image in such cases.

The *attachment* resources are all specific to the Form widget, and describe how a Form should lay out its children. In this case, the Label's top, bottom, and left sides are all attached to the edge of the Form. Similar attachments are made on the ScrolledText object, as we'll soon see. Note that these special resources that enable the widget's parent to position it are completely ignored by the widget itself. See Chapter 8, *Manager Widgets*, for a complete description of how constraint resources are handled by widgets.

Next, a ScrollText object is created to display the help text. The number of rows and columns is arbitrarily set, but could otherwise be set in the application defaults file or fallback resources:

```
XtSetArg(args[0], XmNscrollVertical,        True);
XtSetArg(args[1], XmNscrollHorizontal,      False);
XtSetArg(args[2], XmNeditMode,              XmMULTI_LINE_EDIT);
XtSetArg(args[3], XmNeditable,              False);
XtSetArg(args[4], XmNcursorPositionVisible, False);
XtSetArg(args[5], XmNwordWrap,              True);
XtSetArg(args[6], XmNvalue,                 buf);
XtSetArg(args[7], XmNrows,                  5);
text_w = XmCreateScrolledText(form, "help_text", args, 8);
/* Attachment values must be set on the Text widget's PARENT,
 * the ScrolledWindow. This is the object that is positioned.
 */
XtVaSetValues(XtParent(text_w),
    XmNleftAttachment,   XmATTACH_WIDGET,
    XmNleftWidget,       label,
    XmNtopAttachment,    XmATTACH_FORM,
    XmNrightAttachment,  XmATTACH_FORM,
    XmNbottomAttachment, XmATTACH_FORM,
    NULL);
```

For `XmCreateScrolledText( )`, we must use the old-style `XtSetArg( )` method of setting the arguments that are passed to the function. This routine actually creates multiple widgets that appear to be a single interface object. In this case, a ScrolledWindow and a Text widget are created simultaneously, and the toolkit returns a handle to the Text widget. However, it is the ScrolledWindow widget, not the Text widget, that is a child of the Paned-Window. Therefore, the constraint (or attachment) resources must be set on the Scrolled-Window, not the Text widget.

This is a small point of programming style: we could have passed these resource-value pairs in the **args** list, but then the resources would have been set on both the ScrolledWindow and the Text widget. Since the attachment constraints would be ignored by the Text widget, there would be no real harm in setting them on both widgets. However, it is really better form to set the resources directly on the ScrolledWindow. Details on Text widgets and ScrolledText objects can be found in Chapter 15, *Text Widgets*. Chapter 9, *ScrolledWindows and Scrollbars*, discusses the ScrolledWindow object and its resources.

The text for the widget is set using the **XmNvalue** resource. The value for this resource is the appropriate help text taken from the **help_texts** array declared at the beginning of the program. The Text and Label widgets are the only two items in the Form widget, so once its children are created and managed, the Form can then be managed using **XtManage-Child( )**.

7.3.3 The Action Area

At this point, the control area of the dialog has been created. Now, it is time to create the action area. In our example, the action area is pretty simple; the only action needed is to close the dialog. This is performed by the **Ok** button. For completeness, we have also chosen to make a **More** button in order to support additional or extended help. However, it is left insensitive because we don't provide any such help or text (although you can extend this example by providing it). By having the **More** widget grayed out, you are telling the user that had more help been available, it would be accessible through this button. In this specific instance, there does not happen to be anything more.

Action areas do not have to be contained in separate widgets, although it is much easier to do so in this particular example. We also continue to do so in other examples. Here, we use a Form widget in order to position the items evenly across all instances spanning the width of the dialog. The **XmNfractionBase** resource of the Form widget is set to five, breaking it down into five separate, equally divided units, as shown in Figure 7-5.

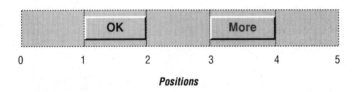

Figure 7-5. The XmNfractionBase resource segments the Form

Position zero is the left edge of the form and position five is the right edge of the form. (Five was chosen because it gave us the best aesthetic layout, but this value may vary.) The region is divided up equally, so you can think of the sections as percentages of the total width (or height, if appropriate) of the Form. By choosing this method for layout, we are not concerned with the width of the form or of the DialogShell itself, since we know that the placement of the buttons will always be proportional.

```
widget = XtVaCreateManagedWidget("Ok",
    xmPushButtonGadgetClass,  form,
    XmNtopAttachment,         XmATTACH_FORM,
    XmNbottomAttachment,      XmATTACH_FORM,
    XmNleftAttachment,        XmATTACH_POSITION,
    XmNrightPosition,         1,
    XmNrightAttachment,       XmATTACH_POSITION,
    XmNrightPosition,         2,
    XmNshowAsDefault,         True,
    XmNdefaultButtonShadowThickness, 1,
    NULL);
```

The **Ok** button's left and right sides are placed at positions one and two, respectively. Because this is the default button for the action area, we want to give visual feedback for this, so we set **XmNshowAsDefault** to **True** and **XmNdefaultButtonShadow-Thickness** to **1**. The value for this latter resource is a pixel width that is used for the area around PushButtons when they are displayed as the default buttons (i.e., those that are activated when the RETURN key is pressed). Default buttons have an extra three-dimensional border that distinguishes them from the other buttons in the action area. If the value for **XmNshowAsDefault** is **False**, the button is not shown as the default, despite the value of the default shadow thickness.[8]

Because this dialog is never reused, we want to set the callback for the **Ok** button to destroy the DialogShell. The callback routine is therefore **DestroyShell()** and the client data to the function is the DialogShell handle, **dialog_help**:

```
static void
DestroyShell(widget, shell)
Widget widget, shell;
{
    XtDestroyWidget(shell);
}
```

Since the dialog we have created is not a predefined Motif dialog widget, the **widget** parameter to the callback routine is not the dialog itself, but the pushbutton that caused the callback to be invoked. (See Chapter 5, *Introduction to Dialogs*, for a discussion of predefined Motif dialog callback routines.) This is a subtle difference that is often overlooked when people begin to break away from the predefined dialogs to build their own.

The callback routine is invoked directly from the widget that was activated. Thus, we pass the dialog as the client data to **XtAddCallback()** so **DestroyShell()** can have easy access to its handle. We could have gotten it using **GetTopShell()**, but is not as readily available as it is through the client data.

---

[8] The resource **XmNshowAsDefault** may also take a numeric value indicating the shadow thickness to use, but its value is only interpreted this way if **XmNdefaultButtonShadowThickness** is set to zero. This is for backwards compatibility with Motif 1.0 and should not be used in this way.

The **More** widget is unused in this application, because we don't provide any more help for this dialog (as discussed earlier):

```
widget = XtVaCreateManagedWidget("More",
    xmPushButtonGadgetClass, form,
    XmNsensitive,            False,
    XmNtopAttachment,        XmATTACH_FORM,
    XmNbottomAttachment,     XmATTACH_FORM,
    XmNleftAttachment,       XmATTACH_POSITION,
    XmNleftPosition,         3,
    XmNrightAttachment,      XmATTACH_POSITION,
    XmNrightPosition,        4,
    XmNshowAsDefault,        False,
    XmNdefaultButtonShadowThickness,   1,
    NULL);
```

In this case, the `XmNshowAsDefault` resource is set to `False`.

The highlight border being drawn in black (the default color) does not affect the visual appearance of the widget because the value for `XmNhighlightOnEnter` defaults to `False`. Even if it were set to `True` by the user's resource database, it doesn't adversely affect the gadget's appearance, so we don't need to hard-code either value; leaving it to the user to specify is fine.

Once all the items in the form have been created and managed, the form and the pane are managed using `XtManageChild()` and the dialog is popped up using `XtPopup()`. Note that, contrary to the way predefined Motif dialogs work, the DialogShell does not automatically pop up when you manage the PanedWindow widget. That special case only happens when the DialogShell's immediate child is a BulletinBoard or Form widget. (Even then, you should never rely on this behavior or expect it to happen.) See Chapter 5, *Introduction to Dialogs*, for a complete discussion of this topic.

7.4 Generalizing the Action Area

While dialogs can change in many respects, the arrangement and structure of the action area usually remain consistent among all dialogs. While Example 7-2 can be used "as is," it is likely that most larger programs are going to make use of many customized dialogs. In the general case, you don't want to rewrite the code to generate action areas for each special case. It is much easier and more efficient to write a generalized routine that generates an arbitrary action area for any dialog.

Whenever we generalize any procedure, we first identify how the situation may change from one case to the next. For example, not all action areas will have only two buttons; you may have any number from one to, say, ten. In this case, you would need to change the number of partitions in the Form widget to any arbitrary value depending on the number of actions there will be. Accordingly, the positions to which the left and right sides of each action button should be adjusted.

One known quantity in this equation is that the action area must be at the bottom of a dialog and must consist of PushButtons. These will be either be widgets or gadgets, but whichever you use may not change from dialog to dialog. That is, you will probably choose to use either a widget or a gadget and maintain this consistency throughout the application. Of course, you may find exceptions to the rule and you can adjust your data structures accordingly. However, consider the following facts about buttons and gadgets.

Gadgets have no colors of their own, per se. They have no background color, since they have no windows. (Their "background" is really transparent and the user really sees the actual parent window's background.) Likewise, their foreground colors are inherited from the parent. The result: all the texts used in PushButton gadgets will be rendered in the same color. This may be a good design, depending on your application. For example, the user can set each of those PushButton's colors using resource specifications like:

```
*action_area.foreground: red
```

Widgets, on the other hand, can have windows, so you can differentiate between them independently, if you like. That is, the **Ok** button could be rendered in blue, with the **Cancel** button in red to emphasize warning:

```
*action_area.ok_button.foreground: blue
*action_area.cancel_button.foreground: red
```

In general, you should try to make all the buttons in the action area a consistent widget class, and make all action areas consistent with one another.

Each button in an action area has its own label and, if selected, its own callback routine (and its own associated client data). So, we can create a new data structure:

```
typedef struct {
    char *label;            /* PushButton's Label */
    void (*callback)();     /* pointer to a callback routine, when activated */
    caddr_t data;           /* client data for the callback routine */
} ActionAreaItem;
```

The new `ActionAreaItem` type is all we need to know in order to create the action area; everything else is either a "predictable value" or a "known value." Note that we use the type `caddr_t` for the `data` field rather than `XtPointer`. This is done because `XtPointer` is specific to Xt and we may want to use this abstraction in a non-GUI interface model like the *curses* library package on UNIX systems.

We can now write a routine that creates an action area.

Example 7-3. The CreateActionArea() function

```
#define TIGHTNESS 20

Widget
CreateActionArea(parent, actions, num_actions)
Widget parent;
ActionAreaItem *actions;
int num_actions;
{
    Widget action_area, widget;
    int i;

    action_area = XtVaCreateWidget("action_area", xmFormWidgetClass, parent,
        XmNfractionBase, TIGHTNESS*num_actions - 1,
      XmNskipAdjust,    True,
        NULL);
```

Example 7-3. The CreateActionArea() function (continued)

```
    for (i = 0; i < num_actions; i++) {
        widget = XtVaCreateManagedWidget(actions[i].label,
            xmPushButtonWidgetClass, action_area,
            XmNleftAttachment,        i? XmATTACH_POSITION : XmATTACH_FORM,
            XmNleftPosition,          TIGHTNESS*i,
            XmNtopAttachment,         XmATTACH_FORM,
            XmNbottomAttachment,      XmATTACH_FORM,
            XmNrightAttachment,
                    i != num_actions-1? XmATTACH_POSITION : XmATTACH_FORM,
            XmNrightPosition,         TIGHTNESS*i + (TIGHTNESS-1),
            XmNshowAsDefault,         i == 0,
            XmNdefaultButtonShadowThickness, 1,
            NULL);
        if (actions[i].callback)
            XtAddCallback(widget, XmNactivateCallback,
                actions[i].callback, actions[i].data);
        if (i == 0) {
            /* Set the action_area's default button to the first widget
             * created (or, make the index a parameter to the function
             * or have it be part of the data structure). Also, set the
             * pane window constraint for max and min heights so this
             * pane in the widget is not resizable.
             */
            Dimension height, h;
            XtVaGetValues(action_area, XmNmarginHeight, &h, NULL);
            XtVaGetValues(widget, XmNheight, &height, NULL);
            height += 2 * h;
            XtVaSetValues(action_area,
                XmNdefaultButton, widget,
                XmNpaneMaximum,   height,
                XmNpaneMinimum,   height,
                NULL);
        }
    }

    XtManageChild(action_area);

    return action_area;
}
```

The purpose of the function is to create and return a Composite widget that contains a number of PushButtons that are evenly distributed horizontally throughout the widget. The actions and number of actions are specified in the **actions** and **num_actions** parameters. We use a Form widget to lay out the actions and give it the name **action_area**. This is not only descriptive for you, the programmer, but the user can also identify this particular anatomy of the dialog in resource files (e.g., to select colors as described earlier).

In order to distribute the PushButtons evenly across the action area, we use the Form widget's **XmNfractionBase** resource to set the number of positions that will be used to segment the Form widget used as the action area. The resource is set to a value that determines how closely the items are placed. This is hard-coded by the definition TIGHTNESS because the relationship between buttons in the action area is not expected to fluctuate from one to the next. The value of **20** was chosen purely for aesthetic reasons and no other. You may choose other values if your tastes are different, although the value should remain constant for all dialogs to maintain consistency. The higher the value, the closer together the PushButtons appear; the lower the value, the further apart they are.

The buttons are positioned in the Form during the **for** loop. The left side of the first item and right side of the last items are attached to the left and right edges of the Form, respectively. All other left and right edges are attached to positions:

```
XmNleftAttachment,       i? XmATTACH_POSITION : XmATTACH_FORM,
XmNrightAttachment,
    i != (num_actions-1)? XmATTACH_POSITION : XmATTACH_FORM,
```

The callback routines and associated client datas are added using **XtAddCallback( )**. The first item in the loop is set to be the default widget and is shown as default. The value for **XmNdefaultButton** (a BulletinBoard widget resource inherited by the Form) indicates which button is designated as the default button for certain actions that may take place in the control area of the dialog. For example, if a Text widget were placed in the control area, you might choose to hook up the Text's **XmNactivateCallback** to also activate the action area's default button's activation callback. In fact, we will demonstrate just how this can be done in Example 7-4.

Before we get to that, the last thing to mention about our **CreateActionArea( )** function is the section where the resources **XmNpaneMaximum** and **XmNpaneMinimum** are set. These are PanedWindow constraint resources (i.e., they are not used by the Form itself, but by the Form's parent) that are used to specify the maximum height of the action area. The assumption, of course, is that the action area's **parent** is a PanedWindow. If it isn't, these resource-value pairs have no effect.

We now present Example 7-4 to demonstrate everything we've discussed here. The output of the program is shown in Figure 7-6. You should run the program to get a better understanding of how some of the features work and why we made certain design decisions. For example, by using a PanedWindow as the child of the DialogShell, you can resize this dialog all you like, and the layout of the window retains the same fundamental structure.

Example 7-4. The action_area.c program

```
/* action_area.c -- demonstrate how CreateActionArea() can be used
 * in a real application.  Create what would otherwise be identified
 * as a PromptDialog, only this is of our own creation.  As such,
 * we provide a TextField widget for input.  When the user presses
 * Return, the Ok button is activated.
 */
#include <Xm/DialogS.h>
#include <Xm/PushBG.h>
#include <Xm/PushB.h>
#include <Xm/LabelG.h>
#include <Xm/PanedW.h>
#include <Xm/Form.h>
#include <Xm/RowColumn.h>
#include <Xm/TextF.h>

main(argc, argv)
int argc;
char *argv[ ];
{
    Widget toplevel, button;
```

Example 7-4. The action_area.c program (continued)

```
    XtAppContext app;
    extern void do_dialog();

    toplevel = XtVaAppInitialize(&app, "Demos",
        NULL, 0, &argc, argv, NULL, NULL);

    button = XtVaCreateManagedWidget("Push Me",
        xmPushButtonWidgetClass, toplevel, NULL);
    XtAddCallback(button, XmNactivateCallback, do_dialog, NULL);

    XtRealizeWidget(toplevel);
    XtAppMainLoop(app);
}

/* callback routine for "Push Me" button.  Actually, this represents
 * a function that could be invoked by any arbitrary callback.  Here,
 * we demonstrate how one can build a standard customized dialog box.
 * The control area is created here and the action area is created in
 * a separate, generic routine: CreateActionArea().
 */
void
do_dialog(w, file)
Widget w; /* will act as dialog's parent */
char *file;
{
    Widget dialog, pane, rc, label, text_w, action_a;
    XmString string;
    extern Widget CreateActionArea();
    extern void
        activate_cb(), ok_pushed(), close_dialog(), cancel_pushed(), help();
    Arg args[10];
    static ActionAreaItem action_items[ ] = {
        { "Ok",     ok_pushed,     NULL            },
        { "Cancel", cancel_pushed, NULL            },
        { "Close",  close_dialog,  NULL            },
        { "Help",   help,          "Help Button" },
    };

    /* The DialogShell is the Shell for this dialog.  Set it up so
     * that the "Close" button in the window manager's system menu
     * destroys the shell (it only unmaps it by default).
     */
    dialog = XtVaCreatePopupShell("dialog",
        xmDialogShellWidgetClass, XtParent(w),
        XmNtitle,  "Dialog Shell",    /* give arbitrary title in wm */
        XmNdeleteResponse, XmDESTROY, /* system menu "Close" action */
        NULL);

    /* now that the dialog is created, set the Close button's
     * client data, so close_dialog() will know what to destroy.
     */
    action_items[2].data = (caddr_t)dialog;

    /* Create the paned window as a child of the dialog.  This will
     * contain the control area (a Form widget) and the action area
     * (created by CreateActionArea() using the action_items above).
     */
    pane = XtVaCreateWidget("pane", xmPanedWindowWidgetClass, dialog,
        XmNsashWidth,  1,
```

Custom Dialogs

Example 7-4. The action_area.c program (continued)

```
        XmNsashHeight, 1,
        NULL);

    /* create the control area (Form) which contains a
     * Label gadget and a List widget.
     */
    rc = XtVaCreateWidget("control_area", xmRowColumnWidgetClass, pane, NULL);
    string = XmStringCreateSimple("Type Something:");
    XtVaCreateManagedWidget("label", xmLabelGadgetClass, rc,
        XmNlabelString,    string,
        XmNleftAttachment, XmATTACH_FORM,
        XmNtopAttachment,  XmATTACH_FORM,
        NULL);
    XmStringFree(string);

    text_w = XtVaCreateManagedWidget("text-field",
        xmTextFieldWidgetClass, rc, NULL);

    /* RowColumn is full -- now manage */
    XtManageChild(rc);

    /* Set the client data "Ok" and "Cancel" button's callbacks. */
    action_items[0].data = (caddr_t)text_w;
    action_items[1].data = (caddr_t)text_w;

    /* Create the action area -- we don't need the widget it returns. */
    action_a = CreateActionArea(pane, action_items, XtNumber(action_items));

    /* callback for Return in TextField.  Use action_a as client data */
    XtAddCallback(text_w, XmNactivateCallback, activate_cb, action_a);

    XtManageChild(pane);
    XtPopup(dialog, XtGrabNone);
}

/*--------------*/
/* The next four functions are the callback routines for the buttons
 * in the action area for the dialog created above.  Again, they are
 * simple examples, yet they demonstrate the fundamental design approach.
 */
static void
close_dialog(w, shell)
Widget w, shell;
{
    XtDestroyWidget(shell);
}

/* The "ok" button was pushed or the user pressed Return */
static void
ok_pushed(w, text_w, cbs)
Widget w, text_w;            /* the text widget is the client data */
XmAnyCallbackStruct *cbs;
{
    char *text = XmTextFieldGetString(text_w);

    printf("String = %s\n", text);
    XtFree(text);
}

static void
cancel_pushed(w, text_w, cbs)
```

Example 7-4. The action_area.c program (continued)

```
Widget w, text_w;              /* the text field is the client data */
XmAnyCallbackStruct *cbs;
{
    /* cancel the whole operation; reset to NULL. */
    XmTextFieldSetString(text_w, "");
}

static void
help(w, string)
Widget w;
String string;
{
    puts(string);
}
/*---------------*/

/* When Return is pressed in TextField widget, respond by getting
 * the designated "default button" in the action area and activate
 * it as if the user had selected it.
 */
void
activate_cb(text_w, client_data, cbs)
Widget text_w;                 /* user pressed Return in this widget */
caddr_t client_data;           /* action_area passed as client data */
XmAnyCallbackStruct *cbs;      /* borrow the "event" field from this */
{
    Widget dflt, action_area = (Widget)client_data;

    XtVaGetValues(action_area, XmNdefaultButton, &dflt, NULL);
    if (dflt) /* sanity check -- this better work */
        /* make the default button think it got pushed.  This causes
         * "ok_pushed" to be called, but XtCallActionProc() causes
         * the button appear to be activated as if the user selected it.
         */
        XtCallActionProc(dflt, "ArmAndActivate", cbs->event, NULL, 0);
}
```

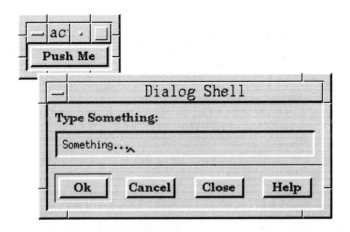

Figure 7-6. Output of action_area.c

The program does nothing substantial, but it does represent a generalized architecture for creating dialogs for applications. That is, the main application has certain control elements that may pop up another dialog. Here, such a control is represented by the **Push Me** button. When activated, it calls **do_dialog( )**, which creates a customized dialog and pops it up. The control area is composed of a RowColumn widget that contains a Label gadget and a TextField widget. The action area is created using **CreateActionArea( )** as described earlier.

7.5 Using TopLevelShells as Dialogs

You don't have to use DialogShell widgets to implement all dialogs. In fact, it is quite common to use TopLevelShells or even ApplicationShells in cases where a particular functionality of a larger application is substantially important. For example, an electronic mail application has a variety of functions that range from reading messages to composing new ones. As shown in Figure 7-7, you can have a completely separate TopLevelShell, complete with a MenuBar, that looks and acts like a separate application, but is still considered a dialog, since it is only a subpart of the whole application.

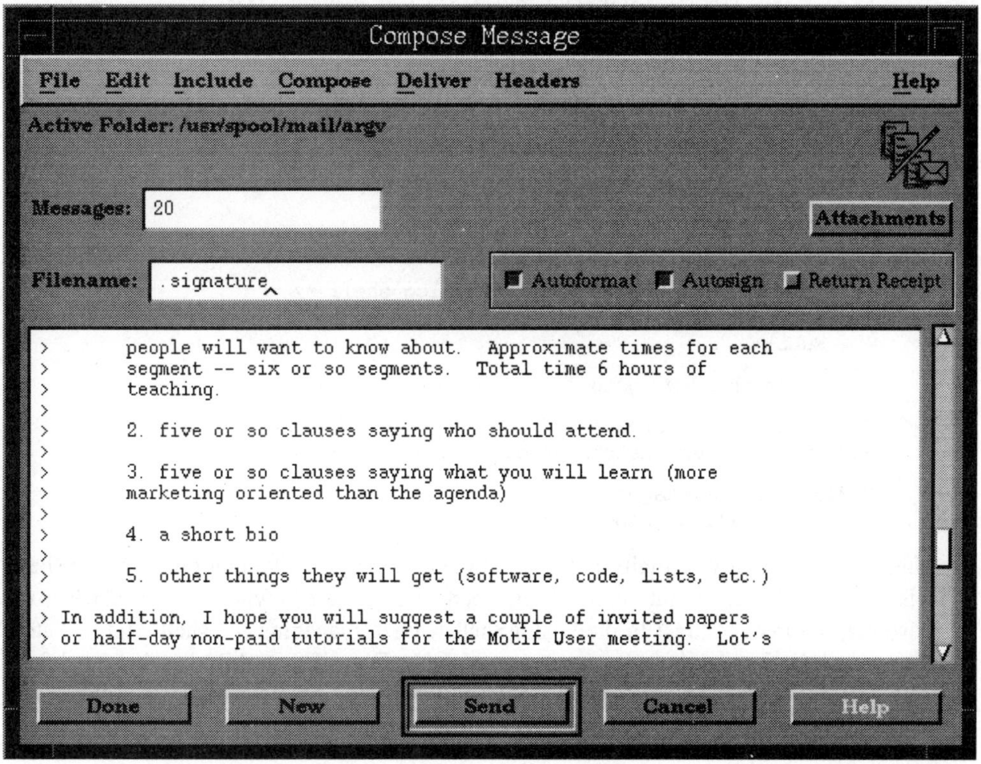

Figure 7-7. A Message composition dialog from an electronic mail application

As you can see, the same elements exist in this dialog: the control area is complete with a ScrolledText region and other controls, while the action area contains common action items. The principal difference is that these TopLevelShells may be iconified separately from the other windows in the program.

In these cases, separate shells are necessary, but should not be regarded or implemented as popup dialogs. For the most part, there is little difference from this approach than the method discussed for regular dialogs. That is, you may still use BulletinBoards, Forms, and RowColumns to manage the inner controls, you still need an action area (provided you want to look and act like a dialog), and you still need to handle the cases where you are popped up and down.

The following code fragment suggests one method for creating a dialog using a TopLevel-Shell:

```
static Widget shell;
Widget manager, action_area;
```

```
/* If dialog is already created, just remap it */
if (shell) {
    XtPopup(shell, XtGrabNone);
    /* call XMapRaised() anyway in case shell was already popped up,
     * but not sitting on the top of the window tree.
     */
    XMapRaised(XtDisplay(shell), XtWindow(shell));
    return;
}

/* Create a topLevelShell as the "dialog" */
shell = XtVaCreateApplicationShell(NULL, "Class",
    topLevelShellWidgetClass, dpy,
    XtNtitle, "Dialog Shell",
    NULL);

/* the main Form widget for the dialog shell */
manager = XtVaCreateWidget("dialog_manager", xmFormWidgetClass, shell,
    NULL);

/* create child widgets */

/* create action area */
action_area = CreateActionArea(manager, ...);

XtManageChild(manager);
XtPopup(shell, XtGrabNone);
```

Although the dialog is actually a TopLevelShell, we treat it like any other DialogShell. By default, the shell will be automatically mapped onto the screen when you call **XtPopup( )**. However, in direct contrast to the DialogShell widget, managing the shell's immediate child does *not* cause the dialog to pop up automatically. Even if that child is subclassed from the BulletinBoard widget, this type of behavior only happens if the shell is a DialogShell widget. The same is true for **XtPopdown( )**.

Since TopLevelShells are not DialogShells, you cannot rely on the special communications that happen between DialogShells and BulletinBoard or Form widgets. Thus, many resources such as **XmNautoUnmanage**, **XmNdialogTitle**, and so forth no longer apply. To achieve the same effects, you must implement those functionalities manually.

The rest of the process is purely mechanical; you can draw the necessary information from Chapter 4, *The Main Window*, and Chapter 17, *Interacting with the Window Manager*.

7.5.1 Using Motif Dialogs Within TopLevelShells

A situation may arise where you would like to have a standard Motif dialog widget such as a MessageDialog or a FileSelectionDialog placed in a shell widget that can be iconified separately from its primary window shell. This can easily be done by creating the TopLevelShell as per the specifications in the previous section, but using the Motif convenience routines to create Dialog*Boxes* as opposed to Dialog*Shells*. An example is shown below:

```
shell = XtVaCreateApplicationShell(NULL, "Class",
    topLevelShellWidgetClass, dpy,
    XtNtitle, "Dialog Shell Title",
    NULL);

dialog = XmCreateMessageBox(shell, "MessageDialog", NULL, 0);

XtAddCallback(dialog, XmNokCallback, callback_func, NULL);
XtAddCallback(dialog, XmNcancelCallback, callback_func, NULL);
XtAddCallback(dialog, XmNhelpCallback, help_func, NULL);
```

7.6 Positioning Dialogs

It is technically simple to automatically position dialogs whenever they are popped up. The difficult part is determining when it is appropriate to do so and the extent to which you should enforce dialog positioning. The default position of a dialog depends on the type of dialog, how it was created, how it was popped up and, ultimately, the whim of the window manager.

When the shell widget is created as a popup shell through `XtVaCreatePopupShell()` or `XtCreatePopupShell()`, the parent determines the placement of the dialog when it is mapped to the screen. Assuming the primary window is visible, the Motif window manager enforces the policy where secondary windows are always initially positioned directly on top of their primary windows. If the parent is unmapped or unmanaged, the dialog will not be displayed at all. In other words, secondary windows are always displayed over their primary windows; if the primary window goes away, it takes its secondary windows with it.

So far, all the examples using DialogShells in this chapter, in Chapter 5, *Introduction to Dialogs*, and in Chapter 6, *Selection Dialogs*, have demonstrated this. However, the initial position of these shells can be modified using the `XmNmapCallback` resource supported by all Motif manager widgets, as shown in Example 7-5.

Example 7-5. Using XmNmapCallback to position a dialog widget
```
/* popup() --the callback routine that pops up a dialog.
 * Attach a callback for the XmNmapCallback so we can position
 * the dialog manually when it is popped up.
 */
void
popup(w, data)
Widget w;
XtPointer data; /* The client_data parameter passed by XtAddCallback */
{
    Widget dialog;
    Arg arg[2];
    extern void map_dialog();

    XtSetArg(arg[0], XmNautoUnmanage, False);
    XtSetArg(arg[1], XmNdefaultPosition, False);
    dialog = XmCreateMessageDialog(w, "dialog", arg, 2);
```

```
    XtAddCallback(dialog, XmNmapCallback, map_dialog, NULL);

    XtManageChild(dialog);
    XtPopup(XtParent(dialog), XtGrabNone);
}

/* callback function for XmNmapCallback.  Position dialog in 200 pixel
 * "steps".  When the edge of the screen is hit, start over.
 */
static void
map_dialog(dialog, client_data, cbs)
Widget dialog;
XtPointer client_data;
XmAnyCallbackStruct *cbs;
{
    static Position x, y; /* always remember current x, y position */
    Dimension w, h;

    /* get the current position of the dialog on the screen */
    XtVaGetValues(dialog, XmNwidth, &w, XmNheight, &h, NULL);
    /* see if the current x position + width exceeds screen width */
    if (x + w >= WidthOfScreen(XtScreen(dialog)))
        x = 0;
    /* same with y position (and height) */
    if (y + h >= HeightOfScreen(XtScreen(dialog)))
        y = 0;
    /* position dialog accordingly, and add new values for next time */
    XtVaSetValues(dialog, XmNx, x, XmNy, y, NULL);
    x += 200, y += 200;
}
```

Each time the Motif dialog is mapped to the screen, the **XmNmapCallback** list is invoked, causing **map_dialog()** to be called. This particular routine merely places the dialog at 200 pixel increments from the place where it placed it last time. The intent is for **map_dialog()** to be invoked on a number of different dialogs simultaneously.

In **map_dialog()**, the **XmNwidth**, **XmNheight**, **XmNx**, and **XmNy** resources may be extracted from the dialog widget. Because this is a predefined Motif dialog, these values are taken from the DialogShell. Similarly, the position of the DialogShell can be set anywhere on the screen by inverting the process; that is, by calling **XtVaSetValues()** using the same resources.

If you are using an ApplicationShell or TopLevelShell, rather than a DialogShell, the position of the dialog is subject to various resources that the user and/or window manager controls. For example, if the user is using *mwm*, he can set the resource **interactive-Placement**, allowing him to position the shell interactively. While it is acceptable for the application to control where DialogShells are placed when they are displayed, you should never try to control where TopLevelShells are placed. This should be left for the user.

However, if you feel you must, you can position shell widgets directly by setting their **XmNx** and **XmNy** resources to the desired position. For example, you can pop up a dialog in the middle of the screen by following the code fragment below:

```
Widget shell;

shell = XtVaCreatePopupShell("dialog", xmDialogShellWidgetClass, parent,
    XmNtitle,            "User Error",
    XmNdeleteResponse,   XmDESTROY,
    XmNx,                DefaultWidthOfScreen(XtScreen(parent)) / 2,
    XmNy,                DefaultHeightOfScreen(XtScreen(parent)) / 2,
    NULL);

/* Create manager child and all subwidgets */

XtPopup(XtWindow(shell), XtGrabNone);
```

While this code fragment demonstrates how you can position the dialog at a particular x,y coordinate on the screen at creation time, you can also use **XtVaSetValues( )** to position the dialog later. The Motif toolkit passes along the coordinate values to the window manager and allows it to position the dialog at the intended location.

This brings up an important dilemma in user-interface design. If you are going to provide a dialog that pops up and down on the screen, even for DialogShells, where you can hard-code its position, chances are that you will not want to position it there *each time the dialog is popped up*.

Imagine using an application for the first time: you pop up a dialog, interact with it for a while, move it to an uncluttered area on your screen and then pop it down. If you want to use it again, you'd probably like (or expect) it to pop back up in the same spot it was last time you used it. The best way to handle this problem is to avoid doing any of your own automatic dialog placement. The only possible exception to this might be the first time a dialog is popped up, as demonstrated in the previous example.

7.6.1 Popup Notification

Whether or not you want to automatically position a dialog when it is displayed, it may still be useful to be informed when a dialog is popped up or down. However, you should not necessarily use the **XmNmapCallback** for this purpose, since it does not reflect each time the dialog's *popped_up* state changes. A better way to be notified of this state is to install **Xt-NpopupCallback** and **XtNpopdownCallback** functions.

These resources are defined and implemented by X Toolkit Intrinsics. Each represents a callback list of functions that are invoked when the programmer calls **XtPopup( )** on a shell widget (which, of course, includes DialogShells). Similarly, you can install a function [list] for **XtNpopdownCallback**. Note that neither of these callbacks are invoked if the shell is already up (for **XtPopup( )**) or down (for **XtPopdown( )**).

7.6.2 Popped Down or Iconified?

As an aside, people often get confused between the terminology of a dialog being *popped down* and a shell that is *iconified*. Remember that whether or not a shell is "up" or "down" has no effect on its iconic state. Although DialogShells cannot be iconified, other shells can be. (Some dialogs that you create yourself may fall into this category.) These shells may also be popped up and down using **XtPopup( )** and **XtPopdown( )** independent of their iconic state. **XtPopup( )** will cause a shell to de-iconify while **XtPopdown( )** causes the dialog and its icon to be withdrawn from the screen, regardless of its iconic state. Ths subject of window iconification is discussed in Chapter 17, *Interacting with the Window Manager*.

7.7 Summary

Obviously, it is impossible to cover all possible scenarios for how dialogs can or should be used, but you should have come away from Chapters 5, 6, and 7 with a general feeling for the design approach we encourage. You should be able to adapt the information we've presented to whatever particular situation you may need to support.

The next logical step is to fully understand manager widgets, since they are very important to all dialogs. While there is a circular dependency between dialogs and manager widgets, the use of managers in the past three chapters has been limited to their most essential features.

Once you have understood dialogs and manager widgets, you should come full circle by understanding the material in Chapter 17, *Interacting with the Window Manager*.

For a final look at some particularly thorny issues in using dialogs, you should see Chapter 20, *Advanced Dialog Programming*.

8

Manager Widgets

This chapter provides detailed descriptions of the various classes of Motif manager widgets. Useful examples explore the limits of the various methods of Form and RowColumn positioning.

In This Chapter:

8
Manager Widgets

As their name implies, manager widgets manage other widgets. That is, they control the size and location (or *geometry*) and input focus policy for one or more widget children (possibly including other manager widgets). The relationship between managers and the widgets they manage is commonly referred to as the *parent-child* model. The manager acts as the parent and the other widgets are its children. Since manager widgets can also be children of other managers, this model provides for the widget-tree hierarchy, a framework for how widgets are laid out visually on the screen and how resources are specified in the resource database (e.g., in the *.Xdefaults* and application defaults files).

While managers are used and explained in different contexts throughout this book, this chapter discusses the gory details of these widgets. Chapter 2, *The Motif Programming Model*, discusses the general concepts behind manager widgets and how they fit into the broader application model. You are encouraged to review material in these and other chapters for a wider spectrum of examples and discussion, since it is impossible to deal with all possibilities here. For an explicit, in-depth discussion on the X Toolkit Composite and Constraint widget classes, from which managers are subclassed, see Volume Four, *X Toolkit Intrinsics Programming Manual*.

8.1 Manager Widget Types

The Manager widget class is a superclass for a number of subclasses listed below. One never instantiates a Manager class widget; the functionality it provides is inherited by each of the subclasses. The following list introduces some of the manager widget classes:

BulletinBoard

> The BulletinBoard is the most basic of the conventional manager widgets. The geometry management is, as the widget's class name implies, like a bulletin board. A child is "pinned up" on the BulletinBoard in a particular location and remains there until it moves itself or someone else moves it. The BulletinBoard has translation tables and callback routines that are designed to be used as a template for predefined Motif dialog boxes. Internally implemented dialogs in the Motif toolkit use the BulletinBoard widget class to handle all the input mechanisms, but the geometry management is handled by the specific dialog widget class. A pure BulletinBoard widget does not impose any layout policy for its children, but it does provide input modes that support keyboard traversal. These basic mechanisms are

ideal for the BulletinBoard's role as a superclass for more sophisticated and useful managers and dialogs alike. For more discussion on dialogs, see Chapter 5, *Introduction to Dialogs*.

Form

Subclassed from the BulletinBoard class, Form extends the capabilities of the class by introducing a sophisticated geometry management policy that involves both absolute and relative positioning and sizing of its children. For example, Forms may lay out their children in a grid-like manner, anchoring edges of each child to specific positions on the grid, or they may attach them to one another in a chain-like fashion.

RowColumn

The RowColumn Widget lays out its children in row and/or column format. Through resources, the programmer (or the user) can have the RowColumn use a specified number of rows or columns, it can pack the widgets it contains into identically sized boxes, or it can simply chain them together side by side, wrapping to new rows or columns as necessary. The Motif toolkit also uses the RowColumn internally to implement many objects that are not implemented as individual widgets. Examples include popup and pulldown menus, MenuBars, RadioBoxes, CheckBoxes, and more. You will find resources specific to these objects in reference pages associated with the RowColumn class.

Frame

The purpose of a Frame widget is to provide a visible, three-dimensional border for objects such as RowColumns or Labels that do not provide one for themselves. The Frame widget may have only one child, which it manages by automatically shrink-wrapping itself to match its child's exact dimensions.

PanedWindow

The PanedWindow manages its children in a vertically tiled format. Its width is taken from the widest widget in its list of children.[1] PanedWindows also provide *control sashes* or *grips* that enable the user to adjust the individual heights of the PanedWindow's children. Constraint resources for the PanedWindow allow each child to specify its desired maximum and minimum height and whether or not it may be resized.

DrawingArea

The DrawingArea widget is subclassed from the manager widget class, but it is not generally used in the way that conventional managers are used. It does no drawing and defines no keyboard or mouse behavior, although it does provide callbacks for user input. It is basically a free-form widget that programs can use in whatever odd way is necessary in order to implement application-specific needs. There are callback resources you may use to handle keyboard, mouse, exposure, and resize events. While the DrawingArea widget can have children, it does not manage them in any defined way (much like the BulletinBoard widget). Because the DrawingArea

---

[1] Currently, there is a bug with the PanedWindow widget in that it uses the width of the widest widget in *all* its children, not just the managed children. Technically, a manager widget is not supposed to consider the geometries of unmanaged widgets.

widget is typically used for drawing, rather than for geometry management of other widgets, it is discussed separately in Chapter 10, *The DrawingArea Widget*.

8.2 Creating Manager Widgets

A manager may be created and destroyed like any other widget. The main difference between managers and other widgets is *when* they are declared to be managed in the creation process.

Normally one creates widgets using `XtVaCreateManagedWidget()`, but it is worthwhile to get into the habit of creating manager widgets using `XtVaCreate-Widget()` and managing them later using `XtManageChild()`. To understand why this can be important, let's review what *widget management* means and the difference between a parent and a child widget.

A parent (a manager widget) is said to manage a child if it controls the child's size and position. In actuality, though, the process of widget layout only happens when the child *and* the parent are both in the state called "managed."

If a child is created as an unmanaged widget, the parent skips over that widget in its managing duties (until such time that the child is finally managed).[2] However, if a manager widget is not itself managed, it does not perform geometry management on any of its children regardless of whether those children are managed.[3]

Let's consider what happens when a manager is created as a managed widget before any of its children are created.

Let's say that a manager is going to have a set of PushButtons as its children. When the first child is added using `XtVaCreateManagedWidget()`, the manager widget negotiates the size and position of the PushButton. Depending on the type of manager widget being used, the parent will probably either change its size to accommodate the new child, or it changes the child's size to its own size. In either case, these calculations are not necessary because the geometry will change again as more buttons are added. The problem becomes complicated by the fact that when the manager's size changes, it must also negotiate its new size with its own parent. This will, of course, cause that parent to negotiate with its parent all the way up to the highest-level shell. If the new size is accepted, the result goes back down

---

[2] There is currently a bug with the PanedWindow widget which causes it to consider even its unmanaged children.

[3] To be precise, a manager doesn't actually manage its children until it is both managed and realized. If you realize all your widgets at once, order is not important. However, if you are adding to a tree of already-realized widgets, the principles set forth in this section are important. We recommend that you get in the habit of creating managers as unmanaged widgets, so that you won't run into trouble in the corner cases.

If you are adding children to an already-realized parent, the child will automatically be realized when it is managed. However, if you are adding a manager widget as a child of a raelized widget, you should explicitly *realize* it (with `XtRealizeWidget()`) before you manage it. Otherwise, the resize calculations will be performed in the wrong order. In a case such as this, it is essential to use `XtManageChild()` rather than `XtVaCreateManaged-Widget()`, since doing so allows you to make the explicit realize call before managing the widget.

the widget tree with each manager widget resizing itself on the way down. Repeating this process each time a child is added will almost certainly affect performance.

Because of the different geometry management methods used by the different manager widgets, there is the possibility that all of this premature negotiation will result in a different layout design than originally intended. The RowColumn widget, for example, lays out its children in a row-column format; as children are added to the widget, the RowColumn checks to see if there is enough room to place the new child on the same row or column. If there isn't, then a new row or column is created. This behavior depends heavily on whether the RowColumn is in a managed state and its size has been established (whether the widget has been realized).

If the manager parent is not itself managed yet, this whole process can be avoided, yet you still have the convenience of using **XtVaCreateManagedWidget( )** for all of the widget children. Only when the manager is itself finally managed does it query its children for their size and position requests, calculate its own size requirements, and communicate that one size back up the widget tree.

Primitive widgets such as Labels, PushButtons, Text, and List widgets do not contain any widget children, so they are typically created as managed widgets. Creating primitive widgets as unmanaged widgets serves no purpose, unless you explicitly want the widget's parent (a manager widget) to ignore it for some reason. Since manager widgets can also be children of other manager widgets, the same principle can apply to managers if they are children. (That is, their sizes and positions are managed by their parents.)

In short, the creation process of an entire widget tree is top down, but the management process is bottom up.

For best results, you should use **XtVaCreateWidget( )** to create manager widgets and **XtVaCreateManagedWidget( )** to create primitive widgets. If you are adding another manager as a child, the same principle applies; you should also create them as an unmanaged widgets until all *their* children are added as well. The idea is to descend as deeply into the widget tree and create as many children as possible before managing the manager parents as you ascend back up. Once all the children have been added, **XtManageChild( )** can then be called for the managers so that they only have to negotiate with their parents once, thus saving time, improving performance, and probably producing better results.

Despite all we've just said, realize that the entire motivating factor behind this principle is to optimize the method by which managers negotiate size and positions of their children. If you only have one child, it doesn't matter if you create the manager widget as managed or not. Also, certain widgets' geometry management constraints are such that no negotiation is required between the parent and the children, anyway. Therefore, you may see some examples where we create certain managers as managed widgets even though they have children. In such cases, we will explain why that particular widget or case is an exception.

Let's now examine some basic manager widget classes and see some examples of how managers can be used. Keep in mind that geometry management is only one aspect of manager widgets. While it is the most obvious and widely used part of the widget class, managers are also responsible for keyboard traversal and gadget display and event handling. In fact, many of the resources intrinsic to the manager superclass (the one that you never instantiate) are inherited by each of its subclasses (the ones you do instantiate).

8.3 The BulletinBoard Widget

The BulletinBoard is the most basic of the manager widget subclasses. BulletinBoard widgets do not enforce position or size policies on their children, so they are rarely used by applications as a general geometry manager for widgets. Rather, they are more commonly used internally by the Motif toolkit as the superclass for Form widgets and all the dialog widgets discussed in Chapter 5, *Introduction to Dialogs*, and Chapter 6, *Selection Dialogs*. To support these roles, BulletinBoards have a number of resources that are used specifically for communicating with DialogShells. (See the aforementioned chapters for details on how BulletinBoards are used as dialog widgets.)

BulletinBoard resources include callbacks for events such as **FocusIn**, **FocusOut**, **Map-Notify**, and so on. These events correspond to noninteractive actions invoked by the user indirectly (e.g., by moving a mouse or using the TAB key to traverse the widget tree). These events are not intended to cause much visual feedback or prompt you to service them with application-specific callback routines. They are mostly informative events that your application can use to set internal states and the like. Their callback routines, such as **XmNfocus-Callback** and **XmNmapCallback**, are used extensively by DialogShells.

Despite the BulletinBoard's low profile as a manager widget, there is a lot to be learned from it, since the principles also apply to most other dialog and manager widgets. In this spirit, let's take a closer look at BulletinBoard widgets and examine the different things that can be done with them as manager widgets.

Applications that wish to create BulletinBoard widgets directly must include the file *<Xm/BulletinB.h>*. To create and manage a BulletinBoard widget, you can use the following calls:

```
Widget  bboard;

bboard = XtVaCreateWidget("name", xmBulletinBoardWidgetClass, parent,
    resource-values,
    NULL);

/* Create children */

XtManageChild(bboard);
```

The **parent** parameter is the parent of the BulletinBoard, which may be another manager widget or a shell. The resources that may be specified may be any of those specific to the BulletinBoard widget class, but unless you are using it as a dialog box, your choices are quite limited.

Of the few BulletinBoard resources not tied to DialogShells, the only visual one is **Xm-NshadowType**. When used in conjunction with the manager's **XmNshadowThickness** resource, you can affect the three-dimensional appearance of the widget. There are four possible values for **XmNshadowType**:

```
XmSHADOW_IN
XmSHADOW_OUT
XmSHADOW_ETCHED_IN
XmSHADOW_ETCHED_OUT
```

The default value for `XmNshadowThickness` is 0, except when the BulletinBoard is the child of a DialogShell, in which case the default value is 1. Either way, it may be reset by the application or the user. Coincidentally, this resource is also used by the Frame widget discussed in Section .

The resource `XmNbuttonFontList` may be set to a fontlist as described in Chapter 19, *Compound Strings*. This fontlist is used for all PushButton and ToggleButton children in the BulletinBoard. Each of these widgets may set its own fonts, of course. But unless it sets its fonts explicitly, its fonts are taken from the `XmNbuttonFontList` resource of the BulletinBoard. If the resource is unspecified, its value is initialized by looking up the parent hierarchy until it finds a BulletinBoard widget (or subclass) or a shell widget. In the latter case, the resource `XmNdefaultFontList` is used.

Similarly, the `XmNlabelFontList` and `XmNtextFontList` resources can be set for the Labels and Text widgets, respectively, that are direct children of BulletinBoards (and subclasses).

8.3.1 BulletinBoard Geometry Management

Since BulletinBoards provide no geometry management by default, you must be prepared to manage the positions and sizes of the widgets within them. This means that you must set the `XmNx` and `XmNy` resource for each child. You may also have to set the `XmNwidth` and `XmNheight` resources if consistent or predetermined sizes for the children are necessary. In order to maintain this size and position layout, you must add an event handler for resize (**ConfigureNotify**) events so that the new size and positions of the child widgets can be calculated. Example 8-1 shows an example of a resize handler.

Example 8-1. The corners.c program

```
/* corners.c -- demonstrate widget layout management for a
 * BulletinBoard widget.  There are four widgets each labeled
 * top-left, top-right, bottom-left and bottom-right.  Their
 * positions in the bulletin board correspond to their names.
 * Only when the widget is resized does the geometry management
 * kick in and position the children in their correct locations.
 */
#include <Xm/BulletinB.h>
#include <Xm/PushBG.h>

char *corners[ ] = {
    "Top-Left", "Top-Right", "Bottom-Left", "Bottom-Right",
};

static void resize();

main(argc, argv)
int argc;
char *argv[ ];
{
    Widget toplevel, bboard;
    XtAppContext app;
    XtActionsRec rec;
    int i;
```

Example 8-1. The corners.c program (continued)

```
    /* Initialize toolkit and create toplevel shell */
    toplevel = XtVaAppInitialize(&app, "Demos", NULL, 0,
        &argc, argv, NULL, NULL);

    /* Create your standard BulletinBoard widget */
    bboard = XtVaCreateManagedWidget("bboard",
        xmBulletinBoardWidgetClass, toplevel, NULL);

    /* Set up a translation table that captures "Resize" events
     * (also called ConfigureNotify or Configure events).  If the
     * event is generated, call the function resize().
     */
    rec.string = "resize";
    rec.proc = resize;
    XtAppAddActions(app, &rec, 1);
    XtOverrideTranslations(bboard,
        XtParseTranslationTable("<Configure>: resize()"));

    /* Create children of the dialog -- a PushButton in each corner. */
    for (i = 0; i < XtNumber(corners); i++)
        XtVaCreateManagedWidget(corners[i],
            xmPushButtonGadgetClass, bboard, NULL);

    XtRealizeWidget(toplevel);
    XtAppMainLoop(app);
}
/* resize(), the routine that is automatically called by Xt upon the
 * delivery of a Configure event.  This happens whenever the widget
 * gets resized.
 */
static void
resize(w, event, args, num_args)
CompositeWidget w;     /* The widget (BulletinBoard) that got resized */
XConfigureEvent *event;  /* The event struct associated with the event */
String args[]; /* unused */
int *num_args; /* unused */
{
    WidgetList children;
    int width = event->width;
    int height = event->height;
    Dimension w_width, w_height;
    short margin_w, margin_h;

    /* get handle to BulletinBoard's children and marginal spacing */
    XtVaGetValues(w,
        XmNchildren, &children,
        XmNmarginWidth, &margin_w,
        XmNmarginHeight, &margin_h,
        NULL);

    /* place the top left widget */
    XtVaSetValues(children[0],
        XmNx, margin_w,
        XmNy, margin_h,
        NULL);
    /* top right */
    XtVaGetValues(children[1], XmNwidth, &w_width, NULL);
```

Example 8-1. The corners.c program (continued)

```
XtVaSetValues(children[1],
    XmNx, width - margin_w - w_width,
    XmNy, margin_h,
    NULL);
/* bottom left */
XtVaGetValues(children[2], XmNheight, &w_height, NULL);
XtVaSetValues(children[2],
    XmNx, margin_w,
    XmNy, height - margin_h - w_height,
    NULL);
/* bottom right */
XtVaGetValues(children[3],
    XmNheight, &w_height,
    XmNwidth, &w_width,
    NULL);
XtVaSetValues(children[3],
    XmNx, width - margin_w - w_width,
    XmNy, height - margin_h - w_height,
    NULL);
}
```

There are four widgets, labeled Top-Left, Top-Right, Bottom-Left, and Bottom-Right. Their positions in the BulletinBoard correspond to their names. Since the widgets are not positioned at the time they are created, the geometry management only happens when the widget is resized. Figure 8-1 shows the program before a resize event.

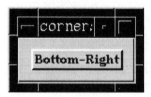

Figure 8-1. corners.c before a resize event

Figure 8-2 shows the program after a resize event.

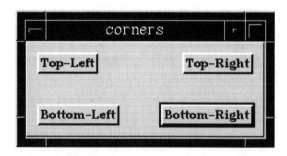

Figure 8-2. corners.c after a resize event

When resizing does occur, X generates a **ConfigureNotify** event, which is interpreted by Xt. The translation table for the widget corresponding to the resized window is searched to see if the application is interested in being notified of the event. We have indicated interest in this event by calling `XtAddActions()` and `XtOverrideTranslations()`:

```
XtActionsRec rec;
. . .
rec.string = "resize";
rec.proc = resize;
. . .
XtAddActions(&rec, 1);
XtOverrideTranslations(bboard,
    XtParseTranslationTable("<Configure>: resize()"));
```

As described in Volume Four, *X Toolkit Intrinsics Programming Manual*, a translation table describes a sequence of one or more events paired with a sequence of one or more functions to call should the event-sequence occur. In this case, the event is **ConfigureNotify** and the function to call is `resize()`. This event-action pair is specified as a `String` value for the ease of the programmer. The function `XtParseTranslationTable()` parses this string and creates an internal structure of real events to look for and real functions to call. Xt provides the table for translating event strings such as **Configure** to the actual **Configure-Notify** event.

Xt cannot convert the string `resize()` to an actual function unless we provide a lookup table. The `XtActionsRec` type is used to do this. It is defined as follows:

```
typedef struct _XtActionsRec{
    String      string;
    XtActionProc proc;
} XtActionsRec;
```

This data structure provides a `String` field that specifies an event or sequence of events that the user may generate. The translation mechanism converts X events into a string representation and attempts to match this string against the one specified in the action record. If a match is successful, the function pointed to by the `proc` field is called. In the example, we only need one record because we are only looking for one event. The action list is initialized to have the string `resize` map to the actual function `resize()`.

We install the translation table on the widget using `XtOverrideTranslations()` so that when a **ConfigureNotify** event occurs, the `resize()` function is called. `XtParse-TranslationTable()` is required to compile the string form of the translation table into Xt's internal format.[4]

---

[4] Translations are always defined as strings to allow them to be set by users in resource files.

The `resize()` function only uses two of the four possible parameters passed to the function.[5] They are a `Widget` and a pointer to an `XConfigureEvent` type:

```
static void
resize(w, event, args, num_args)
    CompositeWidget w;
    XConfigureEvent *event;
    char *args[ ]; /* array of size *num_args */
    int *num_args;
```

Since the function is called as a result of the event happening on the BulletinBoard widget, we know that the parameter is of type `CompositeWidget`. And we also know that there is only one event type that could have caused the function to be called, so we declare the `event` parameter accordingly.

The task of the function is to position the children—one per corner. The first thing to do is get a handle to all the children of the BulletinBoard. Since we are going to place the children around the perimeter of the widget, we need to know how far from the edge to place them. This distance is taken from the values for `XmNmarginWidth` and `XmNmarginHeight`. (The user may have changed these values using his own resources.) All three resource values are retrieved in one call:

```
XtVaGetValues(w,
    XtNchildren,      &children,
    XmNmarginWidth,   &margin_w,
    XmNmarginHeight,  &margin_h,
    NULL);
```

The remainder of the function simply places the children at the appropriate places within the BulletinBoard. This is a very simple method for geometry management, but it demonstrates the process.

The general issue of geometry management for composite widgets is not trivial. If you plan on doing your own geometry management for BulletinBoards or other composite widgets, you should be very careful to consider all the resources that could possibly affect layout. In our example, we considered the margin width and height, but there is the matter of `XmNallowOverlap`, `XtNborderWidth` (a general Core widget resource), `XmNshadowThickness` (a general manager widget resource) and, of course, the same values associated with the BulletinBoard's children. On top of that, there are issues about what to do if a child decides to resize itself (e.g., if a label widget gets wider). In this case, you must first evaluate what the geometry layout of the widgets would be like if you were to grant the Label permission to resize itself as it wants. This is done by asking each of the children how big they want to be, and calculating the new hypothetical layout. The result of this is that the BulletinBoard will either accept or reject the new layout. Of course, it may have to make itself bigger too, which will require the BulletinBoard to ask its parent for a new size, and so on. And then there is the issue of what to do when you can't resize yourself. Do you force other children to be certain sizes or do you reject the resize request of the child that started all this negotiation?

---

[5] The missing parameters are the `args` and `num_args` parameters. They are ignored because we did not specify any extra parameters to be passed to the function when we installed it using `XtParseTranslationTable( )`.

Geometry management is by no means a simple task; it is explained more completely in Volume Four, *X Toolkit Intrinsics Programming Manual.*

8.4 The Form Widget

Forms are subclassed from the BulletinBoard class, so they inherit all the resources that BulletinBoards have to offer. Accordingly, children of Forms can be placed at specific x,y coordinates and geometry management can be performed identically to Example 8-1. However, the added geometry management features that Forms provide allows them to generalize the layout of their children so that they may be positioned relative to one another as well as to specific and absolute locations in the Form.

In order to use Forms, you must include the file *<Xm/Form.h>*. Otherwise, they are created in a similar way to other manager widgets:

```
Widget form;

form = XtVaCreateWidget("name", xmFormWidgetClass, parent,
    resource-value pairs,
    NULL);

/* create children */

XtManageChild(form);
```

The most interesting part of the Form widget is its geometry management capabilities. Geometry management is done using resources referred to as *attachments*.

8.4.1 Form Attachments

Form resources provide various ways of specifying the positions of the Form's children (i.e., the spacing between them and/or their sizes). The basic concept behind this geometry management is the notion of *widget attachment*. Each of the four sides of a widget is attached to something—to another widget, to a fixed position on the Form, to a flexible position on the Form, to the Form itself, or to no attachment at all. These attachments could be considered as hooks, rods, and anchor points, as shown in Figure 8-3.

In this figure, there are three arbitrary widgets — they can be of any size or type. What's important is the relationship between them with respect to their positions in the Form. The top-left widget is attached to the top and left sides of the Form. This is done by creating two attachments. The top side of the widget is hooked to the top of the Form. It can "slide" from side to side, but it cannot be moved up or down (just like a shower curtain). The left side can slide up and down, but not right-to-left. Given these two attachment constraints, the top and left sides of the widget are fixed. The right and bottom edges of the widget are not specified to be attached to anything. However, other widgets are attached to those edges.

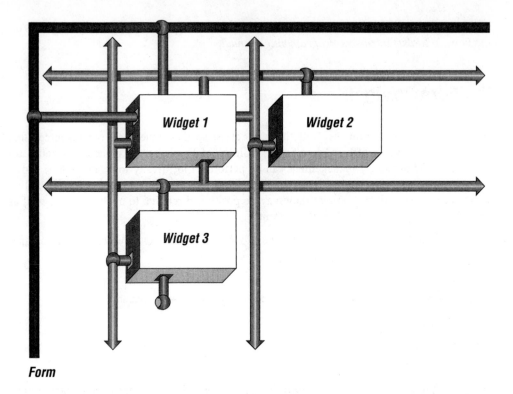

Form

Figure 8-3. Attachments in Forms

The left side of *widget-2* is attached to the right side of *widget-1*. Similarly, the top side of *widget-2* is attached to the top side of *widget-1*. Thus, the top and the left sides of the widget cannot be moved, unless *widget-1* moves.

The same kind of attachments hold for *widget-3*: its top side is attached to the bottom of *widget-1*, and its left side is attached to the left side of *widget-1*. Given these constraints, no matter how large each of the widgets may be, or however the Form may be resized, their positional relationship is maintained.

In general, you must attach at least two adjacent edges of a widget to keep it from moving unpredictably. If you attach opposing sides of the widget to things, then the widget will probably be resized by the Form in order to satisfy the attachment policies.

The following resources represent the four types of attachments:

```
XmNtopAttachment
XmNbottomAttachment
XmNrightAttachment
XmNleftAttachment
```

For example, if we were to specify that the top of a widget is attached to something, we would use the resource **XmNtopAttachment**. What the top of the widget is attached to is described by the following list of resources.

XmATTACH_FORM

> The specified side is attached to the Form as shown in Figure 8-4.

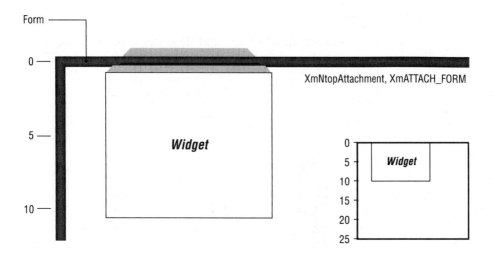

Figure 8-4. A widget's XmNtopAttachment set to XmATTACH_FORM

> If the resource that has this value is **XmNtopAttachment,** then the top side of the widget will be attached to the top of the Form. This is the shower curtain effect. The top attachment will not guarantee that the widget does not move from side to side. If **XmNbottomAttachment** were also set to **XmATTACH_FORM**, the bottom of the widget would be attached to the bottom side of the Form. If the top and bottom attachments were both set to **XmATTACH_FORM**, the widget would be resized to the height of the Form itself. The same would be true for the right and left edges of the widget.

XmATTACH_OPPOSITE_FORM

> This side of the widget is attached to the opposite side of the Form. If **XmNtop-Attachment** is set to **XmATTACH_OPPOSITE_FORM**, then the top side of the widget is attached to the bottom side of the Form. This resource must be used with a negative offset value (discussed in the next section); otherwise, the widget is placed off the edge of the Form (and will not be visible). While it may seem confusing, this value is the only one that can be applied to an attachment resource that allows you to specify a constant offset from the edge of a Form.

XmATTACH_WIDGET

This value indicates that a side of the widget is attached to another widget. That other widget must be specified using an additional resource-value pair. The resource must be one of:

XmNtopWidget
XmNbottomWidget
XmNleftWidget
XmNrightWidget

The value for this resource must be the widget ID to attach to. For example, Figure 8-5 shows how to attach the right side of *widget1* to the left side of *widget2*.

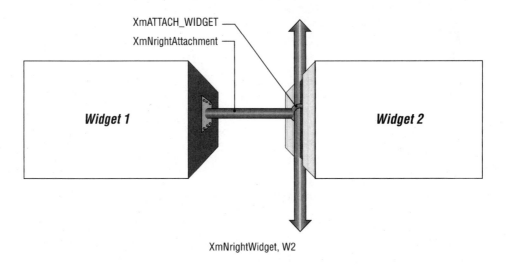

Figure 8-5. XmNrightAttachment set to WXmATTACH_WIDGET

This attachment method is commonly used to *chain* together a series of adjacent widgets. Be careful; this does not guarantee to align widgets vertically. (Remember the shower curtain effect.)

XmATTACH_OPPOSITE_WIDGET

This value is just like **XmATTACH_WIDGET**, except that the widget is attached to the same edge of the specified widget as shown in Figure 8-6.

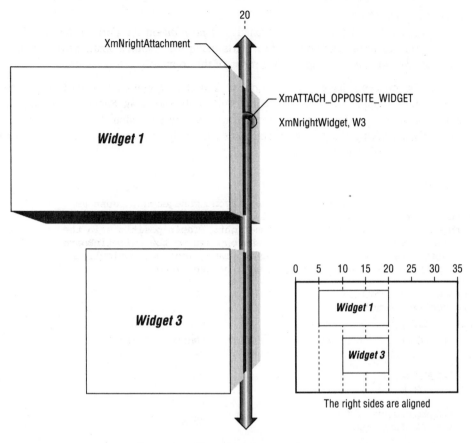

Figure 8-6. XmNrightAttachment set to XmATTACH_OPPOSITE_WIDGET

XmATTACH_NONE

What the top of the widget is attached to is described by the following resources.

XmATTACH_SELF

The widget is attached to its initial position in the Form. In this case, the rod that the hook is anchored to is the vertical or horizontal coordinate on the Form itself. It can slide up and down, or left and right depending on which side of the widget is set to **XmATTACH_SELF**. This is mostly used if you give specific (absolute) x or y coordinates for the widget. By using **XmATTACH_SELF** to a particular side of the widget, you can assure that that side of the widget is not moved from its respective x or y position during resizes or by other widget attachments. For example, if the **Xm-NrightAttachment** and **XmNbottomAttachment** resources were both set to **XmATTACH_SELF**, then the bottom right corner of the widget would be anchored to the position on the Form where it was placed when the widget was created.

XmATTACH_POSITION

When a side of a widget is attached to a *position* on the Form, it implies that the Form has been segmented into *n* parts using the resource **XmNfractionBase**. See Section , for a complete discussion of this topic.

Now that the concepts have been introduced and the programmatic interface has been explained, let's reimplement the four corners example shown in Section . As shown in Example 8-2, there is no longer a need for a resize procedure to calculate the positions of the widgets. By specifying the correct attachments, the widgets are placed and managed correctly by the form when it is resized.

Example 8-2. The form_corners.c program

```
/* form_corners.c -- demonstrate form layout management.  Just as
 * in corners.c, there are four widgets each labeled top-left,
 * top-right, bottom-left and bottom-right.  Their positions in the
 * form correspond to their names.  As opposed to the BulletinBoard
 * widget, the Form manages this layout management automatically by
 * specifying attachment types for each of the widgets.
 */
#include <Xm/PushBG.h>
#include <Xm/Form.h>

char *corners[ ] = {
    "Top-Left", "Top-Right", "Bottom-Left", "Bottom-Right",
};

main(argc, argv)
char *argv[ ];
{
    Widget toplevel, form;
    XtAppContext app;

    toplevel = XtVaAppInitialize(&app, "Demos", NULL, 0,
        &argc, argv, NULL, NULL);

    form = XtVaCreateManagedWidget("form",
        xmFormWidgetClass, toplevel, NULL);

    /* Attach the edges of the widgets to the Form.  Which edge of
     * the widget that's attached is relative to where the widget is
     * positioned in the Form.  Edges not attached default to having
     * an attachment type of XmATTACH_NONE.
     */
    XtVaCreateManagedWidget(corners[0],
        xmPushButtonGadgetClass, form,
        XmNtopAttachment,         XmATTACH_FORM,
        XmNleftAttachment,        XmATTACH_FORM,
        NULL);

    XtVaCreateManagedWidget(corners[1],
        xmPushButtonGadgetClass, form,
        XmNtopAttachment,         XmATTACH_FORM,
        XmNrightAttachment,       XmATTACH_FORM,
        NULL);

    XtVaCreateManagedWidget(corners[2],
        xmPushButtonGadgetClass, form,
        XmNbottomAttachment,      XmATTACH_FORM,
```

Example 8-2. The form_corners.c program (continued)

```
        XmNleftAttachment,          XmATTACH_FORM,
        NULL);

    XtVaCreateManagedWidget(corners[3],
        xmPushButtonGadgetClass, form,
        XmNbottomAttachment,        XmATTACH_FORM,
        XmNrightAttachment,         XmATTACH_FORM,
        NULL);

    XtRealizeWidget(toplevel);
    XtAppMainLoop(app);
}
```

In this case, two sides of each widget are attached to the Form (and only the Form). It wasn't necessary to attach other sides of the widgets to anything else (such as each other) unless we wanted to have the widgets resized (since they would have to stretch to meet each other).

A more sophisticated example of attachments is shown in Example 8-3. This example implements the dialog shown in Figure 8-6.

Example 8-3. The attach1.c program

```
/* attach1.c -- demonstrate how attachments work in Form widgets. */

#include <Xm/PushBG.h>
#include <Xm/Form.h>

main(argc, argv)
int argc;
char *argv[ ];
{
    Widget toplevel, parent, one, two, three;
    XtAppContext app;

    toplevel = XtVaAppInitialize(&app, "Demos", NULL, 0,
        &argc, argv, NULL, NULL);

    parent = XtVaCreateManagedWidget("form",
        xmFormWidgetClass, toplevel, NULL);
    one = XtVaCreateManagedWidget("one",
        xmPushButtonGadgetClass, parent,
        XmNtopAttachment,     XmATTACH_FORM,
        XmNleftAttachment,    XmATTACH_FORM,
        NULL);
    two = XtVaCreateManagedWidget("two",
        xmPushButtonGadgetClass, parent,
        XmNleftAttachment,    XmATTACH_WIDGET,
        XmNleftWidget,        one,
        /* attach top of widget to same y coordinate as top of "one" */
        XmNtopAttachment,     XmATTACH_OPPOSITE_WIDGET,
        XmNtopWidget,         one,
        NULL);
    three = XtVaCreateManagedWidget("three",
        xmPushButtonGadgetClass, parent,
        XmNtopAttachment,     XmATTACH_WIDGET,
        XmNtopWidget,         one,
        /* attach left of widget to same x coordinate as left side of "one" */
        XmNleftAttachment,    XmATTACH_OPPOSITE_WIDGET,
```

Example 8-3. The attach1.c program (continued)

```
        XmNleftWidget,        one,
        NULL);

    XtRealizeWidget(toplevel);
    XtAppMainLoop(app);
}
```

There are three PushButton gadgets inside of a Form widget. The gadgets are created with the necessary attachments to maintain the positional layout shown in Figure 8-7.

Figure 8-7. Output of attach1.c

Not quite what you expected? The widgets are somewhat "rammed" together. This is because we need to specify some distance between them. To do this, we need to introduce a new set of resources called *attachment offsets*.

8.4.2 Attachment Offsets

Attachment offsets control the distances between widgets and the objects they are attached to. Attachment offset resources, represented in Figure 8-8, include the following values:

```
    XmNleftOffset
    XmNrightOffset
    XmNtopOffset
    XmNbottomOffset
```

Normally, offsets are set to 0 (zero), which means that there is no offset, as shown in the output for Example 8-3. To produce more interesting output, we need only to set the left offset between widgets **One** and **Two** and the top offset to between widgets **One** and **Three**. This is easily accomplished either by adding hard-coded values in the application or by using an application defaults file:

```
    *form.one.leftOffset:    10
    *form.one.topOffset:     10
    *form.two.leftOffset:    10
    *form.three.topOffset:   10
```

The value of 10 was used arbitrarily, but the widgets are spaced more appropriately, as shown in Figure 8-9.

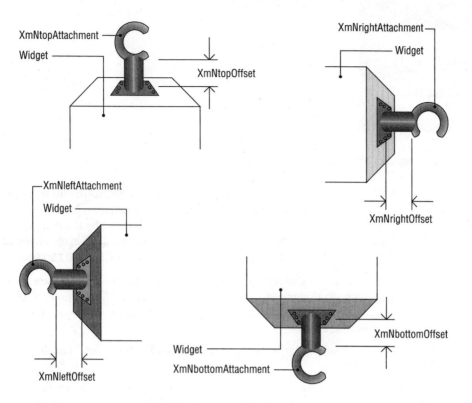

Figure 8-8. Attachment offsets

Figure 8-9. attach1.c with offset resources set to 10

A note of warning: while the layout of the widgets shown can be improved using resource settings, the opposite is also true. Consider what would happen had the resources been specified in the following manner:

```
*form*leftOffset: 10
*form*topOffset:  10
```

It might seem that these resource values are simply a terser way to specify the offsets shown earlier. This is not the case—these resource settings result in Figure 8-10.

Figure 8-10. Output of attach1.c with inappropriately set resources

Obviously, this is not the desired effect. It is the responsibility of the application to set (hard-code) whatever resources may be necessary to prevent the application from becoming non-functional or unaesthetic regardless of the resource values that may be set by the user. Offset resource values can be tricky, because they apply individually to each side of each widget on the Form that uses any of the attachment resources (except for **XmATTACH_POSITION**).

The problem with the particular resources shown in Figure 8-10 is that the offsets are being applied to those widgets whose alignments are intended to be precise. Thus, in order to compensate, we need to specifically hard-code the offsets for those situations. Widgets **Two** and **Three** can be modified as follows:

```
two = XtVaCreateManagedWidget("two", xmPushButtonWidgetClass, parent,
    XmNleftAttachment,   XmATTACH_WIDGET,
    XmNleftWidget,       one,
    /* attach top of widget to same y coordinate as top of "one" */
    XmNtopAttachment,    XmATTACH_OPPOSITE_WIDGET,
    XmNtopWidget,        one,
    XmNtopOffset,        0,
    NULL);

three = XtVaCreateManagedWidget("three", xmPushButtonWidgetClass, parent,
    XmNtopAttachment,    XmATTACH_WIDGET,
    XmNtopWidget,        one,
    /* attach left of widget to same x coordinate as left side of "one" */
    XmNleftAttachment,   XmATTACH_OPPOSITE_WIDGET,
    XmNleftWidget,       one,
    XmNleftOffset,       0,
    NULL);
```

The use of zero-length offsets is important because these values guarantee that the widgets they are associated with are aligned perfectly with the widgets to which they are attached. The general rule of thumb is that whenever you use **XmATTACH_OPPOSITE_WIDGET**, you should also set the appropriate offset to zero so that the alignment remains consistent.

Another way attachment offsets can be tricky is when using them with right or bottom attachments. For example, Figure 8-11 shows that you need a negative value to properly specify a bottom offset when a widget is attached to the bottom of a Form.

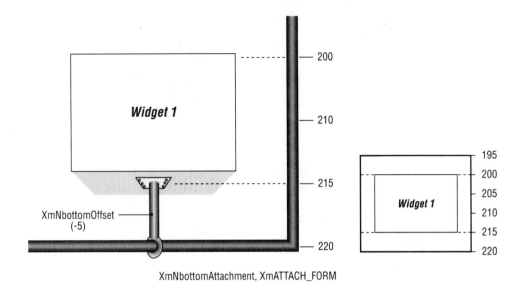

XmNbottomAttachment, XmATTACH_FORM

Figure 8-11. XmNbottomAttachment set to XmATTACH_FORM with negative offset

The lesson here is that attachments in Form widgets are very delicate specifications. You must be specific and, above all, complete in your descriptions of how widgets should be aligned and positioned when using the attachment method. Since resources can be set from many different places, the only way to guarantee that you get the layout you want is to hard-code these resource values explicitly. Remember, though, that it is important to allow the user to specify as many resources as possible (and thus, you should hard-code as few as possible) as long as the integrity of the application is not lost. Attachments and attachment offsets are probably not in that set of resources that should be user-definable.

In order to help determine the best way to attach widgets to one another, it might be helpful to draw pictures first with all hooks and offset values considered. Don't misunderstand the message about attachments and their delicacy. Attachments are a very powerful, convenient, and flexible way to lay out widgets within Forms, especially when widgets are grouped together in some abstract way. Attachments make it easy to chain widgets together, bind them to the edges of the Form, and to allow them to be fixed on specific locations. Don't let their verbosity discourage you.

8.4.3 Extended Example

Let's extend our demonstration of the use of these attachments by examining a common problem encountered by many programmers. Specifically, there are no attachments available to align two widgets horizontally despite their varying heights; we need an `XmNmiddle-Attachment`, but one doesn't exist. Say you have a series of Labels and Text widgets that you want to pair off and stack vertically. The Form constraints that are available to us don't allow for these widgets to be aligned at their midsections; you can attach only their edges.

To solve this problem, let's extrapolate from what we know about manager widgets. We know that by attaching both the top and bottom edges to the Form, the widget will be stretched (resized by the Form) to satisfy the constraints. We also know that managers may contain other manager widgets (like putting smaller boxes into larger ones). Using both of these facts, we can create a Form that contains nothing but smaller Forms. Inside each of the smaller Forms, we place the widgets that are supposed to be aligned with one another. Example 8-4 shows an implementation of this idea.

Example 8-4. The text_form.c program

```
/* text_form.c -- demonstrate how attachments work in Form widgets.
 * by creating a text-entry form type application.
 */

#include <Xm/PushB.h>
#include <Xm/PushBG.h>
#include <Xm/LabelG.h>
#include <Xm/Text.h>
#include <Xm/Form.h>

char *prompts[ ] = {
    "Name:", "Phone:", "Address:",
    "City:", "State:", "Zip:",
};

main(argc, argv)
int argc;
char *argv[ ];
{
    Widget toplevel, mainform, subform, label, text;
    XtAppContext app;
    char buf[32];
    int i;

    toplevel = XtVaAppInitialize(&app, "Demos", NULL, 0,
        &argc, argv, NULL, NULL);

    mainform = XtVaCreateWidget("mainform",
        xmFormWidgetClass, toplevel,
        NULL);

    for (i = 0; i < XtNumber(prompts); i++) {
        subform = XtVaCreateWidget("subform",
            xmFormWidgetClass,    mainform,
            /* first one should be attached for form */
            XmNtopAttachment,     i? XmATTACH_WIDGET : XmATTACH_FORM,
            /* others are attached to the previous subform */
            XmNtopWidget,         subform,
            XmNleftAttachment,    XmATTACH_FORM,
            XmNrightAttachment,   XmATTACH_FORM,
            NULL);
        label = XtVaCreateManagedWidget(prompts[i],
            xmLabelGadgetClass,   subform,
            XmNtopAttachment,     XmATTACH_FORM,
            XmNbottomAttachment,  XmATTACH_FORM,
            XmNleftAttachment,    XmATTACH_FORM,
            XmNalignment,         XmALIGNMENT_BEGINNING,
            NULL);
        sprintf(buf, "text_%d", i);
```

Example 8-4. The text_form.c program (continued)

```
        text = XtVaCreateManagedWidget(buf,
            xmTextWidgetClass,   subform,
            XmNtopAttachment,    XmATTACH_FORM,
            XmNbottomAttachment, XmATTACH_FORM,
            XmNrightAttachment,  XmATTACH_FORM,
            XmNleftAttachment,   XmATTACH_WIDGET,
            XmNleftWidget,       label,
            NULL);
        XtManageChild(subform);
    }
    /* Now that all the forms are added, manage the main form */
    XtManageChild(mainform);

    XtRealizeWidget(toplevel);
    XtAppMainLoop(app);
}
```

The output of the program is shown in Figure 8-12.

Figure 8-12. Output of text_form.c

Notice how the Labels are centered with their corresponding Text widgets. This happened because the Labels were stretched vertically in order to attach to the tops and bottoms of their respective Forms. Of course, if the Labels were higher than the Text widgets (probably due to their having a larger font), the Text widgets would have to be stretched to meet the constraints. Later, we'll show another version of this program that gives better results.

The names given to the Text widgets are **text_**<i> where the *i-th* Text widget can have its resources set externally (by the user or otherwise) if desired. You should be conscientious about the widgets that you want to make available for customization. We are not suggesting that all widgets should be customizable—just that you should think about it and make an intelligent decision.

As you can imagine, there are many other ways for a Form, or any other manager widget to manage the geometry of its children. Later, when we discuss RowColumns, we will take another look at the same type of problem and see how it can be approached differently. Remember, there is no right or wrong way to do things like this; whatever works for your application is the method you should use. However, you should be very careful to experiment with resizing issues as well as with resources that can be set differently by the user (e.g., fonts or strings) and that might affect widget layout.

8.4.4 Common Problems

Because of the intricacies of the Form widget, there are inevitable errors that you might encounter when trying to lay out widgets in a particular format. The most common problem is that of circular dependencies. An example is shown in the following code fragment, which attempts to place two widgets next to each other; the left widget is attached to the right widget and the right widget is attached to the left one.

```
w1 = XtVaCreateManagedWidget("w1", xmLabelGadgetClass, form, NULL);
w2 = XtVaCreateManagedWidget("w2", xmLabelGadgetClass, form, NULL);

/* attach right side of w1 to w2 */
XtVaSetValues(w1,
    XmNrightAttachment, XmATTACH_WIDGET,
    XmNrightWidget,     w2,
    NULL);
/* attach left side of w2 to w1 */
XtVaSetValues(w2,
    XmNleftAttachment, XmATTACH_WIDGET,
    XmNleftWidget,      w1,
    NULL);
```

Most of the time, the Motif toolkit will be able to determine circular dependencies and display an error message if one is found. Unfortunately, we are not able to foretell what kind of situation you may have gotten yourself into if you encounter a circular dependency. Therefore, the only advice we can give is to reconsider your widget layout and try to arrange things such that the relationship between widgets is much simpler and less crowded. Adjacent widgets should be attached in one direction only.

Another common problem is positioning certain Motif composite widgets. For example, `XmCreateScrolledText()` and `XmCreateScrolledList()` both return their corresponding Text and List widgets, but it is the parents of these widgets that need to be positioned within a Form. The following code fragment is an example of positioning a ScrolledList incorrectly:

```
form = XmCreateForm(parent, "form", NULL, 0);

list = XmCreateScrolledList(form, "scrolled_list", NULL, 0);
XtVaSetValues(list,   /* <- WRONG */
    XmNleftAttachment, XmATTACH_FORM,
    XmNtopAttachment,  XmATTACH_FORM,
    NULL);
```

Although a ScrolledList was created as a child of the Form, the List widget itself is a child of a ScrolledWindow object. The attachments specified above will have no effect on the List's positioning within the Form. The correct way to handle this is by setting the resource on the List's parent (which is a ScrolledWindow):

```
XtVaSetValues(XtParent(list),
    XmNleftAttachment, XmATTACH_FORM,
    XmNtopAttachment,  XmATTACH_FORM,
    NULL);
```

The same applies to ScrolledText widgets.

An extremely subtle problem that may arise is the situation where a widget is of fixed size and the Form attempts to resize it. While this may seem obvious most of the time, one particular case that is difficult to find is the case where a List widget (or a ScrolledList) has its **XmNvisibleItemCount** set. This resource implies a specific size requirement; when the List is made part of the Form widget, the negotiation process between the Form and the List may not be resolved. See Chapter 13 for a complete discussion of the List widget.

8.4.5 Form Positions

An alternate way to position widgets within Forms is to use Form *positions*. The concept is similar to the hook and rod principle used in the previous section, but the positions at which widgets are anchored are on imaginary longitude and latitude lines that are used to segment the Form into sections. The resource used to partition the Form into segments is **XmNfractionBase**. Although the name of this resource may suggest complicated calculations, you just need to know that the form is going to be divided horizontally and vertically into the number of partitions represented by its value. For example, Figure 8-13 shows how a Form would be partitioned if **XmNfractionBase** were set to 5.

As you can see, the number of partitions is equal, but the size of the horizontal partitions is not the same as the size of the vertical partitions. It is currently not possible to set the number of horizontal partitions differently than the number of vertical ones. We will explain later how you can compensate for this shortcoming.

Widgets may be placed on the coordinates that represent the partitions by using the same attachment resources used in the previous section. For example, if we wanted to attach the top of a widget to position 1 and the left side of the widget to position 2, the result is shown in Figure 8-14.

The right and bottom attachments are left unspecified, so those edges of the widget are not explicitly positioned by the Form. Had the these edges been specified using some sort of attachment policy (e.g., **XmATTACH_FORM**, **XmATTACH_WIDGET**, etc.) then the widget would have to be resized by the Form in order to satisfy all the attachment constraints.

Manager Widgets

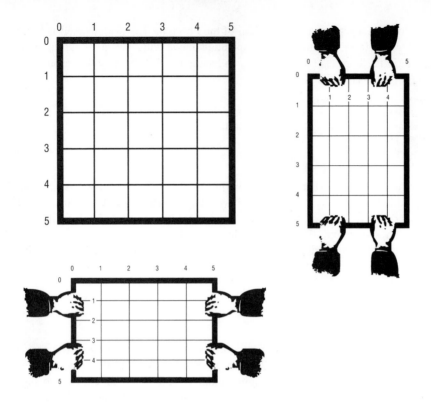

Figure 8-13. Form with XmNfractionBase set to 5

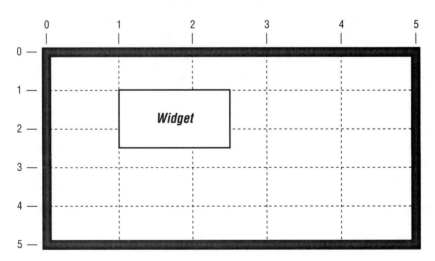

Figure 8-14. Widget with top and left attachments set to positions

The following code fragment would be used to implement the above example:

```
XtVaCreateManagedWidget("name", widgetClass, form_parent,
    XmNtopAttachment,   XmATTACH_POSITION,
    XmNtopPosition,     1,
    XmNleftAttachment,  XmATTACH_POSITION,
    XmNleftPosition,    2,
    NULL);
```

Perhaps the most obvious example of using position attachments is to create a tic-tac-toe board layout (see Example 8-5).

Example 8-5. The tictactoe.c program

```
/* tictactoe.c -- demonstrate how fractionBase and XmATTACH_POSITIONs
 * work in Form widgets.
 */
#include <Xm/PushBG.h>
#include <Xm/Form.h>

main(argc, argv)
int argc;
char *argv[ ];
{
    XtAppContext app;
    Widget toplevel, parent, w;
    int x, y;
    extern void pushed();  /* callback for each PushButton */

    toplevel = XtVaAppInitialize(&app, "Demos", NULL, 0,
        &argc, argv, NULL, NULL);

    parent = XtVaCreateManagedWidget("form", xmFormWidgetClass, toplevel,
        XmNfractionBase,    3,
        NULL);
    for (x = 0; x < 3; x++)
        for (y = 0; y < 3; y++) {
            w = XtVaCreateManagedWidget(" ",
                xmPushButtonGadgetClass, parent,
                XmNtopAttachment,    XmATTACH_POSITION,
                XmNtopPosition,      y,
                XmNleftAttachment,   XmATTACH_POSITION,
                XmNleftPosition,     x,
                XmNrightAttachment,  XmATTACH_POSITION,
                XmNrightPosition,    x+1,
                XmNbottomAttachment, XmATTACH_POSITION,
                XmNbottomPosition,   y+1,
                NULL);
            XtAddCallback(w, XmNactivateCallback, pushed, NULL);
        }

    XtRealizeWidget(toplevel);
    XtAppMainLoop(app);
}

void
pushed(w, client_data, cbs)
Widget     w;           /* The PushButton that got activated */
XtPointer  client_data; /* unused -- NULL was passed to XtAddCallback() */
XmPushButtonCallbackStruct *cbs;
```

Manager Widgets   255

Example 8-5. The tictactoe.c program (continued)

```
{
    char buf[2];
    XmString str;

    /* Shift key gets an O.  (xbutton and xkey happen to be similar) */
    if (cbs->event->xbutton.state & ShiftMask)
        buf[0] = 'O';
    else
        buf[0] = 'X';
    buf[1] = 0;
    str = XmStringCreateSimple(buf);
    XtVaSetValues(w, XmNlabelString, str, NULL);
    XmStringFree(str);
}
```

The output of this program is shown in Figure 8-15.

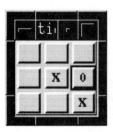

Figure 8-15. Output of tictactoe.c

As you can see, the children of the Form are equally sized because their attachment positions are segmented equally. If the user resizes the Form, all the children maintain their relationship to one another; they simply grow to fill the form.

One of the more common uses of positional attachments is to lay out a number of widgets to be of equal size and equal spacing, such as you might find in the action area of a dialog. Chapter 7, *Custom Dialogs*, goes into detailed discussion of how this might be done.

There may be situations where you want to attach widgets to horizontal positions that do not match up with how you'd like to attach their vertical positions. Since the fraction base cannot be set differently for the horizontal and vertical orientations, you will have to use the highest common denominator as the fraction base value. For example, say you want to position the tops and bottoms of all your widgets to the 2nd and 4th positions as if the Form were segmented vertically into 5 parts. But, you also want to position the left and right edges of those same widgets to the 3rd, 5th, 7th, and 9th positions as if it were segmented into 11 parts. You would have to apply some simple arithmetic and set the value for **Xm-NfractionBase** to (**4x11**) and position the tops and bottoms to the 22nd (**2x11**) and 44th (**4x11**) positions. The left and right edges would have to be set to the 12th (**3x4**), 20th (**5x4**), 28th (**7x4**), and 36th (**9x4**) positions.

As a general note, attachment types need not be used exclusively. It is perfectly reasonable to attach many objects to a single object or to attach widgets to other widgets, the Form, and to positions. However, you should remember that specifying too few attachments might result in misplaced widgets or widgets that "drift" if resized, while too many attachments might cause the Form to be too inflexible.

8.4.6 Other Form Resources

This section describes the other Form resources not covered so far. **XmNhorizontal-Spacing** is used to specify the distance for the left and right attachments between horizontally adjacent widgets, while **XmNverticalSpacing** specifies the distance between vertically adjacent widgets. These values only apply when the left and right offset values are not specified. Therefore, they are intended to be used as offset values global to a Form. A resource-value specification of:

```
*horizontalSpacing: 10
```

is the same as:

```
*leftOffset:    10
*rightOffset:   10
```

The resource **XmNrubberPositioning** specifies the default attachment for widgets in the Form. The default value of **False** indicates that the top and left attachments are, unless otherwise specified, attached to the form. If set to **True**, the attachments are set to **Xm-ATTACH_SELF**. Again, if **XmNtopAttachment** or **XmNleftAttachment** is set to anything other than **XmATTACH_NONE**, then rubber positioning has no effect.

The resource **XmNresizable** is a constraint resource (set on children of Form widgets, not on Forms themselves) and indicates whether children of the Form may be resized by the Form. However, unless a child widget has attachment specifications that may require it to be resized, the Form does not resize its children. If this resource is set and the Form needs to resize the child widget, a warning message is printed. Hint: if you find yourself having to use this resource, you are probably using too many other attachment constraints.

8.5 The RowColumn Widget

The RowColumn widget is a manager widget that, as implied by its name, lays out its children in row and/or column format. Its use, however, is misunderstood by many because it is also used internally by the Motif toolkit to implement a number of special objects not specifically implemented as discrete widgets. For example, RowColumns are used to implement all the Motif menu types such as Popups, Pulldowns, MenuBars, and Option menus. Many of the resources specific to RowColumns are used to implement such objects. However, the Motif convenience functions for creating these objects use most of these resources automatically, so they are generally hidden from the programmer anyway. They are probably of little use to you or the user (in resource files).

One such resource is **XmNrowColumnType,** which indicates how a particular instance of the **XmRowColumn** class is being used. This is always set automatically to one of the following values:

```
XmWORK_AREA — (default)
XmMENU_BAR
XmPULLDOWN
XmMENU_POPUP
XmMENU_OPTION
```

Unless otherwise specified, the type is set to **XmWORK_AREA.** This is also the type that you should use whenever you use RowColumn widgets in your applications. If you want to create a particular menu or MenuBar, you should use one of the appropriate convenience functions rather than try to create them yourself using RowColumns directly. We discuss these special cases in Chapter 4, *The Main Window*, and Chapter 16, *Menus*.

In typical use, RowColumns are very useful for more generic geometry management than the fine tuning necessary for Form and BulletinBoard widgets. RowColumns can be used with a minimum set of resources; the fewer the resources specified for geometry management, the more automatic the geometry management becomes. This automation may or may not be what you want. Consider Example 8-6: several widgets are created inside of a RowColumn widget, yet there are very few constraints specified for how they should be managed.

Example 8-6. The rowcol.c program

```
/* rowcol.c -- demonstrate a simple RowColumn widget.  Create one
 * with 3 pushbutton gadgets.  Once created, resize the thing in
 * all sorts of contortions to get a feel for what RowColumns can
 * do with its children.
 */
#include <Xm/PushBG.h>
#include <Xm/RowColumn.h>

main(argc, argv)
int argc;
char *argv[ ];
{
    Widget toplevel, rowcol;
    XtAppContext app;

    toplevel = XtVaAppInitialize(&app, "Demos", NULL, 0,
        &argc, argv, NULL, NULL);

    rowcol = XtVaCreateManagedWidget("rowcolumn",
        xmRowColumnWidgetClass, toplevel, NULL);

    (void) XtVaCreateManagedWidget("One",
        xmPushButtonGadgetClass, rowcol, NULL);

    (void) XtVaCreateManagedWidget("Two",
        xmPushButtonGadgetClass, rowcol, NULL);

    (void) XtVaCreateManagedWidget("Three",
        xmPushButtonGadgetClass, rowcol, NULL);

    XtRealizeWidget(toplevel);
    XtAppMainLoop(app);
}
```

The output of this simple program is shown in Figure 8-16.

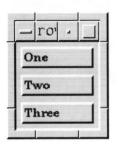

Figure 8-16. Output of rowcol.c

In the default case (with no resources specified), children of RowColumn are laid out vertically. What makes the RowColumn widget unique is that it automates much of the process of widget layout and management. To get a better feel for this, display this application and resize it into many different contortions. Figure 8-17 shows a few of these enumerations.

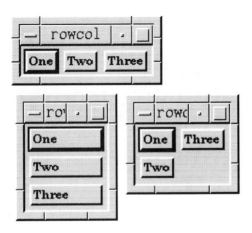

Figure 8-17. Effects of resizing RowColumn widgets

As you can see, if the application is resized just so, the widgets can be oriented horizontally rather than vertically. (This does not necessarily work the other way around. For example, if we were to specify the default orientation to be horizontal, the results are notably different.)

The default orientation can be hard-coded. For C code, the resource is **XmNorientation**:

```
parent = XtVaCreateManagedWidget("rowcolumn",
    xmRowColumnWidgetClass, toplevel,
    XmNorientation,         XmHORIZONTAL,
    NULL);
```

However, for testing purposes, we can specify this value in the resource database instead (to avoid having to recompile the program). To specify this resource, we follow the usual procedure of removing the **XmN** from the resource name (resulting in **orientation**). The resource file could contain:

```
*RowColumn.orientation: horizontal
```

Alternatively, the resource can be specified on the command line:

```
% rowcol —xrm "*orientation: horizontal"
```

The result of setting this resource to the horizontal value is shown in Figure 8-18.

Figure 8-18. Output of rowcol with horizontal orientation set by default

Resizing the widget in various ways renders some interesting results, as shown in Figure 8-19:

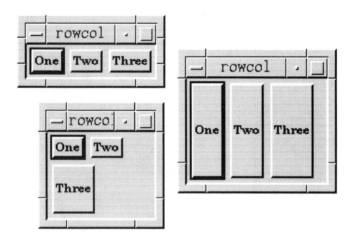

Figure 8-19. Various results from resizing a horizontally oriented RowColumn widget

Generally, you will probably use RowColumn widgets to manage more than just a few objects that can be managed in a singular row or column. It is common to indicate that widgets should be laid out in both rows and columns with additional specifications for whether they should be packed tightly together (where the rows and columns are not necessarily consistent), or whether each object should be placed in an identically-sized box, giving a symmetrical appearance. Of course, as with the Form and BulletinBoard widgets, objects can also be placed in specific x and y locations.

In most cases, the RowColumn widget has no three-dimensional appearance; if you want to provide a visual border for the widget, you should create it as a child of a Frame widget.

8.5.1 Making Rows and Columns

The RowColumn widget can be as flexible or inflexible as your needs require. The advantage to its flexibility is that all the child widgets within it are arranged in an organized fashion no matter what the widget types are, how the RowColumn happens to be resized, or in spite of other constraints imposed by external widgets or resources. The disadvantage is that sometimes a specific layout of children is necessary in order for the user interface to be intuitive or make sense. Let's demonstrate by examining how we would create the layout shown in Figure 8-20.

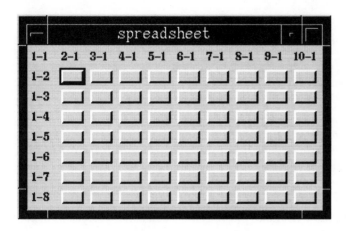

Figure 8-20. Spreadsheet type output (output of spreadsheet.c)

This implementation requires that each of the widgets be of the same size and spaced equally in a predetermined set of rows and columns. Example 8-7 shows how this particular layout can be accomplished using a RowColumn.

Example 8-7. The spreadsheet.c program

```
/* spreadsheet.c -- This demo shows how the most basic use of
 * the RowColumn widget.  It displays a table of widgets in a
 * row-column format similar to a spreadsheet.  This is accomplished
 * by setting the number ROWS and COLS and setting the appropriate
 * resources correctly.
 */
#include <Xm/LabelG.h>
#include <Xm/PushBG.h>
#include <Xm/RowColumn.h>

#define ROWS  8
#define COLS 10

main(argc, argv)
int argc;
char *argv[ ];
{
    Widget toplevel, parent;
    XtAppContext app;
    char buf[16];
```

Example 8-7. The spreadsheet.c program (continued)

```
    int i, j;

    toplevel = XtVaAppInitialize(&app, "Demos", NULL, 0,
        &argc, argv, NULL, NULL);

    parent = XtVaCreateManagedWidget("rowcolumn",
        xmRowColumnWidgetClass, toplevel,
        XmNpacking,      XmPACK_COLUMN,
        XmNnumColumns,   COLS,
        XmNorientation,  XmVERTICAL,
        NULL);

    /* simply loop thru the strings creating a widget for each one */
    for (i = 0; i < COLS; i++)
        for (j = 0; j < ROWS; j++) {
            sprintf(buf, "%d-%d", i+1, j+1);
            if (i == 0 || j == 0)
                XtVaCreateManagedWidget(buf,
                    xmLabelGadgetClass, parent, NULL);
            else
                XtVaCreateManagedWidget("",
                    xmPushButtonGadgetClass, parent, NULL);
        }

    XtRealizeWidget(toplevel);
    XtAppMainLoop(app);
}
```

The number of rows is defined by the ROWS macro and the number of columns is defined by COLS. In order to force the RowColumn to lay out its children in a RowColumn format, we set the resources XmNpacking, XmNnumColumns, and XmNorientation.

The value for XmNpacking is set to XmPACK_COLUMN to indicate that each widget in the rows and columns should be of identical size. All the other widgets will be resized to fit the largest widget(s) in the RowColumn.[6] This is very important to consider when mixing different widget types within a RowColumn. This is one reason why it is common to set Xm-PACK_COLUMN when the widgets are either exactly the same, or similar in nature (as is the case here). The default value of XmPACK_TIGHT will produce variable results, depending on the size of the RowColumn widget, as demonstrated by the earlier examples.

Since we are packing the widgets in a row/column format, we indicate how many columns (or rows) we are going to use by setting the value of XmNnumColumns to the number of columns, whatever that happens to be. In this case, the program defines COLS to be 10. This indicates that the RowColumn should pack its children such that there are 10 columns. It will create as many rows as necessary to provide enough space for all the child widgets.

Whether XmNnumColumns specifies the number of columns or of rows is dependent on the orientation of the RowColumn. That is, in this program, XmNorientation is set to Xm-VERTICAL to indicate that the value of XmNnumColumns indicates the number of columns to use. Had XmNorientation been set to XmHORIZONTAL, then XmNnum-Columns would instead indicate the number of rows. The orientation also dictates how

---

[6] The heights and widths of the widgets are evaluated independently. The largest height and the largest width are used to determine the ultimate size.

children are added to the RowColumn; when the orientation is vertical, children are added vertically as well (e.g., each column is filled up before the next one is started).

In the program, the value of **XmNorientation** is set to the default value of **Xm-VERTICAL** purposely; had we not done so, an external resource specification could have reset it. And unless that external source had also set the value for **XmNnumColumns**, the two values would be inconsistent with one another. Thus, whenever either of these resources are to be set to a value other than its default, both resources should be set. (Whether you choose to hard-code the resources, use the fallback mechanism, or use application defaults files, the important thing to keep in mind is that each resource, if specified, should be in the same place.)

In our example, to achieve the same effect as the vertical orientation using a horizontal one, we could alter the values of the two resources:

```
XmNnumColumns,    ROWS,
XmNorientation,   XmHORIZONTAL,
```

Here, the RowColumn has a horizontal orientation and will create ROWS of widgets (the number of columns may vary). In this case, the two orientations are interchangeable. However, orientation may be significant in other situations. For example, consider a text-entry form as shown in Figure 8-21.

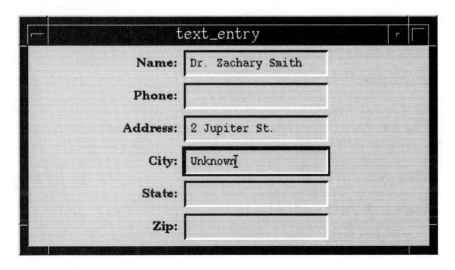

Figure 8-21. Output of text_entry.c

In this case, the order of the widgets may be important. The number of columns is two, and the number of rows is dependent on the number of text entry fields provided by the application. Therefore, we switch the orientation of the RowColumn to **XmHORIZONTAL** and specify **XmNnumColumns** (which now represents *rows*) to the number of entries provided by the application. Thus, we have the program as shown in Example 8-8.

Example 8-8. The text_entry.c program

```
/* text_entry.c -- This demo shows how the RowColumn widget can be
 * configured to build a text entry form.  It displays a table of
 * right-justified Labels and Text widgets that extend to the right
 * edge of the Form.
 */
#include <Xm/LabelG.h>
#include <Xm/RowColumn.h>
#include <Xm/Text.h>

char *text_labels[ ] = {
    "Name:", "Phone:", "Address:", "City:", "State:", "Zip:",
};

main(argc, argv)
int argc;
char *argv[ ];
{
    Widget toplevel, rowcol;
    XtAppContext app;
    char buf[ 8 ];
    int i;

    toplevel = XtVaAppInitialize(&app, "Demos", NULL, 0,
        &argc, argv, NULL, NULL);

    rowcol = XtVaCreateWidget("rowcolumn",
        xmRowColumnWidgetClass, toplevel,
        XmNpacking,        XmPACK_COLUMN,
        XmNnumColumns,     XtNumber(text_labels),
        XmNorientation,    XmHORIZONTAL,
        XmNisAligned,      True,
        XmNentryAlignment, XmALIGNMENT_END,
        NULL);

    /* simply loop thru the strings creating a widget for each one */
    for (i = 0; i < XtNumber(text_labels); i++) {
        XtVaCreateManagedWidget(text_labels[i],
            xmLabelGadgetClass, rowcol,
            NULL);
        sprintf(buf, "text_%d", i);
        XtVaCreateManagedWidget(buf,
            xmTextWidgetClass, rowcol,
            NULL);
    }

    XtManageChild(rowcol);
    XtRealizeWidget(toplevel);
    XtAppMainLoop(app);
}
```

The labels for the text fields are initialized by the **text_labels** string array.[7] When the RowColumn is created, it is set to a horizontal orientation and the number of rows is set to the number of items in **text_labels**. As you can see, this program is similar to

---

[7] The Text widgets themselves are strictly managed by the RowColumn widget. See Chapter 15, *Text Widgets*, for more details on installing callback routines for text-entry type situations.

text_form.c, shown in Section 8.7.3. While the results are slightly different, you can see that Motif provides many ways to solve the same type of problem.

Two new resources found in Example 8-8 are `XmNisAligned` and `XmNentry-Alignment`. These resources control the text positioning for Label and PushButton widgets or gadgets that are children of RowColumn widgets. By default, the text is left justified. While this problem could be solved by setting the Labels' and/or PushButtons' `Xm-Nalignment` resources, it is a convenience to be able to set this same resource on the RowColumn and have it automatically propagate to its children.

When `XmNisAligned` is `True` (the default), the alignment is taken from the `Xm-NentryAlignment` resource. The possible alignment values are the same as those that can be set by the Label's `XmNalignment` resource:

```
XmALIGNMENT_BEGINNING (default)
XmALIGNMENT_CENTER
XmALIGNMENT_END
```

In the case of Example 8-8, we set the alignment to be right justified by using `Xm-ALIGNMENT_END`. This way, the labels' texts are right justified such that they appear to be attached to the Text widgets. See Chapter 11, *Labels and Buttons*, for further examples on how these resources can be used.

8.5.2 Homogeneous RowColumn Children

RowColumns can be set up so that they manage one particular type of widget or gadget. In many cases, this facilitates layout and callback management. For example, MenuBars consist entirely of CascadeButtons that all act virtually the same way. This is also true of certain Popup menus.

The resource `XmNisHomogeneous` indicates whether or not the RowColumn should enforce this restriction among the items it contains. The widget class that is allowed to be managed is specified by the `XmNentryClass` resource. These resources are useful as consistency checkers; if you attempt to add a widget as a child of a RowColumn whose homogeneity does not permit that widget class, then an error message is printed and the widget is not accepted.

Consistency checking in this manner is done internally by the Motif toolkit to prevent you from doing silly things like adding a List widget to a MenuBar, for example. The `Xm-NentryClass` in this case would be set to `xmCascadeButtonWidgetClass`. As another example, when `XmNradioBehavior` is set, the RowColumn only allows Toggle-Button widgets and gadgets to be added. The convenience function `XmCreateRadio-Box()` creates a RowColumn widget with these resources set automatically. (See Chapter 12, *Toggle Widgets*.)

You may not need to use `XmNisHomogeneous` unless you are providing a mechanism that will be exported to other programmers (just as `XmCreateRadioBox()` is provided to you through the Motif toolkit). If you were writing an interactive user-interface builder or a program that creates widgets by scanning text files, you might be concerned that new widgets were of a particular type before adding them to a RowColumn widget. In such cases, you may need to use **XmNisHomogeneous** or **XmNentryClass**. But, unless you are going to provide some method for your application to dynamically create widgets during runtime, these resources will be of little use to you.

Note that **XmNisHomogeneous** can be set at creation-time only. Once a RowColumn is created, you cannot reset this resource although you can always get its value.

8.5.3 RowColumn Callbacks

While the RowColumn inherits those callbacks intrinsic to the manager class, it does not have any specific callback routines associated with it that react to user input. There is no callback for **FocusIn** or **FocusOut** events, but it does have the **XmNmapCallback** and **XmNunmapCallback** callback lists that act identically to the BulletinBoard's. However, the RowColumn is not tuned especially to be a child of DialogShells, although there is no restriction against using them as such.

The only other callback specifically associated with the RowColumn is the **XmNentry-Callback**. This callback resource makes it possible to install a single callback function to act as the *activation callback* for each of a RowColumn widget's children:

```
Widget rowcol;
extern void my_func( );
extern XtPointer data;
XtCallbackRec callbacks[ 2 ];

callbacks[ 0 ].callback = my_func;
callbacks[ 0 ].closure = data;
callbacks[ 1 ].callback = NULL;

XtVaCreateWidget("name", xmRowColumnWidgetClass, parent,
    XmNentryCallback,  callbacks,
    /* other resource-value pairs? */
    NULL);

CreateChildren(rowcol);

XtManageChild(rowcol);
```

Because **XmNentryCallback** is set on the RowColumn parent, the function (or list of functions) specified by this resource will override all **XmNactivateCallback** functions for any PushButton or CascadeButton (widget or gadget) children. It will also reset the **XmNvalueChanged** callback for ToggleButtons. Providing this function is a convenience to the programmer, using the common callback, you don't have to install separate callbacks for each entry in the RowColumn separately. **XmNentryCallback** functions must be installed before children are added or it won't work; therefore, the callback [list] must be specified when the RowColumn is created as shown above, or via **XtAddCallback( )**:

```
XtAddCallback(rowcol, XmNentryCallback, my_func, client_data);
```

The form of the callback procedure is no different from that of any other Motif callback function with the exception of the type of the last parameter:

```
        void
        entry_callback_func(widget, client_data, cbs)
            Widget     widget;
            XtPointer client_data;
            XmRowColumnCallbackStruct *cbs;
```

The **widget** parameter is the RowColumn widget parent of the object that was activated. The **client_data** is the value that was installed in the **closure** field of the **Xt-CallbackRec** data structure, or the value passed to **XtAddCallback( )**. The **cbs** parameter is a pointer of type **XmRowColumnCallbackStruct**:

```
        typedef struct {
            int      reason;
            XEvent   *event;
            Widget   widget;
            char     *data;
            char     *callbackstruct;
        } XmRowColumnCallbackStruct;
```

The **reason** field of this data structure is set to **XmCR_ACTIVATE**. The **event** indicates the event that caused the notification. The entry callback function is called regardless of which widget within the RowColumn was activated. Since entry callbacks override previously-set callback lists for PushButtons, CascadeButtons, and ToggleButtons, the parameters that would have been passed to their callback routines (had they not been overridden) are stuffed into the RowColumn's callback structure. The **widget** field indicates which of the RowColumn's children was activated, the widget-specific callback structure is set in the **callbackstruct** field, and the client data that was set for the widget is set in the **data** field.

For example, Example 8-9 shows how entry callbacks are installed and demonstrates how the normal callback functions are overridden.

Example 8-9. The entry_cb.c program

```
/* entry_cb.c -- demonstrate how the XmNentryCallback resource works
 * in RowColumn widgets.  When a callback function is set for this
 * resource, all the callbacks for the RowColumn's children are reset
 * to point to this function.  Their original functions are no longer
 * called had they been set in favor of the entry-callback function.
 */
#include <Xm/XmP.h>
#include <Xm/PushBG.h>
#include <Xm/PushB.h>
#include <Xm/RowColumn.h>

char *strings[ ] = {
    "One", "Two", "Three", "Four", "Five",
    "Six", "Seven", "Eight", "Nine", "Ten",
};

void
called(widget, client_data, child_data)
Widget widget;
XtPointer client_data; /* data specific to the RowColumn */
XmRowColumnCallbackStruct *child_data;
{
```

Example 8-9. The entry_cb.c program (continued)

```
    Widget pb = child_data->widget;

    printf("%s: %d\n", XtName(pb), child_data->data);
}

static void
never_called()
{
    puts("This function is never called");
}

main(argc, argv)
int argc;
char *argv[ ];
{
    Widget toplevel, parent, w;
    XtAppContext app;
    int i;

    toplevel = XtVaAppInitialize(&app, "Demos",
        NULL, 0, &argc, argv, NULL, NULL);

    parent = XtVaCreateManagedWidget("rowcolumn",
        xmRowColumnWidgetClass, toplevel,
        NULL);
    XtAddCallback(parent, XmNentryCallback, called, NULL);

    /* simply loop thru the strings creating a widget for each one */
    for (i = 0; i < XtNumber(strings); i++) {
        w = XtVaCreateManagedWidget(strings[i],
            xmPushButtonGadgetClass, parent, NULL);
        /* Call XtAddCallback() to install client_data only! */
        XtAddCallback(w, XmNactivateCallback, never_called, i+1);
    }

    XtRealizeWidget(toplevel);
    XtAppMainLoop(app);
}
```

In **main( )**, the RowColumn is created with its **XmNentryCallback** set to **called( )**. That function ignores the **client_data** parameter (none was provided). However, we do use the **data** field of the **child_data** because that is the same data set in the call to **Xt-AddCallback( )** for each of the children.

When the PushButton's activate callback function was installed, we passed a **client_data** value of **(i+1)**, and the function **never_called( )** as the callback function. You may ask, "If I'm going to call **XtAddCallback( )** for a child widget whose callback is not going to be called anyway, just to install client data, why don't I just install the same callback function that is used for the **XmNentryCallback**?"

The most compelling reason for this is that you might want to provide client data for the RowColumn as well as the per-widget client data. See Chapter 12, *Toggle Widgets*, for further examples of using **XmNentryCallback** and other RowColumn-specific resources. That chapter also addresses two more uses for RowColumns: RadioBoxes and CheckBoxes. While these are implemented using RowColumn widgets, they are specific to the management of ToggleButtons and are better explained in that context.

Please remember that the RowColumn widget is used for a great number of objects implemented internally by the Motif toolkit, the foremost being the Motif menu system. Because of this, there are many resources that are not discussed here because they are useless outside of the menu system's context. For more information, see Chapter 4, *The Main Window* and Chapter 16, *Menus*.

8.6 The Frame Widget

Frames are very simple composite widgets that may only contain one child. The sole purpose of a Frame is to draw a visual (three-dimensional) border around its child. The Frame does no geometry management; rather, it "shrink wraps" itself around its child. The child is responsible for setting a Frame's size.

Frames are very useful for grouping related control elements together so they appear conceptually separated from the other elements in a window. Thus, RowColumn widgets, which normally have no three-dimensional border and serve as the parent manager for RadioBoxes, are commonly used as children of Frame widgets. Figure 8-22 shows an example of a dialog where a Frame is used to segregate three toggles from the rest of a dialog box.

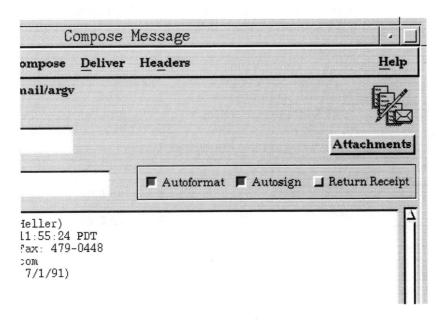

Figure 8-22. A Frame widget containing a RowColumn that in turn contains toggles

To use Frame widgets in an application, you must include the file *<Xm/Frame.h>*. Creating Frame widgets is similar to creating other manager widgets, although you can create Frame widgets as managed:

```
Widget frame;

frame = XtVaCreateManagedWidget("name", xmFrameWidgetClass, parent,
    resource-value pairs,
    NULL);
```

Contrary to the preachings earlier in the chapter, we do not create Frames as unmanaged widgets; we use **XtVaCreateManagedWidget( )** because Frames can only have one child. There is no performance loss because the Frame never has to negotiate anything with its child.

The principal resource used by the Frame widget is **XmNshadowType**. Its value may be any of the following:

```
XmSHADOW_IN
XmSHADOW_OUT
XmSHADOW_ETCHED_IN
XmSHADOW_ETCHED_OUT
```

If the Frame's parent is a shell widget, the default value for **XmNshadowType** is set to **Xm-SHADOW_OUT** and the value for **XmNshadowThickness** is set to 1 (although these values may be overridden by the application or user defaults). Figure 8-23 shows how frames can take different appearances.

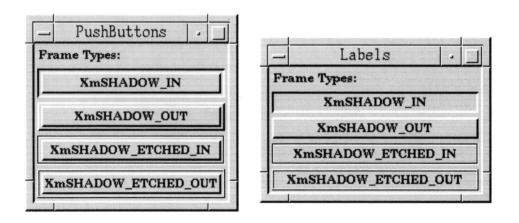

Figure 8-23. Frames managing PushButtons

The program that generated Figure 8-23 is shown in Example 8-10.

Example 8-10. The frame.c program

```
/* frame.c -- demonstrate the Frame widget.
 * Create 4 Labels or PushButtons (depending on an optional -p
 * command line argument) each with a Frame widget as its parent.
 */
#include <Xm/XmP.h>
#include <Xm/PushBG.h>
#include <Xm/LabelG.h>
#include <Xm/RowColumn.h>
#include <Xm/Frame.h>

main(argc, argv)
int argc;
char *argv[ ];
{
    Widget toplevel, rowcol, frame;
    WidgetClass class = xmLabelGadgetClass;
    XtAppContext app;

    /* Initialize toolkit and create TopLevel shell widget */
    toplevel = XtVaAppInitialize(&app, "Demos",
        NULL, 0, &argc, argv, NULL, NULL);

    /* "-p" specifies whether to use PushButton widgets or Labels */
    if (argv[1] && !strcmp(argv[1], "-p"))
        class = xmPushButtonGadgetClass;

    /* Make a RowColumn to contain all the Frames */
    rowcol = XtVaCreateWidget("rowcolumn",
        xmRowColumnWidgetClass, toplevel,
        XmNspacing, 5,
        NULL);

    /* Create different Frames each containing a unique shadow type */
    XtVaCreateManagedWidget("Frame Types:",
        xmLabelGadgetClass, rowcol, NULL);
    frame = XtVaCreateManagedWidget("frame1",
        xmFrameWidgetClass, rowcol,
        XmNshadowType,      XmSHADOW_IN,
        NULL);
    XtVaCreateManagedWidget("XmSHADOW_IN", class, frame, NULL);

    frame = XtVaCreateManagedWidget("frame2",
        xmFrameWidgetClass, rowcol,
        XmNshadowType,      XmSHADOW_OUT,
        NULL);
    XtVaCreateManagedWidget("XmSHADOW_OUT", class, frame, NULL);

    frame = XtVaCreateManagedWidget("frame3",
        xmFrameWidgetClass, rowcol,
        XmNshadowType,      XmSHADOW_ETCHED_IN,
        NULL);
    XtVaCreateManagedWidget("XmSHADOW_ETCHED_IN", class, frame, NULL);

    frame = XtVaCreateManagedWidget("frame4",
        xmFrameWidgetClass, rowcol,
        XmNshadowType,      XmSHADOW_ETCHED_OUT,
        NULL);
    XtVaCreateManagedWidget("XmSHADOW_ETCHED_OUT", class, frame, NULL);

    XtManageChild(rowcol);
```

Example 8-10. The frame.c program (continued)

```
    XtRealizeWidget(toplevel);
    XtAppMainLoop(app);
}
```

The program creates four Frames, each containing a different **XmNshadowType** value. Inside each frame is a Label that identifies the shadow type used for the Frame. An optional command-line option, **-p**, specifies that PushButtons rather than Labels should be used in the Frames. This is to give you an idea of what PushButtons look like within a Frame. Since PushButtons already have the same type of shadows, having the additional border may be an effective technique for providing a pronounced visual cue. Note that Labels should almost never have three-dimensional borders; this implies selectability, and you will probably confuse the user.

8.7 The PanedWindow Widget

The PanedWindow widget lays out its children in a vertically tiled format.[8] The window's width expands to that of its widest managed child and all other children are resized to match that width. The height of the PanedWindow is set to the sum of all its children's heights (plus the spacing between them, and the size of the top and bottom margins).

Applications that wish to use the PanedWindow must include the file *<Xm/PanedW.h>*. An instance of the widget may be created as usual for manager widgets:

```
    Widget paned_w;

    paned_w = XtVaCreateWidget("name", xmPanedWindowWidgetClass, parent,
        resource-value pairs,
        NULL);
    . . .
    XtManageChild(paned_w);
```

The idea behind PanedWindows is that the user can adjust the individual panes to resize the heights of the children providing more or less space as needed on a per-child basis. For example, if the user wants to see more text in a Text widget, he can use the *control sashes* (sometimes called *grips*) to resize the area for the Text widget. This always implies that another widget, either above or below the one being resized, must be resized smaller to compensate for the area size change.

Through constraint resources, children of the PanedWindow may indicate their preferred maximum and minimum sizes. Example 8-11 shows three widgets that are set in a Paned-Window. The output of the program is shown in Figure 8-24.

---

[8] The *Motif Style Guide* also provides for a horizontally-oriented paned window, but the Motif toolkit does not yet support it.

Example 8-11. The paned_win1.c program

```
/* paned_wind1.c --there are two Label widgets that are positioned
 * above and below a Text widget.  The Labels' minimum and maximum
 * sizes are set to 25 and 45 respectively, preventing those
 * panes from growing beyond those bounds.  The Text widget has its
 * minimum size set to 35 preventing it from becoming so small that
 * its text cannot be read.
 */
#include <Xm/Label.h>
#include <Xm/PanedW.h>
#include <Xm/Text.h>

main(argc, argv)
char *argv[ ];
{
    Widget          toplevel, pane;
    XtAppContext  app;

    toplevel = XtVaAppInitialize(&app, "Demos", NULL, 0,
        &argc, argv, NULL, NULL);

    pane = XtVaCreateWidget("pane",
        xmPanedWindowWidgetClass, toplevel,
        NULL);

    XtVaCreateManagedWidget("Hello", xmLabelWidgetClass, pane,
        XmNpaneMinimum,    25,
        XmNpaneMaximum,    45,
        NULL);

    XtVaCreateManagedWidget("text", xmTextWidgetClass, pane,
        XmNrows,           5,
        XmNcolumns,        80,
        XmNpaneMinimum,    35,
        XmNeditMode,       XmMULTI_LINE_EDIT,
        XmNvalue,    "This is a test of the paned window widget.",
        NULL);

    XtVaCreateManagedWidget("Goodbye", xmLabelWidgetClass, pane,
        XmNpaneMinimum,    25,
        XmNpaneMaximum,    45,
        NULL);

    XtManageChild(pane);

    XtRealizeWidget(toplevel);
    XtAppMainLoop(app);
}
```

Figure 8-24. Output of paned_win1.c

In this program, there are two Label widgets that are positioned above and below a Text widget. The Labels' maximum and minimum sizes are set to **25** and **45** pixels respectively using the resources **XmNpaneMinimum** and **XmNpaneMaximum**. That is, no matter how the PanedWindow or any of the other widgets may be resized, the two Labels may not grow or shrink beyond these bounds. The Text widget, however, only has a minimum size restriction, so it may be resized as large or small as the user prefers, provided that it does not get smaller than the 35-pixel minimum. Figure 8-25 shows various sizes of this application. Notice how the "Goodbye" widget is always positioned on the bottom of the pane and is never too big to appear unreasonable.

One problem with setting the maximum and minimum resources for widgets is determining exactly what those extents should be. Had other resources been set on either of the Label widgets that made their sizes grow beyond the maximum bounds, the application would definitely look unbalanced. For example, some extremely high resolution monitors might require users to use unusually large fonts in order for text to appear "normal." The maximum size of **45** for the Label widgets in Example 8-11 was an arbitrary value that was selected for demonstration purposes only. It would not be considered the "correct" thing to do in the general case. There are basically two choices available at this point. One is to specify the maximum and minimum values in a resolution-independent way, and the other is to ask the Label widget itself what height it wants to be. Let's address these two approaches separately.

Specifying resolution-independent dimensions requires you to carefully consider the type of application you are using because the values you specify may only be given in millimeters, inches, points, or font units.

This is demonstrated in Example 8-12.

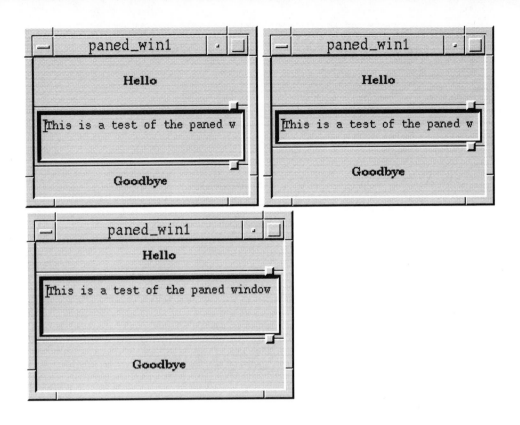

Figure 8-25. Various resizing positions of a PanedWindow

Example 8-12. The paned_win2.c program

```
/* paned_wind2.c --there are two label widgets that are positioned
 * above and below a Text widget.  The labels' desired heights are
 * queried using XtQueryGeometry() and their corresponding maximum
 * and minimum sizes are set to the same value.  This effectively
 * prevents those panes from being resized.  The Text widget has its
 * minimum size set to 35 preventing it from becoming so small that
 * its text cannot be read.
 */
#include <Xm/Xm.h>
#include <Xm/Label.h>
#include <Xm/PanedW.h>
#include <Xm/Text.h>

main(argc, argv)
char *argv[ ];
{
    Widget          toplevel, pane, label;
    XtWidgetGeometry  size;
    XtAppContext  app;

    toplevel = XtVaAppInitialize(&app, "Demos", NULL, 0,
        &argc, argv, NULL, NULL);

    pane = XtVaCreateWidget("pane",
```

Example 8-12. The paned_win2.c program (continued)

```
        xmPanedWindowWidgetClass, toplevel, NULL);

    label = XtVaCreateManagedWidget("Hello",
        xmLabelWidgetClass, pane, NULL);
    size.request_mode = CWHeight;
    XtQueryGeometry(label, NULL, &size);
    XtVaSetValues(label,
        XmNpaneMaximum, size.height,
        XmNpaneMinimum, size.height,
        NULL);
    printf("hello's height: %d\n", size.height);

    XtVaCreateManagedWidget("text", xmTextWidgetClass, pane,
        XmNrows,          5,
        XmNcolumns,       80,
        XmNresizeWidth,   False,
        XmNresizeHeight,  False,
        XmNpaneMinimum,   35,
        XmNeditMode,      XmMULTI_LINE_EDIT,
        XmNvalue,         "This is a test of the paned window widget.",
        NULL);

    label = XtVaCreateManagedWidget("Goodbye",
        xmLabelWidgetClass, pane, NULL);
    size.request_mode = CWHeight;
    XtQueryGeometry(label, NULL, &size);
    XtVaSetValues(label,
        XmNpaneMaximum, size.height,
        XmNpaneMinimum, size.height,
        NULL);
    printf("goodbye's height: %d\n", size.height);

    XtManageChild(pane);

    XtRealizeWidget(toplevel);
    XtAppMainLoop(app);
}
```

In order to query the heights of the two labels, we use the Xt function, `XtQuery-`
`Geometry( )`. The intent of the function is to ask a widget what size it would like to be. It
takes the form:

```
    XtGeometryResult
    XtQueryGeometry(widget, intended, reply)
        Widget widget;
        register XtWidgetGeometry *intended; /* may be NULL */
        XtWidgetGeometry *reply;     /* child's preferred geometry */
```

Since we have no desire to actually resize the widget, we pass `NULL` as the `intended`
parameter. Also, we are not interested in the return value of the function. When the function
returns, the child will tell us what we want to know in the `reply` parameter. We tell the
widget what we want to know by setting the `request_mode` field of the `size` variable,
which is of type `XtWidgetGeometry`. This data structure takes the form:

```
typedef struct {
    XtGeometryMask request_mode;
    Position x, y;
    Dimension width, height, border_width;
    Widget sibling;
    int stack_mode;
} XtWidgetGeometry;
```

The **request_mode** field is checked by the **query_geometry** function within the called widget (a Label widget in this case). Depending on which bits were specified, the appropriate fields are set within the data structure. In Example 8-12, we set **request_mode** to be **CWHeight**, hinting to the Label's **query_geometry** function to return its desired height in the **height** field of the data structure. Had we wanted to know its width as well, we would have set:

```
size.request_mode = (CWHeight | CWWidth);
```

In this case, the **width** and the **height** fields would have been filled in by the Label widget.

Now that we have the Label's desired height, we can set the constraint resources **XmNpane-Maximum** and **XmNpaneMinimum** to the same value: the height of the Label. By making these two values the same, the pane associated with the Label cannot be resized. In most cases, the **XtQueryGeometry( )** method should be used to more reliably determine the minimum and maximum pane extents (if desired).[9]

In most cases, you will find that setting extents is useful, since without them, the user could create unreasonable or unaesthetic widget sizes. When setting the extents for scrolled objects (ScrolledText, ScrolledList, etc.), you are probably not going to be concerned as much about the maximum extents, since scrolling objects are prepared to handle the larger sizes appropriately. Minimum states are certainly legitimate, though. You would probably want to set the height of a font as minimums for Text and Lists, for example.

PanedWindow widgets are very useful for building your own dialogs because there is usually a control area whose size should never be changed and whose position is usually located at the bottom of the shell. See Chapter 7, *Custom Dialogs*, for a complete discussion of how PanedWindows can be used in in this manner.

8.7.1 PanedWindows' Sashes

The PanedWindow widget's sashes are widgets that are not described or defined publicly, and are therefore not technically supported (or may change in the future). While the *Motif Style Guide* says that these objects are part of the PanedWindow widget, the Motif toolkit doesn't happen to make these objects publicly available. However, it is possible to get handles to them if you absolutely need to have them. To do so, you first need to include the header file *<Xm/SashP.h>*. The fact that the file ends in a capital *P* indicates that this is a private header file, and that application programs should technically not include them. The

---

[9] Currently, many of the Motif widgets do not have **query_geometry** methods or do not return sensible values for **XtQueryGeometry( )** calls.

problem is that there is no public header file for Sash widgets, since the widget class is not publicly defined. Therefore, everything there is to know about the Sash widget, including its class declaration and macros, unless you include this private header file. This is necessary as shown in the following code fragment:

```
#include <Xm/SashP.h>
    .
    .
    .
Widget *children;
int num_children;

XtVaGetValues(pane,
    XmNchildren,     &children,
    XmNnumChildren, &num_children,
    NULL);
while (num_children-- > 0)
    if (XmIsSash(children[num_children])) {
        /* it's a sash widget. */
    }
```

The `XmIsSash( )` macro is defined in *<Xm/SashP.h>* as:

```
#define XmIsSash(w)    XtIsSubclass(w, xmSashWidgetClass)
```

Although `XtIsSubclass( )` is a public function, `xmSashWidgetClass` is not publicly declared. Both `XmIsSash( )` and `XtIsSubclass( )` require including the private header file. An example of why it might be important to get handles to the Sash widgets in a PanedWindow is demonstrated in the next section.

8.8 Tab Groups

The *Motif Style Guide* specifies methods by which the user can interact with applications without using the mouse. That is, the user can navigate through applications and/or activate user-interface elements on the desktop using only the keyboard. Such activity is also known as *keyboard traversal*, and is based on the Common User Access (CUA) interface specifications from Microsoft Windows and Presentation Manager. These specifications make heavy use of the TAB key to move between elements in a user interface. (Other keys and modifiers are also used to perform button activation, etc.)

Primitive user-interface controls that have been grouped together with some sort of conceptual consistency are typically also treated as members of a single *tab group*. Just as only one shell on the screen has *keyboard focus*, there may also be one manager or primitive widget that currently has the *input focus*. When keyboard activity occurs in a window, the tookit knows which tab group is current and directs focus or the input mechanisms to the active item within that group. Using the arrow keys, the user moves from one item to the next within the same tab group (like a set of ToggleButtons or a collection of PushButtons). Using the TAB key, the user moves from one tab group to the next.

Certain key combinations take special action on the traversal mechanism. For example, SHIFT+TAB traverses the tab group in the reverse direction. The CTRL key is used to differentiate between an actual *tabbing* traversal command and the TAB key is used as input for a Text widget. The $\boxed{\text{RETURN}}$ and $\boxed{\text{SPACEBAR}}$ keys *activate* or *select* items. (The differing terminology is dependent on the class of widget used.)

To illustrate what happens in a tab group, let's re-examine *tictactoe.c* (shown earlier as Example 8-5 in Section). This program contains one tab group, the Form widget. Because the PushButtons inside of it are elements within the tab group, the user can move between the items in the tic-tac-toe board using the arrow keys on the keyboard as illustrated in Figure 8-26.

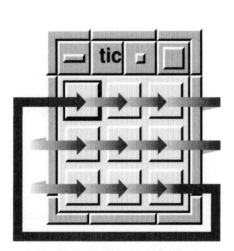
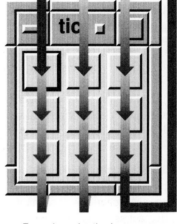

Traversing using the right arrow   Traversing using the down arrow

Figure 8-26. Keyboard traversal for tictactoe.c

Pressing the $\boxed{\text{TAB}}$ key causes the input focus to be directed to the next tab group and set to the first item in the group. (This is also known as the *home* element.) This happens regardless of how many tab groups there are. Since there is only one tab group in this application, the traversal mechanism sets the input focus on the first element in that same group. Thus, pressing the $\boxed{\text{TAB}}$ key in this program always causes the home item to be the current input item.

The conceptual model of the tab group mechanism corresponds to the user's view of the application. That is, in tab groups, the widget tree is flattened out to two simple layers: the first layer contains tab groups, and the second layer contains the elements of those groups. In this design, there is no concept of managers and children or any sort of widget hierarchy. There is only one continuous array of tab groups that contain a set of widgets as its elements.

But, as you know, applications are based on a very structured widget hierarchy. Therefore, tab groups are based on another list of widget pointers that actually refer to the existing group of widgets in the widget tree. These lists, known as *navigation groups*, are maintained by the VendorShell and MenuShell widgets, and are accessed by the input-handling mechanisms of the Motif toolkit.

Each widget class (or predefined object type) in the Motif toolkit is usually initialized as either a tab group leader, or as a member. Managers, Lists and Text widgets are usually tagged as tab groups leaders, since they usually have subelements that can be traversed. Lists, for example, can be traversed using the arrow keys on the keyboard; the up arrow moves the selection to the previous element in the List widget. Text widgets are somewhat different in that the arrow keys move to other characters in the widget's window. Other, simpler widgets such as PushButtons and ToggleButtons are usually tagged as group members.

Output-only widgets are not tagged at all, and are excluded from the tab group mechanism, since you can't traverse to an output-only widget.

None of these default settings are permanent. For example, PushButtons and Toggles can be tagged as being tab group leaders, but this is less common and is only done when the programmer has a special reason for forcing the widget to be recognized as a separate tab group.

When the TAB key is pressed, the next tab group leader becomes the *current* tab group. Because managers are normally tab group leaders, tabbing from one group to the next is typically based on the order the manager widgets were created. This entire process is automated by the Motif toolkit and no interaction from the application is required, unless a different system of tab groups is needed for some reason. In order to maintain Motif compliance, it is recommended that you avoid interfering with the default behavior.

So, why is all this discussed in the chapter on manager widgets? Primarily because manager widgets play the most visible role in keyboard traversal from the application programmer's perspective. Managers, by their nature, contain other widgets, which are typically primitive widgets that act as tab group members. Furthermore, manager widgets must handle all input (events) for gadgets. As a result, a great deal of the functionality supporting keyboard traversal is written into the Manager widget class.

Before we discuss the details of dealing with tab groups, there are a few things we should mention. First, the implementation of tab groups has changed from earlier versions of the toolkit. To maintain backwards compatibility, remnants of the older implementation are still resident in the current implementation. (This may cause some confusion in the current API.) Second, the technology is still being worked on, and although later implementations may not change the existing API, new versions of the toolkit will probably optimize this process substantially. Since the current implementation of tab groups is currently not "perfect," some people want to change the default behavior and control it entirely on their own. This is not recommended. For best results, you should avoid interfering with the keyboard traversal mechanisms. This will help you maintain compatibility with other Motif applications, and require no changes when new versions of the toolkit are available. If you're going to tread on this turf, be careful of what you're doing and test your changes thoroughly.

8.8.1 Tab Group Modification

As we mentioned earlier, the default behavior of the Motif widget set is to add widgets to the traversal list as they are created. Whether a widget is a tab group leader or a member depends on the type of widget it is. If you are going to modify the traversal list, the first thing to learn is how to explicitly prevent a widget from being a part of the traversal list. The mechanism it the same regardless of whether the widget is a tab group leader or member.

By setting a widget's **XmNtraversalOn** resource to **False**, the widget is removed from the traversal list. If the widget is a tab group member, the widget is simply removed from the list and the user cannot traverse to it. If it is a tab group leader, are all its elements are also all removed. Let's experiment with tab group members by modifying *tictactoe.c*. Here, we can modify the **pushed( )** callback routine to remove the selected PushButton from the traversal list as it is selected. If the keyboard is used to traverse and select the items on the tictactoe board, the toolkit automatically skips over those that have already been selected.

```
void
pushed(w, client_data, cbs)
Widget      w;
XtPointer   client_data;
XmPushButtonCallbackStruct *cbs;
{
    .
    .
    .
    str = XmStringCreateSimple(buf);
    XtVaSetValues(w,
        XmNlabelString,    str,
        XmNuserData,       letter,
        XmNshadowThickness, 0,
        XmNtraversalOn,    False,  /* item selected, turn off traversal */
        NULL);
    XmStringFree(str);
}
```

The user can still click on the item with the mouse button, but an error bell will sound.

Output-only widgets, like Labels and Separators (widgets and gadgets), always have their **XmNtraversalOn** resource initialized to **False**. In most cases, setting them value to **True** would present an annoyance to the user, since these objects cannot be respond to keyboard input anyway. The user would have to traverse many unimportant widgets to get to a desired item. However, it is commonly overlooked that Labels can have **XmNhelp-Callback** routines associated with them. (Separators can't.) If the keyboard traversal mechanism were to allow the user to traverse to Labels, he could get help on them by traversing to them and pressing the HELP or F1 keys. It may be considered a design flaw in Motif that a non-mouse driven interface is not supported when getting help for these objects. However, this is not generally regarded as a problem, since most people don't try to get help on Labels, nor do programmers install help for them.

Aside from the possible exception with Labels, turning off the **XmNtraversalOn** resource is generally not something that should be done on a per-widget-class basis. That is, it would not be very useful to have the following resources set in an application defaults file:

```
*XmPushButtonGadget.traversalOn: false
```

This resource setting would not be necessary unless you had a very uncommon program. It is usually the case that if keyboard traversal is something you wish to modify in your application, you should probably hard-code **XmNtraversalOn** values directly into individual widgets as you create them.

Modifying PanedWindows' Sashes

Along these lines, there is a general problem that people tend to have with PanedWindow widgets. That is, as manager widgets, the PanedWindow is a tab group leader, which implies that as its children are added, each child is a member of the tab group and can be traversed accordingly. If you run the program in Example 8-12 and use the ⟶TAB⟵ key to move from one widget to the next, you'll find that the traversal also includes the Sash widgets. Many people find this to be an annoyance, since chances are more likely that, when using keyboard traversal, they'll want to skip over the Sashes than use them to resize any of the panes. (That is, while it is common to resize panes, people usually do so using the mouse.)

When a PanedWindow is created, it does not yet contain any Sashes. Only when new children are added to the PanedWindow are new panes and Sash widgets added. This presents several problems: first, you cannot override the traversability of the Sashes in a Paned-Window using either hard-coded values in the PanedWindow's widget creation call, or in the app-defaults resource settings. In the first case, this is because the Sashes aren't created yet, so hard-coded resources would have no effect. (Hard-coded resources can only affect widgets that are created *at the time of the creation call*.) Second, and more importantly, the internals of the PanedWindow widget *hard-code* its Sash widgets' **XmNtraversalOn** resources to **True** as they are created! This eliminates your ability to turn traversal off using resources.

The only thing to do is reset all the PanedWindow's sashes after all its children have been added (or at least, after each sash is created). Example 8-13 demonstrates a convenient method for doing this based on the code fragment from Section .

Example 8-13. Resetting XmNtraversalOn on all the Sashes in a PanedWindow

```
void
TurnOffSashTraversal(pane)
Widget pane;
{
    Widget *children;
    int num_children;

    XtVaGetValues(pane,
        XmNchildren,     &children,
        XmNnumChildren, &num_children,
        NULL);
    while (num_children-- > 0)
        if (XmIsSash(children[num_children]))
            XtVaSetValues(children[num_children], XmNtraversalOn, False, NULL);
```

}

Note that there are some applications that might actually have to be used without a mouse, so you should be careful about turning off keyboard traversal for PanedWindow widgets. (Be especially careful about hard-coding **XmNtraversalOn** to **False**.) Therefore, we cannot necessarily recommend this type of behavior, but chances are you'd be doing your users more good than bad.

As noted earlier, **XmNtraversalOn** can be set on tab group leaders (which tend to be manager widgets) as well as group members. If traversal is off for a group leader, none of its members can be traversed.

8.8.2 Navigation Types

Whether a widget is a tab group leader or a member is controlled by its **XmNnavigation-Type** resource. When set to **XmNONE**, the widget is not a tab group, so it defaults to being a member of one. As a member, its **XmNtraversalOn** resource indicates whether or not the user can direct input focus to the widget using the keyboard. This is the default value for most primitive widgets. When set to **XmTAB_GROUP**, the widget is a tab group leader, so it is included in keyboard navigation. This is the default value for managers, Lists and Text widgets.

It is possible to specify that a primitive widget is a tab group, and as a result, the user can only get to it using the TAB key, not one of the arrow keys. You can demonstrate this for yourself by modifying *tictactoe.c* and setting each PushButton's **XmNnavigationType** to **XmTAB_GROUP** and running the program.

Backwards Compatibility

There are two other values for **XmNnavigationType** that are used for backwards compatibility with older versions of the toolkit. They are generally unused unless you are porting programs from Motif version 1.0. In this earlier version of the toolkit, a widget was made a tab group leader by calling **XmAddTabGroup( )**. It used to be that this call had to be done by the application for all manager widgets, but now it is no longer necessary. However, older programs written for Motif 1.0 were written according to the older specifications, which required the programmer to specify precisely which widgets were group leaders, which were group members, and which weren't even traversable. To maintain backwards compatibility, whenever **XmAddTabGroup( )** is called, the toolkit assumes the programmer is using the old Motif 1.0 specifications and disables the new, automatic behavior. Unless you are already familiar with the old behavior and your application is currently using the old API, you can probably skip to the next section.

Manager Widgets

Calling **XmAddTabGroup( )** is equivalent to setting **XmNnavigationType** to **Xm-EXCLUSIVE_TAB_GROUP**. If this value is set on a widget (or if **XmAddTabGroup( )** is called), then new widgets are no longer added as tab groups automatically. (Thus, you get the old behavior.) An "exclusive tab group" is much the same as a normal tab group, but Motif recognizes this special value, and if so, ignores all widgets that have the newer **Xm-TAB_GROUP** resource set. In other words, think of this new value as setting exclusivity on the tab group behavior.

If **XmSTICKY_TAB_GROUP** is used on a widget, it is included automatically in keyboard traversal navigation, even if another widget has its navigation type set to **Xm-EXCLUSIVE_TAB_GROUP** or if **XmAddTabGroup( )** has been called. This is the slight workaround towards the new behavior, but not exactly. That is, you can set a widget to be a "sticky tab group" without completely eliminating the old behavior, but it also doesn't interfere with the new behavior.

Again, these two particular values should be ignored for all intents and purposes. If you are worried about porting your old code to new Motif code, you might consider removing all calls to **XmAddTabGroup( )** and just go with the new behavior. For best results, and only if you need to change the default behavior, you should use **XmNONE** or **XmTAB_GROUP** to control whether or not a widget is a tab group (as manager widgets tend to be) or as a member of one (primitives). To control whether the widget is part of the whole keyboard traversal mechanism, use the **XmNtraversalOn** resource.

8.8.3 Event Translations

In order for manager widgets to implement the keyboard traversal, they have their own event translation tables that specify what happens when certain events occur. As discussed in Chapter 2, *The Motif Programming Model*, the translation table specifies a series of one or more *events* and a corresponding *action* to execute if that event occurs. This is all handled automatically by the X Toolkit Intrinsics; when the user presses TAB the Intrinsics look up the event **<Key>Tab** in this table, and executes the corresponding action procedure. In this case, that procedure is responsible for advancing the current tab group to the next one on the list.

This mechanism is also dependent on the window hierarchy of the widget tree. That is, events are first delivered to the widget associated with the window where the event took place. If that widget (or its window) does not handle the event type delivered, it passes the event up the window tree to its parent, which then has the option of dealing with the event. Assuming that the parent is a manager widget of some kind, it now has the option to process the event. If it happens to be a keyboard traversal event, that processing is handled by the appropriate action routine. Obviously, this makes the strong assumption that the primitive widget does not specify any event translations that might conflict with the manager's translations that implement keyboard traversal.

The default event translations that manager widgets use to handle keyboard traversal are currently set as follows:[10]

```
<Key>osfBeginLine:        ManagerGadgetTraverseHome( )
<Key>osfUp:               ManagerGadgetTraverseUp( )
<Key>osfDown:             ManagerGadgetTraverseDown( )
<Key>osfLeft:             ManagerGadgetTraverseLeft( )
<Key>osfRight:            ManagerGadgetTraverseRight( )
Shift ~Meta ~Alt <Key>Tab: ManagerGadgetPrevTabGroup( )
~Meta ~Alt <Key>Tab:      ManagerGadgetNextTabGroup( )
<EnterWindow>:            ManagerEnter( )
<LeaveWindow>:            ManagerLeave( )
<FocusOut>:               ManagerFocusOut( )
<FocusIn>:                ManagerFocusIn( )
```

Note that the OSF-specific keysyms (key symbols) are vendor-defined, which means that the directional arrows must be defined by the user's system at runtime. Note that values like **<Key>osfUp** and **<Key>osfDown** may not be the same as **<Key>Up** and **<Key>Down**.

The routines that handle keyboard traversal are prefixed by **ManagerGadget***. These functions, despite their names, are not necessarily specific to gadgets; they are used to handle keyboard traversal for all children in the manager. As noted earlier, it is important for widgets not to have any translations that conflict with the manager's translations defined previously. If any do, and that widget also has the input focus, the user cannot use those events to do keyboard traversal.

To demonstrate this problem, the following code fragment shows how a primitive (PushButton) widget's translation table can interfere with the keyboard traversal mechanism in its parent:

```
Widget pb;
XtActionRec action;
extern void do_tab( );

actions.string = "do_tab";
actions.proc = do_tab;
XtAddActions(&actions, 1);

pb = XtVaCreateManagedWidget("name", xmPushButtonWidgetClass, parent,
    resource-value pairs,
    NULL);
XtOverrideTranslations(pb, XtParseTranslationTable("<Key>Tab: do_tab"));
```

The translation table that is merged into the existing translations for the PushButton widget is not interfering with the actual translation table in the manager widget, but it is interfering with the events that allow the manager's translation table to do what it's supposed to do. That is, when TAB is pressed, the action-function **do_tab( )** is called, and the event is consumed by the PushButton widget—it is not propagated up to the manager widget so it can do keyboard traversal. This is potentially a problem, but there is a workaround: **do_tab( )** can actually process the keyboard traversal on its own (in addition to whatever else it's doing with the TAB key). This is discussed in the next section.

---

[10] This table is accurate as of Motif version 1.1.3.

Since managers may also have gadgets, manager widgets must also handle input destined for gadgets. Recall that since gadgets have no windows, they can't receive events. Only the manager widget acting as the gadget's parent can receive events destined for gadgets. The manager widget therefore has the following additional translations to handle input on behalf of gadgets:

```
<Key>osfActivate:                   ManagerGadgetSelect( )
<Key>osfSelect:                     ManagerGadgetSelect( )
<Key>osfHelp:                       ManagerGadgetHelp( )
~Shift ~Meta ~Alt <Key>Return:      ManagerGadgetSelect( )
~Shift ~Meta ~Alt <Key>space:       ManagerGadgetSelect( )
<Key>:                              ManagerGadgetKeyInput( )
<BtnMotion>:                        ManagerGadgetButtonMotion( )
<Btn1Down>:                         ManagerGadgetArm( )
<Btn1Down>,<Btn1Up>:                ManagerGadgetActivate( )
<Btn1Up>:                           ManagerGadgetActivate( )
<Btn1Down>(2+):                     ManagerGadgetMultiArm( )
<Btn1Up>(2+):                       ManagerGadgetMultiActivate( )
```

Unlike the default translations, widget translations cannot interefere with those that handle events destined for gadgets. Obviously, if a widget had the input focus, the user's actions could not be destined for a gadget. (The user would have to traverse to the gadget first, in which case the manager would really have the input focus, even though a gadget may be the "current" item in the tab group.)

In Chapter 10, *The DrawingArea Widget*, there is a discussion of the problems with handling input events on the DrawingArea widget. These may be events that you want to process in your application, but they could also be processed by the DrawingArea itself. This is really a semantic problem because there is no way to determine which action-procedure should be invoked for each event—the DrawingArea's manager-based actions, or the application-specified actions defined by the program.

Also note that the last two specifications involving `<Btn1Down>(2+)` and `<Btn1-Up>(2+)` cannot be processed because there is a conflict with the specifications for `<Btn1Down>,<Btn1Up>`. Due to current bugs with the X11 Release Four version of the Toolkit Intrinsics, the translation mechanism's state machine is not robust enough to determine when a double-click event happens because the down-up event has already been consumed by the earlier translation entry. This has been fixed in X11R5, but you should be aware of it for backwards compatibility. For a discussion on using double-button clicks, see Chapter 11, *Labels and Buttons*; for a further discussion of translation tables and action routines, see Chapter 3, *Overview of Motif Widgets*, and Volume Four, *X Toolkit Intrinsics Programming Manual*.

8.8.4 Processing Traversal Manually

At times, it becomes either convenient or necessary to invoke a traversal of some kind as a result of something the user has done. For example, say you have an action area where each PushButton executes a callback function and then sets the input focus to the home item in that tab group (presumably to protect the user from inadvertently reselecting the same item twice). The three frames in Figure 8-27 show this sequence of operations.

Figure 8-27. Changing item focus on button activation

In this figure, the current input focus is on the **Cancel** button; when it is selected, the input focus is changed to the **Ok** button. Example 8-14 demonstrates how this can be accomplished.

Example 8-14. The proc_traversal.c program

```
/* proc_traverse.c -- demonstrate how to process keyboard traversal
 * from a PushButton's callback routine.  This simple demo contains
 * a RowColumn (a tab group) and three PushButtons.  If any of the
 * PushButtons are activated (selected), the input focus traverses
 * to the "home" item.
 */
#include <Xm/PushBG.h>
#include <Xm/RowColumn.h>

main(argc, argv)
int argc;
char *argv[ ];
{
    Widget toplevel, rowcol, pb;
    XtAppContext app;
    void do_it();

    toplevel = XtVaAppInitialize(&app, "Demos", NULL, 0,
        &argc, argv, NULL, NULL);

    rowcol = XtVaCreateManagedWidget("rowcolumn",
        xmRowColumnWidgetClass, toplevel,
        XmNorientation, XmHORIZONTAL,
        NULL);

    (void) XtVaCreateManagedWidget("Ok",
        xmPushButtonGadgetClass, rowcol, NULL);

    pb = XtVaCreateManagedWidget("Cancel",
        xmPushButtonGadgetClass, rowcol, NULL);
    XtAddCallback(pb, XmNactivateCallback, do_it, NULL);

    pb = XtVaCreateManagedWidget("Help",
        xmPushButtonGadgetClass, rowcol, NULL);
    XtAddCallback(pb, XmNactivateCallback, do_it, NULL);

    XtRealizeWidget(toplevel);
    XtAppMainLoop(app);
}

/* callback for pushbuttons */
void
do_it(w)
Widget w;
```

Example 8-14. The proc_traversal.c program (continued)

```
{
    /* do stuff here for PushButton widget */
    (void) XmProcessTraversal(w, XmTRAVERSE_HOME);
}
```

The callback routine associated with the PushButtons does whatever it needs, and then calls
XmProcessTraversal( ) to change the input item to the home item, which happens to
be the **Ok** button. This function can be used when the application needs to set the current
item in the tab group to another widget or gadget, or it can be used to traverse to a new tab
group. The function takes the following form:

```
Boolean
XmProcessTraversal(widget, direction)
    Widget widget;
    int    direction;
```

The function returns **False** if the VendorShell associated with the widget has no tab groups,
the input focus policy doesn't make sense, or if there are other extenuating circumstances
that would be considered unusual. It is unlikely that you'll ever have this problem.

The **direction** parameter can be any of the following values:

```
XmTRAVERSE_CURRENT
XmTRAVERSE_NEXT
XmTRAVERSE_PREV
XmTRAVERSE_HOME
XmTRAVERSE_UP
XmTRAVERSE_DOWN
XmTRAVERSE_LEFT
XmTRAVERSE_RIGHT
XmTRAVERSE_NEXT_TAB_GROUP
XmTRAVERSE_PREV_TAB_GROUP
```

All but the last two cases are for traversing to items within the current tab group; the last two
are for traversing to the next or previous tab group relative to the current one. In the particular case for Example 8-14, the call to **XmProcessTraversal( )** forces the home element to be the current item in the current tab group.

Using what we know about callback routines, we can actually pass the function **Xm-
ProcessTraversal( )** as a callback routine for a widget. Recall how callback routines
work: they take a widget parameter as their first argument and a client data as the second
parameter. **XmProcessTraversal( )** also works in the same way: it takes a widget and
a traversal-direction as its two parameters, so this model conveniently fits into the way callback functions are called. Thus, the following call does the same thing as the code fragment
above, but does not require the existing callback routine to call **XmProcess-
Traversal( )**:

```
XtAddCallback(pb, XmNactivateCallback, XmProcessTraversal, XmTRAVERSE_HOME);
```

For a more sophisticated example of how this is done using Text widgets, see the program
text_box.c, which can be found in Section 15.7, *Single-line Text Widget Callbacks*.

Setting Input Focus Explicitly

The problem with `XmProcessTraversal()` is that you can only move in a relative direction from the item that has the input focus. This is good enough in most cases, since you should try to avoid controlling the user's actions so tightly. That is, the logic of your application should not rely on the user following any particular input sequence. However, it is often the case where you cannot determine where any particular widget is in the widget tree relative to the current input item, what the current item is, or how to traverse to a specific widget regardless of the current item.

In many cases, you can make the following call:

```
XmProcessTraversal(desired_widget, XmTRAVERSE_CURRENT);
```

This sets the `desired_widget` to take the input focus, but *only if the shell that contains the widget already has focus*. If it doesn't, nothing happens—at least, not until the shell obtains keyboard focus. Once it does, then `desired_widget` should have the input focus.

Certain conditions could exist that make this function appear not to work. For example, if you just create a dialog and want to set the keyboard focus directly onto one of its subwidgets, then you may or may not get this to happen, depending on whether or not the dialog has been realized, mapped to the screen and keyboard focus has been accepted.

Unfortunately, there is no general solution to the problem because the Motif toolkit isn't very robust about the programmer changing input focus out from under it. You cannot call generic X functions like `XSetInputFocus()` to force a widget to take input focus, or you will undermine Motif's attempt at monitoring and controlling the input policy on its own.

8.9 Summary

Manager widgets are the backbone of an application. Without them, widgets have no way of controlling their sizes, layout, and input focus model. While the Motif toolkit provides many different manager widget classes, you may find there are lots of things you can't do with them. Those who are experienced toolkit programmers have found that it is possible to port other Constraint class widgets from other toolkits by subclassing them from the generic Manager widget class, but this is beyond the scope of this book.

Manager widgets are a fundamental part of any Xt-based toolkit, so you should be familiar enough with them that this chapter is somewhat of a review process and an introduction to Motif-based widget classes. If the basic concepts presented in this chapter are still somewhat foreign to you, see Volume Four, *X Toolkit Intrinsics Programming Manual*, for a more in-depth discussion of geometry management and the philosophy behind toolkits in general.

Manager Widgets

9

ScrolledWindows and Scrollbars

This chapter describes the ins and outs of scrolling, with particular attention to application-defined scrolling, which is often required when the simple scrolling provided by the ScrolledWindow widget is insufficient.

In This Chapter:

9

ScrolledWindows and Scrollbars

The ScrolledWindow widget provides a viewing area into some other (usually larger) visual object. This *viewport* may be adjusted by the user through the use of Scrollbars attached to the ScrolledWindow. While the Motif MainWindow, ScrolledList, and ScrolledText objects use ScrolledWindows to implement their respective user-interface objects, the Scrolled-Window can also be used independently to provide a viewport into other "large" objects such as a DrawingArea or a manager widget that contains another large group of widgets. We will explore all of these scenarios throughout this chapter.

9.1 ScrolledWindow Design Model

To the user, there is only one way to interact with ScrolledWindows—through Scrollbars. Internally, however, there are several ways to implement what the user sees. These methods are based on two different kinds of scrolling models: automatic and application-defined scrolling. In both cases, the ScrolledWindow is given a *work window* that contains the visual data to be viewed. In automatic scrolling mode, the ScrolledWindow operates entirely on its own, adjusting the viewport as necessary in response to Scrollbar activity. The application simply creates the desired data (say, a Label widget containing a large pixmap) and makes that widget the work window for the ScrolledWindow. When the user operates the Scrollbars to change the visible area, the ScrolledWindow adjusts the Label so that the appropriate portion is visible. This design has been demonstrated in Chapter 4, *The Main Window*, and Chapter 10, *The DrawingArea Widget*.

For application-defined scrolling, the ScrolledWindow does not consider the work window to be "complete"; it assumes that another entity (the application or the internals of another widget) controls the data within the work window, and that the data may change dynamically as the user scrolls around. In order to control the data (scroll), the application must also control all aspects of the Scrollbars. This level of control is necessary when it is impossible or impractical for the application to provide the ScrolledWindow with a sufficiently large work window (or the data for it) at any one time.

We will address each of the two scrolling models separately in the next two sections. However, keep in mind that they share many of the same concepts and features.

9.1.1 Automatic ScrolledWindows Model

Most of the time, ScrolledWindows are used in automatic scrolling mode. The general design of the automatic ScrolledWindow widget is illustrated in Figure 9-1.

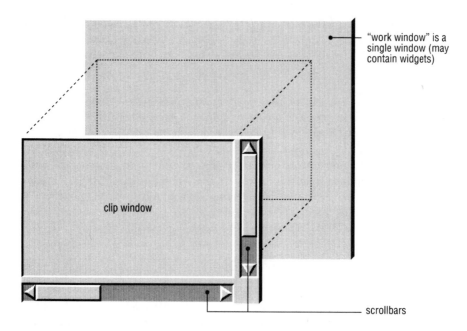

Figure 9-1. Design of an automatic ScrolledWindow

The ScrolledWindow contains at most three internal widgets: two Scrollbars and a *clip window*, which is internally implemented as a DrawingArea widget. The "work area" is an external widget (specified by the `XmNworkWindow` resource) that is "clipped" by the clip window. This widget *is* a child of the ScrolledWindow, but it is provided by the application; it is not created automatically by the ScrolledWindow as the others are. When the user interacts with the Scrollbars, the work window is adjusted so that a different part is visible through the clip window. The work window can be almost any widget, but there may only be *one* work window per ScrolledWindow. If you want to give the illusion that there is more than one widget inside the ScrolledWindow, you can place all the widgets you like in a manager widget and make that manager the work window.

The clip window is always the size of the *viewport* portion of the ScrolledWindow (that is, the ScrolledWindow's size minus the Scrollbars and any borders and margins.) The clip window is never adjusted in size unless the ScrolledWindow is resized, and it is always "fitted" at the origin. That is, you cannot use `XtMoveWidget( )` or change its `XmNx` and `XmNy` resources to reposition it in the ScrolledWindow. The internals of the ScrolledWindow are solely responsible for changing the view in the clip window, although you have the ability to affect this behavior. While you can get a handle to the clipping window, you cannot remove it or replace it with another window.

9.1.2 Application-defined ScrolledWindow Model

In the *application-defined* model (the default), the ScrolledWindow makes itself the same size as the work window, whatever size that happens to be. Just as for automatic scrolling, the application must provide the work window as a widget-child of the ScrolledWindow. (The data for the work window widget is irrelevant to the ScrolledWindow.) You would choose the application-defined scrolling model if the work window contains more data than can possibly be loaded in the automatic scrolling mode. Your application may also require different scrolling behavior than the default pixel-by-pixel increments provided by the automatic scrolling mode. And finally, application-defined scrolling is also best used when the contents of the work window changes dynamically and you don't want to rely on the ScrolledWindow to scroll new data into view.

The disadvantage to application-defined scrolling is that you, not the ScrolledWindow, is responsible for the creation and management of the Scrollbars as well as responding to the scrolling actions that take place within them. Since what is displayed in the clip window and the work window are identical, the ScrolledWindow widget doesn't even bother to create a clip window. There are some limitations to what the ScrolledWindow can support, however, so it is important that you understand them before designing your application. Let's look at two examples.

For the first example, consider a classic example of application-defined scrolling: a Text widget that displays the contents of an arbitrarily large file. Under the automatic scrolling model, the ScrolledWindow widget might possibly have to create a work window large enough to render thousands of lines of text in order to make them all immediately available to the user. An object of such proportions would be prohibitive for reasonable performance and resource consumption. (A List widget with thousands of items would have the same problem.) For these widgets, since the work window cannot be as large as it would need to be for automatic scrolling, the window might as well be as small as possible: the size of the clip window. For example, if a Text widget is a child of a ScrolledWindow, it creates its own Scrollbars and attaches callback routines to them so that it can be notified of scrolling actions. When the user scrolls, the Text widget changes the text in the work window with the text that corresponds to the new (hypothetical) region that just scrolled into view. Here, the user has the illusion that scrolling is taking place, but in reality, the data in the work window has simply changed, thereby saving a great deal of overhead in system and server resources. Remember, the work window is exactly the same size as the clip window. None of the automatic scrolling techniques can be used by the ScrolledWindow or by the application (or portions of the toolkit).

The Text and List widgets are the only examples of application-defined scrolling supported by the current implementation of the ScrolledWindow. However, there is another scenario, in which a large amount of data is retrieved dynamically, and is not all available at the same time. Even though the ScrolledWindow doesn't really support this scenario, there are some workarounds possible, which we'll discuss later in the chapter. At the least, you should be familiar with the problem, since it may come up in many large applications.

Let's say that the Pacific Gas and Electric Company has an on-line database containing all the pipeline information for California, and that an operator wants to view the data for San Francisco county. To display this information, the application must read the data from the database, and convert that data into an image that can be presented in a ScrolledWindow. However, while the database cannot get all the information for the whole county all at once, it can get more information than the window can display. Let's say the window can display 10% of the county, and the database can return information on 20% of the county in a reasonable amount of time. The application would still need to use the application-defined mechanisms because 100% of the data is not available for automatic scrolling. The fact that more than what can be displayed *is* available just means that the application could optimize itself by avoiding unnecessary retrieval of data from the database whenever scrolling takes place. The application would be reusing the existing work window as a *cache*; if the user scrolls in amounts that are small enough, the work window should be redisplayed in ways similar to the automatic scrolling mechanisms. (The application would still have to do this "manually," though).

Unfortunately, the ScrolledWindow does not support this behavior. The ScrolledWindow always expands to the size of its work window in application-defined scrolling mode. In other words, you can't have a work window that is a different size from the clip window. So, you are left with several design decisions in your application. You could reduce the amount of data obtained from a database query, throw away excess information not used in your display, make the viewport of the automatic ScrolledWindow large enough for each query, or use some other method for making the size of the work window conform to that of the clip window. However, the best approach is the *if you can't beat 'em, join 'em* attitude. Make the work window exactly as large as the clip window. This may present some logistical problems with your application's design, but we'll discuss some workarounds for this situation later on in this chapter.

In the two preceding examples, we have defined two fundamentally similar methods of scrolling: *semi-automatic scrolling* and *true application-defined* scrolling. In the first case, Text and List widgets handle their own scrolling internally through special-case routines attached to the Scrollbars. We call this semi-automatic scrolling, since you (the application programmer) are not responsible for the scrolling of these widgets. The ScrolledWindow is still, nevertheless, in an application-defined scrolling mode. This is in contrast to true application-defined scrolling, where you must handle the Scrollbars and the associated scrolling actions entirely on your own. This method is more intricate and requires a significant amount of code to properly implement.

Obviously, the automatic scrolling mechanism provided by the ScrolledWindow is much simpler than the application-defined mechanisms and requires much less application intervention. However, there are some drawbacks in the implementation of automatic scrolling. The fact is, automatic ScrolledWindows only scroll in *single pixel increments*. If other scrolling behavior is required, you must use application-defined scrolling. And while the application-defined scrolling is far more complicated, the advantage is that it provides more flexibility in the ways that the object is scrolled. Now that we have made a distinction between the forms of scrolling mechanisms, we can examine how to implement them. We begin the discussion by describing the method for creating ScrolledWindows.

9.2 Simple ScrolledWindows

Creating ScrolledWindows is no different from creating other kinds of Motif widgets. Applications that wish to use ScrolledWindows must include the header file *<Xm/ScrolledW.h>* in those files where they are created. The process of creating a ScrolledWindow is shown in the following code fragment:

```
Widget  canvas;

canvas = XtVaCreateManagedWidget("name",
    xmScrolledWindowWidgetClass, parent,
    resource-values,
    NULL);
```

The **parent** can be a Shell or any manager widget. The ScrolledWindow should be created as a *managed* widget, since the addition of its child does not cause it to renegotiate its size with itself, its children or any other entity. (See Chapter 8, *Manager Widgets*, for a discussion on whether widgets that have children should be created as managed or unmanaged widgets.) The resource-value pairs control the behavior of the ScrolledWindow as well as its visual effects, and are initialized at creation-time. The most important resources are **Xm-NscrollingPolicy**, **XmNvisualPolicy**, and **XmNscrollBarDisplay-Policy**. These resources control the visual and behavioral attributes for the Scrolled-Window. The value for **XmNscrollingPolicy** can be set to **XmAUTOMATIC** or **XmAPPLICATION_DEFINED**, depending on the scrolling method you want. The use of other ScrolledWindow resources vary depending on this scrolling behavior.

9.2.1 Automatic Scrolling

In automatic-scroll mode, the ScrolledWindow assumes that all of the data is already available in the work window and the size of the work window represents the entire size of the viewable data. Even if the data changes and the work window is modified, the Scrolled-Window can still manage its display automatically. The ScrolledWindow should never resize itself due to changes in the work window. Hence, **XmNvisualPolicy** is typically set to **XmCONSTANT**. This value tells the ScrolledWindow not to resize itself when the work window grows or shrinks. If **XmNvisualPolicy** is set to **XmVARIABLE**, then the Scrolled-Window always expands itself to fit the entire work window. This obviously nullifies the need for an automatic ScrolledWindow. Like any other widget, the only time a Scrolled-Window should resize is when the parent resizes it, presumably because:

- The shell has been resized.

- The ScrolledWindow is a child of a PanedWindow that the user has resized.

- Adjacent (sibling) widgets have been resized, added, removed, etc.

- Application-controlled changes in widget size have been made.

The default size of the ScrolledWindow is never the size as the work area, unless it's a coincidence. This will be a problem if you want the ScrolledWindow to initialize itself to the size of the work window *and* have it be in automatic scrolling mode. The internals to the

ScrolledWindow widget happen to set the width and height to **100** pixels, although this is not officially documented by OSF. Unless you specifically set the **XmNwidth** and **Xm-Nheight** resources, the default size is not very useful. (To make the ScrolledWindow the same size as the work window, you must use application-defined scrolling.) For automatic scrolling, the only thing for you to decide is how you want the Scrollbars to be displayed if the work window dynamically grows or shrinks. You may have situations where the work window is the same size or actually *smaller* than the clip window. In this case, you may not want to display the Scrollbars, since they are not needed. If so, you can set **XmNscroll-BarDisplayPolicy** to **XmAS_NEEDED**. Otherwise, if you always want the Scrollbars to be visible whether or not they are needed, you can set the resource to **XmSTATIC**. Some people prefer static Scrollbars so that a consistency is maintained in the interface; having Scrollbars appear and disappear frequently may be confusing. Perhaps the best thing to do is leave scrollbar display for users to define for themselves. You can always set your preferences in the application's fallback resources:

```
*XmScrolledWindow.scrollBarDisplayPolicy: static
```

Note that the string version of **XmSTATIC** does not have the **Xm** prefix and the string can be represented in lower-case letters.

9.2.2 Application-defined Scrolling

In application-defined scrolling, **XmNscrollingPolicy** is set to **Xm-APPLICATION_DEFINED**. In this case, the work window must be the same size as the ScrolledWindow's clip window. (In fact, this is enforced by the toolkit). Thus, **Xm-NvisualPolicy** has the value of **XmVARIABLE**, indicating that the work window will grow and shrink with the ScrolledWindow, and the other way around. (The ScrolledWindow will grow and shrink with the work window.) (The ScrolledWindow will resize with the work window.) As long as the two windows are the same size, the ScrolledWindow doesn't need to have a clip window, so it doesn't create one. This may cause a savings in resources, but not a substantial one.

Because application-defined scrolling implies that you are responsible for the creation and management of the Scrollbars, the toolkit also forces the **XmNscrollBarDisplay-Policy** to **XmSTATIC**. This means that the ScrolledWindow will always display the Scrollbars if they are managed. The ScrolledWindow has no choice in the matter—it cannot know how large the *hypothetical* work window is because there is no mechanism (resource) for telling the ScrolledWindow that object's size. This means that you cannot get the same *automated* behavior from the Scrollbars' visibility that you can with the automatic scrolling mode. If you want your application to emulate the **XmAS_NEEDED** behavior, you must monitor the size of the ScrolledWindow and the work area and manage the Scrollbars manually.

9.2.3 Other ScrolledWindow Resources

Another ScrolledWindow resource is `XmNworkWindow`, which is used to identify the widget that acts as the ScrolledWindow's work window. Each ScrolledWindow may only have one work window, and a work window may only be associated with one Scrolled-Window. In other words, you can't assign the same widget ID to multiple ScrolledWindows to get multiple views into the same object. There are ways of achieving that effect, though, that will become apparent as we go through the chapter.

The resource `XmNclipWindow` specifies the widget ID for the clip window. This is a get-only resource, so it is illegal to attempt to set the clip window manually or to attempt to reset it to `NULL`. For practical purposes, this resource should be left alone.

The `XmNverticalScrollBar` and `XmNhorizontalScrollBar` resources have values that are widget IDs,[1] and allow you to set and get the Scrollbars on the work window. These come in handy later when we discuss monitoring scrolling actions and setting up application-defined scrolled windows.

Other miscellaneous resources include margin widths and heights and various other "details" that are not particularly interesting. You can refer to Appendix B, *Xt and Motif Widget Classes*, for more information.

9.2.4 Automatic ScrolledWindow Example

Automatic scrolling is the simpler of the two types of scrolling policies available. Fortunately, it is also the more common of the two. However, don't let this simplicity sway you too much—it is a common design error for programmers to use the automatic scrolling mechanisms for designs that are more suited to the application-defined model. On the other hand, if you merely want to monitor scrolling without necessarily controlling it, you can still install your own callback routines to the Scrollbars on automatic ScrolledWindows. We'll get into that in the next section when we talk about Scrollbars.

In automatic mode, ScrolledWindows automatically create their own Scrollbars and handle their callback procedures to position the work window behind the clipping window. All of the examples throughout this book that use ScrolledWindows (like those in Chapter 10, *The DrawingArea Widget*, and Chapter 4, *The Main Window*) use the automatic scrolling mode. (The exception being this chapter, which addresses with all kinds of scrolling.) The only exceptions are the ScrolledList and ScrolledText objects, but the List and Text widgets handle the application-defined scrolling internally. These are discussed again later in the chapter.

Example 9-1 shows a large "panel" of widgets (Labels, PushButtons and Text widgets) placed in a collection of Form and RowColumn widgets, all managed by a ScrolledWindow widget.

---

[1] The OSF documentation mistakenly identifies these values as being of type `Window`.

Example 9-1. The getusers.c program

```
/* getusers.c -- demonstrate a simple ScrolledWindow by showing
 * how it can manage a RowColumn that contains a vertical stack of
 * Form widgets, each of which contains a Toggle, two Labels and
 * a Text widget.  The program fills the values of the widgets
 * using various pieces of information from the password file.
 * Note: there are no callback routines associated with any of the
 * widgets created here -- this is for demonstration purposes only.
 */
#include <Xm/PushBG.h>
#include <Xm/LabelG.h>
#include <Xm/ToggleB.h>
#include <Xm/ScrolledW.h>
#include <Xm/RowColumn.h>
#include <Xm/Form.h>
#include <Xm/Text.h>
#include <pwd.h>

typedef struct {
    String      login;
    int         uid;
    String      name;
    String      homedir;
} UserInfo;

/* use getpwent() to read data in the password file to store
 * information about all the users on the system.  The list is
 * a dynamically grown array, the last of which has a NULL login.
 */
UserInfo *
getusers()
{
    /* extern struct *passwd getpwent(); */
    extern char *strcpy();
    struct passwd *pw;
    UserInfo *users = NULL;
    int n;

    setpwent();

    /* getpwent() returns NULL when there are no more users */
    for (n = 0; pw = getpwent(); n++) {
        /* reallocate the pointer to contain one more entry.  You may choose
         * to optimize by adding 10 entries at a time, or perhaps more?
         */
        users = (UserInfo *)XtRealloc(users, (n+1) * sizeof(UserInfo));
        users[n].login = strcpy(XtMalloc(strlen(pw->pw_name)+1), pw->pw_name);
        users[n].name = strcpy(XtMalloc(strlen(pw->pw_gecos)+1), pw->pw_gecos);
        users[n].homedir = strcpy(XtMalloc(strlen(pw->pw_dir)+1), pw->pw_dir);
        users[n].uid = pw->pw_uid;
    }
    /* allocate one more item and set its login string to NULL */
    users = (UserInfo *)XtRealloc(users, (n+1) * sizeof(UserInfo));
    users[n].login = NULL;
    endpwent();
    return users; /* return new array */
}

main(argc, argv)
```

Example 9-1. The getusers.c program (continued)

```
int argc;
char *argv[ ];
{
    Widget toplevel, sw, main_rc, form, toggle;
    XtAppContext app;
    UserInfo *users;

    toplevel = XtVaAppInitialize(&app, "Demos", NULL, 0,
        &argc, argv, NULL, NULL);

    /* Create a 500x300 scrolled window.  This value is arbitrary,
     * but happens to look good initially.  It is resizable by the user.
     */
    sw = XtVaCreateManagedWidget("scrolled_w",
        xmScrolledWindowWidgetClass, toplevel,
        XmNwidth,               500,
        XmNheight,              300,
        XmNscrollingPolicy, XmAUTOMATIC,
        NULL);

    /* RowColumn is the work window for the widget */
    main_rc = XtVaCreateWidget("main_rc", xmRowColumnWidgetClass, sw, NULL);
    /* load the users from the passwd file */
    if (!(users = getusers())) {
        perror("can't read user data info");
        exit(1);
    }
    /* for each login entry found in the password file, create a
     * form containing a toggle button, two labels and a text widget.
     */
    while (users->login) { /* NULL login terminates list */
        char uid[8];
        form = XtVaCreateWidget(NULL, xmFormWidgetClass, main_rc, NULL);
        XtVaCreateManagedWidget(users->login, xmToggleButtonWidgetClass, form,
            XmNalignment,            XmALIGNMENT_BEGINNING,
            XmNtopAttachment,        XmATTACH_FORM,
            XmNbottomAttachment, XmATTACH_FORM,
            XmNleftAttachment,       XmATTACH_FORM,
            XmNrightAttachment,      XmATTACH_POSITION,
            XmNrightPosition,        15,
            NULL);
        sprintf(uid, "%d", users->uid);
        XtVaCreateManagedWidget(uid, xmLabelGadgetClass, form,
            XmNalignment,            XmALIGNMENT_END,
            XmNtopAttachment,        XmATTACH_FORM,
            XmNbottomAttachment, XmATTACH_FORM,
            XmNleftAttachment,       XmATTACH_POSITION,
            XmNleftPosition,         15,
            XmNrightAttachment,      XmATTACH_POSITION,
            XmNrightPosition,        20,
            NULL);
        XtVaCreateManagedWidget(users->name, xmLabelGadgetClass, form,
            XmNalignment,            XmALIGNMENT_BEGINNING,
            XmNtopAttachment,        XmATTACH_FORM,
            XmNbottomAttachment, XmATTACH_FORM,
            XmNleftAttachment,       XmATTACH_POSITION,
            XmNleftPosition,         20,
```

Example 9-1. The getusers.c program (continued)

```
                XmNrightAttachment,  XmATTACH_POSITION,
                XmNrightPosition,    40,
                NULL);
        /* Although the home directory is readonly, it may be longer
         * than expected, so don't use a Label widget.  Use a Text widget
         * so that left-right scrolling can take place.
         */
        XtVaCreateManagedWidget(users->homedir, xmTextWidgetClass, form,
                XmNeditable,           False,
                XmNcursorPositionVisible, False,
                XmNtopAttachment,      XmATTACH_FORM,
                XmNbottomAttachment,   XmATTACH_FORM,
                XmNleftAttachment,     XmATTACH_POSITION,
                XmNleftPosition,       45,
                XmNrightAttachment,    XmATTACH_FORM,
                XmNvalue,              users->homedir,
                NULL);
        XtManageChild(form);
        users++;
    }
    XtManageChild(main_rc);

    XtRealizeWidget(toplevel);
    XtAppMainLoop(app);
}
```

Those of you familiar with UNIX programming techniques will find the use of **getpwent( )** and **endpwent( )** quite familiar. If you are not aware of these functions, you should consult the documentation for your UNIX system. In short, they can be used to return information about the contents of the password file (typically */etc/passwd*), which contains information about all the users on the system. The first call to **getpwent( )** opens the password file and returns a data structure describing the first entry. Subsequent calls return consecutive entries. When the entries have been exhausted, **getpwent( )** returns NULL and **getpwend( )** closes the password file (so we don't leave an open file descriptor hanging around). In Example 9-1, the information is taken from the password file and represented using Toggles, Labels, and Text widgets, as shown in Figure 9-2. This particular program has no "meaning," per se. It is used solely to demonstrate how "panels" of arbitrary widgets may be displayed in ScrolledWindows. The widget hierarchy is irrelevant to the Scrolled-Window's design model. In this particular case, the ScrolledWindow happens to be a child of the top-level shell. The immediate child of this shell might have been a MainWindow widget which, in this case, is interchangeable with the ScrolledWindow. This is because the MainWindow is subclassed from the ScrolledWindow. See Chapter 4, *The Main Window*, for more details on how the MainWindow widget fits into the application design.

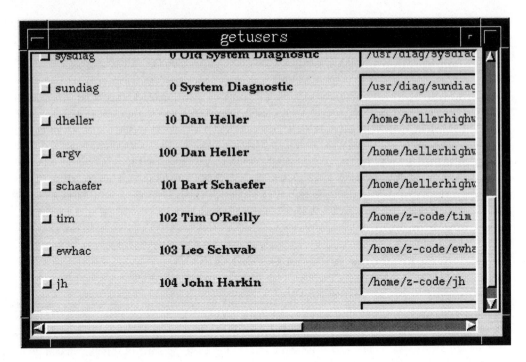

Figure 9-2. Output of getusers.c

The dimensions of the ScrolledWindow are 500 pixels wide by 300 pixels high.[2] These values are completely arbitrary and was chosen for this program because it seemed to work best. The size you choose should usually be based on the aesthetic quality of whatever it is that you are displaying in your ScrolledWindow. The widget itself does not have a sensible default size to rely on, so you will almost always provide a default geometry of some sort. You may not have to do this if you are allowing the ScrolledWindow's parent or siblings to control its size. That is, the ScrolledWindow's default dimensions usually have nothing to do with the type of object it scrolls. Normally, the ScrolledWindow is an extremely flexible object—the "rubber band" of widgets. You stick them in wherever they can fit, and if any resizing of the window occurs, it is usually the ScrolledWindow that changes.

Therefore, you should rarely set the actual dimensions of a ScrolledWindow. Instead, allow its sibling (surrounding) widgets that are less flexible to help define the layout design. ScrolledWindows fit quite nicely in PanedWindows, since they can be adjusted so easily.

In Example 9-1, the ScrolledWindow's child is the **main_rc** widget, a RowColumn that contains all the children that represent the password file information. After **getusers()** is called, we loop through each item in the array of **UserInfo** sturctures, creating a Form widget with a ToggleButton, two Labels and a Text widget. All of these are placed in the

---

[2] We could have set the dimensions using resolution-independent values using the **XmNunitType** resource, but there is a bug with Motif toolkit up to version 1.1.0 where unit types other than **XmPIXEL** are improperly calculated. In 1.1.1, only **Xm100TH_MILLIMETERS** are not handled correctly. Version 1.1.2 works correctly for the Scrollbar's **XmNunitType**.

single Form widget, which in turn, are stacked vertically on top of one another in the Row-Column. Once complete, the user can scroll around and access any of the elements without the host application having to support any of the scrolling mechanisms. It is completely automated by the Motif toolkit.

Basically, that's it for automatic scrolling. In many cases, applications need to do nothing more than what was described in this section. As mentioned earlier, there are many other examples in this book that demonstrate how ScrolledWindows are used in this fashion. However, if you want to monitor scrolling, or just fine-tune the way scrolling is handled (adjust the number of pixels for each scrolling increment), then you need to learn about Scrollbars. If you need to do application-defined scrolling, then you definitely need to learn about Scrollbars, plus a little bit more. The rest of this chapter, therefore, focuses on the use of Scrollbars for all kinds of scrolling models.

9.3 Working Directly with Scrollbars

The Scrollbar is the backbone of the ScrolledWindow. Yet the Scrollbar, in and of itself, is a standalone widget that can be created and manipulated entirely without the aid of a Scrolled-Window as its parent. We aren't going to discuss this kind of use, since it isn't consistent with the *Motif Style Guide* and is no more interesting than the sorts of things you can do with them as children of ScrolledWindows, anyway. What we are going to discuss is how to control a Scrollbar directly from your application in the context of a ScrolledWindow widget.

Before we begin, it is very important to understand that the Scrollbar does *not* handle scrolling—it merely reports scrolling actions through its callback routines. It is up to the internals of the application (or widget) to install callback procedures on the Scrollbar to repaint or adjust the work window appropriately. The Scrollbar manages its own display in accordance with scrolling actions. You needn't ever update the Scrollbar's display unless the underlying data of the object being scrolled changes. This is accomplished by resetting resource values associated with each of the Scrollbar's elements.

Figure 9-3 illustrates the design of a Scrollbar and identifies its elements. This figure represents a vertical Scrollbar, but a Scrollbar may also have a horizontal orientation.

The Scrollbar's appearance and functional behavior is directly related to the object it scrolls. If you think of the relationship between the Scrollbar and the object it scrolls as being "proportional," then the size of the Scrollbar's slider represents how much of the object being scrolled is visible in the clip window.

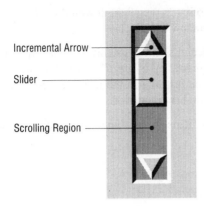

Incremental Arrow ——————

Slider ——————

Scrolling Region ——————

Figure 9-3. Elements of a Scrollbar

The terms associated with the Scrollbar are defined below:

Unit Length An abstraction of the size of the object is broken down into equally sized *units*. When the user clicks on the Incremental Arrows (also called *directional arrows*), the Scrollbar scrolls in the direction indicated by the arrow in unit increments. *The unit length is always stored and interpreted internally by the object being scrolled; it is of no interest to the Scrollbar itself, since it does not affect the display of the Scrollbar.* This is an important point to make here, since it is one of the most misunderstood aspects of the Scrollbar. While this value is not set on the Scrollbar itself, it plays a key role in understanding how Scrollbars work.

All other resource values are measured in these abstract units. A Text widget might have its unit length equal the height of the tallest character in the Text's font set (plus some margin for whitespace on the top and bottom of the character) for its vertical Scrollbar. However, it is the Text widget's responsibility to know this value. Thus, vertical scrolling adjusts the window so that the text is always consistently displayed without lines being partially obscured. Its horizontal Scrollbar unit length might be the average width of the characters in the font being used.

Value The offset, measured in unit lengths, of the data in the clip window from the object's "origin." For example, if the top of the clip window displays the fourth line of text in a Text widget, the Scrollbar is said to have a value of 3 (since it's offset from 0). Clicking and dragging on the slider directly changes the Scrollbar's value to an absolute number; clicking on either of the directional arrows changes the Scrollbar's value incrementally; and clicking on the area in the scrolling region, but not on the Scrollbar itself changes the Scrollbar's value by *page* lengths (see below). Note that the *value* is measured in units, not pixels.

View Length The size of the viewable area (clip window), as measured in unit lengths. The vertical Scrollbar for a Text widget displaying 15 lines of text would have a

view length of **15**. The horizontal Scrollbar's view length would be the number of columns of characters the clip window can display.

Page Length The page length is measured in unit lengths and is usually one less than the view length. If the user scrolls the window by a "page" increment, the first line from the old view is retained as the last line in the new view for visual reference. Otherwise, the user might lose his orientation.

Figure 9-4 illustrates the relationship between the elements listed above and introduces the Scrollbar resources that correspond to these values.

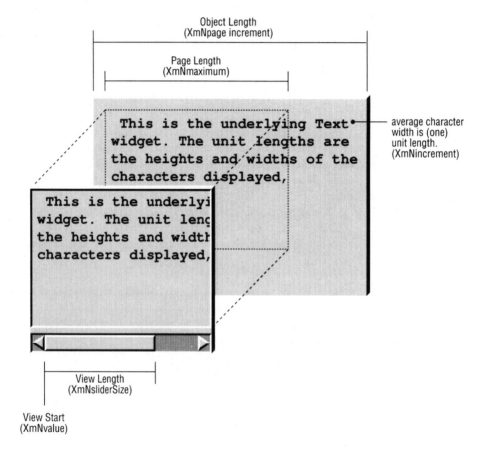

Figure 9-4. Conceptual relationship between a Scrollbar and the object it scrolls

The following resources used in that figure correlate directly with the terms we just described:

XmNincrement

This value represents the number of units that the Scrollbar will report having scrolled when the user clicks on its incremental arrows. The value for **Xm-Nincrement** in Figure 9-5 is **1** because each incremental scroll on the horizontal Scrollbar should scroll one character width. Internally, the Text widget knows that the number of pixels associated with **XmNincrement** is the average width of all the glyphs in the font being used. (It is rare to set **XmNincrement** to any other value for automatic or semi-automatic ScrolledWindows.)

XmNmaximum

The largest size (measured in unit increments) that the object can have. For the text widget shown above, the value for **XmNmaximum** is the number of characters in the widest line shown in the clip window.[3]

XmNminimum

The smallest size (measured in unit increments) that the object will ever have.

XmNpageIncrement

The number of units that the Scrollbar should appear to move the underlying object when the user *pages* the Scrollbar. Again, the Scrollbar doesn't actually perform the Scrolling, it just reports scrolling actions. The Scrollbar itself, however, uses this value to know the new visual position for the slider within the scrolling area so it can update its own display. The application can use this value (multiplied by pixels-per-unit) to determine the new data to display in the work window.

XmNsliderSize

The size of the clip window in unit lengths for the orientation corresponding to the Scrollbar. If the Text widget can display 60 characters (columns), then **XmNsliderSize** is **60**.

XmNvalue

The number of units the data in the clip window is offset from the beginning of the work window. For example, if the Text widget has been scrolled down by four lines from the top, the value of the vertical Scrollbar's **XmNvalue** resource would be **4**. Example 9-2 demonstrates how the vertical Scrollbar resources get their values from a typical ScrolledText object (which is made up of a Text widget inside of a ScrolledWindow widget).

Example 9-2. The simple_sb.c program

```
/* simple_sb.c -- demonstrate the Scrollbar resource values from
 * a ScrolledText object.  This is used as an introductory examination
 * of the resources used by Scrollbars.
 */
#include <Xm/RowColumn.h>
#include <Xm/PushBG.h>
#include <Xm/Text.h>

/* print the "interesting" resource values of a scrollbar */
void
get_sb(pb, scrollbar)
Widget pb, scrollbar;
{
    int increment=0, maximum=0, minimum=0, page_incr=0, slider_size=0, value=0;
```

---

[3] The fact that the Motif Text widget sets its horizontal Scrollbar's **XmNmaximum** to the number of characters in its widest *visible* line is a shortcoming of the widget. It would perhaps be better if the Text widget used the widest of *all* its lines, but it does not happen to be implemented that way.

ScrolledWindows and Scrollbars

Example 9-2. The simple_sb.c program (continued)

```
    XtVaGetValues(scrollbar,
        XmNincrement,       &increment,
        XmNmaximum,         &maximum,
        XmNminimum,         &minimum,
        XmNpageIncrement,   &page_incr,
        XmNsliderSize,      &slider_size,
        XmNvalue,           &value,
        NULL);
    printf("increment=%d, max=%d, min=%d, page=%d, slider=%d, value=%d\n",
        increment, maximum, minimum, page_incr, slider_size, value);
}

main(argc, argv)
int argc;
char *argv[ ];
{
    Widget        toplevel, rowcol, text_w, pb, sb;
    XtAppContext  app;
    Arg           args[5];

    toplevel = XtVaAppInitialize(&app, "Demos",
        NULL, 0, &argc, argv, NULL, NULL);

    /* RowColumn contains ScrolledText and PushButton */
    rowcol = XtVaCreateWidget("rowcol",
        xmRowColumnWidgetClass, toplevel, NULL);

    XtSetArg(args[0], XmNrows,           10);
    XtSetArg(args[1], XmNcolumns,        80);
    XtSetArg(args[2], XmNeditMode,       XmMULTI_LINE_EDIT);
    XtSetArg(args[3], XmNscrollHorizontal,  False);
    XtSetArg(args[4], XmNwordWrap,       True);
    text_w = XmCreateScrolledText(rowcol, "text_w", args, 5);
    XtManageChild(text_w);

    /* get the scrollbar from ScrolledWindow associated with Text widget */
    XtVaGetValues(XtParent(text_w), XmNverticalScrollBar, &sb, NULL);

    /* provide a bushbutton to obtain the scrollbar's resource values */
    pb = XtVaCreateManagedWidget("Scrollbar Values",
        xmPushButtonGadgetClass, rowcol, NULL);
    XtAddCallback(pb, XmNactivateCallback, get_sb, sb);

    XtManageChild(rowcol);

    XtRealizeWidget(toplevel);
    XtAppMainLoop(app);
}
```

This program simply displays a ScrolledText object and a PushButton that, when activated, gets some resource values from the Text widget's ScrolledWindow's vertical Scrollbar. The graphical output of this program is displayed in Figure 9-5.

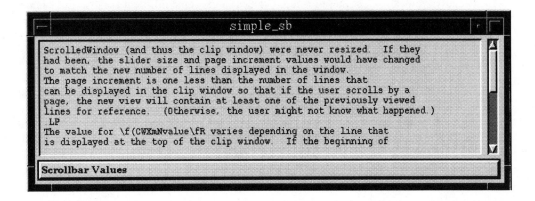

Figure 9-5. Output of simple_sb.c

By activating the PushButton at random times while text is entered into the text widget, the following output might appear on your *xterm* window:

```
increment=1, max=28, min=0, page=9, slider=10, value=18
increment=1, max=28, min=0, page=9, slider=10, value=0
increment=1, max=28, min=0, page=9, slider=10, value=1
increment=1, max=28, min=0, page=9, slider=10, value=2
increment=1, max=28, min=0, page=9, slider=10, value=3
increment=1, max=28, min=0, page=9, slider=10, value=4
increment=1, max=28, min=0, page=9, slider=10, value=10
increment=1, max=37, min=0, page=9, slider=10, value=11
increment=1, max=47, min=0, page=9, slider=10, value=21
```

The value for **XmNincrement** is always **1**, indicating that the incremental arrow buttons will scroll the text by one unit in either direction.

The value for **XmNmaximum** changes according to how many lines are in the window. The values of **28**, **37** and **47** indicate that new text was added in between the times the Push-Button was activated. The value of **XmNminimum** is always **0** because this object can have as few as zero text lines.

The values for **XmNsliderSize** and **XmNpageIncrement** are **10** and **9**, respectively. The values never changed because the ScrolledWindow (and thus the clip window) were never resized. If they had been, the slider size and page increment values would have changed to match the new number of lines displayed in the window. The page increment is one less than the number of lines that can be displayed in the clip window so that if the user scrolls by a page, the new view will contain at least one of the previously viewed lines for reference. (Otherwise, the user might not know what happened.)

Scrolled Windows
and Scrollbars

The value for **XmNvalue** varies depending on the line that is displayed at the top of the clip window. If the beginning of the text is displayed, **XmNvalue** is 0. As the user scrolls through the text, the value for **XmNvalue** increases or decreases, but is always a positive value.

Incidentally, you can adjust these resource values to get some different results. For example, you could set the **XmNincrement** resource to 2 on a ScrolledText's vertical Scrollbar in order to modify the number of lines scrolled by the user's selection of the incremental arrow keys. However, you should not do this arbitrarily; you could really confuse the user by setting these values to unrealistic numbers or even simply by *changing* them.

As mentioned at the beginning of this section, the most important thing to remember about the Scrollbar widget is that it does not cause any actual scrolling of the object in the work window. It merely reports scrolling activity through its callback routines. When scrolling occurs, it is the callback routines that are responsible for modifying the data in the work window (by adjusting elements or redrawing the image). The Scrollbar updates its own display according to the scrolling action. If the widget or the application (whichever owns the callback routines) fails to modify the display, the user will see an inconsistency between what the Scrollbar is displaying and the data seen in the clip window.

9.3.1 Scrollbar Orientation

Two resources that relate very closely to one another are **XmNorientation** and **XmNprocessingDirection**. These resources specify the horizontal or vertical orientation of the scrollbar, and its normal processing direction. The values for **XmNorientation** can be **XmHORIZONTAL** or **XmVERTICAL**. When horizontal, the normal processing direction for the Scrollbar is such that the minimum value is on the left and the maximum is on the right. When vertical, the minimum is on the bottom and the maximum is on the top. You can affect these values using **XmNprocessingDirection**. This resource can have the following values:

```
XmMAX_ON_LEFT
XmMAX_ON_RIGHT
XmMAX_ON_TOP
XmMAX_ON_BOTTOM
```

These values are similar to those set in for the Scale widget. These values should be changed when the user's environment is such that the natural language for his "locale" is read from right-to-left. Similarly, the ScrolledWindow resource **XmNscrollBarPlacement** would be used to match the processing direction. This resource can have the following values:

```
XmTOP_LEFT
XmTOP_RIGHT
XmBOTTOM_LEFT
XmBOTTOM_RIGHT
```

9.3.2 Scrollbar Callback Routines

The callback routines associated with the Scrollbar are its only links into the internal mechanisms that actually scroll the data. You can use these callback routines in various contexts, depending on what you want to accomplish. For example, you can:

- Monitor scrolling in automatic ScrolledWindows.

- Monitor scrolling in semi-automatic ScrolledWindows, such as ScrolledText and ScrolledList widgets.

- Actually *implement* application-defined scrolling.

The first two cases are identical when it comes to the implementation of what we are about to describe. The third case, however, will require intimate knowledge about the internals of the object being scrolled. Let's begin by examining how to monitor scrolling actions.

There are different parts to the Scrollbar that the user can use to cause a scrolling action. In fact, each part of the Scrollbar has a callback routine associated with it. This callback routine is used to both monitor automatic (or semi-automatic) scrolling and to implement application-defined scrolling. Callback functions are passed the usual three parameters, as shown in the following example:

```
void
scrollbar_callback(sbar, client_data, cbs)
    Widget sbar;
    XtPointer client_data;
    XmScrollBarCallbackStruct *cbs;
```

The form of **XmScrollBarCallbackStruct** is:

```
typedef struct {
    int       reason;
    XEvent    *event;
    int       value;
    int       pixel;
} XmScrollBarCallbackStruct;
```

The **reason** field corresponds to the callback resource invoked by its corresponding callback routine.

Table 9-1 lists the possible callback resources for the Scrollbar widget.

Table 9-1. Callback Resources for the ScrollBar Widget

Resource Name	cbs->reason	Location Clicked
XmNincrementCallback	XmCR_INCREMENT	Top or Right directional arrows.
XmNdecrementCallback	XmCR_DECREMENT	Bottom or Left directional arrows.
XmNpageIncrementCallback	XmCR_PAGE_INCREMENT	Area above or right of slider.

Table 9-1. Callback Resources for the ScrollBar Widget (continued)

Resource Name	cbs->reason	Location Clicked
XmNpageDecrementCallback	XmCR_PAGE_DECREMENT	Area below or left of slider.
XmNtoTopCallback	XmCR_TO_TOP	CTRL+Click on increment arrow.
XmNtoBottomCallback	XmCR_TO_BOTTOM	CTRL+Click on decrement arrow.
XmNdragCallback	XmCR_DRAG	Slider is *dragged*.
XmNvalueChangedCallback	XmCR_VALUE_CHANGED	See notes.

(Note: the location clicked may be inverted depending on the value of **XmNprocessing-Direction.**)

The **XmNvalueChangedCallback** is invoked after the user has released the mouse button after dragging the slider. This is a special callback that is also invoked for each of the other scrolling actions if their corresponding callback resources are not set (with the exception of the **XmNdragCallback**). This is convenient for the cases where you are handling your own scrolling and you are not concerned with the *type* of scrolling the user invoked. We'll examine this more closely when we discuss application-defined scrolling.

The **value** field of the callback structure indicates the new position of the Scrollbar that resulted from the callback routine. This value can range from **XmNminimum** to **XmNmaximum**. The **pixels** field indicates the **x,y** coordinates of the mouse location relative to the origin of the Scrollbar. The origin is the top of the vertical Scrollbar or the left side of the horizontal Scrollbar, regardless of the value of **XmNprocessingDirection**. The value for **pixels** isn't very interesting and does not have anything to do with the scrolling action.

Example 9-3 demonstrates how the callback routines can be hooked up to each of the callback resources to allow you to monitor a List widget's scrolling more precisely. For Text and List widgets, you really shouldn't be changing the default scrolling behavior. The next example gets more detailed about how to *affect* scrolling.

Example 9-3. The monitor_sb.c program

```
/* monitor_sb.c -- demonstrate the Scrollbar callback routines by
 * monitoring the Scrollbar for a ScrolledList.  Functionally, this
 * program does nothing.  However, by tinkering with the Scrolled
 * List and watching the output from the Scrollbar's callback routine,
 * you'll see some interesting behavioral patterns.  By interacting
 * with the *List* widget to cause scrolling, the Scrollbar's callback
 * routine is never called.  Thus, monitoring the scrolling actions
 * of a Scrollbar should not be used to keep tabs on exactly when
 * the scrollbar's value changes!
 */
#include <Xm/List.h>

/* print the "interesting" resource values of a scrollbar */
void
```

Example 9-3. The monitor_sb.c program (continued)

```
scroll_action(scrollbar, client_data, cbs)
Widget scrollbar;
XtPointer client_data;
XmScrollBarCallbackStruct *cbs;
{
    printf("cbs->reason: %s, cbs->value = %d, cbs->pixel = %d\n",
        cbs->reason == XmCR_DRAG? "drag" :
        cbs->reason == XmCR_VALUE_CHANGED? "value changed" :
        cbs->reason == XmCR_INCREMENT? "increment" :
        cbs->reason == XmCR_DECREMENT? "decrement" :
        cbs->reason == XmCR_PAGE_INCREMENT? "page increment" :
        cbs->reason == XmCR_PAGE_DECREMENT? "page decrement" :
        cbs->reason == XmCR_TO_TOP? "top" :
        cbs->reason == XmCR_TO_BOTTOM? "bottom" : "unknown",
        cbs->value, cbs->pixel);
}

main(argc, argv)
int argc;
char *argv[ ];
{
    Widget        toplevel, list_w, sb;
    XtAppContext  app;
    char *items = "choice0, choice1, choice2, choice3, choice4, \
                    choice5, choice6, choice7, choice8, choice9, \
                    choice10, choice11, choice12, choice13, choice14";

    toplevel = XtAppInitialize(&app, "Demos",
        NULL, 0, &argc, argv, NULL, NULL, 0);

    list_w = XmCreateScrolledList(toplevel, "list_w", NULL, 0);
    XtVaSetValues(list_w,
        /* Rather than convert the entire list of items into an array
         * of compound strings, let's just let Motif's type converter
         * do it for us and save lots of effort (altho not much time).
         */
        XtVaTypedArg, XmNitems, XmRString, items, strlen(items)+1,
        XmNitemCount, 15,
        XmNvisibleItemCount, 5,
        NULL);
    XtManageChild(list_w);

    /* get the scrollbar from ScrolledWindow associated with Text widget */
    XtVaGetValues(XtParent(list_w), XmNverticalScrollBar, &sb, NULL);
    XtAddCallback(sb, XmNvalueChangedCallback, scroll_action, NULL);
    XtAddCallback(sb, XmNdragCallback, scroll_action, NULL);
    XtAddCallback(sb, XmNincrementCallback, scroll_action, NULL);
    XtAddCallback(sb, XmNdecrementCallback, scroll_action, NULL);
    XtAddCallback(sb, XmNpageIncrementCallback, scroll_action, NULL);
    XtAddCallback(sb, XmNpageDecrementCallback, scroll_action, NULL);
    XtAddCallback(sb, XmNtoTopCallback, scroll_action, NULL);
    XtAddCallback(sb, XmNtoBottomCallback, scroll_action, NULL);

    XtRealizeWidget(toplevel);
    XtAppMainLoop(app);
}
```

The program displays a simple ScrolledList that contains 15 hypothetical entries as shown in Figure 9-6.

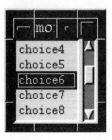

Figure 9-6. Display for monitor_sb.c

The entries themselves aren't important; it's the way the Scrollbar reacts to the user's interaction that's interesting. You'll notice that if you use the keyboard to select elements or scroll around in the list, the Scrollbar's callbacks are *not* invoked, because the List widget is stealing all the keyboard events from the Scrollbar. Actually, the Scrollbar, like any other widget, can get keyboard events, and it even has translations to map certain key sequences to scrolling actions. However, the List widget sets its Scrollbar's **XmNtraversalOn** to **False** so that the List can process its own keyboard actions, some of which scroll the window. (The Text widget does the same thing with its Scrollbar(s)). Alas, there is a limit to what you can accomplish by monitoring the Scrollbar's actions on semi-automatic scrolling objects like List and Text widgets.

Therefore, we move on to another, more interesting use of the Scrollbar.

9.4 True Application-defined ScrolledWindows

In this section, we pull together what we've learned in this chapter and put it to work to implement application-defined scrolling. Example 9-4 displays a large number of individual bitmaps in a ScrolledWindow, allowing the user to view them arbitrarily by scrolling around freely. The intent is to make the appearance and functionality of the ScrolledWindow mimic the automatic scrolling mode as much as possible. The bitmaps may be specified on the command line as in:

```
% app—scroll /usr/include/X11/bitmaps/*
```

The output of this command is shown in Figure 9-7.

Figure 9-7. Output of app-scroll.c

There are actually several ways to go about writing this program, depending on the constraints we impose. The simplest is to render each bitmap into one large pixmap, and use that pixmap as the **XmNlabelPixmap** for a Label widget. The Label widget can then be used as the work window for an automatic ScrolledWindow. This design is similar to most of the other examples of ScrolledWindows used throughout the book. However, let's say we want to add a constraint such that each incremental scrolling action causes the display to shift by exactly one bitmap *cell* so that the top and left sides of the viewport always have a fully displayed bitmap—no partially displayed bitmaps are allowed. Furthermore, smooth-scrolling actions that take place when the user "drags" the slider must not scroll pixel-by-pixel, but must jump in cell-increments.

The constraints just described define precisely the behavior that the List and Text widgets use for their own displays. Like those widgets, our example program has a single conceptual unit size that is represented by the "objects" they scroll. For the Text and List widgets, those unit sizes are the heights and widths of the fonts used by the text entries. But this interaction is where the similarity between our bitmap viewer and the List and Text widgets ends—the actual implementation of the two are quite different. For our display, the heights and widths of the bitmaps vary more dramatically than the characters in a font. Thus, for our display, the unit size is set to the largest of all the bitmaps for consistency. We'll explore this a little more towards the end of the section.

Unlike the Text and List widgets, the design of our program is based on the same principles used by the ScrolledWindow's automatic scrolling method. Only in this case, we are going to do the work ourselves (plus a few twists). The reason for doing this type of implementation is that the automatic scrolling method cannot support the scrolling constraints described above, since there is no way to tell the ScrolledWindow the number of pixels there are per scrolling unit.

In our implementation, the work window is a DrawingArea widget whose size is not constrained by the size of the pixmap or the number of bitmap entries. Rather, it is constrained by the size of the viewport in the ScrolledWindow. Initially, the ScrolledWindow sizes itself to the size of the DrawingArea widget, but once the program is running, the DrawingArea is resized by the ScrolledWindow as it is resized. We'll see how this works when we run the program.

The bitmaps are rendered into a large pixmap, which is rendered into the DrawingArea in connection to scrolling actions. The offset of the pixmap and how much of it is copied into the DrawingArea is controlled by the application, but it follows the same algorithms the ScrolledWindow uses when in automatic scrolling mode. The only difference is that we can adjust for the pixels-per-unit value, whereas the ScrolledWindow's automatic scrolling mode is only aware of single-pixel units.

Proper scrolling is not a particularly difficult problem to solve; it only involves simple arithmetic. The real problem is handling the cases where the user or application causes the ScrolledWindow to *resize*, since this changes all the variables in your calculations. When resizing happens, the ScrolledWindow passes that resizing onto the DrawingArea widget, which then must recalculate its sizes and update the Scrollbars' resources so that the display and the graphic representation match.

In short, the program has to solve four independently simple problems:

1. Read the bitmaps and load them into a sufficiently large pixmap.

2. Create the ScrolledWindow, a DrawingArea widget, and two Scrollbars, and initialize each of these widgets' resources so that the ratio between their own sizes and the size of the pixmap are consistent.

3. Set up a callback routine to the Scrollbars to respond to scrolling actions.

4. Provide a callback routine for the DrawingArea widget's **XmNresizeCallback** that updates all the widgets' resources according to the new ratio between them and the pixmap. (The pixmap never changes size.)

Although each of these problems has a simple solution, when combined, the general solution becomes quite complex. However, rather than trying to solve each problem individually, a well-designed application would integrate all the problems into a single elegant design. In the first step, we must be able to read bitmap filenames successfully and report any errors. Each bitmap may have a different size, so we must save all the information about them for comparison after they are all loaded. At that time, the largest bitmap is found and a single pixmap is created based on the formula:

```
pixmap_width = largest_bitmap_width * columns;
pixmap_height = largest_bitmap_height * rows;
```

This pixmap is used as the "virtual" work window, which is used to render into the real work window: the DrawingArea widget.

This is a very long program, but you can follow along with the comments embedded within the code to understand what's going on. Additional explanation follows the program listing.

Example 9-4. The app-scroll.c program

```
/* app-scroll.c - Displays bitmaps specified on the command line.  All
 * bitmaps are drawn into a pixmap, which is rendered into a DrawingArea
 * widget, which is used as the work window for a ScrolledWindow.  This
 * method is only used to demonstrate application-defined scrolling for
 * the motif ScrolledWindow.  Automatic scrolling is much simpler, but
 * does not allow the programmer to impose incremental scrolling units.
 *
 * The bitmaps are displayed in an equal number of rows and columns if
 * possible.
 *
 * Example:
 *   app-scroll /usr/include/X11/bitmaps/*
 */

#include <stdio.h>
#include <Xm/ScrolledW.h>
#include <Xm/DrawingA.h>
#include <Xm/ScrollBar.h>

#ifdef max   /* just in case--we don't know, but these are commonly set */
#undef max   /* by arbitrary unix systems.  Also, we cast to int! */
#endif
/* redefine "max" and "min" macros to take into account "unsigned" values */
#define max(a,b) ((int)(a)>(int)(b)?(int)(a):(int)(b))
#define min(a,b) ((int)(a)<(int)(b)?(int)(a):(int)(b))

/* don't accept bitmaps larger than 100x100 .. This value is arbitrarily
 * chosen, but is sufficiently large for most images.  Handling extremely
 * large bitmaps would eat too much memory and make the interface awkward.
 */
#define MAX_WIDTH   100
#define MAX_HEIGHT  100

typedef struct {
    char *name;
    int len; /* strlen(name) */
    unsigned int width, height;
    Pixmap bitmap;
} Bitmap;

/* get the integer square root of n -- used to calculate an equal
 * number of rows and colums for a given number of elements.
 */
int_sqrt(n)
register int n;
{
    register int i, s = 0, t;
    for (i = 15; i >= 0; i--) {
        t = (s | (1 << i));
        if (t * t <= n)
            s = t;
    }
```

Example 9-4. The app-scroll.c program (continued)

```
    return s;
}

Widget drawing_a, vsb, hsb;
Pixmap pixmap; /* used as the image for DrawingArea widget */
Display *dpy;
Dimension view_width = 300, view_height = 300;
int rows, cols;
unsigned int
    cell_width, cell_height, pix_hoffset, pix_voffset, sw_hoffset, sw_voffset;
void redraw();

main(argc, argv)
int argc;
char *argv[ ];
{
    extern char *strcpy();
    XtAppContext app;
    Widget toplevel, scrolled_w;
    Bitmap *list = (Bitmap *)NULL;
    GC gc;
    char buf[128], *p;
    XFontStruct *font;
    int i = 0, total = 0;
    unsigned int bitmap_error;
    int j, k;
    void scrolled(), expose_resize();

    toplevel = XtAppInitialize(&app, argv[0], NULL, 0,
        &argc, argv, NULL, NULL, 0);
    dpy = XtDisplay(toplevel);

    font = XLoadQueryFont(dpy, "fixed");

    /* load bitmaps from filenames specified on command line */
    while (*++argv) {
        printf("Loading \"%s\"...", *argv), fflush(stdout);
        if (i == total) {
            total += 10; /* allocate bitmap structures in groups of 10 */
            if (!(list = (Bitmap *)XtRealloc(list, total * sizeof (Bitmap))))
                XtError("Not enough memory for bitmap data");
        }
        /* read bitmap file using standard X routine.  Save the resulting
         * image if the file isn't too big.
         */
        if ((bitmap_error = XReadBitmapFile(dpy, DefaultRootWindow(dpy),
                *argv, &list[i].width, &list[i].height, &list[i].bitmap,
                &j, &k)) == BitmapSuccess) {
            if (list[i].width > MAX_WIDTH || list[i].height > MAX_HEIGHT) {
                printf("%s: bitmap too big\n", p);
                XFreePixmap(dpy, list[i].bitmap);
                continue;
            }
            /* Get just the base filename (minus leading pathname)
             * We save this value for later use when we caption the bitmap.
             */
            if (p = rindex(*argv, '/'))
                p++;
```

Example 9-4. The app-scroll.c program (continued)

```
                else
                    p = *argv;
                list[i].len = strlen(p);
                list[i].name = p;   /* we'll be getting it later */
                printf("size: %dx%d\n", list[i].width, list[i].height);
                i++;
        } else {
                printf("couldn't load bitmap: \"%s\": ", *argv);
                switch (bitmap_error) {
                    case BitmapOpenFailed : puts("open failed."); break;
                    case BitmapFileInvalid : puts("bad file format."); break;
                    case BitmapNoMemory : puts("not enough memory."); break;
                }
        }
    }
    if ((total = i) == 0) {
        puts("Couldn't load any bitmaps.");
        exit(1);
    }
    printf("Total bitmaps loaded: %d\n", total);
    /* calculate size for pixmap by getting the dimensions of each. */
    printf("Calculating sizes for pixmap..."), fflush(stdout);
    for (i = 0; i < total; i++) {
        if (list[i].width > cell_width)
            cell_width = list[i].width;
        if (list[i].height > cell_height)
            cell_height = list[i].height;
        /* the bitmap's size is one thing, but its caption may exceed it */
        if ((j = XTextWidth(font, list[i].name, list[i].len)) > cell_width)
            cell_width = j;
    }
    /* compensate for font in the vertical dimension; add a 6 pixel padding */
    cell_height += 6 + font->ascent + font->descent;
    cell_width += 6;
    cols = int_sqrt(total);
    rows = (total + cols-1)/cols;

    printf("Creating pixmap area of size %dx%d (%d rows, %d cols)\n",
        cols * cell_width, rows * cell_height, rows, cols);

    /* Create a single, 1-bit deep pixmap */
    if (!(pixmap = XCreatePixmap(dpy, DefaultRootWindow(dpy),
            cols * cell_width + 1, rows * cell_height + 1, 1)))
        XtError("Can't Create pixmap");

    if (!(gc = XCreateGC(dpy, pixmap, NULL, 0)))
        XtError("Can't create gc");
    XSetForeground(dpy, gc, 0); /* 1-bit deep pixmaps use 0 as background */
    /* Clear the pixmap by setting the entire image to 0's */
    XFillRectangle(dpy, pixmap, gc, 0, 0,
        cols * cell_width, rows * cell_height);
    XSetForeground(dpy, gc, 1); /* Set the foreground to 1 (1-bit deep) */
    XSetFont(dpy, gc, font->fid); /* to print bitmap filenames (captions) */

    /* Draw the grid lines between bitmaps */
    for (j = 0; j <= rows * cell_height; j += cell_height)
        XDrawLine(dpy, pixmap, gc, 0, j, cols * cell_width, j);
    for (j = 0; j <= cols * cell_width; j += cell_width)
```

Example 9-4. The app-scroll.c program (continued)

```
            XDrawLine(dpy, pixmap, gc, j, 0, j, rows*cell_height);

    /* Draw each of the bitmaps into the big picture */
    for (i = 0; i < total; i++) {
        int x = cell_width * (i % cols);
        int y = cell_height * (i / cols);
        XDrawString(dpy, pixmap, gc, x+5, y+font->ascent,
            list[i].name, list[i].len);
        XCopyArea(dpy, list[i].bitmap, pixmap, gc,
            0, 0, list[i].width, list[i].height,
            x+5, y + font->ascent + font->descent);
        /* Once we copy it into the big picture, we don't need the bitmap */
        XFreePixmap(dpy, list[i].bitmap);
    }
    XtFree(list); /* don't need the array of structs anymore */
    XFreeGC(dpy, gc); /* nor do we need this GC */

    /* Create automatic Scrolled Window */
    scrolled_w = XtVaCreateManagedWidget("scrolled_w",
        xmScrolledWindowWidgetClass, toplevel,
        XmNscrollingPolicy, XmAPPLICATION_DEFINED, /* default values */
        XmNvisualPolicy,    XmVARIABLE,            /* specified for clarity */
        NULL);

    /* Create a drawing area as a child of the ScrolledWindow.
     * The DA's size is initialized (arbitrarily) to view_width and
     * view_height.  The ScrolledWindow will expand to this size.
     */
    drawing_a = XtVaCreateManagedWidget("drawing_a",
        xmDrawingAreaWidgetClass, scrolled_w,
        XmNwidth,       view_width,
        XmNheight,      view_height,
        NULL);

    XtAddCallback(drawing_a, XmNexposeCallback, expose_resize, NULL);
    XtAddCallback(drawing_a, XmNresizeCallback, expose_resize, NULL);

    /* Application-defined ScrolledWindows won't create their own
     * Scrollbars.  So, we create them ourselves as children of the
     * ScrolledWindow widget.  The vertical Scrollbar's maximum size is
     * the number of rows that exist (in unit values).  The horizontal
     * Scrollbar's maximum width is represented by the number of columns.
     */
    vsb = XtVaCreateManagedWidget("vsb", xmScrollBarWidgetClass, scrolled_w,
        XmNorientation, XmVERTICAL,
        XmNmaximum,     rows,
        XmNsliderSize,  min(view_height / cell_height, rows),
        NULL);
    if (view_height / cell_height > rows)
        sw_voffset = (view_height - rows * cell_height)/2;
    hsb = XtVaCreateManagedWidget("hsb", xmScrollBarWidgetClass, scrolled_w,
        XmNorientation, XmHORIZONTAL,
        XmNmaximum,     cols,
        XmNsliderSize,  min(view_width / cell_width, cols),
        NULL);
    if (view_width / cell_width > cols)
        sw_hoffset = (view_width - cols * cell_width)/2;
```

Example 9-4. The app-scroll.c program (continued)

```
        /* Allow the ScrolledWindow to initialize itself accordingly...*/
        XmScrolledWindowSetAreas(scrolled_w, hsb, vsb, drawing_a);

        /* use same callback for both Scrollbars and all callback reasons */
        XtAddCallback(vsb, XmNvalueChangedCallback, scrolled, XmVERTICAL);
        XtAddCallback(hsb, XmNvalueChangedCallback, scrolled, XmHORIZONTAL);
        XtAddCallback(vsb, XmNdragCallback, scrolled, XmVERTICAL);
        XtAddCallback(hsb, XmNdragCallback, scrolled, XmHORIZONTAL);

        XtRealizeWidget(toplevel);
        XtAppMainLoop(app);
}

/* React to scrolling actions.  Reset position of Scrollbars; call redraw()
 * to do actual scrolling.  cbs->value is Scrollbar's new position.
 */
void
scrolled(scrollbar, orientation, cbs)
Widget scrollbar;
int orientation; /* XmVERTICAL or XmHORIZONTAL */
XmScrollBarCallbackStruct *cbs;
{
    if (orientation == XmVERTICAL)
        pix_voffset = cbs->value * cell_height;
    else
        pix_hoffset = cbs->value * cell_width;
    redraw(XtWindow(drawing_a));
}

/* This function handles both expose and resize (configure) events.
 * For XmCR_EXPOSE, just call redraw() and return.  For resizing,
 * we must calculate the new size of the viewable area and possibly
 * reposition the pixmap's display and position offsets.  Since we
 * are also responsible for the Scrollbars, adjust them accordingly.
 */
void
expose_resize(drawing_a, unused, cbs)
Widget drawing_a;
XtPointer unused;
XmDrawingAreaCallbackStruct *cbs;
{
    Dimension new_width, new_height, oldw, oldh;
    int do_clear = 0;

    if (cbs->reason == XmCR_EXPOSE) {
        redraw(cbs->window);
        return;
    }
    oldw = view_width;
    oldh = view_height;

    /* Unfortunately, the cbs->event field is NULL, so we have to have
     * get the size of the drawing area manually.  A misdesign of
     * the DrawingArea widget--not a bug (technically).
     */
    XtVaGetValues(drawing_a,
        XmNwidth,  &view_width,
        XmNheight, &view_height,
```

Example 9-4. The app-scroll.c program (continued)

```
        NULL);

    /* Get the size of the viewable area in "units lengths" where
     * each unit is the cell size for each dimension.  This prevents
     * rounding error for the pix_voffset and pix_hoffset values later.
     */
    new_width = view_width / cell_width;
    new_height = view_height / cell_height;

    /* When the user resizes the frame bigger, expose events are generated,
     * so that's not a problem, since the expose handler will repaint the
     * whole viewport.  However, when the window resizes smaller, no
     * expose event is generated.  The window does not need to be
     * redisplayed if the old viewport was smaller than the pixmap.
     * (The existing image is still valid--no redisplay is necessary.)
     * The window WILL need to be redisplayed if:
     *  1) new view size is larger than pixmap (pixmap needs to be centered).
     *  2) new view size is smaller than pixmap, but the OLD view size was
     *     larger than pixmap.
     */
    if (new_height >= rows) {
        /* The height of the viewport is taller than the pixmap, so set
         * pix_voffset = 0, so the top origin of the pixmap is shown,
         * and the pixmap is centered vertically in viewport.
         */
        pix_voffset = 0;
        sw_voffset = (view_height - rows * cell_height)/2;
        /* Case 1 above */
        do_clear = 1;
        /* scrollbar is maximum size */
        new_height = rows;
    } else {
        /* Pixmap is larger than viewport, so viewport will be completely
         * redrawn on the redisplay.  (So, we don't need to clear window.)
         * Make sure upper side has origin of a cell (bitmap).
         */
        pix_voffset = min(pix_voffset, (rows-new_height) * cell_height);
        sw_voffset = 0; /* no centering is done */
        /* Case 2 above */
        if (oldh > rows * cell_height)
            do_clear = 1;
    }
    XtVaSetValues(vsb,
        XmNsliderSize,     max(new_height, 1),
        XmNvalue,          pix_voffset / cell_height,
        XmNpageIncrement, max(new_height-1, 1),
        NULL);

    /* identical to vertical case above */
    if (new_width >= cols) {
        /* The width of the viewport is wider than the pixmap, so set
         * pix_hoffset = 0, so the left origin of the pixmap is shown,
         * and the pixmap is centered horizontally in viewport.
         */
        pix_hoffset = 0;
        sw_hoffset = (view_width - cols * cell_width)/2;
        /* Case 1 above */
```

Example 9-4. The app-scroll.c program (continued)

```
            do_clear = 1;
            /* scrollbar is maximum size */
            new_width = cols;
        } else {
            /* Pixmap is larger than viewport, so viewport will be completely
             * redrawn on the redisplay.  (So, we don't need to clear window.)
             * Make sure left side has origin of a cell (bitmap).
             */
            pix_hoffset = min(pix_hoffset, (cols-new_width)*cell_width);
            sw_hoffset = 0;
            /* Case 2 above */
            if (oldw > cols * cell_width)
                do_clear = 1;
        }
        XtVaSetValues(hsb,
            XmNsliderSize,    max(new_width, 1),
            XmNvalue,         pix_hoffset / cell_width,
            XmNpageIncrement, max(new_width-1, 1),
            NULL);

        if (do_clear) {
            /* XClearWindow() doesn't generate an ExposeEvent */
            XClearArea(dpy, cbs->window, 0, 0, 0, 0, True);
                                /* all 0's means the whole window */
        }
}

void
redraw(window)
Window window;
{
    static GC gc; /* static variables are *ALWAYS* initialized to NULL */
    if (!gc) { /* !gc means that this GC hasn't yet been created. */
        /* We create our own gc because the other one is based on a 1-bit
         * bitmap and the drawing area window might be color (multiplane).
         * Remember, we're rendering a multiplane pixmap, not the original
         * single-plane bitmaps!
         */
        gc = XCreateGC(dpy, window, NULL, 0);
        XSetForeground(dpy, gc, BlackPixelOfScreen(XtScreen(drawing_a)));
        XSetBackground(dpy, gc, WhitePixelOfScreen(XtScreen(drawing_a)));
    }
    /* Some X servers might require a call to XClearWindow() here in order
     * to clean up "dirty" parts of the ScrolledWindow's viewport.  So far,
     * this only happens on the black and white screen for Sun's with enable
     * planes (sun3/60, sun4/110, etc).
    XClearWindow(dpy, window);
     */
    if (DefaultDepthOfScreen(XtScreen(drawing_a)) > 1)
        XCopyPlane(dpy, pixmap, window, gc, pix_hoffset, pix_voffset,
            view_width, view_height, sw_hoffset, sw_voffset, 1L);
    else
        XCopyArea(dpy, pixmap, window, gc, pix_hoffset, pix_voffset,
            view_width, view_height, sw_hoffset, sw_voffset);
}
```

The program begins by loading the bitmaps into an array of `Bitmap` structures especially designed for this application. Each bitmap is stored into an allocated list of structures, which can be evaluated again after they are all loaded to establish the size of the pixmap. The pixmap is created with only a single-plane (a bitmap), since no color was used to render the standard X11 bitmaps when they were originally created. This saves lots of memory on color displays.

After the bitmaps are loaded, the ScrolledWindow and DrawingArea are created. The DrawingArea has `XmNexposeCallback` and `XmNresizeCallback` callbacks installed so that the pixmap can be rendered or repositioned within the DrawingArea at any time. Resizing does not cause the *pixmap* to change, but it may cause its origin to be repositioned relative to the DrawingArea widget. We'll get into this later when we examine `expose_resize( )`.

The Scrollbars are created separately from the ScrolledWindow (as required by the specifications for `XmAPPLICATION_DEFINED`), but they are still created as children of the ScrolledWindow.

```
vsb = XtVaCreateManagedWidget("vsb", xmScrollBarWidgetClass, scrolled_w,
    XmNorientation, XmVERTICAL,
    XmNmaximum,     rows,
    XmNsliderSize,  min(view_height / cell_height, rows),
    NULL);
if (view_height / cell_height > rows)
    sw_voffset = (view_height - rows * cell_height)/2;
```

They are each initialized so that their `XmNmaximum` values are set to the number of rows (vertical) and columns (horizontal) generated by the number of bitmaps. Similarly, the `XmNsliderSize` is set to the number of bitmap cells that can fit in the viewport in the horizontal or vertical dimensions. Internally, the application knows how many pixels each scrolling unit represents; there is no Scrollbar resource to set for this value. The variables `sw_hoffset` and `sw_voffset` are used when the pixmap is smaller than the actual ScrolledWindow. Under these circumstances, these variables indicate the origin of the pixmap into the DrawingArea so that the pixmap appears centered, as shown in Figure 9-8.

The call to `XmScrolledWindowSetAreas( )` ties it all together for the internals of the ScrolledWindow. This function assigns the Scrollbars and the DrawingArea widget to internal variables within the ScrolledWindow in order for it to function properly. This is basically an opaque call to the programmer, but it must be done for application-defined scrolling.

The Scrollbars are then assigned callback routines for the `XmNvalueChangedCallback` and `XmNdragCallback` callbacks. Here, we will be able to handle all scrolling actions, including incremental and page scrolling, that cause the Scrollbar's value to change. We pass the values `XmHORIZONTAL` and `XmVERTICAL` as the callback data values so the routine knows which of the two Scrollbars invoked it.

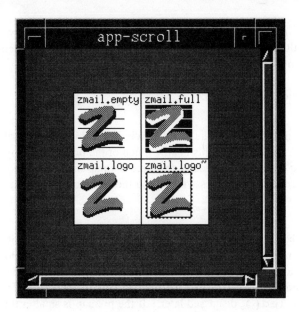

Figure 9-8. app-scroll.c when the display is larger than the data

Finally, the top-level widget is realized and the main loop is started. At this point, the DrawingArea is realized, so the **XmNexposeCallback** is activated, causing the Drawing-Area to draw itself, thus displaying the first image of the pixmap. The function **expose_resize()** handles both the **Expose** and **ConfigureNotify** (resize) events. It determines which was delivered by checking the **reason** field of the callback structure passed to the function:

```
if (cbs->reason == XmCR_EXPOSE) {
    redraw(cbs->window);
    return;
}
```

For **Expose** events, no recalculation of variables is necessary. All we need to do is redraw the display. When **redraw()** is called, it merely calls **XCopyArea()** or **XCopy-Plane()** to copy the relevant portions of the full pixmap directly into the DrawingArea. The fact that the pixmap is one bit deep may require the use of **XCopyPlane()** if the program is running on a color screen. (The DrawingArea cannot create a 1-bit deep window on a color screen because Motif widgets always create windows of the same depth as the screen on which they reside.) If the application is run on a monochrome screen, we can use **XCopyArea()**. We determine whether the screen can support color by using **Default-DepthOfScreen()**.

The position at which the pixmap is rendered into the DrawingArea's window is somewhat complicated to calculate. There are two cases to consider:

1. The pixmap is larger than the clip window, in which case the clip window acts as a view into the work window, so only a portion of it can be seen.

2. The pixmap is smaller than the clip window, so the entire pixmap can be seen along with some surrounding *whitespace* (although it may not be white). In this case, for aesthetic reasons, the pixmap should be centered in the middle of the viewable area.

This behavior is controlled by the following variables:

`view_width`, `view_height`
> These values represent the dimensions of the ScrolledWindow, which are also the dimensions of the DrawingArea window. This is how much of the pixmap `XCopy-Area( )` or `XCopyPlane( )` is going to copy from the pixmap into the window. For case two above, the fact that these values will exceed the width of the pixmap is handled correctly by the X server.

`pix_hoffset`, `pix_voffset`
> These values represent the horizontal and vertical offsets into the pixmap when it is rendered into the DrawingArea. In the first case, if the user has scrolled the window several bitmap cells into the image, then these variables will have calculated these offsets into pixel offsets and passed them onto the pixmap copying routine. (This calculation occurs in `scrolled( )`, discussed later.) If the pixmap is smaller than the ScrolledWindow/DrawingArea (case two), then these values will be set to 0, because the pixmap's origin will always be visible.

`sw_hoffset`, `sw_voffset`
> These variables are used when the pixmap is smaller than the ScrolledWindow and DrawingArea windows (case two). They indicate the top and left offsets into the DrawingArea where the entire pixmap can be rendered so that it appears centered in the viewport.

The `redraw( )` routine depends on those variables already having been set. The way to maintain their values is to monitor the size of the ScrolledWindow continuously. This brings us back to the routine `expose_resize( )`, which is the callback for both `XmNexpose-Callback` and `XmNresizeCallback`. This routine is called whenever the Drawing-Area is resized, which will be any time the user (or the window manager) resizes the ScrolledWindow. The ScrolledWindow passes its resize events onto its children, which includes the Scrollbars and the DrawingArea.

In the case where the DrawingArea is resized, we need to get its new dimensions so we can update those other six variables mentioned above. Normally, we could get the new dimensions directly from the **event** field of the callback structure, but the DrawingArea widget does not invoke the `XmNresizeCallback` callback list from an action routine as it does for other sorts of events. The routine is instead invoked internally within the *resize method* of the DrawingArea widget, which does not have an **Xevent** structure associated with it.[4] This could be considered a design error by the Motif toolkit, since the **event** field of the callback structure is set to NULL. But, it's currently specified this way by the Motif toolkit,

---

[4] All widget internals have *methods* that are invoked automatically by the X Toolkit Intrinsics, and are not associated with the translation tables normally used to handle events. **Resize( )** is one such method. See Volume Four, *The X Toolkit Intrinsics Programmer's Manual*, for more information.

so are forced to resort to other means to get the window's size. Namely, we use `XtVaGet-Values()`:

```
XtVaGetValues(drawing_a,
    XmNwidth,  &view_width,
    XmNheight, &view_height,
    NULL);
```

Once the dimensions are obtained, the program now needs to recalculate each of the remaining four variables' values. These variables all represent pixel units, as opposed to the abstract unit size used by the Scrollbars. So, we must convert such units into pixels by multiplying them by the values for `cell_width` and `cell_height`. These are the internally-used pixels-per-unit values that are meaningless to the Motif toolkit and all its widgets. (This is also why we can't use the automatic scrolling method and why we do all these calculations ourselves.) The variables `new_width` and `new_height` represent the new viewport width and height in Scrollbar units. Since we manage the Scrollbars, we now have many different variables and resources to manage here.

If the new viewport height exceeds the total number of rows (of bitmaps), then we know that the height of the viewport exceeds the height of the pixmap. Thus, the value for `sw_voffset` is calculated to determine the point at which the pixmap will be vertically centered in the viewport. Since centering it will cause the viewport to be completely redisplayed, we set the local variable `do_clear` to 1. (We do this instead of calling `XClearWindow()` directly because we may have to do it again later when we calculate the values for the horizontal Scrollbar.) The value for `new_height` is also going to be used later to set the vertical Scrollbar's `XmNsliderSize`, so it must not exceed its `XmNmaximum` value.

On the other hand, if the new viewport height does not exceed the total number of rows, then we know that the pixmap is still larger than the viewport (at least vertically), so it will be completely redrawn on a redisplay. This means that we don't need to clear the window and that the pixmap is not going to be centered in the DrawingArea. Thus, `sw_voffset` is set to 0, indicating that the pixmap is rendered at the origin of the viewport. `pix_voffset` is set to the minimum of its existing value or difference between the total number of rows and the new height of the viewport. In other words, the case we are testing for is if the viewport *used to be bigger* than the pixmap, but now it got resized significantly smaller. Also, for this case, we still need to do a complete redisplay in order to clear up any blank spots on the DrawingArea that might be left over from the previous view. This is the sort of thing you can only pick up when you test your program thoroughly.

The exact same calculations are done for the horizontal Scrollbar, so there's nothing more to explain in that area. The only thing left is to set the Scrollbar's `XmNsliderSize`, `XmNvalue` and `XmNpageIncrement` resources to account for the new window sizes.

Incidentally, while we did not use it, **XmScrollBarSetValues()** could have been used to set these same resource values. This function takes the following form:

```
void
XmScrollBarSetValues(w, value, slider_size, increment, page_increment, notify)
    Widget w;                /* the Scrollbar widget */
    int value;               /* value for XmNvalue */
    int slider_size;         /* value for XmNsliderSize */
    int increment;           /* value for XmNincrement */
    int page_increment;      /* value for XmNpageIncrement */
    Boolean notify;          /* Notify Scrollbar's XmNvalueChangedCallback? */
```

The **notify** parameter can be **True** or **False** depending on whether you want the Scrollbar's **XmNvalueChangedCallback** to be invoked. Using this interface is probably slightly faster than using the **XtVaSetValues()** method we employed, but only by a small margin. We instead chose to maintain consistency with our own style.

The companion function for **XmScrollBarSetValues()** is **XmScrollBarGetValues()**. This function is almost the same, but it retrieves the values from the Scrollbar widget. For this function, you pass the addresses of integers:

```
void
XmScrollBarGetValues(w, value, slider_size, increment, page_increment)
    Widget w;
    int *value;
    int *slider_size;
    int *increment;
    int *page_increment;
```

Finally, the **scrolled()** function is the callback routine for the Scrollbars. This short routine is only used to determine the new offsets into the pixmap where it should be rendered into the DrawingArea. These values (vertical and horizontal) are calculated by multiplying the Scrollbar's value by the pixels-per-unit for the pixmap.

While Example 9-4 might seem complex and confusing, it does work. However, nothing explains this better than trying to implement it yourself. (Experience is the best teacher.)

9.4.1 Scrolling Text and List Widgets

Before closing this section, let's re-examine what the Text and List widgets do, and compare them with what we have done in Example 9-4. Earlier, we stated that while we mimic much of what these widgets do internally, the implementation is quite different. Indeed, the major difference is that we were fortunate enough to have all the bitmaps to be displayed loaded into a large statically sized pixmap that we can render at will using the **redraw()** function. That function is clearly a convenience, since it does not do anything more than call **XCopyArea()** or **XCopyPlane()** onto the DrawingArea using pre-calculated internal variables. The Text and List widgets don't have this luxury; they must re-render their respective texts directly into their work windows each time they need to redisplay. To do this type of thing in our program, we would have move the functionality of the main **for** loop in **main()** into **redraw()** and calculate each individual bitmap's location into the DrawingArea, taking into account all six variables' values.

Sound painstaking? It is—and very error-prone. You might also run into some X performance issues if you do not take into account multiple exposures, exposure regions and other sorts of low-level Xlib functionality. Indeed, we didn't even take these issues into account in our program. For example, our `redraw( )` method completely repaints the entire window for each and every **Expose** event (which is also generated on scrolling events). Strictly speaking, repainting is inefficient and may not perform adequately for all applications, especially graphic-intensive ones. However, you could come up with a generic set of routines to handle this, so all your applications could use the same methodology. Of course, that's what a toolkit is supposed to be for.

In closing, let's take another look at the PG&E scenario we discussed at the beginning of the chapter. As you recall, the problem with that particular situation was that the database could retrieve 20% of the county (the "work window"), but the graphic resolution was such that only 10% of it could be displayed at one time (the "viewport"). The fundamental problem with the application-defined scrolling mode is that the work window cannot be a different size from the viewport. However, we can work around this problem by complying with the restriction that the work window and viewport are the same size, but we can use the enlarged pixmap idea from Example 9-4 to accomplish the task. Each database query can be converted and rendered into a sufficiently large pixmap, which can then be rendered into the work window as necessary. If the scrolling is small enough, then another part of the pixmap can be rendered into the work window rather than having to do a completely new database lookup.

9.5 Summary

ScrolledWindows are extremely convenient interfaces for displaying large amounts of data when you have limited screen real estate. For most situations, the automatic scrolling mode is all you really need, and in this mode, ScrolledWindows require very little care and feeding. By installing callback routines on the Scrollbars, you can even monitor the scrolling actions. However, there are several drawbacks to the automatic scrolling mode: you must have all the data available already rendered into the work window widget, and you must accept single-pixel scrolling increments. If the size of the work window you need for automatic scrolling is prohibitively large, or if you need to support scrolling in other than single-pixel increments, you must use application-defined scrolling.

As demonstrated in Example 9-4, there is quite a bit of work involved in supporting real application-defined scrolling because of the different states in the relationship between the sizes of the work window and the clip window. You must be able to support not only the underlying data, but the way it's rendered into the work window, the Scrollbars, and all the auxiliary variables required for all the calculations. And that's just to support the functionality—when you introduce the complexity of a "real" application, there is a greater chance of a poor design model. The *xshowbitmap.c* program in Appendix D, *More Example Programs*, shows fundamentally the same program as *app-scroll.c*, but it has been "productized" into more of a real-world program.

9.6 Exercises

The following exercises focus on the concepts and methods described in this chapter.

1. In Chapter 10, *The DrawingArea Widget*, the program *color_draw.c* used a Scrolled-Window to support a DrawingArea widget that allows the user to draw different colored lines. Although this program uses an automatic ScrolledWindow, the work window is constantly updated as new lines are drawn. However, the lines are actually drawn into a background pixmap, rather than into the drawing area. (This pixmap is copied into the DrawingArea dynamically, giving the illusion that the user draws directly into it.) This method of indirection can be used to provide a method for the user to have two different views into the same pixmap. Write a program that uses two automatic ScrolledWindows and two DrawingArea widgets to draw into a single pixmap.

2. The first example in the chapter (*getusers.c*) uses an automatic ScrolledWindow to display a manager widget that contains many widgets and gadgets. Modify the program to use application-defined scrolling so that the scrolling increment for the vertical Scrollbar is the size of the height of one of the Forms. (Each Form will always be the same height.)

10

The DrawingArea Widget

This chapter describes the Motif DrawingArea widget, which provides a canvas for interactive drawing. Rather than trying to teach Xlib drawing, the chapter simply highlights, with numerous code examples, the difficulties that may be encountered when working with this widget. (Some knowledge of Xlib is assumed; we direct the user to Volume One, Xlib Programming Manual, for additional information.)

In This Chapter:

10
The DrawingArea Widget

The DrawingArea widget provides a blank canvas for interactive drawing using basic Xlib drawing primitives. The widget does no drawing of its own, nor does it define or support any Motif user-interface design. Subclassed from the Manager widget class, the DrawingArea widget may also contain other children, although there is frequently no assumed or regimented layout policy. In short, the DrawingArea is a free-form widget that you can use for various interactive drawing routines or object placement where conventional user-interface rules do not apply.

Why then should you use the DrawingArea widget? The most intuitive application is a drawing or painting program. Here, the user interactively draws geometric objects or paints arbitrary colors. Another interesting application demonstrated at a recent trade show used a DrawingArea widget to display a map of the United States with dynamically drawn line segments representing the flight paths taken by an airplane. The actual airplane that follows the path was represented by a PushButton widget displaying a pixmap. The airplane icon moved dynamically along the flight path unless the user grabbed and moved it interactively (in order to change the flight path). Both of these examples demonstrate how certain applications require visual or interactive interfaces that go beyond the scope of the structured interface employed by Motif.

In order to support the widest range of uses for the DrawingArea widget, the toolkit provides callback resources for Expose, Configure (resize), and input (Button or Key press) events. Each of these resources allow you to install very simple drawing routines without doing substantial event-handling of your own. Unfortunately, this level of event-handling support is usually insufficient for most robust applications. Thus, you will probably want to install many of your own direct event handlers or action routines to manage user input. The "free-form" nature of the DrawingArea makes it one of the few Motif widgets where you can do this without risking Motif incompliance. (Most Motif widgets either do not allow programmer-installed translations or (silently) accept only a few override translations for fear that you might inadvertently interfere with Motif GUI specifications.)

The DrawingArea widget never draws into itself except to paint its own three-dimensional shadow borders. Repainting of the window's contents is the responsibility of the application alone. However, because of the three-dimensional shadowing the widget handles, you should take care not to draw onto those parts of the widget.

The DrawingArea widget is subclassed from the Manager widget class, which means that it can have other widgets or gadgets as children. When using a DrawingArea as a manager widget, there are two important things to keep in mind: translation tables (input event model) and widget layout management.

As a Manager widget subclass, the DrawingArea inherits certain translation and action tables that pass events to gadget children (since gadgets have no windows of their own to receive events) and that handle tab group traversal. Because of the inherited translations, you must be careful about application-specific translations that you may introduce into particular instances of the DrawingArea. If you are planning to use the DrawingArea to contain children *and* to have those children follow the standard Motif keyboard traversal motions, you must be careful not to override the existing translations.

However, if you need a manager widget in the conventional sense, you should probably choose something other than a DrawingArea widget. The DrawingArea widget has no geometry management policy of its own. It should probably be used to manage children only when no structured widget layout policy is needed (as in the airline application from the trade show).

Because a manager widget assumes the dual responsibility of managing children and allowing for application-defined interaction, there are going to be some complexities and inconveniences with event handling if you try to exploit both aspects of the widget simultaneously.

10.1 Creating a DrawingArea Widget

Applications that wish to create DrawingArea widgets must include the file *<Xm/Drawing-A.h>*. To create a DrawingArea widget, you can use the following call:

```
Widget  drawing_a;

drawing_a = XtVaCreateManagedWidget("name",
    xmDrawingAreaWidgetClass, parent,
    resource-values,
    NULL);
```

The **parent** of the DrawingArea must be either a Shell of some kind or a manager widget. It is quite common to find a DrawingArea widget as a child of a ScrolledWindow (or of a MainWindow, which more or less amounts to the same thing), since drawing surfaces tend to be quite large, or at least dynamic in their growth potential.

If the DrawingArea widget is to have children, one might want to follow the rules set forth in Chapter 8, *Manager Widgets*, which states that managers are created as *unmanaged* widgets. They are managed by a call to **XtManageChild( )** after their own children have been created. However, we won't demonstrate this, since we are not going to use the widget as a traditional manager. There is not going to be a great deal of parent-child interaction involving geometry management.

10.1.1 Choices in DrawingArea Event Handling

The DrawingArea widget provides virtually no visual resources and very few functional ones. The most important resources are those that allow you to provide callback functions for handling expose, resize, and input events. After all, the DrawingArea is typically input-intensive and, unlike most of the other Motif widgets, requires the host application to provide all the necessary redrawing. For example, the callback for `XmNexposeCallback` is called whenever an **Expose** event is generated. In this callback function, the application must repaint all or part of the contents of the DrawingArea widget. Unless the application does this, the widget is cleared automatically. Similarly, the `XmNresizeCallback` is called whenever a **ConfigureNotify** event occurs as a result of the DrawingArea being resized. The generalized callback `XmNinputCallback` is invoked upon receipt of any keyboard or button event (down and up, but not button-motion (*drag*) events).

As discussed in Chapter 2, *The Motif Programming Model*, callback routines are invoked by internal *action routines*, which are an integral part of all Motif widgets. Translation tables are used to specify X event sequences that invoke action routines, which are intermediate functions usually implemented by the internals of a widget set such as the Motif toolkit. Action functions in turn typically invoke the appropriate application callback functions associated with the widget's resources.

Most Motif widgets do not allow the application to override or replace their default translations; the input model that allows the application to conform to the Motif specifications is not to be overridden by the application. However, because of the free-form nature of the DrawingArea widget, you are at liberty to override or replace the default translation tables used for event-handling and notification without risking Motif incompliance.

If you install your own translation tables, you can have your actions call callback routines (as is done by the existing DrawingArea actions), or you can have your own action functions do their drawing directly. For even tighter control over your event-handling, you can install event handlers at the X Toolkit Intrinsics level.

There are a number of techniques available for doing event management, and we only demonstrate a few of them in this chapter. The technique you choose is a matter of personal preference and the intended extensibility of your application. Event handlers involve less overhead, but translations are user-configurable. Either approach provides more flexibility than the DrawingArea widget's default translation table and set of callback resources. See Volume Four, *X Toolkit Intrinsics Programming Manual*, for a detailed discussion of translation tables and action routines and how they are associated with callback functions.

Let's begin with a demonstration of the callback approach.

10.1.2 DrawingArea Callback Functions

Example 10-1 shows an extremely simple drawing program that associates a line drawing function with the `XmNinputCallback` resource. Pressing any of the pointer buttons marks the starting point of a line; releasing the button marks the endpoint. Only straight lines can be drawn. Note that even though the default translation table for the DrawingArea widget selects key events as well, and they too are passed to the callback function; the callback function itself ignores them. Key events thus have no effect.

To demonstrate the complications inherent in using the DrawingArea widget as a manager, the program also displays a PushButtonGadget that clears the window (including the **Clear** button itself!) The single callback function, `drawing_area_callback()`, exploits both the `reason` field of the `XmDrawingAreaCallbackStruct` and the event itself, which are passed in to the callback routine, to identify whether to draw or to clear the window.

This very simple application draws directly into the DrawingArea widget, and the contents of its window are not saved anywhere. This may be a problem if the window is exposed due to the movement of other windows, for example. The *drawing.c* program does not support redrawing, since its purpose is to demonstrate the way input handling can be managed using strictly the `XmNinputCallback` resource. (This is a shortcoming of the application, not of the DrawingArea widget. The correct technique is demonstrated later in this chapter, when the drawing area is placed into a ScrolledWindow widget.)

A more realistic drawing application would need code to handle resize actions. The current application simply clears the window on resize to further illustrate that the DrawingArea does not retain what is in its window.

Example 10-1. The drawing.c program

```
/* drawing.c -- extremely simple drawing program that introduces
 * the DrawingArea widget.  This widget provides a window for
 * drawing and some callbacks for getting input and other misc
 * events.  It's also a manager, so it can have children.
 * There is no geometry management, tho.
 */
#include <Xm/DrawingA.h>
#include <Xm/PushBG.h>
#include <Xm/RowColumn.h>

main(argc, argv)
int argc;
char *argv[ ];
{
    Widget toplevel, drawing_a, pb;
    XtAppContext app;
    XGCValues gcv;
    GC gc;
    void drawing_area_callback();

    toplevel = XtVaAppInitialize(&app, "Demos", NULL, 0,
        &argc, argv, NULL,
        XmNwidth,   400,
        XmNheight, 300,
        NULL);

    /* Create a DrawingArea widget. */
    drawing_a = XtVaCreateWidget("drawing_a",
        xmDrawingAreaWidgetClass, toplevel,
        NULL);
    /* add callback for all mouse and keyboard input events */
    XtAddCallback(drawing_a, XmNinputCallback, drawing_area_callback, NULL);
```

Example 10-1. The drawing.c program (continued)

The DrawingArea Widget

```
    /* Since we're going to be drawing, we will be using Xlib routines
     * and therefore need a graphics context.  Create a GC and attach
     * to the DrawingArea's XmNuserData to avoid having to make global
     * variable. (Avoiding globals is a good design principle to follow.)
     */
    gcv.foreground = BlackPixelOfScreen(XtScreen(drawing_a));
    gc = XCreateGC(XtDisplay(drawing_a),
        RootWindowOfScreen(XtScreen(drawing_a)), GCForeground, &gcv);
    XtVaSetValues(drawing_a, XmNuserData, gc, NULL);

    /* add a pushbutton the user can use to clear the canvas */
    pb = XtVaCreateManagedWidget("Clear",
        xmPushButtonGadgetClass, drawing_a,
        NULL);
    /* if activated, call same callback as XmNinputCallback. */
    XtAddCallback(pb, XmNactivateCallback, drawing_area_callback, NULL);

    XtManageChild(drawing_a);
    XtRealizeWidget(toplevel);
    XtAppMainLoop(app);
}
/* Callback routine for DrawingArea's input callbacks and the
 * PushButton's activate callback.  Determine which it is by
 * testing the cbs->reason field.
 */
void
drawing_area_callback(widget, data, cbs)
Widget widget;
XtPointer data;
XmDrawingAreaCallbackStruct *cbs;
{
    static Position x, y;
    XEvent *event = cbs->event;

    if (cbs->reason == XmCR_INPUT) {
        /* activated by DrawingArea input event -- draw lines.
         * Button Down events anchor the initial point and Button
         * Up draws from the anchor point to the button-up point.
         */
        if (event->xany.type == ButtonPress) {
            /* anchor initial point (i.e., save its value) */
            x = event->xbutton.x;
            y = event->xbutton.y;
        } else if (event->xany.type == ButtonRelease) {
            /* draw full line; get GC and use in XDrawLine() */
            GC gc;
            XtVaGetValues(widget, XmNuserData, &gc, NULL);
            XDrawLine(event->xany.display, cbs->window, gc, x, y,
                event->xbutton.x, event->xbutton.y);
            x = event->xbutton.x;
            y = event->xbutton.y;
        }
    }

    if (cbs->reason == XmCR_ACTIVATE)
        /* activated by pushbutton -- clear parent's window */
```

Example 10-1. The drawing.c program (continued)

```
        XClearWindow(event->xany.display, XtWindow(XtParent(widget)));
}
```

The output of the program is shown in Figure 10-1.

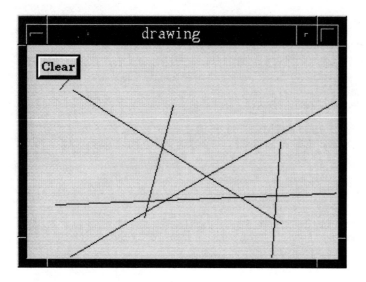

Figure 10-1. Output of drawing.c

The callback routine that is used for **XmNinputCallback** takes the following parameters:

```
drawing_area_callback(widget, data, cbs)
    Widget widget;
    XtPointer data;
    XmDrawingAreaCallbackStruct *cbs;
```

The **widget** parameter is the DrawingArea widget that received the event. The **data** parameter is provided by the application in the call to **XtAddCallback( )** used in **main( )**. In this case, the parameter is unused, so we passed **NULL**. The **XmDrawing-AreaCallbackStruct** is provided by the DrawingArea widget for all its callbacks. It has the form:

```
typedef struct {
    int       reason;
    XEvent    *event;
    Window    window;
} XmDrawingAreaCallbackStruct;
```

The **reason** field identifies the type of occurrence that caused the callback to be invoked. However, since the event itself is passed in as part of the callback structure, we can also look at the **type** field of the event for more specific information. (See Volume One, *Xlib Programming Manual*, for a detailed description of **XEvent** structures and how to use them.) In fact, since there are many possible events that can be associated with the reason **Xm-CR_INPUT**, you have to look at the event structure if you need to get down to that detail.

Table 10-1 shows what the event possibilities are for each of the callback reasons.

Table 10-1. Callback Reasons and Event Types

Callback	cbs->event->xany.type	cbs->reason
XmNexposeCallback	Expose	XmCR_EXPOSE
XmNresizeCallback	ConfigureNotify	XmCR_RESIZE
XmNinputCallback	ButtonPress, ButtonRelease KeyPress, KeyRelease	XmCR_INPUT

The **event** field of the callback structure describes the event that caused the callback to be invoked.[1] The **window** field is the window associated with the DrawingArea widget—this is the same value returned by calling **XtWindow( )** on the widget.

A common convention we've included in this program is the double use of the **drawing_area_callback( )** function. (This is also known as *function overloading*, since the same function is used by more than one source.) That is, we used it as the callback for the input callback for the DrawingArea widget, as well as the activate callback for the Push-Button gadget. Whenever the PushButton is activated, the callback function is invoked with the **reason** field set to **XmCR_ACTIVATE**.

Note that in function overloading, the callback structure (the third parameter) is different for each type of callback resource. It is therefore necessary to typecast the pointer into the appropriate data type for the callback structure used. For example, if the **reason** is **XmCR_ACTIVATE**, then we know that the PushButton was activated and that the callback structure is of type **XmPushButtonCallbackStruct**. As it turns out, all we want to do is clear the window, and that doesn't require any information from that particular callback structure. We only need to call **XClearWindow( )**:

```
XClearWindow(cbs->event->xany.display, XtWindow(XtParent(widget)));
```

The **widget** parameter is the PushButton, while the window we want to clear is the DrawingArea. We can obtain this information by nesting the **XtParent( )** and **XtWindow( )** macros.

Xlib Drawing

It is beyond the scope of this book to discuss at length or even introduce the use of Xlib; for that, see Volume One, *Xlib Programming Manual*. However, there are a couple of details concerning the use of Xlib functions that are worthy of note.

For efficiency in use of the X Protocol, Xlib drawing calls typically don't carry a lot of information about the drawing to be done. Instead, drawing characteristics such as the foreground and background colors, fill style, line weight, and so on, are defined in a Graphics Context

---

[1] *Note:* in older versions of the Motif toolkit, this pointer is **NULL** if **reason** is **XmCR_RESIZE**.

(GC), which is cached in the X server. Any drawing function that wishes to use a particular GC must include the handle returned by a GC creation call.

If many different routines are going to use the same GC, the programmer should try to make the handle to it generally available. The natural thing to do for most people is to declare the GC as a global variable. However, as programs get large (as any program that has a graphical user interface will), most programmers get carried away with the use of global variables. As a result, programs tend to get overly complicated and decentralized. To avoid this problem, you can exploit the **XmNuserData** resource (inherited from the Manager widget class) as a temporary holding area for arbitrary pointers and values. You may be asking, "Is a global variable so bad that it's worth the overhead of a call to *XtGetValues( )*?" In this case, probably not; but programs also tend not to be as small as this one. It's up to you how you want to use the **XmNuserData**; this particular example just shows one way.

All of the other information required by the drawing call is obtained from the event structure passed in to the callback function.

10.1.3 Redrawing a DrawingArea

There is a wide open hole in Example 10-1: the drawing is not retained in the DrawingArea whenever an **Expose** or **Resize** event occurs. As a result, the DrawingArea is always cleared. This was intentional for the first example because we wanted to focus on the use of the callback routines, especially the input mechanism. However, when using the Drawing-Area widget, you must always be prepared to "repaint" whatever is supposed to be displayed in the widget at any time.

As you may already know, most X servers support a feature called *backing store*, which saves the contents of windows, even when they are obscured by other windows, and repaints them when they are exposed. When backing store is enabled and there is enough memory available for the server, X will repaint all "damaged" windows without ever notifying the application that anything happened. However, you should never rely on this behavior, since you never know if the X server supports backing store, or has enough memory to save the contents of your windows. All applications are ultimately responsible for redrawing their windows' contents whenever necessary.

For a painting application, like that in Example 10-1, the easiest way to make sure that a window can be repainted whenever necessary is to draw both into the window and into an offscreen pixmap. The contents of the pixmap can be copied back into the window as needed.

Example 10-2 demonstrates such a program. The offscreen pixmap is copied back to the window with **XCopyArea( )** to redisplay the drawing when an **XmNexposeCallback** is called.

Example 10-2. The draw2.c program

```
/* draw2.c -- extremely simple drawing program that demonstrates
 * how to draw into an off screen pixmap in order to retain the
 * contents of the DrawingArea widget.  This allows us to redisplay
 * the widget if it needs repainting (expose events).
 */
#include <Xm/DrawingA.h>
#include <Xm/PushBG.h>
#include <Xm/RowColumn.h>

#define WIDTH 400     /* arbitrary width and height values */
#define HEIGHT 300

Pixmap pixmap; /* used to redraw the DrawingArea */

main(argc, argv)
int argc;
char *argv[ ];
{
    Widget toplevel, drawing_a, pb;
    XtAppContext app;
    GC gc;
    void drawing_area_callback();

    toplevel = XtVaAppInitialize(&app, "Demos", NULL, 0,
        &argc, argv, NULL,
        XmNwidth,  WIDTH,
        XmNheight, HEIGHT,
        NULL);

    /* Create a DrawingArea widget. */
    drawing_a = XtVaCreateWidget("drawing_a",
        xmDrawingAreaWidgetClass, toplevel,
        NULL);
    /* add callback for all mouse and keyboard input events */
    XtAddCallback(drawing_a, XmNinputCallback, drawing_area_callback, NULL);
    XtAddCallback(drawing_a, XmNexposeCallback, drawing_area_callback, NULL);

    gc = XCreateGC(XtDisplay(drawing_a),
        RootWindowOfScreen(XtScreen(drawing_a)), 0, NULL);
    XtVaSetValues(drawing_a, XmNuserData, gc, NULL);

    XSetForeground(XtDisplay(drawing_a), gc,
        WhitePixelOfScreen(XtScreen(drawing_a)));
    /* create a pixmap the same size as the drawing area. */
    pixmap = XCreatePixmap(XtDisplay(drawing_a),
        RootWindowOfScreen(XtScreen(drawing_a)), WIDTH, HEIGHT,
        DefaultDepthOfScreen(XtScreen(drawing_a)));
    /* clear pixmap with white */
    XFillRectangle(XtDisplay(drawing_a), pixmap, gc, 0, 0, WIDTH, HEIGHT);
    /* drawing is now drawn into with "black"; change the gc for future */
    XSetForeground(XtDisplay(drawing_a), gc,
        BlackPixelOfScreen(XtScreen(drawing_a)));

    /* add a pushbutton the user can use to clear the canvas */
    pb = XtVaCreateManagedWidget("Clear",
        xmPushButtonGadgetClass, drawing_a,
        NULL);
    /* if activated, call same callback as XmNinputCallback. */
    XtAddCallback(pb, XmNactivateCallback, drawing_area_callback, NULL);
```

Example 10-2. The draw2.c program (continued)

```
    XtManageChild(drawing_a);
    XtRealizeWidget(toplevel);
    XtAppMainLoop(app);
}

/* Callback routine for DrawingArea's input and expose callbacks
 * as well as the PushButton's activate callback.  Determine which
 * it is by testing the cbs->reason field.
 */
void
drawing_area_callback(widget, data, cbs)
Widget widget;
XtPointer data;
XmDrawingAreaCallbackStruct *cbs;
{
    static Position x, y;
    XEvent *event = cbs->event;
    Display *dpy = event->xany.display;

    if (cbs->reason == XmCR_INPUT) {
        /* activated by DrawingArea input event -- draw lines.
         * Button Down events anchor the initial point and Button
         * Up draws from the anchor point to the button-up point.
         */
        if (event->xany.type == ButtonPress) {
            /* anchor initial point (i.e., save its value) */
            x = event->xbutton.x;
            y = event->xbutton.y;
        } else if (event->xany.type == ButtonRelease) {
            /* draw full line; get GC and use in XDrawLine() */
            GC gc;
            XtVaGetValues(widget, XmNuserData, &gc, NULL);
            XDrawLine(dpy, cbs->window, gc, x, y,
                event->xbutton.x, event->xbutton.y);
            /* draw into the pixmap as well for redrawing later */
            XDrawLine(dpy, pixmap, gc, x, y,
                event->xbutton.x, event->xbutton.y);
            x = event->xbutton.x;
            y = event->xbutton.y;
        }
    }

    if (cbs->reason == XmCR_EXPOSE || cbs->reason == XmCR_ACTIVATE) {
        GC gc;
        if (cbs->reason == XmCR_ACTIVATE) /* Clear button pushed */
            widget = XtParent(widget); /* get the DrawingArea widget's... */
        XtVaGetValues(widget, XmNuserData, &gc, NULL);
        if (cbs->reason == XmCR_ACTIVATE) { /* Clear button pushed */
            /* to clear a pixmap, reverse foreground and background ... */
            XSetForeground(dpy, gc, WhitePixelOfScreen(XtScreen(widget)));
            /* ...and fill rectangle the size of the pixmap */
            XFillRectangle(dpy, pixmap, gc, 0, 0, WIDTH, HEIGHT);
            /* don't forget to reset */
            XSetForeground(dpy, gc, BlackPixelOfScreen(XtScreen(widget)));
        }
        /* Note: we don't have to use WIDTH and HEIGHT--we could pull the
         * exposed area out of the event structure, but only if the reason
```

Example 10-2. The draw2.c program (continued)

```
         * was XmCR_EXPOSE... make it simple for the demo; optimize as needed.
         */
        XCopyArea(dpy, pixmap, event->xany.window, gc,
            0, 0, WIDTH, HEIGHT, 0, 0);
    }
}
```

10.1.4 DrawingArea Children

After playing with the program a little, you will soon find that you can draw right through the PushButton gadget in the DrawingArea. Because gadgets have no windows (they use their parent's window), the DrawingArea widget will indiscriminately allow you to draw through any gadget children it may be managing.

Similarly, activating the PushButton clears the DrawingArea window, but it does not repaint the PushButton. None of the manager widgets, including DrawingArea, check that the user (or the application) is overwriting or erasing gadgets.

Changing the PushButton from a gadget to a widget solves the immediate problem, but the fact remains: It is generally not a good idea to use a DrawingArea widget as both a drawing canvas and as a place to have user-interface elements such as PushButtons, except in special cases such as the example demonstrating the airplane's flight-path.

For conventional geometry management involving DrawingArea widgets, you have two choices: you can write your own geometry management routine(s) (as demonstrated for BulletinBoard widgets in Chapter 8, *Manager Widgets*,) or you can place the DrawingArea inside another manager that does more intelligent geometry management. The nice part about this alternative is that the other manager widgets are no more or less intelligent about graphics and repainting than the DrawingArea widget. They don't provide a callback for **Expose** events, but you can always add translations for those events, if you need them. How to add translations is addressed in the next section.

10.2 Using Translations on the DrawingArea

As mentioned earlier, it is generally permissible to override or replace the default translation table of the DrawingArea widget with new translations. The only potential problem is if you plan to use the DrawingArea as a manager for other widgets and you expect it to follow the keyboard traversal mechanisms described by the *Motif Style Guide*. In fact, handling keyboard traversal is pretty much what the DrawingArea's default translations *do*. For example, the following is a subset of the default translations for the DrawingArea widget:[2]

```
<Key>osfSelect:                   DrawingAreaInput( ) ManagerGadgetSelect( )
<Key>osfActivate:                 DrawingAreaInput( ) ManagerGadgetSelect( )
<Key>osfHelp:                     DrawingAreaInput( ) ManagerGadgetHelp( )
~Shift ~Meta ~Alt <Key>Return:    DrawingAreaInput( ) ManagerGadgetSelect( )
~Shift ~Meta ~Alt <Key>space:     DrawingAreaInput( ) ManagerGadgetSelect( )
<KeyDown>:                        DrawingAreaInput( ) ManagerGadgetKeyInput( )
<KeyUp>:                          DrawingAreaInput( )
<BtnMotion>:                      ManagerGadgetButtonMotion( )
<Btn1Down>:                       DrawingAreaInput( ) ManagerGadgetArm( )
<Btn1Down>,<Btn1Up>:              DrawingAreaInput( ) ManagerGadgetActivate( )
```

These translations demonstrate that the manager widget part of the DrawingArea is responsible for tracking events for its gadget children. It is not necessary to support these translations if you are not going to use the DrawingArea to manage children. Most user-generated events also invoke `DrawingAreaInput( )`, which does not do any drawing, but simply invokes the `XmNinputCallback`.

As you can see, the `BtnMotion` translation is not passed to `DrawingAreaInput( )`; you are not notified of pointer motion events (whether or not a mouse button is down). When it comes to more complex drawing than shown in Example 10-3, this is a serious deficiency. To support rubberbanding or free-hand drawing techniques (both of which require pointer motion events), you must install either an event handler or a translation entry to handle them.

The simplest approach would be to replace the translation table entry for `<BtnMotion>`. However, this is not possible, due to a bug in the X Toolkit Intrinsics.[3] That is, the correct thing to do is the following:

```
String translations =
    "<Btn1Motion>: DrawingAreaInput( ) ManagerGadgetButtonMotion( )";
    .
    .
    .

drawing_a = XtVaCreateManagedWidget("drawing_a",
    xmDrawingAreaWidgetClass, main_w,
    ...
    NULL);
XtOverrideTranslations(drawing_a, XtParseTranslationTable(translations));
XtAddCallback(drawing_a, XmNinputCallback, draw, NULL);
```

With these new translations, the `XmNinputCallback` function (`draw( )`) would be notified of pointer motion while Button 1 is down.

`XtOverrideTranslations( )` would normally be the preferred method for installing a new translation into the DrawingArea widget because it is *nondestructive*. That is, it only replaces translations for which identical events are specified. (All other translations are still

---

[2] Note that this translation table is only a subset of the current translations in the DrawingArea widget, and that there is no guarantee that they will remain the same in future revisions of the toolkit.

[3] Reportedly due to be fixed in X11 Release 5.

in place.) However, this does not work because there is already a translation for the Button 1 down-up sequence from the translation table shown earlier:

```
<Btn1Down>,<Btn1Up>:              DrawingAreaInput( ) ManagerGadgetActivate( )
```

In the current implementation, once Button 1 goes down, the Xt event translator waits for the Button 1 up event to match the partially finished translation. Therefore, no Button 1 motion events can be caught. If we want to get pointer motion events while the button is down, we have to resort to other alternatives.

One such alternative is to replace the *entire* translation table, regardless of whether we are adding new entries or overriding existing ones. This is known as a *destructive* override because the existing translation table is thrown out. (An override will have the desired effect, because the offending Button 1 translation will be thrown out. However, we must then take steps to re-install any other default translations that are still required.)

To completely replace the existing translations, the **XmNtranslations** resource can be hard-coded when the widget is created using **XtVaCreateManagedWidget( )**, or later using **XtVaSetValues( )**. The following code fragment demonstrates how this is done:

```
String translations =
    "<Btn1Motion>: DrawingAreaInput( ) ManagerGadgetButtonMotion( )";
    .
    .
    .
drawing_a = XtVaCreateManagedWidget("drawing_a",
    xmDrawingAreaWidgetClass, main_w,
    XmNtranslations,  XtParseTranslationTable(translations),
    NULL);
XtAddCallback(drawing_a, XmNinputCallback, draw, NULL);
```

Once you go to the trouble of replacing the translation table, you might want to install your own action functions as well. Doing so will allow you to do the drawing directly from the action function, rather than using it as an intermediate function to call an application callback. This "direct drawing" approach is demonstrated in Example 10-3. Here, the program uses pointer motion to draw lines as the pointer is dragged with the button down, rather than when the button is pressed and released. You'll notice that we have used much the same design as in Example 10-2, but have moved some of the code into different callback routines and have placed the DrawingArea widget into a MainWindow widget for flexibility. None of these changes were required; nor do they enhance performance in any way. They merely point out different ways of providing the same functionality.

Example 10-3. The free_hand.c program

```
/* free_hand.c -- simple drawing program that does freehand
 * drawing.  We use translations to do all the event handling
 * for us rather than using the drawing area's XmNinputCallback.
 */
#include <Xm/MainW.h>
#include <Xm/DrawingA.h>
#include <Xm/PushBG.h>
#include <Xm/RowColumn.h>

GC gc;
Pixmap pixmap;
```

Example 10-3. The free_hand.c program (continued)

```
/* dimensions of drawing area (pixmap) */
Dimension width, height;

main(argc, argv)
int argc;
char *argv[ ];
{
    Widget toplevel, main_w, drawing_a, pb;
    XtAppContext app;
    XGCValues gcv;
    void draw(), redraw(), clear_it();
    XtActionsRec actions;
    String translations = /* for the DrawingArea widget */
        /* ManagerGadget* functions are necessary for DrawingArea widgets
         * that steal away button events from the normal translation tables.
         */
        "<Btn1Down>:    draw(down) ManagerGadgetArm()   \n\
         <Btn1Up>:      draw(up)   ManagerGadgetActivate()  \n\
         <Btn1Motion>: draw(motion) ManagerGadgetButtonMotion()";

    toplevel = XtVaAppInitialize(&app, "Demos", NULL, 0,
        &argc, argv, NULL, NULL);

    /* Create a MainWindow to contain the drawing area */
    main_w = XtVaCreateManagedWidget("main_w",
        xmMainWindowWidgetClass, toplevel,
        XmNscrollingPolicy, XmAUTOMATIC,
        NULL);

    /* Add the "draw" action/function used by the translation table */
    actions.string = "draw";
    actions.proc = draw;
    XtAppAddActions(app, &actions, 1);

    /* Create a DrawingArea widget.  Make it 5 inches wide by 6 inches tall.
     * Don't let it resize so the Clear Button doesn't force a resize.
     */
    drawing_a = XtVaCreateManagedWidget("drawing_a",
        xmDrawingAreaWidgetClass, main_w,
        XmNtranslations, XtParseTranslationTable(translations),
        XmNunitType,      Xm1000TH_INCHES,
        XmNwidth,        5000, /* 5 inches */
        XmNheight,       6000, /* 6 inches */
        XmNresizePolicy, XmNONE,  /* remain this a fixed size */
        NULL);
    /* When scrolled, the drawing area will get expose events */
    XtAddCallback(drawing_a, XmNexposeCallback, redraw, NULL);

    /* convert drawing area back to pixels to get its width and height */
    XtVaSetValues(drawing_a, XmNunitType, XmPIXELS, NULL);
    XtVaGetValues(drawing_a, XmNwidth, &width, XmNheight, &height, NULL);
    /* create a pixmap the same size as the drawing area. */
    pixmap = XCreatePixmap(XtDisplay(drawing_a),
        RootWindowOfScreen(XtScreen(drawing_a)), width, height,
        DefaultDepthOfScreen(XtScreen(drawing_a)));

    /* Create a GC for drawing (callback).  Used a lot -- make global */
    gcv.foreground = WhitePixelOfScreen(XtScreen(drawing_a));
    gc = XCreateGC(XtDisplay(drawing_a),
```

Example 10-3. The free_hand.c program (continued)

```
                RootWindowOfScreen(XtScreen(drawing_a)), GCForeground, &gcv);
    /* clear pixmap with white */
    XFillRectangle(XtDisplay(drawing_a), pixmap, gc, 0, 0, width, height);
    /* drawing is now drawn into with "black"; change the gc */
    XSetForeground(XtDisplay(drawing_a), gc,
        BlackPixelOfScreen(XtScreen(drawing_a)));

    pb = XtVaCreateManagedWidget("Clear",
        xmPushButtonGadgetClass, drawing_a, NULL);
    /* Pushing the clear button calls clear_it() */
    XtAddCallback(pb, XmNactivateCallback, clear_it, drawing_a);

    XtRealizeWidget(toplevel);
    XtAppMainLoop(app);
}

/* Action procedure to respond to any of the events from the
 * translation table declared in main().  This function is called
 * in response to Button1 Down, Up and Motion events.  Basically,
 * we're just doing a freehand draw -- not lines or anything.
 */
void
draw(widget, event, args, num_args)
Widget widget;
XButtonEvent *event;
String *args;
int *num_args;
{
    static Position x, y;

    if (*num_args != 1)
        XtError("Wrong number of args!");

    if (strcmp(args[0], "down")) {
        /* if it's not "down", it must either be "up" or "motion"
         * draw full line from anchor point to new point.
         */
        XDrawLine(event->display, event->window, gc, x, y, event->x, event->y);
        XDrawLine(event->display, pixmap, gc, x, y, event->x, event->y);
    }

    /* freehand is really a bunch of line segments; save this point */
    x = event->x;
    y = event->y;
}

/* Clear the window by clearing the pixmap and calling XCopyArea() */
void
clear_it(pb, drawing_a, cbs)
Widget pb, drawing_a;
XmPushButtonCallbackStruct *cbs;
{
    /* clear pixmap with white */
    XSetForeground(XtDisplay(drawing_a), gc,
        WhitePixelOfScreen(XtScreen(drawing_a)));
    XFillRectangle(XtDisplay(drawing_a), pixmap, gc, 0, 0, width, height);
    /* drawing is now done using black; change the gc */
    XSetForeground(XtDisplay(drawing_a), gc,
        BlackPixelOfScreen(XtScreen(drawing_a)));
```

Example 10-3. The free_hand.c program (continued)

```
    XCopyArea(cbs->event->xbutton.display, pixmap, XtWindow(drawing_a), gc,
        0, 0, width, height, 0, 0);
}

/* redraw is called whenever all or portions of the drawing area is
 * exposed.  This includes newly exposed portions of the widget resulting
 * from the user's interaction with the scrollbars.
 */
void
redraw(drawing_a, client_data, cbs)
Widget      drawing_a;
XtPointer client_data;
XmDrawingAreaCallbackStruct *cbs;
{
    XCopyArea(cbs->event->xexpose.display, pixmap, cbs->window, gc,
        0, 0, width, height, 0, 0);
}
```

The output of the program is shown in Figure 10-2.

Figure 10-2. Output of free_hand.c.

In Example 10-3, the DrawingArea widget is given the following translation string:

```
String translations =
    "<Btn1Down>:   draw(down) ManagerGadgetArm( )        \n\
     <Btn1Up>:     draw(up)   ManagerGadgetActivate( ) \n\
     <Btn1Motion>: draw(motion) ManagerGadgetButtonMotion( )";
```

Here, the translation describes two actions (functions) for each of the specified events:

1. The **draw( )** action is our own function that actually draws into the DrawingArea. (Note that this is now an action function rather than a callback as demonstrated earlier.)

2. The **ManagerGadget*** actions are standard DrawingArea actions (inherited from the Manager widget class) for passing events to a gadget child, as described earlier. We keep them in place because we still maintain the PushButton gadget. Note that we are not keeping the routines for managing keyboard traversal, but simply those required to arm and activate the button.

In this example, the gadget functions won't do anything if the pointer is not inside the **Clear** button, so the translation is relatively safe. However, you should be sure to remember that *both* actions will be called. If you press Button 1 inside the pushbutton, and doodle around a bit before releasing it, the drawing is still done, even though the result is hidden by the gadget. In other applications, the fact that actions for both the drawing area itself and its gadget children were both called might lead to indeterminate results.

In short, the `draw( )` action does not (and cannot) know if the gadget is also going to react to the button event. This was not a problem with the standard `DrawingAreaInput( )` action routine used in the previous examples, because that routine is implemented by the Motif toolkit and uses its own internal mechanisms to determine if the gadget is (or will be) activated. If the DrawingArea does process the event on the gadget, then the `Drawing-AreaInput( )` action knows that it should not invoke the callback function. This internal mechanism is not available outside of the widget code. Reordering the action functions will not help, since there is still no way to know, without making an educated guess, whether or not the DrawingArea acted upon it an event on behalf of a gadget child.

Thus, `draw( )` will start drawing a line, even if it starts in the middle of the pushbutton, because the DrawingArea processes all the action functions in the list. If you drag the pointer out of the gadget before releasing it, the starting point of the line you draw will be inside the gadget, but it will be hidden when the gadget repaints itself. In *this* particular situation, you can do some guesswork; by installing an `XmNarmCallback` function, you can tell whether or not the DrawingArea activated a button, and by setting an internal state (variable), you can decide whether the `draw( )` action routine should do its drawing.

This confusing behavior is yet another reason why it would be best not to include children in DrawingArea widgets that are intended for interactive graphics. If the DrawingArea had no gadget children, installing these auxiliary actions in the translation string would not be necessary.

Since the `ManagerGadget*` actions are self-contained and can manage themselves adequately, let's focus our attention on the `draw( )` function.

This action function tests whether it was called from a button up, down, or motion event. Since the action function is passed the event that invoked it (just as was the callback function in the last example), we could simply test the type field of the event. However, this example gives us a chance to exercise the Xt feature that supports string arguments passed to action functions.

Accordingly, the `draw( )` function determines what action to take by examining its `args[0]` parameter, which contains the string passed as the single parameter in the translation table. For example, `draw(up)` passes the string "up" as the `args[0]` parameter in response to the `<Btn1Up>` event.

Lines are drawn for both the **ButtonRelease** and **ButtonMotion** events, but not the **Button-Press** event. A line is drawn from the last "anchor point" to the mouse's current location. As the pointer moves from one point to the next, the "anchor point" is always one step behind, and a line segment is drawn from that location to the current location. The only time a line segment isn't drawn is on the initial button press (and any motion events that occur while the button is not down). The coordinate values are relative to the current location of the pointer within the DrawingArea widget, no matter how it is positioned in the MainWindow.

This point leads us into the next phase of discussion. The `draw( )` function draws not only into the window but also into a pixmap. When the MainWindow widget is configured to have its `XmNscrollingPolicy` set to `XmAUTOMATIC`, Scrollbars are automatically installed over the DrawingArea when it is larger than the MainWindow, allowing the user to view different parts of the canvas interactively. These scrolling actions cause the contents of the newly exposed portions of the canvas to be erased by default. Unless we provide a mechanism by which the DrawingArea can redraw itself, scrolling the DrawingArea will lose previously drawn contents. To handle this problem, we employ the same principle we used in *draw2.c*—a pixmap is installed and is used by both the `draw( )` and `redraw( )` functions.

`redraw( )` is installed as the callback function for `XmNexposeCallback`:

```
XtAddCallback(drawing_a, XmNexposeCallback, redraw, NULL);
```

The function itself merely uses `XCopyArea( )` to copy the pixmap onto the DrawingArea's window. We were not concerned with the position of the DrawingArea with respect to the MainWindow in the `draw( )` function; this information is not particularly important at this time either. All we need to do is copy the pixmap directly into the window. X will insure that the visible portion of the window will be clipped as necessary.

10.3 Using Colors

In this section, we expand on our previous examples by incorporating color. The choice of colors is primarily supported by a function we define called `set_color( )`, which takes a widget and an arbitrary color name and sets the global **GC**'s foreground color. Just provide an array of colors (in the form of colored PushButtons) and you've got a color paint program. We've also removed the PushButton gadget from the DrawingArea, and created a proper control panel to the left of the drawing area proper. The program uses a RowColumn widget (see Chapter 8, *Manager Widgets*) to manage a set of eighteen pushbuttons "labeled" with pixmaps in various colors.[4]

The output of the program, shown in Example 10-4, is shown in Figure 10-3.

---

[4] On a black and white screen, the program will run, but the buttons will be either black or white, depending on which is closer to the RGB values corresponding to the color names chosen. You can only draw with the black buttons, since the background is already white.

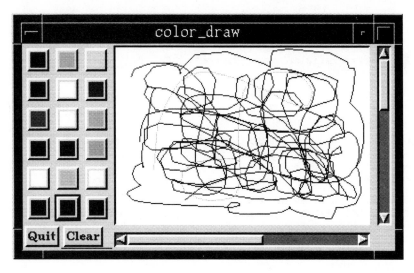

Figure 10-3. Output of color_draw.c

Example 10-4. The color_draw.c program

```
/* color_draw.c -- simple drawing program using predefined colors.  */
#include <Xm/MainW.h>
#include <Xm/DrawingA.h>
#include <Xm/PushBG.h>
#include <Xm/PushB.h>
#include <Xm/RowColumn.h>
#include <Xm/ScrolledW.h>
#include <Xm/Form.h>

GC gc;
Pixmap pixmap;
/* dimensions of drawing area (pixmap) */
Dimension width, height;

String colors[ ] = {
    "Black", "Red", "Green", "Blue", "White", "Navy", "Orange", "Yellow",
    "Pink", "Magenta", "Cyan", "Brown", "Grey", "LimeGreen", "Turquoise",
    "Violet", "Wheat", "Purple"
};

main(argc, argv)
int argc;
char *argv[ ];
{
    Widget toplevel, main_w, sw, rc, form, drawing_a, pb;
    XtAppContext app;
    XGCValues gcv;
    void draw(), redraw(), set_color(), exit(), clear_it();
    int i;
    XtActionsRec actions;
    String translations = /* for the DrawingArea widget */
        "<Btn1Down>:    draw(down)\n\
         <Btn1Up>:      draw(up)  \n\
```

Example 10-4. The color_draw.c program (continued)

```
        <Btn1Motion>: draw(motion)";
    toplevel = XtVaAppInitialize(&app, "Demos", NULL, 0,
        &argc, argv, NULL, NULL);

    /* Create a MainWindow to contain the drawing area */
    main_w = XtVaCreateManagedWidget("main_w",
        xmFormWidgetClass, toplevel, NULL);

    /* Create a GC for drawing (callback).  Used a lot -- make global */
    gcv.foreground = WhitePixelOfScreen(XtScreen(main_w));
    gc = XCreateGC(XtDisplay(main_w),
        RootWindowOfScreen(XtScreen(main_w)), GCForeground, &gcv);

    /* Create a 3-column array of color tiles */
    rc = XtVaCreateWidget("rc", xmRowColumnWidgetClass, main_w,
        XmNnumColumns,        3,
        XmNpacking,           XmPACK_COLUMN,
        XmNleftAttachment,    XmATTACH_FORM,
        XmNtopAttachment,     XmATTACH_FORM,
        NULL);
    for (i = 0; i < XtNumber(colors); i++) {
        /* Create a single tile (pixmap) for each color */
        pixmap = XCreatePixmap(XtDisplay(rc), RootWindowOfScreen(XtScreen(rc)),
            16, 16, DefaultDepthOfScreen(XtScreen(rc)));
        set_color(rc, colors[i]); /* set the gc's color according to name */
        XFillRectangle(XtDisplay(main_w), pixmap, gc, 0, 0, 16, 16);
        pb = XtVaCreateManagedWidget(colors[i], xmPushButtonWidgetClass, rc,
            XmNlabelType, XmPIXMAP,
            XmNlabelPixmap, pixmap,
            NULL);
        /* callback for this pushbutton sets the current color */
        XtAddCallback(pb, XmNactivateCallback, set_color, colors[i]);
    }
    XtManageChild(rc);

    pb = XtVaCreateManagedWidget("Quit",
        xmPushButtonGadgetClass, main_w,
        XmNleftAttachment,      XmATTACH_FORM,
        XmNtopAttachment,       XmATTACH_WIDGET,
        XmNtopWidget,           rc,
        NULL);
    XtAddCallback(pb, XmNactivateCallback, exit, NULL);

    /* Clear button -- wait till DrawingArea is created so we can use
     * it to pass as client data.
     */
    pb = XtVaCreateManagedWidget("Clear",
        xmPushButtonGadgetClass, main_w,
        XmNleftAttachment,      XmATTACH_WIDGET,
        XmNleftWidget,          pb,
        XmNtopAttachment,       XmATTACH_WIDGET,
        XmNtopWidget,           rc,
        NULL);

    sw = XtVaCreateManagedWidget("scrolled_win",
        xmScrolledWindowWidgetClass, main_w,
        XmNwidth,               300,
        XmNscrollingPolicy,     XmAUTOMATIC,
```

Example 10-4. The color_draw.c program (continued)

The DrawingArea Widget

```
                XmNscrollBarDisplayPolicy,  XmAS_NEEDED,
                XmNtopAttachment,           XmATTACH_FORM,
                XmNbottomAttachment,        XmATTACH_FORM,
                XmNleftAttachment,          XmATTACH_WIDGET,
                XmNleftWidget,              rc,
                XmNrightAttachment,         XmATTACH_FORM,
                NULL);

        /* Add the "draw" action/function used by the translation table
         * parsed by the translations resource below.
         */
        actions.string = "draw";
        actions.proc = draw;
        XtAppAddActions(app, &actions, 1);

        /* Create a DrawingArea widget.  Make it 5 inches wide by 6 inches tall.
         * Don't let it resize so the Clear Button doesn't force a resize.
         */
        drawing_a = XtVaCreateManagedWidget("drawing_a",
            xmDrawingAreaWidgetClass, sw,
            XmNtranslations, XtParseTranslationTable(translations),
            XmNunitType,      Xm1000TH_INCHES,
            XmNwidth,         5000, /* 5 inches */
            XmNheight,        6000, /* 6 inches */
            XmNresizePolicy, XmNONE,  /* remain this a fixed size */
            NULL);
        /* When scrolled, the drawing area will get expose events */
        XtAddCallback(drawing_a, XmNexposeCallback, redraw, NULL);
        /* Pushing the clear button clears the drawing area widget */
        XtAddCallback(pb, XmNactivateCallback, clear_it, drawing_a);

        /* convert drawing area back to pixels to get its width and height */
        XtVaSetValues(drawing_a, XmNunitType, XmPIXELS, NULL);
        XtVaGetValues(drawing_a, XmNwidth, &width, XmNheight, &height, NULL);
        /* create a pixmap the same size as the drawing area. */
        pixmap = XCreatePixmap(XtDisplay(drawing_a),
            RootWindowOfScreen(XtScreen(drawing_a)), width, height,
            DefaultDepthOfScreen(XtScreen(drawing_a)));
        /* clear pixmap with white */
        set_color(drawing_a, "White");
        XFillRectangle(XtDisplay(drawing_a), pixmap, gc, 0, 0, width, height);

        XtRealizeWidget(toplevel);
        XtAppMainLoop(app);
}

/* Action procedure to respond to any of the events from the
 * translation table declared in main().  This function is called
 * in response to Button1 Down, Up and Motion events.  Basically,
 * we're just doing a freehand draw -- not lines or anything.
 */
void
draw(widget, event, args, num_args)
Widget widget;
XButtonEvent *event;
String *args;
int *num_args;
{
```

Example 10-4. The color_draw.c program (continued)

```
    static Position x, y;

    if (*num_args != 1)
        XtError("Wrong number of args!");

    if (strcmp(args[0], "down")) {
        /* if it's not "down", it must either be "up" or "motion"
         * draw full line from anchor point to new point.
         */
        XDrawLine(event->display, event->window, gc, x, y, event->x, event->y);
        XDrawLine(event->display, pixmap, gc, x, y, event->x, event->y);
    }

    /* freehand is really a bunch of line segements; save this point */
    x = event->x;
    y = event->y;
}

/* Clear the window by clearing the pixmap and calling XCopyArea() */
void
clear_it(pb, drawing_a, cbs)
Widget pb, drawing_a;
XmPushButtonCallbackStruct *cbs;
{
    /* clear pixmap with white */
    XSetForeground(XtDisplay(drawing_a), gc,
        WhitePixelOfScreen(XtScreen(drawing_a)));
    /* this clears the pixmap */
    XFillRectangle(XtDisplay(drawing_a), pixmap, gc, 0, 0, width, height);
    /* drawing is now done using black; change the gc */
    XSetForeground(XtDisplay(drawing_a), gc,
        BlackPixelOfScreen(XtScreen(drawing_a)));
    /* render the newly cleared pixmap onto the window */
    XCopyArea(cbs->event->xbutton.display, pixmap, XtWindow(drawing_a), gc,
        0, 0, width, height, 0, 0);
}

/* redraw is called whenever all or portions of the drawing area is
 * exposed.  This includes newly exposed portions of the widget resulting
 * from the user's interaction with the scrollbars.
 */
void
redraw(drawing_a, client_data, cbs)
Widget    drawing_a;
XtPointer client_data;
XmDrawingAreaCallbackStruct *cbs;
{
    XCopyArea(cbs->event->xexpose.display, pixmap, cbs->window, gc,
        0, 0, width, height, 0, 0);
}

/* callback routine for when any of the color tiles are pressed.
 * This general function may also be used to set the global gc's
 * color directly.  Just provide a widget and a color name.
 */
void
set_color(widget, color)
Widget widget;
```

Example 10-4. The color_draw.c program (continued)

```
String color;
{
    Display *dpy = XtDisplay(widget);
    Colormap cmap = DefaultColormapOfScreen(XtScreen(widget));
    XColor col, unused;
    if (!XAllocNamedColor(dpy, cmap, color, &col, &unused)) {
        char buf[32];
        sprintf(buf, "Can't alloc %s", color);
        XtWarning(buf);
        return;
    }
    XSetForeground(dpy, gc, col.pixel);
}
```

There should be no surprises here, but there are several things of interest. First, the **Clear** button's callback function was passed the DrawingArea widget as the client data when the callback was installed. This saved us from having to declare a global variable, yet still makes the handle to the DrawingArea available to the button's callback routine.

Secondly, the installation of the **draw( )** action routine was done at the point in the program where it is used by the DrawingArea widget. There are no rules about when or where actions are loaded, but for clarity, we chose to install them where they are used.

10.4 Summary

The DrawingArea widget is probably most useful when used as a canvas for displaying raster images, animation, a mixture of text and graphics, or for tasks that require interactive user input. The widget provides some rudimentary input mechanisms in the form of callbacks invoked by button events.

The translation and action tables supported by the X Toolkit Intrinsics provide a simple mechanism for notifying applications of user events such as double-mouse clicks, keyboard events, and so on. By creatively modifying the default translations and actions, you could build a rather intricate system of action functions that produces interesting graphics based on various forms of user input sequences.

However, what you can do with actions is simplistic given the complexities that are involved in true paint or draw applications. Applications that require a graphic front end should probably dig deeper into the lower levels of Xt for event-handling and into Xlib for image rendering.

10.5 Exercises

There are a number of different possibilities you could explore in extending the DrawingArea widget. The following exercises are intended to shine the light down some interesting paths you can take.

1. As we have demonstrated, DrawingArea widgets need to redisplay the contents of their windows. For the programs in this chapter, redisplay was implemented by duplicating in a pixmap all the drawing done in the window. If there is ever a need for repainting the window, the pixmap can simply be copied into it. Now consider *draw2.c*: if the application is resized bigger, parts of the window will not respond to drawing, since the figure that the user is painting was not expected to grow dynamically. If you wanted to support a dynamically grown canvas, you would also have to resize the off-screen pixmap. Modify *draw2.c* so that the pixmap resizes along with the DrawingArea. Hint: You need to add a callback for **XmNresizeCallback**. When that callback is invoked, query the size of the DrawingArea, and create a new pixmap that is the new size, **XCopyArea( )** the old pixmap into the new one, and then destroy the old pixmap.

2. The resource **XmNcolormap** can be used to set and get the colormap associated with a DrawingArea widget (using **XtVaSetValues( )** and **XtVaGetValues( )**). Modify *color_draw.c* to use the colormap values rather than predefined colors.

3. A paint program and a draw program differ in the way they internally represent their graphical displays. Paint programs usually maintain background pixmaps as demonstrated by *free_hand.c*, whereas draw programs maintain geometric information about the shapes that are drawn. For example, circles are represented using a center (x,y coordinate) and a radius; rectangles are represented by an origin coordinate with width and height values; and freehand drawings are represented by a list of coordinates (line segments). Entire pictures are represented by a list of geometric shape definitions. Do you notice a pattern relating geometric shapes and the parameters passed to Xlib functions that draw such objects? E.g. **XArc**, **XRectangle**, and **XSegment**.

    Modify *free_hand.c* or *color_draw.c* to use a list of **XSegment** structures to represent the lines that are drawn by the user. Instead of using a pixmap and **XCopyArea( )** to repaint the DrawingArea widget on expose events, repaint the picture by calling **XDrawSegments( )** using the data stored in your internal list of **XSegment** structures.

In this last exercise, you are given a hint about how you might go about building an interactive drawing application. For those of you that really want to dig into this subject, you can extend the program by giving the user a choice of which kind of geometric shape to draw. You will have to provide a user interface to support an array of object types (arcs, circles, squares, rectangles, lines, and of course, freehand drawings). Based on the user's choice, you will then have to maintain a *state machine* indicating how much of a geometric figure has been drawn. A translation table should be used to monitor the events that correspond to the state machine; and internal data structures (extrapolated from the predefined Xlib data structures mentioned above) can be used to record the coordinates of the key points in the geometric data. Granted, this is no small feat—but it is a great way to kill a weekend!

11

Labels and Buttons

This chapter provides an in-depth look at labels and buttons, the most commonly-used primitive widgets. It also suggests techniques for interpreting multiple button clicks, which are not supported by the default translations for the PushButton widget.

In This Chapter:

11
Labels and Buttons

Labels and buttons are among the most widely used interface objects in GUI-based applications. They are also the simplest in concept and design. Labels provide the basic resources necessary to render and manage text or images (pixmaps) by controlling color, alignment, and other visual attributes. PushButtons are subclassed from the Label and extend its capabilities by adding callback routines that respond to user interaction from the mouse or keyboard. These visual and interactive features provide the cornerstone for many widgets in the Motif toolkit such as CascadeButtons, DrawnButtons, and ToggleButtons.

While the ArrowButton is not subclassed from the Label or PushButton in its implementation, it provides a subset of the PushButton's interactive capabilities. ArrowButtons may not contain user- or programmer-defined text or graphical labels; they only display directional arrows for up, down, left, and right. These widgets usually act as companions to other interface objects whose values or displays may be controlled or changed incrementally by the user. For example, the endpoints of a Scrollbar have directional arrows like ArrowButtons that increment or decrement the viewport of a window. Another example might be four ArrowButtons used to represent directional movement for the display of a bitmap editor.

Although CascadeButtons are subclassed from the Label widget, they are specifically used in Motif menus and are not addressed in this chapter. The menu system used by Motif is a completely separate module that is treated specifically in Chapter 4, *The Main Window*, and Chapter 16, *Menus*. Since menus represent menu items using Labels and PushButtons, there are certain resources within these widgets that are useless in buttons outside of menus. Therefore, such resources are not discussed in this chapter either.

Because of the wide range of uses that Labels and PushButtons can have and the number of other widgets they can affect, Labels and Buttons are discussed throughout this book. However, this chapter provides a basic discussion of the main resources and callbacks used by these objects. We also provide examples of common usage and attempt to address problem areas.

11.1 Labels

Labels are simply "props" for the stage. They are not intended to be interactive with the user although a help-callback can be attached in case the HELP key is pressed. It is equally common to find Labels displaying either text or graphics, yet they cannot display both simultaneously in the conventional sense. (We'll talk more about this later.)

Since Labels can display text, it may not be obvious whether to use Labels or Text widgets to display textual information. The *Motif Style Guide* suggests that Labels always be used when noneditable text is displayed, even if the text is longer than what you might think of as a label. If a Label is large, you can always place it in the work area of an automatic Scrolled-Window widget as discussed in Chapter 9, *ScrolledWindows and Scrollbars*. Even if the text is expected to change frequently, your needs can often be accomodated by a Label widget or gadget.

Even so, choosing between a Label widget and a Text widget may not be as simple as it may seem. For example, you may have text that isn't editable by the user, but you may wish to provide the ability to *select* all or part of the Label's text. Such interaction requires the use of Text widgets rather than Labels.

Labels have a number of added visual advantages over Text widgets in that they can *turn gray* when they are insensitive and they can display text in multiple fonts. Such visual feedback is not available in Text widgets. Labels are also much lighter weight objects than Text widgets; there is little overhead in maintaining or displaying them and there is no need to handle event processing on them to the same degree as for Text widgets. All things considered, in a toss-up there is a tendency is to choose Label widgets over Text widgets.

When it comes to interactive objects, however, Labels may not be the best choice. In most cases where you want to allow the user to *click* on a Label, PushButtons or Toggles are more appropriate. In fact, there are many widgets and gadgets subclassed from Labels that may be more useful than trying to use something so primitive and unsophisticated as a Label. In short, the best thing to do with Label widgets is the most simple and obvious: display labels.

11.1.1 Creating Labels

Applications that use Labels must include the header file *<Xm/Label.h>* where the type **xm-LabelWidgetClass** is defined. This type is a pointer to the actual widget structure used by **XtVaCreateManagedWidget( )**.

```
Widget   label;

label = XtVaCreateManagedWidget("name",
    xmLabelWidgetClass, parent,
    resource-value list,
    NULL);
```

The previous example shows the most common way to create Labels; since they have no children, there is no reason to create them as unmanaged widgets first and then manage them later.

Label *gadgets* are also available. Recall that gadgets are windowless objects that rely on their parents to display their visual attributes and to provide them with events generated either by the system or by the user. Since gadgets have no windows, background colors and patterns cannot be set individually; they are provided by the parent.

The Label gadget is an entirely different class from its widget counterpart. To use a gadget, you must include the header file *<Xm/LabelG.h>* and use the gadget pointer `xmLabel-GadgetClass` in the call to `XtVaCreateManagedWidget( )`.

```
Widget    label;

label = XtVaCreateManagedWidget("name",
    xmLabelGadgetClass, parent,
    resource-value list,
    NULL);
```

The only difference between this function and the one used for widgets is the *class* specified.

11.1.2 Text Labels

Label widgets and gadgets can display either text or images. The resource `XmNlabelType` governs which type to use and can be set to `XmSTRING` or `XmPIXMAP`. The default value is `XmSTRING`, so if you want to display text in Labels, you do not need to set this value explicitly.

The resource used to indicate the string displayed in Labels is `XmNlabelString`. The value for this resource must be a compound string; common C strings are not allowed. For example:

```
Widget    label;
XmString  str = XmStringCreateSimple("A Label");

label = XtVaCreateManagedWidget("label",
    xmLabelWidgetClass, parent,
    XmNlabelString,  str,
    NULL);

XmStringFree(str);
```

If the `XmNlabelString` resource is not given, the Label automatically converts its *name* into a compound string and uses that as its label. Therefore, the above code fragment can be implemented in a similar manner using:

```
Widget    label;

label = XtVaCreateManagedWidget("A Label",
    xmLabelWidgetClass, parent,
    NULL);
```

This method of creating a label string for the widget is much simpler than using compound strings. You also avoid the overhead of creating and destroying compound strings (which allocate and free memory—both of which are expensive operations). The problem with the name of the widget (`"A Label"`) acting as the Label's label string, as shown by the latter example, is that the widget's name may be "illegal." Technically, widget names should only be composed of alphanumerics (letters and numbers), hyphens, and underscores. Characters such as the dot (.) and the asterisk (*) are disallowed because they may make it impossible for the user to specify these widgets in resource files. On the other hand, using characters such as these may be to your advantage if you want to *prevent* the user from changing resource values of certain widgets. The decision you make here should be well-informed.

If you decide to use separate values as the widget's name and the **XmNlabelString**, you can still avoid creating a compound string by using the **XtVaTypedArg** feature of Xt:

```
label = XtVaCreateManagedWidget("widget_name",
    xmLabelWidgetClass, parent,
    XtVaTypedArg, XmNlabelString, XmRString,
        "A Label", 8, /* 8 = strlen("A Label") + 1 */
    NULL);
```

The C string **"A Label"** (which is 7 chars long, plus 1 NULL byte) is converted into a compound string is automatically converted by the toolkit. This method can also be used to change the label for a widget using **XtVaSetValues( )**.

One final word about setting a label's value using compound strings: Since these strings are dynamically created and destroyed, you cannot statically declare *arglists* that contain pointers to compound string objects. For example, it would be an error to do the following:

```
static Arg list[ ] = {
    ...
    XmNlabelString,  XmStringCreateSimple("A label"),
    ...
};
label = XtCreateManagedWidget("name", xmLabelWidgetClass, parent,
    list, XtNumber(list));
```

This is an error because you cannot create compound strings in statically declared arrays. For a complete discussion of compound strings, see Chapter 19, *Compound Strings*.

11.1.3 Images as Labels

Label widgets and gadgets can display images instead of text by setting the **XmNlabel-Type** resource to **XmPIXMAP**. By doing so, the Label widget uses the pixmap associated with the resource **XmNlabelPixmap**. Example 11-1 demonstrates how pixmaps can be used as labels.

Example 11-1. The pixmaps.c program

```
/* pixmaps.c -- demonstate simple label gadgets in a row column.
 * Each command line argument represents a bitmap filename.  Try
 * to load the corresponding pixmap and store in a RowColumn.
 */
#include <Xm/LabelG.h>
#include <Xm/RowColumn.h>

main(argc, argv)
int argc;
char *argv[ ];
{
    XtAppContext app;
```

Example 11-1. The pixmaps.c program (continued)

```
    Pixel fg, bg;
    Widget toplevel, rowcol;

    toplevel = XtVaAppInitialize(&app, "Demos", NULL, 0,
        &argc, argv, NULL, NULL);

    if (argc < 2) {
        puts("Specify bitmap filenames.");
        exit(1);
    }
    /* create a RowColumn that has an equal number of rows and
     * columns based on the number of pixmaps it is going to
     * display (this value is in "argc").
     */
    rowcol = XtVaCreateWidget("rowcol",
        xmRowColumnWidgetClass, toplevel,
        XmNnumColumns,   int_sqrt(argc),
        XmNpacking,      XmPACK_COLUMN,
        NULL);

    /* Get the foreground and background colors of the rowcol to make
     * all the pixmaps appear using a consistent color.
     */
    XtVaGetValues(rowcol,
        XmNforeground, &fg,
        XmNbackground, &bg,
        NULL);

    while (*++argv) {
        Pixmap pixmap = XmGetPixmap(XtScreen(rowcol), *argv, fg, bg);
        if (pixmap == XmUNSPECIFIED_PIXMAP)
            printf("couldn't load %s\n", *argv);
        else
            XtVaCreateManagedWidget(*argv, xmLabelGadgetClass, rowcol,
                XmNlabelType, XmPIXMAP,
                XmNlabelPixmap, pixmap,
                NULL);
    }

    XtManageChild(rowcol);
    XtRealizeWidget(toplevel);
    XtAppMainLoop(app);
}

/* get the integer square root of n -- used to determine the number
 * of rows and columns of pixmaps to use in the RowColumn widget.
 */
int_sqrt(n)
register int n;
{
    register int i, s = 0, t;
    for (i = 15; i >= 0; i--) {
        t = (s | (1 << i));
        if (t * t <= n)
            s = t;
    }
    return s;
}
```

Example 11-1. The pixmaps.c program (continued)

The program displays a two-dimensional array of pixmaps based on the bitmap files listed on the command line. For example, the following command produces Figure 11-1.

    % pixmaps flagup letters wingdogs woman xlogo64 cross_weave

Figure 11-1. Output of pixmaps.c

To optimize the amount of space used by the RowColumn widget, the number of rows and columns is set to the square root of the number of images. For example, if there are nine pixmaps to load, there should be a 3x3 grid of items. Since the number of files to be loaded corresponds to the number of arguments in `argv`, then `argc` can be passed to `int_sqrt( )` to get the integer square root of its value. This will tell us the number of columns to specify for `XmNnumColumns`. The files are read using `XmGetPixmap( )` which is a function that creates a pixmap from the file specified. This file must be in X11 bitmap format. The function needs a foreground and background color for the pixmap it creates, so we use the RowColumn's colors in order to make the Label and RowColumn be color compatible. If the file can't be found or does not contain a bitmap, the function returns the constant, `Xm-UNSPECIFIED_PIXMAP`.[1] If this error condition is returned, the file is skipped and we go on to the next. More detailed information on `XmGetPixmap( )` and other supporting functions is available later in the chapter in Section 11.6, *Pixmaps and Color Issues*.

---

[1] `XmUNSPECIFIED_PIXMAP` is *not* 0 or `NULL`. Many people have a tendency to test for these values upon return of functions that return opaque objects. The literal value is two.

Insensitive Pixmaps

Labels can have their **XmNsensitive** resource set to **False** to indicate that the Label is inactive. At first this may seem frivolous since Labels are never "active." However, it is very common for the user to associate Labels with other interactive elements such as List widgets, ToggleButtons, TextFields, or even composite items such as RadioBoxes. It is useful to desensitize the Labels along with their corresponding logical user-interface elements to stress the message that a portion of the interface is inactive. In the same vein, the routine **XtSetSensitive( )**, when applied to a Manager widget, will sensitize or desensitize all of its children, Labels included.

XmNlabelInsensitivePixmap can be set to a special pixmap to use when the Label has been set insensitive. By default, this resource is set to **XmUNSPECIFIED_PIXMAP**, which causes whatever label or pixmap associated with the Label to be "grayed out" by bitwise AND-ing a stipple pattern over the text or image used. The pixmap associated with the **XmNlabelInsensitivePixmap** resource is *not* "grayed out" as described; Motif assumes that you want to use a completely new and/or unique pixmap of your own to indicate label insensitivity. For example, your insensitive pixmap for a Label in your application could be the identical label overlaid with a circle that has a diagonal line through the center.

11.1.4 Label Alignment

Within the boundaries of the Label widget or gadget, the text or image used within a Label is either left-justified, right-justified, or centered. This alignment corresponds to the value of **XmNalignment**, which may be any one of the following:

```
XmALIGNMENT_BEGINNING
XmALIGNMENT_END
XmALIGNMENT_CENTER
```

The default value is **XmALIGNMENT_CENTER**, which causes the text or pixmap to be centered vertically and horizontally within the widget or gadget area. The values for **XmALIGNMENT_BEGINNING** and **XmALIGNMENT_END** refer to the left and right edges of the widget or gadget boundaries when the value for **XmNstringDirection** is set to **XmSTRING_DIRECTION_L_TO_R**. That is, if the text used within a Label is read from left-to-right (the default), then the beginning of the string is on the left. However, if the text used is read from right-to-left, the alignment values are inverted (as should be the value for **XmNstringDirection**). Note that these values also apply to Labels that display pixmaps. If you have a set of Labels associated with strings of text that are right-justified, then each Label should assume the same alignment and string direction settings for consistency with one another. Typically, however, these resource settings are set universally (as a class-based resource) for all Labels and subclasses of Labels. That is, if your application is written for a language that displays its text from right-to-left, you may choose to have the following lines in your fallback resources or in an apps-defaults file:

```
*XmLabel.stringDirection: string_direction_r_to_l
*XmLabelGadget.stringDirection: string_direction_r_to_l
```

Notice that the resource must be set for the gadget class as well as for the widget class. Also, be aware that the string direction does not imply that the compound strings you use are automatically converted to the right direction. That is, labels that use compound strings that have right-to-left directions do not automatically affect the **XmNstringDirection** resource of Labels. Similarly, setting **XmNstringDirection** in Labels does not cause their compound strings to automatically have a right-to-left direction. These are important internationalization issues if you are thinking of supporting languages that are justified either left-to-right or right-to-left.

Label Alignment in RowColumns

The RowColumn manager widget can be used to control the geometry management of its children using whatever means are necessary to enforce consistency. If you are using a Row-Column to lay out a group of objects subclassed from Labels (PushButtons, ToggleButtons, etc.) you can tell the RowColumn to align each of its children (entries) in a consistent manner using **XmNentryAlignment**. This resource takes the same values as the **XmNalignment** resource for Labels. If the parent of a Label widget or gadget is a Row-Column whose **XmNisAligned** resource is **True**, each of the Label widget or gadget children of the RowColumn will have its **XmNalignment** forced to the same value as the Row-Column's **XmNentryAlignment** resource.

Note that this change in alignment value only happens when the RowColumn resource **XmNrowColumnType** is **XmWORK_AREA**. Whenever you use a RowColumn, its type will always be a work area, except when the internals of Motif use a RowColumn for their own purposes. Thus, you may or may not see similar effects on Labels that reside in menus, MenuBars, or other predefined Motif objects where RowColumns are treated specially.

11.1.5 Multilined and Multifont Labels

The fonts used within Labels are directly associated with those used in the compound strings set in the **XmNlabelString** resource. The Label's **XmNfontList** resource contains the mapping between the character set and the font name to use when displaying the text. Since compound strings may contain multiple character set combinations, Labels may display any number of fonts as specified in the Label's **XmNlabelString**. Similarly, compound strings may also have embedded newlines (or *separators*) in them. An example of this is shown in Example 11-2, where a single compound string is used to display a monthly calendar.

Example 11-2. The xcal.c program

```
/* xcal.c -- display a monthly calendar.  The month displayed is a
 * single Label widget whose text is generated from the output of
 * the "cal" program found on any UNIX machine.  popen() is used
 * to run the program and read its output.  Although this is an
 * inefficient method for getting the output of a separate program,
 * it suffices for demonstration purposes.  A List widget displays
 * the months and the user can provide the year as argv[1].
 */
```

Example 11-2. The xcal.c program (continued)

```
#include <stdio.h>
#include <Xm/List.h>
#include <Xm/Frame.h>
#include <Xm/LabelG.h>
#include <Xm/RowColumn.h>
#include <Xm/SeparatoG.h>

int year;
XmStringTable ArgvToXmStringTable();
void XmStringFreeTable();

char *months[ ] = {
    "January", "February", "March", "April", "May", "June",
    "July", "August", "September", "October", "November", "December"
};

main(argc, argv)
int argc;
char *argv[ ];
{
    Widget toplevel, frame, rowcol, label, w;
    XtAppContext app;
    Display *dpy;
    extern void set_month();
    XmFontList fontlist;
    XFontStruct *font;
    int i, month_no;

    toplevel = XtVaAppInitialize(&app, "Demos", NULL, 0,
        &argc, argv, NULL, NULL);

    /* Create a fontlist based on the fonts we're using.  These are the
     * fonts that are going to be hardcoded in the Label and List widgets.
     */
    dpy = XtDisplay(toplevel);
    font = XLoadQueryFont(dpy, "-*-courier-bold-r-*--18-*");
    fontlist = XmFontListCreate(font, "charset1");
    font = XLoadQueryFont(dpy, "-*-courier-medium-r-*--18-*");
    fontlist = XmFontListAdd(fontlist, font, "charset2");

    if (argc > 1)
        year = atoi(argv[1]);
    else {
        long time(), t = time(0);
        struct tm *today = localtime(&t);
        year = 1900 + today->tm_year;
        month_no = today->tm_mon+1;
    }

    /* The RowColumn is the general layout manager for the application.
     * It contains two children: a Label gadget that displays the calendar
     * month, and a ScrolledList to allow the user to change the month.
     */
    rowcol = XtVaCreateWidget("rowcol",
        xmRowColumnWidgetClass, toplevel,
        XmNorientation, XmHORIZONTAL,
        NULL);

    /* enclose the month in a Frame for decoration. */
```

Example 11-2. The xcal.c program (continued)

```
    frame = XtVaCreateManagedWidget("frame",
        xmFrameWidgetClass, rowcol, NULL);
    label = XtVaCreateManagedWidget("month",
        xmLabelGadgetClass, frame,
        XmNalignment, XmALIGNMENT_BEGINNING,
        XmNfontList,  fontlist,
        NULL);

    /* create a list of month names */
    {
        XmStringTable strs =
            ArgvToXmStringTable(XtNumber(months), months);
        w = XmCreateScrolledList(rowcol, "list", NULL, 0);
        XtVaSetValues(w,
            XmNitems,       strs,
            XmNitemCount,   XtNumber(months),
            XmNfontList,    fontlist,
            NULL);
        XmStringFreeTable(strs);
        XtAddCallback(w, XmNbrowseSelectionCallback, set_month, label);
        XtManageChild(w);
        XmListSelectPos(w, month_no, True); /* initialize month */
    }

    XtManageChild(rowcol);
    XtRealizeWidget(toplevel);
    XtAppMainLoop(app);
}

/* callback function for the List widget -- change the month */
void
set_month(w, label, list_cbs)
Widget w;
Widget label;
XmListCallbackStruct *list_cbs;
{
    register FILE *pp;
    char text[BUFSIZ];
    register char *p = text;
    XmString str;

    /* Ask UNIX to execute the "cal" command and read its output */
    sprintf(text, "cal %d %d", list_cbs->item_position, year);
    if (!(pp = popen(text, "r"))) {
        perror(text);
        return;
    }
    *p = 0;
    while (fgets(p, sizeof(text) - strlen(text), pp))
        p += strlen(p);
    pclose(pp);

    /* display the month using the "charset1" font from the
     * Label gadget's XmNfontList.
     */
    str = XmStringCreateLtoR(text, "charset1");
    XtVaSetValues(label, XmNlabelString, str, NULL);
    XmStringFree(str);
```

Example 11-2. The xcal.c program (continued)

```
}

/* Convert an array of string to an array of compound strings */
XmStringTable
ArgvToXmStringTable(argc, argv)
int argc;
char **argv;
{
    XmStringTable new =
        (XmStringTable)XtMalloc((argc+1) * sizeof(XmString));

    if (!new)
        return (XmStringTable)NULL;

    new[argc] = 0;
    while (--argc >= 0)
        new[argc] = XmStringCreate(argv[argc], "charset2");
    return new;
}

/* Free the table created by ArgvToXmStringTable() */
void
XmStringFreeTable(argv)
XmStringTable argv;
{
    register int i;

    if (!argv)
        return;
    for (i = 0; argv[i]; i++)
        XmStringFree(argv[i]);
    XtFree(argv);
}
```

The output of this program is shown in Figure 11-2.

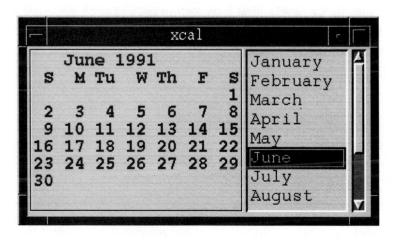

Figure 11-2. Output of xcal.c

The principal function in Example 11-2 is `set_month( )`. This is where we call `popen( )` to run the UNIX program *cal* and read its input into a buffer. We know ahead of time how much text we are going to read, so `text` is declared with ample space (`BUFSIZ`). Each line is read consecutively until `EOF` is reached (when `fgets( )` returns `NULL`), at which time we close the opened process using `pclose( )` and convert the text buffer into a compound string. This compound string specifies both a character set to use and separators (newlines) because `fgets( )` does not strip newline characters from the strings they get.

The month corresponding to the selected item in the List is displayed, but only as a single Label widget. If we wanted to display individual days using a different font (with Sundays grayed out, for example), then the text buffer would have to be parsed individually. Here, separate compound strings would be created using separate fonts for the Sunday dates only. This is more of an exercise for manipulating compound strings than it is for Label widgets. See Chapter 19, *Compound Strings*, for a detailed discussion on the use of multiple fonts in compound strings.

However, say you wanted to provide the user with the ability to select individual days from the month displayed. For this, not only must you parse the dates from the text buffer, you might want to use separate PushButton widgets for each date.

11.1.6 Other Resources

There are many other resources associated with Labels, yet most of them are used by other Motif objects or widget classes that are subclassed from Labels. For example, menus use Labels and PushButtons extensively as menu items—as such, Labels and PushButtons can have accelerators, mnemonics, and other visual resources set to provide the appropriate functionality for menus. However, these resources do not apply to Labels and PushButtons that are not used as menu items.

The only callback routine for the Label widget is the **XmNhelpCallback** associated with all Primitive widgets. That is, if the user presses the HELP key on a Label widget, its help callback is called.[2]

---

[2] Whether Labels will get the **Help** event is dependent on the type of input policy the user is using and whether keyboard traversal is on. Since it may not be possible to use the **Help** button on Labels, we do not strongly recommend providing a help callback routine for them. But it doesn't hurt. If you do, you should probably make the same help text available from another location as well.

11.2 PushButtons

PushButtons and Labels are similar in many ways; they both display either text or graphics, can be set insensitive, and so on. In fact, since the PushButton is subclassed from the Label, it can do everything the Label can. Unlike Labels, however, the PushButton can interact with the user and invoke functions internal to the underlying application through callback routines. This interactivity is the principal difference between PushButtons and Labels. There are other visual differences, but these are adjusted automatically by the PushButton widget using Label resources.

The header files for PushButton widgets and gadgets are *<Xm/PushB.h>* and *<Xm/PushBG.h>*, respectively. These objects can be created using `XtVaCreateManaged-Widget( )`:

```
Widget    pushb_w, pushb_g;

pushb_w = XtVaCreateManagedWidget("name",
    xmPushButtonWidgetClass, parent,
    resource-value list,
    NULL);

pushb_g = XtVaCreateManagedWidget("name",
    xmPushButtonGadgetClass, parent,
    resource-value list,
    NULL);
```

11.2.1 PushButton Callbacks

The major callback routine associated with PushButtons is `XmNactivateCallback`. The functions associated with this resource are called whenever the user presses and releases the left mouse button (by default). Example 11-3 demonstrates how this is done.

Example 11-3. The pushb.c program

```
/* pushb.c -- demonstrate the pushbutton widget.  Display one
 * PushButton with a single callback routine.  Print the name
 * of the widget and the number of "multiple clicks".  This
 * value is maintained by the toolkit.
 */
#include <Xm/PushB.h>

main(argc, argv)
int argc;
char *argv[ ];
{
    XtAppContext app;
    Widget toplevel, button;
    void my_callback();
    XmString btn_text;

    toplevel = XtVaAppInitialize(&app, "Demos",
        NULL, 0, &argc, argv, NULL, NULL);

    btn_text = XmStringCreateSimple("Push Here");
```

Example 11-3. The pushb.c program (continued)

```
    button = XtVaCreateManagedWidget("button",
        xmPushButtonWidgetClass, toplevel,
        XmNlabelString, btn_text,
        XmNwidth,       50,
        XmNheight,      25,
        NULL);
    XmStringFree(btn_text);
    XtAddCallback(button, XmNactivateCallback, my_callback, NULL);

    XtRealizeWidget(toplevel);
    XtAppMainLoop(app);
}

void
my_callback(w, client_data, cbs)
Widget w;
XtPointer client_data;
XmPushButtonCallbackStruct *cbs;
{
    printf("%s: pushed %d times\n", XtName(w), cbs->click_count);
}
```

The callback structure associated with the PushButton's callback routine is `XmPush-ButtonCallbackStruct`:

```
    typedef struct {
        int     reason;
        XEvent *event;
        int     click_count;
    } XmPushButtonCallbackStruct;
```

The `reason` parameter is set to `XmCR_ACTIVATE`. The event that caused the PushButton to be activated is referenced by the `event` field. While a PushButton is typically activated by a press of the leftmost mouse button, you can't just assume this. For example, pressing RETURN while the pointer is in the button also activates a PushButton. Furthermore, the user could define translation settings that may enable other events to activate PushButtons.

The `click_count` reflects how many times the PushButton has been clicked *repeatedly*. A repeated button click is one that occurs during a predefined time segment since the last button click. Only button clicks may be done repeatedly; pressing RETURN repeatedly does not cause the `click_count` to grow, although it will invoke the activate callback list.

The time segment that determines whether a button click is "repeated" is defined by the resource `multiClickTime`. This is not a Motif-defined resource, but a per-display value and should be left to the user to specify independently from the application. You can get or set this value using the functions `XtGetMultiClickTime()` or `XtSetMulti-ClickTime()`. The time interval is used by Xt's translation manager to determine when multiple events are interpreted as a repeat event. The default value is 200 milliseconds (1/5 of a second).

The other callback routines associated with the PushButton are the *arm* and *disarm* callbacks. (There are also arm and disarm actions, which highlight and unhighlight the PushButton when the pointer enters or leaves it; the action functions call the associated callback lists, which allows you to interpose functions of your own at these points.) The arm callback is set using the resource `XmNarmCallback`. Each function in this callback list is called whenever the user has pressed the **select** mouse button. Note: this does not indicate that the button has been released. If the user releases it within the widget, then the activate callback list is invoked. Whether or not this happens (and before it happens), the arm callback is always called and processed before continuing.

When the user releases the button, the disarm callback list is invoked. This callback list is set using the `XmNdisarmCallback` resource and, like the arm callback list, does not guarantee that the activate callbacks have been invoked. The user could change his mind before releasing the button and move (drag) the mouse outside of the widget area before releasing it. The most common case is that the user will actually select and activate the button, in which case, the arm callback is called first, followed by the activate callback, followed by the disarm callback.

We can modify Example 11-3 to demonstrate how arm and disarm callback functions are used by registering the appropriate callbacks:

```
XtAddCallback(button, XmNarmCallback, my_callback, NULL);
XtAddCallback(button, XmNdisarmCallback, my_callback, NULL);
XtAddCallback(button, XmNactivateCallback, my_callback, NULL);
```

We also modify `my_callback( )` to handle the new callback reasons:

```
void
my_callback(w, client_data, cbs)
Widget w;
caddr_t *client_data;
XmPushButtonCallbackStruct *cbs;
{
    if (cbs->reason == XmCR_ARM)
        printf("%s: armed\n", XtName(w));
    else if (cbs->reason == XmCR_DISARM)
        printf("%s: disarmed\n", XtName(w));
    else
        printf("%s: pushed %d times\n", XtName(w), cbs->click_count);
}
```

The callback structure in the callback routine for the arm and disarm callbacks is of type `XmAnyCallbackStruct`, which means that only the **reason** and **event** fields are valid. However, the callback structure passed to this routine is `XmPushButtonCallbackStruct`. The reason for the discrepancy is that the same function is used for all three callbacks: arm, disarm, and activate. Since the `XmAnyCallbackStruct` is a subset of the `XmPushButtonCallbackStruct`, there is no harm in declaring the pointer as the latter type because we will only use the field that is unique to that structure (the `click_count` field) when we know the function was called as a result of `XmNactivateCallback`. In other words, when **reason** is `XmCR_ACTIVATE`, the structure must be of type `XmPushButtonCallbackStruct`.

Since the activate callback function is only called if the user actually activates the PushButton, it is generally unnecessary to register arm and disarm callback functions unless your application has a specific need to know when the button was pushed and released, even if it wasn't activated. We provide examples where these callbacks are used later in the chapter.

11.2.2 Multiple Button Clicks

Unfortunately, there is no way to determine whether you are about to receive multiple button clicks from a PushButton's callback function. Each time the user activates the PushButton, the arm callback is invoked, followed by the activate callback, followed by the disarm callback. These three callbacks are invoked regardless of whether multiple clicks occurred. The best way to determine whether you have (or will have) multiple button clicks would be for the disarm callback to be called only when there are no more button clicks queued. This way, the same callback function can be used to determine the end of a multiple button click sequence.

Since this is not the case for the Motif toolkit, we must approach the task of handling multiple button clicks differently. We do this by setting up our own timeout routines independently of Motif and handling multiple clicks through the timeout function. Even though we are going to use an alternate method for handling multiple timeouts, we still use the `click_count` parameter in the callback structure of the PushButton's callback routine. This is demonstrated in Example 11-4.

Example 11-4. The multi_click.c program

```
/* multi_click.c -- demonstrate handling multiple PushButton clicks.
 * First, obtain the time interval of what constitutes a multiple
 * button click from the display and pass this as the client_data
 * for the button_click() callback function.  In the callback, single
 * button clicks set a timer to expire on that interval and call the
 * function process_clicks().  Double clicks remove the timer and
 * just call process_clicks() directly.
 */
#include <Xm/PushB.h>

XtAppContext app;

main(argc, argv)
int argc;
char *argv[ ];
{
    Widget toplevel, button, WidgetCreate();
    void button_click();
    XmString btn_text;
    int interval;

    toplevel = XtVaAppInitialize(&app, "Demos",
        NULL, 0, &argc, argv, NULL, NULL);

    /* get how long for a double click */
    interval = XtGetMultiClickTime(XtDisplay(toplevel));
    printf("interval = %d\n", interval);

    btn_text = XmStringCreateSimple("Push Here");
    button = XtVaCreateManagedWidget("button",
        xmPushButtonWidgetClass, toplevel,
        XmNlabelString, btn_text,
        XmNwidth,       50,
        XmNheight,      25,
        NULL);
    XmStringFree(btn_text);
```

Example 11-4. The multi_click.c program (continued)

```
    XtAddCallback(button, XmNactivateCallback, button_click, interval);

    XtRealizeWidget(toplevel);
    XtAppMainLoop(app);
}
/* Process button clicks.  Single clicks set a timer, double clicks
 * remove the timer, and extended clicks are ignored.
 */
void
button_click(w, interval, cbs)
Widget w;
int interval;
XmPushButtonCallbackStruct *cbs;
{
    static XtIntervalId id;
    void process_clicks();

    if (cbs->click_count == 1)
        id = XtAppAddTimeOut(app, interval, process_clicks, False);
    else if (cbs->click_count == 2) {
        XtRemoveTimeOut(id);
        process_clicks(True);
    }
}

/* This function won't be called until we've established whether
 * or not a single or a double click has occurred.
 */
void
process_clicks(double_click)
int double_click;
{
    if (double_click)
        puts("Double click");
    else
        puts("Single click");
}
```

The program displays the same basic PushButton widget. First, it obtains the time interval that constitutes a multiple button click from the display. This value is passed as the client_data for the PushButton's callback function, **button_click( )**. When the user clicks on the PushButton, the callback function is called normally and, since it was a single-click (at least so far), a timer is set to expire on the given time interval. If the timer expires, the function **process_clicks( )** is called with **False** as its parameter (thus, a single-click has indeed occurred). However, if a second button click occurs before the timer expires, the timer is removed (before it has a chance to expire) and **process_clicks( )** is called directly, passing **True** as its data.

The function **process_clicks( )** can be any function that processes single, double, or multiple clicks depending on how you modify the example we've provided.

If you've tried running Example 11-5 and found that you were getting mixed messages about whether there was a single or double mouse click, you have just experienced a very common problem found with trying to interpret double (multiple) button clicks.

NOTE

> A multiple mouse "click" means that the user has both *pressed and released* the mouse button more than once. It is very common for a user that intended to "double click" a widget only to find that he really invoked a "double press". That is, he quickly pressed the mouse button twice, but failed to *release* it before the required time interval.

It is important to inform the user of the proper double-clicking method in any accompanying documentation you may provide with your application. Attempting to program around this problem will definitely cause you great distress.

If you are going to provide multiple button clicks for PushButtons, you might also consider displaying some visual cue to the user about the nature of the PushButton's interactivity. For example, you could use a multilined label in a PushButton such as:

```
XmStringCreateLtoR("Delete\nUndelete", "charset");
```

When this compound string is used as the label for a PushButton, the word "Delete" will appear to be over the word "Undelete," reflecting the fact that the PushButton can invoke one of two actions. It is the responsibility of your documentation to inform the user how to invoke either of the two commands.

Not Using Multiple Clicks

While double-clicking is a popular interface technique among application programmers and is certainly useful for computers with single button mice, it may not be the best interface for all occasions. Possible error conditions may arise when the user is unfamiliar with single- and double-clicking techniques. Users often trip on mouse buttons, causing unintentional multiple clicks. Also, users frequently intend to do one double-click yet succeed in doing two single-clicks. As a result, they get very upset with applications when they invoke the wrong action twice as opposed to the right action once. Rather than subjecting your user to possible misinterpretation, it may be better to define an alternate method for providing separate actions for the same PushButton widget.

For example, the action **Shift+ButtonClick** is easy enough for the user to do, is less subject to ambiguity or accidental usage, and is much easier to program. The callback function only needs to check the **event** data structure and see if the SHIFT key is down in the activate callback:

```
if (cbs->event->xbutton.state & ShiftMask)
    /* shift key down too */
```

The PushButton looks for and reports multiple button-click actions by default, so if you are not interested in multiple button clicks, you should set the resource **XmNmultiClick** to **XmMULTICLICK_DISCARD**. When multiple clicks are discarded, only the first of a series of clicks are processed; the rest are discarded without notifying the callback routine. To turn multiple clicks back on, set the resource to **XmMULTICLICK_KEEP**.

11.3 ArrowButtons

ArrowButtons are just like PushButtons, but they only display one of four directional arrow symbols: up, down, right, and left as shown in Figure 11-3.

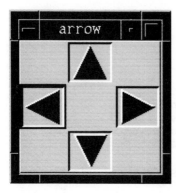

Figure 11-3. The four icons used by ArrowButtons

These arrow button images are not fixed, but are calculated dynamically based on the size of the widget itself. If the widget is resized for some reason, the directional arrow will always grow or shrink to fill its container. Other than this feature, most things ArrowButtons can do can also be handled by some other user-interface element. For example, the callback routines for an ArrowButton may increment or decrement the viewport of a ScrolledList or ScrolledText widget, or modify the value indicators for a Slider. However, ArrowButtons are still useful if you want to provide redundant interface methods to certain widgets or if you want to build your own interfaces for objects that are not part of the Motif widget set. Redundancy, when used appropriately, can be an important part of a graphical user interface. Many users may not adapt well to certain interface controls such as pulldown menus in MenuBars or keyboard accelerators, while they are perfectly comfortable with iconic controls such as ArrowButtons and PushButtons displaying pixmaps.

Which of the four directional arrows an ArrowButton displays is controlled by the value of **XmNarrowDirection**. This resource may have one of the following values:

```
XmARROW_UP
XmARROW_DOWN
XmARROW_LEFT
XmARROW_RIGHT
```

The output from Figure 11-3 was generated from the program listed in Example 11-5.

Example 11-5. The arrow.c program

```
/* arrow.c -- demonstrate the ArrowButton widget.
 * Have a Form widget display 4 ArrowButtons in a
 * familiar arrangement.
 */
#include <Xm/ArrowBG.h>
#include <Xm/Form.h>
```

Example 11-5. The arrow.c program (continued)

```
main(argc, argv)
int argc;
char *argv[ ];
{
    XtAppContext app;
    Widget toplevel, form;
    XmString btn_text;
    Display *dpy;

    toplevel = XtVaAppInitialize(&app, "Demos",
        NULL, 0, &argc, argv, NULL, NULL);

    dpy = XtDisplay(toplevel);
    /* Rather than listing all these resources in an app-defaults file,
     * add them directly to the database for this application only. This
     * would be virtually equivalent to hardcoding values, since these
     * resources will override any other specified external to this file.
     */
    XrmPutStringResource(&dpy->db, "*form*topAttachment", "attach_position");
    XrmPutStringResource(&dpy->db, "*form*leftAttachment", "attach_position");
    XrmPutStringResource(&dpy->db, "*form*rightAttachment", "attach_position");
    XrmPutStringResource(&dpy->db, "*form*bottomAttachment", "attach_position");

    form = XtVaCreateWidget("form", xmFormWidgetClass, toplevel,
        XmNfractionBase,     3,
        NULL);

    XtVaCreateManagedWidget("arrow1",
        xmArrowButtonGadgetClass, form,
        XmNtopPosition,        0,
        XmNbottomPosition,     1,
        XmNleftPosition,       1,
        XmNrightPosition,      2,
        XmNarrowDirection,     XmARROW_UP,
        NULL);

    XtVaCreateManagedWidget("arrow2",
        xmArrowButtonGadgetClass, form,
        XmNtopPosition,        1,
        XmNbottomPosition,     2,
        XmNleftPosition,       0,
        XmNrightPosition,      1,
        XmNarrowDirection,     XmARROW_LEFT,
        NULL);

    XtVaCreateManagedWidget("arrow3",
        xmArrowButtonGadgetClass, form,
        XmNtopPosition,        1,
        XmNbottomPosition,     2,
        XmNleftPosition,       2,
        XmNrightPosition,      3,
        XmNarrowDirection,     XmARROW_RIGHT,
        NULL);

    XtVaCreateManagedWidget("arrow4",
        xmArrowButtonGadgetClass, form,
        XmNtopPosition,        2,
        XmNbottomPosition,     3,
        XmNleftPosition,       1,
```

Example 11-5. The arrow.c program (continued)

```
        XmNrightPosition,    2,
        XmNarrowDirection,   XmARROW_DOWN,
        NULL);

    XtManageChild(form);
    XtRealizeWidget(toplevel);
    XtAppMainLoop(app);
}
```

ArrowButton widgets and gadgets use the following resources in exactly the same way that PushButtons use them:

```
    XmNactivateCallback
    XmNarmCallback
    XmNdisarmCallback
    XmNmultiClick
```

The callback routines take a parameter of type **XmArrowButtonCallbackStruct**:

```
    typedef struct {
        int     reason;
        XEvent  *event;
        int     click_count;
    } XmArrowButtonCallbackStruct;
```

This callback structure is identical to the one used for PushButtons.

ArrowButtons are commonly used to increment values, positions, and other data by some arbitrary amount. If the amount being incremented (or decremented) is sufficiently small in comparison to the total size of the object, it would be convenient for the user if you give him the ability to iterate through such increments quickly. For example, by holding the mouse button down over an ArrowButton widget, we can emulate its activate callback routine being called continuously. This is not a feature of the ArrowButton; this is something we have to do ourselves. To implement this feature, we use the Xt timer demonstrated in Example 11-6.

Example 11-6. The arrow_timer.c program

```
/* arrow_timer.c -- demonstrate continuous callbacks using
 * ArrowButton widgets.  Display up and down ArrowButtons and
 * attach arm and disarm callbacks to them to start and stop timer
 * that is called repeatedly while the button is down.  A label
 * that has a value changes either positively or negatively
 * by single increments while the button is depressed.
 */
#include <Xm/ArrowBG.h>
#include <Xm/Form.h>
#include <Xm/RowColumn.h>
#include <Xm/LabelG.h>

XtAppContext app;
Widget label;
XtIntervalId arrow_timer_id;
typedef struct value_range {
    int value, min, max;
} ValueRange;

main(argc, argv)
```

Example 11-6. The arrow_timer.c program (continued)

```
int argc;
char *argv[ ];
{
    Widget w, toplevel, rowcol;
    XmString btn_text;
    void start_stop();
    ValueRange range;

    toplevel = XtVaAppInitialize(&app, "Demos",
        NULL, 0, &argc, argv, NULL, NULL);

    rowcol = XtVaCreateWidget("rowcol",
        xmRowColumnWidgetClass, toplevel,
        XmNorientation, XmHORIZONTAL,
        NULL);

    w = XtVaCreateManagedWidget("arrow_up",
        xmArrowButtonGadgetClass, rowcol,
        XmNarrowDirection,   XmARROW_UP,
        NULL);
    XtAddCallback(w, XmNarmCallback, start_stop, 1);
    XtAddCallback(w, XmNdisarmCallback, start_stop, 1);

    w = XtVaCreateManagedWidget("arrow_dn",
        xmArrowButtonGadgetClass, rowcol,
        XmNarrowDirection,   XmARROW_DOWN,
        NULL);
    XtAddCallback(w, XmNarmCallback, start_stop, -1);
    XtAddCallback(w, XmNdisarmCallback, start_stop, -1);

    range.value = 0;
    range.min = -50;
    range.max = 50;
    label = XtVaCreateManagedWidget("label",
        xmLabelGadgetClass, rowcol,
        XtVaTypedArg, XmNlabelString, XmRString, "0    ", 3,
        XmNuserData, &range,
        NULL);

    XtManageChild(rowcol);
    XtRealizeWidget(toplevel);
    XtAppMainLoop(app);
}
/* start_stop is used to start or stop the incremental changes to
 * the label's value.  When the button goes down, the reason is
 * XmCR_ARM and the timer starts.  XmCR_DISARM disables the timer.
 * Keypresses are special cases since they do not generate disarm
 * callbacks (fixed in a later version of the toolkit).  For backwards
 * compatibility, change_value() must be called with a 0 id to
 * prevent the timer from starting at all.
 */
void
start_stop(w, incr, cbs)
Widget w;
int incr;
XmArrowButtonCallbackStruct *cbs;
{
    void change_value();
```

Example 11-6. The arrow_timer.c program (continued)

```
    if (cbs->reason == XmCR_ARM)
        /* pass either 0 or 1 as "id" to change_value */
        change_value(incr, cbs->event->type == ButtonPress);
    else if (cbs->reason == XmCR_DISARM)
        XtRemoveTimeOut(arrow_timer_id);
}

/* change_value is called each time the timer expires.  This function
 * is also used to initiate the timer.  The "id" represents that timer
 * ID returned from the last call to XtAppAddTimeOut().  If id <= 1,
 * the function was called from start_stop(), not a timeout.  If it's
 * 0, don't start the timer, just change the value.  If the value has
 * reached its maximum or minimum, don't restart timer, just return.
 * If id == 1, this is the first timeout so make it be longer to allow
 * the user to release the button and avoid getting into the "speedy"
 * part of the timeouts.
 */
void
change_value(incr, id)
int incr;
XtIntervalId id;
{
    ValueRange *range;
    char buf[8];

    XtVaGetValues(label, XmNuserData, &range, NULL);
    if (range->value + incr > range->max ||
        range->value + incr < range->min)
        return;
    range->value += incr;
    sprintf(buf, "%d", range->value);
    XtVaSetValues(label,
        XtVaTypedArg, XmNlabelString, XmRString, buf, strlen(buf),
        XmNuserData, range,
        NULL);
    if (id > 0)
        arrow_timer_id =
            XtAppAddTimeOut(app, id==1? 100: 500, change_value, incr);
}
```

The output of this program is shown in Figure 11-4.

Figure 11-4. Output of arrow_timer.c

The program creates up and down ArrowButtons and attaches arm and disarm callbacks to them to start and stop an internal timer. Each time the timer expires, a Label gadget's value changes incrementally by one. The timer remains on as long as the button is down. We know the button is released when the disarm event occurs.

The function responsible for this is **start_stop( )**, which is installed as both the arm and disarm callback. When the button goes down, the **reason** is **XmCR_ARM**, and the timer starts. When the button is released, the disarm callback is invoked, the **reason** is **Xm-CR_DISARM**, and the timer is disabled. Key presses are special cases since they only invoke the arm callback; they currently do not generate the disarm callbacks.[3]   Therefore, **change_value( )** must be called with a **0** as the **id** parameter to prevent the timer from starting.

The timer is initiated from **start_stop( )** by calling **change_value( )**. Each time the timer expires, it also calls this function and does so repeatedly while the button is down. The **id** represents the ID of the timer that recently expired from the last call to **XtAppAdd-TimeOut( )**. If this value is less than or equal to one, the function was called from **start_stop( )**, not as a timeout. If the value is zero, this is our hint that the timer should not be restarted; just change the value and return. We also don't restart the timer if the value has reached its maximum or minimum values. If the **id** is one, this is the initiating call, so make the first timeout last longer to allow the user to release the button before getting into the "speedy" timeouts. Otherwise, time out every 100 milliseconds.

By experimentation, you can get a feel for how the functions work and modify some of the hard-coded values (such as the timeout values). This procedure could also apply to Push-Buttons or any other widget that provides arm and disarm callbacks.

11.4 DrawnButtons

DrawnButtons are similar to PushButtons except that they also have callback routines for **Expose** and **ConfigureNotify** events. Whenever the widget is exposed or resized, your callback routines can redisplay its contents rather than relying on the widget to handle its own repainting. These callbacks are invoked anytime the widget needs to redraw itself, even if it is a result of changes to certain resources such as **XmNshadowType**, **XmNshadow-Thickness**, or the foreground or background colors of the widget.

The intent of the widget is to allow you to draw into it or, more likely, provide a dynamically changing pixmap while maintaining complete control over what the widget should display. Unlike the PushButton widget, you are in control of the repainting of the surface area of the widget (not including the beveled edges that give it a 3D effect). To do the same thing using PushButton widgets, you would have to change the **XmNlabelPixmap** resource using **XtVaSetValues( )**. Unfortunately, this causes an annoying flickering effect because the PushButton redisplays itself entirely whenever its pixmap changes. By using the Drawn-Button widget, you can dynamically change its display by rendering graphics directly onto the window of the widget using any Xlib routines such as **XDrawLine( )** or **XCopy-Area( )**. This tight control may require more work on your part, but the feedback to the user is greatly improved over the behavior of the PushButton.

---

[3] Key presses not generating disarm callbacks is regarded as a bug and may be fixed in a future release.

DrawnButtons are created similarly to PushButtons and ArrowButtons. However, because
the widget provides you with its own drawing area, there is no corresponding gadget version
of this object. The associated header file is *<Xm/DrawnB.h>* and must be included by files
that create the widget. Example 11-7 shows a simple example of how a DrawnButton can be
created.

Example 11-7. The drawn.c program

```
/* drawn.c -- demonstrate the DrawnButton widget by drawing a
 * common X logo into its window.  This is hardly much different
 * from  a PushButton widget, but the DrawnButton isn't much
 * different, except for a couple more callback routines...
 */
#include <Xm/DrawnB.h>
#include <Xm/RowColumn.h>

main(argc, argv)
int argc;
char *argv[ ];
{
    XtAppContext app;
    Widget toplevel, rowcol, button;
    Pixmap pixmap;
    Pixel fg, bg;
    void my_callback();

    toplevel = XtVaAppInitialize(&app, "Demos",
        NULL, 0, &argc, argv, NULL, NULL);

    rowcol = XtVaCreateManagedWidget("_rowcol",
        xmRowColumnWidgetClass, toplevel, NULL);

    XtVaGetValues(rowcol,
        XmNforeground, &fg,
        XmNbackground, &bg,
        NULL);
    pixmap = XmGetPixmap(XtScreen(rowcol), "xlogo64", fg, bg);
    button = XtVaCreateManagedWidget("button",
        xmDrawnButtonWidgetClass, rowcol,
        XmNlabelType,    XmPIXMAP,
        XmNlabelPixmap,  pixmap,
        NULL);
    XtAddCallback(button, XmNactivateCallback, my_callback, NULL);
    XtAddCallback(button, XmNexposeCallback, my_callback, NULL);
    XtAddCallback(button, XmNresizeCallback, my_callback, NULL);

    XtRealizeWidget(toplevel);
    XtAppMainLoop(app);
}

void
my_callback(w, client_data, cbs)
Widget w;
XtPointer client_data;
XmDrawnButtonCallbackStruct *cbs;
{
    if (cbs->reason == XmCR_ACTIVATE)
        printf("%s: pushed %d times\n", XtName(w), cbs->click_count);
    else if (cbs->reason == XmCR_EXPOSE)
```

Example 11-7. The drawn.c program (continued)

```
        puts("Expose");
   else /* XmCR_RESIZE */
        puts("Resize");
}
```

The program simply displays the X Window System logo as shown in Figure 11-5.

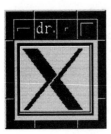

Figure 11-5. Output of drawn.c

A single callback routine handles the activate, expose, and resize callbacks. This is done using **XtAddCallback( )** on the resources **XmNactivateCallback**, **XmNexpose-Callback**, and **XmNresizeCallback**. The callback routine **my_callback( )** demonstrates the possible values that the callback structure's **reason** can have. It may be one of the following values:

```
XmCR_ACTIVATE
XmCR_EXPOSE
XmCR_RESIZE
```

The callback structure associated with the DrawnButton is called the **XmDrawnButton-CallbackStruct**:

```
typedef struct {
    int      reason;
    XEvent   *event;
    Window   window;
    int      click_count;
} XmDrawnButtonCallbackStruct;
```

The **window** field of the structure is the window ID of the DrawnButton widget whose associated callback routine was invoked. This value is the same as that returned by **Xt-Window( )**.

NOTE

Due to bugs in the Motif toolkit, the **event** field of this callback structure is NULL when the reason is **XmCR_RESIZE**. This means that you cannot use the **event** structure to provide you with the new dimensions of the widget. To query the widget's size, you must use **XtVaGetValues( )** or possibly **Xt-QueryGeometry( )**. The **event** field is also NULL when the user activates the button using the keyboard rather than the mouse.

The resource **XmNpushButtonEnabled** indicates whether the DrawnButton should look and act like a PushButton. When the value is **False** (the default), the DrawnButton displays itself and whatever contents you put in it. It does not provide feedback to the user concerning the button's state including the times when the button is insensitive. Since all the rendering is the responsibility of the application, you must decide whether you want to render the graphics (or text) differently when the pixmap is insensitive. However, keep in mind that the DrawnButton is subclassed from the Label class and you can therefore provide a **XmNlabelPixmap** and **XmNlabel-InsensitivePixmap** if you like. In this case, you might as well use a PushButton instead of a DrawnButton.

When the value of **XmNpushButtonEnabled** is set to **False**, the edges of the Drawn-Button are drawn according to the style described by the **XmNshadowType** resource. This is a resource used to help you differentiate DrawnButtons from PushButtons. This resource can be set to one of the following values:

```
XmSHADOW_IN
XmSHADOW_OUT
XmSHADOW_ETCHED_IN
XmSHADOW_ETCHED_OUT
```

The value of **XmNshadowType** only has an effect when the value of **XmNpushButton-Enabled** is **True**.

Example 11-8 demonstrates how all the pieces of the DrawnButton can be used to construct an *application manager*. This is a program that contains a set of icons where each corresponds to a program. When the user pushes one of the buttons (a DrawnButton), a program is executed. The button deactivates itself so that only one instance of each application can run at a time. (There is no particular reason for this design restriction aside from the fact that it demontrates how the widget's visual resources can be used to make subtle suggestions to the user.)

Example 11-8. The app_box.c program

```c
/* app_box.c -- make an array of DrawnButtons that, when activated,
 * executes a program.  When the program is running, the drawn button
 * associated with the program is insensitive.  When the program dies,
 * reactivate the button so the user can select it again.
 */
#include <Xm/DrawnB.h>
#include <Xm/RowColumn.h>
#include <signal.h>

#ifndef SYSV
#include <sys/wait.h>
#else
#define SIGCHLD SIGCLD
#endif /* SYSV */

typedef struct {
    Widget drawn_w;
    char *pixmap_file;
    char *exec_argv[6]; /* 6 is arbitrary, but big enough */
    int pid;
} ExecItem;
```

Example 11-8. The app_box.c program (continued)

```
ExecItem prog_list[ ] = {
    { NULL, "terminal",   { "xterm", NULL },                0 },
    { NULL, "flagup",     { "xterm", "-e", "mush", NULL }, 0 },
    { NULL, "calculator", { "xcalc", NULL },                0 },
    { NULL, "woman",      { "bitmap", "64x64", NULL },      0 },
    { NULL, "xlogo64",    { "foo", NULL },                  0 },
};

XtAppContext app; /* application context for the whole program */
GC gc; /* used to render pixmaps in the widgets */
static void reset(), reset_btn(), redraw_button(), exec_prog();

main(argc, argv)
int argc;
char *argv[ ];
{
    Widget toplevel, rowcol;
    Pixmap pixmap;
    Pixel fg, bg;
    int i;

    /* we want to be notified when child programs die */
    signal(SIGCHLD, reset);

    toplevel = XtVaAppInitialize(&app, "Demos",
        NULL, 0, &argc, argv, NULL, NULL);

    rowcol = XtVaCreateWidget("rowcol", xmRowColumnWidgetClass, toplevel,
        XmNorientation, XmHORIZONTAL,
        NULL);

    /* get the foreground and background colors of the rowcol
     * so the gc (DrawnButtons) will use them to render pixmaps.
     */
    XtVaGetValues(rowcol,
        XmNforeground, &fg,
        XmNbackground, &bg,
        NULL);
    gc = XCreateGC(XtDisplay(rowcol),
        RootWindowOfScreen(XtScreen(rowcol)), NULL, 0);
    XSetForeground(XtDisplay(rowcol), gc, fg);
    XSetBackground(XtDisplay(rowcol), gc, bg);

    for (i = 0; i < XtNumber(prog_list); i++) {
        /* the pixmap is taken from the name given in the structure */
        pixmap = XmGetPixmap(XtScreen(rowcol),
            prog_list[i].pixmap_file, fg, bg);

        /* Create a drawn button 64x64 (arbitrary, but sufficient)
         * shadowType has no effect till pushButtonEnabled is false.
         */
        prog_list[i].drawn_w = XtVaCreateManagedWidget("dbutton",
            xmDrawnButtonWidgetClass, rowcol,
            XmNwidth,             64,
            XmNheight,            64,
            XmNpushButtonEnabled, True,
            XmNshadowType,        XmSHADOW_ETCHED_OUT,
            NULL);
        /* if this button is selected, execute the program */
```

Example 11-8. The app_box.c program (continued)

```
        XtAddCallback(prog_list[i].drawn_w,
            XmNactivateCallback, exec_prog, &prog_list[i]);

        /* when the resize and expose events come, redraw pixmap */
        XtAddCallback(prog_list[i].drawn_w,
            XmNexposeCallback, redraw_button, pixmap);
        XtAddCallback(prog_list[i].drawn_w,
            XmNresizeCallback, redraw_button, pixmap);
    }

    XtManageChild(rowcol);
    XtRealizeWidget(toplevel);
    XtAppMainLoop(app);
}

/* redraw_button() draws the pixmap (client_data) into its DrawnButton
 * using the global GC (gc).  Get the width and height of the pixmap
 * being used so we can either center it in the button or clip it.
 */
static void
redraw_button(button, pixmap, cbs)
Widget button;
Pixmap pixmap;
XmDrawnButtonCallbackStruct *cbs;
{
    int srcx, srcy, destx, desty, pix_w, pix_h;
    int drawsize, border;
    Dimension bdr_w, w_width, w_height;
    short hlthick, shthick;
    Window root;

    /* get width and height of the pixmap. don't use srcx and root */
    XGetGeometry(XtDisplay(button), pixmap, &root, &srcx, &srcx,
        &pix_w, &pix_h, &srcx, &srcx);

    /* get the values of all the resources that affect the entire
     * geometry of the button.  Hint: we can't use XGetGeometry()
     */
    XtVaGetValues(button,
        XmNwidth,            &w_width,
        XmNheight,           &w_height,
        XmNborderWidth,      &bdr_w,
        XmNhighlightThickness, &hlthick,
        XmNshadowThickness,  &shthick,
        NULL);

    /* calculate available drawing area, width 1st */
    border = bdr_w + hlthick + shthick;

    /* if window is bigger than pixmap, center it; else clip pixmap */
    drawsize = w_width - 2*border;
    if (drawsize > pix_w) {
        srcx = 0;
        destx = (drawsize - pix_w)/2 + border;
    } else {
        srcx = (pix_w - drawsize)/2;
        pix_w = drawsize;
        destx = border;
    }
```

Example 11-8. The app_box.c program (continued)

```
    /* now the height ... */
    drawsize = w_height - 2*border;
    if (drawsize > pix_h) {
        srcy = 0;
        desty = (drawsize - pix_h)/2 + border;
    } else {
        srcy = (pix_h - drawsize)/2;
        pix_h = drawsize;
        desty = border;
    }

    XCopyArea(XtDisplay(button), pixmap, cbs->window, gc,
        srcx, srcy, pix_w, pix_h, destx, desty);
}

/* exec_proc() --the button has been pressed; fork() and call
 * execvp() to start up the program.  If the fork or the execvp
 * fails (program not found?), the sigchld catcher will get it
 * and clean up.  If the program is successful, set the button's
 * sensitivity to False (to prevent the user from execing again)
 * and set pushButtonEnabled to False to allow shadowType to work.
 */
static void
exec_prog(drawn_w, program, cbs)
Widget drawn_w;
ExecItem *program;
XmDrawnButtonCallbackStruct *cbs;
{
    switch (program->pid = fork()) {
        case 0:   /* child */
            execvp(program->exec_argv[ 0 ], program->exec_argv);
            perror(program->exec_argv[ 0 ]); /* command not found? */
            _exit(255);
        case -1:
            printf("fork() failed.\n");
    }

    /* The child is off executing program... parent continues */
    if (program->pid > 0) {
        XtVaSetValues(drawn_w,
            XmNsensitive,          False,
            XmNpushButtonEnabled, False,
            NULL);
    }
}

/* reset() -- a program died, so find out which one it was and
 * reset its corresponding DrawnButton widget so it can be reselected
 */
static void
reset()
{
    int pid, i;
#ifdef SYSV
    int status;
#else
    union wait status;
```

Example 11-8. The app_box.c program (continued)

```
#endif /* SYSV */

    if ((pid = wait(&status)) == -1)
        /* an error of some kind (fork probably failed); ignore it */
        return;

    for (i = 0; i < XtNumber(prog_list); i++)
        if (prog_list[i].pid == pid) {
            /* program died -- now reset item.  But not here! */
            XtAppAddTimeOut(app, 0, reset_btn, prog_list[i].drawn_w);
            return;
        }

    printf("Pid #%d ???\n", pid); /* error, but not fatal */
}

/* reset the sensitivity and "pushButtonEnabled" resources on the
 * drawn button passed.  This cannot be done within the signal
 * handler or we might step on an X protocol packet since signals are
 * asynchronous.  This func is safe because it's called from a timer.
 */
static void
reset_btn(drawn_w)
Widget drawn_w;    /* client_data from XtAppAddTimeOut() */
{
    XtVaSetValues(drawn_w,
        XmNsensitive, True,
        XmNpushButtonEnabled, True,
        NULL);
}
```

The output of the program is shown in Figure 11-6.

Figure 11-6. Output of app_box.c

In this particular case, the icons and applications they invoke are hard-coded to a limited set of programs.[4] Internally, the program is quite simple; in fact, it may be too simple for actual use in a product-quality application. However, it serves our demonstration purposes here. The program's main feature from the user-interface perspective is the use of DrawnButton widgets. They are simple widgets and, as such, are used minimally in the application.

---

[4] The design of the program is such that it can be easily modified to support user configurability to specify which programs he'd like to execute and the icons associated with them.

A more important reason for presenting this example is to explore the use of the `fork( )` system call and the delivery of the `SIGCHLD` signal. For System V, this signal number is `SIGCLD`. Signal numbers are defined in *<signal.h>* on UNIX systems.[5] When `fork( )` is used to spawn a new process, it is imperative that the new process does not attempt to interact with the widgets in its parent application or attempt to read events associated with the same display connection as its parent process. In general, child processes must close their connection to the X server and reopen a new connection if interaction with the X display is necessary.

In our application, we are playing it safe by executing a completely new application using `execvp( )`. This system call executes a program provided it is found in the user's `PATH`. This is why we don't need to specify full pathnames to the applications we want to execute. If the program cannot be found (which might be the case with one of the programs used by Example 11-8), the child process immediately dies and the signal handler `reset( )` is immediately called by the operating system. Details of how `reset( )` is implemented are provided in the next section.

11.5 Signal Handling

In Example 11-8, the `reset( )` function was used to notify us that a child process that we had executed from a `fork( )` system call had terminated. Before we continue discussing the reasons why `reset( )` reacts in the way that it does, let us take a step back and examine exactly what UNIX signals are.

Think of signals as "events from the operating system." Operating system events include `SIGINT`, which indicates that the user interrupted the program somehow; `SIGTSTP`, which indicates that the user used job control to "stop" the application temporarily; or `SIGTERM`, which indicates that the application is being terminated. One of these operating system events is `SIGCHLD`, which is generated when the application is being notified that one of its child processes has terminated (as is the case in Example 11-8). What we'd like to do in this case is reset the sensitivity and the `XmNpushButtonEnabled` resources on the Drawn-Button associated with this process so that the user can activate it again. However, what we did was add a timeout using `XtAppAddTimeOut( )`, with a zero-length time interval. What this appears to do is return back to the top-level event processing loop (`XtAppMain-Loop( )`) and immediately call the callback routine placed on the timer (`reset_btn( )`). In fact, this is precisely what happens. But you then may ask, "Why not just reset those values at the time of the signal handler?"

The answer to this question is perhaps one of the most frequently misunderstood concepts in X-based application programming. Signals are asynchronous events that happen on the operating system level; X events occur in the window system. Since the operating system takes precedence over the window system, signals may *interrupt* the windowing system, regardless of the state it is in. If you think of signals as "operating system events," then you can think of signal handlers as "callback routines" for these events. When an operating

---

[5] Non-UNIX operating systems that do not have signals will not be able to compile and run this program.

system event is delivered, it could interrupt another routine that is communicating with the X Window System. The user may be pressing another button at the time, or a repaint routine internal to the Motif widget set could be sending Xlib requests to the X server to redraw another button. Whatever may be going on, that function may be interrupted by the operating system, which may result in unpredictable (and often undesirable) effects.

Because the operating system takes priority, it is very important that signal handlers be very careful not to do anything that may invoke a communication with the X server. The signal handler may set internal variables, flags, or virtually anything else not involving the window system. This is why we don't call `XtVaSetValues()` on the DrawnButton to reset its sensitivity—such a call would ultimately invoke the DrawnButton's repaint procedure and would, in turn, call an Xlib routine.

One of the few things we can do is call `XtAppAddTimeOut()`. This function is strictly client-side (no calls to Xlib functions result) and control is immediately returned to the calling function (the signal handler, in this case). By registering a timeout callback and returning from the signal handler, we allow whatever X-based calls that may be in progress to finish, at which time the program returns to the top level (`XtAppMainLoop()`). The timer expires immediately and the callback function associated with that timer is called. Since this callback came from the Xt layer, we know that Xt and Xlib calls are safe to call again. Thus, `XtVaSetValues()` is finally called to reset the sensitivity and the `XmNpushButton-Enabled` resource.

11.5.1 Xt Timers

One final loose end that should be addressed is the way "timers" are implemented. Many of you may be thinking, "Isn't a timer another signal in UNIX?" The answer is "Yes." But Xt timers are not implemented using UNIX signals; they are implemented by using a feature of the `select()` system call. `select()` is used to determine if there are events being sent to the application from the X server (although no events are actually read). However, `select()` can also be told only to wait a certain amount of time before returning, whether or not there are events queued. By setting the amount of time to wait for events to a specified value, we can implement what appears to the programmer and the user as a *timer*. As long as there are events to read from the server, however, the timers are inactive. This is why timers in Xt may only be set in *intervals* rather than as real-time values.

Timers are not implemented using UNIX signals for the same reasons that we did not call `XtVaSetValues()` from within the `SIGCHLD` signal handler. It is also for this reason that you should be sure not to use UNIX-based functions such as `sleep()` or `setitimer()` to modify widgets or make Xlib calls. This does not imply that you should not use these functions at all; it's just that the same restrictions apply to UNIX timers as they do to other UNIX signals: if you need to do any X- or Xt-related function calls, you should set a simple zero-interval timer function and call those X functions from within the corresponding timeout callback.

11.6 Pixmaps and Color Issues

In this section, we are going to take a closer look at **XmGetPixmap( )**, since it is commonly used to provide graphic images for Labels and its subclasses. The primary purpose of **XmGetPixmap( )** is to provide a caching mechanism for pixmaps. Whenever a new pixmap is created using this function, it retains a handle to this pixmap in case another call is made requesting the same image. If this occurs, the function returns the exact same pixmap that was returned to the original requestor and increments an internal reference counter. In order to provide good housecleaning, whenever **XmGetPixmap( )** is used to "get" a pixmap (which may cause it to be created), the caller must use **XmFreePixmap( )** when the pixmap is no longer needed. This function decrements the reference count; if it reaches zero, then **XmFreePixmap( )** actually uses **XFreePixmap( )** to discard the pixmap.

It is important to note that this caching mechanism is handled on a per-client (per-application) basis. Different processes cannot share pixmaps.

The form of **XmGetPixmap( )** is as follows:

```
Pixmap
XmGetPixmap(screen, image_name, foreground, background)
    Screen *screen;
    char    *image_name;
    Pixel   foreground;
    Pixel   background;
```

The **image_name** can be either a filename or the name of a previously registered image using **XmInstallImage( )**; we'll talk about images in a moment. The pixmap that is created from **XmGetPixmap( )** has the same depth as the given **screen**, and its foreground and background colors are specified by the corresponding parameters. Obviously, this implies that you cannot rely on **XmGetPixmap( )** to create single-plane bitmaps. In fact, if the user is on a color display, **XmGetPixmap( )** will *never* create single-bit deep images. If you need single-plane pixmaps,[6] then you'll have to use one of **XCreateBitmapFromData( )** or **XCreatePixmapFromBitmapData( )** and specify the appropriate depth value. However, the Label and its subclasses have similar drawbacks in that they cannot have pixmaps whose depths are other than their own (which are ultimately taken from the screen's depth). This process is particularly annoying if you want to dynamically change the color of Labels or PushButtons that display pixmaps. To solve that problem, you must dispose of the existing pixmap and create a new one with the appropriate colors. This process is demonstrated in Chapter 4, *The Main Window*.

Whenever **XmGetPixmap( )** is called, it looks in its cache for previously-created pixmaps that match the given name and colors. If a match is found, the previously-created pixmap is returned and the reference count incremented. Here, two separate parts of the application could have a handle to the same pixmap.

---

[6] The terms *single-bit* and *single-plane* are interchangable; they imply a pixmap with only two colors: 0 and 1. While the term *bitmap* usually refers to single-bit deep pixmaps, this is not necessarily true outside of the X Windows social culture.

The `image_name` parameter is the key to where to get the data for the pixmap about to be created. As mentioned above, it can take one of two forms: a filename or a symbolic name previously registered using `XmInstallImage( )`, which we'll get to later. `XmGet-Pixmap( )` uses the following algorithm to determine what pixmap to return or create.

1. Look in cache and return any images already created that have the same name, foreground and background colors.

2. If no pixmap is found, look in its own internal cache of predefined images.

3. If there is still no match, match the name against image names installed by `Xm-InstallImage( )`.

4. If all else fails, interpret the `image_name` as a filename that contains standard X11 bitmap information and read the bitmap data directly out of that file.

The first step is straightforward. The second step is usually used by the internals to the Motif toolkit, but are available to the programmer as a convenience. The following table lists the current image names predefined by the toolkit.

Table 11-1. Predefined Image Names in the Motif Toolkit

Image Name	Description
background	A tile of solid background.
25_foreground	A tile of 25% foreground, 75% background.
50_foreground	A tile of 50% foreground, 50% background.
75_foreground	A tile of 75% foreground, 25% background.
horizontal	A tile of horizontal lines of the two colors.
vertical	A tile of vertical lines of the two colors.
slant_left	A tile of slanting lines of the two colors.
slant_right	A tile of slanting lines of the two colors.

Many other images are installed at runtime by the Motif toolkit to support Motif-specific dialog images as well as random pixmaps used by other widget classes. None of these image names are publicly available, so you should be aware of this. It is possible, although not likely, that you call `XmGetPixmap( )` and pass it a filename expecting the data in that file to be loaded. If a preinstalled image exists in the cache that has the same "name" as the one you're checking for, you won't get the expected image.

If no name matches, the image is loaded from a file—if `image_name` starts with a slash character (/), it is taken as a full pathname. Otherwise, the file is extracted from a file whose pathname is constructed based on the values of various user-defined environment variables. On POSIX systems, the environment variable `XBMLANGPATH` can be set to specify a desired directory in which to search for bitmap files; if this variable is not set, a search path is based on the value of the `XAPPLRESDIR HOME` and `LANG` (as well as various permutations of the path */usr/lib/X11 ... /bitmaps*). See the Motif reference page *XmGetPixmap.3X* for full details.

In any event, this lookup is sufficiently complex, and, like most things having to do with internationalization, sufficiently untested, that at present you should not depend on any of these environment variables to be set at all, let alone set to anything sensible. If you want to rely on the existence of a bitmap file, you should either use hard-coded pathnames or, if this portion of your program is interactive, require the user to input the desired pathname.

In all cases, whenever **XmGetPixmap( )** looks in its cache for a image name, a complete pattern match must occur in order for a match to exist; calling **XmGetPixmap( )** for the file:

    xlogo64

will not match a previously loaded pixmap with the name:

    /usr/include/X11/bitmaps/xlogo64

In short, it is highly-recommended that you always specify full pathnames to **XmGet-Pixmap( )** to be assured that you get the desired file, and not some random file or match against a predefined Motif image name.

11.6.1 Installing Your Own Images

It is possible to predefine your own images and load them directly into the cache for **Xm-GetPixmap( )** using **XmInstallImage( )**. The form of the function is:

```
Boolean
XmInstallImage(image, image_name)
    XImage   *image;
    char     *image_name;
```

The **image** parameter is a pointer to an **XImage** data structure that has been previously created or, more commonly, statically initialized by the application. It is possible to create an image dynamically from an existing window or pixmap using **XGetImage( )**, but this is not the way the function is typically used. It is conceivable for portions of a dialog or a window and store the image using **XGetImage( )**, but this would be extremely application-specific.

The following code fragment demonstrates how the function is used in most cases:

```
#define bitmap_width 16
#define bitmap_height 16
static char bitmap_bits[ ] = {
    0xFF, 0x00, 0xFF, 0x00, 0xFF, 0x00, 0xFF, 0x00,
    0xFF, 0x00, 0xFF, 0x00, 0xFF, 0x00, 0xFF, 0x00,
    0x00, 0xFF, 0x00, 0xFF, 0x00, 0xFF, 0x00, 0xFF,
    0x00, 0xFF, 0x00, 0xFF, 0x00, 0xFF, 0x00, 0xFF
};

static XImage ximage = {
    ximage.width = bitmap_width;
    ximage.height = bitmap_height;
    ximage.data = bitmap_bits;
    ximage.xoffset = 0;
    ximage.format = XYBitmap;
    ximage.byte_order = MSBFirst;
```

```
        ximage.bitmap_pad = 8;
        ximage.bitmap_bit_order = LSBFirst;
        ximage.bitmap_unit = 8;
        ximage.depth = 1;
        ximage.bytes_per_line = 2;
        ximage.obdata = NULL;
    };

        .
        .
        .

    XmInstallImage(&ximage, "image_name");
        .
        .
        .
```

Here, standard X11 bitmap data is declared directly in the code. If this particular bitmap were declared in an external file somewhere, we could just have easily included it using the preprocessor macro:

```
    #include "filename"
```

The point is that the **XImage** structure is initialized to contain the bitmap information and then it is installed in the internal cache shared by the **XmGetPixmap( )**. If you attempt to install a new image with the same name, the function returns **False** and the image is not installed. Otherwise, the function returns **True**.

You can "uninstall" an image by calling **XmUninstallImage( )**:

```
    Boolean
    XmUninstallImage(ximage)
        XImage *ximage;
```

Once the image is uninstalled, it cannot be referenced by name anymore and a new image may be installed with the same name. Note that **XmCreatePixmap( )** creates pixmaps based on image data, not on the images themselves. Any pixmap created by an image is not affected by the image being uninstalled by **XmUninstallImage( )**. Also note that the **XImage** structure is *not* copied by **XmInstallImage( )**, so if the image pointer you pass has been allocated using **XCreateImage( )** or **XGetImage( )**, then you must not free this data until after you call **XmUninstallImage( )**. The **name**, however, is copied to internal storage, so you don't have to worry about that.

Remember that the rationale for using this function (to cache images) is to reuse and share the same images among many parts of the application. If you aren't doing image replication, then it's probably not worth the effort to use these functions.

11.6.2 Color

Color plays an important role in a graphical user interface. It appeals to the senses, so it can provide aesthetic beauty, while at the same time it can be used to influence the user about his course of action. However, for all the power of color, it is frequently abused by an application designer. One color combination can appeal to some, while the same color scheme can offend others. Thus, the safest bet is to avoid forcing (hard-coding) any use of color in your application; rather, provide enough flexibility for the user to configure colors through resource databases or interactively in the application.

Of course, many applications are based on the use of color, so the sweeping generalization made above is intended to apply to those parts of the application that are not dependent on color. In short, this is a judgment call that only you can make. While color is used in various ways throughout this book, this particular section only deals with Labels and Buttons.

There are two things to keep in mind about color when dealing with Motif user-interface controls: gadgets and the 3D effect. As you may recall, gadgets are "windowless widgets," so they do not render themselves—their manager parents do that for them. The Motif toolkit happens to have a restriction that all gadgets in a common manager widget must share the same foreground and background colors.[7] Manager widgets use their foreground and background color resources to determine the colors for rendering their gadget children. The manager's background is usually a solid color (unless it has a background pixmap for its window; see the exercises in this chapter) and its foreground color is unused unless it is managing gadgets. In the latter case, that foreground color is used to render the contents of the gadget. If you change the foreground color of a manager widget, all its gadget children will uniformly change to that color. Similarly, if the manager's background color changes, all the gadgets' backgrounds change to that color. This may or may not be the desired effect; it depends on the nature of your application whether this is appropriate. For example, using Label gadgets is frequently more advantageous than Label widgets in applications whose colors can change dynamically because the Label's colors will change along with its parent. Thus, gadgets provide more consistency in color flow, while widgets provide more flexibility.

Widgets, on the other hand, retain their own foreground and background colors, so the foreground and background colors of a manager widget do not affect its widget-based children.

The **XmNforeground** and **XmNbackground** resources are commonly used by virtually all Motif widgets. (Motif gadgets do not use these resources.) Although each widget makes different use of these resource values, text is typically rendered in the foreground color and everything else in the background color. Exceptions are ToggleButtons, which have a **XmNselectColor** for the square/diamond selection indicator, and the Scrollbar widget, which has **XmNtroughColor** to set the area behind its slider and directional arrows.

Other color resources include **XmNarmColor**, which is used to display the color of an object when it is *armed* (as discussed earlier) and the **XmNborderColor**, which colors the "border" of a window. (All X windows have borders; this is not a Motif- or Xt-specific quality.) Motif widgets typically have a border width of **0**, so this resource is rarely noticed (and should probably remain that way). There is also the **XmNhighlightColor**, which is used to indicate which object on the display has the keyboard focus. The widget that displays this color can be dynamically changed whenever the user selects a new object with the mouse or traverses the widget tree using the tab group mechanism (discussed in Chapter 8, *Manager Widgets*).

Perhaps the most troublesome of all the auxiliary color resources are **XmNtopShadowColor** and **XmNbottomShadowColor**. These are the colors that give Motif widgets their 3D appearance on color displays. If set inappropriately, these colors can ruin the aesthetics of a user-interface display. Normally, these resources are set automatically by the

---

[7] This is not true for all Xt-based toolkits. People porting applications from other widget sets that use gadgets with different colors in the same Manager widget might have to convert them to widgets.

toolkit based on the background color of the object. Therefore, these colors are normally not a problem. That is, if the background color of a PushButton is blue when it is created, the toolkit automatically calculates the **XmNtopShadowColor** to be a slightly lighter shade of blue and the **XmNbottomShadowColor** to be slightly darker. However, if you want to change the PushButton's background dynamically, the toolkit does not automatically recalculate these colors and resources for you. So, for example, if you change the **XmNbackground** for a PushButton to red, the top and bottom shadow colors remain the different shades of blue.

Note: these resources are strictly used by *widgets*, not gadgets. Dynamically changing the background of a manager causes it to automatically recalculate the new top and bottom shadow colors and redisplay its gadgets correctly. Many consider that the fact that this process is not automated for widgets to be a design flaw in the Motif toolkit. However, you can do the work yourself by recalculating the new shading colors and setting the resources directly. This is done using **XmGetColors( )**:

```
void
XmGetColors(screen, cmap, bg, newfg, newtop, newbot, newselect)
    Screen  *screen;
    Colormap cmap;
    Pixel    bg;
    Pixel    *newfg;
    Pixel    *newtop;
    Pixel    *newbot;
    Pixel    *newselect;
```

XmGetColors( ) takes a colormap and a background color and calculates and returns an appropriate foreground color, top and bottom shadow colors, and a "select" color (for the ToggleButton). So, for example, the following code fragment demonstrates how to change the background color of a PushButton to "red."

```
XColor color, unused;
Pixel  bg_color, top_shadow, bottom_shadow, fg, select_color;

/* Get the colormap */
XtVaGetValues(widget, XmNcolormap, &cmap, NULL);

/* convert the color "red" to a pixel value from the given colormap. */
XAllocNamedColor(XtDisplay(widget), cmap, "red", &color, &unused);
bg_color = color.pixel;

/* Let Motif calculate the new colors based on that one color */
XmGetColors(XtScreen(widget), cmap, bg_color,
    &fg_ret, &top_shadow, &bottom_shadow, &select_color);

/* Set the colors accordingly. */
XtVaSetValues(widget,
    XmNbackground,         bg_color,
    XmNtopShadowColor,     top_shadow,
    XmNbottomShadowColor,  bottom_shadow,
    XmNselectColor,        select_color,
    XmNarmColor,           select_color,
    XmNborderColor,        fg_ret,
    NULL);
```

A basic problem behind setting and getting colors for widgets is that what you get for a given pixel value depends on the colormap. That is, a pixel is simply an index value into an array of color definitions (a colormap). The problem with colormaps is that you never know what colormap is associated with any particular widget.

Most of the time, this is not a problem because the widgets in an application will almost always share the same colormap. But if you have a color-intensive application, you may fill up a colormap before the toolkit needs to allocate new colors for certain widgets. In this case, Motif may or may not allocate a new colormap, depending on whether the existing one contains enough room for new colors.

To be on the safe side, we first get the colormap from the widget and convert the color ourselves using **XAllocNamedColor( )**. The function gets the actual color (RGB values and pixel value from the colormap), which we can pass to **XmGetColors( )** to calculate the rest of the colors. Once all the colors are obtained, we can set all of them simultaneously.

Another approach we can take to the same problem is shown in the following code fragment:

```
Pixel  bg_color, top_shadow, bottom_shadow, fg, select_color;

/* First, set the background color to red... */
XtVaSetValues(widget,
    XtVaTypedArg, XmNbackground, XmRString, "red", 4, /* strlen("red")+1 */
    NULL);

/* Once set, get it again, so we know what pixel value it got.
 * Also get the widget's colormap, since we'll be setting its new
 * colors based on the same colormap.
 */
XtVaGetValues(widget,
    XmNbackground, &bg_color,
    XmNcolormap,   &cmap,
    NULL);

/* Let Motif calculate the new colors based on that one color */
XmGetColors(XtScreen(widget), cmap, bg_color,
    &fg_ret, &top_shadow, &bottom_shadow, &select_color);

/* Set the colors accordingly. */
XtVaSetValues(widget,
    XmNtopShadowColor,    top_shadow,
    XmNbottomShadowColor, bottom_shadow,
    XmNselectColor,       select_color,
    XmNarmColor,          select_color,
    XmNborderColor,       fg_ret,
    NULL);
```

By calling **XtVaSetValues( )** using the type-converting resource, **XtVaTypedArg**, we defer the problem to the toolkit and its string-to-color type converter. The toolkit allocates the color out of the colormap already owned by the toolkit and sets the background color accordingly. Once done, we can "get" the actual pixel value using **XtVaGetValues( )**. along with the colormap and proceed as we did before.

Label and its subclasses cannot display more than one color for text. However, you can, if you like, create a multi-plane pixmap and render various strings directly into it using **XDrawString( )**. You can then get multiple colors by changing the foreground color in the GC using **XSetForeground( )** or **XChangeGC( )**. (You must either do that or use separate GCs for each string you wish to render in a separate color or font.) The resulting pixmap can then be used as the **XmNpixmap** resource for the Label (or subclass) widget or gadget.

11.7 Summary

The Label class acts as a superclass for more widgets than any other in the Motif toolkit. Therefore, its use is rather broad. For detailed information on other widgets that are subclassed from the Label, you should see Chapter 4, *The Main Window*; Chapter 12, *Toggle Widgets*; and Chapter 16, *Menus*. Examples of all these widgets are also liberally spread throughout the rest of the book. As mentioned at the beginning of the chapter, the intent of this chapter is not to discuss all aspects of the widgets discussed here, but to give you the fundamentals.

11.8 Exercises

The following exercises are intended to stimulate and encourage other creative ways for using Labels and Buttons.

1. Generic X windows have a *background pixmap* property that can be set using `XSet-WindowBackgroundPixmap()`.[8] Whenever the background pixmap is set, the image is "tiled" on the window; i.e., if the window is larger than the image, the image is replicated in a checkerboard fashion until the window's background is filled; if the window is the same size or smaller than the image, the image is centered in the window. This image is automatically rendered into the window appropriately by the X Window System whenever necessary. Since widgets have windows, the X Toolkit Intrinsics have a convenience resource that allows you to set the widget's window's background pixmap using `XtNbackgroundPixmap`. (Motif's `XmNbackgroundPixmap` resource is identical except that the naming convention provides consistency among resource names.) Write a program that displays a Label that contains both graphics and a text label by setting both `XmNlabelString` and `XmNbackgroundPixmap` to appropriate values.

2. Write an application that displays a set of Labels and PushButtons in the form of both widgets and gadgets. Next, include a ScrolledList that contains a list of color names. When the user selects a color in the list, set the foreground colors of all the widgets in the application to the given color as described in Section 11.6.2, *Color*. Hint: to affect the "gadgets," you must set the manager widget parent that contains them.

3. Modify the previous example to set the background color for these objects. Don't forget about the top and bottom shadow colors.

---

[8] See Volume One, *Xlib Programmer's Manual*, for details on `XSetWindowBackgroundPixmap()`.

12

Toggle Widgets

This chapter describes both ToggleButtons and the special configurations of the RowColumn widget used to manage Toggles in either a CheckBox or RadioBox format.

In This Chapter:

12
Toggle Widgets

A toggle is a simple user-interface element that represents a Boolean state. Usually, this widget consists of an indicator (a square or diamond) with either text or a pixmap on one side of it. However, the indicator is optional, since the text or pixmap itself can provide the state information of the button.

Individually, a ToggleButton might be used to indicate whether a file should be opened in overwrite mode or append mode, or whether a mail application should update a folder upon process termination. But for the most part, it is when Toggles are grouped together that they become interesting components of a user interface. The way these groups of Toggles are managed provides two discrete user-interface control specifications. A *RadioBox* is a group of Toggles in which only one may be "on" at any given time. Like the old AM car radios, when one button is in, all the others pop out. The other form of Toggle group is called a *CheckBox*; in a CheckBox, each Toggle may be set independently from the others. In a RadioBox, the *selection indicator* is represented by a diamond shape, and in a CheckBox, it is represented by a square. In either case, when the Toggle is "on," the selector is filled with a highlight color and appears to be "pressed in," whereas when it is "off," the selector appears to be "popped out."

CheckBoxes and RadioBoxes can present a set of choices to the user in a way that may be more effective than those employed by List widgets, popup menus, or rows of PushButtons.[1] In fact, these configurations are so common that Motif provides convenience routines for creating them: `XmCreateRadioBox()` and `XmCreateSimpleCheckBox()`. These are really specialized instances of the RowColumn widget introduced in Chapter 8, *Manager Widgets*, but we will discuss them in detail later in this chapter.

In the widget hierarchy, ToggleButtons are subclassed from Labels, so resources from that class may be applied to ToggleButtons. This means that Toggles can have their labels set to compound strings or pixmaps and can be aligned (justified) in the same ways and under the same restrictions as Label widgets.

---

[1] In some cases, the choice may be purely aesthetic: providing different user-interface elements may give a more dynamic quality to your applications. Overuse of the same type of object can be uninteresting to the user. Of course, variety for variety's sake is also to be avoided.

12.1 Creating ToggleButtons

Applications that use ToggleButtons must include the header file *<Xm/ToggleB.h>*. Toggle-Buttons may be created using `XtVaCreateManagedWidget( )`:

```
Widget   toggle;

toggle = XtVaCreateManagedWidget("name",
    xmToggleButtonWidgetClass, parent,
    resource-value list,
    NULL);
```

ToggleButtons are also available in the form of gadgets. Since gadgets have no windows, background colors or patterns, the manager widget acting as the gadget's parent is responsible for redisplaying the object and providing its color. See Chapter 11, *Labels and Buttons*, for a complete discussion of how color can be used with gadgets.

To use a ToggleButton gadget, you must include the header file *<Xm/ToggleBG.h>*. Toggle-Button gadgets may be created using `XtVaCreateManagedWidget( )`:

```
Widget   toggle;

toggle = XtVaCreateManagedWidget("name",
    xmToggleButtonGadgetClass, parent,
    resource-value list,
    NULL);
```

The only difference between this function and the one used for the widget is the *class* specified.

As we'll see later in the chapter, it is also possible to create ToggleButtons at the same time as you create their RowColumn parents. This is commonly done when you create Radio-Boxes and CheckBoxes.

Figure 12-1 shows an example of several different ToggleButtons in various states. Example 12-1 shows how a simple ToggleButton can be created.

Example 12-1. The toggle.c program

```
/* toggle.c -- demonstrate a simple toggle button.  */
#include <Xm/ToggleB.h>
#include <Xm/RowColumn.h>

void
toggled(widget, client_data, state)
Widget widget;
XtPointer client_data; /* unused */
XmToggleButtonCallbackStruct *state;
{
    printf("%s: %s\n", XtName(widget), state->set? "on" : "off");
}

main(argc, argv)
int argc;
char *argv[ ];
{
    Widget toplevel, rowcol, toggle;
    XtAppContext app;
```

Example 12-1. The toggle.c program (continued)

```
    toplevel = XtVaAppInitialize(&app, "Demos", NULL, 0,
        &argc, argv, NULL, NULL);

    rowcol = XtVaCreateWidget("_rowcol",
        xmRowColumnWidgetClass, toplevel, NULL);

    toggle = XtVaCreateManagedWidget("toggle",
        xmToggleButtonWidgetClass, rowcol, NULL);
    XtAddCallback(toggle, XmNvalueChangedCallback, toggled, NULL);

    XtManageChild(rowcol);

    XtRealizeWidget(toplevel);
    XtAppMainLoop(app);
}
```

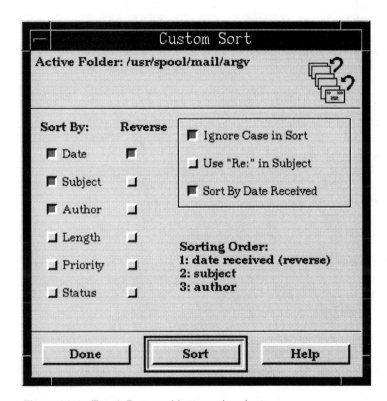

Figure 12-1. ToggleButton widgets and gadgets

The program prints to **stdout** the selection state of the ToggleButton each time its value changes. The details of how this is done are discussed in Section 12.3, *ToggleButton Callbacks*.

Since ToggleButtons are fairly simple objects, there are few resources associated with them aside from those inherited from the Label class.

Probably the most important of these resources is `XmNindicatorType`, which controls whether the toggle button is going to be part of a RadioBox or a CheckBox. The visual result is that its selection indicator will either be a square or a diamond. This resource can set to either `XmN_OF_MANY` (a square, to indicate that multiple toggles in the same group may be selected), or `XmONE_OF_MANY` (a diamond, to indicate that only one toggle in the group may be set). However, an application will rarely set this resource directly, because toggles are so frequently managed in a RadioBox or CheckBox.

When grouping ToggleButtons together in a single manager widget, the Motif toolkit "expects" you to use a RowColumn widget. As the official manager widget for Toggle-Buttons, the RowColumn widget has several resources intrinsic to its class that control the "radio behavior" as opposed to the "checkbox behavior" described earlier. Setting the Row-Column resource `XmNradioBehavior` to `True` automatically changes the `Xm-NindicatorType` resource of every ToggleButton managed by the RowColumn to `Xm-ONE_OF_MANY`, giving the exclusive RadioBox behavior. Setting `XmNradioBehavior` to `False` sets the `XmNindicatorType` to `XmN_OF_MANY`, giving the CheckBox behavior. If you want to use ToggleButtons in a manager widget other than a RowColumn, you must not only set each ToggleButton's `XmNindicatorType` resource individually, but you must also manage (through their callback routines) their toggle states.

Most of the remaining resources (except the `XmNvalueChangedCallback` resource, which identifies the callback routine that toggles the state of the button) are intended mostly for fine-tuning the details of the indicator square or diamond. These details are straight-forward and do not require a great deal of discussion. For example, setting the indicator's width and height is a fairly simple procedure involving `XtVaSetValues( )`, the `Xm-NindicatorSize` resource, and providing a desired value. There is nothing magical about these sorts of resources or their side effects, so most are either set automatically by the ToggleButton or they should be left to the user to configure for herself.

More interesting resources, however, include those that set the Toggle's label string or pix-map and those that define the callback routines. Let's begin by discussing various ways to use pixmaps in the label.

12.2 ToggleButton Pixmaps

The `XmNselectPixmap` resource specifies the pixmap to use when the ToggleButton is *on* (or *selected*)—that is, the `XmNset` resource is set to `True`. The selected pixmap only applies if the `XmNlabelType` resource is set to `XmPIXMAP`.[2] We can modify Example 12-1 to demonstrate how this can be accomplished. The new code for the program is shown in Example 12-2.

Example 12-2. Setting a selected and unselected pixmap for the ToggleButton

```
Pixmap on, off;
Pixel fg, bg;
```

---

[2] `XmNlabelType` is a Label class resource, but it applies to ToggleButtons since they are subclassed from Labels.

```
     .
     .
     .
XtVaGetValues(rowcol,
    XmNforeground, &fg,
    XmNbackground, &bg,
    NULL);
on = XmGetPixmap(XtScreen(rowcol), "switch_on", fg, bg);
off = XmGetPixmap(XtScreen(rowcol), "switch_off", fg, bg);
if (on == XmUNSPECIFIED_PIXMAP || off == XmUNSPECIFIED_PIXMAP)
    puts("couldn't load pixmaps"), exit(1);

toggle = XtVaCreateManagedWidget("toggle",
    xmToggleButtonWidgetClass, rowcol,
    XmNlabelType,    XmPIXMAP,
    XmNlabelPixmap,  off,
    XmNselectPixmap, on,
    NULL);
```

The output for this program is shown in Figure 12-2.

Figure 12-2. Using pixmaps to display toggle states

The toggle on the left shows the output when the toggle is unselected off. The toggle on the right shows the toggle on. The pixmaps illustrate the movement of a simple mechanical switch. The pixmaps shown make the state of the toggle clear, so the square indicator is not really necessary. It can be turned off by setting **XmNindicatorOn** to **False** (its default value is **True**).

In order to create toggle pixmaps, we use the function **XmGetPixmap( )**, which is a general-purpose pixmap loading and caching function. The function needs a foreground and background color for the pixmap it creates, so we retrieve and use these colors from the Row-Column acting as the ToggleButton's parent. **XmGetPixmap( )** loads the pixmaps stored in the files **switch_on** and **switch_off** in the current directory.[3] Those files are defined as:

```
#define switch_on_width 16
#define switch_on_height 16
static char switch_on_bits[ ] = {
    0x00, 0x00, 0x00, 0x00, 0x00, 0x00, 0x00, 0x00, 0x18, 0x00, 0x3c,
    0x00, 0x1e, 0x00, 0x0f, 0x80, 0x07, 0xc0, 0x03, 0xff, 0xff, 0xff, 0xff,
    0xff, 0xff, 0x00, 0x00, 0x00, 0x00, 0x00, 0x00};
```

---

[3] The fact that the pixmap files happen to reside in the current directory is not necessarily the recommended method for using **XmGetPixmap( )**. For a complete discussion of the function, see Chapter 11, *Labels and Buttons*.

```
#define switch_off_width 16
#define switch_off_height 16
static char switch_off_bits[ ] = {
    0x00, 0x00, 0x00, 0x00, 0x00, 0x00, 0x00, 0x00, 0x18, 0x00, 0x3c, 0x00,
    0x78, 0x00, 0xf0, 0x00, 0xe0, 0x01, 0xc0, 0x03, 0xff, 0xff, 0xff, 0xff,
    0xff, 0xff, 0x00, 0x00, 0x00, 0x00, 0x00, 0x00};
```

The **XmNselectInsensitivePixmap** resource can be used to specify a third pixmap
to be used when the widget or gadget is insensitive, but still in a selected state. When insensitive, the user cannot change its value interactively, although the application can do so either
by setting the **XmNsensitive** resource to **False** or by calling the function:

```
XtSetSensitive(widget, False);
```

12.3 ToggleButton Callbacks

There is one callback routine associated with ToggleButton widgets and gadgets aside from
the *arm* and *disarm* callbacks, which are analogous to those in PushButtons.[4] The conventional callback used by the ToggleButton is **XmNvalueChangedCallback**, which is
used for notification when the value of the Toggle has changed. The function installed as the
callback is called with the following parameters:

```
void
my_func(toggle_w, client_data, cbs)
    Widget toggle_w;
    caddr_t client_data;
    XmToggleButtonCallbackStruct *cbs;
```

The **toggle_w** parameter is the ToggleButton widget (or gadget) that was initially created.
The **client_data** value is the same as what was passed as *data* in **XtAddCallback( )**. The **cbs** parameter is a pointer to the callback structure specific to the
ToggleButton widget or gadget whose value was changed. This structure is defined as:

```
typedef struct {
    int     reason;
    XEvent *event;
    int     set;
} XmToggleButtonCallbackStruct;
```

The **reason** field will be set to **XmCR_VALUE_CHANGED**, and the **set** field indicates the
current state of the widget.

---

[4] Arm and disarm callback routines allow you to specify functions to call when a ToggleButton is about to be selected or deselected. For more information, see Chapter 11, *Labels and Buttons*.

You can determine the state of the button at any time using either of the following two functions:

```
Boolean
XmToggleButtonGetState(toggle_w)
    Widget toggle_w;

Boolean
XmToggleButtonGadgetGetState(toggle_w)
    Widget toggle_w;
```

Which function to use depends on whether the ToggleButton is a widget or a gadget. (You can make that determination at runtime using either `XtIsWidget()` or `XmIsGadget()`.)[5]

You can explicitly set the state of a ToggleButton using similar functions:

```
void
XmToggleButtonSetState(toggle_w)
    Widget toggle_w;

void
XmToggleButtonGadgetSetState(toggle_w)
    Widget toggle_w;
```

Unlike the get functions, however, **XmToggleButtonSetState()** determines if its parameter is a widget or gadget internally, so you can use it on either a ToggleButton widget or a ToggleButton gadget. **XmToggleButtonGadgetSetState()** can only be used on a gadget.

One important point to make about ToggleButton gadgets is that unlike PushButtons and DrawnButtons, the callback is not typically used to take an action in the application. This point becomes clearer with groups of ToggleButtons, which are used to set the state of various variables. When the user has set the state as desired, he might tell the application to apply the settings by clicking on an associated PushButton (perhaps labeled "OK").

For this reason, the callback may simply be used to set the state of a global variable, whose value can then be used by some other application function.

Note, of course, that like almost every object in Motif, a ToggleButton can be put to many uses. For example, a single ToggleButton could be used to swap the foreground and background colors of a window as soon as the user selects the button. Or, an application that controls a CD player could have a "Pause" button represented by a ToggleButton. That is, the CD can change from "play" to "pause" and back again by the selection of a ToggleButton.

---

[5] Note that `XtIsWidget()` is an Xt macro, whereas `XmIsGadget()` is a Motif macro.

In user-interface design, you constantly have to balance the twin goals of effectiveness and consistency. Effectiveness often requires imagination, which can run counter to the consistency that breeds user familiarity with your interface.

12.4 Groups of ToggleButtons

When groups of ToggleButtons are used, they may form either a RadioBox or a CheckBox. The primary difference between the two is the selection of the ToggleButtons within. In a RadioBox, only one item may be selected at a time (analogous to old-style AM car radios). You push one button and the previously set button pops out. This behavior does not apply for CheckBoxes.

Examples of exclusive settings in a RadioBox might be baud rate settings for a communications program, or U.S. versus European paper sizes in the page setup dialog of a word processing program. The same word processing program might use a CheckBox for non-exclusive settings, such as whether font smoothing, bitmap smoothing, or both, should be applied.

12.4.1 RadioBoxes

RadioBoxes are implemented using a combination of ToggleButton widgets or gadgets and a RowColumn manager widget. As discussed in Chapter 8, *Manager Widgets*, the RowColumn widget is a general-purpose composite widget that manages the layout of its children. The RowColumn has special resources that allow it to act as a RadioBox for a group of Toggle-Buttons.

In a RadioBox, only one of the toggles may be set at any given time. This functionality is enforced by the RowColumn when the resource **XmNradioBehavior** is set to **True**. For the true RadioBox effect, **XmNradioAlwaysOne** can also be set to tell the RowColumn that one of the ToggleButtons should always be set.[6] Whenever **XmNradioBehavior** is set, the RowColumn automatically sets all of its ToggleButton children's **XmNindicator** resources to **XmONE_OF_MANY** and their **XmNvisibleWhenOff** resources to **True**. (See Chapter 8, *Manager Widgets*.) Furthermore, the **XmNisHomogeneous** resource on the RowColumn is forced to **True** to ensure that no other kinds of widgets can be contained in that RowColumn instance.

---

[6] Since the application always has the freedom to add or delete ToggleButtons from the RowColumn regardless of their selected state, there may exist a case where the radio behavior is violated. Unless you are doing something clever, you shouldn't have this problem. Also, **XmNradioBehavior** is currently not a dynamically settable resource. If you want to use it, you should create the RowColumn widget with this resource set. Setting it using **XtVaSetValues( )** after widget creation may not result in the desired behavior.

Motif provides the convenience function **XmCreateRadioBox( )** to automatically create a RowColumn widget with the following resources set:

```
XmNisHomogeneous,  True,
XmNentryClass,     xmToggleButtonGadgetClass,
XmNradioBehavior,  True,
XmNpacking,        XmPACK_COLUMN,
```

Keep in mind that unless **XmNisHomogeneous** is set to **True**, there is nothing restricting RadioBox-type widgets from containing other classes as well as ToggleButtons. Whether the RowColumn is homogeneous or not, the toggle behavior is not affected. Although the Motif convenience function sets the homogeneity to prevent this from happening, homogeneity is not a requirement.[7] For example, you might want a RadioBox to contain a Label, or perhaps even some other control area, like a Command widget.

An example that creates and uses a RadioBox is shown in Example 12-3.

Example 12-3. The radio_box.c program

```
/* simple_radio.c -- demonstrate a simple radio box.  Create a
 * box with 3 toggles: "one", "two" and "three".  The callback
 * routine prints the most recently selected choice.  Maintain
 * a global variable that stores the most recently selected.
 */
#include <Xm/ToggleBG.h>
#include <Xm/RowColumn.h>

int toggle_item_set;

void
toggled(widget, which, state)
Widget widget;
int which;
XmToggleButtonCallbackStruct *state;
{
    printf("%s: %s\n", XtName(widget), state->set? "on" : "off");
    if (state->set)
        toggle_item_set = which;
    else
        toggle_item_set = 0;
}

main(argc, argv)
int argc;
char *argv[ ];
{
    Widget toplevel, radio_box, one, two, three;
    XtAppContext app;

    toplevel = XtVaAppInitialize(&app, "Demos", NULL, 0,
        &argc, argv, NULL, NULL);

    radio_box = XmCreateRadioBox(toplevel, "radio_box", NULL, 0);
```

---

[7] Prior to 1.1.1, **XmCreateRadioBox** actually set **XmNisHomogeneous** to False rather than True (despite the documentation and the design). This was a bug. If your code relies on the bug, and now breaks, all you need to do is add code to set **XmNisHomogeneous** to False when you create your RadioBox.

Example 12-3. The radio_box.c program (continued)

```
    one = XtVaCreateManagedWidget("One",
        xmToggleButtonGadgetClass, radio_box, NULL);
    XtAddCallback(one, XmNvalueChangedCallback, toggled, 1);

    two = XtVaCreateManagedWidget("Two",
        xmToggleButtonGadgetClass, radio_box, NULL);
    XtAddCallback(two, XmNvalueChangedCallback, toggled, 2);

    three = XtVaCreateManagedWidget("Three",
        xmToggleButtonGadgetClass, radio_box, NULL);
    XtAddCallback(three, XmNvalueChangedCallback, toggled, 3);

    XtManageChild(radio_box);

    XtRealizeWidget(toplevel);
    XtAppMainLoop(app);
}
```

Three ToggleButtons are set inside of a RadioBox. When the user selects one of the buttons, the previously set widget is toggled off and the **XmNvalueChangedCallback** routine is called. Notice that it is called twice for each selection: the first time to notify that the previously set widget has been toggled off, and the second time to notify that the newly set widget has been toggled on. The output of *radio_box.c* is shown in Figure 12-3.

Figure 12-3. Output of radio_box.c

The global variable **toggle_item_set** indicates which of the three selections is on. The value of **toggle_item_set** is accurate at any given time because it is either set to the most currently selected object or it is set to **0**. In a real application, this global variable would convey the state of the buttons to whatever application function was intended to apply them. (Remember that ToggleButtons don't invoke an action, but simply set a Boolean state.)

Beware of lengthy callback lists, however. If you have more than one function in the callback list for the ToggleButtons (unlike the situation shown above), the entire list is going to be called twice. A zero value for **toggle_item_set** indicates that you are in the first of two phases of the toggling mechanism. Fall through your callback lists—the list will be called again with the value set to the recently selected toggle item.

For simple situations where the RadioBox has only one callback associated with it and you only need to know which button was selected, the routine **XmVaCreateSimpleRadio-Box( )** may be used. The form of this function is:

```
XmVaCreateSimpleRadioBox(parent, name, button_set, callback, args...)
    Widget parent;
    String name;
    int    button_set;
    void   *callback;
```

In addition to the specified parameters, the function also accepts a **NULL**-terminated list of resource-value pairs that apply to the RowColumn widget that acts as the RadioBox. You can also specify the value **XmVaRADIOBUTTON** as a convenient method for specifying a button that is to be created inside the RadioBox. This parameter is followed by four additional arguments: a label of type **XmString**, a mnemonic of type **XmKeySym**, an accelerator of type **String**, and the accelerator text (also of type **XmString**) used to display the accelerator in the widget. (Note: only the *label* argument has any effect through release 1.1 and all subreleases.)

Any number of **XmVaRADIOBUTTON** parameters may be given in the same call to **Xm-VaCreateSimpleRadioBox( )**. This is by design, so that you can create an entire group of ToggleButtons in one function call.

Whatever parameters are used to call the function, there must be a terminating **NULL** parameter to indicate the end of the list. An example of this function is shown in Example 12-4. (This program is functionally identical to Example 12-3.)

Example 12-4. The simple_radio.c program

```
/* simple_radio.c -- demonstrate a simple radio box by using
 * XmVaCreateSimpleRadioBox().  Create a box with 3 toggles:
 * "one", "two" and "three".  The callback routine prints
 * the most recently selected choice.
 */
#include <Xm/RowColumn.h>
#include <X11/StringDefs.h>

void
toggled(widget, which, state)
Widget widget;
int which;
XmToggleButtonCallbackStruct *state;
{
    printf("%s: %s\n", XtName(widget), state->set? "on" : "off");
}

main(argc, argv)
int argc;
char *argv[ ];
{
    Widget toplevel, radio_box;
    XtAppContext app;
    XmString one, two, three;

    toplevel = XtVaAppInitialize(&app, "Demos", NULL, 0,
        &argc, argv, NULL, NULL);
```

Example 12-4. The simple_radio.c program (continued)

```
    one   = XmStringCreateSimple("one");
    two   = XmStringCreateSimple("two");
    three = XmStringCreateSimple("three");
    radio_box = XmVaCreateSimpleRadioBox(toplevel, "radio_box",
        0,  /* the inital choice */
        toggled, /* the callback routine */
        XmVaRADIOBUTTON, one,   NULL, NULL, NULL,
        XmVaRADIOBUTTON, two,   NULL, NULL, NULL,
        XmVaRADIOBUTTON, three, NULL, NULL, NULL,
        NULL);
    XmStringFree(one);
    XmStringFree(two);
    XmStringFree(three);

    XtManageChild(radio_box);

    XtRealizeWidget(toplevel);
    XtAppMainLoop(app);
}
```

12.4.2 CheckBoxes

CheckBoxes are similar to RadioBoxes, except that there is no restriction on how many items may be selected at once. Item selection is accomplished by setting `XmNradioBehavior` to `False`. In fact, the convenience routine `XmVaCreateSimpleCheckBox( )` does just that—it creates a simple radio box and turns off the `XmNradioBehavior` resource. Otherwise, it is identical to `XmVaCreateSimpleRadioBox( )`.

Rather than using either of these functions, we can simply create a common RowColumn widget without the aid of convenience functions. In doing this, we have more direct control over which resources are set in the RowColumn, since we can specify exactly which ones we want using the varargs interface for creating the widget.

Since more than one of the toggles may be set at a time in a CheckBox, we can no longer use `toggle_item_set` the way we did in the previous examples. Instead, we are going to change its name to `toggles_set` and its type to `unsigned long`. This time we're going to use the variable as a *mask*—a variable whose individual bits have meaning, rather than the combined value of the variable. The bits indicate which of the ToggleButtons have been set. Each time a ToggleButton changes its value, its corresponding bit in the mask is flipped. We can therefore determine at any given time which toggles are set and which are not.[8]

The program is the same, but the callback routine has changed slightly to reflect the new design. We will also take this opportunity to generalize the main part of the function. The new program is listed in Example 12-5.

---

[8] The `unsigned long` type can only represent up to 32 ToggleButtons. If more toggle buttons are used within the CheckBox, a new mechanism will have to be devised, but the same basic design presented here can still be used.

Example 12-5. The toggle_box.c program

```
/* toggle_box.c -- demonstrate a homebrew ToggleBox.  A static
 * list of strings is used as the basis for a list of toggles.
 * The callback routine toggled() is set for each toggle item.
 * The client data for this routine is set to the enumerated
 * value of the item with respect to the entire list.  This value
 * is treated as a bit which is toggled in "toggles_set" -- a
 * mask that contains a complete list of all the selected items.
 * This list is printed when the PushButton is selected.
 */
#include <Xm/ToggleBG.h>
#include <Xm/PushBG.h>
#include <Xm/SeparatoG.h>
#include <Xm/RowColumn.h>

unsigned long toggles_set; /* has the bits of which toggles are set */

char *strings[ ] = {
    "One", "Two", "Three", "Four", "Five",
    "Six", "Seven", "Eight", "Nine", "Ten",
};

/* A RowColumn is used to manage a ToggleBox (also a RowColumn) and
 * a PushButton with a separator gadget in between.
 */
main(argc, argv)
int argc;
char *argv[ ];
{
    Widget toplevel, rowcol, toggle_box, w;
    XtAppContext app;
    void toggled(), check_bits();
    int i;

    toplevel = XtVaAppInitialize(&app, "Demos",
        NULL, 0, &argc, argv, NULL, NULL);

    rowcol = XtVaCreateManagedWidget("rowcolumn",
        xmRowColumnWidgetClass, toplevel,
        NULL);

    toggle_box = XtVaCreateWidget("rowcolumn",
        xmRowColumnWidgetClass, rowcol,
        XmNpacking,          XmPACK_COLUMN,
        XmNnumColumns,       2,
        NULL);

    /* simply loop thru the strings creating a widget for each one */
    for (i = 0; i < XtNumber(strings); i++) {
        w = XtVaCreateManagedWidget(strings[i],
            xmToggleButtonGadgetClass, toggle_box, NULL);
        XtAddCallback(w, XmNvalueChangedCallback, toggled, i);
    }

    XtVaCreateManagedWidget("_sep",
        xmSeparatorGadgetClass, rowcol, NULL);
    w = XtVaCreateManagedWidget("Check Toggles",
        xmPushButtonGadgetClass, rowcol, NULL);
    XtAddCallback(w, XmNactivateCallback, check_bits, NULL);

    XtManageChild(rowcol);
```

Example 12-5. The toggle_box.c program (continued)

```
    XtManageChild(toggle_box);

    XtRealizeWidget(toplevel);
    XtAppMainLoop(app);
}
/* callback for all ToggleButtons. */
void
toggled(widget, bit, toggle_data)
Widget widget;
int bit;
XmToggleButtonCallbackStruct *toggle_data;
{
    if (toggle_data->set) /* if the toggle button is set, flip its bit */
        toggles_set |= (1 << bit);
    else /* if the toggle is "off", turn off the bit. */
        toggles_set &= ~(1 << bit);
}

void
check_bits()
{
    int i;

    printf("Toggles set:");
    for (i = 0; i < XtNumber(strings); i++)
        if (toggles_set & (1<<i))
            printf(" %s", strings[i]);
    putchar('\n');
}
```

The output of this program is shown in Figure 12-4.

Figure 12-4. Output of toggle_box.c

The PushButton's callback routine prints the strings of those toggles that are "on." This is done by looping through the **toggles_set** variable and checking for bits that have been set by **toggled( )**.

One interesting aspect of this program is that it would work just as well if the CheckBox were a RadioBox. To test this, we can run the program again, but we will set the **radio-Behavior** resource to **True** via the **−xrm** command-line option:

```
toggle_box −xrm "*radioBehavior: True"
```

The result is shown in Figure 12-5.

Figure 12-5. toggle_box.c with radioBehavior set to True

As you can see, simply changing this single RowColumn resource completely changes the appearance of all of the ToggleButtons.

12.5 Summary

As we have seen, ToggleButtons are simple objects that do not require a great deal of attention from the application. When these widgets are incorporated into CheckBoxes or Radio-Boxes, ToggleButton resources are typically set by their RowColumn parents. They are ideal for specifying exclusive (RadioBox) or nonexclusive (CheckBox) configuration settings that will typically be applied by a click on an associated button.

One aspect of ToggleButtons that was not dealt with in this chapter is their role in the Motif menu system. This is discussed in Chapter 4, *The Main Window,* and in more detail in Chapter 16, *Menus.* ToggleButtons are extremely low-maintenance widgets, especially as menu items.

13

List Widgets

This chapter describes yet another method for the user to exert control over an application. List widgets display a series of text choices that the user can select interactively.

In This Chapter:

13
List Widgets

Almost every application needs to display lists of choices to the user. This can be accomplished in many ways, depending on the nature of the choices. For example, a toggle box is ideal for displaying selections such as configuration settings that can be individually set and unset, and then applied all at once. A list of commands can be displayed in a popup menu, or, for a more permanent command "palette," a RowColumn or Form widget can manage a group of PushButton widgets. But for displaying a list of text choices—such as a list of files to be opened or a list of fonts to be applied to text—nothing beats a List widget.

List widgets display a single column of text choices that can be selected or deselected using either the mouse or the keyboard. Each choice is represented by a single-line text element specified as a compound string. Figure 13-1 shows a typical List widget.

Internally, List widgets operate on arrays of compound strings that are defined by the application. (See Chapter 19, *Compound Strings*, for a discussion of how to create and manage compound strings).[1] Each string is an element of the array, with the first position starting at one (as opposed to position zero, which is used in C-style arrays). The user can select any particular choice by clicking and releasing the **select** button on the item.[2] All items in the list are available to the user for selection at all times; you cannot make any one choice insensitive (unselectable). What happens when an item is selected is up to the application callback routines invoked by the List widget.

List widgets are usually displayed with Scrollbars attached to them. This is done by making the List widget a child of a ScrolledWindow widget. The selection mechanism for the List need not change (the user can still select items as before), but the user can use the Scrollbars to adjust which items from the list are visible.

There are four selection policies that may be used in List widgets:

1. **Single Selection.** In single selection mode, selecting an item toggles its selection state and deselects any other selected item. Single-selection Lists are used when only one of many choices may be selected at a time, although there may also be no items selected.

---

[1] Compound strings that use multiple fonts are allowed, but the List widget doesn't render these lists very well.

[2] The default selection model uses the left mouse button, although the user may reassign this action to other buttons or keys.

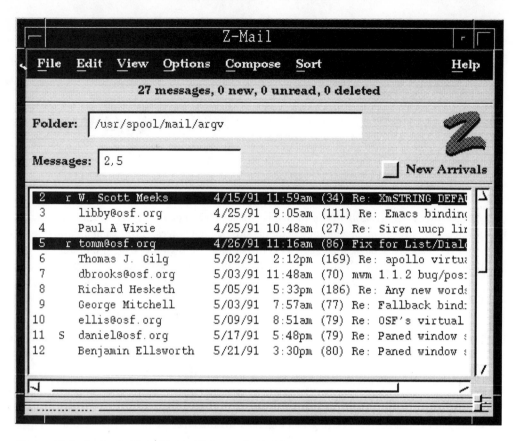

Figure 13-1. A simple List widget with two selected items

For example, there can only be one selection when choosing a font family or style for text input. Single selection would also be important for lists that contained different color choices for an application or bitmap editor.

2. **Browse Selection**. Selecting a new item deselects any other selected item, but there can never be a state where there are no items selected. From the user's perspective, Browse selection is similar to Single selection, except that there is an initial (default) value. There are differences, however, with which callback routines are invoked and when. This is addressed more completely in Section 13.7, *Selecting Items*.

3. **Multiple Selection.** Any number of items can be selected at a time, but the selections are always in contiguous ranges. Items may be toggled on and off by selecting them individually, but no other items are changed when this happens. There may be a state in which no items are selected. Multiple selection mode is advantageous in situations where actions may be taken on more than one item at a time. A user of an electronic mail application, for example, might choose to delete, save, or print multiple messages simultaneously.

4. **Extended Selection**. As an extension of the Multiple selection mode, the extended selection mode can give greater flexibility to the user by allowing any number of items to be selected in noncontiguous ranges.

Which selection policy to use is controlled by the **XmNselectionPolicy** resource. The possible values are:

```
XmSINGLE_SELECT
XmBROWSE_SELECT
XmMULTIPLE_SELECT
XmEXTENDED_SELECT
```

See Section 13.7, *Selecting Items*, for more information on making List widget selections.

13.1 Creating List Widgets

Programmatically, using List widgets is fairly straightforward and is mostly a matter of mechanics. Applications that use the List widget must include the header file *<Xm/List.h>*. This header file declares the types of public List functions and the widget class **XmList-WidgetClass**. The actual variable that refers to this class is **xmListWidgetClass**. We can therefore create a List widget in the following manner:

```
Widget list;

list = XtVaCreateManagedWidget("name", xmListWidgetClass, parent,
    resource-value pairs,
    NULL);
```

Any number of resource-value pairs may be specified. A program that creates a simple List widget is shown in Example 13-1.

Example 13-1. The simple_list.c program

```
/* simple_list.c -- introduce the List widget.  Lists present
 * a number of compound strings as choices.  Therefore, strings
 * must be converted before set in lists.  Also, the number of
 * visible items must be set or the List defaults to 1 item.
 */
#include <Xm/List.h>

char *months[ ] = {
    "January", "February", "March", "April", "May", "June", "July",
    "August", "September", "October", "November", "December"
};

main(argc, argv)
char *argv[ ];
{
    Widget          toplevel;
    XtAppContext    app;
    int             i, n = XtNumber(months);
    XmStringTable   str_list;

    toplevel = XtVaAppInitialize(&app, "Demos", NULL, 0,
        &argc, argv, NULL, NULL);

    str_list = (XmStringTable)XtMalloc(n * sizeof (XmString *));

    for (i = 0; i < n; i++)
        str_list[i] = XmStringCreateSimple(months[i]);
```

Example 13-1. The simple_list.c program (continued)

```
XtVaCreateManagedWidget("Hello",
    xmListWidgetClass,      toplevel,
    XmNvisibleItemCount,    n,
    XmNitemCount,           n,
    XmNitems,               str_list,
    NULL);

for (i = 0; i < n; i++)
    XmStringFree(str_list[i]);
XtFree(str_list);

XtRealizeWidget(toplevel);
XtAppMainLoop(app);
}
```

The program simply creates a List widget as the child of the **toplevel** widget. Its list contains the names of the months as its choices. The output of the program is shown in Figure 13-2.

Figure 13-2. Output of simple_list.c

The program incorporates three basic elements of the List widget: the list of items, the number of items in the list, and the number of items that are visible. Because the items are compound strings, the entire array of choices must be converted from C strings to compound strings before setting. This is done by allocating an array of **XmStrings** that contains the same number of elements (**n**) as the list of months. A compound string for each name of the month is created and stored in the new list, **str_list**. The List widget is then created with **str_list** as the value for **XmNitems**, and **XmNitemCount** is set to **n**.

XmBROWSE_SELECT is the default selection policy for the List widget, which suits this application perfectly, so we don't need to set the **XmNselectionPolicy** resource. But you should be aware that the user could change this policy through resource specifications. If you want to be sure to enforce this selection policy, you might want to do a bit of defensive programming, and hard-code the value for **XmNselectionPolicy** despite its default.

As does every other widget that takes compound strings, the List widget copies the entire table of compound strings into its own internal storage. Therefore, the list of strings must be freed after you've set them into the List widget. When setting items in the list in this manner, the number of items must also be set at the same time or the List widget will not know how many items to copy. For this reason, the value of **XmNitemCount** should never be larger than the number of items in **XmNitems**. If the value for **XmNitemCount** is less than the number of items, the additional items will not be put in the list.

To retrieve the list of items, you can call **XtVaGetValues()** on the same resources as you use when setting values:

```
XmStringTable   choices;
int             n_choices;
extern Widget   list;

XtVaGetValues(list,
    XmNitems,        &choices,
    XmNitemCount,    &n_choices,
    NULL);
```

Since the items returned are compound strings, you must convert them to C-style strings if you care to use any of the standard C library functions to view or manipulate the strings. Otherwise, you can use any of the compound string functions for this purpose. A discussion of compound strings is given in Chapter 19. Since we used **XtVaGetValues()** to obtain the values associated with the **XmNitems** and **XmNitemCount** resources, the returned data should, as always, be considered *read-only*. You should not change any of the items in this list or attempt to free them (or the pointer to them) when you are through examining their values.

Example 13-1 also makes use of the **XmNvisibleItemCount** resource, which sets the height of the list to match the number of items that should be visible. If you want all the items to be visible, you simply set the value to the total number of items in the list. Setting the visible item count to a higher value is acceptable, assuming that the list is expected to grow to at least that size. Otherwise, you may misrepresent the list to the user, leading him to believe that the number of items may grow. If you want to set the number of visible items to be less than the number of items actually in the list, you should use a ScrolledList as described in the next section. This is in fact a more common practice.

13.2 Scrolling Lists

It is unlikely that an application will use a List widget without putting it in a scrolling window. By incorporating a List widget and a ScrolledWindow widget, we create what Motif calls a ScrolledList. Note that there is no ScrolledList widget. Instead, a ScrolledList is a Motif term describing the combination of the two widgets. While this chapter addresses most of the common resources and functions dealing with ScrolledLists, detailed information on ScrolledWindows and Scrollbars can be found in Chapter 9, *ScrolledWindows and Scrollbars*.

Since ScrolledLists are built from the two widget classes, we could create and manage them separately, using two calls to `XtVaCreateManagedWidget()`. However, since ScrolledLists are used so frequently (much more so than List widgets alone), Motif provides the following convenience function to create this compound object:

```
Widget
XmCreateScrolledList(parent, name, args, num_args)
    Widget    parent;
    char      *name;
    Arg       args[ ];
    int       num_args;
```

The `args` parameter is an array of size `num_args` and contains resources to be passed to both the ScrolledWindow widget or the List widget. Generally, the two widgets use different resources that are specific to the widgets themselves, so there isn't usually any confusion about which resources apply to which widget. However, common resources (such as Core resources) will be interpreted by both widgets, so caution is advised. If you wish to make settings on one while ensuring that its values will not be interpreted by the other, you should avoid passing those values into the convenience routine and instead set them separately using `XtVaSetValues()` on each widget individually.

The widget returned by `XmCreateScrolledList()` is the List widget itself. The ScrolledWindow widget is "hidden" in the sense that you can treat the List widget as the entire object, if you like. If you really need to get a handle to the ScrolledWindow, you can use `XtParent()` on the List widget returned by this convenience function:

```
Widget list_w = XmCreateScrolledList(...);

XtVaSetValues(XtParent(list_w),
    ScrolledWindow widget resource values,
    NULL);

XtVaSetValues(list_w,
    List widget resource values,
    NULL);

XtManageChild(list_w);
```

Note the need to call `XtManageChild()` for the new ScrolledList widget. This is necessary because none of the Motif convenience functions manage the widgets they create.

ScrolledLists are useful because they can display a portion of the entire list provided by the widget. This *viewport* into the entire List widget is controlled by the `XmNvisibleItemCount` resource. For example, we can modify our initial program, *simple_list.c*, with the following code segment so that the List widget used is part of a ScrolledList object:

```
/* Create the ScrolledList */
list_w = XmCreateScrolledList(toplevel, "Months", NULL, 0);

/* set the items, the item count, and the visible items */
XtVaSetValues(list_w,
    XmNitems,             str_list,
    XmNitemCount,         n,
    XmNvisibleItemCount,  5,
    NULL);

/* Convenience routines don't create managed children */
XtManageChild(list_w);
```

The output resulting from this change is shown in Figure 13-3.

Figure 13-3. A ScrolledList with five visible items

The ScrolledList manages its vertical and horizontal Scrollbars through the **XmNscroll-BarDisplayPolicy** and **XmNlistSizePolicy** resources.

The default display policy of the ScrolledList is such that if its parent is resized so the entire list is visible, the vertical Scrollbar is unmanaged. In this case, the ScrolledList appears to be exactly the same as a normal List widget. The value for **XmNscrollBarDisplay-Policy** can be either **XmAS_NEEDED** (the default) or **XmSTATIC**. The latter forces the vertical Scrollbar to be displayed at all times. (The horizontal Scrollbar is unaffected by this resource.)

The **XmNlistSizePolicy** resource reflects how the ScrolledList manages its horizontal Scrollbar. (The vertical Scrollbar is unaffected.) The default setting is **XmVARIABLE**, which means that the ScrolledList attempts to grow horizontally to contain its widest item. No horizontal Scrollbar is ever displayed. This may present a problem if the ScrolledList's managing parent constrains its horizontal size. If the value is set to **Xm-RESIZE_IF_POSSIBLE**, the ScrolledList will display a horizontal Scrollbar only if it can't resize itself accordingly. If the value **XmCONSTANT** is used, the horizontal Scrollbar is displayed at all times, necessary or not.

Note that the size of the ScrolledList is ultimately controlled by its parent (i.e., the parent of the ScrolledWindow). In most cases, a manager widget such as a RowColumn or Form will allow its children to be any size they request. Thus, if a ScrolledList is a child of a Form widget, its size will be whatever you specify with either the **XmNheight** resource or the **XmNvisibleItemCount**. However, certain constraints, such as **XmNresizePolicy** in Form widgets, may affect its child's height unexpectedly. For example, if you set **Xm-NresizePolicy** to **XmRESIZE_NONE**, the ScrolledList widget's height request will be ignored, making it look like `XmNvisibleItemCount` doesn't work. Therefore, you should always be aware of the kind of manager widget you have and the constraints in use.

13.2.1 Use of Color

The text of the individual list entries is rendered in the List widget's `XmNforeground` color. However, there is currently a bug in the toolkit where if you change the foreground color dynamically, the List will not update its display until the user interacts with it again or until you change the list entries. The `XmNbackground` of the list affects all areas of the widget not associated with the list entries themselves. When a List widget is the direct child of a ScrolledWindow (i.e., a ScrolledList), the Scrollbar automatically matches the background color of the List widget. And finally, you cannot change the color of individual items in a List widget.

13.2.2 Input Focus

The List widget accepts keyboard input to select items in the list, browse the list, or scroll the list. Like all other Motif widgets, the List has translation functions that facilitate this process. This List is hard-coded into the widget, and it is not recommended to attempt to override this list with new translations.

For ScrolledLists, the List widget automatically sets the Scrollbar's `XmNtraversalOn` resource to `False` so the Scrollbar associated with the ScrolledList will never get keyboard input. It is also recommended that you do not interfere with this process so users are not confused by different applications on the desktop behaving differently from one another.

If the List widget is sensitive, all items in the list are selectable. If insensitive, none of them are selectable. You cannot set certain items to be insensitive to selection at any given time. Furthermore, you cannot set the entire list to be insensitive and allow the user to manipulate the Scrollbars. In short, it is not entirely possible to make a read-only list widget; the user always has the ability to select items in the list, providing that it's sensitive. Of course, you can always choose not to hook up callback procedures to the widget, but this will probably lead to more confusion than anything else. That is, if the user selects an object and the toolkit provides the visual feedback acknowledging his action, he expects the application to respond as well.

13.3 Adding Items

The entire list of choices may not always be available at the time the List is created. In fact, it is not uncommon to have no items available for a new list. In these situations, items can be added to the list dynamically using either `XmListAddItem( )`, `XmListAddItem-Unselected( )`, or `XmListAddItems( )`. These functions have the following form:

```
void
XmListAddItem(list_w, item, position)
    Widget     list_w;
    XmString   item;
    int        position;

void
XmListAddItemUnselected(list_w, item, position)
    Widget     list_w;
    XmString   item;
    int        position;

void
XmListAddItems(list_w, items, item_count, position)
    Widget     list_w;
    XmString   items[ ]; /* array of size item_count */
    int        item_count;
    int        position;
```

One or more items may be added to a List widget at a specified position. Remember that list positions start at 1, not 0. The 0-th position is reserved as the "last" position; specifying position 0 appends the item or items to the end of the list, wherever that may be. If the new item(s) are added to the list in between existing items, then the rest of the items are moved down the list.

The difference between `XmListAddItem( )` and `XmListAddItemUnselected( )` is that `XmListAddItem( )` compares the added item to each item already in the list. If there is another item already in the list *and* if that item is selected, then the newly added item is also selected. `XmListAddItemUnselected( )` simply adds the new item without checking to see if there is already an item in the list that may be selected. For most situations, it is pretty clear which routine you should use. If you know that the new item you are placing in the list does not already exist, then you should add it *unselected*. Or, if you know that your list is a single selection list, then again, you should add new items as unselected. In fact, the only time you should add new items to the list using `XmAddItem( )` is when you expect that there could be duplicate entries, the list can support multiple selections, and you explicitly want to select all new items whose duplicates are already selected.

Example 13-2 shows how items can be added to a ScrolledList dynamically using `XmList-AddItemUnselected( )`.

Example 13-2. The alpha_list.c program

```
/* alpha_list.c -- insert items into a list in alphabetical order.  */

#include <Xm/List.h>
#include <Xm/RowColumn.h>
```

Example 13-2. The alpha_list.c program (continued)

```
#include <Xm/TextF.h>

XmStringCharSet charset = XmSTRING_DEFAULT_CHARSET;

main(argc, argv)
char *argv[ ];
{
    Widget        toplevel, rowcol, list_w, text_w;
    XtAppContext  app;
    Arg           args[1];
    void          add_item();

    toplevel = XtVaAppInitialize(&app, "Demos", NULL, 0,
        &argc, argv, NULL, NULL);

    rowcol = XtVaCreateWidget("rowcol",
        xmRowColumnWidgetClass, toplevel, NULL);

    XtSetArg(args[0], XmNvisibleItemCount, 5);
    list_w = XmCreateScrolledList(rowcol, "scrolled_list", args, 1);
    XtManageChild(list_w);

    text_w = XtVaCreateManagedWidget("text",
        xmTextFieldWidgetClass, rowcol,
        XmNcolumns,     25,
        NULL);
    XtAddCallback(text_w, XmNactivateCallback, add_item, list_w);

    XtManageChild(rowcol);
    XtRealizeWidget(toplevel);
    XtAppMainLoop(app);
}

/* Add item to the list in alphabetical order.  Perform binary
 * search to find the correct location for the new item position.
 * This is the callback routine for the TextField widget.
 */
void
add_item(text_w, list_w)
Widget text_w, list_w; /* list_w is the callback data */
{
    char *text, *newtext = XmTextFieldGetString(text_w);
    XmString str, *strlist;
    int u_bound, l_bound = 0;

    /* newtext is the text typed in the TextField widget */
    if (!newtext || !*newtext) {
        /* non-null strings must be entered */
        XtFree(newtext); /* XtFree() checks for NULL */
        return;
    }
    /* get the current entries (and number of entries) from the List */
    XtVaGetValues(list_w,
        XmNitemCount, &u_bound,
        XmNitems,     &strlist,
        NULL);
    u_bound--;
    /* perform binary search */
    while (u_bound >= l_bound) {
        int i = l_bound + (u_bound - l_bound)/2;
```

Example 13-2. The alpha_list.c program (continued)

```
        /* convert the compound string into a regular C string */
        if (!XmStringGetLtoR(strlist[i], charset, &text))
            break;
        if (strcmp(text, newtext) > 0)
            u_bound = i-1; /* newtext comes before item */
        else
            l_bound = i+1; /* newtext comes after item */
        XtFree(text); /* XmStringGetLtoR() allocates memory ... yuk */
    }
    str = XmStringCreateSimple(newtext); /* convert text to compound string */
    XtFree(newtext);
    /* positions indexes start at 1, so increment accordingly */
    XmListAddItemUnselected(list_w, str, l_bound+1);
    XmStringFree(str);
    XmTextFieldSetString(text_w, "");
}
```

In Example 13-2, the ScrolledList is created with no items. However, we do specify the number of items that would be visible if there were a list. This is done in anticipation of newly created items that will eventually be added to the list. A TextField widget is used to prompt for a new string that is added to the list using the **add_item( )** callback. This function performs a binary search on the list to determine the position where the new item is to be added. A binary search may save quite a bit of time because it is very expensive to scan an entire List widget, constantly converting compound strings into C strings. When the position for the new item is found, it is added using **XmListAddItemUnselected( )**. The output of this program is shown in Figure 13-4.

Figure 13-4. Output of alpha_list.c

13.4 Finding Items

The simplest function for determining whether a particular item exists in a list is **XmList-ItemExists( )**:

```
Boolean
XmListItemExists(w, item)
    Widget   w;      /* List widget */
    XmString item;
```

This function performs a linear search on the list for the specified item. If you are maintaining your list in a particular order, you may choose to search the list yourself using the methods explained in the previous section. However, the List's internal search function does not bother to convert the compound strings to C strings; it does a direct byte-by-byte comparison of the strings using **XmStringByteCompare( )**. This is decidedly more efficient than doing conversions to C strings for comparison. But the linear search method is orders of magnitude slower than a binary search. Unfortunately, **XmStringByteCompare( )** does not return which string is of greater or lesser value; it just returns whether the strings are different. Thus, we could not use it in the *alpha_list.c*.

In the circumstances where you not only need to know whether the item exists, but its actual position in the list, you can use **XmListItemPos( )**:

```
int
XmListItemPos(list_w, item)
    Widget   list_w;      /* List widget */
    XmString item;
```

This function assumes that there is only one instance of the item in the list. If the function returns 0, the element was not found. Otherwise, it returns the position in the list, with 1 being the first position.

If your list possibly contains duplicate entries, you can find all the locations of a particular entry using **XmListGetMatchPos( )**:

```
Boolean
XmListGetMatchPos(list_w, item, pos_list, pos_cnt)
    Widget    list_w;
    XmString  item;
    int       **pos_list;
    int       *pos_cnt;
```

The function normally returns **True** if the specified item is found in the list in one or more locations. The **pos_list** parameter is allocated to contain an array of positions where **item** was found in the list. The number of items found is returned in **pos_cnt**. When **pos_list** is no longer needed, it should be freed using **XtFree( )**.

If the function returns **False**, it may be that there were no items in the list, that memory couldn't be allocated for the **pos_list** returned, or that the specified item simply wasn't found. For any of these cases, **pos_list** does not point to allocated space and should not be referenced or freed. Also, **pos_cnt** will not have any reasonable (or predictable) value.

Example 13-3 shows how **XmListGetMatchPos( )** can be used:

Example 13-3. Getting the positions of a string in a list

```
extern Widget  list_w;
int            *pos_list;
int            pos_cnt, i;
char           *choice = "A Sample Text String";
XmString       str = XmStringCreateSimple(choice);

if (!XmListGetMatchPos(list_w, str, &pos_list, &pos_cnt))
    XtWarning("Can't get items in list");
else {
    printf("%s exists in positions %d:", choice, pos_cnt);
    for (i = 0; i < pos_cnt; i++)
        printf(" %d", pos_list[i]);
    puts("");
    XtFree(pos_list);
}
```

13.5 Replacing Items

There are two functions available for replacing items in a List widget. To replace a contiguous sequence of items in the list, use **XmListReplaceItemsPos( )**:

```
void
XmListReplaceItemsPos(list_w, new_items, item_count, position)
    Widget     list_w;
    XmString  *new_items;
    int        item_count;
    int        position;
```

This function replaces the specified number of items with the new items starting at **position**. However, you can replace arbitrary elements in the list with new elements, whether they are adjacent entries or not, using **XmListReplaceItems( )**:

```
void
XmListReplaceItems(list_w, old_items, item_count, new_items)
    Widget     list_w;
    XmString  *old_items;
    int        item_count;
    XmString  *new_items;
```

The entire list is searched for each element in **old_items**. Every occurrence of each element found is replaced with the corresponding elements from **new_items**. The search continues for each element in **old_items** until **item_count** has been reached.

13.6 Deleting Items

You can delete items from List widgets in many ways. First, to delete a single item, you can use either **XmListDeleteItem()** or **XmListDeletePos()**. These functions have the following form:

```
void
XmListDeleteItem(list_w, item)
    Widget    list_w;
    XmString item;
```

XmListDeleteItem() finds the given item and deletes it from the list.

If you already know the item's position in the list, you can avoid creating a compound string and specify the position to delete using:

```
void
XmListDeletePos(list_w, position)
    Widget list_w;
    int     position;
```

XmListDeletePos() removes an item directly from the given position. After the item is deleted, the items following it are moved up one position.

You can delete multiple items using either **XmListDeleteItems()**, **XmListDeleteItemsPos()**, or **XmListDeleteAllItems()**:

```
void
XmListDeleteItems(list_w, items, item_count)
    Widget    list_w;
    XmString *items;
    int       item_count;
```

Here we see another example where an array of **XmString** types is used. (There are **item_count** strings in the array.) You must create and initialize this array before calling this function, just as you must free it afterwards. The strings do not have to specify a contiguous span of list items, and each item is deleted only if it is found in the list.

If you already know the positions of the items you want to delete, you can avoid creating an array of compound strings and use:

```
XmListDeleteItemsPos(list_w, item_count, position)
    Widget    list_w;
    int       item_count;
    int       position;
```

XmListDeleteItemsPos() deletes **item_count** items from the list starting at **position**. The value for **item_count** is checked and possibly changed in the following manner:

```
if (item_count + position > items_in_list)
    item_count = items_in_list - position;
```

Finally, you can delete all of the items in a List widget using:

```
void
XmListDeleteAllItems(list_w)
    Widget list_w;
```

13.7 Selecting Items

Since the main purpose of List widgets is to allow a user to make a selection from a set of choices, one of the most important tasks for the programmer is to determine which items have been selected by the user. In this section, we present an overview of the resources and functions available to set or get the actual items that are selected in the List widget. Later, in Section 12.3, *ToggleButton Callbacks*, we discuss how to determine the items selected by the user at the time they are selected.

The resources and functions used to set and get the selected items in the List widget are directly analogous to those that set the actual items in the list. For example, just as **Xm-Nitems** represents the entire list, the resource **XmNselectedItems** represents the list of selected items. And just as **XmNitemCount** sets or gets the number of items in the list and is used in conjunction with **XmNitems**, the resource **XmNselectedItemCount** acts on the items that are selected.

The functions **XmSelectItem( )** and **XmSelectPos( )** can be used to select individual items.

```
void
XmListSelectItem(list_w, item, notify)
    Widget   list_w;
    XmString item;
    Boolean  notify;

void
XmListSelectPos(list_w, position, notify)
    Widget   list_w;
    int      position;
    Boolean  notify;
```

These functions cause the specified item (either explicitly or through a position) to be selected. Normally, the indicated item is the only item to be selected; if any other items on the list have previously been selected, they are deselected. The exception is if **Xm-NselectionPolicy** is **XmMULTIPLE_SELECT**; here, the specified item is *added* to the list of currently selected items. Note that this is not the case for **XmEXTENDED_SELECT** or any of the other selection policies. (Hint: if you want to add to the selected list in your extended-select list, dynamically set the selection policy to **XmMULTIPLE_SELECT**, use either of these two functions to add to the selected list, and then reset the selection policy back to **XmEXTENDED_SELECT**.)

The **notify** parameter indicates whether the callback routine for the List widget should be called. If your callback routine does special processing of list items, then you can avoid having redundant code by passing **True** as this parameter. This way, the routine will be called just as if the user had made the selection himself. If you are calling either of these functions from the callback routine, you might want to pass **False** as the **notify** parameter to avoid a possible infinite loop.

There are no functions available for selecting multiple items at the same time. To accomplish this, you must use **XtVaSetValues( )** and set the **XmNselectedItems** and **XmNselectedItemCount** resources to the *entire* list of selected items. These resources are treated the same way as **XmNitems** and **XmNitemCount**. Another alternative is to follow the suggestion made earlier in the chapter: set **XmNselectionPolicy** to **XmMULTIPLE_SELECT** temporarily and use a loop of calls to either of the above functions to select the desired items individually. As long as the List's selection policy is multiple-select, you can add to its selection policy all you like.

If you know the position in the list of the item to be selected, you should use **XmListSelectPos( )** rather than **XmListSelectItem( )**. The latter does a linear search on the entire list trying to find the specified item. Large lists can take quite a long time to search if you are doing frequent list operations.

Items can be deselected in the same manner as they are selected using **XmListDeselectItem( )** and **XmListDeselectPos( )**. These functions, however, do not have an associated **notify** parameter:

```
void
XmListDeselectItem(list_w, item)
    Widget   list_w;
    XmString item;


void
XmListDeselectPos(list_w, position)
    Widget   list_w;
    int      position;
```

When using these functions, the internal selected list is modified, but there is no callback routine called.

You can deselect all items in the list by calling **XmListDeselectAllItems( )**:

```
void
XmListDeselectAllItems(list_w)
    Widget list_w;
```

Note, however, that when using **XmListDeselectAllItems( )**, the function will actually keep *one* item selected. This seems like a bug, but OSF actually defends it as a feature.

Finally, you can get the positions of all the selected items in the list using **XmListGetSelectedPos( )**:

```
Boolean
XmListGetSelectedPos(list_w, pos_list, pos_cnt)
    Widget   list_w;
    int      **pos_list;
    int      *pos_cnt;
```

The use of this function is identical to that of **XmListGetMatchPos( )**. That is, the **pos_list** array is allocated and filled with the positions of those items that are selected. This pointer must be freed after you are done with it. If the function returns **False**, then the `pos_list` parameter does not point to allocated space and should not be referenced. Also, `pos_cnt` may not reflect any reasonable (or predictable) value.

13.8 Collective Example

In this section, we pull together all the functions used in the preceding sections to demonstrate how to select specific items in a rather unique way. We expand on *alpha_list.c*, the program that adds items input by the user to a ScrolledList in alphabetical order. Using another Text widget, the user can also search for items in the list. The searching method uses the regular expression pattern-matching functions intrinsic to UNIX systems. Example 13-4 shows the installation of the new Text widget and its associated callback routine.

Example 13-4. Searching and selecting items in a list

```
/* search_list.c -- search for items in a List and select them */

#include <stdio.h>
#include <Xm/List.h>
#include <Xm/LabelG.h>
#include <Xm/Label.h>
#include <Xm/RowColumn.h>
#include <Xm/PanedW.h>
#include <Xm/TextF.h>

XmStringCharSet charset = XmSTRING_DEFAULT_CHARSET;

main(argc, argv)
char *argv[ ];
{
    Widget         toplevel, rowcol, list_w, text_w;
    XtAppContext   app;
    Arg            args[2];
    XmString       label;
    void           add_item(), search_item();

    toplevel = XtVaAppInitialize(&app, "Demos", NULL, 0,
        &argc, argv, NULL, NULL);

    rowcol = XtVaCreateWidget("rowcol",
        xmPanedWindowWidgetClass, toplevel, NULL);

    label = XmStringCreateSimple("List:");
    XtVaCreateManagedWidget("list_lable", xmLabelWidgetClass, rowcol,
        XmNlabelString,  label,
        NULL);
    XmStringFree(label);
    XtSetArg(args[0], XmNvisibleItemCount, 10);
    XtSetArg(args[1], XmNselectionPolicy, XmEXTENDED_SELECT);
    list_w = XmCreateScrolledList(rowcol, "scrolled_list", args, 2);
    XtManageChild(list_w);

    label = XmStringCreateSimple("Add:");
    XtVaCreateManagedWidget("add_label", xmLabelWidgetClass, rowcol,
        XmNlabelString,  label,
        NULL);
    XmStringFree(label);
```

Example 13-4. Searching and selecting items in a list (continued)

```
    text_w = XtVaCreateManagedWidget("add_text",
        xmTextFieldWidgetClass, rowcol,
        XmNcolumns,      25,
        NULL);
    XtAddCallback(text_w, XmNactivateCallback, add_item, list_w);

    label = XmStringCreateSimple("Search:");
    XtVaCreateManagedWidget("search_label", xmLabelWidgetClass, rowcol,
        XmNlabelString,  label,
        NULL);
    XmStringFree(label);
    text_w = XtVaCreateManagedWidget("search_text",
        xmTextFieldWidgetClass, rowcol,
        XmNcolumns,      25,
        NULL);
    XtAddCallback(text_w, XmNactivateCallback, search_item, list_w);

    XtManageChild(rowcol);
    XtRealizeWidget(toplevel);
    XtAppMainLoop(app);
}

/* Add item to the list in alphabetical order.  Perform binary
 * search to find the correct location for the new item position.
 * This is the callback routine for the Add: TextField widget.
 */
void
add_item(text_w, list_w)
Widget text_w, list_w; /* list_w is the callback data */
{
    char *text, *newtext = XmTextFieldGetString(text_w);
    XmString str, *strlist;
    int u_bound, l_bound = 0;

    if (!newtext || !*newtext) {
        /* non-null strings must be entered */
        XtFree(newtext);
        return;
    }
    XtVaGetValues(list_w,
        XmNitemCount, &u_bound,
        XmNitems,      &strlist,
        NULL);
    u_bound--;
    /* perform binary search */
    while (u_bound >= l_bound) {
        int i = l_bound + (u_bound - l_bound)/2;
        if (!XmStringGetLtoR(strlist[i], "", &text))
            break;
        if (strcmp(text, newtext) > 0)
            u_bound = i-1; /* newtext comes before item */
        else
            l_bound = i+1; /* newtext comes after item */
        XtFree(text);
    }
    str = XmStringCreateSimple(newtext);
    XtFree(newtext);
    /* positions indexes start at 1, so increment accordingly */
```

Example 13-4. Searching and selecting items in a list (continued)

```
    XmListAddItemUnselected(list_w, str, l_bound+1);
    XmStringFree(str);
    XmTextFieldSetString(text_w, "");
}

/* find the item in the list that matches the specified pattern */
void
search_item(text_w, list_w)
Widget text_w, list_w; /* list_w is the callback data */
{
    char *exp, *text, *newtext = XmTextFieldGetString(text_w);
    XmString *strlist, *selectlist = NULL;
    int cnt, j = 0;
    extern char *re_comp();

    if (!newtext || !*newtext) {
        /* non-null strings must be entered */
        XtFree(newtext);
        return;
    }

    /* compile expression into pattern matching library */
#ifdef SYSV
    if (!(exp = regcmp(newtext, NULL))) {
        printf("error with regcmp(%s)\n", newtext);
        return;
    }
#else /* BSD */
    if (exp = re_comp(newtext)) {
        printf("error with re_comp(%s): %s\n", newtext, exp);
        return;
    }
#endif /* SYSV */

    /* get all the items in the list ... we're going to search each one */
    XtVaGetValues(list_w,
        XmNitemCount, &cnt,
        XmNitems,     &strlist,
        NULL);
    while (cnt--) {
        /* convert item to C string */
        if (!XmStringGetLtoR(strlist[cnt], charset, &text))
            break;
        /* do pattern match against search string */
#ifdef SYSV
        /* returns NULL if match failed */
        if (regex(exp, text, NULL)) {
            /* if selection matches, realloc list to contain item */
            selectlist = (XmString *)XtRealloc(selectlist, j+1);
            selectlist[j++] = XmStringCopy(strlist[cnt]);
        }
#else /* BSD */
        /* -1 on error, 0 if no-match, 1 if match */
        if (re_exec(text) > 0) {
            /* if selection matches, realloc list to contain item */
            selectlist = (XmString *)XtRealloc(selectlist, j+1);
            selectlist[j++] = XmStringCopy(strlist[cnt]);
        }
```

List Widgets

Example 13-4. Searching and selecting items in a list (continued)

```
#endif /* SYSV */
        XtFree(text);
    }
#ifdef SYSV
    free(exp);  /* this must be freed for regcmp() */
#endif /* SYSV */
    XtFree(newtext);
    /* set the actual selected items to be those that matched */
    XtVaSetValues(list_w,
        XmNselectedItems,      selectlist,
        XmNselectedItemCount, j,
        NULL);
    while (j--)
        XmStringFree(selectlist[j]);
    XmTextFieldSetString(text_w, "");
}
```

The output of this program is shown in Figure 13-5.

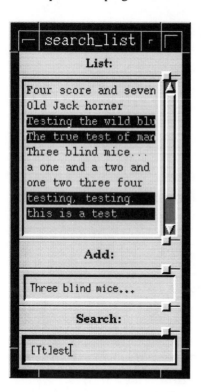

Figure 13-5. Output of search_list.c

The TextField widget used to search for items in the List widget is identical to the one used to add new items. Its callback routine is **search_item( )**, which searches the list for the specified pattern. The version of UNIX you are running (System V or BSD), dictates which kind of regular expression matching is done. System V machines use the function **regcmp( )** to compile the pattern and **regex( )** to search for the pattern within another string while BSD UNIX systems use the functions **re_comp( )** and **re_exec( )** to do the same thing.[3]

The items in the list are retrieved using **XtVaGetValues( )** in the **strlist** parameter. This variable points to the internal list used by the List widget, so it is important that we do not change any of these elements or free these pointers when we are through with them. Changing the value of **XmNselectedItems** causes the internal list to change. This internal list is currently being pointed to by **strlist**, so it is important to copy these values if we want to use them anywhere else. Accordingly, if the pattern matches any of the list items, the item is copied using **XmStringCopy( )** and is later added to the List's **XmNselectedItems**.

13.9 Positioning the List

The items within a ScrolledList can be positioned such that an arbitrary element is placed at the top or bottom of the visible portion of the ScrolledWindow (the *viewport*). The functions that support item positioning within the viewport are **XmListSetItem( )** and **XmListSetBottomItem( )**:

```
void
XmListSetItem(list_w, item)
    Widget     list_w;
    XmString   item;


void
XmListBottomItem(list_w, item)
    Widget     list_w;
    XmString   item;
```

Both of these functions require an **XmString** parameter to reference a particular item in the list. However, if you know the item's position, you can use **XmListSetPos( )** and **XmListSetBottomPos( )** instead:

```
void
XmListSetPos(list_w, position)
    Widget     list_w;
    int        position;


void
XmListBottomPos(list_w, position)
    Widget     list_w;
    int        position;
```

The **position** parameter can be set to **0** to specify that the last item be positioned at the bottom of the viewport. (You can't position the last item at the top.) Through a mixture of resource values and simple calculations, you can position any particular item anywhere in the list. For example, if you have an item that you want to be sure is visible, but you are not

---

[3] Many systems that support both BSD and System V universes may support one, the other, or both methods of regular expression handling. You should consult your system's documentation for more information on these functions.

concerned where in the viewport it is displayed, you can write your own function, as shown in Example 13-5.

Example 13-5. MakePosVisible(): make sure the given position is visible

```
MakePosVisible(list_w, item_no)
Widget list_w;
int item_no;
{
    int top, visible;

    XtVaGetValues(list_w,
        XmNtopItemPosition,   &top,
        XmNvisibleItemCount, &visible,
        NULL);
    if (item_no < top)
        XmListSetPos(list_w, item_no);
    else if (item_no >= top+visible)
        XmListSetBottomPos(list_w, item_no);
}
```

The function gets the number of visible items and the position number of the item in the *top* position of the viewport. It also determines whether the item (`item_no`) lies between `top` and `top+visible`. If it comes before `top`, `item_no` is set to the top using `XmList-SetPos( )`. Otherwise, it is set at the bottom using `XmListSetBottomPos( )`.

If you don't know the item's position in the list, then you can write a new function as shown in Example 13-6.

Example 13-6. MakeItemVisible(): make sure the given item is visible

```
MakeItemVisible(list_w, item)
Widget list_w;
XmString item;
{
    int item_no = XmListItemPos(list_w, item);

    if (item_no > 0)
        MakePosVisible(list_w, item_no);
}
```

`MakeItemVisible( )` simply gets the position of the given item in the list and calls `MakePosVisible( )`.

13.10 List Widget Callback Routines

While the callback routines associated with the List widget are not affected by whether the List is scrollable, they do depend on the selection policy currently in use.

There is a separate callback list resource for each selection policy, plus a separate callback for the default action, which is invoked on either a double-click of the **select** (usually the left) mouse button, or the RETURN key.

The callback list resources are:

        XmNbrowseSelectionCallback
        XmNdefaultActionCallback
        XmNextendedSelectionCallback
        XmNmultipleSelectionCallback
        XmNsingleSelectionCallback

Each of the callback resources takes an **XtCallbackList** value. You can either set the List widget's callback resource explicitly, or you can add callback functions using **XtAdd-Callback( )**. The latter technique is shown in Section 13.10.1, *The Default Action*.

13.10.1 The Default Action

In all of the selection modes, there is the concept of the *default action*. This term refers to a double click of the left mouse button[4] or the RETURN key being pressed while the pointer is in the widget. The default action always indicates that the active item should be selected, regardless of the selection policy. Example 13-7 shows a code fragment that demonstrates how to install a general callback routine for a List widget using the **XmNdefault-ActionCallback** resource as an example.

Example 13-7. Specifying a callback function for a List widget

```
    ...
    list_w = XmCreateScrolledList(toplevel, "months", NULL, 0);
    XtVaSetValues(list_w,
        XmNitems,           str_list,
        XmNitemCount,       n,
        XmNvisibleItemCount, 5,
        NULL);
    XtAddCallback(list_w, XmNdefaultActionCallback, my_proc, NULL);
    ...

void
my_proc(list_w, client_data, cbs)
Widget list_w;
XtPointer client_data;
XmListCallbackStruct *cbs; /* CallBack Structure */
{
    char *choice;
```

_____

[4] The *left* mouse button can be reset by the user to be the *right* mouse button, if desired. Whichever button it is set to is transparent to the application—the default action is called when appropriate.

```
    XmStringGetLtoR(cbs->item, charset, &choice);
    printf("selected item %d (%s)\n", cbs->item_position, choice);
    XtFree(choice);
}
```

Here, we've slightly modified our running example that uses a List widget to display the months of the year. Because the default action may happen on any List widget, it is advisable always to have a callback set for this default action even if there are other callbacks as well.

The callback routine, **my_proc( )**, simply prints the selection made:

```
    selected item 4 (April)
```

The callback routine takes three parameters: the List widget where the selection was made, any client data that may have been registered with the callback routine (via **XtAdd-Callback( )** in this case), and a callback structure defined by Motif. We aren't using the client data, since we passed **NULL** as the last parameter to **XtAddCallback( )**. The callback structure (**cbs**) is used to get information about the nature of the List widget and the selection made.

This structure is provided by the List widget:

```
    typedef struct {
        int         reason;
        XEvent      *event;
        XmString    item;
        int         item_length;
        int         item_position;
        XmString    *selected_items;
        int         selected_item_count;
        int         *selected_item_positions;
        char        selection_type;
    } XmListCallbackStruct;
```

List items are stored as compound strings, so to print this value using **printf( )**, we must convert the string with the compound string function **XmStringGetLtoR( )**.

The Double-click Interval

The default selection is activated when the user *double clicks* on a List item. What determines whether two consecutive button clicks are interpreted as individual clicks or as a double click is the time interval between the clicks. You can set or get this value using the resource **XmNdoubleClickInterval**. The value is stored as milliseconds, so a value of **500** is a half of a second. If this resource isn't set, the value of the **multiClickTime** resource will be used instead. Generally, the double-click interval should be left for the user to specify in his resource database, which he will usually do with the more global resource **multiClickTime**. (Note that this is a fundamental X resource, understood by all X applications. It is not simply an Xt or Motif toolkit resource.)

13.10.2 Browse and Single Selection Callbacks

The browse and single selection modes allow single selection of items only, although the browsing mode is regarded as a simpler interface for the user. While the differences are subtle, the single selection mode allows no items to be selected. Interactively, browse selection allows the user to "drag" the selection over many items; the selection is not made till the mouse button is released. In the single selection mode, the selection is made as soon as the mouse button goes down.

Keyboard traversal through the list is also different between the two modes; if the user uses the keyboard to move from one item to the next in single selection mode, the **XmNsingle-SelectCallback** is not made until the RETURN key is pressed, whereas in browse selection, the **XmNbrowseSelectionCallback** is invoked for each item the user traverses. Visually, these two input modes for the List widget appear identical, so your treatment of the callbacks is very important for maintaining consistency between Lists with different selection modes.

Either of these modes can be set by assigning either **XmSINGLE_SELECT** or **Xm-BROWSE_SELECT** to the **XmNselectionPolicy** resource. For browse selection, the callback list associated with the **XmNbrowseSelectionCallback** is used. Similarly, the **XmNsingleSelectionCallback** is used for the single selection mode.

A simple example of using the browse selection callback is shown in Example 13-8. Here, we simply add a callback routine to the widget's callback list. This time, we add to the **Xm-NbrowseSelectionCallback** resource. For convenience, we specify the same function, **my_proc( )**, as the callback for both the default and browse selections.

Example 13-8. Specifying browse selection and default action callbacks

```
...
list_w = XmCreateScrolledList(toplevel, "months", NULL, 0);
XtVaSetValues(list_w,
    XmNitems,            str_list,
    XmNitemCount,        n,
    XmNvisibleItemCount, 5,
    NULL);
XtAddCallback(list_w, XmNdefaultActionCallback, my_proc, NULL);
XtAddCallback(list_w, XmNbrowseSelectionCallback, my_proc, NULL);
...

void
my_proc(list_w, client_data, cbs)
Widget list_w;
XtPointer client_data;
XmListCallbackStruct *cbs; /* CallBack Structure */
{
    char *choice;

    if (cbs->reason == XmCR_BROWSE_SELECT)
        printf("browse selection: ");
    else
        printf("default action: ");

    XmStringGetLtoR(cbs->item, charset, &choice);
    printf("selected item %d (%s)\n", cbs->item_position, choice);
```

Example 13-8. Specifying browse selection and default action callbacks (continued)

```
    XtFree(choice);
}
```

Because the default selection mode is the *browse* mode, we don't need to specify a literal `XmNselectionPolicy` resource value. As with the default action callback, the only fields of the callback structure that are valid for the browse selection callback routine are `reason`, `event`, `item_length`, and `item_position`. The others are not used because the default, single, and browse selection modes do not support multiple selections.

13.10.3 Multiple Selection Callback

When the `XmNselectionPolicy` is set to `XmMULTIPLE_SELECT`, multiple selections may be made in the widget. This may be accomplished by drag-selecting contiguous items within the List widget. When this occurs, the callback routine associated with the `XmNmultipleSelectionCallback` is invoked (although the `XmNdefaultAction-Callback` list may still be invoked).

Continuing with our example using the months, we increment the selection mode to `XmMULTIPLE_SELECT` and install the modified callback routine in Example 13-9.

Example 13-9. Specifying a multiple selection callback routine

```
    ...
    list_w = XmCreateScrolledList(toplevel, "months", NULL, 0);
    XtVaSetValues(list_w,
        XmNitems,            str_list,
        XmNitemCount,        n,
        XmNvisibleItemCount, 5,
        XmNselectionPolicy,  XmMULTIPLE_SELECT,
        NULL);
    XtAddCallback(list_w, XmNmultipleSelectionCallback, my_proc, NULL);
    XtAddCallback(list_w, XmNdefaultActionCallback, my_proc, NULL);
    ...
static void
my_proc(list_w, client_data, cbs)
Widget list_w;
XtPointer client_data;
XmListCallbackStruct *cbs; /* CallBack Structure */
{
    char *choice;
    int   i;

    printf("reason: %d\n", cbs->reason);
    if (cbs->reason == XmCR_MULTIPLE_SELECT) {
        /* only for multiple selection is the following used */
        printf("%d items selected:\n", cbs->selected_item_count);
        for (i = 0; i < cbs->selected_item_count; i++) {
            XmStringGetLtoR(cbs->selected_items[i], charset, &choice);
            printf("%d (%s)\n",
                cbs->selected_item_positions[i], choice);
            XtFree(choice);
```

```
        }
    } else {
        XmStringGetLtoR(cbs->item, charset, &choice);
        printf("%d (%s)\n", cbs->item_position, choice);
        XtFree(choice);
    }
}
```

By specifying the same callback routine for both the default action callback and the multiple selection callback, we have reduced the number of callback functions we must write. However, the routine must test the callback structure's **reason** field to determine which of the two callbacks was invoked. That is, when the reason is **XmCR_MULTIPLE_SELECT**, we print the list of selected items by looping through **selected_items** and **selected_item_positions**. If the **reason** is **XmCR_DEFAULT_ACTION** (which it must be if it's not the multiple selection), then there must only be one item selected since the default selection action causes all other items to be deselected.

13.10.4 Extended Selection Callback

The most complex of the selection models is *extended selection*. Here, the user has the greatest flexibility to select and deselect individual items or ranges of items. To support this feature, the application must be able to request notification when any such interactions take place.

To enable extended selection, the application must set the **XmNselectionPolicy** to **XmEXTENDED_SELECT** and a callback routine needs to be set for the **XmNextended-SelectionCallback**. In this case, all the fields of the List's callback structure come into play. The code fragment in Example 13-10 demonstrates how this function can be used.

Example 13-10. Specifying an extended selection callback routine

```
    ...
    list_w = XmCreateScrolledList(toplevel, "months", NULL, 0);
    XtVaSetValues(list_w,
        XmNitems,           str_list,
        XmNitemCount,       n,
        XmNvisibleItemCount, 20,
        XmNselectionPolicy, XmEXTENDED_SELECT,
        NULL);
    XtAddCallback(list_w, XmNextendedSelectionCallback, my_proc, NULL);
    XtAddCallback(list_w, XmNdefaultActionCallback, my_proc, NULL);
    ...

static void
my_proc(list_w, client_data, cbs)
Widget list_w;
XtPointer client_data;
XmListCallbackStruct *cbs; /* CallBack Structure */
{
    char *choice;
    int   i;
```

```
    printf("reason: %d\n", cbs->reason);
    if (cbs->reason == XmCR_EXTENDED_SELECT) {
        if (cbs->selection_type == XmINITIAL)
            printf("Initial Selection: ");
        else if (cbs->selection_type == XmMODIFICATION)
            printf("Modification of selection: ");
        else /* selection type = XmADDITION */
            printf("Additional selections: ");
        printf("%d items selected:\n", cbs->selected_item_count);
        for (i = 0; i < cbs->selected_item_count; i++) {
            XmStringGetLtoR(cbs->selected_items[i], charset, &choice);
            printf("%d (%s)\n", cbs->selected_item_positions[i], choice);
            XtFree(choice);
        }
    } else {
        XmStringGetLtoR(cbs->item, charset, &choice);
        printf("%d (%s)\n", cbs->item_position, choice);
        XtFree(choice);
    }
}
```

Most of the callback routine is the same as it was for multiple selection mode, but this time we also test the value of the **selection_type** field. This field can take one of three different values:

XmINITIAL

> This indicates that the selection is the initial selection for the List. All other selected items are deselected and the items selected with this action comprises the entire list of selected items.

XmMODIFICATION

> When the user modifies the selected list (using $\boxed{\text{SHIFT}}$ -left button), then the selected item list contains some items that were already selected before this action took place.

XmADDITION

> The items that are selected are in addition to what was previously selected. When the user selects and drags the left mouse button with the $\boxed{\text{CONTROL}}$ key down, items are toggled on and off.

Regardless of the value for **selection_type**, the **selected_items** and **selected_item_positions** always reflect the set of currently selected items.

13.11 Summary

While the List widget is a powerful user interface tool, its design remains simple and the programming interface mostly mechanical. Although you may be able to present a vast list of choices to the user, the choices themselves must be textual in nature.

Lists are not suitable for all situations; they cannot display any kinds of choices other than text (so pixmaps cannot be used as selection items), and there is no ability to set color on individual items. However, Lists are still one of the most visible and intuitive objects in graphical user-interface designs.

13.12 Exercises

The following exercises expand on some of the ideas expressed in this chapter.

1. Write a program that reads each word from the file */usr/dict/words* into a ScrolledList. Provide a TextField widget whose callback routine searches for the word typed into it from the entries in the List. Once found, make the List widget scroll so that item is centered in the ScrolledList's viewport. (Hint: convert the C string from the TextField into a compound string and use one of the List search routines to find the element.)

2. ScrolledLists frequently confuse the unsuspecting programmer that forgets that the real "parent" of the List widget is the ScrolledWindow, not the List. If you create a ScrolledList as a child of a Form widget, and want to specify "attachment" constraints on the ScrolledList, setting these resources on the List widget does nothing. These values must be set on the ScrolledWindow widget part of the ScrolledList object. Write a program that places two ScrolledList widgets next to each other in a single Form widget. (For more information on the role of the ScrolledWindow widget in ScrolledList objects, see the similar discussion on ScrolledText widgets in Chapter 15, *Text Widgets*, and more discussion in Chapter 9, *ScrolledWindows and Scrollbars*.)

3. Combining the first and second exercises, let's say that you have two List widgets whose items are somewhat dependent on one another. For example, the "left" List contains login names and the right List contains their corresponding user-IDs. (Whatever constraints you want to introduce between the two lists is irrelevant to the problem.) Write a program where the `XmNdefaultSelection` callback routine for each list selects the dependent/corresponding items in the other list. So, because the user ID for "root" is always **0**, selecting "root" from the "login name" list should cause the item **0** in the user-ID list to be selected.

14

Scales

This chapter describes how to use scales to display ranges of data.

In This Chapter:

14
Scales

The Scale widget displays a numeric value with upper and lower bounds and allows the user to change that value interactively using a *slider* mechanism similar to that of a Scrollbar. This style of interface is useful when it is inconvenient or inappropriate to have the user change values using the keyboard. It is also extremely intuitive to use; inexperienced users often understand how Scales work when they first see them. Figure 14-1 shows how a Scale can be used with other widgets in an application.

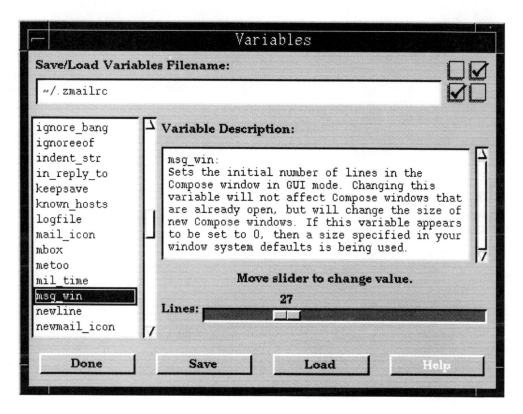

Figure 14-1. A scale widget in an application

The values given to a Scale are stored as integers, but decimal representation of values is possible through the use of a resource that allows you to place a decimal point in the value. Scales can be set to output-only mode (in which mode they are sometimes called *gauges*), implying that the values they display are controlled from some other widget or are used to report information specific to the application. Unfortunately, the internal implementation of read-only Scale widgets requires them to be insensitive, which has the annoying side-effect that they are *grayed out*.

14.1 Creating Scale Widgets

Applications that use the Scale widget must include the header file *<Xm/Scale.h>*. You can then create a Scale widget using:

```
Widget scale;

scale = XtVaCreateManagedWidget("name", xmScaleWidgetClass, parent,
    resource-value pairs,
    NULL);
```

The Scale widget is actually subclassed from the Manager widget. All the parts of a Scale are really made up of other primitive widgets. However, these subwidgets are not accessible through the Motif toolkit. The fact that Scales are Manager widgets means that you can give them children. Each child is evenly distributed along the vertical or horizontal axis parallel to the slider (depending on its orientation). This is used primarily to provide the Slider with "tick marks." (We'll talk about this more later.) In all other respects, Scales are treated just like other primitive widgets.

A program that creates a Scale widget is shown in Example 14-1.

Example 14-1. The simple_scale.c program

```
/* scale.c -- demonstrate a few scale widgets. */

#include <Xm/Scale.h>
#include <Xm/RowColumn.h>

main(argc, argv)
char *argv[ ];
{
    Widget        toplevel, rowcol, scale;
    XtAppContext  app;
    void          new_value(); /* callback for Scale widgets */

    toplevel = XtVaAppInitialize(&app, "Demos", NULL, 0,
        &argc, argv, NULL, NULL);

    rowcol = XtVaCreateWidget("rowcol", xmRowColumnWidgetClass, toplevel,
        XmNorientation, XmHORIZONTAL,
        NULL);

    scale = XtVaCreateManagedWidget("Days",
        xmScaleWidgetClass, rowcol,
        XtVaTypedArg, XmNtitleString, XmRString, "Days", 4,
        XmNmaximum,    7,
```

Example 14-1. The simple_scale.c program (continued)

```
            XmNminimum,    1,
            XmNvalue,      1,
            XmNshowValue,  True,
            NULL);
    XtAddCallback(scale, XmNvalueChangedCallback, new_value, NULL);

    scale = XtVaCreateManagedWidget("Weeks",
        xmScaleWidgetClass, rowcol,
        XtVaTypedArg, XmNtitleString, XmRString, "Weeks", 5,
        XmNmaximum,    52,
        XmNminimum,    1,
        XmNvalue,      1,
        XmNshowValue,  True,
        NULL);
    XtAddCallback(scale, XmNvalueChangedCallback, new_value, NULL);

    scale = XtVaCreateManagedWidget("Months",
        xmScaleWidgetClass, rowcol,
        XtVaTypedArg, XmNtitleString, XmRString, "Months", 6,
        XmNmaximum,    12,
        XmNminimum,    1,
        XmNvalue,      1,
        XmNshowValue,  True,
        NULL);
    XtAddCallback(scale, XmNvalueChangedCallback, new_value, NULL);

    scale = XtVaCreateManagedWidget("Years",
        xmScaleWidgetClass, rowcol,
        XtVaTypedArg, XmNtitleString, XmRString, "Years", 5,
        XmNmaximum,    20,
        XmNminimum,    1,
        XmNvalue,      1,
        XmNshowValue,  True,
        NULL);
    XtAddCallback(scale, XmNvalueChangedCallback, new_value, NULL);

    XtManageChild(rowcol);

    XtRealizeWidget(toplevel);
    XtAppMainLoop(app);
}

void
new_value(scale_w, client_data, cbs)
Widget scale_w;
caddr_t client_data;
XmScaleCallbackStruct *cbs;
{
    printf("%s: %d\n", XtName(scale_w), cbs->value);
}
```

The output of this program is shown in Figure 14-2.

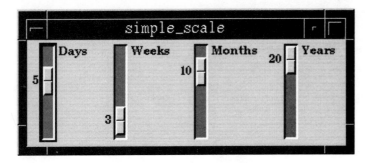

Figure 14-2. Output of simple_scale.c

The four Scales represent a number of days, weeks, months, and years. They all display a title (**XmNtitleString**), a maximum value (**XmNmaximum**), and their current value setting (**XmNshowValue**). The minimum value (**XmNminimum**) is set to **1** for the user's benefit; the minimum value of a Scale defaults to **0**. Note that if you set a minimum value other than **0**, you must also provide a default value for **XmNvalue** that is at least as large as the value of **XmNminimum**. Otherwise, the Motif toolkit will issue a warning message to **stderr**.

Note also that **XmNtitleString** must be set as a compound string, not a normal C string. The easiest way to make the conversion is to use the **XtVaTypedArg** feature, as we've done in the previous example. The use of this conversion method is described in detail in Chapter 19, *Compound Strings*.

14.2 Scale Values

The Scale's value can only be stored as an integer. This restriction is largely based on the fact that variables of type **float** or **double** cannot be passed through **XtVaSetValues( )**, **XtVaGetValues( )**, or any of the widget creation functions.[1] Therefore, if you need to represent fractional values rather than, or in addition to integral values, you must use **XmNdecimalPoints**. This resource's value indicates the number of places to move the decimal point to the left in the displayed value. This gives the user the impression that the value displayed is fractional.

---

[1] While the Toolkit Intrinsics functions mentioned do allow the passing of the *address* of variable of type **float** or **double**, the Scale widget does not happen to support this type of value representation.

For example, a Scale widget used to display the value of a barometer could range from 29 to 31, with a granularity of 1-100th. The Scale widget used to support such a display may be created in the following way:

```
XtVaCreateManagedWidget("barometer", xmScaleWidgetClass, rowcol,
    XtVaTypedArg, XmNtitleString, XmRString,
            "Barometric\nPressure", 19,
    XmNmaximum,        3100,
    XmNminimum,        2900,
    XmNdecimalPoints,  2,
    XmNvalue,          3000,
    XmNshowValue,      True,
    NULL);
```

The value for **XmNdecimalPoints** is 2, indicating that the value displayed will not be **3000**, but **30.00**.

Whenever decimal points are used, it is probably a good idea to set the value of **XmNshow-Value** to **True** since fine tuning is probably necessary.

In this example, the initial value of the Scale (**XmNvalue**) is set arbitrarily, but it must be set within the minimum and maximum values. If the value of the Scale is gotten via **Xt-VaGetValues()** or through a callback routine, it should be divided by 10 to the power of the value of **XmNdecimalPoints** to get the actual (intended) values.

For example, if the value is 2, the multiplication factor is 10 to the power of 2, which is 100.

There is no limit to the ranges of numbers used by the **XmNmaximum**, **XmNvalue**, and **Xm-Nminimum** resources, provided they can be represented by the **int** type. (This includes negative numbers.)

The Scale's value can be set or gotten using **XtVaSetValues()** or **XtVaGet-Values()**, using the **XmNvalue** resource, of course. However, Motif also provides the functions **XmScaleSetValue()** and **XmScaleGetValue()** to serve the same purpose. These functions take the following form:

```
void
XmScaleSetValue(scale_w, value)
    Widget  scale_w;
    int     value;

void
XmScaleGetValue(scale_w, value)
    Widget  scale_w;
    int     *value;
```

The advantage of using these Motif routines rather than the Xt *set* and *get* routines is that the former do not go through the internals of the Toolkit Intrinsics to determine the *set* and *get* methods of the Scale widget, so there is less overhead involved. These routines go into the widget and manipulate data directly. However, the added overhead of the Xt method is negligible.

14.3 The Scale's Label

The `XmNtitleString` resource represents the label on the Scale. The value associated with this resource is a compound string; regular C strings cannot be used. They must either be converted automatically by Xt, or you must convert them yourself using any of the Motif routines that handle this for you. Since real estate for labels is limited in Scale widgets, you should take care to use smaller strings. If the situation makes this difficult, you may choose to include a separator so that the text will print on two lines; otherwise, the label may be too wide and look awkward.

See Section 14.6, *Tick Marks*, for information on adding additional labels to a scale widget.

Scales may not have pixmaps as their labels.

14.4 Scale Orientation and Movement

The scale itself can be either vertical or horizontal, with the maximum and minimum values being on either end of the Scale. By default, as shown by the examples so far, Scales are vertically oriented with the maximum on the top and the minimum on the bottom. The `XmNorientation` resource can also be set to `XmHORIZONTAL` to get a horizontal orientation. The `XmNprocessingDirection` resource controls which end of the Scale the maximum and minimum values are on. The possible values are:

```
XmMAX_ON_TOP
XmMAX_ON_BOTTOM
XmMAX_ON_LEFT
XmMAX_ON_RIGHT
```

Unfortunately, you cannot set the processing direction unless you know the orientation of the Scale beforehand. This is another case where if you hard-code one resource, you should set both or an inconsistency (if not an error) may occur. If the scale is vertically oriented, the default value is `XmMAX_ON_TOP`, but if it is horizontal, the default depends on the value of `XmNstringDirection`. Therefore, if you are using a font that is read from right-to-left as the `XmNfontList` for this widget (which affects all labels), then the maximum value will be displayed on the left rather than on the right. This may or may not be what you want, so use caution if you are implementing an international version of your software.

As the user drags the slider, the value changes incrementally in the direction of the movement. If the user clicks the middle mouse button inside the scale widget, but not on the slider itself, the slider jumps to the point that was clicked on. (Unfortunately, in a small scale widget, the slider takes up a lot of space, so this method gives very poor control in moving the slider close to its current location. Scrollbars are better suited for this type of interaction.)

If the user clicks the left mouse button inside the slider area, but not on the slider itself, the slider moves in increments determined by the value of `XmNscaleMultiple`. This resource defaults to the difference between the maximum and minimum values divided by $10.^2$ Thus, a Scale widget whose maximum value is `250` will have a scale increment of

---

[2] As of Release 1.1 of the Motif toolkit, you should set `XmNscaleMultiple` explicitly if the difference between `XmNmaximum` and `XmNminimum` is less than 10. Otherwise, incremental scaling won't work.

25—by holding down the left mouse button over the area above or below the slider, the Scale's value will change by 25 in the positive or negative direction depending on whether the button went down above or below the slider. This movement continues until the button is released even if the slider moves past the pointer's location.

14.5 Scale Callbacks

The scale widget provides two callback specifications for monitoring the Scale's value. The callback list for `XmNdragCallback` is invoked whenever the user drags the slider. This does not imply that the Scale's value has actually changed or will change—it just indicates that the slider is being moved. The callback list for `XmNvalueChangedCallback` is invoked when the user releases the slider, resulting in an actual change of the Scale's value. This callback is not called while the user is moving the slider.

It is possible for the `XmNvalueChangedCallback` list to be called without the `XmNdragCallback` list being called. For example, when the user moves the slider using the keyboard or incrementally (by clicking in the slider area, but not on the slider itself), only the `XmNvalueChangedCallback` is invoked.

The form of either of these callback routines is no different than that for any other Xt-based callback function:

```
void
scale_callback(scale_w, client_data, call_data)
    Widget      scale_w;
    XtPointer client_data;
    XmScaleCallbackStruct *call_data;
```

Just as with all Motif callback routines, Motif defines its own callback structure depending on the widget class that owned the callback routine invoked. In this case, `call_data` is of type `XmScaleCallbackStruct`:

```
typedef struct {
    int         reason;
    XEvent   *event;
    int         value;
} XmScaleCallbackStruct;
```

The **reason** field of this structure may be set to `XmCR_DRAG` or `XmCR_VALUE_CHANGED` depending on the action that invoked the callback. The `value` field represents the value of the Scale widget regardless of the reason. The value stored internally within the widget changes dynamically with the value reported by the `value` field.

Example 14-2 shows another example of how the Scale widget can be used. In this case, we create a color previewer using Scales to control the red, green, and blue values of the color being edited. This example demonstrates how the `XmNvalueChangedCallback` can be used to automatically adjust colors as the scale is being dragged. For a discussion of the Xlib color setting routines used in this program, see Volume One, *Xlib Programming Manual*.

Example 14-2. The color_slide.c program

```
/* color_slide.c -- Use scale widgets to display the different
 * colors of a colormap.
 */
#include <Xm/LabelG.h>
#include <Xm/Scale.h>
#include <Xm/RowColumn.h>
#include <Xm/DrawingA.h>

Widget colorwindow; /* the window that displays a solid color */
XColor color;        /* the color in the colorwindow */

main(argc, argv)
char *argv[ ];
{
    Widget          toplevel, rowcol, scale;
    XtAppContext    app;
    Pixel           background;
    void            new_value();
    XtVarArgsList   arglist;

    toplevel = XtVaAppInitialize(&app, "Demos", NULL, 0,
        &argc, argv, NULL, NULL);

    if (DefaultDepthOfScreen(XtScreen(toplevel)) < 2) {
        puts("You must be using a color screen.");
        exit(1);
    }

    color.flags = DoRed|DoGreen|DoBlue;
    /* initialize first color */
    XAllocColor(XtDisplay(toplevel),
        DefaultColormapOfScreen(XtScreen(toplevel)), &color);

    rowcol = XtVaCreateManagedWidget("rowcol",
        xmRowColumnWidgetClass, toplevel, NULL);

    colorwindow = XtVaCreateManagedWidget("colorwindow",
        widgetClass,   rowcol,
        XmNheight,     100,
        XmNbackground, color.pixel,
        NULL);

    /* use rowcol again to create another RowColumn under the 1st */
    rowcol = XtVaCreateWidget("rowcol", xmRowColumnWidgetClass, rowcol,
        XmNorientation, XmHORIZONTAL,
        NULL);

    arglist = XtVaCreateArgsList(NULL,
        XmNshowValue, True,
        XmNmaximum, 255,
        XmNscaleMultiple, 5,
        NULL);

    scale = XtVaCreateManagedWidget("Red",
        xmScaleWidgetClass, rowcol,
        XtVaNestedList, arglist,
        XtVaTypedArg, XmNtitleString, XmRString, "Red", 4,
        XtVaTypedArg, XmNforeground, XmRString, "Red", 4,
        NULL);
    XtAddCallback(scale, XmNdragCallback, new_value, DoRed);
```

Example 14-2. The color_slide.c program (continued)

```
    XtAddCallback(scale, XmNvalueChangedCallback, new_value, DoRed);

    scale = XtVaCreateManagedWidget("Green",
        xmScaleWidgetClass, rowcol,
        XtVaNestedList, arglist,
        XtVaTypedArg, XmNtitleString, XmRString, "Green", 6,
        XtVaTypedArg, XmNforeground, XmRString, "Green", 6,
        NULL);
    XtAddCallback(scale, XmNdragCallback, new_value, DoGreen);
    XtAddCallback(scale, XmNvalueChangedCallback, new_value, DoGreen);

    scale = XtVaCreateManagedWidget("Blue",
        xmScaleWidgetClass, rowcol,
        XtVaNestedList, arglist,
        XtVaTypedArg, XmNtitleString, XmRString, "Blue", 5,
        XtVaTypedArg, XmNforeground, XmRString, "Blue", 5,
        NULL);
    XtAddCallback(scale, XmNdragCallback, new_value, DoBlue);
    XtAddCallback(scale, XmNvalueChangedCallback, new_value, DoBlue);

    XtFree(arglist);

    XtManageChild(rowcol);

    XtRealizeWidget(toplevel);
    XtAppMainLoop(app);
}

void
new_value(scale_w, rgb, cbs)
Widget scale_w;
int rgb;
XmScaleCallbackStruct *cbs;
{
    Colormap cmap = DefaultColormapOfScreen(XtScreen(scale_w));

    switch (rgb) {
        case DoRed :
            color.red = (cbs->value << 8);
            break;
        case DoGreen :
            color.green = (cbs->value << 8);
            break;
        case DoBlue :
            color.blue = (cbs->value << 8);
    }

    /* reuse the same color again and again */
    XFreeColors(XtDisplay(scale_w), cmap, &color.pixel, 1, 0);
    if (!XAllocColor(XtDisplay(scale_w), cmap, &color))
        puts("Couldn't XallocColor!"), exit(1);
    XtVaSetValues(colorwindow, XmNbackground, color.pixel, NULL);
}
```

The **XmNdragCallback** is used to display the current color values at all times. The output of this program is shown in Figure 14-3.

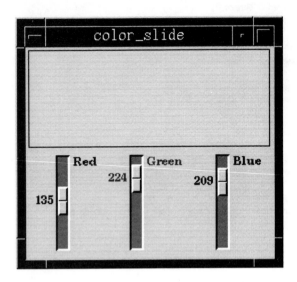

Figure 14-3. Output of color_slide.c

Obviously, a black and white book makes it difficult to show how this application really looks. However, when you run this program, it should provide a useful and intuitive introduction to using Scale widgets.

Another interesting part of this program is the use of **XtVaCreateArgsList()**. We use this function to build a single argument list that we would otherwise have to duplicate for each call to **XtVaCreateManagedWidget()**. The function allocates and returns a pointer to an object of type **XtVarArgsList**, which is an opaque pointer to an array of **XtVaTypedArgList** objects. This means that you can specify either normal resource-value pairs or the quadruplet used by **XtVaTypedArg**. These latter values are used to specify resource values that are not in the appropriate type, yet you may still avoid doing the type conversion yourself. For a discussion on type conversion and the use of **XtVaTyped-Arg**, see Volume Four, *X Toolkit Intrinsics Programming Manual.*

14.6 Tick Marks

The *Motif Style Guide* suggests that Scale widgets can have "tick marks" representing the incremental positions when their values change. The Scale widget does not provide these tick marks by default, but you can add them yourself by creating Label gadgets as children of the Scale widget. This is demonstrated in Example 14-3. Each tick mark is represented by a Label gadget that is added as a child of the Scale widget. In this case, all of the label gadgets are given the same name (a dash), since if the `XmNlabel` resource isn't set, the widget or gadget name will be used instead. Obviously, in a more complex application, labels could be supplied that specified ascending numeric values, or other information that would help the user to read the scale.

Example 14-3. The tick_marks.c program

```
/* tick_marks.c -- demonstrate a scale widget with tick marks. */

#include <Xm/Scale.h>
#include <Xm/LabelG.h>

#define MAX_VAL 20 /* arbitrary value */

main(argc, argv)
char *argv[ ];
{
    Widget         toplevel, scale;
    XtAppContext   app;
    int            i;

    toplevel = XtVaAppInitialize(&app, "Demos", NULL, 0,
        &argc, argv, NULL, NULL);

    scale = XtVaCreateManagedWidget("Days",
        xmScaleWidgetClass, toplevel,
        XtVaTypedArg,       XmNtitleString, XmRString, "Process load", 4,
        XmNmaximum,         MAX_VAL * 100,
        XmNdecimalPoints,   2,
        XmNshowValue,       True,
        NULL);

    for (i = 0; i < MAX_VAL; i++)
        XtVaCreateManagedWidget("-", xmLabelGadgetClass, scale, NULL);

    XtRealizeWidget(toplevel);
    XtAppMainLoop(app);
}
```

The Scale can take any kind of widget as a child, but it usually takes Labels so as to represent actual tick marks. All children are evenly distributed either vertically or horizontally parallel to the slider. No other layout method is possible.

As you can see in Figure 14-4, the labels (i.e., the tick marks) are placed all the way to the left of the Scale widget, leaving space for the value indicator. It is not possible (for example, by using the Label widget's `XmNalignment` resource) to force the tick marks or other labels up against the scale itself.

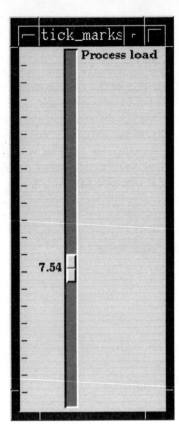

Figure 14-4. A scale with tick marks

14.7 Summary

The Scale widget is as simple in concept as it is in practical use. You may find particular uses for Scales not represented here, but the task of the Scale should never be too complicated.

15

Text Widgets

This chapter explains how the Text and TextField widgets can be used to provide anything from a single data-entry field to a full-fledged text editor. Special attention is paid to problems such as how to mask or convert data input by the user so as to control its format.

In This Chapter:

15
Text Widgets

Despite all that you can do with menus, buttons, and lists, there are times when the user can best interact with the application by typing at the keyboard. The Text widget is usually the best choice for providing this style of interface. It provides full-featured text editing capabilities that can be used anywhere the user might be expected to type free-form text (such as in a mail application's "compose" window). Yet, unlike standard text editors, the user can still rely on the point-and-click model most people expect from GUI-based applications. The TextField widget provides a single-line data entry field with the same full set of editing commands as the Text widget, but requires less overhead. Text Widgets can also be used in output-only mode, whenever it is necessary to display more detailed and precise information than can be expressed by iconic buttons or labels.

Text widgets provide the following mechanisms for program control:

- Resources that access the widget's text.

- Callback routines that enable "interposition" on events that add new text, delete text, and change input positions or input focus.

- Keyboard management methods that control input (editing style), output (paging style), character positioning, and word-breaks or line-wrapping.

- Convenience routines that enable quick and simple access to the clipboard.

The Text widget does have its limitations. For example, it cannot use multiple colors or fonts. (Only one color and font per Text widget is supported.) There is also no support for text formatting such as paragraph specifications, automatic line numbering, or indentation. Consequently, you cannot create WYSIWYG[1] documents. The Text widget is not a terminal emulator and cannot be used to run interactive programs. And finally, Text widgets cannot display multi-media objects—it is not possible to insert graphics into the text stream.

There may be some cases where the Text widget is not the most appropriate user-interface element, even though you are displaying text. For example, Text widgets should not be used to display lists whose items can be individually selected. That is the job of the List widget. Text that can neither be edited nor selected should be displayed in a Label widget. See

---

[1] WYSIWYG stands for *What You See Is What You Get*—a term commonly used to describe page formatting programs that can produce camera-ready documents that match what is displayed on the screen.

Chapter 11, *Labels and Buttons*, and Chapter 13, *List Widgets*, for better solutions to these problems.

If you have not used the Motif Text widget, you should familiarize yourself with one before getting too involved with this chapter. Running some of our introductory examples should provide an adequate platform for experimentation.

Figure 15-1 shows an application displaying several Text widgets.

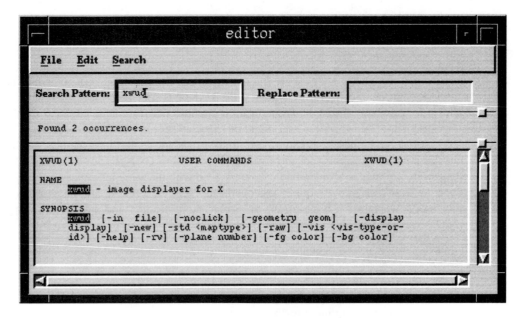

Figure 15-1. An editor application with two different styles of Text widgets

Here, we see four Text widgets taking several different forms. There are widgets used for single-line data entry and for editing multiple lines. The largest of the group has Scrollbars attached to it.

The standard Text widget supports single-line editing. (That is, newlines are ignored.) In fact, that is the Text widget's default behavior. However, single-line text entry is usually done in the TextField widget class. This is a completely separate widget class (not a subclass of Text) that is lighter-weight because it only supports single-line text editing. We should mention, however, that the TextField widget is a newborn in the Motif widget set and consequently has a number of bugs in it that have still to be worked out—especially in older versions of the toolkit. If the version of Motif you're using is 1.1.1 or later, you shouldn't have a problem, but at the time of this printing, many people are using an older version of the toolkit.

Although they are two separate widget classes, the Text and TextField widgets share common resources and convenience routines. We will point these out as we go, but you should be aware now of the two widget classes to avoid possible confusion later as we discuss them throughout this chapter.

Motif Programming Manual

Since the TextField widget cannot handle multiline editing, you must use the standard Text widget for this purpose. However, whenever multiple lines are used for editing, chances are that the number of lines may grow or shrink dynamically as the user edits text. Multiline Text widgets are therefore used frequently in scrollable windows, allowing the user to view portions of the underlying text. The combination of a Text widget and a ScrolledWindow widget is called *ScrolledText*. Although it is not a widget class, ScrolledText is commonly referred to as if it were, and there is a convenience routine, `XmCreateScrolled-Text( )`, that allows you to create both widgets at once.

15.1 The Text Interface Model

The user interface for Text widgets is commonly referred to as the "point and click" model. The *insertion cursor* (^) (also called a *caret*) indicates where the next character typed will be inserted. Using the left mouse button, the user can click on a new location in the widget to move the insertion cursor to that position. Newly typed text may be inserted at arbitrary locations in the Text widget.

The Text widget has predefined action routines (as opposed to callback routines) that allow the user to do simple editing commands such as "move one character to the right" or "delete backwards to the beginning of the line," and so on. The user can use translations specified in resource files to modify the text input behavior to his tastes. Because the Text widget is *stateless* or *modeless*, the user is always in text-insertion mode. Using the action routines, the user can set up his translation tables to mimic editors such as *emacs*. (Since the Text widget does not insert nonprintable characters, users typically bind control-character sequences to editing action routines.) Editors like *vi* cannot be emulated because there is no distinction between "command" mode and "text entry" mode. Although there is no "overstrike" mode, *per se*, through the combination of multiple action routines (such as "delete forward one character" and "insert new character"), it is programmatically possible to emulate such a mode. The input mechanism is not sophisticated enough to allow the user to emulate that style of text entry using resources alone.

Given the level of sophistication for both the programmer and the user, Text widgets should not be taken lightly or underestimated. Similarly, the ease of configurability should not tempt you to enforce your personal ideas about how a text editor should work. The best thing to do with Text widgets is to configure them as minimally as possible to suit the needs of your programs and let the user have ultimate control over as many details of its display and interoperability as possible. By employing this laissez-faire approach, your applications will be more compatible with each other and with other Motif programs.

15.1.1 Selecting Text

Over the years, people have gotten accustomed to the ability to "cut and paste" text between windows in GUI-based applications. In the X Window System, cut and paste is made more difficult for the programmer to implement because the nature of the X Window System requires a more "general" solution than on systems where a single vendor controls all the variables. For example, applications running on the same display may actually be executing on different systems, perhaps even systems with different byte orders, or other differences in the underlying data format.[2]

In order to insulate cut and paste operations from dependencies like these, all communication between applications, including cut and paste, is implemented via the X server. Data that is "cut" is stored in a *property* on the X server. A property is simply a named piece of data associated with a window and stored on the server.

The *Interclient Communications Conventions Manual* (ICCCM)[3] defines a set of standard property names to be used for such operations such as cut and paste, and lays out rules for how applications should interact with these properties. According to the ICCCM, text that is selected is typically stored in the PRIMARY property; the SECONDARY property is defined as an alternate storage area for use by applications that wish to support more than one simultaneous selection operation or that wish to support operations that would require two selections (such as switching the contents of the two selections); the CLIPBOARD property is defined as a longer-term holding area for data that is actually cut (rather than simply copied) from the application's window. (In the remainder of this discussion, when we refer to the primary, secondary, or clipboard selection, you may take this to mean the property of the same name.)

The most common implementation of the selection mechanism is provided by the X Toolkit Intrinsics. The low-level routines to implement selections are described in detail in Volume Four, *X Toolkit Intrinsics Programming Manual*. In general, applications such as *xterm* and widgets such as the Motif Text widget encapsulate this functionality in action routines that are invoked by the user with mouse button or key combinations, as follows:

- A portion of text is selected by pressing the left mouse button, and dragging the pointer across the text. The selected text is displayed in reverse video, and when the button is released, the text is copied into the PRIMARY property.

- An existing selection can be extended (in the Motif Text widget) either by pressing the SHIFT key and then dragging the pointer with the left mouse button down, or by pressing any of the arrow keys while holding down the SHIFT key. (Here implementations diverge. For example, in *xterm* and Athena-widget based applications, selections are typically extended with the right mouse button; however, in standard MIT applications, all of this behavior is subject to customization by the user in any case.)

- In addition to the click-and-drag technique for text selection, the Text widget also supports multiple-clicking techniques, in which a double-click selects a word, triple-clicking selects the current line, and quadruple-clicking selects all the text in the widget.

An important constraint imposed by the ICCCM is that only one window may "own" a selection property at one time. This means that once the user makes another primary selection, the original selection is lost.

---

[2] At the moment, only text selections are implemented, which makes byte order unimportant. However, the mechanism is designed to allow transparent transfer of any kind of data.

[3] Reprinted as Appendix L in Volume Zero, *X Protocol Reference Manual*.

The user can copy text directly from the primary selection into the Text widget (the reverse action) by clicking the middle mouse button at the location where the text is to be inserted. This is also called *stuffing* the selection into the widget. The user can stuff text anywhere in the text stream that is not already selected. It is important to understand that this only happens when the middle mouse button is *clicked*, which is defined as a quick succession of press and release actions; stuffing does not take place simply because the middle mouse button was pressed down. This distinction is important for *secondary selections*.

Secondary selections are not supported by MIT clients or the Athena widgets. However, they are used in the Motif Text widget to copy text directly to and from the same Text widget. The way this is accomplished is by *first* selecting the location where the copied text will go (left mouse button click to place the insertion point), *then* going to the text that needs to be copied and pressing and dragging the middle mouse button. The selected text is underlined rather than highlighted in reverse video. When the button is released, the selected text is immediately stuffed wherever the insertion cursor was placed before. Unlike primary selections, which may be retrieved many times, secondary selections are immediate and can only be stuffed once (at the time the selection is made).

The third location for holding text from Text widgets is the *clipboard* selection. The general idea of the clipboard selection is that it can be used as a longer-term storage area for data. For example, MIT provides a client called *xclipboard*, which asserts ownership of the CLIPBOARD property and provides a user interface to it. *xclipboard* not only allows selections to survive the termination of the window where the data was originally selected, it also allows for storage of multiple selections, which the user can "page through" before deciding which to paste.

OSF's implementation of the clipboard is incompatible with *xclipboard*. If *xclipboard* is running, any Motif routines that attempt to store data to the clipboard will not succeed. (The Motif routines temporarily try to lock the clipboard, and *xclipboard* will not give up its own lock.)

Motif treats the clipboard as a two-item cache; only Motif applications using the clipboard routines described in Chapter 18, *The Clipboard*, can interoperate using this selection.

On the other hand, Motif provides "cut and paste" functionality far ahead of that provided by the standard MIT clients. In *xterm* and the Athena widgets, selections can really only be used for "copy and paste." The selected text is unchanged. The Motif Text widget, by contrast, allows you to cut, copy, clear, or type over a selection.

While there is a translation and action-based interface defined for these operations, it is typically not implemented. As described in Chapter 3, *Overview of Motif Widgets*, Motif defines translations in terms of "virtual key bindings." By default, the virtual keys **osfCut**, **osfCopy**, **osfPaste**, and so on, are not bound to any actual keys. The user must bind these keys (typically in a *.motifbind* file in his home directory) before this interface can be used. Instead, the interface for these features is typically provided by menus associated with the Text widget, and that is how we will demonstrate them in this chapter.

One of the confusing things about working with the Text widget is that selected text is automatically stored in the primary selection; but when one of the Text widget functions, such as **XmTextCut( )**, is used, it is also stored in the clipboard selection. It is important to remember that the user is most likely oblivious to the fact that there are separate holding areas for selected text. If your application gets heavily into cutting and pasting, you'll find that the fusion of the primary and clipboard selections in the single convenience routines might get confusing.

The section on the Text widget in Appendix B, *Xt and Motif Widget Classes*, lists the default translations for the Text widget. See Volume Four, *X Toolkit Intrinsics Programming Manual*, for a description of how to program translation tables; see Volume Three, *X Window System User's Guide*, for a description of how a user can customize widget translations. See Chapter 18, *The Clipboard*, for a discussion of the lower-level Motif clipboard functions.

15.2 The Basics of Text Widgets

To understand and appreciate most of the material in this chapter, we must address some of the basic resources and functions provided by all Text widgets. The Text values, dimensions of the widget, and the ability to choose between single-line and multiline editing are among the most important. We begin with how to create a standard Text widget.

Applications that wish to use Text widgets need to include the file *<Xm/Text.h>*. TextField widgets use the file *<Xm/TextF.h>*. You can create a standard Text widget using **XtVaCreateManagedWidget( )** as usual:

```
Widget text_w;

text_w = XtVaCreateManagedWidget("name", xmTextWidgetClass, parent,
    resource-value pairs,
    NULL);
```

To create a TextField widget instead, specify the class as **xmTextFieldWidgetClass**.

The *resource-value pairs* can be any number of resources specific to the Text widget or its superclasses; note that the Text widget is subclassed from the Primitive widget class.

15.2.1 The Text Widget's Text

The first thing to learn about the Text widget is how to access its internal text storage. While there are many ways to do this, we begin using the most basic and simple method: the **XmNvalue** resource. Unlike the other widgets in the Motif toolkit that use text, the Text widget does not use compound strings for its value. Instead, the value is specified as a regular C string as shown in Example 15-1.

Example 15-1. The simple_text.c program

```
/* simple_text.c -- Create a minimally configured Text widget */
#include <Xm/Text.h>

main(argc, argv)
int argc;
char *argv[ ];
{
    Widget        toplevel;
```

Example 15-1. The simple_text.c program (continued)

```
    XtAppContext   app;

    toplevel = XtVaAppInitialize(&app, "Demos",
        NULL, 0, &argc, argv, NULL, NULL);

    XtVaCreateManagedWidget("text", xmTextWidgetClass, toplevel,
        XmNvalue,        "Now is the time...",
        NULL);

    XtRealizeWidget(toplevel);
    XtAppMainLoop(app);
}
```

This short program simply creates a Text widget whose initial value is set to `"Now is the time . . . "` (see Figure 15-2).

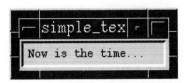

Figure 15-2. simple_text.c: a minimally configured Text widget

Setting a Text Widget's Text

The initial value of the **XmNvalue** resource may be set either at initialization time (as in Example 15-0) or by using **XtVaSetValues( )**:

```
    XtVaSetValues(text_w, XmNvalue, text, NULL);
```

This resource's value always represents the entire text of the widget.

Another method for setting the text in a Text widget is by using the Motif convenience routine, **XmTextSetString( )**:

```
    void
    XmTextSetString(text_w, value)
        Widget   text_w;
        char     *value;
```

Although the two methods produce the same results, the convenience routine may be more efficient since it accesses the internals of the widget directly. (The **XtVaSetValues( )** method involves going through the X Toolkit Intrinsics.) On the other hand, if you are also setting many other resources at the same time, the **XtVaSetValues( )** method is better since it saves the overhead of multiple function calls. (All resources can be set in a single function call.)

Whichever function you use, the *value* (however it is provided) is copied into the internals of the widget. When the user edits the text, the value changes accordingly.

Getting a Text Widget's Text

While the functions for getting a Text widget's text, **XmTextGetString( )** and **Xt-VaGetValues( )**, are parallel in name to those for setting the text, there are more substantial differences between them.

XmTextGetString( ) allocates enough space (using **XtMalloc( )**) to contain all the text in the widget and returns a pointer to this newly allocated area. While the pointer can be modified any way you like, you must free it using **XtFree( )** when you are through using it. The code fragment below demonstrates how this function may be used:

```
char *text;

if (text = XmTextGetString(text_w)) {
    /* allocated memory returned */
    /* we can write into "text" if we want... */
    XtFree(text);
    /* we *must* free "text" or there will be a memory leak */
}
```

The alternative to **XmTextGetString( )** is the Xt function **XtVaGetValues( )**:

```
char *text_p;

XtVaGetValues(text_w, XmNvalue, &text_p, NULL);
```

This method returns a pointer to internal data stored in the Text widget that should be treated as read-only data. In reality, the Text widget responds to **XtVaGetValues( )** by allocating memory and returning a copy of the text just like **XmTextGetString( )**. Currently, this data must be freed after use, but Motif's treatment of the GetValues method in Xt for Text widgets is a design misfeature and should be fixed in a future release of the Motif toolkit. Eventually, this new data will probably be cached and possibly reused over multiple calls to **XtVaGetValues( )**. However, the current implementation requires you to free this data when you are through with it. And although you are given allocated data, you should not get into the practice of modifying this data so your applications will port easily into future releases of the toolkit.

If you want to modify a Text widget's internal text, or you just want a copy of the text that you can modify for other reasons, you should probably use **XmTextGetString( )**. If you use the **XtVaGetValues( )** method as described previously (or call a function that uses it), then you should copy the text into your own local dataspace. For example:

```
char *text_p, buf[BUFSIZ];

XtVaGetValues(text_w, XmNvalue, &text_p, NULL);

(void) strncpy(buf, text_p, sizeof(buf));
XtFree(text_p);

/* modify "buf" all you want */
```

Here, we don't know how much text **text_p** points to, but for purposes of this demonstration, we assume it's not more than the value of **BUFSIZ**.[4] Just to be sure that we don't overrun array segments, we use **strncpy( )** to prevent an overflow of **buf**. Unless you are

---

[4] **BUFSIZ** is typically defined as 1024 in *<stdio.h>* on most modern UNIX systems.

intimately familiar with the nature of the Text widget you are using, it is unwise to make general assumptions about the amount of text you are getting.

Getting the value of a Text widget is potentially an expensive operation if the widget contains large amounts of text. Both methods return allocated data, so they are currently equivalent in performance. If the Motif internals change so that `XtVaGetValues()` returns cached data, it will definitely outperform `XmTextGetString()`. In all situations, whenever text is retrieved from the Text widget using any function, the length of time the data is valid is only guaranteed until the next Toolkit Intrinsics call into the same Text widget; it is undefined what any particular call might do to the internal text stream, and that information will not be reflected in the current character pointer handle you may have.

As suggested earlier, the TextField widget has corresponding routines that closely follow those of the Text widget. The routines `XmTextFieldGetString()` and `XmText-FieldSetString()` get and set the value of a TextField widget exactly the same way as their Text widget counterparts.

A Text widget may contain arbitrarily large amounts of text provided there is enough memory on the computer running the client application. The text stored by widgets is not stored on the X server; only the client computer stores widget-specific information. (The X server only displays a bitmap rendition of what the Text widget chooses to display.) Assuming there is enough memory on the computer, the upper limit on the number of bytes a Text widget may have is determined by the value of the `XmNmaxLength` resource. The default value of this resource is the largest size a `long` value can hold, so it is more likely that the user's computer will run out of memory before the Text widget's maximum capacity is reached. You can reset the resource's value to a lower limit to restrict the number of characters the user should be able to input to any particular Text widget.

Text widgets do not use temporary files to store their text data; all data resides in memory on the machine. Therefore, you cannot use Text widgets to browse or edit files. Instead, you load the contents of files into Text widgets and allow the user to edit the internal buffers. It is up to the application to decide (or to provide an interface that allows the user to decide) when to rewrite files with the updated information. For this reason, applications that use Text widgets to edit vital information should make provisions for system failure or other types of unexpected application termination to write Text widget buffers into recovery files. The Text widget will not support this type of recovery.

Example 15-2 shows an example program that demonstrates how files may be browsed using Text widgets. Later in the chapter, Section 15.6, *A Complete Editor*, demonstrates how Text widgets can be used to implement a full text editor.

15.2.2 Editing Modes

Let's return to Example 15-1 and examine more closely what is exposed to the user. The output of the program was shown in Figure 15-2. The Text widget defaults to the single-line editing style with a 20-column width (the width of each column is based on the font). This means that if the user presses RETURN , a newline is not inserted into the text. In fact, nothing visual happens at all. If you try running the program, you will find that typing more text than can be displayed causes the text to "scroll" to the left. Since newlines are not interpreted when typed by the user, the value of the text will most likely be one line long.[5] You may find that resizing the widget may allow it to appear large enough to display multiple lines, but this does not affect the operation of the widget or the way it handles input.

Multiline editing allows the user to enter newlines into the text of the widget, thereby providing a virtual full-screen editor. This simple change implies a great many other changes that need to be addressed separately. For example, widget geometry needs to be considered in order to establish the amount of text visible or acceptable at one time. This might require the use of Scrollbars to manage the viewing of the text. The callback routines invoked are also affected by which editing mode is used.

Single or multiline editing is controlled through the resource **XmNeditMode**. Its value can be either **XmSINGLE_LINE_EDIT** or **XmMULTI_LINE_EDIT**.

All in all, the two edit modes are quite different in concept, but their use in applications should be quite intuitive. Single-line edit fields are commonly used to display or prompt for file and directory names, short phrases, or single words. They are also quite handy as command-line fields that are interpreted by applications that were originally based on a tty interface. Multiline editing is mainly used to edit files or to display a message area whose entire contents can be viewed at any time, probably through a ScrolledWindow.

15.2.3 Scrollable Text

When multiline Text widgets are used, there can be quite a problem in managing how many lines they display, how they are managed when resized, and what sort of output model to use when new text is added. (Should the widget grow in size?) Multiline widgets cannot easily restrict the actual number of lines they display, especially if the text is editable by the user. For these reasons, most editable multiline Text widgets are usually created as *ScrolledText* objects. ScrolledText is not a widget class in and of itself, but as a combination of two widgets: a Text widget and a ScrolledWindow widget. The two widget classes have hooks and procedures that allow them to cooperate intelligently with each other. As the programmer, you can create each widget yourself and put them together, or you can use the Motif convenience routine, **XmCreateScrolledText( )**:

```
Widget text_w;

text_w = XmCreateScrolledText(parent, "name", args, num_args);

XtManageChild(text_w);
```

Note: this is *not* a variable-argument list function. It requires the old-style method using the **XtSetArg( )** macro and building the argument lists before the actual function call is

---

[5] It is possible to set **XmNvalue** to a string that contains newline characters on single-line Text widgets, but the interaction with the user is undefined; the widget will produce confusing behavior.

made. Typically, this function is adequate for most situations where ScrolledText objects are necessary. An example follows:

```
text = "This is a multiline Text widget.\nIt contains two lines.";

scrolled_text = XmCreateScrolledText(parent, "name2", NULL, 0);
XmTextSetString(scrolled_text, text);
```

This simple code fragment demonstrates the basic principle behind these widgets: you can create a ScrolledText object and assign any stream of text to it, and it will be displayed properly. Later, we'll examine more realistic examples where multiple lines are added to ScrolledText objects by reading in entire files.

While `XmCreateScrolledText()` creates both a Text widget and a ScrolledWindow widget, the handle to the Text widget is returned. You can get a handle to the Scrolled-Window using the function `XtParent(text_w)`. The widget returned by this function is important in many situations, especially ones involving widget layout formats. For example, if you wanted to place two ScrolledText objects next to one another in a Form widget, you would have to use code similar to that in the following fragment:

```
form = XmCreateForm(...);

scrolled_text1 = XmCreateScrolledText(form, "name1", ...);

scrolled_text2 = XmCreateScrolledText(form, "name2", ...);
XtVaSetValues(XtParent(scrolled_text2),
    XmNleftAttachment,    XmATTACH_WIDGET,
    XmNleftWidget,        XtParent(scrolled_text1),
    NULL);
```

Since the parents of the Text widgets are really the widgets we want to place next to one another, we must use `XtParent()` rather than the Text widgets themselves.

For purposes of specifying resources, the name the ScrolledWindow takes is the same as that of the Text widget with the suffix `"SW"`.[6] That is, the name of the Text widget in the `scrolled_text2` object from the previous code fragment is `name2`, and its Scrolled-Window parent widget has the name `name2SW`.

`XmCreateScrolledText()` is adequate for most situations, but in those cases where you do not want to set up the `args` list beforehand, or where you want to name the Scrolled-Window parent yourself, the convenience routine may not be suitable. You can emulate the same functionality using the following code fragment:

```
Widget scrolled_w, text_w;

scrolled_w = XtVaCreateManagedWidget("scrolled_w",
    xmScrolledWindowWidgetClass, parent,
    XmNscrollingPolicy,        XmAPPLICATION_DEFINED,
    XmNvisualPolicy,           XmVARIABLE,
    XmNscrollBarDisplayPolicy, XmSTATIC,
    XmNshadowThickness,        0,
    NULL);
```

---

[6] The "SW" suffix is unsupported, but is not expected to change. Nevertheless, this is for your information only and you should not necessarily write code that relies on this feature.

```
text_w = XtVaCreateManagedWidget(name, xmTextWidgetClass, scrolled_w,
    resource-value pairs,
    NULL);

/* may or may not want to do this... */
XtAddCallback(text_w, XmNdestroyCallback, destroy_parent, NULL);
```

Here, we are creating the ScrolledWindow widget with the same resources that the Motif function uses. However, because we create the ScrolledWindow ourselves, we can give it our own name. In this situation, it is more clear that it is the parent of the ScrolledWindow, not of the Text widget, that controls the position of the combined objects.

The Text widget itself is created in the usual manner as a child of the ScrolledWindow.

By using this method instead of the Motif convenience routine for creating a ScrolledText widget, you assume the responsibility for managing both widgets for as long as they exist. More precisely, you may need to handle the case in which the widget is destroyed. This is why you may or may not want to handle the **XmNdestroyCallback** for the Text widget. **XmCreateScrolledText( )** handles this for you by installing an **XmNdestroy-Callback** automatically on the returned Text widget. This callback destroys its Scrolled-Window parent. Creating the ScrolledWindow explicitly leaves that responsibility with you. In this case, **destroy_parent( )** needs only to look like the following:

```
void
destroy_parent(widget)
Widget widget;
{
    XtDestroyWidget(XtParent(widget));
}
```

The only time you may need to provide this callback function is if you want the Scrolled-Window to be destroyed automatically when you destroy the Text widget. Unless you are creating and destroying ScrolledText objects dynamically, this should not be a concern.

Note that if you use **XmCreateScrolledText( )**, you must be very careful about calling **XtRemoveAllCallbacks( )**, since this function will remove the widget's pre-installed destroy callback function.

You should never attempt to assign a single-line Text widget (or a TextField widget) to a ScrolledWindow. The results are undefined in the toolkit, but it also makes no sense logically. This would be a good place to start looking if you find you are getting unusual and unexplained results in your ScrolledText windows.

15.3 Rudimentary Examples

Now that we have introduced the basics of the Text widget and some simple resources, let's walk through some rudimentary examples that demonstrate real-world scenarios. These examples will also introduce more Text widget resources.

15.3.1 A File Browser

Example 15-2 shows a simple file browser that displays the contents of files using a Text widget. The user chooses which file to display by typing a filename in the single-line Text widget below the **Filename**: prompt, or by selecting a file from the FileSelectionDialog that is popped up by the **New** entry on the **File** menu. (FileSelectionDialogs are described in detail in Chapter 6, *Selection Dialogs*, so we won't say much about them here.) The specified file is displayed immediately in the application's Text widget. If another file is subsequently selected, that file is loaded instead.

Example 15-2. The file_browser.c program

```
/* file_browser.c -- use a ScrolledText object to view the
 * contents of arbitrary files chosen by the user from a
 * FileSelectionDialog or from a single-line text widget.
 */
#include <X11/Xos.h>
#include <Xm/Text.h>
#include <Xm/TextF.h>
#include <Xm/FileSB.h>
#include <Xm/MainW.h>
#include <Xm/RowColumn.h>
#include <Xm/LabelG.h>
#include <sys/types.h>
#include <sys/stat.h>
#include <stdio.h>

main(argc, argv)
int argc;
char *argv[ ];
{
    Widget        top, main_w, menubar, menu, rc, text_w, file_w;
    XtAppContext  app;
    XmString      file, new, quit;
    extern void   read_file(), file_cb();
    Arg           args[ 4 ];

    /* initialize toolkit and create toplevel shell */
    top = XtVaAppInitialize(&app, "Demos",
        NULL, 0, &argc, argv, NULL, NULL);

    /* MainWindow for the application -- contains menubar
     * and ScrolledText/Prompt/TextField as WorkWindow.
     */
    main_w = XtVaCreateManagedWidget("main_w",
        xmMainWindowWidgetClass, top,
        /* XmNscrollingPolicy,   XmVARIABLE, */
```

Example 15-2. The file_browser.c program (continued)

```
            NULL);

     /* Create a simple MenuBar that contains one menu */
     file = XmStringCreateSimple("File");
     menubar = XmVaCreateSimpleMenuBar(main_w, "menubar",
         XmVaCASCADEBUTTON, file, 'F',
         NULL);
     XmStringFree(file);

     /* Menu is "File" -- callback is file_cb() */
     new = XmStringCreateSimple("New ...");
     quit = XmStringCreateSimple("Quit");
     menu = XmVaCreateSimplePulldownMenu(menubar, "file_menu", 0, file_cb,
         XmVaPUSHBUTTON, new, 'N', NULL, NULL,
         XmVaSEPARATOR,
         XmVaPUSHBUTTON, quit, 'Q', NULL, NULL,
         NULL);
     XmStringFree(new);
     XmStringFree(quit);

     /* Menubar is done -- manage it */
     XtManageChild(menubar);

     rc = XtVaCreateWidget("work_area", xmRowColumnWidgetClass, main_w, NULL);
     XtVaCreateManagedWidget("Filename:", xmLabelGadgetClass, rc,
         XmNalignment, XmALIGNMENT_BEGINNING,
         NULL);
     file_w = XtVaCreateManagedWidget("text_field",
         xmTextFieldWidgetClass, rc, NULL);

     /* Create ScrolledText -- this is work area for the MainWindow */
     XtSetArg(args[0], XmNrows,      12);
     XtSetArg(args[1], XmNcolumns,    70);
     XtSetArg(args[2], XmNeditable,  False);
     XtSetArg(args[3], XmNeditMode,  XmMULTI_LINE_EDIT);
     text_w = XmCreateScrolledText(rc, "text_w", args, 4);
     XtManageChild(text_w);

     /* store text_w as user data in "File" menu for file_cb() callback */
     XtVaSetValues(menu, XmNuserData, text_w, NULL);
     /* add callback for TextField widget passing "text_w" as client data */
     XtAddCallback(file_w, XmNactivateCallback, read_file, text_w);

     XtManageChild(rc);

     /* Store the filename text widget to ScrolledText object */
     XtVaSetValues(text_w, XmNuserData, file_w, NULL);

     XmMainWindowSetAreas(main_w, menubar, NULL, NULL, NULL, rc);
     XtRealizeWidget(top);
     XtAppMainLoop(app);
}

/* The "File" menu item was selected; popup a FileSelectionDialog. */
void
file_cb(menu_item, item_no)
Widget menu_item;
int item_no; /* the index into the menu that menu_item is */
{
     static Widget dialog;
```

Example 15-2. The file_browser.c program (continued)

```
    Widget text_w;
    extern void read_file();

    if (item_no == 1)
        exit(0);  /* user chose Quit */

    if (!dialog) {
        Widget menu = XtParent(menu_item);
        dialog = XmCreateFileSelectionDialog(menu, "file_sb", NULL, 0);

        /* Get the text widget handle stored as "user data" in File menu */
        XtVaGetValues(menu, XmNuserData, &text_w, NULL);
        XtAddCallback(dialog, XmNokCallback, read_file, text_w);
        XtAddCallback(dialog, XmNcancelCallback, XtUnmanageChild, NULL);
    }
    XtManageChild(dialog);

    XtPopup(XtParent(dialog), XtGrabNone);
    /* If dialog is already popped up, XtPopup does nothing.
     * Call XMapRaised() anyway to make sure it's visible.
     */
    XMapRaised(XtDisplay(dialog), XtWindow(XtParent(dialog)));
}

/* callback routine when the user selects Ok in the FileSelection
 * Dialog or presses Return in the single-line text widget.
 * The specified file must be a regular file and readable.
 * If so, it's contents are displayed in the text_w provided as the
 * client_data to this function.
 */
void
read_file(widget, text_w, cbs)
Widget widget;  /* file selection box or text field widget */
Widget text_w; /* passed the text_w as client_data */
XmFileSelectionBoxCallbackStruct *cbs;
{
    char *filename, *text;
    struct stat statb;
    FILE *fp;
    Widget file_w;

    if (XtIsSubclass(widget, xmTextFieldWidgetClass)) {
        filename = XmTextFieldGetString(widget);
        file_w = widget; /* this *is* the file_w */
    } else {
        /* file was selected from FileSelectionDialog */
        XmStringGetLtoR(cbs->value, XmSTRING_DEFAULT_CHARSET, &filename);
        /* the user data stored the file_w widget in the text_w */
        XtVaGetValues(text_w, XmNuserData, &file_w, NULL);
    }

    if (!filename || !*filename) { /* nothing typed? */
        if (filename)
            XtFree(filename);
        return;
    }

    /* make sure the file is a regular text file and open it */
    if (stat(filename, &statb) == -1 ||
```

Example 15-2. The file_browser.c program (continued)

```
                (statb.st_mode & S_IFMT) != S_IFREG ||
                !(fp = fopen(filename, "r"))) {
        if ((statb.st_mode & S_IFMT) == S_IFREG)
            perror(filename); /* send to stderr why we can't read it */
        else
            fprintf(stderr, "%s: not a regular file\n", filename);
        XtFree(filename);
        return;
    }

    /* put the contents of the file in the Text widget by allocating
     * enough space for the entire file, reading the file into the
     * allocated space, and using XmTextFieldSetString() to show the file.
     */
    if (!(text = XtMalloc((unsigned)(statb.st_size+1)))) {
        fprintf(stderr, "Can't alloc enough space for %s", filename);
        XtFree(filename);
        fclose(fp);
        return;
    }

    if (!fread(text, sizeof(char), statb.st_size+1, fp))
        fprintf(stderr, "Warning: may not have read entire file!\n");

    text[statb.st_size] = 0; /* be sure to NULL-terminate */

    /* insert file contents in Text widget */
    XmTextSetString(text_w, text);

    /* make sure text field is up to date */
    if (file_w != widget) {
        /* only necessary if activated from FileSelectionDialog */
        XmTextFieldSetString(file_w, filename);
        XmTextFieldSetCursorPosition(file_w, strlen(filename));
    }

    /* free all allocated space and we're outta here. */
    XtFree(text);
    XtFree(filename);
    fclose(fp);
}
```

The output of the program is shown in Figure 15-3.

The Text widget is quite simple and does not require a great deal of setup or maintenance. We use the convenience routine **XmCreateScrolledText( )** to create a ScrolledText area with 12 lines by 70 columns of displayable text. This is done by setting the values for **XmNrows** and **XmNcolumns**, but these settings are used only at initialization. Once the application is up and running, the user can resize the windows and effectively change those dimensions.

The resource **XmNeditable** is set to **False** to prevent the user from editing the contents of the Text widget. Because we do not provide the user with the ability to write changes back to the file (or any other file), there is no sense in misleading him into thinking that the file is editable too.

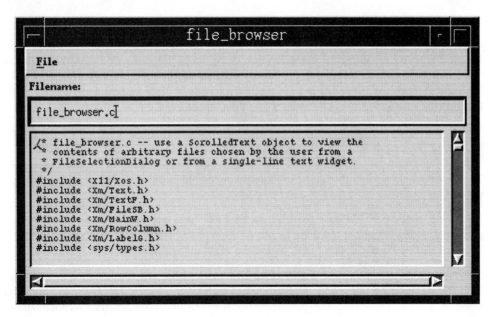

```
┌─────────────────────────────────────────────────────────┐
│ ─       │              file_browser              │ □ │ □ │
├─────────────────────────────────────────────────────────┤
│  File                                                     │
│  Filename:                                                │
│ ┌───────────────────────────────────────────────────────┐│
│ │ file_browser.c                                        ││
│ └───────────────────────────────────────────────────────┘│
│ ┌─────────────────────────────────────────────────────┬─┐│
│ │ /* file_browser.c -- use a ScrolledText object to   │▲││
│ │ view the                                            │ ││
│ │  * contents of arbitrary files chosen by the user   │ ││
│ │    from a                                           │ ││
│ │  * FileSelectionDialog or from a single-line text   │ ││
│ │    widget.                                          │ ││
│ │  */                                                 │ ││
│ │ #include <X11/Xos.h>                                │ ││
│ │ #include <Xm/Text.h>                                │ ││
│ │ #include <Xm/TextF.h>                               │ ││
│ │ #include <Xm/FileSB.h>                              │ ││
│ │ #include <Xm/MainW.h>                               │ ││
│ │ #include <Xm/RowColumn.h>                           │ ││
│ │ #include <Xm/LabelG.h>                              │ ││
│ │ #include <sys/types.h>                              │▼││
│ ├─────────────────────────────────────────────────────┴─┤│
│ │◄│                                                  │►││
│ └─────────────────────────────────────────────────────┘ │
└─────────────────────────────────────────────────────────┘
```

Figure 15-3. Output of file_browser.c

Since noneditable Text widgets should not display an insertion cursor, it is removed by setting **XmNcursorPositionVisible** to **False**.

The FileSelectionDialog is created and managed when the user selects the **New** button in from the **File** menu in the MenuBar. The user exits the program by selecting the **Quit** button from this menu as well. In the FileSelectionDialog, the **Ok** button's callback is **read_file( )**, which is activated when the user either presses the **Ok** button or enters RETURN in the file selection Text widget. This function gets the value of the filename specified and checks its type. If the file chosen is not a *regular* file (e.g., if it is a directory, device, tty, etc.) or if it cannot be opened, an error is reported and the function returns.[7]

Assuming the file checks out, its contents are loaded into the Text widget. Rather than loading the file by reading each line using functions like **fgets( )**, we just allocate enough space to contain the entire file and read it all in with one call to **fread( )**. The text is then loaded into the Text widget using **XmTextSetString( )**. The Scrollbars are automatically updated and the text is positioned so that the beginning of the file is displayed first. Nothing more needs to be done to the Text widget itself.

---

[7] If you are unfamiliar with the use of the *stat( )* system call, or any other aspect of UNIX programming used in examples in this book, a good source of information is the Nutshell Handbook *Using C on the UNIX System*, by Dave Curry (O'Reilly & Associates, 1988).

15.3.2 Line Wrapping and Scrollbar Placements

Despite its seeming simplicity, there is more going on in *file_browser.c* than meets the eye. For example, the ScrolledText object has two Scrollbars that were automatically installed; the vertical Scrollbar is needed in case the text exceeds 24 lines and the horizontal Scrollbar is needed in case any of those lines are wider than 80 columns.

We can make adjustments to serve specific needs. For example, most users grow accustomed to having Text windows be a fixed width (typically 80 columns), especially if they've ever used ASCII terminals. It can be annoying to have text be scrollable in the horizontal direction, since people need both ends of the lines to be visible in order to read smoothly through a page of text.

By setting **XmNscrollHorizontal** to **False**, lines are automatically broken at the point where they would overrun the width of the widget. However, one problem is that the lines are broken exactly at that point, regardless of word breaks.

The companion resources for **XmNscrollHorizontal** are **XmNscrollVertical**, **XmNscrollLeftSide**, and **XmNscrollTopSide**. The latter two resources take Boolean values controlling the placement of the Scrollbars within the ScrolledWindow. Unlike **XmNscrollHorizontal** and **XmNscrollVertical**, these resources should not be set by the application, but should be left to users to specify themselves.

Note that linebreaking is fine for previewing files and other output-only Text widgets, but you should not enforce such policies for Text widgets that are used for text editing. The user may want to edit "wide" files.

Automatic Resizing

The resources **XmNresizeWidth** and **XmNresizeHeight** control whether or not Text widgets should resize themselves vertically or horizontally in order to fit the entire text stream. For example, if **XmNresizeWidth** is **True** and new text is added such that the number of columns would have to grow, the widget's width would grow to fit the new text width. Similarly, if **XmNresizeHeight** is **True** and the number of lines increases, the height of the widget would grow until all of them are displayable.

These resources have no effect in ScrolledText objects since the Scrollbars already manage the widget's size. Also, if linebreaking is active, **XmNresizeWidth** has no effect.

You should use these resources sparingly in Text widgets. It is generally regarded as poor user-interface design to have Text widgets dynamically resizing as they are being edited. This is especially true of widgets in a Shell or Dialog with other elements in it. It is also impolite for windows to resize themselves except as the result of an explicit user action.

An example of an acceptable use of these resources would be when using a Text widget to display text for a Help dialog (although not necessarily an InformationDialog). The Text widget would resize itself silently (before it is ever mapped to the screen) so that by the time it is visible, its size would be constant. This makes it appear to the user that a different dialog is displayed each time it is used.

15.3.3 Output-only Text Areas

Our next example addresses a common need for many developers: a method for displaying continual text messages during runtime. This may include error messages from Xlib or Xt as well as from any function internal to the host application. Such a feature is an important part of the main window of many applications, as discussed in Chapter 4, *The Main Window*. In Motif terminology, this is called the Message Area of an application. And, while a message area can be implemented as a Label widget, ScrolledText objects are usually best suited for this type of feature, since the user has the ability to scroll back to previously displayed messages. This is especially useful when many messages must be displayed.

Assuming we want to use a ScrolledText object to display this information, the following checklist will help us derive a design for the function that we might require:

- The function should act like `printf( )` in that it takes variable arguments and understands the standard string formatting characters.

- The text output should go into a ScrolledText widget so the user can review previously displayed messages.

- All new text should be appended to the end of the output and should be immediately visible so that the user does not have to manually scroll to the end of the display.

Despite these requirements, the implementation of such a function is quite simple and the demands on the Text widget itself are minimal. Example 15-3 shows the function `wprint( )` (which stands for *window-print*).

Example 15-3. The wprint() function

```
#include <stdio.h>
#include <X11/VarargsI.h> /* includes <stdarg.h> or <varargs.h> */

static Widget text_w; /* widget for text output */

    /* Create text_w as a ScrolledText window */
    Arg             args[9];
    ...
    XtSetArg(args[0], XmNrows,              6);
    XtSetArg(args[1], XmNcolumns,           80);
    XtSetArg(args[2], XmNeditable,          False);
    XtSetArg(args[3], XmNeditMode,          XmMULTI_LINE_EDIT);
    XtSetArg(args[4], XmNwordWrap,          True);
    XtSetArg(args[5], XmNscrollHorizontal,  False);
    XtSetArg(args[6], XmNblinkRate,         0);
    XtSetArg(args[7], XmNautoShowCursorPosition, True);
    XtSetArg(args[8], XmNcursorPositionVisible, False);
    text_w = XmCreateScrolledText(parent, "text_w", args, 9);
    XtManageChild(text_w);
    ...

/*VARARGS*/
void
wprint(va_alist)
va_dcl
{
```

Example 15-3. The wprint() function (continued)

```
        char msgbuf[BUFSIZ]; /* we're not getting huge strings */
        char *fmt;
        static XmTextPosition wpr_position; /* maintain text position */
        va_list args;

        va_start(args);
        fmt = va_arg(args, char *);
#ifndef NO_VPRINTF
        (void) vsprintf(msgbuf, fmt, args);
#else /* !NO_VPRINTF */
        {
            FILE foo;
            foo._cnt = BUFSIZ;
            foo._base = foo._ptr = msgbuf; /* (unsigned char *) ?? */
            foo._flag = _IOWRT+_IOSTRG;
            (void) _doprnt(fmt, args, &foo);
            *foo._ptr = ' '; /* plant terminating null character */
        }
#endif /* NO_VPRINTF */
        va_end(args);

        XmTextInsert(text_w, wpr_position, msgbuf);
        wpr_position += strlen(msgbuf);
        XtVaSetValues(text_w, XmNcursorPosition, wpr_position, NULL);
        XmTextShowPosition(text_w, wpr_position);
}
```

Because the function acts like **printf( )**, it takes a variable argument list of parameters. This requires the inclusion of *<X11/VarargsI.h>*.[8] The function **wprint( )** uses **va_alist** as its sole parameter—this is a pointer to the first of a list of arguments passed to the function. It is declared as **va_dcl** in accordance with the standards for functions that take varargs lists.

The **va_start( )** and **va_arg( )** macros are used to extract the first parameter from the variable argument list. Since **wprint( )** is supposed to act like **printf( )**, we know that the first parameter is going to be a **char** pointer:

```
        fmt = va_arg(args, char *);
```

fmt now points to the format string to be used. This may or may not contain **%** formatting characters that expand to other strings depending on the other arguments to the function.

The rest of the arguments are read and parsed by either **vsprintf( )** or **_doprnt( )**, depending on your C library. **vsprintf( )** is a varargs version of **sprintf( )** that exists on most modern UNIX machines.[9] If your machine does not have **vsprintf( )**, you will need to use **_doprnt( )**—a function that can be used in the same manner.

---

[8] The *I* in *VarargsI.h* indicates that it is the *I*mplementation file used by the Toolkit Intrinsics whenever *varargs* is used.

[9] System V has **vsprintf( )**, as does **SunOS**, but Ultrix and older BSD machines typically use **_doprnt( )**. This may or may not be the case in newer editions of an arbitrary operating system.

Both of these functions consume all of the arguments on the list and leave the result in `msgbuf`. Note that the size of this variable does not exceed `BUFSIZ` for this demonstration. If you expect to get larger strings, you should raise its size. We are now ready to append `msgbuf` to the end of the Text widget, `text_w`.

To keep a running count of the end of `text_w`, we maintain the value in `wpr_position`. Each time `msgbuf` is concatenated to the end of the text, the value of `wpr_position` is incremented appropriately. The new text is added using the convenience routine `XmText-Insert( )`.

The format of the function is:

```
void
XmTextInsert(text_w, position, buf)
    Widget          text_w;
    XmTextPosition  position;
    char            *buf;
```

The function simply inserts the given text at the specified position. The type `XmText-Position` is a `long` value to match the type of the value for `XmNmaxLength`.

Finally, the call to `XmTextShowPosition( )` makes that position visible within the Text's viewport. This may require the ScrolledWindow to reposition itself so that the newly printed text is visible. This is a convenience to the user so that he does not have to scroll the window to view new messages.

With the aid of `wprint( )`, we now have a very useful utility for paging the output of just about any text-based utility. One particularly helpful application of this function is shown in Example 15-4. Here, we can reset the error handling functions for Xlib and Xt so that they can be printed in a Text widget rather than to `stderr`.

Example 15-4. The error_handlers() function

```
extern void wprint();

static void
x_error(dpy, err_event)
Display      *dpy;
XErrorEvent  *err_event;
{
    char                 buf[ BUFSIZ ];

    XGetErrorText(dpy, err_event->error_code, buf, sizeof buf);

    wprint("X Error: <%s>\n", buf);
}

static void
xt_error(message)
char *message;
{
    wprint("Xt Error: %s\n", message);
}

main(argc, argv)
int argc;
char *argv[ ];
{
```

Example 15-4. The error_handlers() function (continued)

```
    XtAppContext app;

    XtVaAppInitialize(&app, ... );

    /* catch Xt errors */
    XtAppSetErrorHandler(app, xt_error);
    XtAppSetWarningHandler(app, xt_error);
    /* and Xlib errors */
    XSetErrorHandler(x_error);

    ...
    XtAppMainLoop(app);
}
```

By using **XtAppSetErrorHandler( )**, **XtAppSetWarningHandler( )**, and **XSetErrorHandler( )**, all X-related error messages can be sent to a Text widget through **wprint( )**. You can also use **wprint( )** throughout your application to send random messages to that ScrolledText area.

15.4 Text Positions

By definition, a *position* in the Text widget indicates the number of characters from the beginning of the text in the widget. All whitespace and newline characters are considered part of the text; as such, each is counted as a single character. For example, the insertion cursor in the following display is at position 20:

```
    Now is the time
    for all ...
      ^
```

When the user types in a Text widget, the new text is always added at the insertion cursor's position. Insertions also cause the cursor to advance the same number of characters that are added. If the cursor is never repositioned (either by the user or through Motif functions), then the insertion cursor will always be positioned at the end of the text in the widget. The **wprint( )** function discussed in the previous section makes use of this fact when it calls **XmTextShowPosition( )**. Since text is never deleted from the widget and the user cannot edit it, the insertion cursor is always at the end of the text, and so **XmTextShow-Position( )** always causes the window to scroll to the end of the widget's text.

You can set the cursor's position explicitly using `XmTextSetInsertion-Position()`:

```
void
XmTextSetInsertionPosition(text_w, position)
    Widget          text_w;
    XmTextPosition position;
```

This function is identical to `XmTextSetCursorPosition()`. (There is absolutely no difference between them.) Similarly, you can get the current cursor position using `XmTextGetInsertionPosition()` or `XmTextGetCursorPosition()`.

As with all the Text widget functions, there are corresponding TextField functions called `XmTextFieldSetInsertionPosition()` and `XmTextFieldSetCursorPosition()`.

A good use for these functions might be in a routine that searches for a specified pattern, as shown in Example 15-5.

Example 15-5. The search_text.c program

```
/* search_text.c -- demonstrate how to position a cursor at a
 * particular location.  The position is determined by a search_pat-
 * match search.
 */
#include <Xm/Text.h>
#include <Xm/LabelG.h>
#include <Xm/RowColumn.h>
#include <X11/Xos.h>    /* for the index() function */

Widget text_w, search_w, text_output;

main(argc, argv)
int argc;
char *argv[ ];
{
    Widget        toplevel, rowcol_v, rowcol_h;
    XtAppContext  app;
    int           i;
    void          search_text();
    Arg           args[5];

    toplevel = XtVaAppInitialize(&app, "Demos",
        NULL, 0, &argc, argv, NULL, NULL);

    rowcol_v = XtVaCreateWidget("rowcol_v",
        xmRowColumnWidgetClass, toplevel, NULL);

    rowcol_h = XtVaCreateWidget("rowcol_h",
        xmRowColumnWidgetClass, rowcol_v,
        XmNorientation,  XmHORIZONTAL,
        NULL);
    XtVaCreateManagedWidget("Search Pattern:",
        xmLabelGadgetClass, rowcol_h, NULL);
    search_w = XtVaCreateManagedWidget("search_text",
        xmTextWidgetClass, rowcol_h, NULL);
    XtManageChild(rowcol_h);

    text_output = XtVaCreateManagedWidget("text_out",
        xmTextWidgetClass, rowcol_v,
```

Example 15-5. The search_text.c program (continued)

```
        XmNeditable,            False,
        XmNcursorPositionVisible, False,
        XmNshadowThickness,     0,
        XmNsensitive,           False,
        NULL);

    XtSetArg(args[0], XmNrows,      10);
    XtSetArg(args[1], XmNcolumns,   80);
    XtSetArg(args[2], XmNeditMode,  XmMULTI_LINE_EDIT);
    XtSetArg(args[3], XmNscrollHorizontal, False);
    XtSetArg(args[4], XmNwordWrap,  True);
    text_w = XmCreateScrolledText(rowcol_v, "text_w", args, 5);
    XtManageChild(text_w);

    XtAddCallback(search_w, XmNactivateCallback, search_text, NULL);

    XtManageChild(rowcol_v);

    XtRealizeWidget(toplevel);
    XtAppMainLoop(app);
}

void
search_text()
{
    char *search_pat, *p, *string, buf[32];
    XmTextPosition pos;
    int len;
    Boolean found = False;

    /* get the text that is about to be searched */
    if (!(string = XmTextGetString(text_w)) || !*string) {
        XmTextSetString(text_output, "No text to search.");
        XtFree(string); /* may have been ""; free it */
        return;
    }
    /* get the pattern we're going to search for in the text. */
    if (!(search_pat = XmTextGetString(search_w)) || !*search_pat) {
        XmTextSetString(text_output, "Specify a search pattern.");
        XtFree(string); /* this we know is a string; free it */
        XtFree(search_pat); /* this may be "", XtFree() checks.. */
        return;
    }
    len = strlen(search_pat);

    /* start searching at current cursor position + 1 to find
     * the -next- occurrence of string.  we may be sitting on it.
     */
    pos = XmTextGetCursorPosition(text_w);
    for (p = &string[pos+1]; p = index(p, *search_pat); p++)
        if (!strncmp(p, search_pat, len)) {
            found = True;
            break;
        }
    if (!found) { /* didn't find pattern? */
        /* search from beginning till we've passed "pos" */
        for (p = string;
                (p = index(p, *search_pat)) && p - string <= pos; p++)
            if (!strncmp(p, search_pat, len)) {
```

Example 15-5. The search_text.c program (continued)

```
                found = True;
                break;
            }
    }
    if (!found)
        XmTextSetString(text_output, "Pattern not found.");
    else {
        pos = (XmTextPosition)(p - string);
        sprintf(buf, "Pattern found at position %ld.", pos);
        XmTextSetString(text_output, buf);
        XmTextSetInsertionPosition(text_w, pos);
    }
    XtFree(string);
    XtFree(search_pat);
}
```

In this example, a main ScrolledText object displays arbitrary text in which the user can search for arbitrary strings, as shown in Figure 15-4.

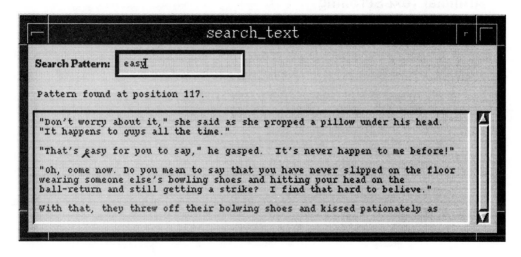

Figure 15-4. Output of search_text.c

Note that this program doesn't include code for loading a file, so if you want to experiment, you will first have to type or paste some text into the widget. Otherwise, you will see the message "No text to search." At any rate, once there is some text to search, type a string pattern in the "Search Pattern" Text widget and press RETURN to activate the search. The main text is searched starting at the position immediately following the current cursor position. If the pattern isn't found by the time the end of the Text's string is reached, the searching resumes at the beginning of the Text widget and continues until either the pattern is found or the original position is reached. If the pattern is found, the insertion point is moved to that location; otherwise, an error message is printed and the insertion cursor does not move.

Parenthetically speaking, you might notice that the `text_output` widget is also a Text widget. However, by setting the shadow thickness to 0 and setting its sensitivity to `False`, the widget looks (and acts) just like a Label widget. The user cannot edit or make selections on the widget's text, and the borders are not typical for other Text widgets. We demonstrate this not to advocate such usage, but to point out the versatility of this widget class.

When experimenting with Example 15-5, try selecting a large amount of text from another window on the screen (perhaps from an *xterm*) and pasting it into the main Text widget. Insert enough text so that the visible text is less than the widget's total contents. Now, search repeatedly for a frequently-occurring pattern (continue to press RETURN). You'll notice that as each occurrence of the pattern is found, the Text widget may automatically scroll to bring the new cursor position into view. This is the default action controlled by `XmNauto-ShowCursorPosition`. When set to `False`, the ScrolledWindow will not scroll to compensate for the cursor's invisibility. This resource has a similar effect on single-line Text widgets. That is, while text does not scroll vertically, single-line Text and TextField widgets may scroll their displays horizontally to display the insertion cursor.

15.4.1 Artificial Text Scrolling

We can artificially scroll Text widgets to any particular position in the text stream by setting the cursor position and then calling `XmTextShowPosition( )`. To scroll directly to the end of the Text widget, you need to scroll directly to the last position of the widget:

```
XmTextShowPosition(text_w, XmTextGetLastPosition(text_w));
```

Relative scrolling can be accomplished using the function `XmTextScroll( )`:

```
void
XmTextScroll(text_w, n)
    Widget text_w;
    int    n;
```

A positive **n** causes a ScrolledText object to scroll upward **n** lines while a negative value causes downward scrolling.

15.4.2 Text Replacement

The next logical step from a function that searches for text is one that performs "search and replace." To accomplish this, we use the Motif function `XmTextReplace( )`:

```
void
XmTextReplace(text_w, frompos, topos, value)
    Widget          text_w;
    XmTextPosition  frompos, topos;
    char            *value;
```

This function replaces the text in the Text widget starting at `frompos` up to and including the position `topos` with the text in `value`. If `value` is NULL or an empty string, the text between the two positions is simply deleted. To remove the entire text of the widget, call `XmTextSetString( )` with a NULL string as the text value.

The **XmTextReplace( )** function would fit in well in Example 15-5 since we already know the **frompos** and **topos** values. We only need to add a new Text widget that prompts for replacement text. Example 15-6 shows the new function, **search_and_replace( )**.

Example 15-6. The search_and_replace() function

```
    ...
    replace_w = XtVaCreateManagedWidget("replace_text",
        xmTextWidgetClass, rowcol_h, NULL);
    ...
void
search_and_replace()
{
    char *search_pat, *p, *string, *new_pat, buf[ 32 ];
    XmTextPosition pos;
    int search_len, pattern_len;
    int nfound = 0;

    if (!(string = XmTextGetString(text_w)) || !*string) {
        XmTextSetString(text_output, "No text to search.");
        XtFree(string);
        return;
    }
    if (!(search_pat = XmTextGetString(search_w)) || !*search_pat) {
        XmTextSetString(text_output, "Specify a search pattern.");
        XtFree(search_pat);
        XtFree(string);
        return;
    }
    new_pat = XmTextGetString(replace_w);
    search_len = strlen(search_pat);
    pattern_len = strlen(new_pat);

    /* start at beginning and search entire Text widget */
    for (p = string; p = index(p, *search_pat); p++)
        if (!strncmp(p, search_pat, search_len)) {
            nfound++;
            /* get the position where pattern was found */
            pos = (XmTextPosition)(p-string);
            /* replace the text from our position + strlen(new_pat) */
            XmTextReplace(text_w, pos, pos + search_len, new_pat);
            /* "string" has changed -- we must get the new version */
          XtFree(string);
          string = XmTextGetString(text_w);
            /* continue search for next pattern -after- replacement */
            p = &string[pos + pattern_len];
        }
    if (!nfound)
        strcpy(buf, "Pattern not found.");
    else
        sprintf(buf, "Made %d replacements.", nfound);
    XmTextSetString(text_output, buf);
    XtFree(string);
    XtFree(search_pat);
    XtFree(new_pat);
}
```

Here, the pattern search starts at the beginning of the text and continues throughout the entire contents of the widget. In this case, we are not interested in the cursor position of the Text widget, nor do we attempt to move it. The main loop of the function only needs to find the specified pattern and replace each occurrence with the new text. Once replaced, the widget's text needs to be reread since the old value is no longer valid. This must occur at each iteration of the loop.

15.5 Text Clipboard Functions

All forms of the Text widget have convenience routines that support communication with the clipboard. Using these functions, you can implement *cut, copy,* and *paste* functionality as well as support communication with other windows or applications on the desktop. If you are not familiar with the clipboard and how it works, see Chapter 18, *The Clipboard*. Briefly, the clipboard is one of three transient locations where arbitrary data (such as text) can be stored so other windows or applications can copy the data. For Text widgets, we are only interested in copying data of type *text* and providing visual feedback within the Text widget. The Text widget sends and receives data from all three of these locations depending on the interface style you are using.

As described earlier in this chapter, a typical action for selecting text using the mouse is the "click-drag" technique. When text is selected, it is rendered in reverse video and automatically copied into the *primary selection*. The user can then *paste* text from the primary selection into any Text widget (or other application that accepts text input from selections) on the desktop by clicking the middle mouse button. The insertion cursor is moved to the location of the middle mouse button click and the data is automatically copied into the Text widget at the insertion cursor's position.

All this clipboard functionality works by default within the Text widget. (Your application needn't do anything to support it.) However, these actions act solely on the primary selection and not the clipboard selection. Furthermore, they allow you only to copy the data to and from the primary selection. You can also type over the selection, but you can't cut it (prior to pasting it) or clear it.

To provide these additional features, most applications provide other user-interface controls such as a pulldown menu and appropriate menu items that call Text widget cut and paste routines. These routines store text on the clipboard, and allow the user to move text between the clipboard and the primary selection as well as between windows that are interested only in the clipboard selection. The typical menu entries include *Cut, Copy, Paste,* and *Clear*.

Example 15-7 demonstrates how these common editing actions can be done. The program *cut_paste.c* creates a MenuBar with a single "Edit" Pulldown menu.

Example 15-7. The cut_paste.c program

```
/* cut_paste.c -- demonstrate the XmText* functions that handle
 * clipboard operations.  These functions are convenience routines
 * that relieve the programmer of the need to use clipboard functions.
 * The functionality of these routines already exists in the Text
 * widget, yet it is common to place such features in the interface
```

Example 15-7. The cut_paste.c program (continued)

```
 * via the MenuBar's "Edit" pulldown menu.
 */
#include <Xm/Text.h>
#include <Xm/LabelG.h>
#include <Xm/PushBG.h>
#include <Xm/RowColumn.h>
#include <Xm/MainW.h>

Widget text_w, text_output;

main(argc, argv)
int argc;
char *argv[ ];
{
    Widget        toplevel, main_w, menubar, rowcol_v, rowcol_h, pb;
    XtAppContext  app;
    int           i;
    void          cut_paste();
    XmString      label, cut, clear, copy, paste;
    Arg           args[5];

    toplevel = XtVaAppInitialize(&app, "Demos",
        NULL, 0, &argc, argv, NULL, NULL);

    main_w = XtVaCreateWidget("main_w",
        xmMainWindowWidgetClass, toplevel, NULL);

    /* Create a simple MenuBar that contains a single menu */
    label = XmStringCreateSimple("Edit");
    menubar = XmVaCreateSimpleMenuBar(main_w, "main_w",
        XmVaCASCADEBUTTON, label, 'E',
        NULL);
    XmStringFree(label);

    cut = XmStringCreateSimple("Cut");       /* create a simple   */
    copy = XmStringCreateSimple("Copy");     /* pulldown menu that */
    clear = XmStringCreateSimple("Clear");   /* has these menu     */
    paste = XmStringCreateSimple("Paste");   /* items in it.       */
    XmVaCreateSimplePulldownMenu(menubar, "edit_menu", 0, cut_paste,
        XmVaPUSHBUTTON, cut, 'C', NULL, NULL,
        XmVaPUSHBUTTON, copy, 'o', NULL, NULL,
        XmVaPUSHBUTTON, paste, 'P', NULL, NULL,
        XmVaSEPARATOR,
        XmVaPUSHBUTTON, clear, 'l', NULL, NULL,
        NULL);
    XmStringFree(cut);
    XmStringFree(clear);
    XmStringFree(copy);
    XmStringFree(paste);

    XtManageChild(menubar);

    /* create a standard vertical RowColumn... */
    rowcol_v = XtVaCreateWidget("rowcol_v",
        xmRowColumnWidgetClass, main_w, NULL);

    text_output = XtVaCreateManagedWidget("text_out",
        xmTextWidgetClass, rowcol_v,
        XmNeditable,                False,
        XmNcursorPositionVisible, False,
```

Example 15-7. The cut_paste.c program (continued)

```
            XmNshadowThickness,        0,
            XmNsensitive,              False,
            NULL);

        XtSetArg(args[0], XmNrows,         10);
        XtSetArg(args[1], XmNcolumns,      80);
        XtSetArg(args[2], XmNeditMode,     XmMULTI_LINE_EDIT);
        XtSetArg(args[3], XmNscrollHorizontal,  False);
        XtSetArg(args[4], XmNwordWrap,     True);
        text_w = XmCreateScrolledText(rowcol_v, "text_w", args, 5);
        XtManageChild(text_w);

        XtManageChild(rowcol_v);
        XtManageChild(main_w);

        XtRealizeWidget(toplevel);
        XtAppMainLoop(app);
    }

    /* the callback routine for the items in the edit menu */
    void
    cut_paste(widget, num)
    Widget widget;  /* the menu item (pushbutton) that was selected */
    int num;        /* the menu item number */
    {
        Boolean result = True;

        switch (num) {
            case 0 : result = XmTextCut(text_w, CurrentTime); break;
            case 1 : result = XmTextCopy(text_w, CurrentTime); break;
            case 2 : result = XmTextPaste(text_w);
            case 3 : XmTextClearSelection(text_w, CurrentTime); break;
        }
        if (result == False)
            XmTextSetString(text_output, "There is no selection.");
        else
            XmTextSetString(text_output, NULL);
    }
```

The application first creates a MainWindow widget because it is the only object that may contain a MenuBar. The MenuBar and the pulldown menu are both created using their respective convenience routines described in Chapter 4, *The Main Window*, and Chapter 16, *Menus*. The output of *cut_paste.c* is shown in Figure 15-5.

Again, you will have to enter some text, or select it from another window if you want to experiment with this application. The callback function for all the menu items in the Edit menu is `cut_paste()`. The rest of the main window contains the same Text widgets we've used in previous examples. However, the user's ability to interact with the clipboard is now available through the **Edit** pulldown menu.

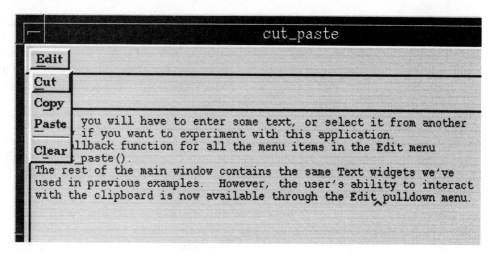

Figure 15-5. Output of cut_paste.c

The `cut_paste()` function makes use of four Text convenience routines. It can be very tricky how these work because of the presence of the primary selection, so pay close attention:

```
Boolean
XmTextCut(text_w, cut_time)
    Widget    text_w;
    Time      cut_time;

Boolean
XmTextCopy(text_w, copy_time)
    Widget text_w;
    Time    copy_time;

Boolean
XmTextPaste(text_w)
    Widget text_w;

void
XmTextClearSelection(text_w, clear_time)
    Widget text_w;
    Time    clear_time;
```

Both `XmTextCopy()` and `XmTextCut()` copy the text that is selected in the Text widget and place it in the clipboard. The selection includes text that may be in either the primary or the clipboard selection. Thus, if the user selects text using the mouse interface (i.e., click and drag) the text is copied from the primary selection. However, the text may also have been selected programmatically through other clipboard functions discussed later. Once the user selects the **Copy** button from the **Edit** menu, the text will be copied into the clipboard selection.

XmTextCut( ) is similar to **XmTextCopy( )** except that the holder of the selection is instructed to delete the text that it used as a copy in the selection.[10] The **copy_time** and **cut_time** should probably be set to **CurrentTime** to avoid collisions with other clipboard operations that might be occurring at the same time. Each function returns **True** if the operation was successful; **False** may be returned if there is no selected text or an error occurs in attempting to communicate with the clipboard.

XmTextPaste( ) gets the current selection from the clipboard and inserts it wherever the insertion cursor happens to be. If there is text already selected in the Text widget (presumably because it is a PRIMARY text selection), that text is replaced by the selection from the clipboard. Like the other two functions, **XmTextPaste( )** returns a **True** if there is a selection in the clipboard and it can be retrieved from the clipboard.

XmTextClearSelection( ) deselects the text selection in the **text_w**. If nothing is selected, nothing happens (there is no audio or visual feedback and the function doesn't return anything special). The location of the text selection is transparent—both the primary and the clipboard selections are cleared if the specified Text widget is holding either of them.

One function that was not used and is not covered elsewhere in this chapter but is worth noting is **XmTextRemove( )**. This function is like **XmTextCut( )** in that it removes selected text from a Text widget, but it does not place the removed text into a selection area. The form of the function is as follows:

```
void
XmTextRemove(text_w)
    Widget text_w;
```

15.5.1 Text Selection Details

You can get the details about the selected text from a Text widget using **XmTextGetSelection( )** and **XmTextGetSelectionPosition( )**. These routines take the following forms:

```
char *
XmTextGetSelection(text_w)
    Widget text_w;
```

XmTextGetSelection( ) returns allocated data containing the selected text. This text must be freed using **XtFree( )** when you are through with it. NULL is returned if there is no text selected in the specified Text widget:

---

[10] This is accomplished by sending a "DELETE" protocol to the window holding the selection. Note, this is not the same as a "WM_DELETE" protocol, which indicates that the window is being deleted. See Chapter 17, *Interacting with the Window Manager*, for more information on Window Manager protocols.

```
Boolean
XmTextGetSelectionPosition(text_w, &left, &right)
    Widget          text_w;
    XmTextPosition *left, *right;
```

If **XmTextGetSelectionPosition( )** returns **True**, the values for **left** and **right** are filled in with the positions where the beginning and ending of the selected text exists. If **False** is returned, **text_w** does not contain any selected text, and the values for **left** and **right** are undefined.

None of the Motif functions deal with secondary text selection since it is so transient (the action is completed before the application can do anything about it). However, the **XmNmodifyVerifyCallback** function(s) can intercept text that is stuffed into the widget and modify or even veto the insertions.

15.5.2 Modifying the Selection Mechanism

While it is unlikely that you would need to alter either of the selection methods (click-drag or multi-click), the one more likely to be altered is the click-selection method. The default selection mechanism in the Text widget is as shown in Table 15-1.

Table 15-1. Default Selection Actions for Multiple Clicks

Action	Feedback
Single click	Resets insertion caret to position.
Double click	Selects a word (bounded by whitespace).
Triple click	Selects a line (bounded by newlines).
Quadruple click	Selects entire text.

This table can be modified using the resource **XmNselectionArray**. This resource corresponds to an array of size **XmNselectionArrayCount** where each element in the array is of type **XmTextScanType**. This is an enumerated type whose values may be one of the following:

```
typedef enum {
    XmSELECT_POSITION,
    XmSELECT_WHITESPACE, [11]
    XmSELECT_WORD,
    XmSELECT_LINE,
    XmSELECT_ALL,
    XmSELECT_PARAGRAPH
} XmTextScanType;
```

---

[11] **XmSELECT_WHITESPACE** is technically unsupported.

When a new **XmNselectionArray** is installed, each successive button click selects the text according to its corresponding index into the array. The default array maps to the entries in Table 15-1 and is defined with the following values:

```
XmSELECT_POSITION
XmSELECT_WORD
XmSELECT_LINE
XmSELECT_ALL
```

Usually, the entries in the table should be in ascending order so as not to confuse the user. That is, it would not be a good idea to have a single-button-click select everything and a double-button-click select a word.

For example, an acceptable change to this array might be as follows:

```
XmTextScanType selection_array[5];

selection_array[0] = XmSELECT_POSITION;
selection_array[1] = XmSELECT_WORD;
selection_array[2] = XmSELECT_LINE;
selection_array[3] = XmSELECT_PARAGRAPH;
selection_array[4] = XmSELECT_ALL;

XtVaSetValues(text_w,
    XmNselectionArray,       selectionArray,
    XmNselectionArrayCount, 5,
    NULL);
```

The maximum time interval that must occur between button clicks is determined by the resource **multiClickTime**. This is not a Motif resource; it is set for all applications in X because it is maintained by the X server. Its value can be gotten via **XtGetMultiClick-Time( )**. Similarly, the value can be changed using **XtSetMultiClickTime( )**. For more discussion on this value, see Chapter 11, *Labels and Buttons*.

You can alter the drag-select method with the resource **XmNselectThreshold**. This resource specifies the number of pixels of motion that is required to determine that the next character should be selected. The default value of 5 means that the user must move the mouse at least 5 pixels before the Text widget determines if the next character has been selected. If you are using extremely large fonts, you may want to increase this value in order to cut down on the number of calculations necessary to determine if another character should be added (or deleted) from the selection.

15.6 A Complete Editor

Before we continue with the chapter, let's take a short time-out to introduce an example that combines all the information we've addressed so far. The sections that follow will discuss Text widget callback routines and some more advanced material.

The example we are going to look at is a full-featured text editor that was built from examples used earlier in this chapter. In fact, virtually every function and code fragment we've used has been modified in some way to produce the program in Example 15-8. You should be able to recognize much of the code. The parts you do not recognize should be clear from the context in which it is used. The output of the program is shown in Figure 15-6.

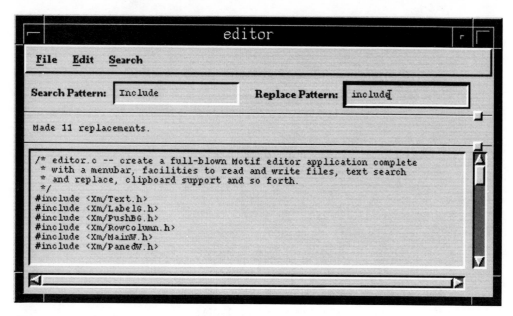

Figure 15-6. Output of editor.c

Example 15-8. The editor.c program

```
/* editor.c -- create a full-blown Motif editor application complete
 * with a menubar, facilities to read and write files, text search
 * and replace, clipboard support and so forth.
 */
#include <Xm/Text.h>
#include <Xm/LabelG.h>
#include <Xm/PushBG.h>
#include <Xm/RowColumn.h>
#include <Xm/MainW.h>
#include <Xm/PanedW.h>
#include <Xm/FileSB.h>
#include <X11/Xos.h>
#include <stdio.h>
#include <sys/types.h>
#include <sys/stat.h>

Widget text_w, search_w, replace_w, text_output;

main(argc, argv)
int argc;
char *argv[ ];
{
    XtAppContext    app;
    Widget          toplevel, main_w, menubar, pane, rowcol, pb;
    void            file_cb(), cut_paste(), search_cb();
    Arg             args[5];
    XmString        new, save, quit, quit_acc, file, edit, cut,
                    clear, copy, paste, search, next, find, replace;

    toplevel = XtVaAppInitialize(&app, "Demos",
```

Example 15-8. The editor.c program (continued)

```
        NULL, 0, &argc, argv, NULL, NULL);

    main_w = XtVaCreateWidget("main_w",
        xmMainWindowWidgetClass, toplevel, NULL);

    /* Create a simple MenuBar that contains three menus */
    file = XmStringCreateSimple("File");
    edit = XmStringCreateSimple("Edit");
    search = XmStringCreateSimple("Search");
    menubar = XmVaCreateSimpleMenuBar(main_w, "menubar",
        XmVaCASCADEBUTTON, file, 'F',
        XmVaCASCADEBUTTON, edit, 'E',
        XmVaCASCADEBUTTON, search, 'S',
        NULL);
    XmStringFree(file);
    XmStringFree(edit);
    XmStringFree(search);

    /* First menu is the File menu -- callback is file_cb() */
    new = XmStringCreateSimple("New ...");
    save = XmStringCreateSimple("Save ...");
    quit = XmStringCreateSimple("Quit");
    quit_acc = XmStringCreateSimple("Ctrl-C");
    XmVaCreateSimplePulldownMenu(menubar, "file_menu", 0, file_cb,
        XmVaPUSHBUTTON, new, 'N', NULL, NULL,
        XmVaPUSHBUTTON, save, 'S', NULL, NULL,
        XmVaSEPARATOR,
        XmVaPUSHBUTTON, quit, 'Q', "Ctrl<Key>c", quit_acc,
        NULL);
    XmStringFree(new);
    XmStringFree(save);
    XmStringFree(quit);
    XmStringFree(quit_acc);

    /* ...create the "Edit" menu --  callback is cut_paste() */
    cut = XmStringCreateSimple("Cut");       /* create a simple     */
    copy = XmStringCreateSimple("Copy");     /* pulldown menu that   */
    clear = XmStringCreateSimple("Clear");   /* has these menu       */
    paste = XmStringCreateSimple("Paste");   /* items in it.         */
    XmVaCreateSimplePulldownMenu(menubar, "edit_menu", 1, cut_paste,
        XmVaPUSHBUTTON, cut, 'C', NULL, NULL,
        XmVaPUSHBUTTON, copy, 'o', NULL, NULL,
        XmVaPUSHBUTTON, paste, 'P', NULL, NULL,
        XmVaSEPARATOR,
        XmVaPUSHBUTTON, clear, 'l', NULL, NULL,
        NULL);
    XmStringFree(cut);
    XmStringFree(copy);
    XmStringFree(paste);

    /* create the "Search" menu -- callback is search_cb() */
    next = XmStringCreateSimple("Find Next");
    find = XmStringCreateSimple("Show All");
    replace = XmStringCreateSimple("Replace Text");
    XmVaCreateSimplePulldownMenu(menubar, "search_menu", 2, search_cb,
        XmVaPUSHBUTTON, next, 'F', NULL, NULL,
        XmVaPUSHBUTTON, find, 'S', NULL, NULL,
        XmVaPUSHBUTTON, replace, 'R', NULL, NULL,
```

Example 15-8. The editor.c program (continued)

```
            XmVaSEPARATOR,
            XmVaPUSHBUTTON, clear, 'C', NULL, NULL,
            NULL);
    XmStringFree(next);
    XmStringFree(find);
    XmStringFree(replace);
    XmStringFree(clear);

    XtManageChild(menubar);

    /* create a standard vertical PanedWindow... */
    pane = XtVaCreateWidget("pane",
        xmPanedWindowWidgetClass, main_w, NULL);

    /* create horizontal RowColumn inside the pane... */
    rowcol = XtVaCreateWidget("rowcol",
        xmRowColumnWidgetClass, pane,
        XmNorientation,  XmHORIZONTAL,
        XmNpacking,      XmPACK_TIGHT,
        NULL);
    /* Create two Text widgets with Labels... */
    XtVaCreateManagedWidget("Search Pattern:",
        xmLabelGadgetClass, rowcol, NULL);
    search_w = XtVaCreateManagedWidget("search_text",
        xmTextWidgetClass, rowcol, NULL);
    XtVaCreateManagedWidget("    Replace Pattern:",
        xmLabelGadgetClass, rowcol, NULL);
    replace_w = XtVaCreateManagedWidget("replace_text",
        xmTextWidgetClass, rowcol, NULL);
    XtManageChild(rowcol);

    text_output = XtVaCreateManagedWidget("text_out",
        xmTextWidgetClass, pane,
        XmNeditable,             False,
        XmNcursorPositionVisible, False,
        XmNshadowThickness,      0,
        XmNsensitive,            False,
        NULL);

    XtSetArg(args[0], XmNrows,    10);
    XtSetArg(args[1], XmNcolumns, 80);
    XtSetArg(args[2], XmNeditMode, XmMULTI_LINE_EDIT);
    text_w = XmCreateScrolledText(pane, "text_w", args, 3);
    XtManageChild(text_w);

    XtManageChild(pane);
    XtManageChild(main_w);

    XtRealizeWidget(toplevel);
    XtAppMainLoop(app);
}
/* callback routine for "Ok" button in FileSelectionDialogs */
void
open_file(dialog, save, cbs)
Widget dialog;
int save;        /* actually, item_no from "new" or "save" */
XmFileSelectionBoxCallbackStruct *cbs;
{
```

Text Widgets

Example 15-8. The editor.c program (continued)

```
    char buf[BUFSIZ], *filename, *text;
    struct stat statb;
    long len;
    FILE *fp;

    if (!XmStringGetLtoR(cbs->value,
        XmSTRING_DEFAULT_CHARSET, &filename))
        return; /* must have been an internal error */

    if (!*filename) {
        XtFree(filename);
        XBell(XtDisplay(text_w), 50);
        XmTextSetString(text_output, "Choose a file.");
        return; /* nothing typed */
    }

    if (save) {
        if (!(fp = fopen(filename, "w"))) {
            perror(filename);
            sprintf(buf, "Can't save to %s.", filename);
            XmTextSetString(text_output, buf);
            XtFree(filename);
            return;
        }
        /* saving -- get text from Text widget... */
        text = XmTextGetString(text_w);
        len = XmTextGetLastPosition(text_w);
        /* write it to file (check for error) */
        if (fwrite(text, sizeof(char), len, fp) != len)
            strcpy(buf, "Warning: did not write entire file!");
        else {
            /* make sure a newline terminates file */
            if (text[len-1] != '\n')
                fputc(fp, '\n');
            sprintf(buf, "Saved %ld bytes to %s.", len, filename);
        }
    } else {
        /* make sure the file is a regular text file and open it */
        if (stat(filename, &statb) == -1 ||
                (statb.st_mode & S_IFMT) != S_IFREG ||
                !(fp = fopen(filename, "r"))) {
            perror(filename);
            sprintf(buf, "Can't read %s.", filename);
            XmTextSetString(text_output, buf);
            XtFree(filename);
            return;
        }
        /* put the contents of the file in the Text widget by
         * allocating enough space for the entire file, reading the
         * file into the space, and using XmTextSetString() to show
         * the file.
         */
        len = statb.st_size;
        if (!(text = XtMalloc((unsigned)(len+1)))) /* +1 for NULL */
            sprintf(buf, "%s: XtMalloc(%ld) failed", len, filename);
        else {
            if (fread(text, sizeof(char), len, fp) != len)
```

Example 15-8. The editor.c program (continued)

```
                    sprintf(buf, "Warning: did not read entire file!");
            else
                    sprintf(buf, "Loaded %ld bytes from %s.",
                        len, filename);
            text[ len ] = 0; /* NULL-terminate */
            XmTextSetString(text_w, text);
        }
    }
    XmTextSetString(text_output, buf); /* purge output message */

    /* free all allocated space. */
    XtFree(text);
    XtFree(filename);
    fclose(fp);
}
/* a menu item from the "File" pulldown menu was selected */
void
file_cb(w, item_no, cbs)
Widget w;
int item_no;   /* pulldown menu item number */
XmAnyCallbackStruct *cbs;   /* unused here */
{
    static Widget open_dialog, save_dialog;
    Widget        dialog = NULL;
    XmString      str, title;

    if (item_no == 2)
        exit(0);

    if (item_no == 0 && open_dialog)
        dialog = open_dialog;
    else if (item_no == 1 && save_dialog)
        dialog = save_dialog;

    if (dialog) {
        XtManageChild(dialog);
        /* make sure that dialog is raised to top of window stack */
        XMapRaised(XtDisplay(dialog), XtWindow(XtParent(dialog)));
        return;
    }
    dialog = XmCreateFileSelectionDialog(text_w, "Files", NULL, 0);
    XtAddCallback(dialog, XmNcancelCallback, XtUnmanageChild, NULL);
    XtAddCallback(dialog, XmNokCallback, open_file, item_no);
    if (item_no == 0) {
        str = XmStringCreateSimple("Open");
        title = XmStringCreateSimple("Open File");
        open_dialog = dialog;
    } else {
        str = XmStringCreateSimple("Save");
        title = XmStringCreateSimple("Save File");
        save_dialog = dialog;
    }
    XtVaSetValues(dialog,
        XmNokLabelString, str,
        XmNdialogTitle,   title,
        NULL);
    XmStringFree(str);
```

Example 15-8. The editor.c program (continued)

```
    XmStringFree(title);
    XtManageChild(dialog);
}

/* a menu item from the "Search" pulldown menu was selected */
void
search_cb(w, item_no, cbs)
Widget w;
int item_no;  /* pulldown menu item number */
XmAnyCallbackStruct *cbs;  /* unused here */
{
#define FIND_NEXT 0
#define FIND_ALL  1
#define REPLACE   2
#define CLEAR     3
    char *search_pat, *p, *string, *new_pat, buf[32];
    XmTextPosition pos = 0;
    int len, nfound = 0;
    int search_len, pattern_len;

    if (item_no == CLEAR) {
        pos = XmTextGetLastPosition(text_w);
        XmTextSetHighlight(text_w, 0, pos, XmHIGHLIGHT_NORMAL);
        return;
    }

    if (!(string = XmTextGetString(text_w)) || !*string) {
        XmTextSetString(text_output, "No text to search.");
        return;
    }
    if (!(search_pat = XmTextGetString(search_w)) || !*search_pat) {
        XmTextSetString(text_output, "Specify a search pattern.");
        XtFree(string);
        return;
    }

    new_pat = XmTextGetString(replace_w);
    search_len = strlen(search_pat);
    pattern_len = strlen(new_pat);

    /* start searching at current cursor position + 1 */
    if (item_no == FIND_NEXT)
        pos = XmTextGetCursorPosition(text_w) + 1;
    for (p = &string[pos]; p = index(p, *search_pat); p++)
        if (!strncmp(p, search_pat, search_len)) {
            nfound++;
            /* get the position where pattern was found */
            pos = (XmTextPosition)(p-string);
            if (item_no == REPLACE) {
                /* replace the text position + strlen(new_pat) */
                XmTextReplace(text_w, pos, pos + search_len, new_pat);
                /* "string" has changed -- get the new value */
            XtFree(string);
            string = XmTextGetString(text_w);
                /* continue search -after- replacement */
                p = &string[pos + pattern_len];
            } else if (item_no == FIND_ALL)
                XmTextSetHighlight(text_w, pos, pos+search_len,
```

Example 15-8. The editor.c program (continued)

```
                        XmHIGHLIGHT_SELECTED);
            else
                break;
        }
    if (item_no == FIND_NEXT && nfound == 0) {
        /* search from beginning till we've passed "pos" */
        for (p = string; p = index(p, *search_pat); p++)
            if (p - string > pos ||
                    !strncmp(p, search_pat, search_len)) {
                nfound++;
                break;
            }
    }
    if (nfound == 0)
        XmTextSetString(text_output, "Pattern not found.");
    else {
        switch (item_no) {
            case FIND_NEXT :
                pos = (XmTextPosition)(p - string);
                sprintf(buf, "Pattern found at position %ld.", pos);
                XmTextSetInsertionPosition(text_w, pos);
                break;
            case FIND_ALL :
                sprintf(buf, "Found %d occurrences.", nfound);
                break;
            case REPLACE :
            default :
                sprintf(buf, "Made %d replacements.", nfound);
        }
        XmTextSetString(text_output, buf);
    }
    XtFree(string);
    XtFree(search_pat);
    XtFree(new_pat);
}
/* the callback routine for the items in the edit menu */
void
cut_paste(widget, num)
Widget widget;    /* the menu item (pushbutton) that was selected */
int num;          /* the menu item number */
{
    Boolean result = True;

    switch (num) {
        case 0 : result = XmTextCut(text_w, CurrentTime); break;
        case 1 : result = XmTextCopy(text_w, CurrentTime); break;
        case 2 : result = XmTextPaste(text_w); break;
        case 3 : XmTextClearSelection(text_w, CurrentTime); break;
    }
    if (result == False)
        XmTextSetString(text_output, "There is no selection.");
    else
        XmTextSetString(text_output, NULL);
}
```

15.7 Single-line Text Widget Callbacks

Fundamentally, Text widget callback routines are no different from callbacks used in any other Motif widget. However, Text widget callbacks may be invoked rather frequently, especially those that monitor keyboard input. In the next few sections, we will introduce several of the callback routines for the Text widget. We begin by exploring the basic callback routines most commonly used for single-line Text widgets.

The first callback we're going to examine is **XmNactivateCallback**. This callback is invoked when the user presses ⟪RETURN⟫ in a TextField widget or a single-line Text widget. (It is never called for multiline editing widgets.) Example 15-9 shows a template for how the callback resource and corresponding function can be used.

Example 15-9. How XmNactivateCallback works for Text widgets

```
#include <Xm/TextF.h>

    void my_func();
    ...
    text_w = XtVaCreateManagedWidget("text_w", xmTextFieldWidgetClass, parent,
        ...
        NULL);
    XtAddCallback(text_w, XmNactivateCallback, my_func, data);
    ...

void
my_func(text_w, data, cbs)
Widget      text_w;
XtPointer   data;
XmAnyCallbackStruct *cbs;
{
    char *text_typed;

    text_typed = XmTextGetString(text_w);
    ...
    XtFree(text_typed);
}
```

The callback routine for **XmNactivateCallback** uses the common **XmAny-CallbackStruct** as the call_data (third) parameter to the function. The callback reason is always **XmCR_ACTIVATE**.

For example, as shown in Example 15-10, two callback functions are installed for some Text-Field widgets.

Example 15-10. The text_box.c program

```
/* text_box.c -- demonstrate simple use of XmNactivateCallback
 * for Text widgets.  Create a rowcolumn that has rows of Form
 * widgets, each containing a Label and a Text widget.  When
 * the user presses Return, print the value of the text widget
 * and move the focus to the next text widget.
 */
#include <Xm/TextF.h>
#include <Xm/LabelG.h>
#include <Xm/Form.h>
```

Example 15-10. The text_box.c program (continued)

```
#include <Xm/RowColumn.h>

char *labels[ ] = { "Name:", "Address:", "City:", "State:", "Zip:" };

main(argc, argv)
int argc;
char *argv[ ];
{
    Widget         toplevel, text_w, form, rowcol;
    XtAppContext   app;
    int            i;
    void           print_result();

    toplevel = XtVaAppInitialize(&app, "Demos",
        NULL, 0, &argc, argv, NULL, NULL);

    rowcol = XtVaCreateWidget("rowcol",
        xmRowColumnWidgetClass, toplevel, NULL);

    for (i = 0; i < XtNumber(labels); i++) {
        form = XtVaCreateWidget("form", xmFormWidgetClass, rowcol,
            XmNfractionBase,    10,
            NULL);
        XtVaCreateManagedWidget(labels[i],
            xmLabelGadgetClass, form,
            XmNtopAttachment,     XmATTACH_FORM,
            XmNbottomAttachment,  XmATTACH_FORM,
            XmNleftAttachment,    XmATTACH_FORM,
            XmNrightAttachment,   XmATTACH_POSITION,
            XmNrightPosition,     3,
            XmNalignment,         XmALIGNMENT_END,
            NULL);
        text_w = XtVaCreateManagedWidget("text_w",
            xmTextFieldWidgetClass, form,
            XmNtraversalOn,       True,
            XmNrightAttachment,   XmATTACH_FORM,
            XmNleftAttachment,    XmATTACH_POSITION,
            XmNleftPosition,      4,
            NULL);

        /* When user hits return, print the label+value of text_w */
        XtAddCallback(text_w, XmNactivateCallback,
            print_result, labels[i]);

        /* Also advance focus to next Text widget, which is in the
         * next Tab Group because each Text widget is in a Form by
         * itself.  If there were all in the same manager, we'd just
         * use XmTRAVERSE_NEXT instead.
         */
        XtAddCallback(text_w, XmNactivateCallback,
            XmProcessTraversal, XmTRAVERSE_NEXT_TAB_GROUP);
        XtManageChild(form);
    }
    XtManageChild(rowcol);

    XtRealizeWidget(toplevel);
    XtAppMainLoop(app);
}

/* callback for when the user his return in the Text widget */
```

Example 15-10. The text_box.c program (continued)

```
void
print_result(text_w, label)
Widget text_w;
char  *label;
{
    char *value = XmTextFieldGetString(text_w);

    printf("%s %s\n", label, value);
    XtFree(value);
}
```

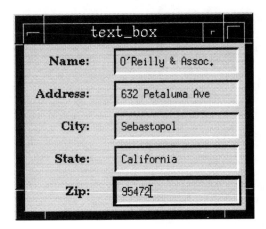

Figure 15-7. Output of text_box.c

The program displays a "Form" consisting of labels and fill-in text fields. This is done by creating a RowColumn widget that manages several rows of Form widgets, each containing a Label and a Text widget, as shown in Figure 15-7.[12]

The user enters values for each field in the form and then presses RETURN . Here, the entry is "accepted" and the callback routines are invoked. Two activation callbacks are invoked: the first calls **print_result( )** and the second advances the keyboard focus to the next TextField widget. The **print_result( )** function is really a place holder for where a real application's callback would be, so let's focus on the second callback. The intent of the RETURN key, in this case, is also to advance the keyboard focus to the next Text field, but this won't happen automatically. We must move the keyboard focus manually using **Xm-ProcessTraversal( )**. This function takes a widget and a traversal-direction as its two

---

[12] The term *form* is used because this program is intended to resemble a "data sheet" of sorts; it should not be confused with the **Form** widget.

parameters, so this model conveniently fits into the way callback function parameters are called. Thus, the following call does the trick:

```
XtAddCallback(text_w, XmNactivateCallback,
    XmProcessTraversal, XmTRAVERSE_NEXT_TAB_GROUP);
```

Just to clarify why this works, recall how Tab Groups work. Each Manager widget is a Tab Group in and of itself; thus, each Form widget is a Tab Group. If all the Text widgets were in the same Form widget together, then we could use `XmTRAVERSE_NEXT` for `XmProcess-Traversal( )`. But since each Text widget is in a separate Form widget, there is only one item within each Tab Group. Thus, we must move to the next Tab Group rather than to the next item in the same Tab Group.

15.7.1 Activation Callbacks in Dialogs

Since Text widgets are frequently active participants in Motif dialog widgets, we should mention that the Motif toolkit introduces some automation of the `XmNactivate-Callback` resource in some cases. When Text or TextField widgets are part of the prede-fined Motif dialogs, the activate callback for the Text widget is automatically hooked up to the **Ok** button in that dialog. Whether the user presses $\boxed{\text{RETURN}}$ in the TextField widget or selects the **Ok** button with the mouse, the same callback is called.

This "convenience" often confuses unsuspecting programmers who are unaware of this and find that their callbacks are being called twice. Ironically, others who *are* aware of this auto-mation subsequently overestimate what the Motif toolkit is going to do and expect their call-backs to be invoked when they aren't supposed to be. The point is that you should be careful with these callback functions and make sure that they are getting invoked when you want or need them to be. See Chapter 6, *Selection Dialogs*, for examples of this feature in Selection-Dialogs, PromptDialogs, and CommandDialogs.

15.8 Text Modification Callbacks

In this section, we discuss the callback routines that can be used to monitor, enhance, or pre-vent text modification in Text widgets. Monitoring can occur either as the user types or if the text is changed elsewhere (e.g., with `XmTextInsert( )` or `XmTextReplace( )`). These callbacks are not limited to single-line or multiline editing modes and can be used in TextField widgets. One thing to keep in mind, however, is that text is modified by each key-stroke, so simple typing may cause the modification callbacks to be invoked rather fre-quently. You should also be very careful never to call `XtVaSetValues( )` on the widget being modified, since the widget's state is very unstable during these callbacks. New call-backs should not be added or deleted and resources should not be changed—including the `XmNvalue` of the Text widget. If a recursive loop occurs, you may get very unpredictable results.

There are two kinds of callbacks for text modification: `XmNvalueChangedCallback` is called after text has been modified (inserted or deleted), and `XmNmodifyVerify-Callback` is called before text is modified. Depending on your needs, you may use either or both callbacks on the same widget at the same time. The following sections address all these scenarios. Let's begin with the **XmNmodifyVerifyCallback** resource.

15.8.1 The ModifyVerify Callback

Installing an **XmNmodifyVerifyCallback** function is useful if you plan on monitoring or changing the user's input before it actually gets inserted into a Text widget. In Example 15-11, we demonstrate how we can use a modify-callback function to convert text to upper-case.

Example 15-11. The allcaps.c program

```
/* allcaps.c -- demonstrate the XmNmodifyVerifyCallback for
 * Text widgets by using one to convert all typed input to
 * capital letters.
 */
#include <Xm/Text.h>
#include <Xm/LabelG.h>
#include <Xm/RowColumn.h>
#include <ctype.h>

void allcaps();

main(argc, argv)
int argc;
char *argv[ ];
{
    Widget        toplevel, text_w, rowcol;
    XtAppContext  app;

    toplevel = XtVaAppInitialize(&app, "Demos",
        NULL, 0, &argc, argv, NULL, NULL);

    rowcol = XtVaCreateWidget("rowcol",
        xmRowColumnWidgetClass, toplevel,
        XmNorientation, XmHORIZONTAL,
        NULL);

    XtVaCreateManagedWidget("Enter Text:",
        xmLabelGadgetClass, rowcol, NULL);
    text_w = XtVaCreateManagedWidget("text_w",
        xmTextWidgetClass, rowcol, NULL);

    XtAddCallback(text_w, XmNmodifyVerifyCallback, allcaps, NULL);

    XtManageChild(rowcol);
    XtRealizeWidget(toplevel);
    XtAppMainLoop(app);
}

void
allcaps(text_w, unused, cbs)
Widget      text_w;
XtPointer   unused;
XmTextVerifyCallbackStruct *cbs;
{
    int len;
```

Example 15-11. The allcaps.c program (continued)

```
    if (cbs->text->ptr == NULL)   /* backspace */
        return;

    /* convert all input to upper-case if necessary */
    for (len = 0; len < cbs->text->length; len++)
        if (islower(cbs->text->ptr[ len ]))
            cbs->text->ptr[ len ] = toupper(cbs->text->ptr[ len ]);
}
```

The program creates a simple RowColumn widget that contains a Label and a Text widget as shown in Figure 15-8.

Figure 15-8. Output of allcaps.c

The sole Text widget uses **allcaps( )** as its **XmNmodifyVerifyCallback** function. The function that converts the text about to be added is quite simple and easy to follow, but there are a lot of details to examine.

The **call_data** (third) parameter to the function is of type **XmTextVerify-CallbackStruct**. The data structure provides the information about the text that may be added to the Text widget. It may also indicate that text is about to be deleted.

The data structure takes the following form:

```
    typedef struct {
        int           reason;
        XEvent        *event;
        Boolean       doit;
        long          currInsert, newInsert;
        long          startPos, endPos;
        XmTex
Block    text;
    } XmTextVerifyCallbackStruct;
```

The **reason** field will have the value **XmCR_MODIFYING_TEXT_VALUE**. The **event** field will contain the **XEvent** that caused the callback to be invoked. This field will be **NULL** if the new text is being added (or deleted) from a call to **XmTextSetString( )**, **XmTextInsert( )**, **XmTextReplace( )**, or any other convenience routine that modifies text.

The **text** field points to a data structure that describes the new text about to be added to the Text widget. The values for **currInsert** and **newInsert** will always be the same value for modify callbacks. These indicate the insertion cursor's location, so they will be different only for the **XmNmotionVerifyCallback** if the user changes the insertion point.

The values for **startPos** and **endPos** indicate the offsets in the Text's string value that will be affected by the modification. For Text insertion, these values will always be the same unless the text insertion is the result of a clipboard paste (*stuff*) or a secondary selection. For text deletion, however, they indicate the beginning and ending offsets of the text about to be deleted. Thus, if the user selects a stream of text and presses the BACKSPACE key, the **startPos** and **endPos** values will indicate the boundaries of the text about to be deleted. We discuss more about text deletion in Section 15.8.3, *Handling Text Deletion*.

Let's review the simple case of adding new text, as demonstrated by Example 15-11. When new text is inserted into the Text widget, the values for **currInsert**, **newInsert**, **startPos**, and **endPos** will all have the same value: the position within the Text widget where the new text will be added. This new text can be found in the **text** field of the callback structure. It is a pointer of type **XmTextBlock**:

```
typedef struct {
    char        *ptr;    /* Pointer to new text to be inserted. */
    int         length; /* Number of bytes in ptr. */
    XmTextFormat format; /* Representations format. */
} XmTextBlockRec, *XmTextBlock;
```

Note that the new text has not yet been added to the value of the widget. Therefore, if you want to change the text before it does get added, you must change the data in this structure. The actual text being added is accessible through **ptr** and is dynamically allocated via **Xt-Malloc( )** each time the function is invoked. The **ptr** field is not NULL-terminated, so you should not use **strlen( )** or **strcpy( )** to copy this data. The number of bytes that are useful is stored in the **length** parameter, so if you want to copy it, you should use **strncpy( )**:

```
char buf[ ??? ];

strncpy(buf, cbs->text->ptr, sizeof(buf));
if (sizeof(buf) > cbs->text->length)
    buf[cbs->text->length ] = 0;
```

The size you declare for **buf** must not be less than what the value of **cbs->text->length** will be. If the user deletes text, then there is not going to be any new text added, so **ptr** will be NULL and **length** will be 0.

The **format** may be either **FMT8BIT** or **FMT16BIT** indicating whether certain wide-character fonts are used (those that extend beyond standard 255-characters).

Let's re-examine the **allcaps( )** function again from Example 15-11. Notice that in order to modify input to be all capital letters, we loop through the valid bytes in the **ptr** field of the text block that is going to be added:

```
for (len = 0; len < cbs->text->length; len++)
    if (islower(cbs->text->ptr[ len ]))
        cbs->text->ptr[ len ] = toupper(cbs->text->ptr[ len ]);
```

The macros **islower( )** and **toupper( )** are found in the header file *<ctype.h>*. Each iteration of the loop potentially modifies the very text about to be added to the Text widget.

Since this function is called each time new text is added to the widget, you might wonder how more than one byte can be added at a time. In other words, how can **length** ever be more than one? This can happen if the user uses cut and paste functions to copy a block of text into the widget. When this happens, the entire block is added at once—thus, `ptr` points to that text and `length` indicates how much text is there. Our loop handles all the cases from single-character typing to large text block paste operations.

15.8.2 Vetoing a Text Modification

The example we just saw merely converts newly inserted text to uppercase. In other situations, however, we might want to filter new text and prevent certain characters from getting through. This may or may not include the entire text block.

The easiest way to veto any modification to the Text widget is to set the `doit` field in the `XmTextVerifyCallbackStruct` to `False`. Upon return of the callback function, Motif checks this field and, if `False`, discards the new text and the widget is left unmodified.

In the cases where text modification is vetoed, the console bell may be sounded to provide audio feedback to the user indicating that his input has been received, but was rejected. This action is dependent on the value of `XmNverifyBell`. This is a Text widget resource and it should be left to users to set for themselves. If they don't want notification of error bells, they can turn off this value (since its default value is `True`). You may confuse users if you set this resource within your application. (You should provide documentation with your application explaining how to set this resource.)

Example 15-12 demonstrates how input can be filtered or completely vetoed. In this case, we want the user to type digits only; all other input should be ignored. The problem is made a little more interesting by the fact that we are prompting for a ZIP code, so the total length of the string should not exceed five digits.

Example 15-12. The check_zip() function

```
void
check_zip(text_w, unused, cbs)
Widget        text_w;
cadr_t        unused;
XmTextVerifyCallbackStruct *cbs;
{
    int len = 0;

    if (cbs->startPos < cbs->currInsert)  /* backspace */
        return;

    len = XmTextGetLastPosition(text_w);

    if (len == 5) {
        cbs->doit = False;
        return;
    }
    /* check that the new additions won't put us over 5 */
    if (len + cbs->text->length > 5) {
        cbs->text->ptr[5 - len] = 0;
        cbs->text->length = strlen(cbs->text->ptr);
    }
    for (len = 0; len < cbs->text->length; len++) {
        /* make sure all additions are digits. */
```

Example 15-12. The check_zip() function (continued)

```
          if (!isdigit(cbs->text->ptr[len])) {
              /* not a digit-- move all chars down one and
               * decrement cbs->text->length.
               */
              int i;
              for (i = len; (i+1) < cbs->text->length; i++)
                  cbs->text->ptr[i] = cbs->text->ptr[i+1];
              cbs->text->length--;
              len--;
          }
      }
      if (cbs->text->length == 0)
          cbs->doit = False;
}
```

For **check_zip( )**, the task becomes slightly more complicated than in the previous examples. The first thing to do is check to see if the user is backspacing, in which case we simply return. (We talk about backspacing and text deletion more in the next section.) If no text is being deleted, then new text is definitely being added. The widget's current text (or the length of it) is not available from any of the fields in the callback structure, so in order to determine the string length of the text within it, we call **XmTextGetLastPosition( )**. If the string is already 5 digits long, we don't want to add more digits. We also set **doit** to **False** so the bell will sound.

Next, we loop through the length of the new text and check for characters that are not digits. If any exist, we remove them by shifting all the characters that follow down one place, thereby overwriting the undesirable character. If we loop through all the characters in the new text and find that none of them are digits, the length will end up being zero and we should set **doit** to **False**.

15.8.3 Handling Text Deletion

We are able to determine when the user backspaces or deletes an arbitrarily large block of text by noticing if **cbs->startPos** is less than **cbs->currInsert**. Alternatively, we could check to see if **cbs->text->ptr** is **NULL**. Until now, our examples were only concerned with additions. In this section, we examine what happens during text deletion. As we mentioned in previous sections, when text is deleted, **startPos** is less than **curr-Insert**. For backspacing, the values will differ by one. However, if the user selects a large block of text and deletes the selection, the callback list associated with the **XmNmodify-VerifyCallback** will be invoked. It may even be invoked twice if the user types new text to replace the selected text. This will also be the case if text is replaced using **XmText-Replace( )**.

The modify callback function(s) will be called at least once to delete the selected (or replaced) text and possibly a second time to add the new text.

Our next example program demonstrates how processing character deletions works within a Text widget's modify callback routine. Example 15-13 displays another single-line Text widget that prompts the user for a password. We don't actually do any encryption on the password; we simply provide an interface that masks what the user is typing, as shown in Figure 15-9. Everything the user types is displayed as an asterisk (*), and the actual data is stored in a separate internal variable. The challenge for this application is to capture the input text, store it internally, and modify the output—even for backspacing.

Example 15-13. The passwd.c program

```
/* passwd.c -- prompt for a passwd.  Meaning, all input looks like
 * a series of *'s.  Store the actual data typed by the user in
 * an internal variable.  Don't allow paste operations.  Handle
 * backspacing by deleting all text from insertion point to the
 * end of text.
 */
#include <Xm/Text.h>
#include <Xm/LabelG.h>
#include <Xm/RowColumn.h>
#include <ctype.h>

void check_passwd();
char *passwd; /* store user-typed passwd here. */

main(argc, argv)
int argc;
char *argv[ ];
{
    Widget         toplevel, text_w, rowcol;
    XtAppContext   app;

    toplevel = XtVaAppInitialize(&app, "Demos",
        NULL, 0, &argc, argv, NULL, NULL);

    rowcol = XtVaCreateWidget("rowcol",
        xmRowColumnWidgetClass, toplevel,
        XmNorientation, XmHORIZONTAL,
        NULL);

    XtVaCreateManagedWidget("Password:",
        xmLabelGadgetClass, rowcol, NULL);
    text_w = XtVaCreateManagedWidget("text_w",
        xmTextWidgetClass, rowcol, NULL);

    XtAddCallback(text_w, XmNmodifyVerifyCallback, check_passwd, NULL);
    XtAddCallback(text_w, XmNactivateCallback, check_passwd, NULL);

    XtManageChild(rowcol);
    XtRealizeWidget(toplevel);
    XtAppMainLoop(app);
}

void
check_passwd(text_w, unused, cbs)
Widget         text_w;
XtPointer      unused;
XmTextVerifyCallbackStruct *cbs;
{
    char *new;
    int len;

    if (cbs->reason == XmCR_ACTIVATE) {
        printf("Password: %s\n", passwd);
        return;
```

Example 15-13. The passwd.c program (continued)

```
    }

    if (cbs->text->ptr == NULL) { /* backspace */
        cbs->endPos = strlen(passwd); /* delete from here to end */
        passwd[ cbs->startPos ] = 0; /* backspace--terminate */
        return;
    }

    if (cbs->text->length > 1) {
        cbs->doit = False; /* don't allow "paste" operations */
        return; /* make the user *type* the password! */
    }

    new = XtMalloc(cbs->endPos + 2); /* new char + NULL terminator */
    if (passwd) {
        strcpy(new, passwd);
        XtFree(passwd);
    } else
        new[ 0 ] = NULL;
    passwd = new;
    strncat(passwd, cbs->text->ptr, cbs->text->length);
    passwd[ cbs->endPos + cbs->text->length ] = 0;

    for (len = 0; len < cbs->text->length; len++)
        cbs->text->ptr[ len ] = '*';
}
```

Figure 15-9. Output of passwd.c

By installing the **XmNactivateCallback**, we can actually see what was typed by pressing $\boxed{\text{RETURN}}$. The function **check_passwd( )** prints what was typed to **stdout**, and is used for both the activate callback and the modify callback. Provided we are not backspacing through the text, we know we can add the new text to the value of **passwd** so that its value can be stored internally (not as part of the Text widget). Once this text is copied, it is converted into asterisks so the user does not see what was typed. You should be able to understand this sufficiently well based on the material we've presented so far.

Now, let's examine how we handle backspacing or other forms of text deletion. We start by testing if `cbs->text->ptr` is NULL:

```
if (cbs->text->ptr == NULL) { /* backspace */
    cbs->endPos = strlen(passwd); /* delete from here to end */
    passwd[cbs->startPos] = 0; /* NULL terminate */
    return;
}
```

Since `startPos` and `endPos` represent the amount of text being deleted, we can change these values and effectively delete *more* text than the user originally intended. In fact, this is potentially what the code may be doing here, depending on the position of the insertion cursor when the backspace event occurred. Consider two cases for text deletion:

1. The insertion cursor is at the end of the typed string and the user simply backspaces.

2. The user first clicks somewhere in the middle of the string of asterisks and presses BACKSPACE .

In the first case, we simply allow the BACKSPACE and RETURN . Although the second case is not as likely, it is possible and therefore must be accounted for. Since the user cannot see what is being typed, he cannot be 100% sure of the character being deleted. So, we delete all the characters from that point in the string to the end.

By setting `cbs->endPos` to the string length of the internal variable, `passwd`, we handle both cases. This also demonstrates how you can delete more characters than originally intended. In fact, we could also have set `cbs->startPos` to 0 and deleted the entire text. As you can imagine, all sorts of methods can be implemented using this callback data structure.

15.8.4 Extending Modifications and the XmNvalueChangedCallback

Let's expand the ZIP code example we used for filtering non-digits from typed input. This time, we're going to provide an input field for an area code and phone number. The format for a US phone number is as follows:

```
123-456-7890
```

We know we want to filter out all non-digits for the phone numbers, but we also want to automatically add the dash character (–) as needed. Thus, when the characters 4, 1, and 5 are typed, the Text widget should automatically insert a - after the 5 so the next character expected from the user is still a digit. This requires additional text to that already being added.

Similarly, when the user backspaces and deletes the - character, we also need to delete the preceding digit in order to maintain consistency for the type-in field. Table 15-2 shows how the situation should work.

Table 15-2. Effect of Backspacing in prompt_phone.c

User Types	Text Widget Displays
4	4
1	41
5	415-
4	415-4
BACKSPACE	415-
BACKSPACE	41

We can continue to use the same type of algorithm used in **check_zip( )** for filtering digits and some code from **check_passwd( )** to handle backspacing. The only problem left is how to add the necessary - characters.

First, let's determine *when* the dashes should be added. Since we are using US phone numbers, the dashes should occur after the third and seventh digits. Therefore, when .hw **currInsert currInsert** is either 2 or 6, the new digit should be added first (which would move the insertion point to 3 or 7), followed by the dash.

How is the dash added? Perhaps the most intuitive way to solve this problem is to use the **XmNvalueChangedCallback** to add the digits as they are typed, and then use **XmTextInsert( )** to add the dash afterwards. The problem with this is that **XmTextInsert( )** will activate the modify callback function again and the dash will be subjected to our strict error checking.

Therefore, the only way to handle this problem is by actually adding the dash right here in the callback function at the same time the digits are added. This requires modifying the **ptr** and **length** fields of the **XmTextBlock** structure in the **XmTextVerifyCallbackStruct**. All that is needed to add the dash is to reallocate **ptr** by one and to increment **lenth** to account for the dash. Given this, we can generate the following code fragment:

```
char c = cbs->text->ptr[ 0 ];
int len = strlen(phone_number);

/* if the input is a digit and we know we must add a hyphen... */
if (isdigit(c) && (len == 2 || len == 6)) {
    cbs->text->ptr = XtRealloc(cbs->text->ptr, 2);
    cbs->text->length = 2;
    cbs->text->ptr[ 0 ] = c;
    cbs->text->ptr[ 1 ] = '-';
}
```

The value of **len** is the length of the current phone number string which we can get using **XtVaGetValues( )**. If the typed character is a digit and the current phone number is either two or six characters long, we must add the new digit plus the dash.

The digit and dash have been added, but there is one remaining problem. The position of the insertion cursor is not affected by how much text is added. As it stands, the insertion cursor will be behind the dash, but after the digit (since that's what the user typed). Unfortunately, setting the value of **cbs->currInsert** or **cbs->newInsert** will not change the insertion cursor (a bug with Motif?). Furthermore, we cannot use

`XmTextSetCursorPosition( )` since it will not have any effect until this function already returns. The only thing we can do is move the cursor *after* the text has been added.

Here is where we can use the **XmNvalueChangedCallback**. Since this function is invoked after the text has been modified through the modify callback, we are now at liberty to change the insertion cursor. Example 15-14 shows the complete program and how the two callback routines work cooperatively to solve the problem.

Example 15-14. The prompt_phone.c program

```
/* prompt_phone.c -- a complex problem for XmNmodifyVerifyCallback.
 * prompt for a phone number by filtering digits only from input.
 * Don't allow paste operations and handle backspacing.
 */
#include <Xm/Text.h>
#include <Xm/LabelG.h>
#include <Xm/RowColumn.h>
#include <ctype.h>

void check_phone();

main(argc, argv)
int argc;
char *argv[ ];
{
    Widget        toplevel, text_w, rowcol;
    XtAppContext  app;

    toplevel = XtVaAppInitialize(&app, "Demos",
        NULL, 0, &argc, argv, NULL, NULL);

    rowcol = XtVaCreateWidget("rowcol",
        xmRowColumnWidgetClass, toplevel,
        XmNorientation, XmHORIZONTAL,
        NULL);

    XtVaCreateManagedWidget("Phone Number:",
        xmLabelGadgetClass, rowcol, NULL);
    text_w = XtVaCreateManagedWidget("text_w",
        xmTextWidgetClass, rowcol, NULL);

    XtAddCallback(text_w, XmNmodifyVerifyCallback, check_phone, NULL);
    XtAddCallback(text_w, XmNvalueChangedCallback, check_phone, NULL);

    XtManageChild(rowcol);
    XtRealizeWidget(toplevel);
    XtAppMainLoop(app);
}

void
check_phone(text_w, unused, cbs)
Widget       text_w;
XtPointer    unused;
XmTextVerifyCallbackStruct *cbs;
{
    char c;
    int len = XmTextGetLastPosition(text_w);

    if (cbs->reason == XmCR_VALUE_CHANGED) {
        XmTextSetInsertionPosition(text_w, len);
        return;
```

Example 15-14. The prompt_phone.c program (continued)

```
    }
    /* no backspacing or typing in the middle of string */
    if (cbs->currInsert < len) {
        cbs->doit = False;
        return;
    }

    if (cbs->text->ptr == NULL) { /* backspace */
        if (cbs->startPos == 3 || cbs->startPos == 7)
            cbs->startPos--; /* delete the hyphen too */
        return;
    }

    if (cbs->text->length > 1) { /* don't allow clipboard copies */
        cbs->doit = False;
        return;
    }

    /* don't allow non-digits or let the input exceed 12 chars */
    if (!isdigit(c = cbs->text->ptr[0]) || len >= 12)
        cbs->doit = False;
    else if (len == 2 || len == 6) {
        cbs->text->ptr = XtRealloc(cbs->text->ptr, 2);
        cbs->text->length = 2;
        cbs->text->ptr[0] = c;
        cbs->text->ptr[1] = '-';
    }
}
```

The **XmNvalueChangedCallback** function is installed at the same time as the **Xm-NmodifyVerifyCallback** function. Both use the function **check_phone( )**, which checks **cbs->reason** to see which callback invoked it. If the reason is **Xm-CR_VALUE_CHANGED**, then it can set the cursor position to the end of the string in the Text widget.

You might also notice some other aesthetic items that help maintain programmer sanity. For example, we do not allow any text insertions or deletions that occur while the insertion cursor is not at the end of the Text's string. While this is not impossible, in order to properly handle such cases, the code becomes a large bowl of spaghetti. We do not allow clipboard copies of more than one character at a time for the same reason. Granted, this case might be a little easier to handle, but for purposes of this demonstration, we only process single character typing that occurs at the end of the string.

15.9 Cursor Movement Callback

In the previous sections, we discussed how to be notified before and after text is inserted into the Text widget. In this section, we introduce the `XmNmotionVerifyCallback` resource to determine if the insertion cursor has changed position. The reasons for this callback to be invoked are:

- The user uses the mouse or the arrow keys to change the cursor location.

- The user drags the mouse or multi-clicks to extend the text selection.

- The application calls any Motif Text function that moves the cursor (e.g., `XmTextSetCursorPosition()`) or any function that adds, deletes, or replaces text (e.g., `XmTextSetString()`).

An exception to this list is if the cursor does not move despite the function being called. For example, if the cursor is already at the end of the text, then the cursor movement callback will not be invoked if the application makes the following call:

```
XmTextSetCursorPosition(text_w, XmTextGetLastPosition(text_w));
```

This functionality is not as complex as the text modify callback, although the same callback structure is used as the `call_data` parameter to the callback function. Again, that structure is defined as follows:

```
typedef struct {
    int            reason;
    XEvent         *event;
    Boolean        doit;
    long           currInsert, newInsert;
    long           startPos, endPos;
    XmTextBlock    text;
} XmTextVerifyCallbackStruct;
```

For motion callbacks, the **reason** is `XmCR_MOVING_INSERT_CURSOR`. The **event** field points to an `XEvent` structure describing the action that caused the cursor position to be modified. However, there is currently a bug with the **event** field *not* being set to the event that caused the motion callback if the cursor position changed as a result of the user clicking in the Text widget. (Thus, the rest of this section may not actually work as expected.) It is not a bug that the pointer will be `NULL` if the cursor moved as a result of the application's call to a Motif Text function that moves the cursor (such as `XmTextSetCursorPosition()`). Checking the **event** field would have been a perfect way to tell the difference between when the Text widget's insertion position changed as a result of the user's action or the application's. As long as that bug exists, however, there is no way to tell.

The fields `startPos`, `endPos`, and `text` are invalid for `XmNmotionVerifyCallback`.

The `doit` field can be set to `False` to reject requests to reposition the insertion cursor. (That is, if there were a way to tell it was the result of a user's action.) Assuming that the bug is eventually fixed, let's look at *prompt_phone.c* again so we can tie up that loose end. That is, we don't want to allow the user to move the insertion cursor to any other place within the phone number; backspacing is required to change a previously typed digit. This is

accomplished by adding the callback function and modifying the appropriate callback routine as shown in the following code fragment:

```
    ...
    XtAddCallback(text_w, XmNmotionVerifyCallback, check_phone, NULL);
    ...

void
check_phone(text_w, unused, cbs)
Widget      text_w;
XtPointer   unused;
XmTextVerifyCallbackStruct *cbs;
{
    int len = XmTextGetLastPosition(text_w);

    if (cbs->reason == XmCR_MOVING_INSERT_CURSOR) {
        if (cbs->newInsert != len && cbs->event)
            cbs->doit = False;
        return;
    }
    ...
}
```

By checking if **cbs>newInsert** is not the same as the length of the current string value,
we know we are not at the end of the text string. If **cbs->event** is NULL, however, then
the cursor motion was artificially caused—the result of the call to **XmTextSetCursor-
Position( )** later in the function.

The **XmNmotionVerifyCallback** function can be used to monitor pointer dragging for
extended text selections, but it cannot be used to monitor secondary selections since they do
not cause the insertion position to change.

15.10 Focus Callbacks

When a Text widget is editable, you may not set **XmNtraversalOn** to **False**. Therefore,
when a Text widget gets input focus, you can assume that the user wants to begin or resume
typing in a Text widget. That is, either the user intentionally switched focus to a widget or
the widget gained focus through the application via **XmProcessTraversal( )**. When
the widget gains input focus and the insertion cursor is not visible, we can make it visible and
cause the widget to automatically scroll to the current cursor location by installing an **Xm-
NfocusCallback** that calls **XmTextShowCursorPosition( )**. For example:

```
{
    Widget text_w;
    extern void gain_focus( );

    ...
    text_w = XmCreateScrolledText(...);
    ...

    XtAddCallback(text_w, XmNfocusCallback, gain_focus, NULL);
    ...
}
void
```

```
gain_focus(text_w, client_data, call_data)
Widget      text_w;
XtPointer client_data;
XmAnyCallbackStruct call_data;
{
    XmTextShowCursorPosition(text_w, XtTextGetCursorPosition(text_w));
}
```

The **XmNlosingFocusCallback** callback can be used to monitor when the Text widget loses its focus. The callback structure passed to the callback function is **XmTextVerify-CallbackStruct**, just as it is for the **XmNmodifyVerifyCallback** and the **Xm-NmotionVerifyCallback** routines.

15.11 Summary

Text widgets function best when they are left alone to do their jobs. For every little bit of fine tuning you add, your code will grow twice as much to accommodate the new features and the necessary error checking. Also, at the time of this writing, not everything in the Text widget works entirely as advertised, so you may find some quirky behavior. You should try not to overcompensate, though, since the bugs will probably be fixed in later releases.

15.12 Exercises

The following exercises are designed to expand on the ideas described in this chapter and possibly introduce some new directions that you can take with Text widgets.

1. Using the **XmNmodifyVerifyCallback**, you can effectively add more data to a Text widget than what was originally typed, as described in Section 15.8.1, *The ModifyVerify Callback*. This technique can be useful for supporting advanced editing features such as file or word completion. For this exercise, let's say that you have a predefined list of words that you obtained by reading in the contents of */usr/dict/words*. As the user enters text, you want to allow the leading part of a word to be entered, followed by a special character that completes the rest of it automatically. To write this program, you need to write an **XmNmodifyVerifyCallback** routine that constantly checks each character typed and, upon receipt of the special character, checks the input queue backwards till it finds a space character (or a newline) and checks this "current word" against the words in your list. If a match is made, complete the word using the methods outlined in Section 15.8.1, *The ModifyVerify Callback*.

2. The function **XmTextHighlight( )** can be used to "highlight" parts of text in the same fashion as if the user had selected it. (That is, the text is displayed in reverse video.) This method can be effective for certain functions such as search and replace, as demonstrated in *editor.c* in Section 15.6, *A Complete Editor*. By using the idea from the previous exercise, write a simple spell-checker program. Here, a PushButton can get all the text from a Text widget, and check it against */usr/dict/words*. All words that are not found in the dictionary should be highlighted for the user to browse.

3. Modify the *allcaps.c* program to use **XmNgainFocusCallback** and **XmNlosing-FocusCallback** callback routines so that when the user "leaves" the window, the characters all convert to lowercase. When input focus is gained, the characters revert back to uppercase.

4. The resource **XmNsource** refers to an abstract data structure, **XmTextSource**. This is an object internal to the Text widget that contains all the information about the text it is editing. You can set or get the value for this resource using **XtVaSetValues( )** and **XtVaGetValues( )**. Since this data type is opaque to the programmer, you cannot create one of your own, but you can get one from an existing Text widget. By getting the **XmNsource** from one Text widget and setting in another, you can effectively have two Text widgets that edit the same text. Write a program that does just that.

16

Menus

This chapter describes the Motif menu system in greater detail than was presented in the simple menus used with the MainWindow widget.

In This Chapter:

16
Menus

Menus provide the user with the choice of an entire set of functions without complicating the normal visual appearance of the application. These convenient "mini-toolboxes" are life-savers for the user who, like an auto mechanic busily working away under the car, needs quick and convenient access to his tools without having to look or move away from his work.

The *Motif Style Guide* actually provides for three different types of menus: *pulldown*, *popup*, and *option* menus.

Pulldown menus like the one displayed in Figure 16-1 are probably the most common. The menu pops up when the user presses the first mouse button[1] on a CascadeButton. As described in Chapter 4, *The Main Window*, CascadeButtons may be displayed as titles in a MenuBar or as menu items of an existing menu. When the CascadeButton is a child of a MenuBar, the menu drops down below the button when the user clicks on it. When the CascadeButton is an item in an existing menu, the new menu pops up to the right of the item; it is sometimes referred to as a "cascading menu" or a "pullright menu."

Under certain conditions, it may be inconvenient for the user to have to stop, pull down a menu from a menu bar, and get back into place. Having to move the mouse away, even to another part of the same window, may be enough to cause a loss in productivity. One solution to this problem is a popup menu, since it can provide immediate access to necessary functionality.

Assume, for example, that the user of a drawing program wants to change the line style in his current editing mode. Rather than having to move the mouse to another part of the screen, he can just press the third mouse button, causing a popup menu to appear on the spot. Popup menus may be displayed anywhere in the application. They need not be associated with any visible user-interface element. In fact, they are usually popped up from work areas or other areas not obviously affiliated with a user-interface element such as a PushButton or Cascade-Button. The only drawback is that there is no "signal" to the novice user that the menu exists, which loses some of the benefit of a graphical user interface. Figure 16-2 shows a popup menu.

---

[1] Which button pops up the menu is typically user-settable, since left-handed users may want to reverse the default button bindings.

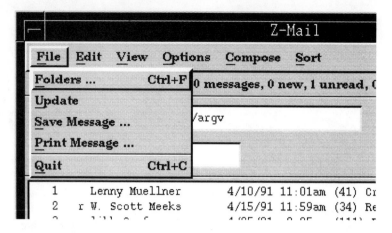

Figure 16-1. A pulldown menu

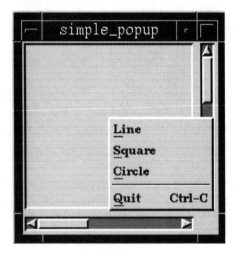

Figure 16-2. A popup menu

Option menus combine the strengths of pulldown and popup menus. Like pulldown menus, they are popped up from visible CascadeButtons, but like popups, they are typically "on the spot." A CascadeButton can be used to display the default choice for a data entry field; but when the value is clicked on by the mouse, alternate choices are displayed, as shown in Figure 16-3.

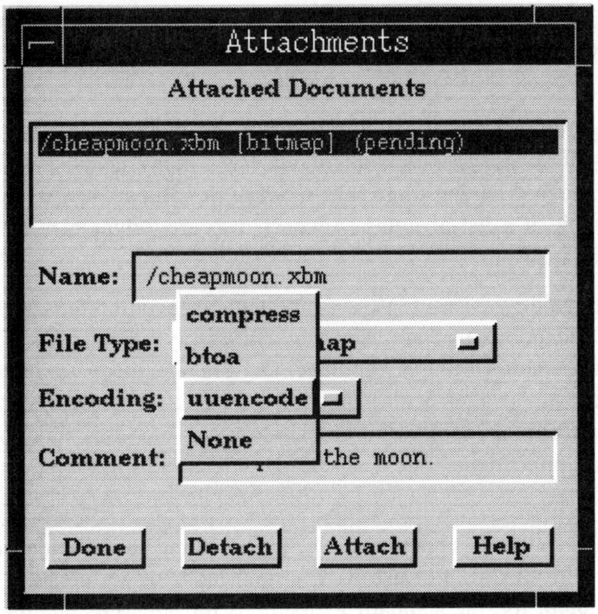

Figure 16-3. An option menu

Like the pulldown menus in MenuBars, option menus are invoked using the first mouse button, but they are displayed on top of their associated CascadeButtons rather than below them. Also, unlike pulldown menus, they may exist anywhere in the application.

The Button 3 (or *menu button*) activation for popup menus is in sharp contrast to pulldown and option menus, which are always invoked by Button 1 (or *select button*). Although it may seem confusing for the user that some menus are invoked by the first mouse button while others are invoked by the third, there is some consistency in the fact that pulldown and option menus are always attached to GUI buttons (CascadeButtons or PushButtons) and are invoked by the first mouse button. Popup menus can be popped up from anywhere. This discrepancy in menu activation frees Button 1 for other activities in application work areas.

Despite the differences between the three types of menu, we never want to lose sight of their common intent: quick, simple, and convenient access to tools.

To make menu functions even more convenient, Motif menus can (and usually do) have *mnemonics* and *accelerators* associated with them. These are keyboard equivalents that enable the user to access menus (and menu items) without having to move from the keyboard to the mouse. For example, in Figure 16-1, the first letter of each menu item is its mnemonic, as indicated by underlining. (The mnemonic need not be the first letter.) Typing that letter while the menu is displayed will activate that entry. Accelerators are keystroke combinations (usually involving Control or Meta keys to distinguish them from ordinary keystrokes to be sent to the application) that invoke a menu or menu item even when the menu is not displayed. For example, again in Figure 16-1, `Ctrl+C` quits the application, without the need to pull down the menu.

Despite their power, you should beware of excessive reliance on popup menus, accelerators, and mnemonics. Menus are never seen unless the user takes the time to find them. Graphical User Interfaces are easy to learn because the controls are visible.

Popup menus are especially dangerous, because they don't correspond to any visible element in the application. And when you do use menus, don't include too many items; the *Motif Style Guide* recommends that you avoid having more than a dozen or so items in a menu. If this is difficult to govern, especially if a list of items is expected to grow dynamically, you should probably use a ScrolledList instead.

Accelerators are convenient, but again, you shouldn't rely on them. They are rarely memorized, except when they execute fucnctions that are used very frequently. If possible, allow accelerators to be externally configurable (through resources) and provide adequate defaults. If the user wants to add an acclerator for a particular function he uses more frequently than you expected, he can modify his resources to add the accelerator himself. This adds to the robustness and flexibility of your applications. We'll discuss how to do this in the course of the chapter.

Before we plunge into the details of menu creation, a word of warning to experienced X Toolkit programmers is in order. Motif does not use Xt's normal methods for creating and managing menus. In fact, you *cannot* use the standard Xt methods for popup menu creation or management without virtually reimplementing the Motif menu design.[2] That is, in Xt, you would typically create an OverrideShell that contains a generic manager widget, followed by a set of PushButtons. You'd then pop up the shell with `XtPopup()` to display the menu. Instead, the Motif toolkit abstracts the menu creation and management process into generic routines that make the menu opaque to the programmer; the internal implementation is irrelevant.

16.1 Simple Menu Creation

In Chapter 4, *The Main Window*, simple menu creation routines were used to build the Menu-Bar and its associated pulldown menus. These simple routines do not require complex data structures or extra function calls in order to work properly. They are designed to be plug-and-play convenience routines, requiring only compound strings for the labels and a single callback function to invoke when the user activates any of the menu items. `XmVaCreate-SimpleMenuBar()` can be used to create a MenuBar and `XmVaCreateSimple-PulldownMenu()` can generate its pulldown menus and their associated items:

```
Widget
XmVaCreateSimpleMenuBar(parent, name, va_alist)
    Widget parent;
    String name;
    va_dcl
```

---

[2] Those of you who wish to port Athena or OPEN LOOK-based applications to Motif should reconsider your menu design right now. It's not going to work.

```
Widget
XmVaCreateSimplePulldownMenu(parent, name, button, callback, va_alist)
    Widget          parent;
    String          name;
    int             button;
    XtCallbackProc  callback;
    va_dcl
```

These *varargs* functions take a *variable argument list* of extra parameters that specify the CascadeButtons (for the MenuBar) or the menu items (for the pulldown menu) followed by a NULL-terminator, indicating the end of the list of items. They are technically a superset of the **XtVaCreateWidget( )** functions because you may also pass RowColumn-specific resource-value pairs to extend the configurability of the RowColumn widget that manages the items in the menu. These functions are really front ends for more primitive routines that actually create the underlying widgets. However, they are convenient for many simple menu creation needs.

You should review Chapter 4, *The Main Window,* for how to use these functions. However, what was not discussed in that chapter are similar simple menu creation functions for creating popup and option menus:

```
Widget XmVaCreateSimplePopupMenu(parent, name, va_alist)
    Widget parent;
    String name;
    va_dcl

Widget XmVaCreateSimpleOptionMenu(parent, name, va_alist)
    Widget parent;
    String name;
    va_dcl
```

Much of the information in Chapter 4 also applies to these functions. For all intents and purposes, the functions for Popup and Option menus are identical to their pulldown menu counterparts. The next few sections demonstrate this through discussion and examples.

16.1.1 Simple Popup Menus

The only difference between **XmVaCreateSimplePopupMenu( )**, which we used in Chapter 4, and **XmVaCreateSimplePulldownMenu( )** is the missing **button** parameter, which was used by the pulldown menu to identify which of the CascadeButtons in a MenuBar or in another popup or pulldown menu was used to display the menu. Since popups are not associated with CascadeButtons, this parameter isn't necessary. (However, if a popup menu is going to have a cascading menu from one of its menu items, then a pulldown menu may be attached to it. This is discussed later in the chapter.) Example 16-1 demonstrates how a simple popup menu can be created.

Example 16-1. The simple_popup.c program

```
/* simple_popup.c -- demonstrate how to use a simple popup menu.
 * Create a main window that contains a DrawingArea widget, which
 * displays a popup menu when the user presses the menu button
 * (typically button 3).
```

Example 16-1. The simple_popup.c program (continued)

```
 */
#include <Xm/RowColumn.h>
#include <Xm/MainW.h>
#include <Xm/DrawingA.h>

main(argc, argv)
int argc;
char *argv[ ];
{
    XmString line, square, circle, quit, quit_acc;
    Widget toplevel, main_w, drawing_a, popup_menu;
    void popup_cb(), input();
    XtAppContext app;

    toplevel = XtVaAppInitialize(&app, "Demos", NULL, 0,
        &argc, argv, NULL, NULL);

    /* Create a MainWindow widget that contains a DrawingArea in
     * its work window. (This happens by default.)
     */
    main_w = XtVaCreateManagedWidget("main_w",
        xmMainWindowWidgetClass, toplevel,
        XmNscrollingPolicy,  XmAUTOMATIC,
        NULL);
    /* Create a DrawingArea -- no actual drawing will be done. */
    drawing_a = XtVaCreateManagedWidget("drawing_a",
        xmDrawingAreaWidgetClass, main_w,
        XmNwidth, 500,
        XmNheight, 500,
        NULL);

    line = XmStringCreateSimple("Line");
    square = XmStringCreateSimple("Square");
    circle = XmStringCreateSimple("Circle");
    quit = XmStringCreateSimple("Quit");
    quit_acc = XmStringCreateSimple("Ctrl-C");
    popup_menu = XmVaCreateSimplePopupMenu(drawing_a, "popup", popup_cb,
        XmVaPUSHBUTTON, line, NULL, NULL, NULL,
        XmVaPUSHBUTTON, square, NULL, NULL, NULL,
        XmVaPUSHBUTTON, circle, NULL, NULL, NULL,
        XmVaSEPARATOR,
        XmVaPUSHBUTTON, quit, NULL, "Ctrl<Key>c", quit_acc,
        NULL);
    XmStringFree(line);
    XmStringFree(square);
    XmStringFree(circle);
    XmStringFree(quit);

    /* after popup menu is created, add callback for all input events */
    XtAddCallback(drawing_a, XmNinputCallback, input, popup_menu);

    XtRealizeWidget(toplevel);
    XtAppMainLoop(app);
}

/* called in responses to events in the DrawingArea; button-3 pops up menu. */
void
input(widget, popup, cbs)
Widget widget;
```

Example 16-1. The simple_popup.c program (continued)

```
Widget popup;    /* popup menu associated with drawing area */
XmDrawingAreaCallbackStruct *cbs;
{
    if (cbs->event->xany.type != ButtonPress ||
        cbs->event->xbutton.button != 3)
        return;

    /* Position the menu where the event occurred */
    XmMenuPosition(popup, cbs->event);
    XtManageChild(popup);
}

/* invoked when the user selects an item in the popup menu */
void
popup_cb(menu_item, item_no, cbs)
Widget menu_item;
int item_no;
XmAnyCallbackStruct *cbs;
{
    if (item_no == 3) /* Quit was selected -- exit */
        exit(0);
    puts(XtName(menu_item)); /* Otherwise, just print the selection */
}
```

In this program, we have a standard MainWindow widget that contains a DrawingArea widget. (Note, however, that the program does no drawing; it is really just a skeleton that shows how to attach a popup menu.) The popup menu is created using `XmVaCreate-SimplePopupMenu( )`, with its parent specified as the DrawingArea widget.

The menu is popped up when the user presses the third mouse button in the DrawingArea. The Motif toolkit does not handle this automatically the way it does with pulldown and option menus, so we must watch for the appropriate events ourselves. To do this, we use the function associated with the `XmNinputCallback` resource of the DrawingArea widget. This function is called whenever keyboard or mouse actions happen in its window. Normally, we'd do our drawing from this function, perhaps using Button 1. However, in this case, all we look for is the menu-request event (Button 3). To facilitate the popping-up process, the menu is passed as the client data to `input( )`, the function installed as the `Xm-NinputCallback`.

When `input( )` is called, the event can be extracted from the callback structure. It is examined to see if it is the correct mouse button and, if so, the Motif utility function `Xm-MenuPosition( )` is used to position the menu at the coordinates specified in the `event` data structure. `XtManageChild( )` is used to pop up the menu.[3] The menu itself is the one that was shown in Figure 16-2. It contains four items, the last of which has the accelerator `Ctrl<Key>C`. Any time the user presses CTRL-C in the menu's parent widget (the DrawingArea), the callback routine associated with the menu will be called as if the menu

---

[3] Technically, this is an incorrect method for popping up menus as far as the X Toolkit Intrinsics are concerned. It is supported by the Motif toolkit because it simplifies the popup menu interface. See the discussion on popping up dialog boxes in Chapter 5, *Introduction to Dialogs*.

had been popped up and the **Quit** item had been selected. If the **Quit** button (the fourth item in the menu) is selected, `popup_cb()` is called and the program exits. Otherwise, the *name* of the widget is printed.

Note that the widget's name does not correspond to the widget's *label*. As described in Chapter 4, *The Main Window*, menu items are automatically given names of the form `buttonn`, where *n* is assigned in order of menu item creation, starting at 0.

Note also that mnemonics are not specified, since they don't make sense in popup menus. Unlike pulldown menus, which can be popped up and left on the screen until a selection is made, popup menus go away as soon as the button is released. A selection must thus be made immediately by dragging the pointer down the menu and releasing the button when the pointer is over the desired item.

16.1.2 Simple Cascading Menus

Cascading menus, also called *pullright menus*, are formally implemented as "pulldown" menus that happen to be displayed from menu items in a menu that's already "up" and in use. Figure 16-4 shows how a typical cascading menu looks in an application.

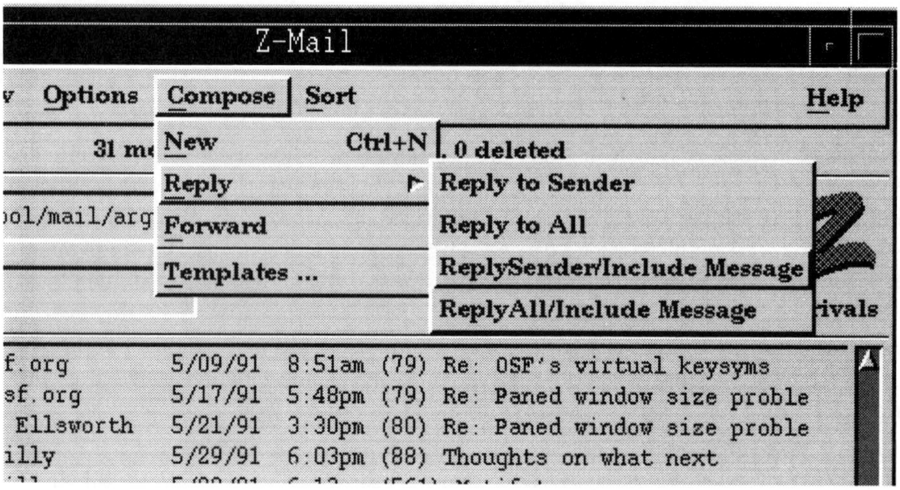

Figure 16-4. A cascading menu

The menu item that is going to pop up the cascading menu must be a CascadeButton widget (or gadget).

Example 16-2 demonstrates how to add a cascading menu using Motif's simple menu routines. This code fragment is based on the previous example, and adds an additional menu item to the popup menu. The **Line Weight** menu item is a CascadeButton that serves as the parent of a pulldown (i.e., pullright) menu created with `XmVaCreateSimplePulldownMenu()`.

Example 16-2. Making a cascading menu

```
                .
                .
                .
line = XmStringCreateSimple("Line");
square = XmStringCreateSimple("Square");
circle = XmStringCreateSimple("Circle");
weight = XmStringCreateSimple("Line Width");
quit = XmStringCreateSimple("Quit");
quit_acc = XmStringCreateSimple("Ctrl-C");
popup_menu = XmVaCreateSimplePopupMenu(drawing_a, "popup", popup_cb,
    XmVaPUSHBUTTON, line, 'L', NULL, NULL,
    XmVaPUSHBUTTON, square, 'S', NULL, NULL,
    XmVaPUSHBUTTON, circle, 'C', NULL, NULL,
    XmVaCASCADEBUTTON, weight, 'W',
    XmVaSEPARATOR,
    XmVaPUSHBUTTON, quit, 'Q', "Ctrl<Key>c", quit_acc,
    NULL);
XmStringFree(line);
XmStringFree(square);
XmStringFree(circle);
XmStringFree(weight);
XmStringFree(quit);

/* create pullright for "Line Width" button -- this is the 4th item! */
w_one = XmStringCreateSimple(" 1 ");
w_two = XmStringCreateSimple(" 2 ");
w_four = XmStringCreateSimple(" 4 ");
w_eight = XmStringCreateSimple(" 8 ");
pullright = XmVaCreateSimplePulldownMenu(popup_menu, "pullright",
    3, /* 3 (offset from 0) is the 4th menu item in the popup_menu! */
    set_weight,  /* callback to call when any of these items are selected */
    XmVaPUSHBUTTON, w_one, '1', NULL, NULL,
    XmVaPUSHBUTTON, w_two, '2', NULL, NULL,
    XmVaPUSHBUTTON, w_four, '4', NULL, NULL,
    XmVaPUSHBUTTON, w_eight, '8', NULL, NULL,
    NULL);
XmStringFree(w_one);
XmStringFree(w_two);
XmStringFree(w_four);
XmStringFree(w_eight);
            .
            .
            .

/* called when items in the Line Weight pullright menu are selected */
void
set_weight(menu_item, item_no, cbs)
Widget menu_item;
int item_no;
XmAnyCallbackStruct *cbs;
{
    printf("Line weight = %d\n", 2 << item_no);
}
```

In the call to **XmVaCreateSimplePulldownMenu( )**, the popup menu is specified as
the parent and the **button** parameter is set to three, indicating that the fourth item in the
popup menu triggers the cascading menu.

Pullright menus can be displayed from either pulldown or popup menus, but they are never displayed from option menus. We'll take a closer look at cascading menus later in the chapter.

16.1.3 Simple Option Menus

Option menus are similar to pulldown menus, in that they are associated with a Cascade-Button. However, there are several major differences:

- In the option menu, the CascadeButton is not a part of a MenuBar. Instead, it is created as a child of a RowColumn widget, which also includes an attached Label. Look at Figure 16-5, which shows the output of the next example. The (invisible) RowColumn widget holds the Label "Draw Mode" and the CascadeButton labeled "Circle."

- The menu does not drop down from the CascadeButton. It pops up on top of the CascadeButton, and the label on the CascadeButton is also one of the elements in the menu. The most recently selected item (or the default item, if the menu has not yet been used) appears as the label of the CascadeButton.

- The management of the pulldown menu is completely automated by the Motif toolkit, so its handle is not available to you (nor does it need to be).

- None of the items in an option menu may have cascading menus.

Example 16-3 shows how `XmVaCreateSimpleOptionMenu( )` can be used. This program uses the same DrawingArea widget, but the user does not pop up a menu from the drawing canvas to select the drawing style. Rather, he can make the selection from the option menu displayed above the canvas as shown in Figure 16-5.

Example 16-3. The simple_option.c program

```
/* simple_option.c -- demonstrate how to use a simple option menu.
 * Display a drawing area (used hypothetically).  The user can select
 * the drawing style from the option menu.  Notice the difference in
 * appearance between the PushButton and the option menu.
 */
#include <Xm/RowColumn.h>
#include <Xm/MainW.h>
#include <Xm/DrawingA.h>
#include <Xm/PushB.h>

main(argc, argv)
int argc;
char *argv[ ];
{
    XmString draw_shape, line, square, circle, quit;
    Widget toplevel, main_w, rc, sw, drawing_a, option_menu, pb;
    void option_cb(), exit();
    XtAppContext app;

    toplevel = XtVaAppInitialize(&app, "Demos", NULL, 0,
        &argc, argv, NULL, NULL);

    /* Create a MainWindow widget that contains a RowColumn
```

Example 16-3. The simple_option.c program (continued)

```
     * widget as its work window.
     */
    main_w = XtVaCreateManagedWidget("main_w",
        xmMainWindowWidgetClass, toplevel, NULL);
    rc = XtVaCreateWidget("rowcol", xmRowColumnWidgetClass, main_w, NULL);

    /* Inside RowColumn is the Quit pushbutton, the option menu and the
     * scrolled window that contains the drawing area.
     */
    pb = XtVaCreateManagedWidget("Quit", xmPushButtonWidgetClass, rc, NULL);
    XtAddCallback(pb, XmNactivateCallback, exit, NULL);

    draw_shape = XmStringCreateSimple("Draw Mode:");
    line = XmStringCreateSimple("Line");
    square = XmStringCreateSimple("Square");
    circle = XmStringCreateSimple("Circle");
    option_menu = XmVaCreateSimpleOptionMenu(rc, "option_menu",
        draw_shape, 'D', 0 /*initial menu selection*/, option_cb,
        XmVaPUSHBUTTON, line, 'L', NULL, NULL,
        XmVaPUSHBUTTON, square, 'S', NULL, NULL,
        XmVaPUSHBUTTON, circle, 'C', NULL, NULL,
        NULL);
    XmStringFree(line);
    XmStringFree(square);
    XmStringFree(circle);
    XmStringFree(draw_shape);

    XtManageChild(option_menu);

    /* Create a DrawingArea inside a ScrolledWindow */
    sw = XtVaCreateManagedWidget("sw", xmScrolledWindowWidgetClass, rc,
        XmNscrollingPolicy, XmAUTOMATIC,
        NULL);
    drawing_a = XtVaCreateManagedWidget("drawing_area",
        xmDrawingAreaWidgetClass, sw,
        XmNwidth, 500,
        XmNheight, 500,
        NULL);

    XtManageChild(rc);

    XtRealizeWidget(toplevel);
    XtAppMainLoop(app);
}

/* invoked when the user selects an item in the option menu */
void
option_cb(menu_item, item_no, cbs)
Widget menu_item;
int item_no;
XmAnyCallbackStruct *cbs;
{
    puts(XtName(menu_item)); /* Otherwise, just print the selection */
}
```

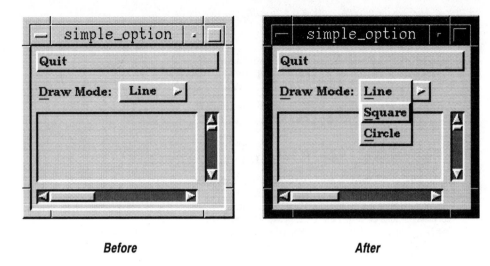

Before   **After**

Figure 16-5. Output of simple_option.c before and after the option menu is popped up

The layout of the application is different from that in the previous examples because a separate ScrolledWindow contains the DrawingArea widget rather than allowing the Main-Window widget to manage the Scrollbar for us. The MainWindow can only have one **Xm-NworkWindow,** so here we create a RowColumn widget (not to be confused with the "invisible" RowColumn that is automatically created as part of the OptionMenu) to contain the **Quit** button, the option menu, and the ScrolledWindow (with DrawingArea).

Notice how the label of the CascadeButton changes as you select alternate values from the menu.

16.1.4 Summary of Simple Menu Routines

The advantages of the simple menu creation routines are clear. Menu creation is simple, the concepts are easily understood, the code is extremely readable, and the job gets done without much room for error. Furthermore, once the code has been written, it can be easily maintained. Strings, mnemonics, accelerators, and the callback function to use can be easily modified by editing the source. However, despite these reasons, there are some disadvantages to using these simple menu creation functions:

*   They require a great deal of "bulk" in order to create one simple menu. If a large number of menus needs to be created (not unusual for a typical application), a great deal of redundant code will have to be generated. The simple menu creation routines make it difficult to build a looping construct or a function to automate the process.

*   Abstraction is difficult due to the non-unique widget names that are given to menus and menu items. The convenience functions name the widgets themselves, so it is difficult for resource files (or fallback resources) to specify alternate labels, mnemonics, or accelerators for menus and menu items alike. Even if the widget hierarchy could be specified,

few resources would actually be applied to actual widgets, since the function parameters imply hard-coded values.

- Separate callback functions (and client data parameters) cannot be individually specified for menu items because of the nature of the callback routines.

Therefore, the rest of this chapter addresses the more advanced functions for creating Motif menus. As we delve into the innards of the toolkit, we will uncover the lower-level functions as well as the concepts behind the design. The goal will be to build a new system that's just as "simple" as the menu creation routines we've just reviewed, yet more dynamic and more easily modifiable. To do this, we are going to start at the beginning, re-examine the MenuBar and pulldown menus, and work our way up again. As we go, pay close attention to the way we develop menus from one step to the next. Experience shows that different applications will differ in their needs for the three kinds of menus Motif provides. Knowing how a menu system is designed may save you lots of time, effort, and frustration.

16.2 Advanced Menu Methods

We start with the MenuBar because this is the most common place for menus to exist in an application. Furthermore, everything there is to know about menus can be adapted from the pulldown menu design. In this section, we examine the functions behind the "XmCreate-Simple*Menu" convenience routines. Be forewarned: this might seem like a step in the wrong direction at first—the functions we use and the approaches we take may seem less "simple" than those from the previous section—but the purpose of this section is to demonstrate what is going on "under the hood" of those simple routines so we can optimize the methodology later.

Let's begin by examining the steps taken to create a MenuBar:

1. Create an appropriate RowColumn widget as a MenuBar using `XmCreateMenuBar( )`.

2. Create a pulldown menu using `XmCreatePulldownMenu( )`.

3. Create menu items (pushbuttons, gadgets, separators, etc.) to fill the pulldown menu.

4. Create a CascadeButton widget as a MenuBar title and attach the pulldown menu to it.

5. Repeat steps 2 through 4 as needed for each title, and then manage the MenuBar with `XtManageChild( )`.

`XmCreateMenuBar( )` returns a handle to a widget that may be referred to as your MenuBar widget. The code fragment in Example 16-4 shows an example of creating a MenuBar that has a **File** title item.

Example 16-4. Creating a File title item

```
Widget      MenuBar, FilePullDown;
XmString    label_str;

MenuBar = XmCreateMenuBar(MainWindow, "MenuBar", NULL, 0);
```

Example 16-4. Creating a File title item (continued)

```
/* create the "File" Menu */
FilePullDown = XmCreatePulldownMenu(MenuBar, "FilePullDown", NULL, 0);

/* create the "File" button (attach Menu via XmNsubMenuId) */
label_str = XmStringCreateSimple("File");
XtVaCreateManagedWidget("File", xmCascadeButtonWidgetClass, MenuBar,
    XmNlabelString,  label_str,
    XmNmnemonic,     'F',
    XmNsubMenuId,    FilePullDown,
    NULL);
XmStringFree(label_str); /* don't need it any longer */

/* Now add the menu items */
XtVaCreateManagedWidget("Open",
    xmPushButtonGadgetClass, FilePullDown, NULL);

XtVaCreateManagedWidget("Close",
    xmPushButtonGadgetClass, FilePullDown, NULL);

XtVaCreateManagedWidget("separator",
    xmSeparatorGadgetClass, FilePullDown, NULL);

XtVaCreateManagedWidget("Quit",
    xmPushButtonGadgetClass, FilePullDown, NULL);

XtManageChild(MenuBar);
```

The code follows the steps outlined earlier: the MenuBar is created as a child of the Main-Window and the pulldown menu is created as a child of the MenuBar. The CascadeButton acts as the **File** title item in the MenuBar, so it is *also* created as the MenuBar's child. (It is frequently overlooked that both the menu title and the pulldown are children of the Menu-Bar.) The CascadeButton sets its **XmNsubMenuId** resource to the pulldown menu so that when the title is selected, the button knows which pulldown menu to display. (This is just what the simple menu creation routines do behind the scenes for both MenuBar Cascade-Buttons and pullright menu cascades.)

The label is set using the **XmNlabelString** resource. The value is a compound string, just as in the simple creation functions. Had we not set the label string directly, the name of the widget itself would appear as the label, and could be overridden by a setting in an application defaults file, or a user-resource file. In short, we had the *choice* of hard-coding the label for the CascadeButton, where we would not have had this luxury (without causing great confusion) in the simple menu creation routines.

Finally, the MenuBar is managed using **XtManageChild( )**. The result of the above code fragment is shown in Figure 16-6.

 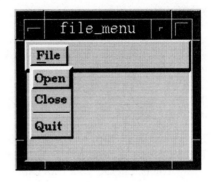

Before   **After**

Figure 16-6. A File menu from a MenuBar

16.2.1 Menu Titles

The titles in MenuBars are CascadeButtons, and each must have a submenu associated with it. You should never attach a callback function directly to a title item in the MenuBar—callback functions should be attached to menu items only.

It is important to note that `XmCreatePulldownMenu()` does not return a pulldown menu *per se*; it returns the RowColumn widget that manages the menu items. This widget's *parent* is the MenuShell. You should keep this in mind if you ever need to specify resources for this widget.[4] Because the function returns a RowColumn widget, the attribute-value list provided to the function sets resources for the RowColumn widget only, not for the Menu-Shell that contains it.

Menu titles should not be dynamically created or destroyed. That is, there should not exist a condition in the program that would cause a MenuBar title to disappear or a new title to be generated. All titles in the MenuBar must be available to the user when the MainWindow is visible. You can, however, deactivate entire menus by toggling the `XmNsensitive` resource on the CascadeButton widgets that act as titles. (You can also set the sensitivity of individual menu items.) This is discussed more fully in Section 16.3, *General Menu Techniques*.

---

[4] Popup and popdown callback functions may be attached to the pulldown menus by calling `XtAddCallback()` on these parents, if necessary, but this is rarely done. See Volume Four, *X Toolkit Intrinsics Programming Manual*, for more information on popup and popdown callbacks.

16.2.2 Menu Items

Unlike the **File** title item in the MenuBar, we chose not to use a hard-coded value for the menu item strings, so the application or the user could reset the labels, if desired. One should strive to limit the use of hard-coded values for menu items and the like, to provide future flexibility for supporting multiple languages, once an internationalization strategy for Motif is clearly articulated.

The menu items themselves are usually PushButton gadgets, although you may also use ToggleButtons, Labels, and Separators, just as you can with the simple menu creation routines. You can install your own callback routines for these objects, or you can install an **XmNentryCallback** for the RowColumn widget (menu) to act on behalf of all the menu items. This resource specifies a callback function that overrides the **XmNactivateCallback** used by Pushbuttons and the **XmNvalueChangedCallback** used by Toggles by replacing them with a single callback used by their managing RowColumn widget. In this case, you could have a design more similar to the simple menu routines described in the beginning of the chapter (although this is not how simple menu functions are actually implemented). See Chapter 8, *Manager Widgets*, for details on this generic RowColumn resource.

As with the title items, menu items are not intended to be dynamically created or destroyed. You should avoid creating or destroying menu items within pulldown menus, since it may not be clear to the user when menus are changing.

16.2.3 Mnemonics

Mnemonics help users traverse menus or select actual menu items without having to use the mouse. In Example 16-4, we used the **XmNmnemonic** resource to attach the mnemonic "F" to the CascadeButton. This allows the user to use the key sequence **Meta-F** to open or close the File menu without using the mouse. The **XmNmnemonic** resource is, in fact, defined by the Label widget and gadget classes, but it is only used by PushButtons, ToggleButtons, and CascadeButtons (which are all subclassed from Labels). Furthermore, mnemonics are only effective when these objects are menu items or contain menus (as in a CascadeButton). The visual representation of the mnemonic is the underlining of the mnemonic character in the label string. In this case, it would be the "F" in the word "File." If the letter is not found, there will be no visual feedback for the mnemonic, although it will still function. The mnemonic specified can be either uppercase or lowercase, but this only affects which letter is underlined. Either way, mnemonics are case insensitive; the user simply types **Meta-<mnemonic>**, and the pulldown menu associated with the CascadeButton is displayed.

Mnemonics can be set on menu items as well. When a pulldown menu is displayed, the user activates a menu item by typing the letter represented by its mnemonic. (The META key does not have to be used once the menu is displayed.) When this happens, the menu item's callback function is called just as if the user had selected it using the mouse. Mnemonics are set on MenuBar titles and menu items in the same way. To illustrate, let's add a mnemonic to the **Quit** PushButton gadget in our example **File** menu. We can set the mnemonic directly in the declaration of the gadget:

```
XtVaCreateManagedWidget("Quit", xmPushButtonGadgetClass, FilePullDown,
    XmNmnemonic, 'Q',
    NULL);
```

While this method accomplishes the task, a problem remains in that this particular mnemonic is hard-coded in the widget, whereas the widget's label is not. Consider what would happen if the user had the following resource specification:

```
*Quit.labelString: Exit
```

This resource sets the label for the quit button to read "Exit." If the mnemonic for the button is hard-coded to "Q," then there would not only be no visual feedback, but the mnemonic itself would be counterintuitive. The best way to handle this particular case is to specify both the label string and the mnemonic in the application defaults file or fallback resources. Thus, if the user changes the item's label, he can also change the mnemonic in the same resource setting. For example:

```
*Quit.labelString: Exit
*Quit.mnemonic:    E
```

Hard-coding the "F" mnemonic in the "File" title discussed earlier was acceptable because we also hard-coded the value for the title string. The basic rule of thumb is: the label string and the mnemonic for buttons should both be set in the same way, either as hard-coded values or in the application defaults file or fallback resources. It doesn't matter which, provided they are specified consistently.

16.2.4 Accelerators

The purpose of *menu accelerators* is to provide the user with the ability to activate menu items in pulldown menus without having to display the menu at all. That is, the user can directly activate a menu item using the keyboard without even displaying the menu. In Figure 16-1, the **Quit** menu item displayed the accelerator **Ctrl+C** to indicate that the user could press the CTRL-C keyboard sequence to activate that menu item and quit the application.

In order to install accelerators on menu items, you need to use the **XmNaccelerator** resource[5] to specify the accelerator translation, and **XmNacceleratorText** to provide visual feedback to the user. The syntax for the accelerator is exactly the same as for translation tables, but you do *not* specify an action function with an event sequence. That is, the accelerator specified in Example 16-1 is **"Ctrl<Key>C"**. (For information on how to specify translation tables, see Volume Four, *X Toolkit Intrinsics Programming Manual*.)

However, the accelerator *text* (the string that is displayed) is not the same string as the accelerator translation because it would be confusing for most users. Instead, you should display something like **"^C"**, **"Ctrl-C"**, or **"Ctrl+C"**, as these make it reasonably clear what

---

[5] The **XmNaccelerator** and **XmNacceleratorText** resources, like the **XmNmnemonic** resource, are defined by the Label class but may only be used by PushButtons and ToggleButtons that are acting as menu items.

the user is expected to type. (The latter is the convention recommended by the *Motif Style Guide*, although all three forms are frequently used.) Since this is displayable text, you cannot use a common C string; the text must be given as a compound string. For example, the following code installs an accelerator for the **Quit** button:

```
char      *accel = "Ctrl<Key>C";
XmString  accel_text = XmStringCreateSimple("Ctrl-C");

XtVaCreateManagedWidget("Quit", xmPushButtonGadgetClass, FilePullDown,
    XmNaccelerator,     accel,
    XmNacceleratorText, accel_text,
    NULL);

XmStringFree(accel_text);
```

After the widget is created, the compound string allocated by **XmStringCreate-Simple( )** must be freed using **XmStringFree( )**.

As with mnemonics, the resources for the accelerator itself and the text used to display the accelerator can be set directly either by using a hard-coded resource-value pair as shown above, or by specifying their values in the application defaults file (or in fallback resources). One should never specify the accelerator one way and the accelerator text another way; they should always be consistent. Either hard-code these values or specify them in the appropriate resource database(s). The decision you have to make is whether you want the user to be able to configure these values.

NOTE

> A side effect of the current implementation of the Motif toolkit (1.1.3) is that you *cannot* install your own accelerators using the standard methods provided by the X Toolkit Intrinsics (such as **XtInstallAccelerators( )** or **Xt-InstallAllAccelerators( )**). These functions will not work, and you may interfere with the Motif accelerator mechanism by attempting to use them.

16.2.5 Help Titles

Motif specifies various ways for the user to get help. He can obtain it using the HELP key on the keyboard,[6] from the help buttons provided in dialog boxes, and from the **Help** MenuBar title item. This title provides the highest level help for your application, and should not provide too much detail about lower-level functions within the program. When you create a pulldown menu for this title, it should have only those essential categories necessary to get the user started. Figure 16-7 shows an example of selections commonly found in a **Help** menu.

---

[6] F1 will also invoke the help functions whether there is a key named Help or not.

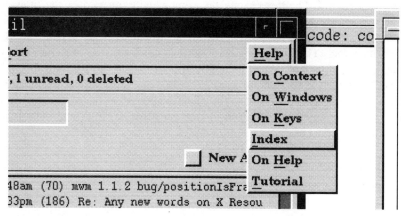

Figure 16-7. A Help menu from a MenuBar

The choices shown in Figure 16-7 are not required, but are recommended by the *Motif Style Guide*; if they apply to your program, use them. It is usually a good idea to have a help item that displays an index of what kind of help is available in a more verbose fashion than the menu itself. An example of a help window is shown in Figure 16-8.

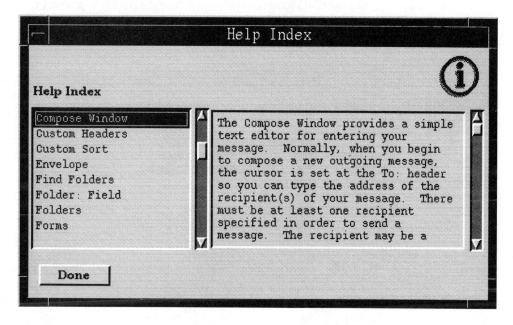

Figure 16-8. A sample help index browser

There is usually an item within the **Help** menu that gives the user a brief overview of how to use the **Help** facility, including the menu and/or other dialog boxes. You should consult the *Motif Style Guide* for details on what kind of help each of the above selections should provide. A complete discussion of how help is provided can be found in Chapter 6, *Selection Dialogs*, and Chapter 7, *Custom Dialogs*.

Creating the pulldown menu for help is exactly the same as with other MenuBar titles with one exception. Once you have created a pulldown menu and CascadeButton, the special resource `XmNmenuHelpWidget` should be set in the MenuBar widget with the **Help** CascadeButton as its value. This tells the MenuBar that this item (the help item) should always be completely right-justified in the menu, even if the menu titles do not fill up the width of the MenuBar. Example 16-5 shows an example of using this attribute within a function that builds a **Help** menu and attaches it to the MenuBar passed as the parameter. In this example, we also present an alternate approach to creating MenuBar titles and their associated pulldown menus.

Example 16-5. The BuildHelpMenu() function

```
BuildHelpMenu(MenuBar)
Widget MenuBar;
{
    Widget HelpPullDown, widget;
    int i;
    static char *h_items[ ] = {
        "Index", "Context", "Keys", "Windows",
        "Tutorial", "Version", NULL, "Help"
    };

    /* Help menu */
    HelpPullDown = XmCreatePulldownMenu(MenuBar, "HelpPullDown", NULL, 0);
    widget = XtVaCreateManagedWidget("Help",
        xmCascadeButtonWidgetClass, MenuBar,
        XmNsubMenuId, HelpPullDown,
        NULL);
    /* tell the MenuBar that this is the help widget */
    XtVaSetValues(MenuBar, XmNmenuHelpWidget, widget, NULL);

    /* Now add the menu items to the pulldown menu */
    for (i = 0; i < XtNumber(h_items); i++) {
        if (h_items[i] != NULL) {
            widget = XtVaCreateManagedWidget(h_items[i],
                xmPushButtonGadgetClass, HelpPullDown, NULL);
            XtAddCallback(widget, XmNactivateCallback,
                do_help, h_items[i]);
        } else
            widget = XtVaCreateManagedWidget(NULL,
                xmSeparatorGadgetClass, HelpPullDown, NULL);
    }
}
```

Much of the work required to create pulldown menus comes in the process of creating its menu items. Therefore, we optimize the code by providing a loop that creates individual items based on the names used in a static array. If you want to add a new help item to the list, you just need to add its name to the **h_items** list. A **NULL** entry causes a Separator gadget to be added.

In Example 16-5, the same callback function is added for each help item in the menu. The **client_data** for the function is the same as the name of the menu item. In the next section, we expand on this approach to build arbitrary menus for the MenuBar.

16.3 General Menu Techniques

Up to this point, we have addressed each of the fundamental elements of the MenuBar and the resources used to provide the user with the appropriate feedback. Using this information, we can now identify each of these elements and generalize the way we build MenuBars. This will enable us to generate arbitrarily large MenuBars, titles, and pulldown menus using a substantially smaller code-set.

In the examples that follow, we use many of the optional or *recommended* elements for a standard Motif MenuBar. You can adjust the algorithms and data structures to fit the needs of your applications. Although we use hard-coded values for each of the widgets' resources, this is by no means a requirement, nor should it be construed as recommended usage. If you choose to implement your application using user-settable resources instead, you should write an appropriate application defaults file that has the correct widget hierarchies and resource values.

Let's begin by identifying each of the elements of a menu item:

- Label.

- Mnemonic.

- Accelerator.

- Accelerator text.

- Callback routine.

- Callback data.

Using this information, you can construct a data structure that comprises all the important aspects of a menu item:

```
typedef struct _menu_item {
    char        *label;         /* the label for the item */
    WidgetClass *class;         /* pushbutton, label, separator... */
    char         mnemonic;      /* mnemonic; NULL if none */
    char        *accelerator;   /* accelerator; NULL if none */
    char        *accel_text;    /* to be converted to compound string */
    void        (*callback)();  /* routine to call; NULL if none */
    XtPointer    callback_data; /* client_data for callback() */
} MenuItem;
```

To create a pulldown menu, all you need to do is initialize an array of **MenuItems** and pass it to a routine that iterates through the array using appropriate information. For example, the following code initializes an array to contain all the elements for a sample **File** menu:

```
MenuItem file_items[ ] = {
    { "New", &xmPushButtonGadgetClass, 'N',
        NULL, NULL, do_open, NEW },
    { "Open ...", &xmPushButtonGadgetClass, 'O',
        NULL, NULL, do_open, OPEN },
    { "Save", &xmPushButtonGadgetClass, 'S',
        NULL, NULL, do_save, SAVE },
    { "Save As ...", &xmPushButtonGadgetClass, 'A',
        NULL, NULL, do_save, SAVE_AS },
    { "Print ...", &xmPushButtonGadgetClass, 'P',
        NULL, NULL, do_print, NULL },
    { "", &xmSeparatorGadgetClass, NULL,
        NULL, NULL, NULL, NULL },
    { "Quit", &xmPushButtonGadgetClass, 'Q',
        "Ctrl<Key>Q", "Ctrl-Q", do_quit, NULL },
    NULL,
};
```

Each element in the **MenuItem** data structure is filled with default values for each menu item. Resource values that are not meaningful or hard-coded are initialized to NULL. The accelerators, for example, are almost all unset except for the **Quit** item. The Separator gadget is completely unspecified, since none of the resources even apply to Separators. The only field that cannot be NULL is the widget class. This design makes modification and maintenance very simple. If you wanted to add an accelerator for the **Save** item, you needn't search through the source code looking for where that item is created; you merely change the appropriate fields within the data structure.

Remember, none of the values are required; if you don't need a callback function or client data for an item, the field may be set to NULL. The final terminating NULL in the `label` field indicates the end of the list. The null string (`""`), used as the name of the Separator, is not the same as NULL. Widgets can have a NULL name or a null string as a name, so this does not adversely affect the widget or the algorithm. It also does not complicate the resource specifications, since one rarely if ever gives resource values for Separators (especially on an individual basis).[7]

One particular point of interest is the way the **WidgetClass** field is initialized. It is declared as a *pointer* to a widget class rather than just a widget class. Because of that, we initialize the field with the *address* of the widget class variable (declared in the widget's header file). The use of **&xmPushButtonGadgetClass** is one such example. The structure must be initialized this way because the compiler must have a specific *value* in order to initialize static data structures. The **xmPushButtonWidgetClass** pointer has no value until the program is actually running. However, the address of the variable does have a value. Once the program is running, the pointer is later dereferenced to access the real PushButton widget class.

---

[7] Technically, the X Toolkit Intrinsics specifications do not define how widgets with NULL names are treated. Currently, however, they are replaced with null strings.

Writing a Generalized Function

We can now put the **MenuItem** data structure to work by writing a routine that pulls it all together to make menus. The **BuildPulldownMenu( )** function, shown in Example 16-6, loops through each element in an array of pre-initialized **MenuItems** and creates menus from that information.

Example 16-6. The BuildPulldownMenu() function

```
Widget
BuildPulldownMenu(parent, menu_title, menu_mnemonic, items)
Widget parent;
char *menu_title, menu_mnemonic;
MenuItem *items;
{
    Widget PullDown, cascade, widget;
    int i;
    XmString str;

    PullDown = XmCreatePulldownMenu(parent, "_pulldown", NULL, 0);
    str = XmStringCreateSimple(menu_title);
    cascade = XtVaCreateManagedWidget(menu_title,
        xmCascadeButtonWidgetClass, parent,
        XmNsubMenuId,    PullDown,
        XmNlabelString, str,
        XmNmnemonic,    menu_mnemonic,
        NULL);
    XmStringFree(str);

    /* Now add the menu items */
    for (i = 0; items[i].label != NULL; i++) {
        widget = XtVaCreateManagedWidget(items[i].label,
            *items[i].class, PullDown,
            NULL);
        if (items[i].mnemonic)
            XtVaSetValues(widget, XmNmnemonic, items[i].mnemonic, NULL);
        if (items[i].accelerator) {
            str = XmStringCreateSimple(items[i].accel_text);
            XtVaSetValues(widget,
                XmNaccelerator, items[i].accelerator,
                XmNacceleratorText, str,
                NULL);
            XmStringFree(str);
        }
        if (items[i].callback)
            XtAddCallback(widget, XmNactivateCallback,
                items[i].callback, items[i].callback_data);
    }
    return cascade;
}
```

The function takes four parameters: the **parent** is (presumably) a handle to a MenuBar widget that must have already been created, the **menu_title** indicates what the title of the menu will be, the **menu_mnemonic** should be set according to its title, and the last parameter is an array of **MenuItems**.

The function first creates a pulldown menu (the RowColumn widget used to manage the menu items). This widget's name is not terribly important, so we use a predefined name, prefixed by an underscore, indicating that it is not intended to be referenced by application defaults files or other methods for resource specification. This is our own convention, by the way, not one adopted by the X Toolkit Intrinsics. We came up with this "unwritten rule" because Xt has no such naming conventions for widgets that do not wish to have their resources specified externally. The only exception is the NULL name, but this is technically undefined.

After the pulldown menu is created, the CascadeButton that acts as the MenuBar's title item is created. Its name is derived from the second parameter, menu_title. Its mnemonic is also set here. (All MenuBar titles should have mnemonics associated with them.)

After the pulldown menu and the associated title item have been created, the function then loops through the array of MenuItems, building new items, until it finds an entry with a NULL label name. We use this as an end-of-menu indicator in our initialization. Each widget is created individually, with its mnemonics, accelerators, and callback functions being added only as specified by the values in the MenuItem structure. The SeparatorGadget is created with no resources specified.

BuildPulldownMenu( ) must be called from another function that passed the appropriate data structures and other parameters. In our design, this is the routine that actually creates the MenuBar itself. Example 16-7 shows the code for the CreateMenuBar( ) routine. This simple function creates a MenuBar widget, calls BuildPulldownMenu( ), manages the MenuBar, and then returns it to the calling function.

Example 16-7. The CreateMenuBar() function

```
Widget
CreateMenuBar(MainWindow)
Widget MainWindow;
{
    Widget      MenuBar, widget, BuildPulldownMenu();

    MenuBar = XmCreateMenuBar(MainWindow, "MenuBar", NULL, 0);

    (void) BuildPulldownMenu(MenuBar, "File", 'F', file_items);
    (void) BuildPulldownMenu(MenuBar, "Edit", 'E', edit_items);
    (void) BuildPulldownMenu(MenuBar, "View", 'V', view_items);
    (void) BuildPulldownMenu(MenuBar, "Options", 'O', options_items);
    widget = BuildPulldownMenu(MenuBar, "Help", 'H', help_items);

    XtVaSetValues(MenuBar, XmNmenuHelpWidget, widget, NULL);

    XtManageChild(MenuBar);
    return MenuBar;
}
```

Each call to BuildPulldownMenu( ) passes an array of preinitialized MenuItem structures. The **Help** menu is a special case, since the MenuBar must know which item it is (if any are to exist). By setting the MenuBar's XmNmenuHelpWidget resource to the CascadeButton returned by the function, it knows that this button should be placed on the far right of the MenuBar. The one and only parameter to the CreateMenuBar( ) function is the MainWindow widget that will manage the MenuBar that is returned.

16.3.1 Building Pullright Menus

Pullright menus can be easily added to our menu creation methodology by expanding on the **MenuItem** data structure and making a slight modification to the **CreatePulldown-Menu()** function. As we learned from the simple menu creation routines, cascading menus are really pulldown menus that are associated with CascadeButtons. We also know that we can attach menus to CascadeButtons by setting the button's **XmNsubMenuId** resource to the handle of the pulldown menu. We begin by modifying the **MenuItem** structure:

```
typedef struct _menu_item {
    char        *label;         /* the label for the item */
    WidgetClass *class;         /* pushbutton, label, separator... */
    char         mnemonic;      /* mnemonic; NULL if none */
    char        *accelerator;   /* accelerator; NULL if none */
    char        *accel_text;    /* to be converted to compound string */
    void        (*callback)();  /* routine to call; NULL if none */
    XtPointer    callback_data; /* client_data for callback() */
    struct _menu_item *subitems; /* pullright menu items, if not NULL */
} MenuItem;
```

The new field at the end of the structure is a pointer to another array of **MenuItems**. If this pointer is not **NULL**, then the menu item points to another (similar) group of menu items that represent a cascading menu. An example of how this field can be used, along with the modified version of **BuildPulldownMenu()**, is shown in Example 16-8. Briefly, **Build-PulldownMenu()** may be called recursively, passing the additional menu items as the information about the cascading menu to be created.

The **MenuItem** declarations initialize a single menu whose items may be Labels, Push-Buttons, or whatever. If the item is a CascadeButton for a cascading menu, then the **sub-items** field contains a pointer to yet another array of items. All the menus and menu items are declared in reverse order because the cascading menu declaration (or initialization) must exist before the menu is actually used.

Example 16-8. The make_pulldown.c program

```
/* build_menu.c -- Demonstrate the BuildPulldownMenu() routine and
 * how it can be used to build pulldown -and- pullright menus.
 * Menus are defined by declaring an array of MenuItem structures.
 */
#include <Xm/RowColumn.h>
#include <Xm/MainW.h>
#include <Xm/DrawingA.h>
#include <Xm/CascadeBG.h>
#include <Xm/PushB.h>
#include <Xm/PushBG.h>

typedef struct _menu_item {
    char        *label;         /* the label for the item */
    WidgetClass *class;         /* pushbutton, label, separator... */
    char         mnemonic;      /* mnemonic; NULL if none */
    char        *accelerator;   /* accelerator; NULL if none */
    char        *accel_text;    /* to be converted to compound string */
    void        (*callback)();  /* routine to call; NULL if none */
    XtPointer    callback_data; /* client_data for callback() */
    struct _menu_item *subitems; /* pullright menu items, if not NULL */
```

Example 16-8. The make_pulldown.c program (continued)

```
} MenuItem;

/* Pulldown menus are built from cascade buttons, so this function
 * also includes pullright menus.  Create the menu, the cascade button
 * that owns the menu, and then the submenu items.
 */
Widget
BuildPulldownMenu(parent, menu_title, menu_mnemonic, items)
Widget parent;
char *menu_title, menu_mnemonic;
MenuItem *items;
{
    Widget PullDown, cascade, widget;
    int i;
    XmString str;

    PullDown = XmCreatePulldownMenu(parent, "_pulldown", NULL, 0);

    str = XmStringCreateSimple(menu_title);
    cascade = XtVaCreateManagedWidget(menu_title,
        xmCascadeButtonGadgetClass, parent,
        XmNsubMenuId,    PullDown,
        XmNlabelString, str,
        XmNmnemonic,     menu_mnemonic,
        NULL);
    XmStringFree(str);

    /* Now add the menu items */
    for (i = 0; items[i].label != NULL; i++) {
        /* If subitems exist, create the pull-right menu by calling this
         * function recursively.  Since the function returns a cascade
         * button, the widget returned is used..
         */
        if (items[i].subitems)
            widget = BuildPulldownMenu(PullDown,
                items[i].label, items[i].mnemonic, items[i].subitems);
        else
            widget = XtVaCreateManagedWidget(items[i].label,
                *items[i].class, PullDown,
                NULL);
        /* Whether the item is a real item or a cascade button with a
         * menu, it can still have a mnemonic.
         */
        if (items[i].mnemonic)
            XtVaSetValues(widget, XmNmnemonic, items[i].mnemonic, NULL);
        /* any item can have an accelerator, except cascade menus. But,
         * we don't worry about that; we know better in our declarations.
         */
        if (items[i].accelerator) {
            str = XmStringCreateSimple(items[i].accel_text);
            XtVaSetValues(widget,
                XmNaccelerator, items[i].accelerator,
                XmNacceleratorText, str,
                NULL);
            XmStringFree(str);
        }
        /* again, anyone can have a callback -- however, this is an
         * activate-callback.  This may not be appropriate for all items.
```

Example 16-8. The make_pulldown.c program (continued)

```
            */
        if (items[i].callback)
            XtAddCallback(widget, XmNactivateCallback,
                items[i].callback, items[i].callback_data);
    }
    return cascade;
}
/* callback functions for menu items declared later... */
void
set_weight(widget, weight)
Widget widget;
int weight;
{
    printf("Setting line weight to %d\n", weight);
}

void
set_color(widget, color)
Widget widget;
char *color;
{
    printf("Setting color to %s\n", color);
}

void
set_dot_dash(widget, dot_or_dash)
Widget widget;
int dot_or_dash;
{
    printf("Setting line style to %s\n", dot_or_dash? "dash" : "dot");
}
MenuItem weight_menu[ ] = {
    { " 1 ", &xmPushButtonGadgetClass, '1', NULL, NULL,
        set_weight, (XtPointer)1, (MenuItem *)NULL },
    { " 2 ", &xmPushButtonGadgetClass, '2', NULL, NULL,
        set_weight, (XtPointer)2, (MenuItem *)NULL },
    { " 3 ", &xmPushButtonGadgetClass, '3', NULL, NULL,
        set_weight, (XtPointer)3, (MenuItem *)NULL },
    { " 4 ", &xmPushButtonGadgetClass, '4', NULL, NULL,
        set_weight, (XtPointer)4, (MenuItem *)NULL },
    NULL,
};

MenuItem color_menu[ ] = {
    { "Cyan", &xmPushButtonGadgetClass, 'C', "Meta<Key>C", "Meta+C",
        set_color, "cyan", (MenuItem *)NULL },
    { "Yellow", &xmPushButtonGadgetClass, 'Y', "Meta<Key>Y", "Meta+Y",
        set_color, "yellow", (MenuItem *)NULL },
    { "Magenta", &xmPushButtonGadgetClass, 'M', "Meta<Key>M", "Meta+M",
        set_color, "magenta", (MenuItem *)NULL },
    { "Black", &xmPushButtonGadgetClass, 'B', "Meta<Key>B", "Meta+B",
        set_color, "black", (MenuItem *)NULL },
    NULL,
};

MenuItem style_menu[ ] = {
```

Example 16-8. The make_pulldown.c program (continued)

```
    { "Dash", &xmPushButtonGadgetClass, 'D', NULL, NULL,
        set_dot_dash, (XtPointer)0, (MenuItem *)NULL },
    { "Dot",  &xmPushButtonGadgetClass, 'o', NULL, NULL,
        set_dot_dash, (XtPointer)1, (MenuItem *)NULL },
    NULL,
};

MenuItem drawing_menus[ ] = {
    { "Line Weight", &xmCascadeButtonGadgetClass, 'W', NULL, NULL,
        0, 0, weight_menu },
    { "Line Color", &xmCascadeButtonGadgetClass, 'C', NULL, NULL,
        0, 0, color_menu },
    { "Line Style", &xmCascadeButtonGadgetClass, 'S', NULL, NULL,
        0, 0, style_menu },
    NULL,
};

main(argc, argv)
int argc;
char *argv[ ];
{
    Widget toplevel, main_w, menubar, drawing_a;
    XtAppContext app;

    toplevel = XtVaAppInitialize(&app, "Demos", NULL, 0,
        &argc, argv, NULL, NULL);

    /* Create a MainWindow widget that contains a DrawingArea in
     * its work window. (This happens by default.)
     */
    main_w = XtVaCreateManagedWidget("main_w",
        xmMainWindowWidgetClass, toplevel,
        XmNscrollingPolicy,  XmAUTOMATIC,
        NULL);

    menubar = XmCreateMenuBar(main_w, "menubar", NULL, 0);
    BuildPulldownMenu(menubar, "Lines", 'L', drawing_menus);
    XtManageChild(menubar);

    /* Create a DrawingArea -- no actual drawing will be done. */
    drawing_a = XtVaCreateManagedWidget("drawing_a",
        xmDrawingAreaWidgetClass, main_w,
        XmNwidth, 500,
        XmNheight, 500,
        NULL);

    XtRealizeWidget(toplevel);
    XtAppMainLoop(app);
}
```

The three new lines added to the function fit in rather nicely with the rest of the routine. Because the function creates and returns a CascadeButton, the return value may be used as the menu item in the menu currently being built. But the menu must exist before it can be attached to a CascadeButton. Recursion handles that problem for us by creating the deepest submenus first and returning to the top later. This ensures that all the necessary submenus are built before their CascadeButtons require them.

The majority of this program is composed of the new version of **BuildPulldown-Menu( )** and the menu and submenu declarations. The rest of the code is basically what was there before in the previous examples. A sample of the output of the program is shown in Figure 16-9.

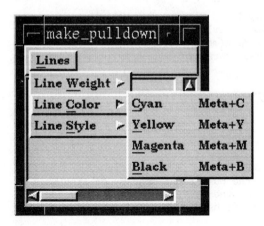

Figure 16-9. Output of make_pulldown.c

16.3.2 Building Popup Menus

To further demonstrate the flexibility of this design and to further exploit the similarity between pulldown, popup, and cascading menus, we can easily modify the **Build-PulldownMenu( )** routine to support any of these menu types. The only thing we need to do is to specify a new parameter indicating which of the two menu types to use. Since Motif already defines the values **XmMENU_PULLDOWN** and **XmMENU_POPUP** in *<Xm/Xm.h>*, we might as well use those values. (Any arbitrary values would do.) We have also given the function the more generic name, **BuildMenu( )**, as shown in Example 16-9.

Example 16-9. The BuildMenu() function

```
/* Build popup and pulldown menus, depending on the menu_type (which
 * may be either XmMENU_PULLDOWN or XmMENU_POPUP).  Pulldowns return
 * the CascadeButton that pops up the menu.  Popups return the menu.
 * Pulldown menus are built from cascade buttons, so the function can
 * be recursive.
 */
Widget
BuildMenu(parent, menu_type, menu_title, menu_mnemonic, items)
Widget parent;
int menu_type;
char *menu_title, menu_mnemonic;
MenuItem *items;
{
    Widget menu, cascade, widget;
    int i;
    XmString str;
```

Example 16-9. The BuildMenu() function (continued)

```
    if (menu_type == XmMENU_PULLDOWN)
        menu = XmCreatePulldownMenu(parent, "_pulldown", NULL, 0);
    else
        menu = XmCreatePopupMenu(parent, "_popup", NULL, 0 );

    if (menu_type == XmMENU_PULLDOWN) {
        str = XmStringCreateSimple(menu_title);
        cascade = XtVaCreateManagedWidget(menu_title,
            xmCascadeButtonGadgetClass, parent,
            XmNsubMenuId,   menu,
            XmNlabelString, str,
            XmNmnemonic,    menu_mnemonic,
            NULL);
        XmStringFree(str);
    }

    /* Now add the menu items */
    for (i = 0; items[i].label != NULL; i++) {
        /* If subitems exist, create the pull-right menu by calling this
         * function recursively.  Since the function returns a cascade
         * button, the widget returned is used..
         */
        if (items[i].subitems)
            widget = BuildMenu(menu, XmMENU_PULLDOWN,
                items[i].label, items[i].mnemonic, items[i].subitems);
        else
            widget = XtVaCreateManagedWidget(items[i].label,
                *items[i].class, menu,
                NULL);
        /* Whether the item is a real item or a cascade button with a
         * menu, it can still have a mnemonic.
         */
        if (items[i].mnemonic)
            XtVaSetValues(widget, XmNmnemonic, items[i].mnemonic, NULL);
        /* any item can have an accelerator, except cascade menus. But,
         * we don't worry about that; we know better in our declarations.
         */
        if (items[i].accelerator) {
            str = XmStringCreateSimple(items[i].accel_text);
            XtVaSetValues(widget,
                XmNaccelerator, items[i].accelerator,
                XmNacceleratorText, str,
                NULL);
            XmStringFree(str);
        }
        /* again, anyone can have a callback -- however, this is an
         * activate-callback.  This may not be appropriate for all items.
         */
        if (items[i].callback)
            XtAddCallback(widget, XmNactivateCallback,
                items[i].callback, items[i].callback_data);
    }
    return menu_type == XmMENU_POPUP? menu : cascade;
}
```

.
.

Example 16-9. The BuildMenu() function (continued)

```
          .
    /* Create a DrawingArea -- no actual drawing will be done. */
    drawing_a = XtVaCreateManagedWidget("drawing_a",
        xmDrawingAreaWidgetClass, main_w,
        XmNwidth, 500,
        XmNheight, 500,
        NULL);

    menu = BuildMenu(drawing_a, XmMENU_POPUP, "Lines", 'L', drawing_menus);

    XtAddCallback(drawing_a, XmNinputCallback, input, menu);
          .
          .
          .

void
input(widget, menu, cbs)
Widget widget;
Widget menu;
XmDrawingAreaCallbackStruct *cbs;
{
    if (cbs->event->xany.type == ButtonPress &&
        cbs->event->xbutton.button == 3) {
        XmMenuPosition(menu, cbs->event);
        XtManageChild(menu);
    }
}
```

All of the original functionality is maintained; we only added a couple of lines to support popup menus. Namely, when **XmMENU_POPUP** is passed as the **menu_type** parameter, the function **XmCreatePopupMenu( )** is used and the menu itself is returned. If any of the menu items have CascadeButtons and cascading menus, then we can continue to do what we were doing before for submenus.

The main routine was modified slightly to move the menu out of the menubar and into the DrawingArea widget as a popup menu. The menu item declarations from Example 16-9 may still be used. In fact, an identical menu is created.

While this does not change the code of **BuildMenu( )**, you should remember that mnemonics are not typically used for popup menus or menu items. If the menu type is **Xm-MENU_POPUP**, the mnemonic field in the data structure should be passed as NULL.

Supporting Toggle Items

As discussed in Chapter 4, *The Main Window*, popup and pulldown menus may contain ToggleButtons as well as Labels, PushButtons, CascadeButtons, and Separators. Yet the current version of **BuildMenu( )** does not account for the possibility that menu items could be ToggleButtons. The menu *class* is fine, but the *callback* function added to each item's callback list may not be right if the item is a ToggleButton. This fact is noted in the comments within the code for the functions `BuildMenu( )` and `BuildPulldownMenu( )`:

```
/* Anyone can have a callback -- however, this is an
 * activate-callback.  This may not be appropriate for all items.
 */
if (items[i].callback)
    XtAddCallback(widget, XmNactivateCallback,
        items[i].callback, items[i].callback_data);
```

Since ToggleButtons use the `XmNvalueChangedCallback` resource rather than the `XmNactivateCallback` used by PushButtons, the solution to the problem is quite simple: check the `class` field of the `MenuItem` being added before calling `XtAddCallback( )`. The new code fragment is shown below:

```
if (items[i].callback)
    XtAddCallback(widget,
        (items[i].class == &xmToggleButtonWidgetClass ||
         items[i].class == &xmToggleButtonGadgetClass)?
            XmNvalueChangedCallback : /* ToggleButton class */
            XmNactivateCallback,        /* PushButton class */
            items[i].callback, items[i].callback_data);
```

The callback *must* be either one or the other, since no other widget classes can be placed in menus. Labels and Separators have no callbacks and CascadeButtons have cascading menus, so that case couldn't (or shouldn't) ever get to this point in the code. (If it does, you have incorrectly initialized a MenuItem structure.)

16.3.3 Using Popup Menus

There are a number of important things to keep in mind about popup menus. The *Motif Style Guide* has very little to say about when and how popup menus should be used, except for the following:

*   When they should pop up is entirely defined by the application.

*   Users should pop up menus using the third mouse button for three-button mice, the "right" mouse button for two-button mice, and the (only) mouse button plus a *modifier key* such as SHIFT for one-button mice.

This leads us to the next problem: how do you get the events necessary on any arbitrary widget so you can pop up a menu? As discussed in Chapter 2, *The Motif Programming Model*, the Motif toolkit generally doesn't permit the user to modify most widgets' translation tables in order to protect the interface specifications of the *Style Guide*.

We have been using the DrawingArea widget because of its ability to track for such input events through the translation mechanism. However, for all other widgets, the problem is not so simple. Unfortunately, the menu system in the Motif toolkit has some shortcomings that require you to dig into the lower level Xt event handing mechanisms in order to provide popup menus to the user. We can continue to *build* menus the same way; it's just how to pop them up that becomes the problem.

Example 16-10 demonstrates how this can be done for an arbitrary widget. Here, we use events in a PushButton widget to display a popup menu, but the popup could be triggered from any type of widget—Lists, Labels, and Text widgets—but not gadgets.

Example 16-10. The popups.c program

```
/* popups.c -- demonstrate the use of popup menus in arbitrary widgets.
 * Display two PushButtons.  The second one has a popup menu
 * attached to it, but it must be activated with the *third*
 * mouse button--you cannot use the second button because of
 * a bug with the Motif toolkit (but that's ok, the Style Guide
 * says to use the third button anyway).  You don't want to use
 * the first mouse button because that activates the PushButton.
 * If you want the first button to display a menu, use an
 * OptionMenu.
 */
#include <Xm/LabelG.h>
#include <Xm/PushBG.h>
#include <Xm/PushB.h>
#include <Xm/SeparatoG.h>
#include <Xm/RowColumn.h>
#include <Xm/MenuShell.h>
#include <Xm/MessageB.h>
#include <Xm/FileSB.h>
#include <Xm/CascadeBG.h>

Widget toplevel;
extern void exit();
void open_dialog_box();

/* dummy callback for pushbutton activation */
void
put_string(w, str)
Widget w;
String str;
{
    puts(str);
}

typedef struct _menu_item {
    char        *label;
    WidgetClass *class;
    char         mnemonic;
    char        *accelerator;
    char        *accel_text;
    void        (*callback)();
    caddr_t      callback_data;
    struct _menu_item *subitems;
} MenuItem;

MenuItem file_items[ ] = {
    { "File Items", &xmLabelGadgetClass, NULL, NULL, NULL, NULL, NULL, NULL },
    { "_sep1", &xmSeparatorGadgetClass, NULL, NULL, NULL, NULL, NULL, NULL },
    { "New", &xmPushButtonGadgetClass, 'N', "Ctrl<Key>N", "Ctrl+N",
        put_string, "New", NULL },
    { "Open ...", &xmPushButtonGadgetClass, 'O', NULL, NULL,
        open_dialog_box, (caddr_t)XmCreateFileSelectionDialog, NULL },
    { "Save", &xmPushButtonGadgetClass, 'S', NULL, NULL,
        put_string, "Save", NULL },
```

Example 16-10. The popups.c program (continued)

```
    { "Save As ...", &xmPushButtonGadgetClass, 'A', NULL, NULL,
        open_dialog_box, (caddr_t)XmCreateFileSelectionDialog, NULL },
    { "Print ...", &xmPushButtonGadgetClass, 'P', NULL, NULL,
        open_dialog_box, (caddr_t)XmCreateMessageDialog, NULL },
    { "Exit", &xmPushButtonGadgetClass, 'E', "Ctrl<Key>C", "Ctrl+C",
        exit, NULL, NULL },
    NULL,
};
main(argc, argv)
int argc;
char *argv[ ];
{
    Widget BuildPopupMenu(), button, rowcol, popup;
    XtAppContext app;
    extern void PostIt();

    toplevel = XtVaAppInitialize(&app, "Demos", NULL, 0,
        &argc, argv, NULL, NULL);

    /* Build a RowColumn to contain two PushButtons */
    rowcol = XtVaCreateManagedWidget("rowcol",
        xmRowColumnWidgetClass, toplevel,
        NULL);

    /* The first PushButton is a -gadget-, so we cannot popup a menu
     * from here!
     */
    button = XtVaCreateManagedWidget("PushMe-1",
        xmPushButtonGadgetClass, rowcol, NULL);
    XtAddCallback(button, XmNactivateCallback, put_string, "button1");

    /* This PushButton is a widget, so it has its own window, so
     * we can pop up a menu from here by adding an event handler
     * specifically for the 3rd mouse button (motif compliance).
     */
    button = XtVaCreateManagedWidget("PushMe-2",
        xmPushButtonWidgetClass, rowcol,
        NULL);
    /* it can still have its callback! */
    XtAddCallback(button, XmNactivateCallback, put_string, "button2");

    /* build the menu... */
    popup = BuildPopupMenu(button, "Stuff", file_items, XmMENU_POPUP);
    /* Add the event handler (PostIt()) and pass the newly created menu
     * as the client_data.  This is done to avoid using unnecessary globals.
     */
    XtAddEventHandler(button, ButtonPressMask, False, PostIt, popup);

    XtRealizeWidget(toplevel);
    XtAppMainLoop(app);
}

/* Event handler for the 3rd mouse button on the PushButton widget's window */
void
PostIt(pb, popup, event)
Widget pb; /* the pushbutton -- unused here */
Widget popup;  /* the client_data passed to XtAddEventHandler() */
XButtonPressedEvent *event; /* We know it's a button press because of how
```

Example 16-10. The popups.c program (continued)

```
                                we registered the event handler. */
{
    if (event->button != 3)
        return;
    /* position the menu at the location of the button press!  If we wanted
     * to position it elsewhere, we could change the x,y fields of the
     * event structure.
     */
    XmMenuPosition(popup, event);
    XtManageChild(popup);
}


/* callback for some of the menu items declared in the MenuItem struct.
 * The client data is a function that creates some sort of Motif dialog.
 * Since the function returns this dialog, associate it with the menu
 * item via XmNuserData so we (a) don't have a to keep a global and
 * (b) don't have to repeatedly create one.
 */
void
open_dialog_box(w, func, cbs)
Widget w;               /* the menu item that was invoked */
Widget (*func)(); /* function that creates and returns a dialog widget */
XmAnyCallbackStruct *cbs; /* unused */
{
    /* initialize in case get values doesn't return anything sensible. */
    Widget dialog = NULL;

    /* first see if this menu item's dialog has been created yet */
    XtVaGetValues(w, XmNuserData, &dialog, NULL);
    if (!dialog) {
        /* menu item hasn't been chosen yet -- create the dialog.
         * Use the toplevel as the parent because we don't want the
         * parent of a dialog to be a menu item!
         *
         * Give the dialog's title the menu item lable (arbitrary, but
         * convenient).
         *
         * Since this is a dummy function, the dialogs does nothing.
         * Attach XtUnmanageChild() as the callback for Ok and Cancel.
         *
         * Obviously, this dialog doesn't have anything in it, but this
         * is a simple example.  You could modify this open_dialog to pass
         * all necessary data in the form of a new data structure as the
         * client data.  This structure should contain the dialog creation
         * function and other stuff as needed.
         */
        dialog = (*func)(toplevel, "dialog", NULL, 0);
        XtVaSetValues(XtParent(dialog), XmNtitle, XtName(w), NULL);
        XtAddCallback(dialog, XmNokCallback, XtUnmanageChild, w);
        XtAddCallback(dialog, XmNcancelCallback, XtUnmanageChild, w);

        /* store the newly created dialog in the XmNuserData for the menu
         * item for easy retrieval next time. (see get-values above.)
         */
        XtVaSetValues(w, XmNuserData, dialog, NULL);
    }
    XtManageChild(dialog);
```

Example 16-10. The popups.c program (continued)

```
    /* call XtPopup() for good form... */
    XtPopup(XtParent(dialog), XtGrabNone);
    /* If the dialog was already open, XtPopup does nothing.  In
     * this case, at least make sure the window is raised to the top
     * of the window tree (or as high as it can get).
     */
    XRaiseWindow(XtDisplay(dialog), XtWindow(XtParent(dialog)));
}
```

The output of the program is shown in Figure 16-10.

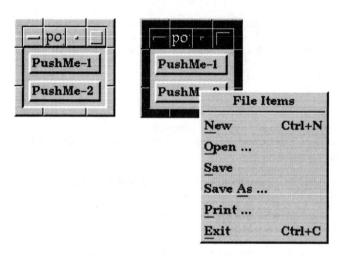

Figure 16-10. Output of popups.c

The program is quite simple: it displays two PushButtons, one of which is a gadget, the other a widget. The only way we can get a **ButtonPress** event is by specifically asking for it using **XtAddEventHandler( )**, which requires a widget, which has a window. To add an event handler for a gadget, you'd have to install it on the gadget's parent, which is a manager widget. But then, anytime a **ButtonPress** event occurs in the manager, the event handler would be called. Of course, the event handler could check the coordinates of the event and see if it happened within the boundaries of the gadget, but this is beyond the scope of this simple demonstration.

Briefly, **XtAddEventHandler( )** takes five arguments:

• The widget on which the event handler is to be installed. Note that the handler must be installed on every widget in which the event might occur.

• A "mask" identifying which events are being handled. The mask values are defined in *<X11/Intrinsic.h>*, which is automatically included by the Motif widget classes. Here, **ButtonPressMask** indicates that button events are of interest. The complete list of event masks is given in Table 16-1.

- A Boolean indicating whether the event handler should be called on "non-maskable events" (**GraphicsExpose**, **NoExpose**, **SelectionClear**, **SelectionRequest**, **Selection-Notify**, **ClientMessage**, and **MappingNotify**). This argument should be `False`, since we are not interested in this list of events.

- The name of the event handler, here `PostIt( )`.

- Client data to be passed to the handler, here the popup menu we wish to post.

Table 16-1. Event Mask Symbols Used by Xt

Event Mask Symbol	Circumstances
NoEventMask	No events.
KeyPressMask	Keyboard down events.
KeyReleaseMask	Keyboard up events.
ButtonPressMask	Pointer button down events.
ButtonReleaseMask	Pointer button up events.
EnterWindowMask	Pointer window entry events.
LeaveWindowMask	Pointer window leave events.
PointerMotionMask	All pointer motion events.
PointerMotionHintMask	Fewer pointer motion events.
Button1MotionMask	Pointer motion while Button 1 down.
Button2MotionMask	Pointer motion while Button 2 down.
Button3MotionMask	Pointer motion while Button 3 down.
Button4MotionMask	Pointer motion while Button 4 down.
Button5MotionMask	Pointer motion while Button 5 down.
ButtonMotionMask	Pointer motion while any button down.
KeymapStateMask	Any keyboard state change on **EnterNotify**, **LeaveNotify**, **FocusIn** or **FocusOut**
ExposureMask	Any exposure (except **GraphicsExpose** and **NoExpose**).
VisibilityChangeMask	Any change in visibility.
StructureNotifyMask	Any change in window configuration.
ResizeRedirectMask	Redirect resize of this window.
SubstructureNotifyMask	Notify about reconfiguration of children.
SubstructureRedirectMask	Redirect reconfiguration of children.
FocusChangeMask	Any change in keyboard focus.
PropertyChangeMask	Any change in property.
ColormapChangeMask	Any change in colormap.
OwnerGrabButtonMask	Modifies handling of pointer events.

`XtAddEventHandler( )` *adds* the event handler to the widget's normal event list of event handlers (there can be more than one). Therefore, you should be careful not to conflict with other possible event handlers that may exist for certain widgets. You needn't worry about whether the Motif toolkit looks for Button 3 events because this button has no place in the Motif specifications so far.

The form of the callback function is as follows:

```
void
event_handler(widget, client_data, event)
    Widget      widget;
    XtPointer   client_data;
    XEvent      *event;
```

In our event handler (**PostIt( )**), we knew that we were only going to get the **ButtonPress** event, and we declared the **event** type to be an **XButtonPressedEvent** structure.[8] Since we want to be Motif-compliant, we are only interested in the third mouse button.

To pop up the menu, we must do two things: position the menu, then manage the menupane. To position it, we use **XmMenuPosition( )**. The form of this function is as follows:

```
void
XmMenuPosition(widget, event)
    Widget                widget;
    XButtonPressedEvent *event;
```

NOTE

The **event** parameter for this function is *defined* to be of type **XButton-PressedEvent**. You may run into Motif toolkit problems if you try to use another type of event than **ButtonPress**. The **x** and **y** fields in the event structure are used to position the menu appropriately. In this case, these fields indicate the position where the mouse button was pressed. However, you could modify these fields so that they match the origin of the button, or are positioned elsewhere on the widget (or the screen, for that matter). Of course, this is highly application-defined, so we recommend restraint.

In order to actually pop up the menu, we call **XtManageChild( )** on the popup menu. Popup menus are treated identically to dialog widgets with respect to their DialogShell parents, as discussed in . The visible popup menu is a RowColumn widget that contains all the menu items; the MenuShell that owns it is the popup's *parent*. As with dialogs, when you call **XtManageChild( )**, the RowColumn checks its **XmNrowColumnType** resource, and if it is a popup menu, it checks to see if its parent is a MenuShell and calls **XtPopup( )** on it automatically. (There is no point in our interfering with this process for dialog shells.)

Here is where the internals to the Motif toolkit take over and where many people run into problems due to some internal bugs. In order to keep the menu popped up, the Motif toolkit makes a server grab on behalf of the menu. In order for it to release the grab, it looks for the mouse Button 3 event. Even if you used another event to pop up the menu, *the menu remains up until it sees a Button 3 release event*.

There is a resource that you can set on popup menus called **XmNmenuPost**, which allows you to specify an alternate button to post the menu. However, this has been known to hang the server. (We don't recommend that you try it.)

---

[8] Note that this is not ANSI-compliant; compilers that use function prototypes should probably declare the **event** parameter as an **XEvent** pointer and typecast it properly in the function.

Further Notes on Popup Menus

There are some more bugs and other facts about the Motif menu system that we haven't mentioned yet:

- It is not possible to have several popups (activated by different mouse buttons) on the same widget. You can have different popups on each child, but if you put a popup on the manager as well, that is the only popup you will get. This is another reason why you shouldn't attempt to install popup menus on gadgets; you would only be able to install one popup per manager widget, since you'd have to install the event handler on the manager itself.

- Destroying a widget with an associated popup menu results in a warning message sent to the user's terminal:

  `"Warning: Attempt to remove non-existant passive grab"`

  Aside from the misspelling of the word "existent," the warning message can be ignored.

- You may have noticed that the popup menu shown in Figure 16-10 has accelerators associated with it. These accelerators will only take affect if the input focus is in the widget that contains the menu. This may take some experimentation to fully understand. Run the program and have the input focus be on `PushMe-1` (the black highlight will be on that gadget). Now type `Ctrl+N`. Nothing should happen. Then press the "down" arrow key and type `Ctrl+N` again. The word "New" is sent to `stdout`.

- The only time you should ever add an event handler to pop up a menu is when you are using *popup menus* specifically. You should not attach pulldown menus or option menus to arbitrary Motif widgets. It is also inappropriate to use popup menus on objects that already have menus (CascadeButtons).

Clearly, the popup menu mechanism is not entirely complete or bug-free. However, if you follow the suggestions made in this section, the system should work adequately. Problems will only plague you if you do things you shouldn't be doing. (Except for the warning message, which may plague you anyway!)

16.3.4 Building Option Menus

In this, the final section on generalized menu methods, we examine how we can create option menus using the `BuildMenu()` function. Here, the underlying function is `XmCreate-OptionMenu()`. This is another convenience routine provided by the Motif toolkit. It creates a RowColumn widget that manages the Label and CascadeButton widgets that define the option menu. However, we must create the actual pulldown menu ourselves. In order to support this functionality while maintaining consistency in our interface technique, we present the final version of the `BuildMenu()` function in Example 16-11.

Example 16-11. The build_option.c program

```
/* build_option.c -- The final version of BuildMenu() is used to
 * build popup, option, pulldown -and- pullright menus.  Menus are
 * defined by declaring an array of MenuItem structures as usual.
 */
#include <Xm/MainW.h>
#include <Xm/PanedW.h>
#include <Xm/RowColumn.h>
#include <Xm/DrawingA.h>
#include <Xm/CascadeBG.h>
#include <Xm/ToggleB.h>
#include <Xm/ToggleBG.h>
#include <Xm/PushB.h>
#include <Xm/PushBG.h>

typedef struct _menu_item {
    char         *label;        /* the label for the item */
    WidgetClass *class;         /* pushbutton, label, separator... */
    char          mnemonic;     /* mnemonic; NULL if none */
    char         *accelerator;  /* accelerator; NULL if none */
    char         *accel_text;   /* to be converted to compound string */
    void         (*callback)(); /* routine to call; NULL if none */
    XtPointer     callback_data; /* client_data for callback() */
    struct _menu_item *subitems; /* pullright menu items, if not NULL */
} MenuItem;

/* Build popup, option and pulldown menus, depending on the menu_type.
 * It may be XmMENU_PULLDOWN, XmMENU_OPTION or  XmMENU_POPUP.  Pulldowns
 * return the CascadeButton that pops up the menu.  Popups return the menu.
 * Option menus are created, but the RowColumn that acts as the option
 * "area" is returned unmanaged. (The user must manage it.)
 * Pulldown menus are built from cascade buttons, so this function
 * also builds pullright menus.  The function also adds the right
 * callback for PushButton or ToggleButton menu items.
 */
Widget
BuildMenu(parent, menu_type, menu_title, menu_mnemonic, items)
Widget parent;
int menu_type;
char *menu_title, menu_mnemonic;
MenuItem *items;
{
    Widget menu, cascade, widget;
    int i;
    XmString str;

    if (menu_type == XmMENU_PULLDOWN || menu_type == XmMENU_OPTION)
        menu = XmCreatePulldownMenu(parent, "_pulldown", NULL, 0);
    else if (menu_type == XmMENU_POPUP)
        menu = XmCreatePopupMenu(parent, "_popup", NULL, 0);
    else {
        XtWarning("Invalid menu type passed to BuildMenu()");
        return NULL;
    }

    /* Pulldown menus require a cascade button to be made */
    if (menu_type == XmMENU_PULLDOWN) {
        str = XmStringCreateSimple(menu_title);
        cascade = XtVaCreateManagedWidget(menu_title,
```

Example 16-11. The build_option.c program (continued)

```
                xmCascadeButtonGadgetClass, parent,
                XmNsubMenuId,    menu,
                XmNlabelString, str,
                XmNmnemonic,     menu_mnemonic,
                NULL);
        XmStringFree(str);
    } else if (menu_type == XmMENU_OPTION) {
        /* Option menus are a special case, but not hard to handle */
        Arg args[2];
        str = XmStringCreateSimple(menu_title);
        XtSetArg(args[0], XmNsubMenuId, menu);
        XtSetArg(args[1], XmNlabelString, str);
        /* This really isn't a cascade, but this is the widget handle
         * we're going to return at the end of the function.
         */
        cascade = XmCreateOptionMenu(parent, menu_title, args, 2);
        XmStringFree(str);
    }

    /* Now add the menu items */
    for (i = 0; items[i].label != NULL; i++) {
        /* If subitems exist, create the pull-right menu by calling this
         * function recursively.  Since the function returns a cascade
         * button, the widget returned is used..
         */
        if (items[i].subitems)
            if (menu_type == XmMENU_OPTION) {
                XtWarning("You can't have submenus from option menu items.");
                continue;
            } else
                widget = BuildMenu(menu, XmMENU_PULLDOWN,
                    items[i].label, items[i].mnemonic, items[i].subitems);
        else
            widget = XtVaCreateManagedWidget(items[i].label,
                *items[i].class, menu,
                NULL);

        /* Whether the item is a real item or a cascade button with a
         * menu, it can still have a mnemonic.
         */
        if (items[i].mnemonic)
            XtVaSetValues(widget, XmNmnemonic, items[i].mnemonic, NULL);

        /* any item can have an accelerator, except cascade menus. But,
         * we don't worry about that; we know better in our declarations.
         */
        if (items[i].accelerator) {
            str = XmStringCreateSimple(items[i].accel_text);
            XtVaSetValues(widget,
                XmNaccelerator, items[i].accelerator,
                XmNacceleratorText, str,
                NULL);
            XmStringFree(str);
        }

        if (items[i].callback)
            XtAddCallback(widget,
                (items[i].class == &xmToggleButtonWidgetClass ||
```

Example 16-11. The build_option.c program (continued)

```
                     items[i].class == &xmToggleButtonGadgetClass)?
                         XmNvalueChangedCallback : /* ToggleButton class */
                         XmNactivateCallback,       /* PushButton class */
                     items[i].callback, items[i].callback_data);
    }

    /* for popup menus, just return the menu; pulldown menus, return
     * the cascade button; option menus, return the thing returned
     * from XmCreateOptionMenu().  This isn't a menu, or a cascade button!
     */
    return menu_type == XmMENU_POPUP? menu : cascade;
}

/* option menu items... quite simple */
MenuItem drawing_shapes[ ] = {
    { "Lines", &xmPushButtonGadgetClass, 'L', NULL, NULL, 0, 0, NULL },
    { "Circles", &xmPushButtonGadgetClass, 'C', NULL, NULL, 0, 0, NULL },
    { "Squares", &xmPushButtonGadgetClass, 'S', NULL, NULL, 0, 0, NULL },
    NULL,
};

main(argc, argv)
int argc;
char *argv[ ];
{
    Widget toplevel, main_w, pane, sw, drawing_a, menu, option_menu;
    void input();
    XtAppContext app;
    XtWidgetGeometry geom;

    toplevel = XtVaAppInitialize(&app, "Demos", NULL, 0,
        &argc, argv, NULL, NULL);

    /* Create a MainWindow widget that contains a DrawingArea in
     * its work window. (This happens by default.)
     */
    main_w = XtVaCreateManagedWidget("main_w",
        xmMainWindowWidgetClass, toplevel, NULL);

    /* Use a PanedWindow widget as the work area of the main window */
    pane = XtVaCreateWidget("pane", xmPanedWindowWidgetClass, main_w, NULL);

    /* create the option menu --  don't froget to manage it. */
    option_menu =
        BuildMenu(pane, XmMENU_OPTION, "Shapes", 'S', drawing_shapes);
    XtManageChild(option_menu);

    /* Set the OptionMenu (the RowColumn part) so that it can't be resized! */
    geom.request_mode = CWHeight;
    XtQueryGeometry(option_menu, NULL, &geom);
    XtVaSetValues(option_menu,
        XmNpaneMinimum, geom.height,
        XmNpaneMaximum, geom.height,
        NULL);

    /* The scrolled window (which contains the drawing area) is a child
     * of the PanedWindow; it's sibling, the option menu, cannot be resized,
     * so if the user resizes the toplevel shell, *this* window will resize.
     */
    sw = XtVaCreateManagedWidget("sw", xmScrolledWindowWidgetClass, pane,
```

Example 16-11. The build_option.c program (continued)

```
                XmNscrollingPolicy,  XmAUTOMATIC,
            NULL);
    /* Create a DrawingArea -- no actual drawing will be done. */
    drawing_a = XtVaCreateManagedWidget("drawing_a",
        xmDrawingAreaWidgetClass, sw,
        XmNwidth, 500,
        XmNheight, 500,
        NULL);

    XtManageChild(pane);
    XtRealizeWidget(toplevel);
    XtAppMainLoop(app);
}
```

There are two particularly interesting features of this program. First, of course, is the modification for the **BuildMenu( )** function. As the comments in the code indicate, the function can now fully support all Motif menu types as well as both PushButtons and ToggleButtons as menu items. The second feature of this program is the way the main window is laid out. Let's first analyze the new **BuildMenu( )** function.

Since option menus display their menus from CascadeButtons, and the only kind of menus that can be displayed from CascadeButtons are pulldown menus, we use **XmCreate-PulldownMenu( )** to create the menu that will be used. It is then attached to the menu by setting the **XmNsubMenuId** as usual. This is automatically attached to the option menu when **XmCreateOptionMenu( )** is called. The label string is also set here.

As we loop through the menu items that are to be placed in the menu, we prevent any intentional or accidental creation of a pullright menu for option menus. (Having a pullright menu as a submenu of an option menu goes against the Motif specification.)

The function returns the RowColumn widget that was returned from the **XmCreate-OptionMenu( )** function, even though it is not really a CascadeButton as the variable name might indicate. This is what the calling function wants anyway, so it worked out well. Later, in the main program, we see that the caller merely calls **XtManageChild( )** on this item to make sure it is visible. (The call to **XtManageChild( )** might be another automated part of **BuildMenu( )** if you want to modify it.)

In the main program, the MainWindow widget has a single PanedWindow widget as its child because we wish to retain the vertical stacking relationship between the option menu and the DrawingArea. Another advantage of using the PanedWindow is that we can set the maximum and minimum height that each pane may be. The user may resize the entire window, using the window manager. In this case, we don't want the option menu to increase or decrease in size at all, but we want the ScrolledWindow to fluctuate without restriction. (After all, it has its own Scrollbars to maintain its integrity.)

Pulling It All Together

All things said and done, you need only two things to create an arbitrary number of menus: predefined arrays of `MenuItem` structures and the `BuildMenu( )` function. Both of these are straightforward and, since initializing an array of `MenuItem` objects is very simple, the method is convenient, yet more powerful than the simple menu creation routines discussed in the beginning of the chapter. Because we have defined our own data type and generalized the routine to build menus, you can use and modify these functions however you like to conform to the needs of your application.

16.4 Menu and Menu Item Sensitivity

As we mentioned earlier, MenuBar titles and menu items should not be dynamically created or destroyed. They may, however, be activated or deactivated by turning their `Xm-Nsensitive` resources on and off. (This may also be set using `XtSetSensitive( )`.) When insensitive, a CascadeButton or a menu item is *grayed out* and the user is unable to display the associated menu or activate the menu item. For CascadeButtons, this has the additional side effect of preventing the user from accessing *any* of its menu's items. This includes access via mnemonics or accelerators. The menu and all its items are completely unavailable until its sensitivity is reset.

Let's say, for example, that you have an editor program and there is currently no file being edited. In this case, it wouldn't make sense to have the **Save** menu item in the **File** pulldown be selectable. Of course, it is important to remember that the user can not select this item until you reset its sensitivity, so you need to make sure to do so at the appropriate time.

Another, possibly less realistic example (but one that can be easily demonstrated), involves a menu item that pops up a dialog. As long as that dialog is up, the user cannot reselect the menu item again. For purposes of this demonstration, let's say that the **Open** menu item pops up a FileSelectionDialog and desensitizes itself. When the dialog goes away, it resensitizes.[9]

To implement this behavior, we create the callback routine for the **Open** menu item, have that routine create the dialog box to select or open a file, and set a callback routine within the dialog box that resets the menu item's sensitivity. The code fragment below shows how this might be done.

Example 16-12. Setting and resetting menu item sensitivity

```
/* reset_sensitive() -- generalized routine that resets the
 * sensitivity on the widget passed as the client_data parameter
 * in a call to XtAddCallback().  See open_callback() below.
 */
void
```

---

[9] We should note that this is not great application design behavior; the dialog should be "cached," and the menu should remain sensitive. If the menu item is reselected, the dialog should be remapped or raised to the top of the window stack, if necessary.

Example 16-12. Setting and resetting menu item sensitivity (continued)

```
reset_sensitive(w, reset_widget, ignored)
Widget w;
Widget reset_widget; /* client data */
XmAnyCallbackStruct *ignored;
{
    XtSetSensitive(reset_widget, True);
}

/* open_callback() -- the callback routine for when the "Open"
 * menu item is selected from the "File" title in the MenuBar.
 */
void
open_callback(menu_item, client_data, call_data)
Widget menu_item;        /* the menu item that was selected */
XtPointer client_data;   /* ignored */
XtPointer call_data;     /* ignored */
{
    Widget dialog, parent = menu_item;

    /* Get the window manager shell widget associated with item */
    while (!XtIsWMShell(parent))
        parent = XtParent(menu_item);

    /* turn off the sensitivity for the Open button ... */
    XtSetSensitive(menu_item, False);
    dialog = XmCreateFileSelectionDialog(parent, "files", NULL, 0);

    /* Add callback routines to respond to Ok button selection here. */

    /* Make sure that if the dialog is popped down or destroyed, the
     * menu_item's sensitivity is reset.
     */
    XtAddCallback(XtParent(dialog),  /* dialog's _parent_ */
        XmNpopdownCallback, reset_sensitive, menu_item);
    XtAddCallback(dialog, XmNdestroyCallback, reset_sensitive, menu_item);

    XtManageChild(dialog);
    XtPopup(XtParent(dialog), XtGrabNone);
}

MenuItem file_items[ ] = {
    { "New", &xmPushButtonGadgetClass, 'N', NULL, NULL,
        new_callback, 0, NULL },
    { "Open", &xmPushButtonGadgetClass, 'O', NULL, NULL,
        open_callback, 0, NULL },   /* open_callback() when item selected */

    /* etc... */

    { "Quit", &xmPushButtonGadgetClass, 'Q', NULL, NULL,
        0, 0, NULL },
};

main(argc, argv)
int argc;
char *argv;
{
    .
    .
    .
    BuildMenu(menubar, XmMENU_PULLDOWN, "Files", 'F', file_items);
```

Example 16-12. Setting and resetting menu item sensitivity (continued)

·
·
·
}

The `open_callback( )` function is called whenever the user selects the **Open** menu item from the MenuBar. (He may also activate it using an accelerator or mnemonic, possibly set in a resource file, since none was hard-coded here.) The first thing `open_callback( )` does is find the nearest window manager shell widget associated with the menu item. Note: this will *not* return the MenuShell (its grandparent), since that is not a window manager shell. We need some other non-transient widget to act as the appropriate parent for the File-SelectionDialog. (If the menu item or any other widget in the menu itself were the parent for the dialog, once the menu was popped down, the dialog, being a secondary window, would also pop down.)

We also set the menu item's sensitivity to `False,` disabling the user from selecting the item again. A FileSelectionDialog is created, but in order to be notified when the dialog has been dismissed (popped down or destroyed), we add callback routines for `XmNpopdown-Callback` and `XmNdestroyCallback`. In either case, the **Open** menu item should be reset, so that the user may reselect it, popping up the FileSelectionDialog again.

The only thing this design is missing is a callback function that opens the selected file should the user select the **Ok** button. However, this is beyond the scope of this chapter; see Chapter 6, *Selection Dialogs*, for details.

16.5 Summary

Menus are basically simple objects, and they contain many repetitive elements. While the simple menu creation routines are handy for basic prototyping and other simple application constructs, their usefulness is limited once you begin to develop larger-scale applications. For this reason, we encourage the use of abstraction and generalization techniques that are flexible enough to fill the menu requirements of any program.

16.6 Exercises

This chapter could go on forever, discussing more and more things you can do with menus. However, the goal was to present you with the fundamental concepts and design considerations behind menus. From this information, you should be able to teach yourself new techniques that we haven't touched upon. In that spirit, you should be able to do the following exercises based on the material covered in this chapter.

1. Create a MainWindow widget that has a fully loaded MenuBar (containing at least the **File**, **Edit**, and **Help** menus), an option menu and a popup menu that pops up from a DrawingArea widget. This should be implemented first using the simple menu creation routines, and then using `MenuItem` structures and the `BuildMenu( )` function.

2. Initialize a **MenuItem** structure whose fields are all set to NULL except for the menu items' names, callback routines, and widget classes. Now, generate an appropriate resource file (or fallback resources) that generates an actual, usable menu.

3. Modify the **MenuItem** structure and the **BuildMenu** routine to allow yourself to specify the initial menu item sensitivity on any particular menu item. (This should probably be a **Boolean** field.)

4. Modify **BuildMenu( )** to recognize when the menu it is about to build is a RadioBox. You may choose to implement this behavior by passing a new parameter to the function, or by examining each child in the **MenuItem** list to see if they are ToggleButtons. Hint: you're probably going to have to modify the **MenuItem** structure by adding another **Boolean** field to allow each element to indicate whether it is a radio button or a plain toggle button. Review Chapter 4, *The Main Window*, for a discussion of RadioBoxes as menus.

17

Interacting with the Window Manager

This chapter provides additional information on the relationship between shell widgets and the Motif window manager. It discusses shell widget resources, and how to use Motif's functions for adding or modifying window manager protocols.

In This Chapter:

17

Interacting with the Window Manager

This chapter provides technical details about how Motif applications can interact with the window manager. It discusses when and how to interpret special window manager events and client messages, how to set shell resources that act as "hints" to the window manager, and how to add "protocols" for communication between the application and the window manager.

In this course of the discussion, we cover the major features of the X Toolkit Intrinsics' WMShell widget class, which handles basic window manager communication, and Motif's VendorShell widget (subclassed from the WMShell), which handles window manager events that are dealt with in the *Motif Style Guide*.

The material in this chapter is advanced, in that you should not typically interfere with the predefined interactions between applications and the Motif window manager. When you do so, you risk damaging the uniform look and feel that is at the heart of a graphical user interface such as Motif. However, the material in this chapter will give you an understanding of some important concepts, and you may make your applications more robust as a result.

The chapter also discusses the use of protocols and client messages, which are used for window manager communication, but which can also be used for communication between instances of the same application, or between suites of cooperating applications. The latter part of this chapter is thus of interest to developers of these kinds of application.

17.1 Review of Concepts

The X Window System is designed so that any user-interface style can be imposed on the user and the display. The X libraries (Xlib and Xt) provide the mechanisms for applications to decide for themselves how to display information and how to react to user-generated actions (events). It is left up to *graphical user interface specifications* such as Motif to standardize most of these decisions. However, in order to preserve a baseline of interoperability, there are certain standards (referred to as "interclient communication conventions") that applications must conform to if they are to be considered "good citizens" of the desktop. That is, while X makes no suggestions about the way an application should look or act, it does have a lot to say about how it interacts with other applications on the user's display. (This is sort of like saying, "Whatever politics you care to follow is fine with us, provided that you don't break the civic laws laid out by the community as a whole.")

One of the interclient conventions that demonstrates this idea is that all applications must negotiate their windows' sizes and positions with the window manager, rather than with one another. The window manager is, in essence, the ultimate ruler of the desktop. While it is mostly benevolent, its primary function is to prevent "window system anarchy."

Communication with the window manager has various forms. Applications can talk directly to the window manager, or the window manager may initiate a conversation with applications. When the user selects menu items from the *window menu* of the window manager decorations, or issues other window manager commands, he initiates a process of communication between the window manager and the application.

Much of the communication between the window manager and the application is in terms of *properties* and *protocols*.

A property is an arbitrary-length piece of data associated with a window (and thus stored on the server) that is identified by a unique integer value called an Atom.[1] Applications set properties on their windows as a way of communicating with the window manager or other applications. Some properties are referred to as "window manager hints" because the window manager doesn't have to obey them. For example, an application might specify the preferred size of its toplevel window, but the window manager might use this value only in the absence of any other instructions from the user.

A window manager protocol is an agreed-upon procedure for the exchange of messages between the window manager and an application. Protocols are implemented by the window manager sending a ClientMessage event to the application, and the application then taking appropriate action. An example of a protocol exchange occurs when the user uses the **Close** button in a dialog to close a window.

There are low-level Xlib routines for setting and getting the value of window properties. However, the resource mechanism—more specifically, various resources provided by Shell widgets—is the preferred interface to most of the predefined properties of interest in window manager/application interaction.

The WMShell widget defines many of the generic (non-Motif-specific) properties that are used for communication with the window manager. For example, you'd use resources of this widget to specify icon pixmaps and placement, resize increment values, and so on. The VendorShell widget class is defined by Xt as the widget class in which particular vendors can define behavior specific to their own window manager and application look and feel. As such, it is customized by every vendor of Xt-compatible toolkits. In the case of Motif, the VendorShell class provides additional Motif-specific resources—in particular, those that control the layout and operation of the window manager decorations—and supports the Motif window manager protocols.

One never instantiates either the WMShell or VendorShell widgets. They exist only as supporting classes for other shells such as TopLevelShells, ApplicationShells, and DialogShells. Even though you never instantiate these shells, you frequently need to set their resources. Note, however, that MenuShells and other popup shells are not subclasses of VendorShell

---

[1] Atoms are used to avoid the overhead of passing property names between client and server as arbitrary-length strings. See Volume One, *Xlib Programming Manual*, and Volume Four, *X Toolkit Programming Manual*, for a detailed discussion of properties and atoms.

and WMShell, and do not have the same provisions for window manager interaction. The following routine tests whether the shell parent of any widget is a subclass of VendorShell and returns a handle to the Shell:

```
Widget
GetVendorShell(w)
Widget w;
{
    Widget parent = w;

    while (!XtIsVendorShell(parent) && (w = XtParent(parent)))
        parent = w;
    return parent;
}
```

The `XtIsVendorShell( )` macro is defined in *<X11/Intrinsic.h>*. Similarly, the macro `XtIsWMShell( )` is also defined there to determine if a widget is a subclass of WMShell. Both of these macros are part of Xt, and thus completely independent of the Motif widget set, but once you get a handle to the Shell widget, for example, you will probably use Motif-specific resources to modify it. In such cases, you may need to include the files *<Xm/Vendor-E.h>* and/or *<Xm/MwmUtil.h>*, depending on the nature of the resources. We'll get into the Motif-specific resources a little later. But first, we're going to address those resources common to all shells found in Xt-based widget sets. It is important to differentiate between these resources and those that are Motif specific.

17.2 Common Shell Resources

As discussed in Chapter 3, *Overview of Motif Widgets*, the WMShell widget class interprets standard window manager/application communications established by the Inter-Client Communications Conventions Manual (ICCCM). This document, which can be found in Appendix L of Volume Zero, *X Protocol Reference Manual*, describes the standards set forth by the X Consortium for all applications and window managers to follow in order to maintain order in the X world. (This is required reading for anyone seriously interested in how interclient communication really works.) Such conventions are necessary because the window manager. and the host application are two separate programs. In this model, these programs communicate with each other through the X11 protocol.

Just to give you an idea of the kinds of properties that can be set on windows that the window manager would be interested in, Table 17-1 shows a partial list of properties that are automatically handled by Shells through either the X Toolkit Intrinsics or Motif.

Table 17-1. Some Properties of Interest to the Window Manager

Atom	Meaning
WM_NAME	The window's name.
WWM_CLASS	The window's class-name.
WWM_NORMAL_HINTS	Various information about the size of the window.
WWM_ICON_NAME	The label the window manager uses for the window's icon.
WWM_HINTS	Various information about the icon's pixmap and position as well as the window's input model.

There are Xlib functions available for changing the values of these atoms on windows. By doing so, you can affect their visual appearance, size, position, or functionality.[2] However, the WMShell's job is to hide this interface from the programmer and to use the resource-value interface for accomplishing the same thing. The next few sections address how most of the more common resources can be used. Note that while not all of the WMShell resources are listed here, most are intuitive and do not require a great deal of explanation. See Appendix B, *Xt and Motif Widget Classes*, for a complete list of the resources available.

17.2.1 Shell Positions

It is possible to position shells at specific locations on the screen using the **XmNx** and **XmNy** resources. However, immediate children of shell widgets widgets can also have their **XmNx** and **XmNy** resources set to position the shell as well. This is all part of the way Motif dialogs were designed to make their corresponding shells invisible to the programmer. It is usually easier to set these values directly on the shell's composite child, since you are more likely to have a handle to that widget already. For instance, you can position a MessageDialog (or any other Motif dialog box) to specific locations as in the following code fragment:

```
Widget dialog, parent;
Dimension width, height;
Screen screen = XtScreen(parent);
Position x, y;

dialog = XmCreateMessageDialog(parent, "dialog", NULL, 0);

/* get center of screen */
x = WidthOfScreen(screen) / 2;
y = HeightOfScreen(screen) / 2;

/* get width and height of dialog */
XtVaGetValues(dialog, XmNwidth, &width, XmNheight, &height, NULL);
```

---

[2] See Volume Zero, *X Protocol Reference Manual*, for complete details on the properties that can be set on windows. See Volume One, *Xlib Programmer's Manual*, for details on how to set or get properties.

```
/* center the dialog on the screen */
x -= width/2;
y -= height/2;
XtVaGetValues(dialog, XmNx, x, XmNy, y, NULL);
```

This particular code fragment places the dialog in the center of the screen (taking the size of the dialog window into account). You can position dialogs in this way because the Motif BulletinBoard (and subclasses) passes positional information to its shell parent. See Chapter 5, *Introduction to Dialogs*, and Chapter 7, *Custom Dialogs*, for more details and discussion.

In any event, you shouldn't normally be setting the **XmNx** and **XmNy** resources, since it is normally the window manager's job to position shells, and it is the user's option to configure how that placement should be handled. If the user has the *mwm* `interactive-Placement` resource set to **True**, then you might interfere with the positioning method the user prefers.

17.2.2 Shell Sizes

Sometimes, the nature of the application is such that it should always remain within certain geometrical bounds. That is, it should never grow or shrink beyond some specified widths and heights. An example might be a dialog box that should never get so small that any of its elements are clipped. Or, a paint application might want to impose on itself a restriction that prevents its toplevel window from growing larger than the size of its canvas. Another interesting constraint might be the increments by which the user may interactively resize the window (by grabbing the window manager's resize handles). For example, *xterm*, the default terminal emulator for X, can only be resized by increments that are in units defined by the font it's using. This way, the terminal is always an exact width and height according to its font's dimensions.

These sorts of constraints can be set on any widget subclassed from the WMShell using the following resources:

```
XmNminWidth
XmNmaxWidth
XmNminHeight
XmNmaxHeight
XmNwidthInc
XmNheightInc
XmNbaseWidth
XmNbaseHeight
```

The resources **XmNbaseWidth** and **XmNbaseHeight** are used by the window manager's visual feedback mechanism to display the size of the window while the user is interactively resizing the shell. The Motif window manager (*mwm*) provides this visual feedback in a small text area in the middle of the screen as the user resizes the window. For example, when an *xterm* is resized, it always displays the number of rows and columns of the window rather than its width and height in pixels. The **XmNwidthInc** and **XmNheightInc** resources control the incremental steps (in pixels) that the window can change in each dimension. Example 17-1 demonstrates incremental resizing. The application displays a shell widget containing a pushbutton. When you click on the button, it displays the size of the window in pixels, but when you resize the window, the *mwm* size display (in the center of the screen) shows the value as divided by **XmNbaseWidth** and **XmNbaseHeight**. The application cannot be resized larger or smaller than the values specified by the **XmNmin*** and **XmNmax*** resources.

Example 17-1. The resize_shell.c program

```
/* resize_shell.c -- demonstrate the max and min heights and widths.
 * This program should be run to really see how mwm displays the
 * size of the window as it is resized..
 */
#include <Xm/PushB.h>

main(argc, argv)
char *argv[ ];
{
    Widget toplevel, button;
    XtAppContext app;
    extern void getsize();

    toplevel = XtVaAppInitialize(&app, "Demos",
        NULL, 0, &argc, argv, NULL,
        XmNminWidth,      25,
        XmNminHeight,     20,
        XmNmaxWidth,      110,
        XmNmaxHeight,     90,
        XmNbaseWidth,     5,
        XmNbaseHeight,    5,
        XmNwidthInc,      5,
        XmNheightInc,     5,
        NULL);

    /* Pushbutton's callback prints the dimensions of the shell. */
    button = XtVaCreateManagedWidget("Print Size",
        xmPushButtonWidgetClass, toplevel, NULL);
    XtAddCallback(button, XmNactivateCallback, getsize, toplevel);

    XtRealizeWidget(toplevel);
    XtAppMainLoop(app);
}

void
getsize(widget, shell)
Widget widget, shell;
{
    Dimension width, height;

    XtVaGetValues(shell, XmNwidth, &width, XmNheight, &height, NULL);
    printf("width = %d, height = %d\n", width, height);
}
```

The size resources can be set on any shell widget in your application, but if they are used at all, they should be hard-coded rather than set in app-defaults files. In our example, we arbitrarily set the shell to have maximum and minimum extents. The width and height increments are each set to five, indicating that the user cannot resize the window width or height in less than five-pixel increments. For example, if the window was originally 417 pixels wide, if the user resizes it smaller, it can only be changed to 412, 407, 402, etc. (The window will always "snap" to the nearest point.) Because we imposed an increment of five, we also set the **XmNbaseWidth** and **XmNbaseHeight** to the same values to provide appropriate feedback to the user about the size of the window. That is, as the window is resized, rather than displaying the size of the window in pixels, its size is shown according to its incremental units. If you run *resize_shell*, clicking on the PushButton prints the size of the shell in pixels. Compare that output to the dimensions reported by the window manager as you resize the window.

The problem with the approach shown in Example 17-1 is that most real applications are not like *xterm* in that they don't display a single window with a single fixed-width font. They typically contain other elements whose sizes cannot be easily computed to give an accurate indication for exactly how large or small the window should be. PushButtons, Labels, ToggleButtons, and MenuBars all typically have variable-width fonts and resettable strings that make the equation too difficult to calculate before the window is actually created and displayed. Incremental width and height values are even more difficult to estimate. There are Manager widget margins to consider, border widths, and a plethora of other resources that come into play. Even an extremely simple window that contains nothing but a ScrolledText or ScrolledList widget cannot be determined easily because of the ScrollBar's geometry and again, variable window margins and other resources affect it.

However, all is not lost. If it is imperative for the application's size to be constrained, consider whether the application's default initial size can be considered either its maximum or minimum size. If so, you can allow the window to come up as its default size, and trap for **ConfigureNotify** events on the shell widget. You can then use the default width and height reported in the event as your minimums or maximums, as demonstrated in Example 17-2.

Example 17-2. The set_minimum.c program

```
/* set_minimum.c -- demonstrate how to set the minimum size of a
 * window to its initial size.  This method is useful if your program
 * is initially displayed at its minimum size, but it would be too
 * difficult to try to calculate ahead of time what the initial size
 * would be.
 */
#include <Xm/PushB.h>

main(argc, argv)
char *argv[ ];
{
    Widget toplevel, button;
    XtAppContext app;
    extern void getsize(), configure();

    toplevel = XtVaAppInitialize(&app, "Demos",
        NULL, 0, &argc, argv, NULL,
        XmNmaxWidth,     110,
        XmNmaxHeight,    90,
        XmNbaseWidth,    5,
        XmNbaseHeight,   5,
        XmNwidthInc,     5,
        XmNheightInc,    5,
        NULL);

    /* Add an event handler to trap the first configure event */
    XtAddEventHandler(toplevel, StructureNotifyMask, False, configure, NULL);

    /* Pushbutton's callback prints the dimensions of the shell. */
    button = XtVaCreateManagedWidget("Print Size",
```

Example 17-2. The set_minimum.c program (continued)

```
        xmPushButtonWidgetClass, toplevel, NULL);
    XtAddCallback(button, XmNactivateCallback, getsize, toplevel);

    XtRealizeWidget(toplevel);
    XtAppMainLoop(app);
}

void
getsize(widget, shell)
Widget widget, shell;
{
    Dimension width, height;

    XtVaGetValues(shell, XmNwidth, &width, XmNheight, &height, NULL);
    printf("width = %d, height = %d\n", width, height);
}

static void
configure(shell, client_data, event)
Widget shell;
XtPointer client_data;
XConfigureEvent *event;
{
    if (event->type != ConfigureNotify)
        return;
    printf("width = %d, height = %d\n", event->width, event->height);
    XtVaSetValues(shell,
        XmNminWidth, event->width,
        XmNminHeight, event->height,
        NULL);
    XtRemoveEventHandler(shell, StructureNotifyMask, False, configure, NULL);
}
```

The function **XtAddEventHandler( )** is used to add an event handler for **toplevel** specifically for those events that satisfy the **ConfigureNotifyMask**. Those events include, among others, **ConfigureNotify** events, which indicate the window's dimensions. The **configure( )** function is called when the window is initially sized, so we use the **width** and **height** fields of the **XConfigureEvent** structure as the **XmNminWidth** and **XmNminHeight** for the shell. However, because the the event handler will be called whenever the window is resized, we don't want to have the minimum size reset again; the window will only be able to grow! So, we remove the event handler using **XtRemove-EventHandler( )**, passing the same parameters as when it was installed.

All said and done, this function can be used most of the time. However, realize that the user could have the *mwm* resource, **Mwm*interactivePlacement**, set to **True**, enabling him to interactively place *and* set the initial size of the application. In this case, if you use the method of setting the application's minimum size to its initial configuration, the user will never be able to make it smaller than the initial size he made it. Although *mwm*'s interactive placement will heed initially set values (such as the maximum width and height resources that were set in the call to **XtVaAppInitialize( )**), this doesn't help our case—we still have no way to determine the initial size of the window. There is no way to allow interactive placement without allowing him to resize the window.

There is a resource called **XmNallowShellResize**, but it does not affect whether the *user* can resize the window. This resource only affects whether the shell will allow itself to be resized if its widget children are resized. Say that the number of items in a List widget grows—the widget will try to increase its own size, causing a rippling effect that eventually hits the toplevel window, which decides whether it can (or wants to) grow. If **XmNallow-ShellResize** is **True**, then the shell will grow, subject to the window manager's approval, of course. But, if the resource is **False**, the window manager will not be consulted because the shell already knows that it doesn't want to resize.

You may ask, "If this resource can prevent the shell from resizing, why doesn't it prevent resizes as widgets are added to it?" The value of the resource does not take effect if the shell has not yet been realized, which is the case while widgets are added to it. After **Xt-RealizeWidget()** is called and the shell's window has been instantiated, the resizing restrictions are then enforcible. The resource's value is **False** by default, so shells will continue to grow until all their children are added and it is realized. If you want the shell to resize itself after adding new children, reset **XmNallowShellResize** to **True**. If you are concerned about **XmNallowShellResize**, you should probably not concern yourself with maximum, minimum, and incremental width and height values.

17.2.3 The Shell's Icon

Shells can be in one of three states: normal, iconic, or withdrawn. When the shell is in its normal state, the user can interact with the user-interface elements in the expected way. When a shell is withdrawn, it is still active, but the user cannot interact with it directly. This is the case for transient shells such as dialog boxes, which can either be destroyed or simply "unmapped" when they are withdrawn. When a shell is iconic, its window is not mapped to the screen, but it is replaced by a smaller image, or icon. In this state, the application is still running, but the program does expect the user to interact with it. A smaller window is usually placed somewhere on the screen, which displays a visual image that suggests some connection to the window from which it came, although it doesn't have to be an exact (scaled down) duplication. Some window managers, like *mwm*, also allow a label to be attached to the icon's window.

The **XmNiconPixmap** resource specifies the icon's pixmap when the application is in an iconic state. Setting the icon pixmap is demonstrated using the code fragment below:

```
Widget toplevel;
XtAppContext app;
Screen *screen;
Pixmap pixmap;

toplevel = XtVaAppInitialize(&app, "Demos",
    NULL, 0, &argc, argv, NULL, NULL);
screen = XtScreen(toplevel);
pixmap = XmGetPixmap(screen, "mailfull",
    BlackPixelOfScreen(screen), WhitePixelOfScreen(screen));

XtVaSetValues(toplevel,
    XmNiconPixmap, pixmap,
    XmNiconic,     True,
    NULL);
```

First, the `toplevel` (ApplicationShell) widget is initialized and the `pixmap` variable is initialized to contain the bitmap described by the file "mailfull" in the directory */usr/include/X11/bitmaps* (see Section 11.6, *Pixmaps and Color Issues*, for details). Finally, the shell's `XmNiconPixmap` is set to that pixmap.[3] There are other ways to set the icon pixmap, but this fragment demonstrates one common approach.

When the `XmNiconic` resource is set to `True`, the shell is iconified. (Conversely, setting `XmNiconic` to `False` would deiconify the shell.) What is really going on here is that the application is sending *hints* to the window manager that it would like its icon window to display the given pixmap and that it would also like to change to its iconic state. These are called "hints" because the window manager does not have to comply with the request. However, if the icon pixmap or iconic state is ignored, it is most likely a bug in the window manager, or an incomplete implementation of one. This happens to be the case for older versions of *mwm* (Version 1.0) and many other older window managers.

One particular workaround for a window manager ignoring the icon pixmap, (and one that will work for almost any window manager, is to set the `XmNiconWindow` resource. It sets the entire icon *window* rather than just its image. Note: the icon window created by the window manager is not accessible to the application using `XmNiconWindow`. Similarly, the default pixmap that a window manager may use for icons whose pixmaps are not individually set is not accessible using `XmNiconPixmap`. That is, you can't get the value of this resource and then modify it. For the best results in portability into environments where the user may not be running the most up-to-date window manager, it is best to create the icon window directly. Once done, we can paint whatever image we like in that window. Example 17-3 demonstrates how this is done. But while we're at it, we might as well make a reusable function that not only creates a shell's icon window, but may also be called repeatedly to dynamically update its image.

Example 17-3. The SetIconPixmap() function

```
void
SetIconPixmap(shell, image)
Widget shell;
Pixmap image;
{
    Window window, root;
    unsigned int x, y, width, height, border_width, depth;
    Display *dpy = XtDisplay(shell);

    /* Get the current icon window associated with the shell */
    XtVaGetValues(shell, XmNiconWindow, &window, NULL);

    /* If there is no window associated with the shell... */
    if (!window) {
        /* ...create one.  Make it at least as big as the pixmap we're
         * going to use.  The icon window only needs to be a simple window.
         */
        if (!XGetGeometry(dpy, image, &root, &x, &y,
                &width, &height, &border_width, &depth) ||
            !(window = XCreateSimpleWindow(dpy, root, 0, 0, width, height,
```

---

[3] Some systems might not get the expected results because of colormap values; such systems might try using the constants 1 and 0 as the foreground and background colors for `XmGetPixmap( )`.

Example 17-3. The SetIconPixmap() function (continued)

```
                (unsigned)0, CopyFromParent, CopyFromParent))) {
            XtVaSetValues(shell, XmNiconPixmap, image, NULL);
            return;
        }
        /* Now that the window is created, set it ... */
        XtVaSetValues(shell, XmNiconWindow, window, NULL);
    }
    /* Set the window's background pixmap to be the image. Easier to handle */
    XSetWindowBackgroundPixmap(dpy, window, image);
    XClearWindow(dpy, win); /* cause a redisplay of this window, if exposed */
}
```

SetIconPixmap() takes two parameters: a shell and an image. If shell has not yet had its icon window set, a new one is created using XCreateSimpleWindow(). This window's size is set to the same size as the pixmap's, which is assumed to already have been created at this point. XGetGeometry() is used to get the size of the image, but this function can be used on windows as well. In the unlikely event that this function or XCreateSimpleWindow() fails, we fall back on our old method using XmNicon-Pixmap and hope the window manager understands it. Otherwise, we move on by setting the image pixmap as the window's background pixmap. This saves us the hassle of rendering it into the image using XCopyArea() or XCopyPlane(). Note that this is also done if shell already had an icon window and the function was being called to merely install a new image.

The final call to XClearWindow() causes the icon to be repainted. This won't be necessary if the window was just created (although it doesn't hurt), but it is necessary if the window was merely updated with a new image.

Setting the Icon's Position

Similar resources to XmNx and XmNy are available for use with a shell's icon. For example, XmNiconX and XmNiconY can be used to set the explicit x and y coordinates on the screen. However, these are the sorts of resources you probably don't want to set arbitrarily unless your particular application has a specific need. In most cases, these resources are best left for the user to specify on his own, or to let the window manager deal with in its own way.

Shell and Icon Names

The resources XmNtitle and XmNiconName may be set to C strings (not compound strings) to set the strings displayed on the window manager's titlebar and icon, respectively. Typically, these values are the same as the name of the program and both are usually set to the value of argv[0], by default. These values also affect the WM_NAME property for the toplevel window (i.e., the shell). This is important for session managers and other applications that monitor all toplevel windows on a desktop. These programs look for the WM_NAME property to provide menus or interactive icons (PushButtons) that allow the user to control the desktop in a GUI-like fashion rather than through tty-like shells like *xterm* and *csh*.

While they may be set independently, **XmNtitle** and **XmNiconName** are also resources that are best left as user-settable resources, rather than as hard-coded ones. Incidentally, there are also some X Toolkit Intrinsics command-line options such as **−name**, which are parsed by **XtAppInitialize( )** (and the other initialization routines) that can be used to set the titlebar and icon names of the application.

See Volume Four, *X Toolkit Intrinsics Reference Manual*, for additional information on the various WMShell resources and how to use them.

17.3 VendorShell Resources

The VendorShell is subclassed from WMShell, so all Shell widgets subclassed from the VendorShell (including all Motif shells except for the MenuShell) can use the same resources described in the previous section for WMShell. By design, the VendorShell is implemented by individual vendors to specify resources that are supported only by that particular vendor's window manager. For instance, *mwm* has some window manager features that are not found in other window managers. You should be familiar with the Motif Window Manager in order to understand how the discussion and examples that follow can be used.

17.3.1 Window Manager Decorations

Recall that the frame around an application's main window belongs to the window manager, and that the controls and window menu in it are not a part of your application. The window manager decorations for an application look like that shown in Figure 17-1.

Figure 17-1. Motif window manager decorations

NOTE

The user can set his own *mwm* resources to control which of these items are available for particular windows on the desktop. Also, *mwm* automatically controls which elements are visible for certain windows in order to maintain compatibility with the *Motif Style Guide. You are discouraged from interfering with this process.* Nevertheless, the resources are available for use in exceptional cases. Examples might be for those who are interested in internally modifying *mwm* or in learning how it works.

The `XmNmwmDecorations` resource can be set to an integer value that is made up of any of the following values (examples of use are given in a moment):

MWM_DECOR_BORDER

Enables the window manager borders for the frame. These borders are decorative only; they are not resize handles. Except for non-rectangular windows or programs like a *clock*, all Motif-style applications should have decorative borders.

MWM_DECOR_RESIZEH

Enables the resize handles for the frame. If the resize handles are displayed, the decorative borders must also be on (i.e., you can't turn them off).

MWM_DECOR_TITLE

Enables the titlebar for the window.

MWM_DECOR_MENU

Enables the menu from the titlebar. If this item is on, the titlebar is forced on (i.e., you can't turn it off).

MWM_DECOR_MAXIMIZE

Makes the "maximize" button visible. When selected, the window is expanded to the largest size possible. The size of the window is constrained by the values for `XmNmaxWidth` and `XmNmaxHeight`. If those resources are unset, the window is expanded to the size of the screen.

MWM_DECOR_MINIMIZE

Makes the "minimize" button visible. Note that minimizing is not the opposite of the "maximize" button. The window is not shrunk to its smallest size; rather, it is *iconified*. This item is off by default for TransientShell widgets (dialogs), since they cannot be iconified. (They are unmapped or destroyed when their parent Shells are unmapped or destroyed.)

MWM_DECOR_ALL

Used to enable all of the items, avoiding having to specify all values simultaneously.

All these values are declared in *<Xm/MwmUtil.h>*, which must be included before any of them may be used. The values can be used in conjunction with one another and they may be retrieved as well as set. For example, if you have a customized dialog that you do not want to have resize handles, you can use the following code fragment:

```
Widget dialog_shell;
int decor;

dialog_shell = XtAppCreateShell(...);

XtVaGetValues(dialog_shell, XmNmwmDecorations, &decor, NULL);
decor &= ~MWM_DECOR_RESIZEH;
XtVaSetValues(dialog_shell, XmNmwmDecorations, decor, NULL);
```

While the programmatic interface is available to make changes in the form described above, you really don't have to resort to this level of complexity. If you want to do something allowed by the *Motif Style Guide*, chances are that the Motif toolkit provides some convenient method for achieving it. For example, Motif dialogs returned by Motif convenience routines like `XmCreateMessageDialog()` can have their resize handles turned off by setting `XmNnoResize` to `False`:

```
Widget dialog;
Arg args[1];

XtSetArg(args[0], XmNnoResize, True);
dialog = XmCreateFileSelectionDialog(parent, "dialog", args, 1);
```

Similar resources are available for interacting with the "shell" part of a Motif dialog. `XmNdialogTitle` takes a compound string that sets the titlebar's label. (However, this resource takes a compound string, which is an overkill since titlebars cannot display multiple fonts or newlines, both of which are supported by compound strings.)

The rule of thumb is: if Motif doesn't provide a *convenience method* (routine or resource) for doing what you want done, chances are you shouldn't be doing it. On the other hand, you don't *have* to use that convenience method; if it seems appropriate, you can use the methods described here. At the time of this writing, the *Motif Style Guide* is not completely explicit about some issues, while others may be changed in the future. You are left to your own good judgment about how you choose to implement your applications.

17.3.2 Window Manager Menu Functions

The window manager's frame decorations, including the contents of the window menu, can be modified using resources described in this section. The standard settings available in the menu may be modified using the resource `XmNmwmFunctions`. This resource acts much like `XmNmwmDecorations` in that the value is an integer that may be set to one or more of the following values ORed together:

`MWM_FUNC_RESIZE`

Enables the **Size** item in the menu. If this value isn't set, it also disables the resize handles for the window manager frame (and the corresponding value in `XmNmwm-Decorations`).

`MWM_FUNC_MOVE`

Enables the **Move** menu item. Disabling this item does not affect the window manager frame decorations for this window.

`MWM_FUNC_MINIMIZE`

> Enables the **Minimize** menu item. Disabling this item causes the corresponding decoration to be disabled (and the corresponding value in **XmNmwm-Decorations**).

`MWM_FUNC_MAXIMIZE`

> Enables the **Maximize** menu item. Disabling this item causes the corresponding decoration to be disabled (and the corresponding value in **XmNmwm-Decorations**).

`MWM_FUNC_CLOSE`

> Enables the **Close** menu item. Disabling this item does not affect the window manager decorations for this frame.

`MWM_FUNC_ALL`

> Enables all of the standard items in the menu to be displayed and all the default functionality of the window manager to work.

It is extremely important to remember that the user can configure similar settings, even provide *new* settings, from his *.mwmrc* file. (See Volume Three, *X Window System User's Guide*.) You may not always get exactly the menu appearance you were looking for, although your settings will always override any user-settable defaults.

A common misuse of this functionality is to disable the **Close** button. This is not recommended. Users expect this button to be there. If you want to require the user to interact with another control, such as a button in a dialog, there is a more acceptable alternative. That is, decide which dialog button would be conceptually equivalent to the **Close** menu item, and link its functionality to that item. For example, if you are using a standard Motif dialog with an **Ok** and a **Cancel** button, the **Close** button should be equivalent to executing **Cancel**. Example 17-4 demonstrates how to make the link, while at the same time explaining how this information is sent from the window manager to the application.

When you run the application, and click on the button, a dialog is displayed, with a fanciful message about deleting all files. All the application really does is to print a "Yes" or "No" message to standard output, based on whether the **Ok** or **Cancel** button is clicked. If you pull down the window menu on the dialog, though, and select **Close**, you'll notice that not only does the dialog disappear, but the "No" message is printed. What is going on here?

Let's begin at the highest level of abstraction. The VendorShell resource, **XmNdelete-Response**, discussed in Chapter 7, *Custom Dialogs, Dialogs and the Window Manager*, in Section 5.3.5, can be used to control what the application should do in response to the user's selection of the **Close** button. The default behavior is that the window is usually *dismissed*. That is, the value of **Xm_UNMAP** is used and the window is unmapped from the screen. By setting **XmNdeleteReponse** to **XmDESTROY**, the dialog will be destroyed. However, if set to **XmDO_NOTHING**, you are declaring that you are going to handle the action yourself. In this case, you are going to link the **Close** button to execute the **No** callback in the dialog.

In order to explain what's really going on, though, we must abandon the higher level of abstraction used by the Motif toolkit and get into more of the internals of how the **Close** button and other window manager messages are sent to the application. We'll go on to that topic immediately following the example.

Example 17-4. The wm_delete.c program

```
/* wm_delete.c -- demonstrate how to bind the Close button in the
 * window manager's system menu to the "cancel" button in a dialog.
 */
#include <Xm/MessageB.h>
#include <Xm/PushB.h>
#include <Xm/Protocols.h>

#define YES 1
#define NO  0
int answer;

/* main() --create a pushbutton whose callback pops up a dialog box */
main(argc, argv)
char *argv[ ];
{
    Widget toplevel, button;
    XtAppContext app;
    void activate();

    toplevel = XtVaAppInitialize(&app, "Demos",
        NULL, 0, &argc, argv, NULL, NULL);

    button = XtCreateManagedWidget("button", xmPushButtonWidgetClass,
        toplevel, NULL, 0);
    XtAddCallback(button, XmNactivateCallback, activate, NULL);

    XtRealizeWidget(toplevel);
    XtAppMainLoop(app);
}

/* Create and popup an ErrorDialog indicating that the user may have
 * done something wrong.  The dialog contains an Ok and Cancel button,
 * but he can still choose the Close button in the titlebar.
 */
void
activate(w)
Widget w;
{
    Widget dialog, shell;
    void handle_close(), response();
    XmString t = XmStringCreateSimple("Warning: Delete All Files?");
    Atom WM_DELETE_WINDOW;
    Arg args[2];

    /* Make sure the VendorShell associated with the dialog does not
     * react to the user's selection of the Close system menu item.
     */
    XtSetArg(args[0], XmNmessageString, t);
    XtSetArg(args[1], XmNdeleteResponse, XmDO_NOTHING);
    dialog = XmCreateWarningDialog(w, "notice", args, 2);
    XmStringFree(t);

    /* add callback routines for ok and cancel -- desensitize help */
    XtAddCallback(dialog, XmNokCallback, response, NULL);
    XtAddCallback(dialog, XmNcancelCallback, response, NULL);
    XtSetSensitive(XmMessageBoxGetChild(dialog, XmDIALOG_HELP_BUTTON), False);

    XtManageChild(dialog);

    /* Add a callback for the WM_DELETE_WINDOW protocol */
```

Example 17-4. The wm_delete.c program (continued)

```
    shell = XtParent(dialog);
    WM_DELETE_WINDOW = XmInternAtom(XtDisplay(w), "WM_DELETE_WINDOW", False);
    XmAddWMProtocolCallback(shell, WM_DELETE_WINDOW, response, dialog);
}

/* callback for the Ok and Cancel buttons in the dialog -- may also be
 * called from the WM_DELETE_WINDOW protocol message sent by the wm.
 */
void
response(widget, client_data, cbs)
Widget widget;
XtPointer client_data;
XmAnyCallbackStruct *cbs;
{
    Widget dialog;

    if (cbs->reason == XmCR_OK) {
        answer = YES;
        puts("Yes.");
    } else {
        answer = NO;
        puts("No.");
    }
    /* test that "reason" is not the cancel button and not the ok button.
     * It's value is XmCR_PROTOCOLS (6666), but we can't check for that
     * because OSF didn't make that value public.
     */
    if (cbs->reason != XmCR_CANCEL && cbs->reason != XmCR_OK)
        /* we passed the dialog as client data for the protocol callback */
        dialog = (Widget)client_data;
    else
        dialog = widget;

    XtDestroyWidget(dialog);
}
```

17.4 Handling Window Manager Messages

The pure definition of a "protocol" in computer circles is a set of rules governing the communication and the transfer of data. When the window manager sends a message to an application that follows a predefined protocol, the client application should respond accordingly. The ICCCM defines a number of protocols for window managers and applications to follow. One such protocol was demonstrated in the previous example. Whenever the **Close** item in the menu is selected, the window manager sends the application a protocol message. The application must comply. The method for delivering the message is through the normal event-handling mechanisms provided by Xlib. The event that corresponds to this message is called a *client message*. The message itself is of type **Atom**, which is merely a unique integer used as an identifier. (Its value is unimportant, since you only need to reference this value through the preprocessor macro, **WM_PROTOCOLS**.) The protocol itself takes the form of other atoms, depending on the nature of the message. Table 17-2 lists the atoms that are used as values for **WM_PROTOCOL** client messages.

Table 17-2. Protocol Atoms Defined by the ICCCM

Atom	Meaning
WWM_TAKE_FOCUS	The window is getting input focus.
WM_DELETE_WINDOW	The window is about to be deleted.
WWM_SAVE_YOURSELF	The application should save its internal state.

Although this table is complete, it is expected to grow in future editions of the ICCCM.

In Example 17-4, the application is sent a **ClientMessage** event by the window manager indicating that the window is about to be deleted. The value associated with the **WM_PROTO-COLS** message is **WM_DELETE_WINDOW**. The application is now responsible for complying with the protocol in some way. In order to handle this client message ourselves, we must tell the dialog's VendorShell not to do its normal processing for this protocol, which would be to destroy or unmap the window, depending on the type of dialog or shell being used. We can interpose on that default action by setting the VendorShell's **XmNdeleteResponse** resource to **XmDO_NOTHING**, and set up a callback routine that can be called whenever this protocol is sent. This is a two phase process: first, we must get the atom associated with the **WM_DELETE_WINDOW** protcol, and then we must add a callback routine to respond to the client message event generated by that protocol being initiated by the window manager. Therefore, we execute the first step by getting the protocol ID of **WM_DELETE_WINDOW** using **XmInternAtom( )**:

```
Atom
XmInternAtom(dpy, atom_name, dont_create)
    Display *dpy;
    char    *atom_name;
    Boolean dont_create;
```

If the atom name described by the string **atom_name** exists, then the **Atom** ID is returned. If it does not exist, then if **dont_create** is **True**, the function returns **None**. If **False**, it creates the atom and returns its ID. This function is identical to **XInternAtom( )**, with the exception that the Motif version maintains an internal cache of previously accessed atom ID's. Since creating and returning atoms causes a round trip to the server, it is a nice performance improvement to have that cache available for frequently accessed atoms.

The function **XmAddWMProtocolCallback( )** is then used to install a callback routine to be invoked whenever the window manager sends a **WM_PROTOCOLS** client message to the application. If the protocol that was sent in the client message matches the specified protocol passed to **XmAddWMProtocolCallback( )**, the associated function is called. In Example 17-4, **response( )**, which is also used by the dialog's action area items, is used as the protocol's callback function. Thus, the **Close** button's callback will now call the same callback associated with the **Ok** and **Cancel** buttons.

The form of this callback routine is the same as that of any other Motif callback. Specifically, the final parameter is a Motif-defined callback structure of some kind. (Its type depends on the widget that was activated.) More interestingly, the **reason** field of this callback function gives a specific reason why the callback was called. This field is provided *because* the same callback function may be invoked by more than one widget. In this case, the `response( )` function's callback structure may have one of three different values of `reason`: `XmCR_OK` for the **Ok** button, `XmCR_CANCEL` for the **Cancel** button, or `Xm-CR_PROTOCOLS` for the **Close** button in the window menu. However, the Motif toolkit currently has a bug that `XmCR_PROTOCOLS` is not a publicly accessible value, so we can't test for that value directly. The workaround is to test `reason`'s value against the other values.

The `event` field of the callback structure will be an `XClientMessageEvent`.

In addition to the `reason` field, another major difference between the way `response( )` is called from the dialog and the **Close** button is the `widget` parameter. When either **Ok** or **Cancel** is called, the `widget` is the dialog itself. But the protocol callback routines are really processed by special *protocol widgets* that are attached to VendorShells.[4] In this case, the `widget` field will be one of those special widgets. But this widget has no intrinsic meaning and can be subsequently ignored. Since the purpose of the callback routine is to obtain the "answer" to the posted question and to then destroy the dialog, we must be able to access the dialog's widget somehow. Knowing ahead of time that the activation of the `WM_DELETE_WINDOW` protocol would cause the protocol widget to be passed as the `widget` parameter, we also knew to pass a handle to the dialog widget as the client data to `XmAdd-WMProtocolCallback( )` to guarantee that we would have a handle to it.

The purpose, of course, is to destroy the window, but this function can just as easily veto the operation, rendering the **Close** button inoperable. However, this is poor application design; if the **Close** button is not going to unmap the window (presumably for some good reason, like an error somewhere), you should report an error message of some sort, perhaps in another dialog. The point is, never leave the user uninformed about what is going on, especially if you are modifying the default behavior of certain user-interface controls. Also, try not to make the interface inconsistent with other windows; people are used to using the **Close** button—don't take that away from them.

17.4.1 Adding New Protocols

In general, you can attach callback routines to any of the published protocols using the mechanisms described previously. You may also assign new protocols to send yourself special messages that are pertinent only to your application. (Remember, protocol messages can be passed from application to application, not just between the window manager and other clients.)

Handling arbitrary protocols is basically a matter of following these simple steps:

1. Get or create an atom from the X server.

2. Make sure the atom is registered on the shell so the event-handling mechanism can recognize it if it should arrive.

---

[4] Recall that shells may have *any number of widget children* provided that only one of them is managed at a time. In the Motif VendorShell widget's case, these other widgets are not managed, yet they are used to process and manage protocols that are exchanged between the window manager and the application.

3. Install a callback routine for when the protocol is sent to the application.

We have already demonstrated how steps one and three work. For the case of WM_DELETE_WINDOW, step two has already been taken care of by the VendorShell, since it is an established and standardized ICCCM protocol. That is, the VendorShell has already registered interest in the protocol so it can react to it in the method described by its Xm-NdeleteResponse resource. However, other protocols (customized or not) may not be registered. Since it doesn't hurt to register a protocol with a window more than once, it's always a good practice always to do step two. The function used to do this is XmAdd-WMProtocols(), which takes the following form:

```
void
XmAddWMProtocols(shell, protocols, num_protocols)
    Widget shell;
    Atom *protocols;
    int    num_protocols;
```

The function takes a list of protocols, implying that you can add as many as you like at one time. We discuss how this can be done in the next section.

17.4.2 Saving Application State

A *session manager* is an application that acts something like a window manager. However, rather than controlling only the windows on a screen, it monitors the actual applications running on that screen. Frequently, session managers allow the user to start, terminate, or even restart any program automatically, through dialog boxes, or through a variety of interface controls. Session managers may even cause programs to "sleep" by terminating all their keyboard and mouse input. As far as the program is concerned, the user is just not interacting with it.

At the moment, there are not many full session managers available, so much of the possible functionality is uncharted. This section discusses one aspect of proposed session manager behavior, and how it might be implemented. This behavior concerns the ability of applications running under the session manager to restart themselves at the point where they left off in a previous session.

If, for any reason, the session manager decides that it might terminate (which might result in the entire X connection terminating), it may send a request to all its applications for them to save themselves. That is, they should save their internal state so they can be restarted later. In this case, the session manager sends a WM_SAVE_YOURSELF protocol message. According to the ICCCM, client applications that can save their current state and restart from that state should register the atom WM_SAVE_YOURSELF on the WM_PROTOCOLS property on *one* of their top-level windows. (That is, one toplevel window per application.) However, there are some extra constraints for applications that want to restart themselves.

Let's say your application is called *wm_save*, and you want to be able to restart it from a previously saved file. Thus, let's say your application will parse the following command-line option:

```
% wm_save —restart filename
```

The ICCCM states that after sending the WM_SAVE_YOURSELF message to the application, the session manager waits until the program updates its WM_COMMAND property on the same window that received the protocol message. The application *is not permitted to interact with the user in any way* at this time. You cannot prompt for filenames, ask if the user wants to save state, or do anything. The callback routine must save its current state somehow—possibly in a predefined file that can be made known to the user through documentation, rather than a runtime message. It must then update the WM_COMMAND property to reflect what the parameters were that not only *started* the program (how the user originally invoked it), but what additional parameters might be required in order to *restart* the program. This process is demonstrated in Example 17-5.

Example 17-5. The wm_save.c program

```
/* wm_save.c -- demonstrate how to save the state of an application
 * from a WM_SAVE_YOURSELF session manager protocol.  This is not a
 * real program -- just a template.
 */
#include <Xm/Xm.h>
#include <Xm/Protocols.h>
#include <stdio.h>

/* save the original argc and argv for possible WM_SAVE_YOURSELF messages */
int save_argc;
char **save_argv;

main(argc, argv)
char *argv[ ];
{
    Widget toplevel;
    XtAppContext app;
    Atom wm_save_yourself;
    void save_state();
    char *restart_file;

    /* save argc and argv values */
    save_argv = (char **)XtMalloc(argc * sizeof(char *));
    for (save_argc = 0; save_argc < argc; save_argc++)
        /* we don't need to save old -restart options */
        if (!strcmp(argv[save_argc], "-restart"))
            argc -= 2, save_argc--;
        else
            save_argv[save_argc] =
                strcpy(XtMalloc(strlen(argv[save_argc]) + 1), argv[save_argc]);

    /* initialize toolkit normally; argv has its Xt-specific args stripped */
    toplevel = XtVaAppInitialize(&app, "Demos",
        NULL, 0, &argc, argv, NULL,
        XmNwidth, 100,
        XmNheight, 100,
        NULL);

    /* get the WM_SAVE_YOURSELF protocol atom and register it with the
     * toplevel window's WM_PROTOCOLS property.  Also add a callback.
     */
    wm_save_yourself =
        XmInternAtom(XtDisplay(toplevel), "WM_SAVE_YOURSELF", False);
    XmAddWMProtocols(toplevel, &wm_save_yourself, 1);
    XmAddWMProtocolCallback(toplevel, &wm_save_yourself, save_state, toplevel);
```

Example 17-5. The wm_save.c program (continued)

```
    /* create widgets... */

    /* now check to see if we are restarting from a previously run state */
    while (--argc) {
        if (!strcmp(argv[0], "-restart")) {
            /* restarting from a previously saved state */
            restart_file = argv[1];
            argc--;
        }

        /* possibly process other args here, too */
    }

    XtRealizeWidget(toplevel);
    XtAppMainLoop(app);
}

/* called if WM_SAVE_YOURSELF client message was sent... */
void
save_state(widget, toplevel, cbs)
Widget widget;      /* protocol widget -- unused */
Widget toplevel;    /* actual toplevel shell passed as client data */
XmAnyCallbackStruct *cbs; /* unused */
{
    extern char *SaveStateAndReturnFileName();  /* hypothetical function */
    char *filename = SaveStateAndReturnFileName();
    puts("save_state()");

    save_argv = (char **)XtRealloc(save_argv, 2 * sizeof(char *));

    save_argv[save_argc++] = "-restart";
    save_argv[save_argc++] = filename;

    XSetCommand(XtDisplay(toplevel), XtWindow(toplevel),
        save_argv, save_argc); /* notice the order of these args! */
}
```

The only difference in the way this program handles protocol messages (as opposed to
wm_delete.c) is that the WM_SAVE_YOURSELF protocol was hand-registered with the
toplevel widget before the callback routine was registered. This was not done with the
WM_DELETE_WINDOW protocol because, as we mentioned, the VendorShell already handles
that particular protocol. If the session manager sends a WM_SAVE_YOURSELF message to this
program, then the **save_state( )** function is called, which causes the program to save its
internal state somehow in the function **SaveStateAndReturnFileName( )**. This is a
hypothetical function that you would write yourself to save the state of the program (which
would vary greatly depending on its nature) and return the filename to which the information
was written. Next, the *-restart* flag and the new filename are added to the saved **argv** from
the beginning of the program. The function **XSetWMCommand( )** is used to set the
WM_COMMAND property on the window associated with the **toplevel** shell. Thus, we have
completed our obligation to the session manager.

For more information about the session manager and the save-yourself communication protocol, see Section L.5.2.1, *Saving Client State*, in Volume Zero, *X Protocol Reference Manual*. For more information on **XSetWMCommand( )** and other Xlib-based functions that set and get window manager properties on toplevel windows, see Volume One, *Xlib Programmer's Manual* and Volume Two, *Xlib Reference Manual*.

17.5 Customized Protocols

The previous section demonstrates how similar one protocol message is to the next in the way it can be added to a program. Adding new protocols is not difficult either. The only changes we have to make are those that would otherwise interfere with the standard protocols and properties that are registered with the X protocol and ICCCM. For this reason, the convention is to name nonstandard atoms and window properties with at least an underscore prefix and possibly a more detailed prefix to identify the atom as a private protocol or property. Accordingly, Motif provides the property **_MOTIF_WM_MESSAGES** as a private atom specifically for Motif-based applications that wish to send private messages to themselves or one another. Note that "private" does not mean that no one else can see them; it just implies that the atom (or protocol) is not publically available for other third-party applications to use. In other words, don't expect other programs on the desktop to participate in the protocol.

Example 17-6 demonstrates how to register your own protocol with the shell and set up a callback routine for when that protocol is delivered. (Note that, like Example 17-5, this program is a skeletal frame only; it is not functional as a real program.)

Example 17-6. The wm_protocol.c program

```
/* wm_protocol.c -- demonstrate how to add your own protocol to a
 * shell.  The nature of the protocol isn't important; however, it
 * must be registered with the _MOTIF_WM_MESSAGES property on the
 * shell.  We also add a menu item to the window manager frame's
 * window menu to allow the user to activate the protocol, if desired.
 */
#include <Xm/Xm.h>
#include <Xm/Protocols.h>
#include <stdio.h>

main(argc, argv)
char *argv[ ];
{
    Widget toplevel;
    XtAppContext app;
    Atom motif_msgs, my_protocol;
    void my_proto_callback();
    char buf[ 64 ];

    /* initialize toolkit normally; argv has its Xt-specific args stripped */
    toplevel = XtVaAppInitialize(&app, "Demos", NULL, 0, &argc, argv, NULL,
        XmNwidth, 100,
        XmNheight, 100,
        NULL);

    /* get the motif_msgs and my_protocol atoms... if it doesn't exist,
```

Example 17-6. The wm_protocol.c program (continued)

```
        * it'll get created.
        */
    my_protocol = XmInternAtom(XtDisplay(toplevel), "_MY_PROTOCOL", False);
    motif_msgs = XmInternAtom(XtDisplay(toplevel), "_MOTIF_WM_MESSAGES", False);

    /* Add my_protocol to the _MOTIF_WM_MESSAGES VendorShell-defined
     * property on the shell.  Add a callback for this protocol.
     */
    XmAddProtocols(toplevel, motif_msgs, &my_protocol, 1);
    XmAddProtocolCallback(toplevel,
        motif_msgs, my_protocol, my_proto_callback, NULL);

    /* allow the user to activate the protocol through the window manager's
     * window menu on the shell.
     */
    sprintf(buf, "MyProtocol _P Ctrl<Key>P f.send_msg %d", my_protocol);
    XtVaSetValues(toplevel, XmNmwmMenu, buf, NULL);

    /* create widgets... */

    XtRealizeWidget(toplevel);
    XtAppMainLoop(app);
}

/* called if _MY_PROTOCOL was activated, a client message was sent... */
void
my_proto_callback(widget, client_data, cbs)
Widget widget;              /* protocol widget -- unused */
XtPointer client_data;      /* NULL was passed */
XmAnyCallbackStruct *cbs;    /* unused */
{
    puts("my protocol got activated!");
}
```

This program is set up to receive the protocol **_MY_PROTOCOL**. If the message is sent, the function **my_proto_callback( )** is called, passing the appropriate client data and callback structure as before. However, since we just made it up, the only way this protocol can be delivered is by the window manager if (and only if) the user selects the new menu item attached to the window manager frame's window menu as shown in Figure 17-2.

The menu item is added using the **XmNmwmMenu** resource in the call to **XtVaSet-Values( )**:

```
    sprintf(buf, "MyProtocol _P Ctrl<Key>P f.send_msg %d", my_protocol);
    XtVaSetValues(toplevel, XmNmwmMenu, buf, NULL);
```

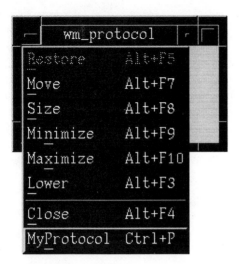

Figure 17-2. Window menu for wm_protocol.c

The syntax for the value for the string used by the **XmNmwmMenu** resource is described completely in the *mwm* documentation. To review: each of the arguments refers to a single entry in the menu that is always added after the last standard protocol in the menu (usually, the **Close** button). The syntax for the resource is:

> *label [mnemonic] [accelerator] function*

Only the label and the window manager function (*mwm*-specific) are required. The label is always first; if a space needs to be embedded in the label, precede it by two backslashes. The next token is parsed as a mnemonic if it starts with an underscore. If an accelerator is given, the Motif toolkit parses this string and creates a corresponding accelerator text string for the menu. Finally, the parser looks for a window manager function as described by the *mwm* documentation. These include, for example, **f.move**, **f.raise** and **f.send_msg**. This last case is where *mwm* will send the specified client message to the application.

One final note: it is possible to deactivate a protocol on the window menu using **XmDeactivateWMProtocol( )**. Deactivation makes a protocol insensitive (unselectable). Protocols may be reactivated by **XmActivateWMProtocol( )**; new protocols are automatically activated when they are added.

XmActivateProtocol( ) and **XmDeactivateProtocol( )** perform an analogous function for non-window manager protocols.

17.5.1 Now What?

Now the question is: what can you do with your own private protocol? These protocols come in handy if you want to attach any application-specific functionality to the window so that it can communicate messages between similar applications on the desktop. Frequently, larger application *suites* that contain multiple programs in a complete set might need to communicate information to one another through this protocol. For example, if a suite of Paint, Draw, and Desktop Publishing products wanted to communicate document information to one another, they could pass messages to one another using their own protocol. Whether you care to allow the window manager (and thus, the user) to participate in the protocol can be controlled by whether you make the protocol handle available in the window menu as shown in Figure 17-2.

However, this advanced work with protocols is getting beyond the scope of this book. Further progress requires Xlib level code that you can research on your own by reading portions of Volume One, *Xlib Programmer's Manual*. However, if you are interested in providing this kind of functionality, you might consider the following design approach:

- If a window cares to communicate with another application on the desktop, you must assume that the other application has extended an invitation for others to communicate with it. This is normally done by interested windows placing an atom on their toplevel windows that identifies themselves as being interested in this particular style of communication. For discussion, let's call this atom _MYAPP_CLIENT_PROP. The atom can be added to the WM_PROTOCOLS property already on the window using XmAddWMProtocol( ), just as we did earlier. Or, you may choose to use XChangeProperty( ) to actually use the atom *as the property itself*. Despite its name, XChangeProperty( ) can be used to add new arbitrary properties to a window's list of existing properties.

- The application that is interested in seeking out other windows that have expressed interest in _MYAPP_PROP can call XQueryTree( ) and start at the root window, searching all of its immediate children for those that have that property. The function XGetWindowProperty( ) can be used to test for the existence of the property itself.

- If a window is found to contain the property, you can use XSendEvent( ) to send an XClientMessageEvent to that window. When sending a client message, you can either do what the Motif toolkit does and send a WM_PROTOCOLS message or you can just send the _MYAPP_CLIENT_PROP atom itself. If you choose the former, the data.1[0] field of the XClientMessageEvent data structure contains the value WM_PROTOCOLS and the atom you want to send is the data.1[1] field. If the receiving window is part of a Motif application and it has registered a callback function for this protocol, then that function will be invoked.[5]

- If the sending application wishes to send any additional data to the receiving application, it should either add or *replace* the receiving window's _MYAPP_CLIENT_PROP property and "upgrade" or change its value.

---

[5] Whether or not the receiving application is a Motif application, it can set up its own event handler to trap for the client message anyway.

17.5.2 Whatever You Like

Remember, since this is your own private protocol, you can do whatever you like in the correspondence process. If you wanted, you could specify that the receiving window would always test for a newly defined property on its window, and if that property is set, obtain further information from the primary selection. Using this process, you could write your own drag and drop methods. However, whatever you come up with is strictly private and no other application will be able to participate with your protocol, unless you tell the developer of the other application what to do.

You can place whatever information you like in properties: a string, an integer, or a data structure. Just make sure that it's not per-process information like a file descriptor. This type of data cannot be shared among separate processes. You should also try not to make the information host-specific because you are not guaranteed that both clients are going to be running on the same computer (although they will be running on the same server). Another thing to avoid is a "continuous" protocol. Do not have programs "chatting" back and forth. This is not a good method for doing interactive talk programs. Your network won't take that kind of traffic for long. To do this kind of communication, it might be better to establish your own TCP or STREAM connection between the two applications. The choice, of course, should attempt to be as network-portable as possible—but again, this is your own personal protocol, so you can do anything you like.

17.6 Summary

With the exception of dealing with `WM_DELETE_WINDOW` protocol messages to link the window menu's **Close** button to other buttons' callback routines already in your dialog, window manager interaction should be regarded as hands-off territory. To stay out of trouble, stay away from the window manager!

The best applications can still function adequately without a window manager. This is especially true for portability's sake; the less you assume that the user is running *mwm*, the better off you'll be. Despite this advice, many nontechnical designers still believe they know better and go head-strong into this area, attempting to redesign Motif on a per-application basis. If you or your organization attempts to go this route, please try to stay conscious of the *Motif Style Guide* and, by all means, do not violate the ICCCM.

Client messages can be extremely powerful tools for large applications that have many toplevel windows that need to interact with each other, or even larger groups of similar applications by the same vendor that needs to have them all talking to one another. The secret to making a private protocol work is establishing a good communication channel and being able to transfer a lot of information without having to transfer a lot of data.

17.7 Exercises

The material in this chapter is quite advanced to begin with, but these questions are very straightforward and you should be able to answer them using material discussed in this chapter.

1. Write a program that always places its error dialogs in the center of the screen.

2. Whenever a shell changes from normal state to iconic state, the window manager changes the shell's **WM_STATE** property. Write a program that gets the **PropertyNotify** event that is generated from this state change so that you can track when a shell is iconified and deiconified. Hint: use **XtAddEventHandler( )** in the same way that we tracked for **ConfigureNotify** events in *set_minimum.c* (You may need to look at the **XPropertyEvent** structure declared in *<X11/Xlib.h>*.)

3. If the user selects the **Close** button from a window menu, have the shell iconify itself if it is a TopLevelShell, or destroy itself if it is a DialogShell.

18

The Clipboard

This chapter describes a way for the application to interact with other applications. Data is placed on the Clipboard, where it can be accessed by other windows on the desktop, regardless of the applications with which they are associated.

In This Chapter:

18
The Clipboard

Imagine a group of people in a room; the only way for them to communicate is by writing messages on paper, placing the paper on a clipboard, and passing the clipboard around. A single person acts as the moderator and holds the clipboard at all times. If someone wants to post a note, he writes the message on a slip of paper and hands the message to the moderator. The note is now available for anyone to read. However, those who read the message do not remove the message from the clipboard; rather, they copy what was written. There is no guarantee that anyone will want to look at any particular message, but it is there nonetheless and will remain there until someone writes a new one.

This is the concept behind the Motif clipboard: a data transfer mechanism that enables widgets to make data available for other widgets, including those in separate applications. Information of any size or type can be passed using the clipboard interface. The most common example of this data transfer model is *cut and paste*, a method by which the user can move or copy text between windows. Here, the user interacts with a Text widget that contains some text that he wishes to transfer to another Text widget. The user first *selects* the text he wants to transfer by clicking the left mouse button and dragging it across the entire area to be copied. Then, he moves the pointer to the target widget and *pastes* the text by clicking the middle mouse button.[1]

This action causes the text to appear to be copied to the new window. However, the text does not actually move; it is copied to the clipboard, from which the second widget then copies it into its own window. The original data may have been changed or destroyed since it was sent to the clipboard, but that is of no concern to the second widget.

An object that wishes to place data on the clipboard or read data from it is called a *client* of the clipboard (one of the people in our imaginary room). Since only one client may access the clipboard at a time, whether it is storing or retrieving data, requesting access to the clipboard implies "locking" it. If another widget already has locked the clipboard, the client must wait and ask for it again later (after the current holder has "unlocked" it).

Now, imagine that the people in the room have all sorts of items besides text messages they wish to make available for copy. Some may have pictures, records, tapes—anything. Their "cargo" must be deliverable by the moderator to anyone who requests it. To deal with this situation, the moderator must know what type of cargo he will be handling. Therefore,

---

[1] This is the default cut and paste user model; the user may override it using resources or keyboard equivalents. The actual method for performing this task is not the point of discussion here.

certain information must be registered with the moderator before cargo may be sent or received through the clipboard mechanism. Once a particular cargo type is registered, anyone may post or request such cargo to or from the moderator.

In the Motif toolkit, different types of cargo are referred to as *formats*. With respect to the X server and client applications, text messages are the most commonly-used format of clipboard messages and are therefore registered by default.[2] Application-specific data structures must be registered separately, perhaps on a per application basis. Once a new data type is registered, even clients that exist on other computer architectures where data is not represented identically (e.g., due to byte swapping) can use that data type, since the clipboard registration handles the proper data conversion.

There are some situations where it is impractical to place complete information on the clipboard. Some people's cargo may be "too heavy" for the clipboard to hold indefinitely. Other people may have perishables that don't last very long. Still others may have information that varies with the state of the world. For these cases, the person with the special cargo may choose to leave only some information about their cargo rather than the cargo itself. This information might include its weight, type, name and/or reference number, for example. Potential recipients may then examine the clipboard and inquire about the cargo without having to get it or even look at it. Only in the event that someone else wishes to obtain the cargo is the original owner called upon to provide it.

In the Motif world, this scenario describes clipboard data that is available *by name*. For example, if a client wishes to place an entire file on the clipboard, he might choose to register it by name without providing the actual contents unless someone requests it. This may save a lot of time and resources, since it's possible that no one will request it. Referencing data this way is very cheap and is not subject to expiration or obsolescence.

When posting messages by name, the client must provide the clipboard with a callback function that returns the actual data. This callback function may be called by the Motif toolkit at any time, provided another client requests the data. If the data is time-dependent or subject to other criteria (someone removed or changed the file), the callback routine may respond accordingly.

The Motif clipboard functions are based on X's Inter-Client Communications Conventions (ICCC). Knowledge of these conventions will aid greatly in your understanding of how these functions are implemented. However, knowledge of the implementation is not required in order to understand the concepts involved here or to be able to use the clipboard effectively through Motif's application interface. This chapter does not address many of the issues involved with the ICCC and the lower-level Xlib properties that implement them. Rather, it will only address the highest level of interaction provided by the Motif toolkit.

Also note that the clipboard is one of three commonly used mechanisms to support interclient communication. There are also the *primary* and *secondary* selections, which are similar in nature, but are handled differently at the application and user level. The Motif toolkit supports convenience routines that interact with clipboard selections only. To use the other selection mechanisms, you must use Tookit Intrinsics functions discussed in Volume Four, *X*

---

[2] There are also other types automatically registered, such as integers. A more complete list is given later.

Toolkit Intrinsics Programming Manual. (Note, however, that the Text widget supports both mechanisms.)

18.1 Simple Clipboard Copy and Retrieval

To introduce the application programmer's interface (API) for the clipboard functions, we demonstrate how simple copy and retrieval may be done with text. Although "cut and paste" functions with Text widgets include copy and retrieval from the clipboard in the manner we are about to describe, they also support interaction with the primary and secondary selection mechanisms that are also supported. However, as Chapter 15, *Text Widgets*, points out, these are usually reserved for interactive actions taken by the user rather than through a programmer's interface discussed here. Fortunately, Motif provides many convenience functions that facilitate the task for Text widgets. This section only discusses the techniques used by the portions of the Text widget that interact with the clipboard.

We'll begin with the short demonstration program in Example 18-1. This program displays two PushButtons that have corresponding callback routines: **to_clipbd( )** copies text to the clipboard and **from_clipbd( )** retrieves text from the clipboard. The text copied to the clipboard is arbitrary; we happened to choose a string that represents the number of times the *Copy to Clipboard* button was pressed.

Example 18-1. The copy_retrieve.c program

```
/* copy_retrieve.c -- simple copy and retrieve program.  Two
 * pushbuttons: the first places text in the clipboard, the other
 * receives text from the clipboard.  This just demonstrates the
 * API involved.
 */
#include <Xm/CutPaste.h>
#include <Xm/RowColumn.h>
#include <Xm/PushBG.h>

static void to_clipbd(), from_clipbd();

main(argc, argv)
int argc;
char *argv[ ];
{
    Widget toplevel, rowcol, button;
    XtAppContext app;

    /* Initialize toolkit, application context and toplevel shell */
    toplevel = XtVaAppInitialize(&app, "Demos", NULL, 0,
        &argc, argv, NULL, NULL);

    /* manage two buttons in a RowColumn widget */
    rowcol = XtVaCreateWidget("rowcol", xmRowColumnWidgetClass, toplevel, NULL);

    /* button1 copies to the clipboard */
    button = XtVaCreateManagedWidget("button1",
        xmPushButtonGadgetClass, rowcol,
        XtVaTypedArg, XmNlabelString, XmRString,
            "Copy To Clipboard", 18, /* strlen() + 1 */
```

Example 18-1. The copy_retrieve.c program (continued)

```
            NULL);
    XtAddCallback(button, XmNactivateCallback, to_clipbd, "text");

    /* button2 retrieves text stored in the clipboard */
    button = XtVaCreateManagedWidget("button2",
        xmPushButtonGadgetClass, rowcol,
        XtVaTypedArg, XmNlabelString, XmRString,
            "Retrieve From Clipboard", 24, /* strlen() + 1 */
        NULL);
    XtAddCallback(button, XmNactivateCallback, from_clipbd, NULL);

    /* manage RowColumn, realize toplevel shell and start main loop */
    XtManageChild(rowcol);
    XtRealizeWidget(toplevel);
    XtAppMainLoop(app);
}

/* copy data to clipboard. */
static void
to_clipbd(widget, data)
Widget widget;
char *data;
{
    unsigned long item_id = 0;   /* clipboard item id */
    int          status;
    XmString     clip_label;
    char         buf[32];
    static int   cnt;
    Display      *dpy = XtDisplayOfObject(widget);
    Window        window = XtWindowOfObject(widget);

    sprintf(buf, "%s-%d", data, ++cnt); /* make each copy unique */

    clip_label = XmStringCreateSimple("to_clipbd");

    /* start a copy.  retry till unlocked */
    do
        status = XmClipboardStartCopy(dpy, window,
            clip_label, CurrentTime, NULL, NULL, &item_id);
    while (status == ClipboardLocked);

    XmStringFree(clip_label);

    /* copy the data (buf) -- pass "cnt" as private id for kicks */
    do
        status = XmClipboardCopy(dpy, window, item_id, "STRING",
            buf, (long)strlen(buf)+1, cnt, NULL);
    while (status == ClipboardLocked);

    /* end the copy */
    do
        status = XmClipboardEndCopy(dpy, window, item_id);
    while (status == ClipboardLocked);

    printf("copied \"%s\" to clipboard.\n", buf);
}

static void
from_clipbd(widget)
Widget widget;
{
```

Example 18-1. The copy_retrieve.c program (continued)

```
    int         status, private_id;
    char        buf[ 32 ];
    Display     *dpy = XtDisplayOfObject(widget);
    Window      window = XtWindowOfObject(widget);

    do
        status = XmClipboardRetrieve(dpy, window,
            "STRING", buf, sizeof buf, NULL, &private_id);
    while (status == ClipboardLocked);

    if (status == ClipboardSuccess)
        printf("retrieved \"%s\" (private id = %d).\n",
            buf, private_id);
}
```

First, we use the header file *<Xm/CutPaste.h>* to include the appropriate function declarations and various constants.[3] Next, we introduce the following clipboard functions which are used in `to_clipbd( )`:

```
    XmClipboardStartCopy( )
    XmClipboardCopy( )
    XmClipboardEndCopy( )
```

Copying data to the clipboard is a three-phase process. Each of the functions locks the clipboard so that other clients cannot access it. Locking a clipboard is done on a per window basis, so the object used to lock the clipboard should contain a window. (Gadgets may not work.)[4] When the clipboard is locked, only lock and unlock requests from objects with the same window ID will be able to access the clipboard. Each time an object requests a lock on the clipboard, a counter is incremented so that matching unlock requests will be honored.

`XmClipboardStartCopy( )` sets up internal storage for the copy to take place. `XmClipboardCopy( )` sends the data to the clipboard and `XmClipboardEndCopy( )` frees the internal supporting structures. When copying data to the clipboard (including copies *by name*), all three functions must be used.

`XmClipboardRetrieveCopy( )` is used to retrieve data from the clipboard. Only the single call is needed for retrieval of short items. However, a three-step process similar to that for copying data to the clipboard is required for incremental retrieval of large amounts of data. We will cover these functions shortly.

The syntax of the functions that copy data to the clipboard is outlined below. Due to the intricacies involved in providing data to the clipboard, these functions take a larger number of parameters than you might expect from the simple examples given so far. Later examples should clarify the intended usage of these functions and their corresponding parameters:

---

[3] Don't let the name of the file confuse you. *CutPaste.h* is derived from the phrase "cut and paste," which historically has been used to describe clipboard-type operations.

[4] Gadgets happen to work in some cases because of their window-based widget parents. However, some of the clipboard functions use `XtWindow( )` rather than `XtWindowOfObject( )` to get the window of an object. The former will not work for gadgets.

The Clipboard

```
     int
     XmClipboardStartCopy(dpy, win, label, timestamp,
                          widget, callback, itemid)
         Display      *dpy;
         Window       win;
         XmString     label;
         Time         timestamp;
         Widget       widget;
         VoidProc     callback;
         long         *itemid;
```

Each of the routines takes a pointer to the **Display** and the **window** associated with the object making the clipboard request. These may be derived from any widget or gaget using **XtDisplayOfObject()** and **XtWindowOfObject()**. The **widget** and **callback** parameters are used only when registering data by name (see Section 18.2, *Copy by Name*). Although the **label** parameter is currently unused, its purpose is to "label" the data so that certain (nonexistent) applications can view the contents of the clipboard.[5] The **timestamp** identifies the server time in which the cut had taken place (**CurrentTime** is the typical value used). The **itemid** parameter is filled in by the toolkit and is returned to the client for subsequent clipboard function calls. This value identifies the item's entry into the clipboard itself:

```
     int
     XmClipboardCopy(dpy, win, itemid, fmt, buf, len, private_id, dataid)
         Display      *dpy;
         Window       win;
         long         itemid;      /* id returned from start copy */
         char         *fmt;        /* Name string for data format */
         caddr_t      buf;         /* Address of buffer holding data */
         unsigned long len;        /* Length of the data */
         int          private_id;  /* application-defined data */
         int          *dataid;     /* Data id returned by clipboard */
```

XmClipboardCopy() copies the data in **buf** to the clipboard. The format of the data is described by the **fmt** parameter. This is not a type, but a string describing the type. (For example, **"STRING"** indicates that the data is a text string.) The **len** parameter is the size of the data. (Text strings, for example, can use **strlen(data)**.)

The **itemid** is the same ID returned by **XmClipboardStartCopy()**. The **dataid** returns the format ID. You may pass **NULL** as this parameter if you are not interested in this value. You may need it for other functions; for example, you will need it if you wish to withdraw an item from the clipboard. This is also discusssed later with registration *by name*.

The **private_id** is an arbitrary number that is application-defined. The value is passed back to various functions, including those called by name, so we'll address it later in Section 18.2, *Copy by Name*.

---

[5] It is silly to include the **label** parameter in the API. Toolkit functions should not be written to support *specific* applications (especially those that aren't even available). Nevertheless, the **label** parameter exists and must be used or an error occurs.

When copying is done, **XmClipboardEndCopy( )** is called to free the internal data structures associated with the **itemid** copy:

```
int
XmClipboardEndCopy(dpy, win, itemid)
    Display *dpy;
    Window  window;
    long    itemid;
```

The three functions described previously may return one of **ClipboardSuccess**, **ClipboardLocked**, or **ClipboardFail** depending on whether the client was successful in gaining access to the clipboard. If another client is already accessing the clipboard (regardless of whether it is cutting to it or pasting from it), the clipboard will be locked. If so, the client may loop repeatedly attempting to gain access.

In Example 18-1, we retrieve the data stored in the clipboard using the function **XmClipboardRetrieve( )**. This function takes the following form:

```
int
XmClipboardRetrieve(dpy, win, fmt, buf, len, outlen, private_id)
    Display         *dpy;
    Window          win;
    char            *fmt;
    char            *buf;       /* Address of buffer to receive data */
    unsigned long   len;        /* size of buf */
    unsigned long   *outlen;    /* Length of the data placed in buf */
    int             *private_id; /* Application-defined value */
```

When using **XmClipboardRetrieve( )**, we must provide buffer space to retrieve the data. In our example, we know that the data space isn't going to be very large, so we declared **buf** to have 32 bytes, which is more than adequate.

The **len** parameter tells the clipboard how much space we can take. The **outlen** parameter is the address of an **unsigned long** variable. This value is filled in by **XmClipboardRetrieve( )** indicating how much data it gave us. The **private_id** is the address of an **int**; its value is the same passed as the **private_id** parameter passed to **XmClipboardCopy( )**. You can pass **NULL** as this parameter if you are not interested in it (the copy-by-name method makes more use of this value, anyway).

If the clipboard is locked, the function returns **ClipboardLocked**; otherwise, it returns **ClipboardSuccess**. A rare internal error may cause the function to return **ClipboardFailed** (in which case you may choose to loop, continuously retrying to retrieve data).

18.1.1 Undoing Copies

Motif keeps a stack of items that have been placed on the clipboard using any of the clipboard functions. As of Release 1.1, the stack depth is set to two. If a third item is added, the older of the other two is removed. Once a copy to the clipboard is complete, you can "undo" it using `XmClipboardUndoCopy( )`:

```
int
XmClipboardUndoCopy(dpy, window)
    Display *dpy;
    Window  window;
```

Calling `XmClipboardUndoCopy( )` twice undoes the last "undo." Thus, "undoing" a copy simply swaps the two elements on the clipboard stack.

You can remove an item you've placed on the clipboard using `XmClipboardWithdraw-Format( )`. This is discussed in Section 18.2.1, *Copying Incrementally*.

18.1.2 Incremental Retrieves

One problem with `XmClipboardRetrieve( )` occurs when there is more data in the clipboard than buffer space to contain it. In this case, the function copies only `len` bytes into `buf` and sets `outlen` to the number of bytes it gave us (which should be the same value as `len` if not enough space is available). If this happens, the function returns `ClipboardTruncate` to indicate that we didn't get everything available. We can't just arbitrarily specify a larger data space without knowing how much data there is. So, we have two choices: query the clipboard to find out how much data there is or copy the data incrementally. There are advantages and disadvantages to each method. Let's start by discussing incremental retrieval.

To do this, we need to introduce two functions: `XmClipboardStartRetrieve( )` and `XmClipboardEndRetrieve( )`.

These functions are similar to the start and end functions used earlier in the copy functions. `XmClipboardStartRetrieve( )` takes the following form:

```
int
XmClipboardStartRetrieve(dpy, window, timestamp)
    Display *dpy;
    Window  window;
    Time    timestamp;
```

This function locks the clipboard and notes the timestamp. Data placed on the clipboard after this timestamp is considered invalid and the function returns `ClipboardFailed`. It is best to provide the constant `CurrentTime` as this value.[6] Internal structures are also allocated to support the incremental copies. Once this function is called, multiple calls to `XmClipboardRetrieve( )` can be made until it returns `ClipboardSuccess`. As long as it returns `ClipboardTruncate`, more data needs to be read and the function should continue to be called. Be careful to save the data already retrieved before each call to the function or you may overwrite the old data and lose information.

---

[6] It is also common to provide the timestamp found in the **event** structure when available. This is usually done when a clipboard retrieval is initiated as a result of an action or callback routine where the **event** structure is available.

Once the data has been completely retrieved, a call to `XmClipboardEndRetrieve()` should be made.

```
int
XmClipboardEndRetrieve(dpy, window)
    Display    *dpy;
    Window     window;
```

This function unlocks the clipboard and frees the internal data structures. Example 18-2 illustrates an incremental retrieve.

Example 18-2. Incrementally retrieving data from the clipboard

```
int           status;
unsigned      total_bytes;
unsigned long received;
char          *data = NULL, buf[ 32 ];
Display       *dpy = XtDisplayOfObject(widget);
Window        window = XtWindowOfObject(widget);

do
    status = XmClipboardStartRetrieve(dpy, window, CurrentTime);
while (status == ClipboardLocked);

/* initialize data to contain at least one byte. */
data = XtMalloc(1);
total_bytes = 1;
do {
    /* retrieve data from clipboard -- if locked, try again */
    if ((status = XmClipboardRetrieve(dpy, window, "STRING",
            buf, sizeof buf, &received, NULL)) == ClipboardLocked)
        continue;
    /* reallocate data to contain enough space for everything */
    if (!(data = XtRealloc(data, total_bytes + received))) {
        XtError("Can't allocate space for data");
        break; /* XtError may or may not return */
    }
    /* copy buf into data.  strncpy() does not NULL terminate */
    strncpy(&data[ total_bytes-1 ], buf, received);
    total_bytes += received;
} while (status == ClipboardLocked || status == ClipboardTruncate);
data[ total_bytes ] = 0; /* NULL terminate */

if (status == ClipboardSuccess)
    printf("retrieved \"%s\" from clipboard.\n", buf);

do
    status = XmClipboardEndRetrieve(dpy, window);
while (status == ClipboardLocked);
```

The code fragment will work regardless of the amount of data held by the clipboard. If the client originally placed an entire file on the clipboard, we will read all of it in 32-byte increments. It would probably be wise to use a larger block size when copying data incrementally; the constant BUFSIZ[7] is a good default choice.

---

[7] BUFSIZ is defined in *<stdio.h>*.

The primary advantage of using the incremental retrieval method is that you needn't allocate a potentially "large" amount of memory at one time. By segmenting memory, you can reuse some of it, or even discard it as each increment is read. (That is, you may be scanning for something, with no intent to actually save everything you are retrieving.)

18.1.3 Querying the Clipboard for Data Size

The problem with incremental retrieval is that numerous round trips to the server may be necessary in order to obtain the entire contents of the clipboard. If you intend to save every bit of information you retrieve, the most economical way to handle it is by reading everything in one fell swoop. Also, a single call to **XmClipboardRetrieve( )** is more convenient than the three-step process involving locking the clipboard.

However, as pointed out earlier, this is a problem if we don't know how much data there is to read. The solution to the problem is to determine exactly how much data there is using **Xm-ClipboardInquireLength( )**:

```
int
XmClipboardInquireLength(dpy, window, format, length)
    Display        *dpy;
    Window          window;
    char           *format;
    unsigned long *length;
```

The function returns the amount of data being held by the clipboard in the given **format**. In Example 18-3, we are looking for data in the **"STRING"** format. If any data on the clipboard is in this format, the function returns **ClipboardSuccess** and the **length** parameter is set to the number of bytes being held. If there is no data on the clipboard in that format, the function returns **ClipboardNoData**. Regardless of what value is returned, no data can be read if **length** is not set to a value other than 0.

If the function is successful, then the number of bytes specified by **length** can be allocated and the data can be retrieved in one call to **XmClipboardRetrieve( )**. Example 18-3 shows how a hypothetical function can find out how much data the clipboard has.

Example 18-3. Getting data from the clipboard, avoiding incremental retrieval

```
int         status, recvd, length;
char        *data;
Display     *dpy = XtDisplayOfObject(widget);
Window      window = XtWindowOfObject(widget);

do status = XmClipboardInquireLength(dpy, window, "STRING", &length);
while (status == ClipboardLocked);

if (length == 0)
    return NULL; /* no data! */

data = XtMalloc(length+1);

do
    status = XmClipboardRetrieve(dpy, window,
        "STRING", data, length+1, &recvd, NULL);
```

```
while (status == ClipboardLocked);

if (status != ClipboardSuccess || recvd != length) {
    XtWarning("failed to receive all clipboard data");
    XtFree(data);
    return NULL;
}

return data;
```

18.2 Copy by Name

As discussed earlier, there may be cases where data should not be copied to the clipboard until it is requested. Instead, it is possible to copy data *by name*. Here, the owner of the data is notified through a callback function when the data is needed by the clipboard. Since copying large amounts of data may be expensive, time-consuming, or even impossible due to other constraints in the application, copying data by name may be the only option available. It is especially advantageous if the data is never requested, since time and resources may be saved.

To copy data by name, one follows a procedure similar to normal copying with only a few exceptions. The new procedure is as follows:

1. The application must have a clipboard callback function.

2. **XmClipboardStartCopy( )** is called, giving valid **callback** and **widget** parameters. These values indicate that the data is to be copied by name. (These parameters were ignored earlier.)

3. **XmClipboardCopy( )** is called with **NULL** as the data to pass.

4. **XmClipboardEndCopy( )** is called as usual.

When a client requests the data from the clipboard, the callback routine provided to **Xm-ClipboardStartCopy( )** is called, and the client adds the actual data using **Xm-ClipboardCopyByName( )**.

The convenience function **XmClipboardBeginCopy( )** can be used rather than **Xm-ClipboardStartCopy( )**. The only difference is that the convenience function does not take a **timestamp** parameter; it simply uses **CurrentTime** as the timestamp value.

The code fragment shown in Example 18-4 shows how copying by name can be accomplished.

Example 18-4. Registering a callback routine to send data to the clipboard

```
/* copy data to clipboard. */
static void
to_clipbd(widget, data)
Widget widget;
char *data;
```

The Clipboard

```
{
    unsigned long item_id = 0;   /* clipboard item id */
    int           status;
    XmString      clip_label;
    Display       *dpy = XtDisplayOfObject(widget);
    Window        window = XtWindowOfObject(widget);
    extern void   copy_by_name();

    clip_label = XmStringCreateSimple("to_clipbd");

    /* indicate copy-by-name by passing NULL as the "data",
     * copy_by_name() as the callback and "widget" as the widget.
     */
    do
        status = XmClipboardBeginCopy(dpy, window,
            clip_label, widget, copy_by_name, &item_id);
    while (status == ClipboardLocked);

    do
        status = XmClipboardCopy(dpy, window, item_id, "STRING",
            NULL, 0L, 0, NULL);
    while (status == ClipboardLocked);

    /* end the copy */
    do
        status = XmClipboardEndCopy(dpy, window, item_id);
    while (status == ClipboardLocked);
}
```

Just as in Example 18-1, the function `to_clipbd( )` is used to initiate copying data to the clipboard. However, rather than passing actual data, we use:

```
    status = XmClipboardBeginCopy(dpy, window,
        clip_label, widget, copy_by_name, &item_id);
```

Passing a valid widget and a callback routine is the way to indicate that the copy-by-name method is being used. Here, the data will be provided through the given callback routine rather than immediately. The `item_id` parameter is filled in by the clipboard function to identify this particular data element. It is used in the call:

```
    status = XmClipboardCopy(dpy, window, item_id, "STRING",
        NULL, size, 0, NULL);
```

Passing `NULL` as the data also indicates that the data is passed by name. The `size` parameter indicates how much data you are going to send should it be requested. This is important in case other clients query the clipboard to find out how much data is available to copy.

Example 18-5 shows the callback routine, `copy_by_name( )`.

Example 18-5. copy_by_name(): sends data to the clipboard on request

```
static void
copy_by_name(widget, data_id, private_id, reason)
Widget widget;
int *data_id, *private_id, *reason;
{
    extern Widget toplevel;
    Display       *dpy = XtDisplay(toplevel);
```

Example 18-5. copy_by_name(): sends data to the clipboard on request (continued)

```
Window        window = XtWindow(toplevel);
int           status;
static char   *data;

if (*reason == XmCR_CLIPBOARD_DATA_REQUEST) {
    data = XtMalloc(size); /* allocate enough memory for data */

    XmClipboardCopyByName(dpy, window, *data_id, data,
        strlen(data)+1, *private_id = cnt);

} else
    /* XmCR_CLIPBOARD_DATA_DELETE */
    if (data)
        XtFree(data);
}
```

The callback function **copy_by_name( )** is called either when someone requests the data
from the clipboard or when another client copies new data (by name or with actual data) to
the clipboard. In the first case, the data must be copied to the clipboard; in the second case,
the clipboard is telling the client that it can now free its data. The callback function takes the
following form:

```
void
by_name_callback(widget, data_id, private_id, reason)
    Widget widget;
    int *data_id, *private_id, *reason;
```

The **widget** parameter is the same as that passed to **XmClipboardStartCopy( )**. The
data_id is the address of the ID of the data, not of the item. The **private_id** is the
address of a variable containing the same value passed as the same parameter to **Xm-
ClipboardCopy( )**. The **reason** parameter is the address of an integer whose value is
either of the following: **XmCR_CLIPBOARD_DATA_REQUEST** or **XmCR_CLIP-
BOARD_DATA_DELETE**.

NOTE

Although the last three parameters are pointers to integer values, changing these
values has no effect whatsoever. They should be considered read-only.

The purpose of the function is either to send the appropriate data to the clipboard or to free it.
The value of ***reason** determines which to do. Since no data is passed to the clipboard
until this callback function is called, either the data must be stored locally (in the application)
or the function must be able to generate it dynamically. The example makes no assumptions
or suggestions about how to create the data. This is entirely subject to the nature of the data
and/or the application.

Once the data is obtained, it is sent to the clipboard using **XmClipboardCopy-
ByName( )**. This function does not need to lock the clipboard since the clipboard is already
being locked by the window that called **XmClipboardRetrieve( )**. At this point in
time, both routines are accessing the clipboard.

If the same application is both retrieving the data and copying the data, the routines `XmClipboardRetrieve()` and `XmClipboardCopyByName()` *must use the same window* in their respective **window** parameters. Otherwise, deadlock will occur and the application will "hang."

18.2.1 Copying Incrementally

There may be cases where you should copy data to the clipboard incrementally. The data may be large enough that allocating one large data space to handle the entire copy is unreasonable; its size may warrant sending it in smaller chunks. Moreover, data may be generated by a slow mechanism such as a database library. If the database only returns data in specific block sizes, then you needn't buffer them all up and send to the clipboard with one call; you can send each block as it comes through.

Incremental copying requires multiple calls to `XmClipboardCopyByName()`. Since `XmClipboardCopyByName()` does not lock the clipboard, you need to do that yourself by calling `XmClipboardLock()`. However, you only need to call it once no matter how much data is transferred (that is, multiple calls to `XmClipboardCopyByName()` do not require multiple calls to `XmClipboardLock()`). When you are through copying, you need to call `XmClipboardUnlock()`. In some cases, you may need to stop sending data before you're done. For example, if the database is not responding to your application or there are other extenuating circumstances, you may terminate the copy using **Xm-ClipboardCancelCopy()**:

```
int
XmClipboardCancelCopy(dpy, window, item_id)
    Display *dpy;
    Window   window;
    long     item_id;    /* id returned by begin copy */
```

When using **XmClipboardCancelCopy**, you should *not* unlock the clipboard using **Xm-ClipboardUnlock()**.

If you have registered a data format to the clipboard, you may withdraw it by calling **Xm-ClipboardWithdrawFormat()**. The function takes the following form:

```
int
XmClipboardWithdrawFormat(dpy, window, data_id)
    Display *dpy;
    Window   window;
    int      data_id;
```

Despite the name of the procedure, its main purpose is not to remove a format specification, but to remove a data element in that format from the clipboard. The **data_id** parameter is the same value that is returned by `XmClipboardCopy()` when the by-name callback was registered. If the specified window holds the clipboard data but it is in a different format than that specified by the **data_id**, then the data is not removed from the clipboard.

18.3 Clipboard Data Formats

As discussed in the introduction, the clipboard may contain messages of arbitrary formats. While the most commonly-used format is text, other formats include integers, pixmaps, and arbitrary data structures. Since all applications on the desktop have access to the clipboard, any of them may register a new format and place items of that type on the clipboard.

When registering a new format, you must also register a corresponding *name*. Determining the type of data on the clipboard is much easier when there is a descriptive name associated with it. Second, along with the name of the format you must register the format length in bits (8, 16, and 32). This will allow applications to send and receive data without suffering from byte-swapping problems due to differing computer architectures.

To register a new format, the following function is used:

```
int
XmClipboardRegisterFormat(dpy, format_name, format_length)
    Display       *dpy;
    char          *format_name;
    unsigned long format_length;
```

The function may return `ClipboardBadFormat` if the format name is NULL or the format length is other than 8, 16, or 32. The format length may be specified as 0, in which case Motif will attempt to look up the default length for the given name. Table 18-1 shows the format lengths for some predefined format names.

Table 18-1. Predefined Format Names and Lengths

User Types	Text Widget Displays
"TARGETS"	32
"MULTIPLE"	32
"TIMESTAMP"	32
"STRING"	8
"LIST_LENGTH"	32
"PIXMAP"	32
"DRAWABLE"	32
"BITMAP"	32
"FOREGROUND"	32
"BACKGROUND"	32
"COLORMAP"	32
"ODIF"	8
"OWNER_OS"	8
"FILE_NAME"	8
"HOST_NAME"	8
"CHARACTER_POSITION"	32
"LINE_NUMBER"	32
"COLUMN_NUMBER"	32
"LENGTH"	32
"USER"	8
"PROCEDURE"	8

Table 18-1. Predefined Format Names and Lengths (continued)

User Types	Text Widget Displays
"MODULE"	8
"PROCESS"	32
"TASK"	32
"CLASS"	8
"NAME"	8
"CLIENT_WINDOW"	32

Although these format names are known, they are not necessarily registered automatically with the server; you may still need to register the one(s) you want to use. If you are specifying your own data structure as a format, you should choose an appropriate name for it and use 32 as the format size.

The code fragment in Example 18-6 shows how you can register an integer format before copying to the clipboard.

Example 18-6. Registering a format type before copying to the clipboard

```
unsigned long item_id;
int         data_id;
Display     *dpy = XtDisplay(widget);
Window      window = XtWindow(widget);
XmString    label = XmStringCreateSimple("my data");

/* register our own data sturcture with clipboard. */
XmClipboardRegisterFormat(dpy, "MY_DATA_STRUCT", 32);

/* use the copy-by-name method to transfer data to clipboard */
do
    status = XmClipboardStartCopy(dpy, window, label, CurrentTime,
        my_data_callback, widget, &item_id);
while (status == ClipboardLocked);

XmStringFree(label); /* don't need this anymore */

/* MY_DATA_SIZE is presumed to be the amount of data to transfer */
do
    status = XmClipboardCopy(dpy, window, item_id, "INTEGER",
        NULL, MY_DATA_SIZE, 0, &data_id); /* save the data_id! */
while (status == ClipboardLocked);

XmClipboardEndCopy(dpy, window, item_id);
```

Once the "MY_DATA_STRUCT" format has been registered with the server, we follow the standard procedure for copying data to the clipboard. Here, we chose to use the *copy-by-name* method discussed earlier. Note that we save the value of the **data_id** returned by XmClipboardCopy( ). This value is used so that we may withdraw the data later using XmClipboardWithdrawFormat( ) if necessary. Note that formats are never removed from the clipboard. (Only data can be removed from the clipboard.) Once a particular format is registered with the clipboard, it is there until the server goes down.

18.3.1 Inquiring About Formats

If you plan on retrieving data held by the clipboard, you may wish to inquire about the format of the data it is holding. To do so, you must use two functions together: `XmClipboard-InquireCount( )` and `XmClipboardInquireFormat( )`. They take the following form:

```
int
XmClipboardInquireCount(dpy, window, count, maxlength)
    Display *dpy;
    Window   window;
    int     *count;
    int     *maxlength;


int
XmClipboardInquireFormat(dpy, window, n, buf, len, outlen)
    Display         *dpy;
    Window           window;
    int              n;
    char            *buf;
    unsigned long    len;
    unsigned long   *outlen;
```

`XmClipboardInquireCount` returns the number of formats the clipboard knows about for all the data items it is currently holding. Also returned is the string length of the longest format name. You can iterate through the formats starting from 1 (one) through `count` calling `XmClipboardInquireFormat`. The iteration number is passed as the `n` parameter. You should use this value to ensure that you can read all the format types in your search for the desired format.

Although there is only one data item stored on the clipboard at any one time, that item may have multiple formats associated with it. While this is unusual, it is possible to handle this case by providing different formats to successive calls to `XmClipboardCopy( )` or `Xm-ClipboardCopyByName( )`.

18.4 The Primary Selection and the Clipboard

Since text is the most commonly-used format in the clipboard, there is a natural interaction between the clipboard and windows that contain text. In most situations, it is usual (even expected) that when the user "selects" text, the selection should be placed on the clipboard. This is known as a "copy" operation. Retrieving text from the clipboard and placing it in another window is known as a "paste" operation. In some cases, after the data is pasted from the clipboard, the original window will delete the data it copied. This is classified as a cut operation. For these reasons, the clipboard is commonly refered to as the *cut and paste model*.

The lower-level implementation of the clipboard mechanism uses the X Toolkit selection mechanism. This model has additional properties that provide for more detailed communication between the clients involved. For example, "cutting" text from a Text widget and placing it in another widget involves more communication between the widgets than that of the clipboard copy and retrieval mechanism. When the text that was selected in the first widget is pasted in the other, the first widget may be notified to "delete" the selected text. This type of communication is usually handled in one of two ways: automatically by the Text widgets themselves, or through lower-level X calls where the corresponding windows of the widgets send real events to one another (called *client messages*).

18.4.1 Clipboard Functions with Text Widgets

In most cases, you never need to access the clipboard functions to perform simple text copy and retrieval ("cut and paste") for Text widgets. If you need to access the clipboard above and beyond the normal selection mechanism in place for the Motif Text widget, there are a number of convenience routines that deal with selections automatically. See Chapter 15, *Text Widgets*, for detailed information. We present a brief overview of these functions below:

```
Boolean
XmTextCut(widget, cut_time)
    Widget widget;
    Time    cut_time;
```

If there is text selected in the Text widget referred to by the **widget** parameter, the selected text is placed on the clipboard and deleted from the Text widget. The function returns **True** if all of these things happen successfully. If **False** is returned, it is usually because the Text widget did not have any selected text.

The **cut_time** parameter may be set to any server timestamp value. If you are calling this function from a callback routine, for example, you may wish to use the **time** field from the **event** pointer in the callback structure provided by the Motif toolkit. (One is provided by all callback structures since Motif passes it as the **call_data** for all predefined Motif callback routines.) The value **CurrentTime** can also be used, but there is no guarantee that this will prevent any race conditions between other clients wanting to use the clipboard. Although race conditions are not likely, the possibility does exist. The result of the race condition is that one widget may appear to have copied (or cut) selected text to the clipboard when in fact another Text widget got there first. This discussion about **cut_time** applies to similar parameters in following text-based clipboard functions:

```
Boolean
XmTextCopy(widget, cut_time)
    Widget widget;
    Time    cut_time;
```

`XmTextCopy( )` is exactly like `XmTextCut( )`, except that the originally selected text is not removed from the Text widget:

```
Boolean
XmTextPaste(widget)
    Widget widget;
```

`XmTextPaste( )` gets the current data from the clipboard and places it into the Text widget. It returns `False` if there is no data on the clipboard.

`XmTextCut( )` and `XmTextCopy( )` only work if there is a current selection in the specified text widget. This may be dependent on whether the user has made a selection. However, you can force a selection in a Text widget using any of the following functions:

```
void
XmTextSetSelection(widget, first, last, set_time)
    Widget          widget;
    XmTextPosition  first, last;
    Time            set_time;
```

`XmTextSetSelection( )` selects the text between the specified positions in the Text widget. Once selected, either of `XmTextCut( )` or `XmTextCopy( )` may be called to place the selection on the clipboard:

```
char *
XmTextGetSelection(widget)
    Widget widget;
```

Although this function does not deal with the clipboard directly, it is a convenient way to get the current selection from the corresponding Text widget. Note that the text returned is allocated data and must be freed by the caller using `XtFree( )`. The function returns `NULL` if the specified widget does not own the text selection:

```
void
XmTextClearSelection(widget, clear_time)
    Widget widget;
    Time   clear_time;
```

If there is selected text in the Text widget given, then it is deselected (cleared).

18.4.2 Who Has the Selection?

Sometimes, if you have a large number of Text widgets, you may need to know which of the widgets has the text selection. You can determine this by using the function `XGet-SelectionOwner( )`:

```
Window
XGetSelectionOwner(dpy, selection)
    Display *dpy;
    Atom selection;
```

The `display` parameter can be taken from any widget using `XtDisplay( )`. However, the selection represents the **Atom** associated with the kind of selection you are looking for. For example, you can determine the Text widget that has the current clipboard selection by calling:

```
Display *dpy = XtDisplay(widget);
Widget text_w;
Atom clipboard_atom = XmInternAtom(dpy, "CLIPBOARD", False);
Window win = XGetSelectionOwner(dpy, clipboard_atom);

text_w = XtWindowToWidget(dpy, win);
```

The `selection` parameter represents any of the Atoms that support selections. The next section takes a closer look at how these properties work in the toolkit.

18.5 How It Works

The following short section is intended to pull together the concepts we've outlined in this chapter and make a connection to how it all works in the X client/server model.

The Motif clipboard mechanism relies on an underlying X mechanism referred to as properties. As you know, windows are data structures maintained by the X server; each window can have an arbitrary list of properties associated with it. Each property consists of a name (called an Atom), an arbitrary amount of data, and a format. (Property formats are not at all the same thing as the higher-level Motif formats—they simply indicate whether the data is a list of 8-bit, 16-bit, or 32-bit quantities, so that the server can perform byte-swapping, if appropriate). Properties are the underlying mechanism for all interclient communication, including interaction between applications and window managers, and interapplication interaction such as the transfer of selections.

In order to simplify communication over the network, property names are not passed as arbitrary-length strings, but as defined integers known as Atoms. A number of standard properties (such as those used for communication between applications and window managers) are predefined and *interned* (made known to, and cached by the server). However, application-defined Atoms can also be interned with the server by calling the Xlib function `XIntern-Atom( )`.

Atoms are used to name not only properties, but any names that may need to be passed back and forth between client and server.

Now, back to selections, and the analogy with which we started this chapter: the Motif toolkit is the moderator, but the clipboard itself is a property (called CLIPBOARD) that is automatically maintained by the X server.

Even though a property is uniquely identified by both an Atom and a Window, and thus it is possible for there to be multiple copies of a given property, in fact there should be only one

CLIPBOARD property active at one time. There are conventions about the use of properties set forth in a document called the *Inter-Client Communication Conventions Manual*[8] (ICCCM) and followed by the deeper layers of X software. Among these conventions are that certain properties should only be set by application top-level windows, for use by the window manager ... and that only one window should own the CLIPBOARD property at any one time.

When an application makes a call to `XmClipboardCopy( )`, the data is actually stored in the CLIPBOARD property of the window that was identified in the call to `XmClipboard-Copy( )`.

The format of the data is defined by another Atom. The standard formats are based on those recommended by the ICCCM. For example, the atom FONT when used as a format might suggest to an application, "I don't want the data of that string the user just selected, I want to know what font it's rendered in." At present, though, Motif doesn't support this functionality. You have to remember that formats (or targets, as they are referred to in the ICCCM) are not really "things"—they are simply names (actually translated into integer "Atoms") whose meaning to applications depends entirely on convention.

At present, most applications support only STRING formats. But eventually, conventions will doubtless be articulated for doing far more with the selection mechanism.

A further complication that needs some mention is how the Motif clipboard implementation relates to the underlying X Toolkit (Xt) implementation of selections. The ICCCM actually defines three separate properties that can be used for selections: PRIMARY, SECONDARY, and CLIPBOARD. Standard Xt applications, including all of the clients distributed by MIT, use the PRIMARY property for storing selections. The SECONDARY property is designed for quicker, more transient selections. That is, applications that make use of this property usually copy data directly to another window instantly when the owner finishes copying data to the property. The Motif Text widget uses the SECONDARY property when the CTRL key is down while the middle button is clicked and dragged or multiple-clicked. As soon as the selection is complete, the selected data is immediately sent to the window that had the input focus (this may be the same window).

In the standard MIT implementation, the CLIPBOARD property is used by an independent client called *xclipboard*. Keep in mind that a property stays around only as long as the window with which it is associated. When you terminate a client, closing its windows, any data in that client's window properties is lost. If the CLIPBOARD property is associated with a client that is kept around between invocations of other applications, it embodies a consistent repository for information to be passed between applications.

Note, however, that the ICCCM blesses either approach. However, you should be aware that the difference between the Motif use of the CLIPBOARD property and the use of the PRIMARY selection property by other Xt applications will make interoperability questionable, unless you take care also to handle the PRIMARY selection. The X Toolkit mechanisms for handling selections are described in Volume Four, *X Toolkit Intrinsics Programming Manual*.

---

[8] Reprinted as Appendix L of Volume Zero, *X Protocol Reference Manual*.

The Motif Text widget supports both the Xt mechanism, which uses the PRIMARY selection, and the Motif clipboard, depending on the interaction. You should probably do the same for your application.

While you can manipulate properties and Atoms directly using Xlib, the higher-level API provided by Motif and Xt should insulate you from many of the details, and ensure that your applications interoperate well with others. Eventually, toolkits and applications will doubtless support numerous extensions of the current clipboard and selection mechanisms.

18.6 Summary

The clipboard is a convenient method for allowing applications to interact with one another in a way that is independent of the application, operating system, and system architecture. Currently, it is not very widely used because of the recent introduction of Motif and X windows into the marketplace. The clipboard is one of two common mechanisms used to handle data transfer between objects: the primary selection is still regarded as the most common method for transfer between applications, but this is mostly because text data is used more often between terminal emulators like *xterm* using standard cut and paste methods. The secondary selection method is also available, but is not very widely used.

Because of the various methods available for transferring data between objects, the Motif toolkit tries to compensate for the *de facto* method that users use—the primary selection used by mouse clicking—by integrating both selections into the same set of functions. This has the unfortunate side effect of confusing programmers, although users seem to be oblivious to the differences.

19

Compound Strings

This chapter describes Motif's technology for encoding font changes and character directions (for use with foreign languages) in the strings that are used by almost all Motif widgets.

In This Chapter:

☞

19
Compound Strings

Compound strings are designed to address two issues frequently encountered by application designers: the use of foreign character sets to display text in other languages and the use of multiple fonts when rendering text.

Many character sets used by foreign languages are too large for the characters to be represented by the `char` type, as English can be. Compound strings solve this problem by representing the text in an internally defined format that takes into account the character set and font conventions of a particular language. Also, since some languages such as Hebrew and Arabic are read from right-to-left, compound strings also store directional information.

A compound string is made of three elements: a character set, a direction, and text. The character set is an arbitrary name that the programmer can choose to correlate a compound string with a particular font. The character set-to-font mapping is done on a per-widget basis, so the same name (e.g., "charset-1") may map to different fonts for different widgets. The binding between character set names and actual fonts is defined as part of each widget's `fontList` resource, which can be set in an application's resource files.

Compound strings that incorporate multiple fonts are achieved by concatenating separate compound strings with different character sets to produce a single (longer) compound string. Concatenating compound strings with different fonts can be a powerful way to create graphically interesting labels and captions. More importantly, because fonts are "loosely bound" to compound strings via resources, you can dynamically associate new fonts with widgets as the application runs. This process simplifies the task of internationalization, and can also be used to change text "styles" on the fly.

19.1 Simple Compound Strings

Almost all Motif widgets require a compound string when specifying text. Labels, Push-Buttons, Lists—all require their text to be given in compound string format, whether or not you require the additional flexibility compound strings provide. The only exception is the Text widget; it does not use compound strings. This will have direct impact on applications that need to support right-to-left string display and editing. There is currently no workaround for this lack in Text widgets. However, you can request that a Text widget uses any particular font, although it can only display text using one font at a time. For a complete discussion on the use of compound strings in Text widgets, see Chapter 15, *Text Widgets*.

The most common use for the Motif compound string functions in English-language applications is to convert standard C-style NULL-terminated text strings for use in a widget.

The most basic form of C string to compound string conversion is done using the function XmStringCreateSimple( ), as demonstrated in examples throughout this book:

```
XmString
XmStringCreateSimple(text)
    char *text;
```

The text parameter is a common C char string. The value returned is of type XmString which is an opaque type to the programmer.

XmStringCreateSimple( ) converts a C string into a compound string using the default character set and direction defined for that particular widget. The actual font is not bound to a character set when the compound string is created; rather, it is dependent on resources intrinsic to the widget. You cannot specify a font, a string direction, or have multiple lines. Common usage might be as follows:

```
XmString str = XmStringCreateSimple("Push Me");

widget = XtVaCreateManagedWidget("widget_name",
    xmPushButtonGadgetClass, parent,
    XmNlabelString,  str,
    NULL);

XmStringFree(str);
```

XmStringCreateSimple( ), along with the other functions that create compound strings, allocates memory to store the strings created. Widgets whose resources take compound strings as values always allocate their own space and store copies of the compound string values you give them, so you must free your copy of the string after having set it in the widget resource. Compound strings are freed using XmStringFree( ).

This three-step process is typical of the type of interaction you will have with compound strings: you create a string, set it in a widget, then free the string (unless you want to use it in another widget). However, this process involves quite a bit of overhead; memory is allocated by the string creation function, then again by the internals of the widget for its own storage, and then your copy of the string must be deallocated. (Freeing memory is also an expensive operation.)

The programmatic interface to this process can be simplified by using the XtVaTypedArg feature in Xt. This special resource is used in variable argument list specifications for functions like XtVaCreateManagedWidget( ), XtVaSetValues( ), or XtVaGet-Values( ). It allows you to specify resources in any type—most likely a more convenient one—and have Xt do the conversion for you. In the case of compound strings, this method can be used to convert between C strings and compound strings without having to do it yourself. The following code fragment has the same effect as the previous example:

```
widget = XtVaCreateManagedWidget("widget_name",
    xmPushButtonWidgetClass, parent,
    XtVaTypedArg, XmNlabelString, XmRString,
        "Push Me", 8, /* or, strlen("Push Me") + 1 */
    NULL);
```

Specifically, **XtVaTypedArg** takes four additional parameters: the resource whose value is going to be set, the type of the value we are giving the resource, the value itself, and the size of the value's data.

The resource is **XmNlabelString**, and its value is normally of type **XmString** (a compound string). We want to avoid doing the conversion explicitly, and so we are giving it a **char *** (string) resource. Thus, we specify **XmRString** as the type of the value we are going to provide.[1]

The string **"Push Me"** is in fact that value and it is of type **char *** (otherwise known as **String**), and thus of conversion type **XmRString**. The length of the string plus the NULL terminating byte is 8, so that is used as the last parameter.

It should be noted that the interface to the **XtVaTypedArg** method discussed above is only a programmatic convenience provided by Xt. There is no work being saved or performance gained by using this interface over the three-step process of creating, setting, and freeing the compound string. This process still takes place, but it happens within Motif's compound string resource converter. In fact, having to go through this automatic conversion is actually slower than doing it manually. Unless you are creating hundreds of strings, however, the difference is negligible. The convenience and elegance of the **XtVaTypedArg** method may be worth it from the maintenance and readability perspective of managing your software, but it is really just a programmer preference.

Parenthetically speaking, the reason most of the examples in the book do not make heavy use of the feature is that the intent of this book is to demonstrate good programming habits and procedures that are tuned to a large-scale, production-size, and quality application. Using the **XtVaTypedArg** method for *compound strings* is painfully slow when repeated over hundreds of Labels, PushButtons, Lists, and other widgets. The **XtVaTypedArg** method is perfectly adequate and reasonable for other types of conversions, however, (i.e., converting resources of other types besides compound strings). If you are doing a lot of conversion from one type to another, it is in your own best interests to evaluate this conversion process yourself by testing the automatic versus the manual conversion methods.

Motif automatically converts all strings specified in resource files into compound strings. There is nothing you need to do to support this behavior, although you should realize that there is currently no way to provide 16-bit character sets ("wide characters") in resource files without additional operating system support. This is one of the difficulties involved with completely internationalizing applications.

---

[1] This terminology may be confusing to the new Motif programmer. Xt uses the typedef **String** for **char ***. The representation type used by Xt resource converters for this datatype is **XtRString** (**XmRString** in Motif). A compound string, on the other hand, is of type **XmString**, with the representation type used with resource converters specified as **XmRXmString**. You just have to read the symbols carefully. And it helps if you have a good understanding of the underlying mechanism of resource converters, which are described in detail in Chapter 11, *Resource Management and Type Conversion*, in Volume Four, *X Toolkit Intrinsics Programming Manual*.

19.2 Character Sets and Font Lists

In order to use any of the Motif compound string creation functions other than **XmString-CreateSimple( )**, you need to know a bit more about the concept of character sets.

Strictly speaking, the term *character set* in X refers to a particular mapping between byte values and characters.[2] Character sets are often defined by standards bodies such as the International Standards Organization (ISO). For example, the ISO Latin-1 character set (ISO8859-1) defines encoding for the characters used in all Western languages. The first half of Latin-1 is standard ASCII, and the second half (with the eighth bit set) contains accented characters needed for Western languages other than English. Character 65 in ISO Latin-1 is an uppercase "A", while 246 is a lowercase "o" with an umlaut.

The jisx0208.1983 character set, on the other hand, encodes the familiar ASCII characters in the lower seven bits, and Japanese kanji characters in the eight-bit values.

There is a connection between this use of the term character set and its use in Motif compound strings, in that compound strings were designed to support future Motif internationalization. However, at present, and for most practical purposes, you can think of the character set simply as an arbitrary identifier that enables Motif widgets to pick their font at runtime from a list of fonts.

Here's how it works:

1. Except for **XmStringCreateSimple( )**, the Motif compound string creation functions take as one of their arguments an arbitrary character set identifier. For example:

   ```
   XmStringCreate(text, charset)
       char *text;
       XmStringCharSet charset;
   ```

   (**XmStringCharSet** is actually just a typedef for **char ***, so the *charset* parameter is a typical C string like **"charset-4"**.)

2. Motif widgets have an **XmfontList** resource that specifies a list of fonts for the widget, together with optional, associated character set identifiers. For example, an application defaults file might specify a font list as follows:

   ```
   *fontList: -*-courier-*-r-*--12-*=charset1, \
              -*-courier-*-r-*--14-*=charset2, \
              -*-courier-*-r-*--18-*=charset3
   ```

3. At runtime, the compound string is rendered in the first font in the widget's fontList that matches the character set identifier specified in the compound string creation function.

---

[2] Note that this is different from the definition of a font, which is a collection of glyphs used to represent the characters corresponding to each value encoded in a character set. In fact, each X font name includes a description of its encoding, along with other font information such as the font family, point size, weight, slant, and so on. (For a full description of X font naming conventions, see Chapter 5, *Font Specification*, in Volume Three, *X Window System User's Guide*.)

This loose binding between the compound string and the font used to render it is useful in a number of ways:

- It allows the same compound string with the same character set identifier to be rendered in a different font in individual widgets, simply by specifying a different font=charset association in each widget. For example:

      XmPushButton.fontList: --courier-*-r-*--12-*=charset1
      XmPushButtonGadget.fontList: --courier-*-r-*--12-*=charset1
      XmList.fontList: --helvetica-*-r-*--12-*=charset1

  These resource settings indicate that "charset1" maps to the 12-point Courier font for all PushButton widgets and gadgets, and to 12-point Helvetica font for all List widgets. That is, a single compound string may be rendered in two separate fonts if the font specification for the character set differs between two widgets.

- Compound strings rendered in different fonts can be concatenated together to create multi-font strings, with the font for each segment selected from the widget's font list by means of its unique charset identifier.

- Compound strings can be language-independent, with the charset identifier used to select between fonts with different character set encodings. It is this last use that gives the charset parameter its name, though this is perhaps the least common use, at least in current applications.

19.2.1 The Default Character Set

In the current implementation of the Motif toolkit, the first character set specified in a widget's font list becomes the default character set for that widget. If the widget has no font list, the widget uses a "universal" character set referred to in applications by the constant **XmSTRING_DEFAULT_CHARSET**. If the user has his **"LANG"** environment variable set,[3] its value becomes the definition of the universal character set. If this value is invalid or its associated font cannot be used, Motif uses the value of **XmFALLBACK_CHARSET** (which is currently defined to be "ISO8859-1", although particular vendors may change this).

If a character set is listed more than once in a font list, then the first matching font is used. If a compound string specifies a character set that is not listed in the widget's **XmNfontList**, no error message is produced and the default character set for the widget is used.

There is one font list per widget instance (of those widgets that use fonts). This is important to know because it is possible to create two character sets with the same name referring to two different fonts. We'll examine this more closely in a moment. For example, the user could set the default font for all widgets using the resource setting:

      fontList: --courier-*-r-*--18-*

---

[3] See *Volume Three, X Window System User's Guide,* for specifics on how to set this variable.

This specifies that an 18-point normal courier font is used as the default font for all the widgets in an application. Because there is no character set associated with this font specification, it is the default character set.

Since the resource setting is specified such that it applies to all widgets (`*fontList`), there is no opportunity for the universal character set to be used.

To add fonts to a font list, the user can specify character set names associated with fonts as in:

```
*fontList: -*-courier-*-r-*--12-*=charset1, \
           -*-courier-*-r-*--14-*=charset2, \
           -*-courier-*-r-*--18-*=charset3
```

This resource specification sets the font list for all widgets to include the character sets `charset1`, `charset2`, and `charset3`. The default character set will be `charset1` because it is listed first. In general, the **XmNfontList** resource may take any number of character set and font name pairs. Since each widget instance may have its own resource, it is important not to confuse one widget's font list with another's.

Special Default Character Sets

In order to maintain a consistent appearance in applications, there are certain resources that may be applied to various high-level objects. The VendorShell widget class has an **XmNdefaultFontList** resource, which controls the fonts used by Text, Labels, and Buttons that are descendents of the Shell parent. The MenuShell widget class has the same resource, which controls all PushButton, Label, and Toggle menu items. This resource affects menus of all kinds (popup, pulldown, option).

For dialog boxes, **XmNbuttonFontList** is specific to the BulletinBoard widget class and controls the font used in dialog widgets (i.e., when the BulletinBoard's immediate parent is a DialogShell widget). The font list specified in this resource is applied to all PushButtons in the dialog, provided that those strings request the *default charset* from the widget. Similarly, the resource **XmNtextFontList** applies to all Text widgets in a dialog. See Chapter 5, *Introduction to Dialogs*, for a complete description of how dialog widgets are used.

In each of these cases, the default font list can be applied to all widgets that are under a particular type of widget class, so you and the user don't have to be more specific about the fonts used by particular strings or the widgets that use them. These resources are currently understood by the BulletinBoard class only, but a future version of the toolkit will extend these resources to all the Manager classes. Note that a default *string direction* (as opposed to a font list) can be set for compound strings by all of the Manager widget subclasses, not just the BulletinBoard class. This is discussed in more detail in the next section and in

19.3 Creating Compound Strings

In order to specify a character set other than the default, you can use any of the following functions:

```
XmStringCreate(text, charset)
    char *text;
    XmStringCharSet charset;


XmStringCreateLtoR(text, charset)
    char *text;
    XmStringCharSet charset;


XmStringLtoRCreate(text, charset) /* identical to ...CreateLtoR */
    char *text;
    XmStringCharSet charset;


XmStringSegmentCreate(text, charset, direction, add_separator)
    char *text;
    XmStringCharSet charset;
    XmStringDirection direction;
    Boolean add_separator;
```

XmStringCreate() creates a compound string that has no direction specified. The *default direction* of a string may be taken from the widget's parent's **XmNstring-Direction** resource value. This is a Manager widget resource that determines the string direction for all of that parent's children. If a direction other than the default is desired, the function **XmStringDirectionCreate()** can be used to create a compound string specifying an explicit direction. The resulting string can then be concatenated to the one containing the text, creating a new compound string rather than an extension of the original one. Compound string concatenation and string direction are discussed later.

XmStringCreateLtoR() and **XmStringLtoRCreate()** create a compound string in which the direction is hard-coded as left-to-right. These functions are useful not only if you want to hard-code the direction, but also, in some special cases, for reading newline-separated strings from a file. (This subject is addressed in .) Note that there is no corresponding "RtoL"-type function. To create right-to-left compound strings, you can use **Xm-StringSegmentCreate()**. Alternatively, you can create simple compound strings using **XmStringCreate()** and specify the direction using **XmStringDirection-Create()** as discussed previously.

XmStringSegmentCreate() gives detailed control over the creation of a compound string. The name is something of a misnomer, since any compound string can be treated as a segment of a larger one. We'll talk more about this function in a moment.

Each of these functions creates (allocates) a new compound string and associates the **charset** parameter with that string. The **charset** is of type **XmStringCharset**, which is defined to be a **char** pointer (a typical C string). Since the character set is dependent on the widget that will ultimately render the string, the font associated with the character set will not be accessed (and possibly not loaded) until the string needs to be drawn.

Example 19-1 demonstrates this concept.

Example 19-1. The charset.c program

```
/* charset.c --
 * Create a compound string using a charset which defaults to
 * the "9x15" font.  Three pushbuttons are created: pb1, pb2
 * and pb3.  The user can specify resources so that each of the
 * widgets have different fonts associated with the "charset"
 * specified in the compound string.
 */
#include <Xm/RowColumn.h>
#include <Xm/PushBG.h>

String fallbacks[ ] = { "*fontList:9x15=charset", NULL };

main(argc, argv)
int argc;
char *argv[ ];
{
    Widget          toplevel, rowcol;
    XtAppContext    app;
    XmString        text;
    Display         *dpy;

    toplevel = XtVaAppInitialize(&app, argv[0], NULL, 0,
        &argc, argv, fallbacks, NULL);

    text = XmStringCreateSimple("Testing, testing...");

    rowcol = XtVaCreateWidget("rowcol",
        xmRowColumnWidgetClass, toplevel,
        NULL);

    XtVaCreateManagedWidget("pb1", xmPushButtonGadgetClass, rowcol,
        XmNlabelString, text,
        NULL);

    XtVaCreateManagedWidget("pb2", xmPushButtonGadgetClass, rowcol,
        XmNlabelString, text,
        NULL);

    XtVaCreateManagedWidget("pb3", xmPushButtonGadgetClass, rowcol,
        XmNlabelString, text,
        NULL);

    XmStringFree(text);
    XtManageChild(rowcol);
    XtRealizeWidget(toplevel);
    XtAppMainLoop(app);
}
```

This simple program creates three PushButton gadgets, each of which uses the exact same compound string as its label. Accordingly, as Figure 19-1 shows, each of the buttons' labels are identical.

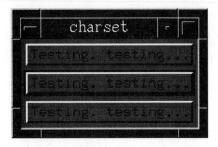

Figure 19-1. Output from charset.c

However, Figure 19-2 shows what happens to the output when the following resources are specified:

```
*pb1.fontList: -*-courier-*-r-*--12-*=charset
*pb2.fontList: -*-courier-*-r-*--14-*=charset
*pb3.fontList: -*-courier-*-r-*--18-*=charset
```

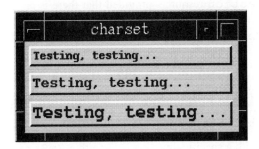

Figure 19-2. Output from charset.c with font list resources set

Notice that each PushButton specifies its font list resource differently from the others. Despite the fact that the character set "charset" is the same for each button, the actual X font associated with the character set is different.

19.3.1 Compound String Segments

A string *segment* is a compound string that contains a continuous sequence of text with no change in character set or direction. A segment of a compound string may also be terminated by a *separator*[4] (similar to the effect of a "newline" within a Text window). Segments are usually thought of as strings that are glued together with other compound strings or segments to form longer strings. Since compound strings that are used to incorporate multiple fonts are built up from smaller compound strings, each of those strings can be thought of as segments.

---

[4] *Separators* in compound strings are not to be confused with the Separator widget and gadget class.

When creating segments, you (the programmer, not the user) can specify the direction of the text (left-to-right or right-to-left) or whether there should be a separator at the end of the segment.

Let's address string direction and separators one at a time.

String Directions

Compound strings are rendered either from left-to-right or from right-to-left. There are several ways you can build a compound string that is rendered from right-to-left. The best method is dependent on the nature of your application.

For applications that wish to use left-to-right strings uniformly in their applications, this section will be of little interest. For those whose programs will use languages read from right-to-left uniformly across all widgets, you may choose to use the Manager widget resource **XmNstringDirection**. This resource controls the default direction for compound strings used by widgets that are immediate children of the Manager widget. For example, a PushButton that is the child of a Form will have its label printed in the direction specified by the Form's **XmNstringDirection** resource, provided that there is no hardcoded direction stored directly in the compound string itself. This resource provides the convenience of continuing to use **XmStringCreate( )** and **XmStringCreate-Simple( )** for most compound strings.

You should be aware, however, that most right-to-left languages still read certain things like numbers from left-to-right. In these cases, you will have to create compound string segments that have their directional information hard-coded directly into the compound string. It is details like this that make true internationalization so difficult.

You can create individual string segments with a specific direction using either **XmString-DirectionCreate( )** or **XmStringSegmentCreate( )**. Let's explore both methods.

When using **XmStringSegmentCreate( )**, you may use either of the definitions **Xm-STRING_DIRECTION_R_TO_L** or **XmSTRING_DIRECTION_R_TO_L** as the *direction* specifier. For example, by changing the line in Example 19-1 that reads:

```
text = XmStringCreateSimple("Testing, testing...");
```

to:

```
text = XmStringSegmentCreate("Testing, testing...", "charset",
    XmSTRING_DIRECTION_R_TO_L, False);
```

you get the output shown in Figure 19-3.

Obviously, you would normally do this only if you were using a font that was meant to be read from right-to-left, such as Hebrew or Arabic.

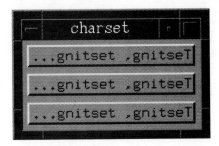

Figure 19-3. charset.c using a right-to-left string direction

You can also use the function **XmStringDirectionCreate( )** to create a new compound string segment that contains directional information. The form of the function is:

```
XmString
XmStringDirectionCreate(direction)
    XmStringDirection direction;
```

The type **XmStringDirection** is defined to be an **unsigned char**. Its value can be either of the following:

```
XmSTRING_DIRECTION_L_TO_R
XmSTRING_DIRECTION_R_TO_L
```

While the function returns a compound string, it is thought of as a string segment because it implies a directional change. You can concatenate another compound string to the end of such a string segment using **XmStringConcat( )** to produce a new compound string (this is discussed later in Section).

String Separators

Separators are used to break strings into multiple lines, in much the same way that a newline character does in a Text widget. To demonstrate its use, let's change the same line again to now read:

```
text = XmStringCreateLtoR("Testing,\ntesting...", "charset");
```

In this case, we use **XmStringCreateLtoR( )** not because we explicitly need to specify the left-to-right string direction, but because this function (and **XmStringLto-RCreate( )**) interprets embedded newline characters (\n) as separators. The effect of this change is shown in Figure 19-4, where the PushButtons display multiple lines of text.

The resulting string is thus made up of two segments: "the string **"Testing,\n"** and the string **"testing . . . "**.

Neither **XmStringCreateSimple( )** nor **XmStringSegmentCreate( )** interpret newline characters as separators; they create one compound string segment in which the **'\n'** is treated no differently than any other character value from within the associated character set (see Figure 19-5).

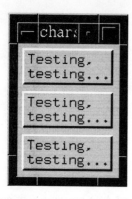

Figure 19-4. charset.c utilizing separators to render multiple lines

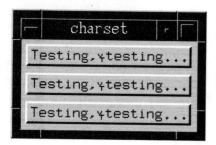

Figure 19-5. A compound string with \n not interpreted as a separator

XmStringSegmentCreate( ), however, can be told to append a separator at the end of the compound string it creates. The separator is thus part of a string segment.

It is important to recognize when you need newline characters to be interpreted as separators (which will probably be most of the time). Certain algorithms use a loop involving **fgets( )** or use **read( )** to load the (partial) contents of a file which is then converted into a compound string. If newlines are read into a buffer, you should use **XmString-CreateLtoR( )** so that newlines are interpreted into separators appropriately. Example 19-2 shows a function that reads the contents of a file into a buffer and then converts that buffer into a compound string.

Example 19-2. Converting the contents of a file into a compound string

```
XmString
ConvertFileToXmString(filename, &lines)
char *filename;
int *lines;
{
    struct stat  statb;
    int          fd, len, lines;
    char         *text;
    XmString     str;

    *lines = 0;
    if (!(fd = open(filename, O_RDONLY))) {
        XtWarning("internal error -- can't open file");
```

```
            return NULL;
        }
        if (fstat(fd, &statb) == -1 ||
                !(text = XtMalloc((len = statb.st_size) + 1))) {
            XtWarning("internal error -- can't show text");
            close(fd);
            return NULL;
        }
        (void) read(fd, text, len);
        text[ len ] = 0;

        str = XmStringCreateLtoR(text, "charset");

        XtFree(text);
        close(fd);

        *lines = XmStringLineCount(str);
        return str;
}
```

Since separators are considered to be line breaks, you can count the number of lines in a particular compound string using the function, **XmStringLineCount( )**.

None of this implies that separators terminate compound strings or cause character set changes. As shown in Figure 19-4 and Figure 19-5, a separator can be inserted into the middle of a compound string without terminating it. The fact that separate segments are created has little significance unless you need to convert compound strings back into C strings (see Section).

19.4 Strings with Multiple Fonts

Once multiple character sets are specified in a font list, you can use the list to display more than one font in a single compound string. You can do this one of two ways: create the compound text in *segments* or create separate compound strings. Either way, once the segments or strings have been created, they must be concatenated together to form a new compound string. This new string will have information embedded in it to indicate character set changes (and thus, font changes). Example 19-3 demonstrates how a compound string is created to contain three fonts.

Example 19-3. The multi_font.c program

```
/* multi_font.c --
 * Create three compound strings using 12, 14 and 18 point fonts
 * The user can specify resources so that each of the strings
 * use different fonts by setting resources similar to that shown
 * by the fallback resources.
 */
#include <Xm/Label.h>

String fallbacks[ ] = {
    "multi_font*fontList: \
        -*-courier-*-r-*--12-*=courier-12, \
```

Example 19-3. The multi_font.c program (continued)

```
            -*-courier-bold-o-*--14-*=courier-bold-14, \
            -*-courier-medium-r-*--18-*=courier-18",
    NULL
};

main(argc, argv)
int argc;
char *argv[ ];
{
    Widget          toplevel;
    XtAppContext    app;
    XmString        s1, s2, s3, text, tmp;
    String          string1 = "This is a string ",
                    string2 = "that contains three ",
                    string3 = "separate fonts.";

    toplevel = XtVaAppInitialize(&app, argv[0], NULL, 0,
        &argc, argv, fallbacks, NULL);

    s1 = XmStringCreate(string1, "courier-12");
    s2 = XmStringCreate(string2, "courier-bold-14");
    s3 = XmStringCreate(string3, "courier-18");

    /* concatenate the 3 strings on top of each other, but we can only
     * do two at a time.  So do s1 and s2 onto tmp and then do s3.
     */
    tmp = XmStringConcat(s1, s2);
    text = XmStringConcat(tmp, s3);

    XtVaCreateManagedWidget("widget_name",
        xmLabelWidgetClass, toplevel,
        XmNlabelString,     text,
        NULL);

    XmStringFree(s1);
    XmStringFree(s2);
    XmStringFree(s3);
    XmStringFree(tmp);
    XmStringFree(text);

    XtRealizeWidget(toplevel);
    XtAppMainLoop(app);
}
```

The output of this code fragment is shown in Figure 19-6.

Figure 19-6. multi_font.c shows how compound strings can use multiple fonts

The **XmNfontList** resource is initialized to have three character set and font name pairs. Each string is created using **XmStringCreate( )** with the appropriate text and character set specified. Then, the strings are concatenated together using **XmStringConcat( )**, two at a time, until we have a single compound string that contains all the texts and includes all the character set changes. `XmStringConcat( )` does not work like `strcat( )` in C. Rather, the function creates a new compound string rather than appending to an existing string. Details of this function and other related functions are discussed in Section .

It is possible to specify compound text strings (such as the `XmNlabelString` resource of the Label widget) in resource files as normal strings. This is possible because Motif takes care of the conversion to compound strings. However, when you want font changes within a string, you need to create compound strings or segments explicitly within the application as illustrated in Example 19-3.

19.4.1 Creating Font Lists

Font lists, as we have demonstrated, can be set in resource files. If your application is robust enough to handle any particular font that the user may specify, you are encouraged to use fallback resources and application defaults files for all font list specifications. You will also find that maintenance for your application is greatly simplified. By using resource files, you avoid the bother of opening fonts, maintaining handles to them, or freeing them. You should still provide a fallback mechanism for when certain fonts cannot be opened, but most of the dirtywork is avoided.

However, if you specifically don't want the user to override your font specifications, you can hard-code fonts within the application. Be aware, though, that you are also taking on the responsibility to create, maintain, and destroy fonts as necessary. This is primarily what this section is about.

There are several functions that deal with font list specification:

```
XmFontListCreate( )
XmFontListAdd( )
XmFontListFree( )
```

Each of these functions deal with a font list object of type `XmFontList`. This is intended to be an opaque type, so you should never attempt to access this data structure's internal fields. It also implies that the internals to this datatype are subject to change in future releases of the toolkit, although no such changes are currently planned. As compared to the resource specifications we've been using, there is a one-to-one correspondence between fonts and character set names. We'll address the details of how these functions work in a moment. First, let's show how the font list specification we've used before can be created using hard-coded font lists. Previously, we used:

```
*fontList: -*-courier-*-r-*--12-*=charset1, \
           -*-courier-*-r-*--14-*=charset2, \
           -*-courier-*-r-*--18-*=charset3
```

The same list can be created using **XmFontListCreate( )** and **XmFontListAdd( )**:

```
XFontStruct *font1, *font2, *font3;
XmFontList   fontlist;

font1 = XLoadQueryFont(XtDisplay(widget), "-*-courier-*-r-*--12-*");
font2 = XLoadQueryFont(XtDisplay(widget), "-*-courier-*-r-*--14-*");
font3 = XLoadQueryFont(XtDisplay(widget), "-*-courier-*-r-*--18-*");

fontlist = XmFontListCreate(font1, "charset1");
fontlist = XmFontListAdd(fontlist, font2, "charset2");
fontlist = XmFontListAdd(fontlist, font3, "charset3");

    . . .

XtVaCreateManagedWidget("widget_name", xmLabelWidgetClass, toplevel,
    XmNlabelString,     text,
    XmNfontList,        fontlist,
    NULL);

XmFontListFree(fontlist);
```

Since all the functions that deal with font lists require the application to load fonts, this is the first thing we do (although we didn't have to do *all* of them, it happened to be more convenient this way).

NOTE

While we did not explicitly check for errors, **XLoadQueryFont( )** may have failed, returning a **NULL** font. If this is the case, you should choose one of the following courses of action depending on how badly your application needs the particular fonts it asked for: terminate the program with an error message; display a warning message, but load a backup font that is known to exist; or display no error message and quietly use a backup font. **XtDefaultFont** is an adequate choice, as it is the name of a predefined font that is guaranteed to exist at runtime. (It is a *name*, not an actual font.)

Once fonts are loaded, a font list is created using **XmFontListCreate( )**. The form of the function is:

```
XmFontList
XmFontListCreate(font, charset)
    XFontStruct     *font;
    XmStringCharSet  charset;
```

Simply, a new font list of type **XmFontList** is created based on the font and character set specified. (Note that if you just want to create a font for a widget's default character set, you can use the constant **XmSTRING_DEFAULT_CHARSET** as the **charset**.) For each of the other fonts that we want to use in the font list, we add them using `XmFontListAdd( )`. The form of this function is:

```
XmFontList
XmFontListAdd(fontlist, font, charset);
    XmFontList        fontlist;
    XFontStruct       *font;
    XmStringCharSet   charset;
```

The function takes a font list and adds the new font and character set specification to the end of its list. The function returns a new font list that replaces the old. Most of the time, this will probably be the exact same list, but it may not be. Motif builds internal caches of font lists so that when a new font and character set pair is added to a list, it could be that the new list already exists elsewhere in the cache. If it does, the old font list is automatically freed and you are returned a copy of the list from the cache. Since this font list management is handled automatically, the interface is simple: just set the old **fontlist** equal to the new list returned.

We repeat this process for each font with which we want to associate a character set. When we are done building the list, we can assign the list to the **XmNfontList** resource when creating a widget:

```
XtVaCreateManagedWidget("widget_name", xmLabelWidgetClass, parent,
    ...
    XmNfontList,        fontlist,
    ...
    NULL);
```

Whenever font lists are assigned to widgets, the widget will copy this list using `XmFont-ListCopy( )`. After such an assignment, the list should be freed using `XmFontList-Free( )` unless the same list is going to be used in other widgets. The forms of these functions are:

```
XmFontList
XmFontListCopy(fontlist);
    XmFontList fontlist;

void
XmFontListFree(fontlist);
    XmFontList fontlist;
```

When a font is copied, the **XFontStruct** is also copied, but new memory is not allocated for it. Therefore, you should not call **XFreeFontInfo( )**, **XFreeFont( )**, or **XUnloadFont( )**; the toolkit will do this when the fonts are no longer needed. Since **XLoadQueryFont( )** returns a pointer to a font that may be cached in the server,[5] calling it multiple times for the same font that is to be applied to many different widgets may not be particularly wasteful. However, it would probably be more efficient to reuse the same pointer, if it is available. Whether a font list for a widget is obtained using resources or

---

[5] The proposed font server for X11R5 will support this same interface.

through the font list creation routines described previously, these font lists can be retrieved directly from widgets using `XtVaGetValues( )`:

```
XmFontList fontlist;

XtVaGetValues(widget, XmNfontList, &fontlist, NULL);
```

Once obtained, the font list can be used with other widgets, for example:

```
XtVaSetValues(another_widget, XmNfontList, fontlist, NULL);
```

Values returned by `XtVaGetValues( )` (and `XtGetValues( )`) should always be considered as *read-only* values; you should never alter these values or free them. Because the font list that was set on **another_widget** was obtained through a get-values call, the list is not freed afterwards.

The way `XtVaGetValues( )` is used for font lists is in direct contrast to the way it is used for compound strings. Compound strings are an exception to the rule that values returned by `XtVaGetValues( )` are never freed. That is, for compound strings, these values *must* be freed in the current release of the Motif toolkit. Here is an example of correct usage:

```
XmString str;
extern Widget pushbutton;
char *text;

XtVaGetValues(pushbutton, XmNlabelString, &str, NULL);
XmStringGetLtoR(str, XmSTRING_DEFAULT_CHARSET, &text);

XmStringFree(str);  /* <- must free compound strings from GetValues */

printf("PushButton's label is %s\n", text);
XtFree(text); /* <- this must be freed when you are through as documented */
```

This is really a design error in Motif, not a fault of the X Toolkit Intrinsics.

19.5 Manipulating Compound Strings

Most C programmers are used to dealing with functions such as `strcpy( )`, `strcmp( )`, and `strcat( )` to copy, compare, and modify strings. However, these functions are ineffective with compound strings since they are not based on a byte-per-character format and they may have NULL characters as well as other types of information (character sets, directions, and separators) embedded within them. In order to accomplish some of these common tasks, you can either convert the compound string back into C strings, or use the Motif-provided functions to manipulate compound strings directly. Your choice depends largely on the complexity of the compound strings you have and/or the complexity of the manipulation you need to do.

This section discusses both approaches, starting with the functions provided by Motif.

19.5.1 Motif String Functions

Motif provides the following functions to allow you to treat compound strings in much the same way that you treat C-style character arrays:

```
XmStringByteCompare( )
XmStringCompare( )
XmStringConcat( )
XmStringCopy( )
XmStringHasSubstring( )
XmStringLength( )
XmStringNConcat( )
XmStringNCopy( )
```

These functions are designed especially for the common task of creating compound strings with multiple fonts. For example, by concatenating two strings with different character sets, you can create a compound string with multiple fonts or separators.

Let's address each of the functions individually.

XmStringCompare()

```
Boolean
XmStringCompare(str1, str2)
    XmString str1, str2;
```

If the strings have the same text components, directions, and separators, then the evaluation returns **True**. This is simpler and more frequently used than **XmStringByte-Compare( )** below.

XmStringByteCompare()

```
Boolean
XmStringByteCompare(str1, str2)
    XmString str1, str2;
```

A byte-by-byte comparison is made on two compound strings that are assumed to have the same character set and string direction. If not, the result is undefined (which means you cannot trust the results you get). Provided that the character sets and string directions are identical, the function returns **True** if each string contains the same embedded **char** string internally. Note that mapping between *character sets* and *fonts* does not happen until the string is associated with a widget; that is, whether the same character set maps to different fonts when rendered in two different widgets does not affect the results of this function.

XmStringConcat() and XmStringNConcat()

```
XmString
XmStringConcat(str1, str2)
    XmString str1, str2;

XmString
XmStringNConcat(str1, str2, n)
    XmString str1, str2;
    int n;
```

Both functions create a new compound string and copy the concatenation of `str1` and `str2` into the newly allocated string. `XmStringNConcat()` copies all of `str1`, but only `n` bytes from `str2` into the new string. The original strings are preserved. You are responsible for freeing the string returned by either of these functions using `XmString-Free()`.

XmStringCopy() and XmStringNCopy()

```
XmString
XmStringCopy(str)
    XmString str;

XmString
XmStringNCopy(str, n)
    XmString str;
    int n;
```

Both functions copy `str1` into a newly allocated compound string. `XmStringNCopy()` copies `n` bytes from `str`.

XmStringHasSubstring()

```
int
XmStringHasSubstring(string, substring)
    XmString string, substring;
```

For this function, `substring` must be a single segment compound string. If its text is completely contained within any single segment of `string`, the function returns `True`. The same constraints about similar character sets described for `XmStringByteCompare()` apply here:

```
int
XmStringLength(str)
    XmString str;
```

This function returns the number of bytes in the compound string including all tags, direction indicators and separators. If the string is invalid, zero is returned. This function cannot be used to get the length of the text represented by the compound string (i.e., it's not the same as `strlen()`).

19.5.2 Converting Compound Strings to Text

If the functions provided by the Motif routines in the previous section are inadequate for your needs, you can convert compound strings back into C strings and manipulate them using the conventional C functions. This process can be simple or complicated depending on the complexity of the compound string to be converted. If the compound string has one character set associated with it and it has a left-to-right orientation, the process is quite simple. Fortunately, this is likely to be the case most of the time.

To make the conversion, you can use the following function:

```
Boolean
XmStringGetLtoR(string, charset, text)
    XmString         string;
    XmStringCharSet  charset;
    char             **text;
```

`XmStringGetLtoR( )` takes a compound string and a character set and converts it back into a C character string. If successful, the function returns **True** and the **text** parameter will point to a newly allocated pointer to a string (therefore, this pointer must be freed when you are through with it). An example of usage:

```
extern XmString  string;
char             *text;

if (XmStringGetLtoR(string, "charset", &text)) {
    printf("text = %s\n", text);
    XtFree(text);
}
```

The function only gets the *first* text segment from the compound string that is associated with the character set specified in **charset**. If the string contains multiple character sets, you must traverse the compound string retrieving each segment individually in order to obtain the entire string.

As its name implies, this function gets only left-to-right oriented text. In order to convert compound strings that have either a right-to-left orientation or multiple character sets, you will have to use an algorithm similar to that described for querying font lists (see Section). That is, you must scan through the elements of a compound string segment by segment.

A new type, **XmStringContext**, is used to identify and maintain the position within the compound string being scanned. The sequence of operations required to cycle through a compound string is:

1. Initialize a string context (**XmStringContext**) based on a compound string (**XmString**).

2. Iterate through the string getting each character set, C string, direction, and separator associated with that particular segment.

3. Dispose of (free) the string context.

The functions that enable the above sequence of steps are:

```
XmStringInitContext( )
XmStringGetNextSegment( )
XmStringFreeContext( )
```

XmStringInitContext()

```
Boolean
XmStringInitContext(context, string)
    XmStringContext   *context;
    XmString          string;
```

`XmStringInitContext( )` initializes a context that allows applications to read out the contents of a compound string segment by segment. The function allocates a new **Xm-StringContext** type and sets the pointer passed by the calling function in the **context** parameter to this data. If the allocation was successful and the string is a valid **XmString**, the function returns **True**.

XmStringGetNextSegment()

Once the context has been initialized, the contents of the string can be scanned using:

```
Boolean
XmStringGetNextSegment(context, text, charset, direction, separator)
    XmStringContext       context;
    char                  **text;
    XmStringCharSet       *charset;
    XmStringDirection     *direction;
    Boolean               *separator;
```

Notice that there is no **XmString** parameter identifying the compound string being scanned. This is because the **context** parameter must have already been initialized using `XmStringInitContext( )`. (The context is associated with the compound string during initialization.) The function reads the next segment. (The current segment is held in the **context**.) When a character set or directional change is found, the segment terminates. If a separator is found at the end of the segment, the **separator** boolean is set to **True**.

The values for **text, charset,** and **direction** are always filled in. The **text**, however, points to allocated data and should be freed by the caller using **XtFree( )**.

XmStringFreeContext()

Once you are through scanning the string, you need to free the string context using:

```
void
XmStringFreeContext(context)
    XmStringContext context;
```

An example of how these functions can be used is shown in Example 19-4.

Example 19-4. Converting from compound strings to C text

```
XmString           str;
XmStringContext    context;
char               *text, buf[128], *p;
XmStringCharSet    charset;
XmStringDirection  direction;
Boolean            separator;

XtVaGetValues(widget, XmNlabelString, &str, NULL);

if (!XmStringInitContext(&context, str)) {
    /* compound strings from GetValues still need to be freed! */
    XmStringFree(str);
    XtWarning("Can't convert compound string.");
    return;
}

/* p keeps a running pointer thru buf as text is read */
p = buf;

while (XmStringGetNextSegment(context, &text, &charset,
                             &direction, &separator)) {
    /* copy text into p and advance to the end of the string */
    p += (strlen(strcpy(p, text)));
    if (separator == True) { /* if there's a separator ... */
        *p++ = '\n';
        *p = 0;   /* add newline and null-terminate */
    }
    XtFree(text);    /* we're done with the text; free it */
}
XmStringFreeContext(context);

XmStringFree(str);

printf("Compound string:\n%s\n", buf);
```

This code fragment can be used to convert the compound string from a widget's label to a regular C string whether it has multiple lines, fonts, or directions.

19.6 Advanced Material

The rest of the sections in this chapter contain advanced material. Widget writers and those who are building extensions to widgets might find this information useful. You might also take interest in the functions described here if you want to have an in-depth understanding of how compound strings work.

19.6.1 Querying Font Lists

Since the **XmFontList** type is opaque to the programmer, getting information from lists requires using certain Motif-specific functions. This internal information may be useful if you wish to extract specific font handles or character set names, or to get relationships between the two. Motif provides a number of routines to cycle through the font list. The task is slightly complicated by the opacity of the **XmFontList** type. That is, we cannot get the beginning, ending, or any arbitrary element in the list without having a reference to any particular element in it. Therefore, a new type, **XmFontContext**, is used to identify and maintain arbitrary positions in a font list. The sequence of operations required to cycle through a font list and access its elements is:

1. Obtain access to a font list (**XmFontList**).

2. Initialize a font context (**XmFontContext**) from the font list.

3. Iterate through the list, accessing whatever information is desired.

4. Dispose of (free) the font context.

There are three functions used to carry out these steps: **XmFontListInitContext( )**, **XmFontListGetNextFont( )**, and **XmFontListFreeFontContext( )**.

XmFontListInitContext()

```
Boolean
XmFontListInitFontContext(context, fontlist)
    XmFontContext   *context;
    XmFontList      fontlist;
```

To initialize a font list, we must pass the address of a **XmFontContext** variable and a font list. The routine will allocate a new font context structure based on the font list and return **True**. If the font list is not valid or not enough memory is available to allocate a new context, **False** is returned.

XmFontListGetNextFont()

```
Boolean
XmFontListGetNextFont(context, charset, font)
    XmFontContext    context;
    XmStringCharSet  *charset;
    XFontStruct      **font;
```

Once the font context has been initialized, **XmFontListGetNextFont( )** accesses the next character set and font in the font list associated with the font context. The **charset** parameter is the *address* of a **char** pointer (e.g., **char ****). Similarly, the **font** parameter is the address of a **XFontStruct** pointer (e.g., **XFontStruct ****).

If **XmFontListGetNextFont( )** is called for the first time since **XmFontListInitFontContext( )**, the function returns the first character set and font from the list. If the function returns **True**, the character set and font pointers will be set to the appropriate values. Note that the **charset** returned is a pointer to *allocated* data that must be freed when no longer needed. The value for ***font** will point to the actual **XFontStruct** data used in the font list and should not be freed (or changed in any way). If the end of the list has been reached, the function returns **False**.

```
void
XmFontListFreeFontContext(context)
    XmFontListFontContext context;
```

Once a font list has been searched, the context must be freed using this function. If, during the search through a font list, it becomes necessary to back up in the list or to start again, the entire process must be redone. In such a case, the current context must be freed, a new one must be created and the loop of calls to **XmFontListGetNextFont( )** must be redone.

19.6.2 Rendering Compound Strings

Motif always renders compound strings automatically within its widgets. More precisely, the widgets themselves manage this type of activity and you should never find yourself in a situation where you need to render a compound string manually. The exception to this rule is if you are writing your own widgets or extensions of widgets and you need to incorporate the same type of functionality into the new widget.

There are three Motif functions that provide compound string rendering into arbitrary X windows. They are:

```
XmStringDraw( )
XmStringDrawImage( )
XmStringDrawUnderline( )
```

Each function, as you will see, requires a great deal of information in order to actually render the string. Specifically, you will need to provide a pointer to the **Window** to render in and the **Display** associated with that window. If you are rendering into a widget, these are easy since Xt provides **XtWindow( )** and **XtDisplay( )**. Each function returns the **Window** and **Display** associated with a widget. Since gadgets have no windows, you must use **XtWindowOfObject( )**. This function returns the window that actually contains the gadget. (The function also works for widgets.)

You are also going to have to provide your own graphics context (**GC**) so that certain rendering attributes such as color may be applied. This **GC** is generally not available in widgets—it certainly isn't available in the common **core** widget. If you are writing your own widgets, you will probably use a **GC** returned by **XtGetGC( )** that is cached by the X Toolkit Intrinsics (See *Volume Four, X Toolkit Intrinsics Programming Manual*). Also, if you are writing your own widgets, you might want to consider exposing the **GC** to the programmer in the form of a gettable resource. Experience with the Motif toolkit suggests that this would be a highly appreciated convenience.

The most basic rendering function is **XmStringDraw( )**:

```
XmStringDraw(dpy, drawable, fontlist, string, gc, x, y, width,
             alignment, layout_direction, clip);
    Display       *dpy;
    Drawable      drawable;
    XmFontList    fontlist;
    XmString      string;
    GC            gc;
    Position      x, y;
    Dimension     width;
    unsigned char alignment;
    unsigned char layout_direction;
    XRectangle    *clip;
```

The `fontlist` parameter may be constructed using any of the functions listed in Section , or you can use a font list associated with another widget using:

```
XmFontList fontlist;
XtVaGetValues(widget, XmNfontList, &fontlist, NULL);
```

The **x**, **y**, and **width** parameters specify the coordinates and width of the rectangle that will contain the compound string. You may notice that there is no height parameter. This is because the font list may specify fonts that are unknown in size and whose heights are too variable. The appropriate values can be set in the **clip** parameter, which defines the boundaries to which the widget is clipped. (You can pass **NULL** as the **clip** parameter to indicate that no clipping should be done by the rendering routine.) The **width** parameter is used only for alignment purposes.

The **alignment** parameter may be set to any of the following values:

```
XmALIGNMENT_BEGINNING
XmALIGNMENT_CENTER
XmALIGNMENT_END
```

The value identifies the justification for the text. The effect of the value is modified by the value of the **layout_direction** parameter. This value may be either of the following:

```
XmSTRING_DIRECTION_L_TO_R
```

or:

```
XmSTRING_DIRECTION_R_TO_L
```

For right-to-left layout, **XmALIGNMENT_END** implies left justification.

The function **XmStringDrawImage( )** is to **XmStringDraw( )** as **XDrawString( )** is to **XDrawImageString( )**. (The *Image* routines also overwrite the background even in places where the font does not set bits in the character image.)

The function **XmStringDrawUnderline( )** takes the same parameters as **XmStringDraw( )**, with one addition. The last parameter, if it is found to be a substring somewhere within the original compound string, specifies a part of the text that is to be underlined. A compound string can be wholly or partially underlined depending on whether the last parameter is exactly the same or is a subset of the **string** parameter.

19.6.3 Compound String Dimensions

Before rendering compound strings, it may be necessary to get dimensional information about the strings in order to know where to place them within the windows when they are drawn. It may also be important to have this data in order to determine optimal or desired widths and heights of widgets in case you have to provide a geometry callback method. That is, when a call to **XtQueryGeometry** is made, a widget that contains compound strings may need to tell the calling function what dimensions it will need in order to render its compound strings adequately.

The functions that Motif provides to determine these values are:

```
XmStringBaseLine( )
XmStringExtent( )
XmStringHeight( )
XmStringWidth( )
```

Each of these functions must provide a font list (**XmFontList**) and a compound string (**XmString**). The font list is therefore dependent on the widget associated with the string. However, there is no requirement that you must use strings associated with widgets—if you just want to get the dimensions of what certain text might look like given an arbitrary font (or set of fonts), you are certainly free to use font lists that you create manually using **XmFont-ListCreate( )** (see Section). The limitation on font lists is the same as that described for **XmStringByteCompare( )** (see Section).

XmStringBaseline()

```
Dimension
XmStringBaseLine(fontlist, string)
    XmFontList  fontlist;
    XmString    string;
```

This function returns the number of pixels between the top of the character box and the baseline of the first line of text in the string.

XmStringExtent()

```
void
XmStringExtent(fontlist, string, width, height)
    XmFontList  fontlist;
    XmString    string;
    Dimension   *width, *height;
```

This function determines the width and height, in pixels, of the smallest rectangle that encloses the compound string specified in **string**.

```
Dimension
XmStringWidth(fontlist, string)
    XmFontList  fontlist;
    XmString    string;

Dimension
XmStringHeight(fontlist, string)
    XmFontList  fontlist;
    XmString    string;
```

These functions return the width and height, respectively, for the compound string passed as `string`.

19.7 Summary

Compound strings can be very useful for creating multiline or multi-font text for widgets such as Labels, PushButtons, and Toggles. They are also helpful for making internationalized versions of your software. However, the current implementation of compound strings is crude and is highly subject to change in the future versions of the toolkit.

The problem of true internationalization is still being addressed at the time of this printing. It is expected that many different aspects of the operating system, the X Window System and the Motif toolkit will need further development before established practices and recommendations for internationalized applications evolve. Until then, the best practice we can recommend is to avoid hardcoding fonts and compound string resources in your application when runtime localization is desired. The fonts and texts to use for widgets should be isolated into separate resource files that may be edited and loaded upon invocation of the program.

20

Advanced Dialog Programming

This chapter describes Motif features that have not been described (at least not completely) in earlier chapters, including issues involved in creating multi-stage help systems, in creating WorkingDialogs that allow you to interrupt a long-running task, and a method for dynamically changing the pixmaps displayed in a dialog.

In This Chapter:

Advanced Dialog Programming

In one sense, this chapter isn't about dialogs at all, but about various aspects of X programming that become most evident when working with dialogs.

In particular, we address here some issues involved in creating multi-stage help systems, we show how to create WorkingDialogs that allow you to interrupt a long-running task, and we describe a method for dynamically changing the pixmaps displayed in a dialog.

Several of these topics take us far deeper into lower layers of X than anything we've seen so far in this book. You should be armed with a good basic understanding of X event-processing, as implemented both in Xlib and Xt. If you're not, be prepared to refer frequently to Volume One, *Xlib Programming Manual* and Volume Four, *X Toolkit Intrinsics Programming Manual*, when faced with references to lower-level functions.

Nonetheless, this chapter bears study, since the problems it explores are among the most interesting faced in this book.

20.1 Help Dialogs

The *Motif Style Guide* doesn't have much to say about how help is presented to the user, although it does discuss the ways the user can select or request help from the application. When to present help is all rather intuitive—you should provide help whenever the user selects a **Help** button in a dialog box, when he chooses from the help items in the MenuBar, or when he uses the HELP or F1 key on the keyboard. Clearly, help should be presented in a very obvious manner, possibly using larger fonts, or graphical images (pixmaps, other Xlib drawing functions, or even animation); anything that gets the user's attention and provides adequate information is usually sufficient. Whatever method you choose, you should try to maintain consistency so that the user becomes familiar with the style of the help you provide.

The easiest and most straightforward method is to create an InformationDialog (one of the MessageDialog types) with the necessary text displayed as the `XmNmessageString`. Example 20-1 demonstrates how to pop up a HelpDialog when the **Help** button is activated from another dialog box.

Example 20-1. The simple_help.c program

```
/* simple_help.c -- create a pushbutton that posts a dialog box
 * that entices the user to press the help button.  The callback
 * for this button displays a new dialog that gives help.
 */
#include <Xm/MessageB.h>
#include <Xm/PushB.h>

/* main() --create a pushbutton whose callback pops up a dialog box */
main(argc, argv)
char *argv[ ];
{
    Widget toplevel, button;
    XtAppContext app;
    XmString label;
    void pushed();

    toplevel = XtVaAppInitialize(&app, "Demos", NULL, 0,
        &argc, argv, NULL, NULL);

    label = XmStringCreateSimple("???");
    button = XtVaCreateManagedWidget("button",
        xmPushButtonWidgetClass, toplevel,
        XmNlabelString,          label,
        NULL);
    XtAddCallback(button, XmNactivateCallback,
        pushed, "You probably need help for this item.");
    XmStringFree(label);

    XtRealizeWidget(toplevel);
    XtAppMainLoop(app);
}

#define HELP_TEXT "You just got help.\n    Now press 'Ok'"

/* pushed() --the callback routine for the main app's pushbutton. */
void
pushed(w, text)
Widget w;
char *text;
{
    Widget dialog;
    XmString t = XmStringCreateSimple(text);
    Arg args[2];
    extern void help_callback();

    XtSetArg(args[0], XmNautoUnmanage, False);
    XtSetArg(args[1], XmNmessageString, t);
    dialog = XmCreateMessageDialog(XtParent(w), "notice", args, 2);
    XmStringFree(t);

    XtUnmanageChild(
      XmMessageBoxGetChild(dialog, XmDIALOG_CANCEL_BUTTON));

    XtAddCallback(dialog, XmNokCallback, XtDestroyWidget, NULL);
    XtAddCallback(dialog, XmNhelpCallback, help_callback, HELP_TEXT);

    XtManageChild(dialog);
    XtPopup(XtParent(dialog), XtGrabNone);
}
/*
```

Example 20-1. The simple_help.c program (continued)

```
 * The callback routine for the Help button in the original dialog
 * box. This routine displays a HelpDialog based on the help_text
 * parameter.
 */
void
help_callback(parent, help_text, cbs)
Widget parent;
char *help_text;
XmAnyCallbackStruct *cbs;
{
    Widget dialog;
    XmString text;
    void help_done();
    Arg args[2];

    text = XmStringCreateLtoR(help_text, XmSTRING_DEFAULT_CHARSET);
    XtSetArg(args[0], XmNmessageString, text);
    XtSetArg(args[1], XmNautoUnmanage, False);
    dialog = XmCreateInformationDialog(parent, "help", args, 2);
    XmStringFree(text);

    XtUnmanageChild(   /* no need for the cancel button */
        XmMessageBoxGetChild(dialog, XmDIALOG_CANCEL_BUTTON), False);
    XtSetSensitive(    /* no more help is available. */
        XmMessageBoxGetChild(dialog, XmDIALOG_HELP_BUTTON), False);
    /* the Ok button will call help_done() below */
    XtAddCallback(dialog, XmNokCallback, help_done, NULL);

    /* display the help text */
    XtManageChild(dialog);
    XtPopup(XtParent(dialog), XtGrabNone);
}
/* help_done() --called when user presses "Ok" in HelpDialog.
 * Destroy the dialog shell and reset it so that help_callback()
 * will create a new one.
 */
void
help_done(dialog)
Widget dialog;
{
    XtDestroyWidget(dialog);
}
```

The main window contains a PushButton that pops up a simple MessageDialog. This dialog, as you can tell from Figure 20-1, contains a **Help** button, which pops up an Information-Dialog. This dialog is intended to provide help text for the user.

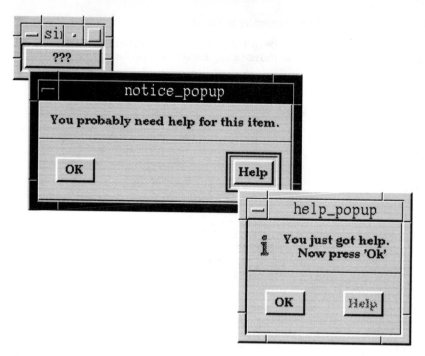

Figure 20-1. Output of simple_help.c

The callback routine for the **Help** button is installed via the **XmNhelpCallback**. This routine pops up an InformationDialog that contains the text predefined in the beginning of the program. Obviously, this text is for demonstration purposes only; it should not be construed as "realistic," but should help you understand the method for how the text was displayed.

The **XmStringCreateLtoR()** function is used to display the text instead of **XmStringCreateSimple()**, since the help message contains newline characters. The difference between these two functions is that the former converts these characters ("\n") into real new lines, while the latter prints them as control characters. Also, **XmStringCreateLtoR()** allows you to specify an alternate character set, which can be encoded in the widget's **XmNfontList**. (We are not taking advantage of this feature, since we specified the special character set, **XmSTRING_DEFAULT_CHARSET**, which defaults to the first character set from the widget's font list.) However, using this function gives you the flexibility of defining whichever font you want to be used within your help system. For example, you could specify that the character set *help-font* is used whenever a HelpDialog is displayed. See Chapter 19, *Compound Strings*, for more information on how you can use compound strings to accomplish this sort of functionality.

The **XmNhelpCallback** resource also serves as the callback for any widget (dialog or otherwise) that wishes to provide help information. All Motif widgets have an **XmNhelpCallback** resource associated with them (although every instance may not have a help callback installed on it). Whenever the user presses the HELP key on the keyboard (if one exists, and the X server is set up correctly[1]), then the **XmNhelpCallback** is invoked for that widget.

The F1 key also serves as a HELP key for compatibility with Microsoft Windows and to compensate for any computer that may not have a HELP key.[2]

If a widget does not have an **XmNhelpCallback** function installed, Motif climbs the widget tree, searching each widget's immediate parent until it finds one with a help callback. In light of this, it is recommended that if you assign help text to widgets, the more primitive widgets (PushButtons, Labels, Lists, etc.) should have explicit help, while more general widgets (managers, dialogs) should have more general help information. You can design a rather elaborate context-sensitive help system for your application if you install the right callback routines to your widgets and assign the correct text with each widget or callback routine.

Let's return to the *simple_help.c* program and examine the sorts of actions the user might take. When the program is first brought up, a single PushButton appears with the label, **???**, which can represent any arbitrary widget in an application where the user might want some help. When activated, the user is then presented with a single MessageDialog with which the user will undoubtedly need help. He selects the **Help** PushButton (or presses the F1 or HELP key) and the InformationDialog appears. Since the dialog providing help is not modal (nor should it be), the user's next action can either be to close the HelpDialog or to close the original MessageDialog it came from. Since the HelpDialog is created as a child of the MessageDialog, if it is destroyed, the HelpDialog is also destroyed. Similarly, if the MessageDialog is dismissed (unmapped, rather than destroyed), so is the InformationDialog. If the HelpDialog remains up, it could confuse the user. Generally, any time a HelpDialog is displayed, it should be removed if the user has unmanaged, destroyed, or otherwise disabled the dialog it came from. This is easily solved by making the HelpDialog the child of the original dialog. The natural interaction between parent and child dialogs facilitate the correct management behavior.

Another interesting question is how to provide additional help once an InformationDialog is already presenting help to the user. One solution would be to display an additional dialog if the user presses HELP in the existing InformationDialog. However, multiple help windows should be avoided, since they will undoubtedly confuse the user. A better solution is to display the new help text in the same InformationDialog. That way, the user can always look to the same place for all his help information. All that's required is the ability to retain state information. Example 20-2 shows one idea for an implementation.

---

[1] By default, Sun workstations do not generate the proper event when the HELP key is pressed. Your mileage may vary for other computers.

[2] The F1 key works by default, but it may be remapped to perform other functions in the user's *.mwmrc* file.

Example 20-2. A multi-stage help system

```
#define MAX_HELP_STAGES 3
char *help_texts[3][5] = {
    {
        "You have reached the first stage of the Help System.",
        "If you need additional help, select the More Help button.",
        "You may exit Help at any time by pressing 'Done'.",
        NULL,
    },
    {
        "This is the second stage of the Help system.  There is",
        "more help available.  Press 'More Help' to see more.",
        "Press 'Previous' to return to the previous Help message.",
        "Or press 'Done' to exit the Help System.",
        NULL,
    },
    {
        "This is the last help message you will see on this topic.",
        "You may either press 'Previous' to return to the previous",
        "Help level, or press 'Done' to exit the Help System.",
        NULL,
    }
};

/*
 * The callback routine for the Help button is in the original dialog
 * box. This routine displays a HelpDialog based on the help_text
 * parameter.  This routine also serves as the callback for the
 * Help button in *this* dialog.  Thus, it is conceptually recursive
 * (altho, not literally).  The client_data, idx_incr, indicates an
 * increment or decrement into the help_texts array declared above.
 * When idx_incr is 0, the MessageDialog called us -- check to see
 * if the dialog has already been created (in which case, don't re-
 * create it.  Otherwise, the value will be -1 or 1.  Increment the
 * "idx" (static int) so the help text changes.
 */
void
help_callback(parent, idx_incr, cbs)
Widget parent;
int idx_incr;
XmAnyCallbackStruct *cbs;
{
    static Widget dialog; /* prevent multiple help dialogs */
    XmString text;
    char buf[BUFSIZ], *p;
    static int idx;
    int i;
    void help_done();

    if (dialog && idx_incr == 0) {
        /* user pressed Help button in MessageDialog again.  We're
         * already up, so just make sure we're visible and return.
         */
        XtPopup(XtParent(dialog), XtGrabNone);
        XMapRaised(XtDisplay(dialog), XtWindow(XtParent(dialog)));
        return;
    }
```

```
        if (dialog)
            idx += idx_incr; /* more/previous help; change index */
        else {
            /* We're not up, so create new Help Dialog */
            Arg args[4];

            /* Action area button labels. */
            XmString done = XmStringCreateSimple("Done");
            XmString cancel = XmStringCreateSimple("Previous");
            XmString more = XmStringCreateSimple("More Help");

            XtSetArg(args[0], XmNautoUnmanage, False);
            XtSetArg(args[1], XmNokLabelString, done);
            XtSetArg(args[2], XmNcancelLabelString, cancel);
            XtSetArg(args[3], XmNhelpLabelString, more);
            dialog = XmCreateInformationDialog(parent, "help", args, 4);

            /* pass help_done() the address of "dialog" so it can reset */
            XtAddCallback(dialog, XmNokCallback, help_done, &dialog);
            /* if more/previous help, recall ourselves with increment */
            XtAddCallback(dialog, XmNcancelCallback, help_callback, -1);
            XtAddCallback(dialog, XmNhelpCallback, help_callback, 1);

            /* If our parent dies, we must reset "dialog" to NULL! */
            XtAddCallback(dialog, XmNdestroyCallback, help_done, &dialog);

            XmStringFree(done);    /* once dialog is created, these */
            XmStringFree(cancel); /* strings are no longer needed. */
            XmStringFree(more);

            idx = 0; /* initialize idx--needed for each new help stuff */
        }

        /* concatenate help texts into a single string with newlines */
        for (p = buf, i = 0; help_texts[idx][i]; i++) {
            p += strlen(strcpy(p, help_texts[idx][i]));
            *p++ = '\n', *p = 0;
        }

        text = XmStringCreateLtoR(buf, XmSTRING_DEFAULT_CHARSET);
        XtVaSetValues(dialog, XmNmessageString, text, NULL);
        XmStringFree(text); /* after set-values, free unneeded memory */

        /* If no previous help msg, set "Previous" to insensitive. */
        XtSetSensitive(
            XmMessageBoxGetChild(dialog,XmDIALOG_CANCEL_BUTTON), idx > 0);
        /* If no more help, set "More Help" insensitive. */
        XtSetSensitive(
            XmMessageBoxGetChild(dialog, XmDIALOG_HELP_BUTTON),
                idx < MAX_HELP_STAGES-1);

        /* display the dialog */
        XtManageChild(dialog);
        XtPopup(XtParent(dialog), XtGrabNone);
}
/* This callback is used to kill ourselves and set the dialog pointer
 * to NULL so it can't be referenced again by help_callback().
 * This function is called from the Done button in the help dialog.
 * It is also our XmNdestroyCallback, so reset our dialog_ptr to NULL.
 */
```

Example 20-2. A multi-stage help system (continued)

```
void
help_done(dialog, dialog_ptr)
Widget dialog, *dialog_ptr;
{
    if (!*dialog_ptr) /* prevent unnecessarily destroying twice */
        return;
    XtDestroyWidget(dialog); /* this might call ourselves... */
    *dialog_ptr = NULL;
}
```

In this scenario, each stage of help produces another text string to display. All help text is displayed in the same InformationDialog. The output of the code is shown in Figure 20-2.

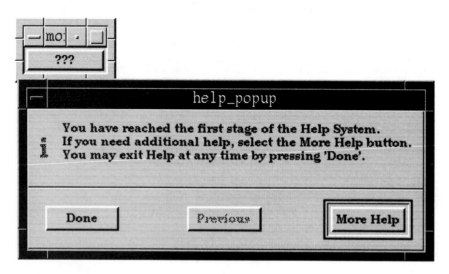

Figure 20-2. Displaying multiple levels of help text

This program addresses several problems that arise due to the added complexity of the multilevel help system. That is, many dialogs (possibly an infinite number of them) may be trying to pop up the same HelpDialog. This particular program prevents multiple instances of the same dialog by keeping a static handle to itself from within its callback routine. This is how we know when the dialog is active and when it is dormant.

Also, as we have seen before, if the parent is unmapped or destroyed, the HelpDialog is also unmapped or destroyed. In order to maintain state information, we install an **Xm-NdestroyCallback** to monitor the InformationDialog's destruction. In this case, we only need to reset the HelpDialog's handle to **NULL** so that we don't try to reference the destroyed dialog again from **help_callback( )** the next time help is requested.

If the HelpDialog box has already been created and the user pressed the **Help** button anyway, it is remapped to the screen and raised to the top using **XMapRaised( )**.

As a final note, if you wish to provide help text that is too lengthy to appear in a single information dialog widget, then you might choose to place a ScrolledText object within your own customized dialog. The information you display can then be an arbitrary length without worrying about screen real estate. This is explained in Chapter 7, *Custom Dialogs*.

20.1.1 Point-and-click Help

In Motif applications, it is not always a simple or intuitive task to activate the HELP key with the pointer over a specific widget. The Motif GUI typically acts somewhat independently of the mouse cursor, and doesn't lend itself well to directing help in a strictly keyboard-driven manner. While the user could use the HELP or F1 keys on the keyboard, this is not the easiest thing to do for many widgets. In fact, it is impossible for Labels, since they do not process input events (not that Labels typically have help associated with them). You can provide a more intuitive interface that allows the user to point-and-click directly on a widget to obtain help.

This is all made possible by the **XmTrackingLocate( )** function. The function takes the following form:

```
Widget
XmTrackingLocate(widget, cursor, confine_to)
    Widget    widget;
    Cursor    cursor;
    Boolean   confine_to;
```

The function invokes a server-grab on the pointer (turning the cursor's image to that specified by the **cursor** parameter) and waits until the user presses a mouse button. The widget on which this event takes place is returned. If the **confine_to** parameter is **True**, then the cursor is confined to the window owned by **widget**. (The **widget**'s window is also used as the owner of the pointer grab.)

This function can be used in the following manner:

```
    ...
    XtAddCallback(widget, XmNactivateCallback, query_for_help, NULL);
    ...

void
query_for_help(widget, client_data, cbs)
Widget widget;
caddr_t client_data;
XmAnyCallbackStruct *cbs;
{
    Widget help_widget;
    Cursor cursor;

    cursor = XCreateFontCursor(XtDisplay(widget), XC_hand2);
    if (help_widget = XmTrackingLocate(widget, cursor, confine_to)) {
        cbs->reason = XmCR_HELP;
        XtCallCallbacks(help_widget, XmNhelpCallback, &cbs);
    }
    XFreeCursor(XtDisplay(widget), cursor);
}
```

This code fragment assumes that the widget whose `XmNactivateCallback` has the `query_for_help( )` callback function is a PushButton, since the callback resource is `XmNactivateCallback`. The **On Context** menu item from the **Help** menu in the Menu-Bar of the application's main window would be an excellent choice. Thus, when the user selects that menu item, `query_for_help( )` is invoked, which calls `XmTracking-Locate( )`. Although the tracking function requires a window from the widget passed to it, you *may* pass a gadget because the function uses `XtWindowOfObject( )`, which obtains the object's parent window if the object is a gadget. (If the object is a widget, the function is identical to `XtWindow( )`.)

The `cursor` is created using `XCreateFontCursor( )`, but this is not required; you may use other functions like `XCreateGlyphCursor( )`, if you like. See Volume One, *Xlib Programmer's Manual*, for more information.

`XmTrackingLocate( )` changes the pointer to the specified cursor in order to provide the user with visual feedback that the program is in a new state. Clearly, it is important to choose an intuitively obvious cursor that indicates that the user is in a help state or that gives him an idea of what is expected of him. `XC_hand2` contains a glyph of a hand as if it were pointing at something; it is an appropriate choice because the user is expected to click on an object.

If the user clicks on any valid widget within the application, `XmTrackingLocate( )` returns that widget handle. The widget itself is not activated, nor does it receive any events indicating that anything has happened at all. If the user does not click on a valid widget or outside of the application, the function returns `NULL`.

Assuming that the user did click on a valid widget, we use `XtCallCallbacks( )` to activate the `XmNhelpCallback` callback functions on the widget returned. At this point, the same scenario takes place as mentioned earlier: if the widget does not have a help callback, its parent is checked, and so on. As far as the `help_widget` is concerned, its help callback was legitimately activated by the user.

The `confine_to` flag makes this function useful in other scenarios as well. For example, you can implement a *very*-modal dialog by using `XmTrackingLocate( )` to force the user to push one of a small set of buttons within a particular dialog or Manager widget. However, you should use this function with caution; once the cursor is confined to the window, the server-grab is not released until the user presses the mouse button. (Caution is advised if you are using a debugger while using this function; if the debugger stops at a breakpoint while this function is being invoked, you will have to log in remotely and kill the debugger process to release the pointer grab. If you can't do that, you will have to shut down the computer.)

20.2 WorkingDialogs

WorkingDialogs are used to inform the user that the application is busy doing something and it doesn't have the time to handle other actions the user may take. For example, if your application is busy trying to figure out the complete value of *pi*, then the user is probably going to have to wait a while before he can expect the program to respond to his next action.

The reason for the delay is that your application code now has control, rather than Xt, which normally processes events. When Xt has control, it processes events and dispatches them to the appropriate widgets in the application. If the widget has a callback installed for an event, it returns control to your application (thus the term, *callback function*) where you can now do whatever it is your application does. While the application has control, there is no way for the window system to service any of the other requests the user may happen to make.

In the meantime, your application is faced with the dilemma of how it is going to process events that happen in the interim. While your application is busily number-crunching, the user is frantically pounding on the **Stop** button, hoping that someone will figure out that he didn't really mean to figure out the complete value of *pi*, but instead to print out the recipe for *cherry pie*.

The problem, restated, is: *how do you do the work necessary for the callback routine and process events at the same time?* The solution to the problem, therefore, is conceptually simple: see if there are X events in the input queue every once in a while; if there are, process and dispatch them. The implementation of this solution, on the other hand, is quite a different story. There are a number of different approaches you can take, but depending on the nature of the work you are trying to do, any one solution may not be appropriate. Let's examine some options:

- If the task can be broken down into tiny chunks, you can set up *work procedures* which are automatically invoked by Xt whenever there are no other events on the event queue. In other words, when there are work procedures installed, Xt thinks in the following manner: "Are there any events waiting? No. Ok, call the work procedures... Done. Ok, are there any events, NOW? No. Ok, call the work procedures again... Done. Ok ...." This type of processing goes extremely quickly, since events are very infrequent when you consider how little time is taken by the simple check to see if there are any events pending. This method is best employed by tasks that are not critical to the application—at least not immediately. These tasks can be done "in the background" and will not interfere with the normal event-processing loop. However, to maintain performance, you should break down the task into very small (time-wise) components. Of course, you can slow down the process by taking a long time in the work procedures, but this is up to you.

- Timer event handlers can be set to go off periodically using `XtAppTimeOut( )`. As each timer fires, another chunk of work can be done before returning control to the Intrinsics. This is similar to using work procedures, but the time intervals might be more in tune with the type of processing you are doing. Timers are typically used when the work being done is synchronous with the system clock or some other regular interval segment. However, as we will see later, timers are *not* associated directly with the system clock and tasks should not rely on their accuracy.

- You may choose not to return control back to the Intrinsics. Instead, bring the Intrinsics to you. In other words, you can use some of the lower-level Xlib and Xt functions to determine whether there are events in the queue, and if so, process them immediately. This type of processing is more appropriate for applications that wish to handle more sophisticated looping constructs, recursion, or to manage complex state information (fractal computation or biological cellular analysis).

- You can also simply choose to ignore events entirely. This is best handled by setting the cursor to a stopwatch image or an hour glass, and/or posting a message indicating that the user *must* wait. This solution is sometimes the only one available if the task is dependent on some outside entity. Examples include communicating with device drivers (printer, disk drives), network communications (NFS), interprocess activity (forks and pipes), or anything that puts the application in a state where it has no control over the object with which it is communicating.

You can mix and match some of these scenarios. For example, say the user wants to send a large PostScript file to a laser printer. When he clicks on the **Print** button in your dialog (assuming you have one), you can post a WorkingDialog reporting that you are going to do the action immediately and the user must wait. Or, you may provide an option where the user can send the file to the printer in the *background*. In such situations, you can do the necessary communication by using work procedures that send little bits and pieces to the printer.

The four points listed can be broken down into two categories: you allow Xt to maintain the control loop (event-handling) and periodically call your internal routines, or you maintain the control loop and periodically call Xlib functions to check the event queue. Work and timer procedures imply returning control back to Xt, allowing it to process events as it normally does. It, in turn, gives control back to you for (presumably) short intervals every now and then. The other two cases imply that you maintain, not relinquish, control to Xt. Instead, you maintain control of the application, querying and processing X events yourself whenever you want (or can). This is a more complicated procedure, but it is simpler to maintain control of your application-specific working loop.

In all four situations, you may or may not wish to display a WorkingDialog. If you want, you can be interactive, giving the user the ability to terminate the work in progress by activating the **Stop** button in its action area. Otherwise, you can simply display it as informational feedback only. We will demonstrate all four cases in the following subsections.

20.2.1 Using Work Procedures

Work procedures in Xt are extremely simple in design. They are mostly used for applications that can process tasks in the "background." When used in conjunction with the WorkingDialog, you can also provide feedback on the status of the task. For example, say the user wants to load a large bitmap into a window. However, the nature of your application requires you to load the file from disk into client-side memory, do some bitmap manipulation, and then send it to the X server to be loaded into a pixmap. If you suspect that this task might take a long time and you want to allow the user to interrupt it at any time, you can use work procedures and a WorkingDialog.

Demonstrating such a task is difficult, due to its extremely complex nature. Activity such as this requires a great deal of code that would make it difficult to keep focused on the issue at hand: installing work procedures while handling user events. However, Example 20-3 provides a short, abstract program demonstrating one approach to the problem. Here, we represent a time-consuming task by simply counting from 0 to 20000 (the macro MAXNUM). The visible portion of the application simply displays a button, labeled with the string "Boy is *this* going to take a long time." Clicking on this button starts the count, and causes a WorkingDialog to be displayed; the user can press **Stop** at any time during the process. This is shown in Figure 20-3.

Figure 20-3. working.c while working

If the user doesn't terminate the program before it completes its task, the WorkDialog's button changes from **Stop** to **Done**, as shown in Figure 20-4. The dialog is automatically popped down when it is done. The program is shown in Example 20-3.

Figure 20-4. working.c after task is finished

Example 20-3. The working.c program

```
/* working.c -- represent a complicated, time-consuming task by
 * counting from 0 to 20000 and provide feedback to the user about
 * how far we are in the process.  The user may terminate the process
 * at any time by selecting the Stop button in the WorkingDialog.
 * This demonstrates how WorkingDialogs can be used to allow the
 * user to interrupt lengthy procedures.
 */
#include <Xm/MessageB.h>
```

Example 20-3. The working.c program (continued)

```
#include <Xm/PushB.h>

#define MAXNUM 20000

/* main() --create a pushbutton whose callback pops up a dialog box */
main(argc, argv)
char *argv[ ];
{
    XtAppContext  app;
    XtWorkProcId  work_id;
    Widget        toplevel, dialog;
    XmString      stop_txt;
    extern void   done();
    Arg           args[1];
    int           count();

    toplevel = XtVaAppInitialize(&app, "Demos",
        NULL, 0, &argc, argv, NULL, NULL);

    /* Create the dialog -- the "cancel" button says "Stop" */
    stop_txt = XmStringCreateSimple("Stop");
    XtSetArg(args[0], XmNcancelLabelString, stop_txt);
    dialog = XmCreateWorkingDialog(toplevel, "working", args, 1);
    XmStringFree(stop_txt);

    work_id = XtAppAddWorkProc(app, count, dialog);
    XtVaSetValues(dialog, XmNuserData, work_id, NULL);

    XtUnmanageChild(  /* no need for the ok button */
        XmMessageBoxGetChild(dialog, XmDIALOG_OK_BUTTON), False);
    XtUnmanageChild(  /* no need for the help button */
        XmMessageBoxGetChild(dialog, XmDIALOG_HELP_BUTTON), False);

    /* Use cancel button to stop counting. True = remove work proc */
    XtAddCallback(dialog, XmNcancelCallback, done, True);

    XtManageChild(dialog);
    XtPopup(XtParent(dialog), XtGrabNone);

    /* XtRealizeWidget(toplevel); */
    XtAppMainLoop(app);
}
/* work procedure -- counts to MAXNUM.  When we hit it, change the
 * "Stop" button to say "Done".
 */
int
count(dialog)
Widget dialog; /* client data for XtAppAddWorkProc() */
{
    static int n;
    char buf[64];
    XmString str, button;
    Arg args[2];

    /* if we printed every number, the flicker is too fast to read.
     * Therefore, just print every 1000 ticks for smoother feedback.
     */
    if (++n % 1000 != 0)
        return False;
```

Example 20-3. The working.c program (continued)

```
        /* display where we are in the counter. */
        sprintf(buf, "Counter: %d", n);
        str = XmStringCreateSimple(buf);
        XtSetArg(args[0], XmNmessageString, str);

        if (n == MAXNUM) {
            button = XmStringCreateSimple("Done");
            XtSetArg(args[1], XmNcancelLabelString, button);
            XtRemoveCallback(dialog, XmNcancelCallback, done, True);
            XtAddCallback(dialog, XmNcancelCallback, done, False);

            XtManageChild(dialog);
            /* or, use:
            if (!XtIsManaged(dialog))
                done(dialog, False);
            */
        }

        XtSetValues(dialog, args, 1 + (n == MAXNUM));

        /* return either True (we're done, remove the work proc)
         * or False (continue working by calling this function).
         */
        return n == MAXNUM;
}

/* User pressed "Stop" or "Done" in WorkingDialog. */
void
done(dialog, remove_work_proc)
Widget dialog;
int remove_work_proc;
{
    if (remove_work_proc) {
        XtWorkProcId work_id;
        XtVaGetValues(dialog, XmNuserData, &work_id, NULL);
        XtRemoveWorkProc(work_id);
    }
    XtDestroyWidget(dialog);
    exit(0); /* for purposes of this demo; remove for general use */
}
```

This program is designed specifically to demonstrate how a work procedure and the Working-Dialog can interact.

The toolkit is first initialized using **XtVaAppInitialize( )**, which returns the **toplevel** Shell of the program and creates the application context. A WorkingDialog is created as a child of **toplevel** using **XmCreateWorkingDialog( )**. The dialog returned is subsequently used as the client data for the work procedure, **count( )**, which is installed using **XtAppAddWorkProc( )**. The form of this function is:

```
XtWorkProcId
XtAppAddWorkProc(app_context, proc, client_data)
    XtAppContext app_context;
    XtWorkProc   proc;
    XtPointer    client_data;
```

In order to allow the user to interrupt the process, we install **done( )** as the **XmNcancel-Callback** resource. In order to actually stop the processing, it must remove the work procedure using **XtRemoveWorkProc( )**. The **XtWorkProcId** created when the work procedure was initialized is installed as the **XmNuserData** to the dialog widget. This is the alternative to creating a global variable, which is something we always try to avoid. However, saving the **XtWorkProcId** as the user data may not be a good thing to do if the actual value would be needed frequently. In other words, if your work procedure needed to get an arbitrary widget's **XmNuserData** value all the time, this would be a tremendous amount of overhead to perform on each iteration. In short, it is generally a good idea to do as little "work" as possible in a work routine. Here is where performance might really slow up or down.

When *working.c* is running, the work procedure is called, incrementing the static n variable. (Static variables are automatically initialized to 0.) Each time n hits an increment of **1000**, the WorkingDialog's **XmNmessageString** is updated, informing the user about how far along the process is. The work procedure returns either **True** or **False**; if **True** is returned, the task is complete and Xt can remove the work procedure from the list of those being called. If at any time during this process, the user clicks on the **Stop** button, the function **done( )** is called (as per the **XmNcancelCallback** function installed earlier), where the work procedure is removed anyway. Either way a work procedure is removed, it is no longer called by Xt, unless it is reinstalled manually.

If the user allows the task to complete, the work procedure changes the action button to say **Done** and removes the old **XmNcancelCallback**. It then installs the callback again, changing the client data from **True** to **False**. (Removing and reinstalling a callback function is the only way to change its client data.) The client data must be set to **False** so that **done( )** will not try to remove the work procedure (because we're going to return **True** at the end of the function, indicating that we are done with the task and that the work procedure can be removed.)

The call to **XtManageChild( )** is made just in case the user covered up the working dialog with other windows or unmapped the dialog completely. Even though we don't know whether the dialog is visible, the call is still made because it is an inexpensive way to ensure that the dialog is indeed visible. Alternatively, we could have just called **done( )** directly from here if we didn't think the user cared to be notified of the job's completion. If you choose to do this, be sure to pass **False** as the client data for the same reason outlined in the previous paragraph. That is, **done( )** checks this parameter to see whether or not it should remove the work procedure.

You can install as many work procedures as you like. The X Toolkit Intrinsics call each work procedure in the opposite order of installation. That is, the last work procedure installed is the first one called in the list. The only exception is if a work procedure installs another work procedure, in which case, the new one is placed before it in the queue; thus, it will always be called *after* the current procedure the next time around. (This represents a standard linked-list insertion algorithm.)

As you can see from running this program, work procedures are called extremely frequently (whenever there are no X events to process). It is assumed, however, that the task you are performing is probably going to be quite a bit more sophisticaed and time-consuming than our example here. We caution you, therefore, that you should not spend inordinate amounts of time in these functions; you should return frequently enough to allow the Intrinsics to process possible user events in order to give the appearance of a smooth-flowing application.

There is one additional thing to mention. Typically, when WorkingDialogs are displayed, you may not want the user to interact with any other dialogs or windows in your application besides the single WorkingDialog. If this is the case, you might want to set the dialog's **Xm-NdialogStyle** resource to **XmDIALOG_FULL_APPLICATION_MODAL**. For more information, see Section 5.7.1, *Implementing Modal Dialogs*.

20.2.2 Using Timers

Using timers to process tasks is virtually identical in design to using work procedures. The main difference is that timers are not called as frequently, allowing the Toolkit Intrinsics to wait longer for user events to be generated and processed. Since timers are used frequently throughout this book in various contexts (like in Chapter 11, *Labels and Buttons*) we leave you with the example given previously using work procedures.

20.2.3 Processing Events Yourself

Let's say you were going to start a lengthy process and you didn't want to return control back to Xt. This might be necessary for some processing tasks that might involve the following type of looping construct:

```
while (still_processing) {
    if (CheckForInterrupt( ))
        break;

    /* do complicated junk */
}
```

In this situation, you never lose control of your own processing loop, but you still check for X events that may need to be processed every once in a while. This is essentially the same sort of situation used by work procedures, but may be more convenient for certain algorithms, since you never really break out of your main control loop unless the user terminated the processing (through a UI object) or the task completes naturally.

The **CheckForInterrupt( )** pseudo-function could check the event queue to see if there are any events destined for the **Stop** button in the popped-up WorkingDialog, as shown in Figure 20-4. Processing events like this is slightly more complicated, not because of the function calls involved or the design required to support it, but because of the annoying decisions you have to make in choosing which events you want to process, which you want to ignore, and which you want to put off till later. For example, say you are generating a complicated graphic directly into an X window (say, a DrawingArea), and you are busily processing away. What do you do if you get an incoming **ButtonPress** event? An **Expose** event? A **ConfigureNotify** event? You might answer, "It depends on the widget or the window."

That's a step in the right direction. So, let's get closer to the problem by analyzing how you actually go about testing for and processing X events yourself. In order to support the code fragment shown above, we need to provide functions that:

1. Turn on *timeout cursors* on all shells with which the user should not be interacting.

2. Post a WorkingDialog that displays an appropriate message and optionally provides a **Stop** button that terminates the job.

3. Process all "important" events, such as those causing widgets to be repainted, or that which calls the callback for the **Stop** button (but for *no* other widgets).

4. Turn off timeout cursors and take down the WorkingDialog.

Looking into the future a little, we will learn that it may be necessary for these functions to retain internal state information so they may be called multiple times without confusion. We'll get to this in a moment. For the time being, the program listed in Example 20-4 supports each of these requirements as well as compacting the API into fewer, more compact functions. The code is as follows:

Example 20-4. The busy.c program

```
/* busy.c -- demonstrate how to use a WorkingDialog and to process
 * only "important" events.  e.g., those that may interrupt the
 * task or to repaint widgets for exposure.  Set up a simple shell
 * and a widget that, when pressed, immediately goes into its own
 * loop.  First, "lock" the shell so that a timeout cursor is set on
 * the shell and pop up a WorkingDialog.  Then enter loop ... sleep
 * for one second ten times, checking between each interval to see
 * if the user clicked the Stop button or if any widgets need to be
 * refreshed.  Ignore all other events.
 *
 * main() and get_busy() are stubs that would be replaced by a real
 * application; all other functions can be used "as is."
 */
#include <Xm/MessageB.h>
#include <Xm/PushB.h>
#include <X11/cursorfont.h>

Widget shell;
void TimeoutCursors();
Boolean CheckForInterrupt();

main(argc, argv)
int argc;
char *argv[ ];
{
    XtAppContext app;
    Widget button;
    XmString label;
    void get_busy();

    shell = XtVaAppInitialize(&app, "Demos",
        NULL, 0, &argc, argv, NULL, NULL);

    label = XmStringCreateSimple(
        "Boy, is *this* going to take a long time.");
    button = XtVaCreateManagedWidget("button",
```

Example 20-4. The busy.c program (continued)

```
            xmPushButtonWidgetClass, shell,
            XmNlabelString,            label,
            NULL);
    XmStringFree(label);
    XtAddCallback(button, XmNactivateCallback, get_busy, argv[1]);

    XtRealizeWidget(shell);
    XtAppMainLoop(app);
}

void
get_busy(widget)
Widget widget;
{
    int n;

    TimeoutCursors(True, True);
    for (n = 0; n < 10; n++) {
        sleep(1);
        if (CheckForInterrupt()) {
            puts("Interrupt!");
            break;
        }
    }
    if (n == 10)
        puts("done.");
    TimeoutCursors(False, NULL);
}

/* The interesting part of the program -- extract and use at will */
static Boolean stopped;   /* True when user wants to stop processing */
static Widget dialog;     /* WorkingDialog displayed when timed out */

/* timeout_cursors() turns on the "watch" cursor over the application
 * to provide feedback for the user that he's going to be waiting
 * a while before he can interact with the application again.
 */
void
TimeoutCursors(on, interruptable)
int on, interruptable;
{
    static int locked;
    static Cursor cursor;
    extern Widget shell;
    XSetWindowAttributes attrs;
    Display *dpy = XtDisplay(shell);
    XEvent event;
    Arg args[1];
    XmString str;
    extern void stop();

    /* "locked" keeps track if we've already called the function.
     * This allows recursion and is necessary for most situations.
     */
    on? locked++ : locked--;
    if (locked > 1 || locked == 1 && on == 0)
        return; /* already locked and we're not unlocking */

    stopped = False; /* doesn't matter at this point; initialize */
```

Example 20-4. The busy.c program (continued)

```
    if (!cursor) /* make sure the timeout cursor is initialized */
        cursor = XCreateFontCursor(dpy, XC_watch);

    /* if "on" is true, then turn on watch cursor, otherwise, return
     * the shell's cursor to normal.
     */
    attrs.cursor = on? cursor : None;

    /* change the main application shell's cursor to be the timeout
     * cursor (or to reset it to normal).  If other shells exist in
     * this application, they will have to be listed here in order
     * for them to have timeout cursors too.
     */
    XChangeWindowAttributes(dpy, XtWindow(shell), CWCursor, &attrs);

    XFlush(dpy);

    if (on) {
        /* we're timing out, put up a WorkingDialog.  If the process
         * is interruptable, allow a "Stop" button.  Otherwise, remove
         * all actions so the user can't stop the processing.
         */
        str = XmStringCreateSimple("Busy.  Please Wait.");
        XtSetArg(args[0], XmNmessageString, str);
        dialog = XmCreateWorkingDialog(shell, "Busy", args, 1);
        XmStringFree(str);
        XtUnmanageChild(
            XmMessageBoxGetChild(dialog, XmDIALOG_OK_BUTTON));
        if (interruptable) {
            str = XmStringCreateSimple("Stop");
            XtVaSetValues(dialog, XmNcancelLabelString, str, NULL);
            XmStringFree(str);
            XtAddCallback(dialog, XmNcancelCallback, stop, NULL);
        } else
            XtUnmanageChild(
                XmMessageBoxGetChild(dialog, XmDIALOG_CANCEL_BUTTON));
        XtUnmanageChild(
            XmMessageBoxGetChild(dialog, XmDIALOG_HELP_BUTTON));
        XtManageChild(dialog);
    } else {
        /* get rid of all button and keyboard events that occurred
         * during the time out.  The user shouldn't have done anything
         * during this time, so flush for button and keypress events.
         * KeyRelease events are not discarded because accelerators
         * require the corresponding release event before normal input
         * can continue.
         */
        while (XCheckMaskEvent(dpy,
                ButtonPressMask | ButtonReleaseMask | ButtonMotionMask
                | PointerMotionMask | KeyPressMask, &event)) {
            /* do nothing */;
        }
        XtDestroyWidget(dialog);
    }
}

/* User Pressed the "Stop" button in dialog. */
void
```

Example 20-4. The busy.c program (continued)

```
stop(dialog)
Widget dialog;
{
    stopped = True;
}

Boolean
CheckForInterrupt()
{
    extern Widget shell;
    Display *dpy = XtDisplay(shell);
    Window win = XtWindow(dialog);
    XEvent event;

    /* Make sure all our requests get to the server */
    XFlush(dpy);

    /* Let motif process all pending exposure events for us. */
    XmUpdateDisplay(shell);

    /* Check the event loop for events in the dialog ("Stop"?) */
    while (XCheckMaskEvent(dpy,
            ButtonPressMask | ButtonReleaseMask | ButtonMotionMask |
            PointerMotionMask | KeyPressMask | KeyReleaseMask,
            &event)) {
        /* got an "interesting" event. */
        if (event.xany.window == win)
            XtDispatchEvent(&event); /* it's in our dialog.. */
        else /* uninteresting event--throw it away and sound bell */
            XBell(dpy, 50);
    }
    return stopped;
}
```

This program is definitely for demonstration purposes only. In order to keep to the subject matter, the main part of the program is quite unrealistic and is only used to support the actual functions we are about to discuss.

We introduce two functions that support the type of functionality outlined earlier. They are `TimeoutCursors( )` and `CheckForInterrupt( )`. In order to demonstrate how the functions are used, the following loop is executed:

```
void
get_busy(widget)
Widget widget;
{
    int n;

    TimeoutCursors(True, True);
    for (n = 0; n < 10; n++) {
        if (CheckForInterrupt()) {
            puts("Interrupt!");
            break;
        }
        sleep(1);
    }
    if (n == 10)
```

```
        puts("done.");
    TimeoutCursors(False, NULL);
}
```

`TimeoutCursors()` is used to turn on and off the "watch" cursor over the main application shell. This is the visual feedback given to the user to let him know that the main window is immune to input. (That is, he should not attempt to interact with objects in areas that have the watch cursor.) In order to make `TimeoutCursors()` aware of the current state of the application, `locked` (a static `int`) remembers how many times the function has been called with **on** being set to `True`. The function does not unlock the windows and take down the WorkingDialog until a matching number of calls has been made with the **on** parameter passed as `False`. This way, lower-level functions in your application can call `TimeoutCursors()` at their beginnings and endings, without affecting higher-level loops that also call the function.

A global variable called `locked` determines whether or not the user clicked on the **Stop** button in the WorkingDialog. It would be better if this were not stored as a global, but associated with a widget (the working dialog, perhaps). But rather than make the example more complicated than it already is, we chose to leave it this way. The `stopped` variable is initialized to `False`. (It won't be reset by subsequent calls, since that has already been checked).

We also store a static `Cursor` object that points to the cursor returned from `XCreateFontCursor()`. This is how the `XC_watch` cursor is loaded from the X server. (This is also why *<X11/cursorfont.h>* is included at the top of the file.) The `shell` widget, which is assumed to be the main ApplicationShell, has its cursor changed to the new watch image using `XChangeWindowAttributes()`. This function is also used to reset the cursor to normal when the **on** parameter is `False`. Here is where you may need to modify the function to support your particular application's needs. For example, if you have multiple ApplicationShells or TopLevelShells, then you might want to construct a loop, setting (or resetting) the watch cursor for each one.

At this point, we need to call `XFlush()` in order to make sure that all our requests are sent to the server. Keep in mind that this function may be called from deep within an application. Many requests to the server may have already been made, so we want to be sure that the server knows about them now. We may need to read the resulting events, if any, in case we are turning off the timeout cursors.

We now determine whether or not we are locking or unlocking the application. If we are locking it, we create and post a WorkingDialog. Note: you don't have to do this; if you do not, then the user will just see the timeout cursor, which should be adequate feedback to indicate that the application is clearly in a "busy" state. Also, since it might take some time, relatively speaking, to actually pop up and down the WorkingDialog, you might want to consider whether or not your task is going to take long enough to warrant the dialog's existence. (You might consider adding a new parameter to the function, indicating whether the dialog is needed.)

The dialog is created with a standard message. (Again, creating dialogs is usually the simplest part of the process.) If the `interruptable` parameter is `True`, then we want to provide a **Stop** button; we do this by changing the label of the **Cancel** button. We also add a callback routine for that item (`XmNcancelCallback`, since it is still the **Cancel** button we're using), which is set to **stop( )**. We'll get back to this in a moment. The other action area buttons needn't be managed.

The application is now in a *busy state*. However, the user has yet to see anything; events need to be processed in order for the dialog to actually be mapped to the screen and the user to interact with it. This is where **CheckForInterrupt( )** comes into play. This function actually tests to see if those events that only require repainting are in the event queue. This is done by calling **XmUpdateDisplay( )**, which is a Motif function that just processes all the **Expose** events in the event queue. If a widget needs repainting, this function will cause the server to flush **Expose** events for windows, possibly causing their associated widgets' redrawing event handlers to be called. While processing all the **Expose** events is useful for most Motif widgets, be careful of those widgets for which you have your own event handlers installed. They will be called at this point, and if they are time-consuming functions, you might find yourself in a bind. You can check to see which windows are going to be repainted before it actually happens (thus, preventing the callback from being called) using **XCheckMaskEvent( )**, described in the next paragraph. We'll return to **Xm-UpdateDisplay( )** in the following section.

After any possible repainting has occurred, we check for "interesting" events in the event queue. Basically, we look for any button or keyboard events. If one has been generated, we extract it directly from the input queue using **XCheckMaskEvent( )**. The form of this function is as follows:

```
Boolean
XCheckMaskEvent(dpy, mask, event)
    Display        *dpy;
    unsigned long   mask;
    XEvent         *event;
```

This is an Xlib function that looks for events in the queue that match the event masks given as the second parameter. The third parameter, a pointer to an **XEvent** structure, is filled in with the event that occurred (provided that one existed). The function returns **False** if no events matching the specified mask were in the queue. In this case, we can return. Otherwise, the event is processed *only* if the event happened within the WorkingDialog window. If it didn't, then the user must have clicked on another widget, or have done something else in the application. Regardless of what he did, it's *illegal* as long as the application is "busy." If he happened to click within the WorkingDialog, then we can process that event because he may have clicked on the **Done** button (provided it was even managed; if it wasn't, it doesn't affect our code here).

Note that **XCheckMaskEvent( )** removes the event from the queue. If you choose not to service an event, you can't stick it back in the queue. If you have gotten an event out of the queue and don't want to service it, then you should set an internal (application-defined) variable or flag that notifies the application that it must eventually deal with the event. You can, if you like, save the event itself (you'll need to allocate a new **Xevent** structure and copy the data) and dispatch it later, when you are prepared to handle it.

Take special note that we do not check for **KeyRelease** events for a very important reason. Consider the following scenario: your application has a pulldown menu item that initiates a long, complicated process. The callback function for this menu item calls **Timeout-Cursors( )** and, subsequently, **CheckForInterrupt( )**. Now, remember how accelerators work: a single keystroke (or sequence thereof) can activate a menu item without the user having to pull down the menu and physically select the menu item. For example, let's say that **Meta-X** is the accelerator for a particular menu item. The user presses the correct key sequence and the callback routine is activated after the initial KeyPresses that triggered the accerlator; *the KeyRelease events associated with the accelerator are still in the queue waiting to be processed.* When we get to `CheckForInterrupt( )`, we would otherwise throw away all those KeyRelease events, since they did not take place in the WorkingDialog. The reason this is a problem is that the X Toolkit Intrinsics keep an internal state machine that determines whether or not any particular sequence of keyboard events is an accelerator or a prefix for one. Since Xt will never get the accompanying KeyRelease events, it will still think the user is in the middle of entering a keyboard accelerator and it will never get out of that state until the matching events are given. The result is that no other keyboard events will work in the application (or, at least, in the Shell where the accelerator took place) until the user happens to type the same accelerator sequence. As obscure as that sounds, it can happen and be considered a bug in your application. There is no bug associated with this behavior, though; the X Toolkit Intrinsics are doing everything they should be. However, it does demonstrate how easily one can get entangled in the intricacies of the X Window System.

Now, back to `CheckForInterrupt( )`...

If the user happens to select the **Stop** button, then the callback routine `stop( )` is called, which merely sets the `stopped` variable to `True`. When `CheckForInterrupt( )` is about to return, `stopped` will have been set and the function will therefore return `True`. As noted earlier, if the WorkingDialog was never created, or if it did not have its **Stop** button managed, then `stopped` will never be set to `True`. Thus, you have all the possibilities for which kind of timeouts you want to provide.

Whether or not `CheckForInterrupt( )` returns `True` or `False`, `TimeoutCursors( )` is called again in order to "unlock" the application. This time, the function does just about the same thing that `CheckForInterrupt( )` does: it looks in the queue for button or keyboard events, but this time, it throws them all away, since there could have been no useful input at all by now. Also, the WorkingDialog is destroyed.

In a sense, the `TimeoutCursors( )` function implements a level of modality, similar to the kind discussed in Chapter 5, *Introduction to Dialogs*, Section 5.7.1, *Implementing Modal Dialogs*. Using the material in that section, however, will not necessarily provide you with what you need to do to process events for long tasks that happen in the background. Modality, however, would certainly simplify some of the work necessary to implement these tasks.

20.2.4 Caveats with XmUpdateDisplay()

As discussed earlier, `XmUpdateDisplay( )` checks the event queue for all **Expose** events and processes them immediately. However, there are problems that may arise under certain conditions. Consider the scenario:

1. Create or pop up a dialog that contains a drawing surface (a DrawingArea widget, for example).

2. Call **XSync( )** and **XmUpdateDisplay( )** to make sure it is up on the screen and fully exposed.

3. Call **XClearWindow( )** to make sure it is clear.

4. Begin drawing.

You faithfully follow this procedure only to find that nothing is drawn. The problem is due to some redirection of events from the window manager and the way events are processed and queued. By creating a dialog, the client program calls **XtManageChild( )** and/or **Xt-Popup( )**, which calls **XMapRaised( )** (so that the window will be raised to the top of the window stack). Calling **XSync( )** causes the **MapRequest** to go to the server, which redirects it to the window manager (e.g., *mwm*). This is where the bottleneck occurs; if the window manager is "swapped out" (a side effect of multi-tasking operating systems such as UNIX), then *mwm* might not react right away to the redirection and may take an indeterminate amount of time to respond. The X server doesn't take this into account; it just thinks that the event has been delivered properly and your application believes that the window has been mapped. You then proceed to clear the window and draw. Unfortunately, the X server's statement of "I've executed your MapWindow request" doesn't mean the same as "I've successfully mapped the window to the screen." As a result, **XmUpdateDisplay( )** doesn't get the **Expose** event that you were expecting, so drawing does no good because the window still hasn't been mapped.

When *mwm* finally gets around to mapping the window to the screen, the server generates the **Expose** event you thought may have been generated before. By now, your application has processed its event queue and is off doing something more useful.

There are several solutions to this problem. First, you could change the design of your application so that you don't start drawing until the server actually generates the **Expose** events you're waiting for. In this case, you should create and/or pop up your dialog and immediately return to the main event-processing loop (**XtAppMainLoop( )**). If you have properly installed an event handler or a translation for the **Expose** event, then it will be called at the appropriate time and you may continue to process your exposure events properly. Another advantage to this design is that your drawing procedure is called *anytime* an **Expose** event occurs, ensuring that your window will always be up-to-date.

The second solution should be used only if you must create, pop up, or manage a dialog and immediately draw into the window. In other words, if you must draw into a window immediately, you can use the methods we employ in **ForceUpdate( )** listed in Example 20-5.

Example 20-5. The ForceUpdate() function

```
/* This function is a superset of XmUpdateDisplay() in that it will
 * ensure that a window's contents are visible before returning.
 * The monitoring of window states is necessary because attempts to
 * map a window is subject to the whim of the window manager -- this
 * introduces a significant delay before the window is actually mapped
 * and exposed.
 *
 * This function is intended to be called after XtPopup(), XtManageChild()
 * or XMapRaised() on a widget (or window, for XMapRaised()).  Don't use
 * this for other situations as it might sit and process other un-related
```

Example 20-5. The ForceUpdate() function (continued)

```
 * events till the widget becomes visible.
 */
ForceUpdate(w)
Widget w; /* This widget must be visible before the function returns */
{
    Widget diashell, topshell;
    Window diawindow, topwindow;
    XtAppContext cxt = XtWidgetToApplicationContext(w);
    Display *dpy;
    XWindowAttributes xwa;
    XEvent event;

    /* Locate the shell we are interested in */
    for (diashell = w; !XtIsShell(diashell); diashell = XtParent(diashell))
        ;

    /* Locate its primary window's shell (which may be the same) */
    for (topshell = diashell; !XtIsTopLevelShell(topshell);
            topshell = XtParent(topshell))
        ;

    /* If the dialog shell (or its primary shell window) is not realized,
     * don't bother ... nothing can possibly happen.
     */
    if (XtIsRealized(diashell) && XtIsRealized(topshell)) {
        dpy = XtDisplay(topshell);
        diawindow = XtWindow(diashell);
        topwindow = XtWindow(topshell);

        /* Wait for the dialog to be mapped.  It's guaranteed to become so */
        while (XGetWindowAttributes(dpy, diawindow, &xwa) &&
                xwa.map_state != IsViewable) {

            /* ...if the primary is (or becomes) unviewable or unmapped,
             * it's probably iconic, and nothing will happen.
             */
            if (XGetWindowAttributes(dpy, topwindow, &xwa) &&
                xwa.map_state != IsViewable)
                break;

            /* we are guaranteed there will be an event of some kind. */
            XtAppNextEvent(cxt, &event);
            XtDispatchEvent(&event);
        }
    }

    /* The next XSync() will get an expose event. */
    XmUpdateDisplay(topshell);
}
```

20.2.5 Avoid Using Forks

Before we close out this section, there is one more method of of executing tasks in the background that we have yet to discuss. Beginning programmers tend to use library functions and system calls such as **system( )**, **popen( )**, **fork( )**, and **exec( )** to solve the problem of executing external commands. Although these functions are perfectly reasonable, they can backfire quite easily on virtually any error condition. Recovering from these errors is the GUI programmer's nightmare, since there are so many different possible conditions to deal with.

The purpose behind using these functions, of course, is to execute some other UNIX program and have it run concurrently with the main application. The **system( )** and **popen( )** functions fork a new process using the **fork( )** system call. They also use some form of **exec( )** so the new child process can execute the external UNIX program. During this procedure, if the new process can't fork, if there is something wrong with the external UNIX command, if there is a communications protocol error, or any one of a dozen other possible error conditions, there is no way for the external program to display error messages as a part of your application. It would be unlikely that the external program would be able to display a dialog box or any sort of reasonable user-interface element. This is because it is illegal for any new process to use any of the widgets or windows in *your* application. Only *one* connection to the server, *per process*, is allowed. If the child process wants to post a dialog, it must establish a new connection to the X server and create an entirely new widget tree. (After all, it is a separate application.) In most cases, this will not happen, since most system utilities do not have graphical user interface front ends. It is also entirely unreasonable to have any expectations whatsoever of the external process, especially since other solutions are much easier.

If a separate process is necessary in order to accomplish a particular task, setting up pipes between the child application and the parent is usually the best alternative. This is superficially done by the **popen( )** function, but that only allows one-way communication and is not the most elegant solution. In any case, it only handles the forking of the new process and setting up half of a two-way pipe. The **popen( )** function is used in several places throughout the book, so you can check the index for those uses.

However, to really handle external processes and pipes properly, you can follow these steps:

1. The parent process calls **pipe( )** to set up entry points for the expected child process' input and output channels (usually, two are needed—one for input and the other for output).

2. The parent process then calls **fork( )** to spawn the new child process.

3. The child side can use **dup2( )** to redirect its own **stdin**, **stdout**, and **stderr** to the other ends of the pipes already set up by the parent. The communication pipeline between the parent and the child are now set up.

4. The parent calls **XtAppAddInput( )** to tell the X Toolkit Intrinsics to monitor an additional file descriptor at the same time it is waiting for input events from the X server.

5. The parent can read any data (e.g., output, error conditions, etc.) sent by the child using **read( )** on the appropriate pipe.

6. Since the parent is still in connection with the X server, it can display the output from the pipe to a dialog, ScrolledText window, or some other widget.

If the child sends data through the pipe to the parent, Xt sees that new data is ready to be read and calls the callback routine associated with **XtAppAddInput( )**. The form of **XtApp-AddInput( )** is as follows:

```
void
XtAppAddInput(app, fd, mask, callback, client_data);
    XtAppContext    app;
    int             fd;
    unsigned long   mask;
    void            (*callback)();
    XtPointer       client_data;
```

The **fd** parameter should be the side of the pipe that the parent uses to read data sent by the child process. The **callback** function is called when there is data to read on the pipe. When the function is called, the **client_data** is passed so that the parent knows the context by which it is being called. You may pass the process ID returned from **fork( )**, for example, so you can use **kill(pid, 0)** to see if the process is still alive. If it is, you can read the data using **read( )** and do whatever you like with it.

This material and discussion is merely presented as an overview, since it is beyond the scope of this book. For example, UNIX signals become a major problem, since the parent is sent signals when the child dies or its process state changes; the child is sent signals that are delivered to the parent by the user or other outside forces; different forms of UNIX require that process groups be set up differently to avoid the rest of the problems with signals. On top of that, you may have problems dealing with file descriptors that are set to be *non-blocking* files, so you may not know whether **read( )** returning 0 means that there is nothing to read, or that the end of file has been reached (the child process has terminated). Incidentally, none of these issues are dealt with appropriately in **popen( )**, so building a new solution would be the best thing to do in the long run. You should really consult your UNIX system's programmer's guide for more information on the techniques used to spawn new processes and to communicate with them appropriately. Once you have a handle on that (most of the work has been done here already), redirecting text from these file descriptors should be relatively easy using the toolkit. That is, just read text from the file descriptor and use that text as the text for arbitrary Motif widgets that display text (like a Text widget).

Further details on **XtAppAddInput( )** and examples of how it can be used are given in Volume Four, *X Toolkit Intrinsics Programming Manual*.

20.3 Dynamic MessageDialog Symbols

Since MessageDialogs are used as the base for many types of predefined Motif dialogs, the identifying element is the image (symbol) displayed in the top-left corner. The pixmaps used by the default dialogs are predefined by the Motif toolkit.

If you are using standard Motif dialogs, it is likely that you would change the dialog's type rather than changing its symbol. Changing the dialog's type effectively changes which of the standard Motif symbols it uses. However, you can change any of the MessageDialog's symbols from its default to one of your own using **XmNsymbolPixmap**:

```
extern Pixmap pix;

XtVaSetValues(dialog, XmNsymbolPixmap, pix, NULL);
```

The value for this resource is a pixmap that must be created beforehand. Once set, however, the pixmap is not copied by the dialog widget. This is in sharp contrast to how Motif widgets deal with **XmStrings**. If the dialog is ever destroyed, you must be sure to free the pixmap it was using unless you are already using it elsewhere. Therefore, if you are going to *knowingly* destroy the dialog (e.g., using **XtDestroyWidget()** on the dialog itself), you should call **XtVaGetValues()** to get the **XmNsymbolPixmap** first. However, the dialog may be destroyed automatically from somewhere else (e.g., you destroy the dialog's *parent*). In this case, you should set up an **XmNdestroyCallback** procedure that is called whenever the dialog is destroyed (no matter who did it).

While this seems rather simple, doing this right probably involves more work that you might have guessed. Example 20-6 shows how a dialog's symbol can be installed in a standard MessageDialog and how it goes about cleaning up after itself.

Example 20-6. The warn_msg.c program

```
/* warn_msg.c -- display a very urgent warning message.
 * Really catch the user's attention by flashing an urgent-
 * looking pixmap every 250 milliseconds.
 * The program demonstrates how to set the XmNsymbolPixmap
 * resource, how to destroy the pixmap and how to use timers
 * (XtAppAddTimeOut()).
 */
#include <Xm/MessageB.h>
#include <Xm/PushB.h>

/* main() --create a pushbutton whose callback pops up a dialog box */
main(argc, argv)
char *argv[ ];
{
    XtAppContext app;
    Widget toplevel, button;
    XmString label;
    void warning();

    toplevel = XtVaAppInitialize(&app, "Demos",
        NULL, 0, &argc, argv, NULL, NULL);

    label = XmStringCreateSimple(
        "Don't Even Think About Pressing This Button");
    button = XtVaCreateManagedWidget("button",
```

Example 20-6. The warn_msg.c program (continued)

```
                xmPushButtonWidgetClass, toplevel,
                XmNlabelString,          label,
                NULL);
        XmStringFree(label);

        /* set up callback to popup warning with random message */
        XtAddCallback(button, XmNactivateCallback, warning,
            "Alert!\nThe computer room is ON FIRE!\n\
            (All your e-mail will be lost.)");

        XtRealizeWidget(toplevel);
        XtAppMainLoop(app);
}

#include "bang0.symbol"
#include "bang1.symbol"

/* define the data structure we need to implement flashing effect */
typedef struct {
    XtIntervalId   id;
    int            which;
    Pixmap         pix1, pix2;
    Widget         dialog;
    XtAppContext   app;
} TimeOutClientData;

/* The callback routine for the push button.  Create a message
 * dialog and set the message string.  Allocate an instance of
 * the TimeOutClientData structure and set a timer to alternate
 * between the two pixmaps.  The data is passed to the timeout
 * routine and the callback for when the user presses "OK".
 */
void
warning(parent, help_text)
Widget parent;
char *help_text;
{
    Widget         dialog;
    XtAppContext   app = XtWidgetToApplicationContext(parent);
    XmString       text;
    extern void    done(), destroy_it(), blink();
    Display        *dpy = XtDisplay(parent);
    int            screen = DefaultScreen(dpy);
    Pixel          fg, bg;
    Arg            args[2];
    TimeOutClientData *data = XtNew(TimeOutClientData);

    /* Create the dialog -- the "cancel" button says OK */
    text = XmStringCreateSimple("OK");
    XtSetArg(args[0], XmNcancelLabelString, text);
    XtSetArg(args[1], XmNdeleteResponse, XmDESTROY);
    dialog = XmCreateMessageDialog(parent, "danger", args, 2);
    XmStringFree(text);

    XtUnmanageChild(  /* no need for the ok button */
        XmMessageBoxGetChild(dialog, XmDIALOG_OK_BUTTON), False);
    XtUnmanageChild(  /* no need for the help button */
        XmMessageBoxGetChild(dialog, XmDIALOG_HELP_BUTTON), False);
    /* The cancel button is the only button left... */
```

Example 20-6. The warn_msg.c program (continued)

```
    XtAddCallback(dialog, XmNcancelCallback, done, NULL);

    XtAddCallback(dialog, XmNdestroyCallback, destroy_it, data);

    /* now that dialog has been created, its colors are initialized */
    XtVaGetValues(dialog,
        XmNforeground, &fg,
        XmNbackground, &bg,
        NULL);

    /* Create pixmaps that are going to be used as symbolPixmaps.
     * Use the foreground and background colors of the dialog.
     */
    data->pix1 = XCreatePixmapFromBitmapData(dpy, XtWindow(parent),
        bang0_bits, bang0_width, bang0_height,
        fg, bg, DefaultDepth(dpy, screen));
    data->pix2 = XCreatePixmapFromBitmapData(dpy, XtWindow(parent),
        bang1_bits, bang1_width, bang1_height,
        fg, bg, DefaultDepth(dpy, screen));
    /* complete the timeout client data */
    data->dialog = dialog;
    data->app = app;

    /* Add the timeout for blinking effect */
    data->id = XtAppAddTimeOut(app, 1000L, blink, data);

    /* display the help text and the appropriate pixmap */
    text = XmStringCreateLtoR(help_text, XmSTRING_DEFAULT_CHARSET);
    XtVaSetValues(dialog,
        XmNmessageString,       text,
        XmNsymbolPixmap,        data->pix2,
        NULL);
    XmStringFree(text);

    XtManageChild(dialog);
    XtPopup(XtParent(dialog), XtGrabNone);
}
/* blink() --visual blinking effect for dialog's symbol.  Displays
 * flashing "!" symbol. Also, restart timer and save timer id.
 */
void
blink(data)
TimeOutClientData *data;
{
    data->id = XtAppAddTimeOut(data->app, 250L, blink, data);
    XtVaSetValues(data->dialog,
        XmNsymbolPixmap,   (data->which = !data->which)?
            data->pix1 : data->pix2,
        NULL);
}
/* done() --called when user presses "Ok" in HelpDialog or
 * if the user picked the Close button in system menu.
 * Remove the timeout id stored in data, free pixmaps and
 * make sure the widget is destroyed (which is only when
 * the user presses the "Ok" button.
 */
void
```

Example 20-6. The warn_msg.c program (continued)

```
done(dialog)
Widget dialog; /* happens to be the same as data->dialog */
{
    XtDestroyWidget(dialog);
}

void
destroy_it(dialog, data)
Widget dialog; /* happens to be the same as data->dialog */
TimeOutClientData *data;
{
    Pixmap symbol;

    XtRemoveTimeOut(data->id);
    XFreePixmap(XtDisplay(data->dialog), data->pix1);
    XFreePixmap(XtDisplay(data->dialog), data->pix2);
    XtFree(data);
}
```

The output of *warn_msg.c* is shown in Figure 20-5 and Figure 20-6.

The dialog is created in **warning( )**, the callback routine for the PushButton in the main window. The routine is set up to be called from anywhere in the program; all it needs is a widget to act as the parent for the dialog it creates and a message to display. The dialog created is a normal MessageDialog whose **XmNsymbolPixmap** is created manually. Since we are not using any other type of MessageDialog (one with a predefined symbol), there is no reason to get a handle to its pixmap and free it. However, should you ever find yourself reusing another MessageDialog type, you should get its pixmap and free it using **XmDestroy-Pixmap( )** rather than **XFreePixmap( )**. This is because the Motif dialogs use **Xm-GetPixmap( )** to generate their images and **XmDestroyPixmap( )** is its companion routine. (One should always be used with the other.) See Chapter 11, *Labels and Buttons*, for a discussion on **XmGetPixmap( )**.

This particular dialog is going to have two symbols, which are exchanged every 250 milliseconds through the use of a timer callback routine. This is the entire design of the program. However, to implement it, we must associate certain information specifically with the dialog itself. For example, the pixmaps must be created and attached to the dialog, a timer callback must be installed so that it can switch between the two alternating pixmaps, the routine must keep track of which pixmap to use, and the dialog must be able to clean up after itself once it's is no longer needed.

Figure 20-5. Output of warn_msg.c (part 1)

Figure 20-6. Output of warn_msg.c (part 2)

By placing all this information into a single data structure, we can create as many of these objects as necessary in order to allow an arbitrary number of dialogs to pop up:

```
typedef struct {
    XtIntervalId    id;
    int             which;
    Pixmap          pix1, pix2;
    Widget          dialog;
    XtAppContext    app;
} TimeOutClientData;
```

The **warning( )** function first allocates a new instance of this structure using **XtNew( )**, since a new dialog is going to be created and there must be a unique structure for each one. The function **XmCreateMessageDialog( )** creates a new instance of a MessageDialog. The **dialog** field of the **TimeOutClientData** points to the new dialog.

Foreshadowing what is to come, we know that the user is going to dismiss the dialog in one of two ways: with the **Ok** button, which is the method we expect, or with the **Close** button from the system menu attached to the MessageDialog. This is a key item that most programmers forget about. This latter case is handled by setting `XmNdeleteResponse` to `XmDESTROY`, indicating that Motif should destroy the dialog if the **Close** button is used.

Since we are not reusing the dialog or its data, we must be sure to handle the cleanup of the pixmaps, release the timer, and free the allocated data structure when the dialog is destroyed. To be sure that all of this gets done when the dialog is destroyed, no matter how its fate may come about, we install a callback function for the `XmNdestroyCallback` resource. The function is `destroy_it( )`.

The dialog's **Ok** and **Help** buttons are unmanaged and the **Cancel** button's label is changed to read **Ok**, since it's the only one we're using and it should be centered. It's callback routine, `done( )`, is called whenever **Ok** is activated. In turn, it calls `XtDestroyWidget( )`, which causes the `XmNdestroyCallback` to be called, which does all the cleanup.

Before we create the pixmaps to be used in the dialog, the dialog's foreground and background colors are retrieved via `XtVaGetValues( )` in order for the new pixmaps to share the same colors. Otherwise, they won't look right. Once the colors are known, we can create the pixmaps and finish initializing the fields in the new `TimeOutClientData` structure:

```
/* now that dialog has been created, its colors are initialized */
XtVaGetValues(dialog,
    XmNforeground, &fg,
    XmNbackground, &bg,
    NULL);

/* Create pixmaps that are going to be used as symbolPixmaps.
 * Use the foreground and background colors of the dialog.
 */
data->pix1 = XCreatePixmapFromBitmapData(dpy, XtWindow(parent),
    bang0_bits, bang0_width, bang0_height,
    fg, bg, DefaultDepth(dpy, screen));
data->pix2 = XCreatePixmapFromBitmapData(dpy, XtWindow(parent),
    bang1_bits, bang1_width, bang1_height,
    fg, bg, DefaultDepth(dpy, screen));
/* complete the timeout client data */
data->dialog = dialog;
data->app = app;
```

At this point, the timer can be started (give it a one-second head start).

Once everything is set up, the function returns (control is returned to the Intrinsics) where normal event-processing resumes. After the initial one-second interval times out, the `blink( )` function is called, which adds another timeout for 250 milliseconds and switches the pixmaps displayed in the dialog. This loop continues until the user either presses the **Ok** button (causing `done( )` to be called) or destroys the window using the **Close** button in the titlebar's system menu. Either way, the dialog is destroyed, causing its `XmNdestroyCallback` function (`destroy_it( )`) to be invoked. This is where the pixmaps are freed, the timer is removed, and the `TimeOutClientData` is freed.

Although the task of changing the symbol pixmap is quite simple, using the feature effectively requires a lot of design and supporting code. Adding the timeouts didn't complicate the program much—everything else had to be there anyway to assure that all possible pointers and data structures were destroyed at the appropriate time. Being meticulous about cleaning up after destroyed widgets and other objects is sometimes a difficult task because of the many ways the user can destroy them. However, filling these possible memory leaks will enable your program to run longer and more efficiently.

20.4 Summary

Real applications produce interesting problems, which cannot necessarily be solved by Motif alone. Motif provides the user interface, but you must make it work with your application. A solid understanding of X window system fundamentals, and how X relates to the underlying operating system, will stand you in good stead when it comes time to face the real world.

A

Motif Functions and Macros

This appendix lists the syntax of every Motif library function.

A
Motif Functions and Macros

This appendix summarizes the routines in the Motif Toolkit. The routines are presented alphabetically, beginning with a brief description and followed by the routine's calling sequence. The calling sequence also lists the include file, unless it is *<Xm/Xm.h>*. Some arguments take defined constants as values, and these values are listed after the calling sequence. Callback structure definitions for particular widget classes are listed in Appendix B, *Xt and Motif Widget Classes*.

Protocols

Motif allows you to define protocols, which are communication channels between applications. Protocols are simply atoms, stored in a property on the top-level shell window for the application. To activate the protocol, a client sends a ClientMessage event containing a property and protocol; the receiving client responds by calling the associated protocol callback routine. A set of predefined protocols for communication between clients and the window manager are stored in the property XA_WM_PROTOCOL.

XmActivateProtocol

Activates the specified *protocol*. (I.e., this routine makes the shell able to respond to Client-Message events containing this protocol.) If *shell* is realized, XmActivateProtocol() updates its protocol handlers and the specified *property*. If *protocol* is active, the protocol atom is stored in *property*; if *protocol* is inactive, the protocol atom is not stored in *property*. *<Xm/MwmUtil.h>* defines some of the possible values for *property*. The protocol must first be added to *shell* with XmAddProtocols(). The inverse routine is XmDeactivateProtocol(). Protocols are automatically activated when they are added.

```
#include <Xm/Protocols.h>
void XmActivateProtocol (shell, property, protocol)
    Widget      shell;        /* widget associated with the protocol property */
    Atom        property;     /* property that will hold protocol data for shell */
    Atom        protocol;     /* atom ID of protocol */
```

XmActivateWMProtocol

A convenience routine that calls XmActivateProtocol() with *property* set to XA_WM_PROTOCOL, the window manager protocol property. The protocol must first be added to *shell* with

XmAddProtocols() or XmWMAddProtocols(). The inverse routine is XmDeactivateWMProtocol(). Protocols are automatically activated when they are added.

```
#include <Xm/Protocols.h>
void XmActivateWMProtocol (shell, protocol)
    Widget          shell;          /* widget associated with the protocol property */
    Atom            protocol;       /* atom ID of protocol */
```

XmAddProtocolCallback

Adds client callbacks for the specified *protocol*. If *protocol* isn't registered, XmAddProtocol-Callback() calls XmAddProtocols(), thereby adding *callback* to the internal callback list. These callback procedures are invoked when a client message event containing the *protocol* atom is received. *<Xm/MwmUtil.h>* defines some of the possible values for *property*. The inverse routine is XmRemoveProtocolCallback(). See also XmSetProtocolHooks().

```
#include <Xm/Protocols.h>
void XmAddProtocolCallback (shell, property, protocol, callback, closure)
    Widget          shell;          /* widget associated with the protocol property */
    Atom            property;       /* property that will hold protocol data for shell */
    Atom            protocol;       /* atom ID of protocol */
    XtCallbackProc  callback;       /* procedure to call when a protocol message is received */
    caddr_t         closure;        /* client data to pass to callback when it's invoked */
```

XmAddProtocols

Registers a list of protocols to be stored in the specified *property* of the specified *shell* widget. *<Xm/MwmUtil.h>* defines some of the possible values for *property*. The inverse routine is Xm-RemoveProtocols(). You must use XmAddProtocolCallback() to add a callback function to be executed when a client message event containing the specified protocol atom is received.

```
#include <Xm/Protocols.h>
void XmAddProtocols (shell, property, protocols, num_protocols)
    Widget          shell;          /* widget associated with the protocol property */
    Atom            property;       /* property that will hold protocol data for shell */
    Atom            *protocols;     /* points to list of protocol atom IDs */
    Cardinal        num_protocols;  /* number of elements in protocols */
```

XmAddTabGroup

Makes the specified widget a separate tab group. This routine is retained for compatibility with Motif 1.0 and should not be used in newer applications. If traversal behavior needs to be changed, this should be done by directly setting the XmNnavigationType resource (defined by Manager and Primitive). A tab group is a group of widgets that can be traversed using the keyboard rather than the mouse. Users move from widget to widget within a single tab group by pressing the arrow keys. Users move between different tab groups by pressing the Tab or Shift-Tab keys. If the *tab_group* widget is a manager, its children will all be members of the tab group (unless they are made into separate tab groups). If the widget is a primitive, it will be its own tab group. Certain widgets must not be included with other widgets within a tab group. For example, each List, Scrollbar, OptionMenu, or multiline Text widget must be placed in a tab group by itself, since these widgets define special behavior for the arrow or

Tab keys (preventing the use of these keys for widget traversal). The inverse routine is Xm-RemoveTabGroup().

```
void XmAddTabGroup (tab_group)
    Widget          tab_group;          /* widget ID of Manager or Primitive widget */
```

XmAddWMProtocolCallback

A convenience routine that calls XmAddProtocolCallback() with *property* set to XA_WM_PROTO-COL, the window manager protocol property. The inverse routine is XmRemoveWMProtocol-Callback().

```
#include <Xm/Protocols.h>
void XmAddWMProtocolCallback (shell, protocol, callback, closure)
    Widget          shell;          /* widget associated with the protocol property */
    Atom            protocol;       /* atom ID of protocol */
    XtCallbackProc  callback;       /* procedure to call when a protocol message is received */
    caddr_t         closure;        /* client data to pass to callback when it's invoked */
```

XmAddWMProtocols

A convenience routine that calls XmAddProtocols() with *property* set to XA_WM_PROTOCOL, the window manager protocol property. The inverse routine is XmRemoveWMProtocols().

```
#include <Xm/Protocols.h>
void XmAddWMProtocols (shell, protocols, num_protocols)
    Widget          shell;          /* widget associated with the protocol property */
    Atom            *protocols;     /* points to list of protocol atom IDs */
    Cardinal        num_protocols;  /* number of elements in protocols */
```

XmCascadeButtonGadgetHighlight

Sets the state of the shadow highlight around the specified cascade button gadget. Xm-CascadeButtonGadgetHighlight() draws the shadow if *highlight* is True and erases the shadow if *highlight* is False.

```
#include <Xm/CascadeBG.h>
void XmCascadeButtonGadgetHighlight (button, highlight)
    Widget          button;         /* button to highlight or unhighlight */
    Boolean         highlight;      /* whether to highlight (True) or to unhighlight (False) */
```

XmCascadeButtonHighlight

Sets the state of the shadow highlight around the specified cascade button or cascade button gadget. XmCascadeButtonHighlight() draws the shadow if *highlight* is True and erases the shadow if *highlight* is False.

```
#include <Xm/CascadeB.h>
void XmCascadeButtonHighlight (button, highlight)
    Widget          button;         /* CascadeButton or CascadeButtonGadget to set */
    Boolean         highlight;      /* whether to highlight (True) or to unhighlight (False) */
```

Clipboard Routines

The Motif toolkit provides 17 cut and paste routines for use with the clipboard. These routines return an integer status constant, expressed as one of the six clipboard constants defined in *<Xm/CutPaste.h>*:

ClipboardSuccess	/* the routine is successful */
ClipboardFail	/* failure for various reasons (see specific routine) */
ClipboardLocked	/* routine failed: clipboard was locked by another application */
ClipboardNoData	/* clipboard is empty, or requested format wasn't found */
ClipboardTruncate	/* data was truncated--specified buffer too small to hold data */
ClipboardBadFormat	/* format name was NULL, or its length wasn't 8, 16, or 32 */

All of these routines can return ClipboardSuccess, but the other possible return values are listed for each clipboard routine.

XmClipboardCancelCopy

Cancels the copy in progress and frees temporary storage. A call to XmClipboardCancelCopy() is valid only between calls to XmClipboardStartCopy() and XmClipboardEndCopy(). XmClipboardCancelCopy() can be called instead of XmClipboardEndCopy() to abort the copying operation. Returns ClipboardFail if XmClipboardStartCopy() wasn't called or if the data item has too many formats; can also return ClipboardLocked.

```
#include <Xm/CutPaste.h>
int XmClipboardCancelCopy (display, window, item_id)
    Display      *display;      /* points to Display structure */
    Window       window;        /* window ID that identifies client to the clipboard */
    long         item_id;       /* ID of data item (from XmClipboardStartCopy()) */
```

XmClipboardCopy

Copies the data item specified by *buffer* to temporary storage. Since the data item is not actually stored in the clipboard until XmClipboardEndCopy() is called, multiple calls to XmClipboardCopy() will add data item formats to the same data item or will append data to an existing format. If *buffer* is NULL, the data is thought of as being passed by name, and a unique number is returned in *data_id* that identifies the data item for later use. When another application requests data that's been passed by name, two things happen: a callback requesting the actual data will be sent to the application that owns it, and the owner must then call XmClipboardCopyByName() to transfer the data to the clipboard. Once data that is passed by name has been deleted from the clipboard, a callback notifies the owner that the data is no longer needed. Returns ClipboardFail if XmClipboardStartCopy() wasn't called or if the data item has too many formats; can also return ClipboardLocked.

```
#include <Xm/CutPaste.h>
int XmClipboardCopy (display, window, item_id, format_name, buffer, length, private_id, data_id)
    Display        *display;        /* points to Display structure */
    Window         window;          /* window ID that identifies client to the clipboard */
    long           item_id;         /* ID of data item (from XmClipboardStartCopy()) */
    char           *format_name;    /* string name of data format */
    char           *buffer;         /* buffer from which data is copied to clipboard */
    unsigned long  length;          /* length (in bytes) of data copied to clipboard */
```

| int | private_id; | /* private data to store with data item */ |
| int | *data_id; | /* returns unique ID for data passed by name */ |

XmClipboardCopyByName

Copies the actual data of a data item previously passed by name. Data is "passed by name" when XmClipboardCopy() is called with a *buffer* value of NULL. This routine is typically used for incremental copying: new data is appended to existing data with each call to XmClipboard-CopyByName(). Copying by name improves performance when there is a large amount of clipboard data and when this data is likely never to be retrieved, since the data itself isn't copied to the clipboard until it's requested with a retrieval operation. Can also return ClipboardLocked.

```
#include <Xm/CutPaste.h>
int XmClipboardCopyByName (display, window, data_id, buffer, length, private_id)
    Display         *display;      /* points to Display structure */
    Window          window;        /* window ID that identifies client to the clipboard */
    int             data_id;       /* data ID previously assigned by XmClipboardCopy() */
    char            *buffer;       /* buffer from which data is copied to clipboard */
    unsigned long   length;        /* length (in bytes) of data copied to clipboard */
    int             private_id;    /* private data to store with data item */
```

Motif Functions and Macros

XmClipboardEndCopy

Locks the clipboard, places data (that has been accumulated by calling XmClipboardCopy()) into the clipboard data structure, and unlocks the clipboard, thus allowing access to it by other applications. XmClipboardEndCopy() frees temporary storage and doesn't need to be called if XmClipboardCancelCopy() has already been called. Returns ClipboardFail if Xm-ClipboardStartCopy() wasn't called; can also return ClipboardLocked.

```
#include <Xm/CutPaste.h>
int XmClipboardEndCopy (display, window, item_id)
    Display     *display;      /* points to Display structure */
    Window      window;        /* window ID that identifies client to the clipboard */
    long        item_id;       /* ID of data item (from XmClipboardStartCopy()) */
```

XmClipboardEndRetrieve

Suspends the incremental copying of data from the clipboard. A call to XmClipboardStart-Retrieve() begins the incremental copy, and calls to XmClipboardRetrieve() incrementally retrieve the data items from clipboard storage. Can also return ClipboardLocked.

```
#include <Xm/CutPaste.h>
int XmClipboardEndRetrieve (display, window)
    Display     *display;      /* points to Display structure */
    Window      window;        /* window ID that identifies client to the clipboard */
```

XmClipboardInquireCount

Returns two pieces of information about the format of the current clipboard item: namely, the number of formats within the data item and the length of its longest format name. Can also return ClipboardLocked or ClipboardNoData.

```
#include <Xm/CutPaste.h>
int XmClipboardInquireCount (display, window, count, max_format_name_length)
    Display      *display;      /* points to Display structure */
    Window       window;       /* window ID that identifies client to the clipboard */
    int          *count;        /* returns number of formats for clipboard's data item */
    int          *max_length;   /* length of longest format name */
```

XmClipboardInquireFormat

Returns a format name for the current data item in the clipboard. The format name returned is specified by *index*, where 0 refers to the first *index*. If *index* exceeds the number of formats contained in the data item, then XmClipboardInquireFormat() returns a value of zero for *copied_len*. Can also return ClipboardLocked, ClipboardNoData, or ClipboardTruncate.

```
#include <Xm/CutPaste.h>
int XmClipboardInquireFormat (display, window, index, format_name_buf, buffer_len, copied_len)
    Display        *display;          /* points to Display structure */
    Window         window;           /* window ID that identifies client to the clipboard */
    int            index;            /* position of queried format name within data item */
    char           *format_name_buf;  /* returns buffer that will hold the format name */
    unsigned long  buffer_len;       /* number of bytes within format_name_buf */
    unsigned long  *copied_len;       /* returns length of string (in bytes) copied to buffer */
```

XmClipboardInquireLength

For the current clipboard item, returns the length of the data stored under the specified *format_name*. If no data is found corresponding to *format_name*, or if there is no item on the clipboard, XmClipboardInquireLength() returns a *length* of zero. (Note that for data passed by name, the data's length is assumed to be passed in a call to XmClipboardCopy(), even though the data has yet to be transferred to the clipboard.) Can also return ClipboardLocked or ClipboardNoData.

```
#include <Xm/CutPaste.h>
int XmClipboardInquireLength (display, window, format_name, length)
    Display        *display;      /* points to Display structure */
    Window         window;       /* window ID that identifies client to the clipboard */
    char           *format_name;  /* string name of data format */
    unsigned long  *length;       /* returns length (in bytes) of queried data item */
```

XmClipboardInquirePendingItems

For the specified *format_name*, returns a list of pending *data_id/private_id* pairs (these arguments are specified in the clipboard functions for copying or retrieving). A data item is considered pending under three conditions: the application that owns the data item originally passed it by name, the requesting application has not yet copied the data, and the data item has not been deleted from the clipboard. An application calls this routine before exiting, to determine whether the data passed by name should be copied to the clipboard. The application must free the memory provided by this function (by calling XtFree(), for example). Can also return ClipboardLocked.

```
#include <Xm/CutPaste.h>
int XmClipboardInquirePendingItems (display, window, format_name, item_list, count)
    Display              *display;        /* points to Display structure */
    Window                window;         /* window ID that identifies client to the clipboard */
    char                 *format_name;    /* string name of data format */
    XmClipboardPendingList *item_list;    /* points to array of data_id/private_id pairs */
    unsigned long        *count;          /* returns number of entries that item_list returns*/
```

XmClipboardLock

Prevents access to the clipboard by other applications, thus ensuring that clipboard data isn't changed by calls to other clipboard functions. All clipboard functions lock or unlock the clipboard; however, an application need not lock the clipboard between calls to XmClipboard-StartCopy() and XmClipboardEndCopy() or between calls to XmClipboardStartRetrieve() and Xm-ClipboardEndRetrieve(), because the clipboard is locked automatically between these calls. When XmClipboardLock() is called and the clipboard is already locked by an application, one of two things can happen: if the call was made by the same application, the lock level is increased, but if the call was made by another application, this function returns Clipboard-Locked. XmClipboardUnlock() allows access again to the clipboard.

```
#include <Xm/CutPaste.h>
int XmClipboardLock (display, window)
    Display        *display;       /* points to Display structure */
    Window          window;        /* window ID that identifies client to the clipboard */
```

XmClipboardRegisterFormat

Registers a new format having the specified name and length. The length must be 8, 16, or 32 bits. This routine is used by applications that support cutting and pasting of arbitrary data types. This routine is not needed for types that are already defined by the ICCCM. Returns ClipboardFail if the format was already registered with the specified length; can also return ClipboardLocked or ClipboardBadFormat.

```
#include <Xm/CutPaste.h>
int XmClipboardRegisterFormat (display, format_name, format_length)
    Display        *display;        /* points to Display structure */
    char           *format_name;    /* string name of data format */
    unsigned long   format_length;  /* format's bit length (8, 16, or 32) */
```

XmClipboardRetrieve

Retrieves the current data item from the clipboard and copies it to the specified *buffer*. Multiple calls to this function (between XmClipboardStartRetrieve() and XmClipboardEndRetrieve()) copy additional data incrementally. Can also return ClipboardLocked, ClipboardTruncate, or ClipboardNoData.

```
#include <Xm/CutPaste.h>
int XmClipboardRetrieve (display, window, format_name, buffer, length, num_bytes, private_id)
    Display        *display;        /* points to Display structure */
    Window          window;         /* window ID that identifies client to the clipboard */
    char           *format_name;    /* string name of data format */
    char           *buffer;         /* buffer to which the clipboard copies data */
    unsigned long   length;         /* length (in bytes) of buffer */
    unsigned long  *num_bytes;      /* returns number of bytes copied to buffer */
    int            *private_id;     /* returns private data that was stored with data item */
```

XmClipboardStartCopy

Establishes storage and data structures that will receive clipboard data. For any cut or copy operation, this routine should be called before any other. Several arguments provide identifying information: *window* identifies the widget's window and should be passed to all clipboard routines called by the same application; *item_id* returns a number that is used by the other clipboard copy routines to identify the data item; *clip_label* identifies the data item by assigning a text string that is used, for example, as the label for a clipboard viewing window. Two additional arguments may be specified to pass data by name: *widget* specifies the ID of the widget that will receive callbacks requesting that data be passed by name; *callback* is the procedure to invoke when the clipboard is ready to receive data that was previously passed to it by name. Can also return ClipboardLocked.

```
#include <Xm/CutPaste.h>
int XmClipboardStartCopy (display, window, clip_label, timestamp, widget, callback, item_id)
    Display     *display;       /* points to Display structure */
    Window       window;        /* window ID that identifies client to the clipboard */
    XmString     clip_label;    /* name for data item, useful when viewing */
    Time         timestamp;     /* time member of event that triggered the copy */
    Widget       widget;        /* widget used for requesting data passed by name */
    VoidProc     callback;      /* called when data has been passed by name */
    long        *item_id;       /* returns an ID for the data item */
```

The callback procedure has the following syntax:

```
void <procedure name> (widget, data_id, private, reason)
    Widget       widget;        /* widget ID from call to XmClipboardStartCopy */
    int         *data_id;       /* points to data passed by name*/
    int         *private;       /* private info passed to XmClipboardCopy */
    int         *reason;        /* XmCR_CLIPBOARD_DATA_DELETE or
                                   XmCR_CLIPBOARD_DATA_REQUEST */
```

XmClipboardStartRetrieve

Begins the incremental copying of data from the clipboard. XmClipboardStartRetrieve() locks the clipboard until XmClipboardEndRetrieve() is called. Between calls to these two routines, multiple calls to XmClipboardRetrieve() (with identical *format_name*) copy data incrementally from the clipboard. Can also return ClipboardLocked.

```
#include <Xm/CutPaste.h>
int XmClipboardStartRetrieve (display, window, timestamp)
    Display        *display;       /* points to Display structure */
    Window         window;         /* window ID that identifies client to the clipboard */
    Time           timestamp;      /* time member of event that triggered the copy */
```

XmClipboardUndoCopy

Deletes the item most recently placed on the clipboard, provided that the application that originally placed the item has matching values for *display* and *window* (if not, no action is taken). This routine also restores any data item that was deleted from the clipboard by previously calling XmClipboardCopy(). Can also return ClipboardLocked.

```
#include <Xm/CutPaste.h>
int XmClipboardUndoCopy (display, window)
    Display        *display;       /* points to Display structure */
    Window         window;         /* window ID that identifies client to the clipboard */
```

XmClipboardUnlock

Unlocks the clipboard, thereby allowing applications to access it. Multiple calls to XmClipboardLock() can increase the lock level, and normally, each XmClipboardLock() call requires a corresponding call to XmClipboardUnlock(). However, by setting *remove_all_locks* to True, nested locks can be removed with a single call. Returns ClipboardFail if the clipboard isn't locked or if it is locked by another application.

```
#include <Xm/CutPaste.h>
int XmClipboardUnlock (display, window, remove_all_locks)
    Display        *display;           /* points to Display structure */
    Window         window;             /* window ID that identifies client to the clipboard */
    Boolean        remove_all_locks;   /* if True, unlock all nested locks */
```

XmClipboardWithdrawFormat

Keeps the application from supplying further data to the clipboard. Can also return ClipboardLocked.

```
#include <Xm/CutPaste.h>
int XmClipboardWithdrawFormat (display, window, data_id)
    Display        *display;       /* points to Display structure */
    Window         window;         /* window ID that identifies client to the clipboard */
    int            data_id;        /* data ID previously assigned by XmClipboardCopy() */
```

XmCommandAppendValue

Appends a null-terminated string (specified by *command*) to the string displayed on the command line of the given Command *widget*.

```
#include <Xm/Command.h>
void XmCommandAppendValue (widget, command)
    Widget         widget;         /* widget ID of Command widget */
    XmString       command;        /* text to append to command line */
```

XmCommandError

Displays an error message in the history region of the specified Command *widget*. The error string remains displayed until the next command takes effect.

```
#include <Xm/Command.h>
void XmCommandError (widget, error)
    Widget        widget;      /* widget ID of Command widget */
    XmString      error;       /* error message string to display */
```

XmCommandGetChild

Returns the widget ID of the specified *child* of the Command widget.

```
#include <Xm/Command.h>
Widget XmCommandGetChild (widget, child)
    Widget          widget;    /* widget ID of Command widget */
    unsigned char   child;     /* component whose widget ID is returned */
```

The values for *child* are defined in *<Xm/Xm.h>* and indicate the corresponding widgets:

XmDIALOG_COMMAND_TEXT   XmDIALOG_HISTORY_LIST   XmDIALOG_PROMPT_LABEL

XmCommandSetValue

Replaces a Command widget's currently displayed command-line text with the string specified by *command*. Specifying a zero-length string clears the command line.

```
#include <Xm/Command.h>
void XmCommandSetValue (widget, command)
    Widget        widget;      /* widget ID of Command widget */
    XmString      command;     /* text with which to replace command line */
```

XmConvertUnits

Converts the value specified in *from_value* into the equivalent value in a different unit of measurement. This function returns the resulting value if successful; it returns 0 if *widget* is NULL or if incorrect values are supplied for orientation or conversion unit arguments. *orientation* matters only when conversion values are font units, which are measured differently in the horizontal and vertical directions. Unit types are XmPIXELS by default.

```
int XmConvertUnits (widget, orientation, from_unit_type, from_value, to_unit_type)
    Widget    widget;          /* widget for which to convert data */
    int       orientation;     /* which screen dimension to use */
    int       from_unit_type;  /* unit of measurement of source value */
    int       from_value;      /* value to convert */
    int       to_unit_type;    /* new unit of measurement desired */
```

The values for *orientation* are defined in *<Xm/Xm.h>*:

XmHORIZONTAL   XmVERTICAL

The values for *from_unit_type* and *to_unit_type* are defined in *<Xm/Xm.h>*:

XmPIXELS   Xm100TH_POINTS
Xm100TH_FONT_UNITS   Xm100TH_MILLIMETERS
Xm1000TH_INCHES

Creation Routines

Motif provides 57 routines for creating widgets and gadgets. All of these routines return a widget ID. Since most routines create only one widget, you can usually tell which widget ID is being returned. However, some of the creation routines create a DialogShell or ScrolledWindow parent along with its child. In these cases, the ID returned is that of the child. (Note also that the widget whose ID is returned is always unmanaged.) The creation routines invariably take four arguments: the parent's widget ID, the name of the new widget or gadget, a list of resource name/value pairs, and the number of name/value pairs. See the XmVaCreate... routines for corresponding creation routines using varargs-style variable argument lists.

For more information on various widgets, see Appendix B, *Xt and Motif Widget Classes*.

XmCreateArrowButton

Creates an instance of an ArrowButton widget, returning its widget ID.

```
#include <Xm/ArrowB.h>
Widget XmCreateArrowButton (parent, name, arglist, argcount)
    Widget        parent;      /* widget ID of the new widget's parent */
    String        name;        /* name of the newly created widget */
    ArgList       arglist;     /* resource name/value pairs used in creating widget */
    Cardinal      argcount;    /* number of name/value pairs in arglist */
```

XmCreateArrowButtonGadget

Creates an instance of an ArrowButtonGadget, returning its gadget ID.

```
#include <Xm/ArrowBG.h>
Widget XmCreateArrowButtonGadget (parent, name, arglist, argcount)
    Widget        parent;      /* widget ID of the new gadget's parent */
    String        name;        /* name of the newly created widget */
    ArgList       arglist;     /* resource name/value pairs used in creating widget */
    Cardinal      argcount;    /* number of name/value pairs in arglist */
```

XmCreateBulletinBoard

Creates an instance of a BulletinBoard widget, returning its widget ID.

```
#include <Xm/BulletinB.h>
Widget XmCreateBulletinBoard (parent, name, arglist, argcount)
    Widget      parent;      /* widget ID of the new widget's parent */
    String      name;        /* name of the newly created widget */
    ArgList     arglist;     /* resource name/value pairs used in creating widget */
    Cardinal    argcount;    /* number of name/value pairs in arglist */
```

XmCreateBulletinBoardDialog

A convenience routine for creating a BulletinBoardDialog. This routine creates a Dialog-Shell and then creates an unmanaged BulletinBoard as its child widget. The routine returns the widget ID of the BulletinBoard. Since XmCreateBulletinBoardDialog() doesn't create any dialog components (e.g., labels and buttons), the application should add these features as children of the BulletinBoard widget once it has been created.

```
#include <Xm/BulletinB.h>
Widget XmCreateBulletinBoardDialog (parent, name, arglist, argcount)
    Widget      parent;      /* widget ID of the new widget's parent */
    String      name;        /* name of the newly created widget */
    ArgList     arglist;     /* resource name/value pairs used in creating widget */
    Cardinal    argcount;    /* number of name/value pairs in arglist */
```

XmCreateCascadeButton

Creates an instance of a CascadeButton widget, returning its widget ID.

```
#include <Xm/CascadeB.h>
Widget XmCreateCascadeButton (parent, name, arglist, argcount)
    Widget      parent;      /* widget ID of the new widget's parent */
    String      name;        /* name of the newly created widget */
    ArgList     arglist;     /* resource name/value pairs used in creating widget */
    Cardinal    argcount;    /* number of name/value pairs in arglist */
```

XmCreateCascadeButtonGadget

Creates an instance of a CascadeButtonGadget, returning its gadget ID.

```
#include <Xm/CascadeBG.h>
Widget XmCreateCascadeButtonGadget (parent, name, arglist, argcount)
    Widget      parent;      /* widget ID of the new gadget's parent */
    String      name;        /* name of the newly created widget */
    ArgList     arglist;     /* resource name/value pairs used in creating widget */
    Cardinal    argcount;    /* number of name/value pairs in arglist */
```

XmCreateCommand

Creates an instance of a Command widget, returning its widget ID.

```
#include <Xm/Command.h>
Widget XmCreateCommand (parent, name, arglist, argcount)
    Widget          parent;        /* widget ID of the new widget's parent */
    String          name;          /* name of the newly created widget */
    ArgList         arglist;       /* resource name/value pairs used in creating widget */
    Cardinal        argcount;      /* number of name/value pairs in arglist */
```

XmCreateDialogShell

Creates an instance of a DialogShell widget, returning its widget ID.

```
#include <Xm/DialogS.h>
Widget XmCreateDialogShell (parent, name, arglist, argcount)
    Widget          parent;        /* widget ID of the new widget's parent */
    String          name;          /* name of the newly created widget */
    ArgList         arglist;       /* resource name/value pairs used in creating widget */
    Cardinal        argcount;      /* number of name/value pairs in arglist */
```

XmCreateDrawingArea

Creates an instance of a DrawingArea widget, returning its widget ID.

```
#include <Xm/DrawingA.h>
Widget XmCreateDrawingArea (parent, name, arglist, argcount)
    Widget          parent;        /* widget ID of the new widget's parent */
    String          name;          /* name of the newly created widget */
    ArgList         arglist;       /* resource name/value pairs used in creating widget */
    Cardinal        argcount;      /* number of name/value pairs in arglist */
```

XmCreateDrawnButton

Creates an instance of a DrawnButton widget, returning its widget ID.

```
#include <Xm/DrawnB.h>
Widget XmCreateDrawnButton (parent, name, arglist, argcount)
    Widget          parent;        /* widget ID of the new widget's parent */
    String          name;          /* name of the newly created widget */
    ArgList         arglist;       /* resource name/value pairs used in creating widget */
    Cardinal        argcount;      /* number of name/value pairs in arglist */
```

XmCreateErrorDialog

A convenience routine for creating an ErrorDialog. This routine creates a DialogShell and then creates an unmanaged MessageBox as its child widget. The routine sets the Message-Box resource XmNdialogType to XmDIALOG_ERROR and returns the widget ID of the Message-Box. An ErrorDialog includes three components: a symbol (by default, an octagon with a diagonal slash), a message, and three buttons (whose labels, by default, are Ok, Cancel, and Help).

```
#include <Xm/MessageB.h>
Widget XmCreateErrorDialog (parent, name, arglist, argcount)
    Widget      parent;      /* widget ID of the new widget's parent */
    String      name;        /* name of the newly created widget */
    ArgList     arglist;     /* resource name/value pairs used in creating widget */
    Cardinal    argcount;    /* number of name/value pairs in arglist */
```

XmCreateFileSelectionBox

Creates an unmanaged FileSelectionBox, returning its widget ID. A FileSelectionBox is a specific kind of SelectionBox in which the items to choose are typically (and by default) the names of files. A FileSelectionBox includes two text fields, a scrollable list of filenames, labels for the text fields and the list, and four buttons. One of the text fields can be used to "filter" the list of filenames, so that the scrollable area displays only the files contained within a named directory (the directory can be specified with wildcard characters). The other text field can be used to type in a desired selection rather than clicking a pointer button. The four buttons have default labels of Ok, Filter, Cancel, and Help.

```
#include <Xm/FileSB.h>
Widget XmCreateFileSelectionBox (parent, name, arglist, argcount)
    Widget      parent;      /* widget ID of the new widget's parent */
    String      name;        /* name of the newly created widget */
    ArgList     arglist;     /* resource name/value pairs used in creating widget */
    Cardinal    argcount;    /* number of name/value pairs in arglist */
```

XmCreateFileSelectionDialog

A convenience routine for creating a FileSelectionDialog. This routine creates a DialogShell and then creates an unmanaged FileSelectionBox as its child widget. The routine sets the SelectionBox resource XmNdialogType to XmDIALOG_FILE_SELECTION and returns the widget ID of the FileSelectionBox. (See previous entry for description of a FileSelectionBox.)

```
#include <Xm/FileSB.h>
Widget XmCreateFileSelectionDialog (parent, name, arglist, argcount)
    Widget      parent;      /* widget ID of the new widget's parent */
    String      name;        /* name of the newly created widget */
    ArgList     arglist;     /* resource name/value pairs used in creating widget */
    Cardinal    argcount;    /* number of name/value pairs in arglist */
```

XmCreateForm

Creates an instance of a Form widget, returning its widget ID.

```
#include <Xm/Form.h>
Widget XmCreateForm (parent, name, arglist, argcount)
    Widget      parent;      /* widget ID of the new widget's parent */
    String      name;        /* name of the newly created widget */
    ArgList     arglist;     /* resource name/value pairs used in creating widget */
    Cardinal    argcount;    /* number of name/value pairs in arglist */
```

XmCreateFormDialog

A convenience routine for creating a FormDialog. This routine creates a DialogShell and then creates an unmanaged Form as its child widget. The routine returns the widget ID of the Form. Since XmCreateFormDialog() doesn't create any dialog components (e.g., labels and buttons), the application should add these features as children of the Form widget once it has been created.

```
#include <Xm/Form.h>
Widget XmCreateFormDialog (parent, name, arglist, argcount)
    Widget          parent;      /* widget ID of the new widget's parent */
    String          name;        /* name of the newly created widget */
    ArgList         arglist;      /* resource name/value pairs used in creating widget */
    Cardinal        argcount;     /* number of name/value pairs in arglist */
```

XmCreateFrame

Creates an instance of a Frame widget, returning its widget ID.

```
#include <Xm/Frame.h>
Widget XmCreateFrame (parent, name, arglist, argcount)
    Widget          parent;      /* widget ID of the new widget's parent */
    String          name;        /* name of the newly created widget */
    ArgList         arglist;      /* resource name/value pairs used in creating widget */
    Cardinal        argcount;     /* number of name/value pairs in arglist */
```

XmCreateInformationDialog

A convenience routine for creating an InformationDialog. This routine creates a DialogShell and then creates an unmanaged MessageBox as its child widget. The routine sets the MessageBox resource XmNdialogType to XmDIALOG_INFORMATION and returns the widget ID of the MessageBox. An InformationDialog includes three components: a symbol (by default, a lowercase *i*), a message, and three buttons (whose labels, by default, are Ok, Cancel, and Help).

```
#include <Xm/MessageB.h>
Widget XmCreateInformationDialog (parent, name, arglist, argcount)
    Widget          parent;      /* widget ID of the new widget's parent */
    String          name;        /* name of the newly created widget */
    ArgList         arglist;      /* resource name/value pairs used in creating widget */
    Cardinal        argcount;     /* number of name/value pairs in arglist */
```

XmCreateLabel

Creates an instance of a Label widget, returning its widget ID.

```
#include <Xm/Label.h>
Widget XmCreateLabel (parent, name, arglist, argcount)
    Widget          parent;      /* widget ID of the new widget's parent */
    String          name;        /* name of the newly created widget */
    ArgList         arglist;      /* resource name/value pairs used in creating widget */
    Cardinal        argcount;     /* number of name/value pairs in arglist */
```

XmCreateLabelGadget

Creates an instance of a LabelGadget, returning its gadget ID.

```
#include <Xm/LabelG.h>
Widget XmCreateLabelGadget (parent, name, arglist, argcount)
    Widget      parent;     /* widget ID of the new gadget's parent */
    String      name;       /* name of the newly created widget */
    ArgList     arglist;    /* resource name/value pairs used in creating widget */
    Cardinal    argcount;   /* number of name/value pairs in arglist */
```

XmCreateList

Creates an instance of a List widget, returning its widget ID.

```
#include <Xm/List.h>
Widget XmCreateList (parent, name, arglist, argcount)
    Widget      parent;     /* widget ID of the new widget's parent */
    String      name;       /* name of the newly created widget */
    ArgList     arglist;    /* resource name/value pairs used in creating widget */
    Cardinal    argcount;   /* number of name/value pairs in arglist */
```

XmCreateMainWindow

Creates an instance of a MainWindow widget, returning its widget ID.

```
#include <Xm/MainW.h>
Widget XmCreateMainWindow (parent, name, arglist, argcount)
    Widget      parent;     /* widget ID of the new widget's parent */
    String      name;       /* name of the newly created widget */
    ArgList     arglist;    /* resource name/value pairs used in creating widget */
    Cardinal    argcount;   /* number of name/value pairs in arglist */
```

XmCreateMenuBar

A convenience routine for creating a MenuBar. This routine creates an instance of a Row-Column widget (returning its widget ID), sets the XmNrowColumnType resource to Xm-MENU_BAR, and sets the resources XmNisHomogeneous and XmNentryClass so as to ensure that all children of the MenuBar are CascadeButtons or CascadeButtonGadgets.

```
#include <Xm/RowColumn.h>
Widget XmCreateMenuBar (parent, name, arglist, argcount)
    Widget      parent;     /* widget ID of the new widget's parent */
    String      name;       /* name of the newly created widget */
    ArgList     arglist;    /* resource name/value pairs used in creating widget */
    Cardinal    argcount;   /* number of name/value pairs in arglist */
```

XmCreateMenuShell

Creates an instance of a MenuShell widget, returning its widget ID.

```
#include <Xm/MenuShell.h>
Widget XmCreateMenuShell (parent, name, arglist, argcount)
    Widget      parent;      /* widget ID of the new widget's parent */
    String      name;        /* name of the newly created widget */
    ArgList     arglist;     /* resource name/value pairs used in creating widget */
    Cardinal    argcount;    /* number of name/value pairs in arglist */
```

XmCreateMessageBox

Creates an unmanaged MessageBox, returning its widget ID. A MessageBox is used to inform, to ask for confirmation of actions, or to report errors. A MessageBox contains an optional symbol, a message, and three buttons (labeled Ok, Cancel, and Help, by default). The default value for the MessageBox's XmNdialogType resource is XmDIALOG_MESSAGE, a value that causes a null message symbol.

```
#include <Xm/MessageB.h>
Widget XmCreateMessageBox (parent, name, arglist, argcount)
    Widget      parent;      /* widget ID of the new widget's parent */
    String      name;        /* name of the newly created widget */
    ArgList     arglist;     /* resource name/value pairs used in creating widget */
    Cardinal    argcount;    /* number of name/value pairs in arglist */
```

XmCreateMessageDialog

A convenience routine for creating a MessageDialog. This routine creates a DialogShell and then creates an unmanaged MessageBox as its child widget. The routine sets the Message-Box resource XmNdialogType to XmDIALOG_MESSAGE (the default) and returns the widget ID of the MessageBox. (See previous entry for description of a MessageBox.)

```
#include <Xm/MessageB.h>
Widget XmCreateMessageDialog (parent, name, arglist, argcount)
    Widget      parent;      /* widget ID of the new widget's parent */
    String      name;        /* name of the newly created widget */
    ArgList     arglist;     /* resource name/value pairs used in creating widget */
    Cardinal    argcount;    /* number of name/value pairs in arglist */
```

XmCreateOptionMenu

A convenience routine for creating an OptionMenu. This routine creates an instance of a RowColumn widget (returning its widget ID) and sets the XmNrowColumnType resource to Xm-MENU_OPTION. As a special RowColumn manager, an OptionMenu contains a label, a selection area, and one pulldown menu pane. XmOptionLabelGadget() can be called to obtain the label's ID, and XmOptionButtonGadget() can be called to obtain the selection area's ID. Whereas the OptionMenu automatically creates both the label (as a LabelGadget) and the selection area (as a CascadeButtonGadget), the pulldown menu pane needs to have been created previously as a child of *parent* (assuming you want the pulldown menu pane to be attached at creation time). This pulldown menu pane is identified in *arglist* by setting the

XmNsubMenuId resource. Other resources that might be set for an OptionMenu include Xm-NmenuPost and XmNmenuHistory. The former determines which mouse button will post the OptionMenu and will make the various selections (default is mouse button 1); the latter determines which item of a pulldown menu pane is displayed as the current choice within the selection area (default is the first item).

```
#include <Xm/RowColumn.h>
Widget XmCreateOptionMenu (parent, name, arglist, argcount)
    Widget      parent;      /* widget ID of the new widget's parent */
    String      name;        /* name of the newly created widget */
    ArgList     arglist;     /* resource name/value pairs used in creating widget */
    Cardinal    argcount;    /* number of name/value pairs in arglist */
```

XmCreatePanedWindow

Creates an instance of a PanedWindow widget, returning its widget ID.

```
#include <Xm/PanedW.h>
Widget XmCreatePanedWindow (parent, name, arglist, argcount)
    Widget      parent;      /* widget ID of the new widget's parent */
    String      name;        /* name of the newly created widget */
    ArgList     arglist;     /* resource name/value pairs used in creating widget */
    Cardinal    argcount;    /* number of name/value pairs in arglist */
```

XmCreatePopupMenu

A convenience routine for creating a popup menu pane. This routine creates first a Menu-Shell and then an instance of a RowColumn widget as its child. The routine sets the XmNrow-ColumnType resource to XmMENU_POPUP and returns the widget ID of the RowColumn. A PopupMenu is the first menu pane of a popup menu system, and the PopupMenu must have a MenuShell parent to operate correctly. The MenuShell is in turn a child of parent.

```
#include <Xm/RowColumn.h>
Widget XmCreatePopupMenu (parent, name, arglist, argcount)
    Widget      parent;      /* widget ID of the new widget's parent */
    String      name;        /* name of the newly created widget */
    ArgList     arglist;     /* resource name/value pairs used in creating widget */
    Cardinal    argcount;    /* number of name/value pairs in arglist */
```

XmCreatePromptDialog

A convenience routine for creating a PromptDialog. This routine creates a DialogShell and an unmanaged SelectionBox as its child. The routine sets the SelectionBox resource Xm-NdialogType to XmDIALOG_PROMPT and returns the widget ID of the SelectionBox. A PromptDialog contains a message, a region for text input, and three managed buttons (whose default labels are Ok, Cancel, and Help). A fourth button, whose default label is Apply, is created as an unmanaged child. An application can remanage this button to build its own dialog box. A dialog box typically remains displayed after the Apply button is pressed.

```
#include <Xm/SelectioB.h>
Widget XmCreatePromptDialog (parent, name, arglist, argcount)
    Widget      parent;      /* widget ID of the new widget's parent */
    String      name;        /* name of the newly created widget */
    ArgList     arglist;     /* resource name/value pairs used in creating widget */
    Cardinal    argcount;    /* number of name/value pairs in arglist */
```

XmCreatePulldownMenu

A convenience routine for creating a Pulldown MenuPane. This routine creates first a Menu-Shell and then an instance of a RowColumn widget. This routine sets the XmNrowColumnType resource to XmMENU_PULLDOWN and returns the widget ID of the RowColumn. If *parent* is a Popup MenuPane or a Pulldown MenuPane, then the MenuShell created is a child of *parent*'s MenuShell; otherwise, the MenuShell created is a child of *parent*.

```
#include <Xm/RowColumn.h>
Widget XmCreatePulldownMenu (parent, name, arglist, argcount)
    Widget      parent;      /* widget ID of the new widget's parent */
    String      name;        /* name of the newly created widget */
    ArgList     arglist;     /* resource name/value pairs used in creating widget */
    Cardinal    argcount;    /* number of name/value pairs in arglist */
```

XmCreatePushButton

Creates an instance of a PushButton widget, returning its widget ID.

```
#include <Xm/PushB.h>
Widget XmCreatePushButton (parent, name, arglist, argcount)
    Widget      parent;      /* widget ID of the new widget's parent */
    String      name;        /* name of the newly created widget */
    ArgList     arglist;     /* resource name/value pairs used in creating widget */
    Cardinal    argcount;    /* number of name/value pairs in arglist */
```

XmCreatePushButtonGadget

Creates an instance of a PushButtonGadget, returning its gadget ID.

```
#include <Xm/PushBG.h>
Widget XmCreatePushButtonGadget (parent, name, arglist, argcount)
    Widget      parent;      /* widget ID of the new gadget's parent */
    String      name;        /* name of the newly created widget */
    ArgList     arglist;     /* resource name/value pairs used in creating widget */
    Cardinal    argcount;    /* number of name/value pairs in arglist */
```

XmCreateQuestionDialog

A convenience routine for creating a QuestionDialog. This routine creates a DialogShell and then creates an unmanaged MessageBox as its child widget. The routine sets the Message-Box resource XmNdialogType to XmDIALOG_QUESTION and returns the widget ID of the MessageBox. A QuestionDialog includes three components: a symbol (by default, a question mark), a message, and three buttons (whose labels by default are Ok, Cancel, and Help).

```
#include <Xm/MessageB.h>
Widget XmCreateQuestionDialog (parent, name, arglist, argcount)
    Widget          parent;         /* widget ID of the new widget's parent */
    String          name;           /* name of the newly created widget */
    ArgList         arglist;        /* resource name/value pairs used in creating widget */
    Cardinal        argcount;       /* number of name/value pairs in arglist */
```

XmCreateRadioBox

A convenience routine for creating a RadioBox. This routine creates an instance of a Row-Column widget, returns its widget ID, and initializes several RowColumn resources. Namely, it sets XmNrowColumnType to XmWORK_AREA (the default), XmNpacking to Xm-PACK_COLUMN, XmNradioBehavior and XmNisHomogeneous to True, and XmNentryClass to xm-ToggleButtonGadgetClass. A RadioBox contains several ToggleButtonGadget children for which the XmNvisibleWhenOff resource is set to True and the XmNindicatorType resource is set to XmONE_OF_MANY (the button will be diamond-shaped).

```
#include <Xm/RowColumn.h>
Widget XmCreateRadioBox (parent, name, arglist, argcount)
    Widget          parent;         /* widget ID of the new widget's parent */
    String          name;           /* name of the newly created widget */
    ArgList         arglist;        /* resource name/value pairs used in creating widget */
    Cardinal        argcount;       /* number of name/value pairs in arglist */
```

XmCreateRowColumn

Creates an instance of a RowColumn widget, returning its widget ID. If the XmNrowColumn-Type resource is not specified in arglist, the RowColumn will be of type XmWORK_AREA.

```
#include <Xm/RowColumn.h>
Widget XmCreateRowColumn (parent, name, arglist, argcount)
    Widget          parent;         /* widget ID of the new widget's parent */
    String          name;           /* name of the newly created widget */
    ArgList         arglist;        /* resource name/value pairs used in creating widget */
    Cardinal        argcount;       /* number of name/value pairs in arglist */
```

XmCreateScale

Creates an instance of a Scale widget, returning its widget ID.

```
#include <Xm/Scale.h>
Widget XmCreateScale (parent, name, arglist, argcount)
    Widget          parent;         /* widget ID of the new widget's parent */
    String          name;           /* name of the newly created widget */
    ArgList         arglist;        /* resource name/value pairs used in creating widget */
    Cardinal        argcount;       /* number of name/value pairs in arglist */
```

XmCreateScrollBar

Creates an instance of a ScrollBar widget, returning its widget ID.

```
#include <Xm/ScrollBar.h>
Widget XmCreateScrollBar (parent, name, arglist, argcount)
    Widget      parent;     /* widget ID of the new widget's parent */
    String      name;       /* name of the newly created widget */
    ArgList     arglist;    /* resource name/value pairs used in creating widget */
    Cardinal    argcount;   /* number of name/value pairs in arglist */
```

XmCreateScrolledList

A convenience routine for creating a ScrolledList. This routine creates a ScrolledWindow and then creates a List as its child widget, returning the widget ID of the List. The name of the ScrolledWindow created by this routine is typically the string formed by adding the letters *SW* to the end of the *name* string.

```
#include <Xm/List.h>
Widget XmCreateScrolledList (parent, name, arglist, argcount)
    Widget      parent;     /* widget ID of ScrolledWindow's parent */
    String      name;       /* name of the new List widget */
    ArgList     arglist;    /* resource name/value pairs used in creating widget */
    Cardinal    argcount;   /* number of name/value pairs in arglist */
```

XmCreateScrolledText

A convenience routine for creating a ScrolledText widget. This routine creates a Scrolled-Window and then creates a Text widget as its child, returning the widget ID of the Text widget. The name of the ScrolledWindow created by this routine is typically the string formed by adding the letters *SW* to the end of the *name* string.

```
#include <Xm/Text.h>
Widget XmCreateScrolledText (parent, name, arglist, argcount)
    Widget      parent;     /* widget ID of ScrolledWindow's parent */
    String      name;       /* name of the new Text widget */
    ArgList     arglist;    /* resource name/value pairs used in creating widget */
    Cardinal    argcount;   /* number of name/value pairs in arglist */
```

XmCreateScrolledWindow

Creates an instance of a ScrolledWindow widget, returning its widget ID.

```
#include <Xm/ScrolledW.h>
Widget XmCreateScrolledWindow (parent, name, arglist, argcount)
    Widget      parent;     /* widget ID of the new widget's parent */
    String      name;       /* name of the newly created widget */
    ArgList     arglist;    /* resource name/value pairs used in creating widget */
    Cardinal    argcount;   /* number of name/value pairs in arglist */
```

XmCreateSelectionBox

Creates an unmanaged SelectionBox, returning its widget ID. The XmNdialogType resource for this widget is set to XmDIALOG_WORK_AREA (the default). A SelectionBox displays a scrollable list of alternatives from which the user chooses. A SelectionBox also contains a text field in which the user can edit a selection, labels for this text field and for the scrollable list, and three buttons whose default labels are Ok, Cancel, and Help. A fourth button, whose default label is Apply, is created as an unmanaged child.

```
#include <Xm/SelectioB.h>
Widget XmCreateSelectionBox (parent, name, arglist, argcount)
    Widget          parent;         /* widget ID of the new widget's parent */
    String          name;           /* name of the newly created widget */
    ArgList         arglist;        /* resource name/value pairs used in creating widget */
    Cardinal        argcount;       /* number of name/value pairs in arglist */
```

XmCreateSelectionDialog

A convenience routine for creating a SelectionDialog. This routine creates a DialogShell and an unmanaged SelectionBox as its child. The routine sets the SelectionBox resource XmNdialogType to XmDIALOG_SELECTION and returns the widget ID of the SelectionBox. See previous entry for a description of a SelectionBox. (However, in a SelectionDialog, the Apply button is managed.)

```
#include <Xm/SelectioB.h>
Widget XmCreateSelectionDialog (parent, name, arglist, argcount)
    Widget          parent;         /* widget ID of the new widget's parent */
    String          name;           /* name of the newly created widget */
    ArgList         arglist;        /* resource name/value pairs used in creating widget */
    Cardinal        argcount;       /* number of name/value pairs in arglist */
```

XmCreateSeparator

Creates an instance of a Separator widget, returning its widget ID. A Separator widget can be a single or double line, solid or dashed. The separator can also appear etched into the screen or raised from it.

```
#include <Xm/Separator.h>
Widget XmCreateSeparator (parent, name, arglist, argcount)
    Widget          parent;         /* widget ID of the new widget's parent */
    String          name;           /* name of the newly created widget */
    ArgList         arglist;        /* resource name/value pairs used in creating widget */
    Cardinal        argcount;       /* number of name/value pairs in arglist */
```

XmCreateSeparatorGadget

Creates an instance of a SeparatorGadget, returning its gadget ID. A SeparatorGadget can be a single or double line, solid or dashed. The separator can also appear etched into the screen or raised from it.

```
#include <Xm/SeparatoG.h>
Widget XmCreateSeparatorGadget (parent, name, arglist, argcount)
    Widget          parent;        /* widget ID of the new gadget's parent */
    String          name;          /* name of the newly created widget */
    ArgList         arglist;       /* resource name/value pairs used in creating widget */
    Cardinal        argcount;      /* number of name/value pairs in arglist */
```

XmCreateSimpleCheckBox

A RowColumn convenience routine that creates a CheckBox with ToggleButtonGadgets as its children. In other words, this routine creates an instance of a RowColumn widget with its XmNrowColumnType resource set to XmWORK_AREA and its XmNradioAlwaysOne resource set to False. The latter resource setting allows more than one button to be selected at the same time—the feature that distinguishes a CheckBox from a RadioBox. Each button's name has the form *button_n*. *n* is the button's number and begins at 0. XmCreateSimpleCheckBox() uses additional RowColumn resources associated with the creation of simple menus. In particular, the XmNbuttonType resource must be set to XmCHECKBUTTON. This routine returns the widget ID of the RowColumn widget.

```
Widget XmCreateSimpleCheckBox (parent, name, arglist, argcount)
    Widget          parent;        /* widget ID of the new widget's parent */
    String          name;          /* name of the newly created widget */
    ArgList         arglist;       /* resource name/value pairs used in creating widget */
    Cardinal        argcount;      /* number of name/value pairs in arglist */
```

XmCreateSimpleMenuBar

A RowColumn convenience routine that creates a MenuBar with CascadeButtonGadgets as its children. In other words, this routine creates an instance of a RowColumn widget with its XmNrowColumnType resource set to XmMENU_BAR. Each button's name has the form *button_n*. *n* is the button's number and begins at 0. XmCreateSimpleMenuBar() uses additional Row-Column resources associated with the creation of simple menus. In particular, the XmNbuttonType resource must be set to XmCASCADEBUTTON. This routine returns the widget ID of the RowColumn widget.

```
Widget XmCreateSimpleMenuBar (parent, name, arglist, argcount)
    Widget          parent;        /* widget ID of the new widget's parent */
    String          name;          /* name of the newly created widget */
    ArgList         arglist;       /* resource name/value pairs used in creating widget */
    Cardinal        argcount;      /* number of name/value pairs in arglist */
```

XmCreateSimpleOptionMenu

A RowColumn convenience routine that creates an OptionMenu along with its submenu of CascadeButtonGadget or PushButtonGadget children. In other words, this routine creates an instance of a RowColumn widget with its XmNrowColumnType resource set to Xm-MENU_OPTION. Each button's name has the form *button_n*, and each separator's name has the form *separator_n*. *n* is the number of the button or separator, and *n* begins at 0. XmCreate-SimpleOptionMenu() uses additional RowColumn resources associated with the creation of simple menus. In particular, the XmNbuttonType resource can have the following values:

| XmPUSHBUTTON | XmSEPARATOR |
| XmCASCADEBUTTON | XmDOUBLE_SEPARATOR |

And the XmNoptionLabel resource can specify a string to use as a label for the OptionMenu. This routine returns the widget ID of the RowColumn widget.

```
Widget XmCreateSimpleOptionMenu (parent, name, arglist, argcount)
    Widget      parent;     /* widget ID of the new widget's parent */
    String      name;       /* name of the newly created widget */
    ArgList     arglist;    /* resource name/value pairs used in creating widget */
    Cardinal    argcount;   /* number of name/value pairs in arglist */
```

XmCreateSimplePopupMenu

A RowColumn convenience routine that creates a popup MenuPane along with its button children. In other words, this routine creates an instance of a RowColumn widget with its XmNrowColumnType resource set to XmMENU_POPUP. The names of buttons, separators, and labels have the forms *button_n*, *separator_n*, and *label_n*, respectively. *n* is the number and begins at 0. XmCreateSimplePopupMenu() uses additional RowColumn resources associated with the creation of simple menus. In particular, the XmNbuttonType resource can have the following values:

XmPUSHBUTTON	XmSEPARATOR
XmCASCADEBUTTON	XmDOUBLE_SEPARATOR
XmRADIOBUTTON	XmTITLE
XmCHECKBUTTON	

This routine returns the widget ID of the RowColumn widget.

```
Widget XmCreateSimplePopupMenu (parent, name, arglist, argcount)
    Widget      parent;     /* widget ID of the MenuShell's parent */
    String      name;       /* name of the newly created widget */
    ArgList     arglist;    /* resource name/value pairs used in creating widget */
    Cardinal    argcount;   /* number of name/value pairs in arglist */
```

XmCreateSimplePulldownMenu

A RowColumn convenience routine that creates a pulldown MenuPane along with its button children. In other words, this routine creates an instance of a RowColumn widget with its XmNrowColumnType resource set to XmMENU_PULLDOWN. For additional description, see XmCreateSimplePopupMenu().

```
Widget XmCreateSimplePulldownMenu (parent, name, arglist, argcount)
    Widget      parent;     /* widget ID of the MenuShell's parent */
    String      name;       /* name of the newly created widget */
    ArgList     arglist;    /* resource name/value pairs used in creating widget */
    Cardinal    argcount;   /* number of name/value pairs in arglist */
```

XmCreateSimpleRadioBox

A RowColumn convenience routine that creates a RadioBox with ToggleButtonGadgets as its children. In other words, this routine creates an instance of a RowColumn widget with its XmNrowColumnType resource set to XmWORK_AREA and its XmNradioBehavior resource set to

True. The latter resource setting enforces button behavior that allows only one button to be selected at a time. Each button's name has the form *button_n*. *n* is the button's number and begins at 0. XmCreateSimpleRadioBox() uses additional RowColumn resources associated with the creation of simple menus. In particular, the XmNbuttonType resource must be set to Xm-RADIOBUTTON. This routine returns the widget ID of the RowColumn widget.

Widget XmCreateSimpleRadioBox (*parent, name, arglist, argcount*)

Widget	*parent*;	/* widget ID of the new widget's parent */
String	*name*;	/* name of the newly created widget */
ArgList	*arglist*;	/* resource name/value pairs used in creating widget */
Cardinal	*argcount*;	/* number of name/value pairs in *arglist* */

XmCreateText

Creates an instance of a Text widget, returning its widget ID.

```
#include <Xm/Text.h>
```
Widget XmCreateText (*parent, name, arglist, argcount*)

Widget	*parent*;	/* widget ID of the new widget's parent */
String	*name*;	/* name of the newly created widget */
ArgList	*arglist*;	/* resource name/value pairs used in creating widget */
Cardinal	*argcount*;	/* number of name/value pairs in *arglist* */

XmCreateTextField

Creates an instance of a TextField widget, returning its widget ID. A TextField widget is essentially a single-line Text widget.

```
#include <Xm/TextF.h>
```
Widget XmCreateTextField (*parent, name, arglist, argcount*)

Widget	*parent*;	/* widget ID of the new widget's parent */
String	*name*;	/* name of the newly created widget */
ArgList	*arglist*;	/* resource name/value pairs used in creating widget */
Cardinal	*argcount*;	/* number of name/value pairs in *arglist* */

XmCreateToggleButton

Creates an instance of a ToggleButton widget, returning its widget ID.

```
#include <Xm/ToggleB.h>
```
Widget XmCreateToggleButton (*parent, name, arglist, argcount*)

Widget	*parent*;	/* widget ID of the new widget's parent */
String	*name*;	/* name of the newly created widget */
ArgList	*arglist*;	/* resource name/value pairs used in creating widget */
Cardinal	*argcount*;	/* number of name/value pairs in *arglist* */

XmCreateToggleButtonGadget

Creates an instance of a ToggleButtonGadget, returning its gadget ID.

```
#include <Xm/ToggleBG.h>
```
Widget XmCreateToggleButtonGadget (*parent, name, arglist, argcount*)

Widget	*parent*;	/* widget ID of the new gadget's parent */
String	*name*;	/* name of the newly created widget */

| ArgList | arglist; | /* resource name/value pairs used in creating widget */ |
| Cardinal | argcount; | /* number of name/value pairs in arglist */ |

XmCreateWarningDialog

A convenience routine for creating a WarningDialog. This routine creates a DialogShell and then creates an unmanaged MessageBox as its child widget. The routine sets the Message-Box resource XmNdialogType to XmDIALOG_WARNING and returns the widget ID of the MessageBox. A WarningDialog includes three components: a symbol (by default, an exclamation point), a message, and three buttons (whose labels, by default, are Ok, Cancel, and Help).

```
#include <Xm/MessageB.h>
Widget XmCreateWarningDialog (parent, name, arglist, argcount)
```
Widget	parent;	/* widget ID of the new widget's parent */
String	name;	/* name of the newly created widget */
ArgList	arglist;	/* resource name/value pairs used in creating widget */
Cardinal	argcount;	/* number of name/value pairs in arglist */

XmCreateWorkArea

Creates an instance of a RowColumn widget with its XmNrowColumnType resource set to Xm-WORK_AREA. This routine returns the widget ID of the RowColumn. As a convenience routine, XmCreateWorkArea() has the same effect as a call to XmCreateRowColumn() with the Xm-NrowColumnType resource set to XmWORK_AREA in arglist.

```
#include <Xm/RowColumn.h>
Widget XmCreateWorkArea (parent, name, arglist, argcount)
```
Widget	parent;	/* widget ID of the new widget's parent */
String	name;	/* name of the newly created widget */
ArgList	arglist;	/* resource name/value pairs used in creating widget */
Cardinal	argcount;	/* number of name/value pairs in arglist */

XmCreateWorkingDialog

A convenience routine for creating a WorkingDialog. This routine creates a DialogShell and then creates an unmanaged MessageBox as its child widget. The routine sets the Message-Box resource XmNdialogType to XmDIALOG_WORKING and returns the widget ID of the MessageBox. A WorkingDialog includes three components: a symbol (by default, an hour-glass), a message, and three buttons (whose labels, by default, are Ok, Cancel, and Help).

```
#include <Xm/MessageB.h>
Widget XmCreateWorkingDialog (parent, name, arglist, argcount)
```
Widget	parent;	/* widget ID of the new widget's parent */
String	name;	/* name of the newly created widget */
ArgList	arglist;	/* resource name/value pairs used in creating widget */
Cardinal	argcount;	/* number of name/value pairs in arglist */

XmCvtCTToXmString

Converts the specified compound *text* string (an MIT X11 text format) to a Motif compound string, returning the result. The result is undefined, however, if *text* contains horizontal tabulation (HT) control characters.

```
XmString XmCvtCTToXmString (text)
    char          *text;              /* compound text to convert to compound string */
```

XmCvtStringToUnitType

Converts the string specified in *from_val* to a different unit of measurement (e.g., font or pixel). The result is returned in *to_val*. This routine shouldn't be called directly; instead, you should install it as a resource converter, using the R3 routine XtAddConverter(). But even then, XmCvtStringToUnitType() should be installed only if a widget must have its XmNunitType resource set by reading data from a resource file. In this case, XmCvtStringToUnitType() must be installed with XtAddConverter() before the widget is created.

```
void XmCvtStringToUnitType (args, num_args, from_val, to_val)
    XrmValuePtr     args;             /* additional XrmValue arguments needed for conversion */
    Cardinal        *num_args;        /* number of additional args */
    XrmValue        *from_val;        /* returns value to convert */
    XrmValue        *to_val;          /* returns converted value */
```

The XmNunitType resource can have the following values, which are defined in *<Xm/Xm.h>*. XmPIXELS is the default.

XmPIXELS	Xm100TH_POINTS
Xm100TH_FONT_UNITS	Xm100TH_MILLIMETERS
Xm1000TH_INCHES	

Here's the XtAddConverter() call that allows the XmNunitType resource to be set through a resource file:

```
XtAddConverter(XmRString, XmRUnitType, XmCvtStringToUnitType, NULL, 0);
```

XmCvtXmStringToCT

Converts the specified Motif compound *string* to a string in X11 compound text format, returning the result. This routine is the complement of XmCvtCTToXmString().

```
char * XmCvtXmStringToCT (string)
    XmString        string;           /* compound string to convert to compound text */
```

XmDeactivateProtocol

Deactivates the specified *protocol* without removing it. If *shell* is realized, XmDeactivateProtocol() updates its protocol handlers and the specified *property*. A protocol may be active or inactive. If *protocol* is active, the protocol atom is stored in *property*; if *protocol* is inactive, the protocol atom is not stored in *property*.

```
#include <Xm/Protocols.h>
void XmDeactivateProtocol (shell, property, protocol)
    Widget          shell;              /* widget associated with the protocol property */
    Atom            property;           /* property that will hold protocol data for shell */
    Atom            protocol;           /* atom ID of protocol */
```

XmDeactivateWMProtocol

A convenience routine that calls XmDeactivateProtocol() with *property* set to XA_WM_PROTO-COL, the window manager protocol property.

```
#include <Xm/Protocols.h>
void XmDeactivateWMProtocol (shell, protocol)
    Widget          shell;              /* widget associated with the protocol property */
    Atom            protocol;           /* atom ID of protocol */
```

XmDestroyPixmap

Removes the specified *pixmap* resource. This routine returns True if successful or False if the specified *screen* or *pixmap* were not matched. The resource ID of *pixmap* can be obtained by calling XmGetPixmap().

```
Boolean XmDestroyPixmap (screen, pixmap)
    Screen          *screen;            /* screen on which pixmap is located */
    Pixmap          pixmap;             /* pixmap to be destroyed */
```

XmFileSelectionBoxGetChild

Returns the widget ID of the specified *child* of the FileSelectionBox widget.

```
#include <Xm/FileSB.h>
Widget XmFileSelectionBoxGetChild (widget, child)
    Widget          widget;             /* widget ID of FileSelectionBox widget */
    unsigned char   child;              /* component whose widget ID is returned */
```

The values for *child* are defined in *<Xm/Xm.h>*:

XmDIALOG_WORK_AREA   XmDIALOG_LIST
XmDIALOG_APPLY_BUTTON   XmDIALOG_LIST_LABEL
XmDIALOG_CANCEL_BUTTON   XmDIALOG_SELECTION_LABEL
XmDIALOG_DEFAULT_BUTTON   XmDIALOG_TEXT
XmDIALOG_OK_BUTTON   XmDIALOG_SEPARATOR
XmDIALOG_FILTER_LABEL   XmDIALOG_DIR_LIST
XmDIALOG_FILTER_TEXT   XmDIALOG_DIR_LIST_LABEL
XmDIALOG_HELP_BUTTON

XmFileSelectionDoSearch

Begins to search for directories and files within the specified FileSelectionBox *widget*. *dirmask* is a text pattern that can include wildcard metacharacters. If non-NULL, *dirmask* restricts the search to directories that match the *dirmask*. (*dirmask* redefines the XmNdirMask resource in *widget* via a callback procedure.)

```
#include <Xm/FileSB.h>
void XmFileSelectionDoSearch (widget, dirmask)
    Widget          widget;              /* widget ID of FileSelectionBox widget */
    XmString        dirmask;             /* directory mask for restricting file display */
```

XmFontListAdd

Adds *font* and its associated *charset* to the list specified by *oldlist*. This routine returns the newly created font list (or returns *oldlist* if either *font* or *charset* is NULL) and deallocates *oldlist*.

```
XmFontList XmFontListAdd (oldlist, font, charset)
    XmFontList      oldlist;             /* font list to which font is to be added */
    XFontStruct     *font;               /* points to a font structure (from XLoadQueryFont()) */
    XmStringCharSet charset;             /* XmSTRING_DEFAULT_CHARSET, for example */
```

XmFontListCopy

Creates a new font list with the same contents as *fontlist* (that is, it makes a copy of *fontlist*).

```
XmFontList XmFontListCopy (fontlist)
    XmFontList      fontlist;            /* list of fonts and character set IDs */
```

XmFontListCreate

Creates a new font list that contains a single entry having the specified *font* and *charset*. This routine allocates the storage for the font list.

```
XmFontList XmFontListCreate (font, charset)
    XFontStruct     *font;               /* points to a font structure (from XLoadQueryFont()) */
    XmStringCharSet charset;             /* XmSTRING_DEFAULT_CHARSET, for example */
```

XmFontListFree

Deallocates storage used by the specified *fontlist*.

```
void XmFontListFree (fontlist)
    XmFontList      fontlist;            /* list of fonts and character set IDs */
```

XmFontListFreeFontContext

Deallocates the specified font list *context*. This is the last of the three font context routines that an application should call if it needs to do its own font list searching. Applications begin by calling XmFontListInitFontContext() and then make repeated calls to XmFontListGetNextFont().

```
void XmFontListFreeFontContext (context)
    XmFontContext   context;             /* font list context used by XmFontListInitFontContext() */
```

XmFontListGetNextFont

Returns the character set and font for the next element of the font list. Applications begin to access the elements of a font list by first calling XmFontListInitFontContext() to create a font list context. Then, repeated calls to XmFontListGetNextFont() using the same context will access successive font list elements. When all elements have been accessed, the application finishes by calling XmFontListFreeFontContext() to free the allocated font list context.

XmFontListGetNextFont() returns True if it accessed valid character set and font values; otherwise, the routine returns False.

```
Boolean XmFontListGetNextFont (context, charset, font)
    XmFontContext    context;          /* font list context used by XmFontListInitFontContext() */
    XmStringCharSet *charset;          /* returns a character set string for current font element */
    XFontStruct      **font;            /* returns a pointer to a font structure */
```

XmFontListInitFontContext

Creates the specified *context*, allowing applications to access the fonts and character sets in *fontlist*. This routine is the first of the three font context routines to call, and the same *context* should be specified for XmFontListGetNextFont() and XmFontListFreeFontContext(). XmFontListInitFontContext() returns True if *context* was allocated and returns False otherwise.

```
Boolean XmFontListInitFontContext (context, fontlist)
    XmFontContext  *context;           /* returns the allocated font list context structure */
    XmFontList     fontlist;           /* list of fonts and character set IDs */
```

XmGetAtomName

Returns the string version for a given *atom*. This routine works like Xlib's XGetAtomName routine, but the Motif routine provides the added feature of client-side caching.

```
#include <Xm/AtomMgr.h>
String XmGetAtomName (display, atom)
    Display      *display;             /* points to Display structure */
    Atom         atom;                 /* atom whose string name you want returned */
```

XmGetColorCalculation

Returns the procedure that calculates the default colors (foreground, top and bottom shadows, and selection highlighting). The procedure calculates these colors based on a background color that has been passed to the procedure. Use XmSetColorCalculation() to change the calculation procedure.

```
XmColorProc XmGetColorCalculation ()
```

XmGetColors

Given a *screen*, *colormap*, and *background* pixel, this routine returns appropriate pixel values for foreground, selection, and shadow colors. If any of *foreground*, *top_shadow*, *bottom_shadow*, or *select* is NULL, XmGetColors() doesn't return a pixel value for that argument.

```
void XmGetColors (screen, colormap, background, foreground, top_shadow, bottom_shadow, select)
    Screen       *screen;              /* screen for which to allocate colors */
    Colormap     colormap;             /* colormap from which to allocate colors */
    Pixel        background;           /* background that the colors should be based on */
    Pixel        *foreground;          /* returns value for foreground pixel */
    Pixel        *top_shadow;          /* returns value for top shadow pixel */
    Pixel        *bottom_shadow;       /* returns value for bottom shadow pixel */
    Pixel        *select;              /* returns value for selection pixel */
```

XmGetDestination

Returns the widget ID of the current destination widget. The destination widget is usually the widget most recently edited via a selection, insertion, paste, etc. XmGetDestination() identifies the widget that serves as the destination for quick-paste operations and some clipboard routines. This routine returns NULL if there is no current destination (e.g., if no edit operations have been performed on a widget).

```
Widget XmGetDestination (display)
    Display         *display;              /* points to Display structure */
```

XmGetMenuCursor

Returns the cursor ID of the menu cursor currently in use by an application on the specified *display*. If the cursor is not yet defined (e.g., the application called this routine before any menus were created), then XmGetMenuCursor() returns the value None.

```
Cursor XmGetMenuCursor (display)
    Display         *display;              /* points to Display structure */
```

XmGetPixmap

Generates a pixmap and returns its resource ID. XmGetPixmap() first checks the pixmap cache for a pixmap that matches the bitmap data specified by *image_name*. If no pixmap is found, XmGetPixmap() checks the image cache for a matching *image_name*. From here, two things can happen. If *image_name* matches an image in the image cache, a pixmap is generated, cached, and returned; however, if no *image_name* matches, then XmGetPixmap() begins a search for an X10 or X11 bitmap file, using *image_name* as the filename. If a file is found, its contents are read, converted into an image, and cached in the image cache. Now, as in the earlier case, the image is used to generate a pixmap that is subsequently cached and returned. If no *image_name* is found, this routine returns XmUNSPECIFIED_PIXMAP. If *image_name* specifies a bitmap, *foreground* and *background* colors can be combined with the image.

```
Pixmap XmGetPixmap (screen, image_name, foreground, background)
    Screen          *screen;               /* screen on which pixmap will be drawn */
    char            *image_name;           /* string name of the image */
    Pixel           foreground;            /* foreground pixel to combine with image */
    Pixel           background;            /* background pixel to combine with image */
```

XmGetPostedFromWidget

A RowColumn routine that returns the widget from which the given *menu* was posted. The value returned depends on the type of *menu*; that is, for a PopupMenu, the routine returns the widget from which *menu* was originally popped up, whereas for a PulldownMenu, the routine returns the MenuBar or OptionMenu widget from which *menu* was pulled down.

```
#include <Xm/RowColumn.h>
Widget XmGetPostedFromWidget (menu)
    Widget          menu;                  /* widget ID of posted menu */
```

XmInstallImage

Stores *image* in an image cache. *image* can then be used later to generate a pixmap, whereas *image_name* can be used in a defaults file so that client applications can access the image (This routine must be called to install the image before the widget is created.) XmInstall-Image() returns True if successful, and it returns False if either argument is NULL or if *image_name* is already stored in the image cache.

```
Boolean XmInstallImage (image, image_name)
    XImage        *image;           /* returns image structure to add */
    char          *image_name;      /* string name of the image */
```

The image-caching routines provide eight preinstalled images. By using their names in a defaults file, you can generate pixmap for resources.

Image Name	Tile That is Generated
background	Solid background
25_foreground	25% foreground, 75% background
50_foreground	50% foreground, 50% background
75_foreground	75% foreground, 25% background
horizontal	Horizontal lines of alternating colors
vertical	Vertical lines of alternating colors
slant_right	Slanting lines of alternating colors
slant_left	Slanting lines of alternating colors

XmInternAtom

Returns an atom identifier corresponding to the given *name*. This routine works like Xlib's XInternAtom routine, but the Motif routine provides the added feature of client-side caching. XmInternAtom() is the inverse of XmGetAtomName(). When no atom exists with the specified *name*, the return value depends on the *only_if_exists* argument. If this argument is True, Xm-InternAtom() will not create a new atom but will simply return None. If *only_if_exists* is False, XmInternAtom() creates the atom and then returns its ID.

```
#include <Xm/AtomMgr.h>
Atom XmInternAtom (display, name, only_if_exists)
    Display       *display;         /* points to Display structure */
    String        name;             /* name of the newly created widget */
    Boolean       only_if_exists;   /* nonexistent name is ignored (True) or created (False) */
```

XmIsMotifWMRunning

Checks the _MOTIF_WM_INFO property to determine whether the Motif window manager is running on the screen containing the specified *shell*. If so, the routine returns True; if not, it returns False.

```
#include <Xm/VendorE.h>
Boolean XmIsMotifWMRunning (shell)
    Widget        shell;            /* shell widget of screen to query */
```

List Routines

Motif provides 25 routines to use in conjunction with List widgets. These routines are used to obtain information, as well as to affect the items in a List widget. Items can be moved, added, deleted, highlighted, etc. Many of the List routines have arguments in common. For example, all of these routines require a List widget ID. Many routines take arguments to specify item names, item counts, or item positions. Item names are specified as compound strings, either as an individual item or as a pointer to an array of items. Item counts are integers, as are item positions: the *position* argument gives the order of an item within a list. A *position* value of 1 indicates the first item, a *position* value of 2 indicates the second item, and so on. A value of 0 specifies the last item of a list.

XmListAddItem

Inserts *item* at the specified *position* within the List widget. A positive *position* sets the corresponding order of *item* in the list (e.g., 1=1st, 2=2nd), whereas a value of 0 designates the end of the list. The new *item* will appear selected if it matches an item in the array of currently selected list items. The List resource XmNselectedItems is a pointer to this array.

```
#include <Xm/List.h>
void XmListAddItem (widget, item, position)
    Widget        widget;       /* widget ID of List widget */
    XmString      item;         /* item to add to list */
    int           position;     /* position at which new item is added */
```

XmListAddItems

Similar to XmListAddItem(), except that more than one item can be added (either selected or unselected). Only the first *item_count* items are added to the specified List widget.

```
#include <Xm/List.h>
void XmListAddItems (widget, items, item_count, position)
    Widget        widget;       /* widget ID of List widget */
    XmString      *items;       /* array of items to add */
    int           item_count;   /* number of items on which to operate */
    int           position;     /* position of first item to be added */
```

XmListAddItemUnselected

Similar to XmListAddItem(), except that *item* does not appear selected, even if it matches a value in the XmNselectItems array.

```
#include <Xm/List.h>
void XmListAddItemUnselected (widget, item, position)
    Widget        widget;       /* widget ID of List widget */
    XmString      item;         /* item to add to list */
    int           position;     /* position at which new item is added */
```

XmListDeleteAllItems

Removes all items from the specified List widget.

```
#include <Xm/List.h>
void XmListDeleteAllItems (widget)
    Widget          widget;            /* widget ID of List widget */
```

XmListDeleteItem

Removes *item* from the specified List widget, shifting up the positions of subsequent items. If *item* doesn't exist, a warning message appears.

```
#include <Xm/List.h>
void XmListDeleteItem (widget, item)
    Widget          widget;            /* widget ID of List widget */
    XmString        item;              /* item to delete */
```

XmListDeleteItems

Removes the *items* from the specified List widget, shifting up the positions of subsequent items. If any of the given *items* don't exist, a warning message appears.

```
#include <Xm/List.h>
void XmListDeleteItems (widget, items, item_count)
    Widget          widget;            /* widget ID of List widget */
    XmString        *items;            /* array of items to delete */
    int             item_count;        /* number of items on which to operate */
```

XmListDeleteItemsPos

Removes (from the specified List widget) a consecutive number of items, with the first such item occurring at *position*. As with all List routines, a positive *position* corresponds to the order of a list item (e.g., 1=1st, 2=2nd), whereas a value of 0 designates the last item of the list. If the last item in the List widget is deleted, XmListDeleteItemsPos() returns, even if the specified *item_count* hasn't been reached. For example, if five deletions are to begin at the second-to-last item, only two deletions will take place.

```
#include <Xm/List.h>
void XmListDeleteItemsPos (widget, item_count, position)
    Widget          widget;            /* widget ID of List widget */
    int             item_count;        /* number of items on which to operate */
    int             position;          /* position of the first list item to delete */
```

XmListDeletePos

Removes the item at *position* from the List widget, shifting up the positions of subsequent items. A positive *position* indicates the order of an item within the list (e.g., 1=1st, 2=2nd), whereas a value of 0 designates the end of the list. If *position* doesn't exist, a warning message appears.

```
#include <Xm/List.h>
void XmListDeletePos (widget, position)
    Widget      widget;          /* widget ID of List widget */
    int         position;        /* position of item to delete */
```

XmListDeselectAllItems

Removes highlighting from all items in the specified List widget, also removing these items from the widget's selected list (the array to which the XmNselectedItems resource points).

```
#include <Xm/List.h>
void XmListDeselectAllItems (widget)
    Widget      widget;          /* widget ID of List widget */
```

XmListDeselectItem

Removes highlighting from *item* in the specified List widget, also removing this item from the widget's selected list (the array to which the XmNselectedItems resource points).

```
#include <Xm/List.h>
void XmListDeselectItem (widget, item)
    Widget      widget;          /* widget ID of List widget */
    XmString    item;            /* item to unhighlight */
```

XmListDeselectPos

Removes highlighting from the item at *position* within the List widget, also removing the item from the widget's selected list (the array to which the XmNselectedItems resource points). A positive *position* corresponds to the order of an item within the list (e.g., 1=1st, 2=2nd), whereas a value of 0 designates the end of the list.

```
#include <Xm/List.h>
void XmListDeselectPos (widget, position)
    Widget      widget;          /* widget ID of List widget */
    int         position;        /* position of item to deselect */
```

XmListGetMatchPos

Determines whether a specified *item* exists within a given List widget. *position_list* returns an array of positional values that indicate the location or locations of *item* (1 = first item; 2 = second item). *position_count* returns the number of values in *position_list*. The routine itself returns a Boolean: if the list contains *item*, XmListGetMatchPos() returns True, allocating memory for the *position_list* array; otherwise, the routine returns False.

```
#include <Xm/List.h>
Boolean XmListGetMatchPos (widget, item, position_list, position_count)
    Widget      widget;              /* widget ID of List widget */
    XmString    item;                /* item whose positions are returned */
    int         **position_list;     /* list of positions containing item */
    int         *position_count;     /* number of positions matched */
```

XmListGetSelectedPos

Determines whether a given List widget has any highlighted items. *position_list* returns an array of positional values that indicate the location or locations of selected items (1 = first item; 2 = second item). *position_count* returns the number of values in *position_list*. The routine itself returns a Boolean: if the list contains at least one selected item, XmListGetMatchPos() returns True, allocating memory for the *position_list* array; otherwise, the routine returns False.

```
#include <Xm/List.h>
Boolean XmListGetSelectedPos (widget, position_list, position_count)
    Widget          widget;            /* widget ID of List widget */
    int             **position_list;   /* list of positions containing selected items */
    int             *position_count;   /* number of positions matched */
```

XmListItemExists

Checks whether the specified List widget contains *item*, returning True if so and False if not.

```
#include <Xm/List.h>
Boolean XmListItemExists (widget, item)
    Widget          widget;   /* widget ID of List widget */
    XmString        item;     /* item whose presence is determined */
```

XmListItemPos

Returns the positional value of the first occurrence of *item* in the specified List widget. If *item* isn't found, XmListItemPos() returns 0.

```
#include <Xm/List.h>
int XmListItemPos (widget, item)
    Widget          widget;   /* widget ID of List widget */
    XmString        item;     /* item whose position is returned */
```

XmListReplaceItems

Replaces each item in a list of *old_items* with the corresponding item from the list of *new_items*. This cycle repeats on an entry-by-entry basis until the number specified by *item_count* is reached.

```
#include <Xm/List.h>
void XmListReplaceItems (widget, old_items, item_count, new_items)
    Widget          widget;       /* widget ID of List widget */
    XmString        *old_items;   /* items that will be replaced */
    int             item_count;   /* number of items on which to operate */
    XmString        *new_items;   /* items that will replace old items */
```

XmListReplaceItemsPos

Replaces a consecutive number of items with the corresponding values in *new_items*. The first item to be replaced occurs at *position*. A positive *position* corresponds to the order of a list item (e.g., 1=1st, 2=2nd), whereas a value of 0 designates the last item of the list. If the last item in the List widget is replaced, XmListReplaceItemsPos() completes its operations, even if the specified *item_count* hasn't been reached. For example, if five replacements are to begin at the second-to-last item, only two replacements will take place.

```
#include <Xm/List.h>
void XmListReplaceItemsPos (widget, new_items, item_count, position)
    Widget      widget;         /* widget ID of List widget */
    XmString    *new_items;     /* items that will replace old items */
    int         item_count;     /* number of items on which to operate */
    int         position;       /* position of first list item to replace */
```

XmListSelectItem

Highlights *item* in the specified List widget. If the widget's XmNselectionPolicy resource is Xm-MULTIPLE_SELECT, this routine adds *item* to the widget's selected list; otherwise, this routine replaces the currently selected item with *item*. The XmNselectedItems resource is a pointer to the selection list. If *notify* is True, XmListSelectItem() invokes the selection callback associated with the item.

```
#include <Xm/List.h>
void XmListSelectItem (widget, item, notify)
    Widget      widget;     /* widget ID of List widget */
    XmString    item;       /* item to highlight */
    Boolean     notify;     /* when True, invokes the callback to process changes */
```

XmListSelectPos

Highlights the item at *position* in the specified List widget. If the widget's XmNselectionPolicy resource is XmMULTIPLE_SELECT, this routine adds the item to the widget's selected list; otherwise, this routine replaces the currently selected item with the specified item. The XmNselectedItems resource is a pointer to the selection list. A positive *position* corresponds to the order of an item within the list (e.g., 1=1st, 2=2nd), whereas a value of 0 designates the end of the list. If *notify* is True, XmListSelectPos() invokes the selection callback associated with the item.

```
#include <Xm/List.h>
void XmListSelectPos (widget, position, notify)
    Widget      widget;     /* widget ID of List widget */
    int         position;   /* position of item to move to top */
    Boolean     notify;     /* when True, invokes the callback to process changes */
```

XmListSetAddMode

Activates Add Mode (if *mode* is True) or deactivates Add Mode (if *mode* is False). Whenever a List widget is in Add Mode, the user can move the insert cursor without disturbing the current selection.

```
#include <Xm/List.h>
void XmListSetAddMode (widget, mode)
    Widget      widget;     /* widget ID of List widget */
    Boolean     mode;       /* turns Add Mode on (True) or off (False) */
```

XmListSetBottomItem

Scrolls the List widget so that the specified *item* appears at the bottom of the list.

```
#include <Xm/List.h>
void XmListSetBottomItem (widget, item)
    Widget        widget;        /* widget ID of List widget */
    XmString      item;          /* item to display as last item */
```

XmListSetBottomPos

Scrolls the List widget so that the item at the specified *position* appears at the bottom of the list. A positive *position* corresponds to the order of an item within the list (e.g., 1=1st, 2=2nd), whereas a value of 0 designates the last item of the list.

```
#include <Xm/List.h>
void XmListSetBottomPos (widget, position)
    Widget        widget;        /* widget ID of List widget */
    int           position;      /* position of item to move to bottom */
```

XmListSetHorizPos

Scrolls to the specified horizontal *location* in the given List widget. Sometimes a list item is too long to fit horizontally inside the viewing area of a List widget. When this happens, the List widget either will expand horizontally or will add a horizontal ScrollBar, depending on the value of the List's **XmNlistSizePolicy** resource. XmListSetHorizPos() scrolls horizontally to the *location* in the List, provided that a horizontal ScrollBar is already present and provided that **XmNlistSizePolicy** is set to **XmCONSTANT** or to **XmRESIZE_IF_POSSIBLE**. This routine accomplishes the scrolling by first setting the ScrollBar's **XmNvalue** resource to the value of *location*.

```
#include <Xm/List.h>
void XmListSetHorizPos (widget, location)
    Widget        widget;        /* widget ID of List widget */
    int           location;      /* horizontal position scrolled to */
```

XmListSetItem

Scrolls the List widget so that the specified *item* appears at the top of the list.

```
#include <Xm/List.h>
void XmListSetItem (widget, item)
    Widget        widget;        /* widget ID of List widget */
    XmString      item;          /* item to display as first item */
```

XmListSetPos

Scrolls the List widget so that the specified *item* appears at the top of the list. A positive *position* corresponds to the order of an item within the list (e.g., 1=1st, 2=2nd), whereas a value of 0 designates the last item of the list.

```
#include <Xm/List.h>
void XmListSetPos (widget, position)
   Widget       widget;        /* widget ID of List widget */
   int          position;      /* position of item to select */
```

XmMainWindowSep1

Returns the widget ID of a MainWindow widget's first Separator. The first Separator is directly below the MenuBar. A MainWindow widget contains three Separator widgets, each of which is visible only when the MainWindow's XmNshowSeparator resource is reset to True.

```
#include <Xm/MainW.h>
Widget XmMainWindowSep1 (widget)
   Widget       widget;        /* widget ID of MainWindow widget */
```

XmMainWindowSep2

Returns the widget ID of a MainWindow widget's second Separator. The second Separator is between the Command widget and the ScrolledWindow widget. A MainWindow widget contains three Separator widgets, each of which is visible only when the MainWindow's XmNshowSeparator resource is reset to True.

```
#include <Xm/MainW.h>
Widget XmMainWindowSep2 (widget)
   Widget       widget;        /* widget ID of MainWindow widget */
```

XmMainWindowSep3

Returns the widget ID of a MainWindow widget's third Separator. The third Separator is located just above the message window. A MainWindow widget contains three Separator widgets, each of which is visible only when the MainWindow's XmNshowSeparator resource is reset to True.

```
#include <Xm/MainW.h>
Widget XmMainWindowSep3 (widget)
   Widget       widget;        /* widget ID of MainWindow widget */
```

XmMainWindowSetAreas

Sets up the standard regions of an application's MainWindow widget (provided that the MainWindow has already been created). Each region may have child widgets, and this routine determines which of those children will be actively managed by the MainWindow.

```
#include <Xm/MainW.h>
void XmMainWindowSetAreas (widget, menu_bar, command_window, horizontal_scrollbar, vertical_scrollbar,
       work_region)
   Widget       widget;              /* widget ID of MainWindow widget */
   Widget       menu_bar;            /* widget ID for MenuBar */
   Widget       command_window;      /* widget ID of Command window */
   Widget       horizontal_scrollbar;/* widget ID for horizontal ScrollBar */
   Widget       vertical_scrollbar;  /* widget ID for vertical ScrollBar */
   Widget       work_region;         /* widget ID for the work window */
```

For the last five arguments, the associated resources are respectively XmNmenuBar and Xm-Ncommand (defined by the MainWindow widget), and XmNhorizontalScrollBar, XmNverticalScroll-Bar, and XmNworkWindow (defined by the ScrolledWindow widget). If the application does not have one of these regions, the corresponding argument can be specified as NULL.

XmMenuPosition

Positions a Popup MenuPane, using the values of the *x_root* and *y_root* members from the specified *event*. An application must call this routine before managing the popup menu, unless the application itself is positioning the MenuPane.

```
#include <Xm/RowColumn.h>
void XmMenuPosition (menu, event)
    Widget                  menu;           /* widget ID of PopupMenu to position */
    XButtonPressedEvent     *event;         /* ButtonPress that marks current position of pointer */
```

XmMessageBoxGetChild

Returns the widget ID of the specified *child* of the MessageBox widget.

```
#include <Xm/MessageB.h>
Widget XmMessageBoxGetChild (widget, child)
    Widget          widget;         /* widget ID of MessageBox */
    unsigned char   child;          /* component whose widget ID is returned */
```

The values for *child* are defined in *<Xm/Xm.h>*:

XmDIALOG_CANCEL_BUTTON   XmDIALOG_OK_BUTTON
XmDIALOG_DEFAULT_BUTTON   XmDIALOG_SEPARATOR
XmDIALOG_HELP_BUTTON   XmDIALOG_SYMBOL_LABEL
XmDIALOG_MESSAGE_LABEL

XmOptionButtonGadget

Returns the widget ID for the internal CascadeButtonGadget that gets created when the *option_menu* widget is created. An OptionMenu is a RowColumn widget containing two gadgets: a LabelGadget that displays the XmNlabelString resource, and a CascadeButtonGadget that displays the current selection.

```
#include <Xm/RowColumn.h>
Widget XmOptionButtonGadget (option_menu)
    Widget          option_menu;    /* widget ID of OptionMenu */
```

XmOptionLabelGadget

Returns the widget ID for the internal LabelGadget that gets created when the given *option_menu* widget is created. An OptionMenu is a RowColumn widget containing two gadgets: a LabelGadget that displays the XmNlabelString resource, and a CascadeButtonGadget that displays the current selection.

```
#include <Xm/RowColumn.h>
Widget XmOptionLabelGadget (option_menu)
    Widget          option_menu;    /* widget ID of OptionMenu */
```

XmProcessTraversal

Causes the input focus to change to another widget under application control, rather than as a result of keyboard traversal events from a user. This routine finds the currently active widget or tab group (i.e., the one receiving keyboard events), and the *direction* argument specifies the nature of the traversal to be made. If the new setting succeeds, XmProcessTraversal() returns True. The routine returns False if the keyboard's focus policy isn't XmEXPLICIT, if no traversible items exist, or if the arguments are invalid.

```
Boolean XmProcessTraversal (widget, direction)
    Widget        widget;        /* widget for which to traverse hierarchy */
    int           direction;     /* direction in which to traverse widget hierarchy */
```

The values for *direction* are defined in *<Xm/Xm.h>*.

```
XmTRAVERSE_CURRENT              /* if tab group is inactive, activate it;
                                   otherwise, activate first item in the tab group */
XmTRAVERSE_NEXT                 /* activate next item in active tab group */
XmTRAVERSE_PREV                 /* activate previous item in active tab group */
XmTRAVERSE_HOME                 /* activate first item in active tab group */
XmTRAVERSE_NEXT_TAB_GROUP       /* activate next tab group */
XmTRAVERSE_PREV_TAB_GROUP       /* activate previous tab group */
XmTRAVERSE_UP                   /* activate item above, wrapping around if needed */
XmTRAVERSE_DOWN                 /* activate item below, wrapping around if needed */
XmTRAVERSE_LEFT                 /* activate item to left, wrapping around if needed */
XmTRAVERSE_RIGHT                /* activate item to right, wrapping around if needed */
```

XmRemoveProtocolCallback

Removes *callback* from the list of callback procedures that are invoked via the given message *protocol*. The inverse routine is XmAddProtocolCallback().

```
#include <Xm/Protocols.h>
void XmRemoveProtocolCallback (shell, property, protocol, callback, closure)
    Widget          shell;      /* widget associated with the protocol property */
    Atom            property;   /* property that will hold protocol data for shell */
    Atom            protocol;   /* atom ID of protocol */
    XtCallbackProc  callback;   /* procedure to call when a protocol message is received */
    caddr_t         closure;    /* client data to pass to callback when it's invoked */
```

XmRemoveProtocols

Removes *protocols* from the protocol manager, deallocating the internal tables. This routine also updates the callback list and the given *property*, provided that at least one of the protocols is active and that *shell* is realized. The inverse routine is XmAddProtocols().

```
#include <Xm/Protocols.h>
void XmRemoveProtocols (shell, property, protocols, num_protocols)
    Widget      shell;           /* widget associated with the protocol property */
    Atom        property;        /* property that will hold protocol data for shell */
    Atom        *protocols;      /* points to list of protocol atom IDs */
    Cardinal    num_protocols;   /* number of elements in protocols */
```

XmRemoveTabGroup

Removes a widget (specified by *tab_group*) from the list of tab groups and sets the widget's XmNnavigationType resource to XmNONE. This routine is retained for compatibility with Motif 1.0 and should not be used in newer applications. If traversal behavior needs to be changed, this should be done by setting the XmNnavigationType resource directly. The inverse routine is XmAddTabGroup().

```
void XmRemoveTabGroup (tab_group)
    Widget          tab_group;          /* widget ID of Manager or Primitive widget */
```

XmRemoveWMProtocolCallback

A convenience routine that calls XmRemoveProtocolCallback() with *property* set to XA_WM_PRO-TOCOL, the window manager protocol property. The inverse routine is XmAddWMProtocol-Callback().

```
#include <Xm/Protocols.h>
void XmRemoveWMProtocolCallback (shell, protocol, callback, closure)
    Widget          shell;              /* widget associated with the protocol property */
    Atom            protocol;           /* atom ID of protocol */
    XtCallbackProc  callback;           /* procedure to call when a protocol message is received */
    caddr_t         closure;            /* client data to pass to callback when it's invoked */
```

XmRemoveWMProtocols

A convenience routine that calls XmRemoveProtocols() with *property* set to XA_WM_PROTOCOL, the window manager protocol property. The inverse routine is XmAddWMProtocols().

```
#include <Xm/Protocols.h>
void XmRemoveWMProtocols (shell, protocols, num_protocols)
    Widget          shell;              /* widget associated with the protocol property */
    Atom            *protocols;         /* points to list of protocol atom IDs */
    Cardinal        num_protocols;      /* number of elements in protocols */
```

XmResolveAllPartOffsets

Ensures that, when an application or a widget is written, it will be upwardly compatible with the records in a widget structure. In other words, if the size of a widget structure changes in the future, this routine can be used to calculate the locations of the new offsets. This routine and XmResolvePartOffsets() are similar. During the creation of a widget, both routines modify the widget structure by allocating an array of offset values. XmResolvePartOffsets() affects only the widget instance record, whereas XmResolveAllPartOffsets() affects the constraint record as well (this means that constraint widget children will also be made upwardly compatible).

```
void XmResolveAllPartOffsets (widget_class, offset, constraint_offset)
    WidgetClass     widget_class;           /* widget class for which to allocate offset record */
    XmOffsetPtr     *offset;                /* returns array of offsets for widget record */
    XmOffsetPtr     *constraint_offset;     /* returns array of offsets for constraint record */
```

XmResolvePartOffsets

See XmResolveAllPartOffsets().

```
void XmResolvePartOffsets (widget_class, offset)
   WidgetClass    widget_class;    /* widget class for which to allocate offset record */
   XmOffsetPtr    *offset;          /* returns array of offsets for widget record */
```

XmScaleGetValue

Returns the value of the slider's current position within the specified Scale widget.

```
#include <Xm/Scale.h>
void XmScaleGetValue (widget, value_return)
   Widget    widget;          /* widget ID of Scale widget */
   int       *value_return;   /* returns the slider's current position */
```

XmScaleSetValue

Within the specified Scale widget, sets the slider's current position to *value*. The *value* argument sets the Scale's XmNvalue resource, whose range is between XmNminimum and Xm-Nmaximum.

```
#include <Xm/Scale.h>
void XmScaleSetValue (widget, value)
   Widget    widget;    /* widget ID of Scale widget */
   int       value;     /* slider's position */
```

XmScrollBarGetValues

Returns current information about the slider of the specified ScrollBar widget. This information consists of the slider's position, size, and increment values.

```
#include <Xm/ScrollBar.h>
void XmScrollBarGetValues (widget, value_return, slider_size_return, increment_return, page_increment_return)
   Widget    widget;                  /* widget ID of ScrollBar widget */
   int       *value_return;           /* returns the slider's current position */
   int       *slider_size_return;     /* returns size of slider */
   int       *increment_return;       /* returns smallest slider movement */
   int       *page_increment_return;  /* returns smallest movement from paging */
```

XmScrollBarSetValues

For the specified ScrollBar widget, sets the slider's position, size, button increment, and page increment values. The minimum value of *value* (the slider's position) is XmNminimum, and the maximum value is XmNmaximum minus XmNsliderSize (you must account for the slider's length). The minimum value of *slider_size* (the length of the slider) is 1, and the maximum value is the absolute value of XmNmaximum minus XmNminimum (i.e., the available range of motion). *increment* (the minimum amount by which the slider moves) has a default value of 1. *page_increment* (slider movement caused by scrolling page by page) has a default value of 10. Specifying each of the above arguments also sets the associated ScrollBar resource (respectively XmNvalue, XmNsliderSize, XmNincrement, and XmNpageIncrement). If *notify* is True, Xm-

ScrollBarSetValues() activates the ScrollBar resource XmNvalueChangedCallback so that the requested slider changes will be made.

```
#include <Xm/ScrollBar.h>
void XmScrollBarSetValues (widget, value, slider_size, increment, page_increment, notify)
    Widget     widget;              /* widget ID of ScrollBar widget */
    int        value;               /* slider's position */
    int        slider_size;         /* size of slider */
    int        increment;           /* smallest movement of slider */
    int        page_increment;      /* smallest slider movement due to ScrollBar paging */
    Boolean    notify;              /* when True, invokes the callback to process changes */
```

XmScrolledWindowSetAreas

Adds or changes the standard regions of an application's ScrolledWindow widget (provided that the ScrolledWindow has already been created). These regions are three child widgets: a horizontal scrollbar, a vertical scrollbar, and a window work region.

```
#include <Xm/ScrolledW.h>
void XmScrolledWindowSetAreas (widget, horizontal_scrollbar, vertical_scrollbar, work_region)
    Widget     widget;                 /* widget ID of ScrollWindow */
    Widget     horizontal_scrollbar;   /* widget ID for horizontal ScrollBar */
    Widget     vertical_scrollbar;     /* widget ID for vertical ScrollBar */
    Widget     work_region;            /* widget ID for the work window */
```

For the last three arguments, the associated resources are XmNhorizontalScrollBar, XmNvertical-ScrollBar, and XmNworkWindow, respectively. If the application does not have one of these regions, the corresponding argument can be specified as NULL.

XmSelectionBoxGetChild

Returns the widget ID of the specified *child* of the SelectionBox widget.

```
#include <Xm/SelectioB.h>
Widget XmSelectionBoxGetChild (widget, child)
    Widget          widget;    /* widget ID of SelectionBox */
    unsigned char   child;     /* component whose widget ID is returned */
```

The values for *child* are defined in *<Xm/Xm.h>*:

XmDIALOG_APPLY_BUTTON	XmDIALOG_OK_BUTTON
XmDIALOG_CANCEL_BUTTON	XmDIALOG_SELECTION_LABEL
XmDIALOG_DEFAULT_BUTTON	XmDIALOG_SEPARATOR
XmDIALOG_HELP_BUTTON	XmDIALOG_TEXT
XmDIALOG_LIST	XmDIALOG_WORK_AREA
XmDIALOG_LIST_LABEL	

XmSetColorCalculation

Sets the procedure called by XmGetColors() that calculates the default colors (foreground, top and bottom shadows, and selection highlighting). The procedure calculates these colors based on a background color that has been passed to the procedure. If *color_proc* is NULL, this routine restores the default procedure.

```
XmColorProc XmSetColorCalculation (color_proc)
    XmColorProc    color_proc;        /* procedure for calculating default colors */
```

The color procedure has the following calling sequence:

```
void (*color_proc) (bg_color, fg_color, select_color, top_shadow_color, bot_shadow_color)
    XColor    *bg_color;              /* background color */
    XColor    *fg_color;              /* foreground color to calculate */
    XColor    *select_color;          /* select color to calculate */
    XColor    *top_shadow_color;      /* top shadow color to calculate */
    XColor    *bot_shadow_color;      /* bottom shadow color to calculate */
```

For each XColor structure, *color_proc* calculates the values for the red, green, and blue structure members. *color_proc* fills in these structure members but shouldn't allocate their color cells.

XmSetFontUnit

Sets the value of the font unit. Applications must call XmSetFontUnit() before creating any widgets that contain resolution-independent data. This routine has been superseded by Xm-SetFontUnits() (which allows the horizontal and vertical units to be set separately).

```
void XmSetFontUnit (display, font_unit_value)
    Display    *display;              /* points to Display structure */
    int        font_unit_value;       /* value to use in conversion calculations */
```

XmSetFontUnits

Sets the value of the horizontal and vertical font units. Applications must call XmSetFont-Units() before creating any widgets that contain resolution-independent data.

```
void XmSetFontUnits (display, h_value, v_value)
    Display    *display;              /* points to Display structure */
    int        h_value;               /* value for converting horizontal units */
    int        v_value;               /* value for converting vertical units */
```

XmSetMenuCursor

Sets the cursor that displays in a Motif menu on the specified *display*.

```
void XmSetMenuCursor (display, cursorId)
    Display    *display;              /* points to Display structure */
    Cursor     cursorId;              /* resource ID of cursor to use in menus */
```

XmSetProtocolHooks

Allows pre- and post-procedures to be invoked in addition to the regular callback procedures that are performed when the Motif window mangager sends a protocol message. The *prehook* procedure is invoked before calling the procedures on the client's callback list, whereas the *posthook* procedure is invoked after calling the procedures on the client's callback list. This routine gives shells more control flow, since callback procedures aren't necessarily executed in any particular order.

```
#include <Xm/Protocols.h>
void XmSetProtocolHooks (shell, property, protocol, prehook, pre_closure, posthook, post_closure)
    Widget          shell;          /* widget associated with the protocol property */
    Atom            property;       /* property that will hold protocol data for shell */
    Atom            protocol;       /* atom ID of protocol */
    XtCallbackProc  prehook;        /* proc to call before client's callbacks have been called */
    caddr_t         pre_closure;    /* data to pass to prehook when it's invoked */
    XtCallbackProc  posthook;       /* proc to call after client's callbacks have been called */
    caddr_t         post_closure;   /* data to pass to posthook when it's invoked */
```

XmSetWMProtocolHooks

A convenience routine that calls XmSetProtocolHooks() with *property* set to XA_WM_PROTO-COL, the window manager protocol property.

```
#include <Xm/Protocols.h>
void XmSetWMProtocolHooks (shell, protocol, prehook, pre_closure, posthook, post_closure)
    Widget          shell;          /* widget associated with the protocol property */
    Atom            protocol;       /* atom ID of protocol */
    XtCallbackProc  prehook;        /* proc to call before client's callbacks have been called */
    caddr_t         pre_closure;    /* data to pass to prehook when it's invoked */
    XtCallbackProc  posthook;       /* proc to call after client's callbacks have been called */
    caddr_t         post_closure;   /* data to pass to posthook when it's invoked */
```

Compound String Manipulation Routines

Motif provides 30 routines for creating, comparing, and manipulating compound strings. A compound string has three main attributes: a character set, a direction, and the text itself. Each attribute, in turn, consists of a tag, a length, and a value.

XmStringBaseline

Returns the distance, in pixels, from the top of the character box to the baseline of the first line of text in *string*. If *string* is created with XmStringCreateSimple() instead of XmStringCreate(), then *fontlist* must begin with the font from the character set of the current language environment (otherwise the result is undefined).

```
Dimension XmStringBaseline (fontlist, string)
    XmFontList      fontlist;       /* list of fonts and character set IDs */
    XmString        string;         /* compound string to use */
```

XmStringByteCompare

Returns True if the compound strings *string1* and *string2* are equivalent, byte for byte; returns False otherwise. Typically, identical character strings are those that are created by the same routine with the same character set or language set. Sometimes, however, when a compound string is placed into a widget, the string is converted to an internal form that allows faster processing, and the conversion strips out some information. As a result, when an application later retrieves the compound string by calling XtGetValues(), the string won't necessarily match byte for byte the string that the widget orginally received.

```
Boolean XmStringByteCompare (string1, string2)
    XmString        string1;            /* compound string to compare with string2 */
    XmString        string2;            /* compound string to compare with string1 */
```

XmStringCompare

Similar to XmStringByteCompare() but less restrictive. XmStringCompare() returns True if the two compound strings are merely "semantically" equivalent. This means that the compound strings have the same text components, directions, separators, and (if specified) character sets.

```
Boolean XmStringCompare (string1, string2)
    XmString        string1;            /* compound string to compare with string2 */
    XmString        string2;            /* compound string to compare with string1 */
```

XmStringConcat

Returns the compound string formed by appending string2 to string1, leaving the original compound strings unchanged. Storage for the result is allocated within this routine and should be freed by calling XmStringFree().

```
XmString XmStringConcat (string1, string2)
    XmString        string1;            /* first compound string */
    XmString        string2;            /* compound string to append to string1 */
```

XmStringCopy

Copies the compound string string and returns the copy, leaving the original unchanged. Storage for the result is managed by the application and should be freed by calling XmStringFree().

```
XmString XmStringCopy (string)
    XmString        string;             /* compound string to use */
```

XmStringCreate

Creates a compound string composed of text and the character set identified by charset.

```
XmString XmStringCreate (text, charset)
    char            *text;              /* null-terminated string to use */
    XmStringCharSet charset;            /* XmSTRING_DEFAULT_CHARSET, for example */
```

XmStringCreateLtoR

Similar to XmStringCreate(), in that they both create a compound string composed of text associated with the character set identified by charset. In addition, this routine searches for newline characters (\n) in text. Each time a newline is found, the characters up to the newline are placed into a segment followed by a separator component. This routine does not add a separator component to the end of the compound string. The default direction is left to right, and the assumed encoding is 8-bit characters rather than 16-bit.

```
XmString XmStringCreateLtoR (text, charset)
    char            *text;              /* null-terminated string to use */
    XmStringCharSet charset;            /* XmSTRING_DEFAULT_CHARSET, for example */
```

XmStringCreateSimple

Similar to XmStringCreate() but doesn't allow a character set to be specified. Instead, this routine obtains the character set from the LANG environment variable or, failing that, from a vendor-specific default (usually ISO8859-1). *text* cannot contain a newline.

```
XmString XmStringCreateSimple (text)
    char          *text;            /* null-terminated string to use */
```

XmStringDirectionCreate

Creates and returns a compound string containing a specified *direction* as its only component.

```
XmString XmStringDirectionCreate (direction)
    XmStringDirection direction;          /* direction of the text */
```

The values for *direction* are defined in *<Xm/Xm.h>*:

XmSTRING_DIRECTION_L_TO_R   XmSTRING_DIRECTION_R_TO_L

XmStringDraw

Draws the compound string specified by *string*. If *string* is created with XmStringCreateSimple() instead of XmStringCreate(), then *fontlist* must begin with the font from the character set of the current language environment (otherwise the result is undefined).

```
void XmStringDraw (display, window, fontlist, string, gc, x, y, width, alignment, layout_direction, clip)
    Display         *display;            /* points to Display structure */
    Window          window;              /* window in which to draw string */
    XmFontList      fontlist;            /* list of fonts and character set IDs */
    XmString        string;              /* compound string to use */
    GC              gc;                  /* graphics context used for drawing string */
    Position        x;                   /* x-coord of rectangle to contain string */
    Position        y;                   /* y-coord of rectangle to contain string */
    Dimension       width;               /* width, in pixels, of rectangle to contain string */
    unsigned char   alignment;           /* how string will align within specified rectangle */
    unsigned char   layout_direction;    /* direction in which to draw segments of string */
    XRectangle      *clip;               /* if non-NULL, drawing area is restricted */
```

The values for *layout_direction* are defined in *<Xm/Xm.h>*:

XmSTRING_DIRECTION_L_TO_R   XmSTRING_DIRECTION_R_TO_L

layout_direction also determines the interpretation of *alignment*, whose values are defined as follows in *<Xm/Xm.h>*:

XmALIGNMENT_BEGINNING   XmALIGNMENT_CENTER
XmALIGNMENT_END

XmStringDrawImage

Draws the compound string specified by *string*, rendering the foreground *and* background pixel values for each character. If *string* is created with XmStringCreateSimple() instead of Xm-StringCreate(), then *fontlist* must begin with the font from the character set of the current language environment (otherwise the result is undefined). See XmStringDraw() for the values of *alignment* and *layout_direction*.

```
void XmStringDrawImage (display, window, fontlist, string, gc, x, y, width, alignment, layout_direction, clip)
    Display         *display;          /* points to Display structure */
    Window          window;            /* window in which to draw string */
    XmFontList      fontlist;          /* list of fonts and character set IDs */
    XmString        string;            /* compound string to use */
    GC              gc;                 /* graphics context used for drawing string */
    Position        x;                 /* x-coord of rectangle to contain string */
    Position        y;                 /* y-coord of rectangle to contain string */
    Dimension       width;             /* width, in pixels, of rectangle to contain string */
    unsigned char   alignment;         /* how string will align within specified rectangle */
    unsigned char   layout_direction;  /* direction in which to draw segments of string */
    XRectangle      *clip;             /* if non-NULL, drawing area is restricted */
```

XmStringDrawUnderline

Similar to XmStringDraw(), but also draws an underline beneath the first matching substring that is contained within *string*. See XmStringDraw() for the values of *alignment* and *layout_direction*.

```
void XmStringDrawUnderline (display, window, fontlist, string, gc, x, y, width, alignment, layout_direction, clip,
                            underline)
    Display         *display;          /* points to Display structure */
    Window          window;            /* window in which to draw string */
    XmFontList      fontlist;          /* list of fonts and character set IDs */
    XmString        string;            /* compound string to use */
    GC              gc;                 /* graphics context used for drawing string */
    Position        x;                 /* x-coord of rectangle to contain string */
    Position        y;                 /* y-coord of rectangle to contain string */
    Dimension       width;             /* width, in pixels, of rectangle to contain string */
    unsigned char   alignment;         /* how string will align within specified rectangle */
    unsigned char   layout_direction;  /* direction in which to draw segments of string */
    XRectangle      *clip;             /* if non-NULL, drawing area is restricted */
    XmString        underline;         /* substring to underline, if contained in string */
```

XmStringEmpty

Returns True if no text segments exist in *string*, and False otherwise.

```
Boolean XmStringEmpty (s1)
    XmString        string;            /* compound string to use */
```

XmStringExtent

Calculates the size of the smallest rectangle that can enclose *string*, returning the width and height (in pixels). If *string* is created with XmStringCreateSimple() instead of XmStringCreate(), then *fontlist* must begin with the font from the character set of the current language environment (otherwise the result is undefined).

```
void XmStringExtent (fontlist, string, width, height)
    XmFontList      fontlist;          /* list of fonts and character set IDs */
    XmString        string;            /* compound string to use */
    Dimension       *width;            /* returns the rectangle's width */
    Dimension       *height;           /* returns the rectangle's height */
```

XmStringFree

Frees memory that was used by *string*.

```
void XmStringFree (string)
    XmString        string;            /* compound string to use */
```

XmStringFreeContext

Deallocates the string context structure specified by *context*. This routine is the last of the string context routines that an application should call. Applications begin by calling Xm-StringInitContext() and then make repeated calls to either XmStringGetNextComponent() or Xm-StringGetNextSegment().

```
void XmStringFreeContext (context)
    XmStringContext  context;          /* string context used by XmStringInitContext() */
```

XmStringGetLtoR

Looks for a text segment in *string* that matches the character set identifier specified by *charset*, and returns True if a text segment is matched. *text* returns a pointer to the matched segment.

```
Boolean XmStringGetLtoR (string, charset, text)
    XmString        string;            /* compound string to use */
    XmStringCharSet charset;           /* XmSTRING_DEFAULT_CHARSET, for example */
    char            **text;            /* pointer to a null-terminated string */
```

XmStringGetNextComponent

Reads the next component in the compound string defined by *context* and returns the type of component found. For some component types, the component's value is returned in the routine's corresponding argument or arguments. That is, for type XmSTRING_COMPO-NENT_CHARSET, the character set identifier is returned in *charset*; for type XmSTRING_COM-PONENT_TEXT, the text string is returned in *text*; for XmSTRING_COMPONENT_DIRECTION, the direction is returned in *direction*. Only one of *charset*, *text*, and *direction* can be valid at any one time. For type XmSTRING_COMPONENT_UNKNOWN, the component's tag, length, and value are returned in the corresponding arguments. Storage for the returned values is allocated by this routine and must be freed by the application. This routine is called after Xm-StringInitContext() and before XmStringFreeContext().

```
XmStringComponentType XmStringGetNextComponent (context, text, charset, direction, unknown_tag,
            unknown_length, unknown_value)
    XmStringContext         context;        /* string context used by XmStringInitContext() */
    char                    **text;         /* pointer to a null-terminated string */
    XmStringCharSet         *charset;       /* returns the character set ID for text */
    XmStringDirection       *direction;     /* returns the direction of the text */
    XmStringComponentType   *unknown_tag;   /* returns an unknown component's tag */
```

| unsigned short | *unknown_length; | /* returns an unknown component's length */ |
| unsigned char | **unknown_value; | /* returns an unknown component's value */ |

The component types can have the following values, defined in *<Xm/Xm.h>*:

XmSTRING_COMPONENT_UNKNOWN	/* next component is of unknown type */
XmSTRING_COMPONENT_CHARSET	/* next component is character set identifier */
XmSTRING_COMPONENT_TEXT	/* next component is a text component */
XmSTRING_COMPONENT_DIRECTION	/* next component is a direction */
XmSTRING_COMPONENT_SEPARATOR	/* next component is a separator */
XmSTRING_COMPONENT_END	/* this is the last component in string */

XmStringGetNextSegment

Obtains the text string, character set identifier, and direction for the next segment of the compound string defined by *context*. XmStringGetNextSegment() returns True if a valid segment was read; otherwise, it returns False. This routine is called after XmStringInitContext() and before XmStringFreeContext().

Boolean XmStringGetNextSegment (*context, text, charset, direction, separator*)

XmStringContext	context;	/* string context used by XmStringInitContext() */
char	**text;	/* pointer to a null-terminated string */
XmStringCharSet	*charset;	/* returns the character set ID for *text* */
XmStringDirection	*direction;	/* returns the direction of the text */
Boolean	*separator;	/* returns True if a separator is next component */

XmStringHasSubstring

Determines whether one compound string (*substring*) is contained within any single segment of another compound string (*string*). (*substring* must also have only a single segment.) Returns True if so; False otherwise. When comparing a compound string created by XmString-Create() with a compound string created by XmStringCreateSimple(), the result is undefined.

Boolean XmStringHasSubstring (*string, substring*)

| XmString | string; | /* compound string to use */ |
| XmString | substring; | /* text portion to search for within larger string */ |

XmStringHeight

Returns the height, in pixels, of the specified compound *string*. If *string* contains multiple lines (a separator component delimits each line), then the total height of all lines is returned. If *string* is created with XmStringCreateSimple() instead of XmStringCreate(), then *fontlist* must begin with the font from the character set of the current language environment (otherwise the result is undefined).

Dimension XmStringHeight (*fontlist, string*)

| XmFontList | fontlist; | /* list of fonts and character set IDs */ |
| XmString | string; | /* compound string to use */ |

XmStringInitContext

Creates the string context structure specified by *context*, thereby allowing applications to read the contents of a compound string. This routine is the first, of the three string context routines to call, and the same *context* should be specified for XmStringGetNextComponent(), XmStringGet-NextSegment(), and XmStringFreeContext(). *string* will be read one component at a time (using XmStringGetNextComponent()) or one segment at a time (using XmStringGetNextSegment()). XmStringInitContext() returns True if *context* was allocated and returns False otherwise.

```
Boolean XmStringInitContext (context, string)
    XmStringContext *context;        /* returns the allocated string context structure */
    XmString        string;          /* compound string to use */
```

XmStringLength

Returns the length, in bytes, of the specified compound *string*. The calculation includes the length of all tags, direction indicators, and separators. This routine returns 0 if the structure of *string* is invalid.

```
int XmStringLength (string)
    XmString        string;          /* compound string to use */
```

XmStringLineCount

Returns the number of lines in the given compound *string* (by counting the number of separators and then adding 1).

```
int XmStringLineCount (string)
    XmString        string;          /* compound string to count */
```

XmStringNConcat

Returns the compound string formed by appending bytes from *string2* to the end of *string1*, leaving the original compound strings unchanged. The number of bytes so appended (*num_bytes*) includes tags, directional indicators, and separators. If *num_bytes* is less than the length of *string2*, the resulting string could be invalid. In this case, XmStringNConcat() appends as many bytes as possible to ensure the creation of a valid string. Storage for the result is allocated within this routine and should be freed by calling XmStringFree().

```
XmString XmStringNConcat (string1, string2, num_bytes)
    XmString        string1;         /* first compound string */
    XmString        string2;         /* compound string to append to string1 */
    int             num_bytes;       /* maximum number of bytes to append */
```

XmStringNCopy

Copies a maximum number of bytes from compound string *string* and returns the resulting copy, leaving the original string unchanged. The number of bytes copied (*num_bytes*) includes tags, directional indicators, and separators. If *num_bytes* is less than the length of *string*, the resulting string could be invalid. In this case, XmStringNCopy() copies as many bytes as possible to ensure the creation of a valid string. Storage for the result is allocated within this routine and should be freed by calling XmStringFree().

```
XmString XmStringNCopy (string, num_bytes)
    XmString        string;          /* compound string to use */
    int             num_bytes;       /* maximum number of bytes to copy */
```

XmStringPeekNextComponent

Checks the next component (without actually reading it) in the compound string defined by *context* and returns the component's type. This routine shows what *would* be returned by a call to XmStringGetNextComponent(), without actually updating *context*. See XmStringGetNext-Component() for possible return values.

```
XmStringComponentType XmStringPeekNextComponent (context)
    XmStringContext  context;              /* string context used by XmStringInitContext() */
```

XmStringSegmentCreate

Returns a compound string formed by assembling the components specified by *text, charset, direction*, and (if True) *separator*.

```
XmString XmStringSegmentCreate (text, charset, direction, separator)
    char            *text;          /* null-terminated string to use */
    XmStringCharSet charset;        /* XmSTRING_DEFAULT_CHARSET, for example */
    XmStringDirection direction;    /* direction of the text */
    Boolean         separator;      /* if True, a separator is added after text */
```

The values for *direction* are defined in *<Xm/Xm.h>*:

XmSTRING_DIRECTION_L_TO_R   XmSTRING_DIRECTION_R_TO_L

XmStringSeparatorCreate

Creates and returns a compound string containing a separator as its only component.

```
XmString XmStringSeparatorCreate ()
```

XmStringWidth

Returns the width, in pixels, of the longest line of text in the specified compound *string*. (A separator component delimits each line.) If *string* is created with XmStringCreateSimple() instead of XmStringCreate(), then *fontlist* must begin with the font associated with the character set of the current language environment (otherwise the result is undefined).

```
Dimension XmStringWidth (fontlist, string)
    XmFontList    fontlist;        /* list of fonts and character set IDs */
    XmString      string;          /* compound string to use */
```

XmTextClearSelection

Cancels the primary selection in the specified Text *widget*. *time* should be the time of the event that triggered the request to clear.

```
#include <Xm/Text.h>
void XmTextClearSelection (widget, time)
    Widget    widget;      /* widget ID of Text widget */
    Time      time;        /* time member from structure of triggering event */
```

XmTextCopy

Copies the primary selection to the clipboard. *time* should be the time of the event that triggered the request to copy. This routine returns **True** if successful; it returns **False** if the primary selection is NULL or is not owned by the Text *widget*, or if the function can't obtain ownership of the clipboard selection.

```
#include <Xm/Text.h>
Boolean XmTextCopy (widget, time)
    Widget      widget;      /* widget ID of Text widget */
    Time        time;        /* time member from structure of triggering event */
```

XmTextCut

Like XmTextCopy() but also deletes the primary selection after copying it to the clipboard. This routine also invokes the Text *widget*'s callback resources XmNmodifyVerifyCallback and XmNvalueChangedCallback.

```
#include <Xm/Text.h>
Boolean XmTextCut (widget, time)
    Widget      widget;      /* widget ID of Text widget */
    Time        time;        /* time member from structure of triggering event */
```

XmTextFieldClearSelection

Deselects the primary selection in the specified TextField *widget*. *time* should be the time of the event that triggered the request to clear.

```
#include <Xm/TextF.h>
void XmTextFieldClearSelection (widget, time)
    Widget      widget;      /* widget ID of TextField widget */
    Time        time;        /* time member from structure of triggering event */
```

XmTextFieldCopy

Copies the primary selected text to the clipboard. *time* should be the time of the event that triggered the request to copy. This routine returns **True** if successful; it returns **False** if the primary selection is NULL or is not owned by the TextField *widget*, or if the function can't obtain ownership of the clipboard selection.

```
#include <Xm/TextF.h>
Boolean XmTextFieldCopy (widget, time)
    Widget      widget;      /* widget ID of TextField widget */
    Time        time;        /* time member from structure of triggering event */
```

XmTextFieldCut

Like XmTextFieldCopy() but also deletes the primary selected text after copying it to the clipboard. This routine also invokes the TextField *widget*'s callback resources XmNmodifyVerifyCallback and XmNvalueChangedCallback.

```
#include <Xm/TextF.h>
Boolean XmTextFieldCut (widget, time)
    Widget          widget;              /* widget ID of TextField widget */
    Time            time;                /* time member from structure of triggering event */
```

XmTextFieldGetBaseline

Returns the *x* position of the first baseline in the specified TextField *widget*. This value is relative to the upper-left corner of *widget* and also accounts for margin height, shadow and highlight thicknesses, and the ascent of the first font in the font list.

```
#include <Xm/TextF.h>
int XmTextFieldGetBaseline (widget)
    Widget          widget;              /* widget ID of TextField widget */
```

XmTextFieldGetEditable

Returns the value of the TextField *widget*'s XmNeditable resource. By default, this resource is True, which means the user can edit the text string.

```
#include <Xm/TextF.h>
Boolean XmTextFieldGetEditable (widget)
    Widget          widget;              /* widget ID of TextField widget */
```

XmTextFieldGetInsertionPosition

Returns the value of the TextField *widget*'s XmNcursorPosition resource. This value locates the insertion cursor by indicating how many characters are between the cursor and the text buffer's beginning. For example, zero is the first character position (as well as the default value for XmNcursorPosition).

```
#include <Xm/TextF.h>
XmTextPosition XmTextFieldGetInsertionPosition (widget)
    Widget          widget;              /* widget ID of TextField widget */
```

XmTextFieldGetLastPosition

Returns the position of the text buffer's last character, within the specified TextField *widget*. The position of the first character is 0.

```
#include <Xm/TextF.h>
XmTextPosition XmTextFieldGetLastPosition (widget)
    Widget          widget;              /* widget ID of TextField widget */
```

XmTextFieldGetMaxLength

Returns the value of the TextField *widget*'s XmNmaxLength resource. This resource limits the length of a text string that a user may type.

```
#include <Xm/TextF.h>
int XmTextFieldGetMaxLength (widget)
    Widget          widget;              /* widget ID of TextField widget */
```

XmTextFieldGetSelection

Returns a pointer to the TextField *widget*'s primary selection (or returns NULL if no text is selected in the TextField widget). The application must call XtFree() to deallocate the storage associated with the returned string.

```
#include <Xm/TextF.h>
char * XmTextFieldGetSelection (widget)
    Widget          widget;              /* widget ID of TextField widget */
```

XmTextFieldGetSelectionPosition

Obtains the primary selection's left and right boundaries. Each boundary value is the number of characters from the text buffer's beginning (with the position of the first character equal to 0). This routine returns True if the specified TextField *widget* owns the primary selection; otherwise, the routine returns False.

```
#include <Xm/TextF.h>
Boolean XmTextFieldGetSelectionPosition (widget, left, right)
    Widget          widget;              /* widget ID of TextField widget */
    XmTextPosition  *left;               /* returns position of primary selection's left boundary */
    XmTextPosition  *right;              /* returns position of primary selection's right boundary */
```

XmTextFieldGetString

Returns a pointer to the TextField *widget*'s currently displayed string (or returns an empty string if the widget's string has a length of 0). The application must call XtFree() to deallocate the storage associated with the returned string.

```
#include <Xm/TextF.h>
char * XmTextFieldGetString (widget)
    Widget          widget;              /* widget ID of TextField widget */
```

XmTextFieldInsert

Inserts a text string at *position* within the specified TextField *widget*. Character positions are numbered sequentially, with 0 marking the start of the text. This routine also invokes the TextField *widget*'s callback resources XmNmodifyVerifyCallback and XmNvalueChangedCallback.

```
#include <Xm/TextF.h>
void XmTextFieldInsert (widget, position, value)
    Widget          widget;              /* widget ID of TextField widget */
    XmTextPosition  position;            /* character position at which to insert string */
    char            *string;             /* text string to insert */
```

XmTextFieldPaste

Inserts the clipboard selection at the current position of the given TextField *widget*'s insert cursor. If the cursor position happens to be within the current selection, the clipboard selection replaces the current selection, provided that *widget*'s XmNpendingDelete resource is True (as it is by default). This routine also invokes *widget*'s callback resources XmNmodifyVerify-Callback and XmNvalueChangedCallback if a selection exists.

```
#include <Xm/TextF.h>
Boolean XmTextFieldPaste (widget)
    Widget          widget;              /* widget ID of TextField widget */
```

XmTextFieldPosToXY

Returns the x- and y- coordinates of a character at *position* within the given TextField *widget*. Character positions are numbered sequentially, with 0 marking the start of the text. Coordinates are relative to the upper-left corner of *widget*. This routine returns True if *position* is valid (i.e., currently displayed in *widget*); otherwise, the routine returns False, and no values are returned in the *x* and *y* arguments.

```
#include <Xm/TextF.h>
Boolean XmTextFieldPosToXY (widget, position, x, y)
    Widget          widget;              /* widget ID of TextField widget */
    XmTextPosition  position;            /* character position whose coordinates are returned */
    Position        *x;                  /* returns x-coord, relative to widget's top left */
    Position        *y;                  /* returns y-coord, relative to widget's top left */
```

XmTextFieldRemove

Deletes the primary selected text from the specified TextField *widget*. Also invokes *widget*'s callback resources XmNmodifyVerifyCallback and XmNvalueChangedCallback if a selection exists. This routine returns True if successful; it returns False if the primary selection is NULL or is not owned by *widget*.

```
#include <Xm/TextF.h>
Boolean XmTextFieldRemove (widget)
    Widget          widget;              /* widget ID of TextField widget */
```

XmTextFieldReplace

Replaces a portion of the text string in the specified TextField *widget*. The character replacement begins at *from_pos* and extends to (but doesn't include) *to_pos*. Character positions are numbered sequentially, with 0 marking the start of the text. If *from_pos* and *to_pos* are equal, then *string* will not replace existing text but will simply be inserted after *to_pos*. This routine also invokes *widget*'s callback resources XmNmodifyVerifyCallback and XmNvalueChanged-Callback.

```
#include <Xm/TextF.h>
void XmTextFieldReplace (widget, from_pos, to_pos, value)
    Widget          widget;              /* widget ID of TextField widget */
    XmTextPosition  from_pos;            /* position of first character to replace */
    XmTextPosition  to_pos;              /* position following last character to replace */
    char            *string;             /* text string whose characters are replaced */
```

XmTextFieldSetAddMode

For the given TextField *widget*, activates Add Mode (if *mode* is True) or deactivates Add Mode (if *mode* is False). Whenever a widget is in Add Mode, this means that users can move the insert cursor without disturbing the primary selection.

```
#include <Xm/TextF.h>
void XmTextFieldSetAddMode (widget, mode)
   Widget         widget;           /* widget ID of TextField widget */
   Boolean        mode;             /* turns Add Mode on (True) or off (False) */
```

XmTextFieldSetEditable

Sets the TextField *widget*'s XmNeditable resource to *editable*. By default, this resource is True, which means the user can edit the text string.

```
#include <Xm/TextF.h>
void XmTextFieldSetEditable (widget, editable)
   Widget         widget;           /* widget ID of TextField widget */
   Boolean        editable;         /* when True, users can edit the text */
```

XmTextFieldSetHighlight

For the given TextField *widget*, highlights text (without actually selecting it) using the given *mode*. *left* and *right* are integers that specify the boundary positions of the text to highlight. Character positions are numbered sequentially, with 0 marking the start of the text.

```
#include <Xm/TextF.h>
void XmTextFieldSetHighlight (widget, left, right, mode)
   Widget           widget;         /* widget ID of TextField widget */
   XmTextPosition   left;           /* left boundary position of text to highlight */
   XmTextPosition   right;          /* right boundary position of text to highlight */
   XmHighlightMode  mode;           /* kind of highlighting to use */
```

mode can have one of three values:

```
XmHIGHLIGHT_NORMAL                  /* text is not highlighted */
XmHIGHLIGHT_SELECTED                /* text is highlighted in reverse video */
XmHIGHLIGHT_SECONDARY_SELECTED      /* text is underlined */
```

XmTextFieldSetInsertionPosition

Sets the position of the TextField *widget*'s insert cursor. This is done by setting the XmNcursorPosition resource to *position*, an integer that indicates how many characters are between the cursor and the text buffer's beginning. Character positions are numbered sequentially, with 0 marking the start of the text. This routine also invokes *widget*'s callback resource XmNmotionVerifyCallback if the insert cursor position changes.

```
#include <Xm/TextF.h>
void XmTextFieldSetInsertionPosition (widget, position)
   Widget           widget;         /* widget ID of TextField widget */
   XmTextPosition   position;       /* character position of insert cursor */
```

XmTextFieldSetMaxLength

Sets the TextField *widget*'s XmNmaxLength resource to *max_length*. This resource limits the length of a text string that a user may type. Text strings will ignore this resource if they are entered via the XmNvalue resource or the XmTextFieldSetString() routine.

```
#include <Xm/TextF.h>
void XmTextFieldSetMaxLength (widget, max_length)
    Widget        widget;          /* widget ID of TextField widget */
    int           max_length;      /* maximum length allowed for text string */
```

XmTextFieldSetSelection

Sets the TextField *widget*'s primary selection to begin at the *first* character position and to end at the *last* character position. Characters in the text string are numbered sequentially, with 0 marking the start of the text. *time* should be the time of the event that triggered the selection request. This routine also sets the position of the insert cursor to *last* and then invokes the widget's XmNmotionVerifyCallback callbacks.

```
#include <Xm/TextF.h>
void XmTextFieldSetSelection (widget, first, last, time)
    Widget         widget;         /* widget ID of TextField widget */
    XmTextPosition first;          /* position of first character to select */
    XmTextPosition last;           /* position of last character to select */
    Time           time;           /* time member from structure of triggering event */
```

XmTextFieldSetString

Sets the current text string in the TextField *widget* to the specified *string*. This routine also invokes the widget's XmNmodifyVerifyCallback and XmNvalueChangedCallback callbacks, sets the position of the insert cursor to the beginning of the string, and invokes the widget's Xm-NmotionVerifyCallback callbacks.

```
#include <Xm/TextF.h>
void XmTextFieldSetString (widget, value)
    Widget        widget;          /* widget ID of TextField widget */
    char          *string;         /* text string to place in edit window */
```

XmTextFieldShowPosition

Forces text at *position* to be displayed in the specified TextField *widget*. Character positions are numbered sequentially, with 0 marking the start of the text. If the TextField resource Xm-NautoShowCursorPosition is True, applications should set the insert cursor to *position* as well.

```
#include <Xm/TextF.h>
void XmTextFieldShowPosition (widget, position)
    Widget         widget;         /* widget ID of TextField widget */
    XmTextPosition position;       /* character position to display */
```

XmTextFieldXYToPos

Returns the position of the character closest to the specified *x* and *y* coordinate within the TextField *widget*. Character positions are numbered sequentially, with 0 marking the start of the text. x- and y- coordinates are relative to the upper-left corner of the TextField widget.

```
#include <Xm/TextF.h>
XmTextPosition XmTextFieldXYToPos (widget, x, y)
    Widget          widget;         /* widget ID of TextField widget */
    Position        x;              /* x-coord, relative to widget's top left */
    Position        y;              /* y-coord, relative to widget's top left */
```

XmTextGetBaseline

Returns the x position of the first baseline in the specified Text *widget*. This value is relative to the upper-left corner of *widget* and also accounts for margin height, shadow and highlight thicknesses, and the ascent of the first font in the font list.

```
#include <Xm/Text.h>
int XmTextGetBaseline (widget)
    Widget          widget;         /* widget ID of Text widget */
```

XmTextGetEditable

Returns the value of the Text *widget*'s XmNeditable resource. By default, this resource is True, which means the user can edit the text string.

```
#include <Xm/Text.h>
Boolean XmTextGetEditable (widget)
    Widget          widget;         /* widget ID of Text widget */
```

XmTextGetInsertionPosition

Returns the value of the Text *widget*'s XmNcursorPosition resource. This value locates the insertion cursor by indicating how many characters are between the cursor and the text buffer's beginning. For example, zero is the first character position (as well as the default value for XmNcursorPosition).

```
#include <Xm/Text.h>
XmTextPosition XmTextGetInsertionPosition (widget)
    Widget          widget;         /* widget ID of Text widget */
```

XmTextGetLastPosition

Returns the position of the text buffer's last character, within the specified Text *widget*. The position of the first character is 0.

```
#include <Xm/Text.h>
XmTextPosition XmTextGetLastPosition (widget)
    Widget          widget;         /* widget ID of Text widget */
```

XmTextGetMaxLength

Returns the value of the Text *widget*'s XmNmaxLength resource. This resource limits the length of a text string that a user may type.

```
#include <Xm/Text.h>
int XmTextGetMaxLength (widget)
    Widget          widget;         /* widget ID of Text widget */
```

XmTextGetSelection

Returns a pointer to the Text *widget*'s primary selection (or returns NULL if no text is selected in the Text widget). The application must call XtFree() to deallocate the storage associated with the returned string.

```
#include <Xm/Text.h>
char * XmTextGetSelection (widget)
    Widget          widget;          /* widget ID of Text widget */
```

XmTextGetSelectionPosition

Obtains the primary selection's left and right boundaries. Each boundary value is the number of characters from the text buffer's beginning (with the position of the first character equal to 0). This routine returns True if the specified Text *widget* owns the primary selection; otherwise, the routine returns False.

```
#include <Xm/Text.h>
Boolean XmTextGetSelectionPosition (widget, left, right)
    Widget          widget;          /* widget ID of Text widget */
    XmTextPosition  *left;           /* returns position of primary selection's left boundary */
    XmTextPosition  *right;          /* returns position of primary selection's right boundary */
```

XmTextGetSource

Returns the source of the specified Text *widget*. When Text widgets share sources, the editing of one widget is reflected in another. Shared sources are useful for providing "splittable views" of the same text. See also XmTextSetSource().

```
#include <Xm/Text.h>
XmTextSource XmTextGetSource (widget)
    Widget          widget;          /* widget ID of Text widget */
```

XmTextGetString

Returns a pointer to the Text *widget*'s currently displayed string (or returns an empty string if the widget's string has a length of 0). The application must call XtFree() to deallocate the storage associated with the returned string.

```
#include <Xm/Text.h>
char * XmTextGetString (widget)
    Widget          widget;          /* widget ID of Text widget */
```

XmTextGetTopCharacter

Returns the value of the XmNtopCharacter resource for the given Text *widget*. This resource gives the position of the character at the top of the widget. Character positions are numbered sequentially, with 0 marking the start of the text.

```
#include <Xm/Text.h>
XmTextPosition XmTextGetTopCharacter (widget)
    Widget          widget;          /* widget ID of Text widget */
```

XmTextInsert

Inserts a text string at *position* within the specified Text *widget*. Character positions are numbered sequentially, with 0 marking the start of the text. This routine also invokes the Text *widget*'s callback resources XmNmodifyVerifyCallback and XmNvalueChangedCallback.

```
#include <Xm/Text.h>
void XmTextInsert (widget, position, value)
    Widget          widget;        /* widget ID of Text widget */
    XmTextPosition  position;      /* character position at which to insert string */
    char            *string;       /* text string to insert */
```

XmTextPaste

Inserts the clipboard selection at the current position of the given Text *widget*'s insert cursor. If the cursor position happens to be within the current selection, the clipboard selection replaces the current selection, provided that *widget*'s XmNpendingDelete resource is True (as it is by default). This routine also invokes *widget*'s callback resources XmNmodifyVerifyCallback and XmNvalueChangedCallback if a selection exists.

```
#include <Xm/Text.h>
Boolean XmTextPaste (widget)
    Widget          widget;        /* widget ID of Text widget */
```

XmTextPosToXY

Returns the x- and y- coordinates of a character at *position* within the given Text *widget*. Character positions are numbered sequentially, with 0 marking the start of the text. Coordinates are relative to the upper-left corner of *widget*. This routine returns True if *position* is valid (i.e., currently displayed in *widget*); otherwise, the routine returns False, and no values are returned in the *x* and *y* arguments.

```
#include <Xm/Text.h>
Boolean XmTextPosToXY (widget, position, x, y)
    Widget          widget;        /* widget ID of Text widget */
    XmTextPosition  position;      /* character position whose coordinates are returned */
    Position        *x;            /* returns x-coord, relative to widget's top left */
    Position        *y;            /* returns y-coord, relative to widget's top left */
```

XmTextRemove

Deletes the primary selected text from the specified Text *widget*. Also invokes *widget*'s callback resources XmNmodifyVerifyCallback and XmNvalueChangedCallback if a clipboard selection exists. This routine returns True if successful; it returns False if the primary selection is NULL or is not owned by *widget*.

```
#include <Xm/Text.h>
Boolean XmTextRemove (widget)
    Widget          widget;        /* widget ID of Text widget */
```

XmTextReplace

Replaces a portion of the text string in the specified Text *widget*. The character replacement begins at *from_pos* and extends to (but doesn't include) *to_pos*. Character positions are numbered sequentially, with 0 marking the start of the text. If *from_pos* and *to_pos* are equal, then *string* will not replace existing text but will simply be inserted after *to_pos*. This routine also invokes *widget*'s callback resources XmNmodifyVerifyCallback and XmNvalueChangedCallback.

```
#include <Xm/Text.h>
void XmTextReplace (widget, from_pos, to_pos, value)
    Widget          widget;        /* widget ID of Text widget */
    XmTextPosition  from_pos;      /* position of first character to replace */
    XmTextPosition  to_pos;        /* position following last character to replace */
    char            *string;       /* text string whose characters are replaced */
```

XmTextScroll

Scrolls text in the specified Text *widget*. Text scrolls upward if *lines* is positive and downward if *lines* is negative.

```
#include <Xm/Text.h>
void XmTextScroll (widget, lines)
    Widget          widget;        /* widget ID of Text widget */
    int             lines;         /* how many lines to scroll (up or down) */
```

XmTextSetAddMode

For the given Text *widget*, activates Add Mode (if *mode* is True) or deactivates Add Mode (if *mode* is False). Whenever a widget is in Add Mode, this means that users can move the insert cursor without disturbing the primary selection.

```
#include <Xm/Text.h>
void XmTextSetAddMode (widget, state)
    Widget          widget;        /* widget ID of Text widget */
    Boolean         mode;          /* turns Add Mode on (True) or off (False) */
```

XmTextSetEditable

Sets the Text *widget*'s XmNeditable resource to *editable*. By default, this resource is True, which means the user can edit the text string.

```
#include <Xm/Text.h>
void XmTextSetEditable (widget, editable)
    Widget          widget;        /* widget ID of Text widget */
    Boolean         editable;      /* when True, users can edit the text */
```

XmTextSetHighlight

For the given Text *widget*, highlights text (without actually selecting it) using the given *mode*. *left* and *right* are integers that specify the boundary positions of the text to highlight. Character positions are numbered sequentially, with 0 marking the start of the text.

```
#include <Xm/Text.h>
void XmTextSetHighlight (widget, left, right, mode)
    Widget          widget;                  /* widget ID of Text widget */
    XmTextPosition  left;                    /* left boundary position of text to highlight */
    XmTextPosition  right;                   /* right boundary position of text to highlight */
    XmHighlightMode mode;                    /* kind of highlighting to use */
```

mode can have one of three values:

```
XmHIGHLIGHT_NORMAL                          /* text is not highlighted */
XmHIGHLIGHT_SELECTED                        /* text is highlighted in reverse video */
XmHIGHLIGHT_SECONDARY_SELECTED              /* text is underlined */
```

XmTextSetInsertionPosition

Sets the position of the Text *widget*'s insert cursor. This is done by setting the XmNcursor-Position resource to *position*, an integer that indicates how many characters are between the cursor and the text buffer's beginning. Character positions are numbered sequentially, with 0 marking the start of the text. This routine also invokes *widget*'s callback resource XmNmotion-VerifyCallback if the insert cursor position changes.

```
#include <Xm/Text.h>
void XmTextSetInsertionPosition (widget, position)
    Widget          widget;                  /* widget ID of Text widget */
    XmTextPosition  position;                /* character position of insert cursor */
```

XmTextSetMaxLength

Sets the Text *widget*'s XmNmaxLength resource to *max_length*. This resource limits the length of a text string that a user may type. Text strings will ignore this resource if they are entered via the XmNvalue resource or the XmTextSetString() routine.

```
#include <Xm/Text.h>
void XmTextSetMaxLength (widget, max_length)
    Widget          widget;                  /* widget ID of Text widget */
    int             max_length;              /* maximum length allowed for text string */
```

XmTextSetSelection

Sets the Text *widget*'s primary selection to begin at the *first* character position and to end at the *last* character position. Characters in the text string are numbered sequentially, with 0 marking the start of the text. *time* should be the time of the event that triggered the selection request. This routine also sets the position of the insert cursor to *last* and then invokes the widget's XmNmotionVerifyCallback callbacks.

```
#include <Xm/Text.h>
void XmTextSetSelection (widget, first, last, time)
    Widget          widget;                  /* widget ID of Text widget */
    XmTextPosition  first;                   /* position of first character to select */
    XmTextPosition  last;                    /* position of last character to select */
    Time            time;                    /* time member from structure of triggering event */
```

XmTextSetSource

Sets the source of the specified Text *widget*, thereby allowing the widget to share another widget's source. When Text widgets share sources, editing of one widget is reflected in another. Setting *source* destroys the previous source when no other Text widget is using it. If *source* is NULL, the Text widget creates a default string source. Character positions are numbered sequentially, with 0 marking the start of the text.

```
#include <Xm/Text.h>
void XmTextSetSource (widget, source, top_character, cursor_position)
    Widget          widget;           /* widget ID of Text widget */
    XmTextSource    source;           /* source for displaying text (obtained by XmTextGetSource) */
    XmTextPosition  top_character;    /* character position to display at top of widget */
    XmTextPosition  cursor_position;  /* character position at which to locate insert cursor */
```

XmTextSetString

Sets the current text string in the Text *widget* to the specified *string*. This routine also invokes the widget's XmNmodifyVerifyCallback and XmNvalueChangedCallback callbacks, sets the position of the insert cursor to the beginning of the string, and invokes the widget's XmNmotionVerifyCallback callbacks.

```
#include <Xm/Text.h>
void XmTextSetString (widget, value)
    Widget     widget;      /* widget ID of Text widget */
    char       *string;     /* text string to place in edit window */
```

XmTextSetTopCharacter

Scrolls the text so that the line containing the character specified by *top_character* appears at the top of the given Text *widget*. Character positions are numbered sequentially, with 0 marking the start of the text. This routine causes vertical scrolling only; the text is not shifted left or right.

```
#include <Xm/Text.h>
void XmTextSetTopCharacter (widget, top_character)
    Widget          widget;         /* widget ID of Text widget */
    XmTextPosition  top_character;  /* character position to display at top of widget */
```

XmTextShowPosition

Forces text at *position* to be displayed in the specified Text *widget*. Character positions are numbered sequentially, with 0 marking the start of the text. If the Text resource XmNautoShowCursorPosition is True, applications should set the insert cursor to *position* as well.

```
#include <Xm/Text.h>
void XmTextShowPosition (widget, position)
    Widget          widget;     /* widget ID of Text widget */
    XmTextPosition  position;   /* character position to display */
```

XmTextXYToPos

Returns the position of the character closest to the specified *x* and *y* coordinate within the Text widget. Character positions are numbered sequentially, with 0 marking the start of the text. x- and y- coordinates are relative to the upper-left corner of the Text widget.

```
#include <Xm/Text.h>
XmTextPosition XmTextXYToPos (widget, x, y)
    Widget          widget;          /* widget ID of Text widget */
    Position        x;               /* x-coord, relative to widget's top left */
    Position        y;               /* y-coord, relative to widget's top left */
```

XmToggleButtonGadgetGetState

Returns True if the ToggleButtonGadget is selected and returns False if the ToggleButton-Gadget is unselected.

```
#include <Xm/ToggleBG.h>
Boolean XmToggleButtonGadgetGetState (widget)
    Widget          widget;          /* ID of ToggleButtonGadget */
```

XmToggleButtonGadgetSetState

Selects the ToggleButtonGadget if *state* is True and deselects the ToggleButtonGadget if *state* is False. If *notify* is True, this routine invokes the callbacks specified by the XmNvalueChanged-Callback resource. As a result, when selecting a ToggleButtonGadget whose parent is a Row-Column with XmNradioBehavior set to True, the other toggle button children will be deselected.

```
#include <Xm/ToggleBG.h>
void XmToggleButtonGadgetSetState (widget, state, notify)
    Widget          widget;          /* ID of ToggleButtonGadget */
    Boolean         state;           /* selects (True) or deselects (False) the button */
    Boolean         notify;          /* when True, invokes the callback to process changes */
```

XmToggleButtonGetState

Returns True if the ToggleButton is selected and returns False if the ToggleButton is unselected.

```
#include <Xm/ToggleB.h>
Boolean XmToggleButtonGetState (widget)
    Widget          widget;          /* ID of ToggleButton widget */
```

XmToggleButtonSetState

Selects the ToggleButton if *state* is True and deselects the ToggleButton if *state* is False. If *notify* is True, this routine invokes the callbacks specified by the XmNvalueChangedCallback resource. As a result, when selecting a ToggleButton whose parent is a RowColumn with Xm-NradioBehavior set to True, the other toggle button children will be deselected.

```
#include <Xm/ToggleB.h>
void XmToggleButtonSetState (widget, state, notify)
    Widget          widget;          /* ID of ToggleButton widget */
    Boolean         state;           /* selects (True) or deselects (False) the button */
    Boolean         notify;          /* when True, invokes the callback to process changes */
```

XmTrackingLocate

Grabs the pointer, waits for the user to press a button, and then returns the ID of the widget in which the button press occurred. This routine supports context-sensitive help: the user clicks on a widget to obtain more information about it, XmTrackingLocate() obtains this widget ID, and a help callback can then be triggered so as to pop up a dialog box containing the appropriate information.

```
Widget XmTrackingLocate (widget, cursor, confine_to)
    Widget          widget;          /* top-level shell in which interaction occurs */
    Cursor          cursor;          /* standard X cursor name to use for pointer */
    Boolean         confine_to;      /* if True, cursor remains inside widget */
```

XmUninstallImage

Removes *image* from the image cache. Returns True if successful, False if *image* is NULL or if *image* isn't found in the image cache.

```
Boolean XmUninstallImage (image)
    XImage          *image;          /* returns image structure to remove */
```

XmUpdateDisplay

Processes any pending exposure events immediately, instead of waiting until all callbacks have been invoked. This routine is useful whenever a time-consuming action might delay the redrawing of the display's windows (for example, when selecting some action from a popup menu pane or from a dialog box).

```
void XmUpdateDisplay (widget)
    Widget          widget;          /* widget or gadget to update */
```

XmVaCreateSimpleCheckBox

A RowColumn convenience routine that creates a CheckBox with ToggleButtonGadgets as its children. This routine is similar to XmCreateSimpleCheckBox() but also uses varargs lists. A varargs list (indicated in the routine's calling sequence by ..., NULL) is composed of several groups of arguments. Within each group, the first argument is a constant, and this argument is followed by zero or more arguments associated with the constant. The varargs list must be NULL-terminated.

```
Widget XmVaCreateSimpleCheckBox (parent, name, callback, ..., NULL)
    Widget          parent;          /* widget ID of the new widget's parent */
    String          name;            /* name of the newly created widget */
    XtCallbackProc  callback;        /* procedure to call when a button's value changes */
```

The following constants can be used for this routine's varargs list:

XmVaCHECKBUTTON   Followed by four arguments:

label	/* label string, of type XmString */
mnemonic	/* mnemonic, of type KeySym */
accelerator	/* accelerator, of type String */
accelerator_text	/* text, of type XmString */

This group specifies one of the CheckBox buttons. (All but the *label* argument are ignored in Release 1.1.)

resource_name   Followed by the resource's value (type XtArgVal). This group specifies a resource name/value pair for the RowColumn widget.

XtVaTypedArg   Followed by four arguments:

name	/* resource name, of type String */
type	/* data type of value, of type String */
value	/* resource value (or pointer to it), of type XtArgVal */
size	/* of value in bytes, of type int */

This group sets a resource's name and value for the RowColumn widget.

XtVaNestedList   Followed by one argument: a nested list of varargs (of type XtVarArgs-List), returned by XtVaCreateArgsList().

XmVaCreateSimpleMenuBar

A RowColumn convenience routine that creates a MenuBar with CascadeButtonGadgets as its children. This routine is similar to XmCreateSimpleMenuBar() but also uses varargs lists. A varargs list (indicated in the routine's calling sequence by ..., NULL) is composed of several groups of arguments. Within each group, the first argument is a constant, and this argument is followed by zero or more arguments associated with the constant. The varargs list must be NULL-terminated.

```
Widget XmVaCreateSimpleMenuBar (parent, name, ..., NULL)
    Widget      parent;      /* widget ID of the new widget's parent */
    String      name;        /* name of the newly created widget */
```

The following constants can be used for this routine's varargs list:

XmVaCASCADEBUTTON   Followed by two arguments:

label	/* label string, of type XmString */
mnemonic	/* mnemonic, of type KeySym */

This group specifies one of the MenuBar buttons.

resource_name   Same as for XmVaCreateSimpleCheckBox().
XtVaTypedArg
XtVaNestedList

XmVaCreateSimpleOptionMenu

A RowColumn convenience routine that creates an OptionMenu along with its submenu of CascadeButtonGadget or PushButtonGadget children. This routine is similar to XmCreate-SimpleOptionMenu() but also uses varargs lists. A varargs list (indicated in the routine's calling sequence by ..., NULL) is composed of several groups of arguments. Within each group, the first argument is a constant, and this argument is followed by zero or more arguments associated with the constant. The varargs list must be NULL-terminated.

Widget XmVaCreateSimpleOptionMenu (*parent, name, option_label, option_mnemonic, button_set, callback,*
    ..., NULL)

Widget	*parent*;	/* widget ID of the new widget's parent */
String	*name*;	/* name of the newly created widget */
XmString	*option_label*;	/* string to use as left-hand label */
KeySym	*option_mnemonic*;	/* keyboard key to use for posting menu */
int	*button_set*;	/* initializes nth PushButtonGadget of varargs list */
XtCallbackProc	*callback*;	/* procedure to call when a button is activated */

The following constants can be used for this routine's varargs list:

XmVaPUSHBUTTON   Followed by four arguments:

label	/* label string, of type XmString */
mnemonic	/* mnemonic, of type KeySym */
accelerator	/* accelerator, of type String */
accelerator_text	/* text, of type XmString */

This group specifies one PushButtonGadget in the OptionMenu's pull-down submenu.

XmVaCASCADEBUTTON   Followed by two arguments:

label	/* label string, of type XmString */
mnemonic	/* mnemonic, of type KeySym */

This group specifies one CascadeButtonGadget in the Option-Menu's pulldown submenu.

XmVaSEPARATOR   Followed by no arguments. Specifies a separator in the Option-Menu's pulldown submenu.

XmVaDOUBLE_SEPARATOR
    Followed by no arguments. Specifies a separator in the Option-Menu's pulldown submenu.

resource_name   Same as for XmVaCreateSimpleCheckBox().
XtVaTypedArg
XtVaNestedList

XmVaCreateSimplePopupMenu

A RowColumn convenience routine that creates a popup MenuPane along with its button children. This routine is similar to XmCreateSimplePopupMenu() but also uses varargs lists. A varargs list (indicated in the routine's calling sequence by ..., NULL) is composed of several groups of arguments. Within each group, the first argument is a constant, and this argument is followed by zero or more arguments associated with the constant. The varargs list must be NULL-terminated.

```
Widget XmVaCreateSimplePopupMenu (parent, name, callback, ... , NULL)
    Widget          parent;          /* widget ID of the MenuShell's parent */
    String          name;            /* name of the newly created widget */
    XtCallbackProc  callback;        /* procedure to call when a button is activated */
```

The following constants can be used for this routine's varargs list:

XmVaPUSHBUTTON   Followed by four arguments:

```
label               /* label string, of type XmString */
mnemonic            /* mnemonic, of type KeySym */
accelerator         /* accelerator, of type String */
accelerator_text    /* text, of type XmString */
```

This group specifies one PushButtonGadget in the popup Menu-Pane.

XmVaCHECKBUTTON   Followed by four arguments (as described above under Xm-VaPUSHBUTTON). This group specifies one ToggleButtonGadget in the popup MenuPane.

XmVaRADIOBUTTON   Followed by four arguments (as described above under Xm-VaPUSHBUTTON). This group specifies one ToggleButtonGadget in the popup MenuPane.

XmVaCASCADEBUTTON Followed by two arguments:

```
label               /* label string, of type XmString */
mnemonic            /* mnemonic, of type KeySym */
```

This group specifies one CascadeButtonGadget in the popup Menu-Pane.

XmVaTITLE   Followed by one argument: a title string of type XmString. This group specifies a LabelGadget in the popup MenuPane.

XmVaSEPARATOR   Followed by no arguments. Specifies a separator in the popup MenuPane.

XmVaDOUBLE_SEPARATOR

Followed by no arguments. Specifies a separator (of type Xm-DOUBLE_LINE) in the popup MenuPane.

resource_name   Same as for XmVaCreateSimpleCheckBox().
XtVaTypedArg
XtVaNestedList

XmVaCreateSimplePulldownMenu

A RowColumn convenience routine that creates a pulldown MenuPane along with its button children. This routine is similar to XmCreateSimplePulldownMenu() but also uses varargs lists. A varargs list (indicated in the routine's calling sequence by ..., NULL) is composed of several groups of arguments. Within each group, the first argument is a constant, and this argument is followed by zero or more arguments associated with the constant. The varargs list must be NULL-terminated.

> Widget XmVaCreateSimplePulldownMenu (*parent, name, post_from_button, callback, . . .* , NULL)
> | Widget | *parent*; | /* widget ID of the MenuShell's parent */ |
> | String | *name*; | /* name of the newly created widget */ |
> | int | *post_from_button*; | /* parent's cascade button that posts the menu */ |
> | XtCallbackProc | *callback*; | /* procedure to call when a button is activated */ |

The varargs list for this routine can have the same constants and associated arguments as for XmVaCreateSimplePopupMenu().

XmVaCreateSimpleRadioBox

A RowColumn convenience routine that creates a RadioBox with ToggleButtonGadgets as its children. This routine is similar to XmCreateSimpleRadioBox() but also uses varargs lists. A varargs list (indicated in the routine's calling sequence by . . . , NULL) is composed of several groups of arguments. Within each group, the first argument is a constant, and this argument is followed by zero or more arguments associated with the constant. The varargs list must be NULL-terminated.

> Widget XmVaCreateSimpleRadioBox (*parent, name, button_set, callback, . . .* , NULL)
> | Widget | *parent*; | /* widget ID of the new widget's parent */ |
> | String | *name*; | /* name of the newly created widget */ |
> | int | *button_set*; | /* initializes nth button of varargs list */ |
> | XtCallbackProc | *callback*; | /* procedure to call when a button's value changes */ |

The following constants can be used for this routine's varargs list:

XmVaRADIOBUTTON   Followed by four arguments:

label	/* label string, of type XmString */
mnemonic	/* mnemonic, of type KeySym */
accelerator	/* accelerator, of type String */
accelerator_text	/* text, of type XmString */

This group specifies one of the RadioBox buttons. (All but the *label* argument are ignored in Release 1.1.)

resource_name
XtVaTypedArg
XtVaNestedList

Same as for XmVaCreateSimpleCheckBox().

B

Xt and Motif Widget Classes

*This appendix describes the resources, callbacks, and translations associ-
ated with every Motif user-interface object.*

In This Chapter:

B

Xt and Motif Widget Classes

This appendix describes the widgets and gadgets available in the Motif toolkit, including various compound objects (such as dialogs, menu bars, and pulldown menus) that are not really separate widget or gadget classes, but can be created as if they were, with a call to a single convenience routine. We will refer to these objects as "convenience widgets." Objects are presented alphabetically, starting with a brief description and then listing information in separate sections. For gadgets, we list only that information that differs from the corresponding widget; for convenience widgets, we present only the description and refer you to the underlying objects. The information is divided into the following sections:

Class Information

This section lists the header file, name, hierarchy, and pointer for this class. For widgets, the class hierarchy begins with Core as the base. For Object, RectObj, and gadget classes, the class hierarchy begins with Object. This section also lists any Motif toolkit routines that are related to the object (such as those used in widget creation or in setting or getting values), as well as the macro that checks the object's class. The creation routine has the general form:

Widget XmCreate*object* (Widget *parent*, String *name*, ArgList *arglist*, Cardinal *argcount*)

and the macro has the general form:

XmIs*object* (w)

where w is the widget whose class is checked, and *object* is the shorthand name for the class. Functions and macros are defined in the header file for the object they relate to.[1]

New Resources

This section presents a table of the resources that are newly defined by each widget class (not inherited from a superclass). In addition to the resource's name, class, data type, and default value, a fifth column lists a code consisting of one or more of the letters C, S, and G. This code indicates whether the resource can be set when the widget is created (C), whether it can be set with XtSetValues() (S), and whether it can be read with XtGetValues()

---

[1] Convenience creation routines are defined in the header file corresponding to the child widget that is created (e.g., XmCreateErrorDialog() is defined in *<Xm/MessageB.h>*). The macros XmIsGadget(), XmIsManager(), and XmIsPrimitive() are defined in *<Xm/Xm.h>*. In addition, some widget classes define macros in their private header file, making the macros unavailable to programmers. As an alternative, you can use XtIsSubClass() directly. We do not list the privately defined macros.

(G). (We've adopted this useful convention from the *Motif Programmer's Reference Manual.*) A brief description of each new resource follows the table. For resources whose values are defined constants, these constants are listed. Unless otherwise noted, they are defined in *<Xm/Xm.h>*.

Callback Resources

This section presents a table of the callback resources that are newly defined by this class. The table lists the name of the resource along with its reason constant.

Callback Structure

This section lists the structure associated with the object's callback functions.

Other New Resources

If present, these sections describe resources associated with specific uses of the widget; for example, RowColumn widget resources for use with simple creation routines, or Text widget resources for use in text input.

Inherited Resources

This section presents an alphabetically arranged table of inherited resources, along with the superclass that defines them.

Translations

This section presents the translations associated with each widget or gadget. Because the button events and key events used in Motif don't necessarily correspond to the events in the X Window System, the Motif toolkit has created a mechanism called *virtual binding*. Virtual binding links the translations used in Motif to their X event counterpart. The "Translations" sections list their events in terms of these virtual bindings. In order to understand the syntax used in the "Translations" sections of this appendix, you must understand the correspondence between virtual bindings and actual keysyms or buttons. The following tables describe the virtual bindings of events.

Table B-1. Virtual Modifier Bindings

Virtual Modifier	Actual Modifier
MAlt	Mod1
MCtrl	Ctrl
MShift	Shift

Table B-2. Virtual Button Event Bindings

Virtual Button	Actual Button Events
BCustom	<Btn3>
BDrag	<Btn2>
BExtend	Shift<Btn1>
BMenu	<Btn3>
BSelect	<Btn1>
BToggle	Ctrl<Btn1>

Table B-3. Virtual Key Event Bindings

Virtual Key	Actual Key Events	Virtual Key	Actual Key Events
KActivate	<Key>Return Ctrl<Key>Return <Key>osfActivate	KPageDown	<Key>osfPageDown
		KPageLeft	Ctrl<Key>osfPageUp
		KPageRight	Ctrl<Key>osfPageDown
KAddMode	<Key>osfAddMode	KPageUp	<Key>osfPageUp
KBackSpace	<Key>osfBackSpace	KPaste	<Key>osfPaste
KBackTab	Shift<Key>Tab		Shift<Key>osfInsert
KBeginData	Ctrl<Key>osfBeginLine	KPrevField	Shift<Key>Tab
KBeginLine	<Key>osfBeginLine		Ctrl Shift<Key>Tab
KCancel	<Key>osfCancel	KPrevMenu	Ctrl<Key>osfUp
KClear	<Key>osfClear		Ctrl<Key>osfLeft
KCopy	<Key>osfCopy Ctrl<Key>osfInsert	KPrimaryCopy	Ctrl<Key>osfPrimaryPaste Mod1<Key>osfCopy Mod1 Ctrl<Key>osfInsert
KCut	<Key>osfCut Shift<Key>osfDelete	KPrimaryCut	Mod1<Key>osfPrimaryPaste Mod1<Key>osfCut Mod1 Shift<Key>osfDelete
KDelete	<Key>osfDelete		
KDeselectAll	Ctrl<Key>backslash	KPrimaryPaste	<Key>osfPrimaryPaste
KDown	<Key>osfDown	KQuickCopy	Ctrl<Key>osfQuickPaste
KEndData	Ctrl<Key>osfEndLine	KQuickCut	Mod1<Key>osfQuickPaste
KEndLine	<Key>osfEndLine	KQuickExtend	Shift<Key>osfQuickPaste
KEnter	<Key>Return	KQuickPaste	<Key>osfQuickPaste
KEscape	<Key>Escape	KReselect	Ctrl Shift<Key>space Ctrl Shift<Key>osfSelect
KExtend	Shift<Key>space Shift<Key>osfSelect	KRestore	Ctrl Shift<Key>osfInsert
KHelp	<Key>osfHelp	KRight	<Key>osfRight
KInsert	<Key>osfInsert	KSelect	<Key>space Ctrl<Key>space <Key>osfSelect
KLeft	<Key>osfLeft		
KMenu	<Key>osfMenu		
KMenuBar	<Key>osfMenuBar	KSelectAll	Ctrl<Key>slash
KNextField	<Key>Tab Ctrl<Key>Tab	KSpace	<Key>space
		KTab	<Key>Tab
KNextMenu	Ctrl<Key>osfDown Ctrl<Key>osfRight	KUndo	<Key>osfUndo Mod1<Key>osfBackSpace
		KUp	<Key>osfUp
		KAny	<Key>

Keysyms that begin with the letters *osf* are not defined by the X server and must be mapped to actual keysyms. Mappings can be specified in four ways:

- In a file named *.motifbind*, in the user's home directory. A sample specification is shown below:

```
osfBackSpace                  :        <Key>BackSpace
osfInsert                     :        <Key>InsertChar
osfDelete                     :        <Key>DeleteChar
```

- By specifying the XmNdefaultVirtualBindings resource in a resource database. In a resource database, the previous specification would be typed as follows:

```
*defaultVirtualBindings:\
osfBackSpace                  :        <Key>BackSpace \n\
osfInsert                     :        <Key>InsertChar \n\
osfDelete                     :        <Key>DeleteChar
```

- Via vendor-specific defaults.

- Via fixed fallback defaults. *osf* keysym strings have the fixed fallback default bindings listed below:

```
osfActivate            <unbound>
osfAddMode             Shift F8
osfBackSpace           Backspace
osfBeginLine           Home
osfClear               Clear
osfCopy                <unbound>
osfCut                 <unbound>
osfDelete              Delete
osfDown                Down
osfEndLine             End
osfCancel              Escape
osfHelp                F1
osfInsert              Insert
osfLeft                Left
osfMenu                F4
osfMenuBar             F10
osfPageDown            Next
osfPageUp              Prior
osfPaste               <unbound>
osfPrimaryPaste        <unbound>
osfQuickPaste          <unbound>
osfRight               Right
osfSelect              Select
osfUndo                Undo
osfUp                  Up
```

Action Routines

This section describes the action routines that are listed in the "Translations" section.

Behavior

This section describes the keyboard and mouse events that affect gadgets, which do not have translations or actions.

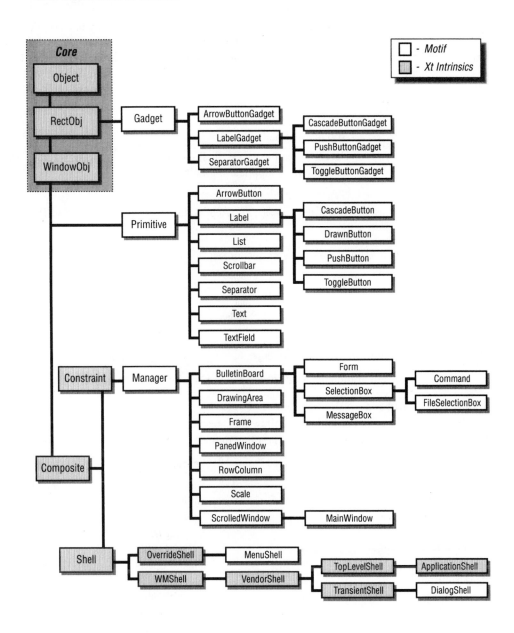

Figure B-1. Class hierarchy of the Motif widget set

Main top-level window for an application. An application should have only one Application-Shell, unless the application is implemented as multiple logical applications. An ApplicationShell is returned by the call to XtVaAppInitialize(). It can also be created explicitly with a call to XtVaAppCreateShell().

Class Information

Include File:	*<X11/Shell.h>*
Class Name:	ApplicationShell
Class Hierarchy:	Core → Composite → Shell → WmShell → VendorShell → Top-LevelShell → ApplicationShell
Class Pointer:	applicationShellWidgetClass
Functions/Macros:	XtAppCreateShell(), XtVaAppCreateShell(), XtIsApplicationShell()

New Resources

ApplicationShell defines the following resources:

Name	Class	Type	Default	Access
XmNargc	XmCArgc	int	0	CSG
XmNargv	XmCArgv	String *	NULL	CSG

XmNargc   Number of arguments in argv.

XmNargv   List of arguments used to start the application (the standard C argv).

Inherited Resources

ApplicationShell inherits the following resources. The resources are listed alphabetically, along with the superclass that defines them.

Resource	Inherited From	Resource	Inherited From
XmNaccelerators	Core	XmNmaxAspectX	WMShell
XmNallowShellResize	Shell	XmNmaxAspectY	WMShell
XmNancestorSensitive	Core	XmNmaxHeight	WMShell
XmNbackground	Core	XmNmaxWidth	WMShell
XmNbackgroundPixmap	Core	XmNminAspectX	WMShell
XmNbaseHeight	WMShell	XmNminAspectY	WMShell
XmNbaseWidth	WMShell	XmNminHeight	WMShell
XmNborderColor	Core	XmNminWidth	WMShell
XmNborderPixmap	Core	XmNmwmDecorations	VendorShell
XmNborderWidth	Core	XmNmwmFunctions	VendorShell
XmNchildren	Composite	XmNmwmInputMode	VendorShell
XmNcolormap	Core	XmNmwmMenu	VendorShell
XmNcreatePopupChildProc	Shell	XmNnumChildren	Composite
XmNdefaultFontList	VendorShell	XmNoverrideRedirect	Shell
XmNdeleteResponse	VendorShell	XmNpopdownCallback	Shell

Resource	Inherited From	Resource	Inherited From
XmNdepth	Core	XmNpopupCallback	Shell
XmNdestroyCallback	Core	XmNsaveUnder	Shell
XmNgeometry	Shell	XmNscreen	Core
XmNheight	Core	XmNsensitive	Core
XmNheightInc	WMShell	XmNshellUnitType	VendorShell
XmNiconic	TopLevelShell	XmNtitle	WMShell
XmNiconMask	WMShell	XmNtitleEncoding	WMShell
XmNiconName	TopLevelShell	XmNtransient	WMShell
XmNiconNameEncoding	TopLevelShell	XmNtranslations	Core
XmNiconPixmap	WMShell	XmNuseAsyncGeometry	VendorShell
XmNiconWindow	WMShell	XmNvisual	Shell
XmNiconX	WMShell	XmNwaitForWm	WMShell
XmNiconY	WMShell	XmNwidth	Core
XmNinitialResourcesPersistent	Core	XmNwidthInc	WMShell
XmNinitialState	WMShell	XmNwindowGroup	WMShell
XmNinput	WMShell	XmNwinGravity	WMShell
XmNinsertPosition	Composite	XmNwmTimeout	WMShell
XmNkeyboardFocusPolicy	VendorShell	XmNx	Core
XmNmappedWhenManaged	Core	XmNy	Core

ArrowButton

A directional arrow that includes a shaded border. The shading changes to make the Arrow-Button appear either pressed in when selected or raised when unselected.

Class Information

Include File:	*<Xm/ArrowB.h>*
Class Name:	XmArrowButton
Class Hierarchy:	Core → XmPrimitive → XmArrowButton
Class Pointer:	xmArrowButtonWidgetClass
Functions/Macros:	XmCreateArrowButton(), XmIsArrowButton()

New Resources

ArrowButton defines the following resources:

Name	Class	Type	Default	Access
XmNarrowDirection	XmCArrowDirection	unsigned char	XmARROW_UP	CSG
XmNmultiClick	XmCMultiClick	unsigned char	dynamic	CSG

XmNarrowDirection

    Sets the arrow direction. Possible values:

XmARROW_UP	XmARROW_LEFT
XmARROW_DOWN	XmARROW_RIGHT

XmNmultiClick

    A flag that determines whether successive button clicks are processed (by incrementing the callback structure's click count argument) or are ignored. Possible values:

XmMULTICLICK_DISCARD	/* ignore successive button clicks; default value in a menu system */
XmMULTICLICK_KEEP	/* count successive button clicks; default value when not in a menu */

Callback Resources

ArrowButton defines the following callback resources:

Callback	Reason Constant
XmNactivateCallback	XmCR_ACTIVATE
XmNarmCallback	XmCR_ARM
XmNdisarmCallback	XmCR_DISARM

Callback Structure

Each callback function is passed the following structure:

```
typedef struct
{
    int       reason;        /* the reason that the callback was called */
    XEvent    * event;       /* points to event structure that triggered callback */
    int       click_count;   /* number of multi-clicks */
} XmArrowButtonCallbackStruct;
```

click_count is meaningful only for XmNactivateCallback. Furthermore, if the XmNmultiClick resource is set to XmMULTICLICK_KEEP, then XmNactivateCallback is called for each click, and the value of *click_count* is the number of clicks that have occurred in the last sequence of multiple clicks. If the XmNmultiClick resource is set to XmMULTICLICK_DISCARD, then *click_count* always has a value of 1.

Inherited Resources

ArrowButton inherits the following resources. The resources are listed alphabetically, along with the superclass that defines them.

Resource	Inherited From	Resource	Inherited From
XmNaccelerators	Core	XmNhighlightPixmap	Primitive
XmNancestorSensitive	Core	XmNhighlightThickness	Primitive
XmNbackground	Core	XmNinitialResourcesPersistent	Core
XmNbackgroundPixmap	Core	XmNmappedWhenManaged	Core
XmNborderColor	Core	XmNnavigationType	Primitive
XmNborderPixmap	Core	XmNscreen	Core
XmNborderWidth	Core	XmNsensitive	Core
XmNbottomShadowColor	Primitive	XmNshadowThickness	Primitive

Resource	Inherited From	Resource	Inherited From
XmNbottomShadowPixmap	Primitive	XmNtopShadowColor	Primitive
XmNcolormap	Core	XmNtopShadowPixmap	Primitive
XmNdepth	Core	XmNtranslations	Core
XmNdestroyCallback	Core	XmNtraversalOn	Primitive
XmNforeground	Primitive	XmNunitType	Primitive
XmNheight	Core	XmNuserData	Primitive
XmNhelpCallback	Primitive	XmNwidth	Core
XmNhighlightColor	Primitive	XmNx	Core
XmNhighlightOnEnter	Primitive	XmNy	Core

Translations

BSelect Press	Arm()
BSelect Click	Activate()
	Disarm()
BSelect Release	Activate()
	Disarm()
BSelect Press 2+	MultiArm()
BSelect Release 2+	MultiActivate()

Action Routines

ArrowButton defines the following action routines:

Activate() Displays the ArrowButton as unselected, and invokes the list of callbacks specified by XmNactivateCallback.

Arm() Displays the ArrowButton as selected, and invokes the list of callbacks specified by XmNarmCallback.

ArmAndActivate()
Displays the ArrowButton as selected, and invokes the list of callbacks specified by XmNarmCallback. After doing this, the action routine displays the ArrowButton as unselected, and invokes the list of callbacks specified by Xm-NactivateCallback and XmNdisarmCallback.

Disarm() Displays the ArrowButton as unselected, and invokes the list of callbacks specified by XmNdisarmCallback.

Help() Invokes the list of callbacks specified by XmNhelpCallback. If the Arrow-Button doesn't have any help callbacks, the Help() routine invokes those associated with the nearest ancestor that has them.

MultiActivate()
Increments the *click_count* member of XmArrowButtonCallbackStruct, displays the ArrowButton as unselected, and and invokes the list of callbacks specified by XmNactivateCallback and XmNdisarmCallback. This action routine takes effect only when the XmNmultiClick resource is set to XmMULTICLICK_KEEP.

Xt and Motif Widget Classes

MultiArm()   Displays the ArrowButton as selected, and invokes the list of callbacks specified by XmNarmCallback. This action routine takes effect only when the XmNmultiClick resource is set to XmMULTICLICK_KEEP.

ArrowButton has additional behavior associated with <EnterWindow> and <LeaveWindow>, which display the ArrowButton as selected or unselected, respectively, if the select button is pressed.

ArrowButtonGadget

The gadget variant of ArrowButton.

Class Information

Include File:	*<Xm/ArrowBG.h>*
Class Name:	XmArrowButtonGadget
Class Hierarchy:	Object → RectObj → XmGadget → XmArrowButtonGadget
Class Pointer:	xmArrowButtonGadgetClass
Functions/Macros:	XmCreateArrowButtonGadget(), XmIsArrowButtonGadget()

ArrowButtonGadget's new resources, callback resources, and callback structure are the same as those for ArrowButton.

Inherited Resources

ArrowButtonGadget inherits the following resources. The resources are listed alphabetically, along with the superclass that defines them.

Resource	Inherited From	Resource	Inherited From
XmNancestorSensitive	RectObj	XmNsensitive	RectObj
XmNborderWidth	RectObj	XmNshadowThickness	Gadget
XmNdestroyCallback	Object	XmNtraversalOn	Gadget
XmNheight	RectObj	XmNunitType	Gadget
XmNhelpCallback	Gadget	XmNuserData	Gadget
XmNhighlightOnEnter	Gadget	XmNwidth	RectObj
XmNhighlightThickness	Gadget	XmNx	RectObj
XmNnavigationType	Gadget	XmNy	RectObj

Behavior

As a gadget subclass, ArrowButtonGadget has no translations associated with it. However, ArrowButtonGadget behavior corresponds to the action routines of the Arrow-Button widget. See the ArrowButton action routines for more information.

Behavior	Equivalent ArrowButton Action Routine
BSelect Press	Arm()
BSelect Click or BSelectRelease	Activate()
	Disarm()

Behavior	Equivalent ArrowButton Action Routine
BSelect Press 2+	MultiArm()
BSelect Release 2+	MultiActivate()
KActivate or KSelect	ArmAndActivate()
KHelp	Help()

ArrowButtonGadget has additional behavior associated with <Enter> and <Leave>, which display the ArrowButtonGadget as selected or unselected, respectively, if the select button is pressed.

BulletinBoard

A general-purpose manager that allows children to be placed at arbitrary x,y positions. The simple geometry management of BulletinBoard can be used to enforce margins and to prevent child widgets from overlapping. BulletinBoard is the base widget for most dialog widgets and defines many resources that have effect only when it is an immediate child of a DialogShell.

Class Information

Include File:	*<Xm/BulletinB.h>*
Class Name:	XmBulletinBoard
Class Hierarchy:	Core → Composite → Constraint → XmManager → XmBulletin-Board
Class Pointer:	xmBulletinBoardWidgetClass
Functions/Macros:	XmCreateBulletinBoard(), XmCreateBulletinBoardDialog()

New Resources

BulletinBoard defines the following resources:

Name	Class	Type	Default	Access
XmNallowOverlap	XmCAllowOverlap	Boolean	True	CSG
XmNautoUnmanage	XmCAutoUnmanage	Boolean	True	CG
XmNbuttonFontList	XmCButtonFontList	XmFontList	dynamic	CSG
XmNcancelButton	XmCWidget	Window	NULL	SG
XmNdefaultButton	XmCWidget	Window	NULL	SG
XmNdefaultPosition	XmCDefaultPosition	Boolean	True	CSG
XmNdialogStyle	XmCDialogStyle	unsigned char	dynamic	CSG
XmNdialogTitle	XmCDialogTitle	XmString	NULL	CSG
XmNlabelFontList	XmCLabelFontList	XmFontList	dynamic	CSG
XmNmarginHeight	XmCMarginHeight	Dimension	10	CSG
XmNmarginWidth	XmCMarginWidth	Dimension	10	CSG
XmNnoResize	XmCNoResize	Boolean	False	CSG
XmNresizePolicy	XmCResizePolicy	unsigned char	XmRESIZE_ANY	CSG
XmNshadowType	XmCShadowType	unsigned char	XmSHADOW_OUT	CSG

Name	Class	Type	Default	Access
XmNtextFontList	XmCTextFontList	XmFontList	dynamic	CSG
XmNtextTranslations	XmCTranslations	XtTranslations	NULL	C

XmNallowOverlap

If True (default), child windows are allowed to overlap.

XmNautoUnmanage

If True (default), the BulletinBoard is automatically unmanaged after a button is activated (unless the button is an Apply or Help button).

XmNbuttonFontList

The font list used for the button children of the BulletinBoard widget. If this value is initially NULL, the font list is derived from the XmNdefaultFontList resource found in the nearest parent.

XmNcancelButton

The widget ID of the Cancel button. The subclasses of BulletinBoard define a Cancel button and set this resource.

XmNdefaultButton

The widget ID of the default button. Some of the subclasses of BulletinBoard define a default button and set this resource. To indicate that it is the default, this button appears different from the others.

XmNdefaultPosition

If True (default) and if the BulletinBoard is the child of a DialogShell, then the BulletinBoard will be centered relative to the DialogShell's parent.

XmNdialogStyle

The BulletinBoard's dialog style, whose value can be set only if the BulletinBoard is unmanaged. Possible values:

```
XmDIALOG_WORK_AREA              /* default when BulletinBoard's parent is not a DialogShell */
XmDIALOG_MODELESS               /* default when BulletinBoard's parent is a DialogShell */
XmDIALOG_PRIMARY_APPLICATION_MODAL
XmDIALOG_FULL_APPLICATION_MODAL
XmDIALOG_SYSTEM_MODAL
XmDIALOG_APPLICATION_MODAL
```

XmNdialogTitle

The dialog title. Setting this resource also sets the resources XmNtitle and XmNnameEncoding in a parent whose superclass is WMShell.

XmNlabelFontList

Like the XmNbuttonFontList resource, but for Label children.

XmNmarginHeight

Minimum spacing between a BulletinBoard's top or bottom edge and any child widget.

XmNmarginWidth

>   Minimum spacing between a BulletinBoard's right or left edge and any child widget.

XmNnoResize

>   If False (default), *mwm* includes resize controls in the window manager frame of the BulletinBoard's shell parent.

XmNresizePolicy

>   How BulletinBoard widgets are resized. Possible values:

> | | |
> |---|---|
> | XmRESIZE_NONE | /* remain at fixed size */ |
> | XmRESIZE_GROW | /* expand only */ |
> | XmRESIZE_ANY | /* shrink or expand, as needed */ |

XmNshadowType

>   The style in which shadows are drawn. Possible values:

> | | |
> |---|---|
> | XmSHADOW_ETCHED_IN | /* double line; widget appears inset */ |
> | XmSHADOW_ETCHED_OUT | /* double line; widget appears raised */ |
> | XmSHADOW_IN | /* widget appears inset */ |
> | XmSHADOW_OUT | /* widget appears outset */ |

XmNtextFontList

>   Like the XmNbuttonFontList resource, but for Text children.

XmNtextTranslations

>   For any Text widget (or its subclass) that is a child of a BulletinBoard, this resource adds translations.

Callback Resources

BulletinBoard defines the following callback resources:

Callback	Reason Constant
XmNmapCallback	XmCR_MAP
XmNunmapCallback	XmCR_UNMAP
XmNfocusCallback	XmCR_FOCUS

Callback Structure

Each callback function is passed the following structure:

```
typedef struct
{
    int      reason;      /* the reason that the callback was called */
    XEvent   * event;     /* points to event structure that triggered callback */
} XmAnyCallbackStruct;
```

Inherited Resources

BulletinBoard inherits the following resources. The resources are listed alphabetically, along with the superclass that defines them. When it is a child of a DialogShell, Bulletin-Board dynamically resets the default XmNshadowThickness from 0 to 1.

Resource	Inherited From	Resource	Inherited From
XmNaccelerators	Core	XmNinitialResourcesPersistent	Core
XmNancestorSensitive	Core	XmNinsertPosition	Composite
XmNbackground	Core	XmNmappedWhenManaged	Core
XmNbackgroundPixmap	Core	XmNnavigationType	Manager
XmNborderColor	Core	XmNnumChildren	Composite
XmNborderPixmap	Core	XmNscreen	Core
XmNborderWidth	Core	XmNsensitive	Core
XmNbottomShadowColor	Manager	XmNshadowThickness	Manager
XmNbottomShadowPixmap	Manager	XmNstringDirection	Manager
XmNchildren	Composite	XmNtopShadowColor	Manager
XmNcolormap	Core	XmNtopShadowPixmap	Manager
XmNdepth	Core	XmNtranslations	Core
XmNdestroyCallback	Core	XmNtraversalOn	Manager
XmNforeground	Manager	XmNunitType	Manager
XmNheight	Core	XmNuserData	Manager
XmNhelpCallback	Manager	XmNwidth	Core
XmNhighlightColor	Manager	XmNx	Core
XmNhighlightPixmap	Manager	XmNy	Core

Translations

The translations for BulletinBoard include those of Manager.

Additional Behavior

The following additional behavior is defined for this widget:

MAny KCancel

> For a sensitive Cancel button, invokes the XmNactivateCallback callbacks.

KActivate For the button that has keyboard focus, invokes the XmNactivateCallback callbacks.

<FocusIn> Invokes the XmNfocusCallback callbacks. The widget receives focus either when the user traverses to it (if XmNkeyboardFocusPolicy = XmEXPLICIT) or when the pointer enters the window (if XmNkeyboardFocusPolicy = Xm-POINTER).

<Map> Invokes the XmNmapCallback callbacks.

<Unmap> Invokes the XmNunmapCallback callbacks.

BulletinBoardDialog

A convenience widget created by a call to XmCreateBulletinBoardDialog() and useful for creating custom dialogs. BulletinBoardDialog consists of a DialogShell with a Bulletin-Board widget as its child. The include file is *<Xm/BulletinB.h>*.

CascadeButton

A button that pops up a menu. CascadeButton links either a menu bar to a menu pane, or a menu pane to another menu pane.

Class Information

Include File:	*<Xm/CascadeB.h>*
Class Name:	XmCascadeButton
Class Hierarchy:	Core → XmPrimitive → XmLabel → XmCascadeButton
Class Pointer:	xmCascadeButtonWidgetClass
Functions/Macros:	XmCascadeButtonHighlight(), XmCreateCascadeButton(), XmIsCascade-Button()

New Resources

CascadeButton defines the following resources:

Name	Class	Type	Default	Access
XmNcascadePixmap	XmCPixmap	Pixmap	dynamic	CSG
XmNmappingDelay	XmCMappingDelay	int	180	CSG
XmNsubMenuId	XmCMenuWidget	Widget	NULL	CSG

XmNcascadePixmap
> The pixmap within the CascadeButton that indicates a submenu. By default, this pixmap is an arrow pointing toward the submenu to be popped up.

XmNmappingDelay
> The number of milliseconds it should take for the application to display a submenu after its CascadeButton has been selected.

XmNsubMenuId
> The widget ID of the pulldown menu pane associated with this CascadeButton (that is, the menu pane to display when the CascadeButton is selected). The pulldown menu pane and the CascadeButton must have a common parent (see discussions of XmCreatePulldownMenu() for clarification of the parent-child hierarchy).

Callback Resources

CascadeButton defines the following callback resources:

Callback	Reason Constant
XmNactivateCallback	XmCR_ACTIVATE
XmNcascadingCallback	XmCR_CASCADING

Callback Structure

Each callback function is passed the following structure:

```
typedef struct
{
    int      reason;       /* the reason that the callback was called */
    XEvent   * event;      /* points to event structure that triggered callback */
} XmAnyCallbackStruct;
```

Inherited Resources

CascadeButton inherits the following resources. The resources are listed alphabetically, along with the superclass that defines them.

Resource	Inherited From	Resource	Inherited From
XmNaccelerator	Label	XmNlabelString	Label
XmNaccelerators	Core	XmNlabelType	Label
XmNacceleratorText	Label	XmNmappedWhenManaged	Core
XmNalignment	Label	XmNmarginBottom	Label
XmNancestorSensitive	Core	XmNmarginHeight	Label
XmNbackground	Core	XmNmarginLeft	Label
XmNbackgroundPixmap	Core	XmNmarginRight	Label
XmNborderColor	Core	XmNmarginTop	Label
XmNborderPixmap	Core	XmNmarginWidth	Label
XmNborderWidth	Core	XmNmnemonic	Label
XmNbottomShadowColor	Primitive	XmNmnemonicCharSet	Label
XmNbottomShadowPixmap	Primitive	XmNnavigationType	Primitive
XmNcolormap	Core	XmNrecomputeSize	Label
XmNdepth	Core	XmNscreen	Core
XmNdestroyCallback	Core	XmNsensitive	Core
XmNfontList	Label	XmNshadowThickness	Primitive
XmNforeground	Primitive	XmNstringDirection	Label
XmNheight	Core	XmNtopShadowColor	Primitive
XmNhelpCallback	Primitive	XmNtopShadowPixmap	Primitive
XmNhighlightColor	Primitive	XmNtranslations	Core
XmNhighlightOnEnter	Primitive	XmNtraversalOn	Primitive
XmNhighlightPixmap	Primitive	XmNunitType	Primitive
XmNhighlightThickness	Primitive	XmNuserData	Primitive
XmNinitialResourcesPersistent	Core	XmNwidth	Core
XmNlabelInsensitivePixmap	Label	XmNx	Core
XmNlabelPixmap	Label	XmNy	Core

Translations

BSelect Press	MenuBarSelect()	(in a menu bar)
	StartDrag()	(in a popup menu or a pulldown menu)
BSelect Release	DoSelect()	
KActivate	KeySelect()	
KSelect	KeySelect()	
KHelp	Help()	
MAny KCancel	CleanupMenuBar()	

Action Routines

CascadeButton defines the following action routines:

CleanupMenuBar()

Unposts any menus and restores the keyboard focus to the group of widgets (tab group) that had the focus before the CascadeButton was armed.

DoSelect()   Posts the CascadeButton's submenu and allows keyboard traversal. If there is no submenu attached to the CascadeButton, this action routine activates the CascadeButton and unposts all the menus in the cascade.

Help()   Similar to CleanupMenuBar() in that the Help() routine unposts any menus and restores keyboard focus. This routine also invokes the list of callbacks specified by XmNhelpCallback. If the CascadeButton doesn't have any help callbacks, the Help() routine invokes those associated with the nearest ancestor that has them.

KeySelect()   Posts the CascadeButton's submenu, provided that keyboard traversal is allowed. If there is no submenu attached to the CascadeButton, this action routine activates the CascadeButton and unposts all the menus in the cascade.

MenuBarSelect()

Unposts any previously posted menus, posts the submenu associated with the CascadeButton, and enables mouse traversal.

StartDrag()   Posts the submenu associated with the CascadeButton and enables mouse traversal.

In a menu bar that is armed, CascadeButton has additional behavior associated with <EnterWindow>, which arms the CascadeButton and posts its submenu, and with <Leave-Window>, which disarms the CascadeButton and unposts its submenu.

CascadeButtonGadget

The gadget variant of CascadeButton.

Class Information

Include File:	*<Xm/CascadeBG.h>*
Class Name:	XmCascadeButtonGadget
Class Hierarchy:	Object → RectObj → XmGadget → XmLabelGadget → XmCascadeButtonGadget
Class Pointer:	xmCascadeButtonGadgetClass
Functions/Macros:	XmCascadeButtonGadgetHighlight(), XmCreateCascadeButtonGadget(), XmOptionButtonGadget(), XmIsCascadeButtonGadget()

CascadeButtonGadget's new resources, callback resources, and callback structure are the same as those for CascadeButton.

Inherited Resources

CascadeButtonGadget inherits the following resources. The resources are listed alphabetically, along with the superclass that defines them.

Resource	Inherited From	Resource	Inherited From
XmNaccelerator	LabelGadget	XmNmarginLeft	LabelGadget
XmNacceleratorText	LabelGadget	XmNmarginRight	LabelGadget
XmNalignment	LabelGadget	XmNmarginTop	LabelGadget
XmNancestorSensitive	RectObj	XmNmarginWidth	LabelGadget
XmNborderWidth	RectObj	XmNmnemonic	LabelGadget
XmNdestroyCallback	Object	XmNmnemonicCharSet	LabelGadget
XmNfontList	LabelGadget	XmNnavigationType	Gadget
XmNheight	RectObj	XmNrecomputeSize	LabelGadget
XmNhelpCallback	Gadget	XmNsensitive	RectObj
XmNhighlightOnEnter	Gadget	XmNshadowThickness	Gadget
XmNhighlightThickness	Gadget	XmNstringDirection	LabelGadget
XmNlabelInsensitivePixmap	LabelGadget	XmNtraversalOn	Gadget
XmNlabelPixmap	LabelGadget	XmNunitType	Gadget
XmNlabelString	LabelGadget	XmNuserData	Gadget
XmNlabelType	LabelGadget	XmNwidth	RectObj
XmNmarginBottom	LabelGadget	XmNx	RectObj
XmNmarginHeight	LabelGadget	XmNy	RectObj

Behavior

As a gadget subclass, CascadeButtonGadget has no translations associated with it. However, CascadeButtonGadget behavior corresponds to the action routines of the CascadeButton widget. See the CascadeButton action routines for more information.

Behavior	Equivalent CascadeButton Action Routine
BSelect Press	MenuBarSelect()
BSelect Release	DoSelect()
KActivate or KSelect	KeySelect()
KHelp	Help()
MAny KCancel	CleanupMenuBar()

In a menu bar that is armed, CascadeButtonGadget has additional behavior associated with <Enter>, which arms the CascadeButtonGadget and posts its submenu, and with <Leave>, which disarms the CascadeButtonGadget and unposts its submenu.

CheckBox

A manager that contains ToggleButtonGadget (or ToggleButton) children, any number of which may be selected at a given time. Like a RadioBox, a CheckBox is a RowColumn widget whose XmNrowColumnType resource is set to XmWORK_AREA. Unlike a RadioBox, a CheckBox sets XmNradioAlwaysOne (from RowColumn) to False. A CheckBox can be created by a call to XmCreateSimpleCheckBox() or XmVaCreateSimpleCheckBox(), which are defined in <Xm/RowColumn.h>.

Command

A composite widget that handles command entry by providing a prompt, a command input field, and a history list region. Many of the Command widget's new resources are in fact renamed resources from SelectionBox.

Class Information

Include File:	<Xm/Command.h>
Class Name:	XmCommand
Class Hierarchy:	Core → Composite → Constraint → XmManager → XmBulletin-Board → XmSelectionBox → XmCommand
Class Pointer:	xmCommandWidgetClass
Functions/Macros:	XmCommandAppendValue(), XmCommandError(), XmCommandGet-Child(), XmCommandSetValue(), XmCreateCommand()

New Resources

Command defines the following resources:

Name	Class	Type	Default	Access
XmNcommand	XmCTextString	XmString	" "	CSG
XmNhistoryItems	XmCItems	XmStringTable	NULL	CSG

Name	Class	Type	Default	Access
XmNhistoryItemCount	XmCItemCount	int	0	CSG
XmNhistoryMaxItems	XmCMaxItems	int	100	CSG
XmNhistoryVisibleItemCount	XmCVisibleItemCount	int	8	CSG
XmNpromptString	XmCPromptString	XmString	dynamic	CSG

XmNcommand

> The text currently displayed on the command line. Synonymous with the XmNtext-String resource in SelectionBox. XmNcommand can be changed using the routines XmCommandSetValue() and XmCommandAppendValue().

XmNhistoryItems

> The items in the history list. Synonymous with the XmNlistItems resource in SelectionBox. A call to XtGetValues() returns the actual list items (not a copy), so don't have your application free these items.

XmNhistoryItemCount

> The number of strings in XmNhistoryItems. Synonymous with the XmNlistItemCount resource in SelectionBox.

XmNhistoryMaxItems

> The history list's maximum number of items. When this number is reached, the first history item is removed before the new command is added to the list.

XmNhistoryVisibleItemCount

> The number of history list commands that will display at one time. Synonymous with the XmNvisibleItemCount resource in SelectionBox.

XmNpromptString

> The command-line prompt. Synonymous with the XmNselectionLabelString resource in SelectionBox.

Callback Resources

Command defines the following callback resources:

Callback	Reason Constant
XmNcommandEnteredCallback	XmCR_COMMAND_ENTERED
XmNcommandChangedCallback	XmCR_COMMAND_CHANGED

Callback Structure

Each callback function is passed the following structure:

```
typedef struct
{
    int      reason;     /* the reason that the callback was called */
    XEvent   * event;    /* points to event structure that triggered callback */
    XmString value;      /* the string contained in the command area */
    int      length;     /* the size of this string */
} XmCommandCallbackStruct;
```

Inherited Resources

Command inherits the resources shown below. The resources are listed alphabetically, along with the superclass that defines them. Note that the Command widget redefines Xm-NautoUnmanage and XmNdefaultPosition to False, XmNdialogType to XmDIALOG_COMMAND, and XmNresizePolicy to XmRESIZE_NONE.

Resource	Inherited From	Resource	Inherited From
XmNaccelerators	Core	XmNlistItems	SelectionBox
XmNallowOverlap	BulletinBoard	XmNlistLabelString	SelectionBox
XmNancestorSensitive	Core	XmNlistVisibleItemCount	SelectionBox
XmNapplyCallback	SelectionBox	XmNmapCallback	BulletinBoard
XmNapplyLabelString	SelectionBox	XmNmappedWhenManaged	Core
XmNautoUnmanage	BulletinBoard	XmNmarginHeight	BulletinBoard
XmNbackground	Core	XmNmarginWidth	BulletinBoard
XmNbackgroundPixmap	Core	XmNminimizeButtons	SelectionBox
XmNborderColor	Core	XmNmustMatch	SelectionBox
XmNborderPixmap	Core	XmNnavigationType	Manager
XmNborderWidth	Core	XmNnoMatchCallback	SelectionBox
XmNbottomShadowColor	Manager	XmNnoResize	BulletinBoard
XmNbottomShadowPixmap	Manager	XmNnumChildren	Composite
XmNbuttonFontList	BulletinBoard	XmNokCallback	SelectionBox
XmNcancelButton	BulletinBoard	XmNokLabelString	SelectionBox
XmNcancelCallback	SelectionBox	XmNresizePolicy	BulletinBoard
XmNcancelLabelString	SelectionBox	XmNscreen	Core
XmNchildren	Composite	XmNselectionLabelString	SelectionBox
XmNcolormap	Core	XmNsensitive	Core
XmNdefaultButton	BulletinBoard	XmNshadowThickness	Manager
XmNdefaultPosition	BulletinBoard	XmNshadowType	BulletinBoard
XmNdepth	Core	XmNstringDirection	Manager
XmNdestroyCallback	Core	XmNtextAccelerators	SelectionBox
XmNdialogStyle	BulletinBoard	XmNtextColumns	SelectionBox
XmNdialogTitle	BulletinBoard	XmNtextFontList	BulletinBoard
XmNdialogType	SelectionBox	XmNtextString	SelectionBox
XmNfocusCallback	BulletinBoard	XmNtextTranslations	BulletinBoard
XmNforeground	Manager	XmNtopShadowColor	Manager
XmNheight	Core	XmNtopShadowPixmap	Manager
XmNhelpCallback	Manager	XmNtranslations	Core
XmNhelpLabelString	SelectionBox	XmNtraversalOn	Manager
XmNhighlightColor	Manager	XmNunitType	Manager
XmNhighlightPixmap	Manager	XmNunmapCallback	BulletinBoard
XmNinitialResourcesPersistent	Core	XmNuserData	Manager
XmNinsertPosition	Composite	XmNwidth	Core
XmNlabelFontList	BulletinBoard	XmNx	Core
XmNlistItemCount	SelectionBox	XmNy	Core

Translations

The translations for Command are inherited from SelectionBox.

Action Routines

Command defines the following action routines:

SelectionBoxUpOrDown(*flag*)

> Selects a command from the history list, replaces the current command-line text with this list item, and invokes the callbacks specified by XmNcommand-ChangedCallback. The value of *flag* determines which history list command is selected. With a *flag* value of 0, 1, 2, or 3, this action routine selects the list's previous, next, first, or last item, respectively.

Additional Behavior

The following additional behavior is defined for this widget:

<KActivate>

> In a Text widget, invokes the callbacks in XmNactivateCallback, appends the text to the Command widget's history list, and invokes the callbacks in Xm-NcommandEnteredCallback.

<Key>

> In a Text widget, any keystroke that changes text invokes the callbacks in Xm-NcommandChangedCallback.

<KActivate> or <DoubleClick>

> In a List widget, invokes the callbacks in XmNdefaultActionCallback, appends the selected item to the Command widget's history list, and invokes the callbacks in XmNcommandEnteredCallback.

<FocusIn> Invokes the XmNfocusCallback callbacks.

<MapWindow>

> Maps a Command widget whose parent is a DialogShell (by calling XmNmap-Callback).

<UnmapWindow>

> Unmaps a Command widget whose parent is a DialogShell (by calling Xm-NunmapCallback).

Composite

A container for other widgets. A Composite widget can have any number of children and can be used for geometry layout of these children[2] and for destroying descendants. Composite is an Intrinsics meta-class and is used internally by the X Toolkit; Composite widgets are never instantiated by the application.

---

[2] Shell widgets are subclasses of Composite but can manage only one child.

Class Information

Include File:	*<X11/Composite.h>*
Class Name:	Composite
Class Hierarchy:	Core → Composite
Class Pointer:	compositeWidgetClass
Functions/Macros:	XtIsComposite()

New Resources

Composite defines the following resources:

Name	Class	Type	Default	Access
XmNchildren	XmCReadOnly	WidgetList	NULL	G
XmNinsertPosition	XmCInsertPosition	(*)()	NULL	CSG
XmNnumChildren	XmCReadOnly	Cardinal	0	G

XmNchildren   List of widget's children.

XmNinsertPosition   Points to the following XtOrderProc() function:

Cardinal (* XtOrderProc) (*widget*)

XmNnumChildren   Length of the list in XmNchildren.

Inherited Resources

Composite inherits the following resources. The resources are listed alphabetically, along with the superclass that defines them.

Resource	Inherited From	Resource	Inherited From
XmNaccelerators	Core	XmNheight	Core
XmNancestorSensitive	Core	XmNinitialResourcesPersistent	Core
XmNbackground	Core	XmNmappedWhenManaged	Core
XmNbackgroundPixmap	Core	XmNscreen	Core
XmNborderColor	Core	XmNsensitive	Core
XmNborderPixmap	Core	XmNtranslations	Core
XmNborderWidth	Core	XmNwidth	Core
XmNcolormap	Core	XmNx	Core
XmNdepth	Core	XmNy	Core
XmNdestroyCallback	Core		

Constraint

Allows constraint resources defined by a manager widget to enforce behavior on its children in some way. For example, a PanedWindow or Form widget's constraint resources may determine a child's maximum width and height, or they may determine how other children should change when one child is resized. Constraint is an Intrinsics meta-class and is used internally by the X Toolkit; Constraint widgets are never instantiated by the application.

Class Information

Include File:	*<Xm/Constraint.h>*
Class Name:	Constraint
Class Hierarchy:	Core → Composite → Constraint
Class Pointer:	constraintWidgetClass
Functions/Macros:	XtIsConstraint()

New Resources

Constraint defines no new resources.

Inherited Resources

Constraint inherits the following resources. The resources are listed alphabetically, along with the superclass that defines them.

Resource	Inherited From	Resource	Inherited From
XmNaccelerators	Core	XmNheight	Core
XmNancestorSensitive	Core	XmNinitialResourcesPersistent	Core
XmNbackground	Core	XmNmappedWhenManaged	Core
XmNbackgroundPixmap	Core	XmNscreen	Core
XmNborderColor	Core	XmNsensitive	Core
XmNborderPixmap	Core	XmNtranslations	Core
XmNborderWidth	Core	XmNwidth	Core
XmNcolormap	Core	XmNx	Core
XmNdepth	Core	XmNy	Core
XmNdestroyCallback	Core		

Core

Fundamental class for windowed widgets. All such widgets are subclasses of Core. Object and RectObj support gadgets (windowless widgets). Core is an Intrinsics meta-class and is normally not instantiated.[3]

Class Information

Include File:	*<Xm/Core.h>*
Class Name:	Core
Class Hierarchy:	Core
Class Pointer:	widgetClass or coreWidgetClass

New Resources

Core defines the following resources:

Name	Class	Type	Default	Access
XmNaccelerators	XmCAccelerators	XtAccelerators	NULL	CSG
XmNancestorSensitive	XmCSensitive	Boolean	dynamic	G
XmNbackground	XmCBackground	Pixel	dynamic	CSG
XmNbackgroundPixmap	XmCPixmap	Pixmap	XmUNSPECIFIED_ PIXMAP	CSG
XmNborderColor	XmCBorderColor	Pixel	XtDefaultForeground	CSG
XmNborderPixmap	XmCPixmap	Pixmap	XmUNSPECIFIED_ PIXMAP	CSG
XmNborderWidth	XmCBorderWidth	Dimension	1	CSG
XmNcolormap	XmCColormap	Colormap	dynamic	CG
XmNdepth	XmCDepth	int	dynamic	CG
XmNheight	XmCHeight	Dimension	dynamic	CSG
XmNinitialResourcesPersistent	XmCInitialResourcesPersistent	Boolean	True	CG
XmNmappedWhenManaged	XmCMappedWhenManaged	Boolean	True	CSG
XmNscreen	XmCScreen	Screen *	dynamic	CG
XmNsensitive	XmCSensitive	Boolean	True	CSG
XmNtranslations	XmCTranslations	XtTranslations	NULL	CSG
XmNwidth	XmCWidth	Dimension	dynamic	CSG
XmNx	XmCPosition	Position	0	CSG
XmNy	XmCPosition	Position	0	CSG

XmNaccelerators

A translation table bound with its actions for a widget. A destination widget can be set up to use this accelerator table.

---

[3] Core is sometimes instantiated for use as a basic drawing area.

XmNancestorSensitive

Tells whether a widget's immediate parent should receive input. Default value is (a) True (if the widget is a top-level shell), (b) copied from the XmNancestorSensitive resource of its parent (if the widget is a popup shell), or (c) the bitwise AND of the XmNsensitive and XmNancestorSensitive resources of the parent (for other widgets).

XmNbackground

Widget's background color.

XmNbackgroundPixmap

Pixmap with which to tile the background, beginning at the upper-left corner.

XmNborderColor

Pixel value that defines the color of the border.

XmNborderPixmap

Pixmap with which to tile the border, beginning at the upper-left corner of the border.

XmNborderWidth

Width (in pixels) of the window's border.

XmNcolormap

Colormap used in converting to pixel values. Previously created pixel values are unaffected. The default value is the screen's default colormap (for top-level shells) or is copied from the parent (for other widgets).

XmNdepth

Number of bits allowed for each pixel. The Xt Intrinsics set this resource when the widget is created. As with the XmNcolormap resource, the default value comes from the screen's default or is copied from the parent.

XmNdestroyCallback

List of callbacks invoked when the widget is destroyed.

XmNheight

Window height (in pixels), excluding the border.

XmNinitialResourcesPersistent

Tells whether resources should be reference counted. If True (default), it is assumed that the widget won't be destroyed while the application is running, and thus the widget's resources are not reference counted. Set this resource to False if your application might destroy the widget and will need to deallocate the resources.

XmNmappedWhenManaged

If True (default), the widget becomes visible (is mapped) as soon as it is both realized and managed. If False, the application performs the mapping and unmapping of the widget. If changed to False after the widget is realized and managed, the widget is unmapped.

XmNscreen

Screen location of the widget. The default value comes either from the screen's default or is copied from the parent.

XmNsensitive

Tells whether a widget receives input (is sensitive). The XtSetSensitive() routine can be used to change a widget's sensitivity and to guarantee that if a parent has its XmNsensitive resource set to False, then its children will have their ancestor-sensitive flag set correctly.

XmNtranslations

Points to a translation table; must be compiled with XtParseTranslationTable().

XmNwidth

Window width (in pixels), excluding the border.

XmNx

The x-coordinate of the widget's upper-left outer corner, relative to the upper-left inner corner of its parent.

XmNy

The y-coordinate of the widget's upper-left outer corner, relative to the upper-left inner corner of its parent.

DialogShell

A Shell parent for dialog boxes. DialogShells cannot be iconified separately, but only when the main application shell is iconified.

Class Information

Include File:	*<Xm/DialogS.h>*
Class Name:	XmDialogShell
Class Hierarchy:	Core → Composite → Shell → WmShell → VendorShell → TransientShell → XmDialogShell
Class Pointer:	xmDialogShellWidgetClass
Functions/Macros:	XmCreateDialogShell(), XmIsDialogShell()

New Resources

Although DialogShell defines no new resources, it redefines the XmNdeleteResponse resource to XmUNMAP.

Inherited Resources

DialogShell inherits the following resources. The resources are listed alphabetically, along with the superclass that defines them.

Resource	Inherited From	Resource	Inherited From
XmNaccelerators	Core	XmNmaxHeight	WMShell
XmNallowShellResize	Shell	XmNmaxWidth	WMShell
XmNancestorSensitive	Core	XmNminAspectX	WMShell
XmNbackground	Core	XmNminAspectY	WMShell
XmNbackgroundPixmap	Core	XmNminHeight	WMShell
XmNbaseHeight	WMShell	XmNminWidth	WMShell
XmNbaseWidth	WMShell	XmNmwmDecorations	VendorShell
XmNborderColor	Core	XmNmwmFunctions	VendorShell
XmNborderPixmap	Core	XmNmwmInputMode	VendorShell
XmNborderWidth	Core	XmNmwmMenu	VendorShell
XmNchildren	Composite	XmNnumChildren	Composite
XmNcolormap	Core	XmNoverrideRedirect	Shell
XmNcreatePopupChildProc	Shell	XmNpopdownCallback	Shell
XmNdefaultFontList	VendorShell	XmNpopupCallback	Shell
XmNdeleteResponse	VendorShell	XmNsaveUnder	Shell
XmNdepth	Core	XmNscreen	Core
XmNdestroyCallback	Core	XmNsensitive	Core
XmNgeometry	Shell	XmNshellUnitType	VendorShell
XmNheight	Core	XmNtitle	WMShell
XmNheightInc	WMShell	XmNtitleEncoding	WMShell
XmNiconMask	WMShell	XmNtransient	WMShell
XmNiconPixmap	WMShell	XmNtransientFor	TransientShell
XmNiconWindow	WMShell	XmNtranslations	Core
XmNiconX	WMShell	XmNuseAsyncGeometry	VendorShell
XmNiconY	WMShell	XmNvisual	Shell
XmNinitialResourcesPersistent	Core	XmNwaitForWm	WMShell
XmNinitialState	WMShell	XmNwidth	Core
XmNinput	WMShell	XmNwidthInc	WMShell
XmNinsertPosition	Composite	XmNwindowGroup	WMShell
XmNkeyboardFocusPolicy	VendorShell	XmNwinGravity	WMShell
XmNmappedWhenManaged	Core	XmNwmTimeout	WMShell
XmNmaxAspectX	WMShell	XmNx	Core
XmNmaxAspectY	WMShell	XmNy	Core

DrawingArea

A manager widget that provides simple geometry management of multiple widget or gadget children. Basically, DrawingArea is an empty widget designed for various purposes. It invokes callbacks that notify applications when it receives input events, exposure events, and resize events.

Class Information

Include File:	*<Xm/DrawingA.h>*
Class Name:	XmDrawingArea
Class Hierarchy:	Core → Composite → Constraint → XmManager → XmDrawing-Area
Class Pointer:	xmDrawingAreaWidgetClass
Functions/Macros:	XmCreateDrawingArea()

New Resources

DrawingArea defines the following resources:

Name	Class	Type	Default	Access
XmNmarginHeight	XmCMarginHeight	Dimension	10	CSG
XmNmarginWidth	XmCMarginWidth	Dimension	10	CSG
XmNresizePolicy	XmCResizePolicy	unsigned char	XmRESIZE_ANY	CSG

XmNmarginHeight
> The spacing between a DrawingArea's top or bottom edge and any child widget.

XmNmarginWidth
> The spacing between a DrawingArea's right or left edge and any child widget.

XmNresizePolicy
> How DrawingArea widgets are resized. Possible values:

XmRESIZE_NONE	/* remain at fixed size */
XmRESIZE_GROW	/* expand only */
XmRESIZE_ANY	/* shrink or expand, as needed */

Callback Resources

DrawingArea defines the following callback resources:

Callback	Reason Constant
XmNexposeCallback	XmCR_EXPOSE
XmNinputCallback	XmCR_RESIZE
XmNresizeCallback	XmCR_INPUT

Callback Structure

Each callback function is passed the following structure:

```
typedef struct
{
    int       reason;        /* the reason that the callback was called */
    XEvent    * event;       /* points to event structure that triggered callback; */
                             /* for XmNresizeCallback, this is NULL */
    Window    window;        /* the widget's window */
} XmDrawingAreaCallbackStruct;
```

Inherited Resources

DrawingArea inherits the following resources. The resources are listed alphabetically, along with the superclass that defines them.

Resource	Inherited From	Resource	Inherited From
XmNaccelerators	Core	XmNinitialResourcesPersistent	Core
XmNancestorSensitive	Core	XmNinsertPosition	Composite
XmNbackground	Core	XmNmappedWhenManaged	Core
XmNbackgroundPixmap	Core	XmNnavigationType	Manager
XmNborderColor	Core	XmNnumChildren	Composite
XmNborderPixmap	Core	XmNscreen	Core
XmNborderWidth	Core	XmNsensitive	Core
XmNbottomShadowColor	Manager	XmNshadowThickness	Manager
XmNbottomShadowPixmap	Manager	XmNstringDirection	Manager
XmNchildren	Composite	XmNtopShadowColor	Manager
XmNcolormap	Core	XmNtopShadowPixmap	Manager
XmNdepth	Core	XmNtranslations	Core
XmNdestroyCallback	Core	XmNtraversalOn	Manager
XmNforeground	Manager	XmNunitType	Manager
XmNheight	Core	XmNuserData	Manager
XmNhelpCallback	Manager	XmNwidth	Core
XmNhighlightColor	Manager	XmNx	Core
XmNhighlightPixmap	Manager	XmNy	Core

Translations

MAny BAny Press	DrawingAreaInput()
MAny BAny Release	DrawingAreaInput()
MAny KAny Press	DrawingAreaInput()
	ManagerGadgetKeyInput()
MAny KAny Release	DrawingAreaInput()

Action Routines

DrawingArea defines the following action routines:

DrawingAreaInput()

> When a widget child of DrawingArea receives a keyboard or mouse event, this action routine invokes the list of callbacks specified by XmNinputCallback.

ManagerGadgetKeyInput()

> When a gadget child of DrawingArea receives a keyboard or mouse event, this action routine processes the event.

DrawingArea has additional behavior associated with <Expose>, which calls XmNexpose-Callback, and with <WidgetResize>, which calls XmNresizeCallback.

DrawnButton

An empty window, surrounded by a shaded border, that provides a graphics area for Push-Buttons whose graphics can be dynamically updated by the application.

Class Information

Include File:	*<Xm/DrawnB.h>*
Class Name:	XmDrawnButton
Class Hierarchy:	Core → XmPrimitive → XmLabel → XmDrawnButton
Class Pointer:	xmDrawnButtonWidgetClass
Functions/Macros:	XmCreateDrawnButton(), XmIsDrawnButton()

New Resources

DrawnButton defines the following resources:

Name	Class	Type	Default	Access
XmNmultiClick	XmCMultiClick	unsigned char	dynamic	CSG
XmNpushButtonEnabled	XmCPushButtonEnabled	Boolean	False	CSG
XmNshadowType	XmCShadowType	unsigned char	XmSHADOW_ETCHED_IN	CSG

XmNmultiClick

> A flag that determines whether successive button clicks are processed (by incrementing the callback structure's click count argument) or are ignored. Possible values:
>
> XmMULTICLICK_DISCARD /* ignore successive button clicks; default value in a menu system */
> XmMULTICLICK_KEEP /* count successive button clicks; default value when not in a menu */

XmNpushButtonEnabled

> If False (default), the shadow drawing doesn't appear three dimensional; if True, the shading provides a pushed in or raised appearance as for the PushButton widget.

XmNshadowType

The style in which shadows are drawn. Possible values:

XmSHADOW_ETCHED_IN   /* double line; widget appears inset */
XmSHADOW_ETCHED_OUT   /* double line; widget appears raised */
XmSHADOW_IN   /* widget appears inset */
XmSHADOW_OUT   /* widget appears outset */

Callback Resources

DrawnButton defines the following callback resources:

Callback	Reason Constant
XmNactivateCallback	XmCR_ACTIVATE
XmNarmCallback	XmCR_ARM
XmNdisarmCallback	XmCR_DISARM
XmNexposeCallback	XmCR_EXPOSE
XmNresizeCallback	XmCR_RESIZE

Callback Structure

Each callback function is passed the following structure:

```
typedef struct
{
    int      reason;        /* the reason that the callback was called */
    XEvent   * event;       /* points to event structure that triggered callback */
    Window   window;        /* ID of window in which the event occurred */
    int      click_count;   /* number of multi-clicks */
} XmDrawnButtonCallbackStruct;
```

event is NULL for XmNresizeCallback and is sometimes NULL for XmNactivateCallback.

click_count is meaningful only for XmNactivateCallback. Furthermore, if the XmNmultiClick resource is set to XmMULTICLICK_KEEP, then XmNactivateCallback is called for each click, and the value of *click_count* is the number of clicks that have occurred in the last sequence of multiple clicks. If the XmNmultiClick resource is set to XmMULTICLICK_DISCARD, then *click_count* always has a value of 1.

Inherited Resources

DrawnButton inherits the following resources. The resources are listed alphabetically, along with the superclass that defines them. DrawnButton sets the XmNlabelString resource to "\0".

Resource	Inherited From	Resource	Inherited From
XmNaccelerator	Label	XmNlabelString	Label
XmNaccelerators	Core	XmNlabelType	Label
XmNacceleratorText	Label	XmNmappedWhenManaged	Core
XmNalignment	Label	XmNmarginBottom	Label
XmNancestorSensitive	Core	XmNmarginHeight	Label
XmNbackground	Core	XmNmarginLeft	Label
XmNbackgroundPixmap	Core	XmNmarginRight	Label
XmNborderColor	Core	XmNmarginTop	Label

Resource	Inherited From	Resource	Inherited From
XmNborderPixmap	Core	XmNmarginWidth	Label
XmNborderWidth	Core	XmNmnemonic	Label
XmNbottomShadowColor	Primitive	XmNmnemonicCharSet	Label
XmNbottomShadowPixmap	Primitive	XmNnavigationType	Primitive
XmNcolormap	Core	XmNrecomputeSize	Label
XmNdepth	Core	XmNscreen	Core
XmNdestroyCallback	Core	XmNsensitive	Core
XmNfontList	Label	XmNshadowThickness	Primitive
XmNforeground	Primitive	XmNstringDirection	Label
XmNheight	Core	XmNtopShadowColor	Primitive
XmNhelpCallback	Primitive	XmNtopShadowPixmap	Primitive
XmNhighlightColor	Primitive	XmNtranslations	Core
XmNhighlightOnEnter	Primitive	XmNtraversalOn	Primitive
XmNhighlightPixmap	Primitive	XmNunitType	Primitive
XmNhighlightThickness	Primitive	XmNuserData	Primitive
XmNinitialResourcesPersistent	Core	XmNwidth	Core
XmNlabelInsensitivePixmap	Label	XmNx	Core
XmNlabelPixmap	Label	XmNy	Core

Translations

BSelect Press	Arm()
BSelect Click	Activate() Disarm()
BSelect Release	Activate() Disarm()
BSelect Press 2+	MultiArm()
BSelect Release 2+	MultiActivate()
KActivate	ArmAndActivate()
KSelect	ArmAndActivate()
KHelp	Help()

Action Routines

DrawnButton defines the following action routines:

Activate() Displays the DrawnButton as unselected, and invokes the list of callbacks specified by XmNactivateCallback.

Arm() Displays the DrawnButton as selected, and invokes the list of callbacks specified by XmNarmCallback.

ArmAndActivate()

Displays the DrawnButton as selected, and invokes the list of callbacks specified by XmNarmCallback. After doing this, the action routine displays the DrawnButton as unselected, and invokes the list of callbacks specified by XmNactivateCallback and XmNdisarmCallback.

Disarm()	Displays the DrawnButton as unselected, and invokes the list of callbacks specified by XmNdisarmCallback.
Help()	Invokes the list of callbacks specified by XmNhelpCallback. If the Drawn-Button doesn't have any help callbacks, the Help() routine invokes those associated with the nearest ancestor that has them.

MultiActivate()
Increments the *click_count* member of XmDrawnButtonCallbackStruct, displays the DrawnButton as unselected, and invokes the list of callbacks specified by Xm-NactivateCallback and XmNdisarmCallback. This action routine takes effect only when the XmNmultiClick resource is set to XmMULTICLICK_KEEP.

MultiArm()	Displays the DrawnButton as selected, and invokes the list of callbacks specified by XmNarmCallback. This action routine takes effect only when the XmNmultiClick resource is set to XmMULTICLICK_KEEP.

DrawnButton has additional behavior associated with <EnterWindow> and <LeaveWindow>, which draw the shadow in the selected or unselected state, respectively.

ErrorDialog

A convenience widget created by a call to XmCreateErrorDialog() and consisting of a Dialog-Shell with a MessageBox widget as its child. The MessageBox resource XmNdialogType is set to XmDIALOG_ERROR. The include file is *<Xm/MessageB.h>*. An ErrorDialog includes three components: a symbol (by default, an octagon with a diagonal slash), a message, and three buttons (whose labels, by default, are Ok, Cancel, and Help).

FileSelectionBox

Used to traverse a directory hierarchy and then select files. FileSelectionBox contains the following: text fields in which you can enter a directory name or a filename, scrollable lists of filenames or subdirectories, and a group of PushButtons.

Class Information
Include File:	*<Xm/FileSB.h>*
Class Name:	XmFileSelectionBox
Class Hierarchy:	Core → Composite → Constraint → XmManager → XmBulletin-Board → XmSelectionBox → XmFileSelectionBox
Class Pointer:	xmFileSelectionBoxWidgetClass
Functions/Macros:	XmCreateFileSelectionBox(), XmFileSelectionBoxGetChild(), XmCreate-FileSelectionDialog(), XmIsFileSelectionBox()

New Resources

FileSelectionBox defines the following resources:

Name	Class	Type	Default	Access
XmNdirectory	XmCDirectory	XmString	dynamic	CSG
XmNdirectoryValid	XmCDirectoryValid	Boolean	dynamic	CSG
XmNdirListItems	XmCDirListItems	XmStringTable	dynamic	CSG
XmNdirListItemCount	XmCDirListItemCount	int	dynamic	CSG
XmNdirListLabelString	XmCDirListLabelString	XmString	"Directories"	CSG
XmNdirMask	XmCDirMask	XmString	dynamic	CSG
XmNdirSearchProc	XmCDirSearchProc	(*)()	default procedure	CSG
XmNdirSpec	XmCDirSpec	XmString	dynamic	CSG
XmNfileListItems	XmCItems	XmStringTable	dynamic	CSG
XmNfileListItemCount	XmCItemCount	int	dynamic	CSG
XmNfileListLabelString	XmCFileListLabelString	XmString	"Files"	CSG
XmNfileSearchProc	XmCFileSearchProc	(*)()	default procedure	CSG
XmNfileTypeMask	XmCFileTypeMask	unsigned char	XmFILE_REGULAR	CSG
XmNfilterLabelString	XmCFilterLabelString	XmString	"Filter"	CSG
XmNlistUpdated	XmCListUpdated	Boolean	dynamic	CSG
XmNnoMatchString	XmCNoMatchString	XmString	" [ ] "	CSG
XmNpattern	XmCPattern	XmString	dynamic	CSG
XmNqualifySearchDataProc	XmCQualifySearchDataProc	(*)()	default procedure	CSG

XmNdirectory

> The base directory that, in combination with XmNpattern, forms the directory mask (the XmNdirMask resource). The directory mask determines which files and directories to display.

XmNdirectoryValid

> A resource that can be set only by the directory search procedure (as specified by the XmNdirSearchProc resource). If the directory search procedure is unable to search the directory that was passed to it, then it will set XmNdirectoryValid to False, and as a result, the file search procedure won't be called.

XmNdirListItems

> The items in the directory list. This resource is set only by the directory search procedure. A call to XtGetValues() returns the actual list items (not a copy), so don't have your application free these items.

XmNdirListItemCount

> The number of items in XmNdirListItems. This resource is set only by the directory search procedure.

XmNdirListLabelString

> The string that labels the directory list.

XmNdirMask

> The directory mask that determines which files and directories to display. This value combines the values of the resources XmNdirectory and XmNpattern.

XmNdirSearchProc

The procedure that performs directory searches. For most applications, the default procedure works just fine. The call to this procedure contains two arguments: the widget ID of the FileSelectionBox and a pointer to an XmFileSelectionCallbackStruct.

XmNdirSpec

The complete specification of the file path. Synonymous with the XmNtextString resource in SelectionBox. It is the initial directory and file search that determines the default value for this resource.

XmNfileListItems

The items in the file list. Synonymous with the XmNlistItems resource in Selection-Box. This resource is set only by the file search procedure. A call to XtGetValues() returns the actual list items (not a copy), so don't have your application free these items.

XmNfileListItemCount

The number of items in XmNfileListItems. Synonymous with the XmNlistItemCount resource in SelectionBox. This resource is set only by the file search procedure.

XmNfileListLabelString

The string that labels the file list. Synonymous with the XmNlistLabelString resource in SelectionBox.

XmNfileSearchProc

The procedure that performs file searches. For most applications, the default procedure works just fine. The call to this procedure contains two arguments: the widget ID of the FileSelectionBox and a pointer to an XmFileSelectionCallbackStruct.

XmNfileTypeMask

Determines whether the file list will display only regular files, only directories, or any type of file. Possible values are XmFILE_DIRECTORY, XmFILE_REGULAR, and XmFILE_ANY_TYPE.

XmNfilterLabelString

The string that labels the field in which the directory mask is typed in by the user.

XmNlistUpdated

A resource that can be set only by the directory search procedure or by the file search procedure. This resource is set to True if the directory or file list was updated by a search procedure.

XmNnoMatchString

A string that displays in the file list when there are no filenames to display.

XmNpattern

The file search pattern that, in combination with XmNdirectory, forms the directory mask (the XmNdirMask resource). The directory mask determines which files and directories to display. If the XmNpattern resource defaults to NULL or is empty, a pattern for matching all files will be used.

XmNqualifySearchDataProc

    The procedure that generates a valid directory mask, base directory, and search pattern to be used by XmNdirSearchProc and XmNfileSearchProc (the search procedures for directories and files). For most applications, the default procedure works just fine. The call to this procedure contains three arguments: the widget ID of the FileSelectionBox, a pointer to an XmFileSelectionCallbackStruct containing the input data, and a pointer to an XmFileSelectionCallbackStruct that will contain the output data.

Callback Structure

    Each callback function is passed the following structure:

```
typedef struct
{
        int        reason;          /* the reason that the callback was called */
        XEvent     * event;         /* points to event structure that triggered callback */
        XmString   value;           /* current value of XmNdirSpec resource */
        int        length;          /* number of bytes in value member */
        XmString   mask;            /* current value of XmNdirMask resource */
        int        mask_length;     /* number of bytes in mask member */
        XmString   dir;             /* current base directory */
        int        dir_length;      /* number of bytes in dir member */
        XmString   pattern;         /* current search pattern */
        int        pattern_length;  /* number of bytes in pattern member */
} XmFileSelectionBoxCallbackStruct;
```

Inherited Resources

    FileSelectionBox inherits the following resources. The resources are listed alphabetically, along with the superclass that defines them. Note that the FileSelection-Box widget resets XmNapplyLabelString to "Filter", XmNautoUnmanage to False, and XmNdialogType to XmDIALOG_FILE_SELECTION.

Resource	Inherited From	Resource	Inherited From
XmNaccelerators	Core	XmNlistItems	SelectionBox
XmNallowOverlap	BulletinBoard	XmNlistLabelString	SelectionBox
XmNancestorSensitive	Core	XmNlistVisibleItemCount	SelectionBox
XmNapplyCallback	SelectionBox	XmNmapCallback	BulletinBoard
XmNapplyLabelString	SelectionBox	XmNmappedWhenManaged	Core
XmNautoUnmanage	BulletinBoard	XmNmarginHeight	BulletinBoard
XmNbackground	Core	XmNmarginWidth	BulletinBoard
XmNbackgroundPixmap	Core	XmNminimizeButtons	SelectionBox
XmNborderColor	Core	XmNmustMatch	SelectionBox
XmNborderPixmap	Core	XmNnavigationType	Manager
XmNborderWidth	Core	XmNnoMatchCallback	SelectionBox
XmNbottomShadowColor	Manager	XmNnoResize	BulletinBoard
XmNbottomShadowPixmap	Manager	XmNnumChildren	Composite
XmNbuttonFontList	BulletinBoard	XmNokCallback	SelectionBox
XmNcancelButton	BulletinBoard	XmNokLabelString	SelectionBox
XmNcancelCallback	SelectionBox	XmNresizePolicy	BulletinBoard
XmNcancelLabelString	SelectionBox	XmNscreen	Core

Resource	Inherited From	Resource	Inherited From
XmNchildren	Composite	XmNselectionLabelString	SelectionBox
XmNcolormap	Core	XmNsensitive	Core
XmNdefaultButton	BulletinBoard	XmNshadowThickness	Manager
XmNdefaultPosition	BulletinBoard	XmNshadowType	BulletinBoard
XmNdepth	Core	XmNstringDirection	Manager
XmNdestroyCallback	Core	XmNtextAccelerators	SelectionBox
XmNdialogStyle	BulletinBoard	XmNtextColumns	SelectionBox
XmNdialogTitle	BulletinBoard	XmNtextFontList	BulletinBoard
XmNdialogType	SelectionBox	XmNtextString	SelectionBox
XmNfocusCallback	BulletinBoard	XmNtextTranslations	BulletinBoard
XmNforeground	Manager	XmNtopShadowColor	Manager
XmNheight	Core	XmNtopShadowPixmap	Manager
XmNhelpCallback	Manager	XmNtranslations	Core
XmNhelpLabelString	SelectionBox	XmNtraversalOn	Manager
XmNhighlightColor	Manager	XmNunitType	Manager
XmNhighlightPixmap	Manager	XmNunmapCallback	BulletinBoard
XmNinitialResourcesPersistent	Core	XmNuserData	Manager
XmNinsertPosition	Composite	XmNwidth	Core
XmNlabelFontList	BulletinBoard	XmNx	Core
XmNlistItemCount	SelectionBox	XmNy	Core

Translations

The translations for FileSelectionBox are inherited from SelectionBox.

Action Routines

FileSelectionBox defines the following action routines:

SelectionBoxUpOrDown(*flag*)

> Replaces the selection text or the filter text, depending on which one has the keyboard focus. That is, this action replaces either:

> - the text string in the selection area with an item from the file list, or
> - the text string in the directory mask (filter) area with an item from the directory list.

> The value of *flag* determines which file list item or which directory list item is selected as the replacement string. A *flag* value of 0, 1, 2, or 3 selects the previous, next, first, or last item, respectively, of the appropriate list.

SelectionBoxRestore()

> Replaces the selection text or the filter text, depending on which one has the keyboard focus. That is, this action replaces either:

> - the text string in the selection area with the currently selected item in the file list (clearing the selection area if no list item is selected), or
> - the text string in the filter area with a new directory mask (which is formed by combining the values of the XmNdirectory and XmNpattern resources).

Additional Behavior

The following additional behavior is defined for this widget:

MAny KCancel   For a sensitive Cancel button, invokes the callbacks in XmNactivateCallback.

KActivate   In selection text, invokes first the callbacks in XmNactivateCallback and then those in either XmNnoMatchCallback or XmNokCallback. In a directory mask, invokes the callbacks in XmNactivateCallback; in a directory list, calls XmNdefaultActionCallback; in either location, also begins a directory and file search and invokes the callbacks in XmNapplyCallback. In a file list, calls XmNdefaultActionCallback and XmNokCallback. When none of these areas nor any button has the keyboard focus, invokes the callbacks in either XmNnoMatchCallback or XmNokCallback.

\<DoubleClick>   In a directory list or a file list, same as KActivate.

\<Single Select> or \<Browse Select>

In a directory list, composes a directory mask using the selected directory item and the current pattern. In a file list, uses the selected file item to replace the selection text.

Each event below invokes a particular set of callbacks:

\<Apply Button Activated>	XmNapplyCallback (after beginning a directory and file search)
\<Ok Button Activated>	XmNnoMatchCallback or XmNokCallback
\<Cancel Button Activated>	XmNcancelCallback
\<Help Button Activated>	XmNhelpCallback

FileSelectionDialog

A convenience widget created by a call to XmCreateFileSelectionDialog() and consisting of a DialogShell with a FileSelectionBox widget as its child. The SelectionBox resource XmNdialogType is set to XmDIALOG_FILE_SELECTION. The include file is *<Xm/FileSB.h>*.

Form

A container widget that constrains its children so as to define their layout and behavior when the Form is resized. Children may be attached to each other, to edges of the Form, or to absolute or relative positions in the Form.

Class Information

Include File:	*<Xm/Form.h>*
Class Name:	XmForm
Class Hierarchy:	Core → Composite → Constraint → XmManager → XmBulletin-Board → XmForm
Class Pointer:	xmFormWidgetClass
Functions/Macros:	XmCreateForm(), XmCreateFormDialog(), XmIsForm()

New Resources

Form defines the following resources:

Name	Class	Type	Default	Access
XmNfractionBase	XmCMaxValue	int	100	CSG
XmNhorizontalSpacing	XmCSpacing	Dimension	0	CSG
XmNrubberPositioning	XmCRubberPositioning	Boolean	False	CSG
XmNverticalSpacing	XmCSpacing	Dimension	0	CSG

XmNfractionBase

> The denominator part of the fraction that describes a child's relative position within a Form. The numerator of this fraction is one of the four positional constraint resources: XmNbottomPosition, XmNleftPosition, XmNrightPosition, or XmNtopPosition. For example, suppose you use the default XmNfractionBase of 100. Then, if you specify XmNtopPosition as 30, the top of the child will remain invariably attached to a location that is 30/100 (or 30 percent) from the top of the Form. (In other words, resizing the Form's height might change the absolute position of the child's top, but not its position relative to the top of the Form.) Similarly, a value of 50 for XmNleftPosition ensures that the left side of the child is attached 50/100 from the left of the Form (or in this case, halfway between the left and right side). Note that these fractions are implemented only when the child's corresponding attachment constraint is set to XmATTACH_POSITION. (The attachment constraints are XmNbottomAttachment, XmNleftAttachment, XmNright-Attachment, and XmNtopAttachment.)

XmNhorizontalSpacing

> The offset for right and left attachments.

XmNrubberPositioning

> Defines the default behavior of a child's top and left side, in the absence of other settings. If this resource is False (default), the child's top and left sides are positioned using absolute values. If True, the child's top and left sides are positioned relative to the size of the Form.

XmNverticalSpacing

> The offset for top and bottom attachments.

New Constraint Resources

Name	Class	Type	Default	Access
XmNbottomAttachment	XmCAttachment	unsigned char	XmATTACH_NONE	CSG
XmNbottomOffset	XmCOffset	int	0	CSG
XmNbottomPosition	XmCAttachment	int	0	CSG
XmNbottomWidget	XmCWidget	Window	NULL	CSG
XmNleftAttachment	XmCAttachment	unsigned char	XmATTACH_NONE	CSG
XmNleftOffset	XmCOffset	int	0	CSG
XmNleftPosition	XmCAttachment	int	0	CSG
XmNleftWidget	XmCWidget	Window	NULL	CSG
XmNresizable	XmCBoolean	Boolean	True	CSG
XmNrightAttachment	XmCAttachment	unsigned char	XmATTACH_NONE	CSG
XmNrightOffset	XmCOffset	int	0	CSG
XmNrightPosition	XmCAttachment	int	0	CSG
XmNrightWidget	XmCWidget	Window	NULL	CSG
XmNtopAttachment	XmCAttachment	unsigned char	XmATTACH_NONE	CSG
XmNtopOffset	XmCOffset	int	0	CSG
XmNtopPosition	XmCAttachment	int	0	CSG
XmNtopWidget	XmCWidget	Window	NULL	CSG

XmNbottomAttachment

The method of attachment for the child's bottom side. Each of the four attachment resources (XmNtopAttachment, XmNbottomAttachment, XmNleftAttachment, and XmNright-Attachment) has the following possible values, defined in *<Xm/Xm.h>*. The comments below refer to a corresponding edge (top, bottom, left, or right) of the child widget within the Form.

XmATTACH_NONE	/* remains unattached */
XmATTACH_FORM	/* attached to same edge of Form */
XmATTACH_OPPOSITE_FORM	/* attached to other edge of Form */
XmATTACH_WIDGET	/* abuts an adjacent widget */
XmATTACH_OPPOSITE_WIDGET	/* attached to other edge of adjacent widget */
XmATTACH_POSITION	/* relative to a dimension of Form */
XmATTACH_SELF	/* relative to its current position and to Form */

XmNbottomOffset

The distance between the child's bottom side and the object it's attached to. Offsets are absolute. A nonzero offset is ignored when XmNbottomAttachment is set to XmATTACH_POSITION, because a resize operation applies relative positioning in this case. Offsets are of type int and may not be resolution-independent.

XmNbottomPosition

Used in conjunction with XmNfractionBase to calculate the position of the bottom of a child, relative to the bottom of the Form. This resource has no effect unless the child's XmNbottomAttachment resource is set to XmATTACH_POSITION. (See Xm-NfractionBase for details.)

XmNbottomWidget

The name of the widget or gadget that serves as the attachment point for the bottom of the child. To use this resource, set the XmNbottomAttachment resource to either XmATTACH_WIDGET or XmATTACH_OPPOSITE_WIDGET.

XmNleftAttachment

The method of attachment for the child's left side.

XmNleftOffset

The distance between the child's left side and the object it's attached to. Offsets are absolute. A nonzero offset is ignored when XmNleftAttachment is set to Xm-ATTACH_POSITION, because a resize operation applies relative positioning in this case. Offsets are of type int and may not be resolution-independent.

XmNleftPosition

Used in conjunction with XmNfractionBase to calculate the position of the left side of a child, relative to the left side of the Form. This resource has no effect unless the child's XmNleftAttachment resource is set to XmATTACH_POSITION. (See Xm-NfractionBase for details.)

XmNleftWidget

The name of the widget or gadget that serves as the attachment point for the left side of the child. To use this resource, set the XmNleftAttachment resource to either XmATTACH_WIDGET or XmATTACH_OPPOSITE_WIDGET.

XmNresizable

If True (default), a child's resize request is accepted by the Form, provided that the child isn't constrained by its attachments. That is, if both the left and right sides of a child are attached, or if both the top and bottom are attached, the resize request fails, whereas if the child has only one horizontal or one vertical attachment, the resize request is granted. If this resource is False, the child is never resized.

XmNrightAttachment

The method of attachment for the child's right side.

XmNrightOffset

The distance between the child's right side and the object it's attached to. Offsets are absolute. A nonzero offset is ignored when XmNrightAttachment is set to Xm-ATTACH_POSITION, because a resize operation applies relative positioning in this case. Offsets are of type int and may not be resolution-independent.

XmNrightPosition

Used in conjunction with XmNfractionBase to calculate the position of the right side of a child, relative to the right side of the Form. This resource has no effect unless the child's XmNrightAttachment resource is set to XmATTACH_POSITION. (See Xm-NfractionBase for details.)

XmNrightWidget

The name of the widget or gadget that serves as the attachment point for the right side of the child. To use this resource, set the XmNrightAttachment resource to either XmATTACH_WIDGET or XmATTACH_OPPOSITE_WIDGET.

XmNtopAttachment

The method of attachment for the child's top side.

XmNtopOffset

The distance between the child's top side and the object it's attached to. Offsets are absolute. A nonzero offset is ignored when XmNtopAttachment is set to Xm-ATTACH_POSITION, because a resize operation applies relative positioning in this case. Offsets are of type int and may not be resolution-independent.

XmNtopPosition

Used in conjunction with XmNfractionBase to calculate the position of the top of a child, relative to the top of the Form. This resource has no effect unless the child's XmNtopAttachment resource is set to XmATTACH_POSITION. (See XmNfractionBase for details.)

XmNtopWidget

The name of the widget or gadget that serves as the attachment point for the top of the child. To use this resource, set the XmNtopAttachment resource to either Xm-ATTACH_WIDGET or XmATTACH_OPPOSITE_WIDGET.

Inherited Resources

Form inherits the following resources. The resources are listed alphabetically, along with the superclass that defines them.

Resource	Inherited From	Resource	Inherited From
XmNaccelerators	Core	XmNinsertPosition	Composite
XmNallowOverlap	BulletinBoard	XmNlabelFontList	BulletinBoard
XmNancestorSensitive	Core	XmNmapCallback	BulletinBoard
XmNautoUnmanage	BulletinBoard	XmNmappedWhenManaged	Core
XmNbackground	Core	XmNmarginHeight	BulletinBoard
XmNbackgroundPixmap	Core	XmNmarginWidth	BulletinBoard
XmNborderColor	Core	XmNnavigationType	Manager
XmNborderPixmap	Core	XmNnoResize	BulletinBoard
XmNborderWidth	Core	XmNnumChildren	Composite
XmNbottomShadowColor	Manager	XmNresizePolicy	BulletinBoard
XmNbottomShadowPixmap	Manager	XmNscreen	Core
XmNbuttonFontList	BulletinBoard	XmNsensitive	Core
XmNcancelButton	BulletinBoard	XmNshadowThickness	Manager
XmNchildren	Composite	XmNshadowType	BulletinBoard
XmNcolormap	Core	XmNstringDirection	Manager
XmNdefaultButton	BulletinBoard	XmNtextFontList	BulletinBoard
XmNdefaultPosition	BulletinBoard	XmNtextTranslations	BulletinBoard
XmNdepth	Core	XmNtopShadowColor	Manager
XmNdestroyCallback	Core	XmNtopShadowPixmap	Manager
XmNdialogStyle	BulletinBoard	XmNtranslations	Core
XmNdialogTitle	BulletinBoard	XmNtraversalOn	Manager
XmNfocusCallback	BulletinBoard	XmNunitType	Manager
XmNforeground	Manager	XmNunmapCallback	BulletinBoard
XmNheight	Core	XmNuserData	Manager

Resource	Inherited From	Resource	Inherited From
XmNhelpCallback	Manager	XmNwidth	Core
XmNhighlightColor	Manager	XmNx	Core
XmNhighlightPixmap	Manager	XmNy	Core
XmNinitialResourcesPersistent	Core		

FormDialog

A convenience widget created by a call to XmCreateFormDialog() and consisting of a Dialog-Shell with a Form widget as its child. The include file is *<Xm/Form.h>*.

Frame

A subclass of Manager that places a three-dimensional border around a single child. This simple widget can be used to give the typical Motif-style appearance to widget classes that don't have a visible frame (e.g., RowColumn).

Class Information

Include File:	*<Xm/Frame.h>*
Class Name:	XmFrame
Class Hierarchy:	Core → Composite → Constraint → XmManager → XmFrame
Class Pointer:	xmFrameWidgetClass
Functions/Macros:	XmCreateFrame(), XmIsFrame()

New Resources

Frame defines the following resources:

Name	Class	Type	Default	Access
XmNmarginWidth	XmCMarginWidth	Dimension	0	CSG
XmNmarginHeight	XmCMarginHeight	Dimension	0	CSG
XmNshadowType	XmCShadowType	unsigned char	dynamic	CSG

XmNmarginHeight
>   The spacing between the top or bottom of a Frame widget's child and the shadow of the Frame widget.

XmNmarginWidth
>   The spacing between the right or left side of a Frame widget's child and the shadow of the Frame widget.

XmNshadowType

The style in which Frame widgets are drawn. Possible values:

XmSHADOW_ETCHED_IN	/* double line; widget appears inset */
XmSHADOW_ETCHED_OUT	/* double line; widget appears raised */
XmSHADOW_IN	/* widget appears inset */
XmSHADOW_OUT	/* widget appears outset */

Inherited Resources

Frame inherits the following resources. The resources are listed alphabetically, along with the superclass that defines them.

Resource	Inherited From	Resource	Inherited From
XmNaccelerators	Core	XmNinitialResourcesPersistent	Core
XmNancestorSensitive	Core	XmNinsertPosition	Composite
XmNbackground	Core	XmNmappedWhenManaged	Core
XmNbackgroundPixmap	Core	XmNnavigationType	Manager
XmNborderColor	Core	XmNnumChildren	Composite
XmNborderPixmap	Core	XmNscreen	Core
XmNborderWidth	Core	XmNsensitive	Core
XmNbottomShadowColor	Manager	XmNshadowThickness	Manager
XmNbottomShadowPixmap	Manager	XmNstringDirection	Manager
XmNchildren	Composite	XmNtopShadowColor	Manager
XmNcolormap	Core	XmNtopShadowPixmap	Manager
XmNdepth	Core	XmNtranslations	Core
XmNdestroyCallback	Core	XmNtraversalOn	Manager
XmNforeground	Manager	XmNunitType	Manager
XmNheight	Core	XmNuserData	Manager
XmNhelpCallback	Manager	XmNwidth	Core
XmNhighlightColor	Manager	XmNx	Core
XmNhighlightPixmap	Manager	XmNy	Core

Translations

The translations for Frame are inherited from Manager.

Gadget

A supporting superclass for other gadget classes. Because Gadget is a meta-class, it is generally not instantiated alone. Gadget can be used to draw border shadows and selection highlighting, as well as to traverse hierarchies. Because gadgets make use of the Manager widget's pixmap and color resources (e.g., XmNforeground), take care when setting these resources via XtSetValues(). If you change such a resource in a manager widget, its gadget children will be affected as well.

Class Information

Include File:	*<Xm/Gadget.h>*
Class Name:	XmGadget
Class Hierarchy:	Object → RectObj → XmGadget
Class Pointer:	xmGadgetClass
Functions/Macros:	XmIsGadget()

New Resources

Gadget defines the following resources:

Name	Class	Type	Default	Access
XmNhighlightOnEnter	XmCHighlightOnEnter	Boolean	False	CSG
XmNhighlightThickness	XmCHighlightThickness	Dimension	2	CSG
XmNnavigationType	XmCNavigationType	XmNavigationType	XmNONE	G
XmNshadowThickness	XmCShadowThickness	Dimension	2	CSG
XmNtraversalOn	XmCTraversalOn	Boolean	True	CSG
XmNunitType	XmCUnitType	unsigned char	dynamic	CSG
XmNuserData	XmCUserData	Pointer	NULL	CSG

XmNhighlightOnEnter

Determines whether to draw a gadget's highlighting rectangle whenever the cursor moves into the gadget. This resource applies only when the shell has a focus policy of XmPOINTER. If the XmNhighlightOnEnter resource is True, highlighting is drawn; if False (default), highlighting is not drawn.

XmNhighlightThickness

The thickness of the highlighting rectangle.

XmNnavigationType

Determines the way in which gadgets are to be traversed during keyboard navigation. Possible values:

```
XmNONE                    /* exclude from keyboard navigation (default for non-shell parent ) */
XmTAB_GROUP               /* include in keyboard navigation (default when parent is a shell) */
XmSTICKY_TAB_GROUP        /* include in keyboard navigation, even if XmAddTabGroup() was called */
XmEXCLUSIVE_TAB_GROUP     /* application defines order of navigation */
```

XmNshadowThickness

The thickness of the shadow border.

XmNtraversalOn

If True (default), traversal of this gadget is made possible.

XmNunitType

The measurement units to use in resources that specify a size or position—for example, any resources of data type Dimension (whose names generally include one of the words "Margin" or "Thickness"). For a gadget whose parent is a Manager subclass, the default value is copied from this parent (provided the value hasn't been explicitly set by the application); otherwise, the default is XmPIXELS. Possible values:

XmPIXELS   Xm100TH_POINTS
Xm100TH_MILLIMETERS   Xm100TH_FONT_UNITS
Xm1000TH_INCHES

XmNuserData
   A pointer to data that the application can attach to the gadget. This resource is
   unused internally.

Inherited Resources

Gadget inherits the following resources. The resources are listed alphabetically, along
with the superclass that defines them. Gadget resets the XmNborderWidth resource from 1
to 0.

Resource	Inherited From	Resource	Inherited From
XmNancestorSensitive	RectObj	XmNsensitive	RectObj
XmNborderWidth	RectObj	XmNwidth	RectObj
XmNdestroyCallback	Object	XmNx	RectObj
XmNheight	RectObj	XmNy	RectObj

Callback Resources

Gadget defines the following callback resources:

Callback	Reason Constant
XmNhelpCallback	XmCR_HELP

InformationDialog

A convenience widget created by a call to XmCreateInformationDialog() and consisting of a
DialogShell with a MessageBox widget as its child. The MessageBox resource XmNdialog-
Type is set to XmDIALOG_INFORMATION. The include file is *<Xm/MessageB.h>*. An
InformationDialog includes three components: a symbol (by default, a lowercase *i*), a
message, and three buttons (whose labels, by default, are Ok, Cancel, and Help).

Label

Provides a text string or a pixmap for labeling other widgets in an application. Label is a superclass for buttons: it supports the button subclasses CascadeButton, DrawnButton, Push-Button, and ToggleButton. That is, a Label widget doesn't allow button or key presses, but it displays accelerators and mnemonics for buttons contained in menus.

Class Information

Include File: *<Xm/Label.h>*

Class Name: XmLabel

Class Hierarchy: Core → XmPrimitive → XmLabel

Class Pointer: xmLabelWidgetClass

Functions/Macros: XmCreateLabel(), XmIsLabel()

New Resources

Label defines the following resources:

Name	Class	Type	Default	Access
XmNaccelerator	XmCAccelerator	String	NULL	CSG
XmNacceleratorText	XmCAcceleratorText	XmString	NULL	CSG
XmNalignment	XmCAlignment	unsigned char	XmALIGNMENT_CENTER	CSG
XmNfontList	XmCFontList	XmFontList	dynamic	CSG
XmNlabelInsensitivePixmap	XmCLabelInsensitivePixmap	Pixmap	XmUNSPECIFIED_PIXMAP	CSG
XmNlabelPixmap	XmCLabelPixmap	Pixmap	XmUNSPECIFIED_PIXMAP	CSG
XmNlabelString	XmCXmString	XmString	dynamic	CSG
XmNlabelType	XmCLabelType	unsigned char	XmSTRING	CSG
XmNmarginBottom	XmCMarginBottom	Dimension	0	CSG
XmNmarginHeight	XmCMarginHeight	Dimension	2	CSG
XmNmarginLeft	XmCMarginLeft	Dimension	0	CSG
XmNmarginRight	XmCMarginRight	Dimension	0	CSG
XmNmarginTop	XmCMarginTop	Dimension	0	CSG
XmNmarginWidth	XmCMarginWidth	Dimension	2	CSG
XmNmnemonic	XmCMnemonic	KeySym	NULL	CSG
XmNmnemonicCharSet	XmCMnemonicCharSet	String	dynamic	CSG
XmNrecomputeSize	XmCRecomputeSize	Boolean	True	CSG
XmNstringDirection	XmCStringDirection	XmStringDirection	dynamic	CSG

XmNaccelerator

A string that describes a button widget's accelerator (the modifiers and key to use as a shortcut in selecting the button). The string's format is like that of a translation but allows only a single key press event to be specified.

XmNacceleratorText

The text that is displayed for an accelerator.

XmNalignment

The alignment (left to right) for a label's text or pixmap. Possible values are Xm-ALIGNMENT_BEGINNING, XmALIGNMENT_CENTER, and XmALIGNMENT_END.

XmNfontList

The font list used for the widget's text. If this value is initially NULL, the font list is derived from the font list resource from the nearest parent that is a subclass of BulletinBoard, MenuShell, or VendorShell.

XmNlabelInsensitivePixmap

The pixmap label for an insensitive button (when XmNlabelType is XmPIXMAP).

XmNlabelPixmap

The pixmap used when XmNlabelType is XmPIXMAP.

XmNlabelString

The compound string used when XmNlabelType is XmSTRING. If this resource is NULL, the application uses the widget's name (converted to compound string format).

XmNlabelType

The type of label (either string or pixmap). Possible values:

```
XmPIXMAP              /* use XmNlabelPixmap or XmNlabelInsensitvePixmap */
XmSTRING              /* use XmNlabelString */
```

XmNmarginTop, XmNmarginBottom,
XmNmarginLeft, XmNmarginRight

The amount of space between one side of the label text and the nearest margin.

XmNmarginHeight
XmNmarginWidth

The spacing between one side of the label and the nearest edge of a shadow.

XmNmnemonic

A keysym that gives the user another way to select a button. In the label string, the first character matching this keysym will be underlined.

XmNmnemonicCharSet

The character set for the label's mnemonic. The default value depends on the current language environment.

XmNrecomputeSize

If True (default), the Label widget changes its size so that the string or pixmap fits exactly.

XmNstringDirection

The direction in which to draw the string. Possible values are XmSTRING_DIRECTION_L_TO_R and XmSTRING_DIRECTION_R_TO_L.

Callback Structure

Each callback function is passed the following structure:

```
typedef struct
{
        int         reason;         /* set to XmCR_HELP */
        XEvent    * event;          /* points to event structure that triggered callback */
} XmAnyCallbackStruct;
```

Inherited Resources

Label inherits the following resources. The resources are listed alphabetically, along with the superclass that defines them. Label resets the resources XmNhighlightThickness and Xm-NshadowThickness from 2 to 0, and resets XmNtraversalOn to False.

Resource	Inherited From	Resource	Inherited From
XmNaccelerators	Core	XmNhighlightPixmap	Primitive
XmNancestorSensitive	Core	XmNhighlightThickness	Primitive
XmNbackground	Core	XmNinitialResourcesPersistent	Core
XmNbackgroundPixmap	Core	XmNmappedWhenManaged	Core
XmNborderColor	Core	XmNnavigationType	Primitive
XmNborderPixmap	Core	XmNscreen	Core
XmNborderWidth	Core	XmNsensitive	Core
XmNbottomShadowColor	Primitive	XmNshadowThickness	Primitive
XmNbottomShadowPixmap	Primitive	XmNtopShadowColor	Primitive
XmNcolormap	Core	XmNtopShadowPixmap	Primitive
XmNdepth	Core	XmNtranslations	Core
XmNdestroyCallback	Core	XmNtraversalOn	Primitive
XmNforeground	Primitive	XmNunitType	Primitive
XmNheight	Core	XmNuserData	Primitive
XmNhelpCallback	Primitive	XmNwidth	Core
XmNhighlightColor	Primitive	XmNx	Core
XmNhighlightOnEnter	Primitive	XmNy	Core

Translations

```
KHelp     Help()
```

For subclasses of Label:

```
KLeft               MenuTraverseLeft()
KRight              MenuTraverseRight()
KUp                 MenuTraverseUp()
KDown               MenuTraverseDown()
MAny KCancel        MenuEscape()
```

Action Routines

Label defines the following action routines:

Help()   Unposts menus, restores keyboard focus, and invokes the callbacks from Xm-NhelpCallback, if there are any.

MenuEscape()

> Unposts the menu, disarms the associated CascadeButton, and restores keyboard focus.

The Label widget has four action routines for traversing menus. Menus can be oriented horizontally or vertically, and the action routines apply differently depending on the menu's orientation. The traversal action routines are described below, first for vertical menus and then for horizontal menus.

When applied within a vertical menu:

MenuTraverseDown()

> Disarms the current menu item and arms the item below it, wrapping around to the top if necessary.

MenuTraverseUp()

> Disarms the current menu item and arms the item above it, wrapping around to the bottom if necessary.

MenuTraverseLeft()

> 1. If the parent menu is horizontal:
>   (a) Unposts the current menu (vertical, in this case), (b) traverses left in the parent menu (wrapping around to the right if necessary), and, if this next item is a CascadeButton, (c) posts its submenu.
>
> 2. If the parent menu is vertical:
>   Unposts the current menu (but does not traverse).

MenuTraverseRight()

> 1. If the current item is a CascadeButton with a submenu:
>   Posts the submenu.
>
> 2. Otherwise, this action finds the nearest ancestor that is a horizontal menu and (like MenuTraverseLeft()):
>   (a) Unposts the current menu (vertical, in this case), (b) traverses right in the parent menu (wrapping around to the left if necessary), and, if this next item is a CascadeButton, (c) posts its submenu.

When applied within a horizontal menu:

MenuTraverseDown()

> 1. If the current item is a CascadeButton with a submenu:
>   Posts the submenu.
>
> 2. Otherwise, this action finds the nearest ancestor that is a vertical menu and does the following:
>   (a) Unposts the current menu (horizontal, in this case), (b) traverses down in the parent menu (wrapping around to the top if necessary), and, if this next item is a CascadeButton, (c) posts its submenu.

MenuTraverseUp()

    1. If the parent menu is vertical:

       (a) Unposts the current menu (horizontal, in this case), (b) traverses up in the parent menu (wrapping around to the bottom if necessary), and, if this next item is a CascadeButton, (c) posts its submenu.

    2. If the parent menu is horizontal:

       Unposts the current menu (but does not traverse).

MenuTraverseLeft()

    Disarms the current menu item and arms the item to its left, wrapping around to the right if necessary.

MenuTraverseRight()

    Disarms the current menu item and arms the item to its right, wrapping around to the left if necessary.

LabelGadget

The gadget variant of Label.

Class Information

Include File:	*<Xm/LabelG.h>*
Class Name:	XmLabelGadget
Class Hierarchy:	Object → RectObj → XmGadget → XmLabelGadget
Class Pointer:	xmLabelGadgetClass
Functions/Macros:	XmCreateLabelGadget(), XmOptionLabelGadget(), XmIsLabelGadget()

LabelGadget's new resources and callback structure are the same as those for Label.

Inherited Resources

LabelGadget inherits the following resources. The resources are listed alphabetically, along with the superclass that defines them. LabelGadget resets the resources XmNhighlightThickness and XmNshadowThickness from 2 to 0, and resets XmNtraversalOn to False.

Resource	Inherited From	Resource	Inherited From
XmNancestorSensitive	RectObj	XmNsensitive	RectObj
XmNborderWidth	RectObj	XmNshadowThickness	Gadget
XmNdestroyCallback	Object	XmNtraversalOn	Gadget
XmNheight	RectObj	XmNunitType	Gadget
XmNhelpCallback	Gadget	XmNuserData	Gadget
XmNhighlightOnEnter	Gadget	XmNwidth	RectObj
XmNhighlightThickness	Gadget	XmNx	RectObj
XmNnavigationType	Gadget	XmNy	RectObj

Behavior

As a gadget subclass, LabelGadget has no translations associated with it. However, LabelGadget behavior corresponds to the action routines of the Label widget. See the Label action routines for more information.

Behavior	Equivalent Label Action Routine
KHelp	Help()
KLeft	MenuTraverseLeft()
KRight	MenuTraverseRight()
KUp	MenuTraverseUp()
KDown	MenuTraverseDown()
MAny KCancel	MenuEscape()

List

Provides a list of choices from which a user can select one or more items. Making a selection invokes a callback, as determined by one of four selection policies: Single Select, Browse Select, Multiple Select, and Extended Select. In Single Select, only one item at a time is selected: a button press toggles the selection state, but a button drag does nothing. In Browse Select, only one item at a time is selected; however, either a button press or a button drag can select the item. In Multiple Select, a button press can select an additional item (i.e., a previously selected item remains selected), but a button drag does nothing. In Extended Select, ranges of items can be selected by combining button presses and button drags. Selections can be made by using either the pointer or the keyboard. Keyboard selection has two modes: Normal Mode and Add Mode. In Normal Mode, a selection can be made either by keyboard selection (akin to a button press) or by keyboard navigation (akin to a button drag). In Add Mode, only a keyboard selection operation affects selection. Browse Select operates in Normal Mode; Single Select and Multiple Select operate in Add Mode; Extended Select can be made to operate in either mode.

Class Information

Include File:	*<Xm/List.h>*
Class Name:	XmList
Class Hierarchy:	Core → XmPrimitive → XmList
Class Pointer:	xmListWidgetClass
Functions/Macros:	XmCreateList(), XmCreateScrolledList(), XmList ... routines, XmIsList()

Xt and Motif
Widget Classes

New Resources

List defines the following resources:

Name	Class	Type	Default	Access
XmNautomaticSelection	XmCAutomaticSelection	Boolean	False	CSG
XmNdoubleClickInterval	XmCDoubleClickInterval	int	dynamic	CSG
XmNfontList	XmCFontList	XmFontList	dynamic	CSG
XmNitemCount	XmCItemCount	int	0	CSG
XmNitems	XmCItems	XmStringTable	NULL	CSG
XmNlistMarginHeight	XmCListMarginHeight	Dimension	0	CSG
XmNlistMarginWidth	XmCListMarginWidth	Dimension	0	CSG
XmNlistSizePolicy	XmCListSizePolicy	unsigned char	XmVARIABLE	CG
XmNlistSpacing	XmCListSpacing	Dimension	0	CSG
XmNscrollBarDisplayPolicy	XmCScrollBarDisplayPolicy	unsigned char	XmAS_NEEDED	CSG
XmNselectedItemCount	XmCSelectedItemCount	int	0	CSG
XmNselectedItems	XmCSelectedItems	XmStringTable	NULL	CSG
XmNselectionPolicy	XmCSelectionPolicy	unsigned char	XmBROWSE_SELECT	CSG
XmNstringDirection	XmCStringDirection	XmStringDirection	dynamic	CSG
XmNtopItemPosition	XmCTopItemPosition	int	1	CSG
XmNvisibleItemCount	XmCVisibleItemCount	short	1	CSG

XmNautomaticSelection

> If **True** (and the widget's XmNselectionPolicy is either XmBROWSE_SELECT or Xm-EXTENDED_SELECT), then this resource calls XmNsingleSelectionCallback whenever the user moves into a new item. If **False**, then the user must release the mouse button before any selection callbacks are called.

XmNdoubleClickInterval

> The time span (in milliseconds) within which two button clicks must occur to be considered a double click rather than two single clicks. By default, this value is the multiclick time of the display.

XmNfontList

> The font list used for the items in the list. If this value is initially NULL, the font list is derived from the font list resource from the nearest parent that is a subclass of BulletinBoard, MenuShell, or VendorShell. This resource, together with the Xm-NvisibleItemsCount resource, is used to calculate the List widget's height.

XmNitemCount

> The total number of items. The widget updates this resource every time a list item is added or removed.

XmNitems

> A pointer to an array of compound strings. The compound strings are the list items to display. A call to XtGetValues() returns the actual list items (not a copy), so don't have your application free these items.

XmNlistMarginHeight
XmNlistMarginWidth

> The height or width of the margin between the border of the list and the items in the list.

XmNlistSizePolicy

> The method for resizing the widget when a list item exceeds the width of the work area. This resizing policy must be set at creation time. Possible values:

XmVARIABLE	/* grow to fit; don't add ScrollBar */
XmCONSTANT	/* don't grow to fit; add ScrollBar */
XmRESIZE_IF_POSSIBLE	/* grow or shrink; add ScrollBar if too large */

XmNlistSpacing

> The spacing between items.

XmNscrollBarDisplayPolicy

> Determines when to display vertical scrollbars in a ScrolledList widget. Possible values:

XmSTATIC	/* vertical ScrollBar always displays */
XmAS_NEEDED	/* add ScrollBar when list is too large */

XmNselectedItemCount

> The number of items in the list of selected items.

XmNselectedItems

> A pointer to an array of compound strings. The compound strings represent the currently selected list items. A call to XtGetValues() returns the actual list items (not a copy), so don't have your application free these items.

XmNselectionPolicy

> Determines the effect of a selection action. Possible values:

XmSINGLE_SELECT	XmBROWSE_SELECT
XmMULTIPLE_SELECT	XmEXTENDED_SELECT

XmNstringDirection

> The direction in which to draw the string. Possible values are XmSTRING_DIRECTION_L_TO_R and XmSTRING_DIRECTION_R_TO_L.

XmNtopItemPosition

> The position of the first item that will be visible in the list. Calling the XmListSetPos() routine is the same as setting this resource. In both cases, the last position is specified as 0.

XmNvisibleItemCount

> The number of items to display in the work area of the list. This value affects the widget's height.

Callback Resources

List defines the following callback resources:

Callback	Reason Constant
XmNsingleSelectionCallback	XmCR_SINGLE_SELECT
XmNmultipleSelectionCallback	XmCR_MULTIPLE_SELECT
XmNextendedSelectionCallback	XmCR_EXTENDED_SELECT
XmNbrowseSelectionCallback	XmCR_BROWSE_SELECT
XmNdefaultActionCallback	XmCR_DEFAULT_ACTION

Callback Structure

Each callback function is passed the structure below; however, some structure members might be unused because they aren't meaningful for particular callback reasons.

```
typedef struct
{
    int       reason;                  /* the reason that the callback was called */
    XEvent    * event;                 /* points to event structure that triggered callback */
    XmString  item;                    /* item that was most recently selected at the time event occurred */
    int       item_length;             /* number of bytes in item member */
    int       item_position;           /* item's position within the XmNitems array */
    XmString  *selected_items;         /* list of items selected at the time event occurred */
    int       selected_item_count;     /* number of items in selected_items */
    int       *selected_item_positions; /* array of integers that mark selected items */
    int       selection_type;          /* type of the most recent selection */
} XmListCallbackStruct;
```

The structure members *event*, *item*, *item_length*, and *item_position* are valid for any value of *reason*. The structure members *selected_items*, *selected_item_count*, and *selected_item_positions* are valid when the *reason* field has a value of XmCR_MULTIPLE_SELECT or XmCR_EXTENDED_SELECT. The structure member *selection_type* is valid only when the reason field is XmCR_EXTENDED_SELECT.

For the strings pointed to by *item* and *selected_items*, as well as for the integers pointed to by *selected_item_positions*, storage is overwritten each time the callback is invoked. Applications that need to save this data should make their own copies of it.

selected_item_positions is an integer array. The elements of the array indicate the positions of each selected item within the List widget's XmNitems array.

selection_type specifies what kind of extended selection was most recently made. One of three values is possible:

XmINITIAL	/* the selection was the initial selection */
XmMODIFICATION	/* the selection changed an existing selection */
XmADDITION	/* the selection added non-adjacent items to an existing selection */

Inherited Resources

List inherits the following resources. The resources are listed alphabetically, along with the superclass that defines them. List resets the XmNnavigationType resource from Xm-NONE to XmTAB_GROUP.

Resource	Inherited From	Resource	Inherited From
XmNaccelerators	Core	XmNhighlightPixmap	Primitive
XmNancestorSensitive	Core	XmNhighlightThickness	Primitive
XmNbackground	Core	XmNinitialResourcesPersistent	Core
XmNbackgroundPixmap	Core	XmNmappedWhenManaged	Core
XmNborderColor	Core	XmNnavigationType	Primitive
XmNborderPixmap	Core	XmNscreen	Core
XmNborderWidth	Core	XmNsensitive	Core
XmNbottomShadowColor	Primitive	XmNshadowThickness	Primitive
XmNbottomShadowPixmap	Primitive	XmNtopShadowColor	Primitive
XmNcolormap	Core	XmNtopShadowPixmap	Primitive
XmNdepth	Core	XmNtranslations	Core
XmNdestroyCallback	Core	XmNtraversalOn	Primitive
XmNforeground	Primitive	XmNunitType	Primitive
XmNheight	Core	XmNuserData	Primitive
XmNhelpCallback	Primitive	XmNwidth	Core
XmNhighlightColor	Primitive	XmNx	Core
XmNhighlightOnEnter	Primitive	XmNy	Core

Translations

Event	Action	Event	Action
BSelect Press	ListBeginSelect()	KBeginLine	ListBeginLine()
BSelect Motion	ListButtonMotion()	KEndLine	ListEndLine()
BSelect Release	ListEndSelect()	KBeginData	ListBeginData()
BExtend Press	ListBeginExtend()	MShift KBeginData	ListBeginDataExtend()
BExtend Motion	ListButtonMotion()	KEndData	ListEndData()
BExtend Release	ListEndExtend()	MShift KEndData	ListEndDataExtend()
BToggle Press	ListBeginToggle()	KAddMode	ListAddMode()
BToggle Motion	ListButtonMotion()	KActivate	ListKbdActivate()
BToggle Release	ListEndToggle()	KSelect Press	ListKbdBeginSelect()
KUp	ListPrevItem()	KSelect Release	ListKbdEndSelect()
MShift KUp	ListExtendPrevItem()	KExtend Press	ListKbdBeginExtend()
KDown	ListNextItem()	KExtend Release	ListKbdEndExtend()
MShift KDown	ListExtendNextItem()	MAny KCancel	ListKbdCancel()
KLeft	ListLeftChar()	KSelectAll	ListKbdSelectAll()
MCtrl KLeft	ListLeftPage()	KDeselectAll	ListKbdDeSelectAll()
KRight	ListRightChar()	KHelp	PrimitiveHelp()
MCtrl KRight	ListRightPage()	KNextField	PrimitiveNextTabGroup()
KPageUp	ListPrevPage()	KPrevField	PrimitivePrevTabGroup()
KPageDown	ListNextPage()		
KPageLeft	ListLeftPage()		
KPageRight	ListRightPage()		

Action Routines

List defines the action routines below. The current selection always appears with its foreground and background colors reversed. Note that many List actions have different effects depending on the selection policy, and note that some actions apply only for a particular selection policy.

ListAddMode()

> Turns Add Mode on or off.

ListBeginData()

> Moves the cursor to the first list item. If keyboard selection is in Normal Mode, this action also selects the first item (after deselecting any earlier selection) and invokes the callbacks specified either by XmNbrowseSelection-Callback or by XmNextendedSelectionCallback (as dictated by the selection policy).

ListBeginDataExtend()

> *Multiple selection*: moves the cursor to the first list item.
>
> *Extended selection*: moves the cursor to the first list item, cancels any current extended selection, selects (or deselects) all items from the first item to the current anchor, and invokes the callbacks specified by XmNextendedSelection-Callback.

ListBeginExtend()

> *Extended selection*: cancels any current extended selection, selects (or deselects) all items from the pointer location to the current anchor, and invokes the callbacks specified by XmNextendedSelectionCallback (if the Xm-NautomaticSelection resource is True).

ListBeginLine()

> Scrolls the List's viewing area horizontally to its beginning.

ListBeginSelect()

> *Single selection*: selects or deselects the item under the pointer (after deselecting any previous selection).
>
> *Browse selection*: selects the item under the pointer (after deselecting any previous selection); invokes the callbacks specified by XmNbrowseSelection-Callback (if the XmNautomaticSelection resource is True).
>
> *Multiple selection*: selects or deselects the item under the pointer (leaving previous selections unaffected).
>
> *Extended selection*: selects the item under the pointer (after deselecting any previous selection); marks this item as the current anchor; invokes the callbacks specified by XmNextendedSelectionCallback (if the XmNautomatic-Selection resource is True).

ListBeginToggle()

> *Extended selection*: keeps the current selection but shifts the anchor to the item under the pointer. This item's selection state is toggled, and (if Xm-NautomaticSelection is True) the extended selection callbacks are invoked.

ListButtonMotion()

Browse selection: selects the item under the pointer (after deselecting any previous selection); invokes the browse selection callbacks (if XmNautomatic-Selection is True and the pointer moved over a new item).

Extended selection: cancels any current extended selection, selects (or deselects) all items from the pointer location to the current anchor, and invokes the extended selection callbacks (if XmNautomaticSelection is True and the pointer moved over a new item).

In addition, when the pointer moves outside a ScrolledList widget, the list scrolls in sync with the pointer motion.

ListEndData()

Moves the cursor to the last list item. If keyboard selection is in Normal Mode, this action also selects the last item (after deselecting any earlier selection) and invokes the appropriate callbacks (browse selection or extended selection).

ListEndDataExtend()

Multiple selection: moves the cursor to the last list item.

Extended selection: moves the cursor to the last list item, cancels any current extended selection, selects (or deselects) all items from the last item to the current anchor, and invokes the extended selection callbacks.

ListEndExtend()

Extended selection: moves the cursor to the last item whose selection state was switched, and invokes the extended selection callbacks if XmNautomatic-Selection is False.

ListEndLine()

Scrolls the List's viewing area horizontally to its beginning.

ListEndSelect()

Single selection or multiple selection: moves the cursor to the last item whose selection state was switched, and invokes the appropriate selection callbacks.

Browse selection or extended selection: same as above, except that the appropriate callbacks are called only if XmNautomaticSelection is False.

ListEndToggle()

Extended selection: moves the cursor to the last item whose selection state was switched, and invokes the extended selection callbacks if XmNautomatic-Selection is False.

ListExtendNextItem()
ListExtendPrevItem()

Extended selection: adds the next/previous item to an extended selection and invokes the extended selection callbacks.

ListKbdActivate()

Invokes the default action callbacks.

ListKbdBeginExtend()

This action is the keyboard's complement to the mouse-activated ListBegin-Extend() action.

Extended selection: cancels any current extended selection and selects (or deselects) all items from the cursor to the current anchor.

ListKbdBeginSelect()

This action is the keyboard's complement to the mouse-activated ListBegin-Select() action.

Single selection: selects or deselects the item at the cursor (after deselecting any previous selection).

Browse selection: selects the item at the cursor (after deselecting any previous selection); invokes the browse selection callbacks if XmNautomatic-Selection is True.

Multiple selection: selects or deselects the item at the cursor (leaving previous selections unaffected).

Extended selection: shifts the anchor to the item at the cursor. In Normal Mode, this item is selected after any previous selection is deselected; in Add Mode, this item's state is toggled, and the current selection remains unaffected. This action calls the extended selection callbacks if Xm-NautomaticSelection is True.

ListKbdCancel()

Extended selection: cancels an extended selection and restores the items to their previous selection state.

ListKbdDeSelectAll()

Deselects all list items and calls the appropriate selection callbacks. This action applies to all selection modes except browse selection because this mode requires one item to remain selected at all times. (Note: in extended selection with keyboard Normal Mode and an XmNkeyboardFocusPolicy of Xm-EXPLICIT, the item at the cursor remains selected after this action is applied).

ListKbdEndExtend()

Extended selection: calls the extended selection callbacks if XmNautomatic-Selection is False.

ListKbdEndSelect()

Single selection or multiple selection: calls the appropriate selection callbacks. If XmNautomaticSelection is False, this action applies under any of the four selection policies.

ListKbdSelectAll()

Single selection or browse selection: selects the item at the cursor and calls the appropriate selection callbacks.

Multiple selection or extended selection: selects all list items and calls the appropriate selection callbacks.

ListLeftChar()
ListLeftPage()
> Scrolls the list either one character or one page to the left.

ListNextItem()
> Moves the cursor to the next list item. Additional operations:
> *Browse selection*: selects this item, deselects any previously selected item(s), and calls the browse selection callbacks.
> *Extended selection (in Normal Mode)*: selects this item and moves the anchor there, deselects any previously selected item(s), and calls the extended selection callbacks. In Add Mode neither the selection nor the anchor is affected.

ListNextPage()
> Moves the cursor (by scrolling the list) to the list item at the top of the next page. *Additional operations*: same as above.

ListPrevItem()
> Same as ListNextItem(), going back one item instead.

ListPrevPage()
> Same as ListNextPage(), going back one page instead.

ListRightChar()
ListRightPage()
> Scrolls the list either one character or one page to the right.

PrimitiveHelp()
> Calls the help callbacks for this widget.

PrimitiveNextTabGroup()
PrimitivePrevTabGroup()
> Moves the keyboard focus to the beginning of the next or previous tab group, wrapping around if necessary.

List has additional behavior associated with <Double Click>, which calls XmNdefaultAction-Callback, and with <FocusIn> and <FocusOut>, which respectively set or remove the focus under an explicit keyboard focus policy.

MainWindow

Provides the standard appearance for an application's primary window. MainWindow is a subclass of ScrolledWindow and can contain up to five areas: a menu bar, a command window, a work region, a message window, and two scrollbars (one horizontal and one vertical). All of these areas are optional. In addition, MainWindow can create up to three Separator widgets for dividing one component from another.

Class Information

Include File:	*<Xm/MainW.h>*
Class Name:	XmMainWindow
Class Hierarchy:	Core → Composite → Constraint → XmManager → XmScrolled-Window → XmMainWindow
Class Pointer:	xmMainWindowWidgetClass
Functions/Macros:	XmCreateMainWindow(), XmMainWindowSep1(), XmMainWindowSep2(), XmMainWindowSep3(), XmMainWindowSetAreas(), XmIsMainWindow()

New Resources

MainWindow defines the following resources:

Name	Class	Type	Default	Access
XmNcommandWindow	XmCCommandWindow	Window	NULL	CSG
XmNcommandWindowLocation	XmCCommandWindowLocation	unsigned char	See below	CG
XmNmainWindowMarginHeight	XmCMainWindowMarginHeight	Dimension	0	CSG
XmNmainWindowMarginWidth	XmCMainWindowMarginWidth	Dimension	0	CSG
XmNmenuBar	XmCMenuBar	Window	NULL	CSG
XmNmessageWindow	XmCMessageWindow	Window	NULL	CSG
XmNshowSeparator	XmCShowSeparator	Boolean	False	CSG

XmNcommandWindow
> The widget ID of the command window child.

XmNcommandWindowLocation
> One of two positions for the command window. Possible values:
>
>   XmCOMMAND_ABOVE_WORKSPACE   /* default; appears below menu bar */
>   XmCOMMAND_BELOW_WORKSPACE   /* appears between work window and message window */

XmNmainWindowMarginHeight
XmNmainWindowMarginWidth
> The margin on the top or bottom (right or left) of the MainWindow widget. This resource overrides the corresponding margin resource in the ScrolledWindow widget.

XmNmenuBar
> The widget ID of the menu bar child.

XmNmessageWindow
> The widget ID of the message window child.

XmNshowSeparator
> If True, separators are displayed between components of the MainWindow widget. If False (default), separators are not displayed.

Inherited Resources

MainWindow inherits the following resources. The resources are listed alphabetically, along with the superclass that defines them.

Resource	Inherited From	Resource	Inherited From
XmNaccelerators	Core	XmNnumChildren	Composite
XmNancestorSensitive	Core	XmNscreen	Core
XmNbackground	Core	XmNscrollBarDisplayPolicy	ScrolledWindow
XmNbackgroundPixmap	Core	XmNscrollBarPlacement	ScrolledWindow
XmNborderColor	Core	XmNscrolledWindowMarginHeight	ScrolledWindow
XmNborderPixmap	Core	XmNscrolledWindowMarginWidth	ScrolledWindow
XmNborderWidth	Core	XmNscrollingPolicy	ScrolledWindow
XmNbottomShadowColor	Manager	XmNsensitive	Core
XmNbottomShadowPixmap	Manager	XmNshadowThickness	Manager
XmNchildren	Composite	XmNspacing	ScrolledWindow
XmNclipWindow	ScrolledWindow	XmNstringDirection	Manager
XmNcolormap	Core	XmNtopShadowColor	Manager
XmNdepth	Core	XmNtopShadowPixmap	Manager
XmNdestroyCallback	Core	XmNtranslations	Core
XmNforeground	Manager	XmNtraversalOn	Manager
XmNheight	Core	XmNunitType	Manager
XmNhelpCallback	Manager	XmNuserData	Manager
XmNhighlightColor	Manager	XmNverticalScrollBar	ScrolledWindow
XmNhighlightPixmap	Manager	XmNvisualPolicy	ScrolledWindow
XmNhorizontalScrollBar	ScrolledWindow	XmNwidth	Core
XmNinitialResourcesPersistent	Core	XmNworkWindow	ScrolledWindow
XmNinsertPosition	Composite	XmNx	Core
XmNmappedWhenManaged	Core	XmNy	Core
XmNnavigationType	Manager		

Translations

The translations for MainWindow are inherited from ScrolledWindow.

Manager

A superclass that supports geometry management by providing resources for visual layout (e.g., setting shadows and highlights) and for keyboard traversal mechanisms. Its subclasses include RowColumn, Form, and BulletinBoard. Because Manager is a meta-class, it is generally not instantiated alone.

Class Information

Include File:	None.
Class Name:	XmManager
Class Hierarchy:	Core → Composite → Constraint → XmManager
Class Pointer:	xmManagerWidgetClass
Functions/Macros:	XmIsManager()

New Resources

Manager defines the following resources. The default values of color resources for foreground, background, and shadows are set dynamically.

Name	Class	Type	Default	Access
XmNbottomShadowColor	XmCBottomShadowColor	Pixel	dynamic	CSG
XmNbottomShadowPixmap	XmCBottomShadowPixmap	Pixmap	XmUNSPECIFIED_ PIXMAP	CSG
XmNforeground	XmCForeground	Pixel	dynamic	CSG
XmNhighlightColor	XmCHighlightColor	Pixel	dynamic	CSG
XmNhighlightPixmap	XmCHighlightPixmap	Pixmap	dynamic	CSG
XmNnavigationType	XmCNavigationType	XmNavigationType	XmTAB_GROUP	CSG
XmNshadowThickness	XmCShadowThickness	Dimension	0	CSG
XmNstringDirection	XmCStringDirection	XmStringDirection	dynamic	CG
XmNtopShadowColor	XmCBackgroundTopShadowColor	Pixel	dynamic	CSG
XmNtopShadowPixmap	XmCTopShadowPixmap	Pixmap	dynamic	CSG
XmNtraversalOn	XmCTraversalOn	Boolean	True	CSG
XmNunitType	XmCUnitType	unsigned char	dynamic	CSG
XmNuserData	XmCUserData	Pointer	NULL	CSG

XmNbottomShadowColor

> The color used in drawing the border shadow's bottom and right sides. (Used only if XmNbottomShadowPixmap is NULL.)

XmNbottomShadowPixmap

> The pixmap used in drawing the border shadow's bottom and right sides.

XmNforeground

> The foreground color used by Manager widgets.

XmNhighlightColor

> The color used in drawing the highlighting rectangle. (Used only if XmNhighlight-Pixmap is XmUNSPECIFIED_PIXMAP.)

XmNhighlightPixmap

> The pixmap used in drawing the highlighting rectangle.

XmNnavigationType

> Determines the way in which a Manager widget is traversed during keyboard navigation. Possible values:

```
XmNONE                    /* exclude from keyboard navigation */
XmTAB_GROUP               /* include in keyboard navigation */
XmSTICKY_TAB_GROUP        /* include in keyboard navigation, even if XmAddTabGroup() was called */
XmEXCLUSIVE_TAB_GROUP     /* application defines order of navigation */
```

XmNshadowThickness

The thickness of the shadow border. This resource is dynamically set to 1 in a top-level window and 0 otherwise.

XmNstringDirection

The direction in which to draw the string. Possible values are XmSTRING_DIRECTION_L_TO_R and XmSTRING_DIRECTION_R_TO_L.

XmNtopShadowColor

The color used in drawing the border shadow's top and left sides. (Used only if XmNtopShadowPixmap is NULL.)

XmNtopShadowPixmap

The pixmap used in drawing the border shadow's top and left sides.

XmNtraversalOn

If True (default), traversal of this widget is made possible.

XmNunitType

The measurement units to use in resources that specify a size or position—for example, any resources of data type Dimension (whose names generally include one of the words "Margin", "Height", "Width", "Thickness", or "Spacing"), as well as the offset resources defined by Form. For a widget whose parent is a manager, the default value is copied from this parent (provided the value hasn't been explicitly set by the application); otherwise, the default is XmPIXELS. Possible values:

XmPIXELS	Xm100TH_POINTS
Xm100TH_MILLIMETERS	Xm100TH_FONT_UNITS
Xm1000TH_INCHES	

XmNuserData

A pointer to data that the application can attach to the widget. This resource is unused internally.

Callback Resources

Manager defines the following callback resources:

Callback	Reason Constant
XmNhelpCallback	XmCR_HELP

Inherited Resources

Manager inherits the following resources. The resources are listed alphabetically, along with the superclass that defines them. Manager resets XmNborderWidth from 1 to 0.

Resource	Inherited From	Resource	Inherited From
XmNaccelerators	Core	XmNheight	Core
XmNancestorSensitive	Core	XmNinitialResourcesPersistent	Core
XmNbackground	Core	XmNinsertPosition	Composite
XmNbackgroundPixmap	Core	XmNmappedWhenManaged	Core
XmNborderColor	Core	XmNnumChildren	Composite
XmNborderPixmap	Core	XmNscreen	Core
XmNborderWidth	Core	XmNsensitive	Core
XmNchildren	Composite	XmNtranslations	Core
XmNcolormap	Core	XmNwidth	Core
XmNdepth	Core	XmNx	Core
XmNdestroyCallback	Core	XmNy	Core

Translations

For Manager widgets that have gadget children:

Event	Action	Event	Action
BAny Motion	ManagerGadgetButtonMotion()	KNextField	ManagerGadgetNextTabGroup()
BSelect Press	ManagerGadgetArm()	KUp	ManagerGadgetTraverseUp()
BSelect Click	ManagerGadgetActivate()	KDown	ManagerGadgetTraverseDown()
BSelect Release	ManagerGadgetActivate()	KLeft	ManagerGadgetTraverseLeft()
BSelect Press 2+	ManagerGadgetMultiArm()	KRight	ManagerGadgetTraverseRight()
BSelect Release 2+	ManagerGadgetMultiActivate()	KBeginLine	ManagerGadgetTraverseHome()
KSelect	ManagerGadgetSelect()	KHelp	ManagerGadgetHelp()
KActivate	ManagerGadgetSelect()	KAny	ManagerGadgetKeyInput()
KPrevField	ManagerGadgetPrevTabGroup()		

Action Routines

The action routines for the Manager widget affect a gadget child that has the keyboard focus. The descriptions below refer to the gadget that has focus. Actions that involve traversal by a relative amount (e.g., ManagerGadgetTraverseLeft()) will wrap around if necessary.

ManagerGadgetActivate()   Activates the gadget.

ManagerGadgetArm()   Arms the gadget.

ManagerGadgetButtonMotion() Triggers the mouse motion event that the gadget received.

ManagerGadgetHelp()   Invokes the list of callbacks specified by the gadget's Xm-NhelpCallback resource. If the gadget doesn't have any help callbacks, the ManagerGadgetHelp() routine invokes those associated with the nearest ancestor that has them.

ManagerGadgetKeyInput()   Triggers the keyboard event that the gadget received.

ManagerGadgetMultiActivate() Processes a multiple click of the mouse.

ManagerGadgetMultiArm()	Processes a multiple press of the mouse button.
ManagerGadgetNextTabGroup() ManagerGadgetPrevTabGroup()	Traverses to the beginning of the next/previous tab group.
ManagerGadgetSelect()	Arms and activates the gadget.
ManagerGadgetTraverseDown() ManagerGadgetTraverseUp()	Within the same tab group, descends/ascends to the item below/above the gadget.
ManagerGadgetTraverseHome()	Changes the focus to the first item in the tab group.
ManagerGadgetTraverseLeft() ManagerGadgetTraverseRight()	Within the same tab group, traverses to the item on the left/right of the gadget.
ManagerGadgetTraverseNext() ManagerGadgetTraversePrev()	Within the same tab group, traverses to the next/previous item.

Manager has additional behavior associated with <FocusIn>, which highlights a gadget and gives it focus, and <FocusOut>, which unhighlights a gadget and removes its focus. These events apply only when the keyboard focus policy is explicit.

MenuBar

A narrow strip (usually horizontal) from which pulldown menus are posted. MenuBar is a RowColumn widget whose XmNrowColumnType resource is set to XmMENU_BAR and whose default orientation is XmHORIZONTAL. Other important RowColumn resources include Xm-NisHomogeneous (set to True), XmNentryClass (set to xmCascadeButtonWidgetClass), and the Xm-Nmenu... resources. A MenuBar can be created by a call to XmCreateMenuBar(), XmCreate-SimpleMenuBar(), or XmVaCreateSimpleMenuBar(), which are defined in <Xm/RowColumn.h>.

MenuShell

A subclass of OverrideShell that is meant to contain only popup or pulldown menu panes. A MenuShell widget doesn't need to be created explicitly, because application writers can use the convenience routines XmCreatePopupMenu() or XmCreatePulldownMenu(). If, however, a MenuShell is created explicitly, the type of menu system being built determines what type of parent to specify for the MenuShell: for a top-level popup, specify the widget from which it will pop up; for a pulldown menu pane, specify the menu pane from which it is pulled down (PopupMenu, PulldownMenu, MenuBar, or OptionMenu).

Class Information

Include File:	*<Xm/MenuShell.h>*
Class Name:	XmMenuShell
Class Hierarchy:	Core → Composite → Shell → OverrideShell → XmMenuShell
Class Pointer:	xmMenuShellWidgetClass
Functions/Macros:	XmCreateMenuShell(), XmIsMenuShell()

New Resources

MenuShell defines the following resource:

Name	Class	Type	Default	Access
XmNdefaultFontList	XmCDefaultFontList	XmFontList	dynamic	C

XmNdefaultFontList

> A default font list for the children of a MenuShell widget. This resource is used by a MenuShell's Text children, Label children or button children for which no font list was specifically set.

Inherited Resources

MenuShell inherits the following resources. The resources are listed alphabetically, along with the superclass that defines them.

Resource	Inherited From	Resource	Inherited From
XmNaccelerators	Core	XmNinitialResourcesPersistent	Core
XmNallowShellResize	Shell	XmNinsertPosition	Composite
XmNancestorSensitive	Core	XmNmappedWhenManaged	Core
XmNbackground	Core	XmNnumChildren	Composite
XmNbackgroundPixmap	Core	XmNoverrideRedirect	Shell
XmNborderColor	Core	XmNpopdownCallback	Shell
XmNborderPixmap	Core	XmNpopupCallback	Shell
XmNborderWidth	Core	XmNsaveUnder	Shell
XmNchildren	Composite	XmNscreen	Core
XmNcolormap	Core	XmNsensitive	Core
XmNcreatePopupChildProc	Shell	XmNtranslations	Core
XmNdepth	Core	XmNvisual	Shell
XmNdestroyCallback	Core	XmNwidth	Core
XmNgeometry	Shell	XmNx	Core
XmNheight	Core	XmNy	Core

Translations

BSelect Press	ClearTraversal()
BSelect Release	MenuShellPopdownDone()

Action Routines

MenuShell defines the following action routines:

ClearTraversal()

> Shuts off keyboard traversal within this menu, turns on mouse traversal, and unposts any submenus that this menu posted.

MenuShellPopdownDone()

> Unposts the menu tree and restores the previous focus.

MenuShellPopdownOne()

> Like MenuShellPopdownDone() except that it unposts only one level of the menu tree. In a top-level pulldown menu pane attached to a menu bar, this action routine disarms the cascade button and the menu bar.

MessageBox

A subclass of BulletinBoard that is typically used as a child of DialogShell for displaying simple, transient, dialog boxes. A MessageBox usually contains a message symbol, a message, and three PushButtons (labeled Ok, Cancel, and Help, by default). The XmNdialogType resource controls the type of message symbol that is displayed.

Class Information

Include File:	*<Xm/MessageB.h>*
Class Name:	XmMessageBox
Class Hierarchy:	Core → Composite → Constraint → XmManager → XmBulletinBoard → XmMessageBox
Class Pointer:	xmMessageBoxWidgetClass
Functions/Macros:	XmCreateErrorDialog(), XmCreateInformationDialog(), XmCreateMessageDialog(), XmCreateQuestionDialog(), XmCreateWarningDialog(), XmCreateWorkingDialog(), XmCreateMessageBox(), XmMessageBoxGetChild(), XmIsMessageBox()

New Resources

MessageBox defines the following resources:

Name	Class	Type	Default	Access
XmNcancelLabelString	XmCCancelLabelString	XmString	"Cancel"	CSG
XmNdefaultButtonType	XmCDefaultButtonType	unsigned char	XmDIALOG_OK_BUTTON	CSG
XmNdialogType	XmCDialogType	unsigned char	XmDIALOG_MESSAGE	CSG
XmNhelpLabelString	XmCHelpLabelString	XmString	"Help"	CSG
XmNmessageAlignment	XmCAlignment	unsigned char	See Below	CSG
XmNmessageString	XmCMessageString	XmString	" "	CSG
XmNminimizeButtons	XmCMinimizeButtons	Boolean	False	CSG
XmNokLabelString	XmCOkLabelString	XmString	"OK"	CSG
XmNsymbolPixmap	XmCPixmap	Pixmap	dynamic	CSG

XmNcancelLabelString

    The string that labels the Cancel button.

XmNdefaultButtonType

    Specifies which PushButton provides the default action. Possible values:

        XmDIALOG_CANCEL_BUTTON
        XmDIALOG_OK_BUTTON
        XmDIALOG_HELP_BUTTON

XmNdialogType

    The type of MessageBox dialog, which also indicates the message symbol that displays by default. Possible values:

XmDIALOG_ERROR	XmDIALOG_QUESTION
XmDIALOG_INFORMATION	XmDIALOG_WARNING
XmDIALOG_MESSAGE	XmDIALOG_WORKING

XmNhelpLabelString

    The string that labels the Help button.

XmNmessageAlignment

    The type of alignment for the message label. Possible values:

        XmALIGNMENT_BEGINNING   /* default */
        XmALIGNMENT_CENTER
        XmALIGNMENT_END

XmNmessageString

    The string to use as the message label.

XmNminimizeButtons

    If False (default), all buttons are standardized to be as wide as the widest button and as high as the highest button. If True, buttons will keep their preferred size.

XmNokLabelString

    The string that labels the Ok button.

XmNsymbolPixmap

    The pixmap label to use as the message symbol.

Callback Resources

MessageBox defines the following callback resources:

Callback	Reason Constant
XmNokCallback	XmCR_OK
XmNcancelCallback	XmCR_CANCEL

Callback Structure

Each callback function is passed the following structure:

```
typedef struct
{
    int       reason;      /* the reason that the callback was called */
    XEvent  * event;       /* points to event structure that triggered callback */
} XmAnyCallbackStruct;
```

Inherited Resources

MessageBox inherits the following resources. The resources are listed alphabetically, along with the superclass that defines them.

Resource	Inherited From	Resource	Inherited From
XmNaccelerators	Core	XmNinsertPosition	Composite
XmNallowOverlap	BulletinBoard	XmNlabelFontList	BulletinBoard
XmNancestorSensitive	Core	XmNmapCallback	BulletinBoard
XmNautoUnmanage	BulletinBoard	XmNmappedWhenManaged	Core
XmNbackground	Core	XmNmarginHeight	BulletinBoard
XmNbackgroundPixmap	Core	XmNmarginWidth	BulletinBoard
XmNborderColor	Core	XmNnavigationType	Manager
XmNborderPixmap	Core	XmNnoResize	BulletinBoard
XmNborderWidth	Core	XmNnumChildren	Composite
XmNbottomShadowColor	Manager	XmNresizePolicy	BulletinBoard
XmNbottomShadowPixmap	Manager	XmNscreen	Core
XmNbuttonFontList	BulletinBoard	XmNsensitive	Core
XmNcancelButton	BulletinBoard	XmNshadowThickness	Manager
XmNchildren	Composite	XmNshadowType	BulletinBoard
XmNcolormap	Core	XmNstringDirection	Manager
XmNdefaultButton	BulletinBoard	XmNtextFontList	BulletinBoard
XmNdefaultPosition	BulletinBoard	XmNtextTranslations	BulletinBoard
XmNdepth	Core	XmNtopShadowColor	Manager
XmNdestroyCallback	Core	XmNtopShadowPixmap	Manager
XmNdialogStyle	BulletinBoard	XmNtranslations	Core
XmNdialogTitle	BulletinBoard	XmNtraversalOn	Manager
XmNfocusCallback	BulletinBoard	XmNunitType	Manager
XmNforeground	Manager	XmNunmapCallback	BulletinBoard
XmNheight	Core	XmNuserData	Manager
XmNhelpCallback	Manager	XmNwidth	Core
XmNhighlightColor	Manager	XmNx	Core
XmNhighlightPixmap	Manager	XmNy	Core
XmNinitialResourcesPersistent	Core		

Translations

The translations for MessageBox include those from Manager.

Additional Behavior

The following additional behavior is defined for this widget:

MAny KCancel For a sensitive Cancel button, invokes the callbacks in XmNactivateCallback.

KActivate   For the button that has keyboard focus (or else the default button), invokes the callbacks in XmNactivateCallback.

Each event below invokes a particular set of callbacks:

<Ok Button Activated>	XmNokCallback
<Cancel Button Activated>	XmNcancelCallback
<Help Button Activated>	XmNhelpCallback
<FocusIn>	XmNfocusCallback
<Map>	XmNmapCallback (if parent is a DialogShell)
<Unmap>	XmNunmapCallback (if parent is a DialogShell)

MessageDialog

A convenience widget created by a call to XmCreateMessageDialog() and consisting of a DialogShell with a MessageBox widget as its child. The MessageBox resource XmNdialog-Type is set to XmDIALOG_MESSAGE. The include file is *<Xm/MessageB.h>*. A Message-Dialog contains an optional symbol (none by default), a message, and three buttons (labeled Ok, Cancel, and Help, by default).

Object

A supporting superclass for widgets and gadgets. An Object encapsulates the mechanisms for resource management and is never instantiated.

Class Information

Include File:	*<X11/Object.h>*
Class Name:	Object
Class Hierarchy:	Object
Class Pointer:	objectClass
Functions/Macros:	XtIsObject()

New Resources

Object defines the following resources:

Name	Class	Type	Default	Access
XmNdestroyCallback	XmCCallback	XtCallbackList	NULL	C

XmNdestroyCallback   List of callbacks invoked when the Object is destroyed.

OptionMenu

A menu system component that lets a user select one of several choices. An OptionMenu contains a label (a LabelGadget), a selection area (a CascadeButtonGadget), and one pulldown menu pane (a PulldownMenu). OptionMenu is a RowColumn widget whose Xm-NrowColumnType resource is set to XmMENU_OPTION. Other important RowColumn resources include XmNmenuHistory, XmNmenuPost, XmNmnemonic, XmNmnemonicCharSet, and XmNsub-MenuId. An OptionMenu can be created by a call to XmCreateOptionMenu(), XmCreateSimple-OptionMenu(), or XmVaCreateSimpleOptionMenu(), which are defined in *<Xm/RowColumn.h>*. Other related routines are XmOptionButtonGadget() and XmOptionLabelGadget().

OverrideShell

A superclass for Motif's MenuShell, allowing popup shell windows (e.g., PopupMenu) to bypass the window manager.

Class Information

Include File:	*<X11/Shell.h>*
Class Name:	OverrideShell
Class Hierarchy:	Core → Composite → Shell → OverrideShell
Class Pointer:	overrideShellWidgetClass
Functions/Macros:	XtIsOverrideShell()

New Resources

Although OverrideShell defines no new resources, it redefines both XmNoverrideRedirect and XmNsaveUnder to True.

Inherited Resources

OverrideShell inherits the following resources. The resources are listed alphabetically, along with the superclass that defines them.

Resource	Inherited From	Resource	Inherited From
XmNaccelerators	Core	XmNinitialResourcesPersistent	Core
XmNallowShellResize	Shell	XmNinsertPosition	Composite
XmNancestorSensitive	Core	XmNmappedWhenManaged	Core
XmNbackground	Core	XmNnumChildren	Composite
XmNbackgroundPixmap	Core	XmNoverrideRedirect	Shell
XmNborderColor	Core	XmNpopdownCallback	Shell
XmNborderPixmap	Core	XmNpopupCallback	Shell
XmNborderWidth	Core	XmNsaveUnder	Shell
XmNchildren	Composite	XmNscreen	Core
XmNcolormap	Core	XmNsensitive	Core

Resource	Inherited From	Resource	Inherited From
XmNcreatePopupChildProc	Shell	XmNtranslations	Core
XmNdepth	Core	XmNvisual	Shell
XmNdestroyCallback	Core	XmNwidth	Core
XmNgeometry	Shell	XmNx	Core
XmNheight	Core	XmNy	Core

PanedWindow

A constraint widget that tiles children vertically from top to bottom. All children will have the same width as that of the widest child. A "control sash" lets users adjust the size of the pane children. The control sash is a small box below the corresponding pane.

Class Information

Include File:	*<Xm/PanedW.h>*
Class Name:	XmPanedWindow
Class Hierarchy:	Core → Composite → Constraint → XmManager → XmPaned-Window
Class Pointer:	xmPanedWindowWidgetClass
Functions/Macros:	XmCreatePanedWindow(), XmIsPanedWindow()

New Resources

PanedWindow defines the following resources:

Name	Class	Type	Default	Access
XmNmarginHeight	XmCMarginHeight	Dimension	3	CSG
XmNmarginWidth	XmCMarginWidth	Dimension	3	CSG
XmNrefigureMode	XmCBoolean	Boolean	True	CSG
XmNsashHeight	XmCSashHeight	Dimension	10	CSG
XmNsashIndent	XmCSashIndent	Position	-10	CSG
XmNsashShadowThickness	XmCShadowThickness	Dimension	dynamic	CSG
XmNsashWidth	XmCSashWidth	Dimension	10	CSG
XmNseparatorOn	XmCSeparatorOn	Boolean	True	CSG
XmNspacing	XmCSpacing	Dimension	8	CSG

XmNmarginHeight
> The spacing between a PanedWindow widget's top or bottom edge and any child widget.

XmNmarginWidth
> The spacing between a PanedWindow widget's right or left edge and any child widget.

XmNrefigureMode

If True (default), children are reset to their appropriate positions following a change in the PanedWindow widget.

XmNsashHeight
XmNsashWidth

The height and width of the sash.

XmNsashIndent

The horizontal position of the sash along each pane. Positive values specify the indent from the left edge; negative values, from the right edge (assuming the default value of XmNstringDirection). If the value is too large, the sash is placed flush with the edge of the PanedWindow.

XmNsashShadowThickness

The thickness of shadows drawn on each sash.

XmNseparatorOn

If True, the widget places a Separator or SeparatorGadget between each pane.

XmNspacing

The distance between each child pane.

New Constraint Resources

The following constraint resources are defined by this widget:

Name	Class	Type	Default	Access
XmNallowResize	XmCBoolean	Boolean	False	CSG
XmNpaneMaximum	XmCPaneMaximum	Dimension	1000	CSG
XmNpaneMinimum	XmCPaneMinimum	Dimension	1	CSG
XmNskipAdjust	XmCBoolean	Boolean	False	CSG

XmNallowResize

If False (default), the PanedWindow widget always refuses resize requests from its children. If True, the PanedWindow widget tries to grant requests to change a child's height.

XmNpaneMaximum
XmNpaneMinimum

The values of a pane's maximum and minimum dimensions for resizing. You can prevent a sash from being drawn by setting these values to be equal.

XmNskipAdjust

If False (default), the PanedWindow widget automatically resizes this pane child. If True, resizing is not automatic, and the PanedWindow may choose to skip the adjustment of this pane.

Inherited Resources

PanedWindow inherits the following resources. The resources are listed alphabetically, along with the superclass that defines them.

Resource	Inherited From	Resource	Inherited From
XmNaccelerators	Core	XmNinitialResourcesPersistent	Core
XmNancestorSensitive	Core	XmNinsertPosition	Composite
XmNbackground	Core	XmNmappedWhenManaged	Core
XmNbackgroundPixmap	Core	XmNnavigationType	Manager
XmNborderColor	Core	XmNnumChildren	Composite
XmNborderPixmap	Core	XmNscreen	Core
XmNborderWidth	Core	XmNsensitive	Core
XmNbottomShadowColor	Manager	XmNshadowThickness	Manager
XmNbottomShadowPixmap	Manager	XmNstringDirection	Manager
XmNchildren	Composite	XmNtopShadowColor	Manager
XmNcolormap	Core	XmNtopShadowPixmap	Manager
XmNdepth	Core	XmNtranslations	Core
XmNdestroyCallback	Core	XmNtraversalOn	Manager
XmNforeground	Manager	XmNunitType	Manager
XmNheight	Core	XmNuserData	Manager
XmNhelpCallback	Manager	XmNwidth	Core
XmNhighlightColor	Manager	XmNx	Core
XmNhighlightPixmap	Manager	XmNy	Core

Translations

The translations for PanedWindow are inherited from Manager. Additional translations are defined for sashes within a PanedWindow widget:

Event	Action	Event	Action
BSelect Press	SashAction(Start)	KUp	SashAction(Key,DefaultIncr,Up)
BSelect Motion	SashAction(Move)	MCtrl KUp	SashAction(Key,LargeIncr,Up)
BSelect Release	SashAction(Commit)	KDown	SashAction(Key,DefaultIncr,Down)
BDrag Press	SashAction(Start)	MCtrl KDown	SashAction(Key,LargeIncr,Down)
BDrag Motion	SashAction(Move)	KNextField	NextTabGroup()
BDrag Release	SashAction(Commit)	KPrevField	PrevTabGroup()
KHelp	Help()		

Action Routines

PanedWindow defines the following action routines:

Help()   Invokes the list of callbacks specified by XmNhelpCallback. If the Paned-Window doesn't have any help callbacks, the Help() routine invokes those associated with the nearest ancestor that has them.

NextTabGroup()

>Traverses to the next tab group. Normally a tab group consists of a pane and its sash.

PrevTabGroup()

>Traverses to the previous tab group. Normally a tab group consists of a pane and its sash.

SashAction(*mouse_action*)

>Controls the placement of the sash (the border of the pane), using the mouse. *mouse_action* can be one of three values:

>Start   Begins the placement operation.
>Move   Causes the sash to move as the mouse moves.
>Commit   Ends the placement operation.

SashAction(Key,*adjustment,direction*)

>Controls the placement of the sash that has keyboard focus, via the keyboard. *adjustment* is either DefaultIncr (increment the sash's position by one line) or LargeIncr (increment the sash's position by one viewing region). *direction* is either Up or Down.

PanedWindow has additional behavior associated with <FocusIn>, which highlights the sash and gives it keyboard focus, and <FocusOut>, which unhighlights the sash and removes its keyboard focus.

PopupMenu

The first menu pane in a popup menu system. PopupMenu is a convenience widget that consists of a MenuShell widget and a RowColumn child whose XmNrowColumnType resource is set to XmMENU_POPUP. Other important RowColumn resources include XmNmenuAccelerator, XmNmenuPost, and XmNpopupEnabled. A PopupMenu can be created by a call to XmCreatePopupMenu(), XmCreateSimplePopupMenu(), or XmVaCreateSimplePopupMenu(), which are defined in *<Xm/RowColumn.h>*. XmMenuPosition() determines a PopupMenu's placement.

Primitive

A supporting superclass that provides Motif-specific resources for border drawing, highlighting, and keyboard traversal mechanisms. Because Primitive is a meta-class, it is generally not instantiated alone; it supports widget subclasses that handle elementary (or "primitive") graphic elements (e.g., buttons, labels, and separators).

Class Information

Include File:	None
Class Name:	XmPrimitive
Class Hierarchy:	Core → XmPrimitive
Class Pointer:	xmPrimitiveWidgetClass
Funtions/Macros:	XmIsPrimitive()

New Resources

Primitive defines the following resources. The default values of color resources for foreground, background, and shadows are set dynamically.

Name	Class	Type	Default	Access
XmNbottomShadowColor	XmCBottomShadowColor	Pixel	dynamic	CSG
XmNbottomShadowPixmap	XmCBottomShadowPixmap	Pixmap	XmUNSPECIFIED_PIXMAP	CSG
XmNforeground	XmCForeground	Pixel	dynamic	CSG
XmNhighlightColor	XmCHighlightColor	Pixel	dynamic	CSG
XmNhighlightOnEnter	XmCHighlightOnEnter	Boolean	False	CSG
XmNhighlightPixmap	XmCHighlightPixmap	Pixmap	dynamic	CSG
XmNhighlightThickness	XmCHighlightThickness	Dimension	2	CSG
XmNnavigationType	XmCNavigationType	XmNavigationType	XmNONE	G
XmNshadowThickness	XmCShadowThickness	Dimension	2	CSG
XmNtopShadowColor	XmCTopShadowColor	Pixel	dynamic	CSG
XmNtopShadowPixmap	XmCTopShadowPixmap	Pixmap	dynamic	CSG
XmNtraversalOn	XmCTraversalOn	Boolean	True	CSG
XmNunitType	XmCUnitType	unsigned char	dynamic	CSG
XmNuserData	XmCUserData	Pointer	NULL	CSG

XmNbottomShadowColor
> The color used in drawing the border shadow's bottom and right sides. (Used only if XmNbottomShadowPixmap is NULL.)

XmNbottomShadowPixmap
> The pixmap used in drawing the border shadow's bottom and right sides.

XmNforeground
> The foreground color used by Primitive widgets.

XmNhighlightColor
> The color used in drawing the highlighting rectangle. (Used only if XmNhighlight-Pixmap is XmUNSPECIFIED_PIXMAP.)

XmNhighlightOnEnter
> Determines whether to draw the widget's highlighting rectangle whenever the cursor moves into the widget. This resource applies only when the shell has a focus policy of XmPOINTER. If the XmNhighlightOnEnter resource is True, highlighting is drawn; if False (default), highlighting is not drawn.

XmNhighlightPixmap

The pixmap used in drawing the highlighting rectangle.

XmNhighlightThickness

The thickness of the highlighting rectangle.

XmNnavigationType

Determines the way in which a Primitive widget is traversed during keyboard navigation. Possible values:

```
XmNONE                      /* exclude from keyboard navigation */
XmTAB_GROUP                 /* include in keyboard navigation */
XmSTICKY_TAB_GROUP          /* include in keyboard navigation, even if XmAddTabGroup() was called */
XmEXCLUSIVE_TAB_GROUP       /* application defines order of navigation */
```

XmNshadowThickness

The thickness of the shadow border.

XmNtopShadowColor

The color used in drawing the border shadow's top and left sides. (Used only if XmNtopShadowPixmap is NULL.)

XmNtopShadowPixmap

The pixmap used in drawing the border shadow's top and left sides.

XmNtraversalOn

If True (default), traversal of this widget is made possible.

XmNunitType

The measurement units to use in resources that specify a size or position—for example, any resources of data type Dimension (whose names generally include one of the words "Margin", "Thickness", or "Spacing"). For a widget whose parent is a manager, the default value is copied from this parent (provided the value hasn't been explicitly set by the application); otherwise, the default is XmPIXELS. Possible values:

XmPIXELS	Xm100TH_POINTS
Xm100TH_MILLIMETERS	Xm100TH_FONT_UNITS
Xm1000TH_INCHES	

XmNuserData

A pointer to data that the application can attach to the widget. This resource is unused internally.

Callback Resources

Primitive defines the following callback resources:

Callback	Reason Constant
XmNhelpCallback	XmCR_HELP

Inherited Resources

Primitive inherits the following resources. The resources are listed alphabetically, along with the superclass that defines them. Primitive resets XmNborderWidth from 1 to 0.

Resource	Inherited From	Resource	Inherited From
XmNaccelerators	Core	XmNheight	Core
XmNancestorSensitive	Core	XmNinitialResourcesPersistent	Core
XmNbackground	Core	XmNmappedWhenManaged	Core
XmNbackgroundPixmap	Core	XmNscreen	Core
XmNborderColor	Core	XmNsensitive	Core
XmNborderPixmap	Core	XmNtranslations	Core
XmNborderWidth	Core	XmNwidth	Core
XmNcolormap	Core	XmNx	Core
XmNdepth	Core	XmNy	Core
XmNdestroyCallback	Core		

Translations

Event	Action	Event	Action
KUp	PrimitiveTraverseUp()	KBeginLine	PrimitiveTraverseHome()
KDown	PrimitiveTraverseDown()	KNextField	PrimitiveNextTabGroup()
KLeft	PrimitiveTraverseLeft()	KPrevField	PrimitivePrevTabGroup()
KRight	PrimitiveTraverseRight()	KHelp	PrimitiveHelp()

Action Routines

Primitive defines the action routines below. Actions that involve traversal by a relative amount (e.g., PrimitiveTraverseLeft()) will wrap around if necessary.

PrimitiveHelp()
: Invokes the list of callbacks specified by the Primitive widget's XmNhelpCallback resource. If the Primitive widget doesn't have any help callbacks, this action routine invokes those associated with the nearest ancestor that has them.

PrimitiveNextTabGroup()
PrimitivePrevTabGroup()
: Traverses to the first item in the next/previous tab group.

PrimitiveTraverseDown()
PrimitiveTraverseUp()
: Within the same tab group, descends/ascends to the item below/above the widget.

PrimitiveTraverseHome()
: Changes the focus to the first item in the tab group.

PrimitiveTraverseLeft()
PrimitiveTraverseRight()
: Within the same tab group, traverses to the item on the left/right of the widget.

PrimitiveTraverseNext()
PrimitiveTraversePrev()
: Within the same tab group, traverses to the next/previous item.

Primitive has additional behavior associated with <FocusIn>, which highlights the widget and gives it focus, and <FocusOut>, which unhighlights the widget and removes its focus. These events apply only when the keyboard focus policy is explicit.

PromptDialog

A convenience widget created by a call to XmCreatePromptDialog() and consisting of a Dialog-Shell with a SelectionBox widget as its child. The include file is *<Xm/SelectioB.h>*. The SelectionBox resource XmNdialogType is set to XmDIALOG_PROMPT. A PromptDialog contains a message, a region for text input, and four buttons (whose default labels are Ok, Cancel, Help, and Apply).

PulldownMenu

A menu pane for pulldown menus. A PulldownMenu combines a MenuShell widget and a RowColumn widget whose XmNrowColumnType resource is set to XmMENU_PULLDOWN. A PulldownMenu can be created by a call to XmCreatePulldownMenu(), XmCreateSimplePulldown-Menu(), or XmVaCreateSimplePulldownMenu(), which are defined in *<Xm/RowColumn.h>*.

PushButton

Displays a label or a pixmap, and invokes an application callback when clicked on with the mouse. The shading of the PushButton changes to make it appear either pressed in when selected or raised when unselected.

Class Information

Include File:	*<Xm/PushB.h>*
Class Name:	XmPushButton
Class Hierarchy:	Core → XmPrimitive → XmLabel → XmPushButton
Class Pointer:	xmPushButtonWidgetClass
Functions/Macros:	XmCreatePushButton(), XmIsPushButton()

New Resources

PushButton defines the following resources:

Name	Class	Type	Default	Access
XmNarmColor	XmCArmColor	Pixel	dynamic	CSG
XmNarmPixmap	XmCArmPixmap	Pixmap	XmUNSPECIFIED_PIXMAP	CSG
XmNdefaultButtonShadow-Thickness	XmCDefaultButtonShadow-Thickness	Dimension	0	CSG
XmNfillOnArm	XmCFillOnArm	Boolean	True	CSG
XmNmultiClick	XmCMultiClick	unsigned char	dynamic	CSG
XmNshowAsDefault	XmCShowAsDefault	Dimension	0	CSG

XmNarmColor

The color with which the armed button is filled. For a color display, the default color is a shade between the bottom shadow color and the background color. For a monochrome display, the default is the foreground color, and label text is switched to the background color. This resource is in effect only when XmNfillOnArm is set to True.

XmNarmPixmap

The pixmap that identifies the button when it is armed (and when its XmNlabelType is XmPIXMAP). For a PushButton in a menu, this resource is disabled.

XmNdefaultButtonShadowThickness

The width of the shadow used to indicate a default PushButton.

XmNfillOnArm

If True (default), the PushButton widget fills the button (when armed) with the color specified by XmNarmColor. If False, the PushButton widget only switches the top and bottom shadow colors. For a PushButton in a menu, this resource is disabled (and assumed to be False).

XmNmultiClick

A flag that determines whether successive button clicks are processed (by incrementing the callback structure's click count argument) or are ignored. Possible values:

```
XmMULTICLICK_DISCARD    /* ignore successive button clicks; default value in a menu system */
XmMULTICLICK_KEEP       /* count successive button clicks; default value when not in a menu */
```

XmNshowAsDefault

Indicates the default PushButton by displaying a shadow. (In a menu, this resource is disabled.) This resource works in different ways:

- If the width of the shadow is already set in the XmNdefaultButtonShadowThickness resource, then XmNshowAsDefault behaves like a Boolean: that is, with a value of 0, no shadow is displayed; with a value greater than 0, a shadow is displayed.

- If the width of the shadow has *not* been set in the XmNdefaultButtonShadowThickness resource (i.e., it has a value of 0), then XmNshowAsDefault performs double duty: that is, a value greater than 0 says to highlight the PushButton as the default button *and* to use this value as the thickness of the shadow.

Callback Resources

PushButton defines the following callback resources:

Callback	Reason Constant
XmNactivateCallback	XmCR_ACTIVATE
XmNarmCallback	XmCR_ARM
XmNdisarmCallback	XmCR_DISARM

Callback Structure

Each callback function is passed the following structure:

```
typedef struct
{
    int      reason;        /* the reason that the callback was called */
    XEvent   * event;       /* points to event structure that triggered callback */
    int      click_count;   /* number of multi-clicks */
} XmPushButtonCallbackStruct;
```

click_count is meaningful only for XmNactivateCallback. Furthermore, if the XmNmultiClick resource is set to XmMULTICLICK_KEEP, then XmNactivateCallback is called for each click, and the value of click_count is the number of clicks that have occurred in the last sequence of multiple clicks. If the XmNmultiClick resource is set to XmMULTICLICK_DISCARD, then click_count always has a value of 1.

Inherited Resources

PushButton inherits the following resources. The resources are listed alphabetically, along with the superclass that defines them.

Resource	Inherited From	Resource	Inherited From
XmNaccelerator	Label	XmNlabelString	Label
XmNaccelerators	Core	XmNlabelType	Label
XmNacceleratorText	Label	XmNmappedWhenManaged	Core
XmNalignment	Label	XmNmarginBottom	Label
XmNancestorSensitive	Core	XmNmarginHeight	Label
XmNbackground	Core	XmNmarginLeft	Label
XmNbackgroundPixmap	Core	XmNmarginRight	Label
XmNborderColor	Core	XmNmarginTop	Label
XmNborderPixmap	Core	XmNmarginWidth	Label
XmNborderWidth	Core	XmNmnemonic	Label
XmNbottomShadowColor	Primitive	XmNmnemonicCharSet	Label
XmNbottomShadowPixmap	Primitive	XmNnavigationType	Primitive
XmNcolormap	Core	XmNrecomputeSize	Label
XmNdepth	Core	XmNscreen	Core
XmNdestroyCallback	Core	XmNsensitive	Core
XmNfontList	Label	XmNshadowThickness	Primitive
XmNforeground	Primitive	XmNstringDirection	Label
XmNheight	Core	XmNtopShadowColor	Primitive
XmNhelpCallback	Primitive	XmNtopShadowPixmap	Primitive
XmNhighlightColor	Primitive	XmNtranslations	Core
XmNhighlightOnEnter	Primitive	XmNtraversalOn	Primitive
XmNhighlightPixmap	Primitive	XmNunitType	Primitive
XmNhighlightThickness	Primitive	XmNuserData	Primitive
XmNinitialResourcesPersistent	Core	XmNwidth	Core
XmNlabelInsensitivePixmap	Label	XmNx	Core
XmNlabelPixmap	Label	XmNy	Core

Translations

For PushButtons outside a menu system:		For PushButtons in a menu system:	
BSelect Press	Arm()	BSelect Press	BtnDown()
BSelect Click	Activate()		
	Disarm()		
BSelect Release	Activate()	BSelect Release	BtnUp()
	Disarm()		
BSelect Press 2+	MultiArm()		
BSelect Release 2+	MultiActivate()		
	Disarm()		
KActivate	ArmAndActivate()	KActivate	ArmAndActivate()
KSelect	ArmAndActivate()	KSelect	ArmAndActivate()
KHelp	Help()	MAny KCancel	MenuShellPopdownOne()

Action Routines

PushButton defines the following action routines:

Activate() Displays the PushButton as unarmed, and invokes the list of callbacks specified by XmNactivateCallback. The button's appearance may depend on the values of the resources XmNfillOnArm and XmNlabelPixmap.

Arm() Displays the PushButton as armed, and invokes the list of callbacks specified by XmNarmCallback. The button's appearance may depend on the values of the resources XmNarmColor and XmNarmPixmap.

ArmAndActivate()

When the PushButton is in a menu, this action unposts the menu hierarchy and invokes the callbacks specified by the resources XmNarmCallback, XmNactivateCallback, and finally, XmNdisarmCallback.

When the PushButton is not in a menu, this action displays the PushButton as armed (as determined by the values of the resources XmNarmColor and XmNarmPixmap) and (assuming the button is not yet armed) invokes the list of callbacks specified by XmNarmCallback. After this occurs, the action displays the PushButton as unarmed and invokes the callbacks specified in XmNactivateCallback and XmNdisarmCallback.

BtnDown() Unposts any menus that were posted by the parent menu of the PushButton, changes from keyboard traversal to mouse traversal, displays the PushButton as armed, and (assuming the button is not yet armed) invokes the callbacks specified by XmNarmCallback.

BtnUp() Unposts the menu hierarchy, activates the PushButton, and invokes first the callbacks specified by XmNactivateCallback and then those specified by XmNdisarmCallback.

Disarm() Invokes the callbacks specified by XmNdisarmCallback.

Help() Unposts the menu hierarchy, restores the previous keyboard focus, and invokes the callbacks specified by the XmNhelpCallback resource.

MenuShellPopdownOne()

Unposts the current menu and (unless the menu is a pulldown submenu) restores keyboard focus to the tab group or widget that previously had it. In a top-level pulldown menu pane attached to a menu bar, this action routine also disarms the cascade button and the menu bar.

MultiActivate()

Increments the *click_count* member of XmPushButtonCallbackStruct, displays the PushButton as unarmed (as determined by the resources XmNfillOnArm and Xm-NlabelPixmap), and invokes first the callbacks specified by XmNactivateCallback and then those specified by XmNdisarmCallback. This action routine takes effect only when the XmNmultiClick resource is set to XmMULTICLICK_KEEP.

MultiArm() Displays the PushButton as armed (as determined by the resources XmNarm-Color and XmNarmPixmap) and invokes the list of callbacks specified by Xm-NarmCallback. This action routine takes effect only when the XmNmultiClick resource is set to XmMULTICLICK_KEEP.

PushButton has additional behavior associated with <EnterWindow> and <LeaveWindow>, which draw the shadow in the armed or unarmed state, respectively.

PushButtonGadget

The gadget variant of PushButton.

Class Information

Include File:	*<Xm/PushBG.h>*
Class Name:	XmPushButtonGadget
Class Hierarchy:	Object → RectObj → XmGadget → XmLabelGadget → XmPush-ButtonGadget
Class Pointer:	xmPushButtonGadgetClass
Functions/Macros:	XmCreatePushButtonGadget(), XmIsPushButtonGadget()

PushButtonGadget's new resources, callback resources, and callback structure are the same as those for PushButton.

Inherited Resources

PushButtonGadget inherits the following resources. The resources are listed alphabetically, along with the superclass that defines them.

Resource	Inherited From	Resource	Inherited From
XmNaccelerator	LabelGadget	XmNmarginLeft	LabelGadget
XmNacceleratorText	LabelGadget	XmNmarginRight	LabelGadget
XmNalignment	LabelGadget	XmNmarginTop	LabelGadget
XmNancestorSensitive	RectObj	XmNmarginWidth	LabelGadget
XmNborderWidth	RectObj	XmNmnemonic	LabelGadget

Resource	Inherited From	Resource	Inherited From
XmNdestroyCallback	Object	XmNmnemonicCharSet	LabelGadget
XmNfontList	LabelGadget	XmNnavigationType	Gadget
XmNheight	RectObj	XmNrecomputeSize	LabelGadget
XmNhelpCallback	Gadget	XmNsensitive	RectObj
XmNhighlightOnEnter	Gadget	XmNshadowThickness	Gadget
XmNhighlightThickness	Gadget	XmNstringDirection	LabelGadget
XmNlabelInsensitivePixmap	LabelGadget	XmNtraversalOn	Gadget
XmNlabelPixmap	LabelGadget	XmNunitType	Gadget
XmNlabelString	LabelGadget	XmNuserData	Gadget
XmNlabelType	LabelGadget	XmNwidth	RectObj
XmNmarginBottom	LabelGadget	XmNx	RectObj
XmNmarginHeight	LabelGadget	XmNy	RectObj

Behavior

As a gadget subclass, PushButtonGadget has no translations associated with it. However, PushButtonGadget behavior corresponds to the action routines of the PushButton widget. See the PushButton action routines for more information.

Behavior	Equivalent PushButton Action Routine
BSelect Press	Arm()
	BtnDown() (in a menu)
BSelect Click or BSelect Release	Activate(), Disarm()
	BtnUp() (in a menu)
BSelect Press 2+	MultiArm()
BSelect Release 2+	MultiActivate(), Disarm()
KActivate or KSelect	ArmAndActivate()
KHelp	Help()
MAny KCancel	MenuShellPopdownOne()

PushButtonGadget has additional behavior associated with <Enter> and <Leave>, which draw the shadow in the armed or unarmed state, respectively.

QuestionDialog

A convenience widget created by a call to XmCreateQuestionDialog() and consisting of a DialogShell with a MessageBox widget as its child. The MessageBox resource XmNdialogType is set to XmDIALOG_QUESTION. The include file is *<Xm/MessageB.h>*. A QuestionDialog includes three components: a symbol (by default, a question mark), a message, and three buttons (whose labels by default are Ok, Cancel, and Help).

RadioBox

A manager that contains ToggleButtonGadget (or ToggleButton) children, only one of which may be selected at a given time. Like a CheckBox, a RadioBox is a RowColumn widget whose XmNrowColumnType resource is set to XmWORK_AREA. Unlike a CheckBox, a Radio-Box sets the RowColumn resource XmNradioAlwaysOne to True (meaning that a button is initially selected as the default) and sets the ToggleButtonGadget resources XmNvisibleWhen-Off to True and XmNindicatorType to XmONE_OF_MANY. A RadioBox can be created by a call to XmCreateRadioBox(), XmCreateSimpleRadioBox(), or XmVaCreateSimpleRadioBox(), which are defined in *<Xm/RowColumn.h>*.

RectObj

A supporting superclass for widgets and gadgets. A RectObj encapsulates the mechanisms for geometry management and is never instantiated.

Class Information

Include File:	*<Xm/RectObj.h>*
Class Name:	RectObj
Class Hierarchy:	Object → RectObj
Class Pointer:	rectObjClass
Functions/Macros:	XtIsRectObj()

New Resources

RectObj defines the following resources:

Name	Class	Type	Default	Access
XmNancestorSensitive	XmCSensitive	Boolean	dynamic	G
XmNborderWidth	XmCBorderWidth	Dimension	1	CSG
XmNheight	XmCHeight	Dimension	dynamic	CSG
XmNsensitive	XmCSensitive	Boolean	True	CSG
XmNwidth	XmCWidth	Dimension	dynamic	CSG
XmNx	XmCPosition	Position	0	CSG
XmNy	XmCPosition	Position	0	CSG

XmNancestorSensitive
> Tells whether a gadget's immediate parent should receive input. Default value is the bitwise AND of the XmNsensitive and XmNancestorSensitive resources of the parent.

XmNborderWidth
> Width (in pixels) of the window's border.

XmNheight

Window height (in pixels), excluding the border.

XmNsensitive

Tells whether a gadget receives input (is sensitive). The XtSetSensitive() routine can be used to change a widget's sensitivity and to guarantee that if a parent has its Xm-Nsensitive resource set to False, then its children will have their ancestor-sensitive flag set correctly.

XmNwidth

Window width (in pixels), excluding the border.

XmNx

The x-coordinate of the widget's upper-left outer corner, relative to the upper-left inner corner of its parent.

XmNy

The y-coordinate of the widget's upper-left outer corner, relative to the upper-left inner corner of its parent.

Inherited Resources

RectObj inherits the following resource.

Resource	Inherited From
XmNdestroyCallback	Object

RowColumn

Provides an area in which children belonging to any widget type are displayed in rows and columns. RowColumn is a general-purpose manager widget class that can be configured into many layouts, such as a MenuBar, PopupMenu, PulldownMenu, or OptionMenu.

Class Information

Include File:	*<Xm/RowColumn.h>*
Class Name:	XmRowColumn
Class Hierarchy:	Core → Composite → Constraint → XmManager → XmRowColumn
Class Pointer:	xmRowColumnWidgetClass
Functions/Macros:	XmCreateMenuBar(), XmCreateOptionMenu(), XmCreatePopupMenu(), XmCreatePulldownMenu(), XmCreateRadioBox(), XmCreateRowColumn(), XmCreateSimpleCheckBox(), XmCreateSimpleMenuBar(), XmCreateSimpleOptionMenu(), XmCreateSimplePopupMenu(), XmCreateSimplePulldownMenu(), XmCreateSimpleRadioBox(), XmCreateWorkArea(), XmVaCreateSimpleCheckBox(), XmVaCreateSimpleMenuBar(), XmVaCreateSimpleOptionMenu(), XmVaCreateSimplePopupMenu(), XmVaCreateSimplePulldownMenu(), XmVaCreateSimpleRadioBox(), XmIsRowColumn()

New Resources

RowColumn defines the following resources:

Name	Class	Type	Default	Access
XmNadjustLast	XmCAdjustLast	Boolean	True	CSG
XmNadjustMargin	XmCAdjustMargin	Boolean	True	CSG
XmNentryAlignment	XmCAlignment	unsigned char	See below	CSG
XmNentryBorder	XmCEntryBorder	Dimension	0	CSG
XmNentryClass	XmCEntryClass	WidgetClass	dynamic	CSG
XmNisAligned	XmCIsAligned	Boolean	True	CSG
XmNisHomogeneous	XmCIsHomogeneous	Boolean	dynamic	CSG
XmNlabelString	XmCXmString	XmString	NULL	C
XmNmarginHeight	XmCMarginHeight	Dimension	dynamic	CSG
XmNmarginWidth	XmCMarginWidth	Dimension	dynamic	CSG
XmNmenuAccelerator	XmCAccelerators	String	dynamic	CSG
XmNmenuHelpWidget	XmCMenuWidget	Widget	NULL	CSG
XmNmenuHistory	XmCMenuWidget	Widget	NULL	CSG
XmNmenuPost	XmCMenuPost	String	NULL	CSG
XmNmnemonic	XmCMnemonic	KeySym	NULL	CSG
XmNmnemonicCharSet	XmCMnemonicCharSet	String	dynamic	CSG
XmNnumColumns	XmCNumColumns	short	1	CSG
XmNorientation	XmCOrientation	unsigned char	dynamic	CSG
XmNpacking	XmCPacking	unsigned char	dynamic	CSG
XmNpopupEnabled	XmCPopupEnabled	Boolean	True	CSG
XmNradioAlwaysOne	XmCRadioAlwaysOne	Boolean	True	CSG
XmNradioBehavior	XmCRadioBehavior	Boolean	False	CSG
XmNresizeHeight	XmCResizeHeight	Boolean	True	CSG
XmNresizeWidth	XmCResizeWidth	Boolean	True	CSG
XmNrowColumnType	XmCRowColumnType	unsigned char	XmWORK_AREA	CG
XmNspacing	XmCSpacing	Dimension	dynamic	CSG
XmNsubMenuId	XmCMenuWidget	Widget	NULL	CSG
XmNwhichButton	XmCWhichButton	unsigned int	dynamic	CSG

Xt and Motif
Widget Classes

XmNadjustLast

> If True (default), the last row (or column) in the RowColumn widget is expanded so as to be flush with the edge.

XmNadjustMargin

> If True (default), text in each row (or column) will align with other text in its row (or column). This is done by forcing the margin resources (defined by the Label widget) to have the same value. For example, in a horizontally-oriented Row-Column widget, all items will have the same value for XmNmarginTop and Xm-NmarginBottom; in a vertically-oriented RowColumn widget, all items will have the same value for XmNmarginLeft and XmNmarginRight.

XmNentryAlignment

> When XmNisAligned is True, this resource tells RowColumn children how to align. The children must be subclasses of XmLabel or XmLabelGadget. Possible values:

```
XmALIGNMENT_BEGINNING        /* default */
XmALIGNMENT_CENTER
XmALIGNMENT_END
```

XmNentryBorder

The border width of a RowColumn widget's children.

XmNentryClass

The widget class to which children must belong when being added to a Row-Column widget. This resource is used only when the XmNisHomogeneous resource is set to True. XmNentryClass ensures that a MenuBar will have only cascade button children and that a RadioBox will have only toggle button children (or gadget variants of each class). XmNentryClass can have one of two default values. For a MenuBar, the default value is xmCascadeButtonWidgetClass. For a RadioBox, the default value is xmToggleButtonGadgetClass. Possible values:

```
xmToggleButtonGadgetClass    /* for type XmWORK_AREA with XmNradioBehavior True */
xmCascadeButtonWidgetClass   /* for type XmMENU_BAR */
```

XmNisAligned

If True, enable the alignment specified in the XmNentryAlignment resource. Alignment is ignored in a label whose parent is a popup or pulldown MenuPane.

XmNisHomogeneous

If True, enforce the condition that all RowColumn children belong to the same class (the class specified by the XmNentryClass resource). When creating a RadioBox or a MenuBar, the default value of this resource is True; otherwise, it's False.

XmNlabelString

A label used only in option menus. A text string displays beside the selection area. By default, there is no label.

XmNmarginHeight
XmNmarginWidth

The spacing between an edge of the RowColumn widget and its nearest child. In popup and pulldown menus, the default is 0; in other types of RowColumn widgets, the default is 3 pixels.

XmNmenuAccelerator

A pointer to a string that specifies an accelerator (keyboard shortcut) for use only in RowColumn widgets of type XmMENU_POPUP or XmMENU_BAR. In a popup menu, typing the accelerator posts the menu; in a menu bar, typing the accelerator highlights the first item and enables traversal in the menu bar. The string's format is like that of a translation but allows only a single key press event to be specified. The default value of this resource is KMenu (for popup menus) and KMenuBar (for menu bars).

XmNmenuHelpWidget

The widget ID of the CascadeButton widget that serves as the Help button. This resource is meaningful only in RowColumn widgets of type XmMENU_BAR.

XmNmenuHistory

The widget ID of the most recently activated menu entry. Since the most recently activated menu entry is also the choice that displays in an OptionMenu, this resource is useful for indicating the current selection in a RowColumn widget of type XmMENU_OPTION. In a RowColumn widget whose XmNradioBehavior resource is set to True, the XmNmenuHistory resource indicates the last toggle button to change from unselected to selected.

XmNmenuPost

The string that describes the event for posting a menu. The default value depends on the type of RowColumn widget: for XmMENU_POPUP, the default is BMenu Press; for XmMENU_OPTION, XmMENU_BAR, and XmWORK_AREA the default is BSelect Press; for XmMENU_PULLDOWN, this resource isn't meaningful.

XmNmnemonic

The keysym of the key to press (in combination with the MAlt modifier) in order to post the pulldown menu associated with an option menu. This resource is meaningful only in option menus. In the label string, the first character matching this keysym will be underlined.

XmNmnemonicCharSet

The character set for the option menu's mnemonic. The default value depends on the current language environment.

XmNnumColumns

The number of columns (in a vertically-oriented RowColumn widget) or the number of rows (in a horizontally-oriented RowColumn widget). This resource is meaningful only when the XmNpacking resource is set to XmPACK_COLUMN.

XmNorientation

The direction for laying out the rows and columns of children of a RowColumn widget. For all RowColumn widgets except a MenuBar, the default value is Xm-VERTICAL. Possible values:

```
XmVERTICAL              /* top-to-bottom creation */
XmHORIZONTAL            /* left-to-right creation */
```

XmNpacking

The method of spacing the items placed within a RowColumn widget. The default value is XmPACK_COLUMN for a RadioBox, and XmPACK_TIGHT for other types of RowColumn widget. Possible values:

```
XmPACK_TIGHT            /* give each box minimum sizing */
XmPACK_COLUMN           /* pad boxes to align if needed */
XmPACK_NONE             /* widget accommodates placement */
```

XmNpopupEnabled

If True (default), keyboard shortcuts are in effect for popup menus. Set this resource to False if you want to disable accelerators and mnemonics in popup menus.

XmNradioAlwaysOne

This resource is effective only when the XmNradioBehavior resource is True. Xm-NradioAlwaysOne, when set to True (default), ensures that one of the toggle buttons is always selected. Once this button is selected, clicking on it will not deselect it; it can be deselected only by selecting another toggle button. If XmNradioAlwaysOne is False, a selected toggle button can be deselected by clicking on it or by selecting another button.

XmNradioBehavior

If True, the RowColumn widget acts like a RadioBox by setting two of the resources for its toggle button children. Namely, the XmNindicatorType resource defaults to XmONE_OF_MANY, and the XmNvisibleWhenOff resource defaults to True. The default value of the XmNradioBehavior resource is False, unless the RowColumn widget was created with the XmCreateRadioBox() routine.

XmNresizeHeight
XmNresizeWidth

If True (default), the widget requests a new height or width when necessary. If False, no resize requests are made.

XmNrowColumnType

The type of RowColumn widget to create. You can't change this resource after it's set. Convenience routines create a RowColumn widget of the appropriate type. Possible values:

XmWORK_AREA	XmMENU_PULLDOWN
XmMENU_BAR	XmMENU_OPTION
XmMENU_POPUP	

XmNspacing

The horizontal and vertical spacing between children in the RowColumn widget. For RowColumn widgets of type XmOPTION_MENU or XmWORK_AREA, the default value is 3 pixels; for other RowColumn types, the default is 0.

XmNsubMenuId

The widget ID for the pulldown menu pane to be associated with an OptionMenu. This resource is meaningful only in RowColumn widgets of type Xm-MENU_OPTION.

XmNwhichButton

This resource has been superseded by the XmNmenuPost resource but is retained for compatibility with older releases of Motif.

Callback Resources

RowColumn defines the following callback resources:

Callback	Reason Constant
XmNentryCallback	XmCR_ACTIVATE
XmNmapCallback	XmCR_MAP
XmNunmapCallback	XmCR_UNMAP

Callback Structure

Each callback function is passed the following structure:

```
typedef struct
{
    int        reason;          /* the reason that the callback was called */
    XEvent    * event;          /* points to event structure that triggered callback */
    Widget     widget;          /* ID of activated RowColumn item */
    char      * data;           /* value of application's client data */
    char      * callbackstruct; /* created when item is activated */
} XmRowColumnCallbackStruct;
```

The structure members *widget*, *data*, and *callbackstruct* are meaningful only when the callback reason is XmCR_ACTIVATE; otherwise, these structure members are set to NULL.

callbackstruct points to a structure that is created by the activation callback of the Row-Column item.

Simple Menu Creation Resources

The following resources are used with the simple menu creation routines.

Name	Class	Type	Default	Access
XmNbuttonAccelerators	XmCButtonAccelerators	StringTable	NULL	C
XmNbuttonAcceleratorText	XmCButtonAcceleratorText	XmStringTable	NULL	C
XmNbuttonCount	XmCButtonCount	int	0	C
XmNbuttonMnemonicCharSets	XmCButtonMnemonicCharSets	XmStringCharSetTable	NULL	C
XmNbuttonMnemonics	XmCButtonMnemonics	XmKeySymTable	NULL	C
XmNbuttons	XmCButtons	XmStringTable	NULL	C
XmNbuttonSet	XmCButtonSet	int	-1	C
XmNbuttonType	XmCButtonType	XmButtonTypeTable	NULL	C
XmNoptionLabel	XmCOptionLabel	XmString	NULL	C
XmNoptionMnemonic	XmCOptionMnemonic	KeySym	NULL	C
XmNpostFromButton	XmCPostFromButton	int	-1	C

XmNbuttonAccelerators

A list of accelerators, containing one item for each created title, separator, and button.

XmNbuttonAcceleratorText

A list of compound strings that represent the accelerators for the created buttons. The list contains one item for each created title, separator, and button.

XmNbuttonCount

The number of titles, separators, and menu buttons to create.

XmNbuttonMnemonicCharSets

A list of character sets to use for displaying button mnemonics. The list contains an item for each created title, separator, and button.

XmNbuttonMnemonics

A list of mnemonics associated with the buttons created. The list contains one item for each created title, separator, and button.

XmNbuttons

A list of compound strings that will serve as labels for the created buttons. The list contains one item for each created title, separator, and button.

XmNbuttonSet

The numeric position of the button to be initially set within a RadioBox or within an OptionMenu's pulldown submenu. The first button is specified as 0.

XmNbuttonType

A list of button types for the created buttons. The list contains one item for each created title, separator, and button. If this resource is not set, the buttons created will be CascadeButtonGadgets in a MenuBar and PushButtonGadgets in other types of RowColumn widget. The XmNbuttonType resource is an enumerated type whose possible values are:

XmPUSHBUTTON   XmCASCADEBUTTON   XmDOUBLE_SEPARATOR
XmCHECKBUTTON   XmRADIOBUTTON   XmSEPARATOR
XmTITLE

XmNoptionLabel

A compound string with which to label the left side of an option menu.

XmNoptionMnemonic

The keysym of the key to press (in combination with the MAlt modifier) in order to post the pulldown menu associated with an option menu.

XmNpostFromButton

The numeric position of the cascade button (in the parent) from which the pulldown submenu is attached and subsequently posted. The first button is specified as 0.

Inherited Resources

RowColumn inherits the following resources. The resources are listed alphabetically, along with the superclass that defines them.

Resource	Inherited From	Resource	Inherited From
XmNaccelerators	Core	XmNinitialResourcesPersistent	Core
XmNancestorSensitive	Core	XmNinsertPosition	Composite
XmNbackground	Core	XmNmappedWhenManaged	Core
XmNbackgroundPixmap	Core	XmNnavigationType	Manager
XmNborderColor	Core	XmNnumChildren	Composite
XmNborderPixmap	Core	XmNscreen	Core
XmNborderWidth	Core	XmNsensitive	Core
XmNbottomShadowColor	Manager	XmNshadowThickness	Manager
XmNbottomShadowPixmap	Manager	XmNstringDirection	Manager
XmNchildren	Composite	XmNtopShadowColor	Manager
XmNcolormap	Core	XmNtopShadowPixmap	Manager
XmNdepth	Core	XmNtranslations	Core
XmNdestroyCallback	Core	XmNtraversalOn	Manager
XmNforeground	Manager	XmNunitType	Manager
XmNheight	Core	XmNuserData	Manager

Resource	Inherited From	Resource	Inherited From
XmNhelpCallback	Manager	XmNwidth	Core
XmNhighlightColor	Manager	XmNx	Core
XmNhighlightPixmap	Manager	XmNy	Core

Translations

The value of the XmNrowColumnType resource determines the available translations.

When XmNrowColumnType is XmWORK_AREA, RowColumn's translations are the traversal translations inherited from the Manager widget.

When XmNrowColumnType is XmMENU_OPTION, RowColumn's translations are the traversal translations inherited from the Manager widget, as well as the following:

BSelect Press	MenuBtnDown()
BSelect Release	MenuBtnUp()
KActivate	ManagerGadgetSelect()
KSelect	ManagerGadgetSelect()
KHelp	Help()

When XmNrowColumnType is XmMENU_BAR, XmMENU_PULLDOWN, or XmMENU_POPUP, RowColumn's translations are the five listed above, as well as the following:

KLeft	MenuGadgetTraverseLeft()
KRight	MenuGadgetTraverseRight()
KUp	MenuGadgetTraverseUp()
KDown	MenuGadgetTraverseDown()
MAny KCancel	MenuGadgetEscape()

Action Routines

RowColumn defines the following action routines:

Help()   Invokes any callbacks specified by the XmNhelpCallback resource.

ManagerGadgetSelect()
Arms and activates the gadget child (in a menu) that has focus. For a CascadeButtonGadget, its submenu is posted; for other gadget children, the menu hierarchy is unposted.

MenuBtnDown()
In a gadget child (in a menu), unposts any menus that were posted by the gadget's parent menu, turns mouse traversal on, and arms the gadget. If the child is a CascadeButtonGadget, its submenu is posted.

MenuBtnUp()
In a gadget child (in a menu), unposts the menu hierarchy and activates the gadget. If the child is a CascadeButtonGadget, this action posts the submenu and turns on keyboard traversal in the submenu.

MenuGadgetEscape()

Unposts the current menu and (unless the menu is a pulldown submenu) restores keyboard focus to the tab group or widget that previously had it (assuming an explicit focus policy). In a top-level pulldown menu pane attached to a menu bar, this action routine also disarms the cascade button and the menu bar.

When applied within a vertical menu:

MenuGadgetTraverseDown()

Disarms the current menu item and arms the item below it, wrapping around to the top if necessary.

MenuGadgetTraverseUp()

Disarms the current menu item and arms the item above it, wrapping around to the bottom if necessary.

MenuGadgetTraverseLeft()

1. If the parent menu is horizontal:
   (a) Unposts the current menu (vertical, in this case), (b) traverses left in the parent menu (wrapping around to the right if necessary), and, if this next item is a CascadeButton, (c) posts its submenu.

2. If the parent menu is vertical:
   Unposts the current menu (but does not traverse).

MenuGadgetTraverseRight()

1. If the current item is a CascadeButton with a submenu:
   Posts the submenu.

2. Otherwise, this action finds the nearest ancestor that is a horizontal menu and (like MenuGadgetTraverseLeft()):
   (a) Unposts the current menu (vertical, in this case), (b) traverses right in the parent menu (wrapping around to the left if necessary), and, if this next item is a CascadeButton, (c) posts its submenu.

When applied within a horizontal menu:

MenuGadgetTraverseDown()

1. If the current item is a CascadeButton with a submenu:
   Posts the submenu.

2. Otherwise, this action finds the nearest ancestor that is a vertical menu and does the following:
   (a) Unposts the current menu (horizontal, in this case), (b) traverses down in the parent menu (wrapping around to the top if necessary), and, if this next item is a CascadeButton, (c) posts its submenu.

MenuGadgetTraverseUp()

1. If the parent menu is vertical:
   (a) Unposts the current menu (horizontal, in this case), (b) traverses up in the parent menu (wrapping around to the bottom if necessary), and, if this next item is a CascadeButton, (c) posts its submenu.

2. If the parent menu is horizontal:
    Unposts the current menu (but does not traverse).

MenuGadgetTraverseLeft()
Disarms the current menu item and arms the item to its left, wrapping around to the right if necessary.

MenuGadgetTraverseRight()
Disarms the current menu item and arms the item to its right, wrapping around to the left if necessary.

RowColumn has additional menu behavior:

KMenuBar In a menu bar or in any menu pane cascaded from it, unposts the menu tree and (under an explicit focus policy) returns keyboard focus to the tab group that had it before entering the menu tree. In other non-popup menu panes, turns on keyboard traversal and sets the focus to the first menu bar item.

KMenu Pops up the menu associated with the keyboard focus and turns on keyboard traversal. In a popup menu system, unposts the menu tree and (under an explicit focus policy) returns keyboard focus to the tab group that had it before entering the menu tree.

Scale

A narrow, rectangular region (similar to a ScrollBar) that contains a slider. The slider's position marks a value within a range of values. Scale is a manager widget that orients its children along its axis. These children (typically labels) can be used to represent tick marks. If the Scale widget is an input-output type (XmNsensitive = True), users can change the displayed value by moving the slider. If the widget is output-only (insensitive), users cannot modify its values.

Class Information

Include File:	*<Xm/Scale.h>*
Class Name:	XmScale
Class Hierarchy:	Core → Composite → Constraint → XmManager → XmScale
Class Pointer:	xmScaleWidgetClass
Functions/Macros:	XmCreateScale(), XmScaleGetValue(), XmScaleSetValue(), XmIsScale()

New Resources

Scale defines the following resources:

Name	Class	Type	Default	Access
XmNdecimalPoints	XmCDecimalPoints	short	0	CSG
XmNfontList	XmCFontList	XmFontList	dynamic	CSG
XmNhighlightOnEnter	XmCHighlightOnEnter	Boolean	False	CSG
XmNhighlightThickness	XmCHighlightThickness	Dimension	2	CSG
XmNmaximum	XmCMaximum	int	100	CSG
XmNminimum	XmCMinimum	int	0	CSG
XmNorientation	XmCOrientation	unsigned char	XmVERTICAL	CSG
XmNprocessingDirection	XmCProcessingDirection	unsigned char	dynamic	CSG
XmNscaleHeight	XmCScaleHeight	Dimension	0	CSG
XmNscaleMultiple	XmCScaleMultiple	int	dynamic	CSG
XmNscaleWidth	XmCScaleWidth	Dimension	0	CSG
XmNshowValue	XmCShowValue	Boolean	False	CSG
XmNtitleString	XmCTitleString	XmString	NULL	CSG
XmNvalue	XmCValue	int	0	CSG

XmNdecimalPoints

A positive integer that determines how the slider's value will be displayed. The decimal point in the slider's value gets shifted to the right, and this resource specifies the number of decimal places to shift. For example, if the slider's value is 1234, then setting the XmdecimalPoints resource to 2 causes the widget to display the value as 12.34.

XmNfontList

The font list used for the text specified by the XmNtitleString resource. If this value is initially NULL, the font list is derived from the font list resource from the nearest parent that is a subclass of BulletinBoard, MenuShell, or VendorShell.

XmNhighlightOnEnter

Determines whether to draw the widget's highlighting rectangle whenever the cursor moves into the widget. This resource applies only when the shell has a focus policy of XmPOINTER. If the XmNhighlightOnEnter resource is True, highlighting is drawn; if False (default), highlighting is not drawn.

XmNhighlightThickness

The thickness of the highlighting rectangle.

XmNmaximum
XmNminimum

The maximum/minimum value of the slider.

XmNorientation

The direction in which the scale is displayed. Possible values:

```
XmVERTICAL          /* top-to-bottom creation */
XmHORIZONTAL        /* left-to-right creation */
```

XmNprocessingDirection

Determines the position at which to display the slider's maximum and minimum values, with respect to the slider. Possible values:

XmMAX_ON_TOP	/* scale increases toward top */
XmMAX_ON_BOTTOM	/* scale increases toward bottom */
XmMAX_ON_LEFT	/* scale increases toward left */
XmMAX_ON_RIGHT	/* scale increases toward right */

For vertically-oriented Scale widgets, the default value is XmMAX_ON_TOP. For horizontally-oriented Scale widgets, the default value is usually XmMAX_ON_RIGHT (depending on the value of the XmNstringDirection resource).

XmNscaleHeight
XmNscaleWidth

The height or width of the slider area.

XmNscaleMultiple

The distance to move the slider when the user moves it by a multiple increment. The default value is calculated as (XmNmaximum – XmNminimum) / 10.

XmNshowValue

If True, the label specifying the slider's current value will be displayed beside the slider. If False, the label isn't displayed.

XmNtitleString

The text string that appears as the title in the Scale widget.

XmNvalue

The current position of the slider along the scale. This resource must have a value between the values of XmNminimum and XmNmaximum.

Callback Resources

Scale defines the following callback resources:

Callback	Reason Constant
XmNdragCallback	XmCR_DRAG
XmNvalueChangedCallback	XmCR_VALUE_CHANGED

Callback Structure

Each callback function is passed the following structure:

```
typedef struct
{
    int      reason;     /* the reason that the callback was called */
    XEvent   * event;    /* points to event structure that triggered callback */
    int      value;      /* new value of the slider */
} XmScaleCallbackStruct;
```

Inherited Resources

Scale inherits the following resources. The resources are listed alphabetically, along with the superclass that defines them.

Resource	Inherited From	Resource	Inherited From
XmNaccelerators	Core	XmNinitialResourcesPersistent	Core
XmNancestorSensitive	Core	XmNinsertPosition	Composite
XmNbackground	Core	XmNmappedWhenManaged	Core
XmNbackgroundPixmap	Core	XmNnavigationType	Manager
XmNborderColor	Core	XmNnumChildren	Composite
XmNborderPixmap	Core	XmNscreen	Core
XmNborderWidth	Core	XmNsensitive	Core
XmNbottomShadowColor	Manager	XmNshadowThickness	Manager
XmNbottomShadowPixmap	Manager	XmNstringDirection	Manager
XmNchildren	Composite	XmNtopShadowColor	Manager
XmNcolormap	Core	XmNtopShadowPixmap	Manager
XmNdepth	Core	XmNtranslations	Core
XmNdestroyCallback	Core	XmNtraversalOn	Manager
XmNforeground	Manager	XmNunitType	Manager
XmNheight	Core	XmNuserData	Manager
XmNhelpCallback	Manager	XmNwidth	Core
XmNhighlightColor	Manager	XmNx	Core
XmNhighlightPixmap	Manager	XmNy	Core

Behavior

Scale has no translations, but button and mouse events affect Scale widgets in a way similar to that of ScrollBar widgets. The only difference is that Scale widgets do not have the callback resources XmNincrementCallback, XmNdecrementCallback, XmNpageIncrementCallback, XmNpageDecrementCallback, XmNtoTopCallback, or XmNtoBottomCallback, so for any event that invokes one of these ScrollBar callbacks, the same event in a Scale widget invokes the callbacks in XmNvalueChangedCallback. For a description of Scale behavior, see the translations and actions described under ScrollBar.

ScrollBar

Although the ScrollBar can be created and used as a standalone widget, it is normally used in a ScrolledWindow widget to allow users to reposition data that doesn't all fit into a viewing window. The ScrollBar consists of a rectangular strip (the "scroll region") with an arrow placed on each end. Within the scroll region is a smaller, movable rectangle called the slider. To scroll the data, users can click one of the arrows, click in the scroll region, or drag the slider. The application typically sets the XmNsliderSize resource such that the size of the slider relative to the size of the scroll region corresponds to the percentage of total data that is currently displayed.

Class Information

Include File:	*<Xm/ScrollBar.h>*
Class Name:	XmScrollBar
Class Hierarchy:	Core → XmPrimitive → XmScrollBar
Class Pointer:	xmScrollBarWidgetClass
Functions/Macros:	XmCreateScrollBar(), XmScrollBarGetValues(), XmScrollBarSetValues(), XmIsScrollBar()

New Resources

ScrollBar defines the following resources:

Name	Class	Type	Default	Access
XmNincrement	XmCIncrement	int	1	CSG
XmNinitialDelay	XmCInitialDelay	int	250	CSG
XmNmaximum	XmCMaximum	int	100	CSG
XmNminimum	XmCMinimum	int	0	CSG
XmNorientation	XmCOrientation	unsigned char	XmVERTICAL	CSG
XmNpageIncrement	XmCPageIncrement	int	10	C
XmNprocessingDirection	XmCProcessingDirection	unsigned char	dynamic	CSG
XmNrepeatDelay	XmCRepeatDelay	int	50	CSG
XmNshowArrows	XmCShowArrows	Boolean	True	CSG
XmNsliderSize	XmCSliderSize	int	dynamic	CSG
XmNtroughColor	XmCTroughColor	Pixel	dynamic	CSG
XmNvalue	XmCValue	int	0	CSG

XmNincrement

    The amount the value changes due to the user's moving the slider one increment.

XmNinitialDelay

    The number of milliseconds a button must remain pressed before triggering continuous slider movement.

XmNmaximum
XmNminimum

    The maximum/minimum value of the slider.

XmNorientation

    The direction in which the scale is displayed. Possible values:

    XmVERTICAL   /* top-to-bottom creation */
    XmHORIZONTAL   /* left-to-right creation */

XmNpageIncrement

    The amount the value changes due to the user's moving the slider one page increment.

XmNprocessingDirection

    Determines the position at which to display the slider's maximum and minimum values, with respect to the slider. Possible values:

XmMAX_ON_TOP	/* scale increases toward top */
XmMAX_ON_BOTTOM	/* scale increases toward bottom */
XmMAX_ON_LEFT	/* scale increases toward left */
XmMAX_ON_RIGHT	/* scale increases toward right */

For vertically oriented ScrollBar widgets, the default value is XmMAX_ON_TOP. For horizontally oriented ScrollBar widgets, the default value is usually Xm-MAX_ON_RIGHT (depending on the value of the XmNstringDirection resource).

XmNrepeatDelay

The number of milliseconds a button must remain pressed before continuing further slider motions, once the XmNinitialDelay time has been triggered.

XmNshowArrows

If True, arrows are displayed; if False, they are not.

XmNsliderSize

The slider's length. The length ranges from 1 to the value of XmNmaximum – XmNminimum. By default, the value is computed to be:

(XmNmaximum – XmNminimum) / 10.

XmNtroughColor

The color of the slider's trough.

XmNvalue

The slider's position. The position ranges from the value of XmNminimum to the value of (XmNmaximum – XmNsliderSize).

Callback Resources

ScrollBar defines the following callback resources:

Callback	Reason Constant
XmNvalueChangedCallback	XmCR_VALUE_CHANGED
XmNincrementCallback	XmCR_INCREMENT
XmNdecrementCallback	XmCR_DECREMENT
XmNpageIncrementCallback	XmCR_PAGE_INCREMENT
XmNpageDecrementCallback	XmCR_PAGE_DECREMENT
XmNtoTopCallback	XmCR_TO_TOP
XmNtoBottomCallback	XmCR_TO_BOTTOM
XmNdragCallback	XmCR_DRAG

Callback Structure

Each callback function is passed the following structure:

```
typedef struct
{
    int      reason;      /* the reason that the callback was called */
    XEvent   * event;     /* points to event structure that triggered callback */
    int      value;       /* value of the slider's new location */
    int      pixel;       /* coordinate where selection occurred */
} XmScrollBarCallbackStruct;
```

pixel is meaningful only when the callback reason is XmCR_TO_TOP or Xm-CR_TO_BOTTOM. The *pixel* member specifies the location at which the mouse button selection occurred, giving the x-coordinate in the case of a horizontal ScrollBar and the y-coordinate in the case of a vertical ScrollBar.

Inherited Resources

ScrollBar inherits the following resources. The resources are listed alphabetically, along with the superclass that defines them. ScrollBar resets XmNhighlightThickness from 2 to 0, XmNnavigationType from XmNONE to XmSTICKY_TAB_GROUP, and XmNtraversalOn to False.

Resource	Inherited From	Resource	Inherited From
XmNaccelerators	Core	XmNhighlightPixmap	Primitive
XmNancestorSensitive	Core	XmNhighlightThickness	Primitive
XmNbackground	Core	XmNinitialResourcesPersistent	Core
XmNbackgroundPixmap	Core	XmNmappedWhenManaged	Core
XmNborderColor	Core	XmNnavigationType	Primitive
XmNborderPixmap	Core	XmNscreen	Core
XmNborderWidth	Core	XmNsensitive	Core
XmNbottomShadowColor	Primitive	XmNshadowThickness	Primitive
XmNbottomShadowPixmap	Primitive	XmNtopShadowColor	Primitive
XmNcolormap	Core	XmNtopShadowPixmap	Primitive
XmNdepth	Core	XmNtranslations	Core
XmNdestroyCallback	Core	XmNtraversalOn	Primitive
XmNforeground	Primitive	XmNunitType	Primitive
XmNheight	Core	XmNuserData	Primitive
XmNhelpCallback	Primitive	XmNwidth	Core
XmNhighlightColor	Primitive	XmNx	Core
XmNhighlightOnEnter	Primitive	XmNy	Core

Translations

The translations for ScrollBar include those from Primitive, plus the following:

Event	Action	Event	Action
BSelect Press	Select()	KRight	IncrementDownOrRight(1)
BSelect Release	Release()	MCtrl KRight	PageDownOrRight(1)
BSelect Press Moved	Moved()	KPageUp	PageUpOrLeft(0)
BDrag Press	Select()	KPageDown	PageDownOrRight(0)
BDrag Release	Release()	KPageLeft	PageUpOrLeft(1)
BDrag Press Moved	Moved()	KPageRight	PageDownOrRight(1)
MCtrl BSelect Press	TopOrBottom()	KBeginLine	TopOrBottom()
MCtrl BSelect Release	Release()	KEndLine	TopOrBottom()
KUp	IncrementUpOrLeft(0)	KBeginData	TopOrBottom()
MCtrl KUp	PageUpOrLeft(0)	KEndData	TopOrBottom()
KDown	IncrementDownOrRight(0)	KNextField	PrimitiveNextTabGroup()
MCtrl KDown	PageDownOrRight(0)	KPrevField	PrimitivePrevTabGroup()
KLeft	IncrementUpOrLeft(1)	KHelp	PrimitiveHelp()
MCtrl KLeft	PageUpOrLeft(1)		

Action Routines

ScrollBar defines the following action routines:

IncrementDownOrRight(*flag*):

Moves the slider by one increment—downward if *flag* is 0; to the right if *flag* is 1. Depending on the value of the XmNprocessingDirection resource, the slider's movement invokes the callbacks listed in either XmNincrementCallback or XmNdecrementCallback (or XmNvalueChangedCallback if the appropriate callback resource is NULL).

IncrementUpOrLeft(*flag*):

Same as IncrementDownOrRight except that the slider moves upward if *flag* is 0 and to the left if *flag* is 1.

Moved()   This action applies when the mouse button is pressed in the slider. When this is done, moving the pointer moves the slider along with it and also invokes the callbacks specified by XmNdragCallback.

PageDownOrRight(*flag*):

Moves the slider by one page increment—downward if *flag* is 0; to the right if *flag* is 1. Depending on the value of the XmNprocessingDirection resource, the slider's movement invokes the callbacks listed in either XmNpageIncrementCallback or XmNpageDecrementCallback (or XmNvalueChangedCallback if the appropriate callback resource is NULL).

PageUpOrLeft(*flag*):

Same as IncrementDownOrRight except that the slider moves upward if *flag* is 0 and to the left if *flag* is 1.

PrimitiveHelp()

Invokes the list of callbacks specified by XmNhelpCallback. If the ScrollBar doesn't have any help callbacks, the Help() routine invokes those associated with the nearest ancestor that has them.

PrimitiveNextTabGroup()
PrimitivePrevTabGroup()

Traverses to the first item in the next/previous tab group, wrapping if necessary.

Release()   If the Moved() action changes the slider's position, then the Release() action invokes the callbacks specified by XmNvalueChangedCallback.

Select()   The results of this action depend on the location in which it's applied.

- Within an arrow, this action is the same as IncrementDownOrRight() or IncrementUpOrLeft()—incrementing or decrementing according to the value of the XmNprocessingDirection resource, and invoking the appropriate increment or decrement callback.

- Within the scrolling area that lies between an arrow and the slider, this action works like the page increment action routines—moving by one page increment according to the value of the XmNprocessingDirection resource, and invoking the appropriate page increment or page decrement callback.

- Within either of these locations, keeping the button pressed repeats the incremental movement of the slider. This behavior is triggered when the duration of the button press exceeds the value of the XmNinitialDelay resource; the slider movement then repeats with a time interval specified by the XmNrepeatDelay resource.

- Within the slider, this action begins slider dragging, which is subsequently affected by the actions Moved() and Release().

TopOrBottom()

Moves the slider to its minimum value and invokes the callbacks specified by XmNtoTopCallback, or moves the slider to its maximum value and invokes the callbacks specified by XmNtoBottomCallback. The direction of the slider's movement depends on the value of the XmNprocessingDirection resource. This action can be applied using either keyboard or mouse events.

ScrolledList

Provides scrollbars for lists that are not visible all at once. ScrolledList is a convenience widget created by a call to XmCreateScrolledList() and consisting of a ScrolledWindow widget with a List widget as its child. The include file is *<Xm/List.h>*.

ScrolledText

Provides scrollbars for text that is not visible all at once. ScrolledText is a convenience widget created by a call to XmCreateScrolledText() and consisting of a ScrolledWindow widget with a Text widget as its child. The include file is *<Xm/Text.h>*.

Provides a scrollable view of data (e.g., text or graphics) that may not be visible all at once. ScrolledWindow widgets can be created to scroll automatically or to respond to user input.

Class Information

Include File:	*<Xm/ScrolledW.h>*
Class Name:	XmScrolledWindow
Class Hierarchy:	Core → Composite → Constraint → XmManager → XmScrolled-Window
Class Pointer:	xmScrolledWindowWidgetClass
Functions/Macros:	XmCreateScrolledWindow(), XmScrolledWindowSetAreas(), XmCreateScrolledList(), XmCreateScrolledText(), XmIsScrolledWindow()

New Resources

ScrolledWindow defines the following resources:

Name	Class	Type	Default	Access
XmNclipWindow	XmCClipWindow	Window	NULL	G
XmNhorizontalScrollBar	XmCHorizontalScrollBar	Widget	NULL	CSG
XmNscrollBarDisplayPolicy	XmCScrollBarDisplayPolicy	unsigned char	dynamic	CSG
XmNscrollBarPlacement	XmCScrollBarPlacement	unsigned char	XmBOTTOM_RIGHT	CSG
XmNscrolledWindowMargin-Height	XmCScrolledWindowMargin-Height	Dimension	0	CSG
XmNscrolledWindowMargin-Width	XmCScrolledWindowMargin-Width	Dimension	0	CSG
XmNscrollingPolicy	XmCScrollingPolicy	unsigned char	See below	CG
XmNspacing	XmCSpacing	Dimension	4	CSG
XmNverticalScrollBar	XmCVerticalScrollBar	Widget	NULL	CSG
XmNvisualPolicy	XmCVisualPolicy	unsigned char	dynamic	CG
XmNworkWindow	XmCWorkWindow	Widget	NULL	CSG

XmNclipWindow

> The widget ID of the clipping area. The clipping window exists only when the Xm-NvisualPolicy resource is set to XmCONSTANT. The XmNclipWindow resource cannot be set to a new value.

XmNhorizontalScrollBar

> The widget ID of the horizontal ScrollBar.

XmNscrollBarDisplayPolicy

> Controls the placement of ScrollBars, depending on the value of the XmNscrolling-Policy resource. Possible values:

> XmSTATIC   /* vertical ScrollBar always displays */
> XmAS_NEEDED   /* add ScrollBar when view is clipped */

If XmNscrollingPolicy is set to XmAUTOMATIC, then XmNscrollBarDisplayPolicy defaults to a value of XmAS_NEEDED, and ScrollBars are displayed only when the workspace cannot fit within the clip area. If XmNscrollingPolicy is set to Xm-APPLICATION_DEFINED, then XmNscrollBarDisplayPolicy defaults to (and must remain with) a value of XmSTATIC. This means that ScrollBars will always be displayed.

XmNscrollBarPlacement

The positions of the ScrollBars relative to the work window. The default value of this resource depends on the value of the XmNstringDirection resource. Possible values:

XmTOP_LEFT	/* vertical ScrollBar on left; horizontal on top */
XmBOTTOM_LEFT	/* vertical ScrollBar on left; horizontal on bottom */
XmTOP_RIGHT	/* vertical ScrollBar on right; horizontal on top */
XmBOTTOM_RIGHT	/* vertical ScrollBar on right; horizontal on bottom */

XmNscrolledWindowMarginHeight

The spacing at the top and bottom of the ScrolledWindow.

XmNscrolledWindowMarginWidth

The spacing at the right and left sides of the ScrolledWindow.

XmNscrollingPolicy

Determines how automatic scrolling occurs. Possible values:

XmAUTOMATIC	/* ScrolledWindow handles scrolling */
XmAPPLICATION_DEFINED	/* application handles scrolling */

XmNspacing

The distance between each ScrollBar and the work window.

XmNverticalScrollBar

The widget ID of the vertical ScrollBar.

XmNvisualPolicy

Possible values:

XmCONSTANT	/* viewing area is clipped if needed */
	/* (default when XmNscrollingPolicy is XmAUTOMATIC) */
XmVARIABLE	/* layout grows or shrinks (default otherwise) */

XmNworkWindow

The widget ID of the viewing area.

Inherited Resources

ScrolledWindow inherits the following resources. The resources are listed alphabetically, along with the superclass that defines them.

Resource	Inherited From	Resource	Inherited From
XmNaccelerators	Core	XmNinitialResourcesPersistent	Core
XmNancestorSensitive	Core	XmNinsertPosition	Composite
XmNbackground	Core	XmNmappedWhenManaged	Core
XmNbackgroundPixmap	Core	XmNnavigationType	Manager
XmNborderColor	Core	XmNnumChildren	Composite

Resource	Inherited From	Resource	Inherited From
XmNborderPixmap	Core	XmNscreen	Core
XmNborderWidth	Core	XmNsensitive	Core
XmNbottomShadowColor	Manager	XmNshadowThickness	Manager
XmNbottomShadowPixmap	Manager	XmNstringDirection	Manager
XmNchildren	Composite	XmNtopShadowColor	Manager
XmNcolormap	Core	XmNtopShadowPixmap	Manager
XmNdepth	Core	XmNtranslations	Core
XmNdestroyCallback	Core	XmNtraversalOn	Manager
XmNforeground	Manager	XmNunitType	Manager
XmNheight	Core	XmNuserData	Manager
XmNhelpCallback	Manager	XmNwidth	Core
XmNhighlightColor	Manager	XmNx	Core
XmNhighlightPixmap	Manager	XmNy	Core

Translations

The translations for ScrolledWindow include those from the Manager widget.

Additional Behavior

ScrolledWindow has additional behavior when the XmNscrollingPolicy resource is Xm-AUTOMATIC:

Event	Scrolls window ...
KPageUp	up
KPageDown	down
KPageLeft	left
KPageRight	right
KBeginLine	horizontally to ScrollBar's minimum value
KEndLine	horizontally to ScrollBar's maximum value
KBeginData	vertically to ScrollBar's minimum value
KEndData	vertically to ScrollBar's maximum value

SelectionBox

A subclass of BulletinBoard that displays a scrollable list of alternatives from which the user chooses one item. A SelectionBox widget contains a text field in which the user can edit a selection, labels for this text field and for the scrollable list, and three buttons whose default labels are Ok, Cancel, and Help. A fourth button, whose default label is Apply, is created as an unmanaged child. Users select an item either by clicking on it with the pointer or by typing the item's name in the text edit area; however, the selection doesn't take effect until the Ok button is pressed.

Class Information

Include File:	*<Xm/SelectioB.h>*
Class Name:	XmSelectionBox
Class Hierarchy:	Core → Composite → Constraint → XmManager → XmBulletin-Board → XmSelectionBox
Class Pointer:	xmSelectionBoxWidgetClass
Functions/Macros:	XmCreateSelectionBox(), XmSelectionBoxGetChild(), XmCreateSelectionDialog(), XmCreatePromptDialog()

New Resources

SelectionBox defines the following resources:

Name	Class	Type	Default	Access
XmNapplyLabelString	XmCApplyLabelString	XmString	"Apply"	CSG
XmNcancelLabelString	XmCCancelLabelString	XmString	"Cancel"	CSG
XmNdialogType	XmCDialogType	unsigned char	dynamic	CG
XmNhelpLabelString	XmCHelpLabelString	XmString	"Help"	CSG
XmNlistItemCount	XmCItemCount	int	0	CSG
XmNlistItems	XmCItems	XmStringTable	NULL	CSG
XmNlistLabelString	XmCListLabelString	XmString	NULL	CSG
XmNlistVisibleItemCount	XmCVisibleItemCount	int	8	CSG
XmNminimizeButtons	XmCMinimizeButtons	Boolean	False	CSG
XmNmustMatch	XmCMustMatch	Boolean	False	CSG
XmNokLabelString	XmCOkLabelString	XmString	"OK"	CSG
XmNselectionLabelString	XmCSelectionLabelString	XmString	"Selection"	CSG
XmNtextAccelerators	XmCTextAccelerators	XtAccelerators	default	C
XmNtextColumns	XmCColumns	short	20	CSG
XmNtextString	XmCTextString	XmString	" "	CSG

XmNapplyLabelString
> The string that labels the **Apply** button.

XmNcancelLabelString
> The string that labels the **Cancel** button.

XmNdialogType
> Determines which children of the SelectionBox widget will be initially created and managed. Possible values:

XmDIALOG_WORK_AREA	/* default, when parent isn't a DialogShell */
XmDIALOG_PROMPT	/* all children except list and label */
XmDIALOG_SELECTION	/* default, when parent is a DialogShell */
XmDIALOG_COMMAND	/* only list, selection label and text field */
XmDIALOG_FILE_SELECTION	/* all standard children */

> Note that in Release 1.1, Command and FileSelectionBox are separate widget classes, and they can no longer be created by setting XmNdialogType.

XmNhelpLabelString

The string that labels the Help button.

XmNlistItems

The items in the SelectionBox list. A call to XtGetValues() returns the actual list items (not a copy), so don't have your application free these items.

XmNlistItemCount

The number of items in the SelectionBox list.

XmNlistLabelString

The string that labels the SelectionBox list. The default string is NULL when the XmNdialogType resource is set to XmDIALOG_PROMPT; otherwise, the default is "Items".

XmNlistVisibleItemCount

The number of items that appear in the SelectionBox list. The default value depends on the height of the list. This resource has a value of 0 when the XmNdialogType resource is set to XmDIALOG_PROMPT.

XmNminimizeButtons

If False (default), all buttons are standardized to be as wide as the widest button and as high as the highest button. If True, buttons will keep their preferred size.

XmNmustMatch

If True, the selection that a user types in the text edit field must match an existing entry in the SelectionBox list. If False (default), the typed selection doesn't need to match a list entry. (When the user activates the Ok button, the widget calls one of two lists of callbacks: if this resource is True but the selections don't match, then the SelectionBox widget calls the callbacks specified by the XmNnoMatchCallback resource; if this resource is False or if the selections do match, then the widget calls the callbacks specified by the XmNokCallback resource.)

XmNokLabelString

The string that labels the Ok button.

XmNselectionLabelString

The string that labels the text edit field.

XmNtextAccelerators

The translations to add to the SelectionBox's Text widget child. The default bindings allow the up and down keys to be used in selecting list items. This resource is meaningful only when the SelectionBox widget is using the default values in the XmNaccelerators resource.

XmNtextColumns

The number of columns in the Text widget.

XmNtextString

The text string that appears in the text edit selection field.

Callback Resources

SelectionBox defines the following callback resources:

Callback	Reason Constant
XmNokCallback	XmCR_OK
XmNcancelCallback	XmCR_CANCEL
XmNapplyCallback	XmCR_APPLY
XmNnoMatchCallback	XmCR_NO_MATCH

Callback Structure

Each callback function is passed the following structure:

```
typedef struct
{
    int       reason;    /* the reason that the callback was called */
    XEvent    * event;   /* points to event structure that triggered callback */
    XmString  value;     /* selection string that was either chosen from the SelectionBox list or typed in */
    int       length;    /* number of bytes of value */
} XmSelectionBoxCallbackStruct;
```

Inherited Resources

SelectionBox inherits the following resources. The resources are listed alphabetically, along with the superclass that defines them.

Resource	Inherited From	Resource	Inherited From
XmNaccelerators	Core	XmNinsertPosition	Composite
XmNallowOverlap	BulletinBoard	XmNlabelFontList	BulletinBoard
XmNancestorSensitive	Core	XmNmapCallback	BulletinBoard
XmNautoUnmanage	BulletinBoard	XmNmappedWhenManaged	Core
XmNbackground	Core	XmNmarginHeight	BulletinBoard
XmNbackgroundPixmap	Core	XmNmarginWidth	BulletinBoard
XmNborderColor	Core	XmNnavigationType	Manager
XmNborderPixmap	Core	XmNnoResize	BulletinBoard
XmNborderWidth	Core	XmNnumChildren	Composite
XmNbottomShadowColor	Manager	XmNresizePolicy	BulletinBoard
XmNbottomShadowPixmap	Manager	XmNscreen	Core
XmNbuttonFontList	BulletinBoard	XmNsensitive	Core
XmNcancelButton	BulletinBoard	XmNshadowThickness	Manager
XmNchildren	Composite	XmNshadowType	BulletinBoard
XmNcolormap	Core	XmNstringDirection	Manager
XmNdefaultButton	BulletinBoard	XmNtextFontList	BulletinBoard
XmNdefaultPosition	BulletinBoard	XmNtextTranslations	BulletinBoard
XmNdepth	Core	XmNtopShadowColor	Manager
XmNdestroyCallback	Core	XmNtopShadowPixmap	Manager
XmNdialogStyle	BulletinBoard	XmNtranslations	Core
XmNdialogTitle	BulletinBoard	XmNtraversalOn	Manager
XmNfocusCallback	BulletinBoard	XmNunitType	Manager
XmNforeground	Manager	XmNunmapCallback	BulletinBoard
XmNheight	Core	XmNuserData	Manager

Resource	Inherited From	Resource	Inherited From
XmNhelpCallback	Manager	XmNwidth	Core
XmNhighlightColor	Manager	XmNx	Core
XmNhighlightPixmap	Manager	XmNy	Core
XmNinitialResourcesPersistent	Core		

Translations

The translations for SelectionBox are inherited from BulletinBoard.

Action Routines

SelectionBox defines the following action routines:

SelectionBoxUpOrDown(*flag*):

> This action applies when the location cursor is within the item list. This action selects a list item from one of four possible positions and uses this item to replace the selection text. A *flag* value of 0, 1, 2, or 3 selects the previous, next, first, or last item, respectively. These four action routines are respectively bound to KUp, KDown, KBeginData, and KEndData, which represent four of the default accelerators in the XmNtextAccelerators resource.

SelectionBoxRestore()

> Like SelectionBoxUpOrDown except that this action replaces the selection text with the current list item. This action clears the selection text if no list item is currently selected. This action routine is bound to KRestore, a default accelerator for XmNtextAccelerators.

Additional Behavior

The following additional behavior is defined for this widget:

MAny KCancel

> For a sensitive Cancel button, invokes the XmNactivateCallback callbacks.

KActivate   For the button that has keyboard focus (or else the default button), invokes the callbacks in XmNactivateCallback. In a List or Text widget, this event calls the associated List or Text action before the associated SelectionBox action.

Each event below invokes a particular set of callbacks:

<Ok Button Activated>	XmNokCallback or XmNnoMatchCallback
<Apply Button Activated>	XmNapplyCallback
<Cancel Button Activated>	XmNcancelCallback
<Help Button Activated>	XmNhelpCallback
<MapWindow>	XmNmapCallback (if parent is a DialogShell)
<UnmapWindow>	XmNunmapCallback (if parent is a DialogShell)

SelectionDialog

A convenience widget created by a call to XmCreateSelectionDialog() and consisting of a DialogShell with a SelectionBox widget as its child. The include file is *<Xm/SelectioB.h>*. The SelectionBox resource XmNdialogType is set to XmDIALOG_SELECTION. A Selection-Dialog displays a scrollable list of alternatives from which the user chooses. A Selection-Dialog also contains a text field in which the user can edit a selection, labels for the text field and for the scrollable list, and four buttons whose default labels are Ok, Cancel, Help, and Apply.

Separator

A subclass of Primitive that draws a horizontal or vertical line[4] between components in an application. Several line styles are available for the Separator.

Class Information

Include File:	*<Xm/Separator.h>*
Class Name:	XmSeparator
Class Hierarchy:	Core → XmPrimitive → XmSeparator
Class Pointer:	xmSeparatorWidgetClass
Functions/Macros:	XmCreateSeparator(), XmIsSeparator()

New Resources

Separator defines the following resources:

Name	Class	Type	Default	Access
XmNmargin	XmCMargin	Dimension	0	CSG
XmNorientation	XmCOrientation	unsigned char	XmHORIZONTAL	CSG
XmNseparatorType	XmCSeparatorType	unsigned char	XmSHADOW_ETCHED_IN	CSG

XmNmargin

> The spacing on either end of the Separator. This would be the left and right margins for a horizontally drawn Separator and the top and bottom margins for a vertically drawn Separator.

XmNorientation

> The direction in which to display the Separator. Possible values:

> XmVERTICAL   /* top-to-bottom creation */
> XmHORIZONTAL   /* left-to-right creation */

---

[4] A pixmap separator can also be made by specifying a pixmap for the Core resource XmNbackgroundPixmap and then setting XmNseparatorType to XmNO_LINE.

XmNseparatorType

The line style in which to draw the Separator. Possible values:

XmNO_LINE	XmSINGLE_DASHED_LINE	XmSHADOW_ETCHED_IN
XmSINGLE_LINE	XmDOUBLE_DASHED_LINE	XmSHADOW_ETCHED_OUT
XmDOUBLE_LINE		

Inherited Resources

Separator inherits the following resources. The resources are listed alphabetically, along with the superclass that defines them. Separator resets XmNhighlightThickness from 2 to 0 and resets XmNtraversalOn to False.

Resource	Inherited From	Resource	Inherited From
XmNaccelerators	Core	XmNhighlightPixmap	Primitive
XmNancestorSensitive	Core	XmNhighlightThickness	Primitive
XmNbackground	Core	XmNinitialResourcesPersistent	Core
XmNbackgroundPixmap	Core	XmNmappedWhenManaged	Core
XmNborderColor	Core	XmNnavigationType	Primitive
XmNborderPixmap	Core	XmNscreen	Core
XmNborderWidth	Core	XmNsensitive	Core
XmNbottomShadowColor	Primitive	XmNshadowThickness	Primitive
XmNbottomShadowPixmap	Primitive	XmNtopShadowColor	Primitive
XmNcolormap	Core	XmNtopShadowPixmap	Primitive
XmNdepth	Core	XmNtranslations	Core
XmNdestroyCallback	Core	XmNtraversalOn	Primitive
XmNforeground	Primitive	XmNunitType	Primitive
XmNheight	Core	XmNuserData	Primitive
XmNhelpCallback	Primitive	XmNwidth	Core
XmNhighlightColor	Primitive	XmNx	Core
XmNhighlightOnEnter	Primitive	XmNy	Core

SeparatorGadget

The gadget variant of Separator.

Class Information

Include File:	*<Xm/SeparatoG.h>*
Class Name:	XmSeparatorGadget
Class Hierarchy:	XmGadget → XmSeparatorGadget
Class Pointer:	xmSeparatorGadgetClass
Functions/Macros:	XmCreateSeparatorGadget(), XmIsSeparatorGadget()

SeparatorGadget's new resources are the same as those for Separator.

Inherited Resources

SeparatorGadget inherits the following resources. The resources are listed alphabetically, along with the superclass that defines them. SeparatorGadget resets XmNhighlightThickness from 2 to 0 and resets XmNtraversalOn to False.

Resource	Inherited From	Resource	Inherited From
XmNancestorSensitive	RectObj	XmNsensitive	RectObj
XmNborderWidth	RectObj	XmNshadowThickness	Gadget
XmNdestroyCallback	Object	XmNtraversalOn	Gadget
XmNheight	RectObj	XmNunitType	Gadget
XmNhelpCallback	Gadget	XmNuserData	Gadget
XmNhighlightOnEnter	Gadget	XmNwidth	RectObj
XmNhighlightThickness	Gadget	XmNx	RectObj
XmNnavigationType	Gadget	XmNy	RectObj

Shell

A supporting superclass that defines the interaction between the application and the window manager. The Shell widget class is never instantiated.

Class Information

Include File:	*<X11/Shell.h>*
Class Name:	Shell
Class Hierarchy:	Core → Composite → Shell
Class Pointer:	shellWidgetClass

New Resources

Shell defines the following resources:

Name	Class	Type	Default	Access
XmNallowShellResize	XmCAllowShellResize	Boolean	False	CG
XmNcreatePopupChildProc	XmCCreatePopupChildProc	(*)()	NULL	CSG
XmNgeometry	XmCGeometry	String	NULL	CSG
XmNoverrideRedirect	XmCOverrideRedirect	Boolean	False	CSG
XmNsaveUnder	XmCSaveUnder	Boolean	False	CSG
XmNvisual	XmCVisual	Visual *	CopyFromParent	CSG

XmNallowShellResize
>   If False (default), the Shell widget refuses geometry requests from its children (by returning XtGeometryNo).

XmNcreatePopupChildProc
>   A pointer to a procedure that creates a child widget—but only when the shell is popped up, not when the application is started. This is useful in menus, for

example, since you don't need to create the menu until it is popped up. This procedure is called after those specified in the XmNpopupCallback resource.

XmNgeometry
This resource specifies the values for the resources XmNx, XmNy, XmNwidth, and XmNheight in situations where an unrealized widget has added or removed some of its managed children.

XmNoverrideRedirect
If True, the widget is considered a temporary window that redirects the keyboard focus away from the main application windows. Usually this resource shouldn't be changed.

XmNsaveUnder
If True, screen contents that are obscured by a widget are saved, thereby avoiding the overhead of sending expose events after the widget is unmapped.

XmNvisual
The visual server resource that is used when creating the widget.

Inherited Resources

Shell inherits the following resources. The resources are listed alphabetically, along with the superclass that defines them.

Resource	Inherited From	Resource	Inherited From
XmNaccelerators	Core	XmNheight	Core
XmNancestorSensitive	Core	XmNinitialResourcesPersistent	Core
XmNbackground	Core	XmNinsertPosition	Composite
XmNbackgroundPixmap	Core	XmNmappedWhenManaged	Core
XmNborderColor	Core	XmNnumChildren	Composite
XmNborderPixmap	Core	XmNscreen	Core
XmNborderWidth	Core	XmNsensitive	Core
XmNchildren	Composite	XmNtranslations	Core
XmNcolormap	Core	XmNwidth	Core
XmNdepth	Core	XmNx	Core
XmNdestroyCallback	Core	XmNy	Core

Text

Provides a text editor that allows text to be inserted, modified, deleted, or selected (for cutting, copying, or pasting via a clipboard). Text widgets provide both single-line and multiline text editing. Like the List widget, a Text widget has two keyboard selection modes: Normal Mode and Add Mode.

Class Information

Include File:	*<Xm/Text.h>*
Class Name:	XmText
Class Hierarchy:	Core → XmPrimitive → XmText
Class Pointer:	xmTextWidgetClass
Functions/Macros:	XmCreateScrolledText(), XmCreateText(), XmText... routines, XmIsText()

New Resources

Text defines the following resources:

Name	Class	Type	Default	Access
XmNautoShowCursorPosition	XmCAutoShowCursorPosition	Boolean	True	CSG
XmNcursorPosition	XmCCursorPosition	XmTextPosition	0	CSG
XmNeditable	XmCEditable	Boolean	True	CSG
XmNeditMode	XmCEditMode	int	See below	CSG
XmNmarginHeight	XmCMarginHeight	Dimension	5	CSG
XmNmarginWidth	XmCMarginWidth	Dimension	5	CSG
XmNmaxLength	XmCMaxLength	int	largest integer	CSG
XmNsource	XmCSource	XmTextSource	default source	CSG
XmNtopCharacter	XmCTextPosition	XmTextPosition	0	CSG
XmNvalue	XmCValue	String	" "	CSG
XmNverifyBell	XmCVerifyBell	Boolean	True	CSG

XmNautoShowCursorPosition

> If True (default), the visible portion of the Text widget will always contain the insert cursor. The Text widget will scroll its contents, if necessary, to ensure that the cursor remains visible.

XmNcursorPosition

> The location at which to place the current insert cursor. Values for this resource are relative to the beginning of the text; the first character position is defined as 0.

XmNeditable

> If True (default), the user is allowed to edit the text string; if False, the user is not allowed to do so.

XmNeditMode

> Determines which group of keyboard bindings to use. Possible values:

> XmMULTI_LINE_EDIT   /* key bindings for multi-line edits */
> XmSINGLE_LINE_EDIT   /* key bindings for single line edits; the default value */

XmNmarginHeight
XmNmarginWidth

> The spacing between the edges of the widget and the text. (Top and bottom edges for height; left and right for width.)

XmNmaxLength

> The maximum length of the text string that a user can enter from the keyboard. This resource doesn't affect strings that are entered via the XmNvalue resource or the XmTextSetString() routine.

XmNsource

> A source that the Text widget uses for displaying text, thereby allowing Text widgets to share the same text source.

XmNtopCharacter

> The location of the text to display at the top of the window. Values for this resource are relative to the beginning of the text, with the first character position defined as 0.

XmNvalue

> The string value to display in the Text widget. Use XtSetValues() to copy string values to the internal buffer, and use XtGetValues() to return the value of the internal buffer.

XmNverifyBell

> If True (default), a bell will sound when a verification produces no action.

Callback Resources

Text defines the following callback resources:

Callback	Reason Constant
XmNvalueChangedCallback	XmCR_VALUE_CHANGED
XmNactivateCallback	XmCR_ACTIVATE
XmNfocusCallback	XmCR_FOCUS
XmNlosingFocusCallback	XmCR_LOSING_FOCUS
XmNmodifyVerifyCallback	XmCR_MODIFYING_TEXT_VALUE
XmNmotionVerifyCallback	XmCR_MOVING_INSERT_CURSOR
XmNgainPrimaryCallback	XmCR_GAIN_PRIMARY
XmNlosePrimaryCallback	XmCR_LOSE_PRIMARY

Callback Structure

Each callback function is passed the following structure:

```
typedef struct
{
        int        reason;        /* the reason that the callback was called */
        XEvent    * event;        /* points to event structure that triggered callback */
} XmAnyCallbackStruct;
```

In addition, the callback resources XmNlosingFocusCallback, XmNmodifyVerifyCallback, and XmNmotionVerifyCallback reference the following structure:

```
typedef struct
{
    int               reason;           /* the reason that the callback was called */
    XEvent            * event;          /* points to event structure that triggered callback */
    Boolean           doit;             /* do the action (True) or undo it (False) */
    XmTextPosition    current_insert;   /* the insert cursor's current position */
    XmTextPosition    new_insert;       /* desired new position of insert cursor */
    XmTextPosition    start_pos;        /* start of text to change */
    XmTextPosition    end_pos;          /* end of text to change */
    XmTextBlock       text;             /* describes the text to insert */
} XmTextVerifyCallbackStruct, *XmTextVerifyPtr;
```

start_pos specifies the location at which to start modifying text. *start_pos* is unused if the callback resource is XmNmotionVerifyCallback, and is the same as the *current_insert* member if the callback resource is XmNlosingFocusCallback.

end_pos specifies the location at which to stop modifying text (however, if no text was modified, *end_pos* has the same value as *start_pos*). *end_pos* is unused if the callback resource is XmNmotionVerifyCallback, and is the same as the *current_insert* member if the callback resource is XmNlosingFocusCallback.

text points to the structure below, which specifies information about the text to be inserted.

```
typedef struct
{
    char          * ptr;      /* pointer to the text to insert */
    int           length;     /* length of this text */
    XmTextFormat  format;     /* text format (e.g., FMT8BIT, FMT16BIT) */
} XmTextBlockRec, *XmTextBlock;
```

Text Input Resources

Name	Class	Type	Default	Access
XmNpendingDelete	XmCPendingDelete	Boolean	True	CSG
XmNselectionArray	XmCSelectionArray	Pointer	default array	CSG
XmNselectionArrayCount	XmCSelectionArrayCount	int	4	CSG
XmNselectThreshold	XmCSelectThreshold	int	5	CSG

XmNpendingDelete
>   If True (default), the Text widget's pending delete mode is on, meaning that selected text will be deleted as soon as the next text insertion occurs.

XmNselectionArray
>   The array of possible actions caused by multiple mouse clicks. Possible values:

```
XmSELECT_POSITION    /* single-click; reset position of insert cursor */
XmSELECT_WORD        /* double-click; select a word */
XmSELECT_LINE        /* triple-click; select a line */
XmSELECT_ALL         /* quadruple-click; select all text */
```

XmNselectionArrayCount

The number of items in the array specified by XmNselectionArray.

XmNselectThreshold

The number of pixels the insertion cursor must be dragged during selection in order to select the next character.

Text Output Resources

Name	Class	Type	Default	Access
XmNblinkRate	XmCBlinkRate	int	500	CSG
XmNcolumns	XmCColumns	short	dynamic	CSG
XmNcursorPositionVisible	XmCCursorPositionVisible	Boolean	True	CSG
XmNfontList	XmCFontList	XmFontList	dynamic	CSG
XmNresizeHeight	XmCResizeHeight	Boolean	False	CSG
XmNresizeWidth	XmCResizeWidth	Boolean	False	CSG
XmNrows	XmCRows	short	dynamic	CSG
XmNwordWrap	XmCWordWrap	Boolean	False	CSG

XmNblinkRate

The time in milliseconds that the cursor spends either being visible or invisible. A value of 0 prevents the cursor from blinking.

XmNcolumns

The number of character spaces that should fit horizontally in the text window. The XmNwidth resource determines the default value of XmNcolumns, but if no width has been set, the default is 20. See also XmNrows.

XmNcursorPositionVisible

If True (default), the text cursor will be visible.

XmNfontList

The font list used for the widget's text. If this value is initially NULL, the font list is derived from the font list resource from the nearest parent that is a subclass of BulletinBoard, MenuShell, or VendorShell.

XmNresizeHeight

If False (default), the Text widget will not expand vertically to fit all of the text (in other words, the widget will need to have scrollbars so that the rest of the text can be scrolled into view). If True, the Text widget always begins its display with the text at the beginning of the source. This resource has no effect in a ScrolledText widget whose XmNscrollVertical resource is set to True.

XmNresizeWidth

If False (default), the Text widget will not expand horizontally to fit its text. If True, the widget tries to change its width. This resource has no effect when the XmNword-Wrap resource is set to True.

XmNrows

The number of character spaces that should fit vertically in the text window. The XmNheight resource determines the default value of XmNrows, but if no height has been set, the default is 1. This resource is meaningful only when XmNeditMode is XmMULTI_LINE_EDIT. See also XmNcolumns.

XmNwordWrap

If False (default), do not break lines automatically between words (in which case text can disappear beyond the window's edge). If True, break lines at spaces, tabs, or newlines. This resource is meaningful only when XmNeditMode is Xm-MULTI_LINE_EDIT.

Text ScrolledText Resources

Name	Class	Type	Default	Access
XmNscrollHorizontal	XmCScroll	Boolean	True	CG
XmNscrollLeftSide	XmCScrollSide	Boolean	dynamic	CG
XmNscrollTopSide	XmCScrollSide	Boolean	False	CG
XmNscrollVertical	XmCScroll	Boolean	True	CG

XmNscrollHorizontal

If True, the Text widget adds a horizontal ScrollBar. The default is True; however, the value changes to False if the widget is in a ScrolledWindow whose XmNscrolling-Policy resource is set to XmAUTOMATIC. This resource is meaningful only when Xm-NeditMode is XmMULTI_LINE_EDIT.

XmNscrollLeftSide

If True, the vertical ScrollBar is placed to the left of the scrolled text window. The default value depends on how the XmNstringDirection resource is set. This resource is meaningful only when XmNeditMode is XmMULTI_LINE_EDIT and when XmNscroll-Vertical is True.

XmNscrollTopSide

If True, the horizontal ScrollBar is placed above the scrolled text window, rather than below by default.

XmNscrollVertical

If True, the Text widget adds a vertical ScrollBar. The default is True; however, the value changes to False if the widget is in a ScrolledWindow whose XmNscrolling-Policy resource is set to XmAUTOMATIC.

Inherited Resources

Text inherits the following resources. The resources are listed alphabetically, along with the superclass that defines them. Text resets XmNnavigationType from XmNONE to Xm-TAB_GROUP.

Resource	Inherited From	Resource	Inherited From
XmNaccelerators	Core	XmNhighlightPixmap	Primitive
XmNancestorSensitive	Core	XmNhighlightThickness	Primitive
XmNbackground	Core	XmNinitialResourcesPersistent	Core
XmNbackgroundPixmap	Core	XmNmappedWhenManaged	Core
XmNborderColor	Core	XmNnavigationType	Primitive
XmNborderPixmap	Core	XmNscreen	Core
XmNborderWidth	Core	XmNsensitive	Core
XmNbottomShadowColor	Primitive	XmNshadowThickness	Primitive
XmNbottomShadowPixmap	Primitive	XmNtopShadowColor	Primitive
XmNcolormap	Core	XmNtopShadowPixmap	Primitive
XmNdepth	Core	XmNtranslations	Core
XmNdestroyCallback	Core	XmNtraversalOn	Primitive
XmNforeground	Primitive	XmNunitType	Primitive
XmNheight	Core	XmNuserData	Primitive
XmNhelpCallback	Primitive	XmNwidth	Core
XmNhighlightColor	Primitive	XmNx	Core
XmNhighlightOnEnter	Primitive	XmNy	Core

Translations

The translations for Text include those from Primitive, as well as the following. (Note that some of the associated actions will be reversed for a language environment in which text is not read from left to right.)

Event	Action	Event	Action
BSelect Press	grab-focus()	KPageRight	page-right()
BSelect Motion	extend-adjust()	KBeginLine	beginning-of-line()
BSelect Release	extend-end()	MShift KBeginLine	beginning-of-line(extend)
BExtend Press	extend-start()	KEndLine	end-of-line()
BExtend Motion	extend-adjust()	MShift KEndLine	end-of-line(extend)
BExtend Release	extend-end()	KBeginData	beginning-of-file()
BToggle Press	move-destination()	MShift KBeginData	beginning-of-file(extend)
BDrag Press	secondary-start()	KEndData	end-of-file()
BDrag Motion	secondary-adjust()	MShift KEndData	end-of-file(extend)
BDrag Release	copy-to()	KTab	process-tab()
MCtrl BDrag Press	secondary-start()	KNextField	next-tab-group()
MCtrl BDrag Motion	secondary-adjust()	KPrevField	prev-tab-group()
MCtrl BDrag Release	copy-to()	KEnter	process-return()
MAlt BDrag Press	secondary-start()	KActivate	activate()
MAlt BDrag Motion	secondary-adjust()	KDelete	delete-next-character()
MAlt BDrag Release	move-to()	KBackSpace	delete-previous-character()
KUp	process-up()	KAddMode	toggle-add-mode()
MShift KUp	process-shift-up()	KSpace	self-insert()
MCtrl KUp	backward-paragraph()	KSelect	set-anchor()
MShift MCtrl KUp	backward-paragraph(extend)	KExtend	key-select()
KDown	process-down()	MAny KCancel	process-cancel()
MShift KDown	process-shift-down()	KClear	clear-selection()

Event	Action	Event	Action
MCtrl KDown	forward-paragraph()	KSelectAll	select-all()
MShift MCtrl KDown	forward-paragraph(extend)	KDeselectAll	deselect-all()
KLeft	backward-character()	KCut	cut-clipboard()
MShift KLeft	key-select(left)	KCopy	copy-clipboard()
MCtrl KLeft	backward-word()	KPaste	paste-clipboard()
MShift MCtrl KLeft	backward-word(extend)	KPrimaryCut	cut-primary()
KRight	forward-character()	KPrimaryCopy	copy-primary()
MShift KRight	key-select(right)	KPrimaryPaste	copy-primary()
MCtrl KRight	forward-word()	KQuickCut	quick-cut-set()
MShiftMCtrl KRight	forward-word(extend)	KQuickCopy	quick-copy-set()
KPageUp	previous-page()	KQuickPaste	quick-copy-set()
MShift KPageUp	previous-page(extend)	KQuickExtend	do-quick-action()
KPageDown	next-page()	KHelp	Help()
MShift KPageDown	next-page(extend)	KAny	self-insert()
KPageLeft	page-left()		

Action Routines

Text defines the action routines below. For actions that involve movement such as *next*, *previous*, *start*, *end*, *back*, *forward*, etc., the actual cursor movement depends on whether the language environment is left-to-right or right-to-left. In addition, some actions accept an optional argument, *extend*. When applied with no argument, these actions move the cursor; when applied with the *extend* argument, these actions move the cursor but also extend the text selection. In all descriptions, the term *cursor* refers to the insertion cursor.

activate()   Invokes the callbacks specified by XmNactivateCallback.

backward-character()
                  Moves the cursor back one character.

backward-paragraph(*extend*)
                  Moves the cursor back to the first non-blank character that follows a blank line (or back to the start of the text if there is no previous blank line). If the cursor is already located at a non-blank character (i.e., if it's already at the beginning of the paragraph), the cursor moves to the start of the previous paragraph. (Multiline edit mode only.)

backward-word(*extend*)
                  Moves the cursor back to the first non-blank character that follows a blank character (or back to the start of the line if there is no previous blank character). If the cursor is already located at a non-blank character (i.e., if it's already at the beginning of a word), the cursor moves to the start of the previous word.

beep()   Makes the terminal beep.

beginning-of-file(*extend*)
                  Moves the cursor to the start of the text.

beginning-of-line(*extend*)
> Moves the cursor to the start of the line.

clear-selection()
> Replaces each character (except a newline) with a space, effectively clearing the current selection.

copy-clipboard()
> Copies the current text selection into the clipboard.

copy-primary()
> Inserts a copy of the primary selection at the cursor location.

copy-to()
> Inserts a copy of the secondary selection at the cursor location, or, if there is no secondary selection, inserts a copy of the primary selection at the pointer location.

cut-clipboard()
> Deletes the current selection and moves it to the clipboard.

cut-primary()
> Deletes the primary selection and inserts it at the cursor.

The next four actions delete the selection when the cursor is inside it and when the XmNpendingDelete resource is True. When this is not the case, these actions do the following:

delete-next-character()
delete-previous-character()
> Deletes the character following/preceding the cursor.

delete-next-word()
delete-previous-word()
> Deletes from the character following/preceding the cursor to the next/previous space, tab, or end of line.

delete-selection()
> Deletes the current selection.

delete-to-end-of-line()
> Deletes forward from the character after the cursor up to and including the end of the line.

delete-to-start-of-line()
> Deletes back from the character before the cursor up to and including the beginning of the line.

deselect-all()
> Deselects the current selection.

do-quick-action()
> Ends a secondary selection and does the action that was started by either of the actions quick-copy-set or quick-cut-set.

end-of-file(*extend*)
> Moves the cursor to the end of the text.

end-of-line(*extend*)
> Moves the cursor to the end of the line.

extend-adjust()
> Selects text that is between the anchor and the pointer location, while deselecting text that is outside this area. As a result of this action, when

the pointer moves past lines of text, these lines are selected and the current line is selected up to the position of the pointer.

extend-end()
Moves the cursor to the pointer location and ends the selection performed by extend-adjust.

extend-start()
Adjusts the anchor in preparation for selecting text via the extend-adjust action.

forward-character()
Moves the cursor forward one character.

forward-paragraph(*extend*)
Moves the cursor forward to the first non-blank character that follows a blank line. If the cursor is already located at a non-blank character (i.e., if it's already at the beginning of the paragraph), the cursor moves to the start of the next paragraph. (Multiline edit mode only.)

forward-word(*extend*)
Moves the cursor forward to the first blank character that follows a nonblank character (or forward to the end of the line if there is no blank character to move to). If the cursor is already located at a blank character (i.e., if it's already at the end of a word), the cursor moves to the end of the next word.

grab-focus()
Processes multiclicks as defined in the XmNselectionArray resource. By default, one click resets the cursor to the pointer location, two clicks select a word, three clicks select a line, and four clicks select all of the text.

Help()
Invokes the list of callbacks specified by XmNhelpCallback. If the Text widget doesn't have any help callbacks, this action routine invokes those associated with the nearest ancestor that has them.

insert-string(*text*)
Inserts *text* at the cursor, or replaces the current selection with *text* (when XmNpendingDelete is True).

key-select(*direction*)
Extends the selection and moves the cursor one character to the right (when *direction* is right), one character to the left (*direction* is left), or not at all (no argument).

kill-next-character()
kill-next-word()
kill-previous-character()
kill-previous-word()
These four actions are similar to their delete action counterparts, but the kill actions have the added feature of storing the deleted text in the cut buffer.

kill-selection()
Deletes the current selection and stores this text in the cut buffer.

kill-to-end-of-line()
> Deletes forward from the character after the cursor up to and including the end of the line; stores this text in the cut buffer.

kill-to-start-of-line()
> Deletes back from the character before the cursor up to and including the beginning of the line; stores this text in the cut buffer.

move-destination()
> Moves the cursor to the pointer location, leaving existing selections unaffected.

move-to()
> Deletes the secondary selection and inserts it at the cursor, or, if there is no secondary selection, deletes the primary selection and inserts it at the pointer location.

The next three actions delete the selection when the cursor is inside it and when the Xm-NpendingDelete resource is True. In addition, these actions do the following:

newline()
> Inserts a newline at the cursor.

newline-and-backup()
> Inserts a newline and then moves the cursor to the previous end of line.

newline-and-indent()
> Inserts a newline and adds blanks (as needed) so that the cursor aligns with the first nonblank character in the previous line.

next-line()
> Places the cursor on the next line.

next-page(*extend*)
> Moves the cursor one page forward.

next-tab-group() Traverses to the next tab group.

page-left() Scrolls the visible area one page to the left or right.
page-right()

paste-clipboard()
> Pastes text from the clipboard to the position before the cursor.

prev-tab-group() Traverses to the previous tab group.

previous-line() Places the cursor on the previous line.

previous-page(*extend*)
> Moves the cursor one page backward.

process-cancel()
> Cancels the extend-adjust() or secondary-adjust() actions that are currently being applied, restoring the selection to its previous state.

process-down() If XmNnavigationType is XmNONE, descends/ascends to the adjacent widget
process-up() in the tab group (single-line edit mode only). Moves the cursor one line down/up (multiline edit mode only).

process-home() Moves the cursor to the start of the line. (Similar to beginning-of-line.)

process-return() Invokes the **XmNactivateCallback** callbacks (in single-line editing) or inserts a newline (in multiline editing).

process-shift-down()
process-shift-up()
         Moves the cursor one line down or up (in multiline editing only).

process-tab() Traverses to the next tab group (in single-line editing) or inserts a tab (in multiline editing).

quick-copy-set() Marks this text location as the start of the secondary selection to use in quick copying.

quick-cut-set() Marks this text location as the start of the secondary selection to use in quick cutting.

redraw-display() Redraws the text in the viewing window.

scroll-one-line-down()
scroll-one-line-up()
         Scrolls the text region one line down or up.

secondary-adjust()
         Extends the secondary selection to the location of the pointer.

secondary-notify()
         Inserts a copy of the secondary selection at the destination cursor.

secondary-start() Marks this text location as the start of a secondary selection.

select-adjust() Extends the selection via the multiple mouse clicks defined by the **Xm-NselectionArray** resource.

select-all() Selects all text.

select-end() Ends the selection made using the **select-adjust()** action.

select-start() Begins a text selection.

self-insert() The basic method of inserting text. Typing at the keyboard inserts new text and (if **XmNpendingDelete** is **True**) replaces selected text that the cursor is in.

set-anchor() Changes the anchor point used when making extended selections; changes the destination cursor used for secondary selections.

set-insertion-point()
         Sets the position of the cursor.

set-selection-hint()
         Sets the selection's text source and the selection's location.

toggle-add-mode()
         Turns Add Mode either on or off.

traverse-home() traverse-next() traverse-prev()	Traverse within the tab group to the first widget, the next widget, and the previous widget, respectively.	
unkill()	Restores the most recently deleted text to the cursor's location.	

Text has additional behavior associated with <FocusIn>, which draws the cursor and begins to make it blink, and with <FocusOut>, which stops the cursor's blinking.

TextField

Like the Text widget class, except that TextField widgets provide only a single-line text editor.

Class Information

Include File:	*<Xm/TextF.h>*
Class Name:	XmTextField
Class Hierarchy:	Core → XmPrimitive → XmTextField
Class Pointer:	xmTextFieldWidgetClass
Functions/Macros:	XmCreateTextField(), XmTextField ... routines, XmIsTextField()

New Resources

TextField defines the following resources:

Name	Class	Type	Default	Access
XmNblinkRate	XmCBlinkRate	int	500	CSG
XmNcolumns	XmCColumns	short	dynamic	CSG
XmNcursorPosition	XmCCursorPosition	XmTextPosition	0	CSG
XmNcursorPositionVisible	XmCCursorPositionVisible	Boolean	True	CSG
XmNeditable	XmCEditable	Boolean	True	CSG
XmNfontList	XmCFontList	XmFontList	dynamic	CSG
XmNmarginHeight	XmCMarginHeight	Dimension	5	CSG
XmNmarginWidth	XmCMarginWidth	Dimension	5	CSG
XmNmaxLength	XmCMaxLength	int	largest integer	CSG
XmNpendingDelete	XmCPendingDelete	Boolean	True	CSG
XmNresizeWidth	XmCResizeWidth	Boolean	False	CSG
XmNselectionArray	XmCSelectionArray	Pointer	default array	CSG
XmNselectionArrayCount	XmCSelectionArrayCount	int	3	CSG
XmNselectThreshold	XmCSelectThreshold	int	5	CSG
XmNvalue	XmCValue	String	" "	CSG
XmNverifyBell	XmCVerifyBell	Boolean	True	CSG

XmNblinkRate

    The time in milliseconds that the cursor spends either being visible or invisible. A value of 0 prevents the cursor from blinking.

XmNcolumns

    The number of character spaces that should fit horizontally in the text window. The XmNwidth resource determines the default value of XmNcolumns, but if no width has been set, the default is 20. See also XmNrows.

XmNcursorPosition

    The location at which to place the current insert cursor. Values for this resource are relative to the beginning of the text, with the first character position defined as 0.

XmNcursorPositionVisible

    If True (default), the text cursor will be visible.

XmNeditable

    If True (default), the user is allowed to edit the text string; if False, the user is not allowed to do so.

XmNfontList

    The font list used for the widget's text. If this value is initially NULL, the font list is derived from the font list resource from the nearest parent that is a subclass of BulletinBoard, MenuShell, or VendorShell.

XmNmarginHeight
XmNmarginWidth

    The spacing between the edges of the widget and the text. (Top and bottom edges for height; left and right for width.)

XmNmaxLength

    The maximum length of the text string that a user can enter from the keyboard. This resource doesn't affect strings that are entered via the XmNvalue resource or the XmTextFieldSetString() routine.

XmNpendingDelete

    If True (default), the TextField widget's pending delete mode is on, meaning that selected text will be deleted as soon as the next text insertion occurs.

XmNresizeWidth

    If False (default), the TextField widget will not expand horizontally to fit its text. If True, the widget tries to change its width.

XmNselectionArray

    The array of possible actions caused by multiple mouse clicks. Possible values:

XmSELECT_POSITION	/* single-click; reset position of insert cursor */
XmSELECT_WORD	/* double-click; select a word */
XmSELECT_LINE	/* triple-click; select a line */

XmNselectionArrayCount

    The number of items in the array specified by XmNselectionArray.

XmNselectThreshold

> The number of pixels the insertion cursor must be dragged during selection in order to select the next character.

XmNvalue

> The string value to display in the TextField widget. Use **XtSetValues()** to copy string values to the internal buffer, and use **XtGetValues()** to return the value of the internal buffer.

XmNverifyBell

> If **True** (default), a bell will sound when a verification produces no action.

TextField does not have an **XmNfocusCallback**, but all other callback resources and callback structures are the same as those for Text.

Inherited Resources

TextField inherits the following resources. The resources are listed alphabetically, along with the superclass that defines them. TextField resets **XmNnavigationType** from **XmNONE** to **XmTAB_GROUP**.

Resource	Inherited From	Resource	Inherited From
XmNaccelerators	Core	XmNhighlightPixmap	Primitive
XmNancestorSensitive	Core	XmNhighlightThickness	Primitive
XmNbackground	Core	XmNinitialResourcesPersistent	Core
XmNbackgroundPixmap	Core	XmNmappedWhenManaged	Core
XmNborderColor	Core	XmNnavigationType	Primitive
XmNborderPixmap	Core	XmNscreen	Core
XmNborderWidth	Core	XmNsensitive	Core
XmNbottomShadowColor	Primitive	XmNshadowThickness	Primitive
XmNbottomShadowPixmap	Primitive	XmNtopShadowColor	Primitive
XmNcolormap	Core	XmNtopShadowPixmap	Primitive
XmNdepth	Core	XmNtranslations	Core
XmNdestroyCallback	Core	XmNtraversalOn	Primitive
XmNforeground	Primitive	XmNunitType	Primitive
XmNheight	Core	XmNuserData	Primitive
XmNhelpCallback	Primitive	XmNwidth	Core
XmNhighlightColor	Primitive	XmNx	Core
XmNhighlightOnEnter	Primitive	XmNy	Core

Translations

Same as for a Text widget whose **XmNeditMode** resource is set to **XmSINGLE_LINE_EDIT** (as it is by default).

Actions

Same as for a Text widget whose **XmNeditMode** resource is set to **XmSINGLE_LINE_EDIT**.

ToggleButton

A button that is either set or unset, typically used within a RadioBox or CheckBox. A ToggleButton can be classified as two types: "one-of-many" (a "radioButton") or "*n*-of-many" (a "checkButton"). *One-of-many* means that only one button among a group of ToggleButtons can be set at a time: setting another ToggleButton will automatically unset a previously set ToggleButton. *n-of-many* means that more than one ToggleButton can be set at a time: such a ToggleButton must be unset explicitly by selecting on it while it's set. The shape of a ToggleButton indicator is either a square (*n*-of-many) or a diamond (one-of-many).

Class Information

Include File:	*<Xm/ToggleB.h>*
Class Name:	XmToggleButton
Class Hierarchy:	Core → XmPrimitive → XmLabel → XmToggleButton
Class Pointer:	xmToggleButtonWidgetClass
Functions/Macros:	XmCreateToggleButton(), XmToggleButtonGetState(), XmToggleButton-SetState(), XmIsToggleButton()

New Resources

ToggleButton defines the following resources:

Name	Class	Type	Default	Access
XmNfillOnSelect	XmCFillOnSelect	Boolean	True	CSG
XmNindicatorOn	XmCIndicatorOn	Boolean	True	CSG
XmNindicatorSize	XmCIndicatorSize	Dimension	XmINVALID_DIMENSION	CSG
XmNindicatorType	XmCIndicatorType	unsigned char	dynamic	CSG
XmNselectColor	XmCSelectColor	Pixel	dynamic	CSG
XmNselectInsensitivePixmap	XmCSelectInsensitivePixmap	Pixmap	XmUNSPECIFIED_PIXMAP	CSG
XmNselectPixmap	XmCSelectPixmap	Pixmap	XmUNSPECIFIED_PIXMAP	CSG
XmNset	XmCSet	Boolean	False	CSG
XmNspacing	XmCSpacing	Dimension	4	CSG
XmNvisibleWhenOff	XmCVisibleWhenOff	Boolean	dynamic	CSG

XmNfillOnSelect
> If True (default), selection of this ToggleButton fills the indicator with the color given by the XmNselectColor resource and switches the button's top and bottom shadow colors. If False, only the top and bottom shadow colors are switched.

XmNindicatorOn
> If True (default), the indicator is visible and its shadows are switched when the button is toggled. If False, the indicator is invisible and no space is set aside for it; in addition, the shadows surrounding the button are switched when it is toggled.

XmNindicatorSize

> The size of the indicator. This value changes if the size of the button's text string or pixmap changes.

XmNindicatorType

> Determines whether the indicator is drawn as a diamond (signifying a one-of-many indicator) or as a square (signifying an *n*-of-many indicator). Possible values:
>
> ```
> XmN_OF_MANY              /* creates a square button */
> XmONE_OF_MANY            /* creates a diamond-shaped button */
> ```
>
> The default value is XmONE_OF_MANY for a ToggleButton in a RadioBox widget, and XmN_OF_MANY otherwise. This resource only sets the indicator; it is Row-Column's XmNradioBehavior resource that actually enforces radioButton or check-Button behavior.

XmNselectColor

> The color with which to fill the indicator when the button is selected. On a color display, the default is a value between the background color and the bottom shadow color; on a monochrome display, the default is the foreground color.

XmNselectInsensitivePixmap

> The pixmap used for an insensitive ToggleButton when it's selected. An unselected, insensitive ToggleButton uses the pixmap specified by the Label resource XmNlabelInsensitivePixmap. However, if this Label resource wasn't specified, it is set to the value of XmNselectInsensitivePixmap. This resource is meaningful only when the Label resource XmNlabelType is set to XmPIXMAP.

XmNselectPixmap

> The pixmap used for a (sensitive) ToggleButton when it's selected. An unselected ToggleButton uses the pixmap specified by the Label resource XmNlabelPixmap. This resource is meaningful only when the Label resource XmNlabelType is set to XmPIXMAP.

XmNset

> If True, the button is displayed only when it is selected. If False (default), the button is displayed whether it is selected or not.

XmNspacing

> The distance between the toggle indicator and its label.

XmNvisibleWhenOff

> If True, the toggle indicator remains visible when the button is unselected. This is the default behavior in a RadioBox. The default is False in a menu.

Callback Resources

ToggleButton defines the following callback resources:

Callback	Reason Constant
XmNactivateCallback	XmCR_ACTIVATE
XmNarmCallback	XmCR_ARM
XmNvalueChangedCallback	XmCR_VALUE_CHANGED

Callback Structure

Each callback function is passed the following structure:

```
typedef struct
{
    int      reason;    /* the reason that the callback was called */
    XEvent   * event;   /* points to event structure that triggered callback */
    int      set;       /* button is selected (True) or unselected (False) */
} XmToggleButtonCallbackStruct;
```

Inherited Resources

ToggleButton inherits the following resources. The resources are listed alphabetically, along with the superclass that defines them.

Resource	Inherited From	Resource	Inherited From
XmNaccelerator	Label	XmNlabelString	Label
XmNaccelerators	Core	XmNlabelType	Label
XmNacceleratorText	Label	XmNmappedWhenManaged	Core
XmNalignment	Label	XmNmarginBottom	Label
XmNancestorSensitive	Core	XmNmarginHeight	Label
XmNbackground	Core	XmNmarginLeft	Label
XmNbackgroundPixmap	Core	XmNmarginRight	Label
XmNborderColor	Core	XmNmarginTop	Label
XmNborderPixmap	Core	XmNmarginWidth	Label
XmNborderWidth	Core	XmNmnemonic	Label
XmNbottomShadowColor	Primitive	XmNmnemonicCharSet	Label
XmNbottomShadowPixmap	Primitive	XmNnavigationType	Primitive
XmNcolormap	Core	XmNrecomputeSize	Label
XmNdepth	Core	XmNscreen	Core
XmNdestroyCallback	Core	XmNsensitive	Core
XmNfontList	Label	XmNshadowThickness	Primitive
XmNforeground	Primitive	XmNstringDirection	Label
XmNheight	Core	XmNtopShadowColor	Primitive
XmNhelpCallback	Primitive	XmNtopShadowPixmap	Primitive
XmNhighlightColor	Primitive	XmNtranslations	Core
XmNhighlightOnEnter	Primitive	XmNtraversalOn	Primitive
XmNhighlightPixmap	Primitive	XmNunitType	Primitive
XmNhighlightThickness	Primitive	XmNuserData	Primitive
XmNinitialResourcesPersistent	Core	XmNwidth	Core
XmNlabelInsensitivePixmap	Label	XmNx	Core
XmNlabelPixmap	Label	XmNy	Core

Translations

The translations for ToggleButton include those from Primitive. In addition, for Toggle-Buttons that aren't in a menu system, the translations are as follows:

BSelect Press	Arm()
BSelect Release	Select()
	Disarm()
KHelp	Help()
KActivate	ArmAndActivate()
KSelect	ArmAndActivate()

For ToggleButtons that are in a menu system, translations include the menu traversal translations inherited from the Label widget, as well as the following:

BSelect Press	BtnDown()
BSelect Release	BtnUp()
KHelp	Help()
KActivate	KeySelect()
KSelect	KeySelect()
MAny KCancel	MenuShellPopdownOne()

Action Routines

ToggleButton defines the following action routines:

Arm()   Sets the button if it was previously unset, unsets the button if it was previously set, and invokes the callbacks specified by XmNarmCallback. Setting the button means displaying it so that it appears selected. The selected state can be shown by:

- Highlighting the indicator so it appears pressed in.
- Filling in the indicator (using the color given by XmNselectColor).
- Highlighting the button so it appears pressed in. This is done only if the indicator isn't displayed.
- Drawing the button face using the pixmap given by XmNselectPixmap.

The unselected state can be shown by:

- Highlighting the indicator so it appears raised.
- Filling in the indicator with the background color.
- Highlighting the button so it appears raised. This is done only if the indicator isn't displayed.
- Drawing the button face using the pixmap given by XmNlabelPixmap.

ArmAndActivate()

Sets the button if it was previously unset, unsets the button if it was previously set, and invokes the callbacks specified by XmNarmCallback (if the button isn't yet armed), XmNvalueChangedCallback, and XmNdisarmCallback. Inside a menu, this action unposts the menu hierarchy. Outside a menu, this action displays the button as selected or unselected, as described for Arm().

BtnDown()   Unposts any menus that were posted by the parent menu of the ToggleButton, changes from keyboard traversal to mouse traversal, draws a shadow to show the ToggleButton as armed, and (assuming the button is not yet armed) invokes the callbacks specified by XmNarmCallback.

BtnUp()   Unposts the menu hierarchy, changes the ToggleButton's state, and invokes first the callbacks specified by XmNvalueChangedCallback and then those specified by XmNdisarmCallback.

Disarm()   Invokes the callbacks specified by XmNdisarmCallback.

Help()   Unposts the menu hierarchy, restores the previous keyboard focus, and invokes the callbacks specified by the XmNhelpCallback resource.

MenuShellPopdownOne()
    Unposts the current menu and (unless the menu is a pulldown submenu) restores keyboard focus to the tab group or widget that previously had it. In a top-level pulldown menu pane attached to a menu bar, this action routine also disarms the cascade button and the menu bar.

Select()   Switches the state of the ToggleButton and invokes the callbacks specified by XmNvalueChangedCallback.

ToggleButton has additional behavior associated with <EnterWindow> and <LeaveWindow>, which draw the shadow in the armed or unarmed state, respectively.

ToggleButtonGadget

The gadget variant of ToggleButton.

Class Information

Include File: *<Xm/ToggleBG.h>*

Class Name: XmToggleButtonGadget

Class Hierarchy: Object → RectObj → XmGadget → XmLabelGadget → Xm-ToggleButtonGadget

Class Pointer: xmToggleButtonGadgetClass

Functions/Macros: XmCreateToggleButtonGadget(), XmToggleButtonGadgetGetState(), XmToggleButtonGadgetSetState(), XmIsToggleButtonGadget()

ToggleButtonGadget's new resources, callback resources, and callback structure are the same as those for ToggleButton.

Inherited Resources

ToggleButtonGadget inherits the following resources. The resources are listed alphabetically, along with the superclass that defines them.

Resource	Inherited From	Resource	Inherited From
XmNaccelerator	LabelGadget	XmNmarginRight	LabelGadget
XmNacceleratorText	LabelGadget	XmNmarginTop	LabelGadget
XmNalignment	LabelGadget	XmNmarginWidth	LabelGadget
XmNancestorSensitive	RectObj	XmNmnemonic	LabelGadget
XmNborderWidth	RectObj	XmNmnemonicCharSet	LabelGadget
XmNfontList	LabelGadget	XmNnavigationType	Gadget
XmNheight	RectObj	XmNrecomputeSize	LabelGadget
XmNhelpCallback	Gadget	XmNsensitive	RectObj
XmNhighlightOnEnter	Gadget	XmNshadowThickness	Gadget
XmNhighlightThickness	Gadget	XmNstringDirection	LabelGadget
XmNlabelInsensitivePixmap	LabelGadget	XmNtraversalOn	Gadget
XmNlabelPixmap	LabelGadget	XmNunitType	Gadget
XmNlabelString	LabelGadget	XmNuserData	Gadget
XmNlabelType	LabelGadget	XmNwidth	RectObj
XmNmarginBottom	LabelGadget	XmNx	RectObj
XmNmarginHeight	LabelGadget	XmNy	RectObj
XmNmarginLeft	LabelGadget		

Behavior

As a gadget subclass, ToggleButtonGadget has no translations associated with it. However, ToggleButtonGadget behavior corresponds to the action routines of the Toggle-Button widget. See the ToggleButton action routines for more information.

Behavior	Equivalent ToggleButton Action Routine
BSelect Press	Arm() BtnDown() (in a menu)
BSelect Release	Select(), Disarm() BtnUp() (in a menu)
KActivate or KSelect	ArmAndActivate()
KHelp	Help()
MAny KCancel	MenuShellPopdownOne()

ToggleButtonGadget has additional behavior associated with <Enter> and <Leave>, which draw the shadow in the armed or unarmed state, respectively.

TopLevelShell

Description
Used for additional top-level windows that an application might need.

Class Information
Include File:	*<X11/Shell.h>*
Class Name:	TopLevelShell
Class Hierarchy:	Core → Composite → Shell → WmShell → VendorShell → Top-LevelShell
Class Pointer:	topLevelShellWidgetClass
Functions/Macros:	XtIsTopLevelShell()

New Resources
TopLevelShell defines the following resources:

Name	Class	Type	Default	Access
XmNiconic	XmCIconic	Boolean	False	CSG
XmNiconName	XmCIconName	String	NULL	CSG
XmNiconNameEncoding	XmCIconNameEncoding	Atom	XA_STRING	CSG

XmNiconic	If True, the widget is realized as an icon, regardless of the value of the XmNinitialState resource.
XmNiconName	The abbreviated name that labels an iconified application.
XmNiconNameEncoding	The property type for encoding the XmNiconName resource.

Inherited Resources
TopLevelShell inherits the following resources. The resources are listed alphabetically, along with the superclass that defines them. TopLevelShell resets XmNinput to True.

Resource	Inherited From	Resource	Inherited From
XmNaccelerators	Core	XmNmaxHeight	WMShell
XmNallowShellResize	Shell	XmNmaxWidth	WMShell
XmNancestorSensitive	Core	XmNminAspectX	WMShell
XmNbackground	Core	XmNminAspectY	WMShell
XmNbackgroundPixmap	Core	XmNminHeight	WMShell
XmNbaseHeight	WMShell	XmNminWidth	WMShell
XmNbaseWidth	WMShell	XmNmwmDecorations	VendorShell
XmNborderColor	Core	XmNmwmFunctions	VendorShell
XmNborderPixmap	Core	XmNmwmInputMode	VendorShell
XmNborderWidth	Core	XmNmwmMenu	VendorShell
XmNchildren	Composite	XmNnumChildren	Composite
XmNcolormap	Core	XmNoverrideRedirect	Shell
XmNcreatePopupChildProc	Shell	XmNpopdownCallback	Shell

Resource	Inherited From	Resource	Inherited From
XmNdefaultFontList	VendorShell	XmNpopupCallback	Shell
XmNdeleteResponse	VendorShell	XmNsaveUnder	Shell
XmNdepth	Core	XmNscreen	Core
XmNdestroyCallback	Core	XmNsensitive	Core
XmNgeometry	Shell	XmNshellUnitType	VendorShell
XmNheight	Core	XmNtitle	WMShell
XmNheightInc	WMShell	XmNtitleEncoding	WMShell
XmNiconMask	WMShell	XmNtransient	WMShell
XmNiconPixmap	WMShell	XmNtranslations	Core
XmNiconWindow	WMShell	XmNuseAsyncGeometry	VendorShell
XmNiconX	WMShell	XmNvisual	Shell
XmNiconY	WMShell	XmNwaitForWm	WMShell
XmNinitialResourcesPersistent	Core	XmNwidth	Core
XmNinitialState	WMShell	XmNwidthInc	WMShell
XmNinput	WMShell	XmNwindowGroup	WMShell
XmNinsertPosition	Composite	XmNwinGravity	WMShell
XmNkeyboardFocusPolicy	VendorShell	XmNwmTimeout	WMShell
XmNmappedWhenManaged	Core	XmNx	Core
XmNmaxAspectX	WMShell	XmNy	Core
XmNmaxAspectY	WMShell		

TransientShell

Used for popup shell widgets, such as dialog boxes, that don't bypass window management. For example, the dialog box can't be iconified separately, but only when the main application shell is iconified.

Class Information

Include File:	*<X11/Shell.h>*
Class Name:	TransientShell
Class Hierarchy:	Core → Composite → Shell → WmShell → VendorShell → TransientShell
Class Pointer:	transientShellWidgetClass
Functions/Macros:	XtIsTransientShell()

New Resources

TransientShell defines the following resources:

Name	Class	Type	Default	Access
XmNtransientFor	XmCTransientFor	Widget	NULL	CSG

XmNtransientFor

The widget from which the TransientShell will pop up. If the value of this resource is NULL or identifies an unrealized widget, then TransientShell uses the value of the WMShell resource XmNwindowGroup.

Inherited Resources

TransientShell inherits the following resources. The resources are listed alphabetically, along with the superclass that defines them. TransientShell resets the resources XmNinput, XmNtransient, and XmNsaveUnder to True.

Resource	Inherited From	Resource	Inherited From
XmNaccelerators	Core	XmNmaxHeight	WMShell
XmNallowShellResize	Shell	XmNmaxWidth	WMShell
XmNancestorSensitive	Core	XmNminAspectX	WMShell
XmNbackground	Core	XmNminAspectY	WMShell
XmNbackgroundPixmap	Core	XmNminHeight	WMShell
XmNbaseHeight	WMShell	XmNminWidth	WMShell
XmNbaseWidth	WMShell	XmNmwmDecorations	VendorShell
XmNborderColor	Core	XmNmwmFunctions	VendorShell
XmNborderPixmap	Core	XmNmwmInputMode	VendorShell
XmNborderWidth	Core	XmNmwmMenu	VendorShell
XmNchildren	Composite	XmNnumChildren	Composite
XmNcolormap	Core	XmNoverrideRedirect	Shell
XmNcreatePopupChildProc	Shell	XmNpopdownCallback	Shell
XmNdefaultFontList	VendorShell	XmNpopupCallback	Shell
XmNdeleteResponse	VendorShell	XmNsaveUnder	Shell
XmNdepth	Core	XmNscreen	Core
XmNdestroyCallback	Core	XmNsensitive	Core
XmNgeometry	Shell	XmNshellUnitType	VendorShell
XmNheight	Core	XmNtitle	WMShell
XmNheightInc	WMShell	XmNtitleEncoding	WMShell
XmNiconMask	WMShell	XmNtransient	WMShell
XmNiconPixmap	WMShell	XmNtranslations	Core
XmNiconWindow	WMShell	XmNuseAsyncGeometry	VendorShell
XmNiconX	WMShell	XmNvisual	Shell
XmNiconY	WMShell	XmNwaitForWm	WMShell
XmNinitialResourcesPersistent	Core	XmNwidth	Core
XmNinitialState	WMShell	XmNwidthInc	WMShell
XmNinput	WMShell	XmNwindowGroup	WMShell
XmNinsertPosition	Composite	XmNwinGravity	WMShell
XmNkeyboardFocusPolicy	VendorShell	XmNwmTimeout	WMShell
XmNmappedWhenManaged	Core	XmNx	Core
XmNmaxAspectX	WMShell	XmNy	Core
XmNmaxAspectY	WMShell		

VendorShell

A vendor-specific supporting superclass for all shell classes that are visible to the window manager and that do not have override redirection. VendorShell defines the subresources that provide Motif's look and feel.

Class Information

Include File:	*<X11/Shell.h>*
Class Name:	VendorShell
Class Hierarchy:	Core → Composite → Shell → WmShell → VendorShell
Class Pointer:	vendorShellWidgetClass
Functions/Macros:	XmIsVendorShell()

New Resources

VendorShell defines the following resources:

Name	Class	Type	Default	Access
XmNdefaultFontList	XmCDefaultFontList	XmFontList	dynamic	C
XmNdeleteResponse	XmCDeleteResponse	unsigned char	XmDESTROY	CSG
XmNkeyboardFocusPolicy	XmCKeyboardFocusPolicy	unsigned char	XmEXPLICIT	CSG
XmNmwmDecorations	XmCMwmDecorations	int	–1	CSG
XmNmwmFunctions	XmCMwmFunctions	int	–1	CSG
XmNmwmInputMode	XmCMwmInputMode	int	–1	CSG
XmNmwmMenu	XmCMwmMenu	String	NULL	CSG
XmNshellUnitType	XmCShellUnitType	unsigned char	XmPIXELS	CSG
XmNuseAsyncGeometry	XmCUseAsyncGeometry	Boolean	False	CSG

XmNdefaultFontList

> The default font list to use for Text children, Label children or button children of the VendorShell that do not have their own font list resource set.

XmNdeleteResponse

> The action to perform when the shell receives a WM_DELETE_WINDOW message. Possible values:

> | | |
> |---|---|
> | XmDESTROY | /* destroy window */ |
> | XmUNMAP | /* unmap window */ |
> | XmDO_NOTHING | /* leave window as is*/ |

XmNkeyboardFocusPolicy

> The method of assigning keyboard focus. Possible values:

> | | |
> |---|---|
> | XmEXPLICIT | /* click-to-type policy */ |
> | XmPOINTER | /* pointer-driven policy */ |

XmNmwmDecorations

This resource corresponds to the values assigned by the decorations field of the _MOTIF_WM_HINTS property. This resource determines which frame buttons and handles to include with a window. The possible values are:

1	/* MWM_DECOR_ALL */	/* remove decorations from full set */
2	/* MWM_DECOR_BORDER */	/* window border */
4	/* MWM_DECOR_RESIZEH */	/* resize handles */
8	/* MWM_DECOR_TITLE */	/* title bar */
16	/* MWM_DECOR_SYSTEM */	/* window's menu button */
32	/* MWM_DECOR_MINIMIZE */	/* minimize button */
64	/* MWM_DECOR_MAXIMIZE */	/* maximize button */

XmNmwmFunctions

This resource corresponds to the values assigned by the functions field of the _MOTIF_WM_HINTS property. This resource determines which functions to include in the system menu. The possible values are:

1	/* MWM_FUNC_ALL */	/* remove functions from full set */
2	/* MWM_FUNC_RESIZE */	/* f.resize */
4	/* MWM_FUNC_MOVE */	/* f.move */
8	/* MWM_FUNC_MINIMIZE */	/* f.minimize */
16	/* MWM_FUNC_MAXIMIZE */	/* f.maximize */
32	/* MWM_FUNC_CLOSE */	/* f.kill */

XmNmwmInputMode

This resource corresponds to the values assigned by the input_mode field of the _MOTIF_WM_HINTS property. This resource determines the constraints on the window's keyboard focus. That is, it determines whether the application takes the keyboard focus away from the primary window or not. The possible values are:

1	/* INPUT_APPLICATION_MODAL */	/* primary window does not have focus */
2	/* INPUT_SYSTEM_MODAL */	/* primary window has keyboard focus */

XmNmwmMenu

The menu items to add at the bottom of the client's window menu. The string has this format:

label [*mnemonic*] [*accelerator*] *mwm_f.function*

XmNshellUnitType

The measurement units to use in resources that specify a size or position. Possible values:

XmPIXELS	Xm100TH_POINTS
Xm100TH_MILLIMETERS	Xm100TH_FONT_UNITS
Xm1000TH_INCHES	

XmNuseAsyncGeometry

If True, the geometry manager doesn't wait to confirm a geometry request that was sent to the window manager. The geometry manager performs this by setting the WMShell resource XmNwaitForWm to False and by setting the WMShell resource

XmNwmTimeout to 0. If **XmNuseAsyncGeometry** is False (default), the geometry manager uses synchronous notification, and so it doesn't change the resources XmNwaitForWm and XmNwmTimeout.

Inherited Resources

VendorShell inherits the following resources. The resources are listed alphabetically, along with the superclass that defines them. VendorShell resets XmNborderWidth from 1 to 0 and resets XmNinput to True.

Resource	Inherited From	Resource	Inherited From
XmNaccelerators	Core	XmNmaxAspectX	WMShell
XmNallowShellResize	Shell	XmNmaxAspectY	WMShell
XmNancestorSensitive	Core	XmNmaxHeight	WMShell
XmNbackground	Core	XmNmaxWidth	WMShell
XmNbackgroundPixmap	Core	XmNminAspectX	WMShell
XmNbaseHeight	WMShell	XmNminAspectY	WMShell
XmNbaseWidth	WMShell	XmNminHeight	WMShell
XmNborderColor	Core	XmNminWidth	WMShell
XmNborderPixmap	Core	XmNnumChildren	Composite
XmNborderWidth	Core	XmNoverrideRedirect	Shell
XmNchildren	Composite	XmNpopdownCallback	Shell
XmNcolormap	Core	XmNpopupCallback	Shell
XmNcreatePopupChildProc	Shell	XmNsaveUnder	Shell
XmNdepth	Core	XmNscreen	Core
XmNdestroyCallback	Core	XmNsensitive	Core
XmNgeometry	Shell	XmNtitle	WMShell
XmNheight	Core	XmNtitleEncoding	WMShell
XmNheightInc	WMShell	XmNtransient	WMShell
XmNiconMask	WMShell	XmNtranslations	Core
XmNiconPixmap	WMShell	XmNvisual	Shell
XmNiconWindow	WMShell	XmNwaitForWm	WMShell
XmNiconX	WMShell	XmNwidth	Core
XmNiconY	WMShell	XmNwidthInc	WMShell
XmNinitialResourcesPersistent	Core	XmNwindowGroup	WMShell
XmNinitialState	WMShell	XmNwinGravity	WMShell
XmNinput	WMShell	XmNwmTimeout	WMShell
XmNinsertPosition	Composite	XmNx	Core
XmNmappedWhenManaged	Core	XmNy	Core

WarningDialog

A convenience widget created by a call to XmCreateWarningDialog() and consisting of a DialogShell with a MessageBox widget as its child. The MessageBox resource XmNdialog-Type is set to XmDIALOG_WARNING. The include file is *<Xm/MessageB.h>*. A Warning-Dialog includes three components: a symbol (by default an exclamation point), a message, and three buttons (whose labels by default are Ok, Cancel, and Help).

WMShell

Top-level widget that serves as a supporting superclass for all shell classes that are decorated by the window manager. (OverrideShell and its subclass MenuShell bypass the window manager.) WMShell is not directly instantiated; instead, it encapsulates the application resources that applications use to communicate with window managers.

Class Information

Include File:	*<X11/Shell.h>*
Class Name:	WMShell
Class Hierarchy:	Core → Composite → Shell → WMShell
Class Pointer:	wmShellWidgetClass
Functions/Macros:	XtIsWMShell()

New Resources

WMShell defines the following resources:

Name	Class	Type	Default	Access
XmNbaseHeight	XmCBaseHeight	int	XtUnspecifiedShellInt	CSG
XmNbaseWidth	XmCBaseWidth	int	XtUnspecifiedShellInt	CSG
XmNheightInc	XmCHeightInc	int	XtUnspecifiedShellInt	CSG
XmNiconMask	XmCIconMask	Pixmap	NULL	CSG
XmNiconPixmap	XmCIconPixmap	Pixmap	NULL	CSG
XmNiconWindow	XmCIconWindow	Window	NULL	CSG
XmNiconX	XmCIconX	int	−1	CSG
XmNiconY	XmCIconY	int	−1	CSG
XmNinitialState	XmCInitialState	int	NormalState	CSG
XmNinput	XmCInput	Boolean	False	CSG
XmNmaxAspectX	XmCMaxAspectX	int	XtUnspecifiedShellInt	CSG
XmNmaxAspectY	XmCMaxAspectY	int	XtUnspecifiedShellInt	CSG
XmNmaxHeight	XmCMaxHeight	int	XtUnspecifiedShellInt	CSG
XmNmaxWidth	XmCMaxWidth	int	XtUnspecifiedShellInt	CSG
XmNminAspectX	XmCMinAspectX	int	XtUnspecifiedShellInt	CSG
XmNminAspectY	XmCMinAspectY	int	XtUnspecifiedShellInt	CSG

Name	Class	Type	Default	Access
XmNminHeight	XmCMinHeight	int	XtUnspecifiedShellInt	CSG
XmNminWidth	XmCMinWidth	int	XtUnspecifiedShellInt	CSG
XmNtitle	XmCTitle	String	dynamic	CSG
XmNtitleEncoding	XmCTitleEncoding	Atom	XA_STRING	CSG
XmNtransient	XmCTransient	Boolean	False	CSG
XmNwaitForWm	XmCWaitForWm	Boolean	True	CSG
XmNwidthInc	XmCWidthInc	int	XtUnspecifiedShellInt	CSG
XmNwindowGroup	XmCWindowGroup	Window	dynamic	CSG
XmNwinGravity	XmCWinGravity	int	dynamic	CSG
XmNwmTimeout	XmCWmTimeout	int	5000 ms	CSG

XmNbaseHeight
XmNbaseWidth

> The base dimensions from which the preferred height and width can be stepped up or down (as specified by **XmNheightInc** or **XmNwidthInc**).

XmNheightInc

> The amount by which to increment or decrement the window's height when the window manager chooses a preferred value. The base height is **XmNbaseHeight**, and the height can decrement to the value of **XmNminHeight** or increment to the value of **XmNmaxHeight**. See also **XmNwidthInc**.

XmNiconMask

> A bitmap that the window manager can use in order to clip the application's icon into a nonrectangular shape.

XmNiconPixmap

> The application's icon.

XmNiconWindow

> The ID of a window that serves as the application's icon.

XmNiconX
XmNiconY

> Window manager hints for the root window coordinates of the application's icon.

XmNinitialState

> The initial appearance of the widget instance. Possible values are defined in `<X11/Xutil.h>`:

```
NormalState          /* application starts as a window */
IconicState          /* application starts as an icon */
```

XmNinput

> A Boolean that, in conjunction with the WM_TAKE_FOCUS atom in the WM_PROTOCOLS property, determines the application's keyboard focus model. The result is determined by the value of **XmNinput** and the existence of the atom, as described below:

Value of XmNinput Resource	WM_TAKE_FOCUS Atom	Keyboard Focus Model
False	Does not exist	No input allowed
True	Does not exist	Passive
True	Exists	Locally active
False	Exists	Globally active

XmNmaxAspectX
XmNmaxAspectY

The numerator and denominator, respectively, of the maximum aspect ratio requested for this widget.

XmNmaxHeight
XmNmaxWidth

The maximum dimensions for the widget's preferred height or width.

XmNminAspectX
XmNminAspectY

The numerator and denominator, respectively, of the minimum aspect ratio requested for this widget.

XmNminHeight
XmNminWidth

The minimum dimensions for the widget's preferred height or width.

XmNtitle

The string that the window manager displays as the application's name. By default, the icon name is used, but if this isn't specified, the name of the application is used.

XmNtitleEncoding

The property type for encoding the XmNtitle resource.

XmNtransient

If True, this indicates a popup window or some other transient widget. This resource is usually not changed.

XmNwaitForWm

If True (default), the X Toolkit waits for a response from the window manager before acting as if no window manager exists. The waiting time is specified by the XmNwmTimeout resource.

XmNwidthInc

The amount by which to increment or decrement the window's width when the window manager chooses a preferred value. The base width is XmNbaseWidth, and the width can decrement to the value of XmNminWidth or increment to the value of XmNmaxWidth. See also XmNheightInc.

XmNwindowGroup

The window associated with this widget instance. This window acts as the primary window of a group of windows that have similar behavior.

XmNwinGravity

> The window gravity used in positioning the widget. Unless an initial value is given, this resource will be set when the widget is realized. The default value is NorthWestGravity (if the Shell resource XmNgeometry is NULL); otherwise, XmNwinGravity assumes the value returned by the XmWMGeometry routine.

XmNwmTimeout

> The number of milliseconds that the X Toolkit waits for a response from the window manager. This resource is meaningful when the XmNwaitForWm resource is set to True.

Inherited Resources

WMShell inherits the following resources. The resources are listed alphabetically, along with the superclass that defines them.

Resource	Inherited From	Resource	Inherited From
XmNaccelerators	Core	XmNinitialResourcesPersistent	Core
XmNallowShellResize	Shell	XmNinsertPosition	Composite
XmNancestorSensitive	Core	XmNmappedWhenManaged	Core
XmNbackground	Core	XmNnumChildren	Composite
XmNbackgroundPixmap	Core	XmNoverrideRedirect	Shell
XmNborderColor	Core	XmNpopdownCallback	Shell
XmNborderPixmap	Core	XmNpopupCallback	Shell
XmNborderWidth	Core	XmNsaveUnder	Shell
XmNchildren	Composite	XmNscreen	Core
XmNcolormap	Core	XmNsensitive	Core
XmNcreatePopupChildProc	Shell	XmNtranslations	Core
XmNdepth	Core	XmNvisual	Shell
XmNdestroyCallback	Core	XmNwidth	Core
XmNgeometry	Shell	XmNx	Core
XmNheight	Core	XmNy	Core

WorkingDialog

A convenience widget created by a call to XmCreateWorkingDialog() and consisting of a DialogShell with a MessageBox widget as its child. The MessageBox resource XmNdialogType is set to XmDIALOG_WORKING. The include file is *<Xm/MessageB.h>*. A WorkingDialog includes three components: a symbol (by default an hourglass), a message, and three buttons (whose labels by default are Ok, Cancel, and Help).

C

Data Types

This appendix describes any special data types used by Motif functions, including Xt or Xlib data types where necessary.

Data Types

This section alphabetically summarizes the Motif, Xt, or Xlib data types (other than widgets and gadgets) that are used as arguments or return values in Motif toolkit routines. Defined symbols (for example, constants used to specify the value of a mask or a field in a structure) or other data types used only to set structure members are listed with the data type in which they are used.

Unless otherwise noted, data types and associated symbols are defined in the header file *<Xm/Xm.h>*.

ArgList

An ArgList is used for setting resources in calls to the widget creation routines. It is defined as follows in *<X11/Intrinsic.h>*:

```
typedef struct {
    String          name;
    XtArgVal        value;
} Arg, *ArgList;
```

The name field is typically a defined constant of the form XmN*resourcename* from either *<Xm/Xm.h>* or a widget public header file. It identifies the name of the argument to be set. The value field is an XtArgVal, a system-dependent typedef chosen to be large enough to hold a pointer to a function. It is often not large enough to hold a float or double.

Atom

To optimize communication with the server, a property is referenced by string name only once, and subsequently by a unique integer ID called an Atom. Predefined atoms are defined in *<X11/Xatom.h>* using defined symbols beginning with XA_; other atoms can be obtained from the server by calling the Motif routine XmInternAtom. Atoms are used in the Motif protocol routines (e.g., XmAddProtocol).

Bool or Boolean

Bool, defined as an int in *<X11/Xlib.h>*, is a Boolean value that indicates True (1) or False (0). Boolean, defined conditionally as an int, char, or long in *<X11/Intrinsic.h>*, indicates TRUE (1) or FALSE (0).

Cardinal

A typedef from *<X11/Intrinsic.h>* used to specify any unsigned integer value; used primarily for specifying the number of name/value pairs used in the Motif creation routines.

Colormap

An XID (server resource ID) from *<X11/X.h>* that identifies a colormap resource maintained by the server; used in calls to XmGetColors.

Cursor

An XID (server resource ID) from *<X11/X.h>* that identifies a cursor resource maintained by the server; used in calls to XmSetMenuCursor and XmTrackingLocate.

Dimension

A typedef from *<X11/Intrinsic.h>* for specifying window sizes; used by the string drawing routines.

Display

A structure defined in *<X11/Xlib.h>* that contains information about the display the program is running on. Display structure fields should not be accessed directly; Xlib provides a number of macros to return essential values. In the Motif toolkit, a pointer to the current Display is returned by calls to the clipboard routines, string drawing routines, and a few others.

GC

Describes a graphics context. A GC is a pointer to a structure defined in *<X11/Xlib.h>* that contains a copy of the settings in a server resource. The server resource, in turn, contains information about how to interpret a graphics primitive. GCs are used by the Motif routines XmStringDraw, XmStringDrawImage, and XmStringDrawUnderline (the string drawing routines). The members of this structure should not be accessed directly.

```
typedef struct _XGC {
    XExtData        *ext_data;     /* hook for extension to hang data */
    GContext        gid;           /* protocol ID for graphics context */
    Bool            rects;         /* True if clipmask is list of rectangles */
    Bool            dashes;        /* True if dash-list is really a list */
    unsigned long   dirty;         /* cache dirty bits */
    XGCValues       values;        /* shadow structure of values */
} *GC;
```

KeySym

A portable representation of the symbol on the cap of a key. Individual KeySyms are symbols defined in *<X11/keysymdef.h>*. The keycode-to-keysym lookup tables are maintained by the server, and hence a KeySym is actually an XID. The XmVaCreateSimpleOptionMenu routine takes a KeySym argument.

Pixel

An unsigned long integer (defined in *<X11/Intrinsic.h>*) that serves as an index to a colormap; specified or returned in calls to XmGetColors and XmGetPixmap.

Pixmap

An XID (server resource ID) returned by a call to XmGetPixmap and representing a two-dimensional array of pixels—a drawable with a specified width, height, and depth (number of planes), but no screen coordinates. A pixmap is also specified in the XmDestroyPixmap routine.

Position

A typedef from *<X11/Intrinsic.h>* used to specify x- and y-coordinates. It is used by the string drawing routines to position the string, and by Text and TextField widget routines (e.g., XmTextPosToXY) for determining a character's coordinates.

Screen

A structure that describes the characteristics of a screen (one or more of which make up a display). A pointer to a list of these structures is a member of the Display structure. A pointer to a structure of this type is returned by XmDestroyPixmap, XmGetColors, and XmGet-Pixmap. Xlib Macros are provided to access most members of this structure.

```
typedef struct {
    XExtData        *ext_data;          /* hook for extension to hang data */
    struct _XDisplay *display;          /* back pointer to display structure */
    Window          root;               /* root window ID */
    int             width, height;      /* width and height of screen */
    int             mwidth, mheight;    /* width and height of in millimeters */
    int             ndepths;            /* number of depths possible */
    Depth           *depths;            /* list of allowable depths on the screen */
    int             root_depth;         /* bits per pixel */
    Visual          *root_visual;       /* root visual */
    GC              default_gc;         /* GC for the root root visual */
    Colormap        cmap;               /* default colormap */
    unsigned long   white_pixel;
    unsigned long   black_pixel;        /* white and black pixel values */
    int             max_maps, min_maps; /* max and min colormaps */
    int             backing_store;      /* Never, WhenMapped, Always */
    Bool            save_unders;        /* should bits under popups be saved */
    long            root_input_mask;    /* initial root input mask */
} Screen;
```

String

A typedef for char *, used by the widget creation routines for specifying the name of the newly created widget.

Time

An unsigned long value (defined in *<X11/X.h>*) containing a time value in milliseconds; used in routines that involve copying and cutting of text. It also specifies the time member of the event structure that corresponds to the operation performed.

VoidProc

A typedef for void *, used to specify the callback procedure that XmClipboardCopy calls when data has been passed by name. VoidProc is defined in *<X11/CutPaste.h>*.

Widget

A structure returned by most Motif toolkit routines to identify the widget on which the routine operates. The members of this structure should not be accessed directly from applications; they should regard it as an opaque pointer. Widget is really a pointer to a widget instance structure. Widget code accesses instance variables from this structure.

WidgetClass

Points to the widget class structure; used in calls to XmResolvePartOffsets and XmResolve-AllPartOffsets.

Data Types

Window

An XID (server resource ID) that identifies the window on which a Motif routine performs an operation; used in calls to the clipboard routines and string drawing routines.

XButtonPressedEvent

A typedef for XButtonEvent, defined in *<X11/Xlib.h>* and used in calls to XmMenuPosition.

XFontStruct

Specifies metric information (in pixels) for an entire font. This structure (defined in *<X11/Xlib.h>*) is filled by means of the Xlib routines XLoadQueryFont and XQueryFont. XListFontsWithInfo also fills it, but with metric information for the entire font only, not for each character. A pointer to this structure is used in the Motif routines XmFontListAdd, XmFontListCreate, and XmFontListGetNextFont.

```
typedef struct {
    XExtData        *ext_data;              /* hook for extension to hang data */
    Font            fid;                    /* font ID for this font */
    unsigned        direction;             /* direction the font is painted */
    unsigned        min_char_or_byte2;     /* first character */
    unsigned        max_char_or_byte2;     /* last character */
    unsigned        min_byte1;             /* first row that exists */
    unsigned        max_byte1;             /* last row that exists */
    Bool            all_chars_exist;       /* flag if all characters have nonzero size*/
    unsigned        default_char;          /* char to print for undefined character */
    int             n_properties;          /* how many properties there are */
    XFontProp       *properties;           /* pointer to array of additional properties*/
    XCharStruct     min_bounds;            /* minimum bounds over all existing char*/
    XCharStruct     max_bounds;            /* maximum bounds over all existing char*/
    XCharStruct     *per_char;             /* first_char to last_char information */
    int             ascent;                /* logical extent of largest character above baseline */
    int             descent;               /* logical descent of largest character below baseline */
} XFontStruct;
```

The direction member is specified by one of the following constants from *<X11/X.h>*:

FontLeftToRight   FontRightToLeft   FontChange

XImage

Describes an area of the screen. This structure (defined in *<X11/Xlib.h>*) is used in XmInstallImage and XmUninstallImage.

```
typedef struct _XImage {
    int             width, height;         /* size of image in pixels */
    int             xoffset;               /* number of pixels offset in X direction */
    int             format;                /* XYBitmap, XYPixmap, ZPixmap */
    char            *data;                 /* pointer to image data */
    int             byte_order;            /* data byte order: LSBFirst, MSBFirst */
    int             bitmap_unit;           /* quant. of scan line 8, 16, 32 */
    int             bitmap_bit_order;      /* LSBFirst, MSBFirst */
    int             bitmap_pad;            /* 8, 16, 32 */
    int             depth;                 /* depth of image */
    int             bytes_per_line;        /* accelerator to next line */
    int             bits_per_pixel;        /* bits per pixel (ZPixmap only) */
    unsigned long   red_mask;              /* bits in z arrangement */
    unsigned long   green_mask;
    unsigned long   blue_mask;
    char            *obdata;               /* hook for the object routines to hang on */
```

```
    struct funcs {                         /* image manipulation routines */
    struct _XImage *(*create_image)();
        int (*destroy_image)();
        unsigned long (*get_pixel)();
        int (*put_pixel)();
        struct _XImage *(*sub_image)();
        int (*add_pixel)();
        } f;
} XImage;
```

The format member is specified by one of the following constants defined in *<X11/X.h>*:

```
XYBitmap                  /* depth 1, XYFormat */
XYPixmap                  /* pixmap viewed as stack of planes; depth == drawable depth */
ZPixmap                   /* pixels in scan-line order; depth == drawable depth */
```

byte_order and bitmap_bit_order are specified by either LSBFirst or MSBFirst, which are defined in *<X11/X.h>*.

XRectangle

Specifies a rectangle. This structure (defined in *<X11/Xlib.h>*) is used in XmStringDraw, XmStringDrawImage, and XmStringDrawUnderline.

```
typedef struct {
    short           x, y;
    unsigned short  width, height;
} XRectangle;
```

XmClipboardPendingList

A structure used in calls to XmClipboardPendingItems for specifying the address of a *DataId/PrivateId* pair. Defined as follows in *<X11/CutPaste.h>*:

```
typedef struct {
    int             DataId;
    int             PrivateId;
} XmClipboardPendingRec, *XmClipboardPendingList;
```

XmColorProc

The prototype for the color calculation procedure that is set by a call to XmSetColorCalculation. This procedure can be obtained by calling XmGetColorCalculation.

```
typedef void (*XmColorProc) ();
```

XmFontContext

A typedef for a font list context that lets applications access fonts and character sets in a font list. This data type is an opaque structure returned by a call to XmFontListInitFontContext, and is used in subsequent calls to XmFontListGetNextFont and XmFontListFreeFontContext. It is defined as follows:

```
typedef struct _XmFontListContextRec *XmFontContext;
```

Data Types

XmFontList

Points to a structure that defines a font list. A font list consists of one or more elements. Each element includes a font and its associated character set. XmFontList is an opaque data type used in calls to font list routines and string manipulation routines; it is defined as follows:

```
typedef struct _XmFontListRec    *XmFontList;
```

To specify a font list in a resource file, use the following syntax:

resource_name: *font_name* [= *charset*] [, *font_name* [= *charset*]] ...

Font list elements consist of a *font_name/charset* pair, each pair separated by a comma. Items within brackets are optional. Only one font list element is required, and for each element, the character set may be omitted (in which case the current language environment determines the character set).

XmHighlightMode

An enumerated type that defines the kind of text highlighting that should result from calls to XmTextFieldSetHighlight or XmTextSetHighlight.

```
typedef enum {
    XmHIGHLIGHT_NORMAL,                    /* no highlighting */
    XmHIGHLIGHT_SELECTED,                  /* highlight in reverse video */
    XmHIGHLIGHT_SECONDARY_SELECTED         /* highlight by underlining */
} XmHighlightMode;
```

XmOffset

A long integer that represents the units used in calculating the offsets into a widget's instance data. Used internally to Motif. See also XmOffsetPtr.

XmOffsetPtr

A pointer to an XmOffset, returned by a call to XmResolveAllPartOffsets or XmResolvePart-Offsets.

```
typedef XmOffset *XmOffsetPtr;
```

XmString

An opaque typedef for char *, used for compound strings. A compound string contains one or more segments. Each segment, in turn, contains three components: text, character set, and direction.

XmStringCharSet

A typedef for char *, used to define the character set of a compound string. Variables of this type can have the following values, among others:

```
XmSTRING_ISO8859_1
XmSTRING_OS_CHARSET
XmSTRING_DEFAULT_CHARSET
```

XmStringComponentType

An unsigned char returned by a call to XmStringGetNextComponent and used for evaluating a component within a compound string. It returns one of the following constants:

```
XmSTRING_COMPONENT_UNKNOWN        /* next component is of unknown type */
XmSTRING_COMPONENT_CHARSET        /* next component is character set identifier */
XmSTRING_COMPONENT_TEXT           /* next component is a text component */
XmSTRING_COMPONENT_DIRECTION      /* next component is a direction */
XmSTRING_COMPONENT_SEPARATOR      /* next component is a separator */
XmSTRING_COMPONENT_END            /* this is the last component in string */
```

XmStringContext

A typedef for a string context that lets applications access components or segments within a compound string. This data type is an opaque structure returned by a call to XmStringInitContext, and is used in subsequent calls to the four other string context routines: XmStringFreeContext, XmStringGetNextSegment, XmStringGetNextComponent, and XmStringPeekNextComponent. This structure is defined as follows:

```
typedef struct __XmStringContextRec *_XmStringContext;
```

XmStringDirection

An unsigned char used for determining the direction in which a compound string will display; returned in calls to XmStringGetNextComponent or XmStringGetNextSegment, and also specified in calls to XmStringDirectionCreate and XmStringSegmentCreate. This data type returns one of the following constants:

```
XmSTRING_DIRECTION_L_TO_R              XmSTRING_DIRECTION_R_TO_L
XmSTRING_DIRECTION_DEFAULT
```

XmStringTable

An opaque typedef for XmString *, used for arrays of compound strings (in other words, arrays of XmString data).

```
typedef XmString *XmStringTable;
```

XmTextPosition

A long integer, used by Text and TextField routines for determining the position of a character inside a text string.

XmTextSource

A pointer to an opaque structure, a text source. The pointer is defined in *<Xm/Text.h>*; it is returned by calls to XmTextGetSource and is used in XmTextSetSource.

```
typedef struct _XmTextSourceRec *XmTextSource;
```

XrmValue

A structure defined in *<X11/Xresource.h>*, used in XmCvtStringToUnitType to return the source value and the value to which it was converted.

```
typedef struct {
    unsigned int        size;
    caddr_t             addr;
} XrmValue, *XrmValuePtr;
```

XrmValuePtr

See XrmValue.

XtCallbackProc

The prototype for callback functions. It is defined as follows in *<X11/Intrinsic.h>*:

```
typedef void (*XtCallbackProc)(
    Widget        /* widget */,
    XtPointer     /* closure */,       /* data the application registered */
    XtPointer     /* call_data */      /* callback specific data */
);
```

D

Additional Example Programs

This appendix provides several additional examples that illustrate techniques not discussed in the body of the book.

In This Chapter:

Additional Example Programs

This appendix contains a number of programs that provide more realistic examples of how Motif is used. Most of these are intended to stimulate further investigation into other X-related topics such as the use of app-defaults files, fallback resources, command line option parsing, more geometry layout and creative uses for dialogs.

D.1 A Postcard Interface for Mail

The first example provides a GUI "wrapper" for a mail program. The user interface model is that of a postcard; there are no facilities for reading mail messages, but simply for composing and sending one message at a time.

Before compiling the program, check the define for **MAIL_CMD**. If you don't have *zmail* on your system, set the value to the name of the mail agent you normally use.

Example D-1. The zcard.c program

```
/*
 * zcard.c -- a "postcard" interface for zmail.
 *
 * Copyright (c) 1991 Z-Code Software Corp.  All rights reserved.
 */
#include <stdio.h>
#include <Xm/List.h>
#include <Xm/LabelG.h>
#include <Xm/PushB.h>
#include <Xm/MessageB.h>
#include <Xm/RowColumn.h>
#include <Xm/Form.h>
#include <Xm/Text.h>

#include "zcard.icon"

/*
 * If you don't have zmail, specify some other mail agent here
 */
#define MAIL_CMD        "zmail"
extern char *strcpy();
Widget list_w, text_w, to_w, subj_w, CreateLabeledTextForm();
static void add_user(), send_it(), add_to_to();
```

```
String fallback_resources[ ] = {
    "*XmText.fontList: -*-courier-medium-r-*--12-*",
    "*XmText.translations: #override \
        Ctrl<Key>D: activate() \n\
        Ctrl<Key>U: kill-to-start-of-line() \n\
        Ctrl<Key>W: delete-previous-word() \n\
        <Key>osfDelete: delete-previous-character()",
    "*msg-text.rows: 15",
    "*msg-text.columns: 60",
    "*XmPushButton.fontList: -*-new century schoolbook-bold-r-*--12-*",
    "*XmPushButtonGadget.fontList: -*-new century schoolbook-bold-r-*--12-*",
    "*XmLabelGadget.fontList: -*-new century schoolbook-bold-r-*--12-*",
    "*XmList.fontList: -*-courier-medium-r-*--12-*",
    "*zcard.labelString: Z-Card",
    "*title.labelString: Quick Message Sender",
    "*actions*leftAttachment: attach_position",
    "*actions*rightAttachment: attach_position",
    "*to-label.labelString: To:",
    "*to-list.visibleItemCount: 6",
    "*subject-label.labelString: Subject:",
    "*add-btn.labelString: Add",
    "*delete-btn.labelString: Delete",
    "*send-btn.labelString: Send",
    "*quit-btn.labelString: Quit",
    "*error.messageString: You must provide at least one message recipient.",
    "*error.cancelLabelString: OK",
    NULL
};

main(argc, argv)
int argc;
char *argv[ ];
{
    Widget toplevel, label, left, heading, icon, titles, actions, rc, w, send_w;
    XtAppContext app;
    Arg args[3];
    Pixel fg, bg;
    Pixmap pixmap;
    extern void exit();

    toplevel = XtVaAppInitialize(&app, "Zcard", NULL, 0,
        &argc, argv, fallback_resources,
        XmNallowShellResize, True,
        NULL);

    /* The form is the general layout manager for the application.
     * It contains two main widgets: a rowcolumn and a scrolled text.
     */
    rc = XtVaCreateWidget("rc", xmRowColumnWidgetClass, toplevel,
        XmNorientation, XmHORIZONTAL,
        NULL);

    /* left side is a RowColumn -- a child of the bigger RowColumn */
    left = XtVaCreateWidget(NULL, xmRowColumnWidgetClass, rc, NULL);

    /* start the left side with a RowColumn to hold the heading */
    heading = XtVaCreateWidget("heading", xmFormWidgetClass, left, NULL);
```

```
    /* create an icon to make things pretty */
    XtVaGetValues(heading, XmNforeground, &fg, XmNbackground, &bg, NULL);
    pixmap = XCreatePixmapFromBitmapData(XtDisplay(heading),
        RootWindowOfScreen(XtScreen(heading)),
        /* these values are defined in "zcard.icon" */
        zcard_logo_bits, zcard_logo_width, zcard_logo_height,
        fg, bg, DefaultDepthOfScreen(XtScreen(heading)));
    icon = XtVaCreateManagedWidget("zcard_icon", xmLabelGadgetClass, heading,
        XmNleftAttachment, XmATTACH_FORM,
        XmNlabelType,       XmPIXMAP,
        XmNlabelPixmap,     pixmap,
        XmNalignment,       XmALIGNMENT_END,
        NULL);

    /* identify the program */
    titles = XtVaCreateWidget(NULL, xmRowColumnWidgetClass, heading,
        XmNrightAttachment,  XmATTACH_FORM,
        XmNleftAttachment,   XmATTACH_WIDGET,
        XmNleftWidget,       icon,
        XmNtopAttachment,    XmATTACH_FORM,
        XmNbottomAttachment, XmATTACH_FORM,
        NULL);
    XtVaCreateManagedWidget("zcard", xmLabelGadgetClass, titles, NULL);
    XtVaCreateManagedWidget("title", xmLabelGadgetClass, titles, NULL);
    XtManageChild(titles);
    XtManageChild(heading);

    /* provide the "To:" prompt (see the resources above) */
    to_w = CreateLabeledTextForm(left, "to-label", "to");

    /* prompt for the subject (see the resources above) */
    subj_w = CreateLabeledTextForm(left,
        "subject-label", "subject-text");
    /* when user hits <Return>, advance caret to next input item */
    XtAddCallback(subj_w, XmNactivateCallback,
        XmProcessTraversal, XmTRAVERSE_NEXT_TAB_GROUP);

    /* Create a ScrolledList of all the recipients entered in To: */
    XtSetArg(args[0], XmNscrollingPolicy, XmAUTOMATIC);
    XtSetArg(args[1], XmNselectionPolicy, XmEXTENDED_SELECT);
    XtSetArg(args[2], XmNlistSizePolicy, XmRESIZE_IF_POSSIBLE);
    list_w = XmCreateScrolledList(left, "to-list", args, 3);
    XtAddCallback(list_w, XmNdefaultActionCallback, add_to_to, to_w);
    XtManageChild(list_w);

    /* Any command line args are recipients */
    while (argc-- > 1) {
        XmString str = XmStringCreateSimple(*++argv);
        XmListAddItemUnselected(list_w, str, 0);
        XmStringFree(str);
    }

    /* Add, Delete, Send and Quit buttons -- space equally */
    actions = XtVaCreateWidget("actions", xmFormWidgetClass, left, NULL);

    send_w = XtVaCreateManagedWidget("send-btn",
        xmPushButtonWidgetClass, actions,
        XmNleftPosition, 0,  /* attachment resources in fallbacks! */
```

Additional Example Programs

```
                XmNrightPosition, 23,
                NULL);
        XtAddCallback(send_w, XmNactivateCallback, send_it, NULL);

        w = XtVaCreateManagedWidget("add-btn",
            xmPushButtonWidgetClass, actions,
            XmNleftPosition, 26, /* attachment resources in fallbacks! */
            XmNrightPosition, 46,
            NULL);
        /* clicking on Add user adds user to scrolled list */
        XtAddCallback(w, XmNactivateCallback, add_user, (caddr_t)1);

        /* Make it appear as tho hitting return in To: text widget
         * is just like clicking on the Add button.
         */
        XtAddCallback(to_w, XmNactivateCallback, add_user, w);

        w = XtVaCreateManagedWidget("delete-btn",
            xmPushButtonWidgetClass, actions,
            XmNleftPosition, 49,  /* attachment resources in fallbacks! */
            XmNrightPosition, 75,
            NULL);
        /* clicking on delete calls add_user() with a 0 client_data */
        XtAddCallback(w, XmNactivateCallback, add_user, (caddr_t)0);

        w = XtVaCreateManagedWidget("quit-btn",
            xmPushButtonWidgetClass, actions,
            XmNleftPosition, 78,  /* attachment resources in fallbacks! */
            XmNrightPosition, 100,
            NULL);
        XtAddCallback(w, XmNactivateCallback, exit, NULL);
        XtManageChild(actions);

        /* right side is a scrolled text region for letter input. */
        XtSetArg(args[0], XmNeditMode,          XmMULTI_LINE_EDIT);
        XtSetArg(args[1], XmNscrollVertical,    True);
        XtSetArg(args[2], XmNscrollHorizontal,  True);
        text_w = XmCreateScrolledText(rc, "msg-text", args, 3);
        XtManageChild(text_w);

        /* Ctrl-D in text_w causes activate() which calls send_it() */
        XtAddCallback(text_w, XmNactivateCallback, send_it, send_w);

        XtManageChild(left);
        XtManageChild(rc);

        /* add tab groups in the order we'd like tabbing to follow */
        XmAddTabGroup(to_w);
        XmAddTabGroup(subj_w);
        XmAddTabGroup(text_w);
        XmAddTabGroup(actions);
        XmAddTabGroup(list_w);

        XtRealizeWidget(toplevel);
        XtAppMainLoop(app);
}
/* user clicked on either Add or Delete buttons, or he hit return in
 * the To: text field.  In the latter case, "data" is the add_btn,
 * so call that widget's ArmAndActivate() action proc.
```

Example D-1. The zcard.c program (continued)

```
 */
static void
add_user(w, data, cbs)
Widget w;
caddr_t data;
XmAnyCallbackStruct *cbs;
{
    if (w == to_w) {
        /* User hit return... make it look as tho he clicked on Add */
        XtCallActionProc(data, "ArmAndActivate", cbs->event, NULL, 0);
        return;
    }
    /* User clicked on Add if data==1, or delete otherwise */
    if (data) {
        /* get the value of the To: text widget */
        char *text = XmTextGetString(to_w);
        XmString str = XmStringCreateSimple(text);
        if (text && *text) /* if not a null string, add to List */
            XmListAddItemUnselected(list_w, str, 0);
        XmStringFree(str);
        XtFree(text);
        XmTextSetString(to_w, NULL); /* reset so user can add more */
    } else {
        /* user clicked on Delete; delete all selected names */
        int *sel, n;
        if (!XmListGetSelectedPos(list_w, &sel, &n))
            return;
        /* Must delete in reverse order or positions get messed up! */
        while (n--)
            XmListDeletePos(list_w, sel[n]);
        XtFree(sel);
    }
}

/* double-clicking a list item causes the selected item to To: text */
static void
add_to_to(list_w, to_w, cbs)
Widget list_w, to_w;
XmListCallbackStruct *cbs;
{
    char *text;

    XmStringGetLtoR(cbs->item, "", &text);
    XmTextSetString(to_w, text);
    XmTextSetCursorPosition(to_w, strlen(text));
    XtFree(text);
    XmListDeletePos(list_w, cbs->item_position);
    /* it's a long way, but traverse to To: text field */
    XmProcessTraversal(list_w, XmTRAVERSE_NEXT_TAB_GROUP);
    XmProcessTraversal(list_w, XmTRAVERSE_NEXT_TAB_GROUP);
    XmProcessTraversal(list_w, XmTRAVERSE_NEXT_TAB_GROUP);
}
/* user clicked on "Send" -- build a command line, use popen() to
 * open pipe to mail command, send text data to it, then exit.
 */
static void
```

```
send_it(w, send_w, cbs)
Widget w, send_w; /* send_w -only- when w == text_w !!! */
XmAnyCallbackStruct *cbs;
{
    char *text, *subj, cmd[ BUFSIZ ], *p, *dummy, *getenv();
    int n, i, status;
    XmString *list;
    FILE *pp;

    if (w == text_w) {
        XtCallActionProc(send_w, "ArmAndActivate", cbs->event, NULL, 0);
        return;
    }

    /* if something was left in the To: field, grab it */
    text = XmTextGetString(to_w);
    if (text != 0 && *text != 0) {
        XmString str = XmStringCreateSimple(text);
        XmListAddItemUnselected(list_w, str, 0);
        XmTextSetString(to_w, "");
        XmStringFree(str);
        XtFree(text);
    }

    /* Get the list of users entered */
    XtVaGetValues(list_w,
        XmNitems, &list,
        XmNitemCount, &n,
        NULL);
    if (n == 0) {
        static Widget dialog;
        /* user goofed -- must provide at least one recipient */
        if (!dialog) {
            Arg args[1];
            XtSetArg(args[0], XmNdialogStyle, XmDIALOG_APPLICATION_MODAL);
            dialog = XmCreateErrorDialog(to_w, "error", args, 1);
            XtUnmanageChild(
                XmMessageBoxGetChild(dialog, XmDIALOG_HELP_BUTTON));
            XtUnmanageChild(
                XmMessageBoxGetChild(dialog, XmDIALOG_OK_BUTTON));
        }
        XtManageChild(dialog);
        return;
    }

    /* get the subject (may be empty) */
    subj = XmTextGetString(subj_w);

    /* build command line */
    if (!(p = getenv("MAIL_CMD")))
        p = MAIL_CMD;
    p = strcpy(cmd, p);
    p += strlen(cmd);
    *p++ = ' ';
    if (subj && *subj) {
        /* if subject not empty, add to mail command */
        sprintf(p, "-s \"%s\" ", subj);
        p += strlen(p);
```

```
    }
    /* Add each user in the List to the command line */
    for (i = 0; i < n; i++) {
        XmStringGetLtoR(list[i], "", &dummy);
        p += strlen(strcpy(p, dummy));
        if (i < n-1) /* more to come yet... */
            *p++ = ',', *p++ = ' '; /* separate addresses w/commas */
    }

    /* open pipe to mail command */
    if (!(pp = popen(cmd, "w"))) {
        fprintf(stderr, "Can't execute");
        perror(cmd);
        return;
    }
    /* give it the text user typed (may be empty) */
    text = XmTextGetString(text_w);
    fputs(text, pp);
    fputc('\n', pp); /* make sure there's a terminating newline */
    status = pclose(pp); /* close mail program */

    XtFree(text);
    XtFree(subj);
    if (status == 0) {
        XmTextSetString(to_w, NULL);
        XmTextSetString(text_w, NULL);
        XmTextSetString(subj_w, NULL);
        XmListDeleteAllItems(list_w);
    }
    /* send complete -- start back at beginning */
    XmProcessTraversal(w, XmTRAVERSE_HOME);
}
/* Create a Form widget that has a label on the left and a Text
 * widget to the right.  Attach perimeter edges to form.
 * We use it twice in the program, so make a function out of it.
 */
Widget
CreateLabeledTextForm(parent, label_name, text_name)
Widget parent;
char *label_name, *text_name;
{
    Widget form, label, ret;

    form = XtVaCreateWidget(NULL, xmFormWidgetClass, parent,
        XmNorientation,      XmHORIZONTAL,
        NULL);
    label = XtVaCreateManagedWidget(label_name, xmLabelGadgetClass, form,
        XmNleftAttachment,   XmATTACH_FORM,
        XmNtopAttachment,    XmATTACH_FORM,
        XmNbottomAttachment, XmATTACH_FORM,
        NULL);
    ret = XtVaCreateManagedWidget(text_name, xmTextWidgetClass, form,
        XmNleftAttachment,   XmATTACH_WIDGET,
        XmNleftWidget,       label,
        XmNtopAttachment,    XmATTACH_FORM,
        XmNrightAttachment,  XmATTACH_FORM,
```

```
        XmNbottomAttachment, XmATTACH_FORM,
        NULL);
    XtManageChild(form);

    return ret;
}
```

Example D-1 uses the following file as the *zcard.icon*:

```
#define zcard_logo_width 50
#define zcard_logo_height 50
static char zcard_logo_bits[ ] = {
    0x00, 0x00, 0x00, 0x00, 0x00, 0x00, 0x00, 0x00, 0x00, 0x00, 0x00, 0x00,
    0x00, 0x00, 0x00, 0x00, 0x00, 0xa0, 0x2a, 0x00, 0x00, 0x00, 0x00, 0x00,
    0x55, 0x55, 0x00, 0x00, 0x00, 0x00, 0xa8, 0xaa, 0xaa, 0x00, 0x00, 0x00,
    0x00, 0x55, 0x55, 0x55, 0x01, 0x00, 0x00, 0xa0, 0xaa, 0xaa, 0xaa, 0x00,
    0x00, 0x00, 0x50, 0x55, 0x55, 0x55, 0x01, 0x00, 0x00, 0xaa, 0xaa, 0xaa,
    0xaa, 0x01, 0x00, 0x00, 0x55, 0x55, 0x55, 0x55, 0x03, 0x00, 0xa0, 0xaa,
    0xaa, 0xaa, 0xaa, 0x03, 0x00, 0x50, 0x55, 0xd5, 0x57, 0xd5, 0x03, 0x00,
    0xa8, 0xaa, 0xfa, 0xaf, 0xea, 0x01, 0x00, 0x54, 0x55, 0xff, 0x57, 0xf5,
    0x01, 0x00, 0xa8, 0xaa, 0x7f, 0xaa, 0xfa, 0x00, 0x00, 0x58, 0xf5, 0x0f,
    0x55, 0x7d, 0x00, 0x00, 0xf8, 0xfa, 0x83, 0xaa, 0x3e, 0x00, 0x00, 0xf8,
    0xff, 0x40, 0x55, 0x1f, 0x00, 0x00, 0xf0, 0x3f, 0xa0, 0xaa, 0x0f, 0x00,
    0x00, 0xc0, 0x0f, 0x50, 0xd5, 0x07, 0x00, 0x00, 0x00, 0x03, 0xa8, 0xea,
    0x03, 0x00, 0x00, 0x00, 0x00, 0x54, 0xf5, 0x01, 0x00, 0x00, 0x00, 0x00,
    0xaa, 0xfa, 0x00, 0x00, 0x00, 0x00, 0x00, 0x55, 0x7d, 0x00, 0x00, 0x00,
    0x00, 0x80, 0xaa, 0x3e, 0x00, 0x00, 0x00, 0x00, 0x40, 0x55, 0x1f, 0x00,
    0x00, 0x00, 0x00, 0xa0, 0xaa, 0x0f, 0x00, 0x00, 0x00, 0x00, 0x50, 0xd5,
    0x07, 0x00, 0x00, 0x00, 0x00, 0xa8, 0xea, 0x03, 0xaa, 0x02, 0x00, 0x00,
    0x54, 0xf5, 0x51, 0x55, 0x05, 0x00, 0x00, 0xa8, 0xfa, 0xaa, 0xaa, 0x0a,
    0x00, 0x00, 0x54, 0x7d, 0x55, 0x55, 0x15, 0x00, 0x00, 0xaa, 0xbe, 0xaa,
    0xaa, 0x2a, 0x00, 0x00, 0x55, 0x5f, 0x55, 0x55, 0x55, 0x00, 0x80, 0xaa,
    0xaa, 0xaa, 0xaa, 0xaa, 0x00, 0x40, 0x55, 0x55, 0x55, 0x55, 0x55, 0x00,
    0x80, 0xaa, 0xaa, 0xaa, 0xaa, 0xaa, 0x00, 0x40, 0x55, 0x55, 0x55, 0x55,
    0x55, 0x00, 0xa0, 0xaa, 0xaa, 0xaa, 0xaa, 0xff, 0xbf, 0x00, 0x40, 0x55, 0x55,
    0xf5, 0xff, 0x7f, 0x00, 0xa0, 0xaa, 0xaa, 0xfe, 0xff, 0x7f, 0x00, 0x40,
    0x55, 0xd5, 0xff, 0x01, 0x60, 0x00, 0xa0, 0xaa, 0xfa, 0x3f, 0x00, 0x00,
    0x00, 0x60, 0x55, 0xfd, 0x03, 0x00, 0x00, 0x00, 0xe0, 0xaa, 0x7f, 0x00,
    0x00, 0x00, 0x00, 0xe0, 0xf5, 0x0f, 0x00, 0x00, 0x00, 0x00, 0xc0, 0xff,
    0x03, 0x00, 0x00, 0x00, 0x00, 0x80, 0xff, 0x00, 0x00, 0x00, 0x00, 0x00,
    0x00, 0x1e, 0x00, 0x00, 0x00, 0x00, 0x00, 0x00, 0x00, 0x00, 0x00, 0x00,
    0x00, 0x00};
```

Figure D-1 shows the output of the program.

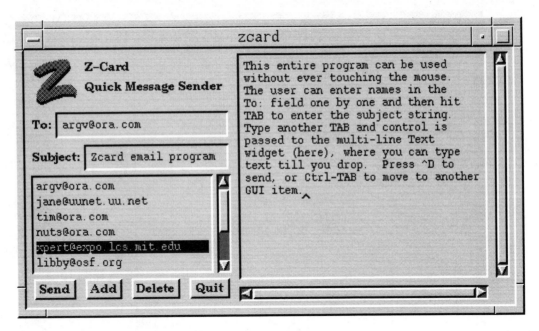

Figure D-1. Sample output of zcard.c

D.2 Displaying a List of Bitmaps

The *xshowbitmap* program is a useful utility for reviewing the contents of a group of bitmaps. It displays a set of bitmaps specified on the command line, from a pipe, or typed into stdin. Bitmaps must be specified as filenames. All the bitmaps are drawn into a pixmap, which is rendered into a DrawingArea widget, which is then used as the work window for a Scrolled-Window. This method is only used to demonstrate application-defined scrolling for the Motif ScrolledWindow. Automatic scrolling is much simpler.

The bitmaps are displayed in an equal number of rows and columns if possible. You may override this by specify either the number of rows (-rows) or the number of columns (-cols) to use. (You can't specify both.)

This example also demonstrates the Xt mechanisms for adding command-line options and application level resources. For an explanation of these Xt features, see Volume Four, *X Toolkit Intrinsics Programming Manual*. For details of the Xlib functions for reading and manipulating bitmaps, see Volume One, *Xlib Programming Manual*.

The output of the example is shown in Figure D-2.

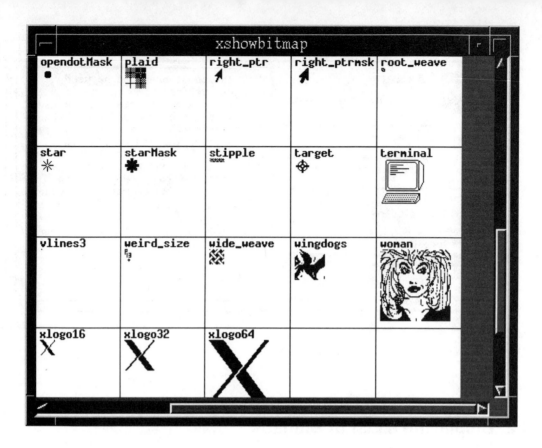

Figure D-2. xshowbitmap.c

Example D-2. The xshowbitmap.c program

```
/* xshowbitmap.c - a bitmap display program
 *
 * Usage: xshowbitmap
 *    -s sorts the bitmaps in order of size (largest first)
 *    -v verbose mode for when input is redirected to stdin.
 *    -w width      (width of viewport window)
 *    -h height     (height of viewport window)
 *    -fg foreground_color
 *    -bg background_color
 *    -label   (labels each bitmap with its corresponding filename; default)
 *    -nolabel (don't label the bitmap with its filename)
 *    -grid N  (line width for grid between bitmaps; defaults to 1)
 *    -rows N  (cannot be used with -cols)
 *    -cols N  (cannot be used with -rows)
 *    -fn font (bitmap filename is printed with bitmap in "font")
 *    -bw max-width  (bitmaps larger than this width are excluded; default 64)
 *    -bh max-height  (bitmaps larger than this height are excluded; default 64)
 *    - indicates to read from stdin.  Piping doesn't require the '-'
 *      argument.  With no arguments, reads from stdin anyway.
 *
```

```
 * Example usage:
 *  xshowbitmap /usr/include/X11/bitmaps/*
 */

#include <stdio.h>
#include <Xm/ScrolledW.h>
#include <Xm/DrawingA.h>
#include <Xm/ScrollBar.h>

#ifdef max
#undef max
#endif
#define max(a,b) ((int)(a)>(int)(b)?(int)(a):(int)(b))
#define min(a,b) ((int)(a)<(int)(b)?(int)(a):(int)(b))

typedef struct {
    char *name;
    int len; /* strlen(name) */
    unsigned int width, height;
    Pixmap bitmap;
} Bitmap;

/* Resrcs is an object that contains "global variables" that we want the
 * user to be able to initialize through resources or command line options.
 * XtAppInitialize() initializes the fields in this data structure to values
 * indicated by the XrmOptionsDescRec structure defined later.
 */
struct _resrcs {
    int         sort;                   /* sort the bitmaps before display */
    int         verbose;                /* be verbose when loading bitmaps */
    int         label_bitmap;           /* whether or not to label bitmaps */
    int         max_width, max_height;  /* largest allowable bitmap size */
    unsigned int grid;                  /* line thickness between bitmaps */
    Pixel       fg, bg;                 /* colors of bitmaps */
    XFontStruct *font;                  /* font to use for bitmap labels */
    Dimension   view_width, view_height; /* initial clip window size */
    int         rows, cols;             /* forcefully set #rows/cols */
} Resrcs;

/* .Xdefaults or app-defaults resources. The values listed here (the last
 * field in each structure) are used as the default values for the fields
 * in the Resrcs struct above.
 */
static XtResource resources[ ] = {
    { "sort", "Sort", XmRBoolean, sizeof (int),
        XtOffsetOf(struct _resrcs,sort), XmRImmediate, False },
    { "verbose", "Verbose", XmRBoolean, sizeof (int),
        XtOffsetOf(struct _resrcs,verbose), XmRImmediate, False },
    { "labelBitmap", "LabelBitmap", XmRBoolean, sizeof (int),
        XtOffsetOf(struct _resrcs,label_bitmap), XmRImmediate, (char *)True },
    { "grid", "Grid", XmRInt, sizeof (int),
        XtOffsetOf(struct _resrcs,grid), XmRImmediate, (char *)1 },
    { "bitmapWidth", "BitmapWidth", XmRInt, sizeof (int),
        XtOffsetOf(struct _resrcs,max_width), XmRImmediate, (char *)64 },
    { "bitmapHeight", "BitmapHeight", XmRInt, sizeof (int),
        XtOffsetOf(struct _resrcs,max_height), XmRImmediate, (char *)64 },
    { XmNfont, XmCFont, XmRFontStruct, sizeof (XFontStruct *),
        XtOffsetOf(struct _resrcs,font), XmRString, XtDefaultFont },
```

*Additional Example
Programs*

```
    { XmNforeground, XmCForeground, XmRPixel, sizeof (Pixel),
        XtOffsetOf(struct _resrcs,fg), XmRString, XtDefaultForeground },
    { XmNbackground, XmCBackground, XmRPixel, sizeof (Pixel),
        XtOffsetOf(struct _resrcs,bg), XmRString, XtDefaultBackground },
    { "view-width", "View-width", XmRDimension, sizeof (Dimension),
        XtOffsetOf(struct _resrcs,view_width), XmRImmediate, (char *)500 },
    { "view-height", "View-height", XmRDimension, sizeof (Dimension),
        XtOffsetOf(struct _resrcs,view_height), XmRImmediate, (char *)300 },
    { "rows", "Rows", XmRInt, sizeof (int),
        XtOffsetOf(struct _resrcs,rows), XmRImmediate, (char *)0 },
    { "cols", "Cols", XmRInt, sizeof (int),
        XtOffsetOf(struct _resrcs,cols), XmRImmediate, (char *)0 },
};

/* If the following command line args (1st field) are found, set the
 * associated resource values (2rnd field) to the given value (4th field).
 */
static XrmOptionDescRec options[ ] = {
    { "-sort", "sort", XrmoptionNoArg, "True" },
    { "-v", "verbose", XrmoptionNoArg, "True" },
    { "-fn", "font", XrmoptionSepArg, NULL },
    { "-fg", "foreground", XrmoptionSepArg, NULL },
    { "-bg", "background", XrmoptionSepArg, NULL },
    { "-w", "view-width", XrmoptionSepArg, NULL },
    { "-h", "view-height", XrmoptionSepArg, NULL },
    { "-rows", "rows", XrmoptionSepArg, NULL },
    { "-cols", "cols", XrmoptionSepArg, NULL },
    { "-bw", "bitmapWidth", XrmoptionSepArg, NULL },
    { "-bh", "bitmapHeight", XrmoptionSepArg, NULL },
    { "-bitmap_width", "bitmapWidth", XrmoptionSepArg, NULL },
    { "-bitmap_height", "bitmapHeight", XrmoptionSepArg, NULL },
    { "-label", "labelBitmap", XrmoptionNoArg, "True" },
    { "-nolabel", "labelBitmap", XrmoptionNoArg, "False" },
    { "-grid", "grid", XrmoptionSepArg, NULL },
};

/* used by qsort to sort bitmaps into alphabetical order (by name)
 * This is used when the "sort" resource is true or when -sort is given.
 */
size_cmp(b1, b2)
Bitmap *b1, *b2;
{
    int n = (int)(b1->width * b1->height) - (int)(b2->width * b2->height);
    if (n)
        return n;
    return strcmp(b1->name, b2->name);
}

/* get the integer square root of n -- used to put the bitmaps in an
 * equal number of rows and colums.
 */
int_sqrt(n)
register int n;
{
    register int i, s = 0, t;
    for (i = 15; i >= 0; i--) {
        t = (s | (1 << i));
```

Example D-2. The xshowbitmap.c program (continued)

```
        if (t * t <= n)
            s = t;
    }
    return s;
}

/* global variables that are not changable thru resources or command
 * line options.
 */
Widget drawing_a, vsb, hsb;
Pixmap pixmap; /* used the as image for Label widget */
GC gc;
Display *dpy;
unsigned int
    cell_width, cell_height, pix_hoffset, pix_voffset, sw_hoffset, sw_voffset;
void redraw();

main(argc, argv)
int argc;
char *argv[ ];
{
    extern char *strcpy();
    XtAppContext app;
    Widget toplevel, scrolled_w;
    Bitmap *list = (Bitmap *)NULL;
    char buf[128], *p;
    XFontStruct *font;
    int istty = isatty(0), redirect = !istty, i = 0, total = 0;
    unsigned int bitmap_error;
    int j, k;
    void scrolled(), expose_resize();

    toplevel = XtAppInitialize(&app, "XShowbitmap",
        options, XtNumber(options), &argc, argv, NULL, NULL, 0);
    dpy = XtDisplay(toplevel);

    XtGetApplicationResources(toplevel, &Resrcs,
        resources, XtNumber(resources), NULL, 0);

    if (Resrcs.rows && Resrcs.cols)
        XtWarning("You can't specify both rows *and* columns.");

    font = Resrcs.font;

    /* check to see if we have to load the bitmaps from stdin */
    if (!argv[1] || !strcmp(argv[1], "-")) {
        printf("Loading bitmap names from input. ");
        if (istty) {
            puts("End with EOF or .");
            redirect++;
        } else
            puts("Use -v to view bitmap names being loaded.");
    } else if (!istty && strcmp(argv[1], "-"))
        printf("%s: either use pipes or specify bitmap names — not both.\n",
            argv[0]), exit(1);

    /* Now, load the bitmap file names */
    while (*++argv || redirect) {
        if (!redirect)
```

More Example Programs 945

```
            /* this may appear at the end of a list of filenames */
            if (!strcmp(*argv, "-"))
                redirect++; /* switch to stdin prompting */
            else
                (void) strcpy(buf, *argv);
        if (redirect) {
            if (istty)
                printf("Bitmap file: "), fflush(stdout);
            if (!fgets(buf, sizeof buf - 1, stdin) || !strcmp(buf, ".\n"))
                break;
            buf[strlen(buf)-1] = 0; /* plug a null at the newline */
        }
        if (!buf[0])
            continue;
        if (Resrcs.verbose)
            printf("Loading \"%s\"...", buf), fflush(stdout);
        if (i == total) {
            total += 10; /* allocate bitmap structures in groups of 10 */
            if (!(list = (Bitmap *)XtRealloc(list, total * sizeof (Bitmap))))
                XtError("Not enough memory for bitmap data");
        }
        if ((bitmap_error = XReadBitmapFile(dpy, DefaultRootWindow(dpy), buf,
                &list[i].width, &list[i].height, &list[i].bitmap,
                &j, &k)) == BitmapSuccess) {
            if (p = rindex(buf, '/'))
                p++;
            else
                p = buf;
            if (Resrcs.max_height && list[i].height > Resrcs.max_height ||
                Resrcs.max_width && list[i].width > Resrcs.max_width) {
                printf("%s: bitmap too big\n", p);
                XFreePixmap(dpy, list[i].bitmap);
                continue;
            }
            list[i].len = strlen(p);
            list[i].name = strcpy(XtMalloc(list[i].len + 1), p);
            if (Resrcs.verbose)
                printf("size: %dx%d\n", list[i].width, list[i].height);
            i++;
        } else {
            printf("couldn't load bitmap: ");
            if (!istty && !Resrcs.verbose)
                printf("\"%s\": ", buf);
            switch (bitmap_error) {
                case BitmapOpenFailed : puts("open failed."); break;
                case BitmapFileInvalid : puts("bad file format."); break;
                case BitmapNoMemory : puts("not enough memory."); break;
            }
        }
    }
    if ((total = i) == 0) {
        puts("Couldn't load any bitmaps.");
        exit(1);
    }
    printf("Total bitmaps loaded: %d\n", total);
    if (Resrcs.sort) {
```

```
            printf("Sorting bitmaps..."), fflush(stdout);
            qsort(list, total, sizeof (Bitmap), size_cmp);
            putchar('\n');
    }
    /* calculate size for pixmap by getting the dimensions of each bitmap. */
    printf("Calculating sizes for pixmap..."), fflush(stdout);
    for (i = 0; i < total; i++) {
        if (list[i].width > cell_width)
            cell_width = list[i].width;
        if (list[i].height > cell_height)
            cell_height = list[i].height;
        if (Resrcs.label_bitmap &&
                (j = XTextWidth(font, list[i].name, list[i].len)) > cell_width)
            cell_width = j;
    }

    /* Compensate for vertical font height if label_bitmap is true.
     * Add value of grid line weight and a 6 pixel padding for aesthetics.
     */
    cell_height +=
        Resrcs.grid + 6 + Resrcs.label_bitmap * (font->ascent + font->descent);
    cell_width += Resrcs.grid + 6;

    /* if user didn't specify row/column layout figure it out ourselves.
     * optimize layout by making it "square".
     */
    if (!Resrcs.rows && !Resrcs.cols) {
        Resrcs.cols = int_sqrt(total);
        Resrcs.rows = (total + Resrcs.cols-1)/Resrcs.cols;
    } else if (Resrcs.rows)
        /* user specified rows -- figure out columns */
        Resrcs.cols = (total + Resrcs.rows-1)/Resrcs.rows;
    else
        /* user specified cols -- figure out rows */
        Resrcs.rows = (total + Resrcs.cols-1)/Resrcs.cols;

    printf("Creating pixmap area of size %dx%d (%d rows, %d cols)\n",
        Resrcs.cols * cell_width, Resrcs.rows * cell_height,
        Resrcs.rows, Resrcs.cols);

    if (!(pixmap = XCreatePixmap(dpy, DefaultRootWindow(dpy),
        Resrcs.cols * cell_width,
        Resrcs.rows * cell_height,
        DefaultDepth(dpy, DefaultScreen(dpy)))))
        XtError("Can't Create pixmap");

    if (!(gc = XCreateGC(dpy, pixmap, NULL, 0)))
        XtError("Can't create gc");
    XSetForeground(dpy, gc, Resrcs.bg); /* init GC's foreground to bg */
    XFillRectangle(dpy, pixmap, gc, 0, 0,
        Resrcs.cols * cell_width, Resrcs.rows * cell_height);
    XSetForeground(dpy, gc, Resrcs.fg);
    XSetBackground(dpy, gc, Resrcs.bg);
    XSetFont(dpy, gc, font->fid);
    if (Resrcs.grid) {
        if (Resrcs.grid != 1)
            /* Line weight of 1 is faster when left as 0 (the default) */
            XSetLineAttributes(dpy, gc, Resrcs.grid, 0, 0, 0);
```

```
            for (j = 0; j <= Resrcs.rows * cell_height; j += cell_height)
                XDrawLine(dpy, pixmap, gc, 0, j, Resrcs.cols * cell_width, j);
            for (j = 0; j <= Resrcs.cols * cell_width; j += cell_width)
                XDrawLine(dpy, pixmap, gc, j, 0, j, Resrcs.rows*cell_height);
        }

        /* Draw each of the bitmaps into the big picture */
        for (i = 0; i < total; i++) {
            int x = cell_width * (i % Resrcs.cols);
            int y = cell_height * (i / Resrcs.cols);
            if (Resrcs.label_bitmap)
                XDrawString(dpy, pixmap, gc,
                    x+5 + Resrcs.grid/2, y+font->ascent + Resrcs.grid/2,
                    list[i].name, list[i].len);
            if (DefaultDepth(dpy, DefaultScreen(dpy)) > 1)
                XCopyPlane(dpy, list[i].bitmap, pixmap, gc,
                    0, 0, list[i].width, list[i].height,
                    x+5 + Resrcs.grid/2,
                    y + font->ascent + font->descent + Resrcs.grid/2,
                    1L);
            else
                XCopyArea(dpy, list[i].bitmap, pixmap, gc,
                    0, 0, list[i].width, list[i].height,
                    x+5 + Resrcs.grid/2,
                    y + font->ascent + font->descent + Resrcs.grid/2);
            XFreePixmap(dpy, list[i].bitmap);
            XtFree(list[i].name);
        }
        XtFree(list);

        /* Now we get into the Motif stuff */

        /* Create automatic Scrolled Window */
        scrolled_w = XtVaCreateManagedWidget("scrolled_w",
            xmScrolledWindowWidgetClass, toplevel,
            XmNscrollingPolicy, XmAPPLICATION_DEFINED,
            XmNvisualPolicy,    XmVARIABLE,
            XmNshadowThickness, 0,
            NULL);

        /* Create a drawing area as a child of the ScrolledWindow.
         * The DA's size is initialized (arbitrarily) to view_width and
         * view_height.  The ScrolledWindow will expand to this size.
         */
        drawing_a = XtVaCreateManagedWidget("drawing_a",
            xmDrawingAreaWidgetClass, scrolled_w,
            XmNwidth,           Resrcs.view_width,
            XmNheight,          Resrcs.view_height,
            NULL);
        XtAddCallback(drawing_a, XmNexposeCallback, expose_resize, NULL);
        XtAddCallback(drawing_a, XmNresizeCallback, expose_resize, NULL);

        /* Application-defined ScrolledWindows won't create their own
         * Scrollbars.  So, we create them ourselves as children of the
         * ScrolledWindow widget.  The vertical Scrollbar's maximum size is
         * the number of rows that exist (in unit values).  The horizontal
         * Scrollbar's maximum width is represented by the number of columns.
         */
```

```
    vsb = XtVaCreateManagedWidget("vsb", xmScrollBarWidgetClass, scrolled_w,
        XmNorientation,    XmVERTICAL,
        XmNmaximum,        Resrcs.rows,
        XmNsliderSize,     min(Resrcs.view_height / cell_height, Resrcs.rows),
        NULL);
    if (Resrcs.view_height / cell_height > Resrcs.rows)
        sw_voffset = (Resrcs.view_height - Resrcs.rows * cell_height)/2;
    hsb = XtVaCreateManagedWidget("hsb", xmScrollBarWidgetClass, scrolled_w,
        XmNorientation,    XmHORIZONTAL,
        XmNmaximum,        Resrcs.cols,
        XmNsliderSize,     min(Resrcs.view_width / cell_width, Resrcs.cols),
        NULL);
    if (Resrcs.view_width / cell_width > Resrcs.cols)
        sw_hoffset = (Resrcs.view_width - Resrcs.cols * cell_width)/2;

    /* Allow the ScrolledWindow to initialize itself accordingly...*/
    XmScrolledWindowSetAreas(scrolled_w, hsb, vsb, drawing_a);

    XtAddCallback(vsb, XmNvalueChangedCallback, scrolled, XmVERTICAL);
    XtAddCallback(hsb, XmNvalueChangedCallback, scrolled, XmHORIZONTAL);
    XtAddCallback(vsb, XmNdragCallback, scrolled, XmVERTICAL);
    XtAddCallback(hsb, XmNdragCallback, scrolled, XmHORIZONTAL);

    XtRealizeWidget(toplevel);
    XtAppMainLoop(app);
}

/* React to scrolling actions. cbs->value is Scrollbar's new position */
void
scrolled(scrollbar, orientation, cbs)
Widget scrollbar;
int orientation; /* XmVERTICAL or XmHORIZONTAL */
XmScrollBarCallbackStruct *cbs;
{
    if (orientation == XmVERTICAL)
        pix_voffset = cbs->value * cell_height;
    else
        pix_hoffset = cbs->value * cell_width;
    redraw(XtWindow(drawing_a));
}

/* This function handles both expose and resize (configure) events.
 * For XmCR_EXPOSE, just call redraw() and return.  For resizing,
 * we must calculate the new size of the viewable area and possibly
 * reposition the pixmap's display and position offset.  Since we
 * are also responsible for the Scrollbars, adjust them accordingly.
 */
void
expose_resize(drawing_a, unused, cbs)
Widget drawing_a;
XtPointer unused;
XmDrawingAreaCallbackStruct *cbs;
{
    Dimension view_width, view_height, oldw, oldh;
    int do_clear = 0;

    if (cbs->reason == XmCR_EXPOSE) {
        redraw(cbs->window);
```

Additional Example Programs

```
        return;
    }
    oldw = Resrcs.view_width;
    oldh = Resrcs.view_height;

    /* Unfortunately, the cbs->event field is NULL, we have to have
     * get the size of the drawing area manually (motif bug?).
     */
    XtVaGetValues(drawing_a,
        XmNwidth,   &Resrcs.view_width,
        XmNheight,  &Resrcs.view_height,
        NULL);

    /* Get the size of the viewable area in "units lengths" where
     * each unit is the cell size for each dimension.  This prevents
     * rounding error for the {vert,horiz}_start values later.
     */
    view_width = Resrcs.view_width / cell_width;
    view_height = Resrcs.view_height / cell_height;

    /* When the user resizes the frame bigger, expose events are generated,
     * so that's not a problem, since the expose handler will repaint the
     * whole viewport.  However, when the window resizes smaller, then no
     * expose event is generated.  In this case, the window does not need
     * to be redisplayed if the old viewport was smaller than the pixmap.
     * (The existing image is still valid--no redisplay is necessary.)
     * The window WILL need to be redisplayed if:
     * 1) new view size is larger than pixmap (pixmap needs to be centered).
     * 2) new view size is smaller than pixmap, but the OLD view size was
     *     larger than pixmap.
     */
    if (view_height >= Resrcs.rows) {
        /* The height of the viewport is taller than the pixmap, so set
         * pix_voffset = 0, so the top origin of the pixmap is shown,
         * and the pixmap is centered vertically in viewport.
         */
        pix_voffset = 0;
        sw_voffset = (Resrcs.view_height - Resrcs.rows * cell_height)/2;
        /* Case 1 above */
        do_clear = 1;
        /* scrollbar is maximum size */
        view_height = Resrcs.rows;
    } else {
        /* Pixmap is larger than viewport, so viewport will be completely
         * redrawn on the redisplay.  (So, we don't need to clear window.)
         * Make sure upper side has origin of a cell (bitmap).
         */
        pix_voffset = min(pix_voffset, (Resrcs.rows-view_height) * cell_height);
        sw_voffset = 0; /* no centering is done */
        /* Case 2 above */
        if (oldh > Resrcs.rows * cell_height)
            do_clear = 1;
    }
    XtVaSetValues(vsb,
        XmNsliderSize,    max(view_height, 1),
        XmNvalue,         pix_voffset / cell_height,
        XmNpageIncrement, max(view_height-1, 1),
```

```
                 NULL);
        /* identical to vertical case above */
        if (view_width >= Resrcs.cols) {
            /* The width of the viewport is wider than the pixmap, so set
             * pix_hoffset = 0, so the left origin of the pixmap is shown,
             * and the pixmap is centered horizontally in viewport.
             */
            pix_hoffset = 0;
            sw_hoffset = (Resrcs.view_width - Resrcs.cols * cell_width)/2;
            /* Case 1 above */
            do_clear = 1;
            /* scrollbar is maximum size */
            view_width = Resrcs.cols;
        } else {
            /* Pixmap is larger than viewport, so viewport will be completely
             * redrawn on the redisplay.  (So, we don't need to clear window.)
             * Make sure left side has origin of a cell (bitmap).
             */
            pix_hoffset = min(pix_hoffset, (Resrcs.cols-view_width)*cell_width);
            sw_hoffset = 0;
            /* Case 2 above */
            if (oldw > Resrcs.cols * cell_width)
                do_clear = 1;
        }
        XtVaSetValues(hsb,
            XmNsliderSize,    max(view_width, 1),
            XmNvalue,         pix_hoffset / cell_width,
            XmNpageIncrement, max(view_width-1, 1),
            NULL);

        if (do_clear)
            /* XClearWindow() doesn't generate an ExposeEvent */
            XClearArea(dpy, cbs->window, 0, 0, 0, 0, True);
}

void
redraw(window)
Window window;
{
    XCopyArea(dpy, pixmap, window, gc, pix_hoffset, pix_voffset,
        Resrcs.view_width, Resrcs.view_height, sw_hoffset, sw_voffset);
}
```

D.3 A Memo Calendar

The next example, *xmemo*, creates a calendar on the left and a list of months on the right. Selecting a month changes the calendar. Figure D-3 shows the output of the program.

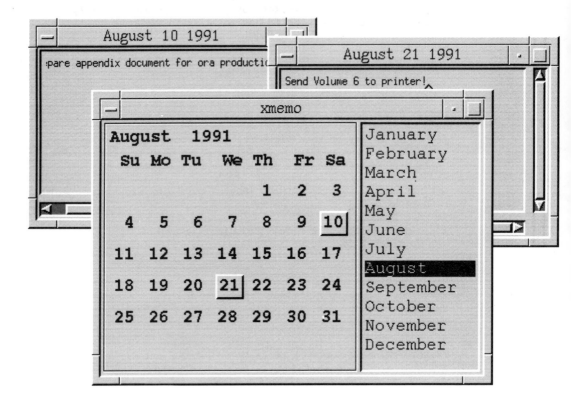

Figure D-3. xmemo.c

Selecting a day causes that date to become activated, and displays a popup window that contains a text widget. This text widget could be used to keep memos for that day (assuming you added code to save and retrieve the memos' contents in one or more files). You can pop up and down the memo window by continuing to select the date on that month.

This program demonstrates a lot of very, very subtle quirks about X and Motif programming. What separates simple programs from sophisticated ones is how well you get around quirks like the ones demonstrated in this example.

For example, the way the dates in the calendar are handled is not as simple as it might appear. Unlike the *xcal* example in Chapter 11, *Labels and Buttons*, which used a single Label widget as the calendar, here each date in each month is a separate PushButton widget. To give the appearance that the month contains a single flat area with days in it, each PushButton's **Xm-NshadowThickness** is initialized to 0. When a date is selected, the shadow thickness for that date's PushButton widget is reset to 2 (the default), giving visual feedback that there is a text-memo associated with it.

This is just the beginning ... along the way, we'll see that there are a number of other snags that we'll have to get around. These are all documented in the code.

Example D-3. The xmemo.c program

```
/* xmemo.c -- a memo calendar. */

#include <stdio.h>
#include <Xm/List.h>
#include <Xm/Frame.h>
#include <Xm/LabelG.h>
#include <Xm/PushB.h>
#include <Xm/RowColumn.h>
#include <Xm/Form.h>
#include <Xm/Text.h>

int year;
void XmStringFreeTable(), date_dialog(), set_month();
Widget list_w, month_label;

typedef struct _month {
    char *name;
    Widget form, dates[6][7];
} Month;

char *day_names[] = {
    "Sun", "Mon", "Tue", "Wed", "Thu", "Fri", "Sat"
};
Month months[] = { /* only initialize "known" data */
    { "January" }, { "February" }, { "March" }, { "April" },
    { "May" }, { "June" }, { "July" }, { "August" }, { "September" },
    { "October" }, { "November" }, { "December" }
};

String fallback_resources[] = {
    "*XmPushButton.fontList: -*-courier-bold-r-*--18-*",
    "*XmLabelGadget.fontList: -*-courier-bold-r-*--18-*",
    "*XmList.fontList: -*-courier-medium-r-*--18-*",
    NULL
};

XtAppContext app;

main(argc, argv)
int argc;
char *argv[];
{
    Widget toplevel, frame, rowcol, rowcol2;
    int month;

    toplevel = XtVaAppInitialize(&app, "Xmemo", NULL, 0,
        &argc, argv, fallback_resources, NULL);

    /* The form is the general layout manager for the application.
     * It will contain two widgets (the calendary and the list of months).
     * These widgets are laid out horizontally.
```

```
        */
    rowcol = XtVaCreateWidget("rowcol",
        xmRowColumnWidgetClass, toplevel,
        XmNorientation, XmHORIZONTAL,
        NULL);

    /* Place a frame around the calendar... */
    frame = XtVaCreateManagedWidget("frame1",
        xmFrameWidgetClass, rowcol, NULL);
    /* the calendar is placed inside of a RowColumn widget */
    rowcol2 = XtVaCreateManagedWidget("rowcol2",
        xmRowColumnWidgetClass, frame, NULL);
    /* the month's label (name of the month) changes dynamically as each
     * month is selected.
     */
    month_label = XtVaCreateManagedWidget("month_label",
        xmLabelGadgetClass, rowcol2, NULL);
    XtVaCreateManagedWidget(" Su Mo Tu  We Th  Fr Sa",
        xmLabelGadgetClass, rowcol2, NULL);

    /* Create a ScrolledText that contains the months.  You probably won't
     * see the scrollbar unless the list is resized so that not all of
     * the month names are visible.
     */
    {
        XmString strs[XtNumber(months)];
        for (month = 0; month < XtNumber(months); month++)
            strs[month] = XmStringCreateSimple(months[month].name);
        list_w = XmCreateScrolledList(rowcol, "list", NULL, 0);
        XtVaSetValues(list_w,
            XmNitems,       strs,
            XmNitemCount,   XtNumber(months),
            NULL);
        for (month = 0; month < XtNumber(months); month++)
            XmStringFree(strs[month]);
        XtAddCallback(list_w, XmNbrowseSelectionCallback, set_month, NULL);
        XtManageChild(list_w);
    }

    /* Determine the year we're dealing with and establish today's month */
    if (argc > 1)
        year = atoi(argv[1]);
    else {
        long time(), t = time(0);
        struct tm *today = localtime(&t);
        year = 1900 + today->tm_year;
        month = today->tm_mon+1;
    }
    XmListSelectPos(list_w, month, True);

    XtManageChild(rowcol);

    /* we're ready to rock-n-roll.  Manage toplevel widget and fly... */
    XtRealizeWidget(toplevel);
    XtAppMainLoop(app);
}

/* Callback routine for when a month is selected.
```

```
 * Each month is a separate, self-contained widget that contains the
 * dates as PushButton widgets.  New months do not overwrite old ones,
 * so the old month must be "unmanaged" before the new month is managed.
 * If the month has not yet been created, then figure out the dates and
 * which days of the week they fall on using clever math computations...
 */
void
set_month(w, client_data, list_cbs)
Widget w;
XtPointer client_data; /* Unused */
XmListCallbackStruct *list_cbs;
{
    char text[ BUFSIZ ];
    register char *p;
    int i, j, m, tot, day;
    static int month = -1;

    if (list_cbs->item_position == month+1)
        return; /* same month, don't bother redrawing */

    if (month >= 0 && months[month].form)
        XtUnmanageChild(months[month].form); /* unmanage last month */
    month = list_cbs->item_position - 1; /* set new month */
    sprintf(text, "%s  %d", months[month].name, year);
    XtVaSetValues(month_label,
        /* too lazy to convert string to compound string.
         * let type converter do it.
         */
        XtVaTypedArg, XmNlabelString, XmRString, text, strlen(text)+1,
        NULL);
    if (months[month].form) {
        /* it's already been created -- just manage and return */
        XtManageChild(months[month].form);
        return;
    }

    /* Create the month Form widget and "dates" pushbutton widgets */
    months[month].form = XtVaCreateWidget("month_form",
        xmRowColumnWidgetClass, XtParent(month_label),
        XmNorientation,     XmHORIZONTAL,
        XmNnumColumns,      6,
        XmNpacking,         XmPACK_COLUMN,
        NULL);

    /* calculate the dates of the month using "science". */
    /* day_number() takes day-of-month (1-31), returns day-of-week (0-6) */
    m = day_number(year, month + 1, 1);
    tot = days_in_month(year, month + 1);

    /* This gets funky -- we are creating a whole bunch of PushButtons,
     * but not all of them have "dates" associated with them.  The buttons
     * that -have- dates get the number sprintf'ed into it.  All others
     * get two blanks.
     */
    for (day = i = 0; i < 6; i++) {
        for (j = 0; j < 7; j++, m += (j > m && --tot > 0)) {
            char *name;
            if (j != m || tot < 1)
```

```
                          name = "   ";
                 else {
                     /* sprintf() returns int on some machines/char * on others */
                     (void) sprintf(text, "%2d", ++day);
                     name = text;
                 }
                 months[month].dates[i][j] =
                     XtVaCreateManagedWidget(name,
                         xmPushButtonWidgetClass, months[month].form,
                         /* this is where we will hold the dialog later. */
                         XmNuserData,      NULL,
                         XmNsensitive,      (j % 7 == m && tot > 0),
                         XmNshadowThickness, 0,
                         NULL);
                 XtAddCallback(months[month].dates[i][j],
                     XmNactivateCallback, date_dialog, day);
             }
             m = 0;
         }
         XtManageChild(months[month].form);

         /* Now, this is *extremely* sneaky.  First, some background: the RowColumn
          * widget creates equally sized boxes (cells) for each child it manages.
          * If one child is bigger than the rest, all children get that big.  The
          * problem with creating all the PushButtons with a 0 shadow thickness is
          * that as soon as one PushButton is selected and its thickness is set to
          * 2 (date_dialog() below), then the entire RowColumn will resize itself.
          * To compensate for the problem, we need to set the shadow thickness of
          * at least -one- of the buttons to 2, so that the entire RowColumn will
          * be initialized to the right size.  But, this will cause the button to
          * have a visible border (which makes it appear "preselected").
          * So, we have to make it appear invisible -- but if it's invisible then
          * it cannot be selectable.  It just so happens that the last 5 days in
          * the month will never have selectable dates, so we can use any one of
          * those.  (Let's choose the last.)  The tricky part is how to make it
          * "invisible."  This can be done by "unmapping" the widget --we can't
          * simply unmanage it or the parent won't consider its size, which defeats
          * the whole purpose.  We can't just create the widget and unmap it
          * because it has no window yet (because it must be realized first).
          * And it that can't happen till its parent has been, and it's parent
          * has been, etc... We don't want to realize and manage this entire
          * application just to make this one widget realized so we can unmap it.
          * So we set XmNmappedWhenManaged to False along with the shadow thickness
          * being set to 2.  Now the form will be created with the appropriate size.
          */
         XtVaSetValues(months[month].dates[5][6],
             XmNshadowThickness, 2,
             XmNmappedWhenManaged, False,
             NULL);
}

/* callback for a date/PushButton widget.  When a date is selected, this
 * function is called.  Create a dialog (toplevel shell) that contains a
 * multiline text widget to save memos about this date.
 */
void
date_dialog(w, date)
```

```
Widget w;
int date;
{
    Widget dialog = 0;
    XWindowAttributes xwa;

    /* the dialog is stored in the PushButton's XmNuserData */
    XtVaGetValues(w, XmNuserData, &dialog, NULL);
    if (!dialog) {
        /* it doesn't exist yet, create it. */
        char buf[ 32 ];
        Arg args[ 3 ];
        int n_pos, *list;

        /* get the month that was selected -- we just need it for its name */
        if (!XmListGetSelectedPos(list_w, &list, &n_pos))
            return;
        (void) sprintf(buf, "%s %d %d", months[list[ 0 ]-1].name, date, year);
        XtFree(list);
        dialog = XtVaCreatePopupShell(NULL,
            topLevelShellWidgetClass, XtParent(w),
            XmNtitle,              buf,
            XmNallowShellResize, True,
            XmNdeleteResponse,    XmUNMAP,
            NULL);
        XtSetArg(args[ 0 ], XmNrows,      10);
        XtSetArg(args[ 1 ], XmNcolumns,   40);
        XtSetArg(args[ 2 ], XmNeditMode, XmMULTI_LINE_EDIT);
        XtManageChild(XmCreateScrolledText(dialog, "text", args, 3));
        /* set the shadow thickness to 2 so user knows there is a memo
         * attached to this date.
         */
        XtVaSetValues(w,
            XmNuserData, dialog,
            XmNshadowThickness, 2,
            NULL);
    }
    /* See if the dialog is realized and is visible.  If so, pop it down */
    if (XtIsRealized(dialog) &&
            XGetWindowAttributes(XtDisplay(dialog), XtWindow(dialog), &xwa) &&
                xwa.map_state == IsViewable)
        XtPopdown(dialog);
    else
        XtPopup(dialog, XtGrabNone);
}

/* the rest of the file is junk to support finding the current date. */

static int mtbl[ ] = { 0,31,59,90,120,151,181,212,243,273,304,334,365 };

int
days_in_month(Year, month)
int Year, month;
{
    int days;

    days = mtbl[month] - mtbl[month - 1];
    if (month == 2 && Year%4 == 0 && (Year%100 != 0 || Year%400 == 0))
```

```
        days++;
    return days;
}

int
day_number(Year, month, Day)
int Year, month, Day;
{
    /* Lots of foolishness with casts for Xenix-286 16-bit ints */

    long days_ctr;      /* 16-bit ints overflowed Sept 12, 1989 */

    Year -= 1900;
    days_ctr = ((long)Year * 365L) + ((Year + 3) / 4);
    days_ctr += mtbl[month-1] + Day + 6;
    if (month > 2 && (Year % 4 == 0))
        days_ctr++;
    return (int)(days_ctr % 7L);
}
```

D.4 Setting Criteria for a List

The following program is incomplete. It displays a List widget that contains all the fonts
available on the server, a CheckBox that sets a text style (normal, bold, italic), and a Toggle-
Box that sets text color. However, there are no callback routines associated with any of the
widgets, so functionally, the program does nothing but display the names of the available
fonts. Figure D-4 displays the output of the program.

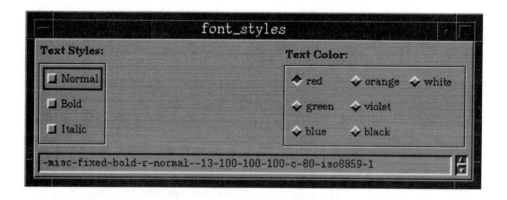

Figure D-4. font_styles.c

Test your understanding of the Motif toolkit by doing the following exercises (in order of difficulty):

1. Provide a default value for the visible number of items in the List widget (other than 1).

2. Add a TextField widget in between the Style and the Colors selections and render a string using the selected font and color. (Hint: use `XmNforeground` to set the color of the Text widget when a new color is selected.)

3. Constrain the list of fonts to those in the "Style" selection. (Hint: determine which of the toggles are selected using either a callback routine on the toggles themselves, or using the RowColumn's `XmNentryCallback` and brush up on `XListFonts( )`.)

4. Implement exercise 2 using a DrawingArea widget instead of a TextField. (Hint: you'll have to create a GC and set its foreground color.)

5. Implement all of the above without adding additional global variables.

Example D-4. The font_styles.c program

```
/*
 * font_styles.c - a program for displaying available fonts
 *
 * This program is incomplete.  It displays a List widget
 * that contains all the fonts available on the server, a CheckBox that
 * sets a text style (normal, bold, italic), and a ToggleBox that sets
 * text color.  However, there are no callback routines associated with
 * any of the widgets, so functionally, the program does nothing but
 * display the names of the available fonts.
 *
 * Actually using the value of the toggles to constrain the
 * values in the list is left as an exercise for the reader.
 */
#include <Xm/LabelG.h>
#include <Xm/RowColumn.h>
#include <Xm/ToggleBG.h>
#include <Xm/Form.h>
#include <Xm/List.h>
#include <Xm/Frame.h>
String colors[ ] = {
    "red", "green", "blue", "orange", "violet", "black", "white"
};
String text_styles[ ] = {
    "Normal", "Bold", "Italic",
};
main(argc, argv)
int argc;
char *argv[ ];
{
    Widget toplevel, radio_box, rowcol, form, frame, w;
    XtAppContext app;
    extern char **XListFonts();
    char **list;
    int i, j;
```

```
    toplevel = XtVaAppInitialize(&app, "Demos",
        NULL, 0, &argc, argv, NULL, NULL);

    form = XtVaCreateWidget("form",
        xmFormWidgetClass, toplevel,
        XmNhorizontalSpacing, 5,
        XmNverticalSpacing,   5,
        NULL);

    w = XtVaCreateManagedWidget("Text Styles:",
        xmLabelGadgetClass, form,
        XmNleftAttachment,  XmATTACH_FORM,
        XmNtopAttachment,   XmATTACH_FORM,
        NULL);
    frame = XtVaCreateManagedWidget("frame1",
        xmFrameWidgetClass, form,
        XmNtopAttachment,   XmATTACH_WIDGET,
        XmNtopWidget,       w,
        XmNleftAttachment,  XmATTACH_FORM,
        NULL);
    rowcol = XtVaCreateWidget("rowcol1",
        xmRowColumnWidgetClass, frame, NULL);
    for (i = 0; i < XtNumber(text_styles); i++)
        XtVaCreateManagedWidget(text_styles[i],
            xmToggleButtonGadgetClass, rowcol, NULL);
    XtManageChild(rowcol);

    rowcol = XtVaCreateWidget("rowcol2",
        xmRowColumnWidgetClass, form,
        XmNtopAttachment,   XmATTACH_FORM,
        XmNrightAttachment, XmATTACH_FORM,
        NULL);
    XtVaCreateManagedWidget("Text Color:",
        xmLabelGadgetClass, rowcol, NULL);
    frame = XtVaCreateManagedWidget("frame2",
        xmFrameWidgetClass, rowcol, NULL);
    radio_box = XmCreateRadioBox(frame, "radio_box", NULL, 0);
    XtVaSetValues(radio_box,
        XmNnumColumns,  3,
        XmNpacking,     XmPACK_COLUMN,
        NULL);
    for (i = 0; i < XtNumber(colors); i++)
        XtVaCreateManagedWidget(colors[i],
            xmToggleButtonGadgetClass, radio_box,
            XmNset, i == 0,
            NULL);
    XtManageChild(radio_box);
    XtManageChild(rowcol);

    w = XmCreateScrolledList(form, "scrolled_list", NULL, 0);
    XtVaSetValues(XtParent(w),
        XmNleftOffset,      5,
        XmNtopOffset,       5,
        XmNtopAttachment,   XmATTACH_WIDGET,
        XmNtopWidget,       rowcol,
        XmNleftAttachment,  XmATTACH_FORM,
        XmNrightAttachment, XmATTACH_FORM,
```

```
            XmNbottomAttachment, XmATTACH_FORM,
            NULL);
    list = XListFonts(XtDisplay(w), "*", 32767, &j);
    for (i = 0; i < j; i++) {
        XmString str = XmStringCreateSimple(list[i]);
        XmListAddItem(w, str, i);
        XmStringFree(str);
    }
    XtManageChild(w);
    XFreeFontNames(list);

    XtManageChild(form);
    XtRealizeWidget(toplevel);
    XtAppMainLoop(app);
}
```

Index

pop-up; building, 557-559
pulldown, 46, 94-95, 553-556;
   (see also pulldown menus.)
pullright; (see menus, cascading)
simple, 532-541
submenus, building, 556
titles, 543, 572
MenuShell, 74, 841
message areas, 67, 111
in main windows, 107
MessageBox, 120, **843**
MessageDialog, 76, 117, **846**
convenience routines for, 137
creating, 123, 142
definition, 121
example, 155
picture of, 118
symbols, 691-697
types of, 124
messages, clipboard, posting by name, 610
Microsoft Windows, and X Windows, 4
Common User Access (CUA) specifications, 9
mnemonics, and menus, 531, 544
case sensitivity of, 544
modal dialogs, 81, 147-159
example, 153-158
implementing, 150
Motif, about, 7-10
and Microsoft Windows, 9
library, 18-19
programming with, 19-41
specifications, 8
toolkit, 8
versus X Toolkit, 532, 546
Motif Style Guide, 45
_MOTIF_WM_MESSAGES property, 601
multiClickTime, 372, 444, 500
multi-colored buttons, 398
multi-colored labels, 398
multi-font strings, 637, 645-650
creating, 651
multi-line editing, and Text widgets, 469,
   476
multiple button clicks, 374
multiple items, deleting from a list, 434
selecting from a list, 436, 446
MWM_DECOR_ALL, 591
MWM_DECOR_BORDER, 591
MWM_DECOR_MAXIMIZE, 591
MWM_DECOR_MENU, 591

MWM_DECOR_MINIMIZE, 591
MWM_DECOR_RESIZEH, 591
MWM_DECOR_TITLE, 591
MWM_FUNC_ALL, 593
MWM_FUNC_CLOSE, 593
MWM_FUNC_MAXIMIZE, 593
MWM_FUNC_MINIMIZE, 593
MWM_FUNC_MOVE, 592
MWM_FUNC_RESIZE, 592
.mwmrc file, 593

N

naming widgets, 33
navigation groups, 278-279
navigation types, tab groups, 283-284
newlines, interpreting as string separators,
   643

O

Object, 846
offsets, attachment, 246-249
data types, 928
zero-length, 248
Open Software Foundation (OSF), 8
option menus, 530
and CascadeButton, 538
building, 567-571
example, 538
OptionMenu, 70, **847**
output-only text, 485
OverrideShell, 74, **847**
overriding translation tables, 344

P

page length, scrollbars, 306
PanedWindow, 230, 272-278, **272**, 571,
   848
and DialogShells, 208
bugs, 63, 208, 230
example, 272-276
resizing, 208
sashes, 277-278, 282
specifying resolution-independent dimensions, 274
use in dialogs, 196